# Family Law, Gender and the State: Text, Cases and Materials

## Second Edition

### Alison Diduck
*University College, London*

### Felicity Kaganas
*Brunel University*

·HART·
PUBLISHING

OXFORD AND PORTLAND, OREGON
2006

Published in North America (US and Canada) by

Hart Publishing
c/o International Specialized Book Services
920 NE 58th Avenue, Suite 300
Portland, OR 97213-3786
USA
Tel: +1 503 287 3093 or toll-free: (1) 800 944 6190
Fax: +1 503 280 8832
Email: orders@isbs.com
Website: www.isbs.com

First edition published 1999
Reprinted 2001, 2004.
Second edition published 2006

Hart Publishing, Salter's Boatyard, Folly Bridge, Abingdon Rd, Oxford, OX1 4LB
Telephone: +44 (0)1865 245533 Fax: +44 (0) 1865 794882
Email: mail@hartpub.co.uk
Website: http//:www.hartpub.co.uk

British Library Cataloguing in Publication Data

Data Available

ISBN-13: 978-1-84113-419-2 (paperback)
ISBN-10: 1-84113-419-8 (paperback)

Typeset by Forewords, Oxford

Printed and bound in Great Britain by Biddles Ltd, Kings Lynn

# Family Law, Gender and the State: Text, Cases and Materials

## Second Edition

The new edition of this popular book of text, cases and materials on family law, as well as providing a firm grounding in family law, sets the law in its social and historical context and encourages a critical approach by students. Legal principle is set against a background which explores, primarily from a feminist perspective, some of the assumptions relating to gender, sexual orientation, class and culture underlying the law. It examines the ideology of the family and, in particular, the role of the law in contributing to and reproducing that ideology. Structured around the themes of welfare, equality and family privacy, the book aims to offer the benefits of a textbook while giving students a wide-ranging set of materials for classroom discussion, and uses the case method to demonstrate how various issues might be resolved.

It has proven to be an ideal introduction to family law for undergraduates, but is equally helpful for postgraduate students of family law for whom it provides a challenging set of materials accompanied by a theoretically rich set of ideas and arguments. Students of social policy, child law or gender studies will also find this book of interest.

'…a stimulating work which attempts to situate family law in its social, historical and political context'.

Mary Childs, *Child and Family Law Quarterly*

'…provocative…and stimulating…the materials amassed strongly support the authors' aim to question the axiomatic allusion what is traditionally designated as family…'

Fiona E Raitt, *Infant and Child Development*

'…offers something that few textbooks seem to offer…this text is a book you can open up virtually anywhere and find an interesting piece on almost any aspect of the broad family law spectrum…a thoroughly sound and stimulating collection of ready-made readings…'

Penny Booth, *The Law Teacher*

'…a wealth of readings and extensive references…as a teaching manual, it is excellent… a coherent feminist perspective across the entire range of family law.'

Marty Slaughter, *Feminist Legal Studies*

# Preface to the Second Edition

One of the first things that a student of law learns is that the law is always changing. Statutes are reinterpreted, repealed and amended and cases are distinguished, applied and overruled by other cases. Nowhere has there been more evidence of this type of legal change in recent years than in the field of family law. Since the first edition of this book was published in 1999, longstanding principles of family law have been revisited by both the courts and the legislature with the result that not only have legal responsibilities between and among family members shifted, but the very meaning of 'family' in law has been recast. As it was in the first edition, the aim of this book is to examine, primarily from a feminist perspective, the way that law constructs and regulates family responsibilities in contemporary British society, but it is also to explore these sometimes quite dramatic shifts in family law and policy that have occurred over the last six years. And, as we did in the first edition, we have continued to rely upon a range of materials that, strictly speaking, may not be considered to be legal, but which we hope will help to shed light upon the social, political and economic aspects of family living and the law that regulates it.

We retain in this edition the format of the last, dividing the book into three parts. The first outlines the nature of families and family roles; the second examines the principles of equality, child welfare and family privacy that we consider to be key in shaping family law and policy; and the third adopts the case method to demonstrate those principles in action. We regret that we have also, for reasons of space as before, had to leave some of the gaps in the previous edition unfilled, most notably elder care and abuse, child abduction, and the financial consequences of death and bankruptcy.

We hope that we have stated the law correctly as at August 2005 and that what we have presented offers critical perspectives and food for thought for students of family law.

We remain indebted to the many people who have given us encouragement and assistance in writing this book. We could not have completed it without the support of Richard Hart and the heroic efforts of his editorial team at Hart Publishing. Nadia Bechai provided research assistance and UCL Faculty of Laws provided funding. And our special thanks must again and always go to our friend and colleague Christine Piper who unstintingly offered both moral support and expertise. Finally, this book could not have been completed without the patience and encouragement shown by our families Mike Rink, David Seymour and Max Seymour.

Alison Diduck and Felicity Kaganas
*London*
*August 2005*

# Contents

# Acknowledgements

The authors and publisher gratefully acknowledge the authors and publishers of extract material which appears in this book, and in particular the following for permission to reprint material from the sources indicated:

**Arena Publishing** for permission to quote from M King, *How the Law Thinks about Children* 2nd edn (1995), and M Roberts *Mediation in Family Disputes.*

**Ashgate Publishing** for permission to quote from F Kaganas 'Contact, Conflict, and Risk' in S Day Sclater and C Piper (eds) *Undercurrents of Divorce* (1999) p 109.

**Blackwell Journals** for permission to quote from K O'Donovan, 'Law's Knowledge: the Judge, the Expert, the battered Woman and the syndrome (1993) *Journal of Law and Society,* Nikolas Rose 'Beyond the public-private division: Law, Power and the Family (1987) *Journal of Law and Society* and C Smart 'The Legal and Moral Ordering of Child Custody' (1991) 18 *Journal of Law and Society,* 485.

**Blackwell Publishing** for permission to quote from J Pryor and B Rodgers *Children in Changing Families* (2001) p 215.

**Buffalo Law Review** for permission to quote from P Bryan, 'Killing us Softly: Divorce Mediation and the Politics of Power' (1992) 441.

**Butterworths, Lexis/Nexis** for permission to quote from C Barton and G Douglas, *Law and Parenthood* (1995) pp 256.

**Cambridge University Press** for permission to quote from A Diduck *Law's Families* (2003)

**Free Press** for permission to quote from RE Dobash and RP Dobash, *Violence Against Wives* (1979) p 31.

**Jessica Kingsley Publishing** for permission to quote from F Kaganas 'Partnership under the Children Act 1989 – an Overview' in F Kaganas, M King and C Piper (eds) *Legislating for Harmony* (1995).

**Jordan Publishing** for permission to quote from A Bainham, *Children: The Modern Law* 3rd edn (2005) pp 226; S Cretney 'Divorce and the Low Income Family' (1990) *Family Law* p 377; A Scully '*Parra v Parra*; Big money cases, judicial discretion and equality of division (2003) 15 *Child and Family Law Quarterly,* pp 213; J Eekelaar 'Rethinking Parental Responsibility' (2001) *Family Law,* 426; F Kaganas and C Piper 'Shared Parenting' (2002) 14 *Child and Family Law Quarterly* pp 272–3; B Lindley and M Richards 'Working Together 2000 – How will Parents Fare under the New Child Protection Process' (2000) 12 *Child and Family Law Quarterly,* p 222; R Deech 'Comment; Not just Marriage Breakdown' (1994) *Family Law,* 121; C Smart and V May 'Residence and Contact Disputes in Court' (2004) *Family Law,* p 37; C Bridge 'Shared Residence in England and New Zealand' (1996) 8 *Child and Family Law Quarterly,* 12; M Hayes 'Re O and N; Re B – Uncertain Evidence and Risk-Taking in Child Protection Cases' (2004) 16 *Child and Family Law Quarterly,* 63; S Gilmore 'The Nature, Scope and Use of the Specific Issue Order' (2004) 16 *Child and Family Law Quarterly,* 367.

**Law and Contemporary Problems** for permission to quote from R Mnookin 'Child Custody Adjudication; Judicial Functions in the face of Indeterminacy' (1975) 226

**Macmillan Press** for permission to quote from S Parker, *Informal Marriage, Cohabitation, and the Law 1750–1989* (1990); D Gittins, *The Family in Question* 2nd edn (1993) pp 2–3; L Fox-Harding *Family, State and Social Policy* (1996) pp 33; J Pahl *Money and Marriage* (1989) pp 3–4; N Parton *Governing the Family; Child Care, Child Protection and the State* (1991) p 20.

**Manchester University Press** for permission to quote from P Hudson and W R Lee 'Women's Work and the Family Economy in Historical Perspective' in P Hudson and W R Lee (eds) _Women's Work and the Family Economy in Historical Perspective_ (1990)

**Modern Law Review** for permission to quote from F Kaganas and A Diduck 'Incomplete Citizens: Changing Images of post-separation Children (2004) _Modern Law Review_ 959; A Diduck and H Orton 'Equality and Support for Spouses' (1994) _Modern Law Review_ p 686; P Symes 'Indissolubility and the Clean Break' (1985) 48 _Modern Law Review_ pp 44; A Bainham 'The Privatization of the Public Interest in Children' (1990) 53 _Modern Law Review_ 206; S Roberts 'Mediation in Family Disputes' (1983) 48 _Modern Law Review_ 537; NV Lowe and S Juss 'Medical Treatment – Pragmatism and the Search for Principle (1993) 56 _Modern Law Review_ 865.

**New Press, New York** for permission to quote from M Fineman, _The Autonomy Myth_ (2004) pp 231–35.

**Oxford University Press** for permission to quote from J Gillis, _For Better or Worse: British Marriages 1600 to the Present_ (1985) pp 233–34; G Douglas _Assisted Reproduction and the Welfare of the Child_ (1993) Current Legal Problems, p 55; G Douglas _An Introduction to Family Law_ 2nd edn (2004) p 203; M Richards 'Divorcing Children: Roles for Parents and the State' in M Maclean and J Kurczewski (eds) _Families, Politics and the Law_ (1995) p 307; L Stone _The Road to Divorce_ (1990) p 374; J Dewar 'Family Law and its Discontents' (2000) 14 _International Journal of Law Policy and the Family_ 59; J Eekelaar 'The Emergence of Children's Rights' 6 _OJLS_, 161.

**Pearson Education** for permission to quote from J Herring _Family Law_ 2nd edn (2004) pp 362.

**Penguin Press** for permission to quote from M Anderson, 'The Relevance of Family History' in M Anderson (ed) _The Sociology of the Family_ (1980).

**Polity Press** for permission to quote from C Smart and B Neale, _Family Fragments?_ (1999) 170–71.

**Sage Publishing** for permission to quote from Beck and Beck-Gernsheim, _Individualization_ (2002) pp 231–35; S Sheldon 'Subject only to the Attitude of the Surgeon Concerned: The Judicial Protection of Medical Discretion' 5 _Social and Legal Studies_ 95; E Stark and A Flitcraft _Women at Risk; Domestic Violence and Women's Health_ (1996) p 270.

**Springer Verlag** for permission to quote from A Diduck: 'Fairness and Justice for All? The House of Lords _in White v White_' (2001) 9 _Feminist Legal Studies_, pp 174–75.

**Taylor and Francis** for permission to quote from R Collier, _Masculinity, Law and the Family_ (1995) p 152; M Fineman, _The Neutered Mother, the Sexual Family, and Other Twentieth Century Tragedies_ (1995), p 228; S Ruddick, 'The Idea of Fatherhood' in NL Nelson (ed) _Feminism and Families_ (1997) pp 85; C Smart _The Ties that Bind_ (1984) pp 89; J Roche 'The Children Act 1989: Once a Parent always a Parent' (1991) _Journal of Social Welfare and Family Law,_ 345; I Thery 'The Interest of the Child' in Smart and Sevenhuijsen (eds) _Child Custody and the Politics of Gender_ (1989) p 81; S Ashenden _Governing Child Sexual Abuse_ (2004) p 55; F Kaganas and C Piper ' Domestic Violence and Divorce Mediation' (1994) _Journal of Social Welfare and Family Law,_ 265

**Thomson, Sweet and Maxwell** for permission to quote from G Douglas _Law, Fertility and Reproduction_ (1991).

**University of Chicago Press** for permission to quote from M Fineman _The Illusion of Equality: the Rhetoric and Reality of Divorce Reform_ (1991) p 180.

**Women's Press** for permission to quote from Backhouse, _Petticoats and Prejudice: Women and Law in Nineteenth Century Canada_ (1999) pp 231–35.

While every effort has been made to establish and acknowledge copyright, and to contact the copyright owners, the publishers apologise for any accidental infringement and would be pleased to come to a suitable agreement with the rightful copyright owner if infringement is found to have occurred.

# Table of Cases

# Table of Legislation

# SECTION 1

## What is a Family?

# 1

# Law and 'The Family'

## I. FAMILIES AND SOCIETIES

In the light of recent family law reforms, it may be provocative, if not downright peculiar, to suggest that the idea of the family in English law is dependent for its meaning on the monogamous sexual relationship (either actually or symbolically) between a man and a woman, or to say that much of the law concerning the formation and adjustment of family relationships highlights the importance of this 'traditional' heterosexual union and retains it, at least symbolically, at its core. Yet, despite recent changes to the laws that constitute and give legal meaning to 'family', 'parent' or 'spouse' that seem to create alternative bases for family formation, we wish to counsel caution in conceding too quickly the decline of the heterosexual norm in family law. We shall make this case in more detail below, and for now wish simply to make the point, by way of introduction, that despite the variety of connections between people that could make their relationship a familial one, there is a particular type of conjugal unit that remains at the foundation of what law understands to be family.

This legal meaning of family sometimes corresponds with and sometimes contradicts popular or personal meanings of family. If you were asked, for example, to define your family, you might include all those people who live in your household whether you were biologically related to them or not, or you might include some or all biological relatives who live outside your household. Your answer may depend upon the reason for the question. Which members of your family do you think you ought legally to be required to support financially? Which members of your family should be required to support you? Which members of your family provide you with emotional and physical security? For whom would you sacrifice most? It is interesting that when children were asked in a recent study to identify members of their families they did not refer simply to those who held a formal status in relation to them, but tended to refer to ties of affection as being the essence of family life and they identified love and the quality of the relationship as being crucial to making someone a 'proper' parent (Smart, Neale and Wade 2001).

So, can we say then that families are created by affective and emotional ties between people? And if we can say this for some purposes, can we say it for all? What if the idea of the family in English law were dependent for its meaning exclusively upon the existence of a parent-child relationship, or were based solely on the giving of mutual affection and emotional support? On the other hand, what if affection and emotion were irrelevant to creating and sustaining a legal family? What if it were an economic interdependence between two or more people that distinguished families from other groups of people?

US scholar Martha Fineman suggests, from a feminist perspective, that the notion of a family should rest upon a 'mother-child' relationship. She is careful to say, however, that men as well as women could perform the 'mother' role:

> In my newly redefined legal category of family, I would place inevitable dependents (sic) along with their caregivers. The caregiving family would be a protected space, entitled to special, pre-ferred treatment by the state.
>
> The new family line, drawn around dependency, would mark the boundaries of the concept of family privacy. The unit would also have legitimate claims on the resources of society. Spe-cifically, I envision a redistribution or reallocation of social and economic subsidies now given to the natural family that allow it to function 'independently' within society. Family and welfare law would be reconceived so as to support caretaking as the family intimacy norm.
>
> (1995 pp 231–32)

> I propose Mother/Child as the substitute core of the basic family paradigm. Our laws and poli-cies would be compelled to focus on the needs of this unit. Mother/Child would provide the structural and ideological basis for the transfer of current societal subsidies (both material and ideological) away from the sexual family to nurturing units. (1995 p 233)

> Two additional theoretical caveats are necessary. First, I believe that men can and should be Mothers. In fact, if men are interested in acquiring legal rights of access to children (or other dependents) (sic), I argue they must be Mothers in the stereotypical nurturing sense of that term—that is, engaged in caretaking. Second, the Child in my dyad stands for all forms of inev-itable dependency—the dependency of the ill, the elderly, the disabled, as well as actual children. (1995 pp 234–35)

> Mothering should be thought of as an ethical practice, as embodying an ideal of social 'good-ness'. As an idealized notion, motherhood should not be confined to women but be a societal aspiration for *all* members of the community. (1995 p 235)

In a later work (Fineman 2004) she argues that a reconceptualisation of family based on the idea of dependency would transform notions about our relationship to the state.

> [I]n our political ideology, dependency is considered to be a private matter. It is the family, not the state or the market, that assumes responsibility for both the inevitable dependent (sic)—the child or other biologically or developmentally dependent person—and the derivative depend-ent (sic)—the caretaker. The institution of the family operates structurally and ideologically to free markets from considering or accommodating dependency. The state is cast as a default institution, providing minimal, grudging and stigmatized assistance should families fail. (p 228)
>
> [But] [i]f the existence of a certain type of family is a prerequisite for the coherent develop-ment of our concepts of the 'public' market and the state, what happens when we are forced to concede that there have been widespread and not easily reversible changes in the way we think about and practice family [...]?
>
> What social expectations apply to the relationships among the state, market and man (out-side his former category as 'husband') or woman (outside her former category as 'wife')? How do we begin to decide what is the appropriate set of social relations and expectations to address the child's claim upon society and its institutions for provision of the goods necessary to meet her or his material, social, and emotional needs? If the family that would have provided the his-toric answer to this latter question no longer exists, our old reliable background begins to crumble. Further complicating this confrontation is the fact that the family is not isolated in its changes. Transformations in the family were provoked by (and further provoke) changes in other institutions. Therefore, our existing ideology about such matters as the appropriateness

of state intervention and regulatory action must also be reconsidered, perhaps shifted, in the context of change. (references omitted, pp 235–36)

In the UK, Patricia Morgan (1995) writing from a 'New Right' perspective, suggests that a parent-child dyad as the basis of 'family' exists already but that the consequences for society are dire. She argues that giving legal recognition as 'family' to a single parent and her child contributes to social ills such as juvenile delinquency, unemployment and poverty.

Irrespective of one's political point of view, then, it seems that the idea that the form or organisation of families is integrally related to the shape and organisation of societies is not contentious. Further, this is not a new insight. Frederick Engels wrote many years ago that the rise in dominance of that which we now know as the conjugal or nuclear family was related to the rise of private property and capitalism and the dominance of men over women. Compare his view of this phenomenon, written in 1884, with that of sociologist Talcott Parsons, who makes many of the same points in 1949, although from a very different political perspective.

As regards the legal equality of man and woman in marriage, the position is no better. Their legal inequality, bequeathed to us from earlier social conditions, is not the cause but the effect of the economic oppression of the woman. In the ancient communistic household, which comprised many couples and their children, the task entrusted to the women of managing the household was as much a public, a socially necessary industry as the procuring of food by the men. With the patriarchal family and still more with the single monogamous family, a change came. Household management lost its public character. It no longer concerned society. It became a *private service*; the wife became the head female servant, excluded from participation in social production. Not until the coming of modern large-scale industry was the road to social production opened to her again—and then only to the proletarian wife. But it was opened in such a manner that, if she carries out her duties in the private service of her family, she remains excluded from public production and unable to earn; and if she wants to take part in public industry and earn independently, she cannot carry out family duties. And the women's position in the factory is the position of women in all lines of business, right up to medicine and the law. The modern individual family is founded on the open or concealed domestic slavery of women, and modern society is a mass composed of these individual families as its molecules. In the great majority of cases today, at least among the possessing classes, it is the husband who is obliged to earn a living and support his family, and that in itself gives him a position of supremacy without any need for special legal privileges. Within the family he is the bourgeois and the wife represents the proletariat. In the industrial world, however, the specific character of the economic oppression burdening the proletariat is visible in all its sharpness only when all the special legal privileges of the capitalist class have been abolished and the complete legal equality of both classes established ... . And in the same way, the peculiar character of the supremacy of the husband over the wife in the modern family, the necessity of creating real social equality between them and the way to do it, will only be seen in the full light of day when both possess complete equality of rights. Then it will be plain that the first condition for the liberation of women is to bring the whole female sex back into public industry, and that this in turn demands the abolition of the monogamous family's attribute of being the economic unit of society. (Engels 1978 pp 84–86)

Monogamy arose from the concentration of larger wealth in the hands of a single individual—a man—and from the need to bequeath this wealth to the children of that man and of no other. For this purpose, the monogamy of the woman was required, not that of the man, so this monogamy of the woman did not in any way interfere with open or concealed polygamy on the part of the man ... .

... With the transfer of the means of production into common ownership, the monogamous family ceases to be the economic unit of society. Private housekeeping is transformed into a social industry. The care and education of the children becomes a public affair; society looks after all children alike, whether they are born of wedlock or not. (Engels 1978 pp 87–88)

Talcott Parsons writes:

What a crucially important structural role is played by the marriage relationship—far more so than in most kinship systems—has already been pointed out. As a structurally unsupported relationship resting largely on emotional attraction, it must be protected against the kind of stresses that go with severe competition for prestige between the members. It is well known that segregation of role is in general one of the main mechanisms for inhibiting potentially disruptive competition. The functional importance of the solidarity of the marriage relationship to our kinship system may therefore be presumed to be a major factor underlying the segregation of the sex roles in American society, since sex is the primary basis of role differentiation for marriage partners ... .

Structurally the most fundamental aspect of the segregation of the sex roles seems to be with reference to the occupational system. Especially in the structurally crucial middle-class area of our society, the dominant mature feminine role is that of housewife or of wife and mother. Apart from the extremely important utilitarian problems of how adequate care of household and children are to be accomplished, the most important aspect of this fact is that it shields spouses from competition with each other in the occupational sphere, which, along with attractiveness to women, is above all the most important single focus of feelings of self-respect on the part of American men. In this sector of society the largest part of the gainful employment of women is that of unmarried girls and of women living outside normal family relationships. There has been a notable check in the tendency for women to enter the higher occupational careers; for example, the proportion of women in the professions of medicine and law has remained approximately constant for more than a generation. Only a minority of such career women carry full normal family responsibilities, including the care of young children. Finally, when in the middle classes married women are gainfully employed, in a large proportion of cases it is in a job rather than in a career. Such employment is ordinarily not in competition with that of men of the same class status and ordinarily does not produce a comparable proportion of the family income. (Parsons 1949 pp 192–94, footnotes omitted)

In the first place, structural analysis clearly shows that, if the United States is to remain and develop further as a democratic, urbanized, industrial society, with a large measure of equality of opportunity, the range of possible family structures which are compatible with its type of society is very narrow. As it is, our family system is responsible for serious limitations on the ideal of equality of opportunity. But any considerable shift in the direction, for instance, of the family types found in peasant societies would undoubtedly entail serious consequences for the rest of the social structure. Such a family type may well be more stable than our own, but if this stability must be purchased at the expense of drastic reduction in the productivity of our economy and drastic limitations of the realizability of our democratic values, is it worth the price? (Parsons 1949 pp 200–1, footnotes omitted)

So we see that, to both of these writers, the organisation of people into traditional, patriarchal nuclear families is a necessary element of industrial and post-industrial capitalist society. Anderson, a more contemporary sociologist, presents yet a different view. He suggests that modern capitalist societies are in many ways antithetical to the values and morality that we consider a part of the 'traditional' family and that the conjugal or nuclear family is neither the result nor the cause of modern industrial or post-industrial capitalism:

We now know, of course, that the fundamental proposition here—family form and process as a functional consequences of the demands of industrial society—is hopelessly over-simple. The historical premise is incorrect, since over most of Britain and much of the rest of Western Europe and North America the typical domestic group has been small and simple in structure, at least since medieval times; where this group was larger and more complex (which was usually only among the more affluent), it was servants and not kin who were responsible. In the European peasant family, as in our own, day-to-day family life was centred around the conjugal pair. While a sense of solidarity with wider kin was clearly present in some sections of the population, and was at times used as an important reference point in social action, at no time in the past one thousand years (with the possible exception of a few remote areas such as Scotland north and west of the Highland Line) has kinship been the dominant basis for social organization, certainly in Britain and probably anywhere in Western Europe; for most of the population, ties even with siblings have probably been of no greater significance than they are today. Indeed, it is a special irony that at least some forms of early industrialization in Britain actually increased people's dependence on kin (and even their ability to live with them and near them) to a level unknown for hundreds of years (at least) before.

Moreover, in as far as the family system did change with industrialization, detailed historically-based analysis of the processes involved suggests that any simple model of industrialization *causing* family change is grossly oversimplified. Firstly, the early methods both of capital accumulation and of labour recruitment were largely extensions of pre-existing social processes. In order to recruit and retain labour, industrial employers often had to adapt to the expectations of their potential labour force by, for example, employing families rather than individuals in the early textile mills and by conniving with parents to ensure the employment of under-age children, by taking on paternal functions for young girls such as guarding their morals and even finding them spouses, and by respecting kinship and community ties in recruitment, promotions and work allocation. Secondly, the association of family change with industrialization obscures the fact that the new features of modern family forms first emerge, not in the early factory towns, but much earlier in the homes of the bourgeoisie and, in the rest of society, in areas like those regions of England where large scale capitalist farming based on hired day labour emerged following enclosure, and in the proto-industrial areas of Europe in the 18th century where domestic production for local use became transformed into domestic production for an anonymous market through the intervention of a capitalist merchant class. In an important sense, therefore, far from industrialization causing changes in the family, changes in production and in domestic life in the direction of modern forms of production and of domestic social organization went together; one without the other was impossible and both were reflections of much more profound structural and value changes. Thus, both can only be understood as a function of this historically specific transformation. It must, therefore, follow that in other societies, with different family traditions and different ideologies of modernization, different outcomes are to be expected in both industrial and family functioning and form.

(1980 pp 35–36, footnotes omitted)

Anderson, therefore, like Engels and Parsons, but without Engels' cause and effect analysis, or Parsons' functionalism, suggests that the 'look' of families and the organisation of society are linked, and that changes in both are linked in turn to changes in society. He lists society's 'structural and value changes' as the family's relationship to production, changes in the roles of children within families, demographic changes, technological developments, the undermining of close community supervision of families and changes in the 'basic values underlying interpersonal relations in the whole society … during the transition from a patriarchal and even feudalistic peasant society to a capitalist industrialised one, based theoretically on principles of citizenship' (p 56). In response to those who wish to return to this historical notion of the 'traditional family', he concludes that

the history of the Western family shows quite clearly that we cannot go back to a strict conformity to the family morality that we have inherited from the past without also—which is clearly
impossible—reverting to the economic and social relations of the past. We are not peasants
anymore and thus cannot sustain a peasant morality. We have to develop new institutions and
new behaviours to cope with new situations. (p 58)

More recent sociological and historical interest in families has also focused upon the
apparent connection between social conditions and family relationships and the view is
that family change 'can be understood in relation to evolving employment patterns,
shifting gender relations, increasing options in sexual orientation and cross-cultural
influences in a multi-cultural society' (Smart, *et al*, 2001 p 17). Families are 'transforming themselves in relation to post-industrialism and the major structural changes of late
modernity' (*Ibid*). To some this means that the individualisation, marketisation and
globalisation of society have transformed intimate relations (Beck and Beck-Gernsheim
1995 and 2002; Giddens 1992; Regan 1999; Beck-Gernsheim 2002; Finch and Mason
1993; Morgan 1996) such that the imperatives associated with the traditional conjugal
bond and conventional familial roles have lost much of their power. On this view, late
modern families and family relationships are in a continual state of flux as we negotiate
responsibilities, obligations and roles according to our individual circumstances.

Whereas, in pre-industrial society, the family was mainly a community of need held together by
an obligation of solidarity, the logic of individually designed lives has come to the fore in the
contemporary world. The family is becoming more of an elective relationship, an association
of individual persons, who each bring to it their own interests, experiences  and plans and who
are each subjected to different controls, risks and constraints.
    As the various examples from contemporary family life have shown, it is necessary to devote
much more effort than in the past to the holding together of these different biographies.
Whereas people could once fall back upon rules and rituals, the prospect now is of a staging of
everyday life, an acrobatics of balancing and coordinating. [...] Since individualization also fos-
ters a longing for the opposite world of intimacy, security and closeness, most people will
continue—at least in the foreseeable future—to live within a partnership or family. But such ties
are not the same as before, in their scope or in their degree of obligation or performance. [...]
As people make choices, negotiating and deciding the everyday details of do-it-yourself relationships, a 'normal chaos' of love, suffering and diversity is growing and developing.
    This does not mean that the traditional family is simply disappearing. But it is losing the
monopoly it had for so long. Its quantitative significance is declining as new forms of living
appear and spread—forms which (at least generally) aim not at living alone but at relationships
of a different kind: for example, without a formal marriage or without children; single
parenting, conjugal succession, or same-sex partnerships; part-time relationships and compan-
ionships lasting for some period in life; living between more than one home or between
different towns. These in all their intermediary and secondary and floating forms represent the
future of families or what I call the contours of the 'post-familial family'.
                    (Beck and Beck-Gernsheim 2002 pp 97–98, references omitted)

Whether or not we agree with this analysis of changes in family structure, obligations
and ties, Beck and Beck-Gernsheim see family as an entity, as a group of people bound
together by choice, biology or marriage. From other sociological perspectives, however,
family is to be seen as 'less of noun and more of an adjective or, possibly, a verb.
"Family" represents a constructed quality of human interaction or an active process
rather than a thing-like object of detached social investigation' (Morgan 1996 p 16;
Morgan 1999). On this view, the object of study becomes what people do rather than the

form of relationships they adopt. The term 'family practices' has been coined to capture the 'family' quality of interactions of everyday living, so that 'activities which on their face seem immediately to be 'about' family are included in this term, but, importantly, so are activities which may not seem so obviously to be family matters. Accessing public transport, eating breakfast, working overtime and voting, for example, can all be studied as family practices' (Diduck 2003 p 28).

> **Q** What are the advantages and disadvantages of understanding family to be a noun or object? What are the advantages and disadvantages of understanding family to be something one does rather than as a unit in which one resides?

Methodological and theoretical problems have been identified in many of the above analyses of family history and family sociology, but despite these problems, as Anderson suggests, we may still fairly conclude that the way in which people choose to structure their affective and economic relationships both affects and is affected by social *mores* and economic conditions in any society. Given this intimate connection, it is reasonable to suppose that a society has a responsibility or an interest in endorsing certain familial structures and roles which conform to what are thought to be the important values in that society. Some idea of this can be gleaned from political or policy statements about families issued or endorsed by government. Consider for example, this recent policy statement from government that clearly promotes a particular view of the good family:

> 10.1 The adult couple, with which this Group is specifically concerned, is the cornerstone of the family. Strong and stable relationships benefit all in society. There is a growing body of evidence in this country which demonstrates the health benefits, and benefits to children, of committed couple relationships. In arguing for greater support for the couple, we do not in any sense question the validity or stability provided by other relationships, such as lone parent families. We are not proposing that there should be some effort to make people marry, or that there should be any criticism of, or penalty for, those who choose not to. But the adverse effects on society of relationship breakdown, and the positive benefits of stable couple relationships, make a strong case for action.
> (Advisory Group on Marriage and Relationship Support, 2002 para 10.1)

Stable couples, then, and ideally married couples, according to government, are good for society and for individuals. Often, though, this ideal, or *idea* of 'the family' does not always accord with the *realities* of our everyday family lives (Smart, *et al*, 2001; Diduck 2003).

## II. FAMILY IDEOLOGY

The *idea* of the family which is dominant in a society has been called an *ideology*[1] of the family. O'Donovan discusses family ideology in this way:

> What is the ideology of the family which contributes to the maintenance of present structures? For evidence of views of law-makers we can turn to the statements of politicians and of the

[1] For a discussion of ideology, see, eg, Eagleton (1991); Purvis and Hunt (1993); Hunt (1985); Easton (1976); Havas (1995); Laclau and Mouffe (1985).

judiciary—the traditional establishment. The family is presented in the Britain of the 1990s as the bedrock of traditional values and common sense ... .

In political rhetoric the family serves many purposes. It is totem, emblem of stability, reassurance and common sense. It can be used to reject challenges to established authority and to castigate critics as 'trendy'. It also serves to be made guilty, to be blamed for crime rates, delinquency, illiteracy. Yet it can stand against the state as bulwark against intrusion and interference. Thus, Ferdinand Mount, one-time Cabinet office advisor:

> The family's most dangerous enemies may not turn out to be those who have openly declared war. It is so easy to fight against the blatant cruelty of collectivist dictators ... . It is less easy to fight against the armies of those who are 'only here to help'—those who claim to come with the best intention but come armed, all the same, with statutory powers and administrative instruments: education officers, children's officers ... welfare workers and all the other councils ... which claim to know best how to manage our private concerns.

The family does not have to establish its credentials, its origins, its sources—it just is whatever it is. It contains, as Goodrich says of law, the tradition of inescapable institutions—repetition ... . As one former government minister puts it, the family:

> poses strength and resilience, not least in adversity. Loyalty to the family ranks highest of all, higher even than loyalty to the state. It is not accident ... that dictatorships, whether of the Left or the Right, seek first to devalue and then to destroy the family.
>
> (1993 pp 39–40, references omitted)

The idea or ideology of the family, then, comprises a timeless, traditional nuclear, private, ideal family form, which may or may not have existed historically in a majority of households, if at all (see Gillis 1997, Diduck 2003 ch 2), and certainly exists only in a shrinking number today. Statistics compiled from the 2001 census and 2002 General Household Survey reveal that 34% of households in Britain in 2002 were made up of (married or cohabiting same or opposite sex) couples living alone, 22% comprised couples with dependent children, 10% of households were made up of lone parents with children and 31% of households were adults living alone (Office for National Statistics 2004). Couples with or without children and lone parents with children make up official 'families' for these purposes, and this means that around 75% of all Britons lived in a family in 2002. Of these, 27% were lone parent families and 0.3% identified themselves as same-sex couples (Duncan and Smith 2004 p 17). Finally, Social Trends (2004) reports that in 2003 60% of married/cohabiting women with a youngest child under 5 were in or looking for paid employment and that this figure increased to 81% for women whose youngest child was between 11 and 15. These statistics demonstrate that the other 'ideal' of the family, a public male head and a private female dependant, is not by any means in the majority. Despite this, however, the ideology of the family informs much of family law and policy-making. Gittins explains:

> [I]t soon becomes evident that a wide gap exists, and has existed, between discourses about 'the family' and how individuals actually live their lives ... . Many studies have failed to differentiate between what preachers, politicians and philosophers say a family should be and how people in fact live and interact in social groups that are defined as families. Much of Lawrence Stone's work (1977), for instance, is really an analysis of changing family ideology rather than a study of actual patterns of family life. Demographers, on the other hand, have tended to concentrate on household structures and demographic events alone without reference to values, discourses

or ideology. Yet both aspects need to be understood.

Linked to this question is the question of what relationship exists between people's material circumstances, the ways in which they live their lives, and discourses and ideologies of how they should live their lives. The extent to which one determines or influences the other is a highly controversial problem which cannot be resolved here (if, indeed, anywhere). What I want to consider, however, is the ways in which a number of sometimes contradictory discourses about 'the family' are exercised in and through the media, religious institutions, the educational system and social policy generally to create an overall 'ideology of the family'.

Discourses within this ideology include prescriptions and proscriptions on gendered behaviour, ethnic relations (eg, social disapproval of mixed marriages), age, masculinities and femininities. Overall, an amalgam of discourses combine to create a dominant representation of what a family should be like. This representation changes over time, but nonetheless is presented as something universal. For the past few decades this ideal has been of a young, married, heterosexual, white, middle-class couple with two children—a boy (older) and a girl, all of whom live together in their own house. The husband is the main breadwinner and the wife is a full-time housewife/mother who may, however, work part-time. The assumption of this ideal family's normality has influenced, and continues to influence, social policy and the ways in which laws are formulated and implemented for the population overall ... (1993 pp 2–3)[2]

One of the themes of this book, then, is that there are close and necessary connections between the way people choose to order their affective relationships, law and the organisation of the social and economic world, and that these connections are mediated through family ideology. In law, just as in business, in the popular media, and in other aspects of modern life, a particular form of 'family' is held out as ideal, even while other forms may in some circumstances be deemed 'good enough'. This is not to say that laws regulating families do not change over time or that changes in family practices do not precede legal change.

Society may be undergoing one such change now. Weeks (2002) found that the term 'family' has become an 'important rallying point' (p 218) for many self-identified non-heterosexuals.

Increasingly, the term is being deployed by many people to denote something broader than the traditional relationships based on lineage, alliance and biology, referring instead to kin-like networks of relationships based on friendship, choice and commitment. ... [U]se of the term suggests a strong perceived need to appropriate the sort of values and comforts that the family is supposed to embody. (2002 p 218)

This could mean that 'the stories many non-heterosexual men and women tell about families of choice are creating a new public space where old and new forms jostle for meaning, and where new patterns of relationships are being invented' (Weeks 2002 p 219). Sociologists tell us, in fact, that there is a wide range of 'new' relationships. These include forms of group marriage, serial monogamy, cohabitation, lesbian and gay partnerships, non co-resident intimate partnerships or living apart together, step-parenthood and lone parenthood (Carling 2002), not to mention non-conjugal homesharers and other household communities as well as long term friends (Budgeon and Roseneil 2004). How, if at all, law should account for these relationships in its definition of family is a contentious issue.

---

[2] On family ideology generally, see Dewar (1992); Collier (1995b); Havas (1995); Barrett and MacIntosh (1991).

Notwithstanding these emergent *social* meanings of family, the ideological family remains a part of 'common sense' and perhaps one of the reasons for its success is the fact that 'family' has always been notoriously difficult to define. We have seen how, not only individuals, but historians, sociologists and anthropologists have had difficulty finding a common definition of family. The diversity of their views demonstrates that all definitions are highly contingent upon social, temporal, geographic and ideological circumstances and do not bode well for law's success in the search.

Founded as it is in a liberal democratic polity, law's various definitions of family have tended to rely upon a number of foundational assumptions, and we now turn to unearthing those assumptions and their implications for families.

## III. THE LIBERAL FAMILY: QUESTIONING SOME ASSUMPTIONS

It has been said that law has moved from a definition of family based on its form, to one based upon its functions. This may be true, but still begs the question of what its appropriate functions are. We have seen Fineman's argument based upon a feminist perspective that the primary function performed by the family is the private and unsubsidised care of dependants. She is concerned to challenge that function. Veitch (1976) has suggested something similar from a liberal perspective, which is descriptive rather than critical. He stated that the characteristics of the modern family are that (1) the family functions as an autonomous economic unit; (2) it is a unit which provides emotional or psychological support and resources for its members; and (3) it is the unit which provides the best medium for the procreation and rearing of children. Fletcher (1973), also from a liberal perspective, would add that at the core of the modern family are relationships that are consciously entered into and voluntarily maintained.

This liberal, functionalist approach to defining families appears to be able to incorporate a diversity of family forms. The number or sex of the family members, for example, is not specified. It is the approach taken by the government for Census purposes (Duncan and Smith 2004), and advocated by some writers for all legal purposes (Bailey-Harris 1999; Glennon 2000; *cf* Diduck 2001a). But it is a testament to the strength of the ideology of the family that, to many who adopt a functionalist approach, the (at least symbolic) heterosexual conjugal relationship remains at the family's core.

In the liberal vision of the family, its social function is to provide a financially autonomous, physically and emotionally fulfilling enclave for its members. This idea of family rests on a few assumptions. First, it assumes a division between that which we know of as the private—the realm of the 'home'—and the public—the realm of politics and market or 'work'. The second assumption is that the need for the type of physical and emotional fulfilment obtained from the liberal family is inherent in human nature, or that we are destined 'naturally' to form private and monogamous heterosexual couples and procreate. The third assumption upon which the functionalist liberal vision of the family rests is that the family is the 'safe' place in which care and nurture dominate over competition and danger.

We will question each of these assumptions in turn.

## 1. Public and Private

This view of a private versus a public sphere of life is reflected in a number of political and social visions as well as legal rules. It emerges in the historical work discussed earlier, from Engels to Parsons to Anderson. One view of the divide is ascribed to German sociologist Ferdinand Tonnies (O'Donovan 1985 pp 4–5). Tonnies contrasted a pre-modern society characterised by social harmony in which relationships were mediated by love, duty, common understanding and purpose—Gemeinschaft—with modern commercial society characterised by individualism, competition and formality—Gesellschaft. His two ideal types of society have come to be used as metaphors for the private realm of family life and the public realm of market relations. Other writers suggest that the origins of a public/private dichotomy can be traced to Aristotle. Freeman (1985), for example, says:

> It can be traced to Aristotle. Men by nature were intended to live in a polis in which the highest good could be attained. Women, slaves and children did not and could not participate in the unfolding of goodness and reason which was the 'common heritage of co-equal participants in perfect association'. They were confined to the oikos, the household, a non-public sphere. The good at which the household aimed was a lesser good. Women, accordingly, achieved only the limited goodness of the 'naturally ruled' a goodness that was, of course, different in kind from that of the naturally ruling. (pp 166–67, endnotes omitted)

Freeman and others (eg, Rose 1987) observe how Aristotle's public/private notion became a part of the more recent liberal philosophy on which contemporary English law is based. O'Donovan describes the separation as follows:

> The idea that private and public can be distinguished is imbued in legal philosophy and informs legal policy. 'One of the central goals of nineteenth-century legal thought was to create a clear separation between constitutional, criminal, and regulatory law—public law—and the law of private transactions—torts, contracts, property and commercial law'. This division is not confined to distinguishing relations between individual and state from relations between individuals. It also draws a line dividing the law's business from what is called private. Although this boundary between the private and public shifts over time, the existence of the distinction and the notion of boundary are rarely questioned.
>
> The dichotomy between private and public as unregulated and regulated has its origins in liberal philosophy. The seventeenth-century liberal tradition as represented by Locke posits a distinction between reason and passion, knowledge and desire, mind and body. This leads to a split between the public sphere in which individuals prudently calculate their own self-interest and act upon it, and a private sphere of subjectivity and desire. As Roberto Unger describes it: 'In our public mode of being we speak the common language of reason, and live under laws of the state, the constraints of the market, and the customs of the different social bodies to which we belong. In our private incarnation, however, we are at the mercy of our own sense impressions and desires'. The liberal conception is of man as a rational creature making rational choices and entering the political sphere for his own ends.
>
> Nineteenth-century liberal thought, as expressed by John Stuart Mill, continued the tradition of the private/public split. In his feminist work On the Subjection of Women the solution for Mill was the grant to women of full equality and formal rights with men in the public sphere. From public equality, he believed, would follow a transformed family, a 'school of sympathy in equality' where the spouses live 'together in love, without power on one side or obedience on the other'. Yet he did not propose the merging of the two spheres but rather sanctioned the division of labour in which women remain in the realm of subjectivity and the

private. Thus he argued: 'When the support of the family depends, not on property but on earnings, the common arrangement, by which the wife superintends the domestic expenditure, seems to me in general the most suitable division of labour between the two persons.' Women's role was to remain that of loving and softening men in the domestic realm. Mill's views on household management overlooked the connection between economic power and dominance in the home. Economic inequality leads to an imbalance of power. The division of labour whereby one spouse works for earnings and the other for love encapsulates the public/private split. (1985 pp 8–9, references omitted)

As each of these writers implies,[3] the separation of life into a public and a private sphere has enormous repercussions for what we believe to be the state's responsibility for assisting families. As more and more types of relationships become subsumed within the private sphere of the family, the state's responsibility for supporting individuals correspondingly lessens (Diduck 2005a). The public/private separation also has political implications for claims to justice made by family members. As Philipps says:

[The public/private divide] functions ideologically to draw boundaries around what properly constitutes the subject of politics and what is considered the legitimate scope of political claims. ... These boundaries, which are shifting, serve to limit arbitrarily the reach of liberal ideals such democracy, equality, justice and liberty. Political claims based on these ideals are effectively confined to a limited public sphere created and defined by marking it off from the family or domestic sphere, and from the market. An expansion of private responsibility for human welfare will therefore tend to depoliticize women's social reproductive labour and to delegitimate any claims to equality based on this work. (2002 p 45, references omitted)

Finally, the public/private split also affects relations between members of families. It enshrines values in legal and social policy, for example, that explain the reluctance, until recently, of police officers to 'intervene' in domestic violence situations,[4] it normalises economic dependence of women upon men,[5] and it has operated to legitimate the 'objectification' of children.[6] Some theorists, however, have been concerned to question the public/private dichotomy and to test its taken-for-granted status. These writers have suggested that a split between public and private is not a naturally occurring social phenomenon but, rather, is socially constructed. It, like the idea of the family, is ideological. Nikolas Rose explains:

Analyses of the legal regulation of marriage, divorce, sexual behaviour and domestic violence are deployed to show that the ideology of individual choice and personal freedom in the private domain of home and family legitimates a refusal by public authorities to intervene into certain places, activities, relationships and feelings. Designating them as personal, private and subjective makes them appear to be outside the scope of law as a fact of nature, whereas in fact non-intervention is a socially constructed, historically variable, and inevitably political decision. The state defines as 'private' those aspects of life into which it will not intervene, then, paradoxically, uses this privacy as the justification for its non-intervention. Like *laissez faire* in the market, the idea that the family can be private in the sense of outside public regulation is a myth. The state cannot avoid intervening in the shaping of familial relations through decisions as to which type of relations to sanction and codify and which types of dispute to regulate or not regulate. (1987 pp 64–65)

---

[3] See also Fineman (2004).
[4] See ch 10.
[5] See ch 5.
[6] See ch 9.

Much has been written on the reification of a public/private divide in the area of family law,[7] including much which questions its usefulness as an analytical device (Collier 1995b pp 66–67). In fact, if we adopt Morgan's (1996) view of family as an adjective or a verb, then all manner of public engagements have 'family' aspects to them, so that laws abut employment, public transportation and political citizenship, for example, all are family matters. We do not have the space here to review the literature in its entirety, but for our purposes we wish to note the assumptions in law about the existence and the propriety of such a separation, and to question how these assumptions inform and affect laws governing families.

Thus, while many take the view that families are private units and are not the business of law unless something 'goes wrong', we, like Rose, take the view that the very definitions of what is a family or what is right or wrong for it is a legal matter. This belies the privacy rhetoric which banishes law from the 'healthy', functioning family. This liberal view of the private family is belied further, not only by law's place relative to the family, but also by the place of other public institutions such as religion and 'the market'. In conjunction with law, each influences the constitution of families in any historical time and place.

## 2. *The Private Nuclear Family as Natural*

The development of the private family and its separation from the social world are often presented as inevitable; writers such as Parsons see a split between a particular form of family and the rest of society as having evolved naturally with increasingly progressive social conditions. However, although we believe that there is a connection between social conditions and family forms, we wish to question the degree to which this version of the family can be assumed to be natural or the product of evolutionary forces.

For early anthropologists and theorists of the family the evolution of capitalist society and hence of the families which formed or were formed by that society was understood in Darwinian terms as a social manifestation of the 'survival of the fittest':

> During the second half of the 19th century, a number of social and intellectual developments—among them the evolutionary researches of Charles Darwin; the rise of 'urban problems' in fast-growing cities; and the accumulation of data on non-Western peoples by missionaries and agents of the colonial states—contributed to what most of us would now recognize as the beginnings of modern social science. Alternately excited and perplexed by changes in a rapidly industrializing world, thinkers as diverse as socialist Frederick Engels and bourgeois apologist Herbert Spencer—to say nothing of a host of mythographers, historians of religion, and even feminists—attempted to identify the distinctive problems and potentials of their contemporary society by constructing evolutionary accounts of 'how it all began'. At base a sense of 'progress' gave direction to their thoughts whether like Spencer they believed 'man' had advanced from the love of violence to a more civilized love of peace or, like Engels, that humanity had moved from primitive promiscuity and incest toward monogamy and 'individual sex-love'. (Collier, *et al.* 1982 pp 36–37)

While later theorists denied a belief in linear social progress toward one universal image of family, many (eg, Linton 1949) continued to have recourse to a belief in what was 'natural' to explain family forms and functions.

---

[7] See eg Eekelaar (2000).

As Barrett and McIntosh (1991 p 26) point out, any appeal to the 'natural' of the idea of the family serves an ideological function by giving legitimacy to the moral and socio-political claims the family is able to make:

> It is in the realm of gender, sexuality, marriage and the family that we are collectively most seduced by appeals to the natural. In this realm the shifting mores of practice are solidified, some to be sanctified and others condemned. The prevailing form of family is seen as inevitable, as naturally given and biologically determined. (p 27).

To make the claim that a certain form of the family is 'natural' gives the claimant a rhetorical advantage. He or she does not have to admit the moral or political aspects of the claim while at the same time can dismiss all opposition as 'unnatural'.

It is our position that the nuclear family's place in the social history of industrialisation, capitalism and liberal political morality is not a result of natural forces. Indeed, its link with that time period is questionable.[8] While humans have most probably always had some need to organise themselves into units which meet needs of affection, sex, safety and nurture, the shape that that unit takes is based upon more than simply 'instinct' or nature. Historians and sociologists alike suggest that there is a direct and dialectical relationship between, for example, 'family' and production, subsistence or labour, and in more modern times, 'family' and taxation policy, and 'family' and immigration, for example, but whether the relationship relies upon the 'naturalness' of this family is debatable. Historians have disagreed, for example, on the timing and causes of the emergence of the intimate, companionate family founded upon romantic love, on the transition from (or indeed existence of) an extended multi-generational family, and on the role of gender and the place of children within the family.[9]

Thus, with the exception perhaps of its place in religious discourse, the 'natural family unit' so eulogised in contemporary political rhetoric can be seen as anything but natural. Mount (1982) even questions the 'naturalness' of the 'traditional' family within the established Church, by suggesting that it has only relatively recently appropriated the 'traditional' family into its discourse.

### 3. The Family as Protection

The third unstated assumption of the liberal view of the family is that emotional, economic, physical and psychological succour are provided in this unit. We saw earlier how Tonnies' Gemeinschaft and Gesellschaft can be used as theoretical models for this view. 'The family' is assumed to be a unit which provides care and allows individual freedom to flourish, and represents the last bastion against the harshness of either individual competition, according to Tonnies, or collectivism, according to more modern theorists like Mount. Prime Minister Margaret Thatcher captured the more modern view when she proclaimed that, '[t]here is no such thing as society. There are individual men and women and there are families' (Woman's Own 1987 p 10). But as cases of child abuse are revealed[10] and as the numbers of battered women continue to outnumber places available for them in refuges,[11] more writers have come to question the idea that individuals

---

[8] See Davidoff, *et al*, (1999) and sources cited therein.
[9] See eg Gillis (1997); Davidoff, *et al*, (1999); and Diduck (2003) and sources cited therein.
[10] See ch 9.
[11] See ch 10.

are necessarily protected within the 'the family' and, accordingly, they argue that it should not be immune from intervention. Freeman, for example, writes:

> [I]f women and children are dependents, all that non-intervention achieves is protection of the dominance of men against women, adults against children. When Goldstein, Freud and Solnit tell us that a policy of minimum coercive intervention by the state accords with their 'firm belief as citizens in individual freedom and human dignity' we have to ask 'whose freedom?' and 'what dignity'? In a world of basic structural inequalities of which the family is a micro-cosm, individual freedom can be so exercised as to undermine not only the liberty of others but also their human dignity. Bill Jordan put the point well when he wrote that 'the case against intervention in family life often rests on the freedom of more powerful members (usually hus-bands in relation to wives and parents in relation to children) to exercise their power without restriction'. (1985 pp 168–69, references omitted)

Certainly in many families mutual respect, affection and nurture prevail. The law no longer permits physical chastisement of a wife by her husband, rape in marriage has been recognised as a crime, and, broadly speaking, the beating of children has come to be called child abuse. We shall explore later in more detail, however, the extent to which the traditional nuclear family lives up to the functional ideal assumed by law, but for our purposes now, we wish to identify the assumption as a problematic one.

## IV. WHAT IS FAMILY LAW?

Thus far we have suggested that that unit which we know of as the family is not capable of any easy definition. Who is included in the definition of 'family' may differ depend-ing upon whether what is being constructed is a sociological model, an anthropological model or an economic or legal model. Perhaps it depends upon what we want the family to represent or to do. Moreover, people in Britain currently arrange their social, eco-nomic and sexual lives in many different ways. Yet, despite this multiplicity of family forms, there is an ideology of the family which relies upon and in turn reinforces assumptions which imply that it is possible to construct a single definition of family. Those assumptions centre on the notion of separate spheres and family privacy, on the image of the family unit as a source of affection and protection, and on the belief in the inherent 'naturalness' of the traditional family form. It is, therefore, as much the ideol-ogy of the family as families themselves which sets the stage for the study of family law. As US family law scholar, Fran Olsen, states:

> the family and roles within the family are constituted by law and state intervention in the family is not an analytical concept but rather an ideological one. Family law is an arena for the ideo-logical struggle over what it means to be a mother, daughter, wife and so forth ... one of the most important questions about any legal decision is how it affects political and ideological struggles. (1992 p 209)

Family law, then, has to address crucial questions: how and in what situations do institutions of the state become involved in our choice of sexual partners, our decisions whether and with whom to have children, and the manner in which we choose to live, share our money or rear our children? In law, just as in sociology, history or anthropol-ogy, the answers to these questions often reflect a judgement about the value of the family unit in question relative to the dominant ideology of the family at any given historical moment. It is an awareness of this judgement which we wish readers to maintain throughout this book. We also wish to underline the relationship between the conditions of families and social conditions as well as that between law and social conditions. Neither families nor law can be conceptually or materially separated from the social and economic context which plays a part in shaping them.

What do these relationships and contingencies mean for the study of family law, especially if, as Katherine O'Donovan suggests, the very 'black box' we construct as 'family law' is part of the ideology of the family (1993 p 25)? They mean, first of all, that the study of 'family law' should encompass more than simply the statutes and cases which regulate relations between husband and wife or parent and child. It is also important to identify those who are not so regulated, and to try to understand reasons for the exclusions and inclusions. Secondly, regulation occurs at normative and informal levels as well as at the level of formal law. Thirdly, family law is also the law of public support, employment, personal taxation, education, immigration, international human rights, housing and crime, and finally, an understanding of the law in each of these areas may be incomplete without further understanding of the economic and social policy affecting each. It is this very broad meaning of 'family law' that we seek to bring to this enterprise, and by drawing readers' attention to these usually neglected parts of 'family law', we hope to undermine to some degree the ideology of the family which keeps the black box closed.

Let us now examine how our relationships are regulated directly by legal definition of them. Law assumes a certain place in society for something called a family, but just as did sociology and anthropology, it has difficulty in defining exactly what that entity looks like.


## V. THE LEGAL FAMILY

There is no statutory definition of family, and there is really no common law definition either. How can law, which demands certainty, cope with this lacuna? The closest thing to a legal definition is a judicial statement that a family is what the ordinary man on the street thinks it is. This reliance upon 'common sense' or popular perception (or ideology?) is illustrated in the case of *Sefton Holdings v Cairns*.[12] The Court of Appeal was called upon to determine whether the relationship between two women who lived as sisters for 45 years was a family relationship for the purposes of the Rent Act 1977. Lloyd LJ said:

> The question is whether the defendant, Miss Florence Cairns, is entitled to protection under the Rent Acts, that is to say, whether she is a statutory tenant under s 2 of the Rent Act 1977. The answer depends on the meaning to be given to the word 'family' in para 7 of Part I of Sch1 to that Act.
>
> The facts are that the plaintiffs, Sefton Holdings Ltd, are the landlords of the premises in question. They let it to Mr Richard Gamble some time between 1939 and 1941 when the house was built. Mr Gamble died in 1965. His daughter, Ada, then succeeded to the tenancy. Miss Ada Gamble died in 1986. The defendant came to live with Mr and Mrs Gamble and their daughter Ada in 1941. She was then 23 and single. Both her parents had died. Her boyfriend

12 [1988] 2 FLR 109.

had just been killed in the war. Miss Ada Gamble asked her parents if they would take the defendant in, which they did. They treated her as their own daughter. She called them 'Mom and Pop'. She has lived in the same house ever since. She is now some 70 years of age.

On 6 June 1986, shortly after Miss Ada Gamble died, the plaintiffs served on the defendant a notice to quit. The defendant claims that she is entitled to remain on in the house as a statutory tenant under para 7 of Part I of the first schedule, which provides as follows:

[The court went on to quote the section which states that a statutory tenancy passes automatically on the death of the first tenant to a member of that tenant's family who was residing with him or her at the time of death.]

... So what we have to decide in this case is whether the defendant is a member of her family who was residing with her at the time of, and for the period of 6 months immediately before, her death. The defendant was clearly residing with Miss Ada Gamble at the time of Miss Ada Gamble's death. But was she a member of Miss Ada Gamble's family? That is the question. The county court judge has decided that she was, and there is now an appeal to this court.

... It has been held over and over again that, in deciding whether a person is a member of another person's family, we must give the word 'family' its ordinary, everyday meaning. We cannot extend that meaning in order to cover what might appear to be a hard case; we must not let affection press upon judgment ... . (pp 109–10)

Various attempts have been made by the courts from time to time to define the word 'family', by identifying various categories within which a person would be a member of another person's family. But Lord Diplock did not embark on that task in *Joram Developments Ltd v Sharratt*, and I do not propose to embark on that task myself. All I would say is that, in approaching this case, I have found it useful to bear two matters in mind. First, there is the distinction drawn by Viscount Dilhorne *in Joram Developments Ltd v Sharratt* ... between being a member of a family and being a member of the household. Secondly, there is the distinction between being a member of the family and living as a member of the family. There is no doubt that the defendant lived as a member of the family, and that may be why the judge decided this case in her favour. But the question we have to ask ourselves is not whether she lived as a member of the family, but whether she was a member of the family. I am clear that she was not, and that the man in the street would take the same view. (p 112)

Sir Roualeyn Cumming-Bruce agreed.

With some feeling of regret, I agree.

I have been aided by the guidance given by Lord Dilhorne in the speech to which Lloyd LJ has referred. It seems to me clear beyond a peradventure that the plaintiff in this case became a member of the household of Mr and Mrs Gamble and, in spite of her age of 23, was offered and accepted a high degree of kindness and support which led the judge to make the finding that she reminded herself that in 1941 young women of 23 did not by and large live in the independent way that so many young women do today. Mr and Mrs Gamble were giving her a home and they took her in as a daughter, and in every way treated her as such.

Like Lloyd LJ, it is with diffidence that I am moved to differ from the view of a county court judge familiar with the local circumstances of the Liverpool environment; but the question is a question of law, although, like all questions of law, it involves a nice appreciation of the relevant factors. Through the now mounting line of cases which deal with the meaning of the word 'family' in the context of the relevant schedule it is to be observed that in no case has the court found it possible to identify the necessary ingredient or quality that distinguishes a familial nexus from a nexus less than familial. The approach of the courts has been to look at all the circumstances and to then seek to answer the question: 'What would an ordinary person characterize the relationship as?' For the reasons explained by Lord Dilhorne, I do not myself think that, putting the test in that way (accepting that it has been so frequently), it really adds very much to the question: 'What is the ordinary meaning of someone being a member of somebody else's family?' To be a member of a family is *different* from being treated as a member of the family ... (p 112)

The court here recognises that circumstances in 1941 may have been different from those in 1987 and also recognises that 'the local circumstances of the Liverpool environment' may have been relevant to the County Court judge who first heard the case. An awareness of these specificities is important in formulating definitions of a concept like 'family' which is so dependent upon social understandings, and yet the court then goes on to say that those specificities must be put aside to determine 'questions of law'. It is possible to criticise this decision on the basis of the court's formal and positivistic separation of law from social conditions, especially as the court then purports to answer the 'legal' question by reference to 'all the circumstances' and 'what an ordinary person would characterise the relationship as'.

> **Q** In your view, could the court have legitimately found that Mrs Cairns was a member of Miss Gamble's family? What about Mr Michalak, who came from Poland and lived with Mr Lul from 1985 to Mr Lul's death in 1998. The judge found that Mr Michalak subsisted on Mr Lul's good graces towards him. They were distantly related, and Mr Michalak addressed Mr Lul by a Polish word which translated to 'Uncle'. M cooked some meals for L, did some of his shopping, and gave him a helping hand with his washing, particularly towards the end of his life when he was incontinent from time to time. The court found that while M was helping to care for L, he was not a full-time carer. It found there was no emotional bond, that theirs was in no sense a loving or caring relationship. Rather, M merely had a relationship of respect for the older man and therefore could not be said to be a part of Mr Lul's family so as to entitle him to remain in the flat on Mr Lul's death. (See *Michalak v LB Wandsworth* [2002] 4 All ER 1136 CA). Do you agree? How would you characterise their relationship?

O'Donovan reviews the *Sefton Holdings* decision and others in which courts have attempted to identify family for different purposes, and finds that 'law privileges certain forms [of family] and denies recognition and benefits to others, while simultaneously denying that a coherent definition of family exists' (1993 p 39). Let us critically analyse this statement by examining some of the cases. First, let us contrast two cases in which same-sex conjugal relationships were at issue.

In *Harrogate Borough Council v Simpson*[13] the court had to decide whether the defendant, who had lived in a lesbian relationship, was entitled to remain in a council house after her partner, the tenant, had died. The court considered the Housing Act 1980 which provided that a secure tenancy vested in a member of the tenant's family on the death of the tenant, and included as family those who lived together as husband and wife. The question was whether the two women, for this purpose, qualified as 'family'. The court below answered no. Counsel for the Respondent argued that cohabitation had become acceptable in society and that, save for the bearing of children, the relationship between the women was characterised by the same factors as heterosexual cohabitation: family values, monogamy and permanence. Watkins LJ said:

[13] [1986] 2 FLR 91 (CA).

That the views of the public have changed with regard to the association of man and woman is to be derived from the judgments in *Dyson Holdings Ltd v Fox* [1976] QB 503. In that case the defendant had lived with the tenant of the house as if she were his wife for 21 years until his death in 1961. They had never married. They had no children. After his death the defendant continued to live in the house, for which she paid rent as if she were his widow. Proceedings were brought to evict her. It was held that the owners of the house were entitled to recover possession of it. On appeal it was held that the question whether the defendant was a member of the tenant's family was to be answered according to the understanding of the ordinary man, using the word 'family' in its popular sense, as at the time of the tenant's death in 1961.

In his judgment Bridge LJ said at page 512G:

It is clear, however, that *Gammans v Ekins*, following *Brock v Wollams* [1949] 2 KB 388, proceeded on the basis that the question who is a 'member of the tenant's family' is to be answered according to the understanding of the ordinary man, and this test has been consistently applied in all the other cases decided on this provision. Now, it is, I think, not putting it too high to say between 1950 and 1975 there has been a complete revolution in society's attitude to unmarried partnerships ... . The ordinary man in 1975 would, in my opinion, certainly say that the parties to such a union, provided it had the appropriate degree of apparent permanence and stability, were members of a single family whether they had children or not ... .

... Counsel for the plaintiffs contends that, if Parliament had wished homosexual relationships to be brought into the realm of the lawfully recognized state of a living together of man and wife for the purpose of the relevant legislation, it would plainly have so stated in that legislation, and it has not done so. I am bound to say that I entirely agree with that. I am also firmly of the view that it would be surprising to the extreme to learn that public opinion is such today that it would recognize a homosexual union as being akin to a state of living as husband and wife. The ordinary man and woman, neither of 1975 nor in 1984, would in my opinion not think even remotely of there being a true resemblance between those two very different states of affairs. That is enough, I think, to dispose of this appeal, which, for the reasons I have provided, I would unhesitatingly dismiss. (pp 94–95)

In this case the court refers to two previous cases of heterosexual cohabitation. Between the time of *Gammans v Ekins*, decided in 1950, and *Dyson Holdings v Fox*, decided in 1976, the view of the 'ordinary man' was said to have changed so as to come to accept unmarried heterosexual cohabitants as a family.

**Q** Do you think that the court could have accepted the position argued by counsel for the Respondent and adopted the same position with respect to same-sex cohabitants?

**Q** Who is the 'ordinary person' to whom the court looked?

The second case is *Fitzpatrick v Sterling Housing Association Ltd.*[14] In this case, F lived for 18 years with T in a 'longstanding, close, loving and faithful, monogamous, homosexual relationship'.[15] When T, the tenant, died, F sought to remain in the flat, either as T's surviving spouse or as a surviving member of his family. The Court was unanimous that for the purposes of the Rent Act 1977 he did not qualify as a surviving

[14] [2001] 1 AC 27.
[15] P 47.

spouse, but the majority found that he was member of T's family. Like the courts before them, they dealt with the issue as a matter of the interpretation of words.

> This expression [family] is not a term of art; that is, it is not a technical term with a specific meaning. It is a word in ordinary usage, with a flexible meaning. The statutory succession provisions have been amended several times, but to this day family has remained unamended, undefined and unparticularised. Parliament has left it to the courts to determine, in any given case, whether a particular individual falls within the description. (p 41)

>   I must also mention the 'ordinary person' test enunciated by Cohen LJ in *Brock v Wollams* [1949] 2 KB 388, 395. He suggested that the trial judge should ask himself this question: would an ordinary person, addressing his mind to the question whether the defendant was a member of the family, have answered 'Yes' or 'No'? This oft-quoted test has tended to bedevil this area of the law. It may be useful as a reminder that family is not a term of art. But the test gives uncertain guidance when, as here, the members of the Court of Appeal and also your Lordships are divided on how the question should be answered. Contrary to what seems implicit in this form of question, the expression family does not have a single, readily recognisable meaning. As I have emphasised, the meaning of family depends upon the context in which it is being used. The suggested question does not assist in identifying the essential ingredients of the concept of family in the present context.

>   The concept of the family has undergone significant development during recent years, both in the United Kingdom and overseas. Whether that is a matter for concern or congratulation is of no relevance to the present case, but it is properly part of the judicial function to endeavour to reflect an understanding of such changes in the reality of social life. Social groupings have come to take a number of different forms. The form of the single parent family has been long recognised. A more open acceptance of differences in sexuality allows a greater recognition of the possibility of domestic groupings of partners of the same sex. The formal bond of marriage is now far from being a significant criterion for the existence of a family unit. While it remains as a particular formalisation of the relationship between heterosexual couples, family units may now be recognised to exist both where the principal members are in a heterosexual relationship and where they are in a homosexual or lesbian relationship. (pp 51–52)

**Q** Do you agree with the way the court explained the ordinary person test?

The next issue was what the essential elements of family were.

> The problem in the present case is to determine what, short of blood or marriage, may evidence the common bond in a partnership of two adult persons which may entitle the one to be in the common judgment of society a member of the other's family. It seems to me that essentially the bond must be one of love and affection, not of a casual or transitory nature, but in a relationship which is permanent or at least intended to be so. As a result of that personal attachment to each other, other characteristics will follow, such as a readiness to support each other emotionally and financially, to care for and look after the other in times of need, and to provide a companionship in which mutual interests and activities can be shared and enjoyed together. It would be difficult to establish such a bond unless the couple were living together in the same house. It would also be difficult to establish it without an active sexual relationship between them or at least the potentiality of such a relationship. If they have or are caring for children whom they regard as their own they would make the family designation more immediately obvious, but the existence of children is not a necessary element. Each case will require to depend eventually upon its own facts. (p 51)

And

The hallmarks of the relationship were essentially that there should be a degree of mutual interdependence, of the sharing of lives, of caring and love, of commitment and support.

And finally,

Where sexual partners are involved, whether heterosexual or homosexual, there is scope for the intimate mutual love and affection and long-term commitment that typically characterise the relationship of husband and wife. This love and affection and commitment can exist in same sex relationships as in heterosexual relationships. In sexual terms a homosexual relationship is different from a heterosexual relationship, but I am unable to see that the difference is material for present purposes. As already emphasised, the concept underlying membership of a family for present purposes is the sharing of lives together in a single family unit living in one house.

(p 44)

> **Q** Can you list the factors required to found a legal family? Why do you suppose conjugality has such central importance? What, in your view are the essential characteristics of the legal family? On this see B Cossman and B Ryder (2001) 'What is Marriage Like? The Irrelevance of Conjugality' 18 Can J Family Law 269.

It seems, then, that law's attempts to define the family now follow a functional approach, but they remain within an ideal in which conjugality and the privatisation of care and dependency are central. In this way, law's model is still the private, heterosexual, traditional family. While the range of people who may be allowed into it may have increased, the norms by which they must live remain the same (Diduck 2001a). Indeed it is ironic that at the same time as policy seems increasingly to be moving away from the view that marriage should be the only state sanctioned intimate relationship, the test for others is the degree to which they are 'marriage-like' (Cossman and Ryder 2001). Law's normative vision of 'the family', with marriage as the benchmark, is reproduced each time a court is called upon to decide whether a particular living arrangement is 'familial' or not, but this vision is said to be that of the 'ordinary public' rather than that of the court. It is also reproduced when courts decide matters which appear to be peripheral to defining 'family'. For example, what vision of family is reproduced in this decision which appeared to be about the living arrangements of a child?

I shall take a great deal of convincing that it is right that an adult male should be permanently unemployed in order to look after one small boy.[16]

> **Q** In the light of all of these cases, consider O'Donovan's assertion regarding law's outward denial that a definition of family is possible. Construct arguments for and against her position.

The concept of family is also important in EU law and the law of the European Convention on Human Rights (ECHR), which has direct effect on domestic law. Salford (2002) examined the case law of the European Court of Justice (ECJ) and the European Court of Human Rights (ECtHR) and found that for both, although less so for the ECtHR, the definition of family or of family life, respect for which is protected under Article 8 ECHR, 'is premised on the traditional and increasingly exclusive notion of the legally married, nuclear and economically functional model'. (p 411)

---

[16] *B v B (Custody of Children)* [1985] FLR 166, 174. The Court of Appeal here was quoting the trial court, and in fact, overturned the trial court's decision by awarding care and control of the child to the father.

The definition of 'family' under EU law was established initially in the 1960s under secondary legislation regulating the free movement of persons within the Union. It arose primarily out of a desire to promote and facilitate the mobility of migrant workers which necessitated extending a right of residence and other valuable social rights to members of their family who would be accompanying them. As such, Regulation 1612/68, which ensures equality of status to migrant workers in their access to and conditions of employment, defines family (in Article 10) to include the worker's '... spouse and their descendants who are under the age of 21 or who are dependants as well as dependant relatives in the ascending line of the worker and his spouse.' The threshold of family life under this regulation is, therefore, firmly set at legal marriage or, in the case of children, a biological link or relationship of dependency with the migrant worker. Furthermore, it is both limited to and restricted by the exercise of free movement.

(pp 412–13, references omitted)

This means that EU law is ambiguous about divorced partners remaining 'family' (pp 414–17); it does not construct cohabitants as family;[17] and social parents of a child are not included as that child's family.

The European Court of Human Rights takes a slightly different approach.

The Strasbourg institutions, for their part, although still limited in their interpretation of 'family' for the purposes of Article 8 ECHR[18] (in that they too favour the legally married, heterosexual union), have gone some way towards acknowledging modern patterns of family life. For instance, they apply what is commonly referred to as the 'reality test' whereby de facto family relationships are taken into account when considering whether or not 'family life' exists. In other words, the Court and Commission draw a distinction between family *relationships* and family *life*, acknowledging that one is not necessarily synonymous with the other to trigger the protection of Article 8. Instead, they assess the reality of the ties between the family members as well as evidence of close personal links such as a relationship of emotional (as opposed to merely economic) dependency between the parties. This contrasts with the ECJ's more formulaic approach whereby the existence of genuine family *life* is irrelevant for the purposes of activating family rights under the free movement provisions.

(Salford 2002 p 413, emphasis in original)

This means that Human Rights law protects the right to family life of divorced parties with children,[19] of unmarried cohabitants with children,[20] and even of unmarried parties with children who have never cohabited,[21] but as yet the ECtHR has not recognized the family life of same sex cohabiting parties with each other.[22] It also agrees that pro-

---

[17] *Netherlands State v Reed* [1987] 2 CMLR 1086 (ECJ); *KB v National Health Service Pensions Agency* [2004] 1 CMLR 28 (ECJ).
[18] Article 8 of the European Convention on Human Rights, now incorporated into the Human Rights Act 1998, states:

1. Everyone has the right to respect for his private and family life, his home and his correspondence.
2. There shall be no interference by a public authority with the exercise of this right except such as is in accordance with the law and as is necessary in a democratic society in the interests of national security, public safety or the economic well-being of the country, for the prevention of disorder or crime, for the protection of health or morals, or for the protection of the rights and freedoms of others.

[19] *Berrehab and Koster v The Netherlands* (1989) 11 EHRR 322.
[20] *Keegan v Ireland* (1994) 18 EHRR 342.
[21] *Boughanemi v France* (1996) 22 EHRR 228.
[22] Although protection might fall under the applicant's 'private life' *Mata Estevez v Spain* (Appn No 00056501/00 Decision 10 May 2001). See also *Salgueiro da Silva Mouta v Portugal* (Appn no 33290/96 Decision 21 December 1999) where the court found a gay father's relationship with his children constituted 'family life' under Article 8.

tection of the 'traditional family' is within a State's margin of appreciation.[23] The Court of Appeal in England, however, has said that the family life of same-sex cohabitants must be provided the same protection as that of opposite-sex cohabitants, and therefore Article 14 prohibits discrimination against them.[24] Neuberger LJ in the majority found that while Convention law does not clearly say this, the fact that it was within a state's margin of appreciation allowed him to include these relationships, while Sedley LJ found that while there were two views, one being inclusion within the margin of appreciation, the better view was that Convention law prohibits discrimination against same-sex couples.

The incorporation of human rights into domestic law has thus had a profound effect upon the law's definition and treatment of families. It has meant that many relationships that previously remained outside the scope of direct legal regulation or protection are now included and therefore has forced the concept of the family to change in accordance with human rights principles. In *Ghaidan v Mendoza*[25]the House of Lords utilised Section 3 HRA to read provisions of the Rent Act compatibly with the Human Rights Act 1998. Lord Nicholls sets out the issue:

4. … Paragraphs 2 and 3 of Schedule 1 to the Rent Act 1977 provide:
2(1) The surviving spouse (if any) of the original tenant, if residing in the dwelling-house immediately before the death of the original tenant, shall after the death be the statutory tenant if and so long as he or she occupies the dwelling-house as his or her residence.
(2) For the purposes of this paragraph, a person who was living with the original tenant as his or her wife or husband shall be treated as the spouse of the original tenant.
3(1) Where paragraph 2 above does not apply, but a person who was a member of the original tenant's family was residing with him in the dwelling-house at the time of and for the period of 2 years immediately before his death then, after his death, that person or if there is more than one such person such one of them as may be decided by agreement, or in default of agreement by the county court, shall be entitled to an assured tenancy of the dwelling-house by succession.
5. On an ordinary reading of this language paragraph 2(2) draws a distinction between the position of a heterosexual couple living together in a house as husband and wife and a homosexual couple living together in a house. The survivor of a heterosexual couple may become a statutory tenant by succession, the survivor of a homosexual couple cannot. That was decided in *Fitzpatrick's* case. The survivor of a homosexual couple may, in competition with other members of the original tenant's 'family', become entitled to an assured tenancy under paragraph 3. But even if he does, as in the present case, this is less advantageous. Notably, so far as the present case is concerned, the rent payable under an assured tenancy is the contractual or market rent, which may be more than the fair rent payable under a statutory tenancy, and an assured tenant may be evicted for non-payment of rent without the court needing to be satisfied, as is essential in the case of a statutory tenancy, that it is reasonable to make a possession order. In these and some other respects the succession rights granted by the statute to the survivor of a homosexual couple in respect of the house where he or she is living are less favourable than the succession rights granted to the survivor of a heterosexual couple.

[23] *Mata Estevez v Spain* (above). In *Karner v Austria* (2004) 38 EHRR 24 the court held that protection of the 'traditional family' is a weighty and legitimate reason to justify a difference in treatment under Article 14's protection from discrimination, but that it was a matter of proportionality. In this case, excluding the surviving member of a same sex relationship from a tenancy was disproportionate to the goal.
[24] *Secretary of State for Work and Pensions v M* [2005] 1 FLR 498; [2004] EWCA Civ 1343. At the time of writing, this case was on appeal to the House of Lords.
[25] [2004] 3 All ER 411; [2004] UKHL 30.

Baroness Hale's words capture the spirit of the majority:

> 142. Homosexual couples can have exactly the same sort of inter-dependent couple relationship as heterosexuals can. Sexual 'orientation' defines the sort of person with whom one wishes to have sexual relations. It requires another person to express itself. Some people, whether hetero-sexual or homosexual, may be satisfied with casual or transient relationships. But most human beings eventually want more than that. They want love. And with love they often want not only the warmth but also the sense of belonging to one another which is the essence of being a couple. And many couples also come to want the stability and permanence which go with sharing a home and a life together, with or without the children who for many people go to make a family. In this, people of homosexual orientation are no different from people of heterosexual orientation.
>
> 143. It follows that a homosexual couple whose relationship is marriage-like in the same ways that an unmarried heterosexual couple's relationship is marriage-like are indeed in an analogous situation. Any difference in treatment is based upon their sexual orientation. It requires an objective justification if it is to comply with article 14. Whatever the scope for a 'discretionary area of judgment' in these cases may be, there has to be a legitimate aim before a difference in treatment can be justified. But what could be the legitimate aim of singling out hetero-sexual couples for more favourable treatment than homosexual couples? It cannot be the *protection* of the traditional family. The traditional family is not protected by granting it a benefit which is denied to people who cannot or will not become a traditional family. What is really meant by the 'protection' of the traditional family is the *encouragement* of people to form traditional families and the *discouragement* of people from forming others. There are many reasons why it might be legitimate to encourage people to marry and to discourage them from living together without marrying. These reasons might have justified the Act in stopping short at marriage. Once it went beyond marriage to unmarried relationships, the aim would have to be encouraging one sort of unmarried relationship and discouraging another. The Act does distinguish between unmarried but marriage-like relationships and more transient liaisons. It is easy to see how that might pursue a legitimate aim and easier still to see how it might justify singling out the survivor for preferential succession rights. But, as Buxton LJ [2003] Ch 380, 391, para 21, pointed out, it is difficult to see how hetero-sexuals will be encouraged to form and maintain such marriage-like relationships by the knowledge that the equivalent benefit is being denied to homosexuals. The distinction between hetero-sexual and homosexual couples might be aimed at discouraging homosexual relationships generally. But that cannot now be regarded as a legitimate aim. It is inconsistent with the right to respect for private life accorded to 'everyone', including homosexuals, by article 8 since *Dudgeon v United Kingdom* (1981) 4 EHRR 149. If it is not legitimate to discourage homosexual relationships, it cannot be legitimate to discourage stable, committed, marriage-like homosexual relationships of the sort which qualify the survivor to succeed to the home. Society wants its intimate relationships, particularly but not only if there are children involved, to be stable, responsible and secure. It is the transient, irresponsible and insecure relationships which cause us so much concern.

The result of this decision was that the Rent Act provision was read as if it said '*as if they were his or wife or husband*'.[26]

This case has been influential in the way the family is defined in English law. In addition, it shows that the *culture* of human rights has influenced family law in more subtle ways and become a part of the 'rules', outside what appears as traditional family law,

---

[26] See also *Nutting v Southern Housing Group Ltd* EWHC 2982 (Ch); [2005] 1 FLR 1066 in which Evans-Lombe, J held that to find that cohabitants in this case of the same sex, qualified as 'spouses' for the purposes of the Housing Act 1988's provisions for succession to tenancies, the important factors were whether the relationship was an 'emotional one of lifetime commitment' (para 9) that was 'openly and unequivocally displayed as such to the outside world' (para 17).

which inform and constitute our familial lives. Criminal laws, for example, regulating male homosexual conduct and social and cultural norms concerning the way in which men and women are supposed to behave sexually tell us that some familial groups are preferred to others. The 'pretended family' of the Local Government Act[27] was a good example, as are provisions of education legislation relating to sex education and 'family life' (Cooper and Herman 1991). At the same time, though, legal language describing 'the family' is framed in terms of public opinion and individual choice. According to this language, we choose to marry or not to marry, to live alone or to live with a partner or to have children or not.

## VI. HOW FREE IS OUR 'FREEDOM' TO CHOOSE HOW TO ORDER OUR FAMILIAL LIVES?

Just as the state, often through law, encourages or discourages certain relationships by reference to family ideology, reproduction within those relationships is mediated by that ideology as well. Children have a central role in the ideology of the family. Sometimes the context in which reproductive decisions are made is an aggressive and obvious state policy like China's one child policy, and sometimes it is only indirectly related to reproduction. The Civil Partnership Act 2004, for example,[28] creates a new legal status for same sex partners who wish to register their partnership. It also allows them to acquire responsibilities for their registered civil partner's children, which can be seen as promoting the welfare of children, but also as promoting the economic interests of society.

> When the social responsibilities of the welfare state are being peeled away, lesbian and gay men are voluntarily offering to take on the responsibilities of other men, women and children. The state interest in conscripting lesbians and gay men, along with the more usual targets of divorced fathers into the taking on the costs of family support has long been clear.
>
> (Adam 2004)

At still other times, the social/legal context is less obviously related to a population or family policy. Gillian Douglas (1991) notes that a state can be described as anti-natalist, such as contemporary China, where overpopulation is perceived as a problem, or it can be pro-natalist, as many western European states have been in the past. Sometimes a pro-natalist policy is eugenic in nature, when it seeks to increase only certain segments of its population. Examples are Britain in the late nineteenth and early twentieth centuries and Nazi Germany in the 1930s and 1940s. As we observed earlier, the reasons that

---

[27] S 28(1) of the Local Government Act 1988 provided:

(1) A local authority shall not—
   (a) intentionally promote homosexuality or publish material with the intention of promoting homosexuality;
   (b) promote the teaching in any maintained school of the acceptability of homosexuality as a pretended family relationship;

This provision was repealed in 2003 by the Local Government Act (2003 c.26), Sch 8(1) Para 1. See further Cooper and Herman (1991); Thomas and Costigan (1990).

[28] See ch 2.

a state might be interested in regulating its population and the units in which that population lives are manifold, and include the fact that rises and falls in population rates and the burden of public and private economic responsibilities have enormous social and economic implications. They also affect the age and size of the population which in turn affects public spending on health, social security and pensions. They also affect education policy and the composition of the labour force. The United Kingdom after World War II, for example, adopted a strong pro-natalist stance with cultural messages and financial rewards encouraging procreation within the traditional nuclear family.

Economic, cultural and social mechanisms which a state may adopt to influence the forms its families take include some of the following (see Douglas, 1991 pp 2–13):[29]

1. Regulation of who, if anyone, has access to medical/technological procedures which control reproduction. For example, a state could render criminal the provision of birth control devices or abortion as part of a pro-natalist stance. Romania in the 1980s under the Ceaucescu regime is an example of this position. Alternatively, a state could selectively enforce such criminal provisions, with the effect of demonstrating a pro-natalist stance for some segments of the population only. Nazi Germany is an example of a state with this policy, and it has been argued that a more contemporary example can be found in the United States, where the feminist demand for women's 'reproductive freedom' means for some, usually white, middle class women, freedom to choose abortion, and for others, usually poor, often African American women, freedom from forced sterilisation or coerced abortion. Related to this policy is also the question of what the state does about infertility. A state's policy on population and family may be determined by examining to whom reproductive treatments are offered and how they are regulated (Langdridge and Blyth 2001). In England and Wales, the Human Fertilisation and Embryology Act 1990 does not provide strict rules regulating decisions regarding eligibility for fertility treatment, preferring to leave such decisions to clinics and medical professional guidelines. The Act does, however, provide that all decisions about treatment must take the welfare of any potential child into account, including the need of a child for a father.[30] This legislative provision clearly promotes one view of family over others in the context of availability of medical treatment.[31]

2. In a society where marriage is revered morally, encouraged socially and privileged legally, the minimum age of legal marriage demonstrates the degree to which the state wishes to encourage people to enter into this privileged form of relationship. It also has a profound effect on the rate of population growth. Although more and more unmarried women are having babies, state policy concerning procreation is reflected in the age at which it approves the formation of a heterosexual relationship through marriage. The age of legal marriage in China, for example, is 20 for women and 22 for men, reflecting China's anti-natalist policy. In England and Wales the minimum age at which men and women can marry is 16, but between the ages of 16 and 18 parental or court permission is required.[32]

---

[29] See ch 3.
[30] Human Fertilisation and Embryology Act 1990, ss 13(5). This section is currently under review. See HFEA 2005.
[31] See ch 3.
[32] See ch 2. Marriage Act 1949, s 3, as amended by Sch 12, para 5 of the Children Act 1989.

3. The state can provide either financial incentives or penalties for a person to have children. The most obvious incentive is some form of family allowance or child benefit provision. Indirect financial reward in the form of tax breaks for children or child care is also an indication of a state's population and family policy, as is the provision of child care and universal free education. England and Wales makes moderate provision only in this category. A small but universal child benefit is paid to carers, a child tax credit is paid to some parents, education is only mandatory until age 16, and only begins at age 5. Child care before the age of 5 is not universally provided by the state, and the state neither requires nor encourages employers to provide either child care or paid time off from work for nursing sick children, visits to schools, or any of the responsibilities that flow from rearing children. It does provide, however, that parents who have completed one year's service with their employers can take up 13 weeks unpaid parental leave to care for their child under the age of 5 and are entitled to take a reasonable amount of time, unpaid, to deal with an emergency situation involving a dependant. Further, up to 2 weeks of paid (at 90% of his average weekly earnings) paternity leave is provided for new fathers and 26 weeks paid (at 90% of her average weekly wage) maternity leave is available for new mothers and for a new parent (either mother or father) on the placement of a child for adoption (adoption leave). Both maternity leave and adoption leave can be extended a further 26 (unpaid) weeks. The government has announced plans to increase paid maternity leave, first to nine months from April 2007 and later, possibly by 2010, to one year. It also will explore the possibility of allowing mothers and fathers to split this time between them.[33] Finally, the law allows for parents of young or disabled children to request flexible working and employers are under a duty to consider the request seriously. While some of these provisions appear to compare favourably with other jurisdictions, the differences in maternity leave and paternity leave do say something about what is considered to be the appropriate division of labour in the family.

4. Cultural factors can influence us in our decision to have children. Frequent vilification in the press of single mothers means that parenthood as a status for women who live without male partners is discouraged. On the other hand, the cultural status of (married) parenthood appears to be high in the UK now. It is interesting to note as well that cultural messages to have children or not to have children tend to be directed at women only, as though men are not involved at all in the process![34]

5. The degree to which a society can be characterised as patriarchal influences population rates as well. In general, there is a correlation between large families and male dominance over women and between small families and societies where women are more economically independent and are more equal decision-makers in society (United Nations, 1996).

**Q** Can you think of any other influences within law or social or popular culture which may have an effect on our decisions how to order our familial lives?

---

[33] 'Blair Puts Focus on Family Friendly Reforms', *The Guardian*, 28 February 2005.
[34] See chs 3 and 4.

## VII.  CONCLUSION

Let us now return to the statement we made at the beginning of this chapter: that attempts in English law to define family revolve around the basic theme of the hetero-sexual conjugal family. Other family forms may be admitted into the family category depending upon the degree to which they appear to be 'marriage-like'.

> **Q** Given the important legal and social consequences of attracting the family label, do you think that law has gone far enough to accommodate new families and new relationships?

In the next chapter we examine English law's almost paradoxical relationship with mar-riage. Marriage is both central and peripheral to family law but arguably remains at the heart of family ideology.

## FURTHER READING AND SELECTED RECENT REFERENCES

BD ADAM, 'Care, Intimacy and Same-sex Partnership in the 21st Century' (2004) 52 *Current Sociology* 265.

U BECK and E BECK-GERNSHEIM, *The Normal Chaos of Love* (Cambridge, Polity, 1995)

——, *Individualization* (London, Sage, 2002).

S BUDGEON and S ROSENEIL, 'Editors' Introduction: Beyond the Conventional Family' (2004) 52 *Current Sociology* 127.

A CARLING, 'Family Policy, Social Theory and the State' in A Carling, S Duncan and R Edwards, (eds), *Analysing Families: Morality and Rationality in Policy and Practice* (London, Routledge, 2002).

B COSSMAN and B RYDER, 'What is Marriage-like Like? The Irrelevance of Conjugality' (2001) 18 *Canadian Journal of Family Law* 269.

L DAVIDOFF, M DOOLITTLE, J FINK and K HOLDEN, *The Family Story: Blood, Contract and Intimacy, 1830–1960* (London, Longman, 1999).

A DIDUCK, *Law's Families* (Cambridge, CUP, 2003).

——, 'Shifting Familiarity' (2005) 58 *Current Legal Problems* 235.

R DINGWALL and J EEKELAAR, 'Families and the State: An Historical Perspective on the Public Regulation of Private Conduct' (1988) 10 *Law and Policy* 341.

S DUNCAN and DP SMITH, 'And then the Lover: Can We All Now Choose Individual Fulfilment?' in *Seven Ages of Man and Woman, A Look at Life in Britain in the Second Elizabethan Era* (London, ESRC, 2004).

J EEKELAAR, 'Uncovering Social Obligations: Family Law and the Responsible Citizen' in M Maclean, (ed), *Making Law For Families* (Oxford, Hart Publishing, 2000).

——, 'What is "Critical" Family Law?' (1989) 105 *LQR* 244.

MA FINEMAN, *The Autonomy Myth* (New York, NY, New Press, 2004).

L FOX-HARDING, *Family, State and Social Policy* (Basingstoke, Macmillan, 1996).

A GIDDENS, *The Transformation of Intimacy* (Cambridge, Polity, 1992).

J GILLIS, *A World of Their Own Making, A History of Myth and Ritual in Family Life* (Oxford, OUP, 1997).

V GILLIS, *Family and Intimate Relationships: A Review of the Sociological Research* (London, Families and Social Capital, ESRC Research Group, South Bank University, 2003).

J HERRING, *Family Law*, 2nd edn, (London, Longman, 2004).

DHJ MORGAN, *Family Connections* (Cambridge, Polity, 1996).

——, 'Risk and Family Practices: Accounting for Change and Fluidity in Family Life' in EB Silva and C Smart, (eds), *The New Family?* (London, Sage, 1999).

LJ NICOLSON, *Gender and History: The Limits of Social Theory in the Age of the Family* (New York, NY, CUP, 1986).

F OLSEN, 'The Politics of Family Law' (1984) 2(1) *Law and Inequality* 1.

——, 'The Myth of State Intervention in the Family' (1984–85)18 *University of Michigan J of Law Reform* 835.

MC REGAN, *Alone Together: Law and the Meanings of Marriage* (Oxford, OUP, 1999).

H SALFORD, 'Concepts of Family under EU Law—Lessons from the ECHR' (2002) 16 *Int J of Law, Policy and the Family* 410.

C SMART, B NEALE and A WADE, *The Changing Experience of Childhood: Families and Divorce* (Cambridge, Polity, 2001).

W STAFFORD, 'Ferdinand Tonnies on Gender, Women and the Family' (1995) XVI *History of Political Thought* 391.

J WEEKS, 'Elective Families: Lesbian and Gay Life Experiments' in A Carling, S Duncan and R Edwards, (eds), *Analysing Families: Morality and Rationality in Policy and Practice* (London, Routledge, 2002).

*Reports*

Advisory Group on Marriage and Relationship Support, *Moving Forward Together: A Proposed Strategy for Marriage and Relationship Support for 2002 and Beyond* (London, Lord Chancellor's Department, The Stationery Office, 2002).

Human Fertilisation and Embryology Authority, *Tomorrow's Children: A Consultation on Guidance to Licensed Fertility Clinics on Taking in Account the Welfare of Children to be Born of Assisted Conception Treatment* (London, HFEA).

Social Trends 34 2004 edn (London, The Stationery Office, 2005).

# 2

# Legal Status and Personal Relationships

Can we say that law and social pressures favour marriage above other family forms? What evidence do we have either for or against such a statement? As we saw in Chapter 1, the, at least, symbolic marital relationship remains central in social and legal ideas of the ideal family. Or perhaps, it is not for marriage *per se* that the most privilege in law is reserved, but rather it is a particular family form, albeit one which is most closely accommodated by marriage, which is favoured by law and encouraged by the state (Smart 1984). As the 'defining family' cases discussed earlier demonstrate, certain roles within relationships attract the legally beneficial 'family' label, while others do not. Parker (1990) also suggests that it is the *form* of the family unit which is important to the state and not whether that form has undergone any formal or religious ritual to legitimate it. He studied patterns of informal marriage and cohabitation in England and Wales from 1750 to 1989 and found that the state at that time appeared increasingly to be recognising unmarried cohabiting relationships as acceptable forms of family. He posits possible reasons for this:

> One can now find some reference to cohabitation in virtually every nook and cranny of law which has an impact on domestic relationships (and I am by no means confining this to 'family law') … .
>
> A common explanation … is to say that it is a response to the increase in informal marriage. Whilst the growth in cohabitation may be a necessary condition, it is not a sufficient one, however. A fuller explanation is obviously because people think that it is right that these references appear. This still leaves the difficult question of why there has been such a shift in the sense of justice to permit juridification of informal marriage in such a relatively short period of time. Why has the space opened up?
>
> In my view the answer is to be found in the changing strategy of family regulation. As marriage is displaced by family, wifedom by motherhood and the support/dependency structures of the patriarchal family assume greater importance than the legal form, it is actually counterproductive to the real purpose of social policy to exclude from regulation a family type that is so obviously here to stay. If income support is paid to a married couple at a lower rate than to two single people then the State loses money if an unmarried couple is treated as two single people. If the allocation of resources, such as public sector housing, ignores informal marriage then the State is manifestly not bolstering the private family (within which children are brought up and women are supported by men). If law-makers are forced to deny what claimants regard as their rights by relying on medieval-sounding arguments about morality then the ideology of justice which gives popular legitimacy to the legal system is severely threatened. Even those judges who have rejected a property claim through preference for individualistic principles of trust law cover themselves by saying that the answer lies with Parliament
>
> (see, for example, Fox LJ in *Burns v Burns* [1984] 1 All ER 244 at 255g). (1990 pp 148–49)

If Parker's observations were correct in 1990, it follows that we should be seeing continued legal accommodation of marriage-like relationships. After all, people are living in these types of relationships in increasing numbers. Statistics show, for example, that unmarried cohabitation between heterosexual partners more than doubled between 1986 and 2001/02: for women the rate was 28% in 2001/02 and for men it was 25% (Social Trends 2004). And in 2001, the first year such statistics were gathered by the Census, between 0.03% (in some parts of the country) and 2.67% (in other parts) of the population reported themselves as living in same-sex relationships (Duncan and Smith 2004 pp 16–17).[1] How has the law responded to these changes in our partnering behaviour? And what of other changes that some see as occurring in patterns of intimate living? Indeed, it seems that people are organising their personal relationships in increasingly diverse ways that do not include monogamous conjugality. According to some sociologists, our 'new' family forms include now (in reality, probably always have included) forms of group marriage, serial monogamy, non co-resident intimate partnerships or living apart together, non-conjugal homesharing and other household communities (Carling 2002; Budgeon and Roseneil 2004), and that all these relationships are important to people in providing intimacy, care, and companionship. They are central to people's core values but fit increasingly uneasily in the category 'family' (Budgeon and Roseneil 2004). Sociologists also tell us that our friendship practices are changing so that there may be a blurring of lines between friends and family (Roseneil and Budgeon 2004; Roseneil 2004). Rather than the romantic love relationship being the basis for care, those more fluid ones, involving the sharing of lives and intimacy, are. In this chapter we will examine Parker's thesis in the light of all these changes in our intimate living.

## I. MARRIAGE AS A SOCIAL INSTITUTION

Before we examine in more detail Parker's analysis of the changing relationship between families and the state and support for, and the law relating to, marriage-like cohabitation, let us first explore the legal and social relationship between marriage and family, for, to many, the two are inextricably linked. Marriage, despite apocalyptic analyses of the 'soaring' divorce rate and the 'death' of the family, is still a (surprisingly, some might say) popular institution. While rates for first marriages have been dropping since 1961 when it was 74.9 per 1000 for men and 83 per 1000 for women (Population Trends 118, 2004), the (provisional) rate in 2002 was still a healthy 25.8 for men and 31.0 for women over the age of 16 (Population Trends 115, 2004). The remarriage rate in 2002 was 34.4 per 1000 widowed or divorced population for men and 15.8 for women (*ibid*). The United Kingdom rate of 4.8 per 1000 population of all ages marrying is the EU average (Social Trends 33, 2004 p 32). Indeed marriage retains such an important place in contemporary consciousness that many of those who are legally excluded from it argue that their exclusion violates their basic human rights (Anderson 1997a p 176).[2]

---

[1] As Duncan and Smith (2004) p 16 note, however, these figures are likely to be a significant underestimation of the actual number of people living in same-sex relationships, as not all would have formally identified themselves as such.

[2] In Canada and the US, for example, prohibitions on same-sex marriage were successfully argued to be a violation of rights (see below), and the European Court of Human Rights accepted arguments in 2002 that the UK's refusal to recognise legally the new gender of a post-operative transsexual person violated that person's right to respect for private and family life and right to marry and found a family under Articles 8 and 12 of the European Convention on Human Rights (*I v UK* and *Goodwin v UK*, see discussion below).

How can we explain the British love affair with marriage, particularly from the point of view of women? Research from the 1970s for example, shows that marriage has different effects for men and women. It has been said to 'endow men with a better life-style, greater freedom and more power, while it has the opposite effect on women, limiting, impoverishing and rendering them vulnerable to abuses of power by their husbands' (Auchmuty 2004 p 105, citing Bernard 1973) There are also statistics which show that for women, at least, poverty is almost as likely an outcome of divorce as financial security (Weitzman 1985; Bailey and Bala 1998; Douglas and Perry 2001).

Nevertheless, it seems that, as a social institution, marriage represents an idealised rite of passage into adulthood. It marks a heterosexual couple's readiness to assume the 'normal' responsibilities of adulthood including home owning, child rearing, legitimate and exclusive sexual activity and financial independence from parents. Further, its ideological status as a desirable precondition for 'family' gives marriage a social legitimacy that other types of relationships do not have. Through a combination of these social factors, the private monogamous couple relationship becomes the model to which we aspire to demonstrate our successful transition into adulthood.

Sociologists of the family Berger and Kellner (1980) provide a comparable explanation for the appeal of marriage in contemporary society. Relying upon the work of French sociologist Emile Durkheim, they suggest that marriage offers a state in which the individual is protected from *anomie*, a state of alienation from and anxiety about what is perceived as a normless and ailing society. They accept psychological research which presents those who are married as happier, more emotionally stable and mature than their unmarried counterparts, but then they argue that the analysis must not stop there; we must look to why married people feel so happy and psychologically healthy. In answer to this question, Berger and Kellner suggest that measuring psychological states such as mental health is misleading without recognition that both one's reality and relationship to it are socially constructed. To them, the compulsion to legitimate the marital world in today's psychological terms of 'emotional stability' is part of the same process as that which was used historically to legitimate it in traditionally religious terms.

> [C]ontemporary psychology functions to sustain this precarious [marital] world by assigning to it the status of 'normalcy', a legitimating operation that increasingly links up with the older religious assignment of the status of 'sacredness' ... . Whether one legitimates one's maritally constructed reality in terms of mental health or of the sacrament of marriage is today largely left to free consumer preference. (pp 320–21)

Berger and Kellner are thus suggesting that we look behind our assumptions about the naturalness or normality of our marriage behaviour and the consequent psychological satisfaction we get from being married and therefore 'normal', to examine the process of how that behaviour *comes to be understood* as normal and therefore satisfying. In earlier times the validation process was achieved through religious discourse, while in modern times it is through the more legitimate (for us) discourses of psychology and sociology.

Gillis' social-historical study of marriage in England and Wales postulates a different explanation for the historical and continued popularity of marriage as an institution. While acknowledging the influence that laws have upon our actions, he suggests that law, at the beginning of the 20th century 'was not enough to explain the rush to marry. In earlier periods working classes had not been afraid to defy church and state so long as economic and social conditions offered viable alternatives' (1985 p 241). The new popularity of marriage in Victorian England, then, resulted from a combination of factors which reduced the number of available alternatives. Those factors included economic changes, revised attitudes toward unmarried sex and maternity, and increased Christian evangelicism, all of which made it more difficult for people to defy the dominant sexual and moral code. To Gillis however, the economic factors were the most important, particularly for women:

> the single greatest factor was the evolution of industrial capitalism which undermined the independence of the family economy and consigned to men the role of principal breadwinner and to women the destiny of dependent wife and mother. From the 1840s onward women lost their place in the economy that offered them the highest wages and the greatest independence.
> (pp 241–42)[3]

Ferdinand Mount, on the other hand, offers yet another perspective from which to view marriage. He equates families with marriage and romantic love.[4] His 1982 book is entitled *The Subversive Family* and is subtitled *An Alternative History of Love and Marriage*. He postulates that the married conjugal union is a subversive institution, one which is based on romantic love and which provides protection and freedom from an interfering Church and state. According to Mount's thesis, men and women have always freely chosen their relationships with one another based upon love, and have always formalised those relationships according to a marriage ritual. The Church and the state only latterly became interested in those relationships in order to exert control over the population, and so, to Mount, the married conjugal family is not the bedrock of church and state, but rather it subverts them. He concludes his book with the following words explaining the appeal of marriage:

> It can only be said, in the most hesitant fashion possible, that it may be because marriage still seems to be the most interesting enterprise which most of us come across. With all its tediums and horrors, it has both more variety and more continuity than any other commitment we can make … . Marriage and the family make other experiences, both pleasant and unpleasant, seem a little tame and bloodless. And it is difficult to resist the conclusion that a way of living which is both so intense and so enduring must somehow come naturally to us, that it is a part of being human. (p 256)

Part of what Mount calls the 'appeal of marriage' may be explained by marriage's link with romantic love and indeed recent research into why people choose to marry confirms this link. Hibbs, *et al*, (2001) found that 30% of their respondents cited love as their primary reason for marrying. Research also shows, however, that people marry for other reasons, including a desire to conform to parent's wishes, religious prescription and cultural norms (Eekelaar and Maclean 2004), a belief that marriage was the natural next step in the progression of their relationship (Hibbs, *et al*, 2001; Lewis 1999), and most importantly because marriage was seen to be an expression of their commitment, not only to each other (Reynolds and Mansfield 1999; Lewis 1999; Hibbs *et al* 2001; Eekelaar and Maclean 2004), but to a way of living (Reynolds and Mansfield 1999).

Alternative explanations for the continuity of marriage in western society, then, rely upon assumptions about the psychological characteristics of individuals and groups, the

---

[3] Gittins (1993) also suggests that the most powerful force inducing people to marry is economic (see ch 5), notwithstanding popular acceptance of what she calls 'the ideology' of romantic love (p 73).
[4] See also Diduck (2003) ch 2 and sources cited therein.

idea that marriage is what people do when they are 'in love', and religious doctrine, law or economic necessity. Marriage is also thought to provide stability to families and to society; it is thought to be the best context in which to rear children (Home Office 1998). Marriage as a social institution is more than the behaviour of actors reacting to either rational or irrational stimuli, however. According to O'Donovan (1993 p 57) the artifacts and ceremonies around marriage give it the status of icon or totem. According to Gillis as well, the married state required and continues to require 'powerful symbolic reinforcement to give it the stability the conjugal bond by itself [does] not provide' (1985 p 259).

According to O'Donovan:

> [M]arriage endures as symbol. The marriage order, like the legal order, is a matter of what is lived, accepted and made familiar, or family. It may be presented as private but it is reinforced everywhere in public and in political discourse. Marriage has its own rituals, children, coupledom, Saturday nights out, reunions, a familiar tradition learned and transmitted at home. It does not have to be rational, its origins are sacred, it can call on mythology, an unconscious reservoir of memories, emblems, a fictive narrative. (1993 p 57)

Despite the number and variability of explanations for why people marry, including those which rely upon the psychological, the mythical-social, the legal, the economic and historical appeals to nature, people still tend to regard marriage as the ultimate commitment one can make to make to a sexual or emotional partner. Marriage, for many, is still the ultimate goal for those wishing to *really* settle down. Is, however, the social and emotional importance attached to marriage an adequate explanation for the level of legal significance which is attached to that form of commitment? Heterosexual couples who choose not to marry tend to express similar levels of commitment and obligation to each other and to share many of the same values as those who marry (Eekelaar and Maclean 2004; Lewis 1999), yet their relationships do not attract the same legal privileges.[5] And even while government policy on the one hand confirms that marriage is a precursor to stable parenting, on the other hand it states:

> It is not for the state to decide whether people marry or stay together. There are strong and mutually supportive families and relationships outside marriage and many unmarried couples remain together throughout their children's upbringing and raise their children every bit as successfully as married parents. (Home Office 1998 p 30)

Marriage thus holds a paradoxical place in English law and policy. It is said to be both important and not important to social stability and children's welfare. The various explanations for the 'good' of marriage, however, do not explain the type of commitment law requires of people, nor do they explain legal exclusions from the categories of potential husbands and wives. It is to these matters that we now turn. If marriage is truly emotionally fulfilling, psychologically and socially stabilising, and economically advantageous for individuals and for society, why are its terms of entry so circumscribed?

[5] See below pp 63–67.

## II. MARRIAGE AS A LEGAL INSTITUTION

Legal scholar Eric Clive questioned in a provocative 1980 article whether marriage was a necessary legal concept at all. He did not comment upon marriage as a social institution, but proposed that the legal concept of marriage is a technical matter which has no real relationship to the social institution of marriage (p 71). He reviewed the relevance of marriage to criminal law, to the law of contract, tort and taxation, as well as the many laws dealing with financial provision for dependants, and concluded that the legal status of marriage added nothing to how justice was done in these areas, and in many cases it only unduly complicated matters (p 77). He agreed that personal commitments between people, or various forms of families, will undoubtedly continue to exist, but that ascribing legal status to those relationships was in most cases unnecessary, and in others unjust.

Martha Fineman has made this argument as well:

> [W]e should abolish marriage as a legal category and with it any privilege based on sexual affiliation. I want to emphasize I am addressing only the *legal* significance of marriage. There would be no special legal rules governing the relationships between husband and wife or defining the consequences of the status of marriage as now exist in family law. In fact, these categories would no longer have any legal meaning at all. Instead, the interactions of female and male sexual affiliates would be governed by the same rules that regulate other interactions in our society—specifically those of contract and property, as well as tort and criminal law. The illusive equality between adults in sexual and all other areas would thus be asserted and assumed, a result that to many will be symbolically appealing. Women and men would operate outside of the confines of marriage, transacting and interacting without the fetters of legalities they did not voluntarily choose. Of course, people would be free to engage in 'ceremonious' marriage; such an event would, however, have no *legal* (enforceable in court) consequences … . Any legal consequences would have to be the result of a separate negotiation. (1995 pp 228–29)

For many, however, Clive's and Fineman's view is unrealistic or, worse, morally wrong. There must, they would argue, be a connection between law and marriage. One of the themes of this chapter is to test Clive's and Fineman's as yet socially unacceptable position by questioning the assumed necessity for society of *legal* marriage.

We shall first examine what marriage is in law and the social and sexual assumptions on which it is based by examining the rules about entry into it.

## III. GETTING MARRIED

Given that marriage remains a popular institution for heterosexual adults who wish to live with one another, how does one go about actually legally doing it, and what does it mean for us legally once we do?

There is no statutory definition of marriage, although the Matrimonial Causes Act (MCA) 1973 defines those marriages which are void or voidable at law. A void marriage is one which is considered to be non-existent *ab initio*. There is no need for a court to render the marriage non-existent; a decree or declaration of nullity by a court is merely declaratory of the parties' status. A void marriage can be attacked by a party to it or a third party even after the death of one of the parties. A void marriage is one where the parties have undergone some form of ceremony of marriage, but there was a fundamental flaw in that ceremony. On granting a decree of nullity the court retains the jurisdiction to make financial provision orders,[6] property adjustment orders[7] and pension sharing orders[8] and a void marriage must thus be distinguished from a non-marriage, in which the parties' ceremony was nothing like a marriage,[9] in which case the court has no powers to make orders for ancillary relief. A voidable marriage is one which is valid until declared otherwise by a court of competent jurisdiction, at which time the court's decree takes retrospective effect. A voidable marriage may not be challenged after the death of one of the parties and may not be challenged by a third party.[10]

Further, there is legislation requiring certain formalities of marriage, breach of some which render a marriage void or voidable.[11]

The MCA 1973:

11. A marriage celebrated after 31 July 1971 shall be void on the following grounds only, that is to say—

(a) that it is not a valid marriage under the provisions of the Marriage Acts 1949–86 (that is to say where—
  (i) the parties are within the prohibited degrees of relationship[12];
  (ii) either party is under the age of sixteen[13]; or
  (iii) the parties have intermarried in disregard of certain requirements as to the formation of marriage)[14];
(b) that at the time of the marriage either party was already lawfully married;
(c) that the parties are not respectively male and female;
(d) in the case of a polygamous marriage entered into outside England and Wales, that either party was at the time of the marriage domiciled in England and Wales.

[6] S 23 MCA 1973.
[7] S 24 MCA 1973.
[8] S 24A MCA 1973.
[9] Contrast *Geries v Yagoub* [1997] 1 FLR 854 which was held to be void marriage because the parties had undergone a religious ceremony in a church and then held themselves out as and believed themselves to be married, with *Ghandi v Patel* [2002] 1 FLR 603 in which a Hindu ceremony in a restaurant was held to be a non-marriage. See also Probert (2002). Where there is doubt as to the validity of the ceremony or there is insufficient evidence as to its validity, a presumption of marriage may be applied and the longer the parties have cohabited assuming they were married, the stronger the presumption and clear and cogent evidence is required to displace it. See *Chief Adjudication Officer v Bath* [2000] 1 FLR 8.
[10] On the history of eligibility to marry see Cretney (2003a) ch 2.
[11] See the Marriage Act 1949, as amended from time to time, most recently by the Marriage Act 1994 regarding acceptable places of solemnisation, the Marriage Ceremony (Prescribed Words) Act 1996 regarding alternatives for the form of words used in marriage ceremonies in certain circumstances, the Immigration and Asylum Act 1999 regarding marriage by certificate, and the Gender Recognition Act 2004 regarding the gender of people within the prohibited degrees of consanguinity and the 'conscientious objection' clause regarding the right of members of the clergy to refuse to solemnise the marriage of a person who has acquired a new gender.
[12] See s 1 Marriage Act 1949 and first schedule to that Act.
[13] The age of capacity to marry at common law was 14 for a boy and 12 for a girl. The minimum age now is 16 (s 2 Marriage Act 1949) but children between the ages of 16 and 18 may marry only with the consent of persons with parental responsibility for them, or a court: see s 3 of the Marriage Act 1949. The capacity to marry of a mentally disabled adult was considered in the case of *Sheffield City Council v E and Another* [2004] EWHC Fam 2808 in which the court held that the relevant questions were (1) did the person understand the nature of the marriage contract (which was in essence, a simple one) and (2) did the person understand the duties and responsibilities that normally attached to marriage? (para 141).
[14] See s 49 Marriage Act 1948.

For the purpose of paragraph (d) of this subsection a marriage is not polygamous if at its inception neither party has any spouse additional to the other.

Section 12 of the Matrimonial Causes Act 1973 provides that a marriage shall be voidable on the following grounds only[15]—

(a) that the marriage has not been consummated owing to the incapacity of either party to consummate it;

(b) that the marriage has not been consummated owing to the wilful refusal of the respondent to consummate it;

(c) that either party to the marriage did not validly consent to it, whether in consequence of duress, mistake, unsoundness of mind or otherwise;

(d) that at the time of the marriage either party, though capable of giving a valid consent, was suffering (whether continuously or intermittently) from mental disorder within the meaning of the Mental Health Act 1983 of such a kind or to such an extent as to be unfitted for marriage;

(e) that at the time of the marriage the respondent was suffering from venereal disease in a communicable form;

(f) that at the time of the marriage the respondent was pregnant by some person other than the petitioner;

(g) that an interim gender recognition certificate under the Gender Recognition Act 2004 has, after the time of the marriage, been issued to either party to the marriage;

(h) that the respondent is a person whose gender at the time of the marriage had become the acquired gender under the Gender Recognition Act 2004.[16]

The judicial definition of marriage most commonly referred to is from a 19th century case, *Hyde v Hyde and Woodmansee*.[17] The court said that marriage is 'the voluntary union for life of one man and one woman to the exclusion of all others' (p 133). This is a deceptively simple definition. Yet, despite its Victorian heritage, it has not been overruled directly and its main principles can be seen to have been incorporated in the MCA above.

The *Hyde v Hyde* definition reveals its western roots in church or canon law,[18] and that it continues in force, and, in effect, is paralleled by sections 11 and 12 above, reveals the continued influence of the established Church in English marriage law.[19] *Hyde v Hyde* and its implicit incorporation into the 1973 MCA raise a number of questions. For example, *Hyde* v *Hyde*'s 'voluntariness' requirement has been recast into the 'valid consent' requirement of subsections 12(c) and (d). What, however, did the court mean by 'voluntary' in 1866, and how has this been translated into the legal meaning of 'valid consent' more than a century later? For example, do social or familial pressures render the choice to marry involuntary or the consent to marriage invalid?

[15] But see s 13 and discussion below regarding bars to relief where these grounds are alleged.

[16] Words inserted by the Gender Recognition Act 2004.

[17] *Hyde v Hyde and Woodmansee* [1866] L Rev 1 P & D 130 where a potentially polygamous marriage contracted in the Mormon faith was not regarded as valid in English law.

[18] Indeed, the court spoke of marriage 'as understood in Christendom' (p 133).

[19] See on this Bradley (1996).

## IV. THE LANGUAGE OF CONSENT

The question of consent has often been raised in the context of arranged marriages in an effort to distinguish them from forced marriages. The traditional view was that for consent to be vitiated the party must have been acting out of fear of an immediate threat to life, limb or liberty. Thus in *Singh v Singh*,[20] and later in *Singh v Kaur*,[21] the Court of Appeal found that intense family pressure to enter into an arranged marriage was not sufficient to render the marriage voidable. In *Hirani v Hirani*,[22] however, the Court of Appeal adopted contract law principles to fashion a different test to determine valid consent. Ormrod LJ said:

> The crucial question ... in these cases is whether the threats, pressure or whatever it is such as to destroy the reality of consent and overbears the will of the individual. It seems to me that ... this is a classic case of a young girl, wholly dependent on her parents being forced into a marriage with a man she has never seen in order to prevent her (reasonably from her parents' point of view) continuing in an association with a Muslim which they would regard with abhorrence. But it is as clear a case as one would want of the overbearing of the will of the petitioner and thus invalidating or vitiating her consent. (p 234)

This alternative test appears to ask whether the party's will was overborne, rather than asking about fear for life or limb. It has been applied recently in *P v R (Forced Marriage: Annulment)*[23] where a young woman was subjected by her family to 'enormous emotional and other pressure' and threats of force.[24] Both tests raise difficult issues, however. How far, for example, should a law premised and reliant upon the existence of a rational individual will, a notion which is itself based upon relatively modern philosophical concepts of liberal individualism, regulate traditional/religious lives based in other philosophical foundations entirely?[25] Neither the *Singh* nor the *Hirani* notion of consent would invalidate a marriage contracted in a context within which marriage is seen as a family or collective event in which the interest/will of the individual becomes subsumed within the interest/will of the group. Neither do these notions acknowledge the gendered notions of the individual and *his* consent which inform contract law[26] as well as the law of duress.

**Q** Does the Court of Appeal's reasoning in *Hirani* and *P v R* mean that the traditional practices of many cultural and religious groups violate English law? On the other hand, does the test merely reproduce in law stereotypical understandings of passive and obedient Asian women who are overcome by coercive traditions?[27]

It is clear that many arranged marriages do not overbear the will of the participants and the law is concerned to distinguish them from forced marriages which do. According to the Home Office:

---

[20] [1971] 2 All ER 828.
[21] (1981) 11 Fam Law 152.
[22] [1982] 4 FLR 232.
[23] [2003] 1 FLR 661.
[24] This reasoning has also been followed in the Scottish courts: see *Mahmood v Mahmood* 1993 SLT 589; and *Mahmud v Mahmud* 1994 SLT 599.
[25] On this and on the gender implications of the test, see Lim (1996). See also Bradney (1994).
[26] See Williams (1991) and Lim's (1996) use of Williams' analysis.
[27] See on this Lim (1996).

A forced marriage is one where one or both parties are coerced into a marriage against their will and under duress. Duress includes both physical and emotional pressure. Forced marriage is an abuse of human rights and cannot be justified on any religious or cultural basis. It is, of course, very different from arranged marriage, where both parties give their full and free consent to the marriage. The tradition of arranged marriages has operated successfully within many communities and many countries for a very long time.

The Government takes forced marriage very seriously. It is a form of domestic violence and an abuse of the human rights (sic). Victims can suffer many forms of physical and emotional damage including being held unlawfully captive, assaulted and repeatedly raped.

(Home Office Community and Race web page, accessed 5 March 2005)

Based on its paper *A Choice by Right*, published in 2000 (Home Office 2000c) the Home Office has issued guidelines for police and, in 2005, with the Foreign and Commonwealth Office, launched a joint Forced Marriage Unit, which is intended to be 'a one stop shop to undertake policy, projects and give practical advice to people at risk of being forced into marriage' (Home Office web page, accessed 5 March 2005). Sometimes, the issue of consent is not so clear, though. Where, for example, is the line to be drawn between concepts such as encouragement and coercion, or social embarrassment and social degradation?

Chapter 8 of John Gillis' (1985) book is entitled 'Better a Bad Husband Than No Husband At All: The Compulsion to Marry, 1850–1914'. He states:

The compulsion to marry was increasingly evident from the 1850's onward. When young Flora Thompson declared that she had no intention of becoming anyone's wife, her brave declaration was met with knowing smiles from the village matrons: 'All right, my girl, I've heard that tale before. You wait until Mr Right comes along. When he says "skip" you'll say "snap" fast enough, I'll warrant ... . Better a bad husband than no husband at all.' Music hall lyrics of the turn of the century expressed the view that, whatever its disadvantages, there was no real alternative to marriage:
When first they come courting,
How nice they behave
For a smile and a kiss
How humbly they crave
But when once a girl's wed,
She's a drudge and a slave
I think we would all prefer
Marriage with strife
Then to be on the shelf
And be nobody's wife.

(pp 233–34, footnotes omitted)

He goes on:

By 1914 the desirability of marriage was evident to virtually everyone. At the beginning of the Great War common-law wives and unwed mothers found to their dismay that they were often excluded from the benefits extended to those dependants of soldiers who could produce proper marriage and baptismal certificates. Women who lived quietly and respectably were told by unsympathetic relief workers that 'you went into this with your eyes open. You will just have to suffer' ... . Common-law husbands, equally desperate, went on leave without permission to marry and ensure that their wives receive the proper benefits. (p 237, footnotes omitted)

Although Gillis' is a historical perspective, it casts doubt upon the degree of voluntariness present in many marriages contracted either by young women afraid of the social repercussions arising from being 'left on the shelf', or by those marrying to bring themselves within dependency relief legislation. It is extremely unlikely, however, that, had the *Hirani* reasoning been applied to them, the consent of these parties would have been found to be invalid. Their will was not overborne by threats of economic suffering or economic pressure.

> **Q** When, in your view, does social pressure or financial or emotional coercion amount to an 'overbearing of the will'?

It is in the light of our earlier discussion of the psycho-social and economic importance to many of marriage that we must evaluate the law which maintains that marriages are entered into by the parties freely and voluntarily. Such a formulation of marriage rests on the liberal assumptions of the exercise of a free and private choice to marry and is reinforced each time courts use the language of 'overbearing of the will' to vitiate consent. Judicial reasoning of this type which preserves the institutional *status quo* and the ideology of marriage and family may, as Smart says, reflect law's concern to preserve marriage as a purely private arrangement construed as being the result of individual choice and freedom to exercise that choice, despite the fact that the terms of the contract are unspecified. It can thus be held up as an example of the 'private sphere *par excellence*' (1984 p 118).

We can unpick the liberal foundations of marriage law further by examining so-called 'immigration marriages'. Immigration law allows husbands or wives of non-British spouses to sponsor their spouses' entry into the UK and provides that as long as this sponsorship remains in effect the non-British spouse is protected from deportation.[28] Until 1997, however, further rules provided that immigration officials assure themselves that the 'primary purpose' of the marriage was not to gain entry into the UK.[29] The primary purpose rule was abolished in June 1997 by the then new Labour government which said that it was 'arbitrary, unfair and ineffective'.[30] Now, immigration officials are expected to focus upon whether the marriage is genuine, whether the couple intends to live together permanently as husband and wife, whether the marriage is subsisting and whether the parties have met.[31] The circumstances of marriages will continue to be scrutinised closely in order to determine whether the marriage is a 'genuine' one or not. 'Genuineness', in these cases, is not related to consent, however, but is related to another of the assumptions underlying marriage which allow it to maintain its status as icon of the private sphere: that, at least in modern times, it is based upon affection or romantic love (Stone 1990; Diduck 2003).

While the genuineness of romantic intentions may be a factor for immigration law, it is not for validity of marriage. In *Vervaeke v Smith*[32] the petitioner, a Belgian national and a prostitute who was about to be deported as a result of her convictions for soliciting, went through a ceremony of marriage with a UK national, a 'down and out' who

---

[28] Statement of Changes in Immigration (HC Paper (1989–90) vol 251, para 50).

[29] See, for interpretation of this rule and the rule that specifies the parties must have met before the marriage, *R v IAT, ex parte Kumar* [1986] Imm AR 446; and *R v IAT, ex parte Bhatia* [1985] Imm AR 50.

[30] Home Office Press Release, 5 June 1997.

[31] Pt 8 Immigration Rules (last updated February 2005). See also Asylum and Immigration (Treatment of Claims) Act 2004.

[32] [1982] 2 All ER 144.

married her allegedly for £50.00 and a ticket to South Africa.[33] Without going through any form of divorce, she later married an Italian national. Her Italian 'husband' died, and at issue was her entitlement, as his widow, to any of his estate. In order to be so entitled she had to prove that her first 'marriage' was invalid. In dismissing her appeal from her petition, Hailsham LC in the House of Lords first approved the words of the trial judge and then extended them:

> Where a man and a woman consent to marry one another in a formal ceremony conducted in accordance with the formalities required by law, knowing that it is a marriage ceremony it is immaterial that they do not intend to live together as man and wife ... . It is immaterial that they intend the marriage to take effect in some limited way ... . To hold otherwise would impair the effect of the whole system of law regulating marriages in this country, and gravely diminish the value of the system of registration of marriages on which so much depends in a modern community.
>
> I have no doubt that [this doctrine] would extend to a marriage as here celebrated between a British to a foreign national in circumstances where the ceremony was intended to achieve the status of British nationality in the foreign national by means of marriage and the private arrangement between the parties was simply to limit their personal relationships to the achievement of the status of married person with a view to acquiring British nationality for the previously alien partner. (pp 148–49)

The House of Lords relied in this passage on the public policy behind the law. It may be argued that in reaching this decision, they identified a conflict between two of the foundations of 'proper' marriage, which meant that the parties to a valid marriage were nonetheless parties to a non-genuine marriage. Apart from the basic question why immigration law should look behind marriage law at all, this clash between two of the ideological bases of marriage, and the laws in respect of them, raises the difficult question phrased by Hayes and Williams as follows:

> [W]here an asylum seeker marries in an attempt to avoid deportation to a country where he reasonably fears that he will be imprisoned, probably tortured, and even killed, is this a sham, [immigration but nonetheless valid] marriage, or a[n invalid] marriage entered into as a result of duress? (1995 p 397)[34]

## V. THE PERMANENT HETEROSEXUAL UNION

The second difficulty raised by Lord Penzance's legal definition of marriage lies in how we are to construe the word 'union'. What kind of union must there be? Is it a physical union? A financial one? An emotional one? Some legal light can be shed upon these questions by reference to the consummation requirement in MCA 1973 subsections 12(a) and (b) which have their basis in Canon law.[35]

---

[33] P 147.

[34] The most recent Rules intended to deal with 'sham' or immigration marriages came into effect in February 2005. One can enter the UK as a fiancé (Pt 8 paras 290–95) or visitor for the purpose of marrying in the UK (Pt 2 paras 56D–F) only if one can satisfy the Entry Clearance Officer of an intention to give notice of the marriage at a designated register office in the UK. Marriage visitors must then obtain a Certificate of Approval to Marry. The rules governing Certificates of Approval to Marry also affect those who are already in the UK but are subject to immigration control. See also Marriage Act 1949 Pt 3.

[35] Note, however, s 13(1)(a) and (b) which states that a marriage in which the parties understood there was not to be a sexual relationship cannot later be avoided on the ground of inability or refusal to consummate.

Notwithstanding that embedded within the ideology of marriage is romantic love, there is no requirement for that in the statute, nor is there one mandating commitment, respect, economic interdependence or emotional fulfilment. It is the physical, heterosexual union which is fundamental to marriage. Cases which have attempted to define the nature of that union-consummation—for the purposes of marriage law have clearly established its heterosexual, and, arguably, phallocentric nature. Even though sexual practices are many and varied, only one particular sex act qualifies as legal consummation. Richard Collier describes the leading case on consummation as follows:

> The case of *D-e v A-g (falsely calling herself D-e)* [1845] 1 Rob Ecc 280 (p 1039) is the cornerstone of the cases on the place of sexual intercourse in marriage. Indeed it was later to be described (Per Willmer LJ in *SY v SY (Orse W)* [1963] p 55) as 'a statement of commanding authority'. In the leading judgement, Dr Lushington declared that the court were 'all agreed that, in order to constitute the marriage bond between young persons, there must be the power, present or to come, of sexual intercourse' (p 1045). He then proceeded, in a passage which is worth quoting at length, to define the legal meaning of sexual intercourse:
>
> Sexual intercourse, in the proper meaning of the term, is ordinary and complete intercourse; it does not mean partial and imperfect intercourse; yet, I cannot go to the length of saying that every degree of imperfection would deprive it of its essential character. There must be degrees difficult to deal with; but if so imperfect as scarcely to be natural, I should not hesitate to say that, legally speaking, it is no intercourse at all. I can never think that the true interest of society would be advanced by retaining within the marriage bonds parties driven to such disgusting practices. Certainly it would not tend to the prevention of adulterous intercourse, one of the greatest evils to be avoided' (p 1045).
>
> This is the crux of Lushington's reasoning in *D-e v A-g*. First, intercourse (giving pleasure) is not in itself sufficient. It is admitted that intercourse has taken place in this case but it was not 'real' (ordinary/proper/natural) intercourse. 'Ordinary' and 'natural' must therefore have some meaning. Second, the 'disgusting practices' which might follow from 'unreal' intercourse are one of the 'greatest evils' against the 'true interest of society'. These are the consequences of a legal recognition of 'imperfect' sexual intercourse in marriage. What sexual intercourse involves is a specific interaction of the male and female body (genital connection, penis/vagina) and what non-marital intercourse (adultery) might lead to is social disorder:
>
> 'Without the power [to consummate] neither of the two principal ends of matrimony can be attained, namely, a lawful indulgence of the passions to prevent licentiousness, and the procreation of children, according to the evident design of Divine Providence' [p 1045].
>
> There is in law a 'true' sexual intercourse which is capable of consummating a marriage. Other 'unnatural' connections and non-penetration, be it due to structural impediment or psychological inability, are not sufficient to consummate a marriage. What such a construction does, of course, is to marginalise sexual practices outside the frames of the heterosexual matrix. It is, simply, penetration which defines sexual intercourse in law (see also O'Donovan 1993 p 46). What constitutes the 'natural' quality of the genitals, however, is far from clear and would appear to vary from case to case ... (1995b pp 152–53)

**Q** What does Dr Lushington's reasoning tell us about the role of marriage in English law and society? Is it to provide a legitimate outlet for one form of sexual expression or is it to procreate? See on this *Cowen v Cowen* [1946] P 36, [1945] 2 All ER 197 (CA) and *Baxter v Baxter* [1948] AC 274, [1947] 2 All ER 886 (HL). How does this judgment fit with the *Vervaeke* case above? Why do you think conjugality or this form of sexual expression of monogamy is so important to law?

The court in *Hyde* spoke of the sexual union in marriage being for life. But, does the phrase 'for life' literally mean that? Does this mean that 'unions', even active heterosexual ones, if they are intended to last only for a limited period, are not legal marriages?[36] In some cases it might not, as *Vervaeke* illustrates. It is true that marriages now are legally dissoluble, but the dominant view is that divorce is a matter of last resort—it is to be resorted to only when the marriage has irretrievably broken down. Most parties believe, and the traditional marriage ceremony reinforces that belief, that marriage is for life, notwithstanding that a 'way out' is offered if things become intolerable. Official Reports over the years on marriage and divorce law have recognised without question the lifetime commitment implied in marriage even when advocating possible forms of divorce. The Royal Commission on Marriage and Divorce reported in 1956, for example, that the basis of its approach to considering possibilities for a new divorce law included reinforcing marriage as a lifetime commitment:

> The Western World has recognised that it is in the best interests of all concerned—the community, the parties to a marriage and their children—that marriage should be monogamous and that it should last for life. It has also always recognised that owing to human frailty, some marriages will not endure for life, and that in certain circumstances it is right that a spouse should be released from the obligations of marriage. (1956 p 7, para 35)

The language of lifetime commitment and individual responsibility for the success or failure of that commitment also pervaded the Law Commission's 1990 Consultation Paper *The Ground for Divorce* which led eventually to the ill-fated Family Law Act 1996.[37]

> The aim of supporting those marriages which can be saved can be distinguished from the aim of upholding the institution of marriage itself. For some of our respondents, as for our predecessors, it was important that divorce law should send the right messages, to the married and the marrying, about the seriousness and the permanence of the commitment involved. We agree. (Law Commission 1990 para 3.4, p 10)

According to these official representations, it is law's business to reinforce 'messages' regarding the desirability of and the responsibility for the permanent heterosexual relationship entered into by the parties. On this view, if marriages fail, rather than looking to outside factors or to the nature of the institution itself as a possible source of the problem, it is the individuals and their failure to negotiate successfully their social and emotional responsibilities—the 'human frailties' identified in the 1956 report—which are believed to be to blame. It is this view which underlines government and popular support for the provision of marriage preparation classes (Advisory Group on Marriage and Relationship Support 2002); for information booklets to be distributed by clergy and registrars on the rights and responsibilities of marriage (Home Office 1999); and counselling and therapy in times of relationship stress (Advisory Group on Marriage and Relationship Support 2002). It may also explain continued demands for retaining notions of fault in divorce law.[38] Arguably this view also exacerbates the feelings of personal failure which are experienced by many when their marriages do not 'work out'. 'If

---

[36] Lack of intention to remain married for life is one of the grounds for annulment in the Catholic Church.
[37] See ch 14.
[38] See ch 14.

counselling or therapy does not help us to see how to mend our relationships, the failure remains ours—it is a failure of our love or our commitment' (Diduck 2003 p 40).[39]

## VI. ONE MAN AND ONE WOMAN

According to *Hyde v Hyde* and subsection 11(c) of the MCA 1973, the union must be between one man and one woman. This requirement is conceptually problematic for a couple of reasons. The first is the exclusivity required. Group marriage, polygamy[40] or, for that matter, certain premarital sexual liaisons[41] may invalidate a marriage on a strict construction of this requirement. Polygamy is also prohibited by the criminal law of bigamy.[42] We can examine some explanations for the monogamy requirement by reference to those jurisdictions in which polygyny[43] is or has been practised on a wider scale than in England.[44]

Examining the prohibition on polygyny that was in force in South Africa in 1991, Kaganas and Murray suggested that the privileging of the Christian companionate model of marriage rested originally on ethno-centric, racist views of 'the heathen society' (Kaganas and Murray 1991 p 119) and on interpretations of Christianity, morality, the evolutionary 'naturalness' of the nuclear family and the 'rightful place of women' (p 121). If we dismiss the first four justifications as remnants of the pernicious effects of colonisation and dominance, we are left with the argument that polygyny is antithetical to the values of equality inherent in a democratic society. Kaganas and Murray addressed these equality-based objections to polygyny:

> The first concern, that there is something inherently unequal in a family structure which comprises one man and many women, is dubious. It is not self-evident that the apparently symmetrical relationship of one woman to one man provides the *only* formula for equality within marriage. A variation of the argument might be that the relationship is unequal and degrading for women because, while each woman in a polygynous marriage is committed to a single man, she has to compete with a number of other women for his attention and a share of the family's material resources. This also fails to withstand scrutiny. It is possible, outside the very specific and historically quite recent notions of romantic love and companionable marriage, that each wife's attentions are also divided among her husband, other members of her family and the community in which she is living. This point is well made in a study on polygyny in Nigeria by Ware when she notes that '[w]hether one considers that women who have to share a husband are underprivileged depends upon the value placed upon husbands'. Furthermore, while it is true that wives are dependent on their husbands for access to resources, they are not necessarily prejudiced by the introduction of new wives; in many polygynous societies, additional wives increase the wealth of the group rather than deplete it.
>
> The power that polygyny may give husbands to introduce new wives and thus to determine

---

[39] See also ch 14 below.
[40] See amended ss 11(d).
[41] See ss 12(e) and (f) of the MCA 1973.
[42] Offences Against the Persons Act 1861 s 57.
[43] The term 'polygamy' is used to denote a marriage in which there is more than one spouse of either sex. The term 'polygyny' refers specifically to marriage in which the law permits the man more than one wife.
[44] On the regulation of polygyny from a rights perspective, see Banda (2003). See also Fox (1992) in which he discusses US courts' approaches to the polygyny of the Mormons of Utah state. Many of his arguments and conclusions are similar to those below.

the composition of the family, raises different issues. On the face of it, the equality objection here is easily dealt with by making the introduction of new wives a matter to be decided jointly by the husband and any existing wives. Indeed, this is already the case in Indonesia. However, a formal requirement of consent may be worth very little and we are likely to mistrust a wife's consent when it is exacted in a society in which men dominate. But this means that the problem lies in the society in which polygyny is practised rather than in the institution itself.

(1991 pp 127–28, footnotes omitted)

They argued that there is nothing inherent in polygyny which requires the oppression of women, and others have agreed that it does not cause the breakdown of the fabric of society (Fox 1992). Rather, it is the patriarchy in any society which can render any family form degrading or oppressive.[45] They concluded that we 'should re-examine the basis of our objections to polygyny' (Kaganas and Murray 1991 p 134).

**Q** How, if at all, would you regulate polygyny or 'group marriages', especially in the light of the sociological work referred to above which suggests that commitment, interdependence, care and support may be shared by more than two people at a time?

The second difficulty with the one man/one woman requirement includes both the subtle issue of determining a precise definition of 'man' and 'woman'—and the far more obvious question of why it is only persons of the opposite sex who are permitted to marry. Let us look first at the man/woman requirement, put in statutory form by section 11(c) of the MCA 1973. We assign sex and gender to people on the basis of a number of different biological, social and psychological factors. In one of the most famous cases in English law, however, the court was called upon to determine the *legal* meaning of 'man' and 'woman', and in effect, therefore, of marriage.

In *Corbett v Corbett (orse Ashley)*[46] the respondent Ashley was a post-operative transsexual. She had undergone male to female sex reassignment surgery before her marriage to Corbett. The marriage failed and the petitioner, Corbett, sought a decree that their marriage was void because both parties at the time of the marriage were persons of the male sex, or, in the alternative, because the marriage was never consummated. Medical and psychological evidence was called and the court found that there were a number of criteria by which we assign the sexual identity of a person. A person could be identified as being of one sex or another by chromosomal factors, by examination of gonads or genitals, by his or her psychological or social identification, or by looking at hormonal or secondary sex characteristics. The issue before the court, then, was which of these factors ought to determine a person's *legal* sex for the purpose of marriage? The decision says much about beliefs in biological determinism and the immutability of sex and their reinforcement through the legitimising authority of law, as well as about the nature of the legal marriage relationship.

---

[45] The law in South Africa has since changed to accord recognition to polygynous marriages entered into in terms of indigenous customary law. The Recognition of Customary Marriages Act 1998 was also intended to remedy the inferior position of women under customary law and gives customary husbands and wives equal status (s 6). In addition, it provides for the fair distribution of assets for the first family when the husband marries a second wife. However, it is reported that in practice, the position of women in customary marriages has not changed in jurisdictions which have attempted to introduce legal equality and doubts have been expressed as to whether the same result will obtain in South Africa (Mamashela 2003).

[46] [1970] 2 All ER 33.

The court in *Corbett* chose only biological indicators to determine sex. It said that the sex of a person was fixed at birth so that later surgical or other intervention could not alter that immutable status. In a case where the first three biological factors are incongruent, the court said that priority ought to be given to one's genetic status. On the test devised by Ormrod LJ, April Ashley was therefore legally a man, notwithstanding surgical and hormonal intervention and the fact that she had lived as a woman for a number of years. The court's view of marriage may help to explain the decision.

[S]ex is clearly an essential determinant of the relationship called marriage, *because it is and always has been* recognised as the union of one man and one woman. It is the *institution on which the family is built*, and in which the capacity for *natural heterosexual intercourse* is an essential element. (p 48, emphasis added)

Let us examine closely the italicised words. First, the court comes to a conclusion about the essential determinants of marriage and goes on to establish the basis on which the conclusion is drawn. How convincing is it, however, in terms of legal argument and proof, to say that something ought to be the case simply (1) because it is and (2) because it always has been, especially where no evidence is relied upon to establish either state of affairs? This form of legal reasoning demonstrates a conservative approach to the judicial role and the power of judicial rhetoric to accept a contention as axiomatic and thus to dismiss any need for evidence to prove it or legal authority to validate it. We can make similar observations about the second assumption connecting, with no stated authority, marriage and the (only legally legitimate, it seems) family. In relation to the kind of sexual behaviour which is essential, the 'natural' is called in aid. That which is 'natural' is one type of heterosex, but more than that, it is heterosex in marriage. A recent judgement of the Supreme Court of Canada provides a less conservative approach to legal reasoning when considering an argument about the historical and natural meaning of marriage:

First, it is argued, the institution of marriage escapes legislative redefinition. Existing in its present basic form since time immemorial, it is not a legal construct, but rather a supra-legal construct subject to legal incidents. In the *Persons* case, Lord Sankey, writing for the Privy Council, dealt with this very type of argument, though in a different context. In addressing whether the fact that women never had occupied public office was relevant to whether they could be considered 'persons' for the purposes of being eligible for appointment to the Senate, he said at p 134:

The fact that no woman had served or has claimed to serve such an office is not of great weight when it is remembered that custom would have prevented the claim being made or the point being contested.

Customs are apt to develop into traditions which are stronger than law and remain unchallenged long after the reason for them has disappeared.

The appeal to history therefore in this particular matter is not conclusive.

Lord Sankey acknowledged, at p 134, that 'several centuries ago' it would have been understood that 'persons' should refer only to men. Several centuries ago it would have been understood that marriage should be available only to opposite-sex couples. The recognition of same-sex marriage in several Canadian jurisdictions as well as two European countries belies the assertion that the same is true today.

Second, some interveners emphasize that while Lord Sankey envisioned our Constitution as a 'living tree' in the *Persons* case, he specified that it was 'capable of growth and expansion within its natural limits' (p 136). These natural limits, they submit, preclude same-sex marriage

...

The natural limits argument can succeed only if its proponents can identify an objective core of meaning which defines what is 'natural' in relation to marriage. Absent this, the argument is merely tautological. The only objective core which the interveners before us agree is 'natural' to marriage is that it is the voluntary union of two people to the exclusion of all others. Beyond this, views diverge. We are faced with competing opinions on what the natural limits of marriage may be. (*Reference Re: Same Sex Marriage* 2004 SCC 79 paras 25–27)

While some may argue that accepting monogamous union as natural is problematic, the point here is that the court acknowledged that there may be differing views about a state of affairs or even an entity that is purported to be 'natural'. The California Supreme Court has also adopted more expansive reasoning in response to arguments about history or tradition justifying law:

The state's protracted denial of equal protection cannot be justified simply because such constitutional violation has become traditional. ... . Advocates of [a ban on interracial marriages] asserted that because historically and culturally blacks had not been permitted to marry whites, the statute was justified. Thus argument was rejected by the Court ... [in *Perez v Sharp* (1948) 32 Cal 2d 711] ... Simply put, same-sex marriage cannot be prohibited simply because California has always done so before.
(Coordination Proceeding, Marriage Cases, San Francisco County Superior Court; Tentative Decision, Kramer, J 14 March 2005 pp 7–8)

Let us continue with the *Corbett* judgment. Once the court declares the legal essence of marriage, it then states:

The question then becomes, what is meant by the word 'woman' in the context of marriage, for I am not concerned to determine the 'legal sex' of the Respondent at large. Having regard to the essentially heterosexual character of the relationship which is called marriage, the criteria must, in my judgment, be *biological* for even the most extreme degree of transsexualism in a male or the most severe hormonal imbalance which can exist in a person with male chromosomes, male gonads and male genitalia cannot reproduce a person who is naturally capable of performing the *essential role of a woman in marriage*. In other words, the law should adopt in the first place, the first three of the doctors' criteria, ie the *chromosomal, gonadal and genital* tests, and if all three are congruent, determine the sex for the purpose of marriage accordingly, and ignore any operative intervention. (p 48, emphasis added))

The italicised parts of this passage make it clear that Ormrod LJ believes that the essential role of a woman in marriage is biological and related in some way to chromosomes, although the precise value of the X chromosome is not made clear, given its post-treatment physical invisibility. One possible conclusion is that chromosomes in some way convey to Ormrod LJ the essence of a person, an essence which, having been engendered by the magical caprice of nature, ought to be respected by humans. The essential role of a woman in marriage is also related, according to Ormrod LJ, to having female gonads, although the non-functioning of these sexual reproductive organs does not preclude a valid marriage being contracted by a person who is sterile. The potential capacity to reproduce, then, in some way, but not finally, determines the role of a woman in marriage. Finally, Ormrod LJ declares that the essential woman in marriage must have the genitals of a woman, implying that having her vagina penetrated is one of the essential roles of woman in marriage.

*Corbett* remained the authority in English law until 2004, despite its reasoning and conclusions having been rejected by courts in other jurisdictions and also despite having

been subjected to criticism by the European Court of Human Rights.[47] Until 2002, however, the court's criticisms did not extend so far as to find that the UK's position on the
immutability of gender violated a person's right to marry and found a family under
Article 12 of the European Convention on Human Rights. Rather, the court said that
while the UK was bound to keep the matter under review in the light of 'scientific and
social developments', designating who was able to marry came within a state's margin
of appreciation.[48] But the Court finally lost patience with the UK in 2002.

In that year the ECtHR decided two cases[49] that set the government in motion toward
legislation that became the Gender Recognition Act 2004. The following extracts from
the ECtHR's judgement in *Goodwin* discuss the interpretation of Articles 8 and 12
ECHR in the context of the marriage of transsexuals.

[92] In the previous cases from the United Kingdom, this Court has since 1986 emphasised the
importance of keeping the need for appropriate legal measures under review having regard to
scientific and societal developments. Most recently in the Sheffield and Horsham case in 1998,
it observed that the respondent State had not yet taken any steps to do so despite an increase in
the social acceptance of the phenomenon of transsexualism and a growing recognition of the
problems with which transsexuals are confronted. Even though it found no violation in that
case, the need to keep this area under review was expressly re-iterated. Since then, a report has
been issued in April 2000 by the Interdepartmental Working Group which set out a survey of
the current position of transsexuals in *inter alia* criminal law, family and employment matters
and identified various options for reform. Nothing has effectively been done to further these
proposals and in July 2001 the Court of Appeal noted that there were no plans to do so. It may
be observed that the only legislative reform of note, applying certain non-discrimination provisions to transsexuals, flowed from a decision of the European Court of Justice of 30 April 1996
which held that discrimination based on a change of gender was equivalent to discrimination
on grounds of sex.
[93] Having regard to the above considerations, the Court finds that the respondent Government can no longer claim that the matter falls within their margin of appreciation, save as
regards the appropriate means of achieving recognition of the right protected under the Convention. Since there are no significant factors of public interest to weigh against the interest of
this individual applicant in obtaining legal recognition of her gender re-assignment, it reaches
the conclusion that the fair balance that is inherent in the Convention now tilts decisively in
favour of the applicant. There has, accordingly, been a failure to respect her right to private life
in breach of Article 8 of the Convention. (P 510)
...
[97] The Court recalls that in the cases of Rees, Cossey and Sheffield and Horsham the inability
of the transsexuals in those cases to marry a person of the sex opposite to their re-assigned gender was not found in breach of Article 12 of the Convention. These findings were based
variously on the reasoning that the right to marry referred to traditional marriage between persons of opposite biological sex, the view that continued adoption of biological criteria in
domestic law for determining a person's sex for the purpose of marriage was encompassed
within the power of Contracting States to regulate by national law the exercise of the right to
marry and the conclusion that national laws in that respect could not be regarded as restricting
or reducing the right of a transsexual to marry in such a way or to such an extent that the very
essence of the right was impaired. Reference was also made to the wording of Article 12 as protecting marriage as the basis of the family.

---

[47] A detailed discussion of the case law and policy can be found in the first edition of this book at pp 51–56.
[48] *Rees v United Kingdom* (1987) 9 EHRR 56; *Cossey v UK* [1991] 2 FLR 492; *Sheffield and Horsham v UK*
[1998] 2 FLR 928.
[49] *Goodwin v UK* [2002] 2 FLR 487; and *I v UK* [2002] 2 FLR 518.

[98] Reviewing the situation in 2002, the Court observes that Article 12 secures the fundamental right of a man and woman to marry and to found a family. The second aspect is not however a condition of the first and the inability of any couple to conceive or parent a child cannot be regarded as *per se* removing their right to enjoy the first limb of this provision.

[99] The exercise of the right to marry gives rise to social, personal and legal consequences. It is subject to the national laws of the Contracting States but the limitations thereby introduced must not restrict or reduce the right in such a way or to such an extent that the very essence of the right is impaired.

[100] It is true that the first sentence refers in express terms to the right of a man and woman to marry. The Court is not persuaded that at the date of this case it can still be assumed that these terms must refer to a determination of gender by purely biological criteria. There have been major social changes in the institution of marriage since the adoption of the Convention as well as dramatic changes brought about by developments in medicine and science in the field of transsexuality. The Court has found above, under Article 8 of the Convention, that a test of congruent biological factors can no longer be decisive in denying legal recognition to the change of gender of a post-operative transsexual. There are other important factors [including] the acceptance of the condition of gender identity disorder by the medical professions and health authorities within Contracting States, the provision of treatment including surgery to assimilate the individual as closely as possible to the gender in which they perceive that they properly belong and the assumption by the transsexual of the social role of the assigned gender. The Court would also note that Article 9 of the recently adopted Charter of Fundamental Rights of the European Union departs, no doubt deliberately, from the wording of Article 12 of the Convention in removing the reference to men and women.

[101] The right under Article 8 to respect for private life does not however subsume all the issues under Article 12, where conditions imposed by national laws are accorded a specific mention. The Court has therefore considered whether the allocation of sex in national law to that registered at birth is a limitation impairing the very essence of the right to marry in this case. In that regard, it finds that it is artificial to assert that post-operative transsexuals have not been deprived of the right to marry as, according to law, they remain able to marry a person of their former opposite sex. The applicant in this case lives as a woman, is in a relationship with a man and would only wish to marry a man. She has no possibility of doing so. In the Court's view, she may therefore claim that the very essence of her right to marry has been infringed.

[102] The Court has not identified any other reason which would prevent it from reaching this conclusion. The Government have argued that in this sensitive area eligibility for marriage under national law should be left to the domestic courts within the State's margin of appreciation, adverting to the potential impact on already existing marriages in which a transsexual is a partner. It appears however from the opinions of the majority of the Court of Appeal judgment in *Bellinger v Bellinger* that the domestic courts tend to the view that the matter is best handled by the legislature, while the Government have no present intention to introduce legislation.

[103] It may be noted from the materials submitted by Liberty that though there is widespread acceptance of the marriage of transsexuals, fewer countries permit the marriage of transsexuals in their assigned gender than recognise the change of gender itself. The Court is not persuaded however that this supports an argument for leaving the matter entirely to the Contracting States as being within their margin of appreciation. This would be tantamount to finding that the range of options open to a Contracting State included an effective bar on any exercise of the right to marry. The margin of appreciation cannot extend so far. While it is for the Contracting State to determine *inter alia* the conditions under which a person claiming legal recognition as a transsexual establishes that gender re-assignment has been properly effected or under which past marriages cease to be valid and the formalities applicable to future marriages (including, for example, the information to be furnished to intended spouses), the Court finds no justification for barring the transsexual from enjoying the right to marry under any circumstances.

[104] The Court concludes that there has been a breach of Article 12 of the Convention in the present case. (pp 511–12, all references omitted)

After these decisions, the matter was again reviewed in domestic law. The *Bellinger* case to which the ECtHR refers above was appealed and in 2003[50] the House of Lords concurred that s.11(c) MCA violated the ECHR, but rather than read that section compatibly with Articles 8 and 12, (as it did the word 'spouse' in the *Mendoza* decision discussed in Chapter 1) it issued a declaration of incompatibility. Neither did the court make the other order sought by the parties, a declaration pursuant to s.55 MCA 1973 that the marriage they celebrated in 1981 (Mrs Bellinger was a post-operative transsexual) was valid. Lord Nicholls thought the matter was one better dealt with by Parliament because of its vast and diverse repercussions:

> Recognition of Mrs Bellinger as female for the purposes of section 11(c) of the Matrimonial Causes Act 1973 would necessitate giving the expressions 'male' and 'female' in that Act a novel, extended meaning: that a person may be born with one sex but later become, or become regarded as, a person of the opposite sex.
>
> This would represent a major change in the law, having far reaching ramifications. It raises issues whose solution calls for extensive enquiry and the widest public consultation and discussion. Questions of social policy and administrative feasibility arise at several points, and their interaction has to be evaluated and balanced. The issues are altogether ill-suited for determination by courts and court procedures. They are pre-eminently a matter for Parliament, the more especially when the government, in unequivocal terms, has already announced its intention to introduce comprehensive primary legislation on this difficult and sensitive subject.
>
> (paras 36–37, p 1052)

He also thought that the issue of when one's gender was changed was too complicated to be dealt with by the courts:

> By what criteria are cases such as these to be decided?
>
> But the problem is more fundamental than this. It is questionable whether the successful completion of some sort of surgical intervention should be an essential prerequisite to the recognition of gender reassignment. If it were, individuals may find themselves coerced into major surgical operations they otherwise would not have. But the aim of the surgery is to make the individual feel more comfortable with his or her body, not to 'turn a man into a woman' or vice versa. As one medical report has expressed it, a male to female transsexual person is no less a woman for not having had surgery, or any more a woman for having had it.
>
> These are deep waters. Plainly, there must be some objective, publicly available criteria by which gender reassignment is to be assessed. (paras 440–42, p 1053)

Finally, the question of recognising an acquired gender went to the fundamental meaning of marriage:

> Marriage is an institution, or relationship, deeply embedded in the religious and social culture of this country. It is deeply embedded as a relationship between two persons of the opposite sex. There was a time when the reproductive functions of male and female were regarded as the primary raison d'être of marriage. The Church of England Book of Common Prayer of 1662 declared that the first cause for which matrimony was ordained was the 'procreation of children'. For centuries this was proclaimed at innumerable marriage services. For a long time now

---

[50] [2003] UKHL 1; [2003] 1 FLR 1043.

the emphasis has been different. Variously expressed, there is much more emphasis now on the 'mutual society, help and comfort that the one ought to have of the other'.

Against this background there are those who urge that the special relationship of marriage should not now be confined to persons of the opposite sex. It should be possible for persons of the same sex to marry. This, it is said, is the appropriate way to resolve problems such as those confronting Mrs Bellinger.

It hardly needs saying that this approach would involve a fundamental change in the traditional concept of marriage. Here again, this raises a question which ought to be considered as part of an overall review of the most appropriate way to deal with the difficulties confronting transsexual people. (paras 46–48, p 1054)

Lords Hope and Rodger thought the words of the statute were important. Lord Hope:

I need hardly say that I entirely agree with the Australian judges that the words 'male' and 'female' in section 11(c) of the 1973 Act, which is the provision with which we are faced in this case, are not technical terms and that they must be given their ordinary, everyday meaning in the English language. But no evidence was placed before us to suggest that in contemporary usage in this country, on whichever date one might wish to select—23 May 1973 when the 1973 Act was enacted, 2 May 1981 when Mr and Mrs Bellinger entered into their marriage ceremony or the date of this judgment, these words can be taken to include post-operative transsexual persons. The definition of 'male' in the *New Shorter Oxford English Dictionary* (1993) tells us that its primary meaning when used as an adjective is 'of, pertaining to, or designating the sex which can beget offspring'. No mention is made anywhere in the extended definition of the word of transsexual persons. The word 'transsexual' is defined as 'having the physical characteristics of one sex but a strong and persistent desire to belong to the other.' I see no escape from the conclusion that these definitions, with which the decision in *Corbett v Corbett* [1971] P 83 and the views of the majority in the Court of Appeal in this case are consistent, are both complete and accurate. The fact is that the ordinary meaning of the word 'male' is incapable, without more, of accommodating the transsexual person within its scope. The Australian cases show that a distinction has to be drawn, even according to the contemporary usage of the word in Australia, between pre-operative and post-operative transsexuals. Distinctions of that kind raise questions of fact and degree which are absent from the ordinary meaning of the word 'male' in this country. Any attempt to enlarge its meaning would be bound to lead to difficulty, as there is no single agreed criterion by which it could be determined whether or not a transsexual was sufficiently 'male' for the purpose of entering into a valid marriage ceremony.

(para 62 pp 1058–59)

And Lord Rodger:

Section 11(c) is a re-enactment of section 1(c) of the Nullity of Marriage Act 1971 which was passed shortly after the decision in *Corbett v Corbett* [1971] P 83. Section 11(c) contains one in a series of grounds of nullity. By section 11(b) a marriage is void if 'at the time of the marriage either party was already lawfully married'. The reference to the situation at the time of the marriage is necessary because a person may have been lawfully married at an earlier time and may be lawfully married at a later time. The situation is one that can change. For purposes of nullity the critical consideration is what the situation was 'at the time of the marriage' in question. Similarly, section 11(d) provides that a polygamous marriage entered into outside England and Wales is void if 'either party was at the time of the marriage domiciled in England and Wales'. Again, when dealing with domicile which can change, Parliament uses the past tense and specifies the time of the marriage. Section 11(c) is different in both respects: a marriage is void if 'the parties are not respectively male and female'. Both the present tense and the omission of any reference to the time of the marriage indicate that, in relation to the validity of marriage, Parliament regards gender as fixed and immutable. (para 83, pp 1064–65)

The proposed legislation to which the Court refers has now become the Gender Recognition Act 2004. This Act provides that a person of at least 18 years of age can make application to a Gender Recognition Panel for a gender recognition certificate on the basis of living in the acquired gender or having changed gender according to the law of another country.[51] If issued, the certificate means that the person's gender becomes, for all purposes, the acquired gender.[52] The application must include reports made by two professionals, one of whom must practice in the field of gender dysphoria and the panel must be satisfied that the applicant has or has had gender dysphoria, has lived in the acquired gender for the immediately preceding two years and intends to live in the acquired gender until death.[53]

In the context of these decisions about the validity of marriage, UK law has thus re-examined the meaning of gender. It is no longer assumed to be biological and therefore immutable. But rather than also re-examining the meaning of (sex in) marriage, the combined effect of the Gender Recognition Act and the *Bellinger* decision seems merely to reinforce old meanings. According to Diduck (2003),[54] while these decisions, along with the Gender Recognition Act 2004, allow that gender is changeable,

> [r]ather than accept a fluid definition of marriage to account for that changeability, [they] require a choice to be made to fix identity so that intimate partners [can] make an orthodox, heterosexual marriage. Further, the basis for choice of gender identity remain[s] rooted in a medical or psychiatric dysfunction. It [is] seen as an abnormality that [can] be remedied by law for the purpose of encouraging 'normal' traditional marriage. (p 204)

Collier (1995b) attempted to deconstruct the law's preoccupation with heterosex in marriage before these changes. He said:

> The transsexual cases, basing marriage on a biological dichotomy, ignore the 'social' aspects of marriage relationship and focus instead on the sexual. If marriage 'depends on sex and not on gender' then legal discourse is valorising one particular medical interpretation of the relationship of sex and gender. Compassion, consideration, empathy and the ability to love and understand are all subordinated within an economy of masculinity which privileges intercourse above all else in the constitution of the marriage relationship. Other forms of human contact and pleasure are denied legal validity within a position which takes it for granted that there is a fundamental difference between men and women, and that heterosexuality is normal ...
>
> (p 130, references omitted)

**Q** Do you think his comments are still relevant?

O'Donovan's (1993) strategy is to analyse marriage law by reference to who is excluded from marriage (pp 49–59). She argues that, by excluding all but one man and one woman from the privileged legal institution of marriage, the law ensures the orderly access of men to women's bodies, and to any children of the union. The political implications of this arrangement for her are clear.

> Legal theorists have deconstructed marriage to point up the gendered nature of its terms. Yet others find a solution in a freely negotiated contract to be agreed by the partners. Contract as

[51] S 1.
[52] S 9.
[53] S 3.
[54] See also Sandland (2003).

the model of political relations and the justification of the state is presented as a solution to marriage difficulties, as a principle of social association, and as a means of creating social relationships, such as couple agreements. This is reinforced by pointing to entry into marriage as free and voluntary. Recent work on family and social contract raises doubts about this line of reasoning. In her powerful book *The Sexual Contract* Carole Pateman criticises the limitations of social contract theory in justifying current political arrangements. The sexual contract, which predated the social contract, gave men conjugal mastery over women, realised through marriage. Readings of major social contract theorists from Hobbes to Rousseau confirm that the family is taken as natural, as pre-given. Marriage, the foundation of family, ensures the subordination of women, which is presented as inevitable. The free individuals who contract in the social contract are male. The issue of whether or not women contract freely into the sexual contract is unresolved, and the way out for political theorists is to tell patriarchal stories in which marriage and family are 'natural' ... .

Although women are taking control of their sexuality and bodies, there remain contradictions surrounding women and contract in relation to political theory and to marriage. The positing of the family as 'natural', pre-dating the state, in political philosophy leaves unspecified social understanding of that unit. There can be no doubt that the fathers of social contract theory wrote in the context of subordination, at a time when married women could not contract, as their legal existence was subsumed under that of their husband. For Pateman the notion of the free, contracting citizen of the modern state remains tainted by its origins in male individualism and female subordination. (pp 58–59, references omitted)

O'Donovan uses Pateman's work to tie together the two underlying premises of English marriage law, that it is a free and voluntary union, but that it is one which only a man and a woman may enter into together. For her, the ideological power of the first masks the political implications of the second.

The other difficulty, of course, with the 'one man and one woman' requirement as it is reproduced in Section 11(c) MCA is that it precludes two people of the same sex from marrying. For many, this exclusion from what can be considered at best a problematic institution is not cause for concern. Auchmuty (2004), for example, highlights that for many feminists, like O'Donovan, Fineman and Pateman above, the institution of marriage is too burdened with historical and ideological baggage and is therefore 'irredeemable'. Many lesbians and gay men who are excluded from marriage thus have no wish to enter into it, claiming that to support same-sex marriage denies legal and social recognition of what is *different* about same-sex relationships; to them the claim for the right to marry is merely a claim for the right to assimilate into a patriarchal institution.[55] Others, however, see same-sex marriage as an opportunity not 'to participate in traditional family life, but to redefine what counts as family' (Auchmuty 2004 p 111 citing Calhoun 2000); it would provide the opportunity to reshape marriage 'into a *genuine* relationship between equals' (Auchmuty 2004 p 109, emphasis in original).

Others still see the issue in terms of rights and discrimination (Hale 2004; Murphy 2004). But as Hale (2004) points out, thus far Article 12 of the ECHR has not been interpreted by any court to permit the marriage of same sex couples. However courts in Canada and the US, which have written constitutions, have done so and may provide guidance on the possible directions European courts may take in the future. The Ontario Court of Appeal put it this way in 2003:

---

[55] See Auchmuty 2004 and sources cited there.

[5] Marriage is, without dispute, one of the most significant forms of personal relationships. For centuries, marriage has been a basic element of social organization in societies around the world. Through the institution of marriage, individuals can publicly express their love and commitment to each other. Through this institution, society publicly recognizes expressions of love and commitment between individuals, granting them respect and legitimacy as a couple. This public recognition and sanction of marital relationships reflect society's approbation of the personal hopes, desires and aspirations that underlie loving, committed conjugal relationships. This can only enhance an individual's sense of self-worth and dignity.

[6] The ability to marry, and to thereby participate in this fundamental societal institution, is something that most Canadians take for granted. Same-sex couples do not; they are denied access to this institution simply on the basis of their sexual orientation. ...

[107] [S]ame-sex couples are excluded from a fundamental societal institution—marriage. The societal significance of marriage, and the corresponding benefits that are available only to married persons, cannot be overlooked. Indeed, all parties are in agreement that marriage is an important and fundamental institution in Canadian society. It is for that reason that the claimants wish to have access to the institution. Exclusion perpetuates the view that same-sex relationships are less worthy of recognition than opposite-sex relationships. In doing so, it offends the dignity of persons in same-sex relationships.

(*Halpern v AG* (2003) 65 OR 3d 161)[56]

On the basis of this rights argument Canada has become one of an increasing number of jurisdictions in the world to allow same-sex marriage.[57]

**Q** Do you agree with the Canadian court that because 'marriage is an important and fundamental institution' in society, exclusion on the basis of sexual orientation constitutes discrimination or a breach of rights? Review the ECtHR's discussion of Article 12, the right to marry and found a family.

Other jurisdictions,[58] on the other hand, including the UK, have chosen to rectify perceived and actual discrimination against same-sex couples by introducing systems of registration of their partnerships, on which couples will obtain many if not all of the rights and responsibilities of marriage. The UK's scheme was, for the Department of Trade and Industry which sponsored the Civil Partnership Bill in Parliament in 2003, an 'important equality measure for same-sex couples' (DTI 2003a p 13 para 1.2). It was said that the proposal, which has now become the Civil Partnership Act 2004, would

provide for the legal recognition of same-sex partners and give legitimacy to those in, or wishing to enter into, interdependent, same-sex couple relationships that are intended to be permanent. Registration would provide a framework whereby same-sex couples could acknowledge their mutual responsibilities, manage their financial arrangements and achieve recognition as each other's partner. Committed same-sex relationships would be recognised and

---

56 www.ontariocourts.on.ca/decisions/2003.

57 As at March 2005, Bill C–38 The Civil Marriage Act had passed its first reading before Parliament. Section 2 of the Act says 'Marriage, for civil purposes, is the lawful union of two persons to the exclusion of all others.'The Netherlands introduced same-sex marriage in 2001, Belgium in 2002, and Spain in 2005. In the United States, Vermont, New York, Massachusetts and California allow same-sex marriage.

58 As at March 2005, within the EU, Denmark, Finland, France, Germany, Ireland (proposed by government in 2005), Luxembourg, Poland (proposed by government in 2004), Slovenia (proposed by government in 2004) and Sweden have registered partnership systems whereby same-sex partners receive some or all of the rights and responsibilities of marriage. Austria, Czech Republic, Hungary and Portugal allow some or all rights and responsibilities of marriage to accrue to same sex partners after a specified period of cohabitation.

registered partners would gain rights and responsibilities which would reflect the significance of the roles they play in each other's lives. This would encourage more stable family life. (*ibid*)

> **Q** Do you agree with the view that a form of registration of partnerships remedies discrimination against same-sex partners?

The California Superior Court took the view that it did not:

> The idea that marriage-like rights without marriage is adequate smacks of a concept long rejected by the courts: separate but equal. In *Brown v Board of Education of Topeka, et al,* (1952) 347 US 483, 494, the Court recognized that the provision of separate but equal educational opportunities to racial minorities 'generates a feeling of inferiority as to their status in the community that may affect their hearts and minds in a way unlikely ever to be undone.' Such logic is equally applicable to the State's structure granting substantial marriage rights but no marriage ... (Coordination Proceeding: Marriage Cases 2005 p 9)

In some jurisdictions, therefore, marriage is no longer an institution reserved for opposite sex partners. To some commentators, reconceptualising marriage as simply a contractual relationship may be another way out from difficulties created by laws reinforcing the 'permanent heterosexual union'.


## VII. MARRIAGE AS CONTRACT?

We have already seen O'Donovan's and Pateman's view of the tainted nature of contract philosophy, but let us examine the case for the contractarians. To many, even the traditional form of marriage is contractual, although it is often spoken of as a 'sacred' contract. It is indeed true that the law insists that marriage, like commercial contracts, must be freely entered into, but that is where the similarities stop. The terms of the marriage contract are not freely negotiable and it may not later be discharged by agreement of the parties. Nonetheless, many advocate alleviating the gender oppressive remnants of traditional marriage by reforming it further along the line of contractarian principles. It is thought that marriage could be divested of its gendered over-garments, and redefined according to modern conceptions of respect for the equal rights of two individuals who choose to make their lives together. David McLellan (1996) examines this argument. The proposal he tests is that 'the state could leave most substantive marital rights and obligations to be defined privately, but make the legal system available to resolve disputes arising under the privately created "legislation"' (p 236 quoting Shuttz, 1982). Intuitively, one might find this proposal attractive.

> [I]t would allow couples to escape from an outmoded legal tradition through an agreement especially tailored to fit their needs, thus respecting the values of privacy and respect for freedom in the ordering of personal relationships; it would give added authority to an anti-patriarchal and egalitarian stance; and it could be used to confer legitimation and structure on other forms of relationships—homosexual, polygamous, and so on.
>
> (McLellan 1996 p 237)

However, McLellan then goes on to present the argument against contract marriage. Most importantly, he reminds us, as did Pateman and O'Donovan, that it is premised upon a particular view of the individual and that individual's relationship with others and with the state: 'it is closely connected with the political doctrine of minimal government and the Adam Smithian optimism that some hidden hand will promote universal well-being through the pursuit by each of economic self-interest' (pp 242–43). It depoliticises the family by removing it into the private sphere of individual bargains where the stronger still rule, but in a non-regulated way (p 242). And finally, it presupposes that the individual bargainers are operating from the proverbial 'level playing field', a presupposition that is belied by the fact that the only women who would be able to negotiate a mutually advantageous relationship with men are those (relatively) few who are economically independent and well educated (p 241). McLellan, therefore, concludes by cautioning against the contractualisation of marriage.

In many jurisdictions, however, prenuptial agreements which set out the parties' intentions about how they wish to organise their relationship during the marriage and how they wish to organise their financial affairs in the event of separation, are permitted. These agreements, while not strictly speaking 'marriage contracts', allow for some autonomy in the parties to opt out of the statutory regulation of the terms of their marriage. These agreements are not enforceable in England and Wales,[59] but in 1998 the government proposed reforming the law to allow for their enforceability (Home Office 1998). Significantly, and perhaps surprisingly, however, half of the respondents to the Home Office consultation document in which it was raised were opposed to the proposal, even if the court would have retained its jurisdiction to disregard the agreement (Home Office 1999), especially where it felt injustice would be done.

[Q] What is your view of the contractualisation of marriage? You may wish to refer to Mary Ann Glendon's work, *The Transformation of Family Law* (1989), in which she suggests that state regulation of marriage has so decreased over the years that it may now be seen as a contractual relationship. See also Cretney (2003b).

[Q] Would it surprise you to learn that cohabitation contracts are enforceable in the courts? Why or why not?

## VIII. ALTERNATIVES TO FORMAL MARRIAGE

We have thus far examined the law regulating entry into marriage, which arguably helps us to understand the meaning and importance of marriage, and we now wish to utilise another approach to examine the meaning of marriage. We wish to consider Parker's (1990) suggestion that an historical perspective may help to move the debate away from a traditional comparison of marriage and cohabitation, to the issue of what is meant by marriage in the first place. He questions whether there was ever historically, or is now, a clear demarcation between marriage and cohabitation. Dire predictions about the breakdown of the fabric of society caused by people marrying less, it seems, have always

---

[59] See discussion below ch 6.

been with us. Usually, as we will see, they are accompanied by predictions of the dire consequences of the removal of women from their homemaking role. Blurring any legal or social distinctions between married and unmarried cohabitation may be society's way of dealing with what are perceived to be the disastrous consequences of cohabitation without marriage. If we look at the debate around the legal regulation of marriage in the 18th and 19th centuries, it may help us to place contemporary debate around the social and legal meaning of marriage into historical and political perspective.

Historically, the status of husband and wife and the regulation of that status were matters only for the individuals concerned, their families and their immediate community. The Church was concerned with peoples' spiritual well being, and so the canons of the Roman Catholic Church declared that marriage was a holy estate. Other than that declaration, though, the Church did not have much to say about how one would enter into that holy estate, other than to say it was by agreement and physical consummation. Rules governing who could enter into it were limited to specifying minimum ages of 12 for girls and 14 for boys and to rules prohibiting marriage within certain degrees of relationship by blood (consanguinity) and by marriage (affinity). Throughout medieval times the consent of the parties, provided it was spoken in the present tense, was sufficient to make a valid marriage. A mutual promise to marry in the future, a betrothal, precluded one from marrying anyone else and became an indissoluble bond once it was accompanied by physical consummation. Here we see the canonical beginnings of the voluntariness and the consummation requirements in the MCA 1973.

The privacy of these arrangements did not cause problems for the majority of people, but when questions of property arose, the private and informal nature of the 'marriage' created difficulties for those concerned about the orderly transmission of their property. Partly to meet the needs of greater certainty required by the propertied classes, the Church then created a set of formal rituals to go along with the exchange of consents. These rituals included the exchange of vows in a church, publicising the intention to marry in the form of banns and placing a ring on the wife's finger. As time went on, the rituals became more strict and included restricting the times of the day during which the vows could be exchanged.

The ecclesiastical rituals became more socially accepted in time, and those who required formal recognition because they wanted to avoid later problems of proof then began to use them more and more. The church rituals were used, then, by that minority of the population who were concerned with the proof of the bond for the purposes of the passing of property. Property disputes were a matter for the common law courts which came to require the evidence of the formal religious ceremony in order to decide questions of property transmission.

The majority of the population for whom property questions were irrelevant had no need to conform to the rituals of the Church, and usually could not afford them anyway. To them, social legitimacy for their unions was achieved in other ways. Gillis (1985) writes, for example, of the ceremonial jumping of the broom and other forms of community rituals which varied from place to place, but which were deeply rooted in custom and authority to provide moral, social and financial legitimacy to unions.

In addition to the 'common' folk, those who were not interested in the church wedding included young people who wished to marry without the parental consent required by the church for those under 21, those who could not afford the Church rituals, couples disparate in age or religion, or those who desired privacy for other personal reasons (Gillis 1985). These people were marrying according to local custom or by using the services of rogue ministers at the Fleet prison in London (Gillis 1985; Parker 1990, 1987; Stone 1990). These 'informal' marriages may not have conformed to church require-ments, but they were all *legal* marriages.

These forms of private ordering of familial lives were tolerated, but by the mid-18th century they became more and more unacceptable to upholders of the propertied and increasingly patriarchal order (O'Donovan 1985). Indeed, as Parker says, 'popular cus-toms of all kinds increasingly came under attack by a ruling class fearful of their public order consequences' (1987 p 144). The consequences for the propertied classes of uncon-trolled marriage were more than simply public-order consequences, however. The legal doctrine of coverture and the rule of primogeniture ensured that propertied men could maintain or indeed increase their wealth through a union with a woman who lost virtu-ally all legal identity upon marriage. By the 18th century, then, the aristocracy realised that the variety of permissible marriage ceremonies and increasing numbers of clandes-tine marriages meant that they lost control over the orderly transmission of their wealth. In this political context, if young people continued to marry whomever they wanted to in these clandestine ceremonies, it was almost seen as a threat to property and patriarchy (O'Donovan 1985 p 48).

Further, it was during this time that the ideal of the nuclear family and the companionate marriage which had divided the middle class and the aristocracy in the 17th century now began to unite them. Their convergence of views of marriage was evident by this time as 'family' began to be seen as a crucial means of capital accumulation and marriage played a central role in mobilising patriarchy and wealth. This 18th century view contrasts with that of the 17th century when 'couples' were rare and personal relationships were always accommodated within larger kin and community relationships (Gillis 1985 pp 11–12). The 17th century aristocracy treated marriage with disdain; neither concubines nor bastards shamed them and marriage was for convenience only. The patterns of family life of the peasant and artisan classes were different but were still characterised by variety. It is interesting that the conjugal family that we take for granted today had its roots in that part of the population Stone calls the 'middling sort' (1990).

The House of Lords had a number of times attempted to promote bills invalidating clandestine marriages, but the House of Commons refused to pass them. Finally, a bill was presented in the Lords by the Lord Chancellor, Lord Hardwicke, in 1753. The debate that accompanied its passage is illustrative. The primary reason for supporting the bill was frankly stated:

> How often have we known of the heir of a good family seduced, and engaged in a clandestine marriage, perhaps with a common strumpet? How often have we known a rich heiress carried off by a man of low birth, or perhaps by an infamous sharper? What distresses some of our best families have been brought into, what ruin some of their sons and daughters have been involved in, by such means, every gentleman from his own knowledge may recollect.
>
> (O'Donovan 1985 p 45)

Lord Hardwicke's bill, therefore, was proposed to meet the perceived needs of the prop-ertied minority. It proposed that all marriages were required to be performed in the Church of England in order to be valid. Oral consent alone no longer constituted a valid marriage. Further, all such church marriages had to be entered in the church regis-ter and no marriage of anyone under the age of 21 years was valid without the consent of parents or guardians. The Act was to apply to all, except members of the Royal Family, Jews and Quakers.

**Q** What aspects of Lord Hardwicke's bill can you see remaining in the MCA 1973? In the Marriage Act 1949?

One of the arguments against the bill was that it would enable the aristocracy to create a closed and increasingly wealthy caste for itself. Another was that it would have a ruinous effect upon the poor; it would be expensive, inconvenient and would therefore result in a rise of concubinage, bastardy and infanticide. Despite these arguments, the bill was passed and became law in 1753.[60] According to O'Donovan, Gillis describes it as 'an undisguised triumph of property, patriarchy and male dominance generally' (1985 p 49), and Cretney notes that it gave the Church of England a virtual monopoly over marriage (2003a p 6).

Enforcement of the law was placed within the jurisdiction of the secular courts, so that any member of the clergy who was convicted of disobeying it was subject to a penalty of 14 years' transportation.

Nevertheless, a number of forms of informal marriage remained popular, and to the people who practised them and to their communities they were respectable and proper. But they left no public record. Perhaps the best known of the evasive tactics was marrying across the border in Scotland in Gretna Green. In the period after the Act to the end of the 18th and beginning of the 19th century, informal marriages were more than just the remnants of 'folk life'; they were actually a powerful challenge to the law of the patriarch, Church and state (Gillis 1985; Parker 1990).

Women in particular often preferred these informal marriages because the doctrine of coverture only applied upon formal marriage. If a woman wished to maintain her separate legal identity an informal marriage would give her legitimacy in the eyes of her community without legally disabling her through a state-sanctioned marriage.

Lord Hardwicke's Act remained the primary law relating to marriage until 1836 when an entirely civil ceremony became legal.[61] This new provision providing for marriage at a Registry Office assisted those who could not meet the 1753 requirements. Initially, the working classes were hesitant to use the civil service because it was associated by them with the Poor Law Administration. But later, by the 1870s, the Registrar became the resort of pregnant women and other persons who did not want the full publicity of a church wedding. But then:

> [b]y the mid-19th century an age of conformity had begun which only began to fragment with the increase in cohabitation after the Second World War. For many working class people in about 1850 alternatives to formal marriage were becoming decreasingly attractive. The amendment to the Poor Law in 1834 made legal marriage increasingly important for women's economic survival. Towns and cities became more anonymous so that there was less effective community pressure on a man to marry or support a woman if she had a child by him. The bourgeois family model slowly filtered down to the working class so that alternative forms became less thinkable. (Parker 1990 pp 74–75)

The 1836 Act completed the move to the secularisation of marriage. The state now had control over marriage. It needed to know clearly who was married to whom for the

---

[60] An Act for the Better Prevention of Clandestine Marriages 1753.
[61] Marriage Act 1836.

purposes of the distribution of benefits and burdens. 'A centralised bureaucratic state could not tolerate the ambiguities of the pre-Hardwicke era' (O'Donovan 1985 p 48).[62]

After 1836, statutes regulating marriage have dealt mainly with the formalities of the wedding itself,[63] with Cretney (2003a) characterising those of the 1990s as demonstrating a Thatcherite approach to administrative efficiency and consumerism: [t]here was an underlying belief in exposing public services to the pressures of consumer demand, competition and market forces, and this led the government to propose giving the public a greater choice of marriage ceremony' (p 30). He observes that the 1994 Marriage Act allowing marriages to be solemnised in 'approved' premises effectively 'privatised' civil marriage (p 31).

Even after its most recent reforms, the legislation retains restrictions on age and proximity of family relationship. Schedule 1 to the Marriage Act 1949 (as amended) lists the following prohibitions based on consanguinity. In Part I, it lists:

—mother or father
—adoptive mother (or father) or former adoptive mother (father)
—daughter (or son)
—adoptive daughter (or son) or former adoptive daughter (or son)
—father's mother (or father)
—mother's mother (or father)
—son's daughter (or son)
—daughter's daughter (or son)
—sister (or brother)
—father's sister (or brother)
—mother's sister (or brother)
—brother's daughter (or son)
—sister's daughter (or son).

The following degrees of affinity are prohibited by Part II unless both partners are at least 21 at the time of the marriage and the younger partner has never been a child of the family in relation to the other partner:

—daughter of former wife; son of former husband
—former wife of father; former husband of mother
—former wife of mother's father; former husband of mother's mother
—daughter of son of former wife; son of son of former husband
—daughter of daughter of former wife; son of daughter of former husband.[64]

And finally, the following degrees of affinity are prohibited, unless both parties are at least 21 years of age at the time of the marriage:

—mother of former wife (unless both former wife and father of former wife are both dead (section 1(5)(a));
—former wife of son (unless both son and mother of son are dead (section 1(5)(b));
—father of former husband (unless both former husband and mother of former husband are dead (section 1(5)(c));

[62] Cretney observes that the 1836 Act met the interests of both the State and the Church: the state had an interest in being able to determine whether or not a person was married, with all the legal consequences that flowed from that status, but its interest in the actual ceremony was limited to ensuring its recognition as binding by both parties (2003a p 9).
[63] See discussion in Cretney (2003a) ch 1.
[64] S 1(2) and (3) of the Marriage Act 1949.

—former husband of daughter (unless both daughter and father of daughter are dead (section 1(5)(d)).[65]

The minimum age for legal marriage now is 18. However, the minimum age is 16 if there is parental consent or the court consents instead.[66]

> **Q** Why was it important that the law allow parents some control over their children's decisions to marry? How real was this control? What were restrictions on age at marriage meant to achieve? What reasons are there today for such control? See also Hamilton (1996) regarding the case of a 13-year-old who contracted a 'marriage' under Islamic law. What were restrictions on marriage between blood relations designed to achieve? What reasons can you think of for such restrictions today?

We raised earlier the effect of the European Convention on Human Rights on marriage law. The historical context in which the Convention was enacted included in part a reaction to the discovery of the atrocities perpetrated by the Nazi regime in Europe, including the Nuremberg laws forbidding certain people from marrying one another. Similarly, former laws in both the United States and South Africa prohibited people of different 'races' from marrying each other.[67] In this light, perhaps Article 12 is better understood as a freedom to marry.

> **Q** Can you make an argument that a freedom to marry does not go far enough, and Article 12 should be interpreted as a right to marry?

## IX. FORMAL AND INFORMAL MARRIAGE

We have dealt so far with how a particular idea of marriage is regulated by legal assignment of eligibility to participate in it and by historical comparisons between formal and informal marriage. Implicit in this discussion was the idea that non-marital relationships between adults entailed little, if any, formal legal regulation. However, the distinct legal consequences of married and non-married cohabitation may serve as a form of *post hoc* regulation of relationships. We turn now to the legal effect that marital status has upon individuals (Clive 1980).

---

[65] S 1(4) and 5. But see now *B and L v UK* (Appn No 36536/02) (13 Sept 2005) in which the ECtHR held that this prohibition on marriage, between parents-in-law and children-in-law, violated Art 12 of the ECHR.

[66] Marriage Act 1949 s 3, as amended by Children Act 1989 Sch 12. The Church of England ceremony itself, although no longer required for validity, still contains elements of the pre-Hardwicke ritual. See generally, Cretney (2003a).

[67] See, eg in South Africa, the Prohibition of Mixed Marriages Act 55 of 1949. The prohibition was removed by the Immorality and Prohibition of Mixed Marriages Amendment Act 72 of 1985. In the United States the Virginia Code prohibited marriage between a 'white' and a 'colored' person. This statute was held to be unconstitutional in 1967. In that year Virginia and 15 other states outlawed interracial marriage. See *Loving v Virginia* 38 US 1; 87 S Ct 1817. See also *McLaughlin v State of Florida* 37 9 US 184, 85 S Ct 283 (1964) where the US Supreme Court held invalid as a denial of the constitutional equal protection provisions in Florida a statute making it a criminal offence for a 'white' and a 'negro' of opposite sexes who were not married habitually to live in and occupy the same room. Finally, see the California Superior Court decision Marriage Cases, referred to above.

The legal effect of marriage is no longer that described by Blackstone in the 18th century whereby husband and wife became one in law and the wife's legal existence was subsumed under that of the husband (1778 p 442). But we can see remnants of this situation in contemporary law (for example, in the question of whether a husband and wife can be co-conspirators[68]), policy (for example, income support policy which is based upon wife-dependence[69]) and custom (for example, the tradition of a wife giving up her name and taking her husband's).

In addition, the remnants of laws which treated unmarried cohabitants in all cases as legal strangers can also be discerned. There is currently no obligation upon unmarried people to support each other financially, and if an unmarried partner dies intestate, the bereaved partner has no automatic right to inherit from the estate.[70] Other examples of legal situations in which married and unmarried people are treated differently include the scope of parental responsibility assigned to unmarried as opposed to married fathers,[71] the lack of legislated proprietary rights in the family home for unmarried partners,[72] the absence of social security rights to 'spousal' contributions for unmarried partners[73] and weaker tax benefits for unmarried partners.[74] On the other hand, there are some situations in which the legal gap between married and unmarried cohabitants is narrowing. Married women may now contract in their own name as if they were unmarried, and we saw in Chapter 1 some similarity of treatment, for example, in the income support cases and the succession to tenancy cases. In addition, spousal benefits are sometimes provided to unmarried partners pursuant to employment contracts or other private contracts, and in some of these situations same sex couples are treated the same as opposite sex couples.[75]

Regulation of legal burdens and benefits to unmarried partners relative to their married counterparts has proceeded in England and Wales on an *ad hoc* or piecemeal basis in response to increasing numbers of heterosexual people who are choosing to live in 'informal' marriage-like arrangements. Recall the statistics with which we opened this chapter: at least 25% of men and women were living in heterosexual unmarried cohabitation in 2001/02, and government sources expect that number to increase steadily over the years (Dyer 2005a). The current *ad hoc* approach whereby in some situations cohabitants are treated in law as though they are married (such as for income support purposes), sometimes as similar but still inferior to married couples (such as for protection from domestic violence under the Family Law Act 1996) and sometimes as legal strangers (such as for the purposes of financial or property division on relationship breakdown) has been described as a 'legislative and judicial lottery' (Barlow and James 2004 p 156).[76] It contrasts with the approach taken in other jurisdictions which have

---

[68] *Midland Bank Trust Co Ltd v Green (No 3)* [1982] Ch 529 (CA); Criminal Law Act 1977 s 2(2)(a).

[69] See Beveridge (1942); Daly (1994).

[70] See Inheritance (Provision for Family and Dependants) Act 1975.

[71] See ch 4.

[72] See ch 5.

[73] See ch 5.

[74] See ch 3. See on this generally Cretney, *et al*, (2002) para 3–007ff; and Herring (2004) p 60ff.

[75] See eg *Mendoza* case, regarding succession to tenancies, discussed in ch 1. Note, however, *Grant v SW Trains* [1998] 1 FLR 839 (ECJ) where it was argued before the ECJ that cohabiting homosexual partners be given the same travel concessions by the employer as heterosexual cohabitants. The court found that it was not a violation of sex equality laws to refuse the concessions.

[76] See Barlow and James (2004) for a comprehensive review of the legal rights and responsibilities of unmarried cohabitants.

adopted comprehensive legislation providing for public and private support and property rights for unmarried cohabitants.[77]

There have been attempts in recent years to remedy the disadvantage suffered by dependent or otherwise vulnerable cohabitants on the death of their partner or breakdown of their relationship. In relation to their home, the Law Commission's discussion paper on the rights of cohabitants and other 'homesharers' in the family home (Law Commission 2002) considered the possibility of devising a scheme which would distribute fairly shares in a shared home. The Commission found it impossible to do so, however, at least through changes in property law. It said:

> [W]e have identified, in the course of this project, a wider need for the law to recognise and to respond to the increasing diversity of living arrangements in this country. We believe that further consideration should be given to the adoption—necessarily by legislation—of broader-based approaches to personal relationships, such as the registration of certain civil partnerships and/or the imposition of legal rights and obligations on individuals who are or have been involved in a relationship outside marriage.
>
> (Law Commission 2002 Executive Summary para 15)

It seemed to be advocating a relationship-based approach which would confer rights and responsibilities upon cohabitants as a result of their cohabitation. This is the approach taken by the Law Society (Law Society 2002b) and by a number of academics.[78] It is also the approach that seems to have been adopted by the government. In March 2005 the Lord Chancellor asked the Law Commission to produce, by 2007, proposals for legislation and a draft bill on the rights of cohabitants. The proposals will almost certainly refer to documents prepared by the Law Society and by Resolution (formerly the Solicitors Family Law Association) as well as to legislation in other jurisdictions. These almost invariably confer at least some rights to support and the family home once a couple live together 'as husband and wife' for a minimum period of time and/or have a child together, and apply to same sex as well as opposite sex partners.

For example, in *Cohabitation: The case for clear law* the Law Society reviewed the historical and current prevalence and context of cohabitation and the uncertain and *ad hoc* nature of the current law. It expressed its concern that some cohabitants 'suffer when their relationships break down because of the inadequate protection in law afforded to them' (2002b p 3). It then reviewed possible approaches that could be taken to a new cohabitation law, and concluded that while any protection afforded by law should not be as great as that provided to married couples, the law should be able to adjust the financial and property arrangements of cohabitants when their relationships break down.[79] It

---

[77] Some of these provisions are over 20 years old. In 1984 New South Wales in Australia passed its *de facto* Relationships Act which provides for the right of unmarried cohabitants to claim either property readjustment or support on the breakdown of the relationship. In Sweden the Law on Cohabitees (Joint Homes) legislation provides for, among other things, a right on separation to division and distribution of property acquired for joint use, and modest succession rights (Bradley 1996 pp 98–100). In both of these jurisdictions it is important to note the class of cohabitants who fall under the jurisdiction of the laws. In New South Wales *de facto* partners for the purposes of a maintenance application are those who have lived in a domestic relationship as husband and wife for not less than two years. The Swedish law applies to 'relationships involving cohabitation in which an unmarried woman and an unmarried man live together in circumstances resembling marriage' (Bradley 1996 p 214).. In contrast to this, the Norwegian Law on Joint Households applies to two or more unmarried persons over 18 who have lived together for at least two years, and so includes relatives, students and friends as well as cohabitees (Bradley 1996 p 214).
[78] See eg Barlow and James (2004).
[79] See Law Society (2002b) for detailed recommendations.

proposed that 'cohabitants' should be defined as two people (either opposite sex or same sex) living together (for a continuous period of at least two years) in the same household in a relationship analogous to that of husband and wife. Alternatively, cohabitants can demonstrate the required 'degree of commitment' (p 4) by having had a 'relevant child' together.

The arguments in favour of a comprehensive scheme protecting vulnerable cohabitants seem clear. First, it would recognise the statistical and social reality that more and more couples are living together without marriage. Second, it would confer at least some social legitimacy upon these relationships by recognising them and their value to society. We noted earlier that the level of commitment to the other person and to the 'family' is not necessarily less in non-marital relationships than in marital ones, and in this way non-marital relationships must be seen to contribute to the good and stable society in the same way as do married relationships. Thirdly, Barlow and James' research confirms an 'astonishing lack of awareness' (2004 p 161) of the legal consequences of marriage and heterosexual cohabitation and therefore that a statutory scheme providing at least some of the benefits of marriage to those who believe they have them already would remedy injustices.

'Over half (56%) of respondents in the BSA survey in England and Wales believed that cohabiting for a period of time gives rise to a "common law marriage" giving cohabitants the same legal rights as married couples. Among cohabitants, this false belief rose to 59%'.
(Barlow and James 2004 p 161)

The arguments against a scheme providing the benefits of marriage to unmarried heterosexual partners range from the traditionally conservative to the critically feminist. The conservative argument is that if those couples want the benefits of marriage they should simply get married. To provide the benefits otherwise would undermine marriage as an institution. The answer to the apparently widespread belief in 'common law marriage' is to provide education about the law, not to change it in line with the mistaken belief.

On the other hand, if law and policy are truly to reflect our new and diverse partnering and living patterns, perhaps conferring rights and benefits only upon those couples who look most like married couples, whether same-sex or different-sex, does not go far enough. A legislative scheme for cohabitants on this view simply reinforces the heterosexual conjugal couple as the paradigm legal and social relationship and the privilege that is and, indeed ought to be, attached to it. The Law Commission recognised the difficulty of accommodating in law our changing family practices that do not conform to that paradigm relationship:

There is also an increasing problem concerning persons who are not in any sense 'a couple', but who live together for mutual support or caring. They may or may not be related, but their financial affairs become somewhat inextricably intertwined. This is not by any means a homogenous group. (Law Commission 2002 para 1.31(4))

It was not able to devise a scheme to accommodate these non-conjugal homesharers, yet arguably that accommodation is precisely what is needed. The Law Commission of Canada observed in 2002 the same growing diversity in Canadian family life and it concluded that recognising and supporting the great variety of caring personal adult relationships is an important state objective, along with valuing equality and autonomy, personal security, privacy, freedom of conscience and religion, while at the same time maintaining coherence and efficiency in the law. In the light of these principles, it concluded that the distinction between conjugal and non-conjugal relationships is inconsistent with the value of equality, since conjugality is not an accurate marker of the qualitative attributes of personal adult relationships that are relevant to practical legislative and policy objectives. Further, it assumed that the state's role should be neutral regarding the roles that people assume in their personal relationships, and therefore instead of simply arguing that some relationships currently excluded should be included in legal recognition, it proposed that we start from square one and look at the way governments have relied upon relational status in allocating rights and responsibilities. It criticised this traditional reliance on status, and instead proposed a legislative regime that accomplishes its goals by relying less on whether people are living in certain kinds of relationships and more on whether a particular characteristic of the relationship was relevant to the particular state goal. Since different laws have different objectives, the characteristics of the relationship deemed to be relevant should differ as we move from one law to another. And while sometimes some characteristics of the relationship would be important and other times they would not be, conjugality would never be important (Law Commission of Canada 2002). As Roseneil observes, the effect of such an approach on law and policy might mean, for example, framing work-life policies 'in terms of the range of important personal relationships and commitments within which people live their lives' (2004 p 415) rather than narrowly with reference to relationship status.

**Q** How would you legislate for the rights and obligations of unmarried partners? Whom would you include within the scope of your legislation? See generally, on the development of the law relating to unmarried cohabitation Cretney (2003a) chapter 13.

## X. THE CIVIL PARTNERSHIP ACT 2004

The alternative course of action to the stark choice between marriage and non-marriage and the rights and responsibilities that ought to come with each is to create a third status for relationships; one where people could register their partnership and thus receive certain rights and responsibilities on registration. A registered partnership scheme exists in many jurisdictions and some apply to both same-sex and opposite-sex partners.[80] The first attempt in Britain to formulate such a scheme, in fact, was intended to apply to both same-sex and opposite-sex partners[81] but partly on the grounds that to do so would undermine marriage, it was withdrawn.

Instead, the UK took the position that registration should be available only for those for whom marriage was unavailable, and, as we saw above, on the basis of equality, promoted and passed the Civil Partnership Act 2004. The Act is expected to come into force in December 2005. A civil partnership is 'a relationship between two people of the same

[80] In France, for example, the PACS or Civil Solidarity Pact is signed in court and commits any two domestic partners of the same or opposite sexes to mutual and material help. Among other EU countries, forms of registered partnerships giving some or all rights of marriage are available in Belgium, Denmark (to same sex partners only), Finland (same sex partners only), Germany (same sex partners only), Luxembourg, the Netherlands, Spain and Sweden. At the time of writing, Poland, Hungary and Ireland were considering proposals or Bills for registered partnerships.
[81] Lord Lester's Civil Partnerships Bill (2002).

sex' (s1(1)) which is formed when they register their partnership in accordance with the Act. The government was keen to distance civil registration from marriage:

> It is a matter of public record that the Government has no plans to introduce same-sex marriage. This consultation document is about a civil partnership registration scheme.
>
> (DTI 2003a p 13 para 1.3)

> We have considered the position of opposite-sex couples, many of whom now choose to cohabit instead of marrying, and other people who live together in a close supportive household environment. The Government believes that these situations are significantly different from that of same-sex couples who wish to formalise their relationships but currently are unable to do so. (*Ibid* para 1.4)

It is not made clear exactly what the 'significant difference' is between the situations of same-sex and opposite-sex cohabitants; certainly protecting against economic vulnerability and providing rights and formal recognition are important in both situations. Perhaps the difference is simply the legal inability of same-sex partners to formalise their relationships, and if so then the government's position seems to reinforce the view that opposite-sex partners should simply get married if they want the legal benefits and protection that comes with that status.

Further, as much as civil partnership is said to be distinct from marriage, a close reading of its terms and the rights and responsibilities it confers reveals that it creates a legal status which displays virtually all the characteristics of a civil marriage. The civil partnership document must be signed by the parties, two witnesses and the registrar before it is registered.[82] Like marriage, a civil partnership is for life, terminating only on death, dissolution or annulment.[83] There are other similarities to marriage as well, including the requirement of monogamy (neither of the partners must already be in a marriage or other civil partnership), legal age (the partners must be over the age of 18 or if between 16 and 18 have parental consent) and exclusion from the prohibited degrees of relationship.[84] There are also requirements as to the formalities of the registration procedure, including the place of registration,[85] the provision of notice of the proposed partnership and a waiting period.[86] And, like marriage, a civil partnership may be void or voidable if defective in certain ways.

49 Grounds on which civil partnership is void
Where two people register as civil partners of each other in England and Wales, the civil partnership is void if

(a)  at the time when they do so, they are not eligible to register as civil partners of each other under Chapter 1 (see section 3),
(b)  at the time when they do so they both know—
    (i)  that due notice of proposed civil partnership has not been given,
    (ii) that the civil partnership document has not been duly issued,
    (iii) that the civil partnership document is void under section 17(3) or 27(2) (registration after end of time allowed for registering),
    (iv) that the place of registration is a place other than that specified in the notices (or notice) of proposed civil partnership and the civil partnership document, or

---

[82] S 2.
[83] S 1(3).
[84] Ss 3 and 4.
[85] S 6.
[86] Ss 8–17.

(v) that a civil partnership registrar is not present, or

(c) the civil partnership document is void under paragraph 6(5) of Schedule 2 (civil partnership between a child and another person forbidden).

50 Grounds on which civil partnership is voidable

(1) Where two people register as civil partners of each other in England and Wales, the civil partnership is voidable if—

(a) either of them did not validly consent to its formation (whether as a result of duress, mistake, unsoundness of mind or otherwise);

(b) at the time of its formation either of them, though capable of giving a valid consent, was suffering (whether continuously or intermittently) from mental disorder of such a kind or to such an extent as to be unfitted for civil partnership;

(c) at the time of its formation, the respondent was pregnant by some person other than the applicant;

(d) an interim gender recognition certificate under the Gender Recognition Act 2004 (c.7) has, after the time of its formation, been issued to either partner;

(e) the respondent is a person whose gender at the time of its formation had become the acquired gender under the 2004 Act.

(2) In this section and section 51 'mental disorder' has the same meaning as in the Mental Health Act 1983 (c. 20).

51 Bars to relief where civil partnership is voidable

(1) The court must not make a nullity order on the ground that a civil partnership is voidable if the respondent satisfies the court—

(a) that the applicant, with knowledge that it was open to him to obtain a nullity order, conducted himself in relation to the respondent in such a way as to lead the respondent reasonably to believe that he would not seek to do so, and

(b) that it would be unjust to the respondent to make the order.

(2) Without prejudice to subsection (1), the court must not make a nullity order by virtue of section 50(1)(a), (b), (c) or (e) unless—

(a) it is satisfied that proceedings were instituted within 3 years from the date of the formation of the civil partnership, or

(b) leave for the institution of proceedings after the end of that 3 year period has been granted under subsection (3)

....

(5) Without prejudice to subsection (1), the court must not make a nullity order by virtue of section 50(1)(d) unless it is satisfied that proceedings were instituted within the period of 6 months from the date of issue of the interim gender recognition certificate.

(6) Without prejudice to subsections (1) and (2), the court must not make a nullity order by virtue of section 50(1)(a) or (e) unless it is satisfied that the applicant was at the time of the formation of the civil partnership ignorant of the facts alleged.

In later chapters we will examine the legal effects of civil partnership, but it seems clear that it is meant to resemble marriage. Indeed, it has been described as 'ingenious' (Stychin 2005)—it is virtually marriage in all but name.[87]

---

[87] See also Auchmuty (2004). Note also that non-consummation is not a ground for voidability.

**Q** Review the position of the US and Canadian Courts on providing a form of part-nership registration short of marriage as a remedy for discrimination or violation of rights. Do you think the Civil Partnership Act 2004 meets the government's aims of being an important equality measure, giving legitimacy to same-sex rela-tionships, and encouraging more stable family life?[88] Do we now have a three tiered system, with marriage at the top, followed by civil registration and then by unmarried cohabitation?

## XI. SUMMARY AND CONCLUSION

The legal approach to regulating relations between intimates is, as we saw, connected with the political and social economy of a state. It is also, however, intimately connected with custom, tradition and religious beliefs held by dominant communities within the state. Perhaps this is what Parker means when he suggests that our study should be focused more upon what we mean by marriage itself, than on any differences between formal and informal marriage. Marriage in England and Wales is accorded a privileged social status which provides a place for the legitimate expression of heterosexual desires, imbuing other types of sexual activity and other relationships with a lesser status. The married unit is the economic unit upon which state financial policy is based and has its modern beginnings in concern for the orderly transmission of property within families. It is the institution which most easily, but not exclusively, accommodates the model of family preferred by other state institutions and is presumed to be the model which best promotes the welfare of children (Home Office 1998). It is, however, also a model which can be adapted in an increasingly egalitarian society, as is demonstrated by recent changes in the law that appear to give legitimacy to other family models, but on closer inspection, do so only if they are sufficiently 'marriage-like' (Cossman and Ryder 2001).

Parker writing in 1990 said:

> It is quite clear that only some kinds of cohabitees fall within the net of rights and regulation; namely those who behave like married people. Every definition of cohabitation in statute law refers to marriage-like behaviour. In case law developments, the judges have paid great atten-tion to whether the couple intended to marry or organised their affairs like a married couple because it is easier then to draw inferences about what the couple intended.
>
> It is tempting to regard this selective assimilation as a grand conspiracy to extend the repres-sive benevolence of marriage to those who approximate to it. Freeman and Lyon (1983, chapter 8) in their extended account of cohabitation law and policy come near to doing this. Such an approach overlooks the disparate nature of law-makers; parliamentarians, judges, Law Com-missioners and so forth. It also overlooks the haphazard way that the law has developed. There is no single piece of legislation devoted solely to cohabitation; instead assimilative rules ride on the back of other measures which chance to be passed.
>
> In my argument, cohabitation law has come about because the displacement of marriage by family, which has been a feature of post-war British social policy, has brought with it and been a part of changing perceptions of justice. (Parker 1990 p 149, emphasis added))

---

[88] See also Murphy (2004); Crompton (2004); Hale (2004).

**Q** How different is the historical attempt to draw dissenters into the net of legal marriage and state regulation of relationships from the modern assimilation of many cohabitants into the laws of marriage? See, on this, Parker 1987 p 150. At what point, if any, can you identify a clear demarcation between formal and informal marriages?

We can now return to Clive's and Fineman's thesis and the subversive question becomes: what is the *legal* value of the religious or social ritual of marriage? Would you feel comfortable living in a society in which decisions to form households were validated socially without the necessity of their legal validation? Why should this religious ritual or social rite of passage confer any more legal status upon a person than a first holy communion, a confirmation, a debutante's 'coming out' or a *bar mitzvah*?

## FURTHER READING AND SELECTED RECENT REFERENCES

R AUCHMUTY, 'Same-sex Marriage Revived: Feminist Critique and Legal Strategy' (2004) 14 *Feminism and Psychology* 101.

F BANDA, 'Global Standards: Local Values' (2003) 17 *International Journal of Law, Policy and the Family*.

A BARLOW and G JAMES, 'Regulating Marriage and Cohabitation in 21st Century Britain' (2004) 67 *Modern Law Review* 143.

W BLACKSTONE, *Commentary on the Laws of England*, 8th edn, (Oxford, Clarendon Press, 1778).

S CRETNEY, *Family Law in the Twentieth Century: A History* (Oxford, OUP, 2003).

——, 'The Family and the Law—Status or Contract?' (2003b) 15 *Child and Family Law Quarterly* 403.

L CROMPTON, 'The Civil Partnerships Bill 2004: The Illusion of Equality' (2004) *Fam Law* 888.

G DOUGLAS and A PERRY, 'How Parents Cope Financially on Separation and Divorce—Implications for the Future of Ancillary Relief' (2001) 13 *Child and Family Law Quarterly* 67.

J EEKELAAR and M MACLEAN, 'Marriage and the Moral Bases of Personal Relationships' (2004) 31 *Journal of Law and Society* 510.

J GILLIS, *For Better or for Worse: British Marriages 1600 to the Present* (Oxford, OUP, 1985).

B HALE, 'Homosexual Rights' (2004) 16 *CFLQ* 125.

S PARKER, *Informal Marriage, Cohabitation and the Law 1750–1989* (Basingstoke, Macmillan, 1990).

R PROBERT, 'When Are We Married? Void, Non-existent and Presumed Marriages' (2002) 22 *Legal Studies* 398.

J REYNOLDS and P MANSFIELD, 'The Effect of Changing Attitudes to Marriage on Its Stability' *Lord Chancellor's Department Research Series* 2/99 vol 1, (London, The Stationery Office, 1999).

S ROSENEIL, 'Why we Should Care about Friends: An Argument for Queering the Care Imaginary in Social Policy' (2004) 3(4) *Social Policy and Society* 409.

S ROSENEIL and S BUDGEON, 'Cultures of Intimacy and Care Beyond "the Family": Personal Life and Social Change in the Early 21st Century' (2004) *Current Sociology* 135.

C SMART, *The Ties That Bind* (London, Routledge and Kegan Paul, 1984).

L STONE, *The Family, Sex and Marriage in England 1500–1800* (London, Harper & Rowe, 1979).

C STYCHIN, 'Family Friendly? Rights, Responsibilities and Relationship Recognition' in A Diduck and K O'Donovan, (eds), *Feminist Perspectives on Family Law* (London, Cavendish, forthcoming, 2006).

*Reports*

Supporting Families: Responses to the Consultation Document (London, The Stationery Office).

Home Office, *A Choice By Right: Report of the working group on forced marriage* (London, Home Office, 2000).

DTI, Women and Equality Unit (2003a), *Civil Partnership: A Framework for the legal recognition of same-sex couples* (London, DTI Home Office, 1999).

J LEWIS, *Marriage, Cohabitation and the Law: Individualism and Obligation* (Lord Chancellor's Department Research Series No 1/99, London, The Stationery Office, 1999).

The Law Commission, *Sharing Homes: A Discussion Paper,* Law Com No 278 (London, The Stationery Office, 2002).

Law Commission of Canada *Beyond Conjugality: Recognizing and supporting close personal adult relationships* (Ottawa, Law Commission of Canada, 2002).

The Law Society, *Cohabitation: The Case for Clear Law* (London, The Law Society, 2002).

# 3

# The Adult–Child–State Relationship:
# Reproduction and Child-Rearing

We have suggested that the couple relationship, based upon the traditional heterosexual relationship, is central to the ideology of the family, and that one of the bases for this centrality is the benefit that relationship is assumed to confer upon society. That relationship is also assumed to confer benefits upon the individuals in it, not least upon children. We have also seen, however, that a great many adults do not arrange their familial lives around this relationship, nor do children live only in heterosexual nuclear family units. We now turn to the relationship between children and adults. Laws concerning those relationships affect not only adult responsibilities for the care of children, but also the regulation of reproduction itself. In this and the next chapter we will examine the social and legal ordering of reproduction and child care, the issues raised in the legal determination of who is a parent and the meaning of parenthood in law. In doing so, we focus as much upon those to whom the label 'parent' may not attach as upon those to whom it may. We also seek to situate the rights and responsibilities assigned to parenthood within the context of equality rights, the ideology of familialism and the public/private divide.

## I. REPRODUCTIVE RIGHTS?

It is one of the characteristics of the liberal state that our relationships with others are often mediated in terms of rights. 18th and 19th century notions of individualism and equality carried with them assumptions about the autonomy of individuals,[1] including assumptions about individual liberties and rights. Within the liberal order, disputes are often framed in terms of individual 'rights' to, for example, bodily autonomy or equality. Some states[2] have facilitated this individualised understanding of disputes by incorporating the protection of individual rights into constitutional documents, and we have also seen the importance of individual rights within EU documents and the Human Rights Act 1998.

   The political and moral desirability of framing disputes in terms of competing individual rights, however, has been questioned, particularly by feminist writers. Kingdom (1991), for example, sees it as particularly unhelpful to place issues of reproduction in a rights framework. She states that because rights arguments always produce counter

---

[1] See eg, discussion in Reece (2003) and for an alternative view of autonomy generally, see Sevenhuijsen (1998) and in the context of reproduction, Jackson (2001) ch 1.
[2] Eg, South Africa, the United States or Canada.

claims to competing rights, they may not serve women's interests. She also says that individual rights based on freedom of choice are problematic in a society where material and social conditions make choice an unrealistic option.[3] Questions about pregnancy and childbirth become further complicated for many and unresolvable for some in the context of a legal or political philosophy which assumes the equality or 'sameness' of autonomous individuals because a pregnant woman is the unique antithesis of an autonomous individual (Diduck 1993 and 1998; Smart 1989b p 157; Fovargue 2002).[4] For these writers, notions of individual rights either cannot be used at all or must be radically reformulated when applied to pregnancy and childbirth. Taking this reasoning further, one could argue that applying notions of competing individual rights may be inappropriate also to relations within collectivities, such as families (Olsen 1983; McLellan 1996).[5] Carol Smart, however, argues that the prevailing political climate makes it difficult to abandon rights arguments, and that until that climate changes, women must resort to rights claims (1989b pp 158–59).

Smart's analysis gains support from the fact that, notwithstanding theoretical arguments over the efficacy of rights discourse generally, or its usefulness when applied in the context of familial relations, domestic and international documents which embody the language of rights are often employed when questions about those relations come to be determined by law. And so, our most intimate and personal decisions about reproduction and their social and legal regulation are often conceptualised in terms of 'reproductive rights'. We will adopt this framework in order to tease out the advantages and disadvantages of reproductive 'rights talk', but before we ask whether we have a *right* to reproduce, or a *right not* to reproduce, we want to question whether reproductive rights can be discussed in gender neutral terms and whether motherhood and fatherhood can be collapsed into a generic notion of parenthood. Whether or not they can is significant in considering how or whether any rights are ascribed.

Disproportionate research into assisting women's reproductive capacities and the plethora of techniques that have been developed for use on women's bodies are examples of how reproduction is seen almost exclusively as a matter of and about women. As Sheldon states, '[r]eproduction has been seen as women's business and it is the bodies of women which have been understood as posing the greatest threat to the foetus. Men's relationship to reproduction has been constructed as distant, and largely vicarious' (Sheldon 1999 p 138). Because of this construction in law, which is linked to the different biological roles in reproduction played by women and men and the different social roles played in caring for children, we must not lose sight of the fact that any rights relating to reproduction, as well as legislation, medical procedures or social or moral discourse concerning reproduction have always and necessarily affected women and men in very different ways.

Historically, the valorisation of maternity was as important to the first wave of the feminist movement as it was to upholders of patriarchy. To both, however, the characteristics of the idealised mother were race-specific (Lewis 1980), class-specific (Lewis 1980; 1992) and status-specific, encouraging motherhood only within marriage (Spensky 1992; Smart 1992). In this context and in the context of an increasingly

---

[3] See also Smart (1989b) pp 150–51; and Sheldon (2004).

[4] 'Himmelweit has argued that we need to reconceptualise pregnancy as a period when women are actually actively nurturing the foetus. This challenges the ideas that the foetus and the mother are simply separate entities which the rights argument does so much to sustain' (Smart 1989b p 157).

[5] For a class analysis of rights see Fudge and Glasbeek (1992).

influential Evangelical movement and other organised movements promoting 'moral purity', advocates for legal and freely available methods of birth control, for example, were often seen to be advancing an 'unnatural' course of action for middle class married women. For women who did not meet the standard of the proper Victorian mother—poor, unmarried and often, not white—birth control and sterilisation were encouraged. In the 21st century, the image of 'traditional' motherhood as woman's 'natural' role remains relatively strong, as does its perceived power to shape the good society (Phoenix 1996; Diduck 1995).

Fatherhood, historically, meant something different. Fatherhood was primarily concerned with the transmission of the family name and property to legitimate heirs. Fathers in the 21st century may not now be so preoccupied with their heirs, and the image of fatherhood is changing somewhat to incorporate the notion of the 'involved' father. Nevertheless Collier (1995b) has argued that a particular form of hegemonic masculinity survives in which masculinity is defined according to a divide between the heterosexual/potent/virile man and the homosexual/impotent/non-virile one; the impotent/non-virile man is constructed as a threat to the institution of marriage, and not really a man at all (pp 150–51). Further, he has argued that the masculinity of the potent/virile man must be manifested in a 'respectable' way—within marriage—so as to create the mature, safe fatherhood of the breadwinner.

> **Q** The above perspectives suggest that motherhood is seen as a natural fulfilment of a woman's instinct, while fatherhood is seen as a necessary expression of appropriate or safe masculinity. Do you agree that these understandings play a part in the gendering of parenthood? How might they differently affect notions of a man's or a woman's right to reproduce?

The notion of gender-neutral reproductive rights is, then, a questionable one. We now go on to consider such rights, beginning with the right to reproduce. If it exists, each of us is free, in theory, to become a parent if we choose to do so. What recourse do we have, however, if the state or another individual decides that we shall not reproduce? Even in the 20th century, this decision was taken for many groups of people (Nash 1991; Bock 1991; Johnson 1997) and continues to be taken for individuals, as a matter of state policy (Douglas 1991; Johnson 1997). Claims based on the right to procreate can be essential in such a context.

A number of international documents[6] appear to recognise reproductive rights in some sense, but their substance is not always entirely clear. How, for example, are we to interpret Article 12 of the European Convention on Human Rights and Fundamental Freedoms, or Article 16 of the Universal Declaration of Human Rights? Article 12 states: 'Men and women of marriageable age have the right to marry and to found a family, according to national laws governing the exercise of this right.'

Article 16 states: 'Men and women of full age, without any limitation due to race, nationality or religion, have the right to marry and found a family.'

And, of course Article 8 of the ECHR, the right to respect for one's private and family life, seems also to be important in the context of reproduction. It is arguable that

---

6 See Douglas (1991) pp 22–25; and generally, Jackson (2001). Further, the Platform for Action agreed at the Fourth World Conference on Women held in Beijing China in September 1995 recognised reproductive rights that 'rest on the recognition of the basic right of all couples and individuals to decide freely and responsibly the number, spacing and timing of their children and to have the information and means to do so, and the right to attain the highest standard of sexual and reproductive health' (1996 para 95).

some right to procreate appears to be protected by these articles, but it also appears that that right is circumscribed to some degree. It may be helpful to recall that these documents were drafted in the aftermath of the atrocities perpetrated by the National Socialist regime in Germany and as a response to Nuremberg laws permitting forced sterilisation of segments of the population deemed undesirable (Bock 1991). In the context of a society practising forced sterilisation, the purpose of a right to reproduce seems clear, but in a society where this kind of treatment is not socially, morally or legally sanctioned, the substance of the right has yet to be determined especially in the light of the margin of appreciation the ECtHR offers to signatory states.[7]

Articles 12 and 8 were considered recently by the Court of Appeal and may give some guidance on the substance of the right to reproduce. In the first set of cases the court was concerned with requests made by prisoners serving life sentences for facilities for artificial insemination of their wives. The Secretary of State's position on according such facilities was to do so only in exceptional circumstances. In *R (Mellor) v Secretary of State for the Home Department*[8] the prisoner claimed that that policy violated his rights under Articles 8 and 12. While the Court of Appeal agreed that both Articles 8 and 12 were engaged by the policy and the refusal to accord the AI pursuant to it, it then said that interference with those rights was justified and proportional under Article 8(2). After looking at the Strasbourg jurisprudence, Lord Phillips MR said:

39. I can summarise the conclusions that I derive from these five decisions as follows:

i)  The qualifications on the right to respect for family life that are recognised by Article 8(2) apply equally to the Article 12 rights.
ii)  Imprisonment is incompatible with the exercise of conjugal rights and consequently involves an interference with the right to respect for family life under Article 8 and with the right to found a family under Article 12.
iii)  This restriction is ordinarily justifiable under the provisions of Article 8(2).
iv)  In exceptional circumstances it may be necessary to relax the imposition of detention in order to avoid a disproportionate interference with a human right.
v)  There is no case which indicates that a prisoner is entitled to assert the right to found a family by the provision of semen for the purpose of artificially inseminating his wife.

45. It does not follow from this that it will always be justifiable to prevent a prisoner from inseminating his wife artificially, or indeed naturally. The interference with fundamental human rights which is permitted by Article 8(2) involves an exercise in proportionality. Exceptional circumstances may require the normal consequences of imprisonment to yield, because the effect of its interference with a particular human right is disproportionate.

In the second case, *Dickson*,[9] the wife was 45 years old. Her husband was serving a life sentence for murder. He had a number of years left to serve before his tariff was up, which meant that the wife would be at least 51 years old before she and her husband might be able to conceive a child. The husband and wife claimed that these circumstances characterised their position as 'exceptional' and they challenged the refusal to grant them facilities for artificial insemination so that they could start a family together. The Court of Appeal found that the *Mellor* case had decided the point and dismissed their claim.

[7] See also Hale J (1996 p 8).
[8] [2001] EWCA Civ 472; [2001] 2 FLR 1158.
[9] *Dickson v Premier Prison Service Ltd, Secretary of State for the Home Department* [2004] EWCA Civ 1477.

These cases raise interesting issues about the way in which the court interprets one's convention rights to reproduction, or, more precisely the way in which it interprets the state's justification for interfering with those convention rights. In *Mellor*, Lord Phillips said:

> By imprisoning the husband the state creates the situation where, if the wife is to have a child, that child will, until the husband's release, be brought up in a single parent family. I consider it legitimate and indeed desirable, that the state should consider the implications of children being brought up in those circumstances, when deciding whether or not to have a general policy of facilitating the artificial insemination of the wives of prisoners … (para 76)

Lord Auld agreed in *Dickson*:

> In so ruling Lord Phillips had in mind, and he set out in the course of his judgment, the provisions of Article 8.2 of the Convention setting out various matters that may justify interference with the right to respect for private and family life, [and now, with the right to marry and found a family] including the protection of health or morals and the protection of the rights and freedoms of others. It seems to me that concern, not only for the public attitude to the exercise by prisoners of certain rights in prison which they would take for granted outside, and concern for the rights of a putative child in the upbringing it would receive depending on the circumstances and the length of imprisonment involved, are highly relevant circumstances, for the purposes of Article 8.2. (para 20)

Concern for the potential child's 'rights' or 'welfare' might, in other words, justify restricting an adult's reproductive decisions. While such a policy may not be intuitively alarming, consider that in *Mellor*, the fact that the child would be raised for a period of years in a single parent family was thought to be important, and in *Dickson*, the fact that the wife was receiving Income Support was important: Lord Auld agreed that 'the seeming insufficiency of resources to provide independently for the welfare of any child who might be conceived' was relevant to legitimate consideration of the interests of the 'yet unborn child' (para 8) as part of Article 8.2.[10]

The second recent case to consider reproductive rights under the ECHR and the HRA 1998 was one in which discrimination was alleged and so the court was required to identify and balance competing rights. In *Evans v Amicus Healthcare and Others*[11] the issues were the meaning of certain provisions of the Human Fertilisation and Embryology Act 1990 and whether those provisions breached any of the claimant's rights under the ECHR. After being diagnosed with ovarian cancer, Ms Evans, together with her then partner Mr Johnston, sought IVF treatment. They executed the required consents and embryos were fertilised and frozen for later implantation in Ms Evans' womb. After treatment for cancer, including the removal of her ovaries, but before implantation, however, the couple split up and Mr Johnston wrote to the Clinic advising them that the embryos should be destroyed; he was, in effect withdrawing his consent for them to be used. Because withdrawal of his consent and destruction of the embryos would have ended any possibility of Ms Evans ever having a child genetically related to her, she sought, among other things, declarations that Mr Johnston could not withdraw his consent, that she could lawfully be treated with the embryos and that the relevant provisions

---

10 On the welfare test as a consideration for assisted reproduction services generally, see Jackson (2002).

11 [2004] EWCA Civ 727; [2005] Fam 1. All refs are to [2005] Fam 1. At the time of writing, Ms Evans' application to the ECtHR was pending.

of the Act allowing a person to withdraw consent at any time up to the 'use' of the embryos breached her rights under Articles and 8, 12 and 14 of the ECHR. She did not allege discrimination between men and women, however. Instead she alleged discrimination between fertile and infertile women.

The Court of Appeal agreed that Ms Evans' Article 8 rights (to respect for her private life—her bodily integrity) were engaged by the state regulating the conditions in which she could have an embryo transferred into her. Even though it was not argued before it, the court also took the opportunity to comment upon the issue of gender, rights and reproduction. It found that just as Ms Evans' rights were engaged by the provisions of the HFEA, Mr Johnson's rights were also affected. Because both parties' rights had to be respected, the policy of requiring ongoing consent satisfied Article 8(2). According to Arden, LJ:

> 110   ... The personal circumstances of the parties are different from what they were at the out-set of treatment, and it would be difficult for a court to judge whether the effect of Mr Johnston's withdrawal of his consent on Ms Evans is greater than the effect that the invalida-tion of that withdrawal of consent would have on Mr Johnston. The court has no point of reference by which to make that sort of evaluation. The fact is that each person has a right to be protected against interference with their private life. That is an aspect of the principle of self-determination or personal autonomy. It cannot be said that the interference with Mr Johnston's right is justified on the ground that interference is necessary to protect Ms Evans's right, because her right is likewise qualified in the same way by his right. They must have equiv-alent rights, even though the exact extent of their rights under article 8 has not been identified.

> 111   The interference with Ms Evans's private life is also justified under article 8(2) because, if Ms Evans's argument succeeded, it would amount to interference with the genetic father's right to decide not to become a parent. Motherhood could surely not be forced on Ms Evans and likewise fatherhood cannot be forced on Mr Johnston, especially as in the present case it will probably involve financial responsibility in law for the child as well.

**Q** Do you agree that the balance of rights between these parties must be 'equivalent'? Are men and women so differently situated with regard to repro-duction that attempting to accord them equal or equivalent rights will be of little use? See on this Sheldon (2004).

It appears from these cases that there may be in English law a right to procreate, as well as a right to not procreate (certainly under Article 8 and possibly under Article 12), but that Article 8(2) allows the state a wide range of actions by which to interfere with those rights.[12]

The right to procreate has also been considered in cases concerning applications to sterilise mentally handicapped women. While many of these cases were decided before the implementation of the HRA 1998, courts used the word 'right' in relation to the patients' reproductive capacity.[13] Use of the terminology is one thing, however, and although it may have demonstrated a 'rights consciousness' in Britain even before the HRA 1998, it is not clear what the courts intended such rights to *mean*, especially in the light of other judicial statements which qualify both the existence and the limits of any such right.

---

[12] See also *Briody v St Helens and Knowsley Health Authority* [2001] EWCA Civ 1010; [2002] QB 856; [2001] 2 FLR 1094.
[13] *Re D (A Minor) (Wardship: Sterilisation)* [1976] Fam 185. See also *Re F (Mental Patient: Sterilisation)* [1990] 2 AC 1.

In *In Re B (A Minor) (Wardship: Sterilisation)*[14] the issue before the House of Lords was whether it was in the best interests of a 17 year old ward of court with a mental age of 6 years to be sterilised. On the issue of whether or not such a procedure would deprive the young woman of a fundamental human right to reproduce, Lord Hailsham said:

> We were invited to consider the decision of Heilbron J in *In re D (A Minor) (Wardship: Sterilisation)* ... when the judge rightly referred to the irreversible nature of such an operation and the deprivation, which it involves, of a basic human right, namely the right of a woman to reproduce. *But this right is only such when reproduction is the result of informed choice of which this ward is incapable.* (p 203, emphasis added)

Lord Oliver on the same issue declared:

> Heilbron J declined to sanction an operation which involved depriving her of her right to reproduce. That, if I may say so respectfully, was plainly a right decision. *But the right to reproduce is of value only if accompanied by the ability to make a choice* and in the instant case there is no question of the minor ever being able to make such a choice or indeed to appreciate the need to make one. (p 211, emphasis added)

Here, their Lordships seem to be saying that a right, or at least the right to reproduce, does not exist, or have any value, unless one has the capacity to exercise it. On this reasoning, they had no hesitation in approving the sterilisation.

**Q** What does this understanding of rights mean for people with physical or mental disabilities?

Lords Bridge and Templeman evinced a slightly different understanding of rights. Lord Templeman appeared to acknowledge that B's right to reproduce existed, even though she may not have had the capacity to exercise it, but he then determined that hers was an appropriate case in which to interfere with that right:

> Sometimes the judge will conclude that a sufficiently overwhelming case has not been established *to justify interference with the fundamental right of a girl to bear a child*; this was the case in *In re D* ... But in the present case the judge was satisfied that it would be cruel to expose the girl to an unacceptable risk of pregnancy which could only be obviated by sterilisation ...
> (p 206)

Similarly, Lord Bridge agreed that the right of a woman to reproduce is a basic human right, but he thought that because B would never be able to exercise that right, the operation was justified in her best interests.

> In *In re D* ... Heilbron J correctly described the right of a woman to reproduce as a basic human right ... . The sad fact in the instant case is that the mental and physical handicaps under which the ward suffers effectively *render her incapable of ever exercising that right* ...
> (p 205, emphasis added)

Whether there is a right to reproduce is therefore not clear from these cases. To Lords Bridge and Templeman, the right always exists, but may be circumscribed in the

---

[14] [1988] AC 199 (HL).

woman's best interests, while to Lords Hailsham and Oliver it exists only in certain cir-cumstances.[15] In any event, the general tenor of the case law seems to be that any right to reproduce can be circumscribed in a mentally incapacitated patient's best interests (Jackson 2001). In contrast, the Canadian Supreme Court found in *In re Eve*[16] that the 'questionable advantages' of sterilisation could not outweigh the 'grave intrusion' of rights that it involved.

**Q** Which approach do you prefer? What makes a right a 'fundamental human right'?

**Q** Notice that many of the judges spoke of a woman's (or girl's) right to reproduce. Do you think the judges would have spoken differently if B, D, F or Eve were a man? There are no reported cases approving sterilisation of a man. In *Re A (medi-cal treatment: male sterilisation)* [2000] 1 FLR 549 an application was made by A's mother and carer for the court's approval of a vasectomy operation. A had Down's syndrome. The court reiterated the best interests test and Dame Eliza-beth Butler Sloss discussed how that test might be different as between men and women:

> An application on behalf of a man for sterilisation is not the equivalent of an application in respect of a woman. It is not a matter of equality of the sexes but a balancing exercise on a case by case basis. There are obvious biological differences and sexual intercourse for a woman carries the risk of pregnancy which patently it does not for a man. Indeed there is no direct consequence for a man of sexual intercourse other than the possibility of sexually transmitted diseases. There may be psychological consequences for him in pregnancy or in the birth of his child. He may be required to take responsibility for the child after birth and may, in certain circumstances attract disapproval and criticism. In the case of a man who is mentally incapacitated, neither the fact of the birth of a child nor disapproval of his conduct is likely to impinge on him to a significant degree other than in exceptional circumstances. His freedom of movement might in certain instances be restricted and consequently his quality of life might be diminished. It is possible that there may be other disadvantages to the person concerned which might lead a court to decide to approve the operation. It may be necessary to evaluate the nature and degree of risk attached to approval of or refusal to approve the operation to sterilise. But the task in each case is to balance all the relevant factors and to decide what are the best interests of the person unable to make his own decision (per Butler-Sloss LJ p 557)

Butler-Sloss LJ seems to be suggesting that the 'best interests' of men and women may be different in the context of reproduction. Can you make an argument that her comments are applicable when considering the 'rights' of men and women as well?

---

[15] See also *Re F* [1989] 2 WLR 1025 in which Lord Brandon referred to the right to bear children as one of the 'fundamental rights of a woman' (p 1068) and *Re X (Adult Sterilisation)* [1998] 2 FLR 1124 where Holman J of the Family Division found that a 31-year-old woman with a mental age of between 4 and 6 had a right to reproduce, but that she was 'unable to make any sensible, informed decision for herself' (p 1128). It was there-fore held to be in her best interests to undergo surgical sterilisation.

[16] (1986) 31 DLR 1.

The sterilisation cases were concerned with interfering with the physical capacity to reproduce, but the search for the meaning of reproductive rights can be still further complicated, and the decisions differently understood, if we think of any right to reproduce as something other than simply a right physically to conceive or bear a child. Many writers suggest that if there is a right to reproduce, it is not an unconditional one because it cannot be understood simply as an issue of physical bodily autonomy at the stage of conception, gestation or delivery. O'Neill, for example, says 'the right to beget or bear [children] is not unrestricted, but contingent upon begetters and bearers having or making some feasible plan for their child to be adequately reared by themselves or by willing others' (1979 p 13). Similarly, Archard argues that 'any right to bear [children] should be conditional upon acceptance of an obligation properly to provide for one's offspring' (1993 p 98). For both of these commentators, then, bearing children cannot be separated from rearing them.[17]

On an intuitive level, one may find this position to be an attractive one. The meaning of a man's right to beget a child, or woman's right to do with her body as she sees fit, including a right to bear children, cannot be assessed in the abstract, divorced from the reality of the lives it affects. In this case, determining the *meaning* or *content* of any right to reproduce must require consideration of the effect of reproduction on the lives of the resulting child and the potential rearers of that child. Indeed, in the context of questions of assisted reproduction, Douglas (1991 pp 20–21) takes this position further by suggesting that the right to reproduce really means protection of the interest in becoming a *social* parent, rather than a biological one.

Douglas expresses the *content* of the right to social parenthood in these terms:

> This is not to say that the state is obliged to provide opportunities to become a parent to those who wish to exercise the right, but only that it should not prevent such opportunities. After all, we do not assume that the state should find suitable partners for single fertile people. But ... where facilities such as donor insemination (AID) are available, there should be equal access to them. Thus, homosexuals or single people should not be prevented from using such techniques, just as fertile homosexuals could not be prevented from exercising their right to procreate.
>
> (1991 p 21)[18]

If the right is concerned with social parenthood, a number of issues are raised. First, if the right to 'found a family' is conditional upon the requirement to consider 'properly' (Archard) providing for a child afterwards, or having a 'feasible' (O'Neill) plan for the rearing of the child, we must bear in mind the importance of any meaning attached to the words 'proper' or 'feasible'. Here, as we saw in the AI prison cases above, historically contingent notions of children's welfare and proper or normal families become relevant. Secondly, we must bear in mind the differential effect protection of such a conditional right may have upon women as the bearers of both children and rights, who are the traditional carers for children, and men as non-bearers and, traditionally, non-carers for children, but bearers of rights. Finally, we must bear in mind any obligations of the state in interpreting the meaning of the right, providing for its equal accessibility and balancing any other rights which may appear to compete with it. We will examine each of

---

[17] See, however, the view of Hale J: '[W]e must be careful not to confuse the right to bear children with the right to rear them: we may be justified in trying to enforce child support and other parental responsibilities, to provide a better life for abused and neglected children, and to punish the abusers. It does not follow that we are entitled to prevent their having children in the first place' (1996) p 9.

[18] See also Hale (1996) p 9.

these issues by continuing our look at whether a right to reproduce includes a right to receive medical or financial assistance to that end.

> **Q** Do you think the right to reproduce is a fundamental human right? If so, what is its content and how do you think that right should be protected? Some suggest that if something is agreed to be fundamental human right the state has a positive obligation to provide access to it, rather than simply to avoid impeding access to it. This requirement goes further than Douglas would go. Would such an understanding of a right be philosophically defensible? Would it be practicable?

## II. DILUTING THE RIGHT TO REPRODUCE: WELFARE AND PRIVILEGING THE NUCLEAR FAMILY

As Kingdom and Smart recognise, the decision to have children, although private, is taken in the context of a number of material social and legal conditions. For the majority of the heterosexual population conceiving a child requires little, if any, medical or legal intervention, and so decisions about embarking upon parenthood appear to remain personal and private. Up to one sixth (Campion 1995) of the population, however, seeks medical-technical assistance in conceiving,[19] rendering the decision to have a baby, and the process of having a baby, a matter of a more apparently public concern, and therefore more amenable to 'rights-talk'. We argue, however, that 'rights-talk' does not necessarily reflect the dominant framework in which these reproductive matters are decided.

When a person seeks medical assistance, the decision becomes more conspicuously public, in the sense that it is shifted to the domain of physicians, donors, scientists, social workers and law-makers. Strict separation between public and private family decisions is particularly inappropriate in such cases. Campion illustrates the public nature of procreation in this situation:

> [T]he private biological process that lay in the natural powers of most men and women has increasingly become a medical and technological process that takes place in clinics and hospitals, arenas of professional power. It has now reached the stage where the very process of conception can be controlled by doctors, with the would-be parents only playing a very subsidiary role. (1995 p 97)

The legal aspects of assisted reproduction are governed by the Human Fertilisation and Embryology Act 1990 and the regulations promulgated under it. The Act regulates research, experimentation and the provision of treatment for infertility. It adopts a disease model of infertility which is often inappropriate for prospective clients. First, framing the services as treatments for 'infertility' ignores those who are medically capable of procreating, but for whom heterosexual intercourse is not an option. Second, infertility is more than a physical matter; it has a strong social component. Morgan writes, for example, of society's 'parenthood mystique' (1989 p 72), a part of which is

---

[19] In 2000–01, approximately 8000 children were born as a result of in vitro fertilisation and approximately 800 as a result of licensed donor insemination Probert (2004) p 274.

society's view of a childless heterosexual couple as a deviant, selfish or incomplete family. The Warnock Report on Human Fertilisation and Embryology, published in 1984 and dealing with the social, ethical and legal implications of human assisted reproduction, put it in these terms:

> Childlessness can be a source of stress even to those who have deliberately chosen it. Family and friends often expect a couple to start a family, and express their expectations either openly or by implication ... . For those who long for children, the realisation that they are unable to found a family can be shattering. It can disrupt the picture of the whole of their future lives. They may feel that they will be unable to fulfil their own and other people's expectations. They may feel themselves excluded from a whole range of human activity and particularly the activities of their child rearing contemporaries. In addition to the social pressure to have children, there is for many a powerful urge to perpetuate their genes through a new generation. This desire cannot be assuaged by adoption. (1984 p 8 para 2.2).

In addition to social pressure upon (married) couples to 'found a family', people face individual pressures as well. For men, fertility is associated with power (Dewar 1989; Morgan 1989) and a hegemonic masculinity (Collier 1995b), and the maternal role for women is valorised as their 'true' or natural role even by the medical profession (Stanworth 1987 p 15). There is a strong argument that, instead of seeking to meet 'demand' by devoting high-tech medical resources to enabling more people to have children, we should instead acknowledge that the demand is at least partly a result of hegemonic ideas about women's 'true' role, and 'promote attitudes which accept childlessness and enable women (especially) to fulfil themselves in other ways than parenthood' (Douglas 1991 p 107).

It may be that the pressures to reproduce are not felt or are resisted by a significant proportion of people, however. Recent statistics on fertility in England and Wales show a trend towards later childbearing and smaller families. The total fertility rate in 2004 was 1.79 children born per woman (Population Trends 120, 2005 p 65) compared with a peak in the UK in 1964 at 2.95 children per woman (National Statistics On-line 2005). The average age of the mother for all live births in England and Wales in 2004 was 29.4 years (Population Trends 2005 p 65) and, while fertility increased in all age groups in 2003 (except for under 20s), the largest increases were for women aged 35–39 and 40+ (National Statistics 2004). Further, completed family size has been steadily declining in the UK from an average of 2.45 children per woman born in the mid 1930s and is expected to level off at around 1.74 in 2021 (Shaw 2004 p 8). Finally, around one in five women currently reaching the end of their fertility are childless, compared with one in ten who were born in the mid 1940s (National Statistics 2004).

> **Q** Are these statistics evidence of individuals not accepting traditional constructions of masculinity and femininity? Are they evidence of a rejection of familialism? Can you identify any social pressures on married couples to have children? Not to have children? What about upon unmarried people? Warnock stated that the urge to have children 'cannot be assuaged by adoption'. Do you agree that the biological connection is important for people? Why do think that might be the case?

Douglas (1993) draws a distinction between 'infertility' and 'childlessness', and suggests that the legislative intention is to treat infertility, rather than childlessness:

The goal of undergoing treatment is to produce a child. But the justification for this can vary. On the one hand a woman may argue that she should receive treatment because she could not conceive otherwise (or could conceive but would pass on a defective gene to the child); in other words, she or her partner is *infertile* … . On the other hand, a person may seek treatment to relieve her state of *childlessness*. She *may* be capable of conceiving through sexual intercourse, but prefers to avoid this, perhaps because she has failed to find a partner with whom she wishes to share her life or bring up a child … . For example, a woman who undergoes a 'premature menopause' at the age of 30 will be regarded as 'infertile'. She is likely to be sympathetically treated if she and her partner seek assisted reproduction; she will be accepted as having a *clinical need* for treatment. A woman who undergoes menopause at the age of 45, on the other hand, and then asks for treatment may be told that she has left it too late. Her childlessness is something she should have done something about sooner; in other words, it is due to her choice. Her desire for a child is nothing more than that—a *desire*. (p 55)

Although the social aspects of infertility, that is the desire to remedy childlessness, are recognised by the medical profession, infertility continues to be seen as a disease and, as such, treatment is available on the NHS. It is arguable that it is childlessness which is in fact being treated, but only if the cause of the childlessness is infertility. As is the case with other non-life-threatening diseases, however, treatment is not universally available. People requesting infertility treatment must 'qualify' for it, and clinics offering such treatment are selective in their decisions about who qualifies. Even private clinics, while adopting less stringent requirements than NHS centres, do not assume treatment to be a right for all to claim. The 'right' to reproduce in this context too is a qualified one.

The Human Fertilisation and Embryology Act 1990 (HFEAct) sets out the requirements for the licensing of clinics, but, with the exception of Sections 13(5) and (6)[20] it does not lay down rules concerning entitlement to treatment. Section 13(5) requires licensed treatment centres to take account 'of the welfare of any child who may be born as a result of the treatment, (including the need of the child for a father), and of any other child who may affected by the birth.'[21]

Jackson (2002) argues that because the principal purpose of this section is to judge, prior to acceptance on a clinic's programme, the fitness of prospective parents, the section is 'incoherent, disingenuous and illegitimate' (p 177). She presents a strong argument for its repeal on this basis. Not only does the section promote discrimination against poor people, as we have seen in the AI prison cases, it also clearly can be interpreted so as to discriminate against single and lesbian women (Wallbank 2004). Wallbank (2004) presents a strong argument for its repeal on the basis of this incompatibility with recent developments in the human rights of same-sex couples, and we can add, with the Civil Partnership Act 2004 and the Adoption and Children Act 2002.[22]

The HFEAct, however, and the regulations provide only a broad framework within which professionals are supposed to exercise their discretion.[23] To give substance to that discretion, the Act created a Human Fertilisation and Embryology Authority, which has

---

[20] Ss (5) is a compromise arising from attempts which were made in Parliamentary debate to ensure that the provisions of the HFEAct and treatment under it were to apply only to married couples. The Warnock Report (1984) stopped short of recommending treatment be limited to married couples, but was clear that it was the patriarchal nuclear family it was supporting through assisted reproduction. '[W]e believe that as a general rule it is better for children to be born into a two parent family with both father and mother although we recognise that it is impossible to predict with any certainty how lasting such a relationship will be' (pp 12–13 para 2.11).

[21] For a discussion of the legislative history of this s, see Douglas (1993); Jackson (2001) and (2002); Wallbank (2004).

[22] See below ch 4.

[23] See Warnock (1984) p 12 para 2.13.

produced a voluntary Code of Practice with a list of guidelines for making selection decisions. This Code of Practice is subject to ministerial approval and is available to the public, but there is no legal sanction if a clinic is found to have violated it. On one hand, this type of regulatory regime provides flexibility which could prove advantageous to individual clients. On the other hand, it leaves individual medical practitioners with almost unfettered discretion over the reproductive lives of many people. The courts, furthermore, are reluctant to police this discretion. Decisions about treatment are not justiciable, so if a person feels aggrieved by a refusal of treatment, her only recourse is judicial review of the decision. In *R v Ethical Committee of St Mary's Hospital*[24] the court refused to look behind the criteria established by the clinic with respect to treatment decisions provided that the rules of administrative law such as procedural fairness were adopted.

The guidelines in the Code of Practice direct centres to bear in mind the requirements of Section 13(5)[25] and direct them to consider a number of factors in this regard, including the prospective parents' commitment to raise children, their ability to provide a stable environment, their immediate and family medical histories, their ages and their ability to provide for the child's needs and the risk of harm to children (HFEA 2003 3.12). In addition, in cases where the child will have no legal father, centres are also required to assess the prospective mother's ability to meet the child's needs and the ability of other persons within her family or social circle willing to share responsibility for those needs (HFEA 2003 3.14). Centres are expected to take medical and social histories of each patient and to make enquiries of their GPs; refusal of patients to provide this information is a factor to be taken into account in the decision to provide treatment (HFEA 2003 3.20).

We see then, that regulation of assisted reproduction is not exclusively legal, medical, moral, financial or bureaucratic, but rather takes a multi-disciplinary approach. We see also that medical professionals must take their decisions after considering two different perspectives: the welfare of the child required by Section 13(5) and the fitness of the patient as assessed by the guidelines (Douglas 1993).

> **Q** What does this multifaceted approach mean for the 'rights' of those who seek treatment? Does practical application of the guidelines promote rights-based decision making at all? Do patients' rights conflict with the welfare test, or do the guidelines merely incorporate a contextual understanding of the right to reproduce as including the 'proper' or 'feasible' care for resulting children?

In her survey of how clinics applied the guidelines, Douglas (1993)[26] demonstrates that any right to procreate is circumscribed by the criteria that they apply. Clinics she studied considered the patient's medical history, her family situation and parenting history, her attitude and commitment to future parenthood, her sexual orientation, age and marital status, the likelihood of success of treatment and prevailing social attitudes to all of the above. Campion, for example, described a decision taken by one NHS centre which denied treatment to a couple who had been living together for six years. 'The consultant, while believing that marriage gave a child a more stable home, was clearly concerned by more than just the welfare of the child: "This treatment is in the public eye. We've got to

---

[24] [1988] 1 FLR 512.
[25] HFEA (2003) s 3.
[26] See also Campion (1995).

be purer than the driven snow" ' (1995 p 108). And there continues to be evidence that clinics discriminate against lesbian women who request services (Wallbank 2004). Access to services may also depend on chance; Probert (2004) notes that the protocols of clinics varied considerably. Finally, the attitudes of the professionals may be more important in access to services than the protocols and the welfare principle (ibid).

The HFEA seems to be aware of the difficulties associated with the possible interpretations of Section 13(5). It launched a 'welfare of the child' review in 2004 and its consultation document *Tomorrow's Children,* was published in 2005 (HFEA 2005). As the introduction to that document makes clear, the HFEA has no power to repeal Section 13(5), but it does have the power to determine how that section should be interpreted by decision-makers (para 1.1). It recognises that over ten years of experience of interpreting Section 13(5) has been accumulated and acknowledges the importance of the psychosocial, ethical, social and legal literature (para 1.2) in those interpretations. It notes in particular the literature that shows that children born to lesbian mother families compare well with other assisted conception children 'in terms of emotional, behavioural and gender development' (para 2.3). As a result of the review, it hopes to have a new set of 'welfare assessment' guidelines by the summer of 2005.[27]

Because there is no direct legal regulation of medical decisions to provide treatment for infertility, it is difficult to adopt a strict rights-based approach which could be guaranteed by law. Moreover, it is clear that the ideology of familialism remains strong in decisions about who is deserving of medical reproductive assistance. To some, this is a missed opportunity, for new reproductive technologies could push the boundaries of those groups socially or legally considered to be family. 'Assisted conception services and the new reproductive technologies are continually redefining family relationships, while regulation and legislation are being used in an attempt to rein in these developments, to try to hold the line' (Langdridge and Blyth 2002 p 47). Same-sex parents in particular may lead the way in the ways in which many mobilise both biological and social parenthood to create new parent-child relationships that are not always, or not yet, acknowledged in law (See Wallbank 2004 and sources cited therein).[28]

**Q** Would you provide in vitro fertilisation treatment for the following (give reasons):

(a) a single, 26 year old unemployed woman who has had a hysterectomy;

(b) a single, 37 year old, fertile, professional woman;

(c) two 30 year old women in a stable, long-standing lesbian relationship;

(d) a married professional couple where the wife has a history of prostitution and the husband, with a low sperm count, has a conviction for living off the earnings of prostitution;

(e) a married heterosexual couple, the husband aged 29 and the wife 50;

(f) a married heterosexual couple in their late 20s, who have two children, where the husband has immotile sperm and has been unemployed for two years.

---

[27] New guidelines, however, would not satisfy Jackson, Wallbank or other critics who have called for the repeal of s 13(5). The government announced in 2004 its intention to review the whole of the HFEA 1990 and DoH will begin a full consultation in 2005.

[28] Wallbank (2004) notes, for example, how the intention to be a social parent is acknowledged in s 28(3) for heterosexual men, but not for lesbian partners, thus ignoring the possibility that a lesbian co-parent is a legally recognised, legitimate family member. See further on this, ch 4.

Do you think the courts and the legislature have struck the right balance between a pure rights-based approach and a pure welfare approach to freedom from interference in reproductive decisions?

## III. REPRODUCTIVE FREEDOM: THE RIGHT NOT TO REPRODUCE

*Contraception*

Like the right to reproduce, the assertion of a right not to reproduce is not a straightforward matter. Different means of contraception have been utilised by men and women for centuries. Throughout the years, however, one can identify a waxing and waning in their social and legal acceptability. Douglas provides a concise history:

> In England, up to 1860, a variety of pamphlets advocating and explaining contraception sold well and enjoyed a wide circulation. In particular, a manual called the *Fruits of Philosophy*, by Charles Knowlton sold for many years, until a bookseller who published an illustrated edition was convicted of distributing obscene literature. To challenge this effective ban on the book, Charles Bradlaugh, who had founded the Malthusian League in 1860 to spread information about the need for birth control, together with Annie Beasant republished Knowlton's book and sold it openly. They were tried for publishing an obscene libel. The jury found that the book was 'calculated to deprave public morals, but entirely exonerated the defendants from corrupt motives in publishing it'. The practice by married couples of birth control increased after the trial, which received enormous publicity, and the birth-rate in Britain actually began to fall from 1877.
>
> At the turn of the century, a new impetus for birth control emerged in the spread of eugenic theory, loosely based on Darwin's theory of evolution. It was argued that the human stock could be improved if 'better' people had children, and less superior specimens did not. This view was adopted particularly in the United States where it was used to sanction the often involuntary sterilisation of those deemed mentally defective, on the ground that this deficiency would be passed on to offspring. Such attitudes never received judicial or legislative formulation in England, although the Brock committee did examine the issue of sterilising the mentally handicapped in 1934.
>
> The 20th century saw the founding of birth control societies which provided both contraceptive information and services, and of the coming to prominence of the contraception campaigners Marie Stopes in Britain and Margaret Sanger (who invented the term 'birth control') in the United States. In 1930, the Minister of Health issued a memorandum allowing local authorities to give contraceptive advice in cases where further pregnancy would be 'detrimental to health'. In fact, this memorandum was ignored, and contraception remained a private matter for individuals themselves, perhaps after consulting their doctor or private birth control clinic, until the late 1960's.
>
> Its practice was, nonetheless, widespread. Surveys carried out from the turn of the century reveal that, beginning with the wealthy and then spreading to the working class, contraception was an increasingly accepted part of married life. (1991 pp 42–44, footnotes omitted)[29]

---

[29] See also Jackson (2001 pp 11–25).

For a time contraception was thought to violate the very purpose of marriage, and this view is still held today by many religions. It was reflected also in early cases. In *Cowen v Cowen*[30] the Court of Appeal found that a marriage could not be consummated if the husband wore a condom during intercourse or withdrew before ejaculation. This decision was eventually overruled,[31] but evidences the importance of maternity, or potential maternity to married women and paternity to married men. In contrast, use of contraceptives was encouraged among the 'lower orders' and, as Douglas states above, many of the 'feminist' pioneers of the birth control movement advocated it for eugenic reasons. Contraception and contraceptive advice are now freely available on the NHS for most sexually active women,[32] but again many feminists have suggested that birth control continues to be viewed differently depending upon whether the patient is poor and black or middle class and white (Cox 1990; Roberts 1993).[33] Smart theorises abortion in a similar way. She suggests that legal concern about abortion increased when married women began having abortions (1992 p 19). Finally, although there is some interest in developing a contraceptive pill for men, comparatively little research is undertaken in this area.

*Abortion*

Abortion is regulated in England and Wales by the criminal law, by the Offences Against the Person Act 1861, the Infant Life Preservation Act 1929 and the Abortion Act 1967 as amended, and by health care policy and practice. The Offences Against the Person Act provides the starting point for the criminal law of abortion. According to sections 58 and 59, all abortions are unlawful.

> 58   Every woman being with child who, with intent to procure her own miscarriage, shall unlawfully administer to herself any poison or other noxious thing, or shall unlawfully use any instrument or other means whatsoever with the like intent, and whosoever, with intent to procure the miscarriage of any woman, whether she be or be not with child, shall unlawfully administer to her or cause to be taken by her any poison or other noxious thing, or shall unlawfully use any instrument or other means whatsoever with the like intent, shall be guilty of felony.
> 59   Whosoever shall unlawfully supply or procure any poison or other noxious thing, or any instrument or thing whatsoever, knowing that the same is intended to be unlawfully used or employed with intent to procure the miscarriage of any woman, whether she be or be not with child, shall be guilty of a misdemeanour.

Similarly, the destruction of a 'viable' foetus is a crime pursuant to the Infant Life Preservation Act 1929.

> 1(1)   Subject as hereinafter in this subsection provided, any person who, with intent to destroy the life of a child capable of being born alive, by any wilful act causes a child to die before it has an existence independent of its mother, shall be guilty of felony, to wit, of child destruction,

---

[30] [1946] P 36, [1945] 2 All ER 197.
[31] See *Baxter v Baxter* [1948] AC 274 and the discussion in Lowe and Douglas (1998 pp 89–90).
[32] See *Gillick v West Norfolk and Wisbech Area Health Authority* [1986] AC 112; [1985] 3 All ER 402; [1985] 3 WLR 830; [1986] 1 FLR 224. Despite this decision which permits doctors to provide contraceptives to children under the age of 16, the UK has the highest rate of teenage pregnancy in Europe (Jackson 2001 p 16).
[33] See Jackson's (2001) discussion of issues of contraception in developing countries.

and shall be liable on conviction thereof on indictment to penal servitude for life:

Provided that no person shall be found guilty of an offence under this section unless it is proved that the act which caused the death of the child was not done in good faith for the purpose only of preserving the life of the mother.

(2) For the purpose of this Act, evidence that a woman had at any material time been pregnant for a period of twenty-eight weeks or more shall be *prima facie* proof that she was at that time pregnant of a child capable of being born alive.

Defences to both of these crimes are provided by the Abortion Act 1967:

1(1) Subject to the provisions of this section, a person shall not be guilty of an offence under the law relating to abortion when a pregnancy is terminated by a registered medical practitioner if two registered medical practitioners are of the opinion, formed in good faith—

(a) that the pregnancy has not exceeded its twenty fourth week and that the continuance of the pregnancy would involve risk, greater than if the pregnancy were terminated, of injury to the physical or mental health of the pregnant woman or any existing children of her family; or

(b) that the termination is necessary to prevent grave permanent injury to the physical or mental health of the pregnant woman; or

(c) that the continuance of the pregnancy would involve risk to the life of the pregnant woman, greater than if the pregnancy were terminated; or

(d) that there is a substantial risk that if the child were born it would suffer from such physical or mental abnormalities as to be seriously handicapped.

(2) In determining whether the continuance of a pregnancy would involve risk of injury to health as is mentioned in paragraph (a) or (b) of subsection (1) of this section, account may be taken of the pregnant woman's actual or reasonably foreseeable environment ....

5(1) No offence under the Infant Life Preservation Act shall be committed by a registered medical practitioner who terminates a pregnancy in accordance with the provisions of this Act.[34]

Apart from the criminal law, abortion is regulated in the way that Health Authorities and Health Trusts negotiate the priority given to abortions as an NHS—funded medical procedure, and in the way in which individual physicians exercise the discretion given to them by the Abortion Act to make decisions about who is entitled to an abortion. So long as their discretion is exercised in good faith, courts usually will not question the decision (Sheldon 1996). Sheldon reviewed the leading cases on abortion in the English courts and concluded:

The court decisions which I have outlined share an acceptance of abortion as a matter for medicine and a consequent judicial reluctance to intervene or to second-guess the decisions made by doctors. What the courts did in these cases is actively to protect and entrench the monopoly of doctors, while policing those marginal cases which did not fall within the bounds of good medical practice. This accords both with the assumption that abortion is a technical matter to be decided by doctors and a long tradition of leaving the regulation and control of medical practice largely to the medical profession itself. (1996 p 106)

As Sheldon has emphasised elsewhere (1993) MPs debating the bill which was to become the Abortion Act 1967 did not question placing the responsibility for decisions

---

[34] Before this amendment was added by the HFEA 1990, the relationship between the ILPA and the Abortion Act was at times unclear. See, eg, *Rance v Mid-Down Health Authority* [1991] 1 QB 587; and *C v S* [1988] QB 134.

regarding termination of pregnancy upon medical practitioners rather than upon the women concerned. Indeed, one MP asked, '[w]ho is the mother to make the judgment?'

Decisions about abortion are also subject to chance, in that the woman's place of residence or her financial situation may affect her case. There is a 'gross disparity in the availability of NHS funding' (Sheldon 1996 p 108) for abortion services.[35]

The regulation of abortion, whether formal or informal, raises a number of issues. The first is the basis upon which abortion is legally and philosophically defensible at all. Defenders of abortion often speak of a woman's right to choose abortion. Does this suggest that what is being advocated is a right to bodily autonomy? Much has been written by ethicists, lawyers and philosophers on the question of abortion and bodily autonomy. One of the most famous is an article by Thompson, in which she likens the pregnant woman to someone who has woken up in hospital to find herself attached to a world famous violinist (1977). Does the hospital patient have the right to disconnect the violinist or is there an obligation to continue to support this other life? She argues that no one can be compelled to sustain the life of another, but the liberal foundations of her analysis have been criticised by many, including feminists who challenge the comparison on the basis of the artificial autonomy of its two protagonists (eg, Kingdom 1991).

Many argue that the legality or morality of abortion cannot be resolved by reference simply to a right to bodily autonomy. As we stated earlier, one person's right usually gives rise to another's competing right, and in the abortion context that competition usually is phrased in terms of women's right to bodily integrity versus a foetus' right to life, and sometimes also places a woman's right to bodily integrity in competition with a man's right to reproduce. Despite the difficulty for many of resolving these contests (eg, Dworkin 1995), both have been resolved legally in England in favour of the woman. In *C v S*[36] a man attempted to obtain an injunction in order to prevent his pregnant girlfriend from having an abortion. The court found that the legislation did not require the consent of anyone but the patient and the doctors and that this procedure did not violate any rights of the 'father'. In *Paton v UK*[37] the married 'father' made the same argument before the European Commission of Human Rights which held with respect to his rights:

> [The Commission] observes that any interpretation of the husband's and potential father's right, under Article 8 of the Convention, to respect for his private and family life, as regards an abortion which his wife intends to have performed on her, must first of all take into account the right of the pregnant woman, being the person primarily concerned in the pregnancy and its continuation or termination, to respect for her private life … . In the present case, the Commission, having regard to the right of the pregnant woman, does not find that the husband and potential father's right to respect for his private and family life can be interpreted so widely as to embrace such potential rights as claimed by the applicant, ie a right to be consulted, or a right to make applications, about an abortion which his wife intends to have performed on her.
> (pp 416–17).[38]

---

[35] Recent research confirms that this is still the case (Abortion Rights 2005 p 10). Further, Francome (2004) points to research which shows that in 1999–2000 at least nine Health Authorities in the UK set their own restrictive criteria for the provision of abortions on the NHS, some of which were intended to be punitive (p 38).

[36] [1988] QB 135; [1987] 1 All ER 1230.

[37] (1981) 3 EHRR 408.

[38] In Canada and the USA notification of or consent by the 'father' is not required either. See *Tremblay v Daigle* (1990) 62 DLR (4th) 634; and *Planned Parenthood v Danforth* 428 US 52 (1976).

**Q** Why do you think the court weighed the balance in favour of the woman? Could it have had something to do with the greater physical risk she takes in the reproductive process?

On the question of the foetus's right to life, the English courts have been consistent in their view that a foetus is not a person until born and so can have no legal rights until then.[39] In *C v S* the plaintiff argued that he was also bringing the action on behalf of the foetus as its next friend, but the court found that such an action was impossible.[40] The European Commission of Human Rights in *Paton* also considered this matter:

> The Commission has considered whether Article 2 [which begins 'Everyone's right to life shall be protected by the law'] is to be construed as recognising an absolute 'right to life' of the foetus and has excluded such an interpretation on the following grounds.
> The life of the foetus is intimately connected with, and cannot be regarded in isolation from, the life of the pregnant woman. If Article 2 were held to cover the life of the foetus and its protection under this Article were, in the absence of any express limitation, seen as absolute, an abortion would have to be considered as prohibited, even where the continuation of the pregnancy would involve a serious risk to the life of the pregnant woman. This would mean the 'unborn life' of the foetus would be regarded as being of a higher value than the life of the pregnant woman ... .
> The Commission finds that such an interpretation would be contrary to the object and purpose of the Convention. It notes that, already at the time of the signature of the Convention (4 November 1950), all High Contracting Parties, with one possible exception, permitted abortion where necessary to save the life of the mother, and that, in the meanwhile, the national law on termination of the pregnancy has shown a tendency towards further liberalisation. (p 415).[41]

Finally, there is the issue of determining the state's responsibility for ensuring meaningful and equal access to a means of securing a right,[42] particularly a right to medical treatment in a state which professes to provide universal and free health care. In the abortion context Sheldon describes the delays, frequent moralising lectures from unsympathetic consultants and variable accessibility to abortions in the NHS system (1996 p 108).[43] It is interesting to note that the criminal law regulating abortion provision in Canada was struck down as unconstitutional precisely because the decision-making mechanism set up by the act created unreasonable and unfair delays for the woman and often resulted in abortions not being available at all in many hospitals in Canada. These circumstances were said to violate a woman's right to 'security of the person' protected under section 7 of the Charter of Rights,[44] and since then there has been no criminal regulation of abortion in Canada. Douglas sums up the multi-faceted arguments around abortion 'rights':

---

[39] See *Re MB (Medical Treatment)* [1997] 2 FLR 426; *St George's Healthcare National Health Service Trust v S, R v Collins, ex parte S*, [1998] 3 WLR 936, [1998] 2 FLR 728. Contrast this view with the Constitution of the Republic of Ireland, for example: Art 40(3) which acknowledges 'the right to life of the unborn'

[40] On the issue of the legal personality of the foetus and competing rights generally, see below.

[41] See also *Kelly v Kelly* [1997] 2 FLR 828 (Ct of Sess) where the Scottish court denied a man an order preventing his estranged wife from having a lawful abortion. It also found that a foetus had no legal persona.

[42] In the USA see *Harris v McRae* 448 US 297 (1980) in which it was held that the state had no obligation to provide abortions, simply that it had an obligation to ensure that no obstacles were placed in the way of women seeking abortions.

[43] See also Francome (2004).

[44] See *Morgentaler, Smoling and Scott v The Queen* (1988) 44 DLR (4th) 385.

The demand for reproductive freedom seems to derive ultimately from the idea of having control over one's own body. This has two aspects. First, there is the right not to have one's body interfered with against one's will. This has received general, though not complete, legal recognition, through tort and criminal law protecting against assault.

The second aspect is less well-established. Here, what is claimed is the right to do with one's body as one wishes. This right has not been generally conceded by the law, which imposes a variety of restrictions upon it ... . However, it may be relied upon where use of contraceptives is in issue, since relatively few nowadays would argue that such use is immoral.

The claim to autonomy in the sense of doing as one wishes with one's body is harder to sustain where abortion or control over childbirth are concerned, for the issue may then become one of competing rights, any right to life of the foetus versus the right to autonomy of the woman. Pro-abortionists may argue that the foetus is akin to an invader, whom the woman has the right to repel. English law has given some recognition to this argument. For example, it permits abortion on the basis that, *inter alia*, the presence of the foetus is a threat to the woman's health or general welfare. Sterilisation of a woman with a severe learning difficulty has been justified by a Law Lord on the basis that pregnancy 'would be an unmitigated disaster' for her.

Anti-abortionists stress the innocence and helplessness of the foetus, imprisoned in the womb, in their calls for its protection from the mother. Such an approach diverts attention away from the interests of the woman who carries the foetus. But viewing the foetus as some hostile invader of the woman's womb is equally unsatisfactory. Neither approach really encompasses the complexity and uniqueness of reproduction. We may ultimately have to conclude that it is not like other life situations, and therefore cannot be dealt with by means of analogies, however ingenious. It may be necessary to find a different way of looking at the question, perhaps by viewing the mother and foetus as a unit.

This is not to argue that the foetus is a part of the mother, like any other bodily organ, to be dealt with by her as she wishes. This view cannot be sustained in the light of our scientific understanding of the development of the foetus. Equally importantly, it is to be doubted whether women view the child they carry merely as a part of themselves, whether they wish to have the child or not. Rather, it is to seek to recognise the intimate connection between the woman and the foetus she carries, based on the immutable reality that, while it remains in her uterus, its growth depends entirely upon her health and strength, and she ultimately is responsible for its nurture. Equally, she, and no one else, is directly affected by the presence of the foetus in her womb. Kant's principle that no one should be used merely as a means, but always as an end in themselves, would seem to be appropriate here. No woman should be required to take on the responsibility and the risks of pregnancy, for the benefit of the foetus, unless she is willing to do so. And no one else is better placed to decide what should happen to that foetus.
(1991 pp 16–18, footnotes omitted)

**Q** To what degree has English law adopted this approach? This approach means that a pregnant woman and a foetus may regarded neither as two autonomous rights-bearing individuals, nor as one, embodied by the woman. What implications does such a view have for our understanding of the liberal legal subject?

Douglas goes on:

This [her argument above] is not an argument which the law has adopted. Rather, it has entrusted decision-making during pregnancy to the medical profession rather than to the woman herself. Legal abortion is dependent upon the certified opinion of two registered medical practitioners. Although English courts have not yet been prepared to sanction control over the movements of a pregnant woman in order to safeguard her foetus, the law offers little freedom to a woman to determine how she will give birth, upholding a medical monopoly on the right to attend a woman in childbirth and hence restricting her choice of attendants and mode of childbirth.

The law therefore gives the woman a right to control her capacity to reproduce through contraception, through its recognition of a right to bodily autonomy in the sense of non-interference. But once the child has been conceived, her freedom to have an abortion depends upon a balance which gradually shifts in the foetus's favour, though never so far as to favour the life of the foetus over that of the woman. (1991 p 18, footnotes omitted)

**Q** In your view, has English law struck an appropriate balance among the woman, the man, the state and the foetus? On the legal history of abortion see Smart 1992 and Douglas 1991. On patient autonomy and abortion generally, see Jackson (2001) chapter 3 in which she argues that 'abortion law should no longer consist in a set of defences to the crime of abortion, but rather should, like the rest of British medical law, be informed by the guiding principle of patient self-determination' (p 72). Finally, see Sheldon (1997) on abortion law generally.

*Conclusion*

Our freedom to make decisions to reproduce, then, must be examined in the context of the extent to which people, particularly women, are able to control their fecundity. We have framed our discussion in terms of rights to control reproduction, not because we suggest that that framework is either the most useful or the most used by law, but because rights have come to dominate the public discourse of reproduction. Indeed, we have attempted to show that legal management of reproduction decisions is not easily, or even usually, made in rights terms. Instead, the state regulates many decisions about reproduction through discourses rooted in problematic notions about welfare and paternalism. When rights language is invoked, the meaning or content of the right is not always clearly articulated. In the abortion context, Clarke (1989) suggests that if anyone at all has any *rights*, it is doctors.

**Q** In what ways are claims to reproductive rights useful for women? For men? What are the disadvantages of 'rights discourse' in the area of reproduction? Would successful claims to rights offer us more or less control in our reproductive lives?

## IV. PARENTHOOD AND SOCIAL POLICY

As we have seen, criminal laws, domestic and international rights documents, health care and social work policy and prevailing moral attitudes all have a direct influence upon decisions to become parents and upon the ability to implement them. Also relevant to child-bearing and child-rearing, although in a less direct way, are other state policies in areas such as childcare, employment, taxation, welfare and housing;[45] they provide the context in which reproductive decisions are taken and either facilitated or complicated. Government policy acknowledges this connection:

---

[45] Also relevant are education policies and law. We will deal in ch 4 with education law, but a good overview can be found in Bainham (2005) and the sources cited therein.

If individuals decide that the challenges of combining work and family are too much, they may choose to have fewer children. In 2003 the fertility rate in the UK was 1.71 children per woman. Fertility rates have been relatively stable in the UK for the last twenty years. They remain below replacement rates (2.075 children per woman), having fallen from the peak of 2.95 children per woman in 1964. (HM Treasury, *et al*, 2004 para 2.55)

Children and 'families' seem to be everywhere in policy reform in recent years (Diduck 2005a). From economic and fiscal policy[46] to employment policy[47] to social security policy, if the goal is to 'help' as many people into work as possible, government now seems to appreciate that a person's caring responsibilities must not be ignored.

### *Childcare*

We stated in chapter 1 that a state's policy respecting the type of families it encourages, in terms both of family form and family privacy, can be demonstrated by, among other things, the support it provides for the care of children. Until recently, policy in England and Wales was based upon and reinforced the assumption that childcare was predominantly the private concern of the conjugal family, in practice, the mother. As a result, very little was done in the public arena about child care,[48] in the form of either financial support or service provision. According to the Family Studies Centre in 1995, this meant that for the 52% of mothers with children under the age of 5 and the 75% of mothers with youngest children aged between 5 and 11 who were employed outside the home, child care was usually arranged privately through the family or a friend or neighbour (Windebank 1996; Hartrais 1994; Rodger 1995; Millar and Worman 1996). Statistics compiled in April 1996 by the National Children's Bureau showed that less than 1% of children aged between 0 and 4 were cared for in local authority day nurseries or family centres, and 9% were cared for by registered childminders. Fox Harding commented on the situation as follows:

> State child-care provision of nurseries, playgroups and nursery schools for younger children, and playschemes out of school hours for older children is restricted in Britain. Not only is provision not universal, but it is mostly limited to children and families deemed to have problems. A contrast is often drawn with the war years when nursery provision was widespread, in order to free women for paid work. Mothers now turn to a range of systems for child care while they are working: husbands, relatives and other informal carers; registered (or unregistered) childminders and nannies; private and employer-provided nurseries, and so on. (1996 pp 33–34)[49]

Since the 1990s, however, policy has shifted. One of the first policy documents published by the new government in 1998 was its National Childcare Strategy. It also launched the Sure Start programme in 1998[50] and in 2004 the government announced its ten year

---

[46] The 2005 Budget Report was entitled *Investing for our future: Fairness and opportunity for Britain's hard-working families* (HM Treasury 2005).

[47] The DTI's most recent proposals for employment law reform are contained in a document entitled *Work and Families, Choice and Flexibility* (DTI 2005).

[48] For a discussion of why feminist mobilisation around the issue of childcare in Britain was so modest, see Randall (1996).

[49] See also Canaan's (1992) work on family centres showing how they were used for 'problem' families only.

[50] Sure Start programmes provide a range of education, health and parenting support in disadvantaged areas.

strategy for childcare (HM Treasury, *et al*, 2004). The aim of that strategy, or the 'vision' at its heart is:

> of a childcare system where: parents are better supported in the choices they make about work and family responsibilities; childcare is available to all families and is flexible to meet their circumstances; childcare services are among the best quality in the world; and all families are able to afford high quality childcare services that are appropriate for their needs.
>
> (HM Treasury, *et al*, 2004 para 1.10)

The strategy document is important and interesting for a number of reasons. First, it is one of the few 'official' statements linking good quality childcare to child development and not merely to parental (or rather, maternal) employment. Second, it concedes that the 'market' may not be appropriate as the exclusive regulator of childcare provision, and finally, it acknowledges that the availability of good quality childcare is an issue with specific relevance for women's well-being. Chapter 2 of the document sets out the government's policy rationale. It is based upon three ideas: that childcare is good for children and for society; that it is good for parents' employability and that it should be based upon parental choice.

The document reviews the literature on the effect of childcare on child development.[51] It points to research confirming the value of 'consistent one to one care' in a child's first year but acknowledges that any negative effects of full time maternal employment in this year can be offset by high quality care from others, including fathers (para 2.15). It also points to the mixed findings with respect to childcare from ages 1–3, but again acknowledges that any negative effects on child development arising from high levels of group care of poor quality can be avoided by good quality care. In fact, good quality care can boost children's cognitive skills, social skills and development (para 2.16). The evidence also shows that involvement in 'high quality early years education [at ages 3 and 4] can lead to better educational and social outcomes for children (para 2.17) and that child care for school age children can improve a child's 'educational attainment and behaviour' (para 2.19). The government concludes that the policy implications of these findings are related to the quality of childcare as much as to its supply.

The document also links childcare with child poverty. It refers to the Child Poverty Review (HM Treasury 2004) issued with the 2004 Spending Review, which states government's goals as halving child poverty by 2010 and eradicating it by 2020 (p 5). Childcare becomes a part of this goal when the government states that 'child poverty is about more than just income' and specifies that government will ensure 'work for those who can and support for those cannot' (*ibid*). Here, the provision of good quality, accessible childcare is part of the strategy to combat child poverty:

> Children's economic well-being is largely determined by the employment status of their parent or parents. (para 3.1)
>
> The likelihood of parents engaging in work depends on a wide range of interlinked factors. Macroeconomic stability and a flexible labour market are key and are complemented by policies to encourage and support people to move off welfare and into work. This can be achieved through a combination of bringing parents into contact with the labour market, improving the financial returns to work and addressing key barriers to work such as problems acquiring childcare ... (para 3.2)

---

[51] Annex A to the document summarises the evidence.

And then the childcare strategy goes one step further. It links not only children's economic wellbeing, but also their social and psychological wellbeing to parental
employment:

> 2.28 Children growing up in households connected to the labour market are likely to have a
> better understanding of the link between educational attainment and its consequences for later
> life. Parental employment is also linked to improved performance in education when a child is
> older. For the adults involved, employment can bring benefits of increased self-esteem,
> extended social networks, a greater sense of control, and reduced mental health problems.
> These can all have positive consequences for children. By contrast, children from workless
> households are less likely to have home environments conducive to learning, and are more
> likely to fail to attain at school and to be workless in later life.
>
> (HM Treasury, *et al*, 2004 para 2.28)

While the childcare strategy is about helping 'parents' and 'households' to connect to the
labour market, it recognises that having children has a far greater impact on the working
lives of mothers than on fathers. It states that maternal employment was at 64% in 2002
(para 2.33), but that around 40% of these women worked part time. Further, while the
percentage of women in professional and managerial roles has increased from 25% to
33% in the last ten years, in 2001 over 70% of those in receipt of the National Minimum
Wage were women (para 2.36). Motherhood clearly matters to a woman's (work) life in a
way that fatherhood does not to a man's (work) life. We will explore further the possible
causes and implications of this difference, but for now, the statistics are sufficiently
revealing. In 2001 86% of all fathers were employed full-time and 3% were employed
part-time. Only 8% were economically inactive. In the same year, 31% of all mothers
were employed full-time, 36% part-time and 30% were economically inactive (O'Brien
and Shemilt 2003 p 8).

> 2.44 .... One study showed that women returning to the labour market after a one year gap
> experienced a 16.1% drop in earnings compared to their previous job, while men experienced a
> drop of about 6.5%. Another study estimated that each year in full-time employment increased
> hourly earnings by three per cent. By contrast, each year of part-time working was found to
> decrease hourly earnings by one per cent, in addition to losing out on the three percent
> increase. Similarly, each year of interruption to employment for child care and family care
> reduced hourly earnings by one per cent, again in addition to losing out on the three per cent
> increase from full-time employment. (HM Treasury, *et al*, 2004)

Comparing figures from other OECD countries the Treasury document observes:

> the reduction in female labour market participation in the UK once women become mothers is
> quite large, although it is falling. It is noticeable that many of the countries where motherhood
> makes little or no difference to labour market participation—like Denmark, Sweden, Finland,
> Norway, Belgium and France—are countries with well developed systems of childcare provi-
> sion. (HM Treasury, *et al*, 2004 para 2.40)

The final point we wish to make about the childcare strategy document is the way in
which it acknowledges that the childcare market cannot be an efficient or effective regulator of childcare services. Contrary to other messages about one's personal and
individual responsibility for children, for work and for family choices, and contrary also
to incentives designed to appeal to that personal responsibility, this part of the

document acknowledges some social responsibility for aspects of those choices. It states that there are benefits to childcare that may not be captured by the market.

> 2.44 … parents do not receive all the benefits generated by their work, but they must meet all the costs of working: parents, as with all workers, capture some of the benefits generated by their work in wages, but the rest is shared with their employers and the rest of society in the form of higher economic growth. Employers may have some incentive to help parents share childcare costs, as if a parent is forced to give up work the employer loses their share of the benefits that were generated by the parent's work. …
> … parents must meet the costs of childcare immediately, whereas the benefits from remaining attached to the labour market when their children are young may extend over many years. …

The government's ten-year strategy for childcare, therefore, includes creating childcare places for all families with children up to age 14 who need it. It has set itself different targets to meet in the years up to 2020. Policy thus seems to be moving closer and closer to the models in countries like Denmark, Norway and Sweden where extensive public day care has been available for many years and state commitment to its provision is seen not only as a policy which advances equality between the sexes by easing women's access to employment, but as one in which the best interests of children are promoted (Bradley 1996 p 171; p 201; p 115).[52] It has come a long way from 1996, when Millar and Warman (1996) examined the provision of day care services in the 15 Member States of the EU plus Norway. This part of their research was aimed at 'how the role of the state is defined *vis à vis* the role of the family' (p 29). Their research shows that at the time, Britain could be grouped with Ireland, Portugal and Spain in assuming that childcare is intended for ' "problem" children, those deemed at risk in some way or with particular needs' (p 31) rather than for 'meeting the needs of mothers (or parents) to combine child-rearing with paid work' or 'as having a primarily educational role for children and so be the entitlement of all children' (p 31).

Fox Harding described the day care debate in the 1990s in these terms:

> Finally, the issue of day care throws into relief the underlying ideological debate about family responsibility, and especially maternal responsibility. The day care debates highlight a struggle over the state-family boundary and over what is properly a public/private area of responsibility. Broadly, the state's expectation in Britain is that parents/mothers will care for young children during the day, and this is conveniently reinforced by post-war theories of child development which suggested that day care outside the family was damaging. However, recent research indicates that much depends on the *quality* of day care; it is not adverse *per se* (National Children's Bureau, 1993). Nevertheless, publicly provided state care is construed as a 'welfare' provision for a minority of families with special problems, for whom it is seen as helpful; otherwise mothers will care (or make their own arrangements). The effects of this are that working parents/mothers must turn to a range of other (possibly unsatisfactory) non-state alternatives, or indeed leave children alone: a situation beginning to attract media attention and public concern in the early 1990s. The assumption that day care is a 'private' matter may be highly damaging to children. (1996 p 171)

**Q** How does the ten year strategy for childcare construct the public/private boundary in terms of responsibility for childcare? How does it influence the construction of motherhood and fatherhood?

[52] But, for the contrary view, see Morgan (1996).

We have seen that many women try to achieve a compromise in their employment and family lives by working outside the home on a part-time basis. Apart from the financial disadvantage this creates for them in terms of their ability to acquire property and pension provision for themselves in later life,[53] part-time work can create a host of other disadvantages. Warren, (2003) for example, suggests that policy that focuses only upon a balance between work and family ignores other important aspects of one's life; we balance other domains in our lives, including leisure and financial security, and that taking these other domains into account shows that female part-timers in lower level jobs showed the least satisfaction with their financial security and with the social aspects of their lives. She concludes that the work-life system is multi and not two dimensional and that policy-makers should take this into account in assessing the benefits and disadvantages associated with working part-time. Morris and Nott also note the complicated moral and financial negotiations undertaken by part-time working mothers:

> Particularly significant are the findings in the Survey on Part-timers on why women choose to work at all. The disadvantages were numerous and obvious: those with children, for example faced horrendous problems of child care, especially in school holidays or when a child was ill. Most of the respondents said they felt guilty about combining work with other responsibilities, continually feeling that one suffered at the expense of the other. Apart from having to juggle their two roles there are also problems concerning the work itself: part time work tends to be in lower skilled jobs and because the pay is also low there are problems with tax and particularly with national insurance.
>
> ...
>
> And yet, despite the multifarious problems, these women still go out to work. Money is clearly an important motivating factor, though the extent to which this was true varied amongst the respondents and it is notable that many referred to the feeling of independence it gave. Other factors mentioned were the social contacts work engenders plus the mental stimulation and self-esteem. (Morris and Nott 1995 p 59)

These complicated negotiations are compounded still further when one factors in the responsibilities of being a 'good mother'. According to Neale and Smart (2002):

> The identities of the mothers in our sample appeared to be bound up primarily with their relationship with their children. They were more likely to start with an imperative to care ... . They also recognised the economic imperatives of raising children and may have extended their role to accommodate this ... . In contrast, the identities of most of the fathers in our study remained bound up primarily with their employment. They were likely to start with an imperative to secure paid work ... . They were also likely to recognise the imperative to care for their children, and some extended their role to accommodate this. (p 196)

Barlow, *et al*, (2002) looked at the 'cost-benefit analysis' employed by lone mothers about their decisions to enter into paid work and found that most saw 'their moral and practical responsibility for their children as their primary duty and for many (although not all) this responsibility to be a good mother is seen as largely incompatible with significant paid work' (p 113).[54] And so, contrary to the 'message' of social security and employment policy, which seems now to have shifted from a male breadwinner model to a dual earner model (Lewis 2002), 'those lone mothers who chose not to take up paid work, far from falling into a deviant sub-culture that abhors self-reliance and social responsibility [and now, the welfare of their children!], did so on the basis of what they

---

[53] See ch 5 below.
[54] See also Duncan, *et al*, (2003); Barlow and Duncan (2000a) and (2000b).

believed to be the morally proper thing to do as a mother' (Barlow, *et al*, 2002 p 113). Given the complicated moral and economic rationalities by which mothers make decisions about their work-life balance, Lewis (2002) suggests that while the dual earner model now adopted in social policy may be better for woman than the male breadwinner model, it is still only aspirational. The reality, she says, may be the one and one-half earner model, the model that is most easily accommodated by women's part-time work.

Other alternatives for working mothers might be to consider flexi-time, job sharing and other 'family friendly' work practices, and since 2003 employers have a legal duty to consider requests for flexible working time arrangements from parents of children under age 6.[55] Research as to the take-up of these provisions will be interesting, as O'Brien and Shemilt's (2003) research indicates that flexible working was generally low before the requirement was introduced.

> Flexitime, part-time and job-sharing were used by 20%, 6% and 2% of fathers respectively. Mothers' use of flexible working practices was always higher than fathers, except in the case of shift work, which was used by 25% of fathers and 18% of mothers. The largest disparities between the two groups were in the use of part-time working (20% of mothers compared with 6% of fathers) and term-time only working (20% of mothers compared with 6% of fathers). Fathers were less likely than mothers to adopt part-time working because of domestic commitments or a desire to spend more time with the family. A majority of fathers thought that working part-time would adversely affect their career progression (66% compared with 45% of mothers). (p 54)

It seems that much of British industry is committed to *flexible* working hours, however, and since the 1980s such patterns have increased. It has usually been driven, however, by competitive pressures, or labour market fluctuations. Brannen, *et al.* note the difference between flexible and family friendly working practices:

> The distinction between 'flexible' and 'family friendly' working practices can easily become blurred. 'Family friendly' practices may be 'flexible'—but not all 'flexible' practices are family friendly'. It has been suggested that
>
> > family friendly practices can be defined as a formal or informal set of employment terms and conditions which are designed to enable an employee to combine family responsibilities with employment … . Whilst family friendly practices are designed to suit both employee and employer, flexible working practices may not be so accommodating towards the former and may be designed more for the employer than the employee.
>
> … 'Flexibility' in patterns of work takes many forms: flexible daily, weekly and annual hours; compressed working weeks; shiftworking; alternatives to full-time permanent working, including temporary contracts, sub-contracting, part-time working and job-sharing; and working part or all of the time at or from home. (1994 p 8, reference omitted)

As it stands now, many employers accommodate men even less than women. Full-time British male workers work the most hours of any of their EU counterparts—a mean of 46 hours per week (O'Brien and Shemilt 2003 p 13). Despite implementation[56] of the EC Working Time Directive[57] which provides, among other things, a limit of 48

[55] Employment Act 2002; and see below.
[56] The Working Time Regs 1998 SI 1998/1833.
[57] Council Dir 93/04/EC.

hours per week on the average time which many employees can be required to work (except by voluntary agreement), British work patterns still tend to be family-unfriendly for all parents, and can be contrasted with Swedish state policy, for example, in which children's interests were material in restructuring employment patterns:

> This [protecting children's interests] is reflected in extensive statutory holiday entitlements and the long term commitment to a six hour day. Employment rights—parental leave, paternity leave, leave for parents of sick children, leave to attend school 'contact' days—are based on the assumption that both parents are employed and that both should have time and energy for their children. (Bradley 1996 p 111)[58]

**Q** To what degree does British policy in this area reflect 'traditional family values'? Which 'traditional family values' are reflected? To what degree can government policy influence the power of 'traditional family values' or even the number of 'traditional families'?

To summarise thus far: reflected by a lack of adequate child care facilities outside the family and a historical lack of interest on the part of business or government to assist workers with family responsibilities, care of children was deemed to be a private matter for the family rather than a matter for universal support by the state. Recently, however, family-friendly work and childcare have appeared on the government agenda. The rationale for this shift is said to include the welfare of children and the welfare of the economy. The government hopes to reduce the number of 'workless' households by providing economic and service incentives for all to work, at least part-time. One's responsibility to society and to one's family, one's very citizenship (Plant 2003),[59] appears to hinge upon one's economic productivity. And yet, while the ideologies of proper motherhood and fatherhood remain entrenched and women tend to resolve the conflict between the imperative to care and the imperative to earn by taking up part-time work, this work often affects not only their levels of stress and feelings of guilt, but also the kind of work they are able to obtain and the hours they are able to work in order to accommodate the dual responsibility which is expected of them. Additionally, many men are deprived of the fulfilment they might have through a stronger relationship, based upon more than 'breadwinning' alone, with their children (O'Brien and Shimelt 2003; Hatten, *et al*, 2002). It is partly these effects upon heterosexual parents and their children which the Scandinavian policy, for example, was designed to counter.[60]

## V. EMPLOYMENT LAW[61]

Related to child care law and policy are some aspects of employment law. Again, the government has made this link in ways that historically were ignored. The most radical

---

[58] The origins of the Swedish policy stem from a number of influences, from pronatalism to acceptance of more state control over reproductive and family matters to feminism (Bradley 1996).

[59] See further below.

[60] Dunne's (2000) research seems to demonstrate that lesbian parents are able to negotiate childcare in a more egalitarian way because they perceived themselves as free of sex role stereotypes and assumptions. See further, ch 4 below.

[61] See generally Pascall (1997) ch 2; Deakin and Morris (1998).

changes were made in the Employment Act 2002, and the government has proposed extending changes to employment law even further (DTI 2005). Let us examine how employment law relates to one's choices about one's reproductive life.

Currently employers in England and Wales are not obliged to provide day care facilities for their workers' children, although they are given tax relief if they do.[62] Further, the *capacity* to reproduce has been and continues to be relevant to work place safety, eligibility for certain kinds of employment and protection of employment rights during pregnancy and maternity or paternity. We will look in chapter 5 at how employment policy and law affect property and wealth acquisition in families; for now let us explore the relationship in law between reproduction/reproductive behaviour and employment.

### Employment and Reproduction

In the 19th century medical warnings about damage to reproductive capacity justified 'protecting' women from various types of employment. It was thought, for example, that prolonged standing was not only cruel and painful for women, but caused irreparable harm to their ability to reproduce and therefore that work as shop assistants could lead to sterility:

> Woman is badly constructed for the purposes of standing eight or ten hours upon her feet. I do not intend to bring into evidence the peculiar position and nature of the organs contained in the pelvis, but to call attention to the peculiar construction of the knee and the shallowness of the pelvis, and the delicate nature of the foot as part of a standing column. *The knee joint of a woman is a sexual characteristic ...*
>
> The Ontario Bureau of Industries also noted in its annual report in 1885 that women were subject to 'fainting spells and spasms' apparently as a direct result of prolonged standing.
> (Backhouse 1991 p 263, reference omitted)

Concern about women's reproductive capacity also excited calls to restrict women's work in factories:

> Specifying the potential for damage to 'internal organs', Dr Bergin shocked the legislators by insisting that because 'her conformation is entirely different from that of a man' a woman factory worker would almost certainly face 'sexual weakness'. He quoted from a leading American physician and public health advocate:
>
> > Amongst the women of factory operatives, much more than among the general population ... deranged states are present, eg, leucorrhea, and too frequent and profuse menstruation; cases also of displacement, flexions and versions of the uterus, arising from the constant standing and the constant heat of and confinement in the mills.
> > (Backhouse 1991 p 270 reference omitted)

Protecting women's reproductive capacity also served as justification for keeping women out of universities:

---

[62] ICT(EP)A 2003 S318. And, from 2005, employers can provide in lieu of income of up to £50.00 per week, child care vouchers. They will be free of tax and NI payments to the parent and to the employer.

The 'horror' of disabled children was presumed to be the obvious consequence of female studies ... [An American doctor] abhorred the prospect of young women studying during menstruation:

> Instead of resting both body and mind for a few days, [the pupil] is expending the nerve-force which should give tone to the uterus, and exhausting menorrhagia occurs, which of course, in turn places the system in a still worse position for the next period ... . This terrible routine may go on til the health is completely broken down ... . Other disturbances of the uterine functions ..., and incomplete or non-development of the reproductive organs take place as a consequence of mental overstrain during early menstruation. The tendency to sterility ... is attributed ... to a diversion of the vital forces from the reproductive system to the brain. (Backhouse p 298, reference omitted)

These excerpts from medical opinions are partly of historical interest only, in the light of modern medical and technological knowledge. But the issues they raise about women's supposed biological imperative to reproduce and the tension this creates with employment are still alive today. Immediately we are faced with the question whether legislation which was, and is, aimed to 'protect' women from industrial health hazards is indeed protective, or is instead exclusionary and discriminatory. Just as contemporary medical knowledge has discredited the notion that studying damages women's reproductive systems, it has also alerted us to new and legitimate hazards to the reproductive health of both women and men, notwithstanding that disproportionate focus remains upon women's reproductive bodies (Sheldon 1999; Thomson 1996). And so, questions of how to understand the equity of protective legislation remain, as does its influence upon the decision and the ability to reconcile childcare responsibilities and earning. As Bacci reminds us:

> [t]he question of the impact of industrial health hazards upon the fetus and the pregnant woman has become even more controversial that earlier in the century. Some companies in America, Britain and elsewhere are excluding women of childbearing age from work processes where there is a known danger to the fetus, unless they can prove themselves sterile.
>
> (1990 p 135)

One interesting point made by Bacci in this context is the assumed exclusivity of the relationship between women and reproduction:

> The suggestion that 'women's' protections be extended to men raises another important theoretical point. On first appearances the fact that some women were forced to undergo sterilisation to save their jobs, to 'sacrifice their "femaleness"' in Joan Bertin's words, seems a prime example of women being compelled to fit into a workplace designed for men. But Bertin also makes the point that 'hazards are often ignored or minimised, except when they involve female aspects of reproduction' and that men are wrongly presumed invulnerable 'to the effects of chemical exposures until conclusive and undeniable evidence of hazard has been amassed' ... . Women have been constructed as *vulnerable* for a multitude of political and economic reasons—to keep them in certain jobs and out of others, and to keep them reproducing—but men have been constructed as *invulnerable* for economic and political reasons as well, mainly to obviate the necessity of creating genuinely healthy working conditions. This may be a 'male norm', but it is probably a norm many men would now prefer to reject. Putting reproduction onto the political agenda has revealed that neither men nor women are the neutered automatons of liberal theory, although the sexual division of labour has made it easier for men to approximate this model. (1990 pp 146–47 references omitted)

Bacci concludes that the solution would be 'to make so-called "women's standards" effective standards for all' (p 142). In other words, '[i]f a workplace is not safe for pregnant workers, therefore, it is not safe' (p 153).

In the 19th century the arguments about women working outside the home rested not only upon biological fears, but also upon the effect of outside work upon the health of the family:

> Coupled with the reproductive argument was the concern that working wives and mothers were not able to attend to their domestic responsibilities, and thus could not provide a proper home-life for their offspring. The point was not that women were doing work other than child care. Women had always done so, especially before industrialisation had moved so much production away from the home. It was rather that in the home women had combined their productive work with child care. In the factories this was virtually impossible.
>
> (Backhouse 1991 p 186)

In the 1844 House of Commons debate over the Hours of Labour in Factories Bill Lord Ashley spoke eloquently about the unnaturalness of working women, leading not only to their usurpation of male privileges, but also to the moral downfall of the family, leading one to speculate about the link between the two. Working women, he said, formed themselves into clubs, where they would come together to drink, sing and smoke, neglecting their children. The effect, he said, was to create within families 'disorder, insubordination and conflict' (Cairns 1965 p 68).

In the 1990s the argument changed slightly; women's employment was said either to be one of the causes or predictors of divorce, or to contribute to the undermining of men as marriage partners, both of which, in turn, are said to be damaging to children and to traditional families.[63] And now, as we have seen, the argument has changed yet again. The policy is work for all, even for lone or married mothers. Whether this policy reflects the reality of women's lives, however, is questionable. Let us begin with pregnancy.

Pregnancy in employment is dealt with in a number of different legislative provisions,[64] many of which were implemented as a result of European law. Included in them is a rule that dismissal from employment as a result of pregnancy is deemed to be unfair dismissal in Britain.[65] Research conducted by the Equal Opportunities Commission in 2004 found, however, that seven per cent of women had either been dismissed, made redundant or treated so badly they felt they had to leave their jobs as a result of their pregnancy, maternity leave or return to work following absence for maternity (Adams, *et al*, 2005 p vii). Further 'forty five per cent had experienced tangible discrimination, such as denial of training opportunities and changes to job descriptions' (*ibid*). Overall, three quarters of mothers of young children had encountered some form of 'discrimination, workplace unpleasantness or poor employer practice either while they were pregnant,

---

[63] See a series of publications from the Institute of Economic Affairs, including Morgan (1995).

[64] See Council Dir. 92/85 on the introduction of measures to encourage improvements in the safety and health at work of pregnant workers and workers who have recently given birth or are breast-feeding; the Sex Discrimination Act 1975; the Employment Protection (Consolidation) Act 1978; the Social Security Act 1986; the Trade Union Reform and Employment Rights Act 1993; the Maternity Allowance and Statutory Maternity Pay Regs, SI 1994/1230; the Social Security Maternity Benefits and Statutory Sick Pay (Amendment) Regs SI 1994/1367; Employment Rights Act 1996; Employment Relations Act 1999; Employment Act 2002; Maternity and Parental Leave (Amendment) Regs SI 2002/2789; Morris and Nott (1995) pp 154–56; and McGlynn (1996).

[65] The Sex Discrimination Act 1975 prohibits employers from dismissing an employee or treating her less favourably because of her pregnancy.

while on maternity leave or on their return to work' (*ibid* p 71). The researchers also found that this treatment has an impact upon the attachment that women feel to the labour market (*ibid* p 73). We see in these statistics the questionable role that law has in influencing behaviour or attitudes.

At present, all woman are entitled to 26 weeks unpaid Ordinary Maternity Leave (OML) regardless of their length of service with their employer. During OML, women retain all the benefits of the terms and conditions of their employment, except for those relating to remuneration. At the end of OML, a woman has the right to return to the same job under the same terms and conditions as before she began her leave. Women who have worked 26 weeks of consecutive service at the fifteenth week before the birth of their expected baby, qualify for Statutory Maternity Pay (SMP) during their OML. According to these current provisions, a woman is entitled to 90% of her average weekly earnings during the first six weeks, and the lesser of £106 or 90% of her average weekly earnings during the subsequent 20 weeks. Women who do not qualify for SMP, including the more recently employed and self-employed women, may be entitled to Maternity Allowance (MA). Under MA, a woman may receive only the lesser of £106 per week or 90% of her average weekly earnings throughout her OML.

Only those women who qualify for SMP are also entitled to take an additional six months unpaid Additional Maternity Leave (AML) following their OML. During AML, the woman is only entitled to some of the terms and conditions of her employment contract. After AML, she may return to the same job on the same terms and conditions as before her leave began unless it is not reasonably practicable for the employer to enable her to do so. Where this is the case, her employer is required to offer her a suitable and appropriate alternative position with terms and conditions only as to remuneration no less favourable than those of her previous position.

The Employment Act 2002, which came into force in 2003, granted fathers statutory paternity leave for the first time.[66] Fathers who have completed six months of service with their employer at the fifteenth week before the baby is due may take one or two consecutive weeks' paternity leave at any time in the eight weeks following the baby's birth. These fathers are entitled to Statutory Paternity Pay (SPP) during their paternity leave, allowing them to receive the lesser of £106 or 90% of their average weekly earnings. Although the introduction of PL is a welcomed provision, the expectation remains that the mother is primarily responsible for the early development of the child as the father is merely entitled to two weeks' leave under PL. Furthermore, although in certain cases fathers may be able to collect Income Support while on PL, given that men in full time employment earn on average 18.4% more than women in full time employment,[67] PL may not be a real option for families where the father will likely only gain the fixed rate of income rather than 90% of his average weekly income.

Adopting parents are now entitled to similar rights to those vesting in natural parents. When a couple adopts a child, they can choose which of them will take Ordinary Adoption Leave (OAL) and the other may take paternity leave and receive SPP. All rights applicable to OML apply to OAL, and all rights which apply to AML equally apply to Additional Adoption Leave (AAL). During the first 26 weeks, the adopter taking OAL may qualify for Statutory Adoption Pay (SAP), thereby becoming entitled to the lesser of £106 per week or 90% of average weekly earnings.

---

[66] The Paternity and Adoption Leave (Adoption from Overseas) Regs 2003 SI 2003/921.
[67] DTI (2005) 11.

Finally, the regulations provide that unmarried parents and parents of the same sex are entitled to equal treatment in leave provisions. They define 'partner' in relation to a child's mother or adopter, as 'a person (whether of a different sex or the same sex) who lives with the mother or adopter and the child in an enduring family relationship but is not a relative of the mother or adopter of a kind specified in paragraph (2)'.[68] This means that an unmarried same or opposite-sex partner may be entitled to paternity or adoption leave.

Parents may also be entitled to unpaid Parental Leave to care for their child or make arrangements for the child's welfare. Both parents may qualify, if they have completed one year's service with their employer by the time they want to take the leave. They are entitled to 13 weeks per child, which can be taken up to the child's fifth birthday (or during the first five years after the child is placed with the adopting family).

Finally, all employees have the right to take a reasonable period of time off work to deal with emergencies involving dependants. Dependants are spouses, partners, children, parents or anyone who lives with the employee as part of his or her family.

Although these allowances reflect a changing attitude toward helping families balance their work and family lives, many mothers continue to find it difficult to take their full leave entitlement due to financial reasons. In 2002, 75% of women surveyed who were entitled to AML returned to work because this portion of their entitlement is unpaid. Only 11% of these said they were ready to return to work (DTI 2005 para 2.4). Further, most new fathers feel that both the level of statutory paternity pay and the time available for leave was inadequate: 80% think the current level of SPP is too low and 56% said that two weeks was too short (Thompson, *et al*, 2005 p ix). 94% of fathers took some leave from work following the birth of their child, however, and 71% took two or more weeks (*ibid* p viii). While two thirds of these fathers took paternity leave, around a quarter took annual or some other type of leave, usually for financial reasons (*ibid*). The evidence seems to show that fathers do wish to be more involved in childcare (70%), although interestingly, 65% also said that women are naturally better at caring for children (*ibid* p vii) and only one in five had made some sort of adjustment to their working pattern in order to spend time with the new baby (p viii). It is also interesting that employers showed support for fathers' involvement with children, but fathers reported feeling that only about half of their employers would be supportive of more than two weeks leave (p ix).

At the time of writing, the Government intends to extend its policy of flexibility regarding work and families. It is currently considering responses to its Consultation Document (DTI 2005) which has proposed to extend paid maternity and adoption leave to nine months from April 2007 toward the goal of a year's paid leave by the end of next Parliament. It also intends to introduce a new law enabling mothers to transfer a proportion of their maternity leave and pay to fathers and to extend the right to request flexible working arrangements to a range of other carers. The exact provisions of the Parental Rights Bill (currently in progress) will depend upon the results of the consultations.

---

[68] The Paternity and Adoption Leave Regulations 2002 SI 2002/2788.

**Q** Comment upon the government's proposals. Millar and Warman (1996) note that parental leave can be used to keep women at home as well as to enable them to work. Why might this be the case?

## VI. TAX AND SOCIAL BENEFITS

How is parenthood supported by the system of taxation of income from employment (assessed on an individual basis) and allocation of income from social benefits (assessed on a family basis)?

The Tax Credits Act 2002 introduced the Child Tax Credit and the Working Tax Credit.[69] Both create tax advantages for those caring for children, but because they come in the form of tax credits, depend upon one having an income against which to credit them. The Child Tax Credit consists of a family element, a child element and a small baby element, payable in the first year of a child's life; the family element is payable to any family responsible for a child, while the child element is payable for each qualifying child for which the carer is responsible. Unlike the Child Tax Credit which is payable even if the carer is on Income Support or income-based Jobseeker's Allowance, the Working Tax Credit requires that the claimant is in paid employment for a minimum of 16 hours per week. It is payable to those who qualify financially, whether they have caring responsibilities or not. The amount received depends on the level of income and caring responsibilities, however, and is designed to provide greater benefits to those with lower incomes. It includes elements that take account of caring responsibilities: there is a lone parent element and, importantly, a child care element to help working carers who spend money on 'approved' or 'registered' child care. At the time of writing, the carer in receipt of the tax credit receives 70% of this expense up to a maximum of £135 for one child and £200 for two or more children. In the Government's 2004 Pre-Budget Report, it announced that it intended to increase both the limitations and the proportion of childcare costs covered.[70] These reforms appear to be designed to encourage more lone parents and second earners in couples to return to work.

The state also provides a universal benefit to carers of children. Child Benefit is seen as an important part of the government's strategy to combat child poverty. It is provided as a universal cash payment[71] paid to the parent with care, assumed to be the mother unless the mother applies for another person to receive it.[72]

**Q** Universality is an issue upon which it is difficult always to find agreement. Many argue, for example, that finite resources should be targeted to the most needy, and that paying child benefit to wealthy parents either does not make financial sense or is inequitable. Others argue that it is the principle of state support for

---

[69] These came into effect in April 2003: The Child Tax Credit (Amendment) Regs SI 2003/738 and The Working Tax Credit (Payment by Employers) (Amendment) Regs SI 2003/715.

[70] See further, ch 13 below.

[71] Social Security Contributions and Benefits Act (SSCBA) 1992.

[72] For a good review of the history and entitlement to Child Benefit, see Wikeley (2002) ch 18.

families that is important, and universality evidences the idea that all children are important to the state and that the state has some responsibility for them. It enhances social integration. Universality has, however, declined in political popularity in Britain over the last two decades. Write a short paragraph identifying the pros and cons of universal child benefit.

**Q** In 2004 The Child Trust Funds Act was passed. The government will issue a voucher worth £250.00 to start an account for all children born on or after 1 September 2002. The voucher will be issued automatically to all carers receiving Child Benefit so that they can start a long-term non-taxable savings fund from which only the child, on turning 18, can withdraw funds. Children in families receiving Child Tax Credit will receive an extra amount. The fund is designed to teach children about finances and the benefits of saving. While this fund is not designed to assist families with the immediate needs of raising children, how might it benefit children and carers in their day to lives?

The state also provides benefits based upon contributions people have made to funds over their working lives. Contributory benefits are based upon insurance-like principles whereby one 'insures' oneself against future contingencies—here, loss of earnings—by making contributions to the National Insurance scheme during one's working life. Contributory benefits are payable when work must stop for short term periods for reasons such as maternity,[73] sickness,[74] incapacity[75] or other short periods of unemployment,[76] provided that the required contributions are made in the appropriate periods.

Contribution-based jobseeker's allowance replaced NI unemployment benefit in 1996. It requires the claimant to be available for and actively seeking work and to sign a jobseeker's agreement before six months' worth of benefit is provided.[77] Until the 1980s it (then called NI unemployment benefit) included extra amounts for child dependants. The Jobseeker's Act (JSA) 1995 also repealed additional allowances for adult dependants of the unemployed.

**Q** In what way might eligibility for or amount of these contributory benefits be affected by gender considerations?

Other benefits are available for people with low incomes. There is a whole group of means-tested benefits which do not require the claimant to have made any previous contributions. Income-based Jobseeker's Allowance (IJSA) is one such means-tested benefit, even though it is intended to be a measure to deal with unemployment rather than low income *per se*. In effect, it merged together NI unemployment insurance and income support for the unemployed under the umbrella of unemployment legislation and is now administered by the newly reorganised Jobcentres Plus with benefits and unemployment dealt with as a single issue. As with contribution-based JSA, claimants must meet the criteria in sections 1 and 3 of the JSA 1995, which include being able to work, being available for work, actively seeking work, signing a jobseeker's agreement, not having a partner who is in work or is eligible for IJSA or IS and not oneself being eligible for

---

73 SSCBA 1992 s 35.
74 SSCBA 1992 ss 31 and 32.
75 Social Security (Incapacity for Work Act) 1994.
76 Jobseeker's Act 1995.
77 JSA 1995 ss 1–3.

income support. In conjunction with claims for IJSA the government has introduced a series of 'New Deals', including the New Deal for Lone Parents, the New Deal for Young People and the New Deal for Partners, the latter being intended to reduce the number of workless households. Joining the New Deals is not mandatory, but if claimants or partners join, they receive enhanced assistance with finding employment. The Welfare Reform and Pensions Act 2000 introduced a third route to JSA: a joint-claim Jobseeker's Allowance, which requires certain unemployed couples with no children to make a joint claim. Both claimants will have to satisfy the conditions for entitlement.

Calculation of IJSA is based upon income support guidelines, including size and composition of family (see below). Income Support is the basic means-tested scheme of benefits for those who are not able or expected to work. Categories of people who are not expected to seek work and who are therefore eligible for IS include lone parents and those with significant caring duties. Various reforms recently, however, have resulted in all claimants for IS (as well as certain other benefits, including Housing Benefit) and their partners to attend a 'work-focused interview' as a condition of eligibility. Only one member of a family may claim income support and, as we saw in chapter 1, cohabitants, same or different-sex, may be included as a family for this purpose.

Both IS and IJSA operate to determine the minimum amount (allowance) it is thought that a person needs in order to live and then to ensure that that person receives that amount through a combination of her other income and capital (if any) and benefits. All income (except certain income which is disregarded) is taken into account, and if it does not meet the level set by the income support guidelines, benefits will be paid to top that person up to the amount specified in the guidelines. Until 2004, children in the claimant's care were taken into account at the determination both of the level of the allowance set for the claimant (her personal allowance) and the income (including income disregards) deducted from that allowance to determine the amount payable to her. Since 2004, however, the child and family elements of IS (and IJSA) have been removed and have become a part of CTC and WTC. IS and IJSA still include a carer's element, however. The total income to be subtracted from someone's basic allowance includes Child Benefit and any maintenance received *or assessed* through the Child Support Agency.

The personal allowance set for each claimant is premised on a determination of how much money that person is said to need on a day-to-day basis. One's personal allowance is affected not only by one's 'marital' status,[78] but also by age and by the number and ages of any children in one's care. In addition to a family premium allowed for parents, and a carer's premium allowed where the claimant or partner receives carer's allowance,[79] single parents who claimed before the 1996 budget are allowed an additional lone parent premium. That premium was abolished in 1996 for new claimants. It was thought that providing state support for single parenthood would only encourage it and would disadvantage two parent, traditional families (Morgan 1995). In assuming an interesting but unsubstantiated direct link between social welfare provision and sexual behaviour, one MP stated: '[t]eenage never-married mothers should not get benefit—then we'd see a

---

[78] This is a nominal distinction. Whether one is married or cohabiting actually makes no difference to the amount allocated. 'Couple' includes unmarried cohabitants and in the light of *Secretary of State for Work and Pensions v M* [2005] 1 FLR 498; [2004] EWCA Civ 1343, arguably also same-sex cohabitants. Note, however, that this case is, at the time of writing, set down for appeal.

[79] Carer's Allowance is available to a person who spends 35 hours or more per week caring for someone who receives Attendance Allowance or Disability Living Allowance. It is not available for those in full-time education and until 2002 it was not available for carers over the age of 65.

massive drop in teenage mums'.[80] It is clear that only certain single-parent families are seen to be undesirable, however: 'I think we have got to look at the very principle of payments to single mothers and separate the widowed and deserted from those who have never married'.[81]

IS is also a 'passport' to other benefits such as free school meals, free prescriptions, and free dental care and eye tests. In addition, once a claimant satisfies the IS requirements, the claimant automatically qualifies for Housing Benefit and Council Tax Benefit.[82] Housing Benefit and Council Tax Benefit[83] are means-tested benefits payable to people on low incomes to assist them in paying rent or council tax. In the Social Security Act 1986 it was provided that up to 100% of eligible rent was provided for, but in 1996 the regulation changed so that local authorities now have a discretion to pay a lesser sum, in the light of 'local considerations'.[84] Both benefits include premiums for children and carers.

Other benefits that may be available for people with children include the Social Fund, and maternity grants. The Social Fund (SF)[85] is a publicly funded source of meeting the cost of single sudden and heavy expenses for those who need them. There is a one-off maternity grant to pregnant women or new mothers, currently £500, which is available to meet all of the costs of a new baby. Further, loans are available for crisis events or high-cost items such as winter coats for children, but these are determined solely at the discretion of the Social Fund officers. There is no right of appeal of an SF officer's decision, only provision for judicial review of the decision.

**Q** Article 26 of the United Nations Convention on the Rights of the Child, to which Britain is a signatory, provides that states parties must:

> recognise for every child the right to benefit from social security ... taking into account the resources and the circumstances of the child and persons having responsibility for the maintenance of the child, as well as any other consideration relevant.

Article 27 requires states to:

> recognise the right of every child to a standard of living adequate to the child's physical, mental, spiritual, moral and social development ....

Construct an argument that Britain has met its international obligations under these provisions. Construct an argument that it has not.

---

[80] *Sunday Telegraph*, 21 July 1996 p 1.

[81] *Ibid*.

[82] See generally Wikeley (2002).

[83] SSCBA 1992 ss 131–33.

[84] Housing Benefit (General) Amendment Regs. 1995 SI 1995/1644, as amended, particularly by SI 1997/852 and SI 1997/1975. See also Social Security Amendment (Lone Parents) Regs 1998/766. Housing benefit is enabled by the SSCBA 1992, s 130, as amended by the Housing Act 1996. The legislation was further amended by the Welfare Reform and Pensions Act 2000 to require claimants to attend a 'work-focused interview'. See also The Housing Benefit and Council Tax Benefit (Abolition of Benefit Periods) Amendment Regs 2004 SI 2004/14.

[85] Part VIII of the SSCBA 1992.

> **Q** Some (Morgan 1995) suggest that the two parent family is discriminated against by Britain's fiscal policies. In what way might this argument be accepted or rebutted?

### Housing Policy

Britain's housing policy[86] has undergone radical changes since the middle of the 20th century. In the 1950s and 1960s, for example, rented accommodation was the primary form of housing, and local authorities provided close to one third of it (Morris and Nott 1995). Throughout the 1980s however, the government's policy was actively to encourage owner occupation of housing through its 'right to buy' legislation. As a result, local authorities now provide only a relatively small proportion of the housing stock.[87] They do have some obligation to house, however, and local authority controlled housing is currently allocated according to rules set out in the Housing Act 1996 as amended. Local authorities are also required to comply with the provisions of the Homelessness Act 2002 and with regulations. In addition, they must take into account the relevant Codes of Guidance.[88]

The Housing Act 1996 was originally drafted under the Conservative government in the context of debates and media coverage about supposed abuses of the system. In particular it was claimed, with little evidence, that the priority accorded to people with dependent children under the homelessness legislation was providing teenagers with an incentive to become pregnant and claim council tenancies (Pascall, *et al*, 2001 p 294). Women, particularly young women, were blamed for 'creating pressures on housing supply, for free-riding and for displacing worthier two-parent families from their place on the housing lists' (Pascall, *et al*, 2001 p 293). The Housing Act 1996 changed the statutory duty upon local housing authorities to provide only temporary rather than permanent accommodation for the homeless, so that permanent accommodation would normally be allocated only through the housing register.

With the advent of the Labour government, policy again changed. The Labour agenda focused less on the promotion of the nuclear family and more on notions of community, need and social exclusion. A Green Paper (DETR and DSS 2000) was published setting out the 'key principles' for housing policy. These concerned choice; an adequate supply of decent housing to meet needs; giving responsibility to individuals who are able to do so to house themselves; improving the quality of housing; reducing barriers to work; supporting vulnerable people; tackling all forms of social exclusion; and promoting sustainable development (para 1.5). The government's proposals specifically in relation to homelessness were intended to 'ensure that unintentionally homeless people in priority need are provided with temporary accommodation until they obtain suitable settled accommodation (in either the public or private sector)' (para 9.42). In addition the aim was to 'ensure our most vulnerable citizens are protected by the homelessness safety net' (para 9.42). The reforms were also designed to open up the possibility of assisting non-priority applicants for housing such as childless couples and homeless single people who are not vulnerable (para 9.58).

---

[86] See generally, Pascall (1997) ch 13.

[87] Registered social landlords are increasingly significant providers of social housing (DETR and DSS 2000 para 1.20).

[88] Housing Act 1996 s 182. The relevant codes are the Homelessness Code of Guidance for Local Authorities and the Revision of the Code of Guidance on the Allocation of Accommodation (ODPM 2002).

The Homelessness Act 2002, including its amendments to the Housing Act 1996, as well as the new Code of Guidance (ODPM 2002) are designed to implement the government's key principles. First, the legislation broadens potential access to housing. Anyone can now apply for accommodation except for specified categories of people from abroad who are designated ineligible,[89] or people whose conduct makes them unsuitable tenants.[90] Second, the legislation has been amended to remove the time limit on the local authority's duty to house those in need of emergency accommodation. Section 193 of the Housing Act 1996 no longer restricts the duration of the duty to two years[91] and simply provides that the authority has a duty to ensure that accommodation is available to an applicant who is eligible, homeless, has a priority need and has not become homeless intentionally.[92] Third, authorities now have a discretion to offer accommodation to those who are not in priority need.[93] Where the applicant has a priority need but is intentionally homeless, there is a duty to provide accommodation for such time as the authority considers will provide him or her a reasonable opportunity to find his or her own accommodation.[94] Housing authorities also have a duty to take reasonable steps to enable those in priority need and threatened with homelessness, but not intentionally so, to remain in their accommodation.[95] However in addition to these duties, housing authorities now have new powers. They are permitted to allocate accommodation to those who are unintentionally homeless but who are not in priority need.[96] They also have a discretion to help those not in priority need but who are not intentionally threatened with homelessness, as well as those who are in priority need but who are intentionally threatened with homelessness to remain in their homes.[97]

Those who have a priority need for accommodation[98] in terms of the statute are people who are homeless or threatened with homelessness as a result of an emergency such as a flood, households with dependent children, and households that include a pregnant woman or a vulnerable person.

The duties of local authorities to provide temporary or emergency accommodation, then, depend on whether the homeless person is in priority need and on whether their plight is the result of an intentional act or omission. The statute also distinguishes between different categories of people in relation to the allocation of settled accommodation. Local Authorities are no longer obliged to keep a housing register. Under the new arrangements, all applicants for housing, including those already in temporary accommodation, are allocated permanent housing in accordance with a housing

---

[89] S 160A Housing Act 1996 as amended. Those subject to immigration control are not eligible unless they fall within prescribed classes, such as people granted refugee status, exceptional leave to remain or indefinite leave to remain. See The Allocation of Housing (England) Regulations 2002, SI 2002 No 3264. See also ODPM (2002) ch 4 on eligibility.

[90] S 160A(7) Housing Act 1996 as amended. Such persons can be treated as ineligible. This extends also to cases where a member of the applicant's household's behaviour is in issue.

[91] The main homelessness duty in s 193 persists until it is brought to an end by circumstances specified in that section. These include an offer of an assured tenancy or a refusal of a final offer of accommodation.

[92] Prior to the 2002 amendments, this duty was limited if the authority was satisfied that other accommodation was available in the area; it was obliged only to provide advice and assistance to enable the applicant to find accommodation him- or herself. Now, this limitation has been repealed.

[93] The statute also places a duty on Authorities to provide advice and assistance to those who are homeless or threatened with homelessness if they are intentionally so or if they do not have priority needs.

[94] S 190(2) Housing Act 1996.

[95] S 195(2) Housing Act 1996 as amended. A person is threatened with homelessness if it is likely that he or she will be homeless within 28 days (s 175(4) Housing Act 1996).

[96] S 192(3) Housing Act 1996 as amended.

[97] See s 195(8)-(9) Housing Act 1996 as amended.

[98] See s 189 Housing Act 1996.

scheme. And the scheme must give 'reasonable preference'[99] to certain categories of people including those who are homeless,[100] those who are homeless and owed a duty under Section 193, those who are threatened with homelessness and owed a duty under Section 195(2), those who are in unsatisfactory housing conditions, those who need to move on medical and welfare grounds, and those who need to move where failure to move will cause them or others hardship.[101] The scheme may also be framed so as to give additional preference to people within the reasonable preference categories who have urgent housing needs.[102]

The effect of the new legislation is to retain the priority status based on pregnancy and dependent children. However, there is a discretion to help unintentionally homeless people who do not qualify for priority status. Moreover, all homeless persons, including those who are single and those who are childless must be given reasonable preference in the allocation of accommodation.

When it comes to securing the housing need of children, it is often social services rather than the housing authority that appears to bear responsibility. Where an application under the housing legislation is made on behalf of the child in an attempt to circumvent the intentional homelessness provisions, the House of Lords has decided that the local authority should find other means of meeting its obligation. (Barton and Douglas 1995 pp 251–52).[103] Parents who are ineligible or intentionally homeless may turn instead to social services. The new section 213A of the Housing Act 1996 is designed to enable social services to be apprised of the situation where a young person is or is likely to be homeless. Where someone applies for housing but is ineligible or intentionally homeless, that person must be asked to consent to social services being notified if a person under 18 lives with him or her. Provided there is consent, social services must be told of the situation so that they can take action.

Local authorities have duties under Part 3 of the Children Act 1989 and it may be necessary for social services and the housing authority to work together to fulfil these. Section 17 provides that:

> (1) It shall be the general duty of every local authority ...
>
> (a)   to safeguard and promote the welfare of children within their area who are in need; and
> (b)   so far as is consistent with that duty, to promote the upbringing of such children by their families, by providing a range and level of services appropriate to those children's needs.

Section 20(1) places a duty upon local authorities to

> provide accommodation for any child in need within their area who appears to them to require accommodation as a result of—
>
> ...

---

[99] S 167(2) Housing Act 1996 as amended.

[100] This includes people who are intentionally homeless and people who cannot show a priority need (ODPM 2002 para 5.8).

[101] S 167 Housing Act 1996 as amended. It is not apparent that the hardship ground would necessarily be appropriate to prioritise victims of domestic violence. See the discussion of these grounds in ODPM (2002) paras 5.16–5.17. However the Code of Guidance provides, as an example under the category of medical or welfare grounds, '[t]he need to recover from the effects of violence (including racial attacks) or threats of violence, or physical, emotional or sexual abuse' (ODPM 2002 Annex 3). See also ch 13.

[102] S 167(2) Housing Act 1996 as amended. The revision of the Code of Guidance gives as an example, people who are victims or at risk of domestic violence (ODPM 2002 para 5.18). See ch 13.

[103] See also *R v Oldham Met BC, ex parte Garlick and Related Appeals* [1993] AC 509; Gilbert (1993); Loveland (1996).

(c) the person who has been caring for him being prevented (whether or not permanently, and for whatever reason) from providing him with suitable accommodation or care.[104]

Social services may ask the housing authority to provide advice and assistance in the exercise of its functions under Part 3 and the housing authority is obliged to provide such 'advice and assistance as is reasonable in the circumstances'.[105] Similarly, section 27 of the Children Act 1989 provides that housing authorities are obliged to respond to a request for help from social services in fulfilling its duties under that Act. So, for example, housing authorities and social services may have to consult in cases where a household includes a child in need who requires accommodation for welfare or medical reasons[106] (ODPM 2002 paras 5.33–5.36).

However, the obligation to co-operate is circumscribed; it applies only where co-operation is compatible with the duties of the authority asked for help and if rendering help would not unduly prejudice the discharge of its functions.[107] And the duty under section 213A(5) of the Housing Act 1996 is limited to what is 'reasonable'. Neither of these provisions, it seems, can be used to force a housing authority to provide accommodation to the carers or family of a child who is in need as a result of the fact that the adults with whom he or she lives are homeless. Social services has the power, but has no obligation under Part 3, to provide housing for the families or carers of children.

A child whose family is homeless and ineligible for help under housing legislation may be assessed as being in need. However section 17, the House of Lords has held,[108] is a general provision and does not confer absolute, enforceable rights on individuals;[109] the only remedy is judicial review. Moreover, section 17 is not primarily designed to deal with the re-housing of children in need to enable them to live with their families: 'housing is the function of the local housing authority'.[110] To use section 17 in this way would have the effect of turning the social services department of a local authority into another kind of housing authority with priorities that differ from those set down in housing legislation.[111]

Section 20 does oblige the local authority to provide children with accommodation if their carers are unable to provide them with suitable accommodation. However, there is no duty in the Children Act[112] to ensure that the carers are given accommodation; the duty is exclusive to the child. And while to place children in accommodation apart from

[104] See also ss 17(1) and 27(2).
[105] S 213A(5) Housing Act 1996 as amended.
[106] Included as one of the categories meriting reasonable preference in s 167(2) Housing Act 1996.
[107] S 27(2) Children Act 1989. See *R v Northaven DC, ex parte Smith* [1994] 2 AC 402, [1994] 3 All ER 313. Having found that a family was intentionally homeless under Part III of the Housing Act 1985 (now Part VII of the Housing Act 1996), the local housing authority refused to rehouse them, but referred them back to the local authority social services department for reconsideration as the children were 'in need' of accommodation under ss 17(1) and 20(1) of the Children Act 1989. The House of Lords found that the refusal to rehouse was correct, and that a fresh consideration of the request for housing was not required under the Children Act once a determination had been made under the Housing Act if the request were incompatible with the functions of the department and/or compliance with the request would be unduly prejudicial to its functions. See Cowan and Fionda (1994) and (1995); Holgate (1993). An attempt to amend the 1996 Housing Bill to include as a priority homeless children in need pursuant to s. 17(10) of the Children Act 1989 was defeated in the House of Commons (Childright 1996 p 6).
[108] *R (on the application of G) v Barnet London Borough Council; R (on the application of W) v Lambeth London Borough Council; R (on the application of A) v Lambeth London Borough Council* [2003] UKHL (2004) 57 1 FLR 454.
[109] See paras 91 and 135.
[110] Para 92.
[111] Para 93.
[112] The court rejected the argument that s 23 created such a duty (paras 102–4).

their parents constitutes an interference with family life,[113] whether a decision taken under Part 3 is compatible with Article 8 of the European Convention on Human Rights depends on the facts of each case.[114]

**Q** Article 27(3) of the United Nations Convention on the Rights of the Child requires states, in the case of need, to provide material assistance and support programmes, particularly with regard to nutrition, clothing and housing.

In your view, has the UK met its obligation under this Article?

## VII. CONCLUSION

We have looked at direct and indirect social and legal ordering of reproduction and the social and legal consequences of our decisions to reproduce. Far from being a private matter, decisions to become parents are either facilitated or frustrated depending upon the degree to which we and our lifestyles are able to conform to the traditional family model, and living as parents is made easier or more difficult according to the same standard. Further, law and policy regarding reproductive choices, employment, social security and child care affect men and women differently at all stages, particularly if reproduction is regulated within a legal framework of individual rights and encouraged within a political and social framework of family ideology.

We have so far examined the social and legal influences upon the decision to become a parent, and the degree of state support once that decision is made. We turn in the next chapter to the questions which arise once a child is born: who in law *are* that child's parents, and what responsibilities does parenthood create?

## FURTHER READING AND SELECTED RECENT REFERENCES

L ADAMS, F McANDREW and M WINTERBROTHAM, *Pregnancy Discrimination at Work: A Survey of Women* (London, Equal Opportunities Commission, 2005).
A BAINHAM, *Children: The Modern Law*, 3rd edn, (Bristol, Jordan, 2005).
A BARLAW and S DUNCAN, 'New Labour's Communitarianism, Supporting Families and the "Rationality Mistake": Part I' (2000) 22(2) *Journal of Social Welfare and Family Law* 23.
——, 'New Labour's Communitarianism, Supporting Families and the "Rationality Mistake": Part II' (2000) 22(2) *Journal of Social Welfare and Family Law* 129.
A BARLAW, S DUNCAN and G JAMES, 'New Labour, the Rationality Mistake and Family Policy in Britain' in A Carling, S Duncan and R Edwards, (eds), *Analysing Families: Morality and Rationality in Policy and Practice* (London, Routledge, 2002).
D BRADLEY, *Family Law and Political Culture* (London, Sweet & Maxwell, 1996).

---

[113] See *Kutzner v Germany* [2003] 1 FCR 249.
[114] *R (on the application of G) v Barnet London Borough Council; R (on the application of W) v Lambeth London Borough Council; R (on the application of A) v Lambeth London Borough Council* [2003] UKHL (2004) 57 1 FLR 454, para 69.

A DIDUCK, 'Conceiving the Bad Mother: "The Focus Should be on the Child to be Born"' (1998) 32 *University of British Columbia Law Review*.

S DUNCAN, *et al*, 'Motherhood, Paid Work and Partnering: Values and Theories' (2003) 17 *Work, Employment and Society* 309.

R DWORKIN, *Life's Dominion: An Argument about Abortion and Euthanasia* (London, Harper Collins, 1995).

S FOVARGUE, 'The Law's Response to Pregnancy and Childbirth: Consistency, Conflict or Compromise?' (2002) 65 *Modern Law Review* 290.

L FOX-HARDING, *Family, State and Social Policy* (Basingstoke, MacMillan, 1996).

Mrs Justice B HALE, *From the Test Tube to the Coffin: Choice and Regulation in Family Life* (London, Sweet & Maxwell, 1996).

W HATTEN, L VINTER and R WILLIAMS, *Dads on Dads: Needs and Expectations at Home and at Work* (London, Equal Opportunities Commission, 2002).

E JACKSON, *Regulating Reproduction: Law, Technology and Autonomy* (Oxford, Hart Publishing, 2001).

——, 'Conception and the Irrelevance of the Welfare Principle' (2002) 65 *Modern Law Review* 176.

J LEWIS, *The Politics of Motherhood: Child and Maternal Welfare in England 1900–1939* (London, Croom Helm, 1980).

——, 'Individualisation, Assumptions about the Existence of an Adult Worker Model and the Shift Towards Contractualism' in A Carling, S Duncan and R Edwards, (eds), *Analysing Families: Morality and Rationality in Policy and Practice* (London, Routledge, 2002).

B NEALE and C SMART, 'Caring, Earning and Changing: Parenthood and Employment after Divorce' in A Carling, S Duncan and R Edwards, (eds), *Analysing Families: Morality and Rationality in Policy and Practice* (London, Routledge, 2002).

M O'BRIEN and I SHEMILT, *Working Fathers: Earning and Caring* (London, Equal Opportunities Commission, 2003).

G PASCALL, *Social Policy: A New Feminist Analysis* (London, Routledge, 1997).

G PASCALL, *et al*, 'Changing Housing Policy: Women Escaping Domestic Violence' (2001) 23 *JSW&FL* 293.

H REECE, *Divorcing Responsibly* (Oxford, Hart Publishing, 2003).

S SEVENHUIJSEN, *Citizenship and the Ethics of Care* (London, Routledge, 1998).

S SHELDON, *Beyond Control: Medical Power and Abortion Law* (London, Pluto, 1997).

——, 'Reconceiving Masculinity: Imagining Men's Reproductive Bodies in Law' (1999) 26 *Journal of Law and Society* 129.

——, 'Gender Equality and Reproductive Decision-Making' (2004) 12 *Feminist Legal Studies* 303.

M THOMSON, 'Employing the Body: The Reproductive Body and Employment Exclusion' (1996) 5 *Social and Legal Studies* 243.

M THOMPSON, L VINTER and V YOUNG, *Dads and their Babies: Leave Arrangements in the First Year: Working Paper Series No 37* (London, Equal Opportunities Commission, 2005).

N WIKELEY, *Wikeley, Ogus and Barendt's: The Law of Social Security* (London, Buterworths, 2002).

## Reports

DTI, *Work and Families, Choice and Flexibility: A Consultation Document* (London, Stationery Office, 2005).

Dame Mary (Chair) Warnock, *A Question of Life: The Warnock Report on Human Fertilisation and Embryology*, Report of the Committee of Inquiry into Human Fertilisation and Embryology (Oxford, Blackwell, 1984).

HFEA, *Code of Practice* (London, HFEA, 2003).

HM Treasury, *Child Poverty Review* (London, The Stationery Office, 2004).

——, *Investing for our future: Fairness and opportunity for Britain's hard-working families, HC 372* (London, The Stationery Office, 2005)

# 4

# Children and their Mothers and Fathers

In this chapter we will examine the way in which legal rules sometimes recognise and sometimes create a connection between adult and child to forge a legal relationship. Although our focus will be on parenthood as a *legal* construct, parenthood (and child-hood) is also a biological phenomenon and a socially constructed category— motherhood and fatherhood themselves are only 'natural' to the extent that it takes genetic material from a male and a female to begin a new life. And the law takes cognisance of understandings of parenthood that span the biological and the social. In addition to the biological parent,[1] it also recognises, for example, the 'psychological parent' (Goldstein, *et al*, 1980a; 1980b),[2] who is that person to whom the child has bonded emotionally and psychologically, and the 'social parent',[3] who is the person who under-takes the day to day care for the child. When thinking about parents and children, then, we may need to distinguish between parentage (the biological link between parent and child), parenthood (legal recognition of that link) and the legal duties and rights that sometimes come with those statuses: parental responsibility (Bainham 1999).

Parental responsibility is a concept created by the Children Act 1989. It encompasses all the rights and duties that parents have with respect to their children.[4] We will discus parental responsibility in more detail below and in chapters 7 and 15, but for now wish to underline that the fragmentation of biological, social and legal parenthood is often fraught with difficulties (Bainham 1999), which, we would suggest, are compounded further when one factors in gender.

Collier (1995b) illustrates the different relationships with a child that a man can have and the role that law plays in those relationships.

> [W]e can, at the outset, distinguish between paternity and fatherhood. 'Fatherhood' is the social construct through which the law has historically sought to attach men to children. It is not a unitary concept and there is (as we shall see) no one fatherhood in law. A distinction may be made therefore, between 'paternity', signifying a biological but not necessarily social connection with a child, 'biological fatherhood', which embraces the biological and social fathering relationship, and 'social fatherhood' in which the 'role' of fathering and all the obligations it involves, occurs but without the presence of a biological relationship between man and child. All of these are instances of men's relationships with children which have been established in law. It is once paternity is proved that there may be a legal relationship between a man and a child ... but the bundle of rights, obligations and duties which make up parenthood do

---

[1] See, eg, s 20(1) Family Law Reform Act 1969.

[2] See *Re M (Child's Upbringing)* [1996] 2 FLR 441 (CA) for an example of a case in which the concept of 'psychological parent' was accepted by the courts: per Ward LJ, pp 54–55.

[3] See, eg, the definition of 'child of the family' s 52(1)(a) of the MCA 1973 which includes a child of one of the parties to a marriage (or, after December 2005, a civil partnership) but who has been treated by both parties as a child of their family. See *Re A (Child of the Family* [1998] 1 FLR 347 and cases cited below.

[4] S 3 Children Act 1989.

not automatically follow from a finding of paternity. Thus although the terms are often used synonymously, *paternity* is different from *fatherhood*. The former refers to the legal status of men who have biologically fathered a certain child or children. In a sense it is the law which 'gives' a man the status of fatherhood through recourse to the concept of paternity.

(1995b pp 184–85, references omitted)

He also reminds us that law can, in other circumstances, override biology in assigning fatherhood: the 'presumption of legitimacy' operates to attach the status of legal father-hood to the husband of the child's mother, even if there is evidence that he is not the biological father (1995b p 184).[5] Finally, legal fatherhood does not necessarily imply that a man has legal responsibility to care for, visit or even acknowledge a child.[6]

Motherhood and maternity have also become categories that are increasingly detached from each other. Advanced techniques of assisted reproduction together with the law of adoption mean that a child may have up to four 'real' mothers (a genetic mother, a gestational mother, a commissioning social mother and an adoptive mother), not to mention social or psychological relationships created through fostering or step-parent situations.

As it does with fatherhood, law accepts some maternal relationships and overrides others in determining legal motherhood and in allocating rights and responsibilities to mothers. Section 27(1) of the Human Fertilisation and Embryology Act (HFEA), which we discuss below, is one example of a choice that law has made between genetic and gestational mothers.

In this chapter we will first outline the ways in which law assigns the status of parent-hood, and explore potential explanations for those assignments. For, as Jackson (2006 forthcoming) states, while it is usually presented as a question of fact, the determination of which of the features that are normally associated with parenthood should be singled out as identifying the 'real' mother or father of a child, is actually a question of judg-ment. We will then examine the legal, social and material meaning of that status. In other words, Part I will address who, in law, is a parent, and Part II what, in law, parenthood means.

## I. WHO IS A PARENT? BECOMING A MOTHER

*Biological Mothers*

Western European culture[7] recognises a link between a child and the woman who has borne that child. In most cases the same woman provides the gametes and bears the child, and the combination of these biological facts usually gives rise to a legal relation-ship with all of its attendant responsibilities.[8] With the advent of methods of assisted reproduction, however, we have seen that an egg may be donated by one woman and implanted in the womb of another, genetically unrelated woman who will then carry and

[5] And see *O v L (Blood Tests)* [1995] 2 FLR 930; *K v M (paternity: contact)* [1996] 1 FLR 312 for applications of this principle.
[6] See ch 7 and pp 153–64 below.
[7] See Kandel (1994) for other possibilities.
[8] There are exceptions, however. See, for example in France *accouchement sous x*, discussed below pp 120–21.

give birth to the child.[9] Both can be called the biological mothers of the child. In such cases, the question becomes whether the law should assign rights and responsibilities to the genetically related mother or the carrying mother.

At present, the law prioritises the carrying woman. Legal motherhood in cases where a woman has received an embryo implant through a licensed clinic is determined by Section 27(1) of the HFEA:

> The woman who is carrying or has carried a child as a result of the placing in her of an embryo or of sperm and eggs, and no other woman, is to be treated as the mother of the child.

This determination shall be for all purposes[10] except for the succession to any dignity or title of honour.[11] Consider, however, s 20(1) of the Family Law Reform Act 1969:

> In any civil proceedings in which the parentage of any person falls to be determined, the court may, either on its own motion or on an application by any party to the proceedings, give a direction—
>
> (a)   for the use of scientific tests to ascertain whether such tests show that a party is or is not the father or mother of that person ...

This section allows for the taking of non-invasive bodily samples in order to perform DNA profiling, which can establish accurately the genetic parentage of a child.

We may thus see two competing priorities at work in determining legal motherhood. When one becomes a mother through sexual intercourse, or without the assistance of a licensed clinic, the genetic connection is deemed most important, and in these cases the genetic mother will always be the carrying mother. When one obtains donated gametes with assistance at a licensed clinic, however, the gestational link takes precedence. A number of explanations are offered for this prioritisation of bearing and delivering a child.

The Warnock Committee appointed to report on various aspects of assisted reproduction considered the ethical, moral, legal and technological issues around the donation of gametes and felt that donations should be encouraged as a means of assisting infertile couples.[12] To this end, it recommended relieving the donors of any legal obligations or responsibilities for children resulting from their donations (1984). The desire to encourage donations may be one reason that the law confers legal status on gestational mothers rather than genetic mothers when licensed assistance is provided. Another might be that the law recognises the commitment and health risks undertaken by the carrying woman (Douglas 1991 p 129). Perhaps a further justification for the rule might be that there should be some recognition of a psychological and physical 'bonding' between woman and foetus, which many suggest takes place in the womb. However, the Warnock Committee, in its discussion of surrogacy,[13] did not consider this factor to

---

[9] See ch 3.

[10] HFEA 1990 s 29(1).

[11] HFEA 1990 ss 29(4)(a).

[12] One of the arguments against legalising egg (or sperm) donation was that the process introduces a third party into marriage, an institution traditionally denoting an exclusive relationship (see ch 2). Donation was thus seen as a moral wrong akin to adultery and as constituting a threat to the 'family unit'. See, eg, Tallin (1956); *MacLennan v MacLennan* 1958 SLT 12; Bartholomew (1958). The Committee did not accept these objections as sufficiently weighty to justify banning the process.

[13] See below pp 122–29.

be significant and appeared to accept arguments that, because little is known about a bonding process *in utero*, 'no great claims should be made in this respect' (1984 p 46).

The Committee's view of maternal-foetal bonding is in sharp contrast to that of some anthropologists and psychologists who suggest that a great deal is indeed known about pre-birth bonding, and that what is known supports the view that bonding—'the intense emotional attachment between two organisms resulting from the totality of the psycho-physical interactions' (Fox 1992 p 74)—begins before birth and continues at parturition. Anthropologist Robin Fox states:

> The emotional bonding of the mother and child starts before birth. This bonding will eventually become essential to the healthy emotional development of the child as the mother's milk (in preformula days) is essential to its physical development. The evolutionary function of the preparturition bonding is presumably to prevent the mother from rejecting the infant at birth … . One of the most important cues in mother-infant bonding is that of voice … . It is not surprising therefore that students of neonate behaviour have noted a marked preference for the mother's voice in the newborn … . (p 78)[14]

On the other hand, many suggest that such connections are only the result of society's 'socio-economic requisites' (Jenks 1996 p 42) or cultural imperatives that have succeeded in constructing women but not men as 'natural caregivers'. Yngvesson (1997) suggests that for law, this means that the mother-child dyad is 'naturalised' as an 'intimate, emotionally charged connection' which patriarchy manifests as 'outside' the boundary of the law, whereas fatherhood, grounded as it is property rights over the child, is fundamentally 'within' the law (pp 38–39).[15] It is ironic, then, that it is the 'naturalised' maternal bond that is automatically accorded legal status, while as we shall see below, the 'rational' paternal bond is not.

As O'Donovan (2000) observes, this means a woman in England and Wales cannot give birth and refuse motherhood, even if only for six weeks (p 73).[16] 'Giving birth makes a woman a mother in English law. Even if the child is to be placed for adoption, or is born to a woman acting as a surrogate for another, or is not genetically related to the birth giver, parturition makes motherhood …' (*ibid*).

In contrast, in France[17] it is perceived as a woman's right to give birth anonymously and remain permanently free from any legal bond with the child (O'Donovan 2000; Lefaucheur 2004), and the ECtHR has upheld her right to do so under Article 8 ECHR. While the child also has a right under Article 8 to know his or her identity and circumstance of birth, in *Odievre v France* the Grand Chamber held that the two had to be balanced along with the general social interest and France's law was within its margin of appreciation.[18]

> The ideal situation is and will remain that even a woman who is pregnant under difficult circumstances—which characterise the situation at issue in the present and similar cases where women today have opted for anonymity when giving birth—should be able to give birth under circumstances that ensure her and her baby's safety and make it possible for the child to know the mother's identity, even if it is immediately adopted by a new family. When however, a

14 For a feminist view of this connection, see Rothman (1989).
15 See also Diduck (1998 and 1999a).
16 A woman may not consent to adoption or to a parental order under the HFEA 1990 in the first six weeks after giving birth. See below pp 123, 137.
17 And Italy and Luxembourg: see *Odievre v France* ECtHR (2004) EHRR 43; [2003] 1 FCR 621 para 19.
18 There was a strong dissenting minority judgment in this case.

woman for whatever reason finds that this is not an option in her case—which it may be difficult for anyone else fully to appreciate—human rights should none the less mediate in favour of
her being able to give birth under circumstances that ensure her and her baby's safety, even if
she insists on remaining anonymous vis-a-vis the child. It would be plainly inhumane to invoke
human rights to force a woman in this situation to choose between abortion or a clandestine
birth; the latter always holds a potential of jeopardising the mother's and/or the child's health
and, if worst comes to worst, could be life threatening and/or result in the child being stillborn.

(Para OIII15 EHRR report)

**Q** In the case of *Re B (Adoption by One Natural Parent to Exclusion of Other)* [2001] I
FLR 589 CA Hale LJ stated that carrying and giving birth to a child is sufficient to
create a 'family life' (for the purposes of Article 8) between a woman and child
even if they are separated at birth (para 38) and this finding was approved by the
House of Lords even though the decision was overturned on other grounds
([2001] UKHL 70; [2002] I FLR 196 at para 30 per Lord Nicholls). How, if at all,
does this decision reflect either of the views on maternal-foetal bonding? How
does the French law do so? Which do you prefer?

**Q** Do you agree with the law's resolution of the priority between genetic and gestational mothers? What arguments can you make for or against Section 27(1)
HFEA?

All of the arguments above assume that the law should designate only one woman as the
child's mother. An alternative view is that the quest for one exclusive legal mother simply reproduces the 'one mother/nuclear family construct', and that instead we ought to
'recognise the maternity of both the genetic mother and the gestational mother and
involve them both in the child's social rearing' (Kandel 1994 p 168).[19] Kandel uses
anthropological literature to establish that child sharing is not uncommon, and that the
theories of bonding and attachment which shaped Goldstein, Freud and Solnit's psychological parent thesis (1980a; 1980b) and Bowlby's maternal deprivation theories
(1953, chapter 8) are linked to the cultural belief that nuclear families are 'natural' so
that a child can have only one mother (and, for that matter, only one father).

The assumption that a nuclear family and/or one mother is essential for a child's stability and
well-being warrants reassessment in light of comparative research. This assumption is
grounded in attachment theory and the concept of the psychological parent which were introduced into child custody law through Goldstein Solnit and Freud's influential book, *Beyond the
Best Interests of the Child*. Attachment theory, also known as the continuous care and contact
model, suggests that continuous interaction between an infant and a single nurturing adult is
critical for the infant's normal motor, cognitive, social and emotional development. This theory
reasons that the strong survival advantages conferred upon helpless newborn humans by
attached interaction, have resulted in adaptive selection over the course of human evolution.
Evidence which supports attachment theory is derived from negative findings: the severe detriment and dysfunction suffered by children who are abandoned, institutionalized or shunted
from foster home to foster home. Ethnographic studies in which multiple mothering results in
shared nurturance, rather than successive abandonment, are relatively rare. Yet, existing studies
compellingly support the positive value of shared mothering. Professors Tronick, Morelli, and
Winn studied the Efe of northeastern Zaire, who 'engage in a system of multiple caretaking'.
Immediately following birth, a newborn infant is passed around and nursed by all women of

[19] See also Langdridge and Blythe (2001) and Jackson (2006 forthcoming).

the camp. When the mother resumes work, childcare responsibilities, including nursing, are shared by individuals at the work site ... . Researchers found that Efe infants were likely to be precocious in their social skills and predisposed to cooperation, mutual support and gregariousness. (Kandel 1994 pp 193–95, footnotes omitted)

One does not even have to examine anthropological literature about family practices in other cultures to accept the possibility that children's understanding of family can healthily accommodate more than one mother.[20] And the Adoption and Children Act 2002 and the Civil Partnership Act 2004 seem to acknowledge this psychological finding legally. Law's demand for exclusivity may, therefore, conflict with the ways in which more people are living their familial lives (see eg, Dunne 2000).

> **Q** How would you determine the legal motherhood of a child? How, if at all, can the law accommodate more than one legal mother? See Jackson (2006) forthcoming; Harrison (1995); Wallbank (2004); Probert (2004); Langdridge and Blyth (2001). This issue arises again in the context of adoption, where the law has difficulty reconciling the privacy of adoptive families with continued contact with birth mothers in 'open adoptions' (see below and Yngvesson 1997), and surrogacy (see below).

In summary, then, in terms of the HFEA 1990, genetic relationships do not necessarily create legal relationships. The woman who carries and gives birth to the child is accorded the status of legal motherhood. This ascription makes sense where the carrying mother is also the intended social mother of the child. Sometimes, however, the woman who carries the foetus to term does not intend to rear the child after its birth, and may be carrying the child as part of a business arrangement or as an act of generosity toward another person. In this case, we introduce another factor into the question of determining legal motherhood: intention and social parenthood.

*Surrogacy*

The persistence of the exclusivity of parenting within the ideal of the nuclear family has led to a search for a 'real' mother in the context of surrogacy arrangements. And so, just as it is thought there is a need to choose between the genetic and the gestational mother, the law in surrogacy cases must also include in its choices the intended social, or commissioning, mother. Complicating the legal issue further is the social understanding of motherhood and surrogacy, as revealed in the language of the discourse itself. Morgan (1989), for example, highlights the social understandings of motherhood revealed by naming the carrying mother instead of the commissioning mother as the surrogate. He defends this use, while recognising that it is another example of 'the use and elision of language to appear to make one set of circumstances more natural, thereby less objectionable, therefore commanding support among right-thinking people' (1989 p 60). The contrary view would be 'that it is the person ... who takes and rears the child rather than she who gives birth who is properly the surrogate. The woman giving birth is *the* mother, not the surrogate' (Morgan 1989 p 56). Surrogacy thus 'fragments motherhood' (Cook, *et al*, 2003a p 4).

---

[20] There is voluminous research on children reared with same-sex parents. For a review of some of the most recent, see Murray (2004).

**Q** Does one's identification of the 'real' mother depend upon one's definition of motherhood or mothering?

Surrogacy can occur where the surrogate receives sperm from the commissioning father, or it can occur where she receives an embryo from both commissioning parents.[21] It is only when surrogacy has been arranged through a licensed clinic and the surrogate has either been artificially inseminated or implanted with an embryo or sperm and egg that the HFEAct is engaged, however. As we have seen, regardless of the surrogate's intention, she is, pursuant to Section 27(1) of the HFEA, the legal mother of the child. In order to give legal effect to the surrogacy arrangement, then, the intended social mother must either adopt the child[22] or, if she is married, she can apply together with her husband under Section 30 of the HFEA for a parental order.[23] The relevant parts of Section 30 read as follows:

30(1) The court may make an order providing for a child to be treated in law as the child of the parties to a marriage (referred to in this section as the 'the husband' and the 'the wife') if—

(a) the child has been carried by a woman other than the wife as the result of the placing in her of an embryo or sperm and eggs or her artificial insemination;

(b) the gametes of the husband or the wife, or both, were used to bring about the creation of the embryo, and

(c) the conditions in subsections (2) to (7) below are satisfied.

(2) The husband and the wife must apply for the order within six months of the birth of the child, or in the case of a child born before the coming into force of this Act, within six months of such coming into force.

(3) At the time of the application and of the making of the order—

(a) the child's home must be with the husband and the wife, and

(b) the husband or the wife, or both of them, must be domiciled in a part of the United Kingdom or in the Channel Islands or in the Isle of Man.

(4) At the time of the making of the order both the husband and the wife must have attained the age of eighteen.

(5) The court must be satisfied that both the father of the child (including a person who is the father by virtue of section 28 of this Act), where he is not the husband, and the woman who carried the child have freely, and with full understanding of what is involved, agreed unconditionally to the making of the order.

(6) Subsection (5) above does not require the agreement of a person who cannot be found or is incapable of giving agreement and the agreement of the woman who carried the child is ineffective for the purposes of that subsection if given by her less than six weeks after the child's birth.

(7) The court must be satisfied that no money or other benefit (other than for expenses reasonably incurred) has been given or received by the husband or the wife for or in consideration of—

---

[21] Statistics on the frequency and success of surrogacy arrangements are difficult to compile due to the informal nature of many surrogacy arrangements..

[22] As in *Re MW (Adoption: Surrogacy)* [1995] 2 FLR 759.

[23] As in *Re Q (Parental Order)* [1996] 1 FLR 369.

(a)   the making of the order,
(b)   any agreement required by subsection (5) above,
(c)   the handing over of the child to the husband and the wife, or
(d)   the making of any arrangements with a view to the making of the order,

unless authorised by the court.

This section, in turn, must be read in conjunction with the Surrogacy Arrangements Act 1985 which prohibits third parties from becoming involved in commercial surrogacy arrangements[24] and provides that no surrogacy arrangement or contract is enforceable by or against any of the parties.[25] Thus any arrangement concerning the care of the child after birth is enforceable only if it is construed as a consent within the meaning of Section 30, rather than as a contractual term agreed when the arrangement was originally made.

You will note that parental orders may only be made in respect of married partners. This section does not apply to cohabitants, nor has it been amended by the Civil Partnership Act 2004 to apply to registered civil partners. In its response to the DTI's Consultation on Civil Partnership, the Human Fertilisation and Embryology Authority drew attention to this anomaly (HFEA, undated, accessed 2005 para 14), and in announcing its review of the HFEA 1990, the government agreed that part of its review would consider the need to 'reflect the wider range of people who seek and receive assisted reproduction treatment in the 21st century' (Select Committee on Science and Technology 2004 para 21).

**Q** How, if at all, would you amend Section 30?

A good review of the law and recent policy on surrogacy is found in Hale LJ's judgment in the case of *Briody v St Helens and Knowsley Health Authority*.[26] The claimant in this case was appealing the rejection at trial of her claim, as a part her damages in a successful action in negligence against the Health Authority, for the costs of making a surrogacy arrangement. Hale LJ took the opportunity to review the law's position on surrogacy:

10 English law on surrogacy is quite clear.

(a) Surrogacy arrangements are not unlawful, nor is the payment of money to a surrogate mother in return for her agreeing to carry and hand over the child.

(b) The activities of commercial surrogacy agencies are unlawful. It is an offence for any person to take part in negotiating surrogacy arrangements on a commercial basis, i e for payment to himself or another (apart from the surrogate mother); for a body of persons negotiating surrogacy arrangements to receive payment from either the proposed surrogate mother or the commissioning parents; or for a person to take part in the management or control of a body of persons which negotiates or facilitates surrogacy arrangements: Surrogacy Arrangements Act 1985, section 2.

(c) It is also a crime to advertise either for surrogate mothers or a willingness to enter into or make surrogacy arrangements: Surrogacy Arrangements Act 1985, Section 3.

[24] S 2.
[25] S 1A.
[26] [2001] EWCA Civ 1010; [2002] QB 856; [2001] 2 FLR 1094.

(d) The surrogate mother is always the child's legal mother, irrespective of whose eggs were used: Human Fertilisation and Embryology Act 1990, Section 27(1).

(e) If the commissioning father supplied the sperm, he will be the child's legal father, unless section 28 of the Human Fertilisation and Embryology Act 1990 applies so as to make someone else the father. It should be possible, by treating him and the surrogate together, to avoid the exclusion from fatherhood of ordinary sperm donors: see the 1990 Act, section 28(6)(a) and Schedule 3, para 5.

(f) If the child is born by IVF (in vitro fertilisation), GIFT (gamete intrafallopian transfer) or artificial (but not natural) insemination to a married surrogate mother, her husband will be the legal father unless it is shown that he did not consent to the treatment: Human Fertilisation and Embryology Act 1990, section 28(2). If the treatment was given 'in the course of treatment services provided for her and a man together' by a licensed clinic, her partner will be the father: 1990 Act, section 28(3). But this can easily be avoided by her partner taking no part in the treatment.

(g) No surrogacy arrangement is enforceable by or against any of the persons making it: Surrogacy Arrangements Act 1985, section 1A, as inserted by section 36 of the 1990 Act (see also the Children Act 1989, section 2(9), reflecting the common law).

(h) The future of any child born, if disputed, will always be governed by the paramount consideration of the welfare of the child: Children Act 1989, section 1(1). It is unlikely, although not impossible, that a court would decide that the child should go to the commissioning parents rather than stay with a mother who had changed her mind: see *A v C* [1985] 1 FLR 445 and *In re P (Minors) (Wardship: Surrogacy)* [1987] 2 FLR 421. If the mother does not want the child and the commissioning parents are able to offer a suitable home, the court is likely to allow them to do so: see *In re C (A Minor) (Wardship: Surrogacy)* [1985] FLR 846.

(i) If the child is handed over in accordance with the arrangement, the court may be prepared retrospectively to authorise, under section 57(3) of the Adoption Act 1976, any payment made to the surrogate mother and grant an adoption order which would otherwise be prohibited by section 24(2) of the 1976 Act: see *In re Adoption Application (Payment for Adoption)* [1987] Fam 81.

(j) There is now a special procedure, similar to adoption, whereby the commissioning parents may become the child's legal parents: they must be married to one another, the child must be born as result of IVF, GIFT or artificial (again not natural) insemination using the gametes of one or both of them, the child must be living with them, the surrogate mother (and any father of the child who is not the commissioning father) must agree, and no payment must have been made unless authorised by the court: Human Fertilisation and Embryology Act 1990, section 30; see *In re Q (Parental Order)* [1996] 1 FLR 369.

(k) If a surrogacy arrangement involves treatment in a clinic licensed by the Human Fertilisation and Embryology Authority (which will be the case in this country unless natural or private artificial insemination is used), this must not be provided 'unless account has been taken of the welfare of any child who may be born as a result of the treatment (including the need of that child for a father), and of any other child who may be affected by the birth': Human Fertilisation and Embryology Act 1990, section 13(5).

(l) Clinics must observe the Code of Practice, 4th ed (1998), promulgated by the Human Fertilisation and Embryology Authority. This provides, in para 3.20: 'The application of assisted conception techniques to initiate a surrogate pregnancy should only be considered where it is physically impossible or highly undesirable for medical reasons for the commissioning mother to carry the child.'

It also gives guidance on the factors to be considered when taking account of the child's welfare (para 3.17); and points out that in a surrogacy arrangement either the surrogate (and her husband or partner if any) or the commissioning parents may become the child's parents and so both should be assessed, along with any risk of disruption should there be a dispute, and the effect on any other children in either the surrogate's or the commissioning parents' family (para 3.19.b).

11 These provisions do not indicate that surrogacy as such is contrary to public policy. They tend to indicate that the issue is a difficult one, upon which opinions are divided, so that it would be wise to tread with caution. This is borne out in the official publications which have considered the matter. If there is a trend, it is towards acceptance and regulation as a last resort rather than towards prohibition.

12 The 'moral and social objections to surrogacy' weighed heavily with the majority of the Warnock Committee: see Report of the Committee of Inquiry into Human Fertilisation and Embryology (1984) (Cmnd 9314), ch 8; *cf* 'Expression of Dissent: Surrogacy' (p 87). They not only made the recommendations which resulted in the 1985 Act, but also recommended criminal liability for 'professionals and others who knowingly assist in the establishment of a surrogate pregnancy': see p 47, para 8.18. This would have resulted in the virtual abolition of safe surrogacy arrangements while leaving private do-it-yourself arrangements untouched. Two members dissented: they thought that public opinion was not yet fully formed on the question and that it would be a mistake to close the door on it completely. They wanted to ban profit-making agencies but regulate the practice of non-profit-making agencies on the analogy of adoption. The 1985 Act took a minimalist course. Yet, only six years later, Parliament made special provision for commissioning parents to become legal parents, in section 30 of the 1990 Act.

13 There was renewed concern in 1997, when Professor Brazier and her colleagues were asked to review the current law and practice. They found 'that the incomplete implementation of the recommendations of either the majority or the minority of the Warnock Committee created a policy vacuum within which surrogacy has developed in a haphazard fashion': see Surrogacy, Review for Health Ministers of Current Arrangements for Payments and Regulations, Report of the Review Team (1998) (Cm 4068), executive summary, para 3. They recommended further regulation, through the registration of non-profit-making agencies, who would have to abide by a Code of Practice, the continued banning of commercial agencies, statutory limitations so that surrogate mothers could only be paid genuine expenses, and the tightening of the section 30 process, with no power retrospectively to authorise illegal payments. These recommendations have not, as yet, been implemented.

14 Thus, while there is general agreement that commercial agencies and advertising should be banned, that surrogacy for convenience or social rather than medical reasons is unacceptable, and that the agreement should be unenforceable, there is little discernible consensus on anything else. Lord Winston's view was that opinion was turning against surrogacy, and that was certainly his experience at his hospital, but if anything the tone of official publications since Warnock has been more sympathetic. Professor Craft's view was certainly different. The British Medical Association has published guidelines for health professionals: see Changing Conceptions of Motherhood, The Practice of Surrogacy in Britain (1996). These begin:

> surrogacy is an acceptable option of last resort in cases where it is impossible or highly undesirable for medical reasons for the intended mother to carry a child herself. In all

cases the interests of the potential child must be paramount and the risks to the surrogate mother must be kept to a minimum.

On the issue of Ms Briody's rights under Arts 8 and 12 ECHR, Hale LJ held:

26 While everyone has the right to try to have their own children by natural means, no one has the right to be provided with a child. Mr Irwin prayed in aid article 12 of the European Convention for the Protection of Human Rights and Fundamental Freedoms: 'Men and women of marriageable age have the right to marry and to found a family, according to the national laws governing the exercise of this right.'

27 So far, the European jurisprudence has linked these two rights: the right to found a family is a family founded by marriage; the right to marry is limited to traditional marriage between persons of opposite biological sex: see *Rees v United Kingdom* (1986) 9 EHRR 56. More importantly, these are freedoms which should not be arbitrarily restricted, for example by preventing prisoners from marrying; this may well preclude placing arbitrary or disproportionate restrictions upon access to the reproductive services which are generally available. But that is quite different from having a right to be supplied with a child (or a spouse): see the recent decision of this court in *R ( Mellor ) v Secretary of State for the Home Department* [2000] QB 13.

The HFEA Code of Practice to which Hale LJ referred has been amended only slightly. It now reads:

3.16 Where the child will not be raised by the carrying mother all involved parties are expected to be made aware that the child's legal parents will be the carrying mother (and in certain circumstances could be her husband or partner) unless relevant court proceedings are carried out. Treatment centres are expected to—where possible—assess the possibility of a dispute in such circumstances and the effect upon the child, and the effect of any proposed arrangement upon a child or children of the family of the carrying mother or commissioning parents.

3.17 Treatment centres are expected to consider the use of assisted conception techniques to produce a surrogate pregnancy only where the commissioning mother is unable for physical or other medical reasons to carry a child or where her health may be impaired by doing so.

(HFEA 2003)

Hale LJ highlights English law's almost reluctant acceptance of surrogacy, but England and Wales are not alone in their apparent ambivalence. There is little international consensus on the legal treatment of surrogacy. As Cook, *et al*, point out, some jurisdictions 'ban surrogacy altogether. Some have opted for partial bans while introducing rules to designate and regulate what is permissible. Some have voluntary guidelines and some have eschewed any form of regulation at all' (2003a p 2). They say that these differences might be evidence of the 'sense of profound anxiety and ambivalence' (p 4) that surrogacy evokes.

Surrogacy is problematic for traditional notions of 'mother', 'father' and 'family' when it introduces a third (or even fourth) party into reproduction, when it introduces contractual or 'public' arrangements into 'private' affairs and when it fragments motherhood. Surrogacy makes motherhood negotiable and confounds both social and biological bases of claims to parenthood. (Cook, *et al*, 2003a p 4)

Many of these concerns are apparent in Hale LJ's review above, and were highlighted by the Warnock Report (1984) which only grudgingly accepted that surrogacy might be acceptable in some cases. In many ways, however, they are real concerns. Surrogacy might indeed disrupt traditional ideas of 'family' and of motherhood. Probert (2004), for example, cites research that shows that most surrogates do not form attachments with the child they bear (p 276) but that many expect to play some role in the child's life as a special aunt or godmother (p 277).

> **Q** Would these disruptions to 'motherhood' or 'family' be consistent with the welfare of children? With the welfare of other members of the 'family'? With changing family practices?

There are other objections one could have to surrogacy.[27] One could, for example, object to it on the grounds that it is exploitative and simply reduces women to the status of incubators—Margaret Atwood's chilling novel, *The Handmaid's Tale* (1985), presents a dystopic vision of established and enforced surrogacy. Conversely, one could view surrogacy as one of the most altruistic acts that one woman can perform for another, and say that to argue that it is 'unnatural' relies upon patriarchal views of motherhood, 'maternal instincts' and 'natural' connections.[28] Or one could put forward arguments focusing on autonomy and say that a woman should be entitled to do as she wishes with her own body.[29] Finally, one may be concerned that surrogacy renders the resulting child a commodity to be 'sold' or given away.[30] Surrogacy is an issue that arouses strong feelings in many, although it may be the case that it is not so shocking to the public consciousness as it was when the first cases were reported in the press[31] in the 1980s resulting in the quick passage of the Surrogacy Arrangements Act 1985.[32]

> **Q** How, if at all, would you regulate surrogacy arrangements? To whom would you assign the status of legal motherhood? See *A v C*.[33]

> **Q** Two of the clauses in the Surrogate Parenting Agreement between Mary Beth Whitehead and William and Elizabeth Stern, the parties in a New Jersey case known as the Baby M case, read as follows:
>
> > MARY BETH WHITEHEAD, Surrogate, represents that she is capable of conceiving children. MARY BETH WHITEHEAD understands and agrees that in the best interests of the child, she will not form or attempt to form a parent-child relationship with any child or children she may conceive, carry to term and give birth to, pursuant to the provisions of this Agreement, and shall freely surrender custody to WILLIAM STERN, Natural Father, immediately upon birth of the child; and terminate all parental rights to said child pursuant to this agreement;
> >
> > (Fox 1992 p 54)

---

[27] See generally, Jackson (2001 ch 6); and Brazier, *et al*, (1998).
[28] But see Ragone (2003).
[29] See Jackson (2001).
[30] On the arguments generally, see Jackson (2001) ch 6 and sources cited therein; Rothman (1989); Fox (1992); Freeman (1989a); Zipper and Sevenhuijsen (1987); Marshall (1994); Smart (1989); Cook, *et al*, (2003b).
[31] In England, see *Re C* [1985] FLR 846; in the USA, see *In the Matter of Baby M* (1988) 537 A 2d 1227 (NJ Sup Ct). Brazier, *et al*, (1998) reported that the public has come to accept surrogacy (para 4.5).
[32] The Warnock Report (1984) also recommended criminalisation of commercial surrogacy. Warnock's view of the arguments against surrogacy can be found in paras 8.10–8.12 of the Report. The Brazier Report (Brazier, *et al*,1998) made a number of recommendations for increased regulation of surrogacy and for new legislation, but none has been implemented.
[33] [1985] FLR 453.

> MARY BETH WHITEHEAD, Surrogate, agrees that she will not abort the child once
> conceived except, if in the professional medical opinion of the inseminating
> physician, such action is necessary for the physical health of MARY BETH
> WHITEHEAD or the child has been determined by the said physician to be physi-
> ologically abnormal ... In the event the ..test reveals that the fetus is
> genetically or congenitally abnormal, MARY BETH WHITEHEAD, Surrogate, agrees
> to abort the fetus upon demand of WILLIAM STERN, Natural Father .... If   MARY
> BETH WHITEHEAD refuses to abort the fetus upon demand of WILLIAM STERN, his
> obligations as stated in this agreement shall cease forthwith, except as to obli-
> gations of paternity imposed by statute. (cited in Fox 1992 p 56)

What view of motherhood is implicit in the first clause? What kind of parent-child
relationship did Whitehead agree to form or not to form? How would this clause
be enforced? Is this a contract for a child or for a 'perfect' child? (see Fox 1992
p 56). Who was entitled to make any decisions concerning abortion? How would
such a clause be enforced?

To what degree does the state regulate the different types of biological motherhood? Refer back to the discussion in chapter 3 of the HFE Authority's discretion
to provide treatment.

*Non-Biological Mothers*

As we have seen, Section 30 of the HFEA enables legal motherhood to be assigned to a
woman who has no biological connection at all with a child, provided that her husband
has such a connection. In this case, it may be said that intention to become a mother, or
social motherhood, is prioritised over biology. Another situation in which intention to
become a mother is given legal effect is adoption, a legal relationship now created by the
Adoption Act 1976 but soon to be regulated by the Adoption and Children Act 2002
which comes fully into force in December 2005. In addition, there are other ways in
which the law recognises one's intention to become a mother and creates something
short of full parental status. These include residence orders which confer parental
responsibility,[34] guardianship, special guardianship and, to a lesser extent, fostering. We
will deal first with adoption. While we proceed with our discussion of adoption in the
context of motherhood, much of it relates to legal fatherhood as well. Adoption creates
the legal status 'parent', but where there are differences between mothers and fathers in
the context of adoption, we will highlight them.

*Adoption*[35]

Adoption in English law is entirely a creature of statute, and a relatively recent one at
that. There is no common law equivalent, and adoption may not be effected in any way

[34] See ch 15.
[35] The Adoption and Children Act 2002, together with the Adoption (Intercountry Aspects) Act 1999, the
Hague Convention (on protection of Children and Co-operation in respect of Intercountry Adoption) 1993,
The Intercountry Adoption (Hague Convention) Regulations SI 2003/118, the Adoption (bringing Children
into the United Kingdom) Regulations 2003 SI 2003/1173 and the Adoptions with a Foreign Element Regulations 2005 SI 2005/392 regulate intercountry adoptions. We will not discuss these in this chapter, but for a good
review see Bainham (2005) pp 767–74 and sources cited therein.

other than by a court order. English law therefore, does not recognise private adoption agreements, or any form of 'customary adoption'.[36] Adoption results in the legal transfer of all rights and responsibilities from one family to another.[37] The Adoption and Children Act 2002[38] Section 67 reads as follows:

(1) An adopted person is to be treated in law as if born as the child of the adopters or adopter.

(2) An adopted person is the legitimate child of the adopters or adopter and, if adopted by—

(a)   a couple, or
(b)   one of a couple under section 51(2),

is to be treated as the child of the relationship of the couple in question.

(3) An adopted person—

(a)   if adopted by one of a couple under section 51(2), is to be treated in law as not being the child of any person other than the adopter and the other one in the couple, and
(b)   in any other case, is to be treated in law, subject to subsection (4),[39] as not being the child of any person other than the adopters or adopter;

but this section does not affect any reference in this Act to a person's natural parent or to any other natural relationship.

The first adoption legislation in England and Wales was the Adoption Act 1926.[40] It was said to evidence a desire to give legal effect to those *de facto* relationships that had developed as a result of family upheaval caused by war and industrialisation (Barton and Douglas 1995), to provide children for childless couples and to relieve the stigma upon unmarried women who had children; in short, it was seen as a solution to the problem of what to do with illegitimate children (Lewis 2004 p 237). Over the next five decades, however, construction of the problem shifted and with it the interests to be prioritised by the legislation shifted as well. In the period after the Second World War, for example, adoption was partly aimed to serve children's interests by enabling them to be raised in 'proper families' and partly to serve adult interests by enabling them to form 'proper families' (Spensky 1992). And by the 1970s social priorities had shifted yet again. The Adoption Act 1976 appeared to prioritise the interests of children over those of adults, but partly because of the changing nature of the pool of adoptable children, a new interest came to the fore, that of the state (Lewis 2004 p 238). Thus, what were once two policy objectives vying for supremacy at different historical moments became three, and by 2002 the third seemed to have won: adoption came to be seen as a solution to the problems of the child care system (Lewis 2004 p 238).

**Q** What changing social conditions may have brought about these policy shifts? Do changing notions of acceptable motherhood or acceptable families have any role to play in this thinking? Spensky (1992), for example, argues that in the 1950s homes for unmarried mothers and the practice of placing their children for

[36] For a discussion of aboriginal child-rearing and adoption philosophies in Australia see Butler (1989).
[37] Adoptive parent–child relationships are also included in the list of prohibited relationships between people lawfully allowed to marry (see Marriage Act 1949, Sch 1 and ch 2).
[38] At the time of writing adoption was governed by the Adoption Act 1976, but because the Adoption and Children Act 2002 is to come into force in December 2005, our discussion will focus on it.
[39] Adoption by natural parent. See discussion below p 140.
[40] For an excellent review of the history of adoption in England and Wales see Cretney (2003a ch 17).

adoption in 'proper' nuclear families functioned to 'legitimate' all three parties: the child, the childless married couple, and the unmarried mother.[41]

Further, the priority given to the interests of either birth parents or adoptive parents has also shifted over time. Lewis (2004) notes that the Houghton Report, which preceded the Adoption Act 1976, is said to have favoured adoption and adoptive parents over birth parents (p 240). By the mid 1980s, she says, favour had swung back toward birth families (p 242). And in the 1990s, a White Paper (Department of Health, *et al*, 1993) and the Adoption Bill 1996 that followed it reflected a mixed view, combining the then Conservative government's commitment to 'family values', family privacy, swift and punitive intervention for families deemed to have failed, and profound suspicion of professions and professional ideology (p 244).[42] The focus of the Adoption and Children Act 2002, in turn, appears to prioritise the interests of yet another party, the state, over those of adopters or birth families.

Leading up to the Adoption and Children Act 2002 was the Prime Minister's Review of Adoption (PIU 2000).[43] It focused clearly upon the potential adoption of children who were 'looked after' by Local Authorities, rather than upon the adoption of babies or of children by step-parents or other relatives. Based upon the assumption that permanence and stability promoted the welfare of looked after children, it promoted adoption, rather than long-term foster care as the preferred method of achieving it (Lewis 2004). It aimed to increase the number of looked after children who were adopted, and recommended changes to social work policy and practice and to the law.

The White Paper that followed[44] stated unequivocally that the government's aim was to promote the wider use of adoption (para 1.13).[45] Included among its recommendations were: to create National Standards for adoption services, including a National Register of adopters and timescales within which decisions for most children should be reached (paras 4.5 and 4.6); to ensure that the welfare of children was paramount in all decisions about their future (para 4.14); to provide a range of permanency options in addition to adoption and long-term fostering (para 5.2); to increase the pool of potential adopters (paras 6.16–6.19); and to provide after adoption support for both adopted people (paras 6.41–6.46) and adopters (paras 6.26–6.40). These recommendations have, for the most part, been incorporated into the Adoption and Children Act 2002,[46] sometimes in controversial ways. What follows is not a detailed review of the Act and the procedures for adoption, but rather is an overview which focuses on these recommendations, the assumptions upon which they are based and the legal form required to implement them.[47]

[41] See also Reeves (1993) who outlines the role played by moral, economic and spiritual discourses to encourage unmarried women to give their children for adoption.

[42] For a discussion of this Bill and the consultations that led to it, see the first edition of this book.

[43] For a discussion of the Review, see Barton (2000).

[44] Secretary of State for Health (2000). Hereafter called 'White Paper'.

[45] Point two of the Executive Summary sets a target of increasing by 40% by 2004–05 the number of looked after children adopted, and to exceed this, if possible, by a 50% increase (Secretary of State for Health 2000 p 5).

[46] And associated legislation, regulations and guidelines. See discussion below.

[47] For a detailed review of adoption law, see Bainham (2005) ch 7; Bridge and Swindells (2003).

*The Goal—Increasing Adoption[48]*

It is clear that the government believes that adoption is beneficial for children, or at least that it is better than being looked after by a Local Authority. Commentators, however, note that the research about the benefits of adoption is ambiguous at best. Eekelaar, for example, reviews the literature and finds that while there is evidence that some children prefer adoption to long term fostering, there is no clear evidence that it provides more advantages for them (2003b pp 262–63).[49] He concludes that the research does not unequivocally support the government's confidence in the benefits of adoption as it was expressed in the White Paper:

> 1.12 … research shows that children who are adopted when they are over six months old gener-
> ally make very good progress through their childhood and into adulthood and do considerably
> better than children who have remained in the care system throughout most of their childhood.
> These children are also better adjusted than children who grow up in institutions. Adoption of
> older children has positive, though to varying degrees, effects on all aspects of their develop-
> ment. (White Paper 2000)

Thoburn (2003) also reviews the literature on outcomes of children in adoptive and long-term foster care. She concludes that

> [O]nly adoption will meet the needs of some children and only foster care or guardianship will
> meet the needs of others. But, for the majority in the middle, what is needed is a family that can
> meet their needs and where they can put down roots knowing that they are not going to be
> moved on. For these children, looking concurrently for either an adoptive or a permanent
> foster family will be the approach most likely to avoid unnecessary delay and avoid the child
> feeling let down if what they are told is the 'best option', adoption, does not materialise.
>
> (2003 p 397)

In effect, the research does seem to show that permanence and stability are important to a child's welfare but it is open to question whether adoption ought to be seen as the preferable means of providing this permanence. Lewis (2004) notes that, in the UK, permanence planning for looked after children[50] tends to focus primarily on adoption rather than rehabilitation with birth families or long-term fostering and observes that promoting adoption serves to divert attention from problems in the care system 'notwithstanding it [the care system] was identified as the problem' (p 249).[51]

Finally, given that Article 8 ECHR has been said to protect one's right to know one's identity,[52] the legal form of adoption, the complete replacement of one family with another, may be out of step with human rights ideals. It may also be out step with changing family practices. As Lewis (2004) comments:

> In the increasingly messy world of family formation and change, children may have a number
> of mother figures and father figures. Furthermore, the messiness is no longer hidden and gives
> rise to less and less stigma. In this context, the notion of giving a child a new legal status in a
> new family looks increasingly anachronistic. (p 251)

---

[48] There were approximately 5000 adoption orders made in England and Wales in the year ending March 2003. In that year 1500 children were adopted by step-parents or relatives. In the year ending March 2004, 510 children were adopted by foster carers. In total that year, 3700 children were adopted from care (BAAF 2005).

[49] See also Lewis (2004).

[50] See ch 17 below.

[51] See also Barton (2000).

[52] See eg *Odievre v France* above.

It may be precisely this new family and new legal status that government is concerned to promote, however. Privileging adoption over long-term fostering or other familial arrangements promotes a version of the traditional, private nuclear family with all of its attendant responsibilities for the care and (financial) support of children. Further, Smith and Logan (2002) found that for adoptive parents, adoption often achieves more than security; it constructs parenthood for them in a certain, traditional way (pp 294, 295). Only a minority of adoptive parents in their study who had been long-term foster parents said they would have been happy to continue fostering rather than adopting their children (p 294), and their concerns were expressed in terms of belonging, and the control and 'ownership' of children.

These issues of changing families, parental identities and control over children were played out in *Re B (a child) (adoption order)*[53] in which the Court of Appeal decision may be seen as supportive of new, 'messy' family practices. The Court had to determine an adoption application by a foster mother. The child, J, had been placed with the foster mother under a care order. With the support of the Local Authority the foster mother applied to adopt the child. The court had three alternatives: it could continue the arrangements then in place (with parental responsibility shared between the Local Authority and the birth parents—in practice the father, as the mother took little part in the proceedings and supported the adoption order); it could make the adoption order (severing all legal ties between J and his birth parents); or it could make a residence order in favour of the foster mother, buttressed by a Section 91(14) order under the Children Act 1989 restraining the father from making an application for a residence order without leave of the court (resulting in parental responsibility being shared between the foster mother and the birth parents). The trial judge made the adoption order, but the Court of Appeal overturned it. It considered that adoption was inconsistent with 'the reality that J was both a member of his foster mother's family and a member of his father's family' (para 19 per Thorpe LJ). Or, as Hale LJ said:

[23] We all understand, as has recently been emphasised in the White Paper, 'Adoption: a new approach' at para 5.1 that 'Children need permanence—a secure, stable and loving family to support them through childhood and beyond'. That, it must be emphasised, this little boy already has. He has a maternal family by which I mean his foster mother and her family and his sisters, and he has a paternal family by which I mean his father, his father's family and his brothers. He has excellent relationships with all of them. The only question in this case is the appropriate legal machinery to recognise those undoubted facts.

[24] It is important, it seems to me, that everyone concerned recognises that there is more than one way of securing legal permanence. One way is adoption. But in a case such as this, there are at least three problems with it. The first is that it takes something away from J. It removes his relationship with his father, his brothers and his father's family. Secondly, it is only a viable solution in a case like this if it is combined with a contact order. That is something which generally the courts are not willing to impose upon the adoptive parents, although there may be cases where it is entirely appropriate to do so. But more importantly, it is designed to maintain a level of continuing contact between J and his whole paternal family which calls into question the appropriateness of the wholesale transfer in legal terms which adoption brings about. ...

(references omitted)

[53] [2001] EWCA Civ 347; [2001] 2 FLR 26.

**Q** Comment upon the government's goal of increasing by 40–50% the number of adoptions. Is adoption consistent with trends toward new, 'messy' family practices? Should adoption be seen as the primary means of achieving security and stability for looked after children?

*National Standards*
Other than certain relatives of a child or people acting pursuant to an order of the High Court, it is only an approved adoption agency that may make arrangements for adoption.[54] Not only are adoption agencies, that is, all Local Authorities and voluntary adoption societies registered under the Care Standards Act 2000,[55] exclusively *permitted* to arrange adoptions, they are *required* to maintain adoption services.[56] In order to achieve the goal of increasing the number of looked after children who are adopted, the White Paper announced the perceived need for further and tighter regulation of the way adoption agencies do this.

> 4.5 The National [Adoption] Standards set out what children, prospective adopters, adoptive parents and birth families can expect from the adoption process, and the responsibilities of adoption agencies and councils, so that all parties receive a fair and consistent service where they live. They are underpinned by a set of values, which stress the importance to each child of having a permanent family, where they are safe. They put the child's needs at the centre of the adoption process.

> 4.6 The Standards include timescales within which decisions for most children should be reached and action taken to ensure that children are not kept waiting for a family.
> (White Paper 2000)

The Adoption and Children Act 2002, Section 3, sets out the basic requirements for the facilities and services that adoption agencies must provide. The way in which adoption services are discharged is regulated by statutory instruments and guidelines, including some which have been in effect since 2001.[57] National Adoption Standards in place since then have taken up the issue of delay in permanence planning by requiring Local Authorities to plan for a permanent home for the child at the four month case review,[58] to set clear timescales for achieving the plan and, where adoption has been identified as the plan, to ensure that the adoption panel will make its recommendation within 2 months of the decision being taken (Department of Health 2001 Section A para 2). All children who are looked after by Local Authorities for four months must, therefore, be considered for adoption. Standards are also set for clear timescales and criteria to be applied at all stages of the adoption process, including assessing prospective adopters

---

[54] Adoption and Children Act 2002 s 92.

[55] *Ibid*, s 2.

[56] *Ibid*, s 3.

[57] A set of National Minimum Standards came into effect in 2003 giving the National Care Standards Commission responsibility for inspecting and regulating all adoption services in England (Department of Health and Welsh Assembly Government 2003). See also Care Standards Act 2000, The Local Authority Adoption Service (England) Regulations 2003 SI 2003/370; The Voluntary Adoption Agencies and the Adoption Agencies (Miscellaneous Amendment Regulations) 2003 SI 2003/367. Actual service provision is regulated by the National Adoption Standards for England (Department of Health 2001). While these provisions are already in effect, a number of new statutory instruments necessary to implement the Adoption and Children Act 2002 have been passed or drafted, to come into effect in December 2005. See in particular The Adoption Agencies Regulations SI 2005/389; The Adoption Contact Register Regulations SI 2005/924; and at the time of writing, the Draft Suitability of Adopters Regulations 2005.

[58] Four weeks plus three months. See ch 17.

(*ibid* Section B), supporting adopters (*ibid* Section C) and supporting birth families (*ibid* Section D).

In addition, efficiency in the adoption process is also improved by the Adoption Register for England and Wales, which links children for whom adoption is considered to be in their best interests with families who have been approved for adoption (Local Authority Circular 2004).[59]

*Adoption and Welfare*

The Adoption and Children Act 2002[60] brings adoption law into line with the principles in the Children Act 1989. Section 1 implements the paramountcy principle, the principle of no delay and the no-order principle:

1 Considerations applying to the exercise of powers

(1) This section applies whenever a court or adoption agency is coming to a decision relating to the adoption of a child.

(2) The paramount consideration of the court or adoption agency must be the child's welfare, throughout his life.

(3) The court or adoption agency must at all times bear in mind that, in general, any delay in coming to the decision is likely to prejudice the child's welfare.

(4) The court or adoption agency must have regard to the following matters (among others) —

(a)  the child's ascertainable wishes and feelings regarding the decision (considered in the light of the child's age and understanding),
(b)  the child's particular needs,
(c)  the likely effect on the child (throughout his life) of having ceased to be a member of the original family and become an adopted person,
(d)  the child's age, sex, background and any of the child's characteristics which the court or agency considers relevant,
(e)  any harm (within the meaning of the Children Act 1989 (c. 41)) which the child has suffered or is at risk of suffering,
(f)  the relationship which the child has with relatives, and with any other person in relation to whom the court or agency considers the relationship to be relevant, including—
   (i)  the likelihood of any such relationship continuing and the value to the child of its doing so,
   (ii)  the ability and willingness of any of the child's relatives, or of any such person, to provide the child with a secure environment in which the child can develop, and otherwise to meet the child's needs,
   (iii) the wishes and feelings of any of the child's relatives, or of any such person, regarding the child.

(5) In placing the child for adoption, the adoption agency must give due consideration to the child's religious persuasion, racial origin and cultural and linguistic background.

(6) The court or adoption agency must always consider the whole range of powers available to it in the child's case (whether under this Act or the Children Act 1989); and the court must not

---

[59] See s 125 Adoption and Children Act 2002.
[60] For the sake of simplicity, what follows treats the 2002 Act as if already in force.

make any order under this Act unless it considers that making the order would be better for the child than not doing so.

The welfare test applies at all stages of the adoption process, from choosing prospective adopters to placing a child for adoption to making the order itself and any conditions for contact to attach to it. We shall consider the effect of the welfare test at each of these stages, beginning with the paramountcy of welfare at the placement and order stages.

This section represents a significant change from the previous legislation. Under the Adoption Act 1976 welfare was only the court's 'first' consideration when making an adoption order and it was not an explicit factor in deciding whether to 'free' a child for adoption.[61] Neither an adoption order (without first freeing) nor a freeing order could not be granted unless the birth parents consented or the court dispensed with their consent on the basis that they were withholding it 'unreasonably.' According to the leading case, *Re W*,[62] the test was an objective one. The court was required to determine whether a reasonable parent in the same situation would withhold agreement to the adoption of her child.

But who is the reasonable mother? Perhaps the reasonable mother ought *never* to agree to give up her child, or perhaps she ought *always* to be supremely altruistic and agree to give up her child whenever a better chance for that child's future can be found. Perhaps reasonable behaviour lies somewhere between these two extremes. In any case, the legal determination of reasonableness was potentially problematic. Our comments in chapter 1 about the gendered nature of the liberal, reasonable individual may be complicated further by research suggesting that 'reasonableness' may also be race- and class-specific. Poor or indigenous mothers may be constructed as unreasonable if they 'cling' to their children, and as reasonable if they give their children up easily (Kline 1995)[63] to be 'properly' cared for. In contrast, middle class, white women may be more easily stigmatised as 'bad' mothers if they contradict their 'maternal instincts' by giving up their children too easily, and classed as reasonable if they put up a fight. The 'unreasonableness' test was objectionable, therefore, on a number of grounds.

The Conservative government's White Paper (DoH, *et al*, 1993) accepted the criticisms of the test that were put forward in the Interdepartmental Review of Adoption Law (DoH, *et al*, 1992 pp 25–26 paras 12.4 and 12.5) and proposed to allow the court to continue to dispense with a parent's agreement to adoption in cases where the court was 'satisfied that adoption is likely to offer a significantly better advantage to the child than any other option' (1993 p 11 para 5.5). But, as we have seen, the Adoption and Children Act 2002 has gone further and incorporated a paramountcy test not only when the court is deciding to make the adoption order, but also when deciding to make a placement order. Placement orders replace freeing orders.

21 Placement orders

(1) A placement order is an order made by the court authorising a local authority to place a child for adoption with any prospective adopters who may be chosen by the authority.

[61] It was, however, considered as part of the reasonableness test: see below and discussion in Bainham (2005) p 291–96 and Choudhry (2003). 'Freeing' for adoption had been the process under the 1976 Act by which Local Authorities obtained the court's approval to place a child for adoption.
[62] [1971] AC 682.
[63] In the context of the reasonable father, see *Re D* [1977] AC 602.

(2) The court may not make a placement order in respect of a child unless—

(a)   the child is subject to a care order,
(b)   the court is satisfied that the conditions in Section 31(2) of the 1989 Act (conditions for making a care order) are met, or
(c)   the child has no parent or guardian.

(3) The court may only make a placement order if, in the case of each parent or guardian of the child, the court is satisfied—

(a)   that the parent or guardian has consented to the child being placed for adoption with any prospective adopters who may be chosen by the local authority and has not withdrawn the consent, or
(b)   that the parent's or guardian's consent should be dispensed with.

This subsection is subject to section 52 (parental etc consent).

(4) A placement order continues in force until—

(a)   it is revoked under section 24,
(b)   an adoption order is made in respect of the child, or
(c)   the child marries or attains the age of 18 years.

52 Parental etc consent

(1) The court cannot dispense with the consent of any parent or guardian [including special guardian] of a child to the child being placed for adoption or to the making of an adoption order in respect of the child unless the court is satisfied that—

(a) the parent or guardian cannot be found or is incapable of giving consent, or
(b) the welfare of the child requires the consent to be dispensed with.

(2) The following provisions apply to references in this chapter to any parent or guardian of a child giving or withdrawing—

(a) consent to the placement of a child for adoption, or
(b) consent to the making of an adoption order (including a future adoption order).

(3) Any consent given by the mother to the making of an adoption order is ineffective if it is given less than six weeks after the child's birth.

(4) The withdrawal of any consent to the placement of a child for adoption, or of any consent given under section 20, is ineffective if it is given after an application for an adoption order is made.

(5) 'Consent' means consent given unconditionally and with full understanding of what is involved; but a person may consent to adoption without knowing the identity of the persons in whose favour the order will be made.

(6) 'Parent' (except in subsections (9) and (10) below) means a parent having parental responsibility.

We can see from these provisions whose consent is required and also whose consent is not required to a placement order or adoption order. First, the consent of arguably the most important person in the process is not required. The child, no matter her or his age, is not required to consent to the proceedings.[64] The Act does, however, require the child's wishes and feelings to be taken into account as a part of the welfare test,[65] and it is likely that the older the child, the more weight will be given to her views. Further, the Regulations require the adoption agency to ascertain the wishes and feelings of the child when it is first considering adoption as an option for him[66] and on its review of a placement for adoption once the child is living in the placement[67] but there is no duty to consult the child on the question of placement itself. In that case, the adoption agency only has the obligation to explain to the child its decision to place her for adoption.[68] Otherwise, there are references throughout the guidance and Standards to adoption agencies' duties, as a matter of practice, to ascertain the wishes and feelings of the child,[69] but none that demand those wishes and feelings to be given effect.[70]

The other obvious gap in the list of persons from whom consent to adoption is required relates to fathers without parental responsibility. While their consent is not required, however, Article 8 ECHR will protect their right to be notified and possibly joined as a party to the proceedings.[71] The Regulations may also protect this right for fathers before the matter proceeds to court. Regulation 14 of the Adoption Agencies Regulations requires agencies, when they are considering adoption for a child, to provide counselling and information for, and to ascertain the wishes and feelings of, the parent or guardian of the child and others, and this requirement extends to a father without parental responsibility if the agency knows his identity,[72] and if the agency is satisfied that it is appropriate to so include him.[73] In this case the agency must also ascertain whether he wishes to acquire parental responsibility for the child or intends to apply for a residence or contact order under the Children Act 1989 s.8.[74] The agency also must, if it considers it appropriate, notify in writing a father to whom Regulation 14(3) applies, of its decision regarding placing a child for adoption.[75]

**Q** Why would it be, or not be, in a child's best interest to have such a father notified? Why would it be, or not be, a child's right, to have such a father notified? Or is it a matter of the father's right? Do these provisions for including the child and the father without parental responsibility go far enough? How, if at all would you change them? On the child's right to know and be brought up by her parents, see Fortin (2003) chapter 14.

**Q** Some argue that the welfare test is too broad a test to use for the dispensation of consent to placement for adoption or for adoption itself; one can always find a

---

[64] This is in contrast to a number of other jurisdictions, including Scotland in which the consent of children over the age of 12 is required.

[64] S 1(4)(a).

[65] The Adoption Agency Regulations 2005 Reg 13.

[66] *Ibid,* Reg 36(5)(a).

[67] *Ibid,* Reg 33(4).

[68] In matching the child with an adoptive family (Standard 2.3 DoH and Welsh Assembly Govt 2003); and where adoption is the plan for a child, his wishes and feelings must be listened to and recorded, and where they are not acted upon, the reasons are to be explained to the child and recorded (National Minimum Standards, DoH 2001 Section A 10).

[69] On incorporating a child's views into the welfare test, see discussion in ch 16 below.

[71] See *Re B (Adoption by One Natural Parent to Exclusion of Other)* [2001] 1 FLR 589 CA and full discussion of the case law in ch 7 below.

[72] The Adoption Agency Regulations 2005 Reg 14(3).

[73] *Ibid,* Reg 14(4)(a).

[74] *Ibid,* Reg 14(4)(b).

[75] *Ibid,* Reg 33(3)(b).

'better' family situation particularly if the birth parents are poor. Do you agree? Bainham (2005 p 291) also raises the question of whether attempting to subsume parent's rights and interests into a general welfare test can withstand a challenge under the Human Rights Act. What is your view? See on this Choudhry (2003) who reviews the case law and academic literature on interpretations of the paramountcy principle in the light of the HRA. She concludes that the current practice, in the context of adoption which acts to sever the legal relationship of birth relatives, may not be consistent with Article 8 ECHR but proposes that a reinterpretation is possible which would be consistent with it. This approach, she says, requires an equal balancing of the interests and claims of all prior to the elevation of any one interest.

The paramountcy of welfare also raises issues about who is considered to be suitable to adopt, and the Adoption and Children Act 2002 changes the previous law in this regard as well. While the Adoption Act 1976 only allowed joint adoptions to be made in favour of married couples, the Adoption and Children Act 2002 states that an adoption order may be made in favour of a couple if both are over 21 years old, or if one of them is the child's mother or father and is at least 18 years old.[76] Section 144(4) states that a 'couple' means a married couple or 'two people (whether of different sexes or the same sex) living as partners in an enduring family relationship'. The symbolic significance of this legal acknowledgment of same-sex parenthood must not be underestimated, but it remains unclear as to what an 'enduring family relationship' might mean. Marshall (2003), for example explores the potential meaning of both 'enduring' and 'family relationship' and concludes that it may be difficult for same-sex couples to meet the test. Consider, for example, our discussion of the meaning of 'family' in chapter 1. If the marriage-like relationship is the basis of the 'normal' family, then considerations of normality may inform considerations of a child's welfare in a same-sex family. In *Frette v France*[77] a majority of the ECtHR held that France's decision to prohibit a single homosexual man from adopting did not infringe his rights under Articles 8 and 14 ECHR. While this case concerned adoption by a single applicant, the court's comments on same-sex parents and children's welfare are relevant here:

42. As the government submitted, at issue here are the competing interests of the applicant and children who are eligible for adoption. The mere fact that no specific child is identified when the application for authorisation is made does not necessarily imply that there is no competing interest. Adoption means 'providing a child with a family, not a family with a child', and the state must see to it that the persons chosen to adopt are those who can offer the child the most suitable home in every respect. The court points out in that connection that it has already found that where a family tie is established between a parent and a child, 'particular importance must be attached to the best interests of the child, which, depending on their nature and seriousness, may override those of the parent' (see *EP v Italy* [1999] ECHR 31127/96 at para 62, and *Johansen v Norway* (1996) 23 EHRR 33 at para 78). It must be observed that the scientific community-particularly experts on childhood, psychiatrists and psychologists—is divided over the possible consequences of a child's being adopted by one or more homosexual parents, especially bearing in mind the limited number of scientific studies conducted on the subject to date. In addition, there are wide differences in national and international opinion, not to mention the fact that there are not enough children to adopt to satisfy demand. ...

---

[76] S 50 Adoption and Children Act 2002.
[77] [2003] 2 FLR 9.

The dissenting judges were no less clear in their view that the ECHR had been infringed:

> 2. b) ... As the government submitted, the decision to deny the applicant authorisation stemmed from a desire to protect the rights and freedoms of the child who might have been adopted. In itself this aim may of course be legitimate, and in fact would even be the only legitimate aim. In the instant case, however, it has to be observed that the applicant's personal qualities and aptitude for bringing up children were emphasised on a number of occasions. The Conseil d'Etat even specified in its statement of reasons that there was no reference in the case-file 'to any specific circumstance that might pose a threat to the child's interests'. The legitimate aim was not therefore effectively established in any way.
>
> In their general and abstract wording, the reasons given by the judicial authorities for their decision to deny the applicant authorisation are based solely on the applicant's homosexuality and therefore on the view that to be brought up by homosexual parents would be harmful to the child at all events and under any circumstances. The Conseil d'Etat failed to explain in any way, by referring for example to the increasing range of scientific studies of homosexual parenthood in recent years, why and how the child's interests militated in the instant case against the applicant's application for authorisation.

The majority held that it was within France's margin of appreciation to prohibit the applicant from adopting, solely on the basis of his sexual orientation. While the Adoption and Children Act 2002 explicitly allows for same-sex adopters, the reasoning in this case may suggest that legal norms and subjective beliefs about 'suitable' families and children's welfare may present an additional hurdle for same-sex adopters to surmount.

The Adoption and Children Act 2002 also allows for one person to adopt a child if he or she is over the age of 21 and is not married[78] or a registered civil partner.[79] A person is also eligible to adopt if he or she is the (same-sex or opposite-sex) partner of a parent of a child.[80] If the lone prospective adopter is married to someone other than the parent[81] or a registered civil partner of someone other than a parent,[82] he or she is eligible if the spouse or partner cannot be found. Similarly a married person or civil partner can adopt alone if he or she is separated and the separation is likely to be permanent or if the spouse or partner is incapable of making a joint application by reason of ill-health. Finally, in limited circumstances,[83] a parent may adopt his or her own child to the exclusion of the other parent. In these cases the purpose of the adoption order would be to 'take away, rather than give, since the focus is on the *termination* of the parental status of the other parent' (Bainham 2005 p 277).

The court recently faced this issue in a case in which the mother of a child had given birth to her without informing the father of the pregnancy. Immediately after the birth she turned the child over to hospital staff requesting that she be adopted. The father found out about the birth only by chance and with the mother's cooperation obtained parental responsibility of the child and began to care for her. He then wished to secure the child's future in his own care and applied, with the mother's consent, for an adoption order. The mother only wanted an annual photo and progress report to be provided through the local authority. The Official Solicitor representing the child at trial opposed

---

[78] S 51((1).

[79] Amendment made by the Civil Partnership Act 2004 s 79(4).

[80] S 51(2). S144(7) states that a person is a partner of a parent if the person and the parent are a couple but the person is not the child's parent'.

[81] S 51(3).

[82] S 51(3A) inserted by the Civil Partnership Act s 79(5).

[83] S 51(4): where the other parent is dead or cannot be found; where there is no other parent by virtue of s 28 HFEA 1990; or there is some other reason justifying the adoption.

the adoption order, as although he regarded the mother's lack of interest in the child as 'lamentable', he submitted that it would not be in the child's best interests to deprive her of a mother. The adoption order was granted at first instance but overturned by the Court of Appeal on a number of grounds.[84] Hale LJ gave the leading judgment finding that an adoption order infringed the mother's Article 8 rights because an adoption did not meet a pressing social need in this case and was a disproportionate response to the child's current needs. She said:

> [40] … it is difficult to argue that there is a pressing social need to deprive A of all legal rela-tionship with one half of her family of birth … she already has a full and secure legal and factual relationship with her father. If there is any need to give her more, it can be provided for in a package of orders along the lines discussed [such as specific issues orders, prohibited steps orders and s.91 orders under the Children Act 1989]. In my view, it would be a disproportionate response to her current needs to turn her from the child of two legal parents, with two legal families, into the child of only one parent, with only one legal family. …

The House of Lords[85] disagreed and restored the adoption order. It said there was no reason to set aside the trial judge's exercise of discretion in finding that A's best interests would be served by adoption. Lord Nicholls stated: 'Given the mother's attitude to A from the moment of A's birth, and her consent, adoption by the father was in A's best interests' (para 27) and on all the evidence, the trial judge was entitled to form this view (para 28).

It is tempting to say that their different conclusions in this case may have been at least in part influenced by the courts' respective assessments of the mother. In the Court of Appeal, Hale LJ regarded the mother's actions as responsible rather than 'lamentable' (para 21). She said

> [h]ard though it may be for many to understand, she has recognised that she is not the maternal type and does not want to have children. She made responsible arrangements for her first child and was planning to do the same for A. She wants what is best for her, understands the father's position, and says that she will not interfere' (para 20).

In contrast, Lord Nicholls in the House of Lords made no direct reference to the mother's actions. His indirect references, however, suggest that he took a different view of them. While acknowledging that 'permanent exclusion of the child's mother' is a 'drastic and detrimental consequence', he stated that 'how serious this loss is likely to be depends on the circumstance of the case' (para 22). He then had to find that there existed the statutory 'other reasons' for making the adoption order, and said that 'aban-donment, or persistent neglect or ill-treatment of the child, could be instances' (para 23) of such 'other reasons'.

**Q** Distinguish this case from *Re B* above, in which the foster mother was not per-mitted to adopt. Besides the fact that Hale LJ's approach appears to be consistent in both, can you make an argument that unstated beliefs and assumptions about the meaning of motherhood and fatherhood inform the decisions in these cases?

---

[84] *Re B (Adoption by One Natural Parent to Exclusion of Other)* [2001] 1 FLR 589 (CA).
[85] *Re B (a child) (sole adoption by unmarried father)* [2001] UKHL 70; [2002] 1 FLR 196.

The Act refers only to general capacity to adopt, and leaves to regulations the role of adoption agencies to determine the suitability of individual adopters, while at the same time stressing that where the potential adopters are a couple, 'proper regard is had to the need for stability and permanence in their relationship'.[86] Adoption agencies are thus mandated to screen and interview all potential adopters and must take medical and social histories, family histories, education, employment and income histories, make personality assessments including asking why that person wants to adopt and their views on child-rearing. They must carry out police and neighbourhood checks and obtain references.[87] Not every person who meets these requirements may become an adoptive parent, however. Exercise of the discretion given by the Act to adoption agencies raises many issues about who, in law as well as in social work theory and practice, is suitable to become a parent. And the focus of investigations may be upon mothers, as in their search for 'normality', social workers may assume that mothers, rather than fathers, will be the primary caretakers of children. Prospective adoptive parents undergo extensive checks and interviews which are more intrusive even than those undergone by applicants for 'fertility treatment'.

While there was evidence that in the past the welfare of the child was perceived to be met best by the traditional nuclear family (Campion 1995), the new policy of promoting adoption for looked after children means that adoption agencies have had to become more accepting of 'non-traditional' applicants, at least for older children and those who would otherwise be difficult to place.[88] This has meant that the old 'benchmarks' are no longer applicable; as Katz comments, 'it is no longer self-evident what is required of a "good enough" parent' (2000 p 218). He says that social workers therefore include a good deal of gut feeling and experience rather than research in their assessments of prospective adopters, which means they tend to favour either the cultural norm or whatever happens to be in current favour at the time (p 219). Adoption practice is, he says suffused with myths, assumptions and cultural values. So, for instance he argues, the stance that openness is vital for children would hold, 'no matter what research demonstrated' (p 227). In general, despite the regulations, guidelines and standards, professionals are faced with a difficult task in trying to 'hold in mind the needs and phantasies of all points in the adoption triangle [child, adopter, birth family] (p 229).

**Q** Consider the wording of the following passage from the White Paper (Department of Health, *et al*, 1993) in the light of our discussion of ideology and common sense in chapter 1:

> 4.28 The judgments that adoption agencies and their staffs need to make are inherently difficult, and do not become any less so as society becomes more complex and varied. Nevertheless, they should be careful always to take approaches which are based on commonsense and objective professional assessment and avoid reliance on ideology. (p 8)[89]

Compare this with the White Paper in 2000:

---

[86] S 45.
[87] See Draft Suitability of Adopters Regulations 2005 and Adoption Agencies Regulations 2005 SI 389/2005, particularly Sch 4 Pt 1.
[88] See also Williams (1994) on the 'price' of 'black' babies versus 'white' in US adoption practice.
[89] See Jolly and Sandland (1994) on this.

2.16 Although the PIU report found little evidence of agencies using arbitrary criteria for assessment, if these are used, children are the losers. There have been cases where potential adopters have been told they cannot adopt solely because they are too old or because they smoke. Blanket bans of this kind are unjust and unacceptable. Each case should be judged on its merits and the needs of the children considered-the important thing is to ensure that adopt - ers can offer children a safe, stable and loving home through childhood and beyond.

6.15 Children's birth heritage, and religious, cultural and linguistic background are all important factors to consider in finding them a new family. [.].How - ever, the child's welfare is paramount, and no child should be denied loving adoptive parents solely on the grounds that the child and the parents do not share the same racial or cultural background.

Do you see a difference in approach?

Placing a child with adopters who do not share the child's ethnic, religious or cultural background is a sensitive and controversial issue.[90] We have seen that Section 1(5) of the Act requires agencies to consider these factors in placing a child for adoption, and there is also reference to these factors in the National Adoption Standards (D of H 2001):

9. Every effort will be made to recruit sufficient adopters from diverse backgrounds, so that each child can be found an adoptive family within the timescales in 3) above, which best meets their needs, and in particular:
   which reflects their ethnic origin, cultural background, religion and language[91];

But the standards also say:

8. Children will be matched with families who can best meet their needs. They will not be left waiting indefinitely for a 'perfect family'.

We see an attempt here to resolve the controversy. Many believe that transracial adoption is not in the best interests of children because it inhibits them from developing a positive racial identity, it subjects them to identity confusion or social ostracism, or because it can be seen as an example of colonialisation of ethnic minorities by the white majority.[92] The evidence of the benefits or otherwise of transracial adoption is inconclusive. Many children fare well in transracial or transcultural placements, while others do not and it seems that current policy is to consider a 'same-ethnicity' placement to be in a child's welfare, but that as a factor, ethnicity should not outweigh other factors.

---

[90] Barn (2000) makes the point that in practice 'transracial' has meant the placement of minority ethnic children in white homes (p 112).

[91] There is also a similar requirement in the National Minimum Standards (DoH and Welsh Assembly Govt 2003). In s 2 'Securing and promoting the child's welfare', Standard 2 requires that 'children are matched with adopters who best meet their assessed needs. Wherever possible this will be with a family which: a) reflects their ethnic origin, cultural background, religion and language', and where children cannot live with such a family 'a clear explanation' must be given to them.

[92] See on this, Barn (2000) above; Murphy (2000); Hayes (2003) and sources cited in therein.

**Q** Do you think the policy strikes the right balance? Hayes (2003) argues that the research on outcomes for children in transracial placements is positive, or at least neutral, and therefore that the requirement to consider ethnicity as a factor in adoption placements is based upon nothing but ideology. Do you agree? Even if it were, does it mean the requirement should be abandoned? For an example of a case in which there was, arguably, too much emphasis placed on a child's 'roots' and ethnic identity, see Re M (child's upbringing) the Zulu boy case, below. After being sent back to his birth family in South Africa, he chose to return to England.

The importance of a child knowing[93] and being secure in his of her identity is also raised in what have come to be known as open adoptions. As we saw above, in many ways the concept of 'open adoption' is contrary to the notion of adoption itself, but studies have demonstrated fairly consistently that adopted children fare better when they are aware of their adopted status, when they have information about their birth parents and, in many cases, when they have the opportunity to make or maintain contact with their birth families. This research, (eg Walby and Symons 1990; Triseliotis 2000; Smith and Logan 2002) suggests that all people have a need to understand or have some knowledge of their identity, history or roots, and that to accommodate this desire is not only compatible with adoption, it is in the best interests of children. This thinking contrasts with that of the 1960s when it was believed that a clean and absolute break from the birth family was in a child's best interests (Rowe 1966), adoption was shrouded in secrecy and it was inconceivable to allow continued contact with birth families. The White Paper (DoH, *et al*, 1993) and the Adoption Bill[94] continued to some extent to reflect the 1960s presumption of the primacy and the privacy of the adoptive family, while at the same time endorsing the giving of more information to the child (para 4.14), and the White Paper (2000) stated also that 'adopted people should be able to find out about their family history if and when they wish to do so' (para 6.44).

The Adoption and Children Act 2002 requires Adoption Agencies to keep information on adoptions, including identifying information about persons involved, and provides for when that information can be disclosed.[95] Further, the Act requires the maintenance of an Adoption Contact Register[96] and an Adopted Children Register.[97] The first is a register that enables adopted persons and their birth relatives to contact each other where they both want to do so, and the second is a register that enables an adopted adult to gain access to her or his birth records. Sometimes just having the information about one's birth family is sufficient, but often adoptees need more. There are, they feel, key aspects of their identity that are missing (Triseliotis 2000). In these situations, and to answer questions about the circumstances of their adoption, they may search for their birth families and the information provided by these registers will assist them. And recent research (Triseliotis, *et al*, 2005) shows that contact and reunion might be good for all parties in the so-called 'adoption triangle'.

---

[93] On the child's right to know his identity, see Fortin (2003) pp 382–98.

[94] And, arguably, some of the judiciary. While the law now favours open adoption, contact will not be forced upon an unwilling adoptive family. See *Re C* [1993] 2 FLR 431; *Re T* [1995] 2 FLR 251.

[95] Ss 56–65. See also The Disclosure of Adoption Information (Post- Commencement Adoptions) Regulations 2005 SI 2005/888 which will apply to adoptions made after the 2002 Act and The Adoption Information and Intermediary Services (Pre-Commencement Adoptions) Regulations 2005 SI 2005/890 which will apply to adults adopted before the 2002 Act came into force.

[96] Ss 80 and 81.

[97] Ss 77–79. See also the Adopted Children and Adoption Contact Registers Regulations 2005 SI 2005/924.

Providing information and encouraging contact is different, however, from making an adoption order with a condition of contact attached to it. Open adoptions of these sorts fly more directly in the face of what an adoption is supposed to be, and the general judicial attitude has been to attach contact conditions only where they have been previously agreed by the adoptive family.[98] As to whether post-adoption contact is in the best interests of the child, Neil (2003)[99] can only conclude after a comprehensive review of the issues and the research that it depends upon the individual child and his or her circumstances. While contact might be beneficial for older children, or help to resolve some children's identity questions or their feelings of rejection, it is by no means of universal benefit.

The White Paper (2000) contained the rather ambiguous statement that 'a child's needs to maintain links to their birth family [...] should always be considered, and [...] where appropriate, the local social services should make arrangements to meet the lifelong needs of the child' (para 6.43). In the result, the Adoption and Children Act 2002 is silent on post-adoption contact, except to require the court, before making an adoption order, to consider whether there should be arrangements made for contact.[100] Before adoption, however, an application for contact may be made with or after a placement order,[101] and regulations also require adoption agencies and adoption panels to consider contact issues throughout each stage of their planning process, from the initial consideration of adoption as a plan,[102] through recommendations made about adoption placements,[103] and on placement.[104] Finally, the National Standards (D o H 2001) ensure that contact is always considered in work with the child (Section A paras 10 and 11), the adoptive parents (Section C para 4) and birth families (Section D para 7).

Post-adoption contact is thus always an issue for adoption agencies and courts and the empirical research about its benefits is uncertain. For those older, looked after children whom government policy now targets, however, it may be important. The difficulty is that adoption still purports to replace one family entirely with another and it is only slowly beginning to be recognised that people often can feel a part of more than one family at a time. Post-adoption contact requires 'an acknowledgement that children are not exclusively "owned" *either* by their birth parents *or*, subsequently, by their adoptive parents' (Smith and Logan 2002 p 290) and promotes the view that adoptive relationships should be based upon 'reciprocal obligations' (Smith and Logan 2002). Smith and Logan observe, however, that this change would represent a fundamental challenge to both adoption legislation and judicial attitudes (*ibid*).

---

[98] Smith and Logan (2002) note, however, that many adoptive families find it a burden to maintain and facilitate contact with birth families.

[99] See also Eekelaar (2003b); and Smith and Logan (2002).

[100] S 46(6).

[101] Ss 26–27. The difficulty with contact during placement before an adoption order is made, however, is that it may frustrate bonding between the child and the prospective adopters. In *Gorgulu v Germany* [2004] 1 FLR 894 the ECtHR held that a German Court which had suspended contact between an unmarried father and his child who had been living with foster parents for two years with a view to eventual adoption, had violated the father's Art 8 rights. The suspension of contact precluded any form of family reunion between the child and the father.

[102] The Adoption Agencies Regulations 2005 Reg 13 requires the agency to ascertain the child's wishes and feelings about contact and Reg 14 the parent or guardian's wishes and feelings about it.

[103] Reg 18(3)(a) requires the adoption panel to consider contact when it makes its recommendation.

[104] Reg 31(2)(c) requires the adoption agency to consider arrangements for contact on placing a child with an adoptive family.

**Q** Do you agree with Smith and Logan's view? Do you think that such a fundamental change would be in the interests of children?

**Q** How has the nature of adoption changed over the years? What, if any, role in a child's life would you reserve for a 'former' mother after adoption? A 'former' father, grandparent or sibling? What, if any, say would you allow the child in this matter? What, if any, say would you allow the adoptive parents?

*Increasing the Range of Permanency Options—Special Guardianship*

Something similar to the new status of special guardianship was created by the now repealed Children Act 1975 and it was rarely used. The 1975 Act was intended to promote adoption and other forms of permanency for children in care with a minimum of stress and delay. In addition to professionalising adoptions it created a legal institution intended to provide 'legal security for those providing long term family care for a child' (Cretney 2003a pp 705–6). This new legal institution was called custodianship, and it remained on the statute book unimplemented until 1985. From 1985 to its repeal by the Children Act 1989 custodianship was little used, mainly, observes Barton (2001), because of its uncertainty and capacity for conflict. The idea of this sort of 'foster-plus' status was revived only a few years later in the Conservative government's White Paper (DoH, *et al*, 1993) which recommended the creation of a new, *inter vivos* guardianship order. It was intended that the order would be used by relatives or other long-term carers of children, including foster parents, who wished to obtain legal recognition of their role as carers, or social parents. The effect of the order would not have been as far-reaching as adoption, but it would have put the long-term carers' relationship with a child on a 'more permanent and clearer basis' (para 5.23). The order would not have severed any legal links with the birth parents (para 5.24), and in this way was consistent with the Children Act policy that parental responsibility can be shared among many, but that legal parenthood can not. The suggestion for this form of new legal status was not taken up in the Adoption Bill 1996, but was yet again revived in the White Paper 2000:

> 5.8 Adoption is not always appropriate for children who cannot return to their birth parents. Some older children do not wish to be legally separated from their birth families. Adoption may not be best for some children being cared for on a permanent basis by members of their wider birth family. Some minority ethnic communities have religious and cultural difficulties with adoption as it is set out in law.[105] Unaccompanied asylum seeking children may also need secure, permanent homes, but have strong attachments to their families abroad. All these children deserve the same chance as any other to enjoy the benefits of a legally secure, stable permanent placement that promotes a supportive, lifelong relationship with their carers, where the court decides that is in their best interests.

The Adoption and Children Act 2002 has created the status of special guardianship. The Children Act 1989 has been amended to include new Sections 14A–G governing the making, variation, discharge, effect, and support of special guardianship orders.[106] They are indeed a form of foster-plus: a special guardianship order does not terminate the status of birth parents; they share parental responsibility with the special guardians(s).

---

[105] Islamic law does not, for example, recognise adoption.
[106] See also the Special Guardianship Regulations 2005 SI 2005/1109.

But, like birth parents who share parental responsibility with each other, special guardians can exercise their parental responsibility to the exclusion of any other person with parental responsibility.[107] Those who are entitled to apply for special guardianship are the same as those who are entitled to apply for Section 8 orders or residence and contact orders pursuant to Section 10(5) of the Children Act 1989[108] and are listed in Section 14A(5). The list specifically includes local authority foster parents with whom the child has lived for at last one year. It is clear that special guardianship is intended to be utilised as part of the focus upon 'looked after' children. It is also thought that special guardianship will be used by extended family members with whom a child has been living for at least three years.[109]

> **Q** Herring believes that 'the success of special guardianship will depend upon the extent to which both children and would-be adopters are satisfied that it will provide them with the sense of security and belonging together as a family which adoption has been said traditionally to provide' (2004 p 614).On this basis, the prognosis for special guardianship may not look good. 78% of Smith and Logan's adoptive mother respondents and 65% of their adoptive father respondents said they would not consider becoming special guardians (2002 p 296).To them, while special guardianship may convey parental responsibility, it did not 'construct parenthood' in the way that adoption did. Adopters 'could not believe that that special guardianship would bestow a sufficient degree of ownership and control to enable effective parenting, security and stability for the child' (ibid p 297). The success of special guardianship may also depend on how the capacity for conflict between all those with parental responsibility can be handled. In what cases do you see special guardianship being used?

*Other Ways to Become a Parent—Guardianship*
A status akin to that of motherhood (or fatherhood) is conferred on a person appointed as guardian of a child. The historical concept of guardianship[110] of children was done away with in the Children Act 1989 and, as Bainham says, '[h]enceforth, parents would just be parents and guardianship would be confined to non-parents who stepped into the shoes of deceased parents' (2005 p 226).[111] Guardianship is provided for in Sections 5 and 6 of the Children Act 1989, which state, *inter alia*, that guardians may be appointed either by a parent with parental responsibility for a child, a guardian or by a court. The guardian, who need not be biologically related to a child, is in a position analogous to, but not identical with, a parent, in that he or she has full parental responsibility for the child.[112] Bainham describes guardianship as follows:

> Guardianship differs significantly from all other forms of social parenthood. It is by far the least regulated, the appointment of guardians being largely a private matter not subject to public scrutiny, judicial or otherwise. It is also the most far-reaching in its legal effects since it

---

[107] Children Act 1989 S 14C.
[108] See ch 16.
[109] Talbot and Kidd (2004) argue that for the purposes of assessing family foster placements, and especially for assessing kin applicants for Special Guardianship orders, Local Authority social workers must adopt a new assessment model. The old one, they say, does not adequately take account of the applicants' already existing sense of attachment to the children.
[110] The married father was the guardian of his children.
[111] See Bainham (2005 pp 225–30) generally on guardianship. See also Law Commission (1985a).
[112] S 5(6).

carries some of the incidents which are normally associated with natural parenthood but which fall outside the concept of parental responsibility. Yet the status of guardianship, although closely resembling parenthood, is not identical. For example, guardians are not liable for child support as parents are. More importantly, they may voluntarily disclaim their appointment, whereas the obligations of parenthood are imposed by operation of law and may not be voluntarily relinquished or transferred. The status of guardianship may also be revoked by court order, whereas parenthood survives all court orders except adoption. (2005 p 226)

> **Q** Does it strike you as incongruous that although guardianship is the most 'far-reaching in its legal effects of all forms of social parenthood', it is also the least regulated? Bainham (2005) further reminds us that the Law Commission reviewed in 1985 the question whether there ought to be restrictions or checks on people appointed as guardians, but it rejected the idea. What do you suppose was the policy behind this decision?

Guardianship only comes into operation where parents with parental responsibility are deceased.

*Parental Responsibility: Residence Orders*
We have seen in the law of guardianship an example of law conferring the responsibilities of parenthood upon people who are not parents at law in order to enable them to carry out the responsibilities of parents. Another category of persons upon whom law confers the responsibility of parents is persons who obtain a residence order under the Children Act 1989. The award of a residence order carries with it parental responsibility[113] which lasts while the order remains in force.[114] However, such an order does not affect the status of a parent: a person with parental responsibility does not lose it simply because another person subsequently also acquires parental responsibility.[115]

*Social Motherhood—No Legal Status*
In addition to forms of social motherhood which are regulated by law there are those relationships between adults and children which do not carry the same degree of legal status, but nevertheless do impose some responsibility upon the adult involved. We include in this category foster mothers and step-mothers, but, again, the rules for acquiring foster parent or step-parent status are generally the same for women as for men. Because the frequency with which they are acquired differs between men and women, however, we will address them in the contexts in which they are most likely to occur. We will discuss foster parenthood in this section under motherhood, and will address step parenthood in the following section on fatherhood.

*Foster Parents*
Foster parents are people who provide substitute care, usually assumed to be temporary, for a child whose parents are unable to do so. But in some situations, long-term fostering is seen as an acceptable permanence plan for a child, usually as a preferable alternative to institutional care, or, as stated in the White Paper (2000 para 5.12): 'It [long-term fostering] has proved particularly useful for older children with strong links to their birth families, who do not want or need the formality of adoption or "special guardianship"'.

---

113 See below, chs 7 and 15.
114 S 12(2) of the Children Act 1989. S 12(3) places some limitations on parental responsibility in these circumstances: it does not confer the right to consent to adoption or to appoint a guardian for the child. See ch 15 for a discussion of recent case law in making residence orders.
115 Children Act 1989 s 2(6).

Generally, fostering reflects the belief that a private family is the better setting in which to care for children. By acting as substitute parents, foster parents take on the role of a child's social parents and are responsible for the day-to-day care of the child, although they do not have parental responsibility for the child. They have only weak legal status, therefore, but are in a position to decide day-to-day matters such as whether to authorise emergency medical treatment for a child. Section 3(5) of the Children Act 1989 states that:

A person who

(a)  does not have parental responsibility for a particular child; but
(b)  has care of the child

may (subject to the provisions of this Act) do what is reasonable for the purpose of safeguarding or promoting the child's welfare.

Informal fostering arrangements have been utilised by parents throughout history, and parents continue to be able to choose informal foster carers privately. The law does not intervene in any way to regulate these fostering arrangements if the parents choose foster carers who are relatives within the meaning of the Children Act. However, if the carers are not relatives, are not applicants for adoption and do not have parental responsibility for the child, they are 'private' foster carers within the meaning of the Act and are regulated by Part IX of the Children Act.

Regulations under the Children Act require private foster carers to notify local authorities either that they intend to act or are acting as private foster carers, and local authorities are then required to ensure that the home meets minimum standards and to monitor the placement to ensure that the welfare of the child is not in danger.[116] While monitoring private foster placements was not high on local authorities' list of priorities (Barton and Douglas 1995 p 107), and so private arrangements were subject to minimal supervision, the 2005 regulations now require the Local Authority to monitor private arrangements closely.[117]

If private foster parents wish to obtain a clearer legal status, they may apply for a residence order which will give them parental responsibility. In order to apply, they need leave of the court[118] unless they have the consent of those with parental responsibility[119] or unless the child has been living with them for at least three years.[120]

Public or local authority foster care is also the subject of direct legal regulation. Regulation of public care originated as a result of the baby-farming scandals of the last century (Barton and Douglas 1995 p 104), and is seen as part of local authorities' duty to care for children in need. Section 23(2)(a) of the Children Act gives local authorities the power to place children in foster care. A person can become a local authority foster parent only after undergoing stringent checks of suitability similar to those carried out

---

[116] S 67 and Sch 8 of the Children Act 1989; The Children (Private Arrangements for Fostering) Regulations 2005 SI 2005/1533.

[117] This is a response to the death of Victoria Climbie at the hands of her aunt and the aunt's partner. Victoria was placed in the care of the aunt pursuant to a private fostering arrangement.

[118] Children Act 1989 S 10(2)(b).

[119] *Ibid*, S 10(5)(c) (iii).

[120] *Ibid*, S 10(5)(b).

for prospective adoptive parents.[121] And a person remains a foster parent only so long as the local authority agrees. The foster carer must be able to work with the local authority, usually with the long term goal of returning the child to her parents or to eventual adoptive parents, and her ability to apply to court for parental responsibility or adoption was therefore circumscribed under the Children Act 1989.

But, as we have seen, the policy announced in the White Paper 2000 identified permanence for looked after children as a priority, and while adoption was seen as the preferred means of achieving that permanence for children, there was also support given to long term fostering for certain children. While 'focused support' and 'better permanence planning' (para 5.13) were seen as necessary for fostered children, the Adoption and Children Act 2002 has also made it easier for local authority foster carers to formalise their 'parental' relationships with their foster children more quickly than was previously the case. Local Authority foster carers may give notice of their intention to adopt the child,[122] or make application for special guardianship of the child,[123] after fostering for one year. Finally, should a local authority foster carer wish to obtain parental responsibility for the child in her care she may only apply for leave of the court to obtain a residence order (which carries parental responsibility—see below), with the consent of the local authority or after the child has lived with her for one year,[124] unless she is a relative of the child.[125]

In the event of a contested application, the court would be faced with deciding whether the best interests of the child lay with her 'social parents'—the foster carers—or with her (usually) biological parents—those with parental responsibility. Although law may be increasing its recognition of biological status in some areas of child law, it is not the case that biology automatically prevails. The welfare test may demand a different outcome.

The most famous, or notorious, case is *J v C*[126] in which the court stated that blood ties were not sufficient determinants of a child's welfare. That case involved a dispute between English 'foster carers' (the term was imprecise as the care arrangements were made privately between the parties) of a 10-year-old boy and his Spanish parents. The boy had lived with his foster parents in England from the age of 3. After receiving a letter from the foster parents suggesting that the boy was becoming an 'English' boy and would be disturbed if he had to return to Spain, the biological parents applied to the court for the return of their child to Spain, and the foster parents applied for an order that the child be brought up in the Protestant faith (his biological parents were Roman Catholic). The trial judge took the view that to return the boy to his family would involve too great an adjustment for him and that, as his welfare was paramount, he should remain with his foster parents.

The House of Lords, in unanimously upholding the trial judge's decision, said that the words of the 1925 Guardianship of Infants Act (then in force) requiring the court to have regard to a child' s welfare was ' the first and paramount consideration' when

---

121 Sch 2, Part II, s 12; Fostering Services Regulations 2002 SI 2002/57. Talbot and Kidd (2004) suggest that the local authority fostering panels who take these decisions are often inflexible and fail to attach sufficient importance to a relative as a potential placement for the child.

122 Adoption and Children Act 2002 s 42(4).

123 Children Act 1989 s 14A(5)(d).

124 S 10(5A) of the Children Act 1989. Introduced by the Adoption and Children Act 2002 to reduce period from three years.

125 S 9(3).

126 [1970] AC 668.

considering the question of custody or upbringing of a child applied between parents and non-parents; there was no presumption that the welfare of the child was best served by allowing him to live with his parents. Lord McDermott went on:

1. Section 1 of the Act of 1925 applies to disputes not only between parents, but between parents and strangers and strangers and strangers.

2. In applying s. 1, the rights and wishes of parents, whether unimpeachable or otherwise, must be assessed and weighed in their bearing on the welfare of the child in conjunction with all other factors relevant to that issue.

3. While there is now no rule of law that the rights and wishes of unimpeachable parents must prevail over other considerations, such rights and wishes, recognised as they are by nature and society, can be capable of ministering to the total welfare of the child in a special way, and must therefore preponderate in many cases. The parental rights, however, remain qualified and not absolute for the purposes of the investigation ...

4. Some of the authorities convey the impression that the upset caused to a child by a change of custody is transient and a matter of small importance. For all I know that may have been true in the cases containing dicta to that effect. But I think a growing experience has shown that it is not always so and that serious harm even to young children may, on occasion, be caused by such a change. I do not suggest that the difficulties of this subject can be resolved by purely theoretical considerations, or that they need to be left entirely to expert opinion. But a child's future happiness and sense of security are always important factors and the effects of a change in custody will often be worthy of the close and anxious attention which they undoubtedly received in this case. (p 715)

Recently, however, courts have become more wary of overriding the parents' wishes in order to choose the 'better' home for the child. Respect for the privacy of the family ensures that courts will be circumspect in their decisions to interfere with the biological relationship. The prevailing attitude is captured by the words of Butler Sloss LJ in *In Re K (a minor)*[127]: 'the mother must be shown to be entirely unsuitable before another family can be considered, otherwise we are in grave danger of slipping into social engineering' (p 62).

**Q** Refer back to our discussion about the paramountcy of welfare in adoption placement orders, and adoption orders. Would the dictum of Butler Sloss LJ in this case be relevant in that context?

In *Re M (Child's Upbringing)*[128] the Court of Appeal had to determine the residence and application for adoption of a 10-year-old boy. In this case the boy was a South African, born of Zulu parents. His mother worked as a live-in maid for the appellant, a woman of Afrikaner descent, and occupied quarters separate from the main house. From the age of 18 months he lived with the appellant's family in the Transvaal until 1992 when, with the agreement of his parents, he came to England with the appellant. In 1994 the appellant made application for an adoption order and a residence order. The parents wished him returned to them as soon as possible. The court made him a ward of court, and decided that although he should be returned to South Africa, he should be

---

[127] [1991] 1 FLR 57.
[128] [1996] 2 FLR 441.

reintroduced to his Zulu language and culture gradually, remaining with the appellant in England for a further two years while the arrangements were made. The appellant appealed the terms of the order, and the parents cross-appealed the two year delay.

In the unanimous Court of Appeal decision to return the boy to South Africa immediately,[129] Ward LJ said:

> ... there is in my judgment an established line of authority which does guide the resolution of competing claims of a psychological parent and a biological parent, and a fortiori, the claims of two psychological mothers, one of whom bore the child ... [citing *Re KD (A Minor) (Ward: Termination of Access)* [1988] AC 806]

> > ... the natural bond and relationship between parent and child gives rise to universally recognised norms which ought not to be gratuitously interfered with and which, if interfered with at all, ought to be so only if the welfare of the child dictates it.

> In Re K (A Minor) (Custody) [1990] 2 FLR 64 ...

> > The question was not where would R get the better home. The question was: was it demonstrated that the welfare of the child positively demanded the displacement of *the parental right*. (p 755, emphasis added)

**Q** What are the relevant differences between Re *M* and *J* v *C*? Can we say that the principle in *J* v *C* has changed? What does the decision in Re *B* (the case we discussed about the foster mother's attempt to adopt) add to the principle? Do you approve of the court legitimating in law the notion of a 'natural bond and relationship' between a parent (here, a mother) and a child but recreating it as a 'right'?[130]

**Q** In what ways does foster caring either conform to or challenge notions of the private nuclear family? What role, if any, is left for the state in caring for children?

**Q** For a good discussion of the case law and interpretation of the paramountcy principle in these cases, see Fortin (2003 pp 419–46). Fortin observes that there appear to be three features common to the way courts treat these disputes between parents and foster carers. First, the blood tie remains significant even long after the actual relationship between the parents and child has been disrupted; second, they apply the same set of principles in cases where a child has not yet formed bonds of attachment with the foster carers as they do in cases where a child is 'happily settled' in the foster home; and third, the courts exploit the language of children's rights in these cases, to support what really are claims to adults' rights to resume caring for their children (Fortin 2003 pp 443–44).

---

129 The boy subsequently returned to England.
130 See also *Re D (Care: Natural Parent Presumption)* [1999] Fam Law 12; and cf *Re B (Residence Order: Leave to Appeal)* [1998] 1 FLR 520.

## II. WHO IS A PARENT? BECOMING A FATHER

Both a biological connection between a man and a child (paternity) and a social connection (fatherhood) can give rise to legal consequences. Historically the law relied upon a combination of both connections to do so. It was thought that the uncertainty of biological paternity (often reinforced by misogynist assumptions about women's predilection for deception in reproductive matters) required presumptions in law to render certain rules about paternal responsibility and the passing of family property in a patrilineal legal order. Carol Smart put it in these terms:

[U]nlike motherhood, fatherhood has posed complicated problems for a legal system that has based the ownership and inheritance of property on descent through the male line—on that is, patrilineal and primogenital ordering. Paternity has been a continuing 'problem' for the patriarchal family in Western Europe ... and this is manifest in the tortuous complexity of the legal system designed to protect the descent of property and privilege. (1987 p 99)

Before DNA testing could establish paternity conclusively, the legal response to this 'problem' was the presumption of legitimacy, or the presumption of paternity (Smart 1984). This presumption, which designates a woman's husband as the father of any children born to her, still remains, but in the light of scientific and social advancements, doubt has been cast upon its usefulness. In *Re H and A (Children)*[131] Thorpe LJ said

[30] ... Twenty years on [from *Serio v Serio* (1983) 4 FLR 756] I question the relevance of the presumption [of legitimacy] or the justification for its application. In the 19th century, when science had nothing to offer and illegitimacy was a social stigma as well as a depriver of rights, the presumption was a necessary tool, the use of which required no justification. That common law presumption, only rebuttable by proof beyond reasonable doubt, was modified by s 26 of the Family Law Reform Act 1969 by enabling the presumption to be rebutted on the balance of probabilities. But as science has hastened on and as more and more children are born out of marriage it seems to me that the paternity of any child is to be established by science and not by legal presumption or inference. ...

In this case the court considered that ascertainment of the 'truth' of the children's biological paternity outweighed even the husband's statement that he would leave the family if he were found not to be their biological father. Law seems to have accepted the value of biological familial relationships (perhaps as a result of the decline in the proportion of children born to married parents or to the increased numbers and power of fathers living separately from their children), but it has also had to reconcile this with the traditional social importance attached to marriage and family. One of the ways in which it has achieved this reconciliation is to suggest that it is in the child's best interests to know,[132] and indeed that he or she may have a right under Article 7 of the UN Convention on the Rights of the Child[133] and Article 8 ECHR[134] to know, the truth about

---

[131] [2002] EWCA Civ 383; [2002] 2 FCR 469.

[132] See eg *Re T (Paternity: Ordering Blood Tests)* [2001] 2 FLR 1190.

[133] *Re H (Paternity: Blood Test)* [1996] 2 FLR 65; *Re G (Parentage: Blood Sample)* [1997] 1 FLR 360; *Re R (A Minor) (Blood Test: Constraint)* [1998] 1 FCR 41. Art 7(1) states: 'The child shall be registered immediately after birth and shall have the right from birth to a name, the right to acquire a nationality and, as far as possible, the right to know and to be cared for by his or her parents'. See also *S v McC* [1972] AC 24; *Re G (A Minor) (Blood Test)* [1994] 1 FLR 495; Fortin (2003).

[134] See eg *Re T (Paternity; Ordering Blood Tests)* above; *Odievre v France*, above.

her or his origins. The trend now appears to be toward biological 'truth' over social arrangements. It appears to have supplanted the older case law that suggests that such tests do not promote the welfare of the child if they are ordered in the face of opposition from the mother, because they would disrupt a settled family relationship.[135]

**Q** Do you think the presumption of legitimacy should be retained?

The man named on the child's birth certificate is also presumed to be the child's father.[136] Both this presumption and the presumption of legitimacy can be rebutted by evidence on a balance of probabilities, but remain in law in order to achieve certainty. They have the effect also of conferring parental responsibility on the presumed father. As we have seen, however, not all biological fathers have social or legal responsibilities for their children.

*Biological Fathers*

Section 56 of the Family Law Act 1986 enables a child to seek a declaration that he or she is the legitimate child of his or her parents. Section 55A of the same Act enables a person to seek a declaration that a person is or was the parent of another person. If the applicant is anyone other than the child, the other parent, the possible parent him or her self,[137] or the Secretary of State in a dispute about child support,[138] the court must determine first that the applicant has sufficient personal interest in the finding.[139] The court may refuse to hear the application if it considers that to determine the application would not be in the best interests of the child.[140] Finally, the declaration, once made, is binding on all persons.[141]

The best evidence the court can have before it to determine parentage is scientific evidence, as Thorpe LJ said in the *Re H and A* case above, and by Section 20 of the Family Law Reform Act 1969 the court has the power to give a direction for the use of scientific tests in order to determine parentage and for the taking of bodily samples to complete those tests. Consents to take the bodily samples are required from all persons over the age of 16[142] and from a person with care and control of a child under 16 in respect of whom bodily samples must be taken. If the person does not give the required consent the bodily sample may be taken from the child anyway if the court considers it would be in the child's best interests.[143] Finally, Section 23(1) of the FLRA 1969 provides that if any person fails to comply with a direction to provide samples for testing, the court may draw whatever inferences it deems appropriate from the refusal. This includes drawing an inference 'as to the very fact which was in issue, namely the child's actual paternity'.[144]

---

[135] See *K v M (Paternity: Contact)* [1996] 1 FLR 312; *Re F (A Minor: Paternity Test)* [1993] 1 FLR 598; *O v L (Blood Tests)* [1995] 2 FLR 930; and Conway (1996).

[136] Births and Deaths Registration Act 1953 s 34(2).

[137] Subs 55A(4).

[138] Child Support Act 1991 s 27.

[139] Family Law Act 1986 s 55A(3).

[140] *Ibid*, s 55A(5).

[141] *Ibid*, s 58(2).

[142] Ss 21(1) and (2).

[143] S 21(3).

[144] *Re A (A Minor) (Paternity: Refusal of Blood Test)* [1994] 2 FLR 463; *Secretary of State for Work and Pensions v Jones* [2003] EWHC 2163; [2004] 1 FLR 282.

It does not automatically follow, however, that a declaration of paternity will carry with it any legal, social or emotional responsibilities or privileges. If the man is married to the legal mother of the child, then this biological confirmation of the presumption of legitimacy merely confirms his status as legal father. If the mother of the child is married to another man, however, the declaration of parentage, even if based upon an adverse inference drawn from a refusal to take the test, may rebut the presumption of legitimacy[145] to place the biological father in the position of an unmarried father under the Children Act with respect to parental responsibility.[146]

These provisions for determining a child's paternity offer a contrast to the former 'bastardy' or affiliation proceedings which were *quasi*-criminal in nature, and which required that a woman's testimony regarding her child's paternity be corroborated. In effect, they appeared to have been designed almost to give the putative father a 'sporting chance to get away with it' (Barton and Douglas 1995 p 200) and their complicated and criminal nature deterred and stigmatised women who were forced to rely upon them (Finer and McGregor 1974). In the past, paternity suits were usually used to determine a support obligation on the part of the father, and it is interesting to note that, while in many cases this is still the case, such declarations are now often sought by men who wish to establish a legal connection to children.

Where an unmarried man[147] is identified as the biological father of a child, he is included within the category 'parent' under a number of statutes. However, that label carries only limited legal rights and responsibilities. He is liable for support of the child pursuant to the Child Support Act 1991, and may as of right make certain applications under the Children Act 1989,[148] for example, but has no parental responsibility under the Children Act unless he agrees with the mother in prescribed form, or obtains an order of the court.[149] As we saw above, he may have the right to be notified about certain proceedings concerning his child, such as adoption proceedings, but, unlike a mother's biological connection to her child, his mere biological connection does not create for him and his child a family life to be recognised under Article 8 ECHR.

In *G v Netherlands*[150] a man, G, donated sperm to a lesbian couple and one of the women gave birth to a child as a result. The mother was the child's legal guardian in Dutch law, and the court later appointed her partner as joint guardian. For several months after the birth, G was able to visit the baby. The guardians subsequently refused to permit him to have regular, staying contact, and their decision was upheld by a Dutch court. G then brought an application before the European Commission alleging that his right to respect for family life under Article 8 of the European Convention had been violated. The Commission was asked to decide whether in this case 'family life' had been created between the man the child. It rejected G's argument that there is always family life between a biological father and his child:

---

[145] See eg *F v Child Support Agency* [1999] 2 FLR 244; *Secretary of State for Work and Pensions v Jones*, above.

[146] See below, and ch 15.

[147] We use this term here to mean unmarried to the child's mother.

[148] See further ch 7.

[149] Children Act 1989 s 4. If he registers the child's birth jointly with the mother, the presumption of paternity will give him parental responsibility. See chs 7 and 15.

[150] [1993] EHRR CD 38. See also discussion in ch 7 and cases cited therein.

The Commission recalls it has previously held that 'family life' in the sense of Article 8 of the Convention implies close personal ties in addition to parenthood. The Commission further recalls that the existence or non-existence of family life will depend on a number of factors, of which cohabitation is only one, and on the circumstances of each case.

...

The Commission considers that the situation in which a person donates sperm only to enable a woman to become pregnant through artificial insemination does not of itself give the donor a right to respect for family life with the child.

As to the applicant's argument that there is family life between him and the child as there have been regular contacts between them for a period of several months after the child's birth, the Commission notes that these contacts were limited in time and intensity. Furthermore, the applicant has apparently not considered making any contribution, financially or otherwise, to the child's upbringing. The Commission is of the opinion that the applicant's contracts [*sic*] with the child, both itself and together with his donorship, form an insufficient basis for the conclusion that as a result thereof such a close personal tie has developed between them that their relationship falls within the scope of 'family life' as referred to Article 8 of the Convention

...

(pp 39–40, footnotes omitted)

**Q** The Commission stated that cohabitation is only one of the factors that might establish the close personal tie necessary for creating 'family life' under Article 8. What others can you infer from this passage to be important? See further on this, chapter 7. Comment on the differences between way law recognises biological connections between men and women and their children.

The legal position of the unmarried father is thus very different from that of the married father and from the unmarried mother. Historically, 'father right' gave married fathers absolute authority over their children while non-marital children were deemed in law to be *filius nullius*, and left to the sole responsibility of their mothers. If a mother were successful in obtaining an affiliation order, she might be able to receive some financial assistance from the biological father, but this order gave him no legal rights over the child. The government was concerned in its pre-Children Act consultations, to find the appropriate place along the continuum between the two extremes of father right and *filius nullius* or mother right, to allocate rights and responsibilities to unmarried fathers. Section 4 of the Children Act 1989 and the ECHR jurisprudence reflect a compromise approaching the 'mother right' side of the continuum.[151] In effect, they give a father some rights, so long as he has a relationship with either the child or the child's mother.

**Q** Comment on this compromise. Do you think the law has struck the right balance?

*Non-Biological Fathers*

In some cases, for example if a declaration of parentage has been made, the biological father may have only a limited legal status. In others, he may have no legal status all. In these situations, the law simply disregards a known biological connection entirely, and ascribes legal fatherhood to the social, or intended social, father. An example of this is

151 See discussion below chs 7 and 15.

the, admittedly now rare, case where the mother or the court does not wish to disturb the presumption of legitimacy by directing scientific tests. Another example of legal rules overriding biological relationships is when a man donates sperm under the auspices of a licensed authority: as sperm donor he has no legal relationship with any resulting children.

The first legal regulation of fatherhood in the context of assisted reproduction, the Family Law Reform Act 1987, provided that where a child was born to a married woman as a result of artificial insemination by donor (AID), no man other than her husband was to be treated as the child's father unless it was shown that the husband did not consent to the insemination.[152] The intention of a man and his consent to act as father remain important in the sections of the HFEA 1990 which have replaced the 1987 provisions. Following the Warnock committee's recommendation that AID was not necessarily ethically objectionable and that donors should have no legal responsibilities toward resulting children (1984 para 4.22), Section 28(6)(a) of the HFEA provides that where the donation is made and used with the consent of the donor, in a manner consented to by the donor, by a licensed clinic under the authority of the HFEA, he is not to be treated as the father of the child. Rather, if she has one, the husband of the woman inseminated with donated sperm or implanted with an embryo brought about by donated sperm is to be treated as the father of the child unless it is shown that he did not consent to the procedure.[153] If she does not have a husband, but a licensed authority provides treatment for her together with a male partner, that unmarried partner is to be treated as the father.[154] If she has no male partner, the resulting child is legally fatherless.

One of the reasons for excluding donors from any legal responsibility for their offspring was to encourage people to donate gametes. And, until 2005 it was thought that for the same reason donations must always remain anonymous, although non-identifying information as to physical and social characteristics could be entered upon a register and disclosed on application[155] to an applicant. From 1 April 2005, identifying information such as the name and date of birth of the donor may also be disclosed to an applicant.[156]

**Q** Recall the discussion above of identity in the context of open adoption. Referring specifically to the welfare of the child, outline the arguments for and against donor anonymity.

It seems that the statutory provisions regulating legal fatherhood embody a 'high-tech' version of the presumption of legitimacy, focusing as they do upon a man's intention and social, marital fatherhood. Sometimes, however, the rules create awkward legalities. They mean, for example, that if the sperm is donated to a surrogate by the intended social father (a commissioning father), he is not the legal father despite his intention; rather the husband of the surrogate is the legal father of the child unless he did not consent to the insemination. If he did not consent, scientific tests would establish a genetic connection with the commissioning father, who would then be in the position of an

---

[152] S 27.

[153] S 28(2). But note that this s. does not override any common law presumption of legitimacy: ss 28(5)(a) and (b), or any adoption order: s 28(5)(c).

[154] S 28(3). But see *Re Q* [1996] 1 FLR 369; and Douglas (1996).

[155] S 31 HFEA 1990.

[156] The Human Fertilisation and Embryology Authority (Disclosure of Donor Information) Regulations SI 2004/1511 para 2(3).

unmarried father with the surrogate as legal mother. If the commissioning (biological) father is married, he and his wife may be granted a Section 30 parental order with the consent of the surrogate and her husband. If he is not married, he must apply to adopt the child or to obtain shared parental responsibility under the Children Act.[157] Where the sperm is donated to a woman by a third party (as opposed to the commissioning father) through a licensed authority, the donor has no legal role as parent, the surrogate is the legal mother, and the surrogate's husband is the legal father unless he did not consent. If he did not consent, or if she has no husband, the child is legally fatherless until an adoption order or a Section 30 parental order (if the surrogate was implanted with gametes from the commissioning wife) is made in favour of the commissioning couple, at which point the male partner becomes a father. There would be no father required to consent to the order.

Generally then, where donated sperm is provided through a licensed authority, a donor will not be treated as a father, but a consenting husband will be so treated. The overriding factor for assigning fatherhood in all of these situations seems to be a man's consent and intention to be, or not to be, a father and no assumptions are made about mystical or biological 'bonds' of fatherhood. But the consent must be clear and unambiguous.

In *Leeds Teaching Hospitals NHS Trust v A*[158] Mr and Mrs A sought IVF treatment together in which his sperm was to be injected into her egg. After a successful pregnancy Mrs A gave birth to twins, but it emerged that her egg had been mistakenly fertilised with Mr B's sperm rather than with her husband's sperm. The question before the court was whether Section 28(2) or Section 28(3) applied to the situation so as to designate Mr A the father of the twins. In observing that the Section 28(2) question revolved around the question of consent to treatment (para 27), Butler Sloss P said:

> 28. Mr A certainly gave his consent to the placing in his wife of 'an embryo'. The embryo actually placed in Mrs A was a fundamentally different embryo from one that might have been created by the use of Mr A's sperm. Mr A has indicated that he does not wish to seek to withdraw his consent and wishes to take advantage of the irrebuttable presumption set out in section 28(2) and become the legal father. It is not, however, a matter of endorsement by the husband of his consent. The question whether the husband consented is a matter of fact which may be ascertained independently of the views of those involved in the process. On the clear evidence provided in the consent forms Mr A plainly did not consent to the sperm of a named or anonymous donor being mixed with his wife's eggs. This was clearly an embryo created without the consent of Mr and Mrs A.

The section 28(3) question revolved around whether the As had received 'treatment together'.

> 31. I have found section 28(3) more difficult to interpret than section 28(2). The first question is whether it was intended to apply to husbands or whether it was designed solely to deal with efforts to have children by those who were not married to each other. Subsection (3) requires in the case of the placing of an embryo in the woman that it was 'in the course of treatment provided for her and a man together by a person to whom a licence applies and the creation of the embryo was not brought about with the sperm of that man'. Subsection (2), although limited to husbands, appears to be broader than subsection (3). The husband is to be treated as the father,

---

[157] As the biological father, he can rely on s 4 of the Children Act 1989.
[158] [2003] EWHC 259; [2003] 1 FLR 1091.

unless it is shown that he did not consent, that he 'opted out.' In subsection (3) the boot is on the other foot. The acceptance of fatherhood has to be shown. The man has to show commitment and that commitment has to be demonstrated by his active involvement. In other words, he must 'opt in.' Further in subsection (2), in contrast to subsection (3), it does not have to be shown that the husband played an active part in the course of treatment provided for his wife and him together by a person to whom a licence applies. ...

37. ... A fundamental error resulting in the use of the sperm of another in place of the use of sperm of the man taking part in the treatment must vitiate the whole concept of 'treatment together' for the purposes of the 1990 Act. I am therefore satisfied, even if section 28(3) could be construed as applying to married couples as well as unmarried couples, that Mr and Mrs A were not being treated together within the meaning of the subsection. Accordingly, section 28(3) cannot cover the present facts.

The result in this case was that Mr B was the legal father of the twins and Mr A would be required to apply for a residence order conferring upon him parental responsibility or, in the alternative to adopt the twins he intended to raise with his wife.

Some assisted reproduction procedures take a very long time, and in *In Re D (a child appearing by her guardian ad litem)*[159] the House of Lords was called upon to interpret Section 28(3) to determine the point at which treatment services were provided for the man and woman together. Was it when the treatment began or when it was completed, or somewhere in between? The issue arose because the unmarried partners separated between the time of the initial consent and first, unsuccessful round of IVF and the second, successful round. Hedley, J at trial found that the original course of treatment continues as treatment services provided to them together, and therefore if a child is conceived at a later date the man will be the father. Hale LJ in the Court of Appeal took a different view[160] and Lord Walker for the majority of the House of Lords approved Hale LJ's observations that treatment services are widely defined and are not limited to a particular cycle or course of treatment (para 39): 'There must be a point in time when the question has to be judged. The simple answer is that the embryo must be placed in the mother at a time when treatment services are being provided for the woman and the man together.'

He went on:

40. Hale LJ considered that this conclusion supported rather than undermined the legislative purpose of regulating treatment services in a way that takes account of the welfare of any child who may be born. She observed (p 139, para 25),

The Act requires that consideration be given to the welfare of the child and that counselling be offered to the prospective parents. If the circumstances which were taken into account when the couple were together change dramatically, it would better serve the purposes of the Act if the matter had to be reconsidered and fresh counselling offered before a further attempt at implantation is offered. That can only be beneficial to the children born as a result. [Counsel then appearing for B] accepted that had the mother not misled the centre, the treatment would have had to stop and a fresh assessment be made. She stopped short of accepting that had the clinic gone ahead regardless of the changed situation the subsection would not have applied. But that must be the inescapable result.

159 [2005] UKHL 33.
160 [2003] EWCA Civ 182; [2003] 1 FLR 1183.

In dismissing the appeal His Lordship recognised that '[i]nfertility treatment may be very protracted and a general rule of "once together, always together" (absent express withdrawal of his acknowledgment by the male partner, or review by the clinic) could produce some very undesirable and unjust consequences' (para 42).

**Q** Hale LJ noted regarding the HFEA:

> [S]ection 28(3) is an unusual provision, conferring the relationship of parent and child on people who are related neither by blood nor by marriage. Conferring such relationships is a serious matter, involving as it does not only the relationship between father and child but also between the whole of the father's family and the child. The rule should only apply to those cases which clearly fall within the footprint of the statutory language (para 20).

Do you agree?

**Q** In this context recall also the Evans case (*Evans v Amicus Healthcare and Others* [2004] EWCA Civ 727; [2005] Fam 1) discussed in chapter 3, where the woman's partner withdrew his consent to her using embryos fertilised with his sperm. Do these cases lend support to the view that consent in matters of parentage cannot be assessed in an ungendered way?

Sperm is relatively easy to collect and to donate and artificial insemination is not a high-tech procedure. AID may occur on an informal basis between friends, and in these cases the HFEA sections above do not apply. In such cases, biological evidence or, if applicable, the presumption of legitimacy will determine legal fatherhood but the social role these fathers play varies from arrangement to arrangement.

Dunne's research (2000) shows, for example, that lesbian mothers overwhelmingly organised donor inseminations informally (p 15) and that it was not unusual for the donors to have regular contact with their offspring (p 160). Fathers sometimes took on the role of 'kindly uncle' (pp 18, 22) and sometimes were actively engaged in parenting (p 28). And finally, this form of AID also had the effect of increasing the child's kin network: sometimes the father's parents enthusiastically accepted the role of grandparents (p 24) while other times they did so less enthusiastically (p 30).

Let us review the implications of the law's apparently mixed pro- and anti-biologism. On the one hand, fatherhood by consent is contrary to law's privileging of biology and things 'natural' but, on the other, it contradicts this position when there is a marriage or marriage-like partnership to privilege above nature. It is still the case, as it was even before the advent of new reproductive technologies, that it is '*marriage* and not the blood tie that confers automatic paternity upon men and creates a legal relationship between children and their fathers' (Smart 1987 p 101). Reliance upon marriage to create a man's legal tie not only to a woman, but to her children, continues to privilege that institution and, by implication, the nuclear family. Smart argued in 1987 that increased assertion by women of 'autonomous' motherhood is disruptive of the idealised nuclear family, and so law has responded by '[extending] the legal concept of paternity and [enhancing] paternal rights' (1987 p 99; see also Diduck 1995):

> The law appears to be moving in two conflicting directions at the same time. ...
> If these apparent contradictory trends are examined more closely it is possible to see that they in fact lend support to a particular family structure, namely one in which there is a

'heterosexual couple living together in a stable relationship, whether married or not'. In other words, the primary aim of law is to link biological fathers to children where it is the biological father who is most likely to reproduce the ideal nuclear family structure. Where the biological father is not available, or is unsuitable (for example the Law Commission's unmeritorious father) the social father will suffice. Where there is a biological father and a social (step) father … the law preserves the rights of the biological father in the 'best interests of the children'. In other cases where there is both a biological and social father (as with AID) the tendency is to ignore the biological father and to invest all the rights of paternity in the social father who will head a two parent family. (Smart 1987 p 114, reference omitted)[161]

**Q** Review the ways we have discussed so far in which fathers are given legal status. How persuasive do you find Smart's position now? Can you reconcile Smart's position with the case of Re *X Y and Z v UK* [1997] 2 FLR 892, where the court refused to allow a female to male transsexual to register as the father of the children born to his partner through AID?

*Adoption*
Men may become adoptive fathers if they apply and qualify jointly with their wives or partners and, in theory, single men can apply to adopt, just as single women can. But, as we saw in the *Frette v France* case above, the norm of the heterosexual two parent family remains strong, even in Human Rights discourse.

*Social Fatherhood: No Legal Status*
This category of fathers encompasses step-fathers and foster fathers. Because much of the discussion above related to foster mothers applies to foster fathers, we will not repeat it here. Conversely, much of the discussion on step-fathers which follows here applies to step-mothers, but we discuss step-parenthood in this section because, according to the 2001 Census 10% of all families with dependent children are step-families and 80% of these are step-fathers (Natinal Statistics Online). Further, the National Stepfamily Association reported in 1996 that a British male is more than 2.5 times more likely to become a full-time step-father than a British woman is to become a full-time step-mother (National Stepfamily Association 1996).

*Step-parents*
A man becomes a step-father by the simple act of either marrying a woman who is the mother of a child and with whom that child lives or entering into a civil partnership with a man who is that child's father. Entry into step-parenthood, therefore, is entirely unregulated by law, other than by the law of marriage or civil partnership.[162] The step-parent is a social parent, but, like a foster parent, he has no automatic parental responsibility for the child. This situation places step-parents in an ambiguous legal position and often an awkward emotional one. Bainham describes it in these terms:

The step parent is in a potentially awkward position from the start. He (or she) is part of a family unit and has a regularised relationship with the natural [*sic*] parent through marriage, but lacks a regularised relationship with the children in the family. Thus while the step parent undoubtedly is in most cases in loco parentis and has de facto care of the children, he lacks the parental responsibility which would put him on an equal footing with his spouse and legitimate his standing to be fully involved in upbringing … . While the relationship between the adult partners may be viewed as a partnership of equals, the relationship between them and the child

---

[161] See also Dewar (1989).
[162] See ch 2.

is clearly not equal in law. In the event of disagreement, the natural [*sic*] parent (by virtue of parental responsibility) has the sole authority on any issues affecting the children. This is a situation which has all the potential for conflict between the spouses and between the step parent and the children. (2005 pp 232–33)

This awkward position may be exacerbated when the couple are not married or registered civil partners, as they may then be perceived to have even less formal status. It also cannot be separated from research which suggests that children from step-families are overrepresented in many negative statistics such as those relating to looked after children, young runaways or child abuse (Smith 2003 p 197). They may experience anger, depression, anxiety and resentment when one of their parents repartners and, particularly in adolescence, they may feel conflicted and disengage from their families.[163] Step-parents also may feel anxious and experience emotional conflict. There is also research, however, which suggests that, like any family living, step-family living is complicated, but that children and adults learn to adapt to its complexities (Smith 2003; Parentline Plus 2005). Their adaptation in practice to become functional families is something that has only relatively recently come to be reflected in the law. Current legal discourse tries to reconcile the competing needs for children for families or social parenthood (in this case recognising the authority and responsibility of the step-father) and their biological ties (in this case recognising the need for contact and on-going parental responsibility of the non-resident father).[164] Its resolution for step-fathers is to provide ways for them to acquire legal status in relation to their step-children, without the non-resident biological father losing his status.

A step-parent can acquire a legal status in relation to the child by applying to the court for a residence order, and, if he is married to, or, after the Civil Partnership Act 2004 comes into force, is the registered civil partner of, the parent with parental responsibility and has treated the child as a 'child of the family', he can do so as of right.[165] A 'child of the family' is one whom the step-parent treats as his or her own. It is defined as follows:

child of the family', in relation to the parties to a marriage,[or to two people who are civil partners of each other] means—

(a)   a child of both of [them] those parties;

(b)   any other child, not being a child who is placed with [them] those parties as foster parents by a local authority or voluntary organisation, who has been treated by both of [them] those parties as a child of their family[166];

---

[163] Parentline Plus 2005.

[164] Edwards, *et al*, (1999) suggest that the law that emphasises biological over social ties is 'seeking to shift people's opinions in a particular direction', one which 'not only ignores the view that children need families, but requires biological parents to construct a social tie that most people feel is unworkable' (p 101). They also suggest that the law exhibits a class bias, as their findings showed a significant class difference in the value people ascribe to each discourse, with working class step-families unanimously adopting a social family preference, none linking emotional relationships to biological status (p 92), and middle class families generally linking emotional connection, parental rights and responsibilities to biological status (p 90).

[165] The Children Act 1989 s 10(5)(a) indicates that any party to a marriage may apply to the court for a residence order in relation to the child of the family, s 10(5)(aa) repeats this provision for civil partners, and s 12(2) provides that anyone who has a residence order in his or her favour has parental responsibility for the duration of the order, although s 12(3) limits the rights which that parental responsibility brings.

[166] S 105 of the Children Act. Words in parentheses substituted by the Civil Partnership Act 2004 s 75(3). The same definition appears in the Matrimonial Causes Act 1973 s 52 and the Domestic Proceedings and Magistrates' Courts Act 1978 s 88.

Courts have interpreted this definition quite broadly in the context of heterosexual step-parents, so that even short-lived relationships will bring a step-parent into this definition.[167] It remains to be seen how same-sex step-parents will be treated. Only the married or civilly registered step-parent may rely upon Section 10(5)(a) of the Children Act, however, and so the cohabiting 'step-parent' remains only a *de facto* carer unless the relationship is formalised legally through an application for a residence order which can be made only with leave of the court, with the consent of those with parental responsibility[168] or after living with the child for three years.[169] Until the Adoption and Children Act 2002, the only other alternative for step-parents was joint adoption with their new spouse, but this alternative meant that not only was the non-resident parent's parental responsibility extinguished, the resident parent had to adopt her own child.

Particularly in the light of the acceptability of 'serial monogamy', some scholars, such as Masson, suggested that the law needed to provide some increased status or rights for step-parents, including automatic parental responsibility on marriage (Masson 1989). In the Conservative government's White Paper (1993) a new scheme was proposed, albeit short of Masson's suggestion, to regularise the step-parent relationship.

5.21 The Government intend that the new legislation will make available a new Parental Responsibility Agreement. This could be entered into by the birth parent with her new spouse, though it would create a new relationship only for the step-parent. It would thus create a joint parental responsibility to be exercised by both, but would not legally sever links with the other birth parent. In cases where the other birth parent registered consent, the agreement would simply be registered with the court. No court hearing and no assessment of suitability or any local authority or adoption agency involvement would be necessary. Even in cases where the other birth parent's consent was not forthcoming and the court needed to judge the issue and decide whether or not to make the order, the process would be simpler and less intrusive than adoption. (DoH, *et al*, 1993 p 12)

The new Section 4A in the Children Act 1989 has adopted this proposal. It allows for a parental responsibility agreement to be made between the step-father and the mother, and the non-resident father, if he has parental responsibility. In some cases, therefore it will be a tripartite agreement. And, as we saw above, the Adoption and Children Act 2002 Section 51(2) also has also made it possible for a step-father (or, indeed any 'partner') to adopt his partner's child.

**Q** Do these reforms, in your view, strike a fair balance between stable family life for children and continued importance of biological relationships?

*Conclusion*

Three themes can be identified in our discussion of becoming a parent in law. The first is the issue of legal and state regulation of the status. Barton and Douglas (1995), drawing on the earlier work of Douglas and Lowe (1992), identify a continuum along which the degree of regulation runs 'from minimal, if any, control in the case of the carrying woman who happens to be unmarried, to a lengthy state investigation into the

---

[167] *See Teeling v Teeling* [1984] FLR 808; *W v W* [1984] FLR 796; *Caron v Caron* [1984] FLR 805.
[168] S 10(5)(c) (iii).
[169] S 10(5)(b).

applicant's suitability to be a parent in the case of adoption' (Barton and Douglas 1995 p 50). Regulation can be in the form of legislation and direct legal coercion, or it can be in the form of control or governance through non-legal agents, such as the social workers who determine the suitability of applicants for adoption and who visit the homes of foster carers or the physicians who decide appropriate candidates for infertility treatment.

The second theme, tied in with the first, focuses on the degree to which regulation operates to reinforce a particular version of the nuclear family in preference to other family forms; the ideology of the family informs the norms by which certain people are considered suitable parents and others are rejected as undesirable.

Finally, there is a theme of intentionality running through this discussion. Barton and Douglas argue that intention is now the 'primary test of legal parentage' (1995 p 51).

**Q** To what extent do you agree with this proposition?

Adoption reforms, the creation of the new legal status of special guardian, and of a new legal status for step-parents appear to give credence to this proposition, even while new biological interventions become available for facilitating much desired biological parenthood and human rights are prayed in aid of acknowledging that identity. As we have maintained, however, these two trends may not be paradoxical; intention is always more relevant to a man's experience of parenting than to a woman's.

It is here, with the possibility of gender differences in mind, that we shall begin our discussion of what being a parent means in law.

## III. WHAT DOES IT MEAN TO BE A PARENT?

*Responsibility to Rear Healthy and Well Adjusted Children*

We usually think of parenthood as entailing rights and responsibilities toward a child as well as the autonomy to exercise those rights and responsibilities. There are other incidents of parenthood, however; incidents that are less readily amenable to legal management, yet are governed directly and indirectly by legal precepts. A parent not only has the responsibility to feed, clothe and educate a child; he or she also has a moral responsibility to care for a child emotionally, socially and psychologically and to prepare the child successfully for assuming the responsibilities of adult life.[170] Barton and Douglas report the results of a 1986 survey in which people were asked to list up to five of the most important qualities parents should try to teach their children. The list from which they were asked to choose, and the resulting choices are reported as follows:

[G]ood manners, cleanness and neatness, independence, hard work, honesty, to act responsibly, patience, imagination, respect for other people, leadership, self-control, being careful with money, determination and perseverance, religious faith and unselfishness. *Honesty* was first with over 85%, followed by *good manners* at 74% and *respect for other people* at 67%.

(1995 p 129, emphasis in original)

---

[170] See O'Neill (1979); Archard (1993); ch 3.

It is as much this aspect of parenthood that we think of when we speak of child-rearing as it is the provision of material nurturance and protection from harm. What does it mean, though, to rear a child 'successfully'? This notion conjures up both the image of the successful child and the successful parent.

Theories from both psychology and sociology emphasise processes of maturation, self-reliance, individuation and socialisation in a child's development, and it is seen primarily as the parents' role to facilitate successfully the child's progression through the various developmental stages. Freud, for example, theorises a series of psycho-sexual stages through which a child progresses, developing from his or her *id*, to heeding an *ego* and *superego*, so that he or she becomes a socially well-adjusted individual. Too much or too little gratification at any of the stages may result in fixation at that stage or regression to it, both of which are pathological (Freud 1905).

**Q** What part do you think a parent plays in producing Freud's normal, well-adjusted children? Are the roles of mother and father the same? In an influential (1980b) publication Goldstein, (Anna) Freud and Solnit adopt Freud's theory of child development to advocate minimal state intervention in parent-child relations:

> [C]onstantly ongoing interactions between parents and children become for each child the starting point for an all-important line of development that leads toward adult functioning. What begins as the experience of physical experience of contentment or pleasure that accompanies bodily care develops into a primary attachment to the person who provides it. This again changes into the wish for a parent's constant presence irrespective of physical wants. Helplessness requires total care and over time is transformed into the need or wish for approval and love. It fosters the desire to please by compliance with a parent's wishes. It provides a developmental base upon which the child's responsiveness to educational efforts rest. Love for the parents leads to identification with them, a fact without which impulse control and socialization would be deficient. Finally, after the years of childhood comes the prolonged and in many ways painful adolescent struggle to attain a separate identity with physical, emotional and moral self reliance.
>
> These complex and vital developments require the privacy of family life under guardianship by parents who are autonomous. The younger the child the greater his need for them. When family integrity is broken or weakened by state intrusion, his needs are thwarted and his belief that his parents are omniscient and all powerful is shaken prematurely. The effect on the child's developmental progress is invariably detrimental.
>
> (1980b pp 8–9, footnotes omitted)

**Q** Do you think Goldstein Freud and Solnit are assuming a particular family form in which roles for parents are clearly delineated? Bowlby (1953 see chapter 8), too, relied upon a Freudian understanding of child development in his theories of maternal deprivation so influential in post 1950s and 1960s custody and child welfare discourse.

Other developmental psychologists who have influenced western thinking (and law: see the discussion of *Gillick* below and Smart, *et al*, 2001) include Kohlberg (1984) who identified stages in the development of moral judgment which, in a healthy individual culminated in individual principles of conscience; Piaget (1952) who characterised child development in terms of cognitive development—the progressive emergence of more logical forms of thought which led ultimately to the development of idealism and the ability to understand the hypothetical; and Erikson (1980) who theorised a child's psychosocial development as the resolution of a series of crises or conflicts through which the individual progresses to a healthy adult personality.[171]

Sociology, too, has had something to say about a parent's proper role in rearing children. One theory, analysed and criticised from a variety of perspectives, is that of *socialisation*. Socialisation has been defined as: 'the process by which an individual incorporates the attitudes and behaviours considered appropriate by any group or society ... . It is learning the culture or the ways of a group; the process encompasses both the teachers and the learners, the socializing agents and the socialized.' (Adams 1975 p 137)

Talcott Parsons, the functionalist sociologist (1949),[172] 'saw society as an organism concerned to ensure its continued perpetuation through time, and socialisation as the process through which this was accomplished' (Diduck 2003 p 78). He placed great responsibility upon families and parents as socialising agents, declaring, for example, that it was in 'the family' that girl children learn how to be women and boy children learn how to be men in contemporary society.[173] Perhaps now, more than ever before, parents are held to be primarily responsible for instilling in their children an 'appropriate' morality and level of industriousness and responsibility. Their employment status is seen as offering a role model for children (chapter 3) and New Deal and other family friendly work practices encourage parents and carers to see themselves as partners with the state and with the market, vested with the responsibility of becoming better citizens by moving from dependency into independence and importantly, also by 'ensuring that their children behave responsibly and are sufficiently informed and educated to become citizen workers themselves' (Williams 2004 p 29). To assist parents in carrying out their roles as socialisers, government has created a National Parenting Helpline and voluntary parenting education classes. There are also mandatory parenting orders,[174] requiring parents to attend parenting programmes if their children are convicted of certain offences.[175]

Socialisation, however, also occurs in the broader societal context as well as in families. Television, school, popular culture and religious involvement, mediated through families, can influence a child's socialisation. And so can direct government involvement. Citizenship classes are now a part of the national curriculum[176] evidencing government's concern with socialising children according to particular precepts. In *Every Child Matters* (DfES, 2003) Government declared its intention of developing a 'strong partnership with [its] stakeholders', which it defined as including 'children and young people' (Executive Summary para 22). As part of this drive, consultation with children and young people has become a priority. The goals identified within the Green

---

171 See also Gilligan (1982) in which the author challenges traditional studies of a child's stages of moral and personality development by suggesting that developmental theories have been built on observations of boys and men, excluding and marginalising the motives and morality of girls and women. See discussion generally in Diduck (2003); Smart, Neale and Wade (2001).
172 See ch 1.
173 See also Chodorow (1978) on mothers and daughters, and Dennis and Erdos (1993) on fathers. Dennis and Erdos present the view that the lack of a father figure in the family harms society.
174 Crime and Disorder Act 1998.
175 See further below pp 175–76. See also Piper, forthcoming 2006.
176 Education Act 2002 s 84 and 85. See further below pp 178–79.

Paper are the product of such a consultation exercise and these goals are described as being important not only for children's well-being but for society as a whole (paras 1.5–1.6). Children's involvement in the 'planning, delivery and evaluation of government services' is said to bring benefits in that it promotes 'citizenship and social inclusion' (CYPU 2001 p 6)[177] and in a document published by the Department of Constitutional Affairs (2003a) children are identified as 'customers' of the department's services. Finally, in *Youth Matters* (DfES 2005), the government builds upon the policy begun in *Every Child Matters* to create and coordinate services to teenagers, with the aim, *inter alia* of encouraging young people to see themselves as 'citizens', by encouraging among them a culture of voluntary work (chapter 4).

Much of this activity aimed at producing responsible citizens can be seen as a response to a perceived 'crisis' in the family and as part of broader social project in which the family is disciplined, or 'remoralised' (Day Sclater and Piper 2000) to cope with this crisis, partly by attributing increased decision-making responsibility to it and by inculcating personal responsibility for those decisions in its members. This view shares something with that of French sociologist Jacques Donzelot (1980). Donzelot relies upon notions of surveillance and tutelage through the realm of the social in which the popular stratum (the working class) is familialised. To him, in the 19th century there was a change from government *of the family* to government *through the family* through increased supervision of and intervention in families. This was not accomplished directly by the state as agent, however, but by various interventions in various different settings, which meant that in the 19th century 'the independent authority of families gave way to social management through families' (Barrett and MacIntosh 1991 p 98). Donzelot's presentation of socialisation then, is as a means of governing or policing families.[178]

Implicit in our discussion which follows are questions about how assumptions about socialisation and about the 'healthy' development of children inform legal assumptions about good mothers, good fathers, good families and the good society.

## IV. DAY-TO-DAY RESPONSIBILITIES OF PARENTS

The law assumes that parents will, for the most part, act in their children's best interests. The law does, however, lay down minimal standards for defining those interests and for parents' responsibilities to maintain them. That the standards have varied over the years reflects ever changing notions of parental rights and responsibilities,[179] children's welfare[180] and private and state responsibility for protecting it.[181]

In his *Commentaries on the Laws of England*, Blackstone divided what we would call parental 'rights and responsibilities' into parental 'duties and powers'. He summarised the duties of parents toward legitimate children as including maintenance, protection and education. The power of parents over their children he summarised as follows:

---

[177] See also P Kirby, et al, *Building a Culture of Participation*, (DfeS, 2003).
[178] See also Vaughan (2000) and further ch 9.
[179] See ch 7.
[180] See ch 8.
[181] See chs 3 and 17.

The power of parents over their children is derived from the former consideration, their duty; this authority being given them, partly to enable the parent more effectually to perform his duty, and partly as a recompense for his care and trouble in the faithful discharge of it. And upon this score the municipal laws of some nations have given a much larger authority to the parents, than others. The Ancient Roman laws gave the father a power of life and death over his children; upon this principle, that he who gave had also the power of taking away ... .

(1778 p 452)

The power of a parent by our English laws is much more moderate, but still sufficient to keep the child in order and obedience. He may lawfully correct his child, being under age, in a reasonable manner, for this is for the benefit of his education. The consent or concurrence of the parent to the marriage of his child under age, was also *directed* by our ancient law to be obtained: but now it is absolutely *necessary*; for without it the contract is void ... . A father has no other authority over his son's *estate*, than as his trustee or guardian; for, though he may receive the profits during the child's minority, yet he must account for them when he comes of age. He may indeed have the benefit of his children's labour while they live with him, and are maintained by him; but this is no more than he is entitled to from his apprentices or servants. The legal power of a father (for a mother, as such, is entitled to no power, but only to reverence and respect) ... over the persons of his children ceases at the age of twenty one; for they are then enfranchised by arriving at years of discretion, or that point which the law has established (as some must necessarily be established) when the empire of the father, or other guardian, gives place to the empire of reason. Yet till that age arrives, this empire of the father continues even after his death; for he may by his will appoint a guardian to his children ... .

(1778 pp 452–53)

**Q** What is the nature of the family relationship and the state-family relationship evoked by Blackstone's description?

*Parental Responsibility*

Prior to the Children Act 1989, the law spoke of 'guardianship', 'parental rights and duties' or the 'rights and authority' of parents (Law Commission 1988b para 2.4). The Law Commission was concerned that the language of rights that predominated at the time reflected an outmoded authoritarian model of parenthood and failed to recognise that contemporary parenthood is characterised by responsibilities rather than rights (1988b para 2.1). The concept of parental responsibility is one of the key innovations of the Children Act 1989 and is designed to shift the emphasis away from rights and to form the basis of a coherent legal framework for the allocation of responsibility and decision-making powers concerning children. As Bainham (1999) has said and we saw above, parental responsibility must be distinguished from parentage and parenthood. All mothers and married parents automatically have parental responsibility, unmarried fathers can acquire it, as can local authorities, step-parents, guardians and special guardians, adopters and those who have a residence order in respect of a child. We have seen above how a number of these 'parents' acquire parental responsibility, and will look at unmarried fathers in chapter 7, but for now wish to note that one of its distinguishing features is that it can be held by any number of people,[182] who do not have to be either biological or social parents of a child. Where parental responsibility vests in more than one person, each of them may act independently in meeting that responsibility, except where, as in the case of the marriage of the child, statute requires the consent of each.[183] When it is held by married parents it can never be lost, except by adoption.

---

[182] Children Act 1989 s 2(5).
[183] *Ibid*, s 2(7).

In any case, parental responsibility cannot be abandoned or transferred although it is possible to arrange for some or all of it to be met by someone, or agencies such as schools, acting on behalf of the person with parental responsibility.[184]

*Parental Responsibility under the Children Act*

Parental responsibility is defined in Section 3(1) of the Children Act 1989: 'In this Act 'parental responsibility' means all the rights, duties, powers, responsibilities and author-ity which by law a parent of a child has in relation to the child and his property.'

Thus, the incidents of parental responsibility were left to the common law, unlike in Scotland, for example, where the incidents of parental responsibility are listed in the Children (Scotland) Act 1995.[185]

The Children Act definition has, in fact, been described as a 'non-definition'.[186] Despite a number of calls for detailed codification of these rights and duties over the years (Barton and Douglas 1995 pp 115–16), the legislature declined to specify in any detail what might be encompassed by this very general definition.

> **Q** How would you define parental responsibility? Why do you think Parliament was reluctant to be more specific?

When debating the possibility of providing a complete list of parental rights and duties, the Law Commission observed that this 'would clearly be a large task involving consid-eration of many difficult and controversial areas ... . We doubt whether the list could ever be comprehensive' (1985b para 1.9). The list would need to change from time to time to meet differing needs and circumstances and to take account of the child's age and maturity (1988b para 2.6). The legislature's decision in favour of a very general defi-nition may therefore be attributable to a perceived need to preserve flexibility and to enable the law to take account of changing circumstances and of differences between children.[187]

The Law Commission acknowledged that the change in terminology from rights to responsibilities would make little difference in substance (1988b para 2.4) and the word-ing of Section 3(1) of the Children Act makes it necessary, in order to interpret it, to look to those rights, duties and powers traditionally recognised by the law. Barton and Douglas, reviewing the literature, conclude that:

> If the legal agenda can be inferred from the conventional lists of issues involving some or all of those with parental authority, it might be itemised, roughly by the age of the child, like this:
>
> (1)  physical possession, home, protection and contact;
> (2)  name;
> (3)  education and religion;
> (4)  discipline and punishment;
> (5)  medical treatment;
> (6)  travel and emigration;
> (7)  property and contracting;

---

[184] S 2(9). In addition, as we saw with foster parents, a person who does not have parental responsibility but who has actual care of a child may do what is reasonable to safeguard or promote the child's welfare (s 3(5)). This would cover, eg, decisions relating to medical treatment in the event of an accident.

[185] S 1(1).

[186] Lord Meston, Hansard (HL), vol 502, col 1172.

[187] Lowe (1997) argues that more clarity along the Scottish lines is needed in England, particularly since the concept of parental responsibility is gaining international acceptance and usage.

(8)  legal proceedings;
(9)  services;
(10) marriage;
(11) disposing of the child's corpse.  (1995 p 114)

The emphasis in the Children Act on responsibilities rather than rights is consonant with the general aim of the law reformers to introduce a legal framework that is fundamentally child-centred. This aim reflected the direction in which the law was already developing; even prior to the enactment of this statute, parental rights were being cast by the courts in terms of the duties owed by parents to children.[188]

> **Q** To what extent does Blackstone's account of parents' duties and powers resemble parental responsibility under the Children Act?

Blackstone's account of paternal authority over children is one illustration of the privacy accorded that relationship by a non-interventionist 18th and 19th century state, in which even the most brutal forms of child abuse became a matter of public concern only in the 19th century (Dingwall and Eekelaar 1988).[189] What type of care does the law require in the 21st century version of the liberal state which privileges both parental autonomy (Blackstone's *powers*) and children's welfare (his *duties*)?

*Criminal Responsibility*
As a general rule, the law only imposes criminal liability as a result of a positive act (Ashworth 1995 pp 104–5; Williams 1983 p 146; *cf* Norrie 1993). It is contrary to notions of the autonomy of the individual to hold a person liable for his or her failures to act, and so, with a few exceptions, omissions cannot form the basis of criminal liability (Ashworth 1995 pp 108–9). One of those exceptions is where there is a pre-existing duty to act, and the parent-child relationship is said to create such a duty. Bainham states that a parent's duty to protect a child arises from his or her parental responsibility (2005 p 617). In addition, others, 'who have "responsibility" for children, in the less technical sense of assuming their physical care' are subject to a duty to protect children, so that their failure to do so can give rise to criminal liability (*ibid*).[190]

Criminal acts committed by parents against children can include any offences against the person, including sexual offences. Parents can be prosecuted under the Sexual Offences Act 2003 for sexual offences against their children in the same way that strangers can, but parents, along with other named relatives and carers, are also subject to special criminal laws respecting sexual offences. The old criminal offence of incest (with respect to children) has been replaced with the offences of sexual activity with a child family member[191] and inciting a child family member to engage in sexual activity.[192] 'Child' means anyone under the age of 18 in these sections, and 'family' is broadly defined to include parent, grandparent, brother, sister, half-brother, half-sister, aunt or uncle, foster parent or former foster parent, and, if they have lived in the same household, step-parent (even if unmarried to the child's parent) cousin, step-brother or sister or someone who has been involved in caring for or training the child.[193] In addition,

---

[188] See *Gillick v West Norfolk and Wisbech Area Health Authority* [1986] 1 AC 112.
[189] See ch 9.
[190] And see Children and Young Persons Act 1933 s 1(1) and (2)(b).
[191] S 25 Sexual Offences Act 2003.
[192] S 26.
[193] S 27.

there are a series of sexual offences that may be committed by people who are in positions of trust respecting a child.[194] These include people who care for children in care homes, institutions, residential homes and the like.[195]

The Offences Against the Person Act 1861 outlaws assault by anyone, including parents against their children, but in some cases the law does permit parents to chastise their children physically. In some cases, parents,[196] unlike strangers, are able to rely upon the right, described by Blackstone, and protected in Section 1(7) of the Children and Young Persons Act (CYPA) 1933, to administer punishment to a child. Until 2005 this defence was available to any charge, but Section 58 of the Children Act 2004 has removed the defence from charges of wounding or causing grievous bodily harm and assault causing actual bodily harm under the Offences against the Person Act 1861 and child cruelty under the Children and Young Persons Act 1933. Even where the defence is available, the corporal punishment must be 'moderate and reasonable'.[197] Once this defence is raised to a charge, the burden of proof is on the prosecution to prove that the assault went beyond those limits.

Views vary greatly on the morality, the legality and indeed the effectiveness, of corporal punishment of children. Supporters say that a 'loving smack' (or more) is effective as a means of discipline and that prohibiting corporal punishment would mean that minor or trivial incidents could be prosecuted as criminal offences. Opponents argue that it teaches children that violence is an appropriate reaction to conflict, that it actually harms children's psychological development and that it can too easily escalate into serious abuse. The clearest argument against hitting children, no matter with what force, is that it infringes their rights under the ECHR and the UN Convention on the Rights of the Child. In *A v UK (Human Rights: Punishment of Child)*[198] the ECtHR heard a case that set in motion changes to the long-standing view in the UK that all corporal punishment was a private matter of child discipline. In this case a step-father beat his 9-year-old step-son with a garden cane on several occasions, causing severe bruising. He raised the defence of lawful chastisement to a charge of assault occasioning actual bodily harm and was acquitted. A took the matter to the European Court of Human Rights alleging, among other things, a violation of his right under Article 3 of the European Convention on Human Rights not to be subjected to torture or to inhuman or degrading treatment or punishment. The European Court held that the law did not provide adequate protection against treatment or punishment contrary to Article 3. The government's response was to issue a Consultation Document (Department of Health 2000a) but it limited its terms of reference immediately:

> 1.5 The Government fully accepts the need for change. The harmful and degrading treatment of children can never be justified. We have made it quite clear, however, that we do not consider that the right way forward is to make unlawful all smacking and other forms of physical rebuke and this paper explicitly rules out this possibility. There is a common sense distinction to be made between the sort of mild physical rebuke which occurs in families and which most loving parents consider acceptable, and the beating of children.

[194] Ss 16–24.

[195] Ss 21–22. For commentary and discussion see Bainham (2005 pp 620–28).

[196] It also protects those to whom parents have delegated the power to chastise: see *Sutton London Borough Council v Davis* [1994] 1 FLR 737. For a good summary see Law Commission (1995) Consultation Paper 139 Part XI and Fortin (2003) pp 276ff.

[197] For changing interpretations of moderate and reasonable see *R v Hopley* (1860) 2 F and F 202; *R v Derriviere* (1969) 53 Cr App R 637; and *R v Smith*, 2 November 1994 (CA); *A v UK* [1998] 2 FLR 959; *R v H* [2001] EWCA Crim 1024; [2001] 2 FLR 431. See also Fortin (2003) pp 278–79; Smith, (2004).

[198] [1998] 2 FLR 959.

The government seemed to be relying upon the results of an ONS survey in 1998 in which 85% of respondents agreed it was sometimes necessary to smack a naughty child over 5 years old; 53% if the child was over 2 year old, and 13% if the child was under 2 years old (DoH 2000a p 21). The English public seems to be quite unequivocal in its support of corporal punishment. Further evidence is provided by an ICM poll, reported in 1996, which indicated that 81% of interviewees nationally supported corporal punishment by parents of their own children, 45% by child carers/nannies or other relatives, 67% by class teachers of pupils, 71% by head teachers of pupils, and a surprising 70% by the courts of children convicted of criminal offences, a criminal punishment which was abolished in 1948.[199] Perhaps it is not surprising that in the light of this popular sentiment, the government went no further than the Children Act 2004 amendments to reform the law directly. It found that more far reaching reform was not required under the ECHR, since the coming into force of the HRA meant that any court considering a reasonable chastisement defence would be bound to take into account the *A v UK* judgment, which said that the factors relevant in determining whether there was a breach of Article 3 were the nature and context of the defendant's behaviour, its duration, its physical and mental effect upon the child and the age and personal characteristics of the child. Since then, there has been some suggestion that a further factor has been added to the list: the reasons given by the defendant for administering the punishment.[200]

> **Q** Do you think the government has responded adequately to the *A v UK* case? In addition to the European Convention on Human Rights, Article 37 of the UN Convention on the Rights of the Child states '[n]o child shall be subjected to cruel, inhuman or degrading treatment or punishment.'[201] Since 1991 corporal punishment has been banned in children's homes[202] and foster placements;[203] it has been outlawed in state schools since 1987;[204] and since 1998[205] in all schools.[206] Finally, since 2003 childminders have not been allowed to administer corporal punishment to children in their care.[207]

In addition to these minimal standards set by the criminal law regarding sexual offences and offences against the person,[208] there are other offences relating to the mistreatment or death of children while in someone's care. The CYPA 1933 creates offences relating to the mistreatment and neglect of children by their carers.[209] The relevant wording of the legislation is as follows:

---

[199] *The Guardian*, 7 November 1996.

[200] *R v H* above. See generally, Smith (2004).

[201] Fortin (2003) p 284 tells us that corporal punishment of children is prohibited in Austria, Croatia, Cyprus, Sweden, Finland, Denmark, Norway, Germany, Latvia, Italy and Israel.

[202] Children's Homes Regs 1991, SI 1991/1506, Reg 8(2)(a).

[203] Foster Placement (Children) Regs 1991, SI 1991/910.

[204] Education (No 2) Act 1986 s 47; Education (Abolition of Corporal Punishment) (Independent Schools) Regs 1987, SI 1987/1183; Education (Abolition of Corporate Punishment) (Independent Schools) (Prescribed Categories of Persons) Regs 1989, SI 1989/1825, which together abolish corporal punishment in schools wholly or partly funded by the state, or where pupils' education is subsidised by the local authority or the government.

[205] Education Act 1996 s 548(1), as amended by School Standards and Framework Act 1998.

[206] The prohibition was upheld by the House of Lords in *R (on the application of Williamson) v Secretary of State for Education and Employment* [2005] UKHL 15; [2005] 1 FCR 498. See further discussion below.

[207] Day Care and Child Minding (National Standards) (England) Regulations 2003 SI 2003/1996, para 5.

[208] See also CYPA s 1(2)(b) regarding death of a child by suffocation while in bed with another who was under the influence of drink.

[209] The Act also deals with employment restrictions for children, begging, sale of tobacco to children and other matters.

1(1) If any person who has attained the age of sixteen years and has responsibility for any child or young person under that age, wilfully[210] assaults, ill-treats, neglects, abandons, or exposes him, or causes or procures him to be assaulted, ill-treated, neglected abandoned or exposed, in a manner likely to cause him unnecessary suffering or injury to health (including injury to or loss of sight, or hearing, or limb, or organ of the body, and any mental derangement), that person shall be guilty of a misdemeanour, and shall be liable—

(a)  on conviction on indictment, to a fine or alternatively, or in addition thereto, to imprisonment for any term not exceeding ten years;

(b)  on summary conviction, to a fine not exceeding [the prescribed sum] or in addition thereto, to imprisonment not exceeding six months.

(2) For the purposes of this section—

(a)  a parent or other person legally liable to maintain a child or young person, or the legal guardian of the young person, shall be deemed to have neglected him in a manner likely to cause injury to his health if he has failed to provide adequate food, clothing, medical aid or lodging for him, or if, having been unable otherwise to provide such food, clothing, medical aid or lodging, he has failed to take steps to procure it to be provided under the enactments applicable in that behalf.

...

(3) A person may be convicted of an offence under this section—

(a)  notwithstanding that actual suffering or injury to health, or the likelihood of actual suffering or injury to health, was obviated by the action of another person ... .

(7) Nothing in this section shall be construed as affecting the right of any parent, or (subject to section 548 of the Education Act 1996) any other person, having the lawful control or charge of a child or young person to administer punishment to him.[211]

And the Domestic Violence, Crime and Victims Act 2004 creates the offence of causing or allowing the death of a child or vulnerable adult:

5  The offence

(1) A person ('D') is guilty of an offence if—

(a)  a child or vulnerable adult ('v') dies as a result of the unlawful act of a person who—
    (i)  was a member of the same household as V, and
    (ii)  had frequent contact with him,

(b)  D was such a person at the time of that act,

(c)  at that time there was a significant risk of serious physical harm being caused to V by the unlawful act of such a person, and

(d)  either D was the person whose act caused V's death or—
    (i)  D was, or ought to have been, aware of the risk mentioned in paragraph (c),

---

[210] In *R v Sheppard* [1981] AC 394 the House of Lords interpreted the word 'wilfully' as including an element of *mens rea* or intention to commit the offence. See the discussion of this in Barton and Douglas (1995) pp 138–39.

[211] Recent examples of prosecutions under this section include *R v AG* [2003] EWCA Crim 3046 (causing unnecessary suffering); *R v L (Yasmin)* [2003] EWCA Crim 1146 (neglect by leaving a young child alone at home); and see also *Re A (Children) (Conjoined Twins: Surgical Separation)* [2001] 2 WLR 480; [2001] 1 FLR 1 for a discussion of the requirement to provide medical treatment.

(ii) D failed to take such steps as he could reasonably have been expected to take to protect v from the risk, and

(iii) the act occurred in circumstances of the kind that D foresaw or ought to have foreseen.

(2) The prosecution does not have to prove whether it is the first alternative in subsection (1)(d) or the second (sub-paragraphs (i) to (iii)) that applies.

(3) If D was not the mother or father of V—

(a)  D may not be charged with an offence under this section if he was under the age of 16 at the time of the act that caused V's death;

(b)  for the purposes of subsection (1)(d) (ii) D could not have been expected to take any such step as is referred to there before attaining that age.

(4) For the purposes of this section—

(a)  a person is to be regarded as a 'member' of a particular household, even if he does not live in that household, if he visits it so often and for such periods of time that it is reasonable to regard him as a member of it;

(b)  where v lived in different households at different times, 'the same household as V' refers to the household in which V was living at the time of the act that caused V's death.

(5) For the purposes of this section an 'unlawful' act is one that—

(a)  constitutes an offence, or

(b)  would constitute an offence but for being the act of—

(i)  a person under the age of ten, or

(ii) a person entitled to rely on a defence of insanity.

Paragraph (b) does not apply to an act of D.

(6) In this section—

'act' includes a course of conduct and also includes omission;
'child' means a person under the age of 16;
'serious' harm means harm that amounts to grievous bodily harm for the purposes of the Offences against the Person Act 1861 (c 100);
'vulnerable adult' means a person aged 16 or over whose ability to protect himself from violence, abuse or neglect is significantly impaired through physical or mental disability or illness, through old age or otherwise.

(7) A person guilty of an offence under this section is liable on conviction on indictment to imprisonment for a term not exceeding 14 years or to a fine, or to both.

This offence is designed to deal with cases in which a child (or vulnerable person) dies as a result of conduct by a member of his or her household which puts him or her at serious risk of physical harm and it is not clear which of two people actually caused the death. An offence is committed if the adult household member actually caused the death, or if they were aware or ought to have been aware of the risk, they foresaw or ought to have foreseen the act causing the death, and they failed to take reasonable steps to protect the child from the risk. The prosecution does not have to prove which of these situations applies to the person(s) charged.

Before leaving the area of criminal law, reference must be made to the government's view about the role parents have in preventing their children from committing criminal offences.[212] In the White Paper (Home Office 1990a) which preceded the Criminal Justice Act 1991, the government said:

> Crime prevention begins in the home. Parents have the most influence on their children's development. From their children's earliest years parents can, and should, help them develop as responsible, law-abiding citizens. They should ensure that their children are aware of the existence of rules and laws and the need for them; and that they respect other people and their property ... .
>
> When young people offend, the law has a part to play in reminding parents of their responsibilities. (paras 8.1 and 8.2 p 40)

Few people would disagree with the first part of this statement. Many, however, disagreed with the latter part, arguing that making someone liable for the criminal behaviour of another constituted a violation of human rights, that the difficulties of proving a 'failure' to prevent behaviour were insurmountable, and that those who were likely to be punished most frequently and most severely were households already in financial or emotional difficulty.[213]

The proposed new offence was not included in the Criminal Justice Act 1991, but the combined effect of its provisions and those in the Criminal Justice and Public Order Act 1994 were to require parents to pay any fines for which their children were liable;[214] to enter into a recognizance of not more than £1,000 if the court deemed it appropriate; to take proper care of and control of their child and to be liable to a fine if they unreasonably refused to enter into such a recognizance;[215] and to be liable to be bound over where children refuse to complete community sentences.[216] Taking further these provisions for parents' responsibility for their children's behaviour, the Crime and Disorder Act 1998 gave the court the power to make a 'parenting order' if it would be desirable to prevent their children's certain anti-social, truanting or criminal behaviour.[217] As we noted above, a parenting order can require parents to attend counseling or parenting classes. And the Anti-social Behaviour Act 2003 extends parenting orders and also makes provision for voluntary parenting contracts to be entered into by parents with Local Education Authorities or youth offending teams.

**Q** Can parental responsibility to rear well-adjusted and law-abiding children be transformed into an enforceable legal duty to do so? What arguments are there for creating such a legal duty? What are the arguments against? Can responsibility for children's criminal behaviour be located with anyone apart from the child him or herself? Bainham (2005 p 657) sees these provisions as reflecting a paradoxical view of children and parents. Apart from seemingly violating basic ideas of

---

[212] See also on this Piper (2006 forthcoming).

[213] On the issue of parental liability for children's actions see Boyd (1990); Barton and Douglas (1995) pp 280–82 and sources cited therein.

[214] The CYPA 1933 s 55 governs the duty of the court to order a parent or guardian to pay a fine in respect of a child, unless to do so is unreasonable or the parent or guardian cannot be found. See further the Criminal Justice Act 1988; the Criminal Justice Act 1991, amending the CYPA 1933 s 55 by adding subs 1B. In *A v DPP, The Times*, 18 April 1996, where the child was being accommodated by a local authority, it was unreasonable to expect the parents to pay the fine. See also Criminal Justice Act 1991 s 57.

[215] Criminal Justice Act 1991 s 58.

[216] Criminal Justice and Public Order Act 1994 (Sch 6, para 50).

[217] S 8. Crime and Disorder Act 1998.

criminal responsibility, these views of children and parents *both* being responsible
for a child's criminal or anti-social behaviour are contrary to the view held elsewhere in child law that a parent has only dwindling control of a child as she gets
older. Parents here are assumed to be in control of their children and responsible
for their behaviour. See also Piper (2006 forthcoming) and Fionda (2001).

*Education*

Most people agree that education is a good in and of itself. Children in England, however, were not required to attend school until 1880. Prior to that, education was
provided on a private fee-paying or charitable basis, with schools often being run by
the Church (Cunningham 1995). Many schools for the poor were run by charities with
the specific aim of teaching children (Protestant) Christian values (Cunningham 1995
pp 119–20)

And the aims of the state were not always child-centred in providing for compulsory
elementary education.

> The state's purpose in making schooling compulsory went beyond a desire to ensure that every
> child was taught the three Rs; it wanted to instil morality, and patriotism, and to train children
> in regular habits. (Cunningham 1995 p 157)

Barton and Douglas also make this point: 'As industrial processes developed in complexity, employers saw the advantages in having a disciplined and at least partly-skilled
labour force and therefore supported the expansion of elementary education.' (1995
p 256)

They go on:

> There were tensions, first, between the needs of the economy for a skilled (or drilled) workforce
> and those of parents to support their families with the help of older offspring, and secondly,
> between the right of the state to assert what should be taught and the right of parents to con-
> trol what their children learnt. Such tensions were reflected in the low leaving age, which
> permitted parents to turn their children into economically productive units, but only as soon as
> industry could make use of them, and the control over the curriculum of Her Majesty's Inspec-
> torate whose annual inspections led to a strong ethos of 'teaching to the test'. (1995 p 266)[218]

The state, then, accepted responsibility in the 19th century for educating its youth, but it
also placed on parents a responsibility to ensure that their children received this education.

Determining a child's education is an incident of parental responsibility. This means
that parents can decide on the type of education their children receive,[219] and the ethos
of the education system since the 1980s has been to encourage parents to exercise a
'choice' in their children's education and to give them more say in the running of
schools. Education has in this way become seen as a consumer commodity amenable to
the 'rules' of the market. The consumer is, however, the parent rather than the child. The
general principle underlying the Education Act 1996 is, in fact, that children shall be
educated in accordance with the wishes of their parents,[220] and this position has the

---

[218] See also Dingwall and Eekelaar (1988).
[219] Where those with parental responsibility disagree about the child's education, they may seek a specific
issue order or a prohibited steps order under s 8 Children Act 1989. See ch 16 for a full discussion.
[220] Education Act 1996 s 9.

backing of the ECHR. Article 2 of the First Protocol of the European Convention on Human Rights states:

> No person shall be denied the right to education. In the exercise of the functions which it assumes in relation to education, and to teaching, the state shall respect the right of parents to ensure such education and teaching in conformity with their own religious and philosophical convictions.

The scope of this article was tested recently in a case in which parents (and teachers) of children at Christian independent schools argued that the prohibition on corporal punishment infringed their rights under it to ensure that their children were educated according to their religious and philosophical convictions.[221] They argued that corporal punishment was required by their religious convictions. The House of Lords agreed that while these rights were engaged, the ban on corporal punishment pursued a legitimate aim, was not disproportionate and therefore was a measure Parliament was entitled to take.

Parents nonetheless have great discretion in determining their children's education. They also have responsibilities, though. After a series of statutory measures, the obligation of parents today to ensure that their children are provided with an education is found primarily in the Education Act 1996. It places parents under a duty to ensure that children of compulsory school age—between the ages of 5 and 16—receive education suitable to their needs, ability, aptitude and age.[222] Some parents attempt to provide this education for their children at home. Where parents fail to secure the regular attendance of a registered pupil at school, they have committed an offence[223] punishable by a fine, three months imprisonment or by the issuing against them of an education penalty notice[224] by the headteacher, his or her delegate or the LEA. The penalty notice requires the parent to pay a fine in lieu of criminal proceedings being brought. If a parent fails to demonstrate that the child is otherwise receiving a suitable education, the LEA may issue a school attendance order[225] and if the parent fails to comply with it he or she has also committed an offence.[226] Otherwise the LEA can apply for a parenting order[227] or request that the parent enter into a parenting contract under the Anti Social Behaviour Act 2003.

> **Q** Should parents be guilty of a criminal offence if children are not sent to school? What about the parents of a 14 year old who regularly truants?

Civil proceedings may also be brought in the event of children's failure to attend school. The LEA can apply for an Education Supervision Order under the Children Act 1989[228] which requires the supervisor to 'advise, assist, befriend and give directions to' the child

---

[221] *R (on the application of Williamson) v Secretary of State for Education and Employment* [2005] UKHL 15; [2005] 1 FCR 498. They also claimed the prohibition violated their right to freedom of religious expression under Art 9 of the ECHR.
[222] Ss 7 and 8.
[223] Education Act 1996 s 444.
[224] *Ibid*, s 444A; Education Penalty Notice Regulations 2004 SI 2004/181.
[225] Education Act 1996 s 437.
[226] *Ibid*, s 443.
[227] Crime and Disorder Act 1998.
[228] S 36 and Part III Sch 3.

and his or her parents so as to secure that the child is properly educated.[229] In extreme circumstance a care order may be made.[230]

You will notice that the first part of Article 2 of Protocol 1 of the ECHR states that 'no person shall be denied the right to education'. This seems to suggest that education is a right belonging to the child, rather than to her parents. And Article 28 of the United Nations Convention on the Rights of the Child requires states to:

> recognise the right of the child to education, and with a view to achieving this right progressively and on the basis of equal opportunity ...
>
> (a)   make primary education compulsory and available free to all ...
> (b)   encourage the development of different forms of secondary education ... make them available and accessible to every child, and take appropriate measures such as the introduction of free education and offering financial assistance in case of need;
> (c)   make higher education accessible to all on the basis of capacity.

> **Q**   What does it mean to have a right to education? Can that right be enforced by children against parents? By children or parents against the state? See on this *R (on the application of Holub) v Secretary of State for the Home Department* [2001] 1 WLR 1359. Against a school? Does Article 2 protect the right of children or the rights of parents? See generally on children's rights and education, Fortin (2003) chapters 6, 11 and 12; Meredith (2001).

In 1988 the National Curriculum was established leading to central government control over what is taught in schools. Barton and Douglas (1995) describe this as a return to Victorian values because, among other reasons, of its emphasis on regular national testing and the publication of league tables. The general requirements of the National Curriculum are to 'promote the spiritual, moral, cultural, mental and physical development' of pupils, and to 'prepare pupils for the opportunities, responsibilities and experiences of later life'.[231] The Education Act 2002 sets out the core and foundation subjects in the National Curriculum for the 'key stages' in education. While not a part of the National Curriculum, the Act also requires the teaching of religious education (which must reflect the fact that 'religious traditions in Great Britain are in the main Christian' while taking account of other principal religions represented in Great Britain)[232] and sex education[233] (which must include, among other things 'the nature of marriage and its importance for family life and the upbringing of children'[234]) and the School Standards Act 1998 requires schools to have a daily act of collective worship[235] which 'shall be wholly or mainly of a broadly Christian character'.[236] Parents have the right to withdraw their children from sex education[237] and from RE or collective worship.[238]

---

[229] Sch 3 Para 12(1)(a).
[230] *Re O (A Minor) (Care Order: Education: Procedure)* [1992] 2 FLR 7.
[231] Education Act 2002 s 78.
[232] Education Act 1996 s 375(3).
[233] S 80.
[234] Education Act 1996 s 403(1A) (a).
[235] S 70.
[236] School Standards and Framework Act 1998 Sch 20 para 3.
[237] Education Act 1996 s 405.
[238] School Standards and Framework Act 1998 s 71.

**Q** How, in your view, does such a National Curriculum fit in with the state's role in socialising children? With a parent's role? With the rights of children to education? Is a parent's right to withdraw a child from sex education or religious education classes consistent with a child's right to education?

**Q** How, in your view, ought the responsibility for educating children to be divided between family members and schools? Does it depend upon what is being taught? Does it depend upon the age of the child? Refer back to the discussion of nursery provision for under fives in chapter 3, where one of the justifications for universal provision was its educational value for younger children.

*Housing and Health Care*

The Children and Young Persons Act 1933 makes it an offence for a parent to fail to provide adequate lodgings for a child, or to fail to procure adequate lodgings according to the appropriate statutory provisions. Those statutory provisions are discussed in chapters 3 and 13 and we will not repeat them here.

The CYPA 1933 also makes specific mention of a parent's duty to provide medical aid for a child, and stipulates that a parent who fails in that duty is deemed to have neglected the child. The state also assumes a responsibility for the medical care of children through the National Health Service, and the court is sometimes called upon to make decisions in respect of medical treatments. As is the case with education, however, the question is how the balance between state responsibilities and parental responsibilities is to be struck. We discuss this in chapter 16 and we also discuss in that chapter the third dimension added to this issue: that of the *child's* role in the decision-making process.

## V. BEING A MOTHER, BEING A FATHER AND BEING A CHILD

*Mothers and Fathers*

Parents' legal responsibilities towards their children are outlined by law in gender-neutral terms. Indeed, reading the statutes, one would not think there is any longer a difference between the responsibilities of mothers and (married) fathers in law. Recent feminist work has suggested, however, that *social* prescriptions about good mothers and good fathers are often reflected in and reinforced by legal prescriptions. Scholars have written, for example, of the ideologies of motherhood and fatherhood and noted that the two bear different meanings when reflected in legal duties and responsibilities of parents.[239]

We argued that this reflection is apparent in, for example, decision-making about prospective adopters and clients for reproductive treatment, and below[240] we will see further differences in interpretations of the welfare principle. What activities or characteristics

---

[239] See eg, Diduck (1993) and (1995); Boyd (1996); Smart (1991); Collier (1995a and b); Smart and Sevenhuijsen (1989); Smart and Neale (1999).

[240] Ch 8.

come to your mind when you think of mothering? What about fathering? Collier (1995a and b) reveals how the absent, authoritarian breadwinner was traditionally the 'father' of law and Smart (1991), Fineman (1995) and Smart and Sevenhuijsen (1989) show how mothering has traditionally meant nurturing and physical care. As all of these writers suggest, however, there is nothing biologically predetermined about these developments. Ruddick (1997) agrees:

> Ruddick (1997) also suggests that in modern Western societies the ideal father is defined by the functions of provision, protection and authority/legitimation (p 207). Crucially, however, while she recognises that mothers also fulfil these functions, they do so in a more immediate way, so that fathers provide 'distantly'—away from home—mothers more closely and intimately; fathers protect against physical intrusion or 'an uncertain and dangerous world', mothers adopt an additional focus on daily dangers or emotional suffering; and fathers represent the reality of the 'world' and its authority to judge and punish while mothers represent the comforts of home and 'soft love' (pp 207–11). Her observations have been confirmed in empirical research which shows that these gendered roles for parents are deeply entrenched in peoples' ideals of family life (Warin, *et al*, 1999, Hatten, *et al*, 2002). She states, of course, that there is nothing inherent about these characteristics, and indeed images of the 'new' caring, sharing father who changes nappies and experiences emotional intimacy with his child have abounded in the last decade or so. That men *can* 'mother' in this way is not disputed (see also Fineman 1995) and presumably this means also that women can 'father', but social and economic conditions and ideologies of motherhood, fatherhood and childhood conspire to make this type of degendered parental work difficult … . (Diduck 2003 p 85)

Despite popular accounts of the 'new' father who cares intimately for children and the 'new' mother who cares distantly for them, fathers, mothers and teenagers involved in empirical research conducted by the Family Policy Studies Centre (Warin, *et al*, 1999; see also Collier 2001 and Hatten, *et al*, 2002) reported that the central role for fathers 'these days' is the provider role, but also that it was important that the father 'be there' for his children. No one was sure, however, what 'being there' meant; it ranged from spending quality time with the children to being on call in case of emergency (Hatten, *et al*, 2002 pp 7–9). Fatherhood seems to have taken on a degree of uncertainty and ambiguity which is fed by current government policy to promote active parenting by both parents (Collier 2001). There is less uncertainty about motherhood, however. Even where parents profess to desire the co-parenting ideal, most settle into the typical pattern where mothers become primary caretakers and fathers provide 'distantly' (Hatten, *et al*, 2002). In Smart, Neale and Wade's study, 'basically fathers were one step removed from their children and their relationship with them was sustained via their relationship with the mother' (Smart, *et al*, 2001 p 47). And children themselves often see mothers as the parent who is 'the main source of physical and emotional care', and fathers as 'someone to do things with' (James 1999 p 192).

The roles that heterosexual parents play in their children's lives may thus be constrained by a gender ideology that arguably is supported by legal and cultural institutions. Dunne (2000) found that when women parent together, however, they redefine the boundaries, meaning and content of parenthood. They do not have to conform to gender scripts and have to 'make it up' as they go along (p 13). Free of the confines of heterosexual gender norms, they were able to 'operationalise their egalitarian ideals' in relation to parenting, routine domestic responsibilities and the right of each parent to an identity beyond the home (p 30–31).

**Q** After reading this chapter and chapter 3, do you see any ways in which law either facilitates or inhibits particular parental roles for mothers and fathers? Do these roles, and their shifts have anything to do with ideas of the 'good family'?

*Children*

Henricson and Bainham argue that it has always been the family that the state has been concerned to support rather than the individual rights of family members (2005 p 11), and on this view the way that motherhood or fatherhood is supported by law and policy does reflect government's ideas of the good family from time to time.[241]

However Henricson and Bainham also note that there is now a 'perceptible trend towards policies that place *children* and their rights much higher up the political agenda' (2005 p 9, emphasis added). This is evident, they say, from the provisions of the UN Convention on the Rights of the Child (p 21), the EU Charter (p 28) and the European Constitution (p 30).[242] This new focus on children's rights[243] implies, and/or stems from, a perception of children as separate and independent persons and legal personalities. 'The story of the acceptance of the notion of children's rights,' they note, 'is very largely one of gradual recognition of [children's] independent status as juristic persons and not mere adjuncts of their parents or constituent members of a family' (p 31).

Traditional ideas of children as objects of concern who can and should be moulded and socialised within the school and the private family have been challenged by researchers who have engaged directly with children. Perceptions of children now encompass the image of the child as an active participant in home and public life. Yet the image of the child as an object of care or concern also persists. Kaganas and Diduck explain:

> The newly complex paradigm child incorporates two previously competing images of the child. The first is the child as incompetent and dependent. This child is vulnerable because he or she is in the process of development toward self or personhood. This child is one whose welfare is to be prioritised over rights because he or she is not yet fully capable of exercising rights competently. This child needs to be protected. The image is rooted in philosophical ideas of the child as 'becoming' a fully rational subject, and incorporates images of the child as evil, innocent or as a blank slate. It also incorporates socialisation theory as well as ideas in developmental psychology suggesting that there is a teleological progression through various and fixed developmental stages of maturation. It can be described as a romantic developmentalist view of the child and has a veneer of common sense about it. It appears to be the dominant paradigm in which educationalists, psychologists and child welfare professionals, including CAFCASS practitioners, work.
>
> However, in contrast to this, sociologists studying childhood have begun to take seriously the idea of the child as 'being'. Rather than seeing childhood as a 'biologically determined' and universal stage, which is characterised by incompetence or irrationality, and through which all children pass on their way to completion as autonomous adults, they see it as a socially constructed space or as a variable concept. On this view, children need not necessarily be conceived of as inactive mounds of clay to be formed by socialising agents, by nature or by structural

---

[241] See also Collier (2001).

[242] See, on the constitution, Schuurman (2003).

[243] Henricson and Bainham (2005) do not regard the primacy accorded to children's rights or welfare as legitimate; they argue that this could lead to the undervaluing of the rights of other family members in contravention of the ECHR They also point out that the CRC recognises the importance to children of their parents and other family members (p 21).

forces over which they have no control. Instead, it becomes possible to put forward alternative images of children and these, according to James and Prout, have gained currency: 'Looking at children not only as outcomes of social processes but as actors within them has gained widespread acceptance'. Indeed, they highlight this as an 'emergent paradigm' for the study of childhood and identify as one of the key features of this approach the need to see children 'as active in the construction and determination of their own social lives, the lives of those around them and of the societies in which they live'. With this kind of paradigm, it becomes possible to ascribe to children the characteristics of reflexivity and agency and to see them as participants in the project of late modern individualisation. In this paradigm, children have the capacity to exercise a form of agency, a type of post-liberal autonomy, and to affect and influence their environment, conditions, attachments, detachments and self-identity. More than this, they are assigned an increasing degree of responsibility for doing so.

Both the romantic developmentalist child and the autonomous reflexive child are idealised constructs. While they are in many ways dichotomous ideals, we suggest that both contribute to the new ideal child of law. Their simultaneous presence reflects an ambivalence within the legal ideal, an ambivalence most clearly apparent in criminal law. And, while there can be little doubt that it is the dependent, romantic child that is still dominant in private family law, we are of the view that it is possible to detect in this field of discourse too increasing references to children's autonomy and responsibility.

This blending of paradigms is more than a way for law to reconcile the long-standing tension between the child as subject and as object. While that attempted reconciliation is important, we suggest that what is also important is the process and the discourse through which it is pursued. It may, in other words, reflect a more general drive to recruit children into a broader social project of promoting 'active citizenship'.

(Kaganas and Diduck 2004 pp 961–62, references omitted)

**Q** Do you agree that law reflects a 'blended paradigm' child? How has law constructed childhood in education law? In adoption law? In determining a child's parentage?

**Q** What do the authors mean by 'active citizenship'? How, if at all does law promote it?

The new way of 'seeing' children is described by Neale as being 'not simply as welfare dependants but as young citizens with an active contribution to make to society' (2004 p 1). She goes on to define children's citizenship as 'an entitlement to recognition, respect and participation' and asserts that these are 'basic needs' which are 'crucial to children's well-being' (*ibid*). Children's citizenship, she says, is 'both a need and a right' (p 9). What needs to be done, she says, is to find ways of integrating citizenship and welfare more effectively into public policy and of extending the principles of citizenship to younger children (p 2).[244]

The concept of citizenship deployed here embraces consultation in the sense of 'listening and responding to children' and entails 'inviting children to communicate and take part in decision making about matters that affect them' (p 3).[245] Those children who wish to participate should be able to do so while the wishes of those who do not should be respected (p 4). This move to participation, she observes, necessitates a change in the way that children are perceived and a change in the relationships between children

---

[244] See also Fortin (2003) ch 19.
[245] See, for example, the National Adoption Standards (DoH 2001) which were drafted after extensive consultations with children.

and adults both in the public and the private arenas. The dominant 'welfare paradigm', she says, constructs children as 'relatively incapable and vulnerable to harm, and therefore in need of strong guidance, control and support from responsible adults', particularly if they are young (p 8). Children's welfare is defined by adults. In contrast, an approach that rests on the idea of citizenship enables children to be seen as people with strengths and competencies, competencies born of experience rather than age and so potentially present in young children (p 8).[246]

Adults, contends Neale, have to recognise that children are people 'in their own right' and that 'they have their own ways of understanding the world and are capable of defining their own needs, rights, interests and responsibilities' (p 9). Adults should not necessarily control children but, instead, support them 'as they begin to take responsibility for their own lives' (*ibid*). At the same time, children do have to be protected.

This tension between welfare and rights/autonomy is apparent in the telling distinction that is made between participation and choice. Children, Neale points out, prefer to make decisions 'collaboratively with supportive adults rather than autonomously' (pp 4, 10). They 'will accept adult responsibilities to make final decisions as long as these are based on open communication and the reasons for particular decisions are made transparent' (*ibid*). 'Granting citizenship to children, then, is not the same thing as granting them autonomous political rights, nor does it detract from their welfare needs' (p 10).

We have seen that there has, indeed, been a move towards eliciting children's views on a number of issues in the public sphere such as adoption, health and education,[247] and children's views are more frequently taken into account in court proceedings impacting on their family lives.[248] Encouraging consultation with young people[249] and facilitating their participation in some form has become an important part of government policy. Whether children's views have a significant influence on decisions is open to doubt, however. Willow, for example, found that, in relation to consultation with children under 12, there was little evidence of noticeable impact and what there was, tended to be 'one-off and small scale' (2004 p 23).[250] Nevertheless the rhetoric of participation is clearly apparent[251] and children are described, like their adult counterparts, as 'customers' of services (DfES 2001 p 6).

What is striking, however, is that much of the talk focuses not only on the benefits to children and young people of being heard, but on the importance of teaching them to become responsible citizens. This is undoubtedly linked to the government's concerns about promoting social inclusion and its 'war on anti-social behaviour' (Henricson and Bainham 2005 p 35).[252] Yet Henricson and Bainham suggest that the government is promoting children's welfare rather than rights in its social exclusion strategy (2005 p 44).

---

[246] See Marchant and Kirby (2004) who contend that even infants' wishes should be taken into account when decisions and plans are made. Of course, young children's wishes might be overridden, they say, but adults should develop ways of communicating with them to enable them to express preferences. Presumably, however, those expressions of preferences are always subject to adult interpretation.

[247] See Willow (2004).

[248] See ch 16. Children's attendance at court may be becoming more acceptable. For example, the model devised for court-based first direction alternative dispute resolution schemes where parents separate envisages the attendance, where the scheme allows for this and where there are the necessary resources, the attendance at court of children aged 9 or over for the appointment. (President of the Family Division 2005 pp 7 and 10).

[249] As Marchant and Kirby (2004) say, it is young people, rather than very young children, who are normally consulted. See DfES (2001) p 5 and see also DfES (2005).

[250] See, on decisions where parents split up, May and Smart (2004); James, *et al*, (2003).

[251] Ssee eg CYPU (2001) pp 1, 6; DCA (2003a) pp 5, 21; (DCA, DfES and DTI 2005 para 52).

[252] See, regarding the government's strategy to reduce poverty and promote social inclusion, Henricson and Bainham (2005) pp 39ff.

And even the remit of the Children's Commissioner, they say, is concerned with outcomes for children rather than children's rights (p 61).

Clearly, then, the image of the child as an autonomous actor is closely constrained within the framework of welfare. The idea of the child as responsible citizen is imbued with ideas of socialisation. And the idea of consulting children does not necessarily include giving effect to their wishes.

**Q** Does government policy on children's citizenship reflect Neale's view of children's citizenship?

Children themselves tend to differ on whether they want to exercise decision-making rights. Those who do want to have some meaningful influence over their social and material lives do not necessarily wish to be independent decision-makers. Nevertheless, they do not want to be shut out from the decision-making process either. They simply wish to have a voice (Smart, Neale and Wade 2001 p 122), both in legal processes concerning them and in their everyday family practices.

> These studies have found that children also see themselves with a degree of autonomy in their construction of family and relationships. They negotiate care and support in a democratic way within their families ... . 'They viewed themselves not simply as children needing care but as young people who wanted to talk to others and be listened to, trust others and be trusted, and engage in open and meaningful communications. ... In other words, children value a democratic style of family life' (Smart, Neale and Wade 2001, p 58) in which they are active participants. (Diduck 2003 p 82)

**Q** How, if at all, can parents accommodate this 'new' child? How can law either support them or inhibit them from doing so? Consider for example, the law on corporal punishment.

## VI. CONCLUSION

We have seen how the law maintains a balance between public and private responsibility for children, but that the balance weighs in favour of private parental responsibility. We have raised questions about how the law assigns parenthood, and raised issues concerning parental autonomy and the public interest in parenting, and have complicated the matter further by introducing issues of gender and of children's autonomy. We have also considered that parents may be the same sex and that this factor may influence parenting in practice and in law. Throughout, we have inferred that much of the law and policy about parents and children is concerned primarily to promote and preserve a particular version of the family. While there are concessions made in law to new and 'messy' family practices, that version still looks remarkably like the heterosexual, nuclear, or traditional, family that we examined in chapter 1. We have also inferred that that family may be perceived as being 'in crisis' and therefore to require discipline, or a form of remoralisation (Day Sclater and Piper 2000), and that law's choices in assigning parenthood and the responsibilities that go with that assignment are a part of that remoralisation project. We shall develop these observations further in the following chapters, in which specific questions arise as to how parents and children negotiate the legal ordering of their day to day lives.

## FURTHER READING AND SELECTED RECENT REFERENCES

A BAINHAM, 'Parentage, Parenthood and Parental Responsibility: Subtle, Elusive, Yet Important Distinctions' in A Bainham, S Day Sclater and M Richards, *What is a Parent?* (Oxford, Hart Publishing, 1999).

R BARN, 'Race, Ethnicity and Transracial Adoption' in A Treacher and I Katz, (eds), *The Dynamics of Adoption* (London, Jessica Kingsley, 2000).

C BRIDGE and QC SWINDELLS, *Adoption: The Modern Law* (Bristol, Jordans, 2003).

S CHOUDHRY, 'The Adoption and Children Act 2002, The Welfare Principle and the Human Rights Act 1998—A Missed Opportunity?' (2003) 15 *CFLQ* 119.

R COLLIER, 'A Hard Time to be a Father? Reassessing the Relationship Between Law, Policy and Family (Practices)' (2001) 28 *Journal of Law and Society* 520.

R COOK, S DAY SCLATER and F KAGANAS, (eds), *Surrogate Motherhood: International Perspectives* (Oxford, Hart Publications, 2003).

G DUNNE, 'Opting into Motherhood: Lesbians Blurring the Boundaries and Transforming the Meaning of Parenthood and Kinship' (2000) 14 *Gender and Society* 11.

R EDWARDS, V GILLIES and J RIBBENS MCCARTHY, 'Biological Parents and Social Families: Legal Discourses and Everyday Understandings of the Position of Step-Parents' (1999) 13 *IJLPF* 78.

J EEKELAAR, 'Contact and Adoption Reform' in A Bainham, *et al*, (eds), *Children and Their Families: Contact, Rights and Welfare* (Oxford, Hart Publishing, 2003).

EH ERIKSON, *Identity and the Life Cycle* (London, Norton, 1980).

M FINEMAN, The Neutered *Mother, the Sexual Family and Other Twentieth Century Tragedies* (London, Routledge, 1995).

M FINEMAN and I KARPIN, (eds), *Mothers In Law* (New York, CUP, 1995).

J FIONDA, 'Youth and Justice' in J Fionda, (ed), *Legal Concepts of Childhood* (Oxford, Hart Publishing, 2001).

——, (ed), *Legal Concepts of Childhood* (Oxford, Hart Publishing, 2001).

J FORTIN, *Children's Rights and the Developing Law*, 2nd edn, (London Butterworths, 2003).

W HATTEN, L VINTER and R WILLIAMS, *Dads on Dads: Needs and Expectations at Home and at Work* (London, Equal Opportunities Commission, 2002).

P HAYES, 'Giving Due Consideration to Ethnicity in Adoption Placements—A Principled Approach' (2003) 15 *CFLQ* 255.

C HENRICSON and A BAINHAM, *The Child and Family Policy Divide* (York, Joseph Rowntree Foundation, 2005).

E JACKSON, 'What is a Parent?' in A Diduck and K O'Donovan, (eds), *Feminist Perspectives on Family Law* (London, Cavendish, 2006 forthcoming).

F KAGANAS and A DIDUCK, 'Incomplete Citizens: Changing Images of Post-Separation Children' (2004) 67 *MLR* 959.

I KATZ, 'Triangles of Adoption The Geometry of Complexity' in A Treacher and I Katz, (eds), *The Dynamics of Adoption* (London, Jessica Kingsley, 2000).

L KOHLBERG, 'The Psychology of Moral Development: The Nature and Validity of Moral Stages' in *Essays on Moral Development*, vol 2 (London, Harper and Row, 1984).

N LEFAUCHEUR, 'The French "Tradition" of Anonymous Birth: The Lines of Argument' (2004) 18 *Int J of Law, Policy and the Family* 319.

J LEWIS, 'Adoption: The Nature of Policy Shifts in England and Wales 1972–2002' (2004) 18 *Int'l J of Law, Policy and the Family* 235.

M MACLEAN and J EEKELAR, *The Parental Obligation* (Oxford, Hart Publishing, 1997).

R MARCHANT and P KIRBY, 'The Participation of Young Children: Communication, Consultation and Involvement' in B Neale, (ed), *Young Children's Citizenship* (York, Joseph Rowntree Foundation, 2004).

A MARSHALL, 'Comedy of Adoption—When is a Parent not a Parent?' (2003) 33 *Fam Law* 840.

P MEREDITH, 'Children's Rights and Education' in J Fionda, (ed), *Legal Concepts of Childhood* (Oxford, Hart Publishing, 2001).

D MORGAN, *Discovering Men* (London Routledge, 1990).

J MURPHY, 'Child Welfare in Transracial Adoptions: Colour-Blind Children and Colour-Blind Law' in J Murphy, (ed), *Ethnic Minorities their Families and the Law* (Oxford, Hart Publishing, 2000).

C MURRAY, 'Same-Sex Families: Outcomes for Children and Parents' (2004) *Fam Law* 136.

B NEALE, 'Executive Summary' in B Neale, (ed) *Young Children's Citizenship* (York, Joseph Rowntree Foundation, 2004).

E NEIL, 'Adoption and Contact: A Research Review' in Bainham, Lindly, et al, (eds), *Children and their Families* (Oxford, Hart Publishing, 2003b).

K O'DONOVAN, 'Constructions of Maternity and Motherhood in Stories of Lost Children' in J Bridgeman and D Monk, (eds), *Feminist Perspectives on Child Law* (London, Cavendish, 2000).

J PIAGET, M COOK, (tran), *The Origins of Intelligence in Children,* (New York, NY, International Universities Press, 1952).

C PIPER, 'Feminist Perspectives on Youth Justice' in A Diduck and K O'Donovan, (eds), *Feminist Perspectives on Family Law* (London, Cavendish, 2006 forthcoming)

A PROUT and A JAMES, 'A New Paradigm for the Sociology of Childhood? Provenance, Promise and Problems' in A James and A Prout, (eds), *Constructing and Reconstructing Childhood* (London, Routledge, 2003).

S RUDDICK, 'The Idea of Fatherhood' in HL Nelson, (ed), *Feminism and Families*, (London, Routledge, 1997).

M SCHUURMAN, 'Children's Rights in the Constitution for Europe' (2003) *Childright* 10.

EB SILVA, (ed), *Good Enough Mothering? Feminist Perspectives on Lone Motherhood* (London, Routledge, 1996).

C SMART, B NEALE and A WADE, *The Changing Experience of Childhood Families and Divorce* (Cambridge, Polity Press, 2001).

C SMITH and J LOGAN, 'Adoptive Parenthood as a "Legal Fiction"—Its Consequences of Direct Post-adoption Contact' (2002) 12 *CFLQ* 281.

M SMITH, 'New Stepfamilies—A Descriptive Study of a Largely Unseen Group' (2003) 15 *CFLQ* 185.

R SMITH, 'Hands-off Parenting?—Towards a Reform of the Defence of Reasonable Chastisement in the UK' (2004) 16 *CFLQ* 261.

C TALBOT and P KIDD, 'Special Guardianship Orders—Issues in Respect of Family Assessment' (2004) 34 *Fam Law* 273.

J TRISELIOTIS, 'Identity Formation and the Adopted Person Revisited' in A Treacher and I Katz, (eds), *The Dynamics of Adoption* (London, Jessica Kingsley, 2000).

J TRISELIOTIS, J FEAST and F KYLE, *The Adoption Triangle Revisited A Study of Adoption, Search and Reunion Experiences (Summary)* (London, BAAF, 2005).

B VAUGHAN, 'The Government of Youth: Disorder and Dependence?' (2000) 9(3) *Social and Legal Studies* 347.

J WARIN, *et al*, *Fathers, Work and Family Life* (London, Family Policy Studies Centre, Joseph Rowntree Foundation, 1999).

F WILLIAMS, *Rethinking Families* (London, Calouste Gulbenkian Foundation, 2004).

C WILLOW, 'Consulting with Under 12s: A Mapping Exercise' in B Neale, (ed), *Young Children's Citizenship* (York, Joseph Rowntree Foundation, 2004).


*Reports*

M BRAZIER, A CAMPBELL and S GOLOMBOK, *Surrogacy: Review for Health Ministers of Current Arrangements for Payments and Regulation, Report of the Review Team* (Cmd 4068, London, HMSO, 1998).
CYPU, *Learning to Listen: Core Principles for the Involvement of Children and Young People* (London, CYPU, 2001).
DfES, *Youth Matters* (Cmd 6629, London, TSO, 2005).
Department of Constitutional Affairs, *Involving Children and Young People: Action Plan 2003–04* (2003).
Department of Health, *Protecting Children, Supporting Parents* (London, TSO, 2000).
——, *National Adoption Standards for England* (London, TSO, 2001).
Department of Health and Welsh Assembly Government, *Adoption: National Minimum Standards* (London, TSO, 2003).
Local Authority Circular (2004) LAC (2004) 27, Department for Education and Skills
Parentline Plus, *Stepfamilies: New relationships new challenges* (London, Parentline Plus, 2005).
Performance and Innovation Unit, *Prime Minister's Review of Adoption* (London, Cabinet Office, 2000).
Secretary of State for Health, *Adoption: A New Approach—A White Paper* (Cmd 5017, London, TSO, 2000).

# 5

# Household Economics

In this chapter we explore the law's impact upon the economic ordering of households, including income generation and distribution, spending and the acquisition of wealth in the form of property and property rights. On the face of it, there is little *direct* legal regulation of the ways in which members of families order their economic and financial affairs, and some attempts at regulation have been considered inappropriate intrusions into the family's privacy and freedom to choose its own means of internal economic ordering. Once again, however, law and social policy play a large part in influencing indirectly both a family's financial arrangements and how its members determine the use of their resources.

We divide this chapter into three main parts. The first will deal with household income. We will examine questions such as how household income is generated and by whom it is generated, while the second deals with how it is distributed among members of the household and who controls that distribution and on what basis. The third part will focus upon the acquisition of property and the determination of interests in property.

There are two themes running through this chapter. The first theme is the significance of the ideology of the family to household economics. While many families do not conform to the ideal of the nuclear family, we examine the extent to which direct and indirect legal ordering of finances assumes that form. The second theme is that of equality, particularly as this principle has been applied to families and family economics. We wish to explore the impact of the principles of formal and substantive equality and of the principles of individualism, cooperation and competition.

## I. FAMILY INCOME

A household's income may come from private or public sources. By private sources, we mean the wages or salaries of those members who engage in paid labour, or income generated by any family business in which a family member has an interest. By public sources we mean income which comes directly from the state in the form of contributory or non-contributory benefits and indirectly in the form of state-provided services.

*Waged Income*

The degree to which law and policy influence the accumulation of a family's income from this outside private source is largely dependent upon the form the family takes. So, because law regulates the labour of adult, able-bodied men less rigorously than it does the labour of women of all ages and men under the age of 16 and over the age of 65,[1] families consisting of adult men only will have less legal 'intervention' to contend with in relation to how they accumulate income and then distribute it between their members. The 'free market' in which these men exchange labour, goods or services for money also constructs few social difficulties or 'barriers' for them, although immigration status, race and racism still play a part in structuring the opportunities of many.[2] On the other hand, families which include women and children, or families which comprise women and children only, will be more affected both by legal regulation of the members' opportunities for employment and by unofficial and social regulation which either inhibits or enhances those opportunities. Similarly, and as we have seen in previous chapters, whether or not the adults in the family are legally attached to each other or to the children also affects the degree of legal intervention in their family finances; some legal relationships create obligations of support.

> **Q** Legal regulation of the 'traditional' (able-bodied male) labour market, the predominant source of household income, is minimal; the National Minimum Wage Act 1998 excludes a number of categories of employees and employers, restriction upon maximum hours of work are limited to those in the Working Time Regulations 1998[3] and there are no occupations from which men are formally excluded. Regulation of the 'non-traditional' labour market (women, children and disabled men), however, is stricter. Statutory limits on the type and hours of work children may undertake are stricter than for adults,[4] and there are legal restrictions on the entry of women and children into certain occupations.[5] What forms of indirect legal or social regulation of the labour market can you think of? How might this indirect regulation affect a household's income?

> **Q** What laws exist to counterbalance the effects of direct and indirect discrimination against some workers? See particularly the Race Relations Acts 1968 and 1976, the Disability Act 1996, the Sex Discrimination Act 1975, the Equal Pay Act 1970 and chapter 3. In your view, how successfully do these laws equalise the labour market?

These forms of direct and indirect regulation are important because English law makes it clear that, at least regarding adults, whoever earns income has all legal rights to it. Further, simply because earners are married to, civilly registered with, or live with other people does not create a legal obligation to share income in any particular way, provided that a 'reasonable maintenance' is given to a spouse, civil partner or child.[6]

---

[1] See below, pp 197–99 on children's work.

[2] According to the Commission for Racial Equality (2005) half of Pakistani and Bangladeshi working households have incomes that are 50% below the average national income. In 2002 the ethnic minority employment rate for Great Britain was 59% compared to an employment rate overall of 75%.

[3] See ch 3.

[4] See below, pp 197–99.

[5] On the employment of women generally, see Whincup (1991); and Fredman (1997).

[6] Matrimonial Causes Act 1973 s 27, Domestic Proceedings and Magistrates' Courts Act 1978 s 1, Civil Partnership Act 2004 Sch 5 part 9; and see below.

*The Historical View*

While contemporary law professes no interest in the manner in which family members organise their household income, historically this was not the case. Marriage, in particular, created its own economic regime. At common law the doctrine of coverture meant that, on marriage, a wife's personal property became her husband's, and this included her earnings from paid work. Indeed, it was for this reason that, both before and after Lord Hardwicke's Act,[7] many working women chose not to marry formally, but rather to enter into informal marriages, or to 'live tally' with their partners (Parker 1987 and 1990). It was not until the Married Women's Property Acts 1870 and 1882, passed after decades of campaigning by women, that married women became entitled to keep their property, including their wages.[8]

These Acts did not pass smoothly. A newspaper editorial in the 1860s argued that such a change in the law would completely alter the relationship between husband and wife, and questioned whether it was sound policy to do this 'for the sake of a particular class of wives' (Pahl 1989 p 20).

The 1882 Married Women's Property Act established the system of separate property for spouses, which remains, in effect, the law today.[9] And, according to Pahl, the legislation 'can be seen as the greatest transfer of resources from married men to married women which has ever taken place' (1989 p 22).

Which members of families are easily able to earn has long been a matter of interest not only from the perspective of traditional family law but also in the context of labour law[10] and welfare law (Beveridge 1942).[11] In the 19th century and first part of the 20th century, it was thought that in families consisting of men, women and children, it was men who contributed income to the family by working outside the home for pay; women maintained the home by working unpaid inside the family. This assumption is still held to some degree today. Not only was this arrangement accepted socially, but global economic figures and gross national products of countries were calculated based upon the assumption that the work that (usually) men did outside the home for remuneration was real work, while the work that (usually) women did in the form of reproduction and homemaking was not.[12] Indeed, as we have seen in chapter 3, such an understanding of historical arrangements leads to statistics which indicate growing numbers of women working outside the home being construed today, just as they were in the 1880s,[13] as revealing a peculiarly modern trend. Recent historical work has suggested, however, that the traditional breadwinner/homemaker arrangement, which has been called the bourgeois family model because of its origins in the middle classes, was dominant only within certain segments of society at particular historical times and was not nearly so pervasive or universal as is popularly thought.

---

[7] An Act for the better prevention of clandestine marriages 1753. See also J Gillis (1985); Lemmings (1996); Parker (1990 and 1987) and ch 2.

[8] See generally Holcombe (1983).

[9] See below pp 212ff.

[10] As in agitation by trade unions for the 'family wage'.

[11] See below and ch 3.

[12] James (1994 p 173) estimates that women's unpaid work—in agriculture, food production, reproduction, and household activities—accounts for as much as 50% of a country's GNP.

[13] See Pahl (1989) p 20.

*Women and Work*

In medieval and early modern societies, for example, women contributed not only to household and farm work, but also to family incomes (Hudson and Lee 1990; Oakley 1985). Further, although industrialisation is often cited as the point at which the sexual division of labour in families became entrenched, even during this period, the bourgeois family model was not universal. Hudson and Lee review the history of female labour in Europe, and they conclude that women's work was persistently under-recorded in historical records (1990 p 20). Nevertheless, they do identify patterns of a 'traditional' division of labour between married men and women, and provide some explanation for the withdrawal of married women from the workplace. With respect to late 18th–early 19th century industrialisation, they indicate that the *ideology* of the family was important.

[F]emale employment during the century or so before 1945 saw greater emphasis on the role of single women and a diminished degree of participation in the formal economy by married women. In Britain in 1911, for example, 69% of all single women worked, but only 9.6% of married women [did] ...

In attempting to explain the long-term determinants of the nature and extent of women's employment, life-cycle and age-related earning patterns were clearly important. Low levels of male wages especially in the less-skilled sectors during the nineteenth century along with large family size made it essential that women earned an income both before marriage and at least during the early years of marriage until children were old enough to replace the wife's income through their own wage-earning activities ...

Changes in the extent of married women's employment in the nineteenth and early twentieth centuries also reflected the growing dominance of the bourgeois family model, in which the breadwinner was the husband and the wife and children the dependants ... . The Victorian ideal of the 'angel in the house', reflecting the influence of evangelicism and the over-riding view of women as domestic beings was clearly evident by the 1830s and 1840s, and this idealisation of femininity ... limited adult women to a narrowly defined role as wives and mothers. Diffusion of the bourgeois family model within nineteenth century European society was underpinned and reinforced by a concept of the sexes which embodied great mental and emotional distinctions. The emergent medical profession, with its image of women as conspicuous consumptives also helped to maintain the view of women as invalid, weak, delicate and invariably prone to illness.

... Formal teaching of girls in schools was equivalent to 'professional mothering' and any higher education was pursued primarily in order to train women for their domestic role ... . Increasing official concern with the potential deleterious effects on family welfare, particularly in relation to infant and child mortality, of full-time work by married women also tended to encourage the primacy placed upon domestic responsibilities. Similarly in the late 1940s and 1950s the emphasis by psychologists on maternal adequacy as the key to 'normal' child development played a role in militating against the active participation of married women in the labour force. (1990 pp 21–22, footnotes omitted)

As regards the working class, the authors point out that [n]otions of respectability were well entrenched within sections of the working class (for example, carding buttons at home was regarded as more respectable than making matchboxes). Status consciousness and increasing social stratification within the working class may well have reinforced the cult of domesticity and contributed to the low profile of women's work and its contribution to the family income.

(1990 p 23, footnotes omitted)

Davidoff, *et al*, (1999) also note how in the 19th century the cult of domesticity permeated both the working classes, perhaps partly as a way to 'lock men, particularly young
men, into steady work' (p 18), and the middle classes in which 'wifely femininity became
associated with being the mistress of a household, and masculinity with elevating the
*need* to work to a moral and respectable *duty* to do so' (Diduck 2003 p 140). The drive
for the 'family wage' and protective labour legislation were also important influences in
the dominance of the 19th century cult of domesticity. An important point to note,
however, is that while women's participation in the *formal* economy was limited, their
place in the *non-formal* economy, doing home or outwork which was not officially recognised, was more prominent (Hudson and Lee 1990 p 29). Women supplemented men's
low or seasonal wages by undertaking work such as childminding, cleaning and wash-
ing, work that could mean the difference between survival and starvation (Hudson and
Lee 1990 pp 30–31).

Married working-class women, then, have always assumed an important role in their
families' economic livelihoods, although the middle-class cult of domesticity which measured a man's status by the idleness of his dependants gradually began to pervade
working-class homes. As a result, women's earnings came to be seen as supplementary
or as their own 'pin money', and these understandings contributed to justifications for
keeping women's wages lower than men's. Even today, women tend to be defined as 'secondary earners'. The importance of these understandings for relationships within
heterosexual families should not be underestimated. In 1989, social policy researcher
Jan Pahl reported on interviews with 102 married couples about their sources of income
and patterns of money management. She found that the power of the 'secondary earner'
assumption continued even when women contributed a greater proportion of their
income to the family coffers than did men. Husbands were perceived by both spouses as
breadwinners and, therefore, as entitled to the privileges that attended this status:

> Inequality in the wider society meshes with inequality within the household. A woman may
> contribute a higher proportion of her earnings to housekeeping than her husband, but her
> income is still likely to be regarded as marginal; a man may contribute a lower proportion of
> his earnings, but he still feels justified in spending more than his wife on leisure because *both
> define him as the breadwinner.* (1989 p 170, emphasis added)

**Q** Do you think this ideology has changed? While heterosexual partners may now
expect to negotiate their respective roles in a context of publicly proclaimed gender equality, gendered norms may continue to affect those negotiations.
According to Hatten, *et al*, (2002) and O' Brien and Shemilt (2003), for example,
the breadwinner role still defines the way in which many men think about being a
good father, although it may, for some, now be tempered with 'being there' for
their children. One father expressed the breadwinner role as being important for
his self-esteem and to provide a role model for his children (Hatten, *et al*, 2002
p 7), while another confessed a 'little bit inside' him that felt he was not doing his
job properly so that [his wife] had to go to work (*ibid*). See also Burgoyne (2004)
in which she observed that in marriages where the woman is the main breadwinner, women were more likely to 'relinquish the power that usually comes to men
with this role', possibly in an attempt to 'minimise the potential discomfort that
the men might feel in occupying a non-normative, dependent position' (p 168).

**Q** What role can or should law play in challenging assumptions about men and women's social identities as workers and breadwinners?

The sources we have cited refer only indirectly to law. Law does not require men to take on the role of family breadwinner, nor is there a statutory requirement that women assume the role of homemaker. Contemporary law professes to be disinterested in relation to the sex of both workers and parents and claims to operate on an assumption of equality between the sexes. It says, in effect, that how men and women choose to order their working lives is a private decision to be made by them alone. We have seen in chapter 3, however, that a combination of low wage work for women and the assumptions in the labour market about both men and women encourages the traditional division of labour in heterosexual households, which, while the relationship is intact, may not be a problem. But, if the partners go their separate ways, the economic consequences for each are very different.

Living outside of these gendered assumptions may allow many same-sex partners to negotiate their respective roles in a more open way (Weeks 2002; Dunne 1999). One of the respondents in Dunne's research with cohabiting lesbian couples expressed it in this way:

> I suppose because our relationship doesn't fit into a social norm, there are no pre-set conditions about how our relationship should work. We have to work it out for ourselves. We've no role models in terms of how we divide our duties, so we've got to work it out afresh as to what suits us … . We try very hard to be just to each other and … not exploit the other person. (p 73)

As in the past, though, we must look today to the non-formal economy to gain a deeper understanding of family income patterns. First, significantly more women than men fall into the category of homeworkers—those engaged in baking, knitting, sewing, computing, clerical work, selling, hairdressing, teaching and childminding (Morris and Nott 1995 p 56). These occupations, which may be unrecorded or under-recorded in formal employment statistics, are less likely to receive employment protection and benefits including national insurance or holiday or sick pay. Further, both formal and informal domestic labour is performed predominantly by women, often by migrant women, and, when unrecorded, or performed by a 'close member of the family', is not subject to statutory protections.[14] Secondly, women may work without pay within a family business, just as they do within the family home, and, it seems this phenomenon is most common among some ethnic minority communities which are characterised by close ties within the extended family (Morris and Nott 1995; Breugel 1994; Anthias and Yuval-Davis 1993 pp 85–86, p 119).

Let us review the picture we have painted so far with regard to the generation of household incomes. Generally, the 'traditional' assumption that in heterosexual households, particularly in married households, men earn and women do not, or that women generally do not earn if they have children, can be challenged with reference to both modern and historical sources. Women do work outside the home, and are therefore able to contribute income as well as services to the household economy. We have also seen, however, that statistics concerning employment may not include many homeworkers, family workers or informal domestic workers. These statistics also do not include unpaid

---

[14] For the 'close relative' exclusion, see Employment Rights Act 1996 s 161. On domestic labour generally, see eg, Gregson and Lowe (1994).

work in the home or family business, which, while not ascribed monetary value, are forms of work that are of crucial importance to the family economy. It is overwhelmingly women who perform this labour, even if they also work for pay. Studies in Britain consistently show that women, even those who work outside the home full-time, retain the bulk of responsibility for organising and performing domestic labour including child care.[15] Although many studies reveal that men are increasing the amount of work they do in the home, their contribution still falls well short of what would be needed to make the division equal. However researchers have identified what they call an 'economy of gratitude', whereby if men demonstrate that they are *aware* of the inequality in the division of unpaid work and compensate with emotional support, their partners might be 'mollified', and both might accept that a 'fair' arrangement had been reached (Lewis, *et al*, 1999 pp 53–57). As the division of household labour is gendered, it may not be surprising that partners of the same sex tend to report more egalitarian negotiations in dividing it (Dunne 1999; Weeks, *et al*, 1999; Weeks 2002).

**Q** Consider these observations in the light of the public-private division and the ideology of the family.

*A Contextual Perspective*

Statistics reflecting earning in families by necessity measure a family's situation at a particular point in time. Patterns of income earning are not static, however. A family member's earnings during his or her lifetime depend upon many factors, including the stage he or she is at in the family's or individual's life cycle. Grassby (1991) identifies three sub-cycles in a household's economic cycle, although we may argue that her model is based upon the patriarchal 'traditional' model of the family which assumes that a worker has no family responsibilities. The first of Grassby's sub-cycles is the employment sub-cycle in which the early years of employment provide a basis for experience or seniority-building, the middle years provide increased revenue and the final years provide the best earning years and the basis upon which pension levels are usually determined.[16] The other two sub-cycles are the saving and spending sub-cycles which are often in direct conflict with each other. Saving is difficult in the early years when income is at its lowest and spending is at its highest, especially if there are children, and so spending predominates at that point, leaving saving for the future and for when income increases.

**Q** Who earns and how the earnings need to be spent may change depending upon the point in the household's economic cycle at which one is looking. What other variables would you suggest influence this model if we were examining a family consisting of a 22-year-old woman, her 50-year-old mother, and her 1-year-old child?

---

[15] The results of studies vary as to the exact split, but they are consistent in their findings that women spend about twice as much of their time as men doing housework. See eg 'Who does what?' (2005). Many full-time earning women have responded to their so-called 'double shift' by buying in the help in the form of (usually female) nannies or cleaners (Brannen, *et al*, 1994; Neale and Smart 2002; Hatten, *et al*, 2002; Warren 2003).

[16] We may also argue here that this 'traditional' cycle may have changed with recent changes in patterns of employment, whereby workers in their later years are more vulnerable to redundancy and where workers are told they must no longer expect 'jobs for life'. See on this Equal Opportunities Commission (1995) p 33.

Added to this view of a household's economic cycle over its life is the particular life stage of the individuals. According to the Equal Opportunities Commission Report (1995):

> The proportions [of women] in employment peak around the late teens and early 20s, followed by a fall in employment rates over the 20s during the main period of family formation. Then there is gradual movement back into work during the 30s and early 40s. From the mid–40s onwards, there is a decline in the proportions of women employed which is linked to women's health and family related reasons. This employment history has been most pronounced for women who are now in their 50s; subsequent generations have had much flatter patterns over the lifecycle.
>
> Men's employment histories are different from women's. The overall pattern is of a move into employment in the teens and early 20s, followed by fairly consistent employment levels into the 40s. Then as men start to leave the labour market, employment levels slowly decline. Younger generations of men show similar patterns of employment to older generations, but with lower levels of employment during the main working years of 30–45. Men in their 40s have experienced declining levels of full-time employment at an earlier age than men in their 50s. With male unemployment is predicted to go on rising, young men can expect less full-time employment, and for increasing numbers, an early departure from the labour market.
>
> Men's employment is mainly full-time, but many women work part-time. Women's full-time and part-time employment histories are very different, and are closely linked with child-care responsibilities. Women's full-time employment peaks in their teens, before the majority of women have started a family. Up to this age, employment patterns are similar for women whether or not they later have children. After having children, women's employment declines sharply during the 20s, only increasing again in the 30s and early 40s. The increase coincides with a move into part-time employment. (p 33)

Let us examine household income in the later life cycle, the time during which income comes through pensions accrued during working life. While the state provides a basic flat rate pension,[17] it is based upon NI contributions made during one's employment. If one is not eligible on this basis, one might be eligible on the basis of contributions made by one's husband, wife or registered civil partner, but that rate is only a proportion of the rate payable (currently 60%) from personal contributions. This basic pension is low and if it is one's only source of income one may be entitled to the means-tested Pension Credit to top it up. There is also a second tier of state pension that increases the amount payable, again based on earnings and again claimable (at a reduced rate) by the widow(er) of the pensioner. It used to be known as SERPs but since 2002 it is the State Second Pension (S2P). These second tier pensions do allow certain carers to build up 'credits' during years out of the workforce; S2P carers who are in receipt of carers' allowance and who remain out of the workforce to care for a child under the age of 6 will build up credits at the low earnings threshold. The S2P scheme is primarily aimed at low earners, however, leaving those on middle or high incomes to join occupational or personal pension schemes. These private schemes are growing in political and economic importance: '[g]overnment hopes to shift the balance in pension provision from 60% public–40% private to 60% private–40% public' (Wikeley 2002 p 625). Occupational and private pension schemes typically provide a retirement income based upon contributions made by the employee and employer during the employee's working life. They assume a model of the full-time forty year employed lifetime in order to calculate the amount

---

[17] Social Security Contributions and Benefits Act 1992 ss 43–55; see also Wikeley (2002) ch 17.

necessary for an adequate retirement income, and typically make no concession for carers (Ginn 2003 p 494). 'Contribution rates, vesting periods, retirement benefits and other terms at the heart of retirement income schemes are all selected on the premise that forty years are available to accumulate enough' for retirement (Smith 2001 p 520). And herein lies the problem for women. While women have the same ability formally to accrue these pensions as men, we have seen that their patterns of work differ markedly from the forty year full-time model on which pension accrual and entitlement are based. If the women was or is married, she may have the benefit derived from her husband's contributions, but if she is single or divorced when she reaches pensionable age, she faces the very real possibility of poverty.

> [T]he different way in which women dispose of their time, divided between the labour force and household production, is crucial [to retirement income]. Because of this most women spend less than half the years spent by men in paid employment. A woman's years in the workforce are broken by child care and shortened by elder care. They are also mostly part-time because of the enduring practice of women doing the greater share of household production even when employed. In truth women oscillate between household production and the labour force. In the former they earn little or nothing towards retirement. What they gain from the latter is diminished further by lower pay rates and lower promotion. (Smith 2001 p 520)

It is clear, therefore, that full-time employment is crucial for building private pension entitlements (Ginn 2003; Ginn and Arber 1996) and women's exclusion from these entitlements has recently come onto the public and political agenda. The Minister responsible for pensions said at the end of 2004:

> Old systems and attitudes have left their mark. Despite increasing recognition of the inequalities that women face, not enough has been done to erode the historical injustices within pension provision.
>
> We must ensure that our pension system evolves concurrently with changes in our society. It must reflect the very different role that women have in comparison to when the pension system was designed, when women were expected to marry, stay at home and raise a family while men went out to work.
>
> ...
>
> Only a half of female pensioners are entitled to a full basic State Pension compared to 90% of men. Of those women, only approximately a third receives the full pension as a result of their own contributions; the remaining having to rely on entitlement through contributions their husbands have made.
>
> On top of this, only 30% of women have additional private pension provision, compared to over 70% of men.
>
> The result of this is obvious. Women pensioners are poorer in retirement than men. It is not by chance that two thirds of those benefiting from Pension Credit are women. It is because they are our poorest pensioners. (Wicks 2004)

Income generation during different parts of a family's life cycle thus affects other parts of the cycle. Attribution of value or money's worth to some types of labour (in the public sphere) and ignoring the value of other types of labour (in the private) means that in the later cycle as well as in the earlier women tend to be poorer relative to men, and the wealth they do 'earn' tends to be derived from their status as a 'wife'. The lack of social and economic recognition of 'home' work obviously has implications for individual women, but it may also say something about the concept of citizenship that is employed in contemporary British society. We will examine this idea again below in the context of social security benefits, but at this point we wish to note one of the recommendations made by Age Concern and the Fawcett Society to remedy the gender-based unfairness of pensions. These two groups suggest that the current state system should be replaced with one that relies upon residency rather than National Insurance Contributions: a 'citizen's pension' (BBC News Online 2005).

> **Q** How would you reform pension law to take into account the many different patterns of work employed by different workers? In what way would a pension derived from residency be a 'citizen's pension'? What model of citizenship does it invoke?

### *Children and Work*[18]

Adult women and men are often not the only members of households to bring in income. We stated earlier that children's employment is relatively strictly regulated by law, but children continue to participate in both the formal and informal economies in Britain. They engage in unpaid labour in the home, by babysitting and helping with household chores. This work, like women's work in the home, has traditionally been ignored when the family economy is studied. In addition, children often contribute to the family's finances by generating their own pocket money or money which becomes a part of the household budget. It has been found that nine tenths of children performed in the non-formal economy by doing household jobs, half performed babysitting duties for families and neighbours, three quarters ran errands, 26% worked in the family business, and many were responsible for light work on family farms (Bond 1996 p 300).

Regulation of children's hours of work and types of work is by both UK domestic law and International instruments.[19] The primary domestic legislation is the Children and Young Persons Act 1933, as amended primarily by the Children (Protection at Work) Regulations 1998[20] which implement the EC Directive on the Protection of Young People at Work.[21] Taken together, they regulate the work of 'children', who are defined as those under the legal school leaving age of 15, and who should be distinguished from 'young people', defined as those between ages 15 and 18.[22] The 1933 Act provides that no child under the age of 14 shall be employed in any work other than as an employee of a parent in light agricultural or horticultural work on an occasional basis.[23] Children are also prohibited from doing any work other than 'light work': work which does not jeopardise a child's safety, health, development, attendance at school or participation in work experience.[24] The Act also provides limits on the hours of work children may work per day and per week, and also for ensuring that they have at least two consecutive weeks off work during school holidays.[25]

---

[18] For an overview, see Bainham (2005) pp 679–88.

[19] See eg. Hamilton and Watt (2004).

[20] SI 1998/276.

[21] Council Dir 94/33/EC.

[22] There are fewer restrictions on the work of young people, who, for the most part, are treated as adults, with the exception of some specific requirements imposed upon their employers regarding health and safety at work. (Health and Safety (Young Persons) Regulations 1997 SI 1997/135. See Bainham 2005 p 688.)

[23] S 18(1).The minimum age at which children can be employed in such work is 13. (Children (Protection at Work) Regulations 2000 (Nos 1 and 2) SI 2000/1333 and SI 2000/2548. See Bainham (2005) p 683.

[24] S 18(1) and (2A).

[25] S 18(1).

Section 18(2), however, empowers the Secretary of State to make regulations providing for exceptions for children aged 13, for certain types of work and in relation to conditions of employment.[26]

Taken together, the UK and EU provisions represent a movement away from historical views of the role of children and of child labour in the family. That view, held by even the most compassionate of reformers in the 19th century, is described by Cunningham as follows:

> The utilitarians did not object to child labour in principle, only to its excess. Time in childhood, they argued, must be set aside for schooling and physical growth. But beyond that, and beyond a certain minimum age, there was no reason why children should not go to work and contribute to the family economy. (1995 p 142)

Cunningham explains the movement away from this view as a type of romanticism captured by and propounded by both the romantic literati such as Wordsworth and Elizabeth Barrett Browning and by campaigners for the emancipation of the slaves who were able to deploy similar arguments about children (1995 p 140). While the state had long regulated the employment of children, they introduced the notion that children had a right not to work at all (1995 p 138).

Bond explains the movement in slightly different terms:

> Whereas the family environment had earlier provided a means of production for peasant families, the process of industrialization demanded that workers move away from the family and compete in the labour market as individuals. Although at first, children continued to be involved in providing the family with a livelihood, the physical separation was reinforced by the gradual imposition upon working-class families of bourgeois ideology, which recognized a man's status by the domesticity of his wife and children and demanded legislation designed to restrict the participation of women and children in the labour market. Several other factors also influenced the legislation: the recognition that the cheap labour of children was undercutting the wages paid to adults; a humanistic concern with the exploitation of children; and an understanding that since children were the key to the country's future economic and military well-being, the preservation of their health was important. (1996 pp 297–98)

She attributes some of this process to an ideology of family privacy whereby the family was separated from the public world of the market, but points out that that same ideology was also responsible for much of the resistance to child labour legislation in the 19th century. For example, it was thought that restricting children's labour in mines and factories was an unwarranted intrusion into parental control over children (Bond 1996 p 298), and she suggests that the ideology of family privacy is what continues to maintain contemporary private exemptions from child labour restrictions, such as those which create exceptions where children are employed by parents in light agricultural work or street trading.

There is a sense in middle class society, that when children work, they do it 'so as to learn the value of an honest day's labour' or 'to learn the value of money', rather than to contribute to the family's finances. Indeed, current understandings of childhood are

---

[26] See also s 20 in relation to street trading and also ss 24, 25, 37 and 39 of the Children and Young Persons Act 1963 regarding children's work in performances, and the Education Act 1996, which requires children's attendance in school between the ages of 5 and 16 (s 8, as amended by the Education Act 1997). Regulations concerning the working time for adolescents—those aged between 15 and 18—are included in the Working Time Regs 1998.

such that the child him- or herself is the antithesis of the worker. Modern childhood is supposed to be the stage at which one does not have the responsibilities of adulthood and when one is supposed to be innocent and free to play and to learn and to mature.[27] In many respects, this is the legacy of the 19th century romantic notions of childhood as a period of innocence. Cunningham quotes one American campaigner as saying 'the term child labor is a paradox for when labour begins ... the child ceases to be' (1995 p 144).

**Q** Does British law reconcile the identities worker and child in a satisfactory way? In your view, can they be reconciled? Is your view influenced by your view of what childhood represents, or an ideology of childhood?

*Other Income*

Income for families may come from another private source in the form of support payments made by non-resident spouses or civil partners, ex-spouses or ex-civil partners and parents. Once again, these obligations stem from the common law duty of a husband to maintain his wife and legitimate children, but now are enshrined in legislation which may extend the obligation beyond both the marriage bond and the old category of legitimacy. Support on separation, divorce or dissolution of civil partnership is at the discretion of a court or may be negotiated between the separating parties. The law is contained in the Matrimonial Causes Act 1973 as amended,[28] the Civil Partnership Act 2004,[29] and the Domestic Proceedings and Magistrates' Courts Act 1978[30] and it provides for interim and final orders, for negotiated agreements and for lump sums as well as periodical payments. Support for children is provided for in the Children Act 1989,[31] the Matrimonial Causes Act 1973 and Civil Partnership Act 2004 (as above), the Domestic Proceedings and Magistrates' Courts Act (as above) and the Child Support Act 1991.[32]

The effect of private maintenance payments on a family's economy varies according to the level of the payment, the proportion of total income it represents, its regularity and enforceability and whether or not the family is in receipt of income support or other state benefits. Any income from maintenance in excess of £10.00 per week is deducted from income support, and this particularly affects lone mothers in receipt of child support because of the large numbers who rely upon income support as their sole or main source of income.

There is no duty of support in Britain between cohabiting partners or former cohabiting partners,[33] but the social security system does take the cohabiting relationship into account for both same and opposite-sex partners. Claimants are treated as members of

---

[27] See, eg, on views of childhood Bar-On (1997); Diduck (1999a); Archard (1993); Jenks (1996); Prout (2005).
[28] Part II ss 21–40.
[29] Sch 5 Pt 9.
[30] Ss 1–8 and 19–32.
[31] S 15.
[32] For good histories of these jurisdictions, see Barton and Douglas (1995); Smart (1984); Cretney (2003a); and Finer and McGregor (1974), and for a clear exposition of the current law see Cretney, *et al*, (2002 ch 14); MacLean and Eekelaar (1997).
[33] But see Law Society 2002b and ch 2 above.

'families' for the purpose of calculating benefits. Children are not obliged to support their parents.[34]

In contrast, many jurisdictions around the world provide for such obligations for cohabitants and for children. In some other common law jurisdictions, for example, there is a statutory obligation to contribute to the support of a former cohabitant in certain circumstances. New South Wales in Australia has enacted such a statute, as have most provinces in Canada. In Canada, this provision extends to same-sex relationships (Bailey and Bala 1998).

> **Q** How, if at all, would you legislate for the support of cohabitants or former cohabitants? For parents or other family members? What would be your rationale for your decision?

We will discuss the law and policy of financial readjustment on divorce or dissolution in chapter 6. We discuss child support here for two reasons: first, because its significance goes beyond marriage to encompass lone parent families as well and, secondly, because child support has been identified by the government as a key aspect of its strategy to combat child poverty. The importance of child support in the lives of so many families means that it crosses the divide between public and private responsibility for family support.

## *Child Support*[35]

Millar (1996) places Britain in the category of states which adopt policies indicating a preference for 'private responsibility' when it comes to child support. Indeed, it was the fact that a relatively high proportion of a lone parent's income came from benefit and a relatively low proportion from private support (and what this ratio meant both ideologically and materially in terms of the state's budget) that formed the primary driving force behind the implementation of the Child Support Act 1991 (CSA).[36] That Act, as it has been amended from time to time, is the primary legislative provision regarding child support. We review the history and policy of the Child Support Act 1991 in chapter 13. Here, we wish simply to review its place as ensuring a source of income for families.

The Child Support Act 1991 was radical in its effects. It appeared at first to remove all decisions about child support from the parties and the courts and to place them in the hands of a *quasi*-governmental agency which itself was tied to an apparently inflexible formula for calculating quantum. It aimed to increase the number of parents who received income from the other parent and to increase the amount they received. The history behind such a drastic move sheds some light on the difficulties the Act was designed to remedy, as well as those that it created.[37]

Most evidence regarding child support awards before the CSA came into force suggested that the awards varied greatly both in terms of their size and in the proportion they represented of the payer's income, although their variation in the proportion they

---

[34] But see Maclean and Eekelaar (2004) in which a considerable variation, according to marital status, gender and ethnicity, was found in how members of couples accepted obligations toward elderly relatives.

[35] And see chs 13 and 15.

[36] See also *Children Come First* (1990); Keating (1995); Diduck (1995); MacLean and Eekelaar (1993); MacLean (1994).

[37] See ch 13.

represented of the recipient's income was not so great (Glendinning, *et al*, 1996). Douglas (2004) observes that by the end of the 1980s:

> Many couples reached settlements (often, it seems, approved by the courts in consent orders) whereby the husband/father provided no ongoing maintenance, not only for the wife, but also for the children, in return for giving up his share in the family home. Moreover, even where child maintenance was ordered or agreed, the amounts payable were all too often based on little more than 'gut feeling' as to what it was appropriate to expect a particular parent to pay, rather than on a rational assessment of what the child needed. To add to the inadequacy of the court regime, the Government found widely differing levels of maintenance being set in similar circumstances. As the final straw, they also found that barely a quarter of those required to pay were making regular payments. (p 203)

Eekelaar (1991b) also found that 54% of registrars[38] deciding child support claims declined to use any kind of guideline to set the amount, relying instead upon what they termed 'common knowledge' about raising children, and that those who did use guidelines favoured income support levels (p 95). For the government, these findings amounted to a crisis over a parent's abdication of personal responsibility for his children and a crisis in the rationality and consistency of the court system (Diduck 2003 p 172). Lone parent recipients of maintenance also were dissatisfied with the low levels of support awarded and its inconsistent enforcement, but they also expressed some satisfaction with the control the system allowed them to keep over decisions to claim and to distribute any money they received informally from the non-resident parent (Clarke, *et al*, 1994 and 1995). Non-resident parents, for their part, also preferred a system which allowed them, even informally, to control the timing and the amount of support paid, and often the way it was spent. These fathers did not view child support as an unconditional obligation, but viewed it as an expression of care for their children, contingent upon the history of the relationship with the mother and thus as mediated through the mother (Bradshaw, *et al*, 1999). They often drew a conceptual distinction between paying informally for specific items or days out and paying day to day maintenance for children, and were often less inclined to pay maintenance.

Eventually, most observers agreed that 'something ought to be done'; justice was clearly not being done for lone parents or for children (or for the taxpayer!). In 1990 the government issued a White Paper (DSS 1990) linking child support with the welfare of the child and with the responsible behaviour of parents. Rather than adopting other solutions such as the issue of guidelines to courts, the Act it proposed was far more radical. Glendinning, *et al.* summarise concisely the main provisions of the original version of the Child Support Act 1991:

> —The establishment of the Child Support Agency, responsible for the assessment of all child maintenance payments and their collection where requested.
> —The creation of a universally applicable but complex formula to calculate liability for child maintenance. The formula was originally based upon income support levels and did not take into account an 'absent parent's actual expenditure', other than some housing costs. Subsequent amendments to the formula have aimed to reduce the levels of hardship reported by some 'absent parents' and their new families.
> —All 'parents with care' claiming means-tested income support, family credit or disability working allowance are *required* to authorize the Secretary of State to recover maintenance from

---

[38] Now district judges.

the 'absent parent', and to co-operate with the Child Support Agency in tracing an 'absent parent', assessing and collecting any maintenance owed. Only where a 'parent with care' can demonstrate 'reasonable grounds' for believing that this would cause her or a child to suffer 'harm or undue distress' is this requirement waived.

—Where a 'parent with care' refuses to co-operate without being able to demonstrate a 'risk of harm or undue distress', the personal allowance element of her benefit is reduced by 20% for six months and 10% for a further twelve months. Both the level and the duration of this deduction are to be increased.

—'Parents with care' on income support have *all* maintenance deducted, pound for pound, from their benefit; 'parents with care' on family credit have £15 maintenance 'disregarded' in calculating their entitlement. (1996 pp 276–77)

This first version of the Act fell into difficulties almost immediately, and was subject to widespread derision. Failures in implementation meant that money was not being assessed or collected for parents with care, and non-resident parents[39] also claimed they were being unfairly treated. As a result of high profile media coverage of opposition to the Act, government made a number of changes to it. Glendinning, *et al*, (1996) summarise the most significant changes made to the Act in the 1995 legislation:

—The introduction of a discretion to 'depart' from the standard maintenance assessment formula in certain closely specified circumstances, to take account of special hardship or other factors.

—Further adjustments to the formula to take greater account of the needs of 'second' partners and children, of an 'absent parent's' travel-to-work costs and of earlier capital property settlements between separating partners.

—From April 1997, lone parents in receipt of income support or the new jobseeker's allowance will be able to build up maintenance 'credits' of £5 a week, which will be repaid as a lump sum when they start working more than sixteen hours a week. (1996 p 285)[40]

In 1998 the government published a Green Paper (Department of Social Security 1998) proposing to reform further the law of child support. It confirmed the government's commitment to ensuring that parents fulfil their responsibilities for their children and to a non-discretionary system of assessing child maintenance, but it acknowledged that too many difficulties continued to beset the administration of the complicated formula then in use. Its primary solution was to simplify the formula.[41]

Even this solution has not worked, however, and the new Child Support Act[42] has also been subjected to criticism (HC Work and Pensions Committee 2005; Chapter 13). Government's commitment to the CSA remains unshaken, though, and the CSA now forms an integral part of the government's plan to eradicate child poverty. In the Child Poverty Review (HM Treasury 2004), government set itself the target of 'increasing the proportion of Parents With Care on Income Support and Income-based Jobseeker's Allowance who receive maintenance for their children to 65% by March 2008' (p 19).

**Q** Comment upon the primary role that private maintenance appears to have in the government's plans to eradicate child poverty. In contrast, Fineman (2004) has argued:

---

[39] They were called 'absent parents' in this Act.
[40] See also Clarke, *et al*, (1996); chs 13 and 15.
[41] For a full discussion see ch 13 below.
[42] The Child Support Act 1991 as amended by the Child Support, Pensions and Social Security Act 2000.

Child support is not a viable solution to the problems of child care and dependency. In fact, the theoretical development of child support stands as a diversion to the development of effective policy. On an ideological level, primarily because it is based on the traditional notion of a nuclear family, child support furthers the assumption that dependency is a private matter. Indeed, insistence on child-support policy is an attempt to reconstruct the gendered complementarity of the traditional family through the imposition of the economically viable male. (p 203)

She then refers to research that demonstrates that on a practical level child support has only a small relationship to child poverty and concludes by saying:

It may be that we want to establish and collect child support orders for reasons other than that they can in fact substitute for governmental of collective assistance to children in poverty, but in doing so, we should not delude ourselves that we are solving the larger problem. (p 204)

Comment on Fineman's position.

The Finer Committee (1974) had envisaged a degree of state responsibility for assisting one parent families living in poverty. The main features of the 'guaranteed maintenance allowance' proposed by the committee were to provide a non-contributory fixed benefit to all one-parent families which would substitute for maintenance payments. Maintenance would be collected by the authority administering the allowance (Finer 1974 vol 1 para 5.104 pp 295–96). In its review of the 'failures' of the new CSA, the HC Work and Pensions Committee (2005) recommended that government explore the possibility creating such an allowance, called 'guaranteed child support' (para 152). The government's response was that to do so would

destabilise the situation and undermine the principle that parents should provide financial support for their children. The government does not support the principle of guaranteed maintenance. This would essentially become an additional benefit payment, no longer linked to the non-resident parent and the support of their children. The danger is that parents on benefit would lose their incentive to comply with the Agency. (Select Committee 2005)

**Q** In arriving at the machinery of the CSA to remedy the perceived injustice to lone parents, how do you think the government viewed the following issues?[43] First, how did it define the problem (was it child poverty or the burden of state expenditure)? Secondly, how should responsibility for children be allocated between public and private?[44]

*State Income*

You will recall from our discussion in chapter 3 that households receive income from 'public' sources as well as private ones. In Britain, the 'contested—and shifting—

---

[43] See Eekelaar (1991b) pp 101–5.
[44] See in this regard *Delaney v Delaney* [1990] 2 FLR 457 and the philosophy espoused in the 1990 and 1999 White Papers.

boundary between state and private responsibility' (Fox Harding 1996 p 108) for support has been negotiated differently at different times. In this section we will not repeat the details of the benefits to which families are entitled, but wish to focus upon their policy implications for families and individuals, and to look particularly at how that policy has resolved the contested boundary between public and private support.

The history begins with the first official legislation providing for public responsibility to support those who were not able to support themselves. The Tudor Poor Law of 1601 was concerned with controlling labour and the movement of people, but also sought to provide for their support by placing obligations upon kin to contribute and to reimburse the parish for support already extended. That law has been called a separate system of family law for the poor (ten Broek 1963–64), or a third system of family law (Finer and McGregor 1974 p 268).[45] According to ten Broek:

> The poor law was thus not only a law *about* the poor but a law *of* the poor. It dealt with a condition, and it governed a class. The special legal provisions were designed not to solve the causes and problems of destitution but to minimise the cost to the public of maintaining the destitute. They were accordingly concomitants of the central concept and great achievement of the poor law—the assumption of public responsibility for the support of the poor—and the necessity it entailed of keeping public expenditure down. (1963–64 p 268)

The modern history of state support for the poor begins with the Poor Law of 1834. Finer and McGregor (1974) say that this Act:

> under the influence of Malthus, imported Elizabethan severities into the society of early industrialism. On this view, poverty was an inescapable part of the natural order of society. Hence it was a leading principle in 1834 to reinforce the distinction between the ordinary poor and paupers, between poverty and destitution, by treating the indigent in accordance with the master formula of 'less eligibility' ... .
>
> ... [L]ess eligibility was to be enforced by abolishing all forms of assistance for able-bodied paupers and their families in their own homes, and by requiring them to be relieved in a workhouse. The workhouse would impose severely deterrent conditions upon its inmates as well as subjecting them to a loss of civil rights, separation from their spouses, and a deliberately imposed stigma of pauperism. It would, therefore, serve both to test the genuineness of destitution—the so-called workhouse test—and to provide an incentive for the pauper to become an independent labourer. In the commission's report, the inmates of the workhouse were to be classified into groups ranging from the impotent aged to the able-bodied and treated with a discriminating severity related to the degree of their moral delinquency. (pp 114–15)[46]

**Q** How would you describe the state's responsibility for supporting families in these laws? Is it closer to the public or the private end of the continuum? Review our discussion of state support for children in chapter 3. Do you see any remnants of the principle of 'less eligibility' in the contemporary law?

This legislation remained in effect until after the Second World War, when legislation based upon Sir William Beveridge's 1942 report was enacted, first in relation to family

---

[45] According to Finer and McGregor (1974), the first two were the common law, which regulated the family lives of the bulk of the population, and the law of trusts and the canon law, which regulated the family lives of the rich and powerful.

[46] And see Finer and McGregor (1974) as well on reactions to the Poor Law and on its break up. For the gendered basis of this law, see Daly (1994).

allowances in 1945[47] and then, as part of the primary foundation of the modern welfare state, the 1946 National Insurance Act and the 1948 National Assistance Act. The idea behind the Beveridge Report was that a compulsory scheme of social insurance paid in return for contributions from earnings was the best way the state could contribute to those families in need. Beveridge did recognise that there would continue to be a residual need for those persons who were not able to work and were therefore not entitled to such contributory benefits, and so he proposed the creation of a 'safety net' of means-tested non-contributory benefits.

Beveridge did not envisage 'workers' to be a gender neutral category.

The welfare and appropriate role of women occupied a central place in the Beveridge schema. The man and his wife as a team, the subsidiary nature of female employment, the sanctity of the family as an economic and moral entity, along with the principles of insurance and subsistence, were the main philosophical tenets underlying Beveridge's proposals. While concerned to give official recognition to the (unpaid) work that women had always done, Beveridge also ensured that women would be retained in their traditional role. 'In the next thirty years housewives as mothers have vital work to do in ensuring the adequate continuance of the British race and of British ideals in the world'. Given this function, it is hardly surprising to find that for Beveridge men's support of their wives was a lifelong obligation, that married women normally did no or negligible paid work and that couples who lived together with regular sexual relations and shared expenses were always heterosexual. Beveridge's fundamental assumption about married women was that public income maintenance was secondary for them because of the security offered by men in marriage. Single women—a minority of women—were, however, to be treated like men. (Daly 1994 p 786)

Daly argues that British income maintenance provisions, then and in the 1990s, displayed a

complex interplay of programmes oriented to the support of families and family obligations. Thus, the family is most commonly the unit of reference, especially in social assistance, and male and female access to welfare is constructed in such a way as to encourage family obligations. Provisions are gendered to the extent that women and men are assigned different roles and responsibilities. Men are, as far as possible, constructed as providers, and maintainers of family well-being. The possibility of them being full-time fathers is more or less eliminated: they are encouraged, if not compelled, to be economically active. Thus, men receive payments mainly if they experience labour market-related contingencies: accident, illness, redundancy, unemployment. British women, in contrast, are encouraged to be carers, although, increasingly on a part-time basis. Provisions at various stages have re-inforced a caring role for women. They have also generally constructed this work as unpaid, although the introduction of contingency, non-contributory benefits for carers in recent years moves some way towards state subsidisation of this form of work. Women have also been typically constructed as dependents of men. The case of widows provides a good example. For long treated more generously than other solo mothers, in effect their privilege derives from the rights of their husbands and traces its roots to the male obligation to maintain. The case of other solo mothers is more complex and appears to be underpinned by an emphasis on their motherhood role. Thus labour market participation for them is not encouraged to the same degree as it is for other people dependent on state support. (1994 p 793)

---

[47] The Family Allowances Act 1945 was passed as a result of decades of campaign, not least by early feminists such as Eleanor Rathbone. See also Pascall (1997).

> **Q** Daly's comments are pertinent to the Beveridge Report itself and to the legisla-
> tion enacted pursuant to it, but to what degree are they accurate in relation to
> contemporary income support provision? Keep Daly's words in mind as we con-
> tinue our review of British welfare provision. Refresh your memory from chapter
> 3 regarding state provision for children in families. Are Daly's ideas supported by
> those rules?

You will recall that the principle that family members are responsible for relatives was
first consolidated in 1601. Since then, there have been changes to that responsibility,[48]
but even the 1948 Act did not derogate from it entirely. Finer and McGregor describe
the changes as follows:

> The National Assistance Act 1948 decreed, 'The existing Poor Law shall cease to have effect',
> and set up the National Assistance Board. It restricted the liable relative obligation to hus-
> bands and wives and to parents and children, but it relieved children of the existing statutory
> duty to support their parents. The Act imposed maintenance obligations equally on both
> spouses, and did not, in its own terms, make these obligations conditional on the continuance
> of cohabitation or the absence of matrimonial offence on the part of the spouse to whom the
> obligation was due. But a decision in the High Court restricted the absolute terms of the statute
> and relieved a spouse of the support obligation in respect of another who was adulterous or in
> desertion. The powers of the National Assistance Board in respect of liable relatives were
> transferred unaltered to the Supplementary Benefits Commission by the Ministry of Social
> Security Act 1966. (1974 p 148)

Supplementary benefits were changed to Income Support in 1988 and since then a number of other changes have been made to the system which, arguably, have rendered it
unrecognisable from its origins.[49] We have seen that the primary policy imperative
behind these changes has been to move people from welfare into work, and that this policy is implemented by setting a number of 'work focused' conditions for entitlement and
by increasing the incentives to 'make work pay'. We have also seen, however, that these
policies have been criticised as relying mistakenly upon the assumption that the benefit
claimant will act as a rational economic actor and consider only the economic implications of his or her actions (Barlow and Duncan 2000a; 2000b; Barlow, *et al*, 2002).
These 'rationality' and 'morality' mistakes not only risk alienating some claimants, particularly mothers, but also have the potential to result in unfairness to them.

　　These welfare reform policies of successive New Labour governments have marked a
significant shift 'away from the traditional social insurance model of social security'
(Wikeley 2002 p 8). The language in which these policies have been promoted mirrors
that by which other policy shifts (such as in Child Support and private pension provision) have been presented: the language of responsibility. In the context of social
security

> These initiatives reflect [...] the [...] government's emphasis on reciprocity or 'welfare
> contractualism' as the basis for a reformed welfare state. In particular, this ideology holds that,
> as a condition of eligibility for benefit, the state may legitimately enforce the citizen's responsi-
> bilities, most notably the responsibility to work or at least to engage in active job search and
> training. (Wikeley 2002 p 8)

---

[48] See, eg, the Poor Law Act 1927.
[49] See ch 3.

Plant (2003) goes further and suggests that the reforms may actually transform political and philosophical notions of citizenship.

> The first view of citizenship is that it is a *status* which is not fundamentally altered by virtue, or lack of it, of the individual citizen, and irrespective of whether the individual citizen is making a recognised contribution to society. As a basic status that comes through membership of a particular political community, citizenship implies a set of rights; these rights are of two sorts: rights to be left alone ... that is to say negative rights; and positive rights to the economic and social conditions of citizenship—health, education and welfare. On this view, status and membership are the crucial issues in relation to rights, not whether a particular citizen makes a positive contribution to society as a whole. ... The rights are linked to the possession of common needs for security, health and education. As common needs their moral force should be recognised by society and the means of their satisfaction financed out of general taxation ...
>
> The second, and alternative, view of citizenship places much less emphasis on rights and focuses instead upon *obligation, virtue and contribution*. On this view, citizenship is not a kind of pre-existing status, but rather something that is developed by contributing to the life of society—it is an *achievement* rather than a *status*. The ideas of reciprocity and contribution are at the heart of this concept of citizenship: that individuals do not and cannot have a right to the resources of society unless they contribute to the development of that society through work or other socially valued activities, if they are in a position to do so. Citizenship has to be earned, it is not a given. (emphasis in original) (Plant 2003 pp 154–55)

If changes to social security are indeed a part of broader changes in ideas of citizenship, it is worthwhile to ask who is most easily accommodated and who is usually excluded from the new model of British citizenship. First, by linking employment to citizenship this policy is dangerously dependent upon the market order in general and the labour market in particular (Plant 2003 p 164). Those whose jobs are most vulnerable in such markets will be most easily excluded from citizenship and those who cannot be active in the labour market for other reasons are equally at risk of social and political exclusion. Disabled people, children[50] or people who care for others outside of the market, that is, on the private side of the public/private divide, are the most obvious candidates for such stigmatisation and exclusion. And as long as women remain the primary source of unpaid care in society, the gender implications of it are clear. We saw these principles in the discussion above on pensions.

Further, attributing as valuable or worthy of earning citizenship rights only *paid* labour is also problematic for women, children and others who face legal, moral, social or physical barriers to entering the workforce. Carers particularly are in a push-pull situation. At the same time as it valorises paid work for all, government also valorises 'the family', an institution, as we have seen, to which roles are clearly assigned. Its primary role is the care of dependants. While carers are also dependent because they depend upon resources in order to undertake that care, those resources are assumed to be subsumed within the self-sufficient family (Fineman 2004 chapter 2) and the recent welfare reforms that prioritise 'workless households' rather than 'workless individuals' collude in this assumption (Bennett 2002).[51] It seems that the reforms aim to reduce 'dependency' but only dependency on the state, not dependency on other individuals (*ibid*).

---

[50] For a discussion of children and young people in social security law, see Wikeley (2001). He describes the ideological underpinning of the poor law as 'mask[ing] both paradoxes and conflicts in the law's treatment of children and young people as nascent full members of the community' (p 223).

[51] See also Bennett (2005).

Finally, basing entitlement to, and the amount of, income support upon the 'family' rather than upon the individual makes the assumption that the money received is distributed equitably among 'family' members. But Lister, *et al*, (1999) studied couples with children in receipt of means-tested social security benefits and found that spending patterns *and* expectations regarding those patterns were highly gendered.

> Men prioritized personal spending money more highly than women, who typically took responsibility for vigilant restraint over both their own and their partners' spending, going without themselves to prioritize their children's needs. In practice, the distinction between 'individual' and 'collective' expenditure was sometimes muddied; men tended to legitimate elements of their 'individual' spending as having a collective benefit and to define women's 'collective' spending on their children as 'individual'. The latter reflected a belief, shared by men and women, that responsibility for meeting children's everyday needs was the woman's domain.
>
> (pp 205–6)

**Q** In what ways is welfare and social security policy consistent with the model of the private family? In what way is it consistent with the individual earner model? Do you think it strikes an appropriate balance between public and private? Is social security law still 'family' law' for the poor? Comment upon Plant's idea of citizenship becoming dependent upon economic productivity in the context of the Fawcett Society and Age Concern's call for a 'citizen's pension' (see above).

## II. DISTRIBUTING INCOME

With the exception of that earned by middle-class children, we tend to assume that money received by individuals from waged work or from the state is usually pooled in the family coffers. We said earlier that the way in which money is distributed from those coffers among family members is only regulated directly to the extent that the law imposes a mutual obligation of support upon civil partners or spouses and upon parents to support their children. The spousal obligation stems from the common law duty of a husband to support his wife (Cretney 2003a; Finer and McGregor 1974), and is now enshrined in statute as a reciprocal obligation between spouses and civil partners.[52] The legislation is limited in scope and effect, however. As we stated, unlike similar legislation in other jurisdictions, it does not apply to cohabitants,[53] and it refers only to 'reasonable maintenance'. The duty imposed on parents to support their legitimate children stems from the common law, although it has been called an 'imperfect duty' and historically was one for which the common law provided no enforcement mechanism (Smart 1987; see also Cretney 2003a). So-called illegitimate children were the responsibility of the parish and the mother until bastardy proceedings for child maintenance were introduced in 1871,[54] which in 1957 became affiliation proceedings.[55] Support for children is now

---

[52] See above, p 199.
[53] And does not automatically apply to void marriages: *J v S-T (Formerly J) (Transsexual: Ancillary Relief)* [1997] 1 FLR 402 (CA).
[54] The Bastardy Act 1733, amended in the Bastardy Laws Amendment Act 1871.
[55] Affiliation Proceedings Act 1957.

enshrined in the Children Act 1989, the MCA 1973 and, most controversially, the Child Support Act 1991.[56]

Distribution of income among family members apart from these duties of support is unregulated by law. Social science research tends to equate the living standards of dependants with those of the breadwinner, assuming that the altruistic and co-operative nature of the family means that income is allocated equally among all. Pahl put it in these terms:

> When a single person lives alone he or she is likely to be both the main earner and the main spender for that household. If an economist were to analyse the consumer behaviour of such an individual there would be a substantial body of economic theory on which to draw. When two or more adults live in the same household economists have traditionally treated that household as though it were an individual and have assumed that the same economic principles of microeconomics apply … . But can we assume that individuals and households behave in similar ways? Where one individual is the main earner and another the main spender what social and economic processes shape the allocation of money within that household?
>
> Certainly households are key economic units, described by a leading economist as 'one of the principal groups of actors on the economic stage': he continued:
>
> > A typical household sells, or attempts to sell, its labour services to employers and receives as proceeds of the sale, labour income. Moreover, the household may own financial assets (such as savings certificates, shares, *etc*) and non-financial assets (such as property) from which it also derives income. The household's income may also include payments from the government in the form of social security payments, old age pensions, *etc*. With this income the household purchases goods and services, pays taxes, and, perhaps, saves.
>
> In reality, of course, income is earned by individuals, not households, and goods and services are purchased not by households but by individuals. However, 'by a heroic simplification the separate identities of men and women are merged into the concept of the household. The inner conflicts and compromises of the household are not explored'.
>
> By treating it as though it were an individual, the household has become a sort of black box, within which the transfer of resources between earners and spenders has been rendered invisible. (1989 pp 3–4 references omitted)

Her research published in 1989 opened up that black box and provided an important source of information for policy makers and theorists on how income is distributed between husbands and wives, how the distribution is explained by them and how it affects power and spending patterns within households. We have alluded to this and other research above. Let us examine first Pahl's groundbreaking research.

Pahl interviewed 102 couples, both separately and together to seek to determine how gender, generation, life course, marriage ideology and trends toward more egalitarian marriages influence the allocation of money and the responsibility for controlling it.

She identified four general systems of money management in families. The first was *wife management* or the *whole wage* system. In families adopting this system one partner, usually the wife, 'is responsible for managing all the finances of the household and is also responsible for all expenditure, except for personal spending of the other partner' (p 67).

---

[56] See, generally, Finer and McGregor (1974); Barton and Douglas (1995); and MacLean and Eekelaar (1997). See also above and ch 13.

The second system was the *allowance* system, where, typically

> the husband gives his wife a set amount every week or month, to which she adds her own earnings, if any. She is then responsible for paying for specific items of household expenditure, while the rest of the money remains in the control of the husband and he pays for other items. Thus he has access to the main source of income, while she only has access to that part of it which he chooses to give her. (p 69)

The third pattern was the *pooling* system or *shared management*. 'Pooling couples have a joint account or common kitty into which both incomes are paid and from which both draw. Thus both have access to the income entering the household and expenditure responsibilities are more or less shared' (p 71).

Finally, she identified the *independent management* system:

> The essential characteristic of this system is that both partners have an income and that neither has access to all the household funds. Each partner is responsible for specific items of expenditure, and though these responsibilities may change over time, the principle of separate control over income and separate responsibility for expenditure is maintained. (p 74)

She then distinguished between *management* (the day-to-day tasks of money management) and *control* (such as decision-making) of finances, and found that although a large number of wives managed money, fewer controlled it (p 90). She drew the following conclusions:

> Where a wife controls the finances she will usually also be responsible for money management; where a husband controls finances he will usually delegate parts of money management to his wife. Thus where a wife controls finances she will usually be responsible for paying the main bills and for making sure that ends meet, as well as for buying food and day-to-day necessities. Where a husband controls finances he will typically delegate to his wife the responsibility for housekeeping expenses, sometimes giving her a housekeeping allowance for this purpose. Marriages where the wife controls the money and the husband manages it are rare. Finally, there is a small number of marriages where the husband both controls and manages the money; Wilson described male control of expenditure as a deviant pattern which has serious consequences for women and children. The evidence suggests that when a husband both controls and manages the money there is likely to be extreme inequality between husband and wife and deprivation on the part of the wife and children. (p 91)

Pahl suggested that the way in which couples choose to allocate income and responsibility depends upon a number of factors, including assumptions about gender roles and the 'natural' marriage and family; psychological characteristics attributed to the partners such as interest and skills in money management; expenditure patterns including which partner is responsible for spending on particular items; practicalities such as who has easiest access to banks and supermarkets and the working hours of the partners; socio-economic variables such as household income level and the wife's proportionate contribution to the total income; and cultural variables such as generation and geographical region of residence (p 122). Further, while the couples themselves tended to give explanations for their particular arrangements in terms of psychological characteristics or practicalities, Pahl's analysis of the results showed that 'the socio-economic circumstances of peoples' lives, and the beliefs which shaped their views of the world, often had greater explanatory power' (p 120):

Household income is an important variable [in explaining patterns of management and control] when income is low: when money is short, so that managing it is a demanding chore rather than a source of power or pleasure, then typically women manage and control finances. At higher incomes the source of that income becomes important. If only the husband is in employment he tends to control the money, and to delegate management of a part of it to his wife ... [Ideology] can be used as a justification: wives are seen as better at management when money is short, while husbands are defined as financially knowledgeable when there is more money and when the wife's work is unpaid ... .

... For some the psychological characteristics appear to dominate: money is controlled by the person with the greatest financial skills. However, being defined as having financial skills can itself be the product of ideological assumptions about the nature of femininity or masculinity. For other couples practicalities appear to dominate, with bills being paid by whoever can get to the bank, or by the partner whose earnings go monthly into the bank rather than by the one who is paid weekly in cash. However, working hours and forms of payment themselves reflect economic forces and social status. (p 121)

Pahl also looked at patterns of spending and her conclusions follow:

Where wives control finances a higher proportion of household income is likely to be spent on food and day-to-day living expenses than is the case where husbands control finances; additional income brought into the household by the wife is more likely to be spent on food than additional money earned by the husband. Additional support for these hypotheses comes from the finding that husbands are more likely to spend more on leisure than wives. (pp 151–52)

More recent research has confirmed Pahl's findings. Mothers tend to exhibit stronger preferences than fathers for putting the children's financial needs before their own individual needs for leisure (Walker, *et al*, 1994; Lister, *et al*, 1999), and women tend generally, compared with men (perhaps because men tend to have more time on their hands?) to minimise their own needs for leisure or personal spending; luxuries such as these tend to be viewed by men as 'needs' and by women as 'wants' (Burgoyne 2004; Walker, *et al*, 1994). Finally, women tend to prioritise spending to benefit children (Ringen and Halpin 1997; Lister, *et al*, 1999)

**Q** Pahl suggested that her results should be seen as having important implications 'for all who are concerned about the living standards of children, about the employment of women and about tax and employment policies which affect families' (p 152). If you were a policy-maker, what would you think are these implications, and how would they influence your recommendations for policy on child poverty and employment law? See also Cantillon and Nolan (1998).

**Q** Pahl studied only married partners, and she questioned whether her results would be consistent for cohabiting partners including same sex partners, and whether there might be any ethnic variations in her results. What do you think?

## III. ACQUIRING PROPERTY

A family's wealth can be measured not only by its income, but also by the value of any real or personal property its members own or control. For most of the history of family law in Britain, however, the regulation of family property was of concern to only a small proportion of the population; the majority did not own any land or other significant assets. Indeed, the histories of both 'traditional' family law and the common law are in many ways the history of the law of property as it was developed by and for the landed and industrialist classes. The ownership of property, particularly of home-ownership, has to some degree been democratised in recent years, but it still remains largely a middle class concern.

Within households, decisions about property, like those about money, tend to remain a matter for private arrangement (Morris and Nott 1995); the law has very little to say about how family members use and allocate their property except in the event of bankruptcy or if the family unit breaks up as a result of separation or death. At that point, the property that family members have accumulated can be redistributed and, in cases of divorce or dissolution of civil partnership, the court has a very broad discretion with respect to redistribution of property among family members. In the absence of such events, there is no scope for the law to intervene. Nevertheless, property ownership may still be significant in the way it affects families, primarily, as we have seen above, in that it may influence dynamics like power and authority in the family. We will discuss financial and property adjustment on separation, divorce and partnership dissolution in later chapters, and will focus now on how wealth in the form of property is accumulated and distributed within households.

Current rules about family property stem from the 19th century Married Women's Property Acts which applied the notion of individual and separate ownership to husband and wife in the same way as it applied between legal strangers. As we noted earlier, this was a radical development at the time, introducing the idea of formal equality which remains the basis of the law of family property today. Separate ownership and formal equality mean that whoever purchases and has legal title to an item of property has all the rights of ownership in it, including the right to keep, mortgage or dispose of it and the right to realise its value on disposition. These property rights apply, in theory, to any item of property, even to those assets which appear to be 'family property' such as the family car or the family home. The strict common law rules of ownership were first tempered only by the gradual development of rules of equity which provide that a beneficial interest in property, as distinct from a legal interest, may be acquired by someone who does not have legal title to it.

We will address the general law of property as it applies to family members, but will not focus upon the intricacies of the common law tenures in land, the legislation such as the Land Registration Act 2002, or the general rules of equity.[57] Our focus instead will be upon the theme of separate ownership of family property and the principle of formal equality which underlies it. We will deal first with intra-familial contracts to regulate property matters, then with the development of the separate property regime as well as

---

[57] For clear and often insightful expositions of the law in respect of the family home see family law texts such as Cretney, *et al*, (2002); and Lowe and Douglas (1998); and The Law Commission discussion paper (Law Commission 2002) which provides an excellent overview of the law..

alternatives to it, and finally, with questions of the 'new property' and of what constitutes property and claims to property in families.

*Contract Law and Families*

In chapter 2 we discussed the concept of the contractual marriage and presented the argument made by some that rights and responsibilities in all marriages ought to be able to be regulated by the parties concerned. Under current law, of course, such extensive regulation is not possible. Married couples or civilly registered couples who wish to define expressly their financial and property obligations to each other during the relationship would find that courts would be reluctant to enforce such an agreement. Contracts made to 'regularise' the couple's financial affairs while they remain married or registered as civil partners are presumed to lack contract law's required 'intention to create relations'[58] and for policy reasons are not strictly enforceable in courts.[59] even though they are given weight when property comes to be divided on separation, divorce or dissolution of civil partnership.[60] The government proposed in 1998 (Home Office 1998) to change this situation, suggesting that prenuptial contracts should become enforceable in courts, but partly because of public opposition to the idea (Home Office 1999), it has not pursued this proposal. Separation agreements, on the other hand, are considered to be agreements made at arm's length, and so are enforceable, and even encouraged. We see in operation here the law's separation of the public and private spheres in which family matters are not supposed to be governed by the materialistic self-interested rules of contract and the market.

Couples who cohabit without marriage or civil registration, on the other hand, may make cohabitation contracts in which they set out their intentions, both during cohabitation and in the event of separation, with respect to property ownership, financial matters and even regarding matters dealing with any children they may have, but agreements respecting children always remain subject to the court's determination of the child's welfare.[61]

> **Q** What is your view of 'contractualising' the financial incidents of marriage? Does it depend upon your view of the nature of the marriage relationship? On the role you see for law in that relationship? Does your view on cohabitation differ? What about civil partnership? Why or why not?

Feminists have criticised too heavy a reliance upon contract principles in family relationships on different bases. One is that these contracts would be unfair because in many cases the parties have unequal bargaining power, given the greater economic power of men over women in many family relationships. Another criticism is that those principles are based upon a particular view of the individual as self-interested and autonomous, a view with which they are uncomfortable. They suggest that many people, particularly many women, do not view their family relationships, or the world for that matter, from

---

[58] *Balfour v Balfour* [1919] 2 KB 571 (CA).
[59] Lowe and Douglas (1998 p 63) cite *Gould v Gould* [1970] 1 QB 275 as authority for this.
[60] See ch 6 below.
[61] Regarding alteration of maintenance agreements, see the Children Act 1989, Sch 1, s 10, and for the overriding authority of the Child Support Agency, see *Crozier v Crozier* [1994] Fam 114; [1994] 2 All ER 362; [1994] 1 FLR 126.

such an individualistic perspective. Rather, they see themselves as related and interdependent subjects who would not easily be able to separate their individual interests from the interests of the group or the family. To apply strict contract principles in these cases, they say, would be to disadvantage such a person and advantage the person who sees himself as an autonomous market actor (Frug 1992; Cossman 1990).[62]

**Q** See also chapter 2. Do you find these arguments convincing?

*Separate Property*

At common law, the owner of property has discretion over how to deal with it, whether the owner lives together with another person in a family relationship or not. This has always been the case for cohabitants, but only in the 19th century did it become so for married individuals. The early history of the law of property as between husbands and wives begins with the common law doctrine of coverture in terms of which the wife's legal personality was subsumed under that of her husband. In exchange, the husband was under an obligation to support his wife for life. Finer and McGregor (1974) describe the law in the 20th and early 19th centuries in these terms:

> [T]he common law virtually stripped a woman, on marriage, both of her existing property and of her capacity to acquire property for herself in the future. All of the wife's personal chattels, including money, which she owned at the date of marriage, or which she acquired thereafter, whether by her own efforts or not, became the husband's absolute property. Any debt owed to the wife became the husband's if he chose to collect it. The husband took the income of the wife's leaseholds; he could sell them in her lifetime and take the proceeds for himself; and they became his property absolutely if his wife predeceased him. The husband was entitled to the sole management of his wife's freeholds, and took a life estate in the whole of them as soon as there was any issue of the marriage born alive. ...
>
> The origins of this regime owed less to biblical metaphor than they did to the practical demands of the feudal overlord. But it was part of the stock-in-trade of the seventeenth century common lawyers to justify it by reference to the Book of Genesis ... .
>
> Theologically sound or not, a doctrine which to so large an extent delivered up a woman's property to her husband was not acceptable to the propertied classes ... .Hence, from the latter part of the sixteenth century onwards, the lawyers busied themselves on behalf of their clients in inventing and refining devices to protect a woman's property from the ravages to which her marriage exposed it. The devices grew up within equity—the system of law developed by the Chancellor to ease the rigidities of the common law—and were recognised and enforced by the court of Chancery ... .
>
> Dicey described these developments by saying 'There came, therefore, to be not in theory but in fact, one law for the rich and another for the poor. The daughters of the rich enjoyed, for the most part, the considerate protection of equity, the daughters of the poor suffered under the severity and injustice of the common law'. This was certainly true; but it is to be remarked that equity served a socio-economic purpose more fundamental than guaranteeing the comforts of rich men's daughters. The essence of the arrangements which equity upheld was the preservation of wealth within the kinship group which had provided it.
>
> (pp 96–97, references omitted)

Thus there was in the 18th century quite a sophisticated system of equity for the property of the rich, the common law of coverture for the wages and small businesses of

---

[62] See also for other feminist perspectives Pateman (1988); Kingdom (1991).

middle classes, and the Poor Law for the labouring or unemployed poor. A clear discrimination between rich and poor was maintained in the law, which was just as clear as the legal discrimination between men and women. Political writers and intellectuals of the time captured the intellectual movement toward equality and liberalism and, at the same time, women lobbied Parliament to change the law (Holcombe 1983). Eventually a series of reforming statutes was enacted. As Finer and McGregor say, however, these did not 'assimilate the property rights of married and single women', but extended 'to all married women the limited advantages of the "separate property" regime which legal ingenuity and private enterprise had until then conferred on the few' (1974 p 110). The Law Reform (Married Women and Tortfeasors) Act 1935 finally enabled a married woman to acquire, hold, and dispose of any property 'in every respect as though she were single'.

These reforms were consistent with the politics of liberalism, individualism, and formal equality in the 19th and early 20th centuries which brought about other political 'revolutions' such as the abolition of the slave trade and the enfranchisement of women and the non-property-holding majority.[63] They meant that men and women, in marriage as in other spheres of life, were to be treated equally in terms of property acquisition and allocation. Whoever acquired the property owned it. This separation of property and formal equality between men and women continues as the foundation of property law within families today.[64]

**Q** What does formal equality mean for the allocation of wealth between men and women in society generally as well as in families? Do men and women have equal access to the wealth needed to acquire property? A quotation from Sir Jocelyn Simon in 1964 is insightful:

> But men can only earn their incomes and accumulate capital by virtue of the division of labour between themselves and their wives. The wife spends her youth and early middle age in bearing and rearing children and in tending the home; the husband is thus freed for his economic activities. Unless the wife plays her part the husband cannot play his. The cock bird can feather his nest precisely because he is not required to spend most of his time sitting on it
> (1964).

In your view, are his remarks still relevant today? Construct an argument that there is symbolic value in the law espousing formal equality between men and women in families. Construct an argument that a legal strategy of formal equality serves simply to mask real inequalities and so to perpetuate them.

Today, proprietary rights in property can be gained pursuant to acquisition of legal ownership, whether sole or joint, or to acquisition of a beneficial interest in property. The law governing the acquisition of legal title to property is formally gender neutral and impervious to marital status. Yet, while it operates on the basis of the principles of formal equality, in the context of the system of separate property, the law may, in effect, prejudice the non-earning partner, usually the woman. As we have seen, women are

---

[63] See, eg, 2nd and 3rd Reform Acts 1867 and 1884 and the Representation of the People Act 1918 extending the franchise to women over 30 and all men.

[64] For a detailed and typically excellent review of the legal history in this field, see Cretney (2003a) ch 3.

usually the primary caretakers of children, and they often give up work to take on this role. When they do earn, their earnings are on average less than those of men. Loss of income and the purchasing power that comes with that income means that women tend to have less money and so less opportunity to acquire property in their own names. In order to ameliorate the plight of women in this position, courts have, in the past, invoked the equitable principles governing the acquisition of beneficial ownership. In this way, courts sought to recognise the contributions women made to families.

## Beneficial Ownership

A beneficial interest in property is created where a person who is not the legal owner has made contributions to its acquisition that the law regards as sufficient. The effect is that the legal owner holds the property in trust for both him- or herself and the non-owning party. This means that the legal owner would have to consult the beneficial owner before selling or mortgaging the property and, if it is sold, that the latter obtains an interest in the proceeds of sale. While these rules of equity apply to all owners of property, the courts have recognised that 'familial' relationships, including same sex relationships,[65] may be amenable to special treatment. Equity in this way ameliorates some of the hardship of the formal equality of the common law, but its discretionary nature means that decisions about the type of contribution sufficient to create the beneficial interest may vary with 'the length of the Chancellor's foot'.

Case law suggests that it may be difficult for a woman to make the kind of contributions that the law regards as relevant to the acquisition of property. Courts have, to a large degree, relied upon gender stereotypes in making their decisions and failed to take account of the disadvantages created for those who conform to traditional gender roles. In effect, courts often refuse to recognise as a relevant contribution anything that a 'normal' husband or wife would do in relation to property. So, for example, while direct financial contributions usually give rise to a beneficial interest, little else does. This means that 'normal' wives who contribute to the running of the household by means of labour and childcare may find these contributions discounted when it comes to determining beneficial ownership property like the family home, because it is money spent on the purchase or the mortgage that is primarily recognised.

## Resulting Trust[66]

A person who is not the legal owner of property can establish that she has a beneficial interest in it by proving that a trust has been created. She[67] can establish a *resulting trust* where she makes a direct financial contribution to the purchase price of the property. Her beneficial ownership then is said to result from the contribution. In *Tinsley v Milligan*[68] these equitable principles were applied in a non-traditional familial situation. The parties were lesbians who, together, had purchased a bed and breakfast establishment. Although Milligan contributed money to the purchase of the house, title to it was

---

[65] See *Tinsley v Milligan* [1994] AC 340.
[66] See also Cretney, *et al*, (2002) and Law Commission (2002) for a comprehensive review of the law.
[67] Reported cases suggest that, where property is not jointly owned, it is usually legally owned by the man and it is usually the woman who has to seek a beneficial interest in it to gain any benefit from it.
[68] [1994] AC 340.

registered in Tinsley's sole name. When the relationship broke down, Milligan was able to establish to the satisfaction of the majority of the House of Lords that she had a proprietary interest in the property by virtue of the trust resulting from her financial contribution to its purchase.

Until recently, there was some uncertainty about the proportion of the interest the contribution created. On the one hand there was a series of cases such as *Springette v Defoe*[69] in which the actual amount, or proportion of the contribution to the price of the property, determined the proportion of the beneficial share. On the other hand, there were cases such as *Stokes v Anderson*[70] and *McHardy*[71] in which the court found that the contribution was not intended to quantify the interest, but rather was evidence of a common intention to share the property, the interests then being determined according to the parties' intentions as could be inferred from all the circumstances and principles of fairness. In 1995 Lord Justice Waite in the Court of Appeal decision of *Midland Bank v Cooke*[72] said:

> I confess that I find the differences of approach in these two cases[73] mystifying. In the one a strict resulting trust geared to mathematical calculation of the proportion of the purchase price provided by cash contribution is treated as virtually immutable in the absence of express agreement; in the other a displacement of the cash-related trust by inferred agreement is not only permitted but treated as obligatory. (p 942)

Where there was no evidence of the parties' intentions as to the amount of the beneficial share, or even where the parties themselves said they had no agreement, the court held that equity still had a role in inferring one. Waite LJ said:

> When people, especially young people, agree to share their lives in joint homes, they do so on a basis of mutual trust and in the expectation that their relationship will endure. ... For a couple embarking on a serious relationship, discussion of the terms to apply at parting is almost a contradiction of the shared hopes that have brought them together. There will inevitably be numerous couples, married or unmarried, who have no discussion about ownership, and who perhaps advisedly make no agreement about it. It would be anomalous, against that background, to create a range of home-buyers who were beyond the pale of equity's assistance in formulating a fair presumed basis for the sharing of beneficial title, simply because they had been honest enough to admit they never gave ownership a thought or reached any agreement about it. (p 927)

On this basis, the court found that the whole course of dealing between the parties, including what took place during the time they cohabited in it, as evidence of what they intended at the time of acquisition of the property.

*Midland Bank v Cooke,* and indeed the bulk of the case law on beneficial ownership, has since been considered by the Court of Appeal. In the case of *Oxhey v Hiscock*[74] the CA reviewed the case law and held that (following *Lloyd's Bank v Rossett*—see below), evidence of a sum of money paid by a non-titled party toward the purchase or mortgage of a property was not only determinative of a resulting trust in the property, but was

---

[69] [1992] 2 FLR 388.
[70] [1991] 1 FLR 391.
[71] *McHardy and Sons v Warren*[1994] 2 FLR 338.
[72] [1995] 2 FLR 915.
[73] Referring to *Springette* and *McHardy.*
[74] [2004] EWCA Civ; [2004] 2 FLR 669.

also evidence of a common intention to share the property, and the relevant question to determine the proportion of the interest (in either case) was 'what would be a fair share for each party having regard to the whole course of dealing between them in relation to the property?' (para 73). As we shall see, this formulation of the issues seems to suggest that the resulting trust has fallen out of favour, with preference to be given to the common intention constructive trust.

## Common Intention Constructive Trust

A party seeking to establish a constructive trust of this nature must show that the parties had a common intention that she would have a share in the property, that she reasonably relied upon (acted upon) that common intention and that her reliance caused her some detriment. In the context of the family home, each of these requirements can present difficulties for the applicant.

### Common Intention

First, a common intention to share must be proved. According to the leading case of *Lloyds Bank plc v Rosset*[75]

> The first and fundamental question which must always be resolved is whether, independently of any inference to be drawn from the conduct of the parties in the course of sharing the house as their home and managing their joint affairs, there has at any time prior to acquisition, or exceptionally at some later date, been any agreement, arrangement or understanding reached between them that the property is to be shared beneficially. The finding of an agreement or an arrangement to share in this sense can only, I think, be based on evidence of express discussions between the parties, however imperfectly remembered and however imprecise the terms may have been. Once a finding to this effect is made it will only be necessary for the partner asserting the beneficial interest against the partner entitled to the legal estate to show that he or she has acted to his or her detriment or significantly altered his or her position in reliance on the agreement in order to give rise to a constructive trust or proprietary estoppel. ...
>
> In sharp contrast with this situation is the very different one where there is no evidence to support a finding of an agreement or an arrangement to share, however reasonable it might have been for the parties to reach such an agreement if they had applied their minds to the question, and where the court must rely entirely on the conduct of the parties both as the basis from which to infer a common intention to share the property beneficially and as the conduct relied on to give rise to a constructive trust. In this situation, direct contributions to the purchase price by the partner who is not the legal owner, whether initially or by payment of mortgage instalments, will readily justify the inference necessary to the creation of a constructive trust. But as I read the authorities, it is at least extremely doubtful whether anything less will do. (pp 132–33)

It is clear, then, that common intention can be established most easily if there is an express agreement between the parties, whether oral or in writing. On occasion, the courts have interpreted a statement by the party as evidencing such an agreement in spite of the fact that, on the face of it, it appears to mean the exact opposite. In *Grant v Edwards*,[76] for example, the owner told his cohabitant that he would have put the house in their joint names, except that to do so would have jeopardised the divorce settlement

---

[75] [1991] 1 AC 107; [1990] 1 All ER 1111. All page references are to the Appeal Cases.
[76] [1986] Ch 638; [1987] 1 FLR 87.

with her previous spouse. Similarly, in *Eves v Eves*[77] the legal owner told his cohabitant that he would have put the house in their joint names, but that he could not because she was under 21 years old. In both of these cases the court found the necessary common intention in these statements. In general, the court will look to see whether, 'at any time prior to the acquisition of the disputed property, or exceptionally at some later date, [there have] been discussions between the parties, leading to any agreement, arrangement or understanding between them that the property is to be shared beneficially'.[78]

The situation is more difficult if there is no agreement. In this case, the court may be asked to infer a common intention from the conduct of the parties. Inferring a state of mind from conduct is always a tricky matter, and these cases are no exception. Direct financial contributions to acquisition or regular payments towards the mortgage will usually be straightforward evidence of a common intention, such as in *Midland Bank v Cooke,* above, where part of the purchase price for the property, which was held in husband's sole name, came from a wedding gift to the parties. The wife's contribution was said to have come from her part of the gift.

Apart from privileging financial contributions, it is in interpreting the effect of so-called 'indirect', and especially non-financial, contributions that the courts have tended to disadvantage women. In *Gissing v Gissing,*[79] although the wife, during the course of a 26–year marriage, paid for furnishings, for laying a lawn and for her own and the children's clothes, these expenditures were not found to evidence a common intention that she should acquire a beneficial interest in the matrimonial home. In *Burns v Burns*[80] the parties cohabited for 19 years. The woman cared for their children full time in the couple's early years together, and her financial contributions began some time after the property was acquired. She contributed to housekeeping, purchased clothes, furniture, a dishwasher and redecorated the interior of the home, while carrying out domestic work in the home. Once again, these contributions were found insufficient to prove a common intention that she should acquire a proprietary interest in the home.

Nevertheless, it seems that if the court considers payment of household expenses to amount to indirect contributions to the mortgage, this could help the person contributing to earn a beneficial interest. A recent decision of the High Court has provided some indication that the courts may be more willing to adopt this analysis than in the past. In *Le Foe v Le Foe and Woolwich PLC,*[81] it held that indirect financial contributions to the mortgage will be sufficient to evidence the requisite common intention. In this case, the wife's contribution to the home was to pay for day-to-day domestic expenditure, while the husband paid the mortgage, service charge and outgoings. It was, as the court found, an 'arbitrary allocation of responsibility' (para 10). It accordingly took the view that, although the wife had made no cash contribution to the mortgage, she had made indirect contributions to the mortgage, sufficient for it to infer the common intention that the wife would have a beneficial interest in the home.

**Q** In the light of *Le Foe*, do you think a case like *Burns* might be decided differently in future? Or is something more required, like regular and substantial responsibility for household expenses?

[77] [1975] 1 WLR 1338 (CA).
[78] *H v M (Property: Beneficial interest)* [1992] 1 FLR 229, 231.
[79] [1971] AC 886; [1970] 3 WLR 255; [1970] 2 All ER 780.
[80] [1984] Ch 317; [1984] FLR 216.
[81] [2001] 2 FLR 970.

In *Burns*, as in *Gissing* before it, the female partners performed traditional 'wifely' labour which did not satisfy the court of the parties' intention to share ownership of their homes.[82] Indeed, in *Burns* the court said:

> If the woman makes no 'real' or 'substantial' financial contributions towards either the purchase price, deposit or mortgage instalments by the means of which the family home was acquired, then she is not entitled to any share in the beneficial interest in that home even though over a very substantial number of years she may have worked just as hard as the man in maintaining the family in the sense of keeping the house, giving birth to and looking after and helping to bring up the children of the union. (FLR p 242)

**Q**   Comment here on the court's use of the words 'real' and 'substantial.'

And in *Rosset* itself,

> Up to 17 December 1982 [Mrs Rosset's] contribution to the venture was: (1) to urge on the builders and to attempt to coordinate their work … . (2) to go to the builders' merchants and obtain material required by the builders … and to deliver the materials to the site … . (3) to assist her husband in planning the renovation and decoration of the house. In this, she had some skill over and above that acquired by most housewives. She was a skilled painter and decorator who enjoyed wallpapering and decorating, and, as her husband acknowledged, she had good ideas about this work. In connection with this, she advised on the position of electric plugs and radiators and planned the design of the large breakfast room and the small kitchen of the house; (4) to carry out the wall papering of Natasha's bedroom and her own bedroom, after preparing the surfaces of the walls and clearing up the rooms concerned before the papering began; (5) to begin the preparation of the surfaces of the walls of her son's bedroom, the den, the upstairs lavatory and the downstairs washroom for papering … . (6) to assist in arranging the insurance of the house … . (7) to assist in arranging a crime prevention survey … . (8) to assist in arranging the installation of burglar alarms … .(Per Lord Bridge, pp 129–30; quoting from Judge Scarlett at trial)

In this case, the wife was attempting to establish a proprietary interest in the property (held in her husband's name alone, and paid for by him alone from trust funds and a bank overdraft) in order to protect her share from the bank which had brought an application for an order of possession. Mr Rosset, had, without his wife's knowledge, executed a charge in favour of the bank in order to obtain an overdraft, on which he subsequently defaulted before the couple separated. Mrs Rosset and her two children, aged 1 and 6, were staying in the house when the bank's application came before the court.

Lord Bridge of Harwich, writing for a unanimous court, gave the judgment. First, he stated the issue before the court.

> The question the judge had to determine was whether he could find that before the contract to acquire the property was concluded they had entered into an agreement, made an arrangement,

---

[82] For a while it seemed that labour of an unusual kind might suffice to establish to the satisfaction of the courts the elusive common intention. In *Cooke v Head* [1972] 1 ELR 518; [1972] 2 All ER 38 the woman demolished a shed and did some building work on the property. This, according to the court, was 'much more than most women would do' and it helped to gain her a one-third interest in the family home. In *Eves v Eves* (above), Lord Denning, but no other members of the Court of Appeal, thought that the fact that she helped with painting and heavy construction-type work including breaking up concrete and demolishing a shed evidenced the requisite common intention (p 1340).

reached an understanding or formed a common intention that the beneficial interest in the property would be jointly owned. I do not think it is of importance which of these alternative expressions one uses. Spouses living in amity will not normally think it necessary to formulate or define their respective interests in property in any precise way. The expectation of parties to every happy marriage is that they will share the practical benefits of occupying the matrimonial home whoever owns it. But this is something quite distinct from sharing the beneficial interest in the property asset which the matrimonial home represents. (pp 127–28)

> **Q** Would parties to a 'happy marriage' ever form a common intention to share beneficial ownership of property as distinct from sharing 'practical benefits' of occupancy? Recall here Chadwick LJ's comments in *Oxhey* above. Do you agree that expectations of sharing the practical benefits of occupancy are distinct from expectations of sharing beneficial interest in the property?

He then went on, first quoting the findings of Judge Scarlett:

I am satisfied that in 1982 the common intention expressed by [Mr and Mrs Rosset] in conversation between themselves was that Vincent farmhouse should be purchased in the name of [Mr Rosset] alone, because funds would not be available from [his] family trust in Switzerland unless the purchase was made only in his name. In addition, however, it was their common intention that the renovation of the house should be a joint venture, after which the house was to become a family home to be shared by [the parties] and their children.

I pause to observe that neither a common intention by the spouses that a house is to be renovated as a 'joint venture' nor a common intention that the house is to be shared by parents and children as the family home throws any light on their intentions with respect to the beneficial ownership of the property. (p 130)

His Lordship went on to determine ownership in the home:

It is clear from these passages in the judgment that the judge based his inference of a common intention that Mrs Rosset should have a beneficial interest in the property under a constructive trust essentially on what Mrs Rosset did in and about assisting in the renovation of the property between the beginning of November 1982 and the date of completion on 17 December 1982. Yet by itself this activity, it seems to me, could not possibly justify any such inference. It was common ground that Mrs Rosset was extremely anxious that the new matrimonial home should be ready for occupation before Christmas if possible. In these circumstances, it would seem the most natural thing in the world for any wife, in the absence of her husband abroad, to spend all the time she could spare and to employ any skills she might have, such as the ability to decorate a room, in doing all she could to accelerate progress of the work quite irrespective of any expectation she might have of enjoying a beneficial interest in the property. The judge's view that some of this work was work 'on which she could not reasonably have been expected to embark unless she was to have an interest in the house' seems to me, with respect, quite untenable. (p 131)

> **Q** What conduct by Mrs Rosset might have sufficed as evidence of a common intention that she should have an interest in the house? Would it be the most 'natural thing in the world' for Mrs Rosset to have hammered nails or knocked down or put up walls?

> **Q** On this analysis, in the absence of an agreement or understanding (the first way in which common intention can be found), can a partner with no income and no

savings ever claim a beneficial interest in the property? What are the implications for men and for women of this analysis? If a partner has an income, would you advise her to pay for food and household bills, or to pay the mortgage? But could it not be said to be the 'most natural thing in the world' for a partner to contribute to the mortgage payments if she is in employment?

**Q** What do these cases tell you about the courts' assumptions about the marriage relationship? In your view, do husbands and wives who conform to traditional gender roles 'intend' common ownership of their home?

*Reliance and Detriment*

In addition to a common intention, evidenced either by an express agreement or by conduct (usually financial contribution to the property), the court must also find that the person seeking to establish the existence of a trust relied upon that intention to her detriment. If the common intention is evidenced by the payment of money, that conduct, ie the payment, acts also as sufficient evidence of the requisite detrimental reliance. If the common intention is evidenced by an agreement, arrangement or understanding, such as in *Grant v Edwards* or *Eves v Eves,* the claimant must have done something else; something she would not have been likely to do unless she believed she had an interest, and the act of reliance must have resulted in detriment to her. The court in *Eves v Eves,* for example, said that the woman would not have wielded a sledgehammer had she not believed she would get an interest in the property and in *Chan Pui Chun v Leung Kam Ho*[83] the court found that by devoting herself to Mr Leung's business affairs and by giving up her own home and moving in with him, all in reliance on his (fraudulent) promise of marriage and a 'dream house', Miss Chan had acted to her detriment and was entitled to a beneficial interest in the property in question.

In *Midland Bank v Dobson,*[84] on the other hand, the court found a common intention, but held that there was no detriment because the wife had not done anything more than the usual domestic duties which were unrelated to the intention that ownership of the house be shared. Similarly, in *Thomas v Fuller-Brown*[85] a man who carried out various pieces of DIY around his partner's home into which he had moved, was found not to have acquired a beneficial interest in the property. His actions were found to be the kinds of things a man would have been expected to have done in his home, and not the kinds of things a man would only do if he believed he had an interest in the property.

**Q** Gender stereotyping can affect whether a party is able to establish detrimental reliance as well as common intention. See on this Lawson (1996). How, if at all, would you reform the requirement for detrimental reliance?

*Quantifying the Beneficial Interest*

The shares to which the parties are entitled once the court finds a constructive trust exists are determined by the parties' intentions. While there was some question about how to infer those intentions, the *Oxley case* seems to have clarified the law, even when there is no evidence about what the parties' intentions may have been at the time of acquisition of the property.

---

[83] [2002] EWCA Civ 1075; [2003] 1 FLR 23.
[84] [1986] 1 FLR 171.
[85] [1988] 1 FLR 237.

[E]ach is entitled to that share which the court considers fair having regard to the whole course of dealing between them in relation to the property. And, in that context, 'the whole course of dealing between them in relation to the property' includes the arrangements which they make from time to time in order to meet the outgoings (for example, mortgage contributions, council tax and utilities, repairs, insurance and housekeeping) which have to be met if they are to live in the property as their home. (para 69)

## Constructive Trust or Proprietary Estoppel?

Proprietary estoppel is a claim made in equity that it would be unconscionable for B to act upon his or her rights in the face of his words or actions and A's detrimental reliance on those words or actions. Formally, it requires that A believe that she has or is going to get an interest in B's property and acts to her detriment on the basis of that belief. It also requires B to have known of and to have encouraged A's belief.[86] We can see that proprietary estoppel does not require any common intention, express or implied, but in other respects it is similar to the common intention constructive trust. The differences between them may be of only historical importance now, however, in the light of the *Oxhey* case. During the course of the court's review of the case law, it considered cases that were said to have been decided on the basis of proprietary estoppel principles and those decided on constructive trust principles. It concluded that 'the time has come to accept that there is no difference in outcome, in cases of this nature, whether the true analysis lies in constructive trust or in proprietary estoppel' (para 71).[87]

## Summary

In property and trust law, then, the court uses gender neutral principles which reflect the formal equality of the partners. What do these principles mean for men and for women and their ownership of matrimonial or household property? The courts are clear that common ownership is not to be inferred simply because the home was meant to be used as the family home. Rather, some sort of valuable contribution must have been made to the home in order to raise equitable principles. But, for non-earning partners, usually women, as long as only money contributions are considered to be valuable for this purpose, the public/private dichotomy is again invoked. Work done in the private sphere is not considered of value, whereas work done in the public, that which can earn wages, is. Okin (1989) has suggested that women are taught to expect to marry and spend their time rearing children, which disadvantages them even before they marry because they set less store in qualifying for well-paid jobs. Women tend to look for flexibility which goes together with low pay. Because of the wage gap, men's higher-paying work is given priority within marriage and there is less leverage to challenge traditional divisions of labour, because to do so would appear to prioritise the 'wrong' (that is, lower) wage.

---

[86] See eg *Gillet v Holt* [2000] 2 FLR 266.

[87] For further reading on trusts, see *Pettit v Pettit* [1970] AC 777; [1969] 2 All ER 385. On rights of third parties to claim charges to disputed property see *Re Citro (A Bankrupt)* [1991] Ch 142; *Barca v Mears* [2004] EWHC 2170; [2005] 1 BPIR 15. See *Jackson v Bell* [2001] EWCA Civ 387; [2001] Fam Law 879 on the use of the Human Rights Act in actions brought against occupiers by trustees in bankruptcy. On the rights and duties of mortgagees in regard to the family home, particularly in relation to undue influence, see *Barclays Bank v O'Brien* [1994] 1 FLR 1; and *Royal Bank of Scotland v Etridge (No 2)* [2001] UKHL 44; [2002] AC 773; and Auchmuty (2003). See generally Herring (2004 pp 149–59).

Wong (2003) suggests that there may be a place for Human Rights law in these cases. She suggests that the Human Rights Act may have indirect horizontal effect such that courts will be required to interpret existing common law or equitable principles in the light of human rights values. This may mean, she argues, that the combination of Articles 8 and 14 may mean that the *Rosset* type test may be seen to be discriminatory. Indeed, human rights values such as non-discrimination have already been applied in family law cases interpreting the distribution of property on divorce (Diduck 2001b).[88]

Sawyer (2004) suggests another route out of the constructive trust's potential unfairness for women. In the light, she says, of the importance of the best interests of children, and the increasingly acceptable idea that it is right to take into account the care of children when considering property rights, an equitable interest could be founded on the shared parental obligation to bring up children. She goes on to say that 'quantification should start with the realistic notion of the costs of childcare, where the parental obligation to care is discharged by one parent on behalf of the other' (pp 46–47).

> **Q** How would a court found a constructive trust on the interests of children and parents' obligations to care for them? How would you construct an argument that the constructive trust complies with human rights principles? That it doesn't? Do you think the property disputes that may arise between same-sex partners after the Civil Partnership Act comes into force could contribute to a change in the way courts determine beneficial entitlement? See Auchmuty (2003).

*Alternatives—1. The Remedial Constructive Trust*

As we have seen, in the same way that the law does not see housework as valuable in terms of wage earning or pension accumulation, it does not see it as valuable in terms of contributions to property ownership. This understanding of value is not only reflected in the law; it is evident in the attitudes of many men and women. In one US study, it was found that divorcing men discuss with their lawyers 'ways to "keep" their property or assets, and women discuss ways to "get" [those] assets' (Gray and Merrick 1996 p 243). This view, defining which contributions are of value in property accumulation, is linked to particular ideas of how families are organised and what marriage means. It is a view which has been challenged in other jurisdictions regarding the value placed upon non-monetary contributions to the acquisition or maintenance of property.

The Canadian case of *Pettkus v Becker*[89] is a good example of how a court was able to adapt trust principles to recognise a different and arguably more realistic view of family relationships in which couples only rarely turn their minds to allocating property ownership. Mr Pettkus and Ms Becker were not married, but lived as husband and wife and worked a bee farm together for 19 years. All of the business and residential property was acquired through Mr Pettkus' funds, which he was able to save during the time that Ms Becker paid their rent from her salary. Legal title was in his name. After the acquisition, Ms Becker used her money to purchase new flooring and helped to lay the floor. They worked the business together. The Supreme Court of Canada said the following:

---

[88] See *White v White* [2001] AC 596; [2000] 2 FLR 976 and ch 6 below.
[89] [1980] 2 SCR 834; (1981) 117 DLR (3d) 257. Page references are to the DLR.

Turning then to the present case and common intention, the evidence is clear that Mr Pettkus and Miss Becker had no express agreement for sharing economic gain. She conceded there was no specific arrangement with respect to the use of her money. She said: 'No, we just saved together. It was meant to be together, it was ours'. The arrangement 'was without saying anything ... there was nothing talked over ...' (p 271)

**Q** Does their arrangement sound to you like a typical or an atypical family arrangement?

The court went on: 'The finances of each were completely separate ... . Uncommitted to marriage or to a permanent relationship it would be difficult to ascribe to Mr Pettkus an intention, express or implied, to share his savings. Miss Becker said they were to "save together" but the truth is that Mr Pettkus saved at the expense of Miss Becker.' (p 271)

The court did not feel that it needed to find or to impute a common intention where it was impossible or unreasonable to do so. But neither did it feel that this barred Ms Becker from any entitlement to the property. It found that it could use equity to assist her. It preferred to abandon the fiction of a common intention and to utilise a concept that focused more accurately on the real issues between the parties. It adopted the constructive trust as a remedy for the unjust enrichment of Pettkus at the expense of Becker. Unjust enrichment has three requirements: an enrichment of one party, a corresponding detriment to the other party and the absence of any juristic reason for the enrichment.

**Q** How do you feel about abandoning the common intention requirement in these cases? How would Mrs Rosset have fared using this approach?

The court went on:

Mr Pettkus has had the benefit of 19 years of unpaid labour, while Miss Becker has received little or nothing in return. As for the third requirement, I hold that where one person in a relationship tantamount to spousal prejudices herself in the reasonable expectation of receiving an interest in property and the other person in the relationship freely accepts benefits conferred by the first person in circumstances where he knows or ought to have known of that reasonable expectation, it would be unjust to allow the recipient of the benefit to retain it.

(p 274)

**Q** Would all wives have a reasonable expectation of receiving an interest in the marital home after doing things that are the 'most natural things in the world' for a wife to do? In 1993 the Supreme Court of Canada again clarified its position regarding household labour as a sufficient contribution to give rise to a constructive trust. The following quote from the case of *Peter v Beblow*[90] captures the court's sentiments:

The notion that household and child care services are not worthy of recognition by the court fails to recognize the fact that these services are of great value, not only to the family, but to the other spouse ... . The notion, moreover, is a pernicious one that systematically devalues the contributions which women tend to make to the family economy. It has contributed to the phenomenon of the feminization of poverty ... (p 346)

---

[90] [1993] 3 WWR 337.

**Q** Boyd (1994) has suggested, however, that, as progressive these decisions appear
to be, they tend to reinforce stereotypes of 'traditional family forms' incorporating a breadwinner-dependant philosophy, so that if a woman conforms to the
dependent role, she is more likely to receive compensation. How can the law be
used to break down such stereotypes while at the same time providing justice for
individual non-property owning women?

*Alternatives—2. Community of Property*

In many jurisdictions, marriage is viewed as a partnership, and so as a reflection of that
philosophy they adopt a system of community of property rather than one of separation of property.[91] It is significant that usually a formal marriage is required to trigger a
community of property regime, and that, while the partners remain unmarried, their
property remains separate; the introduction of a community of property system would
not assist cohabiting women. The community of property regime has been described as
follows:

> The community of property approach is premised on the assumption that marriage, among
> other things, is an economic partnership. As such, the partnership or community owns the
> respective talents and efforts of the spouses. Whatever is acquired as a result of their talents
> and efforts is shared by and belongs to both of them equally.
>     The essence of a community regime is that the earnings and property acquired by the efforts
> of either spouse become community property in which each spouse has a present legal interest.
>                                                                      (Payne 1976 p 296)

A community of property regime usually results in a complicated system in practice, as
elaborate rules tend to be in place governing such matters as the degree to which community property is available to discharge a spouse's contractual obligations or how
management of the community property is allocated between the two spouses.

**Q** What, in your view, are the pros and cons of a community system? Does a community of property system reflect a view of marriage that differs from that
reflected by a separate property regime?

## IV. STATUTORY REFORM

Statutory variations of the separate property regime in England and Wales have been
restricted to two fairly minor amendments: the Married Women's Property Act 1964,
which states that money or property bought by a wife out of a housekeeping allowance
provided by her husband is to be shared equally between the spouses,[92] and Section 37
of the Matrimonial Proceedings and Property Act 1970 which states:

---

[91] A community of property regime was advocated for England and Wales in the 1950s, led by Kahn-Freund
(1955), among others. See also Cretney (2003c); and Eekelaar (2003a).
[92] The Law Commission (1988c) criticised this provision and recommended its repeal.

It is hereby declared that where a husband or wife contributes in money or money's worth to the improvement of real or personal property in which or in the proceeds of sale of which either or both of them has or have a beneficial interest, the husband or wife so contributing shall, if the contribution is of substantial nature and subject to any agreement to the contrary express or implied, be treated as having then acquired by virtue of his or her contribution a share or an enlarged share, as the case may be, in that beneficial interest of such an extent as may have been then agreed, or in default of such agreement, as may seem in all the circumstances just to any court before which the question of the existence or extent of the beneficial interest of the husband or wife arises (whether in proceedings between them or in other proceedings).[93]

Statutory changes with respect to the family home have concentrated upon occupancy rather than ownership. At common law, the owner of a property has rights of occupancy in it, and anyone else living there does so at the owner's discretion. The Family Law Act 1996 provides protection from eviction for non-owner spouses in all cases, and for non-owner domestic partners in cases of domestic violence.[94]

**Q** Do these statutory interventions go far enough, in your view? Scotland has reformed its matrimonial property regime in line with a deferred community scheme. A deferred system is one in which property is held separately by the partners during marriage, but then, on separation of the partners, a 'snapshot' of the family's assets is taken, and the value of all the assets, minus all the debts, is split between them. In Scotland the value is normally split equally, while in others a more complicated formula may be used. Behind both types of system, however, is the notion that both spouses are entitled to an equal share of the value of the assets acquired during the marriage. See *Lightbody (or Jacques) v Jacques* [1997] 1 FLR 748.

**Q** Would this help in cases of same-sex or heterosexual cohabitation?

In 1978, the Law Commission recommended a statutory framework for joint ownership of the family home (Law Commission 1978) and in 1988 it recommended, among other things, that 'the purchase of [moveable] property (with some exclusions) by one or both spouses for their joint use or benefit should give rise to joint ownership of property subject to a contrary intention on the part of the purchasing spouse, known to the other spouse'. It also recommended that 'transfer of property by one spouse to the other for their joint use or benefit should give rise to joint ownership of that property subject to a contrary intention on the part of the transferring spouse, known to the other spouse' (Law Commission 1988c p 101). None of these recommendations has been implemented, and in 2002 the Law Commission reported again on the ownership of the family home (Law Commission 2002). This project was originally intended to include the law relating to cohabitation, but it soon became clear that the Commission was really concerned with rights of 'homesharers'. It covered, therefore, the property rights of a broad range of people, not only 'couples'. This, perhaps, was one of the reasons for its rather woolly (non) conclusions. The Commission considered, for example, whether a property approach or a relationship approach would better solve the problem of determining property interests where there are no express arrangements between homesharers as to how property should be owned. With regard to the property

[93] See *Pettit v Pettit* [1970] AC 777.
[94] Family Law Act 1996 ss 30–34. See chs 10 and 13.

approach, it concluded that: '1.31(1) It is quite simply not possible to devise a statutory scheme for the ascertainment and quantification of beneficial interests in the shared home which can operate fairly and evenly across the diversity of domestic circumstances which are now to be encountered.'

This conclusion may not be surprising given that the Commission considered the wide variety of people's living arrangements. Rather than focus solely upon marriage or marriage-like relationships, it recognised also the possible homesharing rights of 'persons who are not in any sense a "couple", but who live together for mutual support or caring' (para 1.31(4)). In this sense the Commission seemed to be taking our increasingly diverse family practices into account,[95] but just as the law legitimating those relationships as 'family' cannot decide what to do about them,[96] neither could the Law Commission devise a statutory property sharing scheme that would cope. The Commission first reviewed the current common law position, identified problems with it, then recommended that the current trust for land be retained, but highlighted ways in which it thought the common law could be 'usefully developed' (para 1.28). Before we look at these recommendations, let us examine the difficulties in the present law as identified by the Law Commission:

2.106 'Common Intention' constructive trust
Common intention has been described as a 'myth'. It is certainly difficult to explain every decided case on the basis of the parties' intention being 'express' or 'implied', and there is ample evidence of courts taking an inventive approach to the facts and discovering a common intention where none in truth exists. ...

2.107 The relevance of contributions
... Whilst it seems that a qualifying contribution must be financial in nature, it remains unclear whether it must be directly referable to the acquisition of the property, or, indeed, when a contribution is direct or indirect. It does not seem satisfactory to us that the way in which the parties sharing the home have agreed to administer the household budget should have decisive effect on whether the house is treated as beneficially owned by one or both of them. In some cases, the allocation of financial responsibility could even be deliberately contrived to the advantage of the party with legal title.

2.108 Discrimination against home-makers
The decision in *Burns v Burns* highlights the difficulty faced by those who have shared a home for a long time but who cannot establish the requisite 'common intention' nor prove 'financial' contribution as they have been occupied full-time at home, possibly bringing up children. A strong argument can be made to the effect that the current law discriminates against those who do not earn income from employment.

2.109 The quantification of beneficial entitlement
... [T]he principles of quantification are uncertain, with decisions being made which are (not entirely surprisingly) inconsistent and difficult to reconcile. ...

2.110 The unpredictability of estoppel
The unwillingness of the courts to define precisely the scope of proprietary estoppel means that the doctrine is flexible and can be developed as appropriate. However, the corollary is that certain elements of the doctrine remain unclear and that it is difficult to predict when it will operate. ... Furthermore, the extent to which proprietary estoppel and the common intention constructive trust overlap remains a difficult issue.

[95] See ch 1.
[96] See discussion in ch 1.

2.111 The litigation consequences
The lack of coherent principle does not assist parties or their lawyers in attempts to arrive at a compromise. ...

2.112 The current requirements for establishing the existence of an interest under a trust are not ideally suited to the typical informality of s those sharing a home. ... (pp 40–42 references omitted)

**Q** Do you agree with these criticisms? Can you think of any more?

The Commission then made some modest recommendations for useful ways in which the common law could be developed, given these criticisms. First, it suggested that the 'common intention' requirement be kept, despite its highly artificial nature (para 4.24). It thus disagreed with the Canadian unjust enrichment approach discussed above. It then recommended that an indirect contribution to the mortgage, such as that made when one party pays household bills, be sufficient to enable courts to infer common intention to share (para 4.26). Finally, it recommended that beneficial entitlement be quantified in a 'holistic' way, looking at the whole course of dealing between the parties (para 4.28).

**Q** Have any of these recommendations for development of the case law occurred in the courts? Would you recommend any other 'useful development' of the case law?

The Commission also suggested that the 'relationship' or 'status' approach' to homesharing should not be ignored, however. While accepting 'that there is a very strong case for singling out marriage as a status deserving of special treatment' (para 5.42), it also recommended that the law ought to respond to the 'increasing diversity of living arrangements' in Great Britain. It limited its recommendations in this respect, however, to allowing for the 'formal registration of civil partnerships, or, less formally, a power for the court to adjust the legal rights and obligations of individuals who are or have been living together for a defined period or in defined circumstances' (para 5.43).

**Q** To what extent have these recommendations been accepted by the government? Do you feel that any more can be done to ensure fairness in determining owner-ship when people share their home? Do you think the answers lie in a property law approach or in a family/relationship law approach? To what extent are the principles of property law and family law different? To what extent are the divi-sions between the two artificial in the context of the 'home'. See, on this, Sawyer (2004); Miles (2003); Fox (2003); Diduck (2005b).

## V. THE 'NEW' PROPERTY

We have been dealing so far with traditional items of property: houses, household goods and wages, and to some extent also a form of 'new' property: pensions. Pensions can be called a 'new' form of property, first, because it is only relatively recently that courts have agreed that they form part of a person's wealth, but also because of their inchoate nature. They are future rights to something, rather than something one can claim immediately.

Even more controversial than pensions as property, however, is the notion of a person's earning power as a form of property, particularly when that power arises from a specialisation, qualification or licence acquired during a relationship with another. To what degree can one person's contribution to another's earning capacity be quantified or conceptualised as property at all? Professor Nicholas Bala, writing in North America, describes the problem in these terms:

> A young couple marries. One spouse, invariably the man, attends university and obtains a professional degree in law, medicine or business. This is followed by a gruelling period as an intern, articling student or junior associate. Throughout this time, the other spouse has been working hard, perhaps as a secretary or nurse, providing financial and emotional support, sacrificing her career prospects and carrying out almost all the domestic responsibilities. Sometime between the completion of university and the commencement of a lucrative career, the couple separates. At the time of the separation, no tangible or financial assets have been acquired, but both spouses are self-supporting. The issue confronting the courts is whether the spouse who has acquired the degree is obliged to provide some form of compensation to his partner. If so, what is the basis of the claim and how is the compensation to be calculated?
>
> The resolution of this issue is of considerable practical importance. It also raises some fundamental questions. Is a degree or professional licence 'property' which is divisible like other assets? What is the nature of marriage? Is one spouse in effect 'investing' in the career of a partner, or was the support more in the nature of a loan? Or was the support really a gift, provided with the hope of some future advantage, but with no legal entitlement? (1989 pp 23–24)

Bala goes on to argue that there should be some form of compensation for a supportive spouse, but rather than treating degrees, licences or other career assets as property, a remedy should be fashioned 'which is flexible enough to permit an assessment of all the circumstances' (p 25) including the value of the asset and the nature of the sacrifice of the supporting spouse.

> **Q** We will return to the issue of quantifying income and property division on divorce in Chapter 6, but wish at this point to raise the possibility of reconceiving of our notions of property to take such intangibles as career assets or pension rights into account. How would you answer the questions Bala has raised above? How would stereotypes of male and female roles in households affect the answers to those questions?

## VI. CONCLUSION

We have not focused this chapter upon the cases and legislation governing how members of a household earn and distribute income and acquire and hold property. In part, this is because the law does not have much to say about these issues, assuming they are a private matter for family members to decide among themselves unless and until the partners go their separate ways. Legal ordering in this event is discussed in later chapters. Rather, we have raised issues here about the implications of the assumption of family privacy and what it means for non-earning, and therefore, non-powerful members of families. These members rely upon earning and property owning members of families for their financial support, and for the most part, the law remains content with this form of familial organisation.

## FURTHER READING AND SELECTED RECENT REFERENCES

R AUCHMUTY, 'When Equality is not Equity: Homosexual Inclusion in Undue Influence Law' (2003) 11 *Feminist Legal Studies* 163.

A BAINHAM, *Children: The Modern Law*, 3rd edn, (Bristol, Family Law, 2005).

F BENNETT, *Gender and Benefits, Equal Opportunities Commission Working Paper Series No 30* (London, Equal Opportunities Commission, 2005).

S CRETNEY, 'Community of Property Imposed by Judicial Decision' (2003) 119 *Law Quarterly Review* 349.

L DAVIDOFF, *et al*, *The Family Story: Blood, Contract and Intimacy, 1830–1960* (London, Longman, 1989)

A DIDUCK, 'Fairness and Justice for All? The House of Lords in *White v White*' (2001) 9 *Feminist Legal Studies* 173.

G DOUGLAS, *An Introduction to Family Law*, 2nd edn, (Oxford, OUP, 2004).

GA DUNNE, 'A Passion for "Sameness"? Sexuality and Gender Accountability' in EB Silva and C Smart, (eds), *The New Family?* (London, Sage, 1999).

J FINCH and J MASON, *Negotiating Family Responsibilities* (London, Routledge, 1993).

L FOX, 'Reforming Family Property—Comparisons, Compromises and Common Dimensions' (2003) *CFLQ* 1

J GINN, 'Parenthood, Partnership Status and Pensions: Cohort Differences among Women' (2003) 37 *Sociology* 493.

J GINN and S ARBER, 'Patterns of Employment, Pensions and Gender: The Effect of Work History on Older Women's Non-State Pensions' (1996) 10 *Work, Employment and Society* 469.

C HAMILTON and B WATT, 'The Employment of Children' (2004) *Child and Family Law Quarterly* 135.

A LAWSON, 'The Things we Do for Love: Detrimental Reliance in the Family Home' (1996) 16 *Legal Studies* 218.

M MACLEAN and J EEKELAAR, 'The Obligations and Expectations of Couples Within Families: Three Modes of Interaction' (2004) 26 *JSWFL* 117.

MILES, 'Property Law v Family Law: Resolving the Problems of Family Property' (2003) 23 *Legal Studies* 624.

A PROUT, *The Future of Childhood* (London, Routledge Falmer, 2005).

C SAWYER, 'Equity's Children—Constructive Trusts for the New Generation' (2004) 16 *CFLQ* 31.

DK SMITH, 'Superannuating the Second Sex: Law, Privatisation and Retirement Income' (2001) 64 *Modern Law Review* 519.

J WEEKS, 'Elective families: Lesbian and Gay Life Experiments' in A Carling, S Duncan and R Edwards, (eds), *Analysing Families: Morality and Rationality in Policy and Practice* (London, Routledge, 2002).

J WEEKS, C DONOVAN and B HEAPHY, 'Everyday Experiments: Narratives of Non-heterosexual Relationships' in EB Silva and C Smart, (eds), *The New Family?* (London, Sage, 1999).

N WIKELEY, 'Children and Social Security Law' in J Fionda, (ed), *Legal Concepts of Childhood* (Oxford, Hart Publishing, 2001).

S WONG, 'Trusting in Trust(s): The Family Home and Human Rights' (2003) 11 *Feminist Legal Studies* 119.

*Reports*

Home Office, *Supporting Families: Responses to the Consultation Document* (London, The Stationery Office, 1999)

Law Commission, *Third Report on Family Property: The Matrimonial Home (Co-ownership and Occupancy Rights) and Household Goods*, No 86 (London, HMSO, 1978).

——, *Sharing Homes: A Discussion Paper, Report 278* (London, The Stationery Office, 2002).

J LEWIS, J DATTA and S SARRE, 'Individualism and Commitment in Marriage and Cohabitation' in *Lord Chancellor's Department Research Series No 8/99* (London, Stationery Office, 1999).

'Who Does What?' (2005) www.sociology.org.uk

C POND and A SEARLE, *The Hidden Army: Children at Work in the 1990s* (London, Low Pay Unit, 1991).

# SECTION 2

## The Principles Behind the Law

# 6

# Equality: Dividing the Family Assets

## I. INTRODUCTION

Before we introduce our case studies in the next section, we wish to introduce some of the principles with which the law operates to resolve household disputes. We will focus upon the principles of equality, welfare and family privacy. Chapters 6 and 7 will introduce the first of these principles, that of equality between the adult partners to a relationship, and will illustrate it in two contexts.

First, when partners are or have been in a marriage relationship, and, when the Civil Partnership Act comes into force,[1] a civil partnership, the court has jurisdiction to make orders regarding all of their property and finances, no matter how or when acquired. In considering these questions of finances, the court has an extremely broad discretion, which it exercises so as to achieve an economic 'fairness' between the parties. There are no statutory guidelines as to what 'fairness' means, or as to how best to achieve it, although the statutes that govern financial relief on separation, divorce, nullity or dissolution of civil partnerships contain lists of factors for the court to consider when it is deciding if and how to exercise its powers. The courts have also developed principles to guide the exercise of their discretion, and in this chapter we look at the primary principle of fairness in this regard and how, if at all, that principle should be informed by some idea of equality. We note also that when the partners have not married or registered their partnership, a type of formal equality based upon individualism applies. In these cases 'fairness' is not an issue unless it comes into play in equity's determination of beneficial ownership in property. Notwithstanding their affective and economic ties, former cohabitants are assumed to be legal strangers for the purposes of property division and support,[2] and we question whether there is a case for tempering this formal equality with an idea of fairness.

Secondly, questions may arise as between parents, and between parents and third parties, concerning the authority to make decisions about children's upbringing. In addition, when parents separate, arrangements have to be made for their children's residence and care. In relation to parental responsibility in particular, and to some extent residence and contact, the law has been shaped, at least in part, by the principle of equality. Parental responsibility is discussed in chapter 7.[3]

We seek to explore the development of equality as it has been adopted in family law, and present alternative conceptions of what it might mean. We will raise questions about the appropriateness of various notions of individual equality in families and the

---

[1] This is expected to be in December 2005.

[2] At the time of writing, the Law Commission is studying the possibility of introducing obligations for support and some property sharing between cohabitants. Its report is expected in 2006. See ch 2.

[3] See also ch 15. See, on residence and contact, chs 8, 14 and 15.

impact of gender on those notions. The discussion in this chapter will focus on the issue of maintenance and property division on separation/divorce/dissolution.

In both the 'public' sphere of work and wealth creation and the private sphere of family care, the relationship between the sexes has been characterised by increasing formal or liberal equality which, we argue, has had serious implications for women's economic well-being.[4] While we include in our discussion the distribution of income and property on the dissolution of both marriages and civil partnerships, both the legislative scheme regulating that distribution and the principles used to interpret it were developed in the context of heterosexual marriage and divorce and the structural and ideological considerations and assumptions about sex and gender roles that inform(ed) those institutions. The law in this area thus governs finances and property on (heterosexual) divorce and (same-sex) dissolution, but it was, and, we argue to a large degree still is, about the regulation of (gendered) marriage and divorce. Obviously, there is as yet no judicial analysis of the transferability of this law to same-sex relationships, and it will be interesting to see how the courts approach those cases, and what, if any, impact they, in turn, might have upon marriage and divorce.

Further, the law regarding the fair or 'rightful' ownership of, and ways of sharing, family finances and property was, and we suggest still is, impossible to separate from ideas about the ownership and acquisition of property generally, the 'rightful' places of men and women in society and their consequent implications for men's and women's relative abilities to accumulate wealth. And so, while ancillary relief law is about marriage and family roles, it is also about men's and women's relative abilities to engage with the 'public' world of work and wealth generation. Again, given that the legislation dealing with this 'wealth' and the judicial 'glosses' upon it were developed in the context of gendered relationships to work and to earning, it will be interesting to watch the first few ancillary relief disputes between former same-sex partners that come before the courts.

## II. HISTORICAL OVERVIEW

We have seen that marital relationships historically were not considered to be relationships based upon the type of equality we assume today. If there was any idea of equality at all, it was of the (spurious) 'separate but equal' type according to which each partner assumed a particular status as the result of the marriage; the husband's status gave him more economic, public and legal power and the wife's status gave her moral superiority in society and responsibility for the family.[5] The parties' economic statuses were dictated by the doctrine coverture. Cretney reminds us of Blackstone's authoritative view:

> The effect of the marriage contract (declared by statute to be indissoluble) was, for Blackstone, dramatic: the husband and wife became legally a single person, 'the very being or legal existence of the woman is suspended during the marriage' … . And, of course, on marriage, the wife's assets vested in the husband as his 'sole and absolute property', to 'be disposed of at his

4 See ch 5.
5 See, eg, Stone (1990) and the essays in Smart (1992). The 'traditional family' often eulogised today has its roots in this marital relationship in which each party's role was separate and clearly understood (Diduck 2003, Ch.2).

pleasure'. For Blackstone, marriage was accurately classified among the methods of acquiring property. True, it was not quite roses all the way for the husband: he was, for example, liable for the wife's pre-marital debts and for her torts; but for this reason the law gave him the power to restrain his wife by 'moderate correction' ... . Blackstone, nonetheless, assures us that the wife's legal disabilities were 'for the most part intended for her protection and benefit', so 'great a favourite is the female sex of the laws of England'. (Cretney 2003b p 403)

Unmarried heterosexual couples perhaps had more flexibility to order their private affairs, including their economic affairs, differently if they wished, and indeed it was this ability to opt out of the doctrine of coverture which encouraged many women to enter only into informal marriages (Parker 1990).[6] Couples living in lesbian or gay relationships may have kept the nature of their relationships secret, and could, in theory, create a relationship of equality for themselves if they wished.

The husband's economic and legal superiority over the wife, coupled with the moral, if not legal, indissolubility of marriage before the Divorce and Matrimonial Causes Act 1857, meant that, based simply upon his status as husband, he was responsible for maintaining her until her death. She could, however, disentitle herself from maintenance if she committed a matrimonial offence.[7] Finer and McGregor (1974) summarise the state of the law at this time:

The law had two dominant characteristics. First, it subordinated one sex to the other. This was both a cause and an effect of the wider social phenomenon which Mill called the 'subjection of women'—a subjection that was sexual, psychological, economic and domestic, as well as legal, in the midst of which women spent most of their lives (of which they had a far shorter expectation than exists today) occupied with the pains and responsibilities of childbearing and child rearing. The second characteristic of the law, which operated in this respect impartially as between the sexes, was the discrimination its institution created between the rich and the poor. In the sphere of married women's property, the wealthy classes with the aid of their advisors and the Chancery court protected their kin with the marriage settlement, while the common law stripped other women of their possessions. If a marriage broke down, a handful of the richest in the land could win their release from Parliament, and some others, if they could raise the fees and costs, could obtain a legal separation from the Church. The rest had no remedy. The same dichotomy permeated the law related to maintenance. The few women whose marriage was terminated in Parliament obtained—whether themselves guilty or not—a measure of secured financial support. A few others who brought successful petitions to the ecclesiastical courts were awarded decrees of alimony, although these were difficult of enforcement. All the rest of married women who had no separate property—and they were the vast majority—whether living together with or apart from their husbands were, apart from the exiguous protection provided by the doctrine of agency, literally at their husbands' mercy in the financial sense. If the husband was not kind, the wife's only resource was charity, the poor law, or prostitution ... . There developed from this situation, from the mid century onwards, a deliberate legislative drive towards equality: equality within the law for women; equality within the law for people of small means. All major developments in family law from this time onwards have been directed to these ends. (p 101)

---

[6] And see ch 2 above.
[7] On the history of the Matrimonial offence, see ch 14.

## III. THE MOVE TO EQUALITY

Let us develop Finer and McGregor's statement that all major developments in family law from the mid-19th century have been directed towards equality,[8] for equality can have different meanings to different people. 19th century legislative reforms created the possibility of divorce in the common law courts,[9] for the award and enforcement of maintenance (alimony) after divorce,[10] and, as we saw in the previous chapter, the law related to married women's property was reformed in this century as well, replacing the doctrine of coverture with that of formal equality and separate property. At this time, formal discrimination in many spheres of public life[11] and as between husband and wife became less and less socially acceptable. On a day-to-day basis, however, and despite an ethos of social equality, it was still women who required and were entitled to maintenance on divorce, and still men who had the obligation and income to provide it.[12] Even into the 20th century formal equality between the spouses did not translate into economic equality as the practices of mortgage lenders required that property be purchased in the name of the breadwinner or head of the family (Cretney 2003b), and the ideology of the traditional family meant that few middle class wives or mothers earned their own income.

Separation of property thus meant that on divorce, husbands usually were entitled to the(ir) property. They still had an obligation to support their former wives, however, and even before the 1970 reforms, judges had discretion as to how to enforce this obligation. If the wife were deemed to be entitled to support, often decided on moral grounds, the judge would then attempt to assess her needs, based on what he determined were her necessaries, given her station in life (Cretney 2003b). Carol Smart indicates that even until the 1960s maintenance obligations were based upon moral grounds.

> A wife was however legally entitled to claim a portion of a man's wage as a dependent under *certain conditions*. She did not have a right to share his wage, nor even to know what he earned, but as a dependent when the marriage broke down and as long as she met certain moral conditions, she was entitled to apply for maintenance. The maintenance could cease on her remarriage, when she became dependent on another man, or could be reduced to below subsistence level if her husband's circumstances changed. Maintenance awards were therefore not based on the wife's need so much as on what she was morally entitled to and what her husband could afford. The common law held that an adulterous wife lost all her rights to maintenance whether the adultery occurred before or after the breakdown of the marriage. However, in practice, statute law had modified this principle somewhat although it depended on the discretion of the judiciary just how much it was modified ... .
>
> In *M v M*[13] the wife lost her right to maintenance because it was discovered that she had had a child by another man eleven years after she and her husband separated. This was in spite of the fact that she had divorced her husband on the grounds of *his* adultery. ...
>
> This differential response to behaviour of husbands and wives undoubtedly contains a moral element ... . Most husbands were (and are) in a much more powerful financial position than their wives. Maintenance, like housekeeping, was in their *gift*. That is to say, it depended to a very great extent on their benevolence and cooperation. (1984 pp 89–91)

[8] See also The Honourable Mrs Justice (now Baroness) Hale (1998).
[9] Divorce and Matrimonial Causes Act 1857; and see ch 14.
[10] Divorce and Matrimonial Causes Act 1857.
[11] See, eg, Reform Act 1867; Reform Act 1884; Representation of the People Act 1918.
[12] See generally, Cretney 2003a ch 10.
[13] [1962] 2 All ER 895.

In 1970 the Matrimonial Proceedings and Property Act was passed. The Act followed the Law Commission's 1969 Report (Law Commission 1969) which recommended that the primary objective for any reform ought to be that the parties' financial positions 'should so far as possible be unaffected by their divorce' (see Law Commission 1980 para 22).[14] So, in addition to a list of factors for courts to consider in making maintenance determinations, it included a direction to that effect to courts. Among the list of factors for courts to consider when making awards of maintenance were the recipient's needs, the payer's ability to pay and any future obligations or resources each might have. The Act also attempted to address the difficulty with allocating property between the parties and gave the court jurisdiction to make property adjustment orders and orders for the sale of property. The 1970 Act was consolidated in 1973 with the Divorce Reform Act 1969 and the resulting Matrimonial Causes Act 1973 seemed to shift the ground generally to an approach which focused on the needs and means of the parties, but which still assumed that entitlement to maintenance was based upon a wife's dependence upon her husband. Smart described the developments in these terms:

It was suggested that during the 1970s the redistribution of family assets was gradually organised more around the concept of need than moral entitlement. Although such a shift is clearly visible, this formulation of the development of case law is somewhat oversimplistic. The major and overriding consideration to affect levels of maintenance is not so much the recipient's need as the donor's ability to pay. (1984 p 113)

She observed that in order to determine both need and ability to pay the Act directed courts to look to, among other things, the future needs and obligations of the spouses or former spouses as well as their earning power and future earning power. The concept of means and needs, therefore, was very flexibly applied in practice. Writing in 1984, she stated

The concept of need must therefore be seen as a highly flexible tool and over time the courts can prioritise different needs. For example there may now be occurring a shift away from an emphasis on the needs of the first wife towards the needs of a second family, and there has been a clear shift away from the needs of the spouses to the needs of the children. The 'flexibility' of the concept should not obscure the fact that it appears to have developed in response to the increasingly visible economic vulnerability of the dependent wife or mother. The courts as a whole (with the assistance of legislation) have now come to recognise that the division of labour in the family adversely affects the economic viability of women, particularly when they have children. In so doing they have employed private law to protect her but have rapidly begun to realise that the financial burden this may place on individual men is increasingly unacceptable to them. This is particularly the case where the man has remarried and has another family to support. The major issue affecting maintenance in the 1970s (and early 1980s) therefore is the extent to which wives, simply because of their marital status, can rely on their right to maintenance on divorce or separation. The extent to which judges have been willing to extinguish this right is not only a reflection of judicial perception of the changing role of women, it may also have an effect on the institution of marriage itself by challenging the taken-for-granted nature of women's dependency in marriage. (1984 p 114)[15]

---

[14] The 1969 Report's recommendation was enacted in s 25(1) of the MCA 1973 and became known as the principle of 'minimal loss'.
[15] See, further, Eekelaar (1991b).

This extract raises a number of issues. The first is that the legislation left (and still leaves) the determination of all ancillary relief, including maintenance awards, to the discretion of the presiding judge. And, as Smart noted, in the 1970s and 1980s judges were concerned both to ameliorate women's economic vulnerability and to protect men's finances.

> **Q** Apart from the direction in Section 25(1) to exercise their powers so as to put the parties in the financial position in which they would have been had the marriage not broken down—a concession to status-based policy which has now been repealed—there was no direction in the statute to judges to prioritise any of the considerations over others. And while the legislation has since been amended to prioritise the welfare of the children as well as the clean break principle,[16] and case law has provided some guidance,[17] judicial discretion remains wide.
>
> Would different considerations carry different weight depending upon the facts of the case? On the views of the judge? On the conduct of the parties as assessed by the judge?

The second point we wish to highlight from Smart's extract is that even where considerations other than morality were taken into account, the basis of any maintenance claim was, and still is, the fact of there having been a marriage. Smart suggested, however, that the needs/means approach may have had an effect on the ideological nature of marriage, as the status of wife, although a necessary starting point, was no longer sufficient for a successful maintenance claim.

> **Q** Do you agree with Smart's suggestion that, by beginning to question the assumption of female dependency in maintenance awards, judges can have some influence on the nature of marriage as it is currently practised?

In the 1970s, principles of formal equality in the public sphere[18] eventually led to calls for formal equality to be applied in the private sphere. Interest groups such as Campaign for Justice on Divorce (a divorced men's group) lobbied for a change in the law whereby a woman would not be entitled to maintenance from a man simply because she was at one time married to him. Many feminists also thought that entitlement to maintenance based upon status simply perpetuated women's dependency. It was thought that formal equality in the public sphere meant that women and men, during marriage and after divorce, ought to be able to remain financially independent of one another. The image of the 'alimony drone'[19]—the idle woman living off the hard-earned income of her former husband—was invoked to castigate dependent women in the name of equality principles.

In 1980 the Law Commission recommended 'evolutionary' change to the law, advocating the removal of the minimal loss principle and the inclusion of the requirement that courts give consideration to each party's capacity, actual or potential, to become

---

[16] See below pp 245–47.
[17] See below pp 248–71.
[18] The Sex Discrimination Act was passed in 1975, the Equal Pay Act in 1970. The election of a woman Prime Minister and gradual public acceptance of a woman's movement generally led to greater public acceptance of some notions of equality.
[19] 'Divorcees to lose meal ticket', *Guardian*, 3 November 1983, quoted by Smart (1984).

self-sufficient after divorce.[20] In addition, the 1979 House of Lords judgment in *Minton v Minton*[21] had made credible, in the social context of the time, the idea which was already becoming established in lower courts: that spouses, on divorce, ought to have a 'clean break' from one another. According to the frequently cited words of Lord Scarman: '[a]n object of the modern law is to encourage each to put the past behind them and to begin a new life which is not overshadowed by the relationship which has broken down' (p 608). His words, and the Law Commission's recommendations, captured in law the acceptability of social movements toward equality between the sexes, and the Matrimonial Causes Act 1973 was amended in 1984 in accordance with this movement. While the guidelines for the exercise of the court's discretion remained substantially unchanged, the legislation repealed the former Section 25(1) and incorporated new duties upon the court to consider, first, the welfare of any children of the marriage and then to consider whether imposing a 'clean break' between former spouses would be desirable.

The unarticulated model of equality adopted by this new divorce policy was one based upon sameness of treatment, or formal equality. Its liberal origins have been explored in earlier chapters. This approach to equality is based upon the proposition that there are no material differences between men and women in the context of modern, egalitarian marriage, and so any difference in treatment amounts to discrimination and constitutes a violation of equality principles. On this view, to assume that women require support from their husbands perpetuates women's inequality. Many who take this view of equality argue that all maintenance after divorce should therefore be abolished.[22]

This argument, and counter positions to it are summarised as follows:

> While the ultimate goal for many feminists may be to abolish maintenance altogether, such a move must occur only when there is no need for support and not be made merely as a concession to the rhetoric of formal sex equality. In order to abolish need, however, we must restructure fundamentally the relationship between state, family and work. Implicitly, we must not concentrate exclusively upon private support law in order to avoid asking the more basic questions around the division of responsibilities among men, women and society, and around the greater issues of sex equality in the economy generally. O'Donovan has suggested that we must meet five particular conditions in order to abolish the need for maintenance. She advises that the state must: first, ensure the equality of partners during marriage, including financial equality; second, ensure equal participation by both partners in wage earning activities; third, ensure that wages are geared to persons as individuals and not as heads of families; fourth: ensure treatment of persons as individuals and not as dependents by state agencies; and fifth, ensure provision of children by both parents, including financial support, child care, love, attention and stimulation.
>
> Even if one takes a different view and one's goal is not to abolish maintenance entirely, but rather to abolish the systemic economic and social disadvantage for women associated with a systemic gender based division of labour within marriage, similar fundamental changes in the social structure would be necessary. Along with true equity in employment and pay and affordable good quality child care, an adequate valuation of domestic work would mean it would not be necessary that each partner play exactly the same role in wage earning that O'Donovan envisions. Roles in marriage could be adopted based on the partners' actual interests and skills. Maintenance on divorce would still sometimes be necessary, then, but it would no longer

---

[20] See Law Commission (1980) and compare with this the Scottish Law Commission Report (1981).
[21] [1979] AC 593.
[22] See, eg, Deech (1977).

overwhelmingly be women who required it and it would no longer result in economic disadvantage for the recipient. Maintenance would be seen as a right, expected and earned, rather than as a gift, act of benevolence or based on a notion of *women's* dependency on *men*.

(Diduck and Orton 1994 p 686, references omitted)

Equality, then, can be understood or conceived of in law in different ways. The first view in the above passage envisages that men and women are 'similarly situated' in marriage and for the purposes of market activity, and so equality between them is to be achieved by treating them the same. The second view holds that in some cases, in marriage and the traditional workplace, for example, sameness of treatment results not in equality, but in inequality. This view recognises that some differences of treatment might be required in order to achieve equality, but that those differences are not required because of any assumed inherent differences between men and women[23]; instead they are needed to compensate for differences and disadvantage created by *institutions* such as marriage or structural conditions such as lack of public support for child care.[24] In this light, different treatment might be necessary to ensure that disadvantage is not suffered by one group disproportionately to another. This has been called substantive equality.[25]

Eekelaar, seeking in 1988 to theorise a basis for equality in maintenance questions, raised two further notions of equality: equality of outcome and equality of opportunity. He suggested, however, that neither of them could be seen as an appropriate objective for maintenance determinations. He defined equality of outcome as the goal that 'each spouse should exit from the marriage at the same economic level as the other' (1988 p 191) and suggested that the major objections to this principle were that it suffered from 'internal contradiction because, by rewarding people with disparate merits and needs equally, the outcome was an even greater inequality' (p 192). He saw equality of opportunity as the ideal that 'each former spouse should be in an equal position to take advantage of the opportunities to enhance her or his economic position in the labour market' (p 192), but this objective too he found artificial. '[T]he prevailing social structure (including, but not only, the labour market) is such that perfect equality of economic opportunity does not in fact pertain as between the sexes' (p 192). He concluded instead that the principle of 'resource sharing' ought to guide courts, in which the 'total combined income of the adults is shared equally among all the family members' (p 197), including children. This vision of equality, then, can be described as one in which equality between the sexes is subordinated to the claims of any children in the family to equality (p 198), and it still assumes ultimately that sameness of treatment is the answer.

Diduck and Orton comment upon his approach as follows:

In accepting that equality must always mean sameness [either] of treatment or of result, and thus failing to broaden his vision of equality outside of equality in the male patterned market, or to reconceptualise the traditional role of work within the family, it is not surprising that he could not find a basis for equality between the spouses and had to pursue such claims in the name of children. (1994 p 688)

---

[23] As was the case supporting protective labour legislation, for example. See ch 3.
[24] That women may be rendered vulnerable financially as a result of child care responsibilities appears to be recognised by the public. See Maclean and Eekelaar (2005).
[25] For an example of how substantive equality arguments have been used successfully in Canadian courts, see Women's Legal Education and Action Fund (1996).

In other words, Eekelaar's approach can be criticised because it failed to challenge the type of equality which accepts traditionally male characteristics, realities and work patterns as the ones to which all must aspire in order to receive the social advantages that men, as the currently more dominant social group, enjoy. It failed to ask 'equal to whom?' and why the traditionally male work pattern ought to be the one that is rewarded. His approach also failed to challenge the institutions, for example that of marriage, which created the disadvantage for one group as compared with the other (Diduck and Orton 1994). Indeed, he has suggested elsewhere that a woman may mitigate her loss from marriage by remarrying (Eekelaar 1991b p 83).

> **Q** Eekelaar's 'resource sharing' model of equality is based on an acceptance of the currently still dominant model of the husband-provider/wife and children-dependent family. It also entails equal provision for all on divorce. In this respect, the model can be seen as founded on a conception of the family unit as a type of collectivity with shared interests rather than as a group of individuals, each with his or her own individual interests. Indeed, one might suggest that individual equality principles are inappropriate when it comes to family relations, precisely because the family's interests are about the collective welfare of the group and therefore cannot be separated into the rights or interest of the individuals. Which approach do you prefer?

Formal equality approaches have informed family law reform in the past two decades and perhaps the best example of this in action is the reform made in 1984 to the MCA 1973. As we said above, the Matrimonial and Family Proceedings Act 1984 repealed the old Section 25 of the 1973 Act[26] and replaced it with a new Section 25 that made the welfare of the child the first consideration in support cases,[27] and with a new Section 25A which directed courts to consider imposing a clean break between the parties. The MCA 1973 now reads as follows:

25 (1) It shall be the duty of the court in deciding whether to exercise its powers under section 23,[28] 24,[29] 24A[30] or 24B[31] above and, if so, in what manner, to have regard to all the circumstances of the case, first consideration being given to the welfare while a minor of any child of the family who has not attained the age of eighteen.
 (2) As regards the exercise of the powers of the court under section 23(a) (b) or (c), 24, 24A or 24B above in relation to a party to the marriage, the court shall in particular have regard to the following matters—

---

[26] This directed the courts to try to keep the parties in the position they would have been had the divorce not occurred—the so-called principle of 'minimal loss'.

[27] This approach seems to adopt Eekelaar's preferred model.

[28] S 23 enables the court, on granting a decree of divorce, of nullity of marriage, or of judicial separation, to make financial provision orders for a spouse or child of the family, including periodical payments for a specified term, secured periodical payments for a specified term and lump sum payments.

[29] On granting a decree of divorce, a decree of nullity or a judicial separation, the court may make property adjustment orders, including a transfer of property to a spouse or child or other party for the benefit of a child, a settlement of property for the benefit of a spouse or child, and a variation of any ante-nuptial or post-nuptial settlement.

[30] This section gives the court power, where it makes a secured periodical payments order, a lump sum order or a property adjustment order, to order the sale of any property in which or in the proceeds of sale in which either or both spouses has a beneficial interest.

[31] This section gives the court power, on or after granting a decree of divorce or a decree of nullity, to make a pension sharing order.

(a)   the income, earning capacity, property and their financial resources which each of the parties to the marriage has or is likely to have in the foreseeable future, including in the case of earning capacity any increase in that capacity which it would in the opinion of the court be reasonable to expect a party to the marriage to take steps to acquire;

(b)   the financial needs, obligations and responsibilities which each of the parties to the marriage has or is likely to have in the foreseeable future;

(c)   the standard of living enjoyed by the family before the breakdown of the marriage;

(d)   the age of each party to the marriage and the duration of the marriage;

(e)   any physical or mental disability of either of the parties to the marriage;

(f)   the contributions which each of the parties has made or is likely in the foreseeable future to make to the welfare of the family, including any contribution by looking after the home or caring for the family;

(g)   the conduct of each of the parties, if that conduct is such that it would in the opinion of the court be inequitable to disregard it;

(h)   in the case of proceedings for divorce or nullity of marriage, the value to each of the parties to the marriage of any benefit, which, by reason of the dissolution or annulment of the marriage, that party will lose the chance of acquiring.

...

25A (1) Where on or after the grant of a decree of divorce or nullity of marriage the court decides to exercise its powers under section 23(1)(a), (b) or (c), 24, 24A or 24B above in favour of a party to the marriage, it shall be the duty of the court to consider whether it would be appropriate so to exercise those powers that the financial obligations of each party towards the other will be terminated as soon after the grant of the decree as the court considers just and reasonable.

(2) Where the court decides in such a case to make a periodical payments or secured payments order in favour of a party to a marriage, the court shall in particular consider whether it would be appropriate to require those payments to be made or secured only for such term as would in the opinion of the court be sufficient to enable the party in whose favour the order is made to adjust without undue hardship to the termination of his or her financial dependence on the other party.

(3) Where on or after the grant of a decree of divorce or nullity of marriage an application is made by a party to the marriage for a periodical payments or secured payments order in his or her favour, then, if the court considers that no continuing obligation should be imposed on either party to make or secure periodical payments for the other, the court may dismiss the application with a direction that the applicant shall not be entitled to make any future application in relation to that marriage for an order under section 23(1)(a) or (b)[32] above.

So, with the exception of the welfare of children, no factor is prioritised in Section 25 over others and, although there is explicit reference to the aim of a clean break where appropriate, no clear or even coherent model of support or property allocation is apparent. Indeed, the factors can be interpreted as supporting different models. Subsections 25(2)(a), (b), (c), (d) and (e) seem to point to a needs-based or income security model in which the obligation to support arises from the marriage itself and the quantum and duration of support from a simple calculation of the parties' needs and means, regardless of the source of those needs and means. Subsections (f), (g) and (h) contain elements of a compensation model in which maintenance should compensate for financial advantages and disadvantages to each party of the roles they undertook in the marriage. Entitlement is not based on the *fact* of the marriage, but rather is a

[32] Orders for periodical payments and secured periodical payments, respectively.

reimbursement or compensation for needs that were created by the way in which the parties structured their marital roles. Finally, Section 25A points to a clean break model in which maintenance, if awarded at all, is meant to be rehabilitative or temporary in order to recognise the parties' presumptively equal ability to move on financially from the marital relationship. 'Equality', applied in each of these models takes on very different meanings.

Let us continue with the legislation, focusing on the clean break principle.

28 (1) Subject in the case of an order made on or after the grant of a decree of divorce or nullity of marriage to the provisions of sections 25A(2) above and 31(7)[33] below, the term to be specified in a periodical payments or secured periodical payments order in favour of a party to a marriage shall be such term as the court thinks fit, except that the term shall not begin before or extend beyond the following limits, that is to say—

(a)  in the case of a periodical payments order, the term shall begin not earlier than the date of the making of an application for the order, and shall be so defined as not to extend beyond the death of either of the parties to the marriage or, where the order is made on or after the grant of a decree of divorce or nullity of marriage, the remarriage of the party in whose favour the order is made;

(b)  in the case of a secured periodical payments order, the term shall begin not earlier than the date of the making of an application for the order, and shall be so defined as not to extend beyond the death, or where the order is made on or after the grant of such a decree, the remarriage of the party in whose favour the order is made.[34]

(1A) Where a periodical payments or secured periodical payments order in favour of a party to a marriage is made on or after the grant of a decree of divorce or nullity of marriage, the court may direct that the party shall not be entitled to apply under section 31 below for the extension of the term specified in the order.

...

**Q** Why should remarriage of the payee terminate support? What model or 'ground' for support is envisaged by termination on remarriage?

Symes' analysis, published in 1985, remains pertinent. She acknowledged that the clean break principle could be seen as 'arguably a logical step forward in the long march towards liberal divorce and sexual equality' (1985 p 46). She went on to argue, however, that it contains within it an internal contradiction which is in danger of creating severe inequity because, in failing to reconsider the nature of marriage at the time it considered the reform of divorce law, those who framed the 1984 reform which introduced it imposed a consequence of solubility (clean break) upon indissoluble (provider/dependant) marriage. She phrased it this way:

Quite clearly, marriage as it has traditionally been practised, is not intended to be ended by divorce. Indeed, traditional housewife marriage has a most potent feature of indissolubility built right into it—dependency ... . The accumulation of responsibilities and obligations, the consequences of an unequal partnership based on dependency—all mean that an absolute

[33] S 31 gives the court power to vary, discharge or suspend orders for financial relief. S 31(7) states that when the court is considering making such an order, it is to have regard to all the circumstances of the case, including the any changes to the factors listed in s 25(1) and (2).
[34] The effect of this is that an unsecured periodical payments order can continue after the death of the payer.

severance of the bond without massive adjustment would be manifestly unjust, more likely impossible. (Symes 1985 p 57)

And further:

> Divorce in fact takes the lid off marriage, exposes the issue of female dependency and reveals just how much has been taken for granted as appropriate family activity. The process of childrearing was carried out relatively cheaply in the traditional nuclear family, with the mother usually combining her roles of spouse/parent and homemaker with no direct financial reward. Modern divorce with its emphasis on ultimate self-sufficiency has very rightly called in question the underlying assumptions about this role fusion. For example, is there a legitimate role of homemaker when there are no children? Equally, we must ask, is it just to place the general burden of caring (for children and those of society's dependants who are not in institutions) on women without it being rewarded? ...
>
>     Before divorce became pandemic it was possible to avoid these questions of discriminatory role assumptions, although this did not necessarily mean that all was well within the family and that the system worked without injustice. But given our general goal of economic self-sufficiency at the end of marriage, it is imperative that there now be potential if not actual self-sufficiency *throughout* marriage as well. (p 56)

Even if we accept that some notion of equality is appropriate for courts to consider in post-divorce financial adjustment, we are faced with the question of why the husband should have to compensate his wife for all the structural inequalities created by society historically, economically and socially. Symes questioned the appropriateness of trying to rectify systemic inequality through 'private' family law reform. She went on to argue that divorce law cannot provide a substitute for 'humane social policy' incorporating provision for state support. She highlighted female dependency during marriage as a primary reason for the difficulties in adjustment on divorce but maintained that divorce law alone could not provide a solution. For one thing, as she noted, women generally suffer from discrimination in the labour market and with regard to pensions. For another, she said:

> In very few cases will financial provision [on divorce] adequately recompense an ex-wife for the many disadvantages she suffers when her marriage ends and distinguishing between specifically marriage-related disabilities and more general ones is not always a simple exercise ... [Further], [o]nce a party's earning ability has been permanently impaired, clean break divorce is impossible without grave injustice unless adequate state provision (including pensions) compensates for the impairment. The long term effects of such impairment are so profound the task is almost impossible for divorce law in isolation. (p 51)

Others agree that women's equality generally will not be achieved by divorce or family law reform alone, but argue that support law can redress at least some of women's disadvantage on divorce and ought to reflect some fairness as between the parties. '[A]rguing for systemic change does not mean we should continue to tolerate unfairness in the allocation of family resources on separation and divorce. Law must deal with the society it has helped to create and play its part in shaping ideologies it helps to support.' (Diduck and Orton 1994 p 685)

One way to do this is to revise assumptions about the *value* of each party's role in the family enterprise:

To recognize that each spouse is an equal economic and social partner in marriage, regardless of function, is a monumental revision of assumptions. It means, among other things, that caring for children is just as valuable as paying for their food and clothing. It means that organizing a household is just as important as the career that subsidizes this domestic enterprise. It means that the economics of marriage must be viewed qualitatively rather than quantitatively. (Diduck and Orton 1994 pp 699–700 quoting Abella JA, references omitted)

**Q** How does this approach to equality on divorce differ from Eekelaar's? From Symes'? From formal equality?

Recall that the MCA provides the court with a wide discretion on financial matters. The court's discretion has been described in these terms:

> The Family Court takes the rights and obligations of the parties all together—and puts the pieces into a mixed bag. Such pieces are the right to occupy the matrimonial home or to have a share in it, the obligation to maintain the wife and children, and so forth. The court then takes out the pieces and hands them to the two parties—some to one party and some to the other—so that each can provide for the future with the pieces allotted to him or to her. The court hands them out without paying any too nice a regard to their legal rights or equitable interests but simply according to what is the fairest provision for the future, for mother and father and the children ... . (per Lord Denning MR in *Hanlon v The Law Society* [1981] AC 124 p 147.

The English approach, therefore, is to treat all matters, financial and property, as a discretionary part of a 'mixed bag'. There is, consequently, no *right* to receive financial support and no right to any item of property. There is just a right to claim them and then to rely upon the court's determination of the 'fairest provision' for the future of the parties.

By the end of the 1990s, then, a trend had developed in the way that courts exercised their wide statutory discretion to distribute the contents of the 'mixed bag'. In 2000 District Judge Bird put it this way:

Housing is normally the most important issue; the housing of the parent with care of the children normally takes priority over that of the other parent, although his/her needs must be met wherever possible. Once housing has been disposed of the reasonable needs of the parties should be considered. The clean break should only be imposed where there is no doubt that the parties will be self-sufficient. Attention must be given to pensions. Where the reasonable needs of the parties have been met there is no justification for further adjustment by the court.

(2000 p 831)[35]

**Q** Does equality in any of its forms feature in this approach?

---

[35] See also Family Law Committee (1998 para 8.5(a)); Solicitors' Family law Association (SFLA) (1998 para 23); Association of District Judges (1998 p 2).

## IV. ILLUSTRATION OF THE PRINCIPLES 1984–2000

*Example 1: Wealthy Parties*

For high income families, or families with extensive capital, the so-called 'big money cases', application of the principles of welfare, reasonable requirements and clean break usually meant that housing was not an issue. What was in issue was usually the extent of the distribution of the remaining assets and income. On this point, the courts considered primarily the 'needs', or rather 'reasonable requirements', of the claimant spouse. The case of *Dart v Dart*[36] was the leading case and a good example of this principle in action. The parties had been married 15 years. They had lived in England for two years, having moved as tax exiles from the United States. The Dart family fortune had been made in foam cups and Mr Dart was worth at the time of the divorce anywhere from £400 million (his estimate) to £800 million (her estimate). The wife applied for full disclosure of the husband's financial situation but he replied with the *Thyssen*[37] defence 'that since he recognised that he was rich enough to comply with any order that the court might make, detailed financial disclosure was superfluous'.[38] In upholding the trial judgment award of, among other things, a lump sum in favour of the wife in the amount of £9 million, Thorpe LJ in the Court of Appeal discussed the history and context of the Section 25 guidelines, and referred specifically to sex equality principles. He went on:

> The statutory design was to give the judge exercising the power of equitable distribution the widest discretion to do fairness between the parties, reflecting considerations and criteria laid out within the section. Parliament might have opted for a community of property scheme or some fraction approach. It opted instead for a wide judicial discretion that would produce a bespoke solution to fit the infinite variety of individual cases. (p 294)

---

[36] [1996] 2 FLR 286.

[37] So named after the case in which the proposition was established *Thyssen-Bornemisza v Thyssen-Bornemisza (No 2)* [1985] FLR 1069 (CA). Since the court's disapproval of it in *White v White* (see below), this defence has been narrowed significantly, but Coleridge, J has held recently that there still might be place for it. In *J v V (Disclosure: Offshore Corporations)*[2003] EWHC 3110 (Fam); [2004] 1 FLR 1042; [2004] Fam Law 398:

> [128] ... [The so-called Thyssen defence] was a very useful mechanism employed regularly in the 1980s and 1990s for avoiding huge financial enquiries in circumstances where wealth was very considerable and where a respondent was prepared to make an admission as to the overall value of the available wealth and the broad categories into which it fell. It is sometimes said that nowadays, with the greater emphasis placed on fractions and 'contribution' since *White v White* [2001] 1 AC 596, [2000] 2 FLR 981, that this mechanism is no longer apt or useful. I do not agree. [...] Especially where cases involve marriages of short/medium length and the wealth has largely come from sources other than the efforts of the respondent during the course of the marriage, Thyssen defences could still be usefully deployed. An application at the First Appointment stage to the High Court judge allocated to hear such a case might save enormous time and money by adjudicating on this as a preliminary issue.
> [129] Furthermore, I hope I am not being naive in saying that even in the longer marriage cases where a 50/50 split is the aspiration, many applicants would, I feel sure, be prepared to compromise over precision providing sensible admissions at a high figure were made in order to avoid acrimonious, lengthy and very expensive proceedings.

[38] *Dart* p 289. The husband did, however, end up providing disclosure in the form of '19 pages of schedules and 35 ring binders containing approximately 7000 pages of supporting documents' (p 289).

**Q** It is interesting in the light of this comment that before a decision was made in the *Dart* case, Mrs Dart brought an application that the matter be heard in the Michigan courts where a less discretionary property distribution regime applied. Thorpe LJ said at page 288 '[i]t is plain that Mrs Dart thought she would do better in Michigan whilst Mr Dart thought he would do better in London'. Why do you suppose that Mr Dart thought that he would 'do better' under the English discretionary system?

Thorpe LJ continued.

The scheme of the Act must also be set in the wider perspective of history and of the general civil law. In this jurisdiction rights of property are not invaded or reduced by statutory powers save for specific and confined purposes. The purpose of this statute was to make fair financial arrangements on or after divorce in the absence of agreement between the former spouses. Beyond that power was not introduced to reorganise proprietary rights within families. After commencement on 1 January 1971 there was obviously curiosity and speculation amongst practitioners as to how this new power would be interpreted and utilised by the courts. In 1973 Lord Denning MR chose the case of *Wachtel v Wachtel* [39] as a vehicle for the pronouncement of guidelines. He proposed a mathematical solution. If the applicant was to have periodical payments her capital share should be one-third. If she were not to have periodical payments then her capital share should be one half. ... But behind these deferential acknowledgements [by judges of Lord Denning's reasoning over the years] lies the reality that it has been consistently rejected as an authority of general application. The real interpreter of s 25 and its predecessor was Ormrod LJ who between 1976 and 1981 demonstrated in a series of judgements in this court how s 25 should be utilised by practitioners in negotiating or judges in determining the fair result. This was one of his major contributions to the evolution of family law. (p 294)

Thorpe LJ went on to refer to Ormrod LJ's insistence in *O'D v O'D*[40] that the judge should direct himself by reference to the Section 25 criteria and not use fractions other than within the context of a broad analysis of outcome. Counsel for Mrs Dart argued that in the 'big money' cases, the courts were giving undue weight to the consideration of the claimant's need over the other factors listed in Section 25, an approach first established in *Preston v Preston*,[41] where it was held 'there should be a ceiling on the award to the wife based on her spending needs in the form of a capital sum which reduces in income and capital which both expire on the day she dies' (Bennett 1997 p 79).

Thorpe LJ continued, explaining the different ways in which 'needs' had been interpreted, and then saying:

it is implicit that reasonable requirements are more extensive than needs ... There must be an objective appraisal of what the applicant subjectively requires to ensure that it is not unreasonable. But the objective appraisal must have regard to the other criteria of the section, obviously including what is available, the standard of living to which the parties are accustomed, their age and state of health and, perhaps less obviously, the duration of the marriage, contributions, pension rights both as affected by the marriage and as accrued or likely to accrue. (p 296)

---

[39] [1973] 2 WLR 366.
[40] [1976] Fam. 83.
[41] [1982] Fam. 17.

**Q** Would you be happy, if you were Mrs Dart, to rely upon the court's objective determination of your reasonable requirements? Recall that Mrs Dart was awarded approximately £9 million. In your view, was fairness achieved in the *Dart* case? Was any form of equality achieved? Keep in mind that it was never clarified whether or to what extent Mrs Dart contributed to Mr Dart's fortune. In your view, should this matter?

Diduck (2001b) comments on this case:

> It is arguable that the erstwhile 'fairness' of the clean break or needs based models had very little to do with principles of non-discrimination, but relied instead upon principles reflected in what have been called supporting ideologies of the law, including the protection of property and individual liberty. Further, because courts were deciding matters between husbands and wives rather than between autonomous and acontextual legal individuals, those principles also relied upon a particular ideology of the marital relationship in which the relationship itself and the parties to it were gendered in very specific ways. So, for example, in the breadwinner/dependent ideology of marriage the claimant wife (and approximately 70% of claimants are wives) comes to law not as the autonomous rights-bearing individual, but as dependent and supplicant (or potential plunderer of her husband's fortune). The husband/breadwinner's subjectivity, on the other hand, is more easily reconciled with liberal law's subject—he is the autonomous rights-bearing property holder and therefore comes to law as either benefactor or potential victim of plunder. Fairness between *those* subjects, arising out of *that* relationship, in the light of the 'supporting ideologies of law' resulted in a body of case law in which wifely dependency was confirmed and the protection of property interests appeared to be paramount.
>
> In *Dart v Dart*, for example, perhaps the leading 'big money' case before *White*,[42] the Court of Appeal stated 'the scheme of [the Matrimonial Causes Act 1973] must also be set in the wider perspective of history and of the general civil law. In this jurisdiction rights of property are not invaded or reduced by statutory powers save for specific and confined purposes.' This meant that non-propertied wives were required to demonstrate extraordinary or exceptional contribution to the marriage or direct financial contribution to the acquisition of the property in question before they were thought, in fairness, to deserve a share in it. Instead, the breadwinner/dependent ideology prevailed in which so long as her reasonable requirements were met, fairness dictated that she had no further claim to assets, no matter how extensive they were. It was as if the courts felt similar to the way in which many husbands and wives feel when they are negotiating ancillary relief—that it is the husband's money and assets that are being dealt with.
>
> (pp 174–75 references omitted)

Bennett too regarded the outcome in big money cases as unsatisfactory:

> In case legal advisors are still advising wives that if they make contributions this will make a difference, the salutary experience of reading *Gojkovic* is recommended. The court found that the wife had contributed 50% but she was awarded 27% of the assets ... .
>
> The award in such cases ... is out of line with most other non-Islamic jurisdictions. At a recent meeting of the International Bar Association, Family Law Committee, on multi-million dollar divorces ... [t]he conclusion was that the award to the wife in nearly 30 jurisdictions around the world would be from 10% to 50%, with the exception of England where it would be 0.6%. (Bennett 1997 p 79)

---

[42] See below pp 255–58.

*Example 2: Low and Middle Income Families*

The principles were the same for low and middle income families, except that after their housing situation was considered, there was usually little left for redistribution. Like in the big money cases, clean break, welfare, needs and means were the primary factors to be taken into account but, in practice, this meant that the court would often order the transfer of the husband's interest in the home to the wife for her benefit and that of any children in her care, in exchange for dismissing her claim for ongoing support and dismissing or reducing any claim for child support.[43] Priest noted, however, that:

> Such clean break orders, although made in their hundreds by county court registrars/district judges throughout the UK, were overwhelmingly orders made by consent, and were thus not productive of a reported appellate jurisprudence giving them the clear imprimatur of the Court of Appeal (although indirect support might be derived from authorities such as *Ashley v Blackman* ... and *Delaney v Delaney* ...). They thus formed part of a 'submerged' jurisprudence, evolved and endorsed by practice, and one which gave the lie to the Law Commission's expectation, in 1981, that cases in which a clean break for spousal support would be considered appropriate would be 'comparatively few (and where there were infant children almost non-existent)'. (Law Com. No 112, *The Financial Consequences of Divorce, The Response to the Discussion Paper*, para 24) (Priest 1997 p 115)

Transferring the home was only one way in which a clean break was achieved by the courts where it was felt that entitlement to maintenance existed. Lump sums or time limited periodical payments were also awarded (and indeed the court has the obligation to consider them in Section 25A of the MCA 1973), particularly where the wife was seen as able to earn an independent income, where the marriage was of short duration or where the wife intended to remarry in the future. Harcus (1997) summed up the situation respecting time limited periodical payments as follows:

> The conclusion that one must surely draw from a review of the cases is that, whatever the rationale behind the particular decisions,[44] the court has been prepared to make term orders (albeit without prohibition)[45] in cases where:
>
> (1)  the marriage is short;
> (2)  there is evidence of earning capacity;
> (3)  the wife is as old as 38–40 years of age; and
> (4)  notwithstanding that there was a child or children of tender years.
>
> It is apparent also that even if there is some uncertainty as to whether a wife can or cannot adjust without undue hardship to the termination of her maintenance, the court will make an order. It will not, however, in such circumstances make a prohibition. Equally, the cases show that the court is not prepared to make such an order in the case of a long marriage where the wife's earning capacity has been affected by her duties as a wife and mother over a long period of time—and rightly so. (Harcus 1997 pp 341–42)

---

[43] See, eg, *Livesey (formerly Jenkins) v Jenkins* [1985] AC 424 (HL); and the incompatibility of clean break settlements with the philosophy and application of the Child Support Act 1991 as it was originally applied. See *Crozier v Crozier* [1994] Fam 114; [1994] 2 All ER 362; [1994] 2 WLR 444; [1994] 1 FLR 126; and ch 5.

[44] He drew upon *Barrett v Barrett* (1988) 2 FLR 516; *Waterman v Waterman* [1989] 1 FLR 380; and *Mawson v Mawson* [1994] 2 FLR 985.

[45] In terms of s 28(1A).

However, he then cited a number of cases decided in 1996 which, to him, changed the state of the law.[46] In one of these, *C v C*,[47] Ward LJ gave the following guidance on term orders:

(1) The first task is to consider a clean break which pursuant to s 25A(1) requires the court to consider whether it would be appropriate to exercise its powers so that the financial obligations of each party towards the other will be terminated as soon after the grant of the decree as the court considers just and reasonable.
(2) If there is to be no clean break, and a periodcial [*sic*] payments order is to be made, then the court must decide pursuant to s 25 what amount is to be ordered. The duration of the marriage is in fact relevant to the determination of quantum.
(3) If a periodical payments order is made, whether for 5p pa or whatever, the question is whether it would be appropriate to impose a term because in the absence of such a direction, the order will endure for joint lives or until the remarriage of the payee: see s 28(1)(a).
(4) The statutory test is this: is it appropriate to order periodical payments only for such a term as in the opinion of the court would be sufficient to enable the payee to adjust without undue hardship to the termination of financial dependence on the paying party?
(5) What is appropriate must of necessity depend on all the circumstances of the case including the welfare of any minor child and the s 25 checklist factors, one of which is the duration of the marriage. It is, however, not appropriate simply to say, 'This is a short marriage, therefore a term must be imposed'.
(6) Financial dependence being evident from the very making of an order for periodical payments, the question is whether, in the light of all the circumstances of the case, the payee can adjust—and adjust without undue hardship—to the termination of financial dependence and if so when. The question is can she adjust, not should she adjust. In answering that question the court will pay attention not only to the duration of the marriage but to the effect the marriage and its breakdown and the need to care for any minor children has had and will continue to have on the earning capacity of the payee and the extent to which she is no longer in the position she would have been in but for the marriage, its consequence and its breakdown. It is highly material to consider any difficulties that the payee may have in entering or re-entering the labour market, resuming a fractured career and making up any lost ground.
(7) The court cannot form its opinion that a term is appropriate without evidence to support its conclusion. Facts supported by evidence must, therefore, justify a reasonable expectation that the payee can and will become self-sufficient. Gazing into the crystal ball does not give rise to such a reasonable expectation. Hope, with or without pious exhortations to end dependency, is not enough.
(8) It is necessary for the court to form an opinion not only that the payee will adjust, but also that the payee will have adjusted within the term that is fixed. The court may be in a position of such certainty that it can impose a deferred clean break by prohibiting an extension of the term pursuant to s 28(1A). If, however, there is doubt about when self-sufficiency will be attained, it is wrong to require the payee to apply to extend the term. If there is uncertainty about the appropriate length of the term, the proper course is to impose no term but leave the payer to seek the variation and if necessary go through the same exercise, this time pursuant to s 31(7)(a) [regarding variation and discharge applications]. (pp 45–46)

Q Harcus suggested that these new, stricter principles meant that the term order would from then on be used more rarely and that this would do more injustice than justice. He proposed that 'proper evidence of "can" with a bit of "should"

46 See *G v G (Periodical Payments: Jurisdiction)* [1997] 1 FLR 368; *Flavell v Flavell* [1997] 1 FLR 353; and *C v C (Financial Relief: Short Marriage)* [1997] 2 FLR 26.
47 [1997] 2 FLR 26.

and not "will"' (1997 p 344) should be the test for ability to adjust to termination. Do you agree? Which approach appears better to meet the test of fairness? Which approach better conforms to the legislation and its philosophy? Did either the courts' earlier approach or their newer one meet any of the definitions of equality discussed above? See, for example, Grassby (1991) referred to in chapter 5.

In *Clutton v Clutton*[48] the clean break principle was considered in conjunction with considerations of housing and the possible remarriage of the former wife.[49] The parties were married for 20 years before they separated in 1984. The court at the time of their divorce in 1985 made an order transferring the matrimonial home to the wife, subject to a charge in the husband's favour in the amount of £7000, not to be enforced until 1991 when the children would be 23 and 16 years of age. It also made an award of child support and an award of periodical payments for the wife in the amount of £10 per week. The equity in the home, the sole capital asset of the parties, was £50,000. On appeal, the judge took into account the husband's net disposable income of £127 per week, his new wife's income of £2000 per year, the former wife's income of £66 per week and the fact that she was in a stable sexual relationship with another man, and ordered a clean break. Confirming the transfer to the wife, he set aside both the wife's periodical payments order and the husband's charge over the matrimonial home. Lloyd LJ on the husband's further appeal said the following:

An order whereby the sale of the matrimonial home is postponed until the youngest child of the family is 18, or some other age, is usually known as a *Mesher* order: see *Mesher v Mesher and Hall* (1973) [1980] 1 All ER 126n. An order whereby the sale is postponed until the wife dies, remarries or cohabits with another man, is usually known as a *Martin* order: see *Martin v Martin* [1977] 3 All ER 762, [1978] Fam 12. It will be seen that while, in 1984, the wife was asking for an out-and-out transfer of the matrimonial home, she would have been content, in the alternative, with a *Martin* order. (p 342)

The principle of the clean break was, of course, well established long before the Matrimonial and Family Proceedings Act 1984; see eg, *Minton v Minton* … It is now enshrined in section 25A(1) of the Matrimonial Causes Act 1973. But there is perhaps a danger of referring to it as a 'principle', since it might lead courts to strive for a clean break, regardless of all other considerations. This is not what section 25A requires … . (p 343)

Where the judge went wrong, and plainly wrong in my opinion, was in refusing to make a *Martin* order … Why then did the judge not make a *Martin* order? … It cannot surely have been because a *Martin* order would offend against the principle of clean break. A charge which does not take effect until death or remarriage could only be said to offend against the principle of the clean break in the most extended sense of that term. The only clue we have is the argument on behalf of the wife that she did not want to be spied on.

I see some force in that argument … [but] it is far outweighed by the resentment which the husband will naturally feel if the wife remarries within a year or two and continues thereafter to occupy the matrimonial home. She says she has no intention of marrying Mr Davidson. But it remains a distinct possibility … .

It is true that, in the present case, the husband's earning capacity is very much greater than that of the wife. In due course, when he has paid off his debts, he will be able to get back on to the property ladder without insuperable difficulty … . The question is whether the difference in earning capacity, and the severance of the maintenance tie, justified an out and out transfer of the sole capital asset to the wife. In my judgment it did not. The very least which the judge

---

48 [1991] 1 All ER 340.
49 On the relevance of the recipient spouse's new relationship, see Hayes (1994).

should have done was to order a charge in favour of the husband in the event of the wife's death or remarriage ... .

... Not to have made a *Martin* order in this case was therefore manifestly unjust to the husband. (pp 343–45)

Ewebank J agreed, and the court made an order that the proceeds of sale of the house were to be divided one third to the husband and two thirds to the wife (or her estate) on the death, remarriage or cohabitation of the wife.[50]

**Q** To what degree does this solution reflect any of the previously described principles of equality?

Courts were just as concerned to consider a clean break in those cases in which two households simply could not be maintained on the parties' incomes. In some of these cases the question was the interaction of state support with private support for families. In the majority of those cases, it was the former wife, because she had care of children, who became eligible for Income Support,[51] and the question facing both the respondent and the courts was the extent to which maintenance payments from a former spouse ought to be required to reduce the amount of benefit she received. The courts sought to balance achieving a clean break between the spouses and passing the spousal obligation to the taxpayers. Writing in 1990, Cretney highlighted for practitioners some of the factors to be kept in mind when dealing with low income families:

> The courts have traditionally adopted a pragmatic solution. Income support rates are pitched at subsistence level, and the court, therefore, will rarely make a substantive order against a spouse who is on income support ... . Moreover, if both parties have incomes at or near the subsistence level, the court, while not allowing the less impoverished spouse to throw onto the state the cost of supporting his dependents, will allow him and his family to keep not only a subsistence level of income ... but also some additional financial incentive to continue in work: *Barnes v Barnes* [1972] WLR 1381; *Stockford v Stockford* (1982) 3 FLR 58; *Freeman v Swatridge* [1984] FLR 762; *Peacock v Peacock* [1984] FLR 263.
>
> The novelty here is the growing judicial support for using the clean break provisions introduced by the Matrimonial and Family Proceedings Act 1984 as a technique to reconcile the policies of protecting public funds on the one hand, whilst on the other hand enabling the parties to put the past behind them and to begin new lives which are not overshadowed by the relationship which has broken down ... . The principle appears to be that a spouse should be allowed to see light at the end of the tunnel, and hence, in appropriate cases, a periodical payments order should be made for a defined period: *Ashley v Blackman* [1988] 2 FLR 278.
>
> (1990 p 377)

Although appealed specifically on the issue of child support, the case of *Delaney v Delaney*[52] illustrates the court's preference for a clean break where there are other resources, including income support, to support the recipient spouse. The Court of Appeal allowed Mr Delaney and his new girlfriend to remain in their newly purchased three bedroomed semi-detached house (with their total joint income of £212 per week)

---

[50] On registrars' (now district judges) interpretations of the s 25 factors see Eekelaar (1991b). He found that principles or models did not usually underpin registrars' decisions with respect to spouse support, but that they thought in terms of the individual case before them.

[51] See chs. 3, 5 and 13.

[52] [1990] 2 FLR.457 (CA).

and ordered only nominal spouse and child support (£50 *per annum* each for the former wife and three children) whose total family income was £152 per week. Ward LJ said:

> This court is entitled ... to approach the case upon a basis that if, having regard to the reasonable financial commitments undertaken by the husband with due regard to the contribution properly made by the lady with whom he lives, there is insufficient left properly and fully to maintain the former wife and children, then the court may have regard to the fact that in proper cases social security benefits are available to the wife and children of the marriage; that having such regard, the court is enabled to avoid making orders which would be financially crippling to the husband. Benefits are available to this family of which the Judge was not made aware, and I have come to the conclusion that the husband cannot reasonably be expected to contribute at all to the maintenance of his previous family without financially crippling himself. In my judgment, it far better that the spirit of effecting a clean break and starting with a fresh slate be implemented in this case, not by dismissing the claims of the wife and children, but by acknowledging that now, and it is likely, in the foreseeable future he will not be able to honour the obligations he has recognised toward his children ... (pp 462–63)

> **Q** Has there been a clean break in this case? To what extent have equality principles been applied?

## V. RETHINKING FAIRNESS: EQUALITY AND NON-DISCRIMINATION

Thus, in the 1980s and 1990s solicitors were able to advise their clients based upon the above interpretations of the legislation, although they always had to be sure to add that, because the matter was entirely within the discretion of the courts, no outcome could be predicted with any accuracy. In 2000, however, the ground shifted enormously. In *White v White*,[53] the House of Lords can be said to have revolutionised the law of matrimonial property and financial provision. Diduck (2001b) summarises the facts and history of the case:

> *White v White* was about the breakdown of a 34 year marriage. Mr and Mrs White were both farmers; as the House of Lords stated, 'farming was in their blood'.[54] They acquired their farm one year after marriage with 'a more or less equal'[55] contribution of capital of £2000, a mortgage of £21,000 and an interest-free loan from Mr White's father of £14,000. By the time their applications for ancillary relief came before the court in 1996, their farm was worth approximately £3.5 million. They had executed a formal partnership agreement and traded throughout as equal partners in the farming business. They also farmed together a separate holding called Rexton Farm which Mr White acquired in his sole name from his family, but which was financed substantially by payments out of the partnership income.[56] It was worth £1.25 million. The House of Lords summarised their holdings as follows:

53 [2000] 2 FLR 981 (HL).
54 *Ibid*, p 984.
55 *Ibid*.
56 *White v White* [1998] 2 FLR 310 (CA) 316.

[T]he overall net worth of Mr and Mrs White's assets was, in round figures, £4.6 million. This comprised, on the figures found and used by the judge: Mrs White's sole property: £196,300 (mostly pension provision); her share of property owned jointly, either directly or through the partnership: £1,334,000; Mr White's share of jointly-owned property: £1,334,000, and Mr White's sole property: £1,783,5000 (mostly Rexton Farm).[57]

On the bases that he did not want to break up an existing farming enterprise, that the wife's desire to have sufficient funds to enable her to continue to farm was unreasonable, and that her reasonable requirements should determine the award, Holman, J awarded her £984,000, or approximately 20% of the total value of the family's assets.

Mrs White successfully appealed to the Court of Appeal. The Court awarded her a total of £1.69 million worth of assets, or approximately 40% of the whole, primarily because she would have received at least £1.52 million had her application proceeded as a formal dissolution of the partnership, rather than under section 25 of the MCA. Indeed, the Court of Appeal was critical of counsel's presentation of the case on this basis, or as a case of 'contribution' rather than 'entitlement', as they put it.[58] Both Mr and Mrs White appealed to the House of Lords, he asking the Court to restore Holman J's order, and she seeking an equal share in all the assets.

(pp 176–77)

The House of Lords took the opportunity to review the exercise of the discretion given to courts by the MCA. It confirmed that the unstated but nonetheless overriding objective of the legislation was to do 'fairness' between the parties, but it also recognised that 'fairness' was a socially contingent concept; 'fairness' it said, 'like beauty, lies in the eye of the beholder' (p 989).

Generally accepted standards of fairness in a field such as this change and develop, sometimes quite radically, over comparatively short periods of time. ... These wide powers [conferred by Parliament in s 25 of the Matrimonial Causes Act 1973] enable the courts to make financial provision orders in tune with current perceptions of fairness. Today there is greater awareness of the value of non-financial contributions to the welfare of the family. There is greater awareness of the extent to which one spouse's business success, achieved by much sustained hard work over many years, may have been made possible or enhanced by the family contribution of the other spouse, a contribution which also required much sustained hard work over many years. ... In the exercise of these discretions 'the law is a living thing moving with the times and not a creature of dead or moribund ways of thought'. (pp 989–90, references omitted)

Its review of fairness provoked a number of changes in the way courts were meant to exercise their discretion. First, the court challenged specifically the disproportionate weight attached to 'needs' or 'reasonable requirements' that had developed in the case law. It made it clear that this factor was only one among many for the court to consider and should no longer be determinative of a claimant's award.

I can see nothing, either in the statutory provisions or in the underlying objective of securing fair financial arrangements, to lead me to suppose that the available assets of the respondent become immaterial once the claimant wife's financial needs are satisfied. Why ever should they? If a husband and wife by their joint efforts over many years, his directly in his business and hers indirectly at home, have built up a valuable business from scratch, why should the claimant wife be confined to the court's assessment of her reasonable requirements, and the husband left with

[57] *White v White* [2000] 2 FLR 981 (HL) 985.
[58] *White v White* [1998] 2 FLR 310 (CA) 323, per Butler Sloss, LJ.

a much larger share? Or, to put the question differently, in such a case, where the assets exceed the financial needs of both parties, why should the surplus belong solely to the husband? ... [t]he mere absence of financial need cannot, by itself, be sufficient reason. If it were, discrimination would be creeping in by the back door. In these cases, it should be remembered, the claimant is usually the wife. Hence the importance of the check against the yardstick of equal division.[59] (p 992)

The gender implications of this finding are important for wives who too often found their 'reasonable requirements' determined according to gendered assumptions about what it was reasonable for a wife to do or to want.[60]

The Lords' second important clarification or revision of the case law was the explicit injection of principles of non-discrimination in the interpretation of 'fairness'.

In seeking to achieve a fair outcome, there is no place for discrimination between husband and wife and their respective roles. ... [W]hatever the division of labour chosen by the husband and wife, or forced upon them by the circumstances, fairness requires that this should not prejudice or advantage either party when considering para (f), relating to the parties' contributions. ... If, in their different spheres, each contributed equally to the family, then in principle it matters not which of them earned the money and built up the assets. There should be no bias in favour of the money-earner and against the homemaker and the child-carer. (p 989)

Taken together, these two changes are significant. They mean that it is discriminatory and therefore unfair for an earning spouse merely to meet his non-earning wife's needs out of his capital or salary and then keep any balance that is left over.

In effect, Lord Nicholls' words are a challenge to the traditional idea that only work done or money earned in the public sphere (that is, by means of traditionally male or husband conduct) is valuable and is the norm which wives must reach in order to receive financial benefits from a marriage; it challenges the idea that only the person who earns or buys is the *rightful* owner of family property, and that the other spouse is seeking something to which she is not morally entitled.

**Q** What view of equality is the court espousing here?

Finally, the House of Lords introduced what can now be called an additional factor for courts considering ancillary relief claims: the 'yardstick of equality'. The court was clear that it did not want to establish a presumption of equal sharing in ancillary relief cases. But it was equally clear that judges ought to think about equality:

[A] judge would always be well-advised to check his tentative views against the yardstick of equality of division. As a general guide, equality should only be departed from if, and to the extent that, there is good reason for doing so. The need to consider and articulate reasons for departing from equality would help the parties and the court to focus on the need to ensure the absence of discrimination. This is not to introduce a presumption of equal division under another guise. (p 989)

---

[59] See below pp 258–69.

[60] An example can be found in *White* itself. At trial Mrs White's reasonable requirements formed the ceiling for her award, and in determining those requirements the court said that it was not reasonable for her to want to continue to farm and to leave a legacy for her children, but it was reasonable for Mr White to do so. As Butler Sloss LJ said in the Court of Appeal, 'In 1998 why should it be reasonable for him to farm and not for her?' (p 324).

In the result, the House of Lords confirmed the Court of Appeal decision giving Mrs White only approximately 40% of the total assets, at least partly on the basis that the money used to start the business had come from the husband's parents.

> **Q** The Court was clearly concerned with the position of homemakers/carers and its decision can be read not only as important for wealthy divorcing couples, but also as important for social policy and other areas of law. To what degree might this case be of value, for example, in cases about acquiring a beneficial interest in the family home? For revision of policy on pensions? To what degree might it be of symbolic value in thinking about the marital partnership? Refer back to the different 'models' of financial provision. What model of financial provision is adopted in this case? The court did not refer to the Human Rights Act, but to what extent can you see human rights principles or values in its reasoning?

## VI. ILLUSTRATION OF THE PRINCIPLES 2000–2005

The following cases illustrate how the decision in *White v White* may have changed the landscape of ancillary relief. Many of the principles established up to 2000 have changed as a result of this decision, the clearest being the 'reasonable requirements' ceiling for awards.[61] Many of the principles have not changed, however, and therefore remain good law, while others are, at the time of writing, open to question. We shall break down our discussion according to the questions that have arisen about the effect the *White* decision has had on the way in which courts have exercised their MCA discretion. When reading this section, consider the degree to which the yardstick of equality has made a difference as the court tries to achieve fairness between the parties.[62] Consider also whether a (statutory) presumption of equality would have a different effect.[63]

The litigation that resulted in the immediate aftermath of *White* focused primarily upon when a departure from equality would be appropriate and many of these

---

[61] But see *P v P (Inherited property)* [2004] EWHC 1364; [2005] 1 FLR 576 where Munby, J found that due to the nature of the property in question (a farm that had been in the husband's family for generations) fairness required that the property not be sold and only that the wife's reasonable needs be met.

[62] On the merits of a discretionary system see Jackson, *et al*, (1993). On how the discretionary system influences private negotiations between the parties see Davis, *et al*, (1994); and Diduck (1999b) and (2003). For an example of how *White*'s fairness has influenced the exercise of discretion 'in all the circumstances' see *Miller v Miller* [2005] EWCA Civ 984; [2005] 2 FCR 713; (*MSM v AJRM* [2005] EWHC 528) in which the Court of Appeal agreed the judge was entitled to hold that 'fairness' in all the circumstances included consideration of the fact that Mrs Miller was committed to the marriage and that it broke down because Mr Miller had formed an association with another woman, and also that Mr Miller had, by marrying her, given Mrs Miller a reasonable expectation that she would on a long term basis be living on a 'higher economic plane' (*per* Singer J para 48). In these circumstances, Mr Miller could not rely on the fact that the marriage was a short one. At the time of the divorce Mr Miller was a 40 year old investment manager worth at least £17.5 million and Mrs Miller was a 35 year old professional who gave up £85,000 per annum job at the time of the marriage to become a full time homemaker. They had no children, were married for 2¾ years and engaged (although not cohabiting) for one year. Even though this was a short, childless marriage, the Court of Appeal agreed that her award should not be limited to one putting her 'back on her feet', and said the judge's award for Mrs Miller of approximately £5 million was not disproportionate when assessed against Mr Miller's overall wealth. While conduct of the parties is not relevant to ancillary relief unless it is conduct that would be inequitable to disregard (s.25(2)(g)), and the court here said explicitly Mr Miller's was not such conduct (para 38), it is difficult to escape the conclusion that the court took conduct into account in its overall determination of fairness under the category 'all the circumstances of the case'.

[63] See, for example, the Family Law (Scotland) Act 1985 and for a discussion, Hale, *et al*, (2002) pp 329–34.

questions are still unresolved. One question, for example, is whether a departure from equality would be fair if the contribution made by one of the parties could be classified as exceptional, special or 'stellar'. Recall that the court saw the basis for equality as lying in equal contributions. It thus appeared to leave the way open lawyers and courts to dispute the quality of contributions, and as Eekelaar observed, 'search for reasons why division should be unequal' (2001 p 33).

*Can a party's 'Special' contribution to the family justify a departure from equality?*

In *Cowan v Cowan*[64] the Court of Appeal found that where one party's contribution could be considered exceptional or special, a departure from equality would be justified. It seemed to be relying upon a 'market labour desert' theory of property acquisition in which 'property rights are justified [and quantified] as a reward for the expenditure of one's labor' (Regan 1999 p 169). The cases that followed this concerned millionaire husbands who (usually successfully) argued that not only the hard work and long hours they put in to the business, but the very size of the fortune they had amassed was evidence of special skill or exceptional contribution justifying a departure from equality. In *Lambert v Lambert,*[65] however, the Court of Appeal put an end to this line of argument.

> Having now heard submissions, both full and reasoned, against the concept of special contribution save in the most exceptional and limited circumstances, the danger of gender discrimination resulting from a finding of special contribution is plain. If all that is regarded is the scale of the breadwinner's success then discrimination is almost bound to follow since there is no equal opportunity for the homemaker to demonstrate the scale of her comparable success. Examples cited of the mother who cares for a handicapped child seem to me both theoretical and distasteful. Such sacrifices and achievements are the product of love and commitment and are not to be counted in cash. The more driven the breadwinner the less available will he be physically and emotionally both as a husband and father. (para 45)

> **Q** Do you agree? How could a homemaker ever demonstrate exceptional contribution?

> **Q** The court was also concerned to close the forensic 'Pandora's box' that might have been opened by *Cowan* by which courts could be asked to make a minute examination and valuation of each party's contributions over the course of a long marriage. It preferred to see marriage as a genuine partnership. In *Lambert* itself the children attended boarding schools and the family employed staff (para 34). Does this make a difference to the value of the wife's contribution to the family?

Finally, on the issue of whether exceptional contribution could ever be sufficient to justify a departure from equality the court said:

> [G]iven the infinite variety of fact and circumstance, I propose to mark time on a cautious acknowledgement that special contribution remains a legitimate possibility but only in exceptional circumstances. It would be both futile and dangerous even to attempt to speculate on the boundaries of the exceptional. In the course of argument I suggested that it might more readily

---

[64] [2001] EWCA Civ 679; [2001] 2 FLR 192.
[65] *Lambert v Lambert* [2002] EWCA Civ 1685; [2003] 1 FLR 139; [2003] Fam 103.

be found in the generating force behind the fortune rather than in the mere product itself. A number of hypothetical examples were canvassed ranging from the creative artist via the super-star footballer to the inventive genius who not only creates but also develops some universal aid or prescription. All that seems to me to be more safely left to future case by case exploration.

(para 46)

> **Q** Since *Lambert*, there has been no reported case in which special contribution has been argued successfully in court, however, it is always open to the parties to agree that one has been made. Can you think of a case that might now constitute special contribution? In *Parlour v Parlour*[66] where the husband was a professional football player, the parties agreed, and the court did not disturb, a capital division of 63–37 in favour of the husband.

*Does the duration of the marriage matter?*

*White v White* concerned a long marriage—34 years—and most of the cases that have applied it have also involved long—more than 20 years long—marriages.[67] There is some question as to whether the equal valuation of contributions referred to in *White* and its yardstick of equality of division apply to shorter marriages. In *GW v RW*[68] the court thought that to apply these principles to a shorter relationship (in this case a 12 year marriage) was 'problematic', either at the stage of valuing the respective contributions or at the stage of calculating division according to the yardstick of equality.

> It seems to me that the assumption of equal value of contribution is very obvious where the marriage is over 20 years. For shorter periods the assumption seems to me to be more problematic. [...] the entitlement to an equal division must reflect not only the parties (sic) respective contributions but also an accrual over time. ... (para 40)
> Even if I am wrong about this, and I am required [...] to find equality of contributions during this 12 year marriage, this does not necessarily lead to equality of division. (para 42)
> I have to say that whatever intellectual route is adopted I find it to be fundamentally unfair to be required to find that a party who has made domestic contributions during a marriage of 12 years should be awarded the same proportion of the assets as a party who has made the domestic contributions for period in excess of 20 years. (para 43)

> **Q** Do you agree? Why is it 'fundamentally unfair'? The court also held that to disregard the duration of the marriage would be to disregard MCA Section 25(2)(d) which refers to the duration of the marriage. Do you agree?

*M v M*[69] involved a 16 year relationship (4 years of cohabitation which 'moved seamlessly' to a 12 year marriage), and the court in this case also acknowledged that there was no direct authority on whether *White* applied to a medium length marriage such as this one (para 54). As a result, it followed the *GW* reasoning, holding that in a marriage such as this one, 'at the lower end of the bracket of medium to long term', 'equal

[66] *McFarlane v McFarlane; Parlour v Parlour* [2004] EWCA Civ 872; [2004] 2 FLR 893. Mr McFarlane obtained leave to appeal to the House of Lords and at the time of writing, his appeal is pending.
[67] See eg *P v P (Divorce: Financial Provision Clean Break)* [2002] EWCA Civ 1886; [2003] 1 FLR 942; *Lambert v Lambert* [2002] EWCA Civ 1685; [2003] 1 FLR 139; [2003] Fam 103 and cases cited therein.
[68] [2003] EWHC 611; [2003] 2 FLR 108.
[69] [2004] EWHC 688; [2004] 2 FLR 236.

division is not necessarily to be regarded as almost automatic' (para 55.7). The court in this case made an equal division, however, at least partly on the basis that the wife's would have to make an 'extra' contribution to the family in the future because of the special needs of the child in her care (para 77).

> **[Q]** What does the court mean by 'almost automatic'? Is equal division ever 'almost automatic'? More fundamentally, why should length of marriage matter to the value of the domestic, but not the financial, contributions to the marriage?

In these cases the judges were influenced by academic debate, principally between Eekelaar (2001b and 2003a) and Bailey-Harris (2003), on the question of valuing domestic contributions. Mostyn QC refers to it directly in his judgment in *GW* and Baron J refers to it indirectly in *M v M*. Eekelaar (2001b) has suggested that the duration of the relationship builds up, incrementally, entitlement to share, reaching 50% over a specified period. He says that duration is an inherent aspect of the value of non-pecuniary contributions like homemaking: 'homemaking for 1 day, however brilliantly done, is in itself, of relatively little value' (2003a p 831). He points also to Finch's research demonstrating that obligations and shared interests are developed in families over time.[70] Bailey-Harris (2003), on the other hand, suggests that it is discriminatory to require only certain contributions to earn their value over a long period.

The courts in these two cases favoured Eekelaar's position, but we suggest that in doing so they failed to address the discrimination issue. Linking only non-pecuniary contributions to duration has the clear effect of indirect discrimination against women, and accepts without challenge the hierarchically gendered value placed upon one type of contribution over another. It also fails to take into account the corresponding disadvantage to women suffered by even short periods out of the workforce. Further, Eekelaar's linking of this argument to Finch's work is surprising. Finch explores the way in which commitment is negotiated over time in kinship groups. In our view, however, marriage is somewhat different from relationships between extended family members; it represents an already committed relationship. In marriage or civil partnership the parties have expressed their intention at the outset to commitment and at least some sense of obligation to each other, and the issue is how that obligation is expressed when their relationship breaks down. Further, the issue in ancillary relief cases is not necessarily about either of the parties' personal sense of moral obligation to other; rather it is about what society considers to be a fair and just expression of that obligation.

> **[Q]** Which reasoning do you prefer?

Finally, Hale LJ (as she then was) considered in *Foster v Foster*[71] the argument that the *White/Lambert* line of cases is only relevant when evaluating the different contributions of breadwinner and homemaker over a long marriage and are not relevant when evaluating the financial contributions of both parties over a short (in this case, 4 year) marriage. She found this a 'surprising proposition' (para 18). 'If both go out to work and pool their incomes or spend a comparable proportion of their incomes for the benefit of the family, it would be a surprising proposition indeed if they were not to be

---

[70] Finch (1989).
[71] [2003] EWCA Civ 565; [2003] 2 FLR 299.

regarded as having made an equal contribution to the family home or other family assets'. (para 18)

In cases such as this, 'where a substantial surplus had been generated by their joint efforts, it could not matter whether they had taken a short or a long time to do so' (para 19). This case can, however, be distinguished from what has now become the 'classic' *White/Lambert* scenario in which the contributions are made in different realms, and as Herring (2004) states it will be up to the Court of Appeal finally to answer the question of how, if at all, duration of the marriage affects valuation of (domestic) contributions (p 211).[72]

## Does the yardstick of equality apply only to 'big money' cases?

That *White's* yardstick of equality applies to wealthy parties is uncontroversial. It applies as a means of sharing the value of the assets left after the needs of the parties for housing and day-to-day living costs have been met. On the one hand, we can say that this means that it only applies to wealthy families, but on the other, we can say that it applies to all families, but that consideration of the other statutory factors, particularly needs, provides a reason for departing from equality. The yardstick was said to apply, for example in *Elliott v Elliott*[73] and in *B v B (Mesher Order)*.[74]

**Q** Which approach do you prefer?

## To what property and contributions does the yardstick of equality apply?

The MCA directs the court to consider, among other factors, the needs, resources and contributions of the parties at the time of trial as well as in the foreseeable future. It is on this basis that housing needs while the children remain minors, or the potential income of a carer once children begin or finish school, for example, are taken into account. It is also on this basis that courts have recognised contributions to the welfare of the family, so that in *B v B (Mesher Order)* and in *M v M* the court assessed the wife's contributions to the family on the basis of caring for the children in the future. In *B v B*, for example:

> True it is that this was a very short marriage indeed [9 months]. True it is that the wife's contri-butions to the marriage, down to the point at which the marriage ended in divorce, may have been modest. But [...] the wife's major contribution to this marriage [...] is the fact that, for the next 16 years or so, (and I put it that way because W is now approximately 2 years old), she will have the very considerable burden of looking after him and bringing him up. That [...] is a very substantial contribution, albeit a contribution in the future, which has to be brought into the equation. (*B v B (Mesher Order)* p 295)

You will recall that the court's discretion under the MCA extends to all assets of either party, however or whenever they were acquired. In this way the MCA differs from the

---

[72] See also *B v B (Mesher Order)* [2002] EWHC 3106 (Fam); [2003] 2 FLR 285 in which the court applied the yardstick of equality to a nine month marriage, specifically noting that it had been of short duration.
[73] [2001] 1 FCR 477.
[74] [2002] EWHC 3106; [2003] 2 FLR 285.

system in other jurisdictions, such as Scotland, in which only assets acquired during the marriage are available for distribution on divorce or separation. In the light of this very broad discretion to deal with all assets, questions have been raised about the fairness of requiring one party to share an asset that he or she inherited, for example, or that he or she acquired well before or after the marriage. The view of the courts is clear on these points. Generally, all assets must be included in the 'pot' and made available for distribution, but their source and time of acquisition are relevant considerations when it comes time to determine the proportions of the whole pot to be distributed to each party. In other words, their source or time of acquisition may provide a reason to depart from equality. With respect to after acquired assets, the court in *M v M* was clear that the substantial increase in value of the assets between the date of separation and the date of trial was shareable (para 81) and no departure from equality was necessary in their division. The *White*[75]decision itself provides an example of the view taken with respect to pre-acquired assets. It was partly because the income used to purchase the original property came from the husband's family that the court was not moved to increase the wife's share from the 40% the Court of Appeal awarded her.

In *GW* the court went even further than this, however. In justifying its departure from equality, it found first that the husband brought into the marriage substantial assets unmatched by any contribution on the part of the wife (para 50). This is not controversial, as we have seen. It then found, however, that the husband's earning capacity should also be considered an asset brought by him into the marriage and thus taken into account in departing from equal division.

> H also brought into the marriage a developed career, existing high earnings and an established earning capacity. I cannot see why this should not be treated as much as a non-marital asset as the provision of hard cash. … In this aspect also I find that H made a contribution unmatched by any comparable contribution by W. (para 51)

**Q** Does Mostyn QC's ruling here, that earning capacity can be treated as a non-marital asset, open up the possibility of also treating it as a marital asset, and thus as available for distribution? See chapter 5. If so, is it to be accounted for by way of maintenance or by way of a transfer of capital?

In *M v M* Mostyn QC acted for the claimant wife. He submitted on her behalf that:

> 72.1 An earning capacity developed and nurtured during a marital relationship is a thing of value which falls to be fairly or equitably shared at the end of the relationship; [and] 72.2 a non-working party can validly claim by virtue of her domestic contributions to have contributed equally to the creation and development of this earning capacity.

On this basis, the wife claimed a series of 'inchoate lump sums', based upon a percentage of the husband's income in future years.

**Q** Is she claiming capital transfers or periodical payments?

---

[75] See also *Norris v Norris* [2002] EWHC 2996 (Fam); [2003] FCR 245; and *P v P (Inherited Property)* above n 61 in which Munby J took account of the fact that the parties' main asset was the husband's inherited farm. While not 'quarantined' or excluded from consideration, the source of the farm was significant and the court did not wish it to be sold. It awarded the wife only her 'reasonable requirements' which amounted to about 25% of the total value of assets.

The court dismissed her claim:

> I do not consider his future earnings to be a marital asset which falls for division in this case. There may be cases when needs will dictate that future income must be shared because the parties' capital is insufficient. The wife's claims for 'inchoate lump sums' is effectively a claim for maintenance by another name. It is not justified. (para 78)

In this case then, the court did not depart from equality in dividing *those assets it identified as marital assets.* We have seen that these included post-separation increases in the value of assets, but not pre-marriage acquired earning capacity. What, however, is the court saying here about the characterisation of future income? Is the court suggesting that future income, or earning capacity, *may* be a shareable asset, but only if other capital is insufficient to meet the parties' needs? Is it also suggesting that maintenance is not a legitimate claim to make upon marital assets or future income? Indeed, the relationship between maintenance and property adjustment is a tricky one. They are to be decided together, taken from the same 'pot', but the preference for the clean break means that maintenance orders have fallen out of favour with parties and courts alike.[76] As we saw in the pre–2000 case law, however, sometimes periodical payments or lump sum payments of maintenance are required, at least to help the payee in the transition to self-sufficiency;[77] is there a role for the *White* principles in these cases?

*Does the yardstick of equality apply only to capital, or does it apply to income as well?*

The issue of the yardstick of equality and the relationship between it and maintenance and capital transfers is, at the time of writing, before the House of Lords. The issue, as it was put in the Court of Appeal decision of *McFarlane v McFarlane; Parlour v Parlour,* is 'if the decision in *White v White* introduces the yardstick of equality for measuring a fair division of capital why should the same yardstick not be applied as the measure of division of income?' (para 4).

In both cases (heard by the Court of Appeal simultaneously) the wives were not employed outside the home, nor had they any prospects of becoming so employed in the foreseeable future. In both cases the net incomes of the husbands exceeded the expenditures of their two households by great margins. In both cases capital transfers had been agreed by the parties (in *McFarlane* an equal division, in *Parlour* an approximate 60–40 division in favour of the husband) and the only issue before the court was maintenance for the wife. At trial both cases were argued on the basis that the wife would require joint lives periodical payments with the wives each claiming that the yardstick of equality rather than reasonable requirements should apply to the determination of quantum, even if that meant awarding them a sum vastly in excess of their needs, so as to allow them to accumulate capital for their future support. The husbands argued that the purpose of periodical payments was to maintain, and that to award payments sufficient to

---

[76] See Douglas and Perry (2001).

[77] Nominal orders are also available if the circumstances of the parties are liable to change in the future. Nominal orders of, say, £1 per annum leave the court able to vary the periodical payments on an application by one of the parties in the future (see section 31 MCA 1973). See eg *A v A (Ancillary relief: property division)* [2004] EWHC 2818 for a recent example of a case where a clean break was thought to be preferable to a nominal order where the parties were of medium income, and *S v B (Ancillary Relief: Costs)* [2004] EWHC 2089; [2005] 1 FLR 474 where, on appeal, the High Court did not disturb a district judge's nominal order even where it stated it would have exercised its discretion differently.

allow for the accumulation of capital amounted to a further order to share capital and thus subverted the principle that a capital award is made once and for all.[78]

The District Judge awarded Mrs McFarlane £250,000 per annum notwithstanding that she estimated her annual expenses at £128,000 per annum. That figure represented approximately 33% of the husband's present net income. The court went on:

> This reflects her needs, obligations and the contribution that she has made over the years of the marriage. It may well need to be revised in later years for a variety of reasons. It is a matter for her whether she chooses to make pension provision, [...] and it is a matter for her whether she takes out insurance to protect her and the children's position in the event that the husband dies or is ill and unable to work. (para 22)

This decision was overturned on appeal to the High Court, where Bennett J reduced Mr McFarlane's payments to £180,000.

The facts and arguments in *Parlour* were similar, except that while Mr Parlour's income was greater than Mr McFarlane's, it was likely to plummet within a few years when he was no longer able to play premier league football. The case was heard at first instance by Bennett J who assessed the wife and the children's needs at £150,000 per annum before awarding the wife £250,000 per annum, or approximately 28% of the husband's income.

In both cases periodical payments were assessed in amounts in excess of needs, and in both, Bennett J declared that needs should not be a 'glass ceiling' that determined the amount of the awards. It thus appears that *White* applies at least to that extent in cases of maintenance. The Court of Appeal did not take issue with this conclusion. On the question of what test was to be applied, however, if 'the glass ceiling' of reasonable requirements was not the correct one, the court was not entirely clear. On the question of the yardstick of equality, Thorpe LJ said

> Clearly in the assessment of periodical payments, as in capital provision, the overriding objective is fairness. Discrimination between the sexes must be avoided. The crosscheck of equality is not appropriate for a number of reasons. First in many cases the division of income is not just between the parties, since there will be children with a priority claim for the costs of education and upbringing. Second Lord Nicholls suggested the use of the crosscheck in dividing the accumulated fruits of past-shared endeavours. In assessing periodical payments the court considers the division of the fruits of the breadwinner's future work in a context where he may have left the child-carer in the former matrimonial home, where he may have to meet alternative housing costs and where he may have in fact or in contemplation a second wife and a further child. (para 106).

**Q** Why should the overall settlement for the wife be dependent upon the husband's contemplated further wives or children? Upon child support? Is there an argument that the two are based on different philosophical foundations or justifications? What model of financial provision is Thorpe LJ suggesting here? See Eekelaar (2005).

Where the court was clearest was on the issue of the primacy of a clean break. It said that the cases ought to have been argued on the basis of the clean break principle rather than on the basis of the joint lives principle. The court said that Bennett J had failed, in

---

[78] See *Pearce v Pearce* [2003] EWCA Civ 1054; [2003] 2 FLR 1144.

both cases, to give due weight to the imperative to achieve finality between the parties. It ordered the reinstatement of the district judge's decision in *McFarlane* and the award of £444,000 per annum in *Parlour* on the basis of the following reasoning:

> In any case in which, despite a substantial capital base available for division, clean break is not presently practicable, the court has a statutory duty to consider the future possibility. That duty assumes particular prominence in cases where there is a certain and substantial surplus of future income over future needs. If, as in one of the present appeals, the surplus will be predictably short-lived, the first option for consideration should be the planned progress to clean break by means of a substantial term order open to a later application for extension. The obligation on the parties to achieve financial independence is mutual. The earner must give proper priority to making payments on account out of the surplus income. The payee must invest the surplus sensibly, or risk that her failure to do so might count against her on an application for discharge under section 31(7A) and (7B). Given the mutuality of the obligation, the opportunity and responsibility to invest should, in my judgment, be shared. It strikes me as discriminatory, and therefore wrong in principle, for the earner to have sole control of the surplus through the years of accumulation. The preferred mechanism by which the surplus is to be divided annually must be periodical payments. (para 66)

**Q** Mr McFarlane's case is presently before the House of Lords. Draft a summary of the issues that you think the Court ought to consider, including your recommendation for their resolution.[79]

### What understanding of equality does the yardstick of equality imply?

We saw above that equality can have different meanings. Whether the *White* decision requires courts to interpret the notion as formal equality/sameness of treatment, or as substantive equality is not clear from the cases, although most cases seem to assume a formal equality model. We shall illustrate this issue by reference to two cases. The first is *P v P (Divorce: Financial Provision Clean Break)*.[80]

Mr and Mrs Parra together set up a family business in 1987. The business prospered but the couple separated in 2000. They agreed that the husband would buy out the wife's share of the business. Their case came to trial, however, with each claiming entitlement to more than 50% of the value of the marital assets. The wife claimed that she would have to start a new business while the husband had the benefit of the old one. The husband said that the wife would have the benefit of almost £1 million in liquid assets while he would have to shoulder a debt. According to the court, however, during their marriage they had arranged their affairs on the basis of equality, and therefore that arrangement should be reflected in the division of assets on divorce. The court thus did not engage in a Section 25 analysis of the circumstances; its supervisory role over the agreement was to assume that because there was formal equality of contribution, equal division would result in fairness to the parties.

On the face of it, fairness may have been done in this case, but Scully (2003) raises some difficult issues.

---

[79] See also *Q v Q (ancillary relief: periodical payments)* [2005] EWHC (Fam) 402 in which Bennett, J applied the *McFarlane; Parlour* case to another case of a divorcing football player, and awarded the wife 40% of her husband's net income as a 'bridge' along the way to an anticipated clean break.
[80] [2002] EWCA Civ 1886; [2003] 1 FLR 942.

In *Parra*, unlike *Lambert*, the contributions of the partners are capable of being measured against each other. Thorpe LJ directly referred to Mrs Parra's 'equal achievements in creating and building up the company'. The High Court also referred to the working relationship of the spouses. Charles J said of the couple: 'He worked exceptionally hard and has been the major creative force in the business. She too has worked exceptionally hard both in the business and in bringing up the children and maintaining the family home.' It is unclear from these statements exactly what was the division of work in the business and in the home. What is clear though is that neither of the existing definitions of formal equality is pertinent to this case. To balance the couple's breadwinning contributions would be to ignore Mrs Parra's work as wife and mother. To presume they have made different contributions of equal worth is to ignore the breadwinning contributions Mrs Parra has made alongside her husband. Therefore, by relying upon formal equality, in the form of equal division of assets, to achieve a fair outcome, without carrying out the section 25 exercise, the Court of Appeal has stumbled onto a minefield, rather than taken a shortcut to equality. (references omitted pp 212–13)

**Q** Do you agree? How would the Section 25 exercise have achieved fairness?

Scully goes on:

[It may be that] when considering Mrs Parra as a business woman, the court focused on that aspect of her life rather than on her role as a mother. This would seem unlikely but for Thorpe LJ's statement that both parents should be equally responsible for the cost of their children's education. He justifies this by saying that equal division of assets brings with it equal division of obligation. Post-separation, Mrs Parra has taken on the primary care of the children and this should be weighed in the balance when considering the division of obligation. However, it is not. It is also not taken into account when Thorpe LJ sets out the relative hurdles to be crossed by the couple when they pursue their businesses independently of one another. He balances factors in the wife's favour such as liquidity of assets against the advantage the husband holds in the form of the ongoing business. That Mrs Parra will also have the burden of caring for the children for the next few years is not taken into account. ... [P]erhaps he relied too heavily on formal equality as a means of ensuring real fairness without recognising the added, and often invisible, work that is done by women. Moreover, the court has failed to acknowledge the manner in which reliance on formal equality masks the reality of the uneven playing field faced by women. (p 213)

**Q** *White* and *Lambert* were about attributing value to labour done in the private sphere when that was the sole or primary contribution made to the family welfare. Recall the statistics we cited in chapter 5 about the division of household labour in dual earner heterosexual couples. While household labour continues to be performed overwhelmingly by women, is there an argument that it should be taken into account, even where the wife also contributes financially? How can the court take into account the invisible work done by full-time working women; in other words for work done in the public and private spheres simultaneously? Is this an argument for the pursuit of substantive rather than formal equality?

Let us now look at *B v B ( Mesher Order)*,[81] which is an example of an alternative interpretation of equality. In this case the parties married, had a child and separated, all within one year. The husband's net salary was about £5582 per month. The wife was about 30 years old and was caring for the child full-time. Before the marriage she had

---

[81] [2002] EWHC 3106 (Fam); [2003] 2 FLR 285.

worked for a bank and earned approximately £40,000 per annum. She did not plan to return to work until the child was 7 years old, and then perhaps only on a part-time basis. The court found her plans to be sensible and realistic. The court made awards for periodical payments and for a lump sum in order to allow her to rehouse herself.

The husband appealed all parts of the order unsuccessfully. We shall focus here, however, upon his claim that the house purchased with the lump sum should have been subject to a 30% Mesher order. In making this claim the husband relied upon the judgments of Thorpe LJ in two recent cases, including in particular, *Elliott v Elliott*,[82] where it was said that if the court were not inclined to make a Mesher order it should explain why it would be appropriate to 'ignore the husband's reasonable entitlement to deploy capital to house himself at the end of a long marriage during which he worked hard' (p 294).

> **Q** What kind of equality is Thorpe LJ espousing in these cases and the husband claiming in *B v B*?

The court in *B v B* then went on to outline the wife's arguments in response to Thorpe LJ's comments:

> Mr Tod's response [...] is this. True it is that this was a very short marriage indeed. True it is that the wife's contributions to the marriage, down to the point at which the marriage ended in divorce, may have been modest. But [...] the wife's major contribution to this marriage [...] is the fact that, for the next 16 years or so, (and I put it that way because W is now approximately 2 years old), she will have the very considerable burden of looking after him and bringing him up. That [...] is a very substantial contribution, albeit a contribution in the future, which has to be brought into the equation.
>
> Furthermore, says Mr Tod, in the nature of things the performance by the wife of her obligations in this respect, to discharging by her of her responsibility for W's upbringing, will inevitably impact adversely upon her earning capacity. Not merely her capacity to earn an income during that part of her life, during W's early years when she will not be able to work at all; not merely during that part of W's later childhood during which she will be able to work part-time perhaps on an increasing scale. But even after W is off her hands, her continuing earning capacity, even when she is free to work full-time will be significantly reduced, he says, by the fact that for a number of years she will have been out of the job market. She will therefore find herself, when W is 18, in her mid-forties, even if free to work full-time, not able to get the kind of job which will generate the kind of income which by then she could realistically have hoped to obtain had she not had the interruption of looking after W.
>
> Moreover, says Mr Tod, that impacts not merely upon her earning ability in the sense of her income, it impacts seriously (and he suggests decisively) upon her ability, if her return to full-time employment is as delayed as it is likely to be, ever to generate capital, whether by way of acquiring a property on a mortgage, or more particularly by way of building up a pension fund. (p 295)

> **Q** What kind of equality is the wife seeking?

The court made the following decision:

> At the end of the day, it seems to me that there are two factors in particular which point strongly to the conclusion that there should not be a Mesher order. The first is that the wife's

---

[82] [2001] 1 FCR 477. The other was *Dorney-Kingdom v Dorney Kingdom* [2000] 2 FLR 855.

realistic prospects of being able to generate capital of her own between now and the date when one of the Mesher triggers would operate is small, whereas there is every reason to believe with a significant degree of confidence that well before [...] a Mesher trigger operates the husband will be able to generate a substantial degree of capital for himself ... .

That inequality of outcome [...] is an outcome brought about by the fact that this wife will have to devote the best part of those years of her working life which would otherwise enable her to generate capital and earn at a higher rate in later life, to the job of bringing up W.

...

The other point [...] is that as it seems to me, [... a Mesher order] will throw upon her a financial burden much more significant in terms of her financial economy than the corresponding financial advantage will have upon the husband's financial economy.

That again, as it seems to me, would produce an outcome that is unfair rather than fair.

(pp 297–98)

In this case, then, the court adopts a version of fairness that incorporates some element of substantive equality that recognises and attempts to compensate for the difficulties women in general and mothers in particular face in attempting to achieve financial self-sufficiency.

Generally then, we can see that the impact of *White v White* and the cases that have followed it has been substantial, and that its full effect is still being tested in the courts. Cretney (2003b)[83] suggests that it has had the effect of creating a community property regime in all but name and Eekelaar that it has moved 'the basis of the award firmly from a subjective evaluation of desert to a more objective assessment of entitlement'; 'away from the language of welfare and dependence to one of entitlement' (2001a p 32).

> **Q** Do you agree? Has the basis of, or the model for, financial and property awards now shifted from a welfare one, based on moral ideas of worthiness or need, to one based upon entitlement? Or does even the concept of entitlement still encompass some idea of 'evaluation of desert', such as the labour market desert principle discussed above?

> **Q** Bearing in mind all of the previous discussion, how would you resolve the financial affairs of the couple in the following situation? How would you deal with the husband's pension? What if either the wife or the husband were intending to remarry? When considering these questions, bear in mind the models of support and equality you wish to adopt.

> A husband and wife are divorcing after a 28-year marriage. Each is 50 years old. They own their home in joint tenancy. The husband is a partner in a firm of chartered accountants. He has a substantial pension and life assurance as well as an interest in the partnership. He began to work there the year before they got married and now draws an average salary of £6500 per month. The wife is employed as a sales manager in a local dress shop. She began working there four years ago after both their children had finished university and left home. Prior to that she was full-time wife, mother and homemaker. She now earns approximately £200 per week. The parties met at university and each graduated the year before they married. During that year the wife began her first year of graduate studies, but left when she got married.

---

[83] See also Cretney (2003c).

## VI. POSSIBLE REFORM[84]

The Lord Chancellor's Department referred to an Advisory Group the question of reforming the MCA 1973 to include a presumption of a 50–50 split of property on divorce, potentially introducing a notion of compensation and equality into ancillary relief proceedings (Diduck 1999b; 2003). The Advisory Group unanimously rejected the proposal, however, declaring that a presumption of equality would too often do injustice, and that judicial discretion was necessary to do justice in individual cases (Ancillary Relief Advisory Group 1998). As a result, new proposals for reform were published by the government. In order to provide greater clarity to the law, it proposed to add to the Section 25 list of factors 'an over-arching objective and set of guiding principles which could make clear the process a judge now follows in determining the allocation of property on divorce' (Home Office 1998 para 4.48).

The proposed objective was for the court to 'exercise its powers so as to endeavour to do that which is fair and reasonable between the parties and any child of the family' (Home Office 1998 para 4.49). The proposed set of guiding principles would set out the objectives for the court in making property decisions. They are listed in proposed order of precedence:

> First, to promote the welfare of any child of the family under the age of eighteen, by meeting housing needs of any children and the primary carer, and of the secondary carer; both to facilitate contact and to recognise the continuing importance of the secondary carer's role.
>
> Second, the court would take into account the existence and content of any written agreement about financial arrangements … .
>
> Third … the court would then divide any surplus so as to achieve a fair result, recognising that fairness will generally require the value of the assets to be divided equally between the spouses.
>
> Fourth, the court would try to terminate financial relationships between the parties at the earliest date practicable. (Home Office 1998 para 4.49)

**Q** Have these proposals been all but accepted in the case law that followed them? Do you agree that equality could sometimes result in injustice? Diduck (1999b) suggests that a compensation model of support coupled with a presumption of equality in property division would lead to a fairer outcome. Do you agree?

Statutory reform of the MCA no longer appears to be on the government's agenda, but the profession remains concerned that uncertainty continues and that the public does not understand the law. In 2003 the Law Society published recommendations for further reform of the law (Law Society 2003). It suggested the following 'Guideline for the sharing of assets on divorce to be read in conjunction with Section 25':

> 1. Different guidelines apply to cases where assets exceed needs and those where assets do not exceed needs. In deciding what are the needs of the parties, the court must take account of all the factors in section 25 … .
> 2. Paragraphs 3 to 5 below apply to those cases where the assets do not exceed the needs, and paragraphs 6 onwards apply where the assets exceed the needs.
> 3. Where there are minor children the housing of the parent with primary care of the children

---

[84] See also Lord Chancellor's Department (1999) and Law Society (2003) in which options for reforming the court procedure are presented.

will normally be regarded as the first matter to be resolved. The issue will be decided on the basis of what is in the best interest of the children. This may mean that the former matrimonial home will have to be preserved for that parent with the children, but this is not inevitable, and where the housing of the other parent can also be provided from existing resources without having a detrimental effect on the welfare of the children, the court may require the parent with care to move.

4. The anticipated housing needs of the parent with primary care of the children after the children have ceased to be dependent may be a separate issue and would be dealt with in accordance with paragraph 5 below.

5. Where there are assets remaining after the housing needs of the parties have been met they should be distributed in accordance with the remaining needs of the parties and in proportion to their separate abilities to meet those needs.

6. Where assets exceed the needs of the parties those needs will first be (notionally) met. These needs may include a capital fund to provide for the maintenance of one party where continuing financial obligations are appropriate. The court must then consider how the remaining assets should be distributed.

7. Contributions of either party must be taken into account as one of the statutory factors. The non-financial contributions of a homemaker and child carer must be given a weight and significance appropriate to the circumstances of the case; the significance of such contributions relative to any financial contributions of the other party will be within the discretion of the trial judge.

8. Financial contributions may include money or capital introduced into the marriage as a result of an inheritance by a party or a gift to a party.

9. Having dealt with the needs of the children, the housing and other needs of the couple, and having taken into account any pre-marriage agreement, the court must then divide any surplus so as to achieve a fair result. Fairness may frequently require the value of the remaining assets to be divided equally, but this may be affected by one or more of the factors in section 25, such as the length of the marriage, the contributions of the parties, the future obligations to the family of the parties, and their respective overall financial positions. In any event, when a judge, in his final determination, proposes to depart from equality of division, he must specify which of the factors in section 25 have led him to that conclusion.

10. For the avoidance of doubt, these guidelines have precedence over any decided case before the (date). (pp 20–21)

**Q** How, if at all do these recommendations propose to change the law? See particularly, guidelines 3, 4, 7 and 9. How, if at all, would you modify these guidelines?

## VII. CONCLUSION: IS THERE ANY ROLE FOR EQUALITY IN FAMILIES?

Our discussion has proceeded thus far on the basis that equality has had a role to play in the development of rules about the allocation of the economic benefits and burdens of family membership after the partners go their separate ways. We are, in this way, saying something about the nature of the relationship itself. As we said at the beginning of this chapter, rules about the distribution of financial benefits and burdens at the end of a relationship say a great deal about norms in the intact relationship. We saw, for example, how at least three models of property division and financial provision can be distilled from the legislation and we can now link views of marriage and the place of equality within them. Does this mean that the MCA holds all three views of marriage and the proper role of equality in marriage? The first model of property division was a needs-based, income security model, arguably rooted in a breadwinner/dependant 'traditional' view of marriage. It seems that in this model, any notion of equality has little place in determinations of fairness in division of assets. The second was a compensation model, which may be rooted in a partnership philosophy of marriage and in which we can see some idea of substantive equality in determinations of fairness; and the third was a clean break model which may be rooted in a highly individualised model of marriage and in which formal equality until recently dominated in determinations of fairness. That no statutory provision at all is made for non-married or non-registered cohabitants seems to suggest that their relationships are outside the scope of legal concern entirely, or at least that it is fair that their relationships remain governed by the common law of formal equality and separate property. The view, however, that any notion at all of equality should be applied to families is not uncontroversial.

We raised above Eekelaar's (1991) resource sharing approach to family finances in which there seemed to be no place for individual claims to rights. Regan (1999) also identifies this view of marriage as one which can be held by spouses. He identifies two orientations toward marriage. The first is an external orientation that emphasises the discrete individual with his or her own interests and who enters the marriage relationship as a sort of market interaction; the individual with this orientation always retains his or her separate identity in the marriage. It is easy to see how some idea of equality between those individuals might be appropriate in this view of marriage. Regan's second orientation he calls 'internal'. It is a commitment to 'a shared purpose that transcends the self' (p 30). Marriage partners in this orientation are not concerned to maintain independence; the self becomes a part of the other and of the relationship; its interests become the interests of the marital community. Regan advocates this model in which it is less easy to apply any notion of equality. This model is similar to Eekelaar's (1991) idea of the family unit as a collectivity with shared interests rather than as group of individuals, each with her or his own interests and for whom resource sharing is the most equitable way to divide marital assets.[85]

But it is clear that these ideas of marriage, or of relationship, need not be mutually exclusive. Regan, for example, suggests that throughout the course of their everyday lives, spouses move back and forth between the internal and external orientations to marriage (1999 p 29), and we tend to agree. The issue, however, is the model that law adopts. Does it vacillate like its subjects do, or does it express a particular norm?

This question is important, we suggest, because gender may be a factor in one's orientation to one's relationship from time to time. Women's normative role in the family has traditionally been confined to the private sphere and women's primary experience of family has been, and is still, as its caretaker. It may be the case then, that women find it easier to adopt the internal orientation. In contrast, men's experience of family has been, and continues to be, primarily as provider and as mediator between the private family and the public sphere. They may therefore find it easier to adopt an external stance toward marriage in which their individuality and autonomy as rights and property bearing individuals are legitimated. It seems that women are more likely to be successful in achieving recognition for the domestic, private labour they perform for

[85] See above pp 242–43.

their families when their claims are justified on the basis of the external, rights and market-based view, as compensation for services provided (Regan 1999; Diduck 2003). Because, we suggest, the stance adopted by the law toward marriage is an external one, this strategy is the best one that women can adopt in order to alleviate the almost universal economic disadvantage they suffer relative to men on divorce.[86]

Smith (2000) also finds a link between models of marriage and models of financial provision. She says we should expect 'a state's philosophical model of marriage to influence the method it seeks for property division on divorce' (p 215). She identifies five models of marriage:

1. Marriage as Commitment: Marriage is a relationship involving two individuals who have made a lifelong commitment—to each other and to the relationship—that overrides their individual interests in the relationship.
2. Marriage as Partnership: Marriage is a venture designed to promote the interests and development of the individuals who create it.
3. Marriage as Contract: Marriage is a contract of indefinite duration, the continuation of which is subject to the likely changing desires of the individual contracting parties.
4. Marriage as Monarchy: In marriage one must lead and the other must follow, and the leader is accorded the relationship's rights and responsibilities in trust to assure the success of the marriage.
5. Marriage as Democracy: In marriage the spouses are equal to each other in rights, in presumed contributions to the relationship, and in economic and social position; the success of the marriage depends on decisions made by individuals with equal decision-making power. (p 215)

**Q** Which of these models of marriage are reflected in the MCA? Smith also identifies different models of property division, including an equitable distribution model and an equal division model. She suggests that the first, the equitable distribution model, lies between the partnership and commitment models of marriage: it vests the judge with a wide discretion to distribute property according to needs, and needs are defined in a forward looking way (p 218). She contrasts this with a democracy/partnership model or a democracy/contract model of marriage which would best be served by the equal division model. Comment on Smith's categorisation of marriages and methods of property division. Do her observations and conclusions mean that equality can ever be an appropriate model for property division as long as the commitment model of marriage persists?

If the way the law organises post-separation finances reflects the way it views family living, then there is another reason for advocating substantive equality on separation. The symbolic importance of the law, not necessarily as a direct influence on behaviour, but because it has normative force, means that there are social reasons for being concerned with these private family law decisions, and Herring goes so far as to suggest that seeking fairness only between the parties to the divorce may be misguided (Herring 2005). 'Family' law defines not only individuals' obligations towards one another and their obligations to the family unit as a whole, but also their obligations to society at large. It also defines or regulates the public obligation to families and individual family members and thus raises again the hegemony of liberalism with its emphasis on individuals and its divide between public and private. When we adopt a model of commitment and

---

[86] Research in the US (Weitzman 1985), Canada (Bailey 1994) and England (Douglas and Perry 2001) is consistent that women's income tends to drop on divorce and men's tends to increase or stay the same.

life-long marriage we identify a particular role for society to play, or in the case of the private family, not to play, in its support of those individuals. In this context, the part that family law and policy are thought to play to alleviate the disadvantage suffered by less powerful members of families shifts from time to time according to ideas about the nature of the family and its location in society.

Symes (1985) argues that focusing only on private (family) law reform to redress any inequality created by the traditional nuclear family model may not be sufficient. Even a compensatory approach to maintenance and property division which attributes value to previously unvalued or undervalued home-work and which furthers a type of substantive equality between the spouses may indirectly reinforce the traditional nuclear family model and the inequalities associated with it.

Susan Boyd also observes that in cases where compensatory support has been awarded and the feminisation of poverty has been acknowledged, it *appears* that the state has dealt with the problem (1994 p 67). She goes on, however:

> Sociologist Margrit Eichler has pointed out that even if the equality principle were fully implemented in family law and women received the full benefit of recognition for their domestic labour, only a tiny minority of women (and children) living in poverty would be assisted … .
>
> The valuing of women's domestic labour in the family law context is achieved only for a woman who did that work for another person with whom she no longer lives, specifically a male partner. The argument is that her male partner would otherwise be unjustly enriched. Had Ms Peter [see *Peter v Beblow*, referred to in chapter 5] been a single mother doing much the same work for herself and her children, she would not have had recourse to anyone's property to compensate her. The benefit that society as a whole receives from women's (usually unpaid) domestic labour, particularly in the context of raising children, is thus not recognized. This approach fits with the [Canadian and arguably UK] government's generally neo-conservative anti-statist, pro-market, and pro-'family' approach to child care and economic responsibilities. While courts cannot and perhaps should not impose social programmes, the effect of courts appearing to resolve some social problems through decisions such as *Moge* and *Peter* is to lend ideological support to the state's privatization of financial responsibility.
> …
> Increasingly, then, courts and administrative arms of the … (welfare) state are reinforcing certain private familial responsibilities for women's poverty in the name of feminist values and in part in response to feminist struggle in the courts, while diminishing public societal commitment to alleviating that poverty. Individual men are (again) being held financially responsible to the women they used to live with … . Women who live more independently from men, or who do not wish to make a private claim upon a man, will almost certainly not be compensated, and woe betide the single mother who cannot find a well-paying job and childcare, and who must therefore rely on welfare. Ideologically, heterosexual relationships—and women's roles as wives and mothers within them—are thus reproduced. (pp 67–69)

**Q** Do you agree with Boyd's analysis? Do you see any role for equality principles in financial and property adjustment after divorce or after separation of unmarried partners? Where same-sex partners separate and dispute the ownership of property, courts thus far have tended to apply the same basic principles as for opposite-sex couples, and often utilise the same sex-role stereotypes,[87] notwithstanding that same-sex partners often organise their domestic and employment roles in a non-gendered and more egalitarian way (Dunne 2000). Do you see any scope for change in interpretations of the MCA principles after the Civil

---

[87] See ch 5.

Partnership Act comes into force? Further, Edwards (2004) suggests that the law must also take into account aspects of culture and ethnicity as they form an important part of 'all the circumstances' the court must consider in making financial and property awards. She mentions specifically cultural practices with regard to family property and 'the structural position of Asian women within the private and public world and the specific cultural limitations placed on their opportunities for self-sufficiency and for remarriage' (p 814). How might the court consider these factors?

We have directed the discussion in this chapter to how courts determine financial matters between former partners. In many, if not most, separations, however, the parties come to their own mutually agreed settlements. As we shall see in chapters 11 and 15, parties and their representatives bargain in the 'shadow of the law' and in the shadow of the prevailing social climate to come to these agreements.

## FURTHER READING AND SELECTED RECENT REFERENCES

J CARBONE, 'Feminism, Gender and the Consequences of Divorce' in M Freeman, (ed), *Divorce: Where Next?* (Aldershot, Dartmouth, 1996).

A DNES, *The Division of Marital Assets Following Divorce with Particular Reference to Pensions* (Lord Chancellor's Department, Research Series No 7/97, London, LCD, 1997).

S EDWARDS, 'Division of Assets and Fairness—"Brick Lane"—Gender, Culture and Ancillary Relief on Divorce' (2004) 34 *Fam LJ* 809.

J EEKELAAR, 'Back to Basics and Forward into the Unknown' (2001) *Family Law* 30.

——, 'Asset Distribution on Divorce—The Durational Element' (2001) 117 *Law Quarterly Review* 552.

——, 'Shared Income After Divorce: A Step Too Far' (2005) 121 *LQR* 1.

J FINCH, *Family Obligations and Social Change* (Cambridge, Polity Press, 1989).

M FINEMAN, *The Illusion of Equality: The Rhetoric and Reality of Divorce Reform* (Chicago, IL, University of Chicago Press, 1991).

J HERRING, 'Why Financial Orders on Divorce Should be Unfair' (2005) 19 *International Journal of Law, Policy and the Family* 218.

C LITTLETON, Reconstructing Sexual Equality' (1987) 75 *California Law Review* 1279.

MC REGAN, *Alone Together: Law and the Meanings of Marriage* (Oxford, OUP, 1999).

A SCULLY, '*Para v Para*: Big Money Cases, Judicial Discretion and Equality of Division' (2003) 15 *CFLQ* 205.

C SMART, *The Ties That Bind* (London, Routledge and Kegan Paul, 1984).

IM YOUNG, *Justice and the Politics of Difference* (Princeton, NJ, Princeton University Press, 1990).

*Reports*

Association of District Judges, 'Submission of Association of District Judges' Appendix 8 to the *Report to the Lord Chancellor by the Ancillary Relief Advisory Group* (1998).

Family Law Committee of the Law Society, 'Maintenance and Capital Provision on Divorce, The Family Law Committee's Submission to the Ancillary Relief Advisory Group', Appendix 10 to

*Report to the Lord Chancellor by the Ancillary Relief Advisory Group* (London, The Law Society, 1998).

Law Society, *Financial Provision on Divorce: Clarity and Fairness, Proposals for Reform* (London, The Law Society, 2003).

Solicitors Family Law Association, 'Proposals for Reform of Ancillary Relief Law', Appendix 11 to *Report to the Lord Chancellor by the Ancillary Relief Advisory Group,* (Orpington: SFLA, 1998).

# 7

# Equal Status under the Children Act 1989—Parental Responsibility

## I. INTRODUCTION

In chapter 4 we examined the concept of parental responsibility and how it is acquired. We noted that parental authority is now generally conceived of as existing primarily for the benefit of the child, in that it enables parents to carry out their obligations to their children.[1] Nevertheless, 'the notion that parental authority is of real significance remains powerful' (Cretney 1996a p 136), for who is vested with parental authority shows us whom the law regards as entitled to play a part in a child's upbringing and to make decisions about that child. The allocation of parental authority throws light on the model of the family that is dominant in society and that attracts the imprimatur of the law. It is not surprising, therefore, that the history of the law governing parental status has been marked by the struggle of women against a strict patriarchal hierarchy within the family and towards legal parity with men. Nor is it surprising that more recent years have seen campaigns by men's groups which contend that mothers are now favoured and fathers are being marginalised by the law. This has resulted in a change in the law to vest parental responsibility automatically in most fathers. The law has also responded to the changes in family structures to offer the possibility of parental responsibility to step-parents and to same-sex civil partners.[2]

In this chapter, we examine the historical context within which the concept of parental responsibility developed and consider its practical as well as its symbolic significance.

## II. FROM PATERNAL RIGHTS TO SHARED PARENTAL RESPONSIBILITY

Historically, in the eyes of the law, legitimate children[3] belonged to their father, and he had sole rights of custody and control over them. So extensive were these rights that the father was empowered to appoint a guardian, over the mother, to exercise authority over his children on his death.[4] The mother, by contrast, had no parental rights and her legal identity was subsumed under that of her husband.[5] Although by the 19th century, the

[1] For different theoretical explanations for parental responsibility, see Herring (2004) pp 353–56.
[2] S 4A Children Act 1989 (not in force at time of writing). See ch 15.
[3] For discussion of unmarried parents, see below pp 289ff and ch 15.
[4] The Tenures Abolition Act 1660, as amended by the Wills Act 1837.
[5] See, generally, Maidment (1984) 108ff.

courts did sometimes intervene to restrict the father's rights, this was only where his behaviour was 'exceptionally culpable' (Maidment 1984 p 112)[6] so that he forfeited his right to custody.

Mothers' statutory rights emerged piecemeal over the years[7] beginning, in 1839, with the right, on separation, to apply for access to their children up to full age and to seek custody of children up to the age of 7.[8] The Matrimonial Causes Act 1857, which introduced judicial divorce, gave the court wide discretion to deal with the custody, education and maintenance of children. This discretion was partially extended to cases other than those involving divorce or judicial separation by the Custody of Infants Act 1873. That statute also raised the maximum age at which the courts could award custody of children to their mothers from 7 to 16. In addition, it removed the bar, which existed under the 1839 Act, on custody petitions from adulterous mothers.

In 1886, the Guardianship of Infants Act established mothers as sole guardians of their children where the father died without appointing a guardian. Where a guardian had been appointed by the father or by the court, the mother was entitled to act jointly with him. And the Act went even further: it 'destroyed the concept of the family as a domestic kingdom ruled by the father' (Bainham 2005 p 11). It empowered the court to make such order as it thought fit in relation to the custody or access of an infant 'having regard to the welfare of the infant, and to the conduct of the parents, and to the wishes as well of the mother as of the father'.[9]

The statutory erosion of paternal rights continued into the 20th century, and the Guardianship of Infants Act 1925 was passed after vigorous campaigning by a leading women's group.[10] It explicitly stated in its Preamble that its goal was to establish the principle of equality between men and women in relation to their legitimate children. The Act therefore stipulated that in proceedings before the court concerning the custody or upbringing of an infant, or concerning the property of an infant, the court should have regard to the welfare of the child as the first and paramount consideration and should not consider that the claim of the father was superior to that of the mother or vice versa.

> **Q** The Guardianship of Infants Acts 1886 and 1925 both introduced the welfare of the child as a consideration in decisions concerning children. What do you think explains the shift from parental status, and paternal authority in particular, to welfare?

It was during the course of the struggle towards gender equality that the welfare principle became prominent and, indeed, Maidment suggests that it developed as a device to sidestep women's claims:

> The welfare of the child principle was ... used in the nineteenth century to deny a mother any right to custody, or even access, because the judges deemed the welfare of the child to be best

---

[6] See, eg, *R v Greenhill* (1836) 4 Ad & E 624 where Lord Denman CJ noted that 'the right of the father would not be acted upon where the enforcement of it would be attended with danger to the child; as where there was an apprehension of cruelty, or of contamination by some exhibition of gross profligacy' (p 640). The fact that the father was involved in an adulterous relationship was not of itself decisive.

[7] For a detailed account of this process, see Maidment (1984) ch 5.

[8] Custody of Infants Act 1839. For an historical account of the passage of this legislation, see Maidment (1984) 113–16.

[9] S 9.

[10] See for an account of the events leading up to the passing of the legislation Cretney (1996a).

served by upholding the 'sacred rights of the father' to his children. Conversely the welfare principle was used at this time to dilute women's demands for equal parental rights to their children. Indeed the 1925 Act was a political device to actually deny women equality of parental rights. (1984 pp 107–8)

Accordingly, she argues, the welfare principle developed largely in response to women's claims:

The rise of the welfare principle could only come in proportion to the fall in the sacred rights of fathers, but this fall did not come essentially out of concern for the interest of the child but out of the fight of women's groups for equality of legal rights. This is not to dismiss the Victorian concern for the welfare of children as hollow or empty, but to say that in this particular context it was in fact a by-product of the women's movement. It may have happened anyway, because other developments in society emphasised the child as a centre of concern (in the nineteenth century largely philanthropic, and in the twentieth largely social and scientific). But as historical fact the emergence of the Guardianship of Infants Act 1925 owes far more to the women's movement than to the child protection movement. (1984 pp 146–47)

The welfare principle did benefit mothers. Smart explains that shifts in 'the perception of childhood and the construction of modern "scientific" conceptions of child development' (1989a p 5) fortified women's claims. The development of new types of knowledge, particularly in the spheres of psychiatry, psychoanalysis, psychology and pedagogics, together with feminist lobbying, combined to enable mothers to make new claims relating to their children:

These power claims were not rights based like men's claims to children; rather they were formulated around the uniqueness of motherhood and the supposedly natural (biological) bond between the mother and the child she has borne. They also invoked the idea of the interests of the child, interests which were gradually defined as inhering in the quality of physical and emotional care provided for a child. Under this regime the care a mother could provide became valued and hence created a shift in the power nexus of parenthood ... [A]t the point of marital breakdown, if not during a marriage, the valorisation of motherhood gradually modified men's power in relation to children. (Smart 1989a p 6)

Mothering came to be seen in the 20th century as crucial to the welfare of children and mothers therefore tended to be awarded custody by the courts.[11] Still, however, the mother had no automatic parental rights or authority; her rights had to be conferred by means of a court order. With the passing of the Guardianship Act 1973, mothers were eventually given equal rights and authority with the father 'exercisable by either without the other'.[12] Yet even that statute left unchanged the father's status as natural guardian of his legitimate children. It was not until the enactment of the Children Act 1989 that this rule, which admittedly was more of symbolic than practical importance, was finally abolished.[13] Under the Children Act 1989, married parents, both mothers and fathers, acquire parental responsibility automatically; each is entitled to exercise it independently of the other; and neither loses it on divorce.[14]

---

[11] See Smart (1989a) pp 8–9 and ch 8 below.
[12] S 1(1) of the Guardianship Act 1973.
[13] S 2(4) of the Children Act 1989.
[14] See further ch 4.

**Q** Why do you think both parents retain parental responsibility equally irrespective of events such as divorce? Does this tell us anything about the dominant ideology of the family? Does it tell us anything about the way we conceive of the welfare of children?

## III. EXPLANATIONS FOR THE CHANGE TO SHARED AND ENDURING PARENTAL RESPONSIBILITY

The legal framework that existed prior to the Children Act 1989 had become complex and confusing. The reforms were intended to address a number of problems that had been identified and that were considered by the Law Commission (1988b). For example, the kinds of orders available on separation or divorce varied depending on the nature of the proceedings brought (Law Commission 1988b para 4.2). Also, it was not clear what powers and responsibilities were conveyed by the various statutes and court orders (1988b paras 2.10 and 4.3). There were also other concerns. It was observed by professionals that the welfare of children was endangered by parental conflict[15] and it was also felt that court intervention in determining the arrangements for children was of limited use (Hoggett 1994 p 9). In addition, children were increasingly coming to be seen as the victims of the breakdown of adult relationships (Roche 1991 p 346; Piper 1996b). In consequence, there developed a preference for mediation, thought to reduce conflict, and for arrangements which were thought to go some way towards satisfying children's perceived need for continuity in their relationships with both parents.

The Law Commission, therefore, endorsed three principles (1988b para 4.5): the law should intervene as little as possible; in cases of dispute, it should seek to lower the stakes; and court orders should reduce the opportunities for conflict and litigation in the future.[16] It also endorsed the 'fundamental principle … that the primary responsibility for the upbringing of children rests with their parents' (Law Commission 1988b para 2.1).[17] The role of the state in regulating the relationship between parents and children should be a residual one.

**Q** See chapter 1. To what extent does the reasoning of the Law Commission tend to conform with the notion of a public/private divide?

Bainham viewed this philosophy of promoting autonomous parenting with some unease:

> The 1989 Act gives effect to this philosophy of public support for parental responsibility in a number of ways. First, it introduces a general principle of non-intervention [s 1(5)] … . Secondly, it substantially modifies section 41 [of the Matrimonial Causes Act 1973[18]] and … is likely to curtail severely the extent of court involvement in divorce cases … . Thirdly, the Act asserts the primary status of parenthood which is to be characterised by the acquisition of

---

[15] See further Chs 8 and 11.
[16] See, for discussion, King (1987) 186.
[17] See, further, Eekelaar (1991a) and ch 9 below.
[18] Further reform of this section is being considered. See Herring (2004) 421–22.

'parental responsibility' ... . If no order is made (as will increasingly be the case in a system favouring non-intervention) the two parents will, in principle, retain their joint responsibility for the children ... .

The hope appears to be that this scheme will result in a significant number of parents continuing to accept the parental roles of the other by agreement and without needing to have recourse to the courts. A great deal of time and money could be saved and children ought to benefit both from ongoing relationships with each parent and from the removal of one area of dispute during the divorce process. ...

These aims are laudable. I have no quarrel with either the intended marginalisation of the judicial role or with the view that child care arrangements brought about by agreement are more likely to work than those that result from attempts at compulsion. But I want to suggest that this scheme, by regarding private arrangements as sacrosanct, fails to give adequate recognition to the *public* interest in children. In developing this argument it must be conceded that, on one interpretation, the Act has simply re-defined the public interest and has not diluted it. On this view, the public interest is seen as best served by facilitating parental agreements. In other words, the theory would be that it is in children's best interests (and consequently the public interest) that parents should agree on their future care. But ... whichever way the policy shift is described there can be little doubt that an area which hitherto was thought appropriate for legal regulation will in future be substantially de-regulated.

(1990 pp 209–10, emphasis in original, footnotes omitted)

The Law Commission envisaged its reforms as having the effect of providing a realistic framework for decision-making while encouraging the involvement of both parents, even after separation or divorce, in the upbringing of their children. It took the view that the incidents of parenthood could not be realistically divided up into different sized packages and, since '[m]ost parental responsibilities can only be exercised while the parent has the child' (1988b para 4.8), 'power and responsibility should go hand in hand and largely "run with the child"' (1986 para 4.53(d)). This, it stated (1986 para 4.53(d)), would be preferable to joint custody, which was gaining in popularity at the time, where one parent had physical care and the other had ill-defined powers to intervene. Accordingly, the legislation gives both parents equal status and each has the capacity to act independently of the other in the absence of a court order to the contrary. In the event of a dispute, a parent may invoke the provisions of Section 8 in order to seek its resolution by the court. The statute enables a parent[19] to seek a residence order, determining with whom the child shall live; a contact order, determining whether there may be contact with the child and, if so, what form that contact will take; a specific issue order, settling a specific question which arises concerning parental responsibility for a child; or a prohibited steps order, precluding a person, without the consent of the court, from taking a designated step which could be taken by a parent in exercising parental responsibility.

[W]e believe it important to preserve the equal status of parents and their power to act independently of one another unless and until a court orders otherwise. This should be seen as part of the general aim of encouraging both parents to feel concerned and responsible for the welfare of their children. A few respondents suggested that they should have a legal duty to consult one another on major matters in their children's lives, arguing that this would increase parental

---

[19] Among others. See s 10 of the Children Act 1989. This section has been amended to enable step-parents and civil partners who have acquired parental responsibility under s 4A to seek s 8 orders without the leave of the court. The amended version is not in force at the time of writing. Civil partners who have treated a child as a child of the family will be able to apply for residence and contact orders as of right. Step parents already have this capacity.

co-operation and involvement after separation or divorce. This is an objective which we all share. However, whether or not the parents are living together, a legal duty of consultation seems both unworkable and undesirable. The person looking after the child has to be able to take decisions in the child's best interests as and when they arise. ...In practice, where the parents disagree about a matter of upbringing the burden should be on the one seeking to prevent a step which the other is proposing, or to impose a course of action which only the other can put into effect, to take the matter to court.

(Law Commission 1988b para 2.10, footnote omitted)

Roche (1991) points out that it was assumed that the durability of parental responsibility would contribute to a reduction in disputes over children because there would be less to fight over. The court's powers are restricted to the making of Section 8 orders and these do not 'fundamentally disturb' parental responsibility. 'The assumption is that because conflict will be reduced, children will benefit' (p 349). He observes that:

The legislative change was accompanied by a rhetoric of parenthood which stressed the consensual resolution of disputes between parents over their children. ...By definition, parents who fight over such matters are in the wrong. Thus dual-parenting became the new aim of legislation and social policy initiatives and indicated not only how best to resolve disputes over children, but also how the preferred post-divorce arrangements should be organised.

(pp 346–47).

However, according to Bainham, while the Act was intended to promote joint parenting, it is deficient in achieving that aim:

A regime which allows independent decision-making, without prior consultation, may work perfectly well where parents are living together amicably. It is likely that the main issues affecting the child will be discussed and that parents will reach a consensus where they initially disagree. The situation of parental estrangement or divorce is quite different. Here there may well not be harmonious relations or any inclination to co-operate. That this can be so is well-illustrated by the intractable problem of enforcing access orders. It cannot be assumed that an ex-wife will be well disposed to inform her ex-husband (or vice versa) about plans for the child or that, if she does, she will take his views into account when they clash with her own. The chances are that in many (if not most) cases the non-custodial or non-residential parent will be kept at a distance and in the dark.

   If ... a major aim of the reformed legislation is to strengthen and encourage dual parenting we might have expected to see written into the Act provisions relating to co-operation or consultation ... [T]he implication is ... that joint *independent* rather than *co-operative* parenting, is the normative standard approved by society and reflected in the law. I doubt the wisdom of this message even in the context of a functioning family. It is difficult to square with the stated aims and purposes of the reforms which are ostensibly to encourage the practical involvement of two parents where possible. But the message is even less appropriate in the post-divorce context ... .

   Is the reality, perhaps, that parental responsibility can only be exercised meaningfully by a parent who has the physical care of a child? ... If this is right, the focus of attention should really be on what the Act is doing to promote 'time-sharing', a concept alien to English law, whereby the child spends a significant amount of time in the physical care of each parent. If this yardstick is used, the conclusion must again be that there is little real commitment in the legislation to the principle of dual parenting following divorce.

(1990 pp 211–12, emphasis in original, footnotes omitted)

**Q** What do you understand by 'dual parenting'? Would, in your view, provisions relating to consultation and co-operation have better promoted dual parenting? Is there a difference between decision-making and child care? Do you agree that dual parenting was the aim of the legislation? Could it be argued that the retreat of the courts and the 'lowering of the stakes' by ensuring that both parents retain parental responsibility on divorce were intended to reduce conflict and to facilitate the resolution of disputes through agreement?

## IV. PARENTAL RESPONSIBILITY, JOINT PARENTING AND THE REDUCTION OF CONFLICT

Eekelaar took the view that dual parenting was not the main aim of the legislation. The 'stronger imperative', he said, was to promote parental autonomy and the issue of parental co-operation was always meant to be for the parents to work out (1991b p 129).

Yet there are statutory constraints on independent action. These are enumerated by Herring:

1.  [Placement for adoption] and [a]doption can only take place if *all* parents with parental responsibility [and guardians] consent.[20]
2.  If the child aged 16 or 17 wishes to marry then *all* parents with parental responsibility and any guardians must consent.[21]
3.  If the child is to be accommodated by the local authority then *none* of those with parental responsibility must have objected.[22]
4.  Section 13 of the Children Act 1989 states that if a residence order has been made and one party wishes to change the surname of the child then the consent of all those with parental responsibility is required ... .[23]
5.  Section 13 of the Children Act 1989 states that if there is a residence order it is not possible to remove a child from the UK without the consent of all those with parental responsibility ... .

(Herring 2004 pp 362–63)

In addition, the courts appear to have extended the circumstances in which some element of co-operation is required. Parental responsibility apparently does entail a duty to consult in some circumstances and does not merely 'run with the child'. One of these circumstances is where one parent wishes to change the child's surname. This is quite often a source of conflict and, according to Hale LJ, the name of a child has come to have too great a symbolic significance. She regretted that it is often suggested that 'fathers need that outward and visible link in order to retain their relationship with, and commitment to, their child. It is a poor sort of parent whose interest in and commitment to his child depends upon that child bearing his name'.[24] Be that as it may, in the case of

---

[20] S 16 Adoption Act 1976. See also for the new law, Adoption and Children Act 2002 ss 19, 47, 52(2)(6).

[21] Marriage Act 1949 s 3(1A).

[22] See s 20(7) and (8) Children Act 1989.

[23] This applies also if there is no residence order in force: *Re PC (Change of Surname)* [1997] 2 FLR 730. See Bainham (2005) 134.

[24] *Re R (Surname: Using Both Parents)* [2001] EWCA Civ 1344; [2001] 2 FLR 1358 para 18. See further on change of name, *Re S (Change of Names: Cultural Factors)* [2001] 2 FLR 1005; *Re W, Re A, Re B (Change of Name)* [1999] 2 FLR 930; *Re A (A Child) (Change of Name)* [2003] EWCA Civ 56; [2003] 2 FLR 1; *Re H (Child's Name: First Name)* [2002] EWCA Civ 190; [2002] 1 FLR 973.

a change of name, consultation and agreement are required, failing which the matter must be resolved by a court.[25] This applies irrespective of whether the father opposing the change has parental responsibility.[26] Certain forms of medical treatment, namely circumcision[27] and decisions about the MMR vaccine,[28] also require consultation. Changing a child's school too is something that a parent cannot do unilaterally. Glidewell LJ held in *Re G (Parental Responsibility: Education)*[29] that because a mother had parental responsibility, she was 'entitled and indeed ought to have been consulted' by the father, with whom the child was living, about taking this 'important step'. In *Re H (Parental Responsibility)*,[30] Butler Sloss LJ appeared to consider the duty to consult a wide-ranging one. She said that a father with parental responsibility would have a right to be heard in adoption and in Hague Convention abduction proceedings. In addition, he would have the 'right to be consulted on schooling, serious medical problems, and other important occurrences in a child's life'.[31] However, as Eekelaar has observed, the obligation is ill-defined. He points out that it is not clear what amounts to consultation. Nor is it clear whether information suffices or whether agreement is necessary. There is no indication of what qualifies as important or serious. Finally, he questions how the obligation to consult can be enforced (Eekelaar 2001c p 429).

In reality, in the event of a disagreement over any decision, the parent with whom the child is physically present is usually, in practice, in a better position to put her wishes into effect.[32] Moreover, it seems that in law, if there is a residence order in force, the non-resident parent cannot interfere with the day-to-day upbringing of the child.[33] But the non-caretaking parent is not powerless; provided he is not acting in a manner that is incompatible with a court order,[34] he can, while the child is with him, reverse the caretaking parent's decisions or, in any event, he can challenge them in court. Dewar has said that what has been imposed is 'a presumption of joint custody in all but name' (1992 p 355).

> **Q** The Law Commission, commenting on the old joint custody orders, said that these were being described to absent[35] parents as providing 'an important ratification of their continued parental role' and, at the same time, to caregiving parents concerned at the prospect of interference by absent parents as merely 'a matter of words' (1988b para 4.3). Do you think similar criticisms can be made of shared parental responsibility?

---

[26] *Dawson v Wearmouth* [1997] 2 FLR 629.

[27] It seems that if the father does not have parental responsibility, the mother alone can choose the name initially (Bainham 2005 p 134). However changing the name is different. A disputed change should not be made unilaterally without the authorisation of the court, irrespective of parental responsibility: *Dawson v Wearmouth* [1997] 2 FLR 629 (obiter); *Re T (Change of Surname)* [1998] 2 FLR 620; *Re C (Change of Surname)* [1998] 2 FLR 656; *Re R (Surname: Using Both Parents)* [2001] EWCA Civ 1344; [2001] 2 FLR 1358.

[28] *Re J (Specific Issue Orders)* [2000] 1 FLR 571.

[29] *Re B (A Child) (Immunisation)* [2003] EWCA Civ 1148; [2003] 2 FCR 156.

[30] [1994] 2 FLR 964, 967.

[31] [1998] 1 FLR 855, 859.

[31] *Ibid.* See also *Re P (A Minor) (Parental Responsibility Order)* [1994] 1 FLR 578, 585, where parental responsibility was considered analogous to joint custody, which entailed consultation.

[32] This is most often the mother. In over 90% of lone-parent families, it is the mother with whom the child lives. See Blackwell and Dawe (2003) para 1.3; Simpson, *et al*, (1995) 3.

[33] *Re P (A Minor) (Parental Responsibility Order)* [1994] 1 FLR 578, 585.

[34] Children Act 1989, s 2(8).

[35] This term has now been replaced by 'non-resident' parents.

*Parental Responsibility and the Non-Resident Parent*

The Law Commission stated that 'parents should not be regarded as losing their position, and their ability to take decisions about their children, simply because they are separated or in dispute with one another' (1988b para 2.11). But, as it pointed out, in reality, it is only the parent who has 'practical control' over the child who is in a position to implement any decisions (1988b para 2.10). So, while both parents have in law the power of independent action, there are considerable constraints on non-resident parents, many of whom have limited contact with their children, in exercising this power. It is perhaps unlikely that a non-resident parent will be able give effect to a decision made independently and against the wishes of the other parent. And although decisions made by the caretaking parent can be challenged under Section 8, the non-resident parent may not even become aware of a decision until it is too late to reverse it. What is more, probably few parents understand what their rights are under the law (Hoggett 1994 p 10).

Research conducted in California by Maccoby and Mnookin (1992) confirmed that parents might indeed be unaware of what their ex-spouses are doing. They found that while many parents reported discussing matters such as their children's emotional state, their schooling and their extra-curricular activities, there was relatively little discussion about other matters (Table 9.5). They also found that the resident parent was usually the primary decision-maker. Joint decisions were made only in a small number of cases, and then only on major issues (pp 221–22). However, there was a discrepancy in perceptions about the division of tasks, the extent of discussion and the way in which decisions were made. Typically, caretaking parents reported less discussion and joint decision-making than the other parents. The authors concluded from this that parents in their sample were probably ignorant of what went on in each other's homes. They went on to say: '[w]e suspect that residential parents make many routine decisions that the non-residential parent knows nothing about' (p 221). This contention was fortified by their finding that a few years after separation, the most common pattern was what they called 'spousal disengagement' which involved 'parallel parenting' (p 277). Parents avoided conflict by making little or no effort to communicate or to co-operate over child care (pp 233–34). Most importantly, a joint custody order made little difference to the extent of joint decision-making (p 225).

Similar findings were reported in a study carried out in England (Simpson, *et al,* 1995). Three approaches to post-divorce parenting were identified: no contact, with fathers reporting that they had lost all contact or had contact only rarely; parallel parenting, where fathers reported contact with children but no communication with their ex-spouses; and communicative parenting, where fathers reported contact accompanied by communication with their ex-spouses (p 23). Of those fathers in the research sample, 27% reported no contact, 27% reported parallel parenting and 46% reported communicative parenting (p 24). Relationships in the first two categories were characterised by hostility and conflict and there was little exchange of information between parents.[36] Although the study focused on fathers who were divorced prior to the coming into force of the Children Act 1989, the researchers maintained that this did not affect its relevance: 'it is our contention that the experience of being a father post-divorce is

---

[36] However, this was not necessarily a permanent state of affairs. Parents did move between categories and some parents who began in the no contact category moved up to the communicative category, often via the parallel parenting category (p 43).

much the same for fathers today as it was for the fathers who took part in this study' (p xv).

Another study, conducted by Maclean and Eekelaar, revealed that there was little joint decision-making among those parents in their sample who were 'formerly married': '[J]oint decision-making of any serious nature probably occurs only in about one in ten cases where contact is regularly exercised, and then usually only on a limited number of issues.'[37] (1997 p 122)

And it seems that, still, little has changed. The most recent research dealing with this issue reveals low levels of joint decision-making, with 78% of parents never discussing their children's problems together (Trinder, *et al*, 2005 para 5.5).[38]

It is likely, then, that the concept of parental responsibility does not necessarily facilitate co-operative parenting between separated parents in practice or even, in many cases, give rise to parity in relation to decision-making.[39] The parental responsibility vested in the non-resident parent 'legitimates the actual exercise of parenthood by a natural parent' (Maclean and Eekelaar 1997 p 146).[40] However, when the availability of opportunities to engage in such parenting is taken into account, parental responsibility may have no more than symbolic significance for many fathers. This is not to say that it is irrelevant. To vest parental responsibility in non-resident parents may have the intended effect of reducing conflict and encouraging settlement. It may have the effect of mollifying some fathers who would otherwise fight for a court order. It may also persuade resident parents to take cognisance of the non-resident parent's wishes. But the only way those wishes can be enforced in the absence of actual control of the child and in the face of opposition from the carer, is by means of a Section 8 order.[41]

## Parental Responsibility and the Resident Parent

The position of the resident parent is far from impregnable. Conflict and poor communication with the other parent can make it difficult to reach satisfactory arrangements or joint plans relating to children (Cockett and Tripp 1994; 1996 pp 42–43). In such circumstances, the resident parent may be vulnerable to attempts by the non-resident parent to challenge her decisions.

---

[37] Indeed, Maclean and Eekelaar (1997) found little evidence of widespread joint parenting or joint decision-making generally. This was generally true of parents when they were living together and after they separated, whether they were former spouses or former cohabitants. It was also true of those who had never lived together (p 137).

[38] See also Smith (2003).

[39] See Eekelaar (1991b) 135–36.

[40] It also gives the non-resident parent rights in the context of consent to adoption and the right to remove the child from voluntary accommodation against the wishes of the local authority. See above. In addition, it enables the parent to deal with third parties such as doctors. See, generally, Maclean and Eekelaar (1997) 36.

[41] See chs 15 and 16. It is not so much parental responsibility that gives non-resident fathers legal remedies; it is simply parenthood that does so. For parents, the power to challenge decisions in court is not in any way linked in the Act to the concept of responsibility. In terms of s 10(4)(a) of the Act, in addition to persons that have parental responsibility, 'any parent' is entitled to seek a s 8 order. So unmarried fathers without parental responsibility, even the rapist that so exercised the Law Commission (Law Commission (1979) para 3.9), are entitled, without needing to seek the leave of the court, to challenge the caretaking mother's decisions about a child's upbringing. It is arguably, therefore, parenthood coupled with s 8, rather than the possession of parental responsibility, that gives non-resident parents, whether married or unmarried, any real say in relation to their children. See Eekelaar (2001c).

As mentioned above, Section 8 is the most important resource for non-resident fathers wishing to challenge the decisions of resident mothers.[42] Research examining the use of specific issue orders suggests that these are used by non-resident parents to challenge resident parents. The main categories of disputes identified in which the orders are made are children's education, medical treatment, relocation, children's surnames and disclosure of information such as the child's medical details (Gilmore 2004).

While the availability of Section 8 orders is not dependent on the father's having parental responsibility, fathers who do have parental responsibility may be in a better position to acquire information about the child's upbringing and, therefore, to oppose the mothers' decisions.[43] Even the threat of legal proceedings is a potent weapon; a mother who does not have the means to litigate, who is dominated by the father or who is in any way in a weaker bargaining position than he is may feel unable to withstand his demands, however unreasonable.

Grand, a practitioner, has suggested that shared parental responsibility can give rise to adverse consequences. He was worried that the way in which the Act is worded seems to invite excessive interference by the non-resident parent in the decision-making of the resident parent. He pointed out that the Act imposes no constraints on the exercise of parental responsibility by the non-resident parent: '[t]here is no reference to joint responsibility or to sharing responsibility and, on the face of it, what is granted is absolute power, exercisable without reference to the other parent' (1994 p 586).[44] In his view, the legislation could present a real risk that 'irresponsible' non-resident fathers might choose to rely on parental responsibility to reverse the decisions made by resident mothers to the detriment of children's interests (p 587).

Roche's concerns were somewhat different. His disquiet related more to the symbolic force of the status conferred by parental responsibility which could, he said, exacerbate the difficulties resident parents face. He described his concerns in this regard:

> The reality for most mothers is, at best, one of occasional support from their partners in the domestic sphere including those tasks which directly relate to the child. This is not the same thing as shared responsibility for child care, merely assistance. Nevertheless it is still involvement and important. However the father's role is rendered problematic when the adult relationship does break up. ...
>
> If, by symbolically valuing the role of the absent parent, the Act is successful in promoting a continuing and constructive involvement on the part of fathers, it will be of benefit to ex-partners as well as children. ...

---

[42] The fact that the burden of initiating legal proceedings is placed on the non-resident parent might be some deterrent against interference with the resident parent's decisions. However, for a non-resident parent with resources or for one able to negotiate successfully the hurdles of the public funding system, s 8 provides considerable scope for litigation. Indeed, Dewar has pointed out that the Act has increased the opportunity for the 'legalisation' of disputes (1992 p 356). Any aspect of parental responsibility not already regulated by a court order is open to challenge. Cretney, however, comments that fears of increased litigation are unfounded (1996a p 137). But see Eekelaar (2001c) 429, quoted below. The case law seems, on balance, to discourage trivial applications. See *Re C (A Minor) (Leave to Seek S 8 Orders)* [1994] 1 FLR 26; *Re P (A Minor) (Parental Responsibility Order)* [1994] 1 FLR 578. But see *Re HG (Specific Issue Order: Sterilisation)* [1993] 1 FLR 587, 593 where the court stressed the importance of avoiding a restrictive interpretation and of refraining from selecting 'idiosyncratic' situations or events for exclusion from the ambit of a s 8 order. The number of orders made is not inconsiderable. In 2003, there were 9487 prohibited steps orders and 3142 specific issue orders (DfES 2004e Fig 12.1). It is not stated how many of these concerned disputes between parents. The number of applications as opposed to orders is not specified.

[43] See *Re P (Parental Responsibility)* [1998] 2 FLR 96. In this case, the father, who was unmarried and seeking a parental responsibility order, made it clear that he would use it to enable him to monitor the child's health and education. In other words, the court said, he would use it to 'try to interfere with and possibly undermine the mother's care of the child' (p 110). See also *Re M (Contact: Parental Responsibility)* [2001] 2 FLR 342.

[44] But see above for decisions requiring consultation.

While this [parental] responsibility can be exercised independently of the will of the other parent, it is also always potentially open to challenge in the courts via ... Section 8 orders. Whether or not a parent is involved with or has contact with his child, this question of potential involvement, and hence power in relation to the child and the parent the child is living with, is critical.

The argument here is not Bainham's concern over the 'exclusion' of the 'other parent' but whether the Act has made the situation facing the primary carer worse by symbolically re-emphasising the other parent's responsibility and power ... . The parent without day-to-day care of the child will be encouraged to consider himself still involved in the life of the child—indeed this is the very purpose of the new arrangements. However this may operate so as to undermine the position of the primary carer, and the child, whose well-being is inextricably bound up with the well-being of the primary carer economically, emotionally and socially. Mutuality of concerns and action sounds cosy but is this always going to be the case? The family is not an absence of power but, on the contrary, a nexus of a complex and shifting series of power relations involving adults and children.[45] (Roche 1991 pp 355–57)

**Q** Can a non-resident parent be compelled to assist the primary carer in fulfilling the obligations of parenthood? The Law Commission described the old joint custody as carrying the risk of '"power without responsibility" or, what might be worse, responsibility without power' (1986 para 4.41). Might this be an apt description also of shared parental responsibility?

In contrast, Eekelaar seems rather sanguine about shared parental responsibility and the potential for applications under Section 8 to challenge resident parents (Eekelaar 1991b pp 135–36). Indeed, his preference would be for all fathers to have automatic parental responsibility (Eekelaar 2001c p 430). However he has criticised the way in which the concept of parental responsibility has been interpreted by the courts to impose a duty to consult:[46]

However desirable the result which the courts are seeking to achieve might seem to be, it flies in the face of the clear words of s 2(7) of the Children Act 1989. But while I wish to maintain that the outcome is indeed wrong in law, I also wish to argue that it is undesirable. The mistake is to attempt to cast into legal form an aspiration of good conduct. No one could possibly argue that it would not be a 'good thing' for separated parents to co-operate together as far as possible, and as amicably as possible, over their children's upbringing. So also we could not but applaud a parent who lives apart from his child and who visits the child regularly and lovingly. But we do not impose a legal duty to visit. Even if we believed that imposing such a duty would 'send the right message', the risk would be that by clothing the features of co-operative behaviour in the form of legal duty, people would be encouraged to resort to lawyers over perceived infractions. In any case, how could it be enforced? So we wisely leave this to moral persuasion and the dynamics of the relationship. Precisely the same considerations apply to consultation between separated parents. Provided the relationship is good, and especially where contact takes place, either consultation will occur or the non-residential parent will know what is going on. Cases where problems arise tend to be those where the contact has ceased or is rare .... Suppose there was a generalised legal duty to consult, such as that articulated by Butler-Sloss LJ [in *Re H*][47] ... . Will it apply if the non-resident parent has virtually lost touch, or shown no interest in previous communications? What must the parent with the duty do to comply with the duty? What if consultation exacerbates conflict? ... . And what would such parents think

---

[45] See also Smart (1989a) 21.
[46] See also, for discussion, Maidment (2001).
[47] See above p 284.

when they realise that the non-residential parents are under no corresponding duty to take an interest in the children? These are all hard enough questions. They would be made harder by giving the parties an added opportunity for dispute, and incentives to consult solicitors if they believe there has been a failure to comply. In any event, it is difficult to see what enforcement mechanism could be used that is not already available to a non-residential parent who is dissatisfied with how children are being brought up. (Eekelaar 2001c p 429)

   This is not to say that a court could not impose a requirement for consultation appropriate to the circumstances when disposing of a specific dispute within the context of a specific issue order. But a generalised duty is another matter. It threatens to subject parents caring for children to an unnecessary risk of legal harassment and the added anxieties and pressures that would cause in already conflicted situations. (pp 429–30)

The concerns voiced by Grand, Roche and Eekelaar are equally relevant in those cases involving unmarried parents where both have parental responsibility.

## V. UNMARRIED FATHERS AND PARENTAL RESPONSIBILITY

All mothers are automatically vested with parental responsibility as are married fathers.[48] Although the possibility was debated in the past,[49] parental responsibility was not conferred automatically on unmarried fathers because of concern to protect vulnerable mothers (LCD 1998 p 2). Until recently, unmarried fathers could acquire parental responsibility under Section 4 of the Children Act 1989 only through a parental responsibility agreement with the mother or though an order of court. However Section 4 has been amended and an unmarried father can now gain parental responsibility automatically if he registers as the child's father.[50]

   In the case of married parents, there is a duty on both to register the birth within 42 days.[51] Where the parents are not married to each other at the time of the birth, however, the father has no obligation to register and has no independent right to do so. Normally, he can be registered as the father only if he and the mother attend to register together or, if not, then with the consent of the mother. In the latter case, the mother and the father are each required to provide a declaration that he is the father. Independent registration by either mother or father of the father's name is permitted only where there is a parental responsibility agreement or where a relevant court order can be produced, together with a declaration that it is still in force. The relevant court orders include a parental responsibility order and an order made under Schedule 1 of the Children Act 1989 instructing the father to make financial provision for the child.[52] Unless one of these requirements is met, the father's name cannot be entered on the register.[53] However it can be entered at a later stage if the parents jointly request this; if the necessary declarations are made; if there is a parental responsibility agreement; if there is a relevant order of court; or if the parents have married.[54]

---

48 Children Act 1989 s 2(1).
49 See Law Com Report No 118 (1982).
50 See ch 15.
51 Births and Deaths Registration Act 1953 s 2.
52 *Ibid*, s 10.
53 *Ibid*, s 10(1).
54 *Ibid*, ss 10A and 14.

The amendment of Section 4 is significant. Relatively few parents go down the route of parental responsibility agreements or orders. However, the majority of unmarried parents register their children's births jointly. In 2003, for instance, 63.5% of births outside of marriage were registered jointly by parents who lived at the same address and 19% of births outside of marriage were registered jointly by parents living at separate addresses.[55] Similar figures are recorded for the previous few years. If this trend continues, it means that about 80% of unmarried fathers each year will acquire parental responsibility automatically.

Intimations of the change in the law came with a Consultation Paper (LCD 1998), which noted that the lack of parental responsibility might put fathers at disadvantage in situations like adoption. In addition, it said, parental responsibility 'may be important to people as a symbol of the legal status of parenthood, and it may be a particular source of grievance for some unmarried fathers that they may be forced to support their children financially, whether or not they have acquired parental responsibility under the Children Act 1989' (p 2). It was also noted that few fathers actually got parental responsibility under the Act; the number of agreements and orders was small (para 53).

As Sheldon says, the anomaly the law was intended to redress was not that there were large numbers of fathers involved in the long-term day to day care of children who did not have parental responsibility. Rather it was the fact that there were many men who did not have the rights and status of parental responsibility despite being genetic fathers (2001 p 99).[56]

The arguments that prompted the change centred on the issue of fairness and on claims that fathers were being discriminated against.[57] There was also the view that if unmarried fathers were given automatic parental responsibility, this would help to 'promote more involvement by absent fathers in the lives of their children' (Sharp 2001 p 610). Without a change in the law, men would continue to be 'condemned as somehow undeserving' and this would only confirm in them the apathy and detachment that leads them to lose contact with their children (*ibid*). Extra litigation about specific issues would be a price worth paying for justice for fathers and children (*ibid*).

Another impetus for change[58] was a research study exploring the perceptions held by fathers of their legal status (Pickford 1999). Pickford found that, in her sample, three quarters of fathers, whether married or unmarried, were not aware that there was a difference in the legal status of married and unmarried fathers. Nor did they know that unmarried fathers did not have parental responsibility (p 145). The reactions of the unmarried fathers on being told of their legal position ranged from surprise to anger to anxiety, and '[o]ften fathers expressed their dissatisfaction in terms of unfairness or injustice', frequently referring to child support (p 152). 'They tended to feel strongly that fathers should have rights if they were expected to bear responsibilities' (*ibid*). A small number reported difficulties in relation to consent to medical treatment of their children. Few knew of the possibility of entering into a parental responsibility agreement and, in any event, interviewees felt awkward about taking this route as it felt like a betrayal of trust in their partners (*ibid*).

---

[55] ONS (2005) Table 3.2.

[56] But a large number of unmarried fathers appear to live with the mother and child. See above.

[57] See Wallbank (2002) pp 291–92. But note that claims of unjustifiable discrimination under the ECHR failed in *McMichael v UK* (1995) 20 EHRR 205; and *B v UK* [2000] 1 FLR 1.

[58] See Eekelaar (2001c) 426.

Pickford maintained that the law was out of step with society's ideas about father-hood, that it was unfair and that it was potentially 'destabilising of the parental relationship' (p 158). It could also 'undermine the objective of promoting a sense of involvement and responsibility amongst these fathers' (*ibid*). She recommended confer-ring parental responsibility on those fathers who registered the birth jointly with mothers: 'If both parents are prepared to recognise the fact of the man's paternity, it appears in itself a strong argument for such a change, and it would also accord with the views of most people' (p 157). In addition, it would have the effect of giving parental responsibility to most unmarried fathers automatically.

Section 4(1)(a) of the Children Act 1989 now provides that fathers who register the child's birth have parental responsibility for that child. There is implicit in this legis-lation an assumption that registration is evidence of a level of commitment sufficient to warrant the giving of parental responsibility (Wallbank 2002 p 277). However, if paren-tal responsibility is abused it can be revoked.[59] Alternatively, the mother can apply to court to deal with a specific incident. As Wallbank notes, the burden rests on the mother to institute proceedings in either situation (2001 p 281).[60]

Of course, it could be said that most mothers who allow joint registration are willingly allowing their partners to gain parental responsibility; joint registration normally requires the mother's consent. But there is the question of how to ensure that that con-sent is given freely and not under pressure. There is also the question of how to ensure that mothers know what the legal effect of joint registration is. Furthermore, it is open to doubt whether many mothers will know of their right to revoke.

Eekelaar says that biological fathers gain little from obtaining parental responsibility. Their situation is strengthened in some cases such as where children are in local author-ity accommodation and in adoption proceedings.[61] However, he contends, since fathers, as parents, have legal duties to secure their children's education and to safeguard their health, they must also have concomitant rights to make decisions about these things (2001c p 428). He goes on:

> Whatever may have been the experience of some unmarried fathers in Pickford's research, the law must bear some reasonable relationship to social life. The fact that around one million fathers are daily making decisions concerning their children's upbringing cannot surely go unrecognised by the law. The conclusion is irresistible that they do, indeed, have the legal rights necessary to bring up their children … .
>
> It may all boil down to symbolism, but it is unsatisfactory to use scarce legal resources to engage in gestures. It must be remembered that cases where fathers make applications for parental responsibility are invariably those where they are living apart from their children. Sometimes they have been in prison. The truth, therefore, is that they believe they are acquiring rights to be directly involved in their children's upbringing, despite living apart from them: that is, a right to be consulted. (Eekelaar 2001c p 428)

[59] Like parental responsibility acquired through an agreement or through the court, it can be removed by a court (Children Act 1989 s 4(2A)). The parental responsibility of mothers and married fathers can only be lost through adoption.

[60] See also Wallbank (2002) 286. Her complaint that fathers who register escape court scrutiny could be applied to fathers who enter into parental responsibility agreements.

[61] And where the mother appoints a guardian (Children Act 1989 s 5(8)). However local authorities are already obliged to consult unmarried fathers under s 22 because they are parents. The consent of fathers with-out parental responsibility is not needed for adoption. However Adoption agencies are expected to notify fathers, who are not parents under s 52(6) of the Adoption and Children Act 2002, to provide them with infor-mation about the plans for the child. It may also be necessary to notify and involve them in order to comply with Art 8 ECHR (see below). As parents, unmarried fathers have the capacity to apply for s 8 orders as of right (Children Act 1989 10(4)).

If the registration gives the father a generalised legal right to be consulted, the mother could be opening herself up to potential trouble in the future. She would be well advised not to agree to have his name recorded, although this would need to be balanced against any difficulty non-registration of his name might cause in establishing paternity, should she subsequently seek child support. (p 430)

> **Q** Does Eekelaar's distinction between a right to make decisions and a right to be consulted reflect important differences in principle or is it a distinction based on practical considerations, reliant on the fact that many non-resident fathers are not aware in advance (or at all) of mothers' decisions?

So, to summarise, non-resident parents (usually fathers) are entitled to challenge resident parents' (usually mothers) decisions by instituting Section 8 proceedings. Mothers who disagree with decisions made by fathers have to do likewise, although non-resident parents have fewer opportunities to put their decisions into effect. If non-resident fathers abuse their parental responsibility, the burden is on mothers to seek Section 8 orders, perhaps repeatedly. In the case of unreasonable unmarried fathers, mothers might need to apply to court to have parental responsibility revoked.

As a result of the change in the law, most fathers will have parental responsibility. If parental responsibility creates a wide ranging duty to consult (and the courts seem to be saying it does), it seems that resident mothers will be worse off. In order to consult, the parents will have to communicate more often with each other and this could increase opportunities for conflict. In the event that resident mothers do consult, this will mean that fathers, particularly those who do not have good relationships with their former partners and those who are not close to their children,[62] will have more information than they would otherwise have. For this reason they will be in a better position to challenge decisions. Moreover, a failure to consult could lead to litigation by the aggrieved parent.

## VI. PARENTAL RESPONSIBILITY, WELFARE AND EQUALITY

To a large degree, it has been the influence of social science research into the needs of children that has prompted policy-makers to adopt what Maclean and Eekelaar (1997 p 50) have referred to as the 'new orthodoxy': a conviction that it is important for children's welfare that parents are not in conflict and that both parents participate in their children's upbringing. A number of studies have highlighted the adverse effects of divorce for children and have pointed to conflict between parents as one of the primary sources of these difficulties.[63] They have also pointed to the detrimental effects on children of the loss of a parent, usually the father, on the break-up of the family and have suggested that for the child to sustain a relationship with both parents after breakdown is important in ameliorating the effects of divorce.[64]

---

[62] Dunn (2003 p 24) reports that 'contact *per se* was not significantly linked to fathers' knowledge and influence'. Fathers who had 'affectionate and supportive' relationships with their children knew more about their children's lives.

[63] See further chs 8, 11 and 14.

[64] See, eg, Hetherington (1979) pp 855–56.

Probably one of the most influential of these studies round the time the Children Act 1989 was being drafted was that of Wallerstein and Kelly, documented in their book, *Surviving the Breakup* (1980).

> Although the initial breakup of the family is profoundly stressful, the eventual outcome depends, in large measure, not only on what has been lost, but on what has been created to take the place of the failed marriage. In full and proper perspective, the effect of the divorce is an index of the success or failure of the participants, parents and children, to master the disruption, to negotiate the transition successfully, and to create a more gratifying family to replace the family that failed. ..(pp 304–5)

> Taken as a whole our findings point to the desirability of the child's continuing relationship with both parents during the postdivorce years in an arrangement which enables each parent to be responsible for and genuinely concerned with the well-being of the children. For those parents who are able to reach an agreement on child-related matters after divorce and are willing to give the needs of the children priority or a significant role in their decision-making regarding how and where the children reside, joint legal custody may provide the legal structure of choice. . Although the influence of the legal structure on the fabric of family life may be considerably less than many persons believe it to be, nevertheless, there is some evidence that legal accountability may influence and shore up psychological and financial responsibility. Furthermore, there is evidence in our findings, that lacking legal rights to share in decisions about major aspects of their children's lives, that many noncustodial parents withdrew from their children in grief and frustration. ...
>
> [W]e offer a view diametrically opposed to that of our esteemed colleagues Goldstein, Freud and Solnit in their book *Beyond the Best Interests of the Child*. ..Our findings regarding the centrality of both parents to the psychological health of children and adolescents alike leads us to hold that, where possible, divorcing parents should be encouraged and helped to shape postdivorce arrangements which permit and foster continuity in the children's relations with both parents. (pp 310–11)

Indeed, the conclusions reached by Goldstein, Freud and Solnit (1980a) were very different. They drew attention to the limitations of the law in regulating matters such as the parent-child relationship and warned against the unreliable predictive value of the knowledge on which its judgments can be based (pp 50–51). All that can be done, they suggested, is to identify who, amongst the available adults, is or has the capacity to become the child's psychological parent, and so will make the child feel wanted. This would probably be the adult with whom the child has had and continues to have an affectionate bond. Once this decision is made, they argued, it should be final and it should be that parent alone who decides how he or she wishes to raise the child (p 38). The other parent, they said, should therefore have no legally enforceable right to visit the child. Children, they asserted, have difficulty in relating positively to or benefiting from contact with two psychological parents who are not in positive contact with each other. Loyalty conflicts may result which destroy both relationships. And in any event, a non-resident parent is unlikely to serve as a 'true object for love, trust, and identification, since this role is based on his being available on an uninterrupted day-to-day basis' (p 38).

As Maclean and Eekelaar (1997 pp 51–52) observe, this approach was criticised as leading to an imbalance of power between parents. Also the political climate in the 1970s, with the growth of men's groups, was against it and it had little impact. The 'new orthodoxy', in contrast, continues to find support.

Such support is evident, for example, in the Exeter Family Study (Cockett and Tripp 1994, 1996), a study into the effects on children of family breakdown. Like many of the studies before it, it emphasised the detrimental effects on children of parental conflict. Yet it did not endorse the solution, espoused by Goldstein, Freud and Solnit, of excluding the non-resident parent. On the contrary, it identified the loss of a parent figure as a primary source of harm and, accordingly, it affirmed the importance to children of maintaining relationships with both parents, and indicated that parents should avoid disagreements. More recent research favouring contact has tended to be somewhat more qualified, particularly in the light of concerns about domestic violence in the context of contact.[65] Nevertheless, children's well-being is identified with the preservation of ties with both caretaking and non-resident parents. Government policy is emphatically in favour, except in those cases where there are serious problems, of preserving relationships between children and their non-resident parents:[66] 'A child's welfare is usually best promoted by a continuing and constructive **relationship with both parents**, as long as it is in the child's best interests and safe for all concerned' (CDA, DfES and DTI 2005 para 2, emphasis in original).

Parental responsibility is regarded as one of the mechanisms for preserving and enhancing the relationship between the non-resident parent and the child.[67] As we have seen, one of the central justifications for giving non-resident parents, and unmarried fathers, parental responsibility was that this would encourage fathers to feel responsible for their children and to be involved in their children's lives.[68] Another was the perception that fairness and justice demanded the equalising of the legal status of both parents.

Smart, writing in 1989, contended that heightened significance was being accorded to fathers,[69] and it is clear, from the arguments currently dominating the debate, that this still holds true. She observed that the confluence of a changed deployment of the welfare principle with equality claims have combined to make fathers' claims virtually unanswerable. Fathers' rights groups have argued that the law is biased in favour of mothers and that fathers are being denied equal rights. And their claims are

---

[65] See, for example Dunn (2003). See also Sturge and Glaser (2000). See further ch 8.

[66] See ch 8.

[67] Interestingly, this argument appears to have been extended to a non-biological, social parent who had been in a same-sex relationship with the mother. In *Re G (Children) (Shared Residence Order: Parental Responsibility)* [2005] All ER (D) 25 (Apr) the Court of Appeal awarded a shared residence order to the lesbian partner of the mother of children born into the relationship as a result of artificial insemination. The court pointed out that this order was the only way the former partner could gain parental responsibility. Parental responsibility was crucial, said the court, because without it, the former partner would be marginalised from the children's lives. What is notable about the judgment is the idea that the children's welfare is best served by the involvement of both parents, whatever their sex, and the notion that parental responsibility enables parents to play a role in their children's lives. However the decision can be distinguished from decisions relating to applications for parental responsibility for fathers as this woman was clearly already an involved parent. Compare the cases discussed in ch 15. That fathers, rather than social parents, are generally regarded in a special light is apparent from the fact that social parents cannot get parental responsibility automatically or through something akin to registration. There must be an agreement or an order of court.

[68] Yet, as we will see in ch 15, parental responsibility may have little to do with the care of a child or a close relationship. The courts have often approached parental responsibility orders primarily as status conferring devices. They have distinguished between contact and parental responsibility (Herring 2003 p 91) and they have vested parental responsibility in fathers in cases where it has been acknowledged that the father concerned would not be in a position to make any contribution to his child's upbringing. Parental responsibility is seen as a way of 'recognising a man's position as a father, rather than giving the father rights to make decisions over the upbringing of the child' (Herring 2003 p 91). This, Herring says, 'makes some sense' (p 92): 'A father may well deserve a "stamp of approval" for being a committed father, even if it would not promote the welfare of the child for him to have contact with her' (p 92). Compare Kaganas (1996).

[69] See Smart (1989a) 9.

strengthened by the fact that, increasingly, children's welfare has come to be linked more closely with paternal influence. Noting this shift, she stated that:

> [F]or many, to be a father carries very different meanings, emotions and behaviours than in the pre-war period. Such changes have coincided with legal changes in which the father has lost his legal authority whilst being regarded as more and more central to the family in emotional and psychological terms. The father as constituted in legal discourse is no longer the paterfamilias, he is the producer of normal, heterosexual children, the stabilizing anti-delinquency agent, and the bringer of realistic values and the desire for achievement. (1991 pp 485–86)

Drawing on the work of Tronto, she distinguished between 'caring for' and 'caring about' children. Mothers typically do more of the physical work of caring for children and, she said, this 'caring for' can be seen as a 'moral practice'. Yet it is assumed to be 'natural' and it is therefore rendered invisible. There is no legitimate language in which mothers can frame moral claims based on this work; mothers are not heard unless they speak in the language of welfare or equality:

> [T]he central and determining metaphors in family law have become the welfare of the child and the importances [*sic*] of the father as an instrument of welfare and as an individual who earns legal standing. The mother seems to lose her standing. My point is not, of course, that courts or legal policy ignore mothers, nor that mothers have no part to play in the legal proceedings. However, it is not clear to me that there is any longer a language available for mothers to voice their subject position in law. There is an erasure taking place which is based on a form of silencing which arises out of giving the legitimate modes of expression to those who speak of welfare (psy professions now rather than mothers) and those who speak of the significance of fatherhood (fathers and the psy professions—but also many mothers).
>
> (Smart 1991 p 486, footnotes omitted)

> [W]here there is a conflict, there is a tendency for the welfare principle to make the moral claims made by these mothers, based on the work of 'caring for', appear to be statements of self-interest. Equally, the fathers' rights principle makes such claims appear to resemble the unacceptable and 'old-fashioned' appeal to biological motherhood which is now renounced in favour of a policy of equality. The consequence is that such claims are disregarded or silenced. Moreover, the mother is constituted as selfish and self-serving. ...
>
> [W]e view women's caring work as a natural attribute which requires little or no substantive acknowledgement, while men's expression of 'caring about' seems increasingly to occupy a sentimental and sacred place in the dominant moral and legal order. (Smart 1991 p 494)

Collier (2001), writing more recently, also remarks on the way in which talk of equality and welfare obscures the way in which parenting is actually done. Referring to *Supporting Families* (Home Office 1998), a policy document published by the Home Office, he comments that we see portrayed there

> a family marked by the qualities of emotional and sexual equality, mutual rights and responsibilities, a negotiated authority over children, co-parenting and—of particular relevance to discussion of fatherhood—a clear belief in promoting the commitment on the part of both women *and* men to lifelong obligations to children. (p 527)

Men, it is assumed, can parent as well as women and the law, he says, is regarded as having a key role in getting 'men involved' in the family (p 533). Yet, 'there exists a marked disjuncture between the rhetoric of gender convergence and the realities of family practices' (p 537); women remain the primary carers of children (p 542). Indeed men resist change and they resist because it suits them to do so (*ibid*). The debates about law and the family, which emphasise gender neutrality and equality, are unconnected with the realities of care.

For Sheldon (2001 pp 114–16), the realities of child care invalidate the arguments advanced in favour of extending parental responsibility to unmarried fathers who register the birth. She agrees with the contention of the Lord Chancellor's Department that it cannot be assumed that all unmarried fathers are irresponsible and so undeserving of rights. However, she says, there is no evidence that all are playing a useful role. It is easier to generalise about mothers because most unmarried mothers do in fact assume an active parenting role. So as they are in general the primary carers, it makes sense for them to have parental responsibility. The argument that men are unfairly discriminated against is therefore unfounded. Moreover the argument that having parental responsibility will make men play a greater role in child care has no empirical basis. In her view, although the risks to mothers are difficult to assess, they should have given the legislature pause before the law was changed (pp 114–16).

Wallbank (2002) too is critical of the new law for its disregard of the practice of child care. She states that the change is 'based upon the ethics of justice and fairness as opposed to the ethic of care' (2002 p 278). To invoke fairness and justice is to focus on abstract principles and to give prominence to issues of equality and the possession of rights'. This, she says, occurs at the 'expense of a consideration of the practical work that women perform as mothers' (2002 p 280) and, we might add, of the well-being of children.

## VII. THE UNMARRIED FATHER AND HUMAN RIGHTS

There have been attempts to challenge the legal distinction between unmarried fathers and their married counterparts by using rights discourse. In *B v UK*,[70] however, the ECtHR held a complaint of discrimination under Article 14 ECHR inadmissible. The court declared that there was an 'objective and reasonable justification'[71] for the difference in treatment in relation to automatic parental responsibility. The 'relationship between unmarried fathers and their children', said the court, 'varies from ignorance and indifference to a close stable relationship indistinguishable from the conventional family-based unit'.[72] In addition, discrimination against fathers without parental responsibility was justified; fathers with care of their children had different responsibilities from those who merely had contact.[73]

Bainham argues that the position taken by the ECtHR and also the English legislation, even after the reform of s.4 of the Children Act 1989, are 'at odds' with the UN Convention on the Rights of the Child (2005 p 216). He cites Article 7(1), which gives the child, as far as possible, the right, from birth, 'to know and be cared for by his or her parents'. He also refers to Article 18(1) which provides that states should try to 'ensure

---

[70] [2000] 1 FLR 1. See also *McMichael v UK* (1995) 20 EHRR 205.
[71] P 5.
[72] P 5.
[73] P 6. However, some fathers who do not have parental responsibility do live with their children. See Pickford (1999). This may become less common now that s 4 of the Children Act has been amended.

recognition of the principle that both parents have common responsibilities for the upbringing and development of the child' (*ibid*). He says that the Convention requires that proof of paternity should give rise to the child's right to know and have a relationship, if possible, with his or her father. Likewise, he suggests, proof of paternity alone should suffice to confer automatic parental responsibility (pp 216–17).

This argument hinges on a particular interpretation of 'care' and 'responsibility'. It can only be sustained if parental responsibility is, as Bainham says, seen as primarily a 'status-conferring device' (p 207). It is only if one dissociates the notion of care from material, physical caring activity that the Convention can be read in the way Bainham suggests. And if it is emotional care he is concerned with, it is not clear how parental responsibility will enhance emotional bonds. In addition, it is questionable whether giving an uninterested father parental responsibility will ensure that there is recognition of the principle that he is responsible for his child, except in the most abstract and symbolic way.

Nevertheless, as Bainham observes, the courts are moving towards greater rights for unmarried fathers, at least in the context of adoption (p 217). The consent to his child's adoption of a father without parental responsibility is not necessary. However under the Adoption Act 1976, there is a requirement to ascertain whether a father without parental responsibility intends to apply for parental responsibility or a residence order and, if so, whether the application is likely to fail.[74] There is also provision for hearing the father's views[75] and the court has a discretion to join him as a party in the proceedings. Bainham predicts that similar provisions will be included in the rules to be made under the Adoption and Children Act 2002 (2005 p 289).

In any event, as a result of the enactment of the Human Rights Act 1998, the position of unmarried fathers without parental responsibility has been strengthened. In *Re M (Adoption: Rights of Natural Father)*,[76] the court observed that in the majority of cases, the father has to be informed of the adoption, however 'unpalatable' this might be for the mother and however 'problematic' for the adoption agency. The duty arises even when the father is unaware of the child's existence. In that case, however, the child's and the mother's rights under Article 8(2) outweighed the violent father's rights under Article 8 ECHR (right to respect for private and family life) and Article 6 (right to a fair trial).

Of course, whether the father's rights are engaged at all depends on whether there is family life between him and his child that the court deems as worthy of protection under Article 8.[77] The existence of family life is subject to a reality test; it is a matter of fact and depends on the presence of close personal ties.[78] The potential for family life also falls within Article 8. There will be family life if the parents have cohabited and the fact

---

[74] S 18(7) Adoption Act 1976. Regulations made to coincide with the coming into force of the Adoption and Children Act 2002 in December 2005 provide that the adoption agency must, if it considers it appropriate, notify a father without parental responsibility of its decision about whether to place a child for adoption (Adoption Agencies Regulations 2005 Reg 19) and also, if it considers it appropriate, to include him in their requirements to provide information and counselling for and to ascertain the wishes and feelings of parents, guardians and 'others', and to ascertain whether he intends to apply for parental responsibility for or for a residence or contact order with respect to the child (Reg 14).

[75] Adoption Agencies Regulations 1983 Reg 7. See also Adoption Rules 1984, r 4.

[76] [2001] 1 FLR 745, 755.

[77] See *Re J (Adoption: Contacting Father)* [2003] EWHC 199 (Fam); [2003] 1 FLR 933. For an extensive discussion of the concept of family life, see *Singh v Entry Clearance Officer New Delhi* [2004] EWCA Civ 1075; [2004] 3 FCR 72.

[78] *K v United Kingdom* (1987) 50 D&R 199; *K and T v Finland* [2000] 2 FLR 79.

that the relationship subsequently breaks down is irrelevant. It seems that the commitment to the mother demonstrated by cohabitation is considered to extend to the new family member automatically. From the moment of the child's birth there exists between the father and child 'a bond amounting to family life'.[79] And this bond may also come into being even if the parents have not cohabited if there are other factors showing a sufficient degree of constancy.[80] In *Lebbink v The Netherlands*[81] the ECtHR said:

> 35   The Court recalls that the notion of 'family life' under Article 8 of the Convention is not confined to marriage-based relationships and may encompass other *de facto* 'family' ties where the parties are living together out of wedlock. A child born out of such a relationship is *ipso iure* part of that 'family' unit from the moment and by the very fact of its birth. Thus there exists between the child and the parents a relationship amounting to family life.
> 36   Although, as a rule, cohabitation may be a requirement for such a relationship, exceptionally other factors may also serve to demonstrate that a relationship has sufficient constancy to create de facto 'family ties'. The existence or non-existence of 'family life' for the purposes of Article 8 is essentially a question of fact depending upon the real existence in practice of close personal ties. Where it concerns a potential relationship which could develop between a child born out of wedlock and its natural father, relevant factors include the nature of the relationship between the natural parents and the demonstrable interest in and commitment by the father to the child both before and after its birth. (footnotes omitted)

In *Soderback v Sweden*[82] it appears to have sufficed that, although the father did not live with the child, he showed some commitment to contact. In *Re H; Re G ( Adoption: Consultation of Unmarried Father )*,[83] the need for cohabitation, or, in its absence, some sign of commitment to the child rather than simply the mother is clear. The father and mother of H had cohabited and, although the relationship had ended, the father qualified under Article 8 as having a right to respect for his family life with his child. To have the child adopted without notifying him would be a *prima facie* breach of his rights. The father also had rights under Article 6. It was held that he should be made aware of the proceedings and given an opportunity to take part. This right could only be overridden in grave cases such as rape or serious domestic violence.[84] On the other hand, as regards the father of G, his relationship with the mother did not come within the meaning of family life; they had not cohabited and, although it lasted 7 years, the relationship lacked commitment. Because he had no right to respect for family life, no obvious issue arose under Article 8 which engaged Article 6.

## VIII. CONCLUSION

One of the aims of the Children Act 1989, through the creation of the concept of parental responsibility, is to reduce conflict between parents when their relationship breaks down. With its emphasis on non-intervention by the courts and its endorsement of

---

[79] *Keegan v Ireland* (1994) 18 EHRR 342 para 45. See also *Berrehab v The Netherlands* (1989) 11 EHRR 322 para 21.
[80] *Price v United Kingdom*, 55 D&R 224, 234 (Application 12402/86, 9 March 1988). See also *Kroon v The Netherlands* [1995] 19 EHRR 263.
[81] [2004] 3 FCR 59.
[82] (1998) 3 EHRLR 342.
[83] [2001] 1 FLR 646.
[84] Para 48.

autonomy for parents, it promotes a expectation that parents will resolve questions relating to child-rearing by agreement. By enshrining in the law an equal and enduring status for both parents, it seeks to ensure that there is less to fight over and that agreement is more likely to be reached. Moreover, by conferring this equal and enduring status on the non-resident parent (usually the father), the law is said to motivate him to remain involved in his children's lives and to encourage the mother to accept that involvement. This goal is, arguably, also at the heart of the courts' growing preoccupation with consultation. It certainly was a justification put forward for extending parental responsibility to unmarried fathers who register the birth. All these aims, absence of conflict, agreement and continued involvement, are said to promote the best interests of the children concerned.

Yet in most cases, the extent of involvement of mothers and fathers in their children's lives remains very different. And the expectations of mothers and fathers are very different. Indeed, Collier has suggested in the past that the law has been implicated in the construction of the 'good father' as economic provider rather than as carer. The presence expected of fathers, he said, is not physical presence but the presence of 'paternal heterosexual authority' (1995a p 20). In his later work (Collier 2001), he has shown that the rhetoric has shifted to embrace co-parenting and active paternal participation. However, in truth, the involvement facilitated by parental responsibility is primarily concerned with participation in decision-making; the status conferred by parental responsibility lends legitimacy to a non-resident parent's claim to have a say in the upbringing of his children while leaving, often, the responsibility of day-to-day childcare to the mother.

Wallbank, writing of the amendment of Section 4 of the Children Act 1989, alleges that the change is part of a wider movement aimed at tying men to children as well as a move from discretion to rules and rights. Parenthood and parental responsibility can be seen, she says,[85] as a way of creating an illusion of permanence in the face of instability[86] amid fears of the breakdown of the traditional family. According to Wallbank, the change to the law 'will do little to promote the relationships between children and fathers in any practical way. However … significant inroads will be made into the control that women have in relation to their children' (2002 p 278).

The law cannot compel fathers to shoulder the responsibility of the practical care of their children. So the extent to which it can deliver a joint parenting arrangement is limited. What it does do is establish a framework, of which parental responsibility is a part, in terms of which caretaking mothers are by and large expected to accept whatever degree of involvement with their children that fathers choose for themselves. They are expected to sustain the kind of conflict-free relationship that does not undermine the paternal role.

It is true that the impact in practice of parental responsibility may be limited for many fathers. Nevertheless, parental responsibility does have considerable symbolic force. It serves to affirm paternal status and paternal links with children. It may therefore provide some solace to fathers who might otherwise feel aggrieved and, in doing so, may reduce conflict. Conversely, the extension of the duty to consult may increase conflict. In any event, by equalising the status of both parents, the law might be said to be masking the inequality of the contributions of most mothers and fathers to childcare. It could be said to be rendering invisible mothers' work and to sanction traditional gender

---

[85] Citing Dewar (2000).
[86] See Dewar (2000) 63.

roles and child-care patterns. And by promoting an ideal of the post-separation family as one that is conflict-free and in which the non-resident father has an equally important role to that of the mother, it tends to render illegitimate maternal objections to paternal intervention. As a result, it seems, mothers may be expected to bear most of the responsibility for avoiding conflict and to follow the path of acquiescence.

## FURTHER READING AND SELECTED RECENT REFERENCES

R COLLIER, 'A Hard Time to Be a Father? Reassessing the Relationship between Law, Policy and Family (Practices)' (2001) 28 *J of Law and Society* 520.

S CRETNEY, ' "What Will the Women Want Next?" The Struggle for Power Within the Family 1925–75' (1996) 12 *LQR* 110.

S EDWARDS and A HALPERN, 'Parental Responsibility: An Instrument of Social Policy' (1992) *Fam Law* 113.

J EEKELAAR, 'Rethinking Parental Responsibility' (2001) *Fam Law* 426.

S GILMORE, 'The Nature, Scope, and Use of the Specific Issue Order' (2004) 16 *CFLQ* 367.

S MAIDMENT, 'Parental Responsibility—Is there a Duty to Consult?' (2001) *Fam Law* 518.

J MASSON, 'The Impact of the Adoption and Children Act 2002: Part 1—Parental Responsibility' (2003) *Fam Law* 580.

R PICKFORD, 'Unmarried Fathers and the Law' in A Bianham, S Day Sclater and M Richards, (eds), *What is a Parent? A Socio-Legal Analysis* (Oxford, Hart Publishing, 1999).

J ROCHE, 'The Children Act 1989: Once a Parent Always a Parent?' (1991) *JSW & FL* 345.

S SHELDON, 'Unmarried Fathers and Parental Responsibility: A Case for Reform?' (2001) 9 *FLS* 93.

C SMART, 'The Legal and Moral Ordering of Child Custody' (1991) 18 *J of Law and Society* 485.

——, 'The "New" Parenthood: Fathers and Mothers after Divorce' in EB Silva and C Smart, *The New Family?* (London, Sage, 1999).

J WALLBANK, 'Clause 106 of the Adoption and Children Bill: Legislation for the 'Good' Father?' (2002) 22 *Legal Studies* 276.

# 8

# The Welfare Principle

## I. INTRODUCTION

The welfare of children has increasingly claimed the attention of policy-makers and law reformers alike in recent decades. Children are portrayed as victims of divorce[1] and of child abuse and their victimisation is presented as the cause of delinquency, maladjustment and under-achievement. These concerns have led to the elevation of the welfare principle to a central and seemingly unassailable position in the law relating to children. Indeed Article 3 of the United Nations Convention on the Rights of the Child[2] sets out the principle that, in all actions concerning children, whether taken by courts, legislatures, administrative bodies or welfare agencies, 'the best interests of the child shall be a primary consideration'.

In this chapter, we examine the welfare principle in the context of private law.[3] We suggest that the way it is applied and interpreted owes less to scientific 'truths' than to understandings of the welfare of children that accord with prevailing beliefs about how families should be structured and what the roles of family members should be.

## II. LEGISLATION AND THE WELFARE PRINCIPLE

Section 1 of the Children Act 1989 provides:

1. Welfare of the Child

(1) When a court determines any question with respect to—
   (a) the upbringing of a child; or
   (b) the administration of a child's property or the application of any income arising from it,
   the child's welfare shall be the court's paramount consideration.

---

[1] Pryor and Rodgers (2001 p 31) refer to 'trauma theories' which focus on divorce or separation as an event and view that event as potentially traumatic for children. They also describe 'life-course theories' which treat parental separation as part of a process over time and not as a single determining event. The dominant view apparent in government documents appears to be that, although most children emerge unharmed, parental separation is potentially damaging if it is not managed 'correctly'. See below.

[2] Ratified by the UK in 1991. It is not part of UK law but the UK government is bound to follow policies that conform broadly to the Convention. See further Bainham (2005) pp 66–78. Whether the welfare principle as it is currently applied in domestic law is compatible with the Human Rights Act 1998 is contentious. See below.

[3] For discussion of public law, see chs 9 and 17.

(2) In any proceedings in which any question with respect to the upbringing of a child arises, the court shall have regard to the general principle that any delay in determining the question is likely to prejudice the welfare of the child.

Section 1(3) goes on to enumerate a checklist of factors to which the court is obliged to have regard in contested Section 8 proceedings and Part IV proceedings. This checklist, which is reproduced and discussed in chapter 14, includes factors such as the ascertainable wishes and feelings of the child, the needs of the child and the ability of the parents to meet those needs, and the likely effect on the child of any change in his or her circumstances.

> **Q** The UN Convention states that the child's best interests shall be a primary consideration, whereas the Children Act 1989 states that the child's welfare shall be the paramount consideration. How do you interpret each?

In the context of divorce and separation, the Family Law Act 1996 was intended to transform the law in order to uphold what were regarded as fundamental norms, some of which were considered to be important for children's well-being. These norms were enshrined in the general principles set out in Section 1:

1. The general principles underlying Parts II and III

The court and any person, in exercising functions under or in consequence of Parts II and III,[4] shall have regard to the following general principles—

...

(c)  that a marriage which has irretrievably broken down and is being brought to an end should be brought to an end—
    (i)  with minimum distress to the parties and to the children affected;
    (ii) with questions dealt with in a manner designed to promote as good a continuing relationship between the parties and any children affected as is possible in the circumstances. ...[5]
(d)  that any risk to one of the parties to a marriage, and to any children, of violence from the other party should, so far as reasonably practicable, be removed or diminished.

Although this provision is still in force at the time of writing, it has no effect since Part II has never been brought into force and is expected to be repealed, while Part III has already been repealed. Nevertheless it reflects widely held assumptions about children's welfare.[6] Most importantly, the principles continue to drive government policy: 'Since January 2001,[7] the Government has sought to emphasise its continued commitment to the principles underlying the Family Law Act, looking for alternative ways to provide the support that families want and need' (Walker 2004 p 10). This commitment is apparent from the 'key principles' identified by the government as underpinning its 'agenda for change' (DCA, DfES and DTI 2005 para 2):

---

[4] Dealing with divorce and separation and with mediation respectively.

[5] See also s 11(4)(c), which has never been brought into force.

[6] For example, the Law Society's Family Law Protocol (2002a) is, it is said, intended to 'encourage a constructive and conciliatory approach to the resolution of family disputes' and to 'have regard to the interests of the children and long-term family relationships' (www.lawsociety.org.uk, undated, accessed 24 December 2004). See also the Legal Services Commission *Funding Code Guidance* (2003b www.legalservices.gov.uk, accessed 23 December 2004).

[7] When the demise of the Family Law Act 1996 was announced.

The child's welfare must be the **paramount consideration** in any help, support or intervention given.

A child's welfare is usually best promoted by a continuing and constructive **relationship with both parents,** as long as it is in the child's best interests and safe for all concerned.

Both parents have a responsibility to ensure their child has **constructive contact with the other parent** where contact is in the child's best interests.

**Collaborative agreements** made between parents should be favoured, as they are likely to work better than those arrangements that flow from court-based resolutions.

Parental separation needs a long-term and **flexible approach**. It is not an event that can be solved by a single unchanging settlement, whether court-imposed or not.

Help, advice and support for parents should be **readily accessible**.

The **wishes and feelings of children** in light of their age and understanding should be considered and taken fully into account. (DCA, DfES and DTI 2005 para 2, emphasis in original)

One well-established assumption discernible in the White Paper is that it is better for parents to reach agreement than to litigate. Indeed, the Children Act 1989 was partly shaped by the assumption that the intrusion of the law into the family can have damaging effects. The statute therefore includes provisions designed to limit judicial intervention in decision-making in relation to arrangements for children. Whereas the law prior to the Act accorded, at least in principle, a leading role to courts in such decisions, even where the parents were not in dispute,[8] now judicial intervention is itself seen as potentially detrimental to children's welfare.

The Law Commission in 1988, for example, indicated that court orders might have the effect of polarising parents and perhaps alienating the child from one or other of them (Law Commission 1988b paras. 3.2–3.3). Consequently, it said, it should not always be assumed that an order should be made. While it would remain open to courts to invoke their powers in uncontested cases, they should do so only where this would be in the child's best interests (para 3.3).[9] This approach gains expression in Section 1(5) of the Children Act 1989 which states that: 'Where a court is considering whether or not to make one or more orders under this Act with respect to a child, it shall not make the order or any of the orders unless it considers that doing so would be better for the child than making no order at all'.

In addition, the Law Commission was of the view that judicial intervention often served little purpose in securing the welfare of children on divorce. While in the 1950s[10] it was considered essential that the courts oversee arrangements for children lest parents

[8] Courts were required to perform a supervisory function and, before granting a divorce, had to approve any agreement reached by the divorcing parents in relation to their children. In practice, the role of the court was of limited significance. See below.

[9] An order might be needed 'in the child's own interests, so as to confirm and give stability to the existing arrangements, to clarify the respective roles of the parents, to reassure the parent with whom the children will be living, and even to reassure the public authorities responsible for housing and income support that such arrangements have in fact been made' (Law Commission 1988b para 3.2).

[10] See Royal Commission on Marriage and Divorce 1951–55 (1956) paras 366–67. The report noted the potentially detrimental effects of divorce on children (para 361) and the possibility that agreements between parents might not safeguard the best interests of their children (para 366). It was considered necessary to focus the minds of parents on the question of their children's welfare and to provide the courts with control over arrangements. In response to this recommendation, s 41 of the Matrimonial Causes Act 1973 was enacted to provide that arrangements made for children on divorce were reviewed by the courts. Before it could make absolute a decree of nullity or divorce, a court had to declare the proposed arrangements 'satisfactory' or the 'best that can be devised in the circumstances'. For a more detailed account of the background to s 41 of the Matrimonial Causes Act 1973, see Law Commission (1986) paras 4.5–4.6. See further Cretney (1989).

fail to put the interests of their offspring first, it is now acknowledged that the courts cannot effectively carry out this function.[11]

It was therefore decided that the court's duty should be pitched at a more modest level; it should simply be required to consider whether to exercise any of its powers under the legislation (Law Commission 1988b para 3.9). The law was accordingly amended. Where a court decides that it should exercise its powers, it can, in exceptional cases, delay the divorce decree. In the majority of cases, however, said the Commissioners, parents are considered to be the best judges of their children's best interests and there would have to be cogent reasons for setting aside an agreed plan (Law Commission 1988b para 3.10). The relevant law in relation to divorce and separation proceedings is contained in Section 41 of the Matrimonial Causes Act 1973.[12]

41 Restrictions on decrees for dissolution, annulment or separation affecting children

(1)  In any proceedings for a decree of divorce or nullity of marriage, or a decree of judicial separation, the court shall consider—
  (a) whether there are any children of the family to whom this section applies; and
  (b) where there are any such children, whether (in the light of the arrangements which have been, or are proposed to be, made for their upbringing and welfare) it should exercise any of its powers under the Children Act 1989 with respect to any of them.
(2)  Where, in any case to which this section applies, it appears to the court that—
  (a) the circumstances of the case require it, or are likely to require it, to exercise any of its powers under the Act of 1989 with respect to any such child;
  (b) it is not in a position to exercise the power or (as the case may be) those powers, without giving further consideration to the case, and
  (c) there are exceptional circumstances which make it desirable in the interests of the child that the court should give a direction under this section,
  it may direct that the decree of divorce or nullity is not to be made absolute, or that the decree of judicial separation is not to be granted until the court orders otherwise.
(3)  This section applies to—
  (a) any child of the family who has not reached the age of sixteen at the date when the court considers the case in accordance with the requirements of this section; and
  (b) any child of the family who has reached that age at that date and in relation to whom the court directs that this section shall apply.

**Q** Whereas previously it was thought that divorcing parents posed a potential threat to the wellbeing of their children, it is now assumed that they are usually the people best qualified to judge what is good for their children. How do you explain this change? To what extent do you think this 'hands-off' approach reflects a privatisation of decision-making on divorce?

Section 41 of the Matrimonial Causes Act 1973 is being reviewed with the aim of altering the procedure to include some sort of procedure for giving parents information. Attention is also being directed to ways of improving the information available to the

---

[11] The information available to the court was too sparse; the interview with the parent(s) was too perfunctory; the power of the court in practice to produce the desired outcome was limited; and there was no way of guaranteeing that the agreed plan would be observed (Law Commission 1988b para 3.6).

[12] S 11 of the Family Law Act, which has never been brought into force, is similarly worded.

courts and to ways of encouraging informal dispute resolution.[13] At present, the provision applies only in cases of separation and divorce but consideration is also being given to extending any new procedure that might be developed to apply to contact applications more generally.[14]

Section 1 of the Children Act 1989 is broader in scope than the current Section 41. It covers cases where questions relating to the upbringing of children arise between parents and also where parents are in dispute with third parties.[15] In addition, it applies in care proceedings and, in that context, is dealt with in more detail in chapters 9 and 17.[16]

Where applicable, the welfare principle requires the courts to accord overriding importance to the child's best interests.[17] This was not always the criterion by which decisions were made. As Mnookin (1975) observes, the history of the legal standards governing disputes over children reveals a dramatic shift from the application of rules to a discretionary system (p 233) demanding the 'neutral' (p 235) application of the best interests standard. Arguably, now, despite the pre-eminence of the welfare principle, we are seeing something of a return to rule-like regulation.[18]

## III. FROM STATUS TO WELFARE

Until the early 19th century, the common law[19] invested fathers with the sole rights of custody and control over their legitimate children. The Court of Chancery had by then acquired powers to make children Wards of Court or Wards in Chancery, as a result of which paternal rights could be restricted and fathers could be deprived of custody.[20] However, although the court's primary consideration was the benefit of the child, intervention to curtail a father's rights was confined to cases where his conduct was 'exceptionally culpable' (Maidment 1984 p 112).[21] In *Re Agar-Ellis*,[22] for instance, the court found itself bound to uphold the 'natural' and 'sacred' rights of fathers, affirming that these should not be interfered with except in extreme cases.[23] Although in these cases the welfare of the child was relevant, it had to be threatened in some serious way to justify interference with paternal rights. In *Re Fynn*, for example, the Vice-Chancellor stated that a court would not intervene unless satisfied that to do so was 'not merely better for the children, but essential to their safety or to their welfare, in some very

[13] See DCA (2002) Recommendation 13.

[14] *Ibid.* Although this is not mentioned in the White Paper (DCA, DfES and DTI 2005).

[15] It covers situations such as that which arose in *J v C* [1970] AC 668, a case pre-dating the Children Act 1989. See also *Re K (Adoption and Wardship)* [1997] 2 FLR 221.

[16] The welfare principle in the context of assisted reproduction and adoption is dealt with in chs 3 and 4 respectively.

[17] While statutes in the UK use the term 'welfare', the dominant term in North America is 'best interests'. Both terms are used synonymously in the literature in the UK.

[18] See Dewar (2000).

[19] See *Cartlidge v Cartlidge* (1862) 2 Sw & Tr 567; *R v De Manneville* 102 ER 1054, 1055 (KB 1804).

[20] See Pinchbeck and Hewitt (1973) p 363ff.

[21] See also *ibid,* p 364ff.

[22] (1883) 24 Ch D 317.

[23] See also *Re Fynn* (1848) 2 De G & SM 457; *Wellesley v Duke of Beaufort*, 2 Bl NS 124; 1 Dow & Cl 152. In *Cartlidge v Cartlidge*, n 19 above, the court held that the discretionary power conferred on the courts by s 35 of the Divorce and Matrimonial Causes Act 1857 should be exercised with reference to the common law rights of the father. Compare *Barnes v Barnes and Beaumont* (1867) 1 Sw & Tr 567.

serious and important respect'.[24] Generally, the interests of children were deemed to be
best served by paternal custody.

As Maidment observes, the law at this time was less concerned with the wellbeing of
children than with protecting the rights of fathers and thereby the social order:

> [I]t is clear that the law was concerned with the enforcement of patriarchal authority and not
> with the practice of child-care. The common law which gave father absolute rights over wife
> and children was concerned with the social control of the family and its stability, and with the
> orderly devolution of property. ...
>
> That the law's insistence on the sacred rights of fathers had nothing to do with the practice
> of child-care which remained a maternal role, is apparent from the sorts of disputes in which
> the issues of guardianship and custody arose ... [F]rom the mid-century onwards the cases all
> involved fathers who were insistent on controlling the discipline or religious upbringing of the
> children, which in Victorian society was socially approved behaviour. The courts were not in
> the slightest concerned with the proper care of the children. Nor were the fathers; they were
> fighting for higher principles. They were also fighting for control of their sons.
>
> (1984 pp 144–45)

Things did begin to change[25] during the 19th century, largely as a result of the struggle
mounted by women for equal status in relation to their children.[26] Legislation was
passed that enabled mothers to seek custody and access in certain circumstances[27] and,
in 1886, the Guardianship of Infants Act empowered the court to make such order as it
thought fit 'having regard to the welfare of the infant' as well as the conduct and the
wishes of the parents.[28] The divorce courts claimed to apply these principles too.[29] The
Guardianship of Infants Act 1925 provided that the court, in deciding any question
relating to a child's custody or upbringing, should regard the child's welfare as the 'first
and paramount consideration'.[30] While it appears that, initially, the paramountcy principle was introduced to side-step women's calls for equal status,[31] it has continued to
inform child law over the years.

## IV. THE PARAMOUNTCY OF WELFARE

The paramountcy principle, which has been described as the 'golden thread' running
through the Children Act 1989 (Mackay 1989 p 505),[32] is interpreted as enshrining

---

[24] *Re Fynn* (1848) 2 De G & SM 457, 475. See also *Wellesley v Duke of Beaufort* 2 Bl NS, 124; 1 Dow & Cl
152.

[25] For an account of this process, see Maidment (1984), ch 5.

[26] See Maidment (1984) pp 144–46; ch 7 above. Bailey (1994) points out that Caroline Norton, who cam-
paigned for reform of the law, focused not on equality but on the vulnerability of women. Bailey suggests that
this approach, rather than a direct challenge to men's rights, may have been the only way to succeed in getting
the law changed at that time.

[27] Custody of Infants Act 1839, Divorce and Matrimonial Causes Act 1857, Custody of Infants Act 1873.

[28] S 5(4).

[29] See Maidment (1984) p 131.

[30] S 1. See, for a full discussion of the legislation, Cretney (1996a).

[31] See Cretney (1996a); Reece (1996a); ch 7 above.

[32] The paramountcy principle has now been introduced into adoption law as well (s 1(2) Adoption and Children Act 2002). It does not, however apply in committal proceedings where a parent has breached an order of
court relating to the child's upbringing (*A v N (Committal: Refusal of Contact)* [1997] 1 FLR 533). Nor does it
apply in proceedings relating to maintenance (s 105(1) of the Children Act 1989) or to secure accommodation

the welfare of the child[33] as the determining factor in cases concerning children's upbringing, overriding all others.[34] The formula designating the child's welfare 'first and paramount', contained in the then applicable legislation,[35] was said by Lord MacDermott in *J v C*[36] to mean:

> more than that the child's welfare is to be treated as the top item in a list of items relevant to the matter in question. I think [it] connote[s] a process whereby, when all the relevant facts, relationships, claims and wishes of parents, risks, choices and other circumstances are taken into account and weighed, the course to be followed will be that which is most in the interests of the child's welfare as that term has now to be understood. That is the first consideration because it is of first importance and the paramount consideration because it rules upon or determines the course to be followed. (p 710)

Although the word 'first' was omitted from the Children Act 1989 because it was said to cause a certain amount of confusion (Law Commission 1988b para 3.13), the import of Section 1 is much the same. It is intended that the court should be guided 'solely by the children's welfare' (Law Commission 1988b para 3.15) and all relevant factors should be considered in this light.

## V. THE HUMAN RIGHTS ACT AND WELFARE

When the Human Rights Act 1998 was enacted, a number of academics suggested that the paramountcy principle might be displaced; there is a view that it is not strictly compatible with the rights framework introduced by the legislation.[37] For example, Swindells, *et al*, (1999 para 3, 154) suggest that 'Article 8 does not support the notion that paramountcy is to be given to the interests of the child'.

Article 8 of the ECHR is probably the most important article[38] for the purposes of family lawyers. It reads:

> 1. Everyone has the right to respect for his private and family life, his home and his correspondence.
> 2. There shall be no interference by a public authority with the exercise of this right except such

---

(s 25 of the Children Act 1989). Nor does it apply to the provision of services by local authorities in terms of Part III of the Children Act 1989 (*Re M (A Minor) (Secure Accommodation Order)* [1995] Fam 108). The Child Support Act 1991 specifies only that the Secretary of State must 'have regard' to welfare (s 2).

[33] Where the court has to make a decision in a case involving two children, the question of whose interests should prevail may arise. In *Birmingham City Council v H (A Minor)* [1994] 2 AC 212, the mother of a baby was herself a minor. She wanted contact but the court was of the view that, although it was in her best interests to have contact, it was not in the baby's best interests. The House of Lords took the view that it was the child who was the subject of the proceedings whose welfare was paramount. In this case, the baby's welfare dictated the outcome. Where the interests of two children conflict, and they are both subjects of the proceedings, the court will seek to balance the interests of both. See *Re A (Children) (Conjoined Twins: Surgical Separation)* [2001] 1 FLR 1. See further, Herring (2004 pp 371–72).

[34] Whether this was the intention behind the introduction of the 'first and paramount' formula into the law is doubted by Cretney (1996a) pp 129–30.

[35] S 1 of the Guardianship of Minors Act 1971.

[36] [1970] AC 668.

[37] See, for discussion of the tensions in Australian law between rights and utility in the sense of securing the best possible outcome for children, Dewar (1998, 470–73).

[38] Articles 6 and 14 are also significant however.

as in accordance with the law and is necessary in a democratic society in the interests of national security, public safety or the economic well being of the country, for the prevention of disorder or crime, for the protection of health or morals, or for the protection of the rights and freedoms of others.

Any interference must be in accordance with the law, in pursuance of a legitimate aim, necessary and proportionate.[39] It seems that in interpreting Article 8, the European Court of Human Rights and the (now defunct) European Commission have refrained from polarising the concepts of rights and welfare. Their decisions reveal that they have long considered that the legitimate aim of protecting the health and rights of others extends to the aim of safeguarding the welfare of children, including their emotional and psychological well-being.[40] One case that is often cited, for instance, is *Johansen v Norway*.[41] There, the court referred to the need to 'strike a fair balance' between the interests of the parents and the child. In doing so, it said,

> the court will attach particular importance to the best interests of the child,[42] which depending on their nature and seriousness may override those of the parent. In particular ... the parent cannot be entitled under Article 8 of the Convention to have such measures taken as would harm the child's health and development.

Similarly, in *Hokkanen v Finland*,[43] the court stated that. 'Where contacts with the parent might appear to threaten [the child's] interests or interfere with those rights, it is for the national authorities to strike a fair balance between them'. It went on, in effect, to give greatest weight to the child's interests.[44] In *Yousef v The Netherlands*,[45] it was held that where the rights of parents and children conflict, the rights of the children must be the 'paramount consideration'.

Herring (2004) argues that there are important differences between the approach required under the Children Act 1989 and the approach necessitated by the European Convention. He says that in a contact dispute, the starting point under the Convention is the parent's right to family life which will be infringed if contact with his or her child is refused. To justify a breach there must be 'clear and convincing evidence that contact would infringe the rights and interests of the child[46] to such an extent that the infringement was necessary and proportionate' (p 378). Under the Children Act it is assumed that contact is in the child's best interests. He contends that the evidential burden differs depending on which approach is taken and that the nature of the questions asked is different (*ibid*). Fortin (2003 p 59) suggests that the application of the Convention requires the court to consider whether infringement of a parent's rights is proportionate to the child's immediate needs and is concerned that a 'revival of outdated notions of parents' rights' could undermine the spirit of the Children Act.

---

[39] See Kaganas and Piper (2001) p 259.

[40] See Kaganas and Piper (2001) p 258 and references cited in n 61.

[41] (1996) 23 EHRR 33, para 78. See also *L v Finland* [2000] FLR 118, 140; *K and T v Finland* [2000] 2 FLR 79, 107; *Elsholz v Germany* [2000] 2 FLR 486, 497.

[42] See also *Glaser v UK* [2001] 1 FLR 153; *Hoppe v Germany* [2003] 1 FCR 176, para 49; *Hendricks v The Netherlands* (1982) D&R 225.

[43] (1995) 19 EHRR 139, para 58.

[44] See Kaganas and Piper (2001) p 260.

[45] [2000] 2 FLR 118, para 118.

[46] Herring seems to have omitted consideration of the mother's right to family life which could be damaged by contact in some cases.

Yet the UK courts do not discern any conflict between the two approaches and they continue to operate the paramountcy principle. In *Dawson v Wearmouth*,[47] Lord Hobhouse of Woodborough said that nothing in the Convention requires the court to act otherwise than in accordance with the best interests of the child. In *Re F (Adult: Court's Jurisdiction)*,[48] the court clearly prioritised the interests of the child: 'The family life for which Art 8 requires respect is not a proprietary right vested in either parent or child; it is as much an interest of society as of individual family members, and its principal purpose, at least where there are children, must be the safety and the welfare of the child'.

In *Re KD (A Minor) (Ward: Termination of Access)*[49] Lord Oliver said that any conflict between the welfare principle and the human rights jurisprudence was 'semantic only'.[50] And in *CF v Secretary of State for the Home Department*[51] Munby J made it clear that, in his view, the paramountcy principle is entirely compatible with the European Convention and so, also, the Human Rights Act 1998. He referred to an earlier judgment[52] in which he had stated that Strasbourg jurisprudence, like English law, 'has long recognised that, in the final analysis, parental rights have to give way to the child's'. He continued:

> That reflects what the Court of Appeal had earlier said in *Re P & Q*[53] at [84]:
> 'The balance to be struck in these cases is between the rights of the parents and the rights of the child ... . In striking that balance, the European court has repeatedly stressed that the interests of the child are of crucial importance.'
> To this I would only add ... that the court has now made clear that, as between parent and child, the child's interests are paramount. As the court said in *Yousef v The Netherlands* (2003) 36 EHRR 20, [2003] 1 FLR 210 at para 73:

> > The court reiterates that in judicial decisions where the rights under Art 8 of parents and those of a child are at stake, the child's rights must be the paramount consideration. If any balancing of interests is necessary, the interests of the child must prevail.
> > (para 48)

It is clear, then, that the courts will not readily relinquish the welfare principle. It has been suggested that, 'The probability is that under the HRA only those rights of adults involved in disputes that correspond with current understandings of welfare will be upheld' (Kaganas and Piper 2001 p 268). And what falls into that category changes.

That understandings of children's best interests are never fixed is something the court had to consider in *CF v Secretary of State for the Home Department*.[54] The judge was presented with an argument that the notion of the child's best interests is not sufficiently certain to comply with the Convention. He examined the principle in *Olsson v Sweden*[55] that, in order for something to be 'in accordance with the law' in terms of Article 8, the law has to be formulated with enough precision to give the individual adequate

---

47 [1999] 1 FLR 1167, 1182.
48 [2000] 2 FLR 512, 531.
49 [1998] 1 All ER 577, 588.
50 See also *Re B (Adoption by One Natural Parent to Exclusion of Other)* [2002] 1 FLR 196.
51 [2004] EWHC Fam 111; [2004] 2 FLR 517.
52 *Re S (Adult Patient) (Inherent Jurisdiction: Family Life)* [2002] EWHC Fam 2278; [2003] 1 FLR 292, para 42.
53 *R(P) v Secretary of State for the Home Department and Another: R(Q) v Secretary of State for the Home Department* [2001] EWCA Civ 1151; [2001] 2 FLR 1122.
54 N51 above.
55 (1989) 11 EHRR 259.

protection against arbitrary interference. He concluded, obiter, that although what is regarded as in children's best interests changes over time, the welfare principle satisfies this test:

> It may be helpful to bear in mind here Professor Dworkin's distinction between the 'concept' which does not change and changing 'conceptions of the concept' ... . The rule of law demands adequate statement of the 'concept' but recognises and, within appropriate limits, can accommodate the fact that 'conceptions of the concept' may change over time ... . The concept of the child's welfare or best interests as something central to decision-making in respect of the child has of course been part of our law for well over a century ... . Not surprisingly, 'conceptions' of that 'concept'—what Lord Hoffmann would call the 'content'—have changed, and are continuing to change ... . But no one could sensibly suggest that the 'welfare principle' does not meet the *Olsson v Sweden* test. Indeed, it is, as we have seen, a core principle of the Strasbourg jurisprudence ... (paras 101–3)

It is to the idea that welfare is socially constructed and to the problems of indeterminacy that we now turn.


## VI. THE SCOPE OF THE WELFARE PRINCIPLE

What is encompassed by 'welfare' under the legislation is a very particular understanding of that concept. King and Piper remind us that:

> The broad range of factors—genetic, financial, educational, environmental and relational—which science would recognise as capable of affecting the welfare of a child are narrowed by law to a small range of issues which fall directly under the influence of the judge, the social workers or the adult parties to the litigation process. Among social problem construction theorists the issue is usually presented in terms of political ideology. By reconstructing the social dimension of any issue concerning the welfare of the child in such matters as housing, education, health care and financial security in ways which emphasise individual responsibility and the failure to accept that responsibility or perform those duties expected of a child carer, law in capitalist societies effectively depoliticizes social problems and reinforces liberal, individualistic ideology to the detriment of socialist notions of collective or governmental responsibility. (1995 p 50)

Thus the courts confine themselves to consideration of the individual means, behaviour and relationships of the family members involved. The law does not, and indeed King and Piper would argue cannot, attempt to address structural problems such as poverty or gender inequality.


## VII. DECIDING WHAT IS GOOD FOR CHILDREN—THE PROBLEM OF INDETERMINACY

Even this restricted conception of welfare presents decision-makers with considerable difficulties. Bereft of any clear rules, such as the old father-right, they are confronted with making choices on the basis of a principle noted for its indeterminacy. This indeterminacy is attributed by Mnookin (1975) to a number of factors.

First, the court is expected to make 'person-oriented', not 'act-oriented' determinations (p 250). Instead of deciding on the basis of what it sees to be the true facts of the case, the court is required to make a decision based on its evaluation of the people concerned. It must judge 'the attitudes, dispositions, capacities, and shortcomings of each parent to apply the best-interest standard. Indeed, the inquiry centers on what kind of person each parent is, and what the child is like' (p 251).

Secondly, while adjudication usually requires the determination of past facts, the welfare test demands that the court predict the future. And this prediction must encompass the future relationships between all the protagonists (pp 252–53). The future conduct of, say, the father may affect the behaviour of the mother and child. Mnookin highlights the difficulties in operating the welfare test:

[E]ven where a judge has substantial information about the child's past home life and the present alternatives, present-day knowledge about human behaviour provides no basis for the kind of individualized predictions required by the best-interests standard. There are numerous competing theories of human behaviour, based on radically different conceptions of the nature of man, and no consensus exists that any one is correct. No theory at all is considered widely capable of generating reliable predictions about the psychological and behavioural consequences of alternative dispositions for a particular child.

While psychiatrists and psychoanalysts have at times been enthusiastic in claiming for themselves the largest possible role in custody proceedings, many have conceded that their theories provide no reliable guide for predictions about what is likely to happen to a particular child. ...

(pp 258–59)

He goes on:

Even if the various outcomes could be specified and their probability estimated, a fundamental problem would remain unsolved. What set of values should a judge use to determine what is in a child's best interests? If a decision-maker must assign some measure of utility to each possible outcome, how is utility to be determined? ...

[T]he child could be asked to specify those values or even to choose. In some cases, especially those involving divorce, the child's preference is sought and given weight. But to make the child responsible for the choice may jeopardize his future relationship with the other parent. And we often lack confidence that the child has the capacity and the maturity appropriately to determine his own utility.

Moreover, whether or not the judge looks to the child for some guidance, there remains the question whether best interests should be viewed from a long-term or a short-term perspective. The conditions that make a person happy at age seven to ten may have adverse consequences at age thirty. (p 260)

The courts, faced with these imponderables, cannot seek refuge in the certainties of judicial precedent. It is true that the courts have, over time, devised rules of thumb which offer some guidance. So, for example, in disputes between parents and third parties, courts begin with a 'strong supposition' that it is in a child's best interests to be brought up by his or her 'natural', meaning biological, parents.[56] But where the dispute is

---

[56] *Re M (Child's Upbringing)* [1996] 2 FLR 441, 453. See also *Re KD (A Minor) (Access: Principles)* [1988] 2 FLR 139. See also *Re K (Adoption and Wardship)* [1997] 2 FLR 221, 228; *Re D (Care: Natural Parent Presumption)* [1999] 1 FLR 134; *Re O (Adoption: Withholding Agreement)* [1999] 1 FLR 451.

between parents, the courts have abandoned the old formulas. For example, in the past the mother was regarded as the natural caregiver.[57] Although mothers who were adulterous or were considered sexually deviant in other ways were regarded as unfit to care for their children (Brophy 1985 pp 102–3; Boyd 1991 p 87), generally the courts took the view that it was 'better'[58] and in accordance with natural law[59] that small children should be with their mothers. This approach has now, however, been repudiated by the judiciary. Judges have been careful to stress that all considerations must be viewed in the light of the welfare principle; courts are expected to judge each case on its unique merits and to assess the welfare of each child individually without relying on generalisations.[60]

In addition, mindful of the complexities inherent in the exercise of discretion in these cases, appeal courts are reluctant to overturn decisions. *G v G*,[61] a decision of the House of Lords, outlines the limited scope of the appellate jurisdiction in cases concerning children:

> The jurisdiction in such cases is one of great difficulty, as every judge who has had to exercise it must be aware. The main reason is that in most of these cases there is no right answer. All practicable answers are to some extent unsatisfactory and therefore to some extent wrong, and the best that can be done is to find an answer that is reasonably satisfactory. It is comparatively seldom that the Court of Appeal, even if it would itself have preferred a different answer, can say that the judge's decision was wrong, and unless it can say so it will leave his decision undisturbed. ...
>
> [T]he appellate court should only interfere when it considers that the judge of first instance has not merely preferred an imperfect solution which is different from an alternative imperfect solution which the Court of Appeal might or would have adopted, but has exceeded the generous ambit within which a reasonable disagreement is possible. (pp 228–29)

In the absence of defined rules, a court must seek to assess the likely outcomes of the various courses open to it and decide which will best serve the child's interests. Yet these decisions are informed by more than the facts of each particular case. Bradley suggests that the judicial emphasis on the uniqueness of each case is somewhat disingenuous, serving to obscure the values deployed by the court in reaching its conclusions (1987 p 186).[62] Writers have criticised the welfare test as being subjective and as leaving room for personal prejudice in decision-making.[63] Reece (1996a), however, argues that there is a more fundamental problem: 'the indeterminacy of children's welfare has allowed other principles and policies to exert an influence from behind the smokescreen of the paramountcy principle' (pp 295–96). These principles and policies are not so much a reflection of subjective prejudice as of a perceived preference in society for the heterosexual nuclear family. Parents who do not fit into the accepted mould, such as those who

[57] Maidment says there was never a maternal preference rule. However, 'in practice the *prima facie* right of the father gave way to the *prima facie* right of the mother from the early part of this century' (1984 p 156).

[58] *Re L* [1962] 3 All ER 1.

[59] *Re B* [1962] 1 All ER 875.

[60] See *In Re K (Minors) (Children: Care and Control)* [1977] 2 WLR 33, 35; *Re L (Contact: Domestic Violence); Re V (Contact: Domestic Violence); Re M (Contact: Domestic Violence); Re H (Contact: Domestic Violence)* [2000] 2 FLR 334, 342.

[61] [1985] 2 All ER 225.

[62] See, further, King (1987) p 189; Eekelaar (1984); Eekelaar (1985).

[63] See Eekelaar (1984) p 596; King (1987) p 189.

are gay or lesbian, are marginalised.[64] Similarly, Thèry (1989), writing about French child custody law, sees the best interest standard less as an expression of the prejudices of individual judges than as a means of regulating the post-separation family:

> [T]he practice of referring to 'the interest of the child' as a criterion in judicial decision making has been much criticized and disputed. There are three levels of argument that can be distinguished.
>
> 1. For some, it is not so much the principle nor the general criterion as such, but rather the dominant meanings which have been attributed to it. They therefore offer a 'good' interpretation. ... [E]ach position claims its particular version of the 'interest of the child' as the only one in accord with the current state of knowledge. ...
>
> 2. At a second level, there are those who dispute the criterion itself. Its indefinable character is seen as giving free rein to the subjectivity of the decision makers. ...
>
> 3. Finally, ... there is another group who criticize the criterion itself, not as a subjective and 'empty' concept, but, on the contrary, as a concept overflowing with political and social objectives which, further, have very little to do with the person of the child. ...
>
> These three levels of criticism have a common thread in seeing the criterion as an alibi; an alibi for dominant ideology, an alibi for individual arbitrariness, an alibi for family and more general social policies for which the law serves as an instrument. In my opinion we need to go beyond these critiques, which all assume (implicitly or explicitly) that there is such a thing as 'the interest of the child' *per se*. ... Rather we need to examine the relationship between the use of such a criterion and the changing methods of regulation in family affairs. ... (pp 81–82)
>
> The concept of 'the interest of the child' necessarily develops into a general image of what the 'good' post-divorce family organization should be, indicating one or more model(s) of family life after divorce. ... (p 86)
>
> At a more general level, one can distinguish two opposing poles in relation to the 'interest of the child': a logic of substitution which prioritizes the household; and a logic of durability based on the biological family and its history. ... (p 95)
>
> In the substitution theory, the mother (and more generally, the woman, if one includes the second spouse) remains the person who is the principal means of ensuring the permanence of the child's relationships. According to the logic of durability, paternal and maternal roles are assumed to be equally important and thus less gender specific. (p 99)

**Q** Thèry concedes that most cases cannot be neatly categorised as applying one or other model, but argues that one or other of the opposed logics is usually dominant. When reading the case law in chapters 14 and 15, consider whether judicial decisions reflect a preference for either model: the model in terms of which the biological family is substituted by the reconstituted family or the model in terms of which the biological family is preserved but reorganised. Could one argue that ideology or politics might play a part in influencing the selection of the model perceived as the 'good' post-separation family?

Recent developments in law and in policy appear to confirm that the welfare principle is perhaps not as indeterminate as one might think. Dewar (2000) argues that there is a growing interest in shifting family law towards a more rights based model and that there is a move away from discretion towards rules:

---

[64] Arguably this is changing. The Civil Partnership Act 2004 can be seen as endowing same sex relationships with legitimacy and acceptability while the inclusion in the Adoption and Children Act 2002 of same sex couples within the category of adoptive parents endorses their capacity to parent.

The factors leading to this growth in rights claims are complex, and include domestic political pressure from organized groups (such as fathers' rights groups seeking greater 'equality' in legal treatment, especially in matters concerning children) [and] the increased relevance of human rights instruments ... (p 68, footnote omitted)

[T]he liberal State's own commitment to privacy has [in the past] made it impossible to formulate clear rules or principles to govern family dissolution—discretion has allowed the underlying issues to remain unresolved. Yet if that is correct, what has changed? It seems that such is the anxiety surrounding the perceived disintegration or decline in 'family values', as well as the financial costs of divorce itself, that families and family law have become central concerns of political debate. As a result, modern legislators have overcome their traditional respect for 'family privacy' and are now more willing than in the late 1970s to issue prescriptions for a 'good divorce'—in particular, that divorcing or separating couples should be rational, altruistic, settlement minded, co-operative and cost-conscious. Part of this prescription for the new model divorce is enshrined in rules, or norms that are increasingly rule-like. An example of the growing prescriptiveness of family law legislation concerns relationships between children and the non-resident after separation or divorce. A striking feature of family law policy in recent years has been the desire to maintain relations between children and the parent with whom they are not living, a relationship that usually involves preserving in law relations between households. This is evident in the child support scheme ..., in the new emphasis on continuing and shared parental responsibility, and on children's 'right to contact with both parents after parental separation ... (pp 68–69, footnotes omitted)

The prominence given to the maintenance of this parent-child link is a relatively recent phenomenon—and it is noticeable that the relevant legal provisions are rule-like in nature ... . In this way, modern family law increasingly seeks to radiate messages about how to divorce well, or how the fragmented family should re-form itself. (p 69)

## VIII. THE WELFARE PRINCIPLE AND THE 'GOOD' POST-SEPARATION FAMILY

Dewar was writing of Australian law and of the position in England prior to the demise of the Family Law Act 1996. Nevertheless despite the now obscure legal status of Section 1, it can still be seen, along with the White Paper, which also emphasises the continuity of relationships between children and both their parents, as giving some indication of the dominant image in this country of the 'good' post-separation or post-divorce divorce family. Moreover, the legislation simply endorses an already entrenched preference for continuity. For some time now, courts, like child welfare professionals, have considered it a priority, when families split up, to preserve links between children and their non-resident biological fathers. Courts hearing contact disputes begin with an 'assumption' in favour of contact.[65]

The 'good' post-separation family needs a 'good' post-separation mother to sustain it. Carol Smart gives us some insight into the way the preoccupation with continuity has shaped what is expected of mothers. Not only are they expected to care for their children, they are expected to extend that work to encompass the facilitation of contact by

---

[65] *Re L (Contact: Domestic Violence); Re V (Contact: Domestic Violence); Re M (Contact: Domestic Violence); Re H (Contact: Domestic Violence)* [2000] 2 FLR 334, 367.

fathers. When mothers refuse to take on this additional task, they become identified as bad or vindictive mothers (Smart 1991 p 496). Smart suggests that 'it is assumed that children need fathers so badly that mothers must be prepared to tolerate almost any behaviour. In this form of reasoning, the welfare principle ... diverts attention away from the problem of the "bad" father by creating in its place the "bad" mother' (1991 p 497).

The comments of Boyd (1996), writing in Canada, are apt to describe the demands made of British mothers too. She identifies what she calls a 'new ideology of mother-hood' according to which 'good' post separation mothers are expected to be 'reasonable' and to facilitate contact (p 510). This unrealistic and even oppressive arrangement, she says involves an attempt to recreate the nuclear family and it places an enormous responsibility on mothers (pp 514–15). Moreover, it seems that it is not only mothers who are charged with building the 'good' post-separation family. We have argued else-where that some of the responsibility for ensuring that contact 'works' is also now being placed on children; there is an emerging construct of the 'good' child of separation and divorce. This child 'copes' with the upheaval and accedes to contact with the non-resident parent (Kaganas and Diduck 2004).

> [Q] When reading the cases on residence and contact in chapters 14 and 15, consider whether the work of Smart and Boyd accurately describes the attitudes of judges. What factors do you think might be contributing to the construction of these images of 'good' mothers and fathers?

That fathers must be enabled to play a part in their children's upbringing is a conviction that, according to Day-Sclater and Piper, can be seen as part of a project to 're-moralise' the family. Anxieties about what is perceived as a crisis in the family, about uncertainty surrounding the role of the father and about the threat to 'traditional' masculinities are, to some extent assuaged by the new emphasis on the 'rights and responsibilities' of fathers. 'Old' ideas about the biological, two-parent family appear to survive reassur-ingly amidst the flux of changing families and family forms (Day Sclater and Piper 2000 p 147).

The political acceptability of the ideology of the separate but continuing family is also buttressed by the ideas held by diverse groupings for diverse reasons. A number of writers have observed the impact of the image of the new fatherhood, fathers' rights movements and the New Right on the law. The new fatherhood, as Smart (1989a pp 16–19) says, relies on the assumption that fathers are increasingly engaged in the work of child care.[66] Fathers are therefore as capable of looking after their children as moth-ers are. Fathers' rights advocates, in turn, demand greater rights in relation to their children and complain of discrimination.[67] The New Right, less vocal now than in the 1980s and 1990s, aims to restore the traditional hierarchy within the family, giving mothers the role of domesticating men and rendering them responsible.[68] All these fac-tors have had a profound influence on perceptions of the 'good' family and all place fatherhood at the centre of this institution. And, as Fineman (1989 pp 846–47, 861) points out, these claims to the importance of fathers receive crucial support from an apparently neutral source: child welfare science.

---

[66] See DCA, DfES and DTI (2004 Ministerial Foreword p 1 and paras 2, 36). There is evidence that some fathers do become more involved in child care after divorce than they were during their marriages. See Smart (1999); Walker (2004).

[67] See Geldof (2003). See further Kaganas (2006 forthcoming).

[68] See also Pryor and Rodgers (2001 p 7) on what they term the 'conservative' perspective.

## IX. CHILD WELFARE KNOWLEDGE

Fineman (1989), referring to the USA, suggests that child welfare knowledge has been harnessed in support of campaigns by various interest groups. In particular, child welfare knowledge has been coupled with egalitarian arguments to form the basis of a strategy to enhance the position of fathers.

The success in Britain of arguments based on child welfare knowledge and advocating greater emphasis on fatherhood is evidenced by the law governing parental responsibility as well as the law concerning contact and, to a lesser extent, residence. The 'good' post-separation family is portrayed as one that ensures that children's relationships with both parents are preserved. This, it is said, is not just good for parents; child welfare research shows that it is the best arrangement also for children. Claims based on the welfare of children are extremely potent especially if they bear the hallmark of objective, scientific research. They have accordingly led to a preoccupation in social policy and in the law with ensuring the continued participation of both parents in the upbringing of their child.

King (1981) remarks that the ascendancy of child welfare science in the legal arena is hardly surprising given that, with 'the decline of the Church and the growth of pluralism, the only universally accepted truths... appear to be those manufactured by scientists' (p 124).[69] Yet what is accepted as scientific 'truth' changes over time:

This term [welfare], used as a criterion for decision-making, carries with it the implicit assumption that it is both possible and necessary to discover the needs of the child. Yet how does one set about defining and assessing children's needs? In the case of physical needs, the answer is relatively straightforward. ... But what of a child's psychological and social needs? How do we know, in the first place, what they are? In our society, the answer to this question in recent years has been to place our faith in the experts, that is, pediatricians like Dr Spock or child psychiatrists like Anna Freud or Albert Solnit. But this answer raises the further question: how do the child experts determine children's needs? 'A combination of theoretical knowledge and empirical observation' would be an intelligent reply, but hardly a satisfactory one, for it does not begin to explain how different experts may come to completely different conclusions not only about the same individual child, but on the needs of children in general. Moreover, theories of child development seem to move in and out of fashion with alarming regularity. ... Suffice it here to make the point that the kinds of behaviour that the experts choose to observe, the hypotheses they choose to formulate and their interpretations of their findings all depend upon the preconceptions they bring with them to the psychology laboratory or field survey. To these preconceptions are added biases of the funding agencies, university departments and hospitals who sponsor and promote research projects.

This leads us then to something of a truism, which nevertheless ought to be stated: except for the basic physical requirements for healthy development, children's needs are socially defined, socially sustained and socially adjusted to conform with prevailing values and expectations. ... A brief glance at some of the child care theories which have won popularity in this country over the past 50 years and the social conditions from which they emerged and within which they were accepted adds further evidence to support this argument. First there was the Truby King regime of the late thirties and early forties:

'Strict four hour feeds, no unnecessary handling beyond nappy changing and feeding and absolutely no cuddling (molly coddling). ...'

It was probably no coincidence that the end of the war in 1945 saw the passing of the Truby King era. There followed a period when the writings of John Bowlby, a psychiatrist ... were to

---

[69] See also Fineman (1991) pp 110–12.

prove highly influential. ... Bowlby's message was clear and simple. There was no substitute for full-time motherhood. ... It was a message which was rapidly taken up by a popular press critical of the conduct of neglectful working mothers and their 'latch-key' children. It coincided with a widespread feeling that the traditional values associated with the home and family life were under threat, adding the weight of scientific authority to the call for a return to pre-war values. It also coincided with the need for a contraction in the female labour force, made necessary by the return of servicemen and the fact that the government was not in a position to provide day-nurseries for the vast army of potential working mothers.

After King and Bowlby came Dr Spock ... with his emphasis on self-expression and self-indulgence for babies and infants at a time of unprecedented economic growth, confidence and buoyancy in American society. ... More recently, a body of knowledge has emerged disproving Bowlby's more extreme statements about maternal deprivation and suggesting that conflict between parents or growing up in a hostile environment may be far more damaging than the fact of separation of child from mother. Other work has cast doubt on the irreversibility of the effects of damage or deprivation in the early years of life. Significantly perhaps, these ideas are gaining wide dissemination at a time when the number of children affected by divorce has never been higher and state intervention in the family has never been greater.

Three points arise from this discussion of child care theories which are highly relevant to the concept of welfare. ... The first is that doctors and scientists have become authority figures in our society on almost any aspect of human behaviour including the rights and wrongs of child development. In the absence of any absolute morality or universal value system, science and medicine are the only bodies of knowledge which have almost universal appeal. ... It is hardly surprising, therefore, that all the major figures in the recent history of child care have been medically or scientifically qualified.

Secondly, although ideas about what is good or bad for children's healthy mental and social development may be legitimized by the language and trappings of science and medicine, they are neither scientific or medical in the accepted sense. They are rather moralistic and value-laden, emerging from the cauldron of prevailing beliefs and social conditions. ...

The third point is that in order for any particular theory of child development and child care to win recognition, respectability and popular support, the right social conditions must prevail. ... [O]ur society does not consist of a homogeneous collection of people, all sharing the same values and beliefs about child welfare. Bowlby's views on maternal deprivation, for example, were not accepted by working women. ... Yet in a society dominated by men and imbued with the spirit of post-war reconstruction and a desire to return to traditional values, it is not surprising that Bowlby's ideas gained credence despite the opposition of working women. The general principle that one can extract from recent history appears to be that any notion as to what is good or bad for children, above and beyond purely physical matters, if it is to gain popular support and influence policies and practices to a significant degree, must have the backing of powerful groups within society and must be consistent with the objectives of those groups. (King 1981 pp 109–13, footnotes omitted)

Policy-makers therefore make choices between different research findings. And the theories concerning child welfare that are currently most influential in the context of separation and divorce are those that focus on the damaging effect of inter-parental conflict[70] and on children's need to know and to maintain relationships with both parents.[71]

Wallerstein and Kelly (1980), for instance, in their book *Surviving the Breakup*, emphasise the psychological importance of both parents (p 307) and conclude that, 'where possible, divorcing parents should be encouraged and helped to share post divorce arrangements which permit and foster continuity in the children's relationship

---

[70] See Piper (1994).
[71] See also ch 7.

with both parents' (p 311). Richards,[72] who writes extensively in the field of childcare
and development, also stresses the importance of both parents for children. He argues
that a relationship with both parents helps to reduce the emotional trauma of divorce
and to avoid disruption of the child's social connections outside the immediate family.
The damage inflicted on children by divorce can best be mitigated if parents avoid conflict and continue to play a part in their children's lives.

> After divorce most children live with their mothers, and fathers become at best, occasional visi-
> tors in their lives. Research... suggests that within a short time of separation many children
> cease to have a relationship with their father. ... The breaking of established relationships with
> fathers and other family members may have significant effects on a child's social development
> and their capacity to form and sustain relationships. ...
>     Conflict between parents before and after divorce is associated with poorer outcomes for
> children. ...
>     The analysis I have sketched out provides a set of clear issues which could become goals for
> policies related to divorce and children. Such policies should aim to encourage the maintenance
> of a child's existing relationships with parents and the wider family and kin, ensure an adequate
> income to post-divorce households with children, reduce as far as possible conflict between
> divorcing parents or, at least, encourage its expression in areas that do not involve children,
> encourage the provision of emotional and practical support for divorcing parents ... and,
> finally, avoid as far as possible moves of house or school. ... It will not always be desirable to
> strive to maintain relationships with both parents. ... In rare cases, existing relationships may be
> detrimental to children if they continue. However, I suspect that such cases are much less com-
> mon than many professionals ... choose to believe. It is also important to realize that the loss of
> a parent usually means the permanent loss of half of a child's kin relationships which may have
> profound ... consequences. (1994 pp 307–9)

Conflicting views, such as those propounded by Goldstein, Freud and Solnit (1973),
who warned of loyalty conflicts for children and who advocated that the caretaking parent be given the right to decide whether contact should take place, were never widely
accepted. Such an approach would, it was said, encourage blackmail and malice on the
part of the caretaking parent and preclude co-operation between the parents.[73] Other
research highlighting the negative aspects of contact,[74] observing that it allows parents
to continue their battles and that it is often stressful for children, has also not impacted
on policy so as to limit support for contact.

Pryor and Rodgers (2001) review some of these studies in their survey of research into
children's lives after parental separation, and their conclusions are in many ways at odds
with the current dominant discourse. They point out that research does not support the
assumption that contact is necessarily 'good' or that children are damaged if it is not
sustained:

> [W]e have established that, in the main, contact with children is good for men and often desired
> by them, and that children say they want to see their fathers. It is a different question to ask,
> however, whether it is important for children's well-being that they maintain a relationship with
> their fathers, especially as so many grow up apparently unscathed by the absence of a father in
> their day-to-day lives. The view is now widely held that frequency and regularity of father-child

---

[72] See also Burgoyne, Ormrod and Richards (1987), ch 4; Richards (1987); Cockett and Tripp (1994, 1996);
Hooper (1994).
[73] See Foster (1976); Freeman (1983) pp 215–19.
[74] See Maidment (1975).

contact after separation is associated with children's psychological well-being, unless abuse or psychopathology is present. Although positive contact is in itself a good outcome for children who usually want it, the assumption that contact *per se* is measurably good for children does not stand up to close scrutiny. Several studies have found that there is no direct or simple relationship between levels of nonresidential father-child contact and child well-being, while others have reported both positive and negative relationships. This does not mean that contact with fathers is unimportant for children, and these mixed feelings suggest several explanations. First, contact between fathers and children is not necessarily a positive experience for children if the child does not want it or if the relationship is negative. Separation, too, sometimes increases parental conflict, and father-child contact in situations of high parental conflict can be negatively related to well-being, especially for boys. (p 214, references omitted)

[F]requency by itself does not have a consistent link with children's well-being, [and so] attention has more recently been given to the *quality* of the father-child relationship ... [I]t is apparent that, apart from economic provision, fathers' contributions to their children's lives depend on more than their mere presence ... [I]t is those aspects of parenting encompassing monitoring, encouragement, love and warmth, that are consistently linked with child and adolescent well-being. (p 215, references omitted, emphasis in original)[75]

The most recent large-scale research study, headed by Walker (2004), is also circumspect in its support for contact. The report argues that too much stress is placed on 'making contact work'. Instead, there should be a focus on 'promoting and maintaining relationships' (p 176). The authors argue that support for relationships is more important than 'simply noting who does what as a parent' (p 153). The report concludes:

The findings suggest that more attention needs to be given to the processes people go through and to finding ways of ameliorating the emotional distress they experience. An excessive focus on outcomes does little to help people achieve a more conciliatory divorce and work together to develop better relationships in future. (p xxxi)[76]

We would suggest that there has been an over-emphasis on regular physical contact as the only way for parents and children to stay in touch. Undoubtedly parents and children do want to spend time together, but in very sensitive, precarious or conflictual situations other forms of contact may at least keep parent-child relationships alive while other efforts are made to resolve the dispute between parents. (p 314)

This report is published by the Department of Constitutional Affairs and whether it will have any significant influence on policy or law remains to be seen. In any event, the way research findings are used in the policy-making arena has been subject to criticism. For example, Fineman (1991) questions the way in which social science research has been deployed to ascribe increased importance to the role of fathers. She maintains, for instance, that the findings reported by Wallerstein and Kelly have been grossly oversimplified by legal policy-makers; rather than revealing maternal incompetence and children's grief at the loss of a father, the study paints a more qualified and complex picture (pp 119–21).

King and Piper also raise issues relating to the interpretation and oversimplification of research but their work focuses specifically on the difficulties inherent in translating child welfare discourse into legal discourse. They argue that the way the law 'thinks' about children is different from the way that child welfare science does. In order for the law to fulfil its functions, such as that of resolving disputes, it has to reconstruct child

[75] See also Buchanan, *et al*, (2001) p 5; Walker (2004) p 185; Smith (2003) p 198.
[76] See also p 310.

welfare knowledge so that it 'makes sense' within law. This inevitably leads to reductionism[77]:

> The problem for child welfare as science is that, within the legal arena, the information will almost invariably be constructed according to the demands of the legal discourse. ... The law's demand for decisiveness and finality, for winners and losers, for rights and wrongs to be identified and exposed to the public gaze in order to further its normative objectives tend to force legal judgments out of the mouths of child welfare representatives. There is no room in law for suspended judgments. ...
>
> [T]he ... process [of reconstruction] may be seen, not in political terms,[78] but as the inevitable consequence of the autopoietic nature of law and its inability to incorporate external discourses except by reconstructing them. ... Thus the scientific discourse of child welfare in all its richness and complexity is reconstructed as concepts which 'make sense' within law—that is, concepts which further the immediate demands of the law to determine guilt and responsibility, resolve disputes and do justice between litigants. ... This reconstruction process necessarily involves reductionism, and simplification as well as a concentration on the behaviour of individuals. ...
>
> [P]recepts, focusing on mother-child bonding and stability of relationships were used to justify particular outcomes in particular cases, but such outcomes therefore also became the *ratio* for deciding later cases and guidelines for child protection functions. It is consequently easy to trace the emergence and development of a line of cases dealing with 'mother preference' in custody disputes. Similarly, the work of child psychologists concerning the advantages of stability for the child led to the '*status quo principle*'. (King and Piper 1995 pp 50–51)

So, not only does child welfare science continually reinterpret children's best interests, it in turn is simplified by policy-makers and reinterpreted by the law. Moreover the law not only simplifies child welfare science in its search for clear normative principles, it also makes choices from a range of available principles. It has been argued, drawing on Niklas Luhmann's conceptualisation of risks as decisions leading to avoidable loss (Luhmann 1993 pp 21–22), that, in the simplified version of child welfare knowledge adopted by law, to deny children contact with non-resident parents and for parents to go down the road of conflict have been constructed as constituting the primary risks to children's welfare on relationship breakdown. It is those risks, rather than others that might be thought to exist, that are addressed by law (Kaganas 1999):

> [The legal system] could, for example, have chosen to adopt the principle that contact should not be ordered against the wishes of the resident parent but chose, instead, the opposite. The reason for this must be that a decision to give the resident parent a veto would run counter to the dominant discourse surrounding contact which has been informed by political as well as child welfare imperatives. Currently, government and professional groupings, as well as popular culture reflected in the media, all espouse a particular understanding of the consequences of separation and divorce for children. This understanding has been accorded the status of taken-for-granted truth and cannot fail to impact on the legal system if it is to retain credibility. And the law, in making pronouncements consistent with the dominant discourse, confirms its 'rightness'. Within the dominant discourse and so, also, in the legally reconstituted version of child welfare science, children are damaged by divorce and, increasingly, it is thought that the damage or loss they suffer is exacerbated by conflict or lack of contact. The task for law, then, is to establish the rules and to make the decisions that will avoid or minimise this damage; the

---

[77] Compare James (1992).
[78] See p 293 above.

legal system must be able to retain public confidence by giving the impression that it can do what is right for children and avert the risks to which they might be exposed. (1999 pp 109–10)

The use made of the Sturge/Glaser report (Sturge and Glaser 2000) is perhaps instructive. This report was compiled by experts for the court hearing in *Re L*[79] and it drew on 'developmental and psychological knowledge, theory and research' (p 615). Although it focused primarily on contact in cases involving domestic violence, it also dealt more generally with contact. It states that 'contact can only be an issue where it has the potential for benefiting the child in some way' (p 616) and enumerates both the advantages and the risks of direct and indirect contact. Among the risks is abuse, including emotional abuse where the non-resident parent uses contact to get at the other parent. The report refers, in particular, to the continuation of unhealthy relationships, the risk of undermining the child's sense of stability and continuity as well as the potential for stress on children and carers. It suggests that children who do not want contact should be listened to and seems to indicate that it is risky to insist on contact when the parents are implacably at odds. The report also recommends a presumption against contact in domestic violence cases.

This report was extensively cited by the court in *Re L* but affirmed only selectively. The court decided that the effect of violence should be to 'offset' the presumption or, as Thorpe LJ preferred to call it, the 'assumption' in favour of contact.[80] There was mention of other factors that might have the same effect but little prominence was given by the court to the risks mentioned by Sturge and Glaser.[81] Similarly, while the Guidelines for Good Practice on Parental Contact in Cases where there is Domestic Violence (LCD 2002) do advert to some of the issues raised in the Sturge/Glaser report, the document certainly does not favour a presumption against contact in domestic violence cases.

The Sturge/Glaser Report is also quoted in the Consultation Paper, *Making Contact Work* (CASC 2001b p 10) but, although that document lists the benefits of contact, the existence of risks is only briefly acknowledged. The subsequent Green Paper and White Paper both evidence undimmed enthusiasm for promoting contact and they devote almost no space to its risks, except in relation to domestic violence cases.[82]

## X. NEW POLICIES AND RECENT RESEARCH

A number of policy documents have been published in recent years dealing with contact. The first of these, published in response to a number of studies highlighting the problem of domestic violence in the context of contact, was a consultation paper followed by a report on contact in cases where there has been domestic violence (CASC 2000).[83] Another consultation paper followed, entitled *Making Contact Work. The Facilitation of Arrangements for Contact Between Children and their Non-residential Parents; and the Enforcement of Court Orders for Contact* (CASC 2001b). The Report of the

[79] *Re L (Contact: Domestic Violence); Re V (Contact: Domestic Violence); Re M (Contact: Domestic Violence); Re H (Contact: Domestic Violence)* [2000] 2 FLR 334.
[80] P367.
[81] See further Kaganas (2000) pp 321–23.
[82] See DCA, DfES and DTI (2004) paras 46–50.
[83] This issue is dealt with in detail in ch 14.

Committee was then published in 2002: *Making Contact Work. A Report to the Lord Chancellor on the Facilitation of Arrangements for Contact Between Children and their Non-residential Parents and the Enforcement of Court Orders for Contact* (CASC 2002). As the titles suggest, both documents, although they do allude to research on the difficulties surrounding contact, clearly endorse contact as being in the best interests of children. The Government's response likewise prioritises contact (DCA 2002).

The most recent documents, the Green Paper, (DCA, DfES and DTI 2004) and the White Paper (DCA, DfES and DTI 2005) set out the Government's proposals for the future. Separation, the government claims, 'can be permanently damaging, though any adverse effects can be significantly reduced if arrangements for the separation are handled well' (DCA, DfES and DTI 2002, Ministerial Foreword p 1). Both documents go on to make it clear that contact should be central to these arrangements:

> The Government firmly believes that both parents should continue to have a meaningful relationship with their children after separation as long as it is safe and in the child's best interests. Most parents are able to make arrangements between themselves for the care of their children
>
> .... .
>
> We [the government and the judiciary] are working together to ensure that resolutions achieved with or without court intervention are carried through in order to promote the welfare of the affected children.
>
> The proposals in the Green Paper are aimed at helping separating parents to make arrangements in the interests of their child. To help parents more effectively to reach these agreements, the proposals are intended to provide improved access to information, advice and mediation at the time of separation. For those who do ask the courts to decide on arrangements for their children, we intend to improve the legal process and service delivery ... .
>
> We will be resolute in implementing these many changes to the system and will monitor their impact. But changing social expectations, as well as Government action, are both needed. In time, it needs to become socially unacceptable for one parent to impede a child's relationship with its other parent wherever it is safe and in the child's best interests. Equally, it should be unacceptable that non-resident parents absent themselves from their child's development and upbringing following separation. Friends, relatives, the legal profession and the media all have a role to play in emphasizing that children require a good and lasting relationship with both their parents wherever it is safe and in the child's best interest to do so.
>
> (DCA, DfES and DTI 2005 Ministerial Foreword)[84]

> The Human Rights Act 1998 also requires the courts to interpret the law (including the Children Act 1989), in a way that is consistent with the European Convention on Human Rights. Article 8 of the Convention requires respect for private and family life. This includes respect for the rights of both parents who enjoy family life with their children to have contact with those children, provided this is consistent with the welfare of the children, and also the rights of children to have beneficial relationships with their parents. (DCA, DfES and DTI 2004 para 45)

Clearly, the Government remains committed to contact as a general 'good' for children. It does qualify this stance by referring to 'safe', 'meaningful' and 'constructive' contact. This is presumably in response to the work of researchers such as Walker[85] and to the Sturge/Glaser report (Sturge and Glaser 2000),[86] which highlights the risks to children in cases of domestic violence. However it is not clear how significant these qualifications

---

[84] See also DCA, DfES, and DTI (2004) Ministerial Foreword p 2; *ibid* para 6.
[85] Referred to in CASC (2001b).
[86] See further ch 14.

will prove to be in the prevailing 'pro-contact culture'.[87] It is anticipated that there will continue to be some safeguards in cases where there is a history of child abuse or domestic violence, but those that exist at present are criticised as being inadequate and, contact centres and new Gateway forms[88] apart, there seems little likelihood of improvement.[89] As far as the notion of 'meaningful' contact is concerned, it is possible that the term will itself have little meaning, given the tenor of the decided cases and the research findings concerning professional attitudes;[90] contact is thought important even in cases where the relationship is not particularly strong.[91]

The ways in which the Government proposes to promote contact are both coercive and persuasive. The Children and Adoption Bill, published in 2005,[92] contains provisions empowering the courts to make 'contact activity directions'[93] in contested contact proceedings, requiring attendance at information sessions intended to help with making or operating contact arrangements. There is also provision for attendance at programmes, counselling or guidance to assist parents to establish, maintain or improve contact with children. The Bill also empowers courts to make 'contact activity conditions' when making contact orders. These orders are to be monitored by CAFCASS officers and breaches of contact orders, including conditions,[94] can be punished by means of an enforcement order.[95] In terms of an enforcement order, the court can impose an unpaid work requirement. Courts will also be able to award financial compensation. In addition, other measures under consideration include the provision of information, advice, mediation, in-court conciliation, parenting plans and the creation of new contact centres. The combination of these measures is likely to place considerable pressure on parents, particularly mothers, to reach agreement and for that agreement to make provision for some form of contact. The arrangements made for children are thus to be left largely in the hands of the parents, perhaps with some input from children, and family privacy is to be seen to be left largely intact. But considerable efforts will be made by the state to ensure that the arrangements are the 'right' ones, those that conform to the image of the 'good' post-separation family and therefore those that are assumed to be in the best interests of the children.

The Government's proposals, it seems, accord well with Dewar's analysis. The state is seeking to 'radiate' messages about how to separate or divorce well and these messages are rights-oriented and rule-like. The state is seeking to promote 'responsible' decision-making by families, so allowing for the preservation of the liberal ideal of family privacy. At the same time, the state is seeking to promote a particular construction of welfare, one that 'responsible' families will embrace.

---

[87] This phrase is borrowed from Walker (2004 pp xxviii and 267).

[88] These will allow courts to be advised of allegations of domestic violence at the beginning of the case (DCA, DfES and DTI 2005 para 20).

[89] See further ch 14.

[90] See further ch 14.

[91] The assumption in favour of contact appears to weaken in cases where there is no pre-existing relationship between non-resident parent and child (*Re L Contact: Domestic Violence; Re V (Contact: Domestic Violence); Re M (Contact: Domestic Violence); Re H (Contact: Domestic Violence)* [2000] 2 FLR 334, 364. However Smart and May (2004b p 41) found that the courts appear to require substantial proof that children could be harmed by contact before denying or restricting contact.

[92] See further, ch 14.

[93] Cl 1.

[94] The provisions do not appear to apply to failure to comply with contact activity directions.

[95] Cl 3.

This all prompts the question: will it work? Eekelaar, reviewing the proposals for reform in the UK,[96] comments that 'the recommendations ... signal a significant increase in legal coercion over family arrangements' (2002b p 272). Yet, he says, similar measures adopted in Australia do not appear to have led to an increase in joint parenting. He concludes that 'it is important not to jump from the fact that an outcome is optimally desirable to the conclusion that it should, therefore, be legally enforceable' (*ibid*). 'As a general rule', he argues, 'legal coercion should be confined to cases where the actions of a parent threaten to harm a clearly beneficial existing relationship enjoyed by a child' (p 273).

There is also Australian research that suggests that the underlying reasons for conflict over contact are complex and often relate to domestic violence or to one parent's (usually the non-resident parent's) concerns about the other's inability to care adequately for the children, or concerns about issues like substance abuse or mental health problems (Rhoades 2002 p 75ff).[97] It is debatable whether fears like this would be allayed by information imparting the importance of contact or even by parenting classes. Research conducted in the UK suggests that the reason for contact disputes is not that parents lack education and information about the supposed benefits of contact. In many instances it is that parents believe that they need to engage in the dispute in order to protect their children's best interests.

This study,[98] exploring the dynamics of protracted contact disputes, reveals that both mothers and fathers frame their arguments in terms of children's best interests and cast themselves as 'good' parents. Mothers who were interviewed had internalised the view that contact is good for children generally. But they resisted contact with *their* children by ex-partners because were convinced it would not be good for those particular children.[99] For example, some doubted fathers' commitment to their children or capacity to parent. Many recounted incidents of domestic violence.

Fathers who insisted that they should have contact invoked the welfare of their children as a reason. Those who admitted to violence or aggression tended to minimise the impact of their behaviour and still saw themselves as good parents. Some complained about mothers' shortcomings and considered their presence in their children's lives necessary to counteract these perceived faults. Some fathers maintained that it was imperative to fight for contact in order to safeguard their children's best interests generally.

The fact that both mothers and fathers had been to court and some had failed to achieve the outcomes they sought did not deter them from continuing the battle; they simply saw the courts and the legal system as unfair and biased. Whether they would respond any differently if they were advised of the advantages of contact is open to doubt.

---

[96] As they appeared in Making Contact Work (LCD 2000).

[97] See also Smart and May (2004a). They found that other issues such as housing and child support fuelled disputes.

[98] See Kaganas and Day Sclater (2004); Day Sclater and Kaganas (2003).

[99] See also Trinder (2003) p 404.

## XI. ALTERNATIVES TO THE WELFARE PRINCIPLE

That the welfare of children should be paramount has come to be widely accepted as self-evident and beyond question.[100] However, as we have seen, the welfare principle has been criticised by Reece (1996a) who maintains that it conceals policy choices. This objection is one that Eekelaar (2002a) would categorise as the 'lack of transparency objection.' But Reece also challenges the paramountcy principle on grounds consistent with what Eekelaar (*ibid*) terms the 'lack of fairness' objection. Reece (1996a) contends that it is possible to protect children's interests without making their welfare paramount. While more care and attention might be needed to ascertain a child's best interests, since the child may be less able to articulate them, the parents' interests should not be left out of the equation. She finds no justification for allowing adults' rights to be subordinated to children's needs: 'The paramountcy principle must be abandoned, and replaced with a framework which recognizes that the child is merely one participant in a process in which the interests of all the participants count'. (p 303)

Herring (1999) also raises questions about both transparency and fairness. He is particularly concerned about how to reconcile clashes between parents' and children's interests in the light of the HRA. He is also concerned that adults' interests are smuggled into the equation under the guise of children's welfare. He proposes a modification of the welfare test which he calls a relationship-based welfare approach. He contends that, since families are based on mutual co-operation and support, it is important to encourage children to learn altruism. He also maintains that children's welfare is promoted if their relationships with other family members are fair and just and, to this end, it may be necessary for children to make sacrifices. Decisions should be guided by what is considered a proper parent-child relationship, with children's interests at the forefront of the family's concern.

How 'proper' relationships are identified is not specified and Eekelaar (2002a) points out that Herring's approach involves a balancing of interests but leaves unanswered the question of how they should be balanced. Instead, he advocates a different approach:

> The best solution is surely to adopt the course that avoids inflicting the most damage on the well-being of any interested individual ... . Under the proposed test, if the choice was between a solution that advanced a child's well-being a great deal, but also damaged the interests of one parent a great deal, and a different solution under which the child's well-being was diminished, but damaged the parent to a far lesser degree, one should choose the second option, even though it was not the least detrimental alternative for the child. (pp 243–44)

Eekelaar (2002a) qualifies this, however: a solution should not be adopted if the detriments outweigh the benefits to the child unless this is unavoidable. Solutions that harm children are generally unacceptable.

As part of his proposals, Eekelaar (2002a) argues that the notion of welfare should be replaced by that of well-being. He contends that the latter concept can be articulated in a way that gives clearer guidance about the matters to be weighed than the welfare test does. There are some matters, he says, that can be seen as indicators of well-being. For example, for parents to bring up their children serves the well-being of all concerned. However, he goes on, while we can assume that well-being is promoted by maintaining

---

[100] However, there appears to be no obligation on parents to apply the paramountcy principle when making decisions about their children. See Herring (2004: 369–70).

relationships between children and parents, we cannot assume this with regard to establishing a relationship that does not already exist.[101] The problem here is that, as Eekelaar himself concedes, the transparency question persists. Who decides, and on what basis, which relationships are important for parents and children? His evaluation is not uncontentious; the courts have certainly at times insisted that to establish a relationship that does not yet exist with a non-resident parent is good for parents and children.

None of these three commentators challenges the use of judicial discretion[102] in resolving disputes about children. Others have. Writing in the USA in the 1990s, Fineman, like other feminist scholars, advocated the abandonment of the best interests test as unworkable and recommended its replacement, in relation to decisions about the child's residence, with a presumption. The primary caretaker presumption involves a shift from 'person oriented' to 'fact oriented' decision-making as well as a shift from discretion to rules:

> As it has evolved, legal doctrine cannot adequately address the difficult problems inherent in custody decision making. The best-interest-of-the-child test must be replaced. ... [W]hat we need is a more definite rule that will nonetheless have at its core an appreciation of what we as a society agree will be in the best interests of children.
>
> One recent suggestion is that custody courts should apply a 'primary-caretaker' rule. This rule has been characterized in different ways, but the essence of the primary-caretaker standard is that children need day-to-day care, and that the parent who has performed this primary care during the marriage should get custody ...
>
> The primary-caretaker standard would not ignore the less essential, secondary contributions of the other parent. They are rewarded by the establishment of visitation periods with the children. Custody, however, can be viewed as a reward for past caretaking behaviour.
>
> The primary-caretaker rule implicitly recognizes that no expert can confidently make the predictions required under the future-oriented best-interest placement, and that past behaviour may in fact be the best indication we have of commitment to the future care and concern for children. ...
>
> In my opinion, a major advantage of the primary-caretaker rule is that it is particularly susceptible to legal analysis because it involves past fact-finding, an inquiry traditionally performed by courts. It has the benefit, therefore, of being a rule that judges can comfortably apply and that lawyers can easily understand and use ...
>
> The rule may currently operate to the advantage of mothers, but, if we value nurturing behaviour, then rewarding those who nurture seems only fair. If fathers are left out, they can change their behaviour and begin making sacrifices in their careers and devoting their time during the marriage to the primary care and nurturing of children. ... In cases in which both parents acted as true primary caretakers, I predict that few custody battles would ensue. ... The positive message that the rule sends to parents about what is valued by the legal system and by society at large is clear and unambiguous. (Fineman 1991 pp 180–84)[103]

**Q** How great a departure is the primary caretaker presumption from the status quo principle? From the welfare principle? Does it avoid the application of the welfare principle in contact disputes or in care proceedings? Would its adoption address the issues raised by King and Piper?

---

101 See also Eekelaar (2002b).

102 This discretion is, as mentioned above, constrained by an almost rule-like 'assumption' in favour of contact.

103 See, for a more radical proposal, Fineman (1995).

Boyd (1996) points out that the primary caretaker presumption cannot address the concerns of feminists around contact law. However, what is notable about the primary caretaker approach is that it seeks to ground policy in the reality of childcare (Boyd 1996 p 514).

Bainham adopts a very different view,[104] contending that the law should play a normative role and promote the ideal of co-parenting:

> It may readily be agreed that the existing socio-economic structure of British society militates against the adoption of equal parenting roles within the context of a functioning family. It is incontestable that women are frequently expected to take low paid part-time employment with a built-in expectation that they are the primary providers of child care. Conversely, men are expected to act out the role of breadwinners in full-time employment and not to assume any responsibility for daily child care during the working week. The reality in many families is that the man who might conceivably wish to assume a co-parenting role will find it difficult (if not impossible) to do so. ... But it does not follow from any of this that we must accept [the] view that legal reform should be contingent upon a sea-change in socio-economic policy or parental patterns of behaviour during marriage. It may just as validly be argued that it is a function of law to seek to influence and shape attitudes to the respective roles of parents both during marriage and following divorce. As the Law Commission has said, it is 'an important function of law to provide a model of behaviour which is generally believed to be desirable'. While there may be legitimate disagreement about the efficacy of law in influencing social attitudes (in this case parental behaviour) it is surely right that legislation affecting the family should hold up some normative standard of what society regards as good practice in child-rearing. ...
>
> The search for gender-neutral solutions to the problem of child custody has caused some feminists to argue for a 'primary carer' principle ... .
>
> A better gender-neutral concept in my view is quite simply the concept of 'parenthood' which the 1989 Act ostensibly supports. ... It must be conceded that legislative change cannot of itself convince anyone of the sexual equality implicit in parenthood but it could at least give expression to societal expectations of parental co-operation. (1990 pp 218–19)

This argument is rejected by Boyd:

> As for child custody law, recent challenges to feminist work by authors such as Andrew Bainham demonstrate a somewhat simplistic idea of the role of law as positive and expressive. Law is not adequately conceptualized as an instrument of public policy which reacts to social change or dysfunction, and tries to influence the problem. To take this latter view is to ignore the symbolic and discursive effects of law and to treat it as a non-ideological mechanism of social regulation. It omits a consideration of the ways in which law, as a particular discursive field crucial to liberalism and modernism, tends to empower certain discourses over others. (1991 p 113)

Certainly, in Smart's opinion, the tendency to regard the activity of caring for children as a natural expression of maternal instinct, together with the valorisation of fatherhood, have meant that mothers have 'no legitimate voice unless they speak the language of equal rights (for fathers) or welfare (for children)' (1991 p 498). Anything else is interpreted as a manifestation of selfishness. Similarly, Roche points out that the predominant discourse renders invisible the burdens placed on mothers who are expected to conform to the policy of including fathers: '[i]f she fails to do so it is she

---

[104] See also Ziff (1990).

who becomes the problem rather than, for instance, the substance of her well-founded anxieties around contact between the children and their father' (1991 p 358).[105]

Smart and Neale (1999) suggest that an 'ethic of care' could be deployed in disputes about children:

> An ethic of care is based on responsibilities and relationships, is bound to concrete situations, and is an activity. To operate according to this ethic, one would have to have regard for the discharge of responsibilities, the quality of relationships, the actual situation that people find themselves in and the practice that people have been engaged in. The ethic of care allows for changes to occur in decisions because concrete situations change.
>
> The ethic of justice, on the other hand, focuses on the application of abstract principles from an impartial stance, giving primacy to issues of equality and generalizability ... . It would not be concerned with actualities but with concepts of equality (between men and women) and/or ideals about the welfare of children in general. It would not be concerned with who had done what in terms of providing care, but with identifying whose claim to these abstract principles is the highest. In this formulation the just outcome would be one which puts the rights of the child highest, the rights of the father (who has not had equality in childcare) next, and the welfare of children in general as its basic rule. A decisions based on the ethic of justice cannot be easily changed or modified ... .
>
> An ethic of care ... would be concerned with who has held responsibility and established relationships, with the actuality of a specific family life and a specific child and with who had actively done the caring. In this formulation responsibility could be economic as well as nurturing, different children in the same family could be treated differently but *theoretical* claims about ability to care would not take precedence over, nor would they be regarded as being as significant as, *actual* past caring behaviour. The quality of the relationship between the parents and between the parents and children would also be part of the equation and the ability of parents to treat each other with dignity and respect would be considered ... [T]he ethic of care would have a range of different and individuated outcomes while also being just.
>
> (Smart and Neale 1999 pp 170–71, footnotes omitted, emphasis in original)

> The application of an ethic of care might start from the assumption that wrongs cannot always be 'righted' and that they cannot be reversed by judicial utterance. It might therefore promote non-intervention in these cases rather than seeking to coerce. But it could do this in the context of recognizing the loss, supporting the parent who is excluded and providing the means of future communication when circumstances have changed sufficiently to resume contact.
>
> (*ibid*, p 196)

There can be no doubt that the debate about the primary caretaker principle has all but vanished from the public and even the academic agenda. Nor have discussions about the ethic of care[106] featured large of late. On the contrary, the popular imagination has been captured by a notion firmly rooted in the ethic of justice: shared parenting. This is somewhat puzzling, say Kaganas and Piper (2002 pp 368–69), as it amounts to a resurrection of the old discussions about joint custody in the 1980s. A presumption of joint custody was rejected by the Law Commission (1986) on the grounds that it could operate to the detriment of mothers and, in the absence of genuine shared care, would be purely symbolic.

The revival of the issue is largely attributable to the efforts of pressure groups representing fathers. In the submissions made by three organisations, including Families

---

[105] See further ch 7 pp 292–96.
[106] But see, for example Sevenhuijsen (2002).

Need Fathers, to the consultation on *Making Contact Work*, it was agued that there should be a presumption of shared parenting, although not necessarily in the form of a 50–50 split. A presumption would, these groups maintained, counter the idea that 'winner takes all' and promote parental involvement by means of the least adversarial method. It would amount to recognition of the importance of both parents and, if it were to become the norm, would 'set the tone' for negotiations and would 'remove obstacles' to contact.[107] Another organisation, Fathers4Justice has attracted considerable media attention in a bid to publicise its claims of court bias and injustice. Much publicity has also been given to the contention that the legal system is failing to enforce contact orders against obstructive mothers. In addition, proponents of shared parenting suggest that it would solve the problems posed by so-called Parental Alienation Syndrome (PAS), a phenomenon manifested by the child's rejection of one parent caused mainly by 'brainwashing' by the other, hostile, parent (usually the mother).[108]

The claims made by fathers' rights groups are somewhat surprising, given that most children are in contact with their fathers and given the very strong preference for contact shown by the judiciary,[109] lawyers[110] and other professionals[111] involved with separating and divorcing couples.[112]

Moreover, there is no evidence to support the suggestion that it is malevolent mothers who constitute the primary obstacle to contact.[113] Walker's report (2004)[114] indicates that there are many other reasons for lack of contact. Some fathers in the study experienced difficulty with contact because they could not take the children to their new homes, sometimes because of the presence of a new partner. Distance was also a factor as was the father's work commitments. Communication between the parents was significant; contact stopped when communication was bad and resumed when communication improved. Children often played a part in deciding whether contact should take place (p xxv). While some mothers would have preferred their former husbands to disappear from their own and their children's lives, most wanted the fathers to contribute more to

---

107 See CASC (2002 appendix 3 paras 3 and 8).

108 The existence of PAS as a recognised syndrome was rejected in an expert report to the Court of Appeal (Sturge and Glaser 2000). The experts' view was accepted by the court: *Re L (Contact: Domestic Violence); Re V (Contact: Domestic Violence; Re M (Contact: Domestic Violence); Re H (Contact: Domestic Violence)* [2002] 2 FLR 334. See further, Kaganas and Piper (2002 p 367).

109 See, for example, Davis and Pearce (1999).

110 See, for example, Wheeler (2004).

111 See, for example, James, *et al*, (2003).

112 See Kaganas and Piper (2002 pp 370–71). Most fathers are in contact with their children. Walker reports that in her sample, 5% of those asked said the non-resident parent had contact daily; 62% of parents reported that their children saw the non-resident parent at least once a week; 21% said there was contact at least once a month; and only just under 7% said their children never saw the non-resident parent (2004 p xxiv). Dunn reports the results of a longitudinal study into contact: one third of the children in the sample had contact with their fathers at least once a week, 133 out of 162 had some contact and only 29 had no contact (2003 p 18). Office of National Statistics figures show that at least half the children in the study had contact, either direct or indirect, at least once a week. Between a tenth and a quarter had no contact (Blackwell, 2003). About 90% of parents do not resort to court proceedings and, of the applications for contact that are made, fewer than 1% are rejected (see DCA, DfES and DTI 2004 paras 21 and 25). One sixth of applications are made because of an alleged breach of an order (DCA, DfES and DTI 2004 para 26). In the ONS survey, overall, parents were satisfied with their contact arrangements with almost half saying they were 'very satisfied'. One in twenty parents were 'fairly dissatisfied' with their contact arrangements (Blackwell, 2003). Almost two thirds of Walker's sample were satisfied (2004 p xxiii. See also p 168). See further Mitchell (2004).

113 In an analysis of 300 court files by the DCA, it was found that in around half the cases there was a repeat application and one third of those were because of alleged breach of court orders (Draft (Children) Contact and Adoption Bill 2005, Regulatory Impact Assessment, para 17).

114 See also Rhoades (2002).

their children's upbringing (p xxv).[115] Many mothers were disappointed that the fathers made little effort to stay in contact (pp 174, 195) Several mothers explained that contact had ceased because of the father's indifference:

> [T]he father was uninterested in the children and, quite often, they [the mothers] confirmed that this had been the case during the marriage too. Less often, the 'lack of interest' had begun after the separation, sometimes because the father had met a new partner or was leading a new and very different life in which children were not as easily accommodated. Sometimes mothers suggested that the children themselves were not interested in seeing their father, or that the children did not like or wish to spend time with their father's new partner. Some of the children were clearly choosing between seeing their father and seeing their friends, or had part-time or Saturday jobs, so that contact became less frequent as a consequence. (p xxv)[116]

Kaganas and Piper (2002) argue that a presumption of shared parenting would not have the effect of encouraging those fathers who do not want to maintain relationships with their children to do so. It also has potential disadvantages: it might create an imbalance of power between the parents, put pressure on mothers and increase their resentment by downgrading their childcare contributions. It could put mothers as well as children at risk and it would not solve the problem of parental conflict:

> Many mothers might have very good reasons for opposing shared parenting and these may never come to light or may be minimised in the push for a consent order. Buchanan and Hunt, for example, found that, in their sample, at least one parent reported domestic violence, including harassment and intimidation, in 78% of cases, and, in 56%, there were reports of physical violence. The incidents referred to were rarely minor and in almost two-thirds of cases the violence and fear were present after separation. By the time of the court proceedings, sometimes years after separation, the fear/violence persisted in half the cases but only one-quarter of those interviewed cited violence as an issue in the case. So, even if conduct such as domestic violence might be allowed in law to rebut the proposed presumption, evidence of this may not, in practice, come before the court.
>
> In any event, the likelihood that some mothers who oppose contact will be made to agree to it does not necessarily support the claims of the proponents of a presumption of shared parenting that it will be a solution to the problem of conflict over contact. As *Making Contact Work* points out, it is doubtful that the existence of a presumption will prevent acrimonious disagreement between parents who cannot co-operate.
>
> First, it is doubtful whether it will significantly reduce litigation … . Certainly research in the UK shows that 'there has been a remarkable rise both in the number of orders and the number of "disposals" in respect of private law applications under the Children Act'. This would suggest that the existing presumption or assumption in favour of contact has done nothing to stem the tide of litigation and there is no reason to suppose that a statutory presumption of shared parenting will prove more effective in doing so. Mothers who are strongly opposed to any contact at all or who may wish to resist a statutorily mandated split will seek to rebut the presumption in much the same way as they do now.
>
> Secondly, whatever arrangement is embodied in a court order, child care arrangements are unlikely to work or to take place in a conflict-free context, unless the parents espouse this as a goal and are willing to achieve it. A parent might be pressured into agreeing to shared parenting but may resist implementing the arrangement … .
>
> A statutory presumption of shared parenting has, arguably, the potential for an increase in

---

[115] See also Walker (2004) pp 173 and 193. The courts refuse to address a dispute framed in terms of one parent's complaint that the other is insufficiently involved with the children (Pearce, Davis and Barron 1999 p 26).
[116] See also Walker (2004 pp 196, 214); Simpson, *et al*, (2003 pp 204–6).

the use of [enforcement] measures. There will be more court orders for contact and, so, more mothers will be exposed to the risk of imprisonment for defying such orders.

(pp 272–73, references omitted)

Furthermore, there is no consensus that shared parenting is in the best interests of children generally[117] and so a presumption would constitute a departure form the paramountcy principle (Kaganas and Piper 2002 pp 376–77). And, it is argued, the courts are likely to see any presumption as incompatible with the Human Rights Act 1998. In the case of *Payne v Payne*[118] Thorpe LJ observed that to create a presumption in favour of one parent would present a risk to the other's right to private and family life in terms of Article 8 of the European Convention and to the right to a fair trial under Article 6.[119]

The issue of shared parenting is addressed in the Green Paper as well as the White Paper and the Government has declared itself unwilling to introduce a statutory presumption:

Some have proposed that legislative change is needed to introduce 'presumptions of contact', to give parents equal rights to equal time with their child after parental separation. Where such arrangements are best for the child, and are agreed between the parents or determined by a court, such arrangements can and should be put in place. The Government does not, however, believe that an automatic 50:50 division of the child's time between the two parents would be in the best interests of most children. In many separated families, such arrangements would not work in practical terms, owing to living arrangements or work commitments. Enforcing this type of arrangement through legislation would not be what many children want and could have a damaging impact on some of them. Children are not a commodity to be apportioned equally after separation. The best arrangements for them will depend on a variety of issues particular to their circumstances: a one-size-fits-all formula will not work. The assumption that both parents have equal status and value as parents is enshrined in current law. The actual arrangements made by courts start from that position. (DCA, DfES and DTI 2004 para 42)[120]

The welfare principle, it appears, will not easily be displaced.

## XII. CONCLUSION

The welfare principle is a powerful construct, legitimating policy—and decision-making on the basis of apparently neutral, scientifically valid criteria. It operates to privilege the biological nuclear family form over other family structures. This image of the family persists even in instances where the nuclear unit has broken down and it is embodied, often to the detriment of caretaking mothers, in legal norms adopted to regulate the post-separation family which prioritise fathers. Mothers who do not embrace these norms are criticised and, in future, are likely to be given information, education and therapeutic services to encourage them to do so. Those who resist are likely to face a court with a new armoury of punishments at its disposal.

---

117 See Neale, *et al*, (2003).
118 [2001] EWCA Civ 166; [2001] 1 FLR 1052.
119 See Kaganas and Piper (2002) p 378.
120 See also DCA, DfES and DTI (2005) paras 13–15.

# FURTHER READING AND SELECTED RECENT REFERENCES

R BAILEY-HARRIS, J BARRON and J PEARCE, 'From Utility to Rights? The Presumption of Contact in Practice' (1999) 13 *Int J of Law, Policy and the Family* 111.

A BLACKWELL and F DAWE, *Non-Resident Parental Contact* (London, ONS, 2003).

S BOYD, 'Some Postmodernist Challenges to Feminist Analyses of Law, Family and State: Ideology and Discourse in Child Custody Law' (1991) 10 *Canadian J of Family Law* 79.

——, 'Is there an Ideology of Motherhood in (Post) Modern Child Custody Law?' (1996) 5 *Social and Legal Studies* 495.

A BUCHANAN, *et al*, Families in Conflict: Perspectives of Children and Parents on the Family Court Welfare Service (Bristol, Policy, 2001).

G DAVIS and J PEARCE, 'The Welfare Principle in Action' (1999) *Fam Law* 237.

S DAY SCLATER and F KAGANAS, 'Contact: Mothers, Welfare and Rights' in A Bainham, *et al*, (eds), *Children and Their Families: Contact, Rights and Welfare* (Oxford, Hart Publishing, 2003).

S DAY SCLATER and C PIPER, 'Remoralising the Family?—Family Policy, Family Law and Youth Justice' (2000) 12 *CFLQ* 135.

J DEWAR, 'The Normal Chaos of Family Law' (1998) 61(4) *MLR* 467.

——, 'Family Law and its Discontents' (2000) 14 *Int J of Law, Policy and the Family* 59.

J DUNN, 'Contact and Children's Perspectives on Parental Relationships' in A Bainham, *et al*, (eds), *Children and Their Families: Contact, Rights and Welfare* (Oxford, Hart Publishing, 2003).

J EEKELAAR, 'Beyond the Welfare Principle' (2002) 14(3) *CFLQ* 237.

——, 'Contact—Over the Limit' (2002) *Fam Law* 271.

——, ' "Trust the Judges": How Far should Family Law Go?' (1984) 47 *MLR* 593.

J HERRING, 'The Human Rights Act and the Welfare Principle in Family Law—Conflicting or Complementary?' (1999) 11(3) *CFLQ* 223.

AL JAMES and S MCNAMEE, 'Constructing Children's Welfare in Family Proceedings' (2003) *Fam Law* 889.

F KAGANAS, 'Contact, Conflict and Risk' in S Day Sclater and C Piper, (eds), *Undercurrents of Divorce* (Aldershot, Ashgate, 1999).

——, 'Re L (Contact: Domestic Violence); Re V (Contact: Domestic Violence); Re M (Contact: Domestic Violence); Re H (Contact: Domestic Violence)*: Contact and Domestic Violence' (2000) 12(3) CFLQ 311.

——, 'Domestic Violence, Men's Groups and the Equivalence Argument' in A Diduck and K O'Donovan, *Feminist Perspectives on Family Law* (London, Cavendish, 2006 forthcoming).

F KAGANAS and S DAY SCLATER, 'Contact Disputes: Narrative Constructions of "Good" Parents' (2004) 12 *Feminist Legal Studies* 1.

F KAGANAS and A DIDUCK, 'Incomplete Citizens: Changing Images of Post-separation Children' (2004) 67(6) *MLR* 959.

F KAGANAS and C PIPER, 'Grandparents and Contact: "Rights v Welfare" Revisited' (2001) 15(2) *Int J of Law, Policy and the Family* 250.

——, 'Shared Parenting—A 70% Solution?' (2002) 14(4) *CFLQ* 365.

District Judge JOHN MITCHELL, 'Contact in Practice' (2004) *Fam Law* 662.

JB KELLY, 'Children's Post-Divorce Adjustment: Effects of Conflict, Parent Adjustment and Custody Arrangement' (1991) *Fam Law* 52.

M KING, 'Playing the Symbols—Custody and the Law Commission' (1987) *Fam Law* 186.

B NEALE, J FLOWERDEW and C SMART, 'Drifting Towards Shared Residence?' (2003) *Fam Law* 904.

B NEALE and C SMART, 'In Whose Best Interests? Theorising Family Life Following Separation or Divorce' in S Day Sclater and C Piper, (eds), *Undercurrents of Divorce* (Aldershot, Ashgate, 1999).

J PEARCE, G DAVIS and J BARRON, 'Love in a Cold Climate—Section 8 Applications under the Children Act 1989' (1999) *Fam Law* 22.

C PIPER, 'Assumptions About Children's Best Interests' (2000) 22(3) *JSWFL* 261.

J PRYOR and B RODGERS, Children in Changing Families: Life after Parental Separation (Oxford, Blackwell, 2001).

H REECE, 'The Paramountcy Principle: Consensus or Construct?' (1996) 49 *Current Legal Problems* 267.

H RHOADES, 'The "No Contact Mother": Reconstruction of Motherhood in the Era of the "New Father"' (2002) 16 *Int J of Law, Policy and the Family* 71.

J ROCHE, 'The Children Act 1989: Once a Parent Always a Parent?' (1991) *JSW & FL* 345.

S SEVENHUIJSEN, 'A Third Way? Moralities, Ethics and Families' in A Carling, S Duncan and R Edwards, (eds), *Analysing Families* (London, Routledge, 2002).

B SIMPSON, J JESSOP and P MCCARTHY, 'Fathers after Divorce' in A Bainham, *et al,* (eds), *Children and Their Families: Contact, Rights and Welfare* (Oxford, Hart Publishing, 2003).

C SMART and V MAY, 'Why Can't They Agree? The Underlying Complexity of Contact and Residence Disputes' (2004) 26 *JSWFL* 347.

——, 'Residence and Contact Disputes in Court' (2004) *Fam Law* 36.

C SMART and B NEALE, *Family Fragments?* (Cambridge, Polity, 1999).

C STURGE and D GLASER, 'Contact and Domestic Violence—The Experts' Court Report' (2000) *Fam Law* 615.

L TRINDER, 'Working and Not Working Contact after Divorce' in A Bainham, *et al,* (eds) *Children and Their Families: Contact, Rights and Welfare* (Oxford, Hart Publishing, 2003).

J WALKER, Picking up the Pieces: Marriage and Divorce: Two Years After Information Provision (London, Department of Constitutional Affairs, 2004).

D WHEELER, 'Can We Make Contact Work?' (2004) *Fam Law* 601.

*Reports*

CASC, The Advisory Board on Family Law: Children Act Sub-Committee, *A Report to the Lord Chancellor's Department on the Question of Contact in Cases where there is Domestic Violence* (London, The Stationery Office, 2000).

——, Children Act Sub-Committee of the Advisory Board on Family Law, *Making Contact Work: The Facilitation of Arrangements for Contact Between Children and their Non-residential Parents; and the Enforcement of Court Orders for Contact* (London, The Stationery Office, 2001).

——, The Advisory Board on Family Law: Children Act Sub-Committee, *Making Contact Work: A Report to the Lord Chancellor on the Facilitation of Arrangements for Contact Between Children and their Non-residential Parents and the Enforcement of Court Orders for Contact* (London, LCD, 2002).

DCA, *Government Response to the Report of the Children Act Sub-Committee of the Lord Chancellor's Advisory Board on Family Law 'Making Contact Work'* (London, DCA, 2002).

DCA, DfES and DTI, *Parental Separation: Children's Needs and Parents' Responsibilities: Next Steps* Cm 6452 (London, The Stationery Office, 2005).

——, *Parental Separation: Children's Needs and Parents' Responsibilities.* Cm 6273 (London, The Stationery Office, 2004).

Law Society 'What is the Family Law Protocol?'

LCD *Guidelines for Good Practice on Parental Contact in Cases where there is Domestic Violence* (LCD, 2002).

Legal Services Commission *Funding Code Guidance* www.legalservices.gov.uk.

# 9

# A Public or Private Matter—Child Abuse

## I. INTRODUCTION

Child abuse has come to be seen as a social problem[1] demanding the attention of governments and legislators and justifying state intervention in what is regarded as the private realm of the family. Yet this was not always so. It was not until the 19th century that the ill-treatment of children within the family became a matter of public concern. It appears that there were two pre-conditions for this development. First, perceptions of children had to change and, secondly, there had to be a change in attitudes to family privacy. It was in the 18th century that the image of the child as vulnerable and in need of protection began to emerge. And even then, family privacy and parental, specifically paternal, authority largely shielded the family from outside intervention. It was not until the late 19th century that the protection of children came to be regarded as a legitimate reason for intervening in the family. Since then, the ill-treatment of children within the family has been regarded as a matter of public concern. However, the focus of concern has changed over the years; definitions of the harm from which children have been thought to need protection have been shaped by the nature of specific campaigns and by the state of knowledge about children at particular times.

In this chapter, we trace the way in which child abuse has come to be constructed as a social problem so serious that state intervention is seen not only as permissible but, indeed, as a moral and legal imperative. We then explore definitions of child abuse which have come to be accepted as justifying intervention in the family. We go on to

---

[1] Official statistics tend to underestimate the prevalence of abuse. A study published by the NSPCC (Cawson, *et al*, 2000) was devised with the aid of the CTS (see ch 10). A quarter of the sample had experienced at least one form of violent behaviour such as being hit with an implement, punched, kicked, knocked down, shaken or deliberately burned or scalded. 78% of the violent treatment occurred at home, most often at the hands of mothers and fathers. One fifth reported that they had suffered injury on at least one occasion (p 8). 7% were assessed as having been seriously abused and 14% as experiencing intermediate abuse (p 9). 6% were assessed as suffering serious absence of care with 9% experiencing intermediate absence of care (p 11). 6% were considered to have experienced emotional abuse (p 15). Sexual abuse by relatives affected about 4% (p 17). See also Creighton (2004). The NSPCC estimates that an average of 79 children are killed every year in England and Wales and that in 78% of child homicides in 2000/01, the parents were the main suspects (Creighton and Tissier 2003 p 2).

Statistics published by the DfES (2004b) give a total of 572,700 referrals, nearly a quarter of which were repeat referrals, to social services in England in the year ending 31 March 2004. As at that date there were 26,300 children on child protection registers, representing 24 per 10,000 of the population aged under 18.41% were children considered to be at risk of neglect. Physical abuse accounted for 19%, emotional abuse for 18% and sexual abuse for 9%. 14% involved mixed categories (p 5). In 2002/03 there were more girls on the child protection register for sexual abuse and more boys on the register for physical abuse (p 11). See also Creighton (2004) Table 1 for figures on sexual abuse.

The way in which prevalence is gauged depends on the definitions of abuse used. Also, not all children who experience what could be classed as abuse are within the child protection system and not all are placed on the register.

examine the response of the state to the problem of child abuse and the roles of professionals and the law in regulating the family. Finally, we consider contemporary moves to
shift the focus of attention from child protection to the prevention of abuse.

## II. THE CONSTRUCTION OF SOCIAL PROBLEMS

According to social construction theorists, social conditions do not in themselves constitute social problems. Rather, these conditions may or may not be constructed as
problems. Behaviour is categorised as deviant and as presenting a social problem when
policy-makers perceive it as transgressing public morality or as a threat to social order,
and as necessitating social action to control it.[2] The process which leads to this outcome
is described by Manning:

> [T]he promotion of social conditions as social problems typically occurs through perceived
> grievances being organised into claims which various groups bring to the state. The legitimacy
> of those claims is heavily influenced by mass media interpretations of public opinion, and the
> priorities and interests of government departments in terms of existing policies, perceived voter
> preference and major power blocks. (1985a p 22)

Manning's description is a contemporary one but, as we shall see, the process of identifying certain conditions as problems, endeavouring to have them generally accepted as
such and campaigning for change predates the mass media age. Crucial to this process
have been the efforts of individuals or groups of people, those whom Becker refers to as
'moral entrepreneurs':

> Deviance—in the sense … of publicly labeled wrongdoing—is always the result of enterprise.
> Before any act can be viewed as deviant, and before any class of people can be labeled and
> treated as outsiders for committing the act, someone must have made the rule which defines the
> act as deviant. Rules are not made automatically. Even though a practice may be harmful in an
> objective sense to the group in which it occurs, the harm needs to be discovered and pointed
> out. People must be made to feel that something ought to be done about it. Someone must call
> the public's attention to these matters, supply the push necessary to get things done, and direct
> such energies as are aroused in the proper direction to get the rule created. (Becker 1963 p 162)[3]

The emergence of child abuse as a social problem has traditionally been traced to the
efforts of campaigners who, at different times, have included philanthropists,[4] professional groupings[5] and feminist activists. Their success, however, cannot be fully

---

[2] See Gordon (1989) p 27. See also Gusfield (1975).

[3] The activities of an enterprising individual or group 'can properly be called "moral enterprise" for what
they are enterprising about is the creation of a new fragment of the moral constitution of society, its code of
right and wrong' (Becker 1963 p 145). Becker's analysis stresses the crusading spirit of 'moral entrepreneurs',
suggesting that they typically believe that 'their mission is a holy one' (p 148) and that they tend to be members
of a dominant class seeking to improve the status of those 'beneath' them (p 149). However Manning's analysis, based on the work of Spector and Kitsuse, does not imply missionary zeal and refers to the role of pressure
groups other than elites (1985a p 19). While Becker's analysis is apt in relation to 19th century philanthropists,
Manning's better describes 20th century developments.

[4] See Simey (1951); Mowat (1961).

[5] An account of the involvement of professional groupings in the construction of social problems is offered
by Dickson (1968). He argues that agencies have a tendency to extend their power so that their enterprise arises

explained outside the context of changes in political and economic conditions. In particular, their messages would, it seems, have gone unheeded without significant changes in perceptions of children and of the family.


## III. CONSTRUCTIONS OF CHILDHOOD


Parton states that '[v]alues are crucial ... in whether and how a situation is defined as a problem' (1985 p 6). According to Pinchbeck and Hewitt, one of the significant changes in our values over the last two centuries has been in our attitude to children (1973 p 347).

The fact that, for centuries, children lacked statutory protection from abuse, is, they say, explicable in the light of the nature of parent-child relationships in pre-industrial England. Children were regarded as the property of their parents. They were seen as tainted with original sin and harsh discipline and punishment were considered necessary to correct waywardness.[6] Moreover, from about the age of 7, children were gradually initiated into the world of adult work (Cunningham 1995 p 79) and, to that extent, it appears that, as Pinchbeck and Hewitt suggest, they were seen as 'little adults' (1973 p 348).

The French historian Ariès argues that our concept of childhood is a modern invention emanating from 17th century Europe; there was no notion of childhood in medieval times:

> [I]n medieval society, the idea of childhood did not exist; this is not to suggest that children were neglected, forsaken or despised. The idea of childhood is not to be confused with affection for children: it corresponds to an awareness of the particular nature of childhood, that particular nature which distinguishes the child from the adult ... . In medieval society this awareness was lacking. That is why, as soon as the child could live without the constant solicitude of his mother, his nanny or his cradle-rocker, he belonged to adult society. (1962 p 128)

Ariès is criticised for drawing on material that documents the, probably unrepresentative, life of Louis XIII, and because his research was confined to records compiled exclusively by male authors who may have had little contact with children.[7] A more fundamental criticism is that, as Ariès himself acknowledges, childhood has been recognised through the ages as a separate stage of human existence.[8] Instead of interpreting his evidence to show that there was no concept of childhood in the middle ages, he should, says Archard (1993 p 19), have concluded only that what was lacking was our concept of childhood. It is our concept of childhood that demands as a morally appropriate way of treating children that there be a separation of adult and children's worlds (p 20).[9]

---

from bureaucratic pressures. Both Becker's and Dickson's theories are referred to in the context of child abuse by Parton (1985) pp 6–9. He discusses both the crusading efforts of philanthropists in the 19th century and the efforts of groupings within the medical profession to secure their professional status during the 20th century. See further below.

  [6] See also Cunningham (1995) p 55.
  [7] See Freeman (1983) p 12.
  [8] See Cunningham (1995) p 32.
  [9] See generally Archard (1993), chs 2 and 3.

It was during the 18th century that this separation began to occur. There was a shift 'from a prime focus on the spiritual health of the child to a concern for the development of the individual child' (Cunningham 1995 p 62). The key to this shift, says Cunningham (p 61), was the secularisation of attitudes to childhood and children and the decline in belief in original sin.[10] The writings of Locke, Rousseau and the Romantics in turn contributed to an emphasis on the individuality of the child and to a belief that childhood should be a happy, carefree time.[11] According to Cunningham (1995 p 17), the introduction of compulsory schooling in the late 19th century was crucial in transforming the meanings attached to childhood by removing children, in principle at least, from the workforce.[12] Most importantly, mass attendance at school made children 'visible' to medical professionals, sociologists and philanthropic workers, who saw that the school could be used as a 'laboratory' to produce 'scientific' knowledge (Hendrick 2003 p 22). The Child Study movement, formed in the 1890s, subjected childhood to 'scientific' scrutiny, using the techniques of natural history and spearheading the use of 'observation, classification and experiment' (Hendrick 2003 p 23). It popularised the notion that the child's conception of the world differed from that of adults and that there were marked stages in normal development (Hendrick 2003 p 23). During the 19th century, says Hendrick, the child was widely perceived as characterised by 'ignorance, incapacity and innocence' (p 21).[13] Helping children became a priority among charitable organisations: 'Because children were thought to be innocent … they could easily be victimised. Because children were thought to be malleable … they could be molded into good citizens.' (Gordon 1989 p 29)

And as 'scientific' knowledge grew, doctors and psychologists were beginning to define children 'in an apparently "scientific" manner, thereby making it difficult for lay persons to dispute their findings' (Hendrick 2003 p 23). This, perhaps, marked the ascendancy of expertise in the arena of child protection which is so evident today.

## IV. CHILD CONCERN AND THE ROLE OF THE STATE

*Protection through 'Tutelage'*

The protection of family members regarded as vulnerable to cruelty and neglect presents the liberal state with a problem. The question it faces is 'how child-rearing can be made into a matter for public concern and its quality can be monitored without destroying the ideal of the family as a counterweight to state power, a domain of voluntary, self-regulating actions' (Dingwall, *et al*, 1983 pp 214–15).[14] As Dingwall, *et al*, point out, one

---

[10] But see Cox (1996) p 203.

[11] See Cunningham (1995) p 62ff.

[12] Schools, family and youth organisations such as the Scouts and the Boys Brigade were seen as the 'proper' places for children to take them off the street. This 'privatising' of children became a part of the idea of childhood in the 19th century (Prout 2005 p 36).

[13] Rex and Wendy Stainton Rogers (1992) in their discussion of the contemporary construction of children as vulnerable and dependent challenge the assumption that this is necessarily evidence of progress; it was the understanding of children as different from adults that made corporal punishment of children acceptable at a time when it had become unthinkable for adults. To label them as inherently dependent may afford children greater compassion in some respects but there are many children 'for whom their culturally and socially constructed dependency is the root of their suffering and discontent' (p 195).

[14] See further Archard (1993) ch 9, and ch 1 of this book.

possible solution to the abuse of power within the family is to give to vulnerable members greater access to outside agencies. This solution preserves family autonomy because privacy is breached only at the behest of a family member. However, while some abused women may actively seek help from outside agencies, access to outside agencies is a particularly ineffective means of protecting children. In many cases, protection from parental abuse can be gained only by means of surveillance of the family by outside agencies (1983 p 216).

According to the French writer, Donzelot (1980), drawing on Foucault's theoretical ideas, one way in which this has been achieved has been through the operation of what he refers to as 'the tutelary complex'. He observes that during the 19th century, there was a transition from government *of* the family to government *through* the family (p 92). Philanthropy, he says, was a deliberately depoliticised strategy for establishing public services without undermining the liberal definition of the state. Families were used as agents for conveying social norms into the private sphere of the home. Philanthropic organisations penetrated the family in the name of hygienic and educative protection, limiting patriarchal power and placing the family under economic-moral tutelage. By means of the technique of moralisation, charity was made available, but only to those families whose shortcomings were not judged to be the result of moral failure. Through the process of normalisation, families were inculcated with approved norms by means of education and, sometimes, legislation. Complaints, usually by women against men, facilitated entry into the home. Tutelage, involving the monitoring and surveillance of families to assess levels of compliance, made possible coercive intervention. The family's automomy was preserved only if it observed approved norms; resistance or non-compliance were seen as evidence of deviance.[15]

Philanthropic bodies gradually lost their principal role in 'civilising' the family and, according to Cunningham (1995), the state began to take on itself the primary responsibility for child-saving at the end of the 19th century (p 137). Philanthropy was largely replaced by a new series of professions[16] that emerged in the late 19th century and early 20th centuries, including the 'psy' professions[17] and social work. Increasingly, the regulation of the family has fallen to those with professional expertise 'underpinned by the power of a claim to truth' (Rose 1987 p 71) and backed up by legal sanctions. This sphere of activity, termed 'the social' by Donzelot, was seen as enabling the liberal state to maintain its legitimacy while protecting family members.

**Q** In the light of Donzelot's analysis, to what extent can the family be said to constitute a private domain?

*The 'Cruelty Act': Protecting Children or Protecting Society?*

The first major statute regulating the care of children in their families was the Prevention of Cruelty to and Protection of Children Act 1889. Prior to this, the state had intervened little in the family which was seen as being under the rule of the patriarch.[18]

---

[15] See further Dingwall, *et al*, (1983) pp 215–17.
[16] However, many professionals work for charitable bodies.
[17] Such as psychiatry.
[18] But see, on Poor Law children, Frost and Stein (1989) pp 21–24.

Why intervention became a moral and a political possibility is not entirely clear. According to Cunningham (1995), the reasons included 'concern about population levels; worry about the level of "civilization" of the masses; desire to breed a race capable of competing in the 20th century', as well as concern for the children themselves (p 137). He observes that the industrial revolution first brought the 'new ideology of childhood' into play in policy-making (p 138), an ideology at the heart of which lay a commitment to the view that childhood was significant in determining the kind of adult the child would become and that childhood attracted its own rights and privileges (p 41).

Initially, however, the focus was not on abuse within the family, but on those visible 'children without a childhood'[19]: children who were working in factories and in mines.[20] These new workplaces were seen as presenting not only physical but moral dangers; they were seen as sources of 'deprivation and depravity' (Piper 1999a p 37). Pursuant to scandals around baby farming, legislation was also passed against infanticide.[21] This, as Piper (1999a pp 42–43) observes, was directed against single, unmarried mothers and commercial nurses. The reluctance to breach the privacy of the 'normal' family continued. In 1871, for instance, Lord Shaftesbury, a leading philanthropist, condemned the evils of child abuse. Yet he stated that they were 'of so private, internal and domestic a character as to be beyond the reach of legislation'.[22] To change this view, 'it was necessary to show how little of the sacredness of family life existed among the more depraved, and the manner in which a man exercised his right to do what he would with his own'.[23]

Explanations of the concern about child cruelty that emerged during the late 19th century have centred on the social anxiety engendered by social instability.[24] This was linked to disquiet about the urban masses (Piper 1999a p 46). In particular, it was linked to ideas about the socialisation of children. Children who grew up in urban slums were seen as a potential threat to the moral order; they could not but grow up unhealthy and depraved.[25] Intervention in the family came to be seen 'as a lesser evil' than the risk that 'the entire moral framework of society [might be undermined] ... unless selected families were regulated' (Piper 1999a p 46).[26]

Societies for the Prevention of Cruelty to Children were set up locally in the 1880s and the NSPCC was formed in 1889. The NSPCC, says Hendrick:

> was of vital importance in reshaping public opinion away from the view that the family was inviolate, towards a view which recognised that if the ideal of the family were to be realised, then a certain amount of interference by outside bodies was essential for the purposes of education and, occasionally, prosecution. (Hendrick 2003 p 32)

Child protection legislation, modelled on the earlier legislation against cruelty to animals, was promoted by the NSPCC and enacted.[27] The Prevention of Cruelty to and Protection of Children Act 1889 reflects, say Eekelaar, *et al*, (1982), primarily moral rather than welfarist concerns: '[c]hild and animal cruelty were morally corrupting and

---

[19] This phrase was used by Douglas Jerrold in 1840 to describe factory children. Quoted by Cunningham (1995) p 144.

[20] See, eg, the Health and Morals of Apprentices Act 1802.

[21] Infant Life Protection Act 1872.

[22] Quoted in Pinchbeck and Hewitt (1973) p 622.

[23] Gertrude Tuckwell (1894), *The State and Its Children* p 127, quoted by Pinchbeck and Hewitt (1973) p 623.

[24] But see also Hendrick (2003) pp 24–25.

[25] See Hendrick (2003) pp 8–9, 25.

[26] See also Hendrick (2003) pp 24–25.

[27] See *ibid*, p 26.

for such moral delinquency parents were to lose their rights to their children' (p 74). This they did if they committed the offence of wilfully ill-treating, neglecting or abandoning a child so as to cause unnecessary suffering or injury to health.[28] The 1889 Poor Law (Children) Act in turn gave guardians authority to assume parental rights over Poor Law children.[29]

> **Q** Do the analyses discussed above suggest that the primary justification for inter-vention in the family was seen as the protection of children from abuse or the protection of society from moral disintegration?

### Shifting Patterns of Concern

Child cruelty and neglect were now firmly on the political agenda but, in the ensuing years, policies oscillated between prevention and protection, between working with families and rescuing children from their families.

The turn of the century saw concern focusing not only on urban degeneration and child-saving but also on a different aspect of the national interest. This change stemmed largely from anxieties about the fitness of the working class for manual labour and military service; in particular, the Boer War revealed general unfitness among the recruits. The new priorities included all round efficiency, public health, nutrition, hygiene and responsible parenthood (Hendrick 2003 pp 15, 68–69). Children were seen as potential assets of the nation and so state welfare provision for children increased. The state became more interventionist, providing support in the form of school meals[30] for example, while also taking on an active role in rescuing children subject to cruelty. The Prevention of Cruelty to Children Act 1904 and the 1908 Children Act gave local authorities powers to remove children.[31]

There emerged a child guidance movement and, as psychological and psychiatric interest in children grew, treatment of children and their families came to be seen as cru-cial in problem cases; when parents failed to provide the 'correct environment', 'mental disturbance' was thought to ensue (Hendrick 2003 p 107). By 1933, the legislators' gaze had shifted once again to delinquency and this continued to occupy their attention for many years. The Children and Young Persons Act 1933 was concerned more with young offenders than with the victims of cruelty or neglect (Parton 1985 p 39, Hendrick 2003 p 119). Both offenders and non-offenders were thought to need treatment (Hendrick 2003 p 116) and those children who were considered to be at risk were usually removed from the family.

That policy changed with the Second World War. The evacuation of children from the cities revealed to many the scale of deprivation of urban children, and it was argued that this was too widespread to be dealt with by removing children from their families. 'Prob-lem' families could be helped to provide better childcare (Hendrick 2003 p 140). Further, the dislocation of war time led to concern that families should be together. The 1948 Children Act gave expression to this new approach.[32] Prevention, rather than rescue,

---

[28] For the contemporary equivalent, see s 1 of the Children and Young Persons Act 1933.
[29] See Parton (1985) p 35.
[30] Education (Provision of Meals) Act 1906. See also Hendrick (2003) pp 66ff.
[31] See Parton (1985) pp 37–38.
[32] See Parton (1985) pp 42–43; Hendrick (2003) p 139.

became the focal point. Yet concern continued to centre on delinquency rather than protection.[33]

During the 1950s through to the 1970s, coercive intervention was seen as a last resort;
the emphasis was on working with the family (Parton 1991 p 20):

> In effect the newly emerging social welfare model, with its prime concern on the relationship
> between neglect and delinquency saw no clash of interests between the wider society, the state
> and different family members. Everything could be tackled by humane regulation and
> non-coercive welfare intervention techniques. ...
>
> Under the 1969 Children and Young Persons Act, children in trouble with the law were
> treated in virtually the same way as children who were not offenders. In the process of concep-
> tualising and treating all problems to do with children as being essentially the same, any
> reference to children as victims was lost. (Parton 1985 p 45)

Indeed, Hendrick (2003) argues that, running throughout the history of concern to protect children, has also been a thread of concern about what children might become
without intervention: 'The child victim was nearly always seen as harbouring the
possibility of another condition, one that was sensed to be threatening to moral fibre,
sexual propriety, the sanctity of the family, the preservation of the race, law and order,
and the wider reaches of citizenship' (p 7).

> **Q** Does a focus on delinquency imply concern to protect children or to protect
> society from children?

## V. CHILD ABUSE—THE BEGINNINGS OF CONTEMPORARY CONCERN

The image of the child as victim has emerged strongly since the 1970s and, as child welfare knowledge has expanded, the ways in which children are seen to be victimised have
multiplied. Whereas early concerns about children focused on child cruelty and neglect,
more recent concerns have centred on a wider range of harms to children, encompassed
in the term 'child abuse'. The catalyst for the contemporary wave of concern was the
publication in 1974 of the report of the enquiry into the death of Maria Colwell (Secretary of State for Social Services 1974). As Parton notes, however, the groundwork had
already been laid in the preceding decades.[34]

This groundwork was primarily the achievement of members of the medical profession. In the 1940s Dr John Caffey, a specialist in paediatric radiology working in the
USA, observed a connection between the incidence of subdural haematoma in infants
and multiple fractures in the arms and legs. Others in the medical profession began to
draw links between the trauma suffered by young children and parental conduct and, in
1961, the term 'Battered Child Syndrome' was coined by Dr C Henry Kempe. The
following year he and his colleagues published an account of his research (Kempe, *et al*,
1962). The article argued that the syndrome was found in children who had been subjected to severe physical abuse, usually by a parent. As Parton (1985 p 51) points out, the

---

[33] See the report of the Ingleby Committee (1960).
[34] See Parton (1985), ch 3, for a detailed discussion.

label defined abuse as an illness—a syndrome—and it came to be conceptualised as a medical problem. Doctors were seen as having a central role to play in the diagnosis of the 'syndrome' and its treatment (Parton 1985 p 52). Attention was deflected from social and cultural factors that might be considered significant in explaining abuse (*ibid*).

In Britain, this 'syndrome' was first recognised in an article published by two ortho-paedic surgeons in 1963 (Griffiths and Moynihan 1963) and was subsequently publicised by forensic pathologists and paediatricians.[35] Yet although the NSPCC set up a Battered Child Research Unit which gave the issue a higher profile, it was not until the death of Maria Colwell, aged 7, at the hands of her step-father, that child abuse emerged as a major social problem (Parton 1985 p 68).

Reaction to this event, Parton says, 'took on the proportions of a moral panic' (1985 p 70). The case, he suggests, 'provided a focus for the expression of a range of social anxieties'. These anxieties, echoing those expressed during the 19th century, were 'con-cerned with the collapse of the "English way of life", the growth in violence, the decline in individual and social discipline and morality, and the need to re-establish the tradi-tional family' (Parton 1985 p 81).

Whereas previously abuse was conceptualised as a 'medical and social welfare prob-lem' (Parton 1985 p 97) to which the solution was the treatment and rehabilitation of the family, the Maria Colwell case led to a downgrading in the importance of the blood-tie (p 98) and an increased willingness to remove children from their families. In addition, rehabilitation of children with their parents became less of a priority. Research suggesting that children in care tended to be left to 'drift' (Rowe and Lambert 1973) contributed to a move towards permanency, necessitating timely and decisive action to place the child in a new family. The 1975 Children Act reflected this shift and attempted to give local authorities greater powers to intervene between parents and children.[36]

The Children Act 1989 heralded another change, with the emphasis on working with families wherever possible. And, according to Hendrick (2003), the Bulger case has led to a preoccupation with socialisation. That case involved the murder of a toddler by two young boys and it gave rise to concerns within the Labour government about the child-ren of the 'socially excluded'. It has led, says Hendrick, to increasing efforts to ensure that children are ' "protected" from becoming antisocial' and 'early intervention' to achieve this aim is presented as being in children's best interests (Hendrick 2003 p 244).

*Sexual Abuse*

The history of concern about child sexual abuse differs somewhat from that of concern about physical cruelty and neglect. In the 19th century one of the corrupting influences that preoccupied reformers was that of sex. However, concern seems to have centred on moral harm rather than on the child's psychological or even physical state. Controversy surrounding the Contagious Diseases Acts (1864, 1866, 1869), designed to control pros-titution, generated debate about juvenile prostitution (Hendrick 2003 p 34). Purity campaigners turned their attention to this subject and the Criminal Law Amendment Act 1885 was passed to raise the age of consent to 16 for girls and to make it an offence to procure a girl younger than 21 (Hendrick 2003 p 35). The privacy of the family and

---

[35] The 'discovery' of child abuse, says Parton, helped to advance the prestige of these branches of the medical profession (1985 pp 53 and 58).
[36] See Parton (1985) p 116.

Victorian beliefs in the 'almost sacred nature of domesticity' (Hendrick 2003 p 38) meant that legislation outlawing incest was passed only in 1908.[37] This legislation, too, stemmed from concerns about purity and public morality rather than child welfare.[38]

Professional interest in child sexual abuse has been traced by Freeman (1989b p 86) to the publication in 1886 of Krafft-Ebing's *Psychopathia Sexualis*, documenting a number of incest histories. However, allegations of incest were thought to be the product of children's fantasies, a response widely attributed to the writings of Freud which focused on Oedipal fantasies.[39] According to Smart (1999c), the medical profession explained venereal disease in babies and children by reference, for example, to mothers kissing their children's genitals and passing on infections received from their husbands (p 395). Symptoms suffered by children in institutions were attributed to poor hygiene (*ibid*). Smart argues that there was an awareness of adult-child sexual contact but that early feminist campaigners found themselves unable to change medical opinion or legal and common-sense perceptions of harm (p 405) and of childhood. Legal discourse, for instance, characterised children as unreliable witnesses who, in any event, were likely to be 'partly responsible for the minor lapse in adult behaviour' of which they complained (Smart 1999c p 399). Smart suggests that throughout the 1920s and 1930s it was 'assumed that children simply forgot what had happened to them or they were perceived as becoming "vicious"' (1999c p 404); although there was some understanding that they were 'damaged', they were seen as wicked (*ibid*).

Opinions about harm, it seems, remained divided even into the 1950s. The Kinsey Report, published in 1953, revealed that sex between adults and children did take place but said that it was difficult to understand, except in terms of cultural conditioning, how children might be disturbed by sexual contact. The Report went on to suggest that children were harmed more by the reactions of the police and other adults than by the sexual contact itself (1953 p 121). It was only towards the 1980s that child sexual abuse within the family began to be seen as a social problem in the United Kingdom.[40]

The new factors accounting for this included a growing feminist movement in the 1970s and a more general focus on victims and their experiences. It was through the efforts of rape crisis groups and incest survivor groups that sexual abuse began to be brought to public attention, (Smart 1989b p 56; MacLeod and Saraga 1988 p 18) and with the help of prominent figures within medicine and psychiatry, it came to be seen as a child protection issue. The media too contributed to the construction of sexual abuse as a social problem: a BBC progamme, 'Childwatch' was followed by the launch of Childline, a national freephone number set up to help abused children.[41] These events in turn contributed to knowledge about sexual abuse and its prevalence.

---

[37] The Punishment of Incest Act 1908. Smart (1989b p 54) argues that the legislation focused on the unnaturalness of the offence rather than simply the protection of children.

[38] See Hendrick (2003) pp 39–40.

[39] See Freeman (1989b) p 86. See, for an account of Freud's abandonment of his initial explanation of hysteria in terms of childhood sexual abuse in favour of a theory of seduction fantasies, Howitt (1993) p 10ff.

[40] See Parton (1991) p 85.

[41] See Parton (1991) p 91ff.

agenda even though, in the long run, these factors may be just as harmful as a severe beating or emotional deprivation.[52]

### 'Significant Harm'

For the purposes of coercive intervention in the family to protect children from abuse, the legal concept of 'significant harm' marks the threshold.[53] This concept is defined in relatively unspecific terms in Section 31 of the Children Act 1989. However, some indication of what might be covered can be found in the more detailed description of those acts considered abusive provided in *Working Together*, a document devised by government departments in 1999.[54] This enumerates the categories of abuse for the purposes of registration on the child protection register:

Physical Abuse
2.4 Physical abuse may involve hitting, shaking, throwing, poisoning, burning or scalding, drowning, suffocating, or otherwise causing physical harm to a child. Physical harm may also be caused when a parent or carer feigns the symptoms of, or deliberately causes ill health to a child whom they are looking after. This situation is commonly described using terms such as factitious illness by proxy or Munchausen syndrome by proxy.

Emotional Abuse
2.5 Emotional abuse is the persistent emotional ill-treatment of a child such as to cause severe and persistent adverse effects on the child's emotional development. It may involve conveying to children that they are worthless or unloved, inadequate, or valued only insofar as they meet the needs of another person. It may feature age or developmentally inappropriate expectations being imposed on children. It may involve causing children frequently to feel frightened or in danger, or the exploitation or corruption of children. Some level of emotional abuse is involved in all types of ill-treatment of a child, though it may occur alone.

Sexual Abuse
2.6 Sexual abuse involves forcing or enticing a child or young person to take part in sexual activities, whether or not the child is aware of what is happening. The activities may involve physical contact, including penetrative (eg, rape or buggery) or non-penetrative acts. They may include non-contact activities, such as involving children in looking at, or in the production of, pornographic material or watching sexual activities, or encouraging children to behave in sexually inappropriate ways.[55]

Neglect
2.7 Neglect is the persistent failure to meet a child's basic physical and/or psychological needs, likely to result in the serious impairment of the child's health or development. It may involve a

---

[52] See also Birchall (1989) p 10; Archard (1993) p 151.

[53] See ss 31, 43 and 44 of the Children Act 1989. See further ch 17. In relation to the criminal law, see ch 4.

[54] Superseding a version published in 1991.

[55] See, for alternative definitions, Schechter and Roberge (1976) p 129; Freeman (1989b) p 88ff. What kind of sexual contact should be classified as abuse is a contentious question. Howitt questions the assumption that all adult–child sexual contact is harmful to children (1993 p 108). Rex and Wendy Stainton Rogers point out that one of the axioms built into child protection work is that children lack capacity to consent or are so positioned in the power of others that true consent is not possible. This assumption that children lack capacity contradicts the emphasis elsewhere in the law on allowing children to make decisions about their lives. Moreover, this assumption of incapacity becomes difficult to sustain in cases of sexual activity between children (1992 pp 177–78). But see the Sexual Offences Act 2003 below.

parent or carer failing to provide adequate food, shelter and clothing, failing to protect a child from physical harm or danger, or the failure to ensure access to appropriate medical care or treatment. It may also include neglect of, or unresponsiveness to, a child's emotional needs.

> (DoH, Home Office and DfEE 1999)

It has been remarked that the scope for state intervention in the family has widened over time: 'the threshold beyond which child abuse is considered to occur is gradually being lowered' (DoH 1995b p 15). This development has been attributed to a number of factors: 'This is happening for a variety of reasons, including an emphasis on the rights of children as individuals, ease of disclosures, the influence of feminist social theories about victimisation and public expectation that the state should intervene in the privacy of family life.' (DoH 1995b p 15)

Whether any particular instance or instances of ill-treatment will be regarded as falling within the scope of significant harm and as warranting coercive intervention, depends on how the professionals (and the courts) evaluate the behaviour:

> 2.17 There are no absolute criteria on which to rely when judging what constitutes significant harm. Consideration of the severity of ill-treatment may include the degree and the extent of physical harm, the duration and frequency of abuse and neglect, and the extent of premeditation, degree of threat and coercion, sadism, and bizarre or unusual elements in child sexual abuse. Each of these elements has been associated with more severe effects on the child, and/or relatively greater difficulty in helping the child overcome the adverse impact of the ill-treatment. Sometimes, a single traumatic event may constitute significant harm e.g a violent assault, suffocation or poisoning. More often, significant harm is a compilation of significant events, both acute and long-standing, which interrupt, change or damage the child's physical and psychological development. Some children live in family or social circumstances where their health and development are neglected. For them, it is the corrosiveness of long-term emotional, physical or sexual abuse that causes impairment to the extent of constituting significant harm. In each case, it is necessary to consider any ill-treatment alongside the family's strengths and supports. (DoH, Home Office and DfEE 1999)

In any event, the 'state remains selective in its concerns' (DoH 1995b p 15). Although a duty is imposed in terms of Section 17 of the Children Act 1989 to alleviate disadvantages stemming from conditions such as homelessness and poverty,[56] these disadvantages are not of themselves regarded as constituting abuse.

## VII. THE 'CAUSES' OF CHILD ABUSE

Manning explains that an important element in the construction of social problems is the choice of explanations for those problems and of appropriate solutions. Indeed, he suggests, 'a major influence on the emergence of a successful social problem is the availability of a promising solution for it—in many cases the solution determines the problem rather than vice versa' (1985b p 162). The tendency is to designate as a cause that which can be tackled to achieve the desired change in the 'most convenient, economic or efficient way possible' (p 164), a way that typically leaves the broader *status quo* unchanged (p 165). So, the process of constructing child abuse as a social problem

---

[56] See also the government's 'Sure Start' programme (Home Office 1998 paras 1.36–1.44).

has involved not only categorising certain behaviours as abusive, but also selecting those behaviours which are amenable to causal explanations that suggest manageable solutions.

The literature on the 'causation' of child abuse may be seen as postulating two major models: the 'psychological model' and the 'sociological model' (O'Donnell and Craney 1982 p 185). The model of causation espoused naturally determines what strategies for combating abuse appear appropriate. As we shall see, the models that have influenced policy and professional practice have focused on the particular family and the individuals within it.[57] It follows that the 'solution' to the problem is seen as lying within the family; either it can be rehabilitated or the child must be separated from it. This 'solution' appears, on the face of it, more manageable for the state and less disruptive of the *status quo* than the wide-ranging economic, social or cultural reforms suggested by other models of causation. However, as we shall see, it assumes that the problem family or individual can be identified and this is by no means an easy task.

*Neglect, Physical and Emotional Abuse*

The 'psychological model', which locates the principal cause of abuse in the psychological make-up of the abuser and which suggests that there are particular psychiatric categories specifically associated with child abuse, has been largely discounted. For example, Gelles (1973 p 614) points out that of the 19 psychological traits put forward by authors subscribing to this theory, 'there was agreement by two or more authors on only four traits'. Parton, reviewing the literature, also observes that writers who maintain that abusers suffer from personality disorders cannot agree on what these are (1985 p 135).

The 'sociological model' embraces a variety of theoretical positions, but each of the analyses suggest that radical change, whether social, economic or cultural, is necessary to deal with abuse. Straus, Gelles and Steinmetz (1981), writing on violence in families, maintain that it is far from abnormal and arises from the interaction of culture, family structure, stress and social learning. It is argued that it is in the family that people learn to be violent. The prevalence of violence within families is a result of the fact that people tend to see intra-familial violence generally and corporal punishment of children[58] in particular, as normal and acceptable.[59] Freeman (1983 p 124) argues that children are still seen as objects and that it is not surprising therefore that they are abused. Writers such as Parton (1985 p 175) contend that child abuse is strongly related to class, inequality and poverty and, more specifically, the stress and frustration engendered by difficult economic and social conditions.

**Q** Are the two major models mutually exclusive?

---

[57] See also Hendrick (2003) p 169.

[58] But see s 58 Children Act 2004. In *A v United Kingdom (Human Rights: Punishment of Child)* [1998] 2 FLR 952, the European Court of Human Rights held that a boy who had been subjected to severe beatings had suffered ill-treatment within the purview of Art 3 of the Convention for the Protection of Human Rights and Fundamental Freedoms.

[59] See also Gelles (1979) p 39; Gelles (1992).

A number of the various models put forward since the Second World War to explain
why children are maltreated are summarised[60] in a Department of Health document:
*Child Protection. Messages from Research* (1995b pp 21–22).The document goes on to
indicate that single cause explanations, whether relying on pathology, stress, poverty,
environment, or the characteristics of the victim, have largely been supplanted by an 'integrated model': [61]

> *Integrated model*: Today, it is broadly accepted that a combination of social, psychological, eco-
> nomic and environmental factors play a part in the abuse or neglect of children. ...Families
> overwhelmed and depressed by social problems form the greatest proportion of those assessed
> and supported by child protection agencies. Not included in this group is a small proportion
> with very different characteristics, such as those in which a parent has serious psychiatric prob-
> lems or a predisposition to family violence. (DoH 1995b pp 21–22)

*Working Together* (DoH, Home Office and DfEE 1999 paras 2.19–2.24) lists various
'sources of stress for children and families' which could contribute to poor parenting.
These include social exclusion, domestic violence, mental illness of a parent or carer and
substance abuse by the care-taking adults.

**Q**  What 'solutions' do these formulations of the problem suggest?

*Sexual Abuse*

Since sexual abuse has been found to be spread more evenly across social classes than
other forms of abuse,[62] explanations have centred less on factors such as poverty than
on the characteristics of the families themselves. However competing explanations,
emerging from feminist theory, stress male power and suggest strategies entailing social
and cutural change.[63]

Sexual abuse, like other types of abuse, is thought by many to be learned behaviour.[64]
Other explanations have been put forward by proponents of family systems theory.[65]
The family is seen as a system and sexual abuse occurs when that system breaks down:
'sexual abuse is a *symptom* of what is wrong in the family, or even a "solution" to the
dysfunction' (p 33). Furniss (1991), a proponent of systems theory, draws a distinction
between 'conflict-avoiding' and 'conflict-regulating' families. Sexual abuse, he maintains,
functions either to avoid conflict between the parents or to help to regulate it. In conflict-avoiding families, sexual abuse 'takes the pressure off the precarious sexual
relationship between the parents' (p 56); the role of sexual partner is delegated to a
child. In conflict-regulating families, the sexually abusive relationship helps to decrease
conflict and prevents the break-up of the adults' relationship.

Feminist writers point out that this account blames mothers for the abuse of their
children by fathers; they are seen as being responsible for the behaviour of their

---

[60] For detailed discussion of the various models, see Freeman (1983), ch 4; Parton (1985), chs 6 and 7.

[61] See also DoH (2000b) para 2.24.

[62] See Freeman (1989b) p 97.

[63] Eg, Freeman suggests that the 'socialisation processes which construct images of masculinity need to be
re-examined' (1989b p 116) and that the status of children should be improved (*ibid* p 117).

[64] See Briggs (1995).

[65] See, for discussion, MacLeod and Saraga (1988).

menfolk. They are described as withdrawing, being punitive and as denying men their conjugal rights while men are described as acting on uncontrollable sexual urges.[66]

The feminist analysis, in contrast, finds the explanation of sexual abuse in the way in which male sexuality is constructed.[67] Feminist writers emphasise the fact that sexual abusers are predominantly male[68] while their victims are predominantly female[69] and assert that masculinity and male sexuality are associated with dominance:

> Generally boys and men learn to experience their sexuality as an overwhelming and uncontrollable force; they learn to focus their sexual feelings on submissive objects, and they learn the assertion of their sexual desires, the expectation of having them serviced. Obviously this is a crude account of a complex phenomenon ... . Thus all men do not abuse ... .
>
> (MacLeod and Saraga 1988 p 41)

A more sophisticated account is provided by Liddle (1993). Drawing on the concept of 'cathexis', meaning the social organisation of desire, he suggests that 'dominant processes of masculinization ... create a momentum toward the cultivation of sets of desires compatible with adult-child sex' (p 116). This is because male sexual desire is constructed in a way that links it with 'themes of performance, superiority and achievement' (p 112). The feelings and needs of partners and the possible harm caused by a sexual encounter are accorded little significance (p 114). However, there is nothing inevitable about child sexual abuse, he says; men who abuse choose to do so.

It appears that it is the feminist analysis that has, at least to some extent, prevailed. Official documentation indicates that sexual abuse is now seen in terms of power and exploitation. This is apparent from *Protecting the Public*, the White Paper which preceded the enactment of the Sexual Offences Act 2003. Although this relates to the criminal law, it can be seen as reflecting current thinking generally. Children are regarded as vulnerable and abusers are seen as predatory. The assumption that there has been an abuse of power persists in cases involving children irrespective of consent: [70]

> [48] There may be circumstances where sexual activity takes place with the ostensible consent of both parties but where one of the parties is in such a great position of power over the other that the sexual activity is wrong and should come within the realms of the criminal law. The most obvious cases involve children and vulnerable people with learning disabilities or mental disorders. (Home Office 2002)

Section 13 of the Sexual Offences Act 2003 introduces a new offence: 'Child sex offences committed by children or young persons'. Sections 25 and 26 create the new offences of 'Sexual activity with a child family member'[71] and 'Inciting a child family member to engage in sexual activity'[72] respectively. These are also explained in terms of power and exploitation:

> [52] ... While it is recognised that much sexual activity involving children under the age of consent might be consensual and experimental and that, in such cases, the intervention of the

---

[66] See MacLeod and Saraga (1988) pp 36–37.

[67] See Smart (1989b) p 50. Compare Howitt (1993) p 108.

[68] See Finkelhor (1986) p 126ff. See also Briggs (1995), ch 8.

[69] See Finkelhor and Baron (1986) pp 61–64. See also n 1 above.

[70] Piper (2000) argues that children are seen as 'unsexualised' in our society and there is little room, in our conception of childhood, for self-willed sexual activity.

[71] Replacing incest under the Sexual Offences Act 1956.

[72] Replacing the offence of incitement to commit incest, s 54 Criminal Law Act 1977.

criminal law may not be appropriate, the criminal law must make provision for an unlawful sexual activity charge to be brought where the sexual activity was consensual but was also clearly manipulative. (Home Office 2002)

[58] ... **Familial sexual abuse of a child**, will capture the sexual abuse and exploitation of children within the family unit. It is recognised that the balance of power within the family and the close and trusting relationships that exist make children particularly vulnerable to abuse within its environment. (Home Office 2002)

**Q** What response does this explanation suggest is needed?

## VIII. THE 'HIGH RISK' FAMILY

As we have seen, theories of causation entailing radical social, economic or cultural change have had little impact on the law, the politics or the practice of child protection. The perspective that has predominated in shaping policy and social work practice, and which can be discerned in the 'integrated model' and in family systems theory, locates the primary 'causes' of child abuse firmly within the family.[73] This approach differs from the pathological model in that, while it admits of psychiatric disorder or 'defect in character structure'[74] as an explanation in some cases, it does not postulate this as the single 'cause' of abuse; social and economic stress are also included. Nevertheless, child abuse is conceptualised as having its roots in the pathological personalities of parents or in dysfunctional families (Parton 1985 p 152); psychological make-up, responses to stress and family dynamics are crucial.

The child protection system assumes that the family or individual family members can be 'diagnosed'. It assumes that, in consequence, abuse can be predicted or at least identified and abusers can be offered treatment. It places reliance on health and welfare professionals who are seen as having the requisite expertise to fulfil these tasks and so protect children.[75] In particular, it relies on professionals to identify high-risk cases.[76] Indeed, the assumed ability to do so is fundamental to the belief that children can be protected and that this can be achieved without undermining the philosophy underlying the liberal state: 'In theory, the identification of the actual or potentially dangerous individual or family provides the mechanism for both ensuring that children are protected while also avoiding unwarrantable interventions.' (Parton 1992 p 103)

Part of the expertise of professionals charged with identifying high risk cases is their knowledge of 'risk factors' that are said to serve as indicators of such cases. Factors that have been identified in the past have included signs in children; statements from children; unplanned and unwanted pregnancy; abuse of the parent during childhood; a

---

[73] See Parton (1985) pp 132–33. Parton traces the dominant model to the work of Kempe and his team who saw child abuse as a disease and the parents as carriers (1991 pp 57–58).
[74] See Parton (1991) p 58.
[75] Parton (1985) p 149.
[76] See, eg, London Borough of Brent (1985) p 289.

history of violence; emotional neglect; and social and economic stress.[77] And as social science knowledge changes, those factors categorised as risk factors change. So, for example, substance abuse by parents and mental illness are now seen as major risk factors.[78] In addition, it is now accepted that children living in violent families are exposed to increased risk; men who abuse their partners are likely to abuse children as well.[79] Children who witness domestic violence are also considered damaged as a result.

The *Framework for the Assessment of Children in Need and their Families* (DoH 2000b) is the most recent attempt to assist professionals to judge whether a child is in need, whether the child is suffering or likely to suffer significant harm, what action should be taken and what services would best meet the needs of the child and the family (p viii). It embodies what is described as an ecological approach and requires assessments to take account of three domains:

- **The child's developmental needs;**
- **The parents' or caregivers' capacities to respond appropriately;**
- **The wider family and environmental factors.**

(para 1.40, bold in original)

The assessment is therefore one that examines not only the personal characteristics of the parents and children but also highlights factors such as income, employment and community resources. Cooper, *et al*, describe this as 'a psychosocial model for thinking about child and family problems' (2003 p 18) and suggest that it is a positive innovation which 'has the potential to raise the standard of assessment throughout the country' (*ibid*).[80] Nevertheless, it does not make identifying child abuse or the risk of abuse an easy task.

## Identifying and Predicting Child Abuse

The difficulty that besets the child protection system is that, while professional knowledge and expertise are assumed to facilitate the accurate identification or prediction of child abuse, this assumption is, it seems, unfounded.

A number of child abuse inquiries have concluded that child welfare professionals have failed to carry out their tasks satisfactorily. These failures, says Ashenden (2004 pp 11 and 19), are often attributed to lack of resources and inadequate training. They provoke criticisms of workers[81] as well as recommendations for better training[82] and closer supervision.[83] However, at times, a more fundamental problem is identified: an insufficient knowledge base. This deficit, says Ashenden, calls into question the very legitimacy of intervention in the family by child protection agencies. Such crises in child protection lead to calls for more research and the development of better predictive tech-

[77] See Parton (1985) pp 135–36; DoH (1995a) p 14; DoH (1991b) p 63. 'Social exclusion', the terminology used in *Working Together* refers to the disadvantage arising out of poverty (DoH, Home Office and DfEE 1999 para 2.20).
[78] See DoH (2000b) para 2.21; Sinclair and Bullock (2002) p 18.
[79] See DoH (2000b) para 2.22.
[80] See also Sinclair and Bullock (2002) p 26.
[81] See London Borough of Brent (1985) p 289; London Borough of Greenwich (1987) pp 106–7; Laming (2003). See also Sinclair and Bullock (2002) p 40.
[82] See, for example, Laming (2003) Recommendations 14, 31 and 37.
[83] See, for example, Laming (2003) Recommendation 30.

niques.[84] 'Better' experts are summoned before inquiries to evaluate the expertise and professionalism of the experts and professionals involved in the case and who are deemed to have failed. These 'better' experts are seen as offering the promise of more 'reliable' expertise. In this way, says Ashenden, the legitimacy of the system is restored.[85]

King (1995b) suggests that child welfare professionals are faced with an impossible task. They must, however, give the impression that they are able to accomplish their professional goals successfully, he says. He too maintains that the need to give the impression that the child protection system can 'work' leads to the accumulation of ever more extensive 'knowledge' about child abuse which is used to legitimate decisions. And when things go wrong, he says, organisations adopt coping strategies such as the introduction of increasingly detailed regulation.[86] These strategies serve to convince the members of these organisations, as well as the outside world, that mistakes arise from remediable faults, such as inefficiency or failure to observe the proper procedures, rather than the uncertainties inherent in child protection work (1997 pp 439–40).[87]

Yet Cooper, *et al*, (2003 p 13) complain that procedures fail to distinguish between cases which are serious and those which are not. In addition, they come to dominate decision-making (*ibid*),[88] partly because they also operate to give some protection to professionals if things go wrong.[89] But the risk-averseness that these rules represent and that permeates the child protection system, say Cooper, *et al*, has detrimental effects on practice:

> Systems of risk assessment and management are oriented almost entirely to minimising risk of extreme failure, and never to promoting creative and acceptable risk taking in pursuit of good outcomes for children. Equally, the systems of professional accountability which have developed in tandem with the risk-averse culture, are almost exclusively oriented to locating responsibility and blame and accounting for error and failure, and almost never to encouraging responsibility (in the sense of [professional] autonomy) or acknowledging the inevitability of failure. In short, these methodologies are ill adapted to the complexity, uncertainty and indeterminacy of the functions to which they are applied. (Cooper, *et al*, 2003 pp 57)

So failures are inevitable because predicting abuse is very difficult,[90] as a Department of Health publication, *Child Abuse: A Study of Inquiry Reports 1980–1989*, acknowledges:

---

[84] See, eg, London Borough of Brent (1985) pp 288–89. See also Audit Commission (1994).

[85] See Ashenden (2004) p 164.

[86] See further on the proceduralisation of social work, King (1997), ch 4. See, on the use of regulations, Smith (2000).

[87] As Becker (1963) p 157 observes, those charged with enforcing rules devised to deal with social problems must be able to show that their attempts at enforcement are 'effective and worthwhile', while at the same time demonstrating that the problem still exists and that their services are still needed to control it.

[88] See also Cooper, *et al*, (2003) pp 18–19. Cooper, *et al*, (2003) also refer to the mechanisms relied on by professionals in order to cope with the uncertainties inherent in child protection; they tend to 'fall back into denial, optimism, a checklist mentality or the use of other unhelpful defensive risk avoidance techniques' (p 59).

[89] See Cooper, *et al*, (2003) p 11.

[90] See also Sutton (1981); Howitt (1993) p 31. For Howitt, (pp 123–24) though, the problem goes deeper than the possibility of mistaking warning signals. He maintains that it is the child protection process that is at fault and that produces 'errors'. This process involves checking the characteristics of a suspected abuser against a 'social template' to see whether he or she fits a particular pattern ('templating'); the deployment of theories not amenable to testing ('justificatory theorising'—eg, denial of abuse will give rise to an assessment that the family cannot be worked with, even if the denial might be true); and the building up of an irreversible momentum towards intervention ('ratcheting').

It is not possible confidently to predict who will be an abuser, for the potential for abuse is widespread and often triggered by the particular conjunction of circumstances which is unpredictable. Almost anyone with whom the professionals work could be an abuser, and when an incident 'breaks' it is also easy to look back with the confidence of hindsight and to see cues that were missed, small mistakes and tell tale signs. (DoH 1991g p 63)

An examination of 40 serious case reviews involving cases where children died or were seriously injured came to similar conclusions. Of the cases studied, only one was classified as 'highly predictable' and three were 'highly preventable' (Sinclair and Bullock 2002 pp 46 and 96).[91] The authors observe that the predictive value of known indicators of abuse is limited (pp 17–18). The likelihood of abuse depends on an 'interplay of a range of factors' and it is not possible to determine the significance of particular features or characteristics (p 18). They go on to say that: 'Even if the forecasts of future abuse were accurate, attempts to predict which of those children would be murdered or suffer serious injury are virtually impossible' (p 18). As the Foreword to the study says, '[i]n some cases, the abuse occurred out of the blue, in others it occurred in a context of low level need and occasionally it arose in situations where it seemed to have been "waiting to happen"' (p i).

Nevertheless Sinclair and Bullock fall into the category of those calling for more knowledge and better practice. What they say is that, although child deaths are 'unpredictable and unpreventable', more could be known and done (2002 pp 62, 64). Cooper, *et al*, take a different approach, stressing the need to concentrate on outcomes rather than diagnosis and risk (2003 pp 59–60).

We shall see later in this chapter that the most recent child protection policy documents do indeed stress outcomes rather than procedures. But the likelihood is, perhaps, that outcomes will become one of the criteria against which professionals' performance will be evaluated, so increasing accountability.[92] Furthermore, the identification of children at risk is still seen as a central function of child welfare professionals. So it may well be that future child abuse inquiries will focus on professionals' failure to achieve satisfactory outcomes as well as their failure to identify risk. This will, perhaps, in turn, lead to calls for yet further research, greater knowledge and more training in an ongoing effort to secure both objectives.[93]

## IX. THE ROLE OF PROFESSIONALS AND THE LAW

### *The Children Act 1989—The Background*

The Children Act 1989 is part of the continuing drive to show that the child protection system can function effectively to protect children and that it can accomplish this goal with the minimum of coercive state intervention. It was enacted at least in part in response to what were seen as flaws in the practices and procedures adopted by child

---

[91] Twelve of the 40 children were 'completely unknown to their local social services department at the time of the incident' (Sinclair and Bullock 2002 p 27).

[92] See, for example, DfES (2004c) p 2.

[93] Ashenden speculates that, without change in the way we think about child protection, 'crises' will be repeated indefinitely (2004 p 210).

protection personnel as well as deficiencies in the law. Political pressure reflecting concerns about the functioning of the child care system led to the setting up of a working party to consider reform. The report of this body, the *Review of Child Care Law* (DHSS 1985), adverted to a number of factors pointing to the need for change. Among these was the perception that children should be seen as the holders of rights. In addition, there was seen to be a need for clear demarcations of powers between social workers and the courts and for greater accountability of social workers.

The *Review* emphasised that, in most cases, the interests of children are best served by allowing them to be brought up by their families and that parents should be allowed 'to undertake their natural and legal responsibility to care for their own children' (para 2.8).[94] Even where a child could not remain at home, the emphasis should be on working 'in partnership with rather than in opposition to his parents, and to work towards his return to them' (*ibid*). '[T]he state', it went on, 'should only be able compulsorily to intervene where the child is being or is at risk of being harmed if it does not' (para 2.15).

**Q** Is the use of the word 'natural' significant? To what extent does the approach adopted in the Review reflect adherence to the notion of family privacy?

At the same time that these policies promoting the autonomy of the family and voluntary co-operation were being formulated, a number of inquiries into child deaths during the 1980s stressed the need to intervene decisively to protect children at risk. The inquiry into the death of Jasmine Beckford (London Borough of Brent 1985) criticised social workers for operating under the 'rule of optimism'. The operation of this rule, identified by Dingwall, *et al*, (1983), leads professionals to assume that parents love their children and that they are 'honest, competent and caring' (p 89). Instead, the Beckford Report states, social workers should be able to identify 'high risk' cases and, in such cases, '[s]ociety should sanction ... the removal of such children for an appreciable time' (London Borough of Brent 1985 p 289). Similarly, the inquiry into the death of Kimberly Carlile (London Borough of Greenwich 1987),[95] who was abused by her step-father, criticised social workers for failing to be alert to danger signals.

While these inquiries criticised social services for doing too little too late, the Cleveland crisis[96] raised very different issues. During 1987, a paediatrician based in Cleveland, with the help of a colleague, began to use a new and controversial method of diagnosing sexual abuse. Their use of the reflex anal dilatation test, along with other indicators, led to the diagnosis of an unprecedented number of children as having been sexually abused. There were not enough resources to deal with the number of children taken into emergency care as a result. Local newspapers published the story and the local MP asserted that the parents had been subjected to great injustice. Parents in turn set up a pressure group PAIN (Parents Against Injustice) to lobby for their cause. Carol Smart observes that: 'Although it appears on the surface to be a panic about child sexual abuse within the family, it was in fact a panic over parents' rights. ...What appeared to

[94] These principles are echoed in Art 9 of the UN Convention on the Rights of the Child. This states that children should not be separated against their will from their parents, except by process of law, and only where necessary in their best interests. Abuse and neglect are cited as justifiable reasons for separating children from parents. Where so separated, children have a right to contact with their parents except where contrary to their best interests.
[95] See also London Borough of Lambeth (1987).
[96] Like the events in Rochdale and the Orkneys. See SSI (1990); Clyde (1992).

be a concern for children became deflected into a concern to protect the nuclear family from any outside interference.' (1989b p 62)

The report of the inquiry set up as a result of the events in Cleveland (Butler-Sloss 1988) had a significant effect on the content of the Children Act 1989. While there was criticism of the over-reliance on medical evidence in diagnosing abuse, and there was criticism of misunderstandings of their roles between the professionals, the report is perhaps most notable for its emphasis on the importance of the law in cases of child abuse and, in particular, the importance of parents' rights: '[p]arents alone (except possibly in wardship) have inherent rights and obligations in respect of a child' (p 227). It emphasised the need for parents to be kept informed and, where appropriate, to be consulted by the professionals involved in the investigation; it stated that parents should always be advised of their rights of appeal or complaint in respect of any decisions made; and it instructs social services to confirm important decisions in writing and to give parents the opportunity to take legal advice (p 246).

Nevertheless the report, like those that preceded it, went on to affirm that:

Social workers have a duty in law to ensure the protection of children where they have cause to believe that there is a high risk of further immediate abuse. If that risk cannot be mollified by the withdrawal from the home of the person whose behaviour is believed to pose a risk to the child; or the non-abusing parent cannot be relied upon to protect the child; and in the absence of the parents' agreement to the child's admission to hospital, an application to magistrates ... may be inevitable. (Butler-Sloss 1988 para 13.4)

**Q** Are the messages coming out of the Jasmine Beckford inquiry and the Cleveland Report contradictory? How can the law ensure that children are protected while still protecting parents' 'inherent rights'?

## The Children Act 1989

The Children Act 1989 was passed in the context of political pressure favouring a reorientation of policy away from interventionism towards a greater emphasis on family autonomy. Intervention between parent and child was again increasingly becoming conceived of as interference with the natural order of things. Nevertheless, it was considered a necessary evil to prevent or terminate a worse evil: child abuse. The only justification for coercive intervention, therefore, would be 'reliable' evidence of abuse or the risk of abuse.

It has been said that the Act 'strikes a new balance between family autonomy and the protection of children' (DoH 1989b p iii). This balance is most apparent in the stress on 'partnership' with families. At the centre of the notion of partnership is the promotion of co-operation and consultation between all those concerned with child protection,[97] including local authorities, parents and the children themselves.[98] The discussion that follows focuses on partnership between local authorities and parents.

**Q** What do you understand by the term 'partnership'?

---

[97] This is the focus of the Children Act 2004.
[98] See Kaganas (1995); and Masson (1995). See also DoH, Home Office and DfEE (1999) para 3.6.

*Partnership*

We will argue that partnership serves a dual function. First, it promotes the ideology that it is the family, rather than the state, that should be responsible for children. Secondly, it enables the liberal state to maintain its legitimacy by restricting coercive intervention in families while still regulating them. ‾‾‾‾‾‾‾‾‾‾‾‾‾‾‾‾‾‾‾‾‾‾‾‾‾‾‾‾
~~Partnership is discussed extensively in government~~ publications such as the Guidance and Regulations that supplement the Children Act 1989 and, although the legislation itself contains no reference to the term, it includes a number of measures designed to give effect to the partnership philosophy. Local authorities have a duty to promote the upbringing of children within their families and, in order to facilitate this, to provide support for families of children in need.[99] This extends to providing accommodation for children in need[100] in a way that does not stigmatise the parents or restrict their parental responsibility.[101] Section 20(7) provides that a local authority may not provide accommodation against the wishes of a person who has parental responsibility for the child and who is willing and able to provide or to arrange for accommodation. Section 20(8) stipulates that any person who has parental responsibility for a child may at any time remove that child from local authority accommodation. As the White Paper that preceded the Act states, local authority accommodation should:

> be seen as a positive response to the needs of families and not as a mark of failure either on the part of the family or those professionals and others working to support them. An essential characteristic of this service should be its voluntary character, that it should be based clearly in continuing parental agreement and operate as far as possible on a basis of partnership and co-operation between the local authority and parents. (DHSS 1987 para 21)

Even where there is some risk to a child, the policy behind the Act, and articulated in the Guidance and Regulations, is that coercive intervention should be avoided if possible. Schedule 2 to the Act (para 7) directs local authorities to take reasonable steps to reduce the need to bring proceedings for care or supervision orders. *Working Together*, a document containing guidance for agencies and professionals,[102] states that even when there is evidence of abuse or neglect, most children remain with their families (DoH, Home Office and DfEE 1999 para 5.44). 'In the great majority of cases', it says, 'children are safeguarded from harm by working with parents, family members and other significant adults in the child's life to make the child safe, and to promote his or her development, within the family setting' (para 3.8). Alternatively, local authorities must consider whether accommodation on a voluntary basis is sufficient to safeguard the child's safety (DoH 1995a para 5.3).

---

[99] S 17.

[100] S 20.

[101] The only powers that can be exercised by a local authority are those delegated to it by the parents (s 2(9)) or the power to do what is reasonable in the circumstances for the purpose of safeguarding or promoting the child's welfare (s 3(5)). The Act repealed s 3 of the Child Care Act 1980 which enabled local authorities to assume parental rights over children in what was known as 'voluntary care' by means of an administrative process. It also abolished the old statutory requirement that a parent wishing to remove a child from 'voluntary care' give notice to the local authority of this intention.

[102] This document replaces the 1991 version of *Working Together*. Like its predecessor, it was issued under s 7 of the Local Authority Social Services Act 1970. It does not have statutory force but should be complied with in the absence of exceptional circumstances.

Compulsory intervention is seen as a last resort. This approach finds expression in the 'non-intervention principle' embodied in Section 1(5) of the Act which enjoins the court to refrain from making orders unless there is some positive advantage to the child in doing so: 'Where a court is considering whether or not to make one or more orders under this Act with respect to a child, it shall not make the order or any of the orders unless it considers that doing so would be better for the child than making no order at all.'

As far as child welfare professionals are concerned, *Working Together* makes it clear that they should not normally intervene unless invited to do so by the family. The aim is to 'promote access to a range of services for children in need without inappropriately triggering the child protection processes' (DoH, Home Office and DfEE 1999 para 2.26).

> Only in exceptional cases should there be compulsory intervention in family life: for example, where this is necessary to safeguard a child from significant harm. Such intervention should—provided this is consistent with the safety and welfare of the child—support families in making their own plans for the welfare and protection of their children.
>
> (DoH, Home Office and DfEE 1999 para 1.5)

Even in cases where there is a finding of 'significant harm' to the child and compulsory intervention in the form of an emergency protection order, care order or supervision order is necessary, local authority social services are still expected to work in partnership with parents.[103] For example, parents are normally entitled to have contact with their children while they are in local authority care[104] and also to have a say in their upbringing.[105] While the local authority acquires parental responsibility pursuant to an emergency protection order[106] or a care order,[107] the parents still retain their parental responsibility, albeit in a curtailed form, in terms of Section 2(6).

> **[Q]** Why do parents who have been found wanting in respect of their ability to care for their child retain parental responsibility when that child is taken into local authority care? Why are local authorities expected to work in partnership with such parents? What is the practical significance of these measures?

*Partnership—The Emphasis on Parental Responsibility*

Eekelaar (1991a) argues that the Act encompasses two concepts of responsibility. First, what he calls '*responsibility (1)*', refers to the duties parents have to take care of and provide for their children. '*Responsibility (2)*', on the other hand, refers to the idea that parents are entitled to bring up their children without interference from others or the state.

Reviewing the provisions of the Children Act 1989, as well as the official documentation that followed it, he concludes that the legislation evidences an emphasis on '*responsibility (2)*'. In support of this contention, he draws attention to the fact that the

---

[103] See DoH, Home Office and DfEE (1999) para 7.3.
[104] S 34.
[105] See, eg, s 22(4).
[106] S 44(4)(c).
[107] S 33(3)(a).

law conceives of parental responsibility as individual responsibility; it vests in parents, or, in their absence, other individuals in preference to the state. He also notes that parental responsibility may not be voluntarily surrendered to the state and that parental responsibility remains in parents when care of their children is shared with the state.

> The truth of the situation where parental responsibility has been assumed by an authority under a Care Order is that the parent is unable to exercise *responsibility (1)*: indeed, he has been deprived of the opportunity to do so because he has failed to exercise it competently. The 're-sponsibility' which the parent retains under the Act is *responsibility (2)*. But, split from *responsibility (1)*, this second sense of responsibility appears nakedly ideological. ...[I]t is a statement that, despite realities, it remains the parent's rather than the authority's role to look after the child, either because that is what nature ordained ('their very parenthood') or because it is a desirable social ordering. (1991a p 45, emphasis in original)

He goes on to question the suggestion that the reduction of control over parents will encourage them to behave more 'responsibly' towards their children:

> In other words, [it is said] that the promotion of *responsibility (2)* encourages *responsibility (1)*, or, as the Secretary of State put it: 'The Bill's emphasis on the primary function of parent-hood will, we hope, sharpen our perceptions and highlight the obligation on parents to care for their children and bring them up properly' (House of Commons Debates, vol 151, col 1107). ... [The] apparent confinement to parents [of the theory that the more freedom people are given the more likely it is that it will be used wisely] may reflect a deeper belief that, given freedom from state regulation, parents will *naturally* care for their offspring; that the fact of parenthood itself provides sufficient assurance. It may be asked whether the historical record justifies such a view. (pp 49–50, emphasis in original)

**Q** What 'ideology' do you think Eekelaar is referring to? Where does the Children Act 1989 place primary responsibility for children—in the private or the public sphere?

*Partnership—Regulating the Family*

While Eekelaar sees partnership in terms of a withdrawal of the state and the placing of primary responsibility for children on families, official documentation gives prominence to the ideas of family autonomy and empowerment. The most recent guidance on part-nership is contained in *Working Together*: [108]

> 7.2 Family members have a unique role and importance in the lives of children, who attach great value to their family relationships. Family members know more about their family than any professional could possibly know, and well-founded decisions about a child should draw upon this knowledge and understanding. Family members should normally have the right to know what is being said about them, and to contribute to important decisions about their lives and those of their children. Research findings brought together in *Child Protection: Messages from Research* endorse the importance of good relationships between professionals and fami-lies in helping to bring about the best possible outcomes for children.
>
> (DoH, Home Offfice, DfEE 1999)

---

[108] See also DoH (1995a) paras 2.1–2.6; DoH (2000b) paras 1.44–1.47.

The government has again, more recently, endorsed the importance, in order to improve the outcomes for children, of 'listening to children, young people and their families when assessing and planning service provision, as well as in face-to face delivery' (DfES 2004d para 1.2).[109] Partnership, according to this account, is a way of respecting the rights of families and the children in them[110] as well as a way of furthering children's beat interests.

Partnership can take several forms. In the *Challenge of Partnership*, the Department of Health identified four approaches: providing information to families; involvement of family members; participation of family members; and partnership (DoH 1995a para 2.7).[111] It acknowledges that involvement may sometimes be 'predominantly passive and amount to little more than receiving information, having a non-contributory presence at meetings, endorsing other people's decisions or making minor decisions' (para 2.12). When involvement includes contribution to discussions and decision-making on key issues, this makes family members active participants (*ibid*). However, their role is a limited one.

Partnership
2.13 The objective of any partnership between families and professionals must be the protection and welfare of the child; partnership should not be an end in itself. From the outset workers should consider the possibility of a partnership with each family based on openness, mutual trust, joint decision making and a willingness to listen to families and to capitalise on their strengths. However, words such as equality, choice and power have a limited meaning at certain points in the child protection process. There are times when professional agencies have statutory responsibilities that they have to fulfil and powers that they have to use for the benefit of the child. (DoH 1995a para 2.13)[112]

*Working Together* is phrased slightly more strongly, asserting that there should be 'a *presumption* of openness, joint decision making, and a willingness to listen to families'. (DoH, Home Office and DfEE 1999 para 7.6, emphasis added). Families must be told of agencies that give advice and provide advocacy (paras 7.19–7.23); they should be given all the information they need to understand the child protection process (paras 7.22–7.23); and their racial, ethnic and cultural identities should be taken into account (paras 7.24–7.25). However, 'the overarching principle should always be to act ... in the best interests of the child' (para 7.6).

Children's involvement, in particular, is addressed along with that of other family members. Children and young people must be 'made to understand the extent and nature of their involvement in decision-making and the planning processes' (para 7.12). They should be 'helped to understand' how they can contribute to decision-making in accordance with their 'age and understanding' (*ibid*). But they also have to understand that 'ultimately, decisions will be taken in the light of all the available information contributed by themselves, professionals, their parents and other family members, and other significant adults' (*ibid*).

109 See also DfES (2004c) p 2.
110 See, on partnership with children, DoH, Home Office and DfEE (1999) paras 7.11–7.12. See also s 53 Children Act 2004, which amends the Children Act 1989, ss 17, 20 and 47 to place more emphasis on children's wishes and feelings.
111 The term 'partnership' appears to have two meanings in this document, one more general and one more specific.
112 See also DoH, Home Office and DfEE (1999) paras 7.5–7.6.

**Q** You were asked about your understanding of partnership above. Has this understanding changed? Are the partners in the child protection process equals? To what extent are parents empowered? To what extent are children empowered?

Kaganas[113] argues that choice and power lie largely in the hands of the child protection professionals:

> It is this concept of parental responsibility that is the linchpin of the partnership ideology. ... [I]t can be argued that responsibility in the first sense [referring to Eekelaar above], the withdrawal of the state, is made possible by the prevailing assumption that responsibility in the second sense is in fact met by parents, that parents are indeed dutiful and responsible. ...
>
> Because partnership rests on the assumption that parents are responsible and reasonable, difficulties ensue when they do not conform to this model. ...
>
> There are two very serious obstacles to meaningful partnership with parents. On one hand, if workers cling too faithfully to its tenets in practice, partnership might place children at risk. And, on the other hand, the discourse of partnership might be deployed as rhetoric to mask the very real coercive power that responsible authorities have over families judged to be irresponsible. ... (1995 pp 8–9)

> [N]ot all the parties have the freedom to choose whether to enter into a partnership relationship. It is the professional partners who decide whether it is fitting to extend an offer of partnership to the family members. On the basis of their assessment of the family, they decide whether partnership is possible and, if so, to what extent.[114] They also largely determine the tasks that family members must perform in order to sustain the partnership.[115] In all this, they are free to discount the views and wishes of their supposed partners. But a rebellious family that refuses to work with the professionals or attempts to ignore their views will find that it cannot safely do so; it will simply be subjected to coercive measures. For those judged irresponsible and unreasonable, the partnership, if it exists at all, will be of the most rudimentary nature. Clearly, then, the partnership is largely controlled by the professional partners.[116] (1995 p 11)

Lindley and Richards, although they concede that *Working Together* ensures that parents have information, also question whether it is possible for a 'true partnership' to develop (2000 p 222):[117]

> The term 'partnership' implies equality between partners. Yet it is inevitable that when the state intervenes in family life on a compulsory basis such equality is not achievable, because

---

[113] See also Aldgate (2001) p 67.

[114] See, for example, DoH, Home Office and DfEE (1999) para 7.7. The professionals decide what is and is not negotiable.

[115] See, for example, DoH, Home Office and DfEE (1999) para 5.88. Arguably, the proposals for change made by Cooper, *et al*, are susceptible to the same analysis. They advocate giving families the 'opportunity' to change. They must 'cooperate with the professionals or eventually face a less negotiated form of intervention' (2003 p 67).

[116] See, for example, on participation in child protection conferences, DoH, Home Office and DfEE (1999) paras 5.57–5.58.

[117] The authors suggest that advice and advocacy for parents can enhance partnership. They report that parents and social workers find this helpful and that such work can 'ease communication with the parents, and help them to understand the issues and engage in partnership' (Lindley and Richards 2000 p 225). However, it is not apparent from their findings that parents are necessarily empowered as a result; it seems, rather, that they are often persuaded to 'come round' to the professionals' point of view. Indeed in Lindley, *et al*, (2001 p 182), it is reported that most advocates in the study encouraged parents to co-operate in most cases. While parents were, for instance, helped to express themselves and to participate in meetings, they were also helped to understand the risk, to accept the professionals' decisions and to understand the local authority social services view (p 185).

ultimately, such intervention may involve the local authority overriding the parents' wishes.

(Lindley and Richards 2000 p 222)

[Social workers] are expected to make inquiries about the child's safety and welfare, whilst simultaneously empowering parents to be actively involved in the planning and decision-making process. When the inquiries result in a plan being made which is prescriptive about how the parents should care for their child, the local authority is effectively placing restrictions on how they may exercise their parental responsibility. Social workers are therefore being required to empower people whose power they are themselves circumscribing. (p 223)

Parents are expected to co-operate with any assessment, planning and monitoring which the local authority may require following registration [on the child protection register], otherwise they risk an application being made for a compulsory order ... .

Although it may be conducted under the guise of partnership and agreement, the degree of informal coercion exercised in these circumstances can be quite considerable. Indeed, the familiar practice of persuading parents to agree to their child being accommodated, with the threat of a compulsory order being applied for if they do not comply, has been documented.[118]

(p 224, reference omitted)

For King, partnership is a useful device that enables surveillance of the family to be carried out by professionals without disturbing the balance between the family and the state:

To appreciate the importance of this device for politics and thus for government, we need to refer to ... the paradox of child protection and respect for parental rights. Seen in the light of these seemingly incompatible objectives, what the notion of partnership does is to allow officials to intrude upon the privacy of family life, while maintaining intact the structure of parental and family rights. Instead of trampling on the sacred ground of family life, the social worker takes on the status of a third parent, or, in the case of single-parent families, a second or substitute parent, involved with the other parent in a joint enterprise to promote the child's welfare. This is not to suggest in any way that partnership arrangements are necessarily one-sided. The agreements may well place parents or other care-givers in a better position to secure support and services for themselves and for the child than might have been the case if the responsibilities to the social services department had not been specified in a semi-formal manner.

It hardly needs to be stated, however, that local authority social service departments charged by government with the protection of children have much to gain from entering into partnership arrangements with parents. Partnership operates for them as an observation post sited in the midst of family life from where, under ideal conditions, all the activities of the family may be noted, and reported back to case conferences and planning meetings. Partnership then allows the social worker to play the part of an ethologist, while leaving the political environment, the delicate balance between family and state, between private and public, largely undisturbed. (1995a pp 149–50, footnotes omitted)

'Partnership failure' provides proof of the parents' deficiencies and hence the justification for the intrusion into the private sphere and 'all the information that the social services and other agencies acquired during the partnership is now reproduced in court in the form of evidence that the child is being abused or neglected' (King 1995a p 150).

**Q** To what extent do these analyses reflect Donzelot's concept of tutelage?

---

[118] See also Aldgate (2001) p 51.

*Family Group Conferences*

Another, more recent, innovation in the context of child protection that is said to empower families is the family group conference. This is deployed as a mechanism for making decisions about children 'at risk' as well as 'in need'.[119] The composition and the functions of the family group conference are described in *Working Together*:

> 7.14 FGCs are a process through which family members, including those in the wider family, are enabled to meet together to find solutions to difficulties which they and a child or young person in their family are facing. FGCs are not just a one-off meeting. They are an approach to planning and decision-making which uses the skills and experience of the wider family, as well as professionals. The definition of who is in a family should come from the family itself. It includes parents and extended family, as well as friends, neighbours and community members if they are considered part of the child's 'family'.
> 7.15 FGCs may be appropriate in a number of contexts where there is a plan or decision to be made. FGCs do not replace or remove the need for child protection conferences, which should always be held when the relevant criteria are met … . They may be valuable, for example:

> - for children in need, in a range of circumstances where a plan is required for the child's future welfare;
> - where s 47 enquiries[120] do not substantiate referral concerns about significant harm but where there is a need for support and services;
> - where s 47 enquiries progress to a child protection conference,[121] the conference may agree that an FGC is an appropriate vehicle for the core group to use to develop the outline child protection plan into a fully worked-up plan.

> (DoH, Home Office and DfEE 1999)

First introduced in New Zealand and based on traditional Maori practice, the family group conference process gives the task of decision-making to the family rather than the child-care professionals.

**Q** Refer to chapter 11. To what extent is this process similar to mediation? To what extent might it give rise to similar problems?

The procedure evokes some anxiety among professionals about imbalances of power within the family and the risk that some members will be silenced or dominated by others (Lupton, *et al*, 1995 para 5.2.6). One study, conducted by Lupton, *et al*, reveals that this did occur in a minority of cases (1995 para 5.6.4). Some family members interviewed also indicated that family tension and hostility created problems (*ibid*). Nevertheless, the available research indicates that there is general satisfaction among families and professionals with family group conferences.[122] In particular, proponents of the model argue that among its virtues is the fact that it extends the partnership principle and empowers families (Lupton, *et al*, 1995 para 6.1). While parental involvement in the form of partnership can appear 'tokenistic' (Lupton, *et al*, 1995 para 2.2.8), the family group conference procedure is promoted as transferring power 'from the hands of faceless state officials to the family and the community' (King 1997 p 140).

---

[119] See Lupton, *et al*, (1995) para 2.5.3.
[120] See ch 17.
[121] See ch 17.
[122] See Lupton, *et al*, (1995); Crow and Marsh (1997).

Yet, on closer analysis, this transfer is limited. There are certain decisions that the family is not permitted to make. For example, they cannot decide whether to place the child's name on the child protection register or to remove it (Lupton, *et al*, 1995 para 3.5.7). *Working Together* makes it clear that it is the professionals who set the parameters of the discussion:

> 7.16 It is essential that all parties are provided with clear and accurate information, which will make effective planning possible. The family is the primary planning group in the process. Family members need to be able to understand what the issues are from the perspective of the professionals. The family and involved professionals should be clear about:
>
> - what are the professional findings from any core assessment of the child and family;
> - what the family understand about their current situation;
> - what decisions are required;
> - what decisions have already been taken;
> - what is the family's scope of decision-making, and whether there are any issues/decisions which are not negotiable; *and*
> - what resources are or might be available to implement any plan
>
> Within this framework, agencies and professionals should agree to support the plan if it does not place the child at risk of significant harm, and if the resources requested can be provided.
>
> (DoH, Home Office and DfEE 1999)

That it is the professionals who have the final say means that the family unit is allowed to make decisions only within the confines of pre-defined notions of what is harmful to children (King 1997 p 158). The privacy of the family can be preserved only within constraints set by the professionals and the law. Where the child's safety is at stake, the family is not permitted to operate autonomously within its 'black box' (King 1997 p 159).

## X. LOCAL AUTHORITY LIABILITY

### *The Human Rights Act 1998*

Much of the jurisprudence that has developed around the European Convention for the Protection of Human Rights and Fundamental Freedoms 1950 (the European Convention) can be seen as consistent with the notion of partnership and with the aim of family participation in decision-making. It also reinforces the idea that compulsory intervention should be a last resort.

The Human Rights Act 1998 incorporates most of the provisions of the Convention and provides remedies for individuals whose rights have been infringed. Section 6(1) stipulates that it is unlawful for a public authority to act in a way that is incompatible with a Convention right, unless, as a result of the contents of primary legislation, it could not have acted differently.[123] Courts and local authorities are classified as public authorities and so are bound by the Act. A person who claims that a public authority has acted or proposes to act unlawfully in contravention of his or her rights may rely on

---

[123] S 6(2)(a).

the Convention rights within the context of existing legal proceedings or may bring a free-standing application.[124]

The HRA has created a cause of action for those harmed by the failure of a local authority to intervene to protect them. In *Z and Others v United Kingdom*[125] it was held by the ECtHR that the failure of a local authority to protect children from serious, long term neglect and abuse constituted a violation of Article 3, which prohibits torture, or inhuman or degrading treatment or punishment, and which requires the state to intervene to prevent ill-treatment of which the authorities knew or ought to have known.[126]

However, most of the case law focuses on protection of the family from intervention. The rights that are invoked most frequently in child protection cases are those enshrined in Articles 6 and 8. Article 6 states that everyone is entitled to a fair and public hearing in the determination his or her civil rights and obligations, or any criminal charge. This extends to a right to be involved in decisions to make, continue or discharge care orders.[127] Decisions about the child while a care order is in force may or may not affect the child's or the parents' rights.[128] The proceedings have to be examined as a whole to determine whether they were fair.[129]

Article 8 is quoted in full in chapter 8. It gives everyone a right to respect for private and family life. Case law has established that the 'mutual enjoyment by parent and child of each others' company constitutes a fundamental element of family life'.[130] The article also prohibits interference by a public authority with the rights to respect for private and family life, except to the extent that it is in accordance with the law, necessary in a democratic society and for the protection of health or morals, or for the protection of the rights and freedoms of others. The notion of necessity implies that the interference must correspond to a pressing social need and must be proportionate to a legitimate aim.[131] The reasons for interfering must be 'relevant' and 'sufficient'.[132] Protection of the interests of children can, potentially, justify interference as it is a legitimate aim; it falls within the ambit of the expressions 'protection of health' and the 'protection of the rights and freedoms of others'.[133] Consideration of what is in the best interests of the child is of 'crucial importance'.[134]

---

[124] S 7. Remedies are set out in s 8. Proceedings against local authorities under s 7 should be considered a longstop; other mechanisms such as judicial review may be appropriate: *Re S (Minors) (Care Order: Implementation of Care Plan); Re W (Minors) (Care Order: Adequacy of Care Plan)* [2002] UKHL 10; [2002] 1 FLR 815 para 62. Judicial review itself should only be considered when local authority actions cannot be challenged by other means such as through the provisions of the Children Act 1989: *Re M (Care Proceedings: Judicial Review)* [2003] EWHC Admin 850; [2003] 2 FLR 171. See also *Re L (Care Proceedings: Human Rights Claims)* [2003] EWHC Fam 665; [2003] 2 FLR 160.

[125] [2001] 2 FLR 612.

[126] Paras 74–5. This applies only if the local authority should have been aware of the abuse: *DP and JC v United Kingdom* [2003] 1 FLR 50, para 114. Nor is there a failure to protect the child's physical or moral integrity in breach of Art 8 unless the local authority ought to have been aware of the abuse: *DP and JC v United Kingdom* [2003] 1 FLR 50, para 119. See, also, on breach of Art 3 as a result of physical punishment, *A v United Kingdom (Human Rights: Punishment of Child)* [1998] 2 FLR 952.

[127] *Re S (Minors) (Care Order: Implementation of Care Plan); Re W (Minors) (Care Order: Adequacy of Care Plan)* [2002] UKHL 10; [2002] 1 FLR 815, paras 75–76.

[128] *Ibid*, paras 77–79. Decisions about contact and rehabilitation do affect rights.

[129] *Re V (Care: Pre-Birth Actions)* [2004] EWCA Civ 1575; [2005] 1 FLR 627.

[130] *W v United Kingdom* (1987) 10 EHRR 29, para 59; *Johansen v Norway* (1996) 23 EHRR 33, para 52; *K and T v Finland* [2001] 2 FLR 707, para 151; *P, C and S v United Kingdom* [2002] 2 FLR 631, para 113.

[131] *W v United Kingdom* (1987) 10 EHRR 29, para 60; *Re W and B; Re W(Care Plan)* [2001} EWCA Civ 757; [2001] 2 FLR 582, para 54; *Haase v Germany* [2004] 2 FLR 39, para 88.

[132] *K and T v Finland* [2001] 2 FLR 707, para 154; *P, C and S v United Kingdom* [2002] 2 FLR 631, para 114.

[133] *Olsson v Sweden (No 2)* (1992) 17 EHRR 134, para 119 (Commission), and para 84 (Court); *Haase v Germany* [2004] 2 FLR 39, para 87.

[134] *K and T v Finland* [2001] 2 FLR 707, para 154.

Article 8 has been interpreted as not only prohibiting unnecessary interference but also as imposing a positive obligation on the state: 'it must act in a manner calculated to allow those concerned to lead a normal family life'.[135] The provision has also been interpreted as imposing obligations of procedural fairness. For example, the court in *W v United Kingdom*[136] said that when making decisions about children, local authorities should take into account the views and interests of parents and that the parents should be given the opportunity to exercise any remedies available to them.[137] Parents must be involved in the decision-making process, 'seen as a whole', to a degree sufficient to provide them with the requisite protection of their interests, having regard to the circumstances and the serious nature of the decisions.[138] In *Re G (Care: Challenge to Local Authority's Decision)*,[139] the court provided some clarification of the extent of this duty:

[36] So Article 8 requires that parents are properly involved in the decision-making process not merely before the care proceedings are launched, and during the period when the care proceedings are on foot ... but also ... after the care proceedings have come to an end and whilst the local authority is implementing the care order.[140]

Removal of a child from the family is regarded as a drastic measure and should not be undertaken unless 'necessary';[141] consideration has to be given to other means by which the child's welfare and safety can be safeguarded.[142] In particular, there need to be 'compelling reasons' to justify removal of a newly born baby into public care.[143] Unless there are 'wholly exceptional circumstances', parents must be given adequate prior notice of any application for a court order and also be told of the evidence the local authority is relying on.[144] The situation must be shown to be urgent before emergency measures can be justified.[145]

In the event that children have to be removed from their parents, the care order should be regarded as a temporary measure; public authorities should make such efforts to arrange for the family to be reunited as can reasonably be expected.[146] A fair balance has to be struck between the interests of the parents in being reunited and those of the child, which may be best served by remaining in care. Parents are, in any event, not per-

135 *Marckx v Belgium* (1979) 2 EHRR 330, para 31.
136 (1988) 10 EHRR 29.
137 *Ibid*, para 63. See also para 62. This would normally entail attendance at meetings where decisions are being made: see also *Re M (Care: Challenging Decisions by Local Authority)* [2001] 2 FLR 1300, 1309 ff. Compare *C v Bury Metropolitan Borough Council* [2002] EWHC Fam 1438; [2002] 2 FLR 868.
138 *W v United Kingdom* (1988) 10 EHRR 29, para 64; *Re S (Minors) (Care Order: Implementation of Care Plan); Re W (Minors) (Care Order: Adequacy of Care Plan)* [2002] UKHL 10; [2002] 1 FLR 815, paras 55 and 99; *Haase v Germany* [2004] 2 FLR 39, para 94.
139 [2003] EWHC Fam 551; [2003] 2 FLR 42.
140 For detailed instructions, see *Re G (Care: Challenge to Local Authority's Decision)* [2003] EWHC Fam 551; [2003] 2 FLR 42, para 45.
141 *K and T v Finland* [2001] 2 FLR 707, para 172. See also *TP and KM v United Kingdom* [2001] 2 FLR 549.
142 See *Kutzner v Germany* [2003] 1 FCR 249, paras 69 and 75. To sever all links with a parent is especially draconian. See *P, C and S v United Kingdom* [2002] 2 FLR 631, para 118.
143 *K and T v Finland* [2001] 2 FLR 707, para 168; *P, C and S v United Kingdom* [2002] 2 FLR 631, paras 116, 131–33; *Haase v Germany* [2004] 2 FLR 39, para 91.
144 *Re M (Care Proceedings: Judicial Review)* [2003] EWHC Admin 850; [2003] 2 FLR 171, para 44 (iii). See also *Haase v Germany* [2004] 2 FLR 39, para 95.
145 *Haase v Germany* [2004] 2 FLR 39, para 99.
146 *K and T v Finland* [2001] 2 FLR 707, para 178; *Olsson v Sweden (No 2)* (1992) 17 EHRR 134, para 90; *Haase v Germany* [2004] 2 FLR 39, para 93.

mitted to rely on Article 8 in order to have measures taken that would harm the child.[147] Since particular importance is accorded to the best interests of the child, these, 'depending on their nature and seriousness, may override those of the parent'.[148] If the child has been separated from the family for a long period of time, his or her interests in not having to undergo further change might accordingly override the interests of the parents in having the family reunited. In order to preserve family relationships, therefore, it is important for courts to scrutinise strictly any measures that could lead to their attenuation, such as restrictions on contact.[149] Moreover, a local authority is not permitted to change the care plan in any significant way or change the arrangements under which the children are living without 'properly involving the parents in the decision-making process and without giving the parents a proper opportunity to make their case before a decision is made'.[150]

The connections between the partnership principle and Article 8 emerge from the discussion of the court in Re *S (Minors) (Care Order: Implementation of Care Plan)*; Re *W (Minors) (Care Order: Adequacy of Care Plan)*:

> [56] ... The Children Act 1989 imposes on a local authority looking after a child the duty to safeguard and promote the child's welfare. Before making any decision with respect to such a child the authority must, so far as reasonably practicable, ascertain the wishes and feelings of the child and his parents: s 22. Section 26 of the Children Act 1989 provides for periodic case reviews by the authority, including obtaining the views of parents and children. One of the required reviews is that every 6 months the local authority must actively consider whether it should apply to the court for a discharge of the care order ... . Every local authority must also establish a procedure for considering representations, including complaints, made to it by any child who is being looked after by it, or by his parents, about the discharge by the authority of its parental responsibilities for the child.

> [57] If an authority duly carries out these statutory duties, in the ordinary course there should be no question of an infringement by the local authority of the Art 8 rights of the child or his parents.

**Q** Parents and children as individuals, and families as units, are all entitled to protection by the ECHR. What potential is there for these interests to conflict? How can local authorities reconcile them in their day to day practice? Henricson and Bainham (2005) say:

> The obligations under the ECHR in relation to child protection therefore have the potential to pull local authorities in two separate directions. On the one hand, they must devote enough resources to protect children seriously at risk, but, on the other hand, they must commit extensive resources to family support and to working with parents to reunite them with children temporarily looked after by the State. How this balance of resource allocation is struck,

---

[147] *Haase v Germany* [2004] 2 FLR 39, para 93.

[148] *L v Finland* [2000] 2 FLR 118, para 122; *Haase v Germany* [2004] 2 FLR 39, para 93.

[149] *Haase v Germany* [2004] 2 FLR 39, para 92. *K and T v Finland* [2001] 2 FLR 707, para 155. However the obligation to use coercion is limited because the best interests of the child must be taken into account. Where contact threatens the child's best interests, a balance must be struck between those and the interests of the parents (para 194). See also *P, C and S v United Kingdom* [2002] 2 FLR 631, para 117; *L v Finland* [2000] 2 FLR 118, para 118. See on contact with babies, *Re M (Care Proceedings: Judicial Review)* [2003] EWHC Admin 850; [2003] 2 FLR 171, para 44 (iv).

[150] *Re G (Care: Challenge to Local Authority's Decision)* [2003] EWHC Fam 551; [2003] 2 FLR 42, para 43.

already an extremely difficult question for cash-strapped authorities, has become an even more acute problem with the potential for human rights violations if they get it wrong (p 17).

## *Negligence*

Local authorities owe a duty of care to the children for whom they are responsible. They are expected to exercise their discretion in placing children and making decisions about them in a reasonable manner. Failure to do so could result in an action in tort for negligence.[151] In *Barrett v Enfield London Borough Council*,[152] the House of Lords ruled that an action in negligence is available in relation to decisions taken by a local authority about the upbringing of a child while already in care. The negligence alleged in that case consisted of the way the plaintiff was placed with various unsuitable foster parents and in children's homes as a child, without being adopted or placed with his relatives. There were also allegations about the local authority's failure to enable him to see his mother and a failure to provide psychiatric treatment. He argued that as a result he had suffered psychiatric injury. He had experienced behavioural problems, a tendency to self-harm, alcohol problems and a failed marriage. The court held that, in principle, the exercise of a statutory discretion could give rise to a duty of care. The possibility of a viable cause of action in negligence was confirmed by the court in *S v Gloucestershire County Council*,[153] a case in which two adults claimed that the foster fathers with whom they had been placed as children had sexually abused them. They sued in negligence claiming that they had suffered long term damage as a result of their abuse.

## XI. FAMILY SUPPORT AND THE CHILDREN ACT 2004

The Children Act 1989 was shaped in part by child abuse scandals. The Children Act 2004, on the other hand, largely owes its very existence to yet another such scandal.[154] Victoria Climbié died after being subjected to horrific abuse by a great-aunt and her cohabitant. The Report of the inquiry that followed concluded that 'in general, the legislative framework for protecting children is basically sound' (Laming 2003 para 1.30). But it severely criticised the professionals involved in the case for failing to adhere to good practice, for poor investigative standards and for poor communication. The fault, said Lord Laming, who headed the inquiry, lay not in the law but in its implementation (para 1.30). He made a number of recommendations aimed at improving co-operation,

---

[151] Local authorities have a duty of care to the children they deal with. They also have a duty of care to the foster parents with whom they place children. In *W v Essex County Council* [2000] 1 FLR 657, the House of Lords held that the foster parents had an arguable case because the local authority had placed a known sexual abuser with them, without informing them of the boy's history, and in the knowledge that the foster parents had stipulated that they did not want to foster children who were known to be or suspected of being sexual abusers. The boy allegedly abused the foster parents' children. See also *A and B v Essex County Council* [2003] 1 FLR 615.

[152] [1999] 2 FLR 426.

[153] *S v Gloucestershire County Council: Tower Hamlets London Borough Council and Havering London Borough Council* [2000] 1 FLR 825.

[154] See DfES (2004c) p 4. It was also a response to an inspection report.

partnership and the sharing of information between agencies. He also recommended setting up new agencies. And he made it clear that family support was a crucial: 'It is not possible to separate the protection of children from wider support to families. Indeed, often the best protection for a child is achieved by the timely intervention of family support services' (Laming 2003 para 1.30).

A move from a focus on child protection to one on prevention through family support has been the subject of debate for some time. For instance, a consultation paper issued by the government in 1998 pointed to a shift towards concentrating on family support: '[t]he Government wishes to see a new emphasis on early intervention to help children in need and their families' (DoH 1998 para 1.2). But it was after the publication of the Laming Report that the government moved family support much further up the policy agenda. In 2003, it published a Green Paper, *Every Child Matters* (DfES 2003), that contained proposals not only to overhaul the child protection machinery but to increase the services available to families and to promote early intervention:

> 4. As Lord Laming's recommendations made clear, child protection cannot be separated from policies to improve children's lives as a whole. We need to focus both on the universal services which every child uses, and on more targeted services for those with additional needs. The policies set out in the Green Paper are designed both to protect children and to maximise their potential. It sets out a framework for services that cover children and young people from birth to 19 living in England. It aims to reduce the numbers of children who experience educational failure, engage in offending or anti-social behaviour, suffer from ill-health, or become teenage parents.
> 5. We need to ensure we protect children at risk within the framework of universal services ... .
> (DfES 2003 *Executive Summary*)

> 1.2 When we consulted children, young people and families ... [t]hey wanted an approach that was less about intervening at points of crisis or failure, and more about helping every child to achieve his or her potential. They wanted an approach that involved children, families, communities and public services working to a shared set of goals rather than narrow or contradictory objectives.
> 1.3 There was broad agreement that five key outcomes really matter for children and young people's well-being:
>
>> **being healthy:** enjoying good physical and mental health and living a healthy lifestyle
>> **staying safe:** being protected from harm and neglect and growing up able to look after themselves
>> **enjoying and achieving:** getting the most out of life and developing broad skills for adulthood
>> **making a positive contribution:** to the community and to society and not engaging in anti-social or offending behaviour
>> **economic well-being:** overcoming socio-economic disadvantages to achieve their full potential in life. (DfES 2003, emphasis in original)

The Green Paper went on to identify a number of risk factors, such as poor parenting, poor schooling and low income, that are associated with 'poor outcomes' for children (DfES 2003 para 1.10). It also listed 'protective' factors, such as strong family relationships, parental interest in education and positive role models (para 1.12). The aims, then, would be to tackle the risk factors such as poverty,[155] to support children's relationships with their families and to facilitate early intervention: 'We need a greater focus on

[155] The reduction of child poverty is one of the priorities identified in the 2005 Budget (HM Treasury 2005 paras 1.24, 5.15).

ensuring children at risk are identified earlier. We need to be able to share information to identify children who require additional support, and provide a tailored service that safeguards them from abuse and neglect, and enables them to fulfil their potential.' (DfES 2003 para 1.18)

As an aid to identification, and in order to determine children's needs, a Common Assessment Framework was recommended. Preliminary assessments would be made by the agency initially alerted and before referral to another agency. This would mean that children would be dealt with by the appropriate agency and it would avoid social services being overwhelmed with inappropriate cases (DfES 2003 para 4.13). Results of assessments would be shared so as to avoid multiple assessments.[156] Greater accountability, better information sharing and better training would improve protection. (para 1.19).[157] Support for parents was also considered important but, for those who fail, permanence planning would become a reality; their children might well be removed from them permanently (para 3.17–18).

By the time the ensuing White Paper appeared, a new post of Minister for Children, Young People and Families had been created, signifying the importance the government was attaching to family and child issues.[158] The White Paper, *Every Child Matters: Next Steps* (DfES 2004a) outlined new legislation, which was to become the Children Act 2004, and endorsed the contents of the Green Paper generally. Reporting on the consultations that were carried out, it stated:

1.12 There is a strong consensus in support of profound change in the cultures and practices of working with children towards a system organised around children, young people and families with a sharper focus on prevention and early intervention.

3.5 We want to help all children and young people maximise their potential by supporting parents, extending the offer of high quality childcare integrated with nursery education and schools, and ensure that, as they grow up, young people have access to the resources that can help each of them fulfil their potential. This means high quality universal services. It means better access through those universal services (like schools and primary health care) to targeted support for vulnerable groups such as children on the child protection register, looked after children, young carers, disabled children, the children of asylum seekers or prisoners.

3.6 ... [We] need to shift away from associating parenting support with crisis interventions to a more consistent offer of parenting support throughout a child and young person's life. We will work towards a mix of universal and targeted parenting approaches including advice and information, home visiting and parenting classes ... .

3.17 Consultees welcomed the idea of focusing on outcomes rather than processes ... .

3.33 ... Our aim is to achieve a culture change where practitioners and managers focus creatively on whether outcomes have improved rather than whether centrally determined processes have been adhered to. (DfES 2004a)

The Children Act 2004 establishes the legal framework within which these changes are to take place. First, it creates the office of Children's Commissioner.[159] Section 2 stipulates that the function of the commissioner is to promote awareness of the views and interests of children on issues such as health and protection from harm and neglect. Part 2 of the Act focuses on the child protection system and on services for children. Section

[156] See also DfES (2004a), para 3.14.
[157] See also DfES (2004d), paras 3.18–3.28.
[158] See DfES, DoH and Home Office (2003) para 19.
[159] S 1 Children Act 2004.

10 places a duty on all children's services authorities in England[160] to promote co-operation between agencies. The partnership embraces children's services authorities and bodies such as the police, probation and health authorities.[161] The partners are permitted, in terms of Section 10(6), to pool budgets in order to achieve better outcomes for children. Information sharing is promoted as a means of helping to track children and follow up concerns more effectively; Section 12 provides for the setting up of databases containing basic information about children and young people.[162] Section 11 places a duty on a wide range of agencies, including children's services authorities, NHS trusts, youth offending teams, health authorities and the police, to have regard, when discharging their normal functions, to the need to safeguard and promote the welfare of children.[163] Section 13 makes provision for the establishment of Local Safeguarding Children Boards to replace the Area Child Protection Committees, bodies which were criticised in the Laming Report for being ineffective and unwieldy. These Local Safeguarding Children Boards are meant to co-ordinate steps taken to safeguard and promote the welfare of children in the area.[164] To improve accountability, each authority must appoint a Director of Children's Services and a Lead Member to be responsible for, as a minimum, the authority's education and social services functions insofar as they relate to children.[165] The Act also makes provision for the inspection and review of children's services to evaluate the extent to which they improve the well-being of children and young people.[166]

What is perhaps most notable about the legislation, for the purposes of this chapter, is the formulation of Section 10:

10 Co-operation to improve well-being

(1)  Each children's services authority in England must make arrangements to promote co-operation between—
(a) the authority;
(b) each of the authority's relevant partners; and
(c) such other persons or bodies as the authority consider appropriate, being persons or bodies of any nature who exercise functions or are engaged in activities in relation to children in the authority's area.

(2)  The arrangements are to be made with a view to improving the well-being of children in the authority's area so far as relating to—
(a) physical and mental health and emotional well-being;
(b) protection from harm and neglect;
(c) education, training and recreation;
(d) the contribution made by them to society;
(e) social and economic well-being.

(3)  In making arrangements under this section a children's services authority in England must have regard to the importance of parents and other persons caring for children in improving the well-being of children.

---

[160] For the law relating to Wales, see Pt 3 Children Act 2004.
[161] See s 10(4) Children Act 2004.
[162] See further DfES (2004d) paras 3.33–3.36.
[163] Schools are already under a duty to safeguard pupils and promote their welfare (s 175 Education Act 2002).
[164] S 14 Children Act 2004.
[165] Ss 18 and 19 Children Act 2004.
[166] Ss 20–24 Children Act 2004.

So, the legislation incorporates and gives statutory force to the outcomes identified in the Green Paper. However, the government has remarked, to have any effect, the legislation has to be part of a 'wider process of change, focused on outcomes' (DfES 2004d para 1.5). Also, 'if the outcomes are to be really effective in driving change, it is important to be clear what they mean in practice and how progress towards them will be measured' (*ibid* para 2.3). The government has accordingly set out a number of aims for children and young people and has indicated the support needed from parents, carers and families in order to realise them (*ibid* para 2.4). The meanings ascribed to the outcome of staying safe, for example, are:

> Safe from maltreatment, neglect, violence, and sexual exploitation
> Safe from accidental injury and death
> Safe from bullying and discrimination
> Safe from crime and anti-social behaviour in and out of school
> Have security, stability and are cared for (DfES 2004d p 9)

In order to promote this outcome, '[p]arents, carers and families [should] provide safe homes and stability' (*ibid*).

The statutory duty on agencies to co-operate in achieving the five outcomes is to be implemented through the development of children's trust arrangements (DfES 2004c p 1). These are meant to create partnerships involving various professional groupings engaged in providing services for children and young people. They are intended to 'encourage collaborative and coordinated working across agencies' such as those delivering services in health, education and social care (University of East Anglia in association the National Children's Bureau 2005 para 21). They are also supposed to engage other partners such as youth offending teams, Connexions and the voluntary sector. In addition, they are expected to take cognisance of the views of children and families (*ibid*). Each professional grouping retains its normal functions but all are expected to co-operate in matters such as devising strategies for delivering services.

At the time of writing, trust arrangements of this type were being piloted in some areas. The trusts are diverse in size but most coincide with local government administrative divisions such as London Boroughs (University of East Anglia in association the National Children's Bureau 2005 p 19). Almost all are run by children's trust boards on which education, health and social services are represented (*ibid* paras 77–79).

An interim report evaluating the trusts involved in the pilots, known as pathfinder trusts, has already identified problems in the way they are operating. One problem, according to the report, stems from the tension between two different policy imperatives. The first, developed in response to the Laming Report, is concerned, say the authors,[167] primarily with the provision of 'targeted, individualised services focused on protection and support for more vulnerable children, young people and families' (para 34). The second is directed at the provision of universal services, such as those offered by Sure Start and Connexions (*ibid*).[168] Not all pathfinders interpreted their duties in the same way; some, the study showed, were concentrating on targeted rather than universal services (*ibid*).[169] A number of pathfinders were targeting specific, and different, age

---

[167] However Lord Laming's views were interpreted in the Green Paper as suggesting that targeted services should be delivered in the context of universal services. See above.

[168] Sure Start makes provision for help for families with small children, while Connexions provides advice and assistance for the 13–19 age group. See below.

[169] See also Cooper, *et al*, (2003) p 21.

groups (para 71). Perceptions of the relative importance of the five outcomes varied between trusts (paras 74–75). And, while pathfinders were optimistic about the potential for improving efficiency through integration, they complained of inadequate funding (p 59).

The report findings suggest that there are difficulties in interpreting priorities. But it also points to another problem. In addition to differences in priorities between different trust areas, there were differences between the various professional communities: each different group, whether education, health or social care, was interpreting the concept of 'need' differently (para 35). This highlights the difficulty of defining need. However, even if a definition is agreed on, there are other issues. The difficulty, in many cases, is how best to meet children's needs and to assess whether they are being met in the home.

To this end, new mechanisms for assessment are being created for individual professionals working with children. The Common Assessment Framework,[170] which was being developed at the time of writing, is intended to 'provide a national, common process for early assessment' (DfES 2004d para 3.30). It is designed to 'enable practitioners in schools, health settings, children's centres and other early years services to identify with greater accuracy what additional services a child may need' (DfES 2004c p 6). The idea is that the professional who first deals with a child who is thought to be in need or at risk, such as a head-teacher, can make an initial assessment before deciding whether it is necessary to refer the case to children's services. If the case is referred, then there is another guide to assessment, already in use, that must be adhered to by local authority social workers[171]: the *Framework for the Assessment of Children in Need and their Families* (DoH 2000).[172] This sets out an 'ecological' approach which must be adopted by child protection professionals in assessing children to determine whether they are in need or at risk. This approach demands that an understanding of a child should be 'located within the context of the child's family (parents or caregivers and the wider family) and of the community and the culture in which he or she is growing up' (DoH 2000 para 1.39). Assessment requires, therefore, a 'thorough understanding' of children's developmental needs, the capacity of parents or carers to 'respond appropriately to those needs and the impact of 'wider family and environmental factors' (DoH 2000 para 2.1). In assessing developmental needs, professionals are expected to consider, among other things, whether the child responds 'appropriately' to caregivers and how the child presents to the outside world (p 19). In assessing parenting capacity, professionals are directed to a list of criteria including the parents' response to the child, their capacity to adapt and change and the nature of the parent-child relationship (para 2.11). In relation to family and environment, there are a number of factors to be addressed, including how well the family is integrated into the community (p 23). Professionals are told that the 'complex interplay of factors across all three domains should be carefully understood and analysed' (para 2.20).

Sinclair and Bullock point to the challenges of applying this framework.[173] They argue that professionals need to know whether some of the specified factors are more important than others, whether they are more dangerous in combination and what interventions meet particular needs (2003 p 62). It is clear, therefore, that however helpful

[170] See above.
[171] Other agencies which might be involved in helping with assessments under s 27 of the Children Act 1989, such as health authorities, are also required to be aware of the *Framework* (DoH 2000 p ix).
[172] See above. This document is issued under s 7 of the Local Authority Social Services Act 1970. It is not binding but should be complied with in the absence of exceptional circumstances.
[173] See also, for example, DoH (2003a) para 2.2.4.

guidance and frameworks might be, child welfare professionals are still required to exercise considerable judgment and powers of interpretation in the context of a complex knowledge base that offers little certainty. Identifying children who are suffering or likely to suffer significant harm is unlikely to get much easier and the need to do so, while it may diminish with the advent of improved universal services, will certainly remain:

> The social services functions of Local Authorities, for example those arising from the Children Act 1989, remain unchanged but the way that services are delivered will change radically as they become integrated around the child or young person and their family and carers. There will be an increased emphasis on early identification and earlier intervention. (DfES 2004c p 3)

> 13 Abuse and neglect of children will inevitably remain a substantial problem, with children dying at the hands of their parents or carers, albeit in very small numbers, an unavoidable feature. The children's services system must therefore be able to protect and support those children who are at risk of abuse or neglect. Although the Government does not believe that child deaths an be eliminated entirely, action is still needed—by supporting families more effectively, and at an earlier stage, the extent and seriousness of abuse and neglect can and will be lowered.
> (DfEs, DoH and Home Office 2003)

Within the newly established structures for services for children and families, there will still be considerable priority given to child protection. The National Service Framework,[174] for example, requires professionals to attain high standards in assessing and averting risk:

> 2.9 Children and young people who are at risk of achieving poor outcomes need to be identified at an early stage and should be provided with a range of non-stigmatising services which meet their needs if they are to fulfil their potential. Children and young people who may be suffering harm should have their needs assessed and be provided with services to protect them. High quality, holistic assessment of the developmental needs of children and their families can help to ensure timely and appropriate intervention and services. (DoH 2003a)[175]

This too, then, places an expectation on child welfare professionals to predict and to identify harm. It also assumes that professionals know how to ameliorate it. And in a document directed at social workers and social care workers, the government makes their task clear: 'As social workers and social care workers, you have a unique contribution to make in assessing and analysing information in order to make judgements about, for example, risks to a child's welfare' (DfES 2004c p 5).

To summarise, then, the policy is to ensure that children and families are provided with universal services to meet their needs and to prevent the risk of children suffering harm. Within this universal service, targeted services are supposed to meet the more pressing needs of children at risk. To achieve all this, trusts to promote professional co-operation are being set up. Standards are being set which professionals are expected to fulfil and desired outcomes have been specified. Finally, guidance is being provided to show professionals how to assess children in a bid to equip them better to attain those outcomes and standards.

---

[174] The NSF is intended to ensure good quality services for children and young people. It sets standards for services which they have to meet. The government expects that, by 2014, health, social services and educational services meet the standards set out. All professionals delivering such services are expected to adhere to the framework. See *Forewords*, DoH (2004) p 2.See also p 8.

[175] See also DoH 2004 pp 6–7; DfES (2004c) p 3; and DfES (2003) para 1.18, reproduced above, pp 370–71.

**Q** What explanation(s) of child abuse do these measures assume to be the 'correct' one(s)?

*A Programme Based on Prevention*

The government is, clearly, still concerned to impress on professionals the need to iden-tify children who are or may be victimised. But it has declared its intention to 'maximise opportunity and to minimise risk' largely through a strategy based on prevention (DfES 2004d Foreword). It has already taken steps to provide services aimed at promoting chil-dren's well being. For example *Sure Start* makes provision for help for families with small children, while *Connexions* provides advice and assistance for the 13–19 age group, with a view to ensuring that they are in education or employment. Financial help for families is available in the form of increased Child Benefit and child tax credits.[176] A Green Paper has been published (DfES 2005b) setting out proposed services for all young people during their teenage years. It also makes provision for targeted services to be delivered by frontline youth support teams which are designed to intervene early to help those at risk.

Yet, as Hendrick[177] says, the image of the child as victim and the image of the child as threat tend to go in tandem and the services provided are often described as means of preventing social exclusion.[178] The five outcomes listed above, for example, refer to the aim of preventing anti-social activity. The policy documents are replete with references to children as future adults[179] and as future good and responsible parents.[180] They stress the need to ensure that children grow up into good citizens[181] and even Section 10 of the Children Act 2004 refers to children's contribution to society.

So, yet again, the construction of the child embraces two images. And children moulded in both of those images, it seems, must be made increasingly visible. The family remains private but the aim is to draw more and more families and their children into public arenas to take advantage of the services offered. It appears that the tutelary sys-tem is expanding in a bid by the state to ensure that children become neither victims nor threats.

## XII. CONCLUSION

Changes in images of childhood have led to the perception that children must be pro-tected; child abuse has been successfully constructed as a major social problem. Recent years have seen government initiatives to tackle poverty and social exclusion. Efforts are being made to provide universal services for children and to reduce the social and finan-cial stresses on families. However it remains the case that the obligation of the state to intervene in order to protect children from harm is conceived of more narrowly; the

---

[176] See further DfES (2003) para 1.8, HM Treasury (2005) para 1.25; ch 3 above.
[177] See above.
[178] See eg DoH (2000b) p x; DfES (2005) Executive Summary p 4.
[179] See, for example, DoH (2004) Executive Summary p 4.
[180] See DoH (2004) Executive Summary, Forewords.
[181] See DfES (2005b).

notion of abuse is confined to acts perpetrated by individuals.[182] This might be explained, applying Manning's analysis, by the fact that it is in relation to these types of harm that 'entrepreneurial' efforts have been concentrated and that publicity has been greatest. In addition, what are seen as appropriate measures to combat these types of harm have been capable of accommodation within the political agenda of the state.

This accommodation has not been without its difficulties. Measures to protect children potentially threaten the autonomy of the family which, in the liberal state, must also be protected. The history of child protection reveals an ever-present tension between the ideal of family privacy and a perceived need to respond to the problem of abuse. Moreover, the scope of the problem is expanding; child welfare knowledge is constantly changing and leading to the 'discovery' of new categories of abuse.

However, while child welfare knowledge is contributing to the construction of new problems, it also constitutes the modern justification for breaching the privacy of the family to deal with these problems. The state has to be seen to be responding to concerns by 'doing something' about abuse, and this it does through the agency of its social workers. They work within a legal framework which precludes coercive intervention in the absence of 'reliable' evidence of abuse or a risk of abuse. The law sets thresholds and child welfare workers are charged with the almost impossible task of determining whether these have been crossed. Unlike the philanthropists of old, however, they do not rely on moral judgements to justify their actions. Instead, they rely on what is regarded as a more 'scientific' set of principles. Child welfare knowledge enables social workers, and other child welfare professionals working in the child protection arena, to be presented and to present themselves as having the expertise necessary to determine which children are at risk. This apparent ability to judge when intervention is needed allows them to be seen as protecting children without unwarranted intrusions into family life.

We have noted a trend to curtail coercive intervention and to emphasise working with the family. The concept of partnership, said to empower families, is evidence of this trend. And now the aim is to provide help for families and children in an attempt to pre-empt any need at all for coercive intervention. However, it is doubtful whether the trend to minimise coercion implies a lessening in regulation of the family. Partnership can be seen as facilitating surveillance and the expanded services to help families, too, can be seen in this light. These measures could be seen as functioning to strengthen what Donzelot referred to as the 'tutelary complex' and they may serve as a means of inculcating families with approved norms. While the ideology of privacy of the family remains strong and family autonomy is underwritten by the law, the private family will continue to be regulated to encourage it to conform to public norms informing the image of the responsible family.

## FURTHER READING AND SELECTED RECENT REFERENCES

D ARCHARD, 'Can Child Abuse Be Defined?' in M King, (ed), *Moral Agendas for Children's Welfare* (London, Routledge, 1999)

S ASHENDEN, *Governing Child Sexual Abuse: Negotiating the Boundaries of Public and Private, Law and Science* (London, Routledge, 2004).

---

[182] Including, more recently, the behaviour of individuals within institutions. See Report of the National Commission of Inquiry into the Prevention of Child Abuse (1996) para 2.42; Utting (1997).

J EEKELAAR, 'Parental Responsibility: State of Nature or Nature of the State?', (1991) *JSW&FL* 37

B LINDLEY and M RICHARDS, 'Working Together 2000—How Will Parents Fare under the New Child Protection Process?' (2000) 12 *CFLQ* 213.

P MARSH and G CROW, *Family Group Conferences in Child Welfare* (Oxford, Blackwells, 1997).

N PARTON, *The Politics of Child Abuse* (Basingstoke and London, Macmillan Education, 1985).

——, *Governing the Family: Child Care, Child Protection and the State* (Basingstoke, Macmillan Education, 1991).

F ROBERTSON ELLIOT, 'The Family: Private Arena or Adjunct of the State', (1989) 16 *J of Law and Society* 443.

N ROSE, 'Beyond the Public/Private Division: Law, Power and the Family', (1987) 14 *J of Law and Society* 61.

W STAINTON ROGERS, D HEVEY and E ASH (eds), *Child Abuse and Neglect: Facing the Challenge* (London, BT Batsford Ltd in association with The Open University, 1989).

R STAINTON ROGERS and W STAINTON ROGERS, *Stories of Childhood: Shifting Agendas of Child Concern* (London, Harvester Wheatsheaf, 1992).

——, 'What is Good and Bad Sex for Children', in M King, (ed), *Moral Agendas for Children's Welfare* (London, Routledge, 1999).

C WATTAM, 'The Social Construction of Child Abuse for Practical Policy Purposes—A Review of *Child Protection: Messages from Research*', (1996) 8 *CFLQ* 189.

*Reports*

DfES, *Every Child Matters* Cm 5860 (London, The Stationery Office, 2003).

——, *Every Child Matters: Next Steps* (London, The Stationery Office, 2004a).

DfES, DoH and Home Office, *Keeping Children Safe: The Government's Response to the Victoria Climbie Inquiry Report and Joint Chief Inspectors' Report Safeguarding Children* Cmd 5861 (London, The Stationery Office, 2003).

DoH, *Framework for the Assessment of Children in Need and their Families* (London, The Stationery Office, 2000).

——, *National Service Framework for Children, Young People and Maternity Services* (London, The Stationery Office, 2004).

DoH, Home Office and DfEE, *Working Together to Safeguard Children* (London, The Stationery Office, 1999).

# 10

# A Public or Private Matter?
# Domestic Violence

## I. INTRODUCTION

The term 'domestic violence' is widely used, and will be used here,[1] to describe abuse between partners in an intimate relationship.[2] Like child abuse, abuse of women in intimate relationships has not always been seen as a social problem demanding remedial action by the state and its agents. It has come to be constructed as such through the efforts, first, of 'moral entrepreneurs'[3] and, more recently, of feminists. The success of those efforts was a product of social and economic change and, in particular, changes in the way women and their place in the family were seen. Women had to be seen as individuals rather than adjuncts of their husbands before they could be seen as requiring protection from spousal abuse. In addition, the abuse of women in the family had to be constructed as representing so serious a problem that intervention in the private domain of the family to deal with it was justified.

As we noted in chapter 9, until the 19th century, the ideal of family privacy, an ideal central to the philosophy underlying the liberal state, largely shielded the family from state intervention. Feminist writers have frequently pointed to the notion of the family as a private domain as one of the primary obstacles, initially, to the designation of domestic violence as a social problem, and, latterly, to devising a response to it.[4] The ideal of family privacy, as O'Donovan says, rests on certain assumptions about family life; the home 'is thought to be a private place, a refuge from society, where relationships can flourish untrammelled by public interference' (1985 p 107). In order for domestic violence to be seen as a problem justifying, and even demanding, state intervention, these assumptions had to be challenged.

---

[1] This term has been criticised for masking the gendered nature of the violence but, as one writer has pointed out, the other terms frequently used in this context, such as battered wife, are also unsatisfactory (Smith 1989 p 1). The use of 'victim' rather than 'survivor' is criticised by some commentators as well.

[2] This category will be taken to include cohabiting and married couples, ex-partners and couples who have never lived together. This chapter will not, however, address other violence that could be seen as domestic violence, such as abuse of children or elderly or disabled family members (see, on elder abuse, eg, Special Edition on Elder Abuse (1995) 2(3) *Social Work in Europe*; Decalmer and Glendenning 1993). As the Home Office has pointed out, these forms of abuse are different from partner abuse and are dealt with differently (Home Office (2000) para 1.12). Some reference will be made to children in this chapter since child abuse is linked to partner abuse. However child abuse is covered separately in ch 9. To focus on this issue in the context of domestic violence risks marginalising partner abuse (see Home Office 2000 para 1.13).

[3] See ch 9.

[4] See Dobash and Dobash (1997) p 7.

In this chapter, we consider what behaviours are categorised as domestic violence and trace the way in which domestic violence came to be constructed as a social problem. We then go on to examine the law designed to address the problem and the way in which it is implemented.

## II. WHAT IS DOMESTIC VIOLENCE?

### 1. Definition

What is regarded as abusive in the context of intimate relationships has changed over time. Early concern focused on wife-beating but attention is now directed at a broader range of behaviour. For example, Hester and Radford identify 'a range of abusive behaviours' such as 'emotional cruelty, controlling and demeaning behaviour including withholding of money, attempts at strangulation and threats to kill' (1996 p 7). Sev'er (1997) also refers to controlling behaviour and examines tactics such as intimidation, threats, stalking, destruction of property and using children to induce guilt in or to threaten the woman.

The influence of feminism is now discernible within official thinking. The Home Office has adopted as its definition of domestic violence,[5] 'any violence between current or former partners in an intimate relationship, wherever and whenever the violence occurs. The violence may include physical, sexual,[6] emotional and financial abuse' (Home Office 2003 pp 6 and 8). In addition, the law is now beginning to respond to research highlighting the various forms of behaviour that characterise abusive relationships and to research suggesting that these kinds of behaviours often continue, and even escalate, after the victims leave their assailants.[7]

> Typically the violence involves a pattern of abusive and controlling behaviour which tends to get worse over time. It can take a number of forms. Some are directly and indirectly physical, such as assault, indecent assault, rape, destruction of property and threats. Some are non-physical, such as destructive criticism, pressure tactics, belittling, breaking trust, isolation, oppressive control of finances and harassment. The physical manifestations of domestic violence are criminal offences; the non-physical forms may also amount to offences, under the Protection from Harassment Act 1997.[8] (Home Office 2000a para 1.15)

---

[5] Also used by HM Inspectorate of Constabulary. See Home Office (2000a) para 1.10.

[6] Research suggests that between 10% and 14% of married or cohabiting woman have been raped at least once by their partners, and that these rapes are often particularly violent (Paradine and Wilkinson 2004 para 1.2.1).

[7] See, eg, Hester and Radford (1996) p 8; Mahoney (1991), Richards (2004) para 6.2.2. The Crown Prosecution Service regards domestic violence as 'particularly serious because there is often a continuing risk to the victim's safety and in the worst cases, the victim's life and the lives of others (including children) may be at risk' (CPS 2001 para 1.2).

[8] The Protection from Harassment Act 1997 was passed to introduce criminal penalties and a remedy in tort for harassment, a term not defined other than that it includes 'alarming a person or causing a person distress' (s 7(1)(a)). This legislation was primarily intended to deal with acts such as stalking but can be and is being used in cases of domestic violence (see ch 12).

## 2. *Perpetrators and Victims*

Domestic violence is conceived of primarily as a problem of men's abuse of women. Although researchers have documented abuse within same sex relationships,[9] and although there is evidence that, in a comparatively small number of cases, women abuse men,[10] the available research suggests that domestic violence is overwhelmingly directed by men against women.[11]

Mirrlees-Black (1999), in her analysis of a computerised self-completion questionnaire included in the 1996 British Crime Survey, found prevalence figures for violence against men that were similar to those for violence against women: 26% of women and 17% of men in her study had suffered physical (use of force) or non-physical violence (frightening threats) from a partner at some time (p 18). However women tended to suffer more severe abuse than men did. Women were far more likely to be 'chronic' victims, suffering repeated abuse (p 25). Women were 'much more likely to report choking, strangling and suffocation and being forced to have sex' (p 37). In addition, women were more likely to be injured than men (*ibid*). Far more women than men were frightened during the incident and they remained upset by it for longer (p 39); women were more likely to be 'living in fear of their partners' (p 20). Only 11% of 'chronic' male victims and 5% of 'intermittent' male victims, compared with 80% of 'chronic' female victims and 52% of 'intermittent' female victims, said they had been 'very frightened'. These figures suggest that many of the 'threats' reported by men did not make them feel threatened. Mirrlees-Black suggests that it may be that men tend to report more trivial incidents (p 61). She also speculates that men may suffer less serious consequences because of their greater physical strength, or that they are less likely to admit to serious outcomes (p 62). In any event, she says, men are far more likely to be in a position to leave an abusive relationship than women are (*ibid*).

The Scottish Crime Survey in 2000 reported that men were the victims in 1 in 3 incidents where force or threats were used, suggesting that domestic violence affects comparable numbers of men and women. However Gadd, *et al*, (2002) found that, on interviewing those men who responded to the self-completion questionnaire, 1 in 4 denied having experienced domestic abuse (p 1). Some had misunderstood the questionnaire and were referring to vandalism or theft rather than to domestic abuse when they filled it in. About half the men said that they themselves were abusive although some said their acts were retaliatory (p 3). Many of the men described the abuse from their partners as 'rare and relatively inconsequential' and few perceived themselves as victims (p 3).

The 2001 British Crime Survey (Simmons and Colleagues 2002) estimated that one in five women (21%) and one in ten men (10%) were subject to at least one incident of

---

9 See, eg, Eaton (1994) p 195.

10 A recent inspection report reveals that only 1.5% of cases of partner abuse on the Crown Prosecution Service files involved assaults on men by women. However there were numerous counter-allegations by male defendants against women at the time of reporting an incident or at a later interview (HMcpsi and HMIC 2004 para 7.9). The 1996 British Crime Survey recorded that 0.7% of men reported one or more incidents of domestic violence in 1995 and that of these, 45% were perpetrated by partners and 2% by ex-partners (Mirrlees-Black, *et al*,1996). Simmons, *et al*, (2002) found that in their study, women were the victims in 73% of domestic violence incidents, with men being victimised in 27%. The study included incidents between persons other than heterosexual intimates and does not specify perpetrators' sex. Sexual offences appear to be dealt with separately and 93% of rapes were perpetrated on women.

11 See Mirrlees-Black, *et al*,1996; Law Commission (1992a) para 2.1(a); Home Office (2000a) para 1.17, Walby and Allen (2004); Barnish (2004) paras 2.1- 2.3.

domestic violence in the form of a non-sexual threat or force[12] since the age of 16. When emotional and financial abuse were taken into account, the figures rose to 26% and 17% respectively (p vii, p 12). Yet a study conducted by Walby and Allen (2004), examining responses from the computerised self-completion questionnaire which was included in the 2001 Survey, found that 'women are the overwhelming majority of the most heavily abused group' (p vii). The authors report that it is largely women who 'suffer multiple attacks and are subject to more than one form of inter-personal violence' (p 11).[13] Of those respondents who had been subject to four or more incidents of domestic violence,[14] 89% were women (p vii).[15] Women also outnumbered men when it came to severe injury[16] and mental or emotional harm.[17] Ten times more women than men reported potentially life-threatening violence in the form of being choked or strangled (p 19). The number of sexual assaults against women greatly exceeded those against men.[18] Women were more likely to be subjected to aggravated stalking,[19] by an 'intimate or former intimate.'[20] They were more likely to suffer post-separation violence. Also, far more women then men reported being frightened of threats (p 19).

A study carried out by Dobash and Dobash (2004) led them to conclude that it 'is impossible to construe the violence of men and women as either equivalent or reciprocal' (p 343). All the women in the study had been victims of repeated violence inflicted by their male partners yet just under half had not used violence against the men concerned, none had used sexual violence and only a few had used serious violence. The women's violence was often in self-defence. The men usually reported that the women's violence was 'inconsequential', generally infrequent and they experienced few negative consequences (pp 343–44).

All these studies, then, reveal that violence between men and women is asymmetrical.[21] And the reason for gender differences, feminist writers argue, can be found in hierarchical notions about relationships between men and women, notions that have a long historical pedigree.

## III. HISTORICAL BACKGROUND

### 1. The Legal Position of Husbands and Wives

It appears that, until relatively recently, violence by men against their wives, provided it

---

[12] Sexual abuse is excluded from these figures (p 15).

[13] See further pp 18, 29–31.

[14] By the same person who perpetrated the worst incident the respondent could recall happening since the age of 16.

[15] See further Walby and Allen (2004) pp 23, 25. Domestic violence also appears to affect women's health but not men's (*ibid* p 87).

[16] Six per cent compared with one per cent (Walby and Allen 2004 p viii).

[17] Thirty one per cent compared with nine per cent (Walby and Allen 2004 p viii). See further, Walby and Allen (2004) pp 33–37.

[18] See Walby and Allen (2004) vii. Of the women who were raped, 45% were raped by a husband or partner and 9% by a former husband or partner (ix).

[19] Cases where there was violence in addition to stalking.

[20] Thirty seven percent in the case of women compared with eight percent in the case of men (Walby and Allen 2004 pp 61 and ix).

[21] For judicial acknowledgement of this, see Wall (2005) p 30.

fell within permissible bounds, was considered socially acceptable and was condoned by the church and by the law:

> It is impossible to say who first declared that wives could and should be beaten by their hus-
> bands or when this practice began; it is equally difficult to find any historical period in which
> there were no formulas stating the form such beatings should take and specifying the condi-
> tions under which a wife was deserving of a good clout. (Dobash and Dobash 1979 p 31)

The most frequently cited formula is the 'rule of thumb', according to which, it is said, it was lawful for a man to beat his wife provided the 'stick were no thicker than his thumb' (Stone 1977 p 326). While it is doubted that this rule ever actually existed (Doggett 1992 p 8), there is evidence that a certain amount of violence against wives was tolerated. Freeman (1979 p 128), for example, refers to a case decided in 1395 where Margaret Neffield produced witnesses before an ecclesiastical court to show that her husband had attacked her with a dagger, wounding her and breaking a bone, but was refused a sepa-ration order.[22] Doggett (1992 p 5), in turn, quotes from a manual of procedure published by Sir Anthony Fitzherbert in 1516 which indicates that husbands were enti-tled to subject their wives to reasonable chastisement. What was considered reasonable, according to Doggett's review of 17th century authority, appears to have included 'a high degree of violence' (1992 p 6). With the rise of Protestantism, however, wife-beat-ing came to be frowned on by theologians and authors of marriage manuals alike:

> It was ... the 'Homily on Marriage' that was probably the most influential manual,
> reaching the largest audience for the longest period of time. The inferior character,
> rights, and status of wives were clearly stated in this document, which was ordered by
> the crown to be read in church every Sunday from 1562 onward. In it, the wife's subjec-
> tion and obedience were made a primary necessity for a happy Christian marriage, but
> husbands were advised, for the sake of domestic peace, not to exercise the right to beat
> their wives but rather to remember women's weak and inconstant character when deal-
> ing with them ... .
>
> (Dobash and Dobash 1979 p 55, footnotes omitted)

Despite moral injunctions to abjure violence, according to Dobash and Dobash (1979 p 56) wife-beating remained widespread. Yet there does appear to have been a move to deny it legitimacy. This normative shift was manifested both in the law and in the atti-tudes of the community. Violence that went beyond generally accepted limits sometimes provoked a community response and, by the 19th century, rituals[23] of public shaming or ridicule in the form of the *chiavari*[24] or 'rough music'[25] were being directed at abusive husbands (Thompson 1972 p 290). Legal measures to combat violence were also deployed. Doggett (1992 p 11) reports that it had become common for women in the 18th century to swear the peace against their husbands; the aggressor was required to enter into a recognisance, promising to pay a sum of money if he failed to keep the peace.[26] And in the 19th century, legislation was introduced to punish wife-beating.

---

[22] In the form of divorce a *mensa et thoro* (see further below).

[23] These rituals were also used to shame wives who were thought to be dominating their husbands.

[24] In which the offender might be paraded through the town astride a pole or seated backwards on a donkey, pelted with mud, thrown into a pond or beaten (Doggett 1992 p 112).

[25] The offender's home would be surrounded by a crowd beating on pots and chanting verses (Doggett 1992 p 112; Dobash and Dobash 1979 p 58).

[26] This did not mean that wife-beating was a criminal offence, but it did mean that a remedy was provided for

Nevertheless, whatever its limits, and these may never have been precisely defined, reasonable chastisement remained legal and its demise only finally became evident by the 1880s, says Doggett (1992 p 15). Even so, husbands remained immune from prosecution if they raped their wives[27] and were still legally entitled to exercise a right of reasonable confinement. Blackstone (1778 p 445) suggested that the power of correction had come to be doubted in the 'politer reign' of Charles II but that the right to restrain for 'gross misbehaviour' remained. In *Re Cochrane*,[28] the court appeared to go even further, upholding 'the *general* right of the husband to the control and custody of his wife'.[29] Doggett (1992 pp 22–24) suggests that this right was abridged only if the parties entered into a separation agreement (except if the wife was guilty of certain types of misbehaviour) or if the husband behaved unreasonably by, for instance, confining his wife in a madhouse. A wife imprisoned by her husband and who felt herself to be unreasonably confined could be brought before the court pursuant to a writ of habeas corpus. Criminal prosecution was also possible. For wives seeking a more permanent escape, a separation agreement might provide an appropriate remedy. However, for wives whose husbands would not enter into such an agreement, it was necessary to petition the ecclesiastical courts for a separation *a mensa et thoro* on the grounds of cruelty.[30] In 1857 judicial divorce was introduced but for a wife to divorce her husband, she had to show he had committed aggravated adultery.[31]

## IV. EXPLANATIONS FOR THE HUSBAND'S RIGHTS

Doggett (1992 p 74) points out that in the middle ages, common lawyers unabashedly wrote of the husband's power over his wife. For example, one writer observed that the position of a wife 'whilst in the power of her Husband' was such that she could 'in no measure oppose or controvert his will' (de Glanville 1812 p 281).

However, Blackstone, in the 18th century, explained the husband's powers in less forthright terms. He said that the husband's rights of chastisement and confinement arose out of the doctrine of coverture:

> The husband, also, (by the old law) might give his wife moderate correction. For, as he is to answer for her misbehaviour, the law thought it reasonable to intrust him with this power of restraining her, by domestic chastisement, in the same moderation that a man is allowed to correct his apprentices or children; for whom the master or parent is also liable in some cases to answer. But this power of correction was confined within reasonable bounds, and the husband was prohibited from using any violence to his wife [except in so far as he may lawfully and reasonably do so in order to correct and chastise his wife]. (1778 p 445)

This power stemmed from the doctrine of the unity of the spouses: 'By marriage, the

---

abused wives (see Doggett 1992 p 12; Clark 1992 p 192).
   [27] *R v Clarence* (1889) 22 QBD 23, 51.
   [28] (1840) 8 Dowl 630, cited by Doggett (1992) pp 15–16.
   [29] Quoted by Doggett (1992) pp 15–16.
   [30] Cruelty, says Doggett (1992 p 31), was strictly interpreted until the late 18th century. The definition was gradually relaxed and in the mid–19th century the idea of mental cruelty began to develop (Doggett 1992 p 32).
   [31] Adultery coupled with, eg, cruelty, incest, bigamy or rape (s 27 of the Divorce and Matrimonial Causes Act 1857). See further ch 14.

husband and wife are one person in law: that is, the very being or legal existence of the woman is suspended during the marriage, or at least is incorporated and consolidated into that of her husband: under whose wing, protection, and *cover*, she performs every thing' (Blackstone 1778 p 442).

Thus, a 'husband was not simply *permitted* to control his wife's behaviour—he was *expected* to control it. In return for the power over her which the state allowed him, he was required to answer for her conduct' (Doggett 1992 pp 57–58).[32] 'In the eyes of the law, a husband and wife constituted *not two individuals, but one*' (Doggett 1992 p 83) and this doctrine, argues Doggett, served, in the 17th century, to mask the contradiction between the emerging principle of individualism and the subordination of wives (pp 77 and 83).

The right of the husband sexually to coerce his wife, while also rooted in women's subordination, was explained differently. In 1736 Sir Matthew Hale found its origin in a fiction of consent: '[b]ut the husband cannot be guilty of rape committed by himself upon his lawful wife, for by their mutual matrimonial consent and contract the wife hath given up herself in this kind unto her husband, which she cannot retract' (Hale 1971 p 629).

This fiction survived as part of the law, albeit in modified form, until 1991.[33] Law reform to prohibit wife-beating came far earlier, and we now turn to examine the way violence perpetrated by husbands on their wives came to be constructed as a social problem demanding action by the state and its agents.

## V. THE EMERGENCE OF WIFE-BEATING AS A SOCIAL PROBLEM

According to Doggett (1992 p 111), wife-beating became a matter of public concern from about the mid-19th century. Extensive coverage in legal and popular journals of cases of assaults appeared and legislation was enacted to afford some protection to victims. In 1853, the Act for Better Prevention and Punishment of Aggravated Assaults upon Women and Children introduced new penalties for wife-beating.[34]

Clark (1992 p 196) explains the readiness of the state to engage in more extensive regulation of violence in the family in terms of pressure coming from a middle class motivated by evangelicalism and humanitarianism. However, they were also, according other commentators, motivated by anxieties evoked by the urban poor. Doggett[35] (1992 p 20) emphasises the preoccupation of reformers with the idea that the working class

---

[32] The subordinate status of wives was reflected in a number of legal rules. One of these was that, until 1828, a wife who killed her husband was guilty of petit treason but a husband who killed his wife was guilty only of murder 'because of the obedience which in relation of law is due from the wife to the husband' (East 1972 p 336). See also Stephen (1883) pp 34–35.

[33] See pp 393ff.

[34] This gave, one commentator observed, women the same protection that had already been accorded to animals (see Freeman (1979) p 129). It seems that, rather than use their powers of imprisonment, courts continued to prefer the peace bond and deferred sentencing as sanctions. Edward Cox, a London magistrate in his work, The Principles of Punishment (1984, originally 1877), felt that a criminal justice response would exacerbate the tensions between the spouses and make future cohabitation even more difficult (pp 103–4). In any event, most of the men who came before him for beating their wives had been grievously provoked, he thought (p 101). Similar concern with family unity and assertions of provocation have echoed down the years. See pp 392–3, 395–6 and 401 below.

[35] See also Pahl (1985b) p 42.

was degenerate and posed a threat to public order. Whereas previously wife-beating had been seen and tolerated as part of working class family life, now it came to be deplored. In the context of concerns about an increase in public violence generally, wife-beating was, she says, regarded by the upper and middle classes as threatening; it was seen as but one facet of generalised savagery among the working classes. Moreover, it was feared that this savagery might spill over into the streets and that children exposed to it would become delinquent. Doggett's explanation echoes those discussed in chapter 9 relating to concerns about child abuse. Like concern about child abuse, concern about woman abuse is, therefore, largely attributed to social anxiety and the perception that intervention in the family would be a lesser evil than the threat to social order that some families would present unless they were regulated.

Nevertheless, it appears that the movement for women's rights also contributed to change and that the work of liberal reformers such as John Stuart Mill, Harriet Taylor Mill and Frances Power Cobbe had an impact.[36] Cobbe, certainly, is credited with influencing the content of the Matrimonial Causes Act 1878.[37] These reformers shared many of the assumptions held by other commentators, believing, for example, that violent abuse was mainly confined to the working class.[38] But, unlike the parliamentarians seeking reform, these 'moral entrepreneurs' were not simply arguing for the cessation of violence against women. They were challenging what they saw as the causes of violence: patriarchy and women's inferior legal, social and economic status. Mill and Taylor argued that women lacked adequate legal protection because they were deprived of their rights under the social contract.[39] Marriage was seen as curtailing those rights further. For example, in *The Subjection of Women*, published in 1869, John Stuart Mill wrote:

> [A] female slave has (in Christian countries) an admitted right, and is considered under a moral obligation, to refuse to her master the last familiarity. Not so the wife: however brutal a tyrant she may unfortunately be chained to ... he can claim from her and enforce the lowest degradation of a human being, that of being made the instrument of an animal function contrary to her inclinations. (1975 p 463)

> Marriage is not an institution designed for a select few. ...The vilest malefactor has some wretched woman tied to him, against whom he can commit any atrocity except killing her, and, if tolerably cautious, can do that without much danger of the legal penalty. (1975 p 467)

> The law of servitude in marriage is a monstrous contradiction to all the principles of the modern world. ... (1975 p 521)

Cobbe, in 1878, published 'Wife Torture in England' in which she presented a horrifying catalogue of cases of abuse. Her discussion of the causes of wife beating reverberates in the writings of modern feminists, highlighting as it does the proprietary attitudes of husbands to wives and prevailing beliefs in the privacy of the family:

> The general depreciation of women *as a sex* is bad enough, but in the matter we are considering, the special depreciation of *wives* is more directly responsible for the outrages they endure. The notion that a man's wife is his PROPERTY, in the sense in which a horse is his property ...

---

[36] See for a more detailed account, Dobash and Dobash (1979) p 64ff. See also Stark and Flitcraft (1996) pp 43ff.

[37] See Doggett (1992) pp 130–31.

[38] See Doggett (1992) p 126.

[39] See Clark (1992) p 202.

is the fatal root of incalculable evil and misery. Every brutal-minded man, and many a man who in other relations of life is not brutal, entertains more or less vaguely the notion that this wife is his *thing*. ..It is even sometimes pleaded on behalf of poor men, that they possess *nothing else* but their wives, and that, consequently, it seems doubly hard to meddle with the exercise of their power in this narrow sphere! (1878 pp 62–63, emphasis in original)

The inadequacy of the law and the leniency shown to abusers by magistrates came in for criticism and Cobbe set out to draft a Bill designed to give women an escape route from abuse.[40] The Matrimonial Causes Act of 1878, based on that Bill, empowered magistrates to grant judicial separation with maintenance[41] to a wife whose husband had been convicted of an aggravated assault on her, if satisfied that the future safety of the wife was imperilled.[42]

In addition, the 1884 Matrimonial Causes Act removed the power of the court to imprison a spouse for a refusal to obey an order for restitution of conjugal rights.[43] Relying on this new legislation, the Court of Appeal held, in *R v Jackson*,[44] that a husband now had no right, if indeed he ever had, to seize and detain his wife until she agreed to restore to him his conjugal rights. While a husband might be entitled to 're-strain' his wife from dishonouring him by, for example, going with another man, he had no right to imprison her.[45] Moreover, said Lord Esher, he did not believe it had ever been the law that a husband had a right to beat his wife.[46]

## VI. THE MODERN EMERGENCE OF DOMESTIC VIOLENCE AS A SOCIAL PROBLEM

Although in the early years of the 20th century, violence against women was taken up as an issue by both British and American suffragists,[47] 'it virtually disappeared from the agenda of "social" problems between 1920 and 1970' (Smith 1989 p 5).[48] One of the principal reasons for its reappearance on the agenda was the growth of the women's movement in the late 1960s and 1970s. The modern version of the 19th century 'moral entrepreneurs', acting to bring domestic violence to public attention and to present it as a problem requiring amelioration by the state and its agents, were primarily feminists.

In 1971, Chiswick Women's Aid was established in a house made available by the local council (Dobash and Dobash 1979 p 1). It was in the course of conversations there that some women began to reveal that they had been subjected to serious violence at the

---

[40] See Doggett (1992) pp 130–31.

[41] The wife could also be awarded custody of children under the age of 10 (s 4).

[42] In 1895, this proviso was removed by the Summary Jurisdiction (Married Women) Act 1895.

[43] Previously, wives seeking to escape abusive husbands could be imprisoned for failing to return to them. After the 1884 Act was passed, the refusal to comply simply rendered that spouse guilty of desertion.

[44] [1891] 1 QB 671.

[45] *R v Reid* (1972) 56 Cr App R 703 finally established that, on the basis of Jackson, a husband could be convicted of kidnapping his wife, whether or nor the spouses were living apart: '[t]he notion that a husband can, without incurring punishment, treat his wife … with any kind of hostile force is obsolete' (p 707).

[46] P 682.

[47] See Dobash and Dobash (1979) p 74.

[48] Pahl (1985c pp 42–43) suggests that this may be attributable to the low status of women during the period concerned and the 'high degree of regard for the privacy of the home and the sanctity of marriage'.

hands of their male partners.[49] In response to their stories, Chiswick Women's Aid, headed by Erin Pizzey, opened the Chiswick refuge. Feminist activists set out to establish further refuges and to raise public awareness about domestic violence.[50] Pizzey's book, *Scream Quietly or the Neighbours Will Hear* (1974) contributed to this awareness and, by 1974, public pressure demanded that the government respond to the problem. A Parliamentary Select Committee was accordingly set up in 1975 to hear evidence and to make recommendations.[51]

Since the 1970s, the efforts of feminist campaigners and researchers working in the field of domestic violence have been directed at moving it up the political and legal agenda.[52] They have advocated law reform. They have also sought to change the practices and attitudes of those involved in implementing the law as well as the responses of other professionals.[53]

In order to redefine domestic violence as a serious social problem requiring action by public agencies, it has been necessary to transform prevailing perceptions of domestic violence as a relatively uncommon phenomenon and as a private family matter, often trivial in nature. Feminist writers have therefore consistently stressed that, although it has been a largely hidden problem,[54] domestic violence affects significant numbers of women[55] (and their children[56]) in profound ways. The effects of domestic violence have

[49] For a detailed account, see Dobash and Dobash (1992) p 25ff.

[50] See Dobash and Dobash (1992) p 27.

[51] *Ibid*, pp 112–13.

[52] See Itzin (2000). For an account of the efforts of Women's Aid, see Harwin and Barron (2000). For an account of the efforts of Southall Black Sisters, see Patel (2000). Women's Aid, for example, has responded to numerous recent government documents and consultation papers and has published widely in the field of domestic violence.

[53] See generally on the impact of feminist perspectives, Hanmer and Itzin (2000). Most recently, researchers have sought to highlight the links between woman abuse and child abuse as well as the violence that occurs in the context of contact with children. They have also argued for change to the defences for murder in the context of domestic homicide committed by abused women. See Law Commission (2003); Kaganas (2002) McColgan (1993); O'Donovan (1993). See Hester, *et al*, (1994); Harne and Radford (1994) on contact. See further ch 14.

[54] See Stanko (1988); Mooney (2000) pp 24–5. Over half the victims in the British Crime Survey had told no-one of the most recent attack (Mirrlees-Black 1999 p 51). Most who did tell anyone told friends or relatives. Many did not seek help from a professional agency (p 63). The police are told of only 1 in 8 incidents (*ibid*). Underreporting may be explained by a number of factors. Those suggested include a desire to preserve the relationship, a wish to protect privacy, financial dependence on the perpetrator and fear that contact with officialdom could lead to the removal of the victim's children by social services. It is also likely that many victims are physically prevented from reporting and that the fear of reprisals is a strong deterrent. Some may feel that the end result of the process does not justify the ordeal of going through the criminal justice system. There are also suggestions that victims from some ethnic groups as well as lesbian, gay, transgender and bi-sexual victims may fear a hostile response from the authorities. See, on barriers to seeking help, Paradine and Wilkinson (2004) para 1.2.4 and para 5.1.

[55] The government, relying on the figures revealed by the 1996 British Crime Survey, accepts that 1 in 4 women experiences domestic violence during her lifetime (Home Office 2003 p 8). The 1996 British Crime Survey indicates that women were most vulnerable to attacks by current partners (60% of reported incidents) or ex partners (21%) (Mirrlees-Black, *et al*,1996). A study conducted in North London revealed that 12% of women questioned had experienced actual physical violence (including being grabbed, pushed, shaken, punched, slapped, kicked, head-butted, choked and hit with a weapon/object) from their partners during the previous 12 months. 6% had been raped by their partners. A quarter of violent incidents occurring in the previous 12 months had involved former partners (Mooney 1994). Reviewing the literature, Stanko, *et al*, conclude that '[i]n general, the research suggests that many women may experience threats or assaults from partners during their relationships, while a small number (two to five percent) report serious, frequent attacks' (1998 p 14). They estimate in their study of Hackney, that in 1996 1 in 9 women in Hackney suffered domestic violence of some kind (1998 p 22).

[56] Stanko, *et al*, (1998 p 24) estimate that there may have been as many as 5057 children in Hackney in 1996 who witnessed some form of threat, intimidation and violence between parents, step-parents or guardians. Children might suffer physical or sexual assault and many are aware of the violence being meted out to their

been found to range from social isolation, fear and depression to permanent disability[57] or death[58] and, it is argued, it should be taken seriously. Feminist campaigners and scholars have sought to displace the image of the idealised family as a haven from the outside world and to present it as a potentially dangerous arena. And the danger, they contend, is primarily to women. They argue that the roots of domestic violence can be traced to women's inferior status and to dominant constructions of masculinity. For this argument to gain ground, it has been necessary to challenge the view that domestic violence is usually attributable to dysfunctional families or to the individual pathology of the parties.[59]

## VII. THE 'CAUSES' OF DOMESTIC VIOLENCE[60]

Some proponents of theories locating the 'causes' of domestic violence in the individual explain it in terms of an inter-generational cycle of violence.[61] Others seek explanations in biology, citing chromosomal structure or testosterone levels.[62] Yet others look to the character of the abuser. Perpetrators are said to suffer from mental illness; [63] to abuse drugs or alcohol; or to act as a result of frustration or stress brought about by factors such as unemployment or poverty.[64] Alternative explanations are sought in the character of the victim, who might be described as masochistic or addicted to violence.[65] Further, women who are bad housekeepers or who 'nag' might be seen to provoke violence.[66] Indeed, family systems theorists, who adopt what has been termed a 'family violence' approach (Dobash and Dobash 1992 p 258), locate the genesis of violence in the inter-action between family members.[67] According to this view, it is the family that is violent and women are as likely as men to be the aggressors.[68] These claims lead to an under-standing of domestic violence in terms of mutual combat, an understanding that underlies the greater use of arrest of both parties in the USA under mandatory arrest statutes and the use, in the British civil courts, of cross-undertakings[69] in cases where the

mothers (see Paradine and Wilkinson para 1.4.2). See Mullender, *et al*, (2002); Mullender (2000); Humphreys (2000); McGee (2000).

[57] See Paradine and Wilkinson (2004) para 1.4.1; Hester, *et al*, (2000) para 1.8. Humphreys and Thiara's research (2003 p 200) shows that women may fear for their emotional well-being or mental health. Many fear for their lives or for the lives of their children. Some fear they might kill the abuser.

[58] The Home Office (2003 p 9) states that on average, two women per week are killed by a male partner or for-mer partner and that almost half of all female murder victims are killed by a partner or former partner. Of all murders of men, about 8% occur in a domestic context but some women who kill may have done so in self-defence or after a history of abuse. See also Flood-Page and Taylor (2003) p 3; Home Office (2000a) para 1.18; Home Office (2002) paras 8.4–8.5; Paradine and Wilkinson (2004) para 1.2.2.

[59] For a fuller discussion of dominant stereotypes, see Edwards (1996), ch 5, especially pp 178–79). For dis-cussion of the various explanations that have been put forward, see Hearn (1998) pp 17–33.

[60] See also Barnish (2004) para 3.1–3.2.

[61] For a discussion of this theory, see Morley and Mullender (1994) pp 37–38.

[62] Neither explanation is convincing. See Hearn (1998) pp 18–19.

[63] See, for example, *Lomas v Parle* [2003] EWCA Civ 1804; [2004] 1 FLR 812, para 51: 'Those who molest others are usually trapped in an obsessional emotional state …'.

[64] See, eg, Borkowski, *et al*, (1983) ch 5.

[65] See Pizzey and Shapiro (1982). Compare Pahl (1985a) p 5.

[66] See Borkowski, *et al*, ch 5.

[67] See, for an account of this approach, Dobash and Dobash (1992) pp 238–39.

[68] See, eg, Straus (1993). For a discussion of relevant research, see Dobash and Dobash (1992), ch 8.

[69] Undertakings by both parties that they will not molest or interfere with each other.

woman uses violence to protect herself.[70] It also leaves room for the view that mediation between parties to resolve their disputes is appropriate.[71]

Dobash and Dobash (1992 chapter 8; 2004),[72] amongst others, attempt to counter such claims and argue that research focusing on the parity of men's and women's violence, which tends to rely on what is called the 'Conflict Tactics Scale' (CTS), is deficient. In studies which use an 'act-based approach' such as the CTS, respondents are required to indicate whether they had done any of the things referred to in a list of items intended to measure conflict, violence and abuse. The items listed might range from calm discussion, through acts such as throwing things, to the use of a knife or gun. The results of the studies have been interpreted as suggesting that there is little difference in the extent to which men and women engage in these acts (Straus and Gelles 1990).[73]

However, Browne (1987 pp 6–9) indicates that these studies are misleading. Women, she says, underestimate the extent of the violence they have suffered. Moreover, men underreport the extent of the violence they have committed and overestimate their partners' violence in order to justify their own.[74] Dobash and Dobash (1992 pp 275–81; 2004 pp 330–31) in turn say the act-based research is not geared to establishing the context in which acts of violence take place and fails to distinguish between acts of aggression and self-defence.[75] Nor does it discriminate adequately between different types of violence; Dobash and Dobash (1992 p 280) note that two slaps are treated as equivalent to two knife attacks. In addition, they say, it ignores the motives behind actions and therefore does not take account of the possibility that an act, such as throwing something, may not be intended to harm or intimidate. Allied to this is the problem that no attention is paid to determining whether the act causes injury and, if so, whether the injury is serious. Acts of sexual violence, which are almost invariably perpetrated against women, are excluded from some assessments.[76] Finally, act-based research fails to reveal the 'constellation of abuse' that characterises men's violence against women and that includes 'a variety of additional intimidating, aggressive and controlling' behaviour (Dobash and Dobash 2004 p 328).

Stark and Flitcraft (1996) are also critical of family violence research[77] and point out that there is no evidence of a hidden population of battered men in police reports, medical records or clinical samples. They argue that there is a difference between domestic violence against women and other forms of violence:

> Only women attacked by their partners exhibit the syndrome of multiple injuries, medical problems, isolation, psychosocial problems, and almost paralyzing terror we identify with battering … . Battering is not about fighting … . Fighting occurs in many … families and relationships without jeopardizing the liberty of those involved … . In contrast, battering occurs when persons have been forcibly isolated from potentially supportive kin and peer relations and become locked, like hostages, into situations in which objectification, subordination and continued punishment are inevitable. Physical fighting presents a moral concern; battering presents a

---

[70] See, on the use of cross-undertakings, Barron (1990) p 57.

[71] Compare Kaganas and Piper (1994).

[72] See also Kurz (1993).

[73] See generally, on this research, Dobash and Dobash (1992) pp 258–61; Dobash and Dobash (2004); Kurz (1993); Hester, *et al*, (2000) para 1.3. Brush (1993).

[74] See also Dobash and Dobash (2004) p 344.

[75] See also Kurz (1993) p 258.

[76] Mirrlees-Black (1999) reports that it is overwhelmingly women who suffer serious abuse, injury and sexual abuse.

[77] See pp 64–65.

political reality. Unlike the battered husband, the abused woman cannot escape because her situation is mediated by reproduction and enforcement of her dependent status through all society. (Stark and Flitcraft 1996 pp 27–28).

They, like other researchers adopting a feminist perspective, see domestic violence as an extension of male power and control, control that is 'historically and socially constructed' (Dobash and Dobash 1979 p 15).[78] According to Hearn, male violence is intimately bound up with notions of masculinity: 'Men's doing of violence to women simultaneously involves 'being a man' and symbolically showing 'being a man' (1998 p 37). It is a manifestation of dominance and also perpetuates dominance.

Hearn argues that men's use of violence reflects the power relations that exist in 'normal' family life (1998 p 36). As Dobash and Dobash point out, although the status of women has changed, there are still widely held beliefs about the hierarchical nature of family relationships (1979 p 76). These beliefs, coupled with the willingness of many men to use violence because they are taught that it is an appropriate means of problem-solving, are thought to explain domestic violence. Men who use violence, the Dobashes argue, are simply living up to cultural norms that endorse dominance and the enforcement of that dominance (1979 pp 22–24).

That these norms exist is borne out by a research study conducted by Burton, *et al*, (1998).[79] They found that almost one in four young men[80] thought it would be acceptable to hit a woman if she had 'slept with' someone else. A substantial proportion thought it would be acceptable to hit a woman or force her to have sex if she was his wife or girlfriend. Women who nagged or were 'disrespectful' were also seen as deserving of abuse.

Dobash and Dobash contend[81] (1979 p 96) that their research findings[82] demonstrate that abusive husbands exhibit a sense of 'possessiveness, domination and "rightful" control' over their wives. They report that the men they interviewed tended to minimise the seriousness of their violence and to justify it in as being necessary to achieve the purpose of ' "shutting her up", getting a meal or having sex' (Dobash and Dobash 1998 p 167). The women they interviewed reported that the arguments that preceded the first violent incident (Dobash and Dobash, 1979 p 95) and those that followed (p 98) were primarily associated with husbands' possessiveness, their sexual jealousy, their ideas about wives' domestic duties or their ideas about how money should be allocated.[83] In particular, women's resistance to men's demands or failure to fulfil those demands might lead to violence (Hearn 1998 p 36, pp 127–28).[84] For example:

> It would start off with him being angry over trivial little things, a trivial thing like cheese instead of meat on a sandwich, or it might be the way your face just looked for a second at him, or something, and then he'd just give you one across the face, always across the face.
>
> (Dobash and Dobash 1979 p 100)

Women were not expected to challenge their husbands and, if they did, they might be silenced by force:

---

[78] Marital rape too is perceived as an abuse of power. See Russell (1990, originally 1982) p 4 and p 123ff.

[79] See also Mullender, *et al*, (2002) pp 70–74.

[80] Twelve percent of young women concurred.

[81] See also Ptacek (1988).

[82] Arising out of a study conducted in Scotland.

[83] See further Dobash and Dobash (1998) p 144ff See also Pahl (1985b pp 36–39) who found links between control of money by husbands and more general attempts at control and subordination.

[84] However Hearn also found evidence of simple misogyny (1998 p 135).

We were having an argument about something. I think it was money ...  It was the first time he really hit me ...  Before then he used to shout and bawl messages, you know; I wouldn't answer back ...  But this time I started shouting back at him and that was it. He got angry and made a dive for me and started thumping me about.

At what point in the argument did he actually hit you?

When I answered him back, you know. (Dobash and Dobash 1979 p 103)

Similarly:

Q: What made you violent towards her?

A: ....her being clever and cocky with me. (Hearn 1998 p 129)

Campbell's (1992) study of woman killing also focuses on men's proprietariness and dominance[85] and, according to Wilson and Daly (1992), separation increases the risk of woman killing because it challenges male sexual proprietariness; it entails the woman moving out of the man's control. Polk (1994), in a study of violence conducted in Australia, found two 'dominant forms of sexual ownership' (p 56). One category of cases involved violence, fuelled by rage, and aimed at controlling women. The cases he put into this group included cases where women were killed after they ended the relationship and cases where women were killed because they were suspected of infidelity. The other category involved severely depressed men who, before committing suicide, killed their female partners (p 57). In both categories, he notes, the woman is seen as a possession (p 189). Woman killing can be seen as 'an extreme of the more general pattern of male dominance, including physical intimidation, which feminists argue is a feature of men's control of women' (p 211). In contrast, the few women who killed their sexual partners tended to be reacting to abuse by that partner.[86]

**Q** Why do feminist researchers emphasise issues of power and control as well as the predominance of men amongst assailants and women amongst victims?

As we have noted in chapter 9, an important element in the construction of social problems is the designation of their 'causes'. Whether violence is seen as pathological or an expression of uncontrollable rage or sexual jealousy brought on by the conduct of the victim, or whether it is seen as a manifestation of proprietary control, has significant implications for the way it is dealt with by agencies such as the police and the legal system.

Radford's account of a case that went to trial in England in 1982 can be used to illustrate the point. The victim, Mary, was clubbed with a meat tenderiser, smothered with a pillow and strangled. Peter Wood, a former lover, was charged with her murder. On the night of the murder, Peter had gone into the house when she was out and had awaited her homecoming. He told the court that they had made love but that when she rejected his suggestion that they should have a monogamous relationship, he had decided to kill her. In his summing up, the judge endorsed the view that Mary brought her death upon herself.

---

[85] In her Ohio sample, 64% of cases involved male jealousy, which, she suggests, is related to a wish to control and possess the woman concerned. Male dominance was a factor in 18% of cases. Included in this category were a case where the woman refused to fetch the perpetrator more wine and one where the woman rejected her assailant's sexual advances. In only 7% of cases did the victim precipitate the violence by producing a weapon.

[86] See also Browne (1987) pp 9–11, 35, 180–83.

'Mary Bristow,' he said,

> with an IQ of 182, was a rebel from her middle-class background. She was unorthodox in her relationships, so proving that the cleverest people aren't always very wise. Those who engage in sexual relationships should realise that sex is one of the deepest and most powerful human emotions, and if you're playing with sex you're playing with fire ...

In drawing a distinction for the jury between murder and manslaughter, he explained, '... There is a difference between a villain shooting a policeman, and a husband killing his wife or lover at a stage when they can no longer cope.' (Radford 1992 pp 228–32).

> **Q** Wood was convicted of manslaughter. Might a judge adopting a feminist analysis have instructed the jury differently?

What this account illustrates is that the construction of male aggression or male sexuality as uncontrollable and linked to biological make-up serves to normalise violence and to diminish male culpability.[87] It also leads to victim-blaming, in that women who are thought incautiously to inflame male passions are seen to be courting danger. Similarly women who 'provoke' men through their 'nagging' or infidelity are regarded as contributing to their fate.

Feminist commentators reject explanations relying on pathology or on victim blaming. Instead, by explaining violence in terms of male dominance and proprietariness, they seek to locate the blame firmly in the perpetrator and in dominant constructions of masculinity which inform the way in which men are socialised. More fundamentally, by linking violence to women's subordinate status in the family and in society generally, they aim to effect a social transformation.

## VIII. EQUALITY WITHIN MARRIAGE—THE ABOLITION OF THE MARITAL RAPE EXEMPTION

Feminist reformers have met with notable success in campaigning for formal, if not substantive, equality within marriage. However, the last bastion of husbands' legal sovereignty over their wives fell only relatively recently. It was only in 1991, in the case of *R v R (Rape: Marital Exemption)*[88] that it was finally held without qualification[89] that a husband could be convicted of raping his wife.

Apart from Hale's statement,[90] a number of modern justifications for retaining the marital rape exemption were advanced in the literature prior to its abolition. These have been extensively canvassed by other writers[91] and only a brief outline of the debate will be offered here. First, fears existed that, without this protection, husbands would be vulnerable to charges fabricated by malicious wives. Secondly, it was argued that

---

[87] See Stanko (1985) p 9.

[88] [1991] 4 All ER 481. See, now, Sexual Offences Act 2003 ss 1–4. See also Law Commission (1992b).

[89] The exemption was modified in a number of decisions. See, eg, *R v Clarke* [1949] 2 All ER 448; *R v Miller* [1954] 2 QB 282; *R v O'Brien* [1974] 3 All ER 663; *R v Steele* (1976) 65 Crim App R 22; *R v Roberts* [1986] Crim L Rev 188; *R v Sharples* [1990] Crim L Rev 198. See, on sexual acts other than rape, Edwards (1996) pp 187–89.

[90] See p 385.

[91] See, eg, Freeman (1981); Glasgow (1979–80); Scutt (1976); Geis (1978).

evidentiary problems would arise if rape in marriage were a crime. Thirdly, it was contended that prosecution for rape would jeopardise the possibility of reconciliation between the spouses. Fourthly, it was said that adequate remedies already existed in the law and, finally, some commentators took the view that all violence between husband and wife should be dealt with by family law.

The House of Lords in *R v R* took the view quite simply that the exemption was anachronistic, pointing out that women's status had changed since Hale's time and that to say that a woman consented irrevocably to sexual intercourse with her husband was 'unacceptable' in modern times; marriage had come to be regarded as 'a partnership of equals'.[92] The court finally brought down the last legal rule upholding husbands' dominion over the private family.

## IX. GOVERNMENT POLICY AND LAW REFORM

Wife-rape has been declared illegal. The view that domestic violence is an understandable response to 'provocation' or a lapse in self-control is becoming less prevalent. Domestic violence has been firmly established as a serious social problem and the state must therefore be seen to be dealing with it. The involvement of the criminal justice system has increasingly come to be seen as an appropriate response to the problem. The civil law has been reformed in an effort to provide more 'effective' remedies for victims of abuse. Refuges and batterers' programmes have been set up. Yet the notion of family privacy persists to some extent and this, as well as prevailing understandings of violence between intimates, has significantly affected the way in which these measures operate in practice.

Recent years have seen a number of government initiatives intended to address this problem and to tackle domestic violence.[93] A campaign entitled 'Living Without Fear' was launched with the aim of changing attitudes to violence against women generally and domestic violence in particular. A leaflet about domestic violence, *Breaking the Chain*,[94] was issued. A document was published encouraging multi-agency approaches to violence against women (Cabinet Office and Home Office 1999). Guidance was published setting out the issues that agencies are expected to bear in mind and ways in which they might deal with domestic violence (Home Office 2000a). The government indicated that local crime and disorder reduction partnerships established pursuant to the Crime and Disorder Act 1998 should address domestic violence.[95] Special measures were introduced for vulnerable and intimidated witnesses.[96] In 2002 Rape Sentencing Guidelines[97] were published indicating that rape by an assailant known to the victim should be treated no less seriously than stranger rape. A consultation paper was disseminated requesting views on sentencing in domestic violence cases.[98] In 2003 a White Paper,

---

[92] P 484.

[93] See Home Office (1998) para 5.32–5.39 where the government announced its intention to tackle domestic violence.

[94] Now entitled *Loves Me Not*.

[95] See Home Office (2000a) paras 1.6 and 2b.iii.2.

[96] Section 17 Youth Justice and Criminal Evidence Act 1999.

[97] Sentencing Advisory Panel *Advice to the Court of Appeal–9: Rape* (2002). The Court of Appeal followed these in its guidelines issued in *R v Millberry* [2003] 1 WLR 546. See Rumney (2003).

[98] Sentencing Advisory Panel (2004) Sentencing Guidelines on Domestic Violence Cases. Consultation Paper.

*Safety and Justice—the Government's Proposals on Domestic Violence*, was published. And most of the proposals set out in it are now embodied in the Domestic Violence, Crime and Victims Act 2004.

Various strands have shaped government policy: prevention, which includes both preventing violence from happening in the first place and preventing recurrences of violence; justice and protection through legal reform; and support to assist victims to rebuild their lives.[99] The government suggests that, through changing public attitudes, domestic violence can be prevented and that early intervention can help reduce its recurrence. Support is to be delivered in the form of increased availability of accommodation, help to enable victims to stay in their own homes, outreach services and advice. Protection and justice are to be achieved by changes to the civil and the criminal law. In addition, these aims should, in the government's view, be promoted by an 'effective' police response to reports of domestic violence and improved prosecution with appropriate sentencing (Home Office 2003 p 11).

## X. THE CRIMINAL JUSTICE SYSTEM

Some of the acts designated as domestic violence by feminist commentators, such as constant and severe criticism, belittling and withholding money for essentials, do not fall within the criminal law.[100] Nevertheless, abuse can constitute a criminal offence ranging from harassment,[101] common assault, through aggravated assault, assault occasioning actual bodily harm, grievous bodily harm and unlawful wounding to manslaughter or murder.[102] However those involved in implementing the criminal law have traditionally regarded the context of the private relationship within which domestic violence occurs as rendering it less serious or as not warranting a criminal justice response at all.

The police, in particular, have in the past been loath to respond to woman abuse as a crime. They tended to take the view that a criminal justice response was appropriate only in exceptional cases and that domestic violence should be dealt with by social services and family counselling agencies.[103] Police intervention in such cases was seen, first, as a waste of time because women often withdrew their complaints[104] and, secondly, as an unwarranted and potentially damaging invasion into the private sphere of the family. So, for instance, the Association of Chief Police Officers argued before the Select Committee that, '[e]very effort *should be made to re-unite the family*' (House of Commons, Select Committee on Violence in the Family 1975 p 369). It also stated that, '[w]e are, after all, dealing with persons "bound in marriage", and it is important for a host of reasons, to maintain the unity of the spouses' (p 366). The typical response, then, was to refuse to arrest and to treat the assault as a private and/or civil matter (Dobash and Dobash 1979 p 214).

---

[99] See, for example, Home Office (2003) pp 6, 8 and 11. See also Cabinet Office and Home Office (1999) *Introduction*.

[100] See Stanko, *et al*, (1998) p 12.

[101] See Protection from Harassment Act 1997.

[102] See Offences Against the Person Act 1861.

[103] See Dobash and Dobash (1992) p 150.

[104] A joint inspection of police and the CPS revealed that in 44% of cases dealt with by the CPS, the victim made a withdrawal statement (HMcpsi and HMIC 2004 para 6.15). See also Cretney and Davis (1997a).

The view held by many officers that domestic violence cases did not involve 'real crimes'[105] and that they were unlikely to proceed to prosecution gave rise to a reluctance on the part of the police to record them as crimes (Edwards 1996 p 194).[106] Often, the police would see their role as a conciliatory one, calming the situation down.[107] If a woman indicated that she wanted more done, she might be pressed on whether she really wanted to take legal action and might be given time to 'think it over' (Faragher 1985 p 117). These strategies had the effect of leaving the woman unprotected and in a state of fear.[108] Racist attitudes on the part of the police exacerbated matters for ethnic minority women.[109] And a recent study suggests that these may be persisting. Humphreys and Thiara (2002) report complaints from women about 'lack of interpreters, stereotyped attitudes to Asian women; lack of action in relation to the perpetrator; and a dismissive and judgmental attitude towards the woman' (p 49).

Smith (1989), reviewing the earlier research on police practice, comments:

> The view that the police should not be involved in dealing with domestic violence reveals an underlying assumption that such violence is not 'truly' criminal. ...The rationale for this seems to lie in the notion that domestic violence is almost exclusively a 'family matter' or a 'private affair'. ... (p 55)

> Reluctance [by the police] to intervene was, to a large part, shaped by notions and assumptions about the role of women in society and, in particular, within families as wives and mothers; the importance attached to 'family life' and the consequent perceived need for families to stay intact; and the privacy traditionally accorded families in which state intervention is seen as being mainly inappropriate unless it is designed to help families stay together. ... (p 85).

> [A]lthough domestic violence is not *simply* a crime problem, it nevertheless remains such a problem. If the criminal justice system does not treat it as seriously as other crime problems ... then the criminal justice system may signal to other agencies and to the wider public that domestic violence is a problem with which we should not be too concerned. ...Although it seems unlikely that the response of the criminal justice system *on its own*, will be sufficient to combat domestic violence or to deal with the diverse problems it brings in its wake, it is arguable that that response is nevertheless both necessary and potentially very important. The symbolic nature of law—its declaratory and denunciatory functions—is important in shaping climates of opinion. The criminal law is after all a normative statement. It sets the boundaries of acceptable behaviour. (p 89, emphasis in original)

**Q** Should the police be taught more about domestic violence? Should they be deprived of their discretion and instructed to enforce the law strictly? Could police inaction in the face of domestic violence constitute a breach of Article 3 of the European Convention on Human Rights?

Police policy has changed in response to criticism and, officially, domestic violence is no longer viewed as a private matter. For some years now, the police have been expected to

---

[105] See further, Bossy and Coleman (2000) pp 29–31.
[106] For a summary of research, see Edwards (1996) pp 195–96. See also Edwards (1989).
[107] See Borkowski, *et al*, (1983) p 192; London Strategic Policy Unit, Police Monitoring and Research Group (1986) p 3.
[108] See Borkowski, *et al*, (1983) p 192.
[109] For a discussion of the particular problems created by racism, see Mama (1989) p 304.

be more interventionist[110] and pro-arrest policies[111] have been developed along the lines of those introduced in North America.[112] An inspection report published in 2004 focusing on the investigation and prosecution of domestic violence cases noted that considerable strides had been made in the development of policies designed to ensure that incidents are taken seriously (HMcpsi and HMIC 2004 p 6).

Over 90% of police forces now have Domestic Violence Officers/Co-ordinators within established units, playing a mainly supportive role, acting as a point of contact with the police for the victim and liaising with other support services (HMcpsi and HMIC 2004 para 3.1).[113] Among other things, these officers play an important[114] part in carrying out risk assessments and in helping victims through court proceedings.[115]

Other measures are intended to affect the police more generally. The police service has adopted a revised Home Office Circular on domestic violence (Home Office 2000b). This makes it clear that the police should not treat an incident less seriously because has occurred in a domestic setting. It stipulates that an incident should only be 'no-crimed' if there is clear evidence that an offence did not take place. It instructs officers at the scene to speak to the parties separately and in a way that ensures that the victim will not be overheard. It stresses that the police should not act as conciliators. It requires the police to ask the victim if she wishes to take the matter to court. However it also emphasises the importance of gathering photographic and other forensic evidence so as to reduce the need to rely on the victim's willingness and ability to testify. In addition, it creates a presumption in favour of arrest in all but exceptional cases. It states that where the authority to arrest exists,[116] and where evidence is present, the offender should normally be arrested and a decision not to do so should be recorded and justified.

However, the inspectors observed that often these policies were not reflected in practice (p 6). They concluded that, overall, 'the priority given to domestic violence locally was variable' (p 10).[117] The inspectors found that call-handlers in police control rooms lacked training and sometimes failed to prioritise calls appropriately and, as a result, police responses to reports of domestic violence could be too slow. This meant that

---

[110] See Edwards (1996) pp 192–93; Home Office 1990b.

[111] But see, for an overview of other measures adopted by some police forces, such as risk assessment, safety planning, tiered systems of intervention and the provision of alarms to victims, Paradine and Wilkinson (2004) pp 43–45.

[112] In the USA, feminist campaigns centred around increased use of criminal sanctions and included the tactic of suing police departments for failing to implement assault laws. See further Walsh (1995). In response, some states expanded police powers of arrest while others made arrest mandatory. Pro-arrest polices were adopted by police forces, and in some areas 'no-drop' policies prevented the dropping of charges except in exceptional circumstances (see Morley and Mullender (1992) pp 266–68). These pro-arrest policies gained considerable support as a result of a well-publicised research project, the 'Minneapolis Experiment', carried out by Sherman and Berk (1984). On comparing 3 possible police responses to domestic violence—arrest, advice/mediation and separating the parties—the researchers found arrest to be most effective in reducing repeat offending. They therefore recommended that police should operate on the basis of a presumption in favour of arrest. In Canada, researchers reported favourably on the effects of a pro-charge policy adopted in London, Ontario (see further Morley and Mullender (1992) p 267). However, Morley and Mullender point out that attempts to replicate the Sherman and Berk study have failed (1992 p 270).

[113] The police attending an incident generally provide information to victims or make referrals to helping organisations (HMcpsi and HMIC 2004 para 3. 26).

[114] However, within the police service, domestic violence work has low status. (HMcpsi and HMIC 2004 para 3.4).

[115] See HMcpsi and HMIC 2004 para 7.91.The victim can also choose an agency, whether Victim Support/Witness Service or an agency specialising in domestic violence to be present in court to support her.

[116] This power will be widened to cover common assault. S 10 of the Domestic Violence, Crime and Victims Act, when it comes into force, will make this an arrestable offence.

[117] The Metropolitan Police force issued a press release in response to the report stating that it had already put in place most of the measures recommended by the joint inspectorate (Metropolitan Police 2004).

victims' first contact with the police could be unsatisfactory (HMcpsi and HMIC 2004 paras 2.1–2.5). Not all police officers understood force policy and responses to incidents varied with individual officers.[118] Few, with the exception of specialist officers 'had any real understanding of the dynamics of domestic violence' (HMcpsi and HMIC 2004 para 2.18). Police practice relating to arrest varied between forces with arrests being made in 13% to 63% of cases where, potentially, there could have been arrests (HMcpsi and HMIC 2004 para 2.21). Case histories were seldom provided to officers attending incidents and they were seldom made aware of court orders, bail conditions or injunctions unless the victim told them (HMcpsi and HMIC 2004 paras 2.23–2.24). The inspectors noted differences between forces in the percentages of incidents recorded as crimes and concluded that there was 'potentially, a significant under-recording of domestic violence crime' (HMcpsi and HMIC 2004 para 2.28).[119] In particular, potential offences under the Protection from Harassment Act 1997 were being missed and officers showed inadequate understanding of the legislation (HMcpsi and HMIC 2004 para 6.4) Where a crime was recorded, only 21% of offenders were charged (HMcpsi and HMIC 2004 para 6.6).[120] Decisions as to whether a crime would be recorded or a charge preferred were usually based on the victim's wishes and willingness to co-operate (HMcpsi and HMIC 2004 para 6.9). Enhanced, or what the report refers to as 'effective' evidence gathering rarely featured in police practice, with few officers recording injuries or taking photographs of the scene (HMcpsi and HMIC 2004 paras 2.30–2.32).[121] Poor investigation meant that corroborative evidence was lacking, leading to reliance on the victim's testimony. If she proved unwilling to proceed, the CPS would often take the view that the case was unlikely to succeed in court and it was dropped (HMcpsi and HMIC 2004 para 1.16). The inspectors report that, partly because of this, the attrition rates in these cases has been consistently higher than for most other crimes (HMcpsi and HMIC 2004 para 1.16)

Clearly, then, implementation of policy has been patchy and the Domestic Violence, Crime and Victims Act makes provision for of the Secretary of State to issue a code of practice[122] to govern the services, including police services, provided for victims of crime. But in any event, the pro-arrest policies are being criticised by some as having the effect of endangering women. Not only might arrest fail to deter violence,[123] it might put women at risk of reprisals from an irate partner (Morley and Mullender 1992 pp 270–71; Hoyle 1998 pp 189–90).

Hoyle and Sanders (2000) conducted research in 1996–7, interviewing victims of domestic violence to discover what response they wanted when they called the police to

---

[118] Humphreys and Thiara (2000) pp 55ff report that the experiences of the women in their study varied considerably. In particular, while many reported positive change in the attitude of police, this often depended on whether they qualified as 'good' victims in the eyes of the police.

[119] Between 10% and 66% of incidents were recorded as crimes in the different forces, an overall rate of 25%. According to the joint inspection, had all potential crimes been recorded, the figure would have been 46% (HMcpsi and HMIC 2004 para 6.3) As the inspectors point out, not all abusive incidents to which the police are called involve behaviour defined as a crime.

[120] When 'missed' crimes were taken into account, the figure dropped to 10% (HMcpsi and HMIC 2004 para 6.9). Hester, *et al*, (2003) report that in their study, less than a third of arrests led to criminal charges.

[121] See also Hester, *et al*, (2003).

[122] Section 32. There will also be a Commissioner for Victims and Witnesses to promote the interests of victims and witnesses (ss 48 and 49) and a Victim's Advisory Panel (s 55). Not in force at time of writing.

[123] Maxwell, Garner and Fagan (2002) found a correlation between arrest and a consistent but modest reduction in repeat offences against the victim (p 70). However they concede that many offenders are not deterred by police involvement or arrest (p 71–72). See also Hanmer, *et al*, (1999) p 37. Generally, however, research on this is inconclusive (Paradine and Wilkinson 2004 para 5.2).

an incident. Over half the women interviewed wanted the offender to be arrested but a significant minority did not. Furthermore, most of the women who wanted an arrest did not want a prosecution. (p 22).[124] The authors concede that the choice not to pursue arrest or prosecution was often a result of being in a coercive relationship. However these were rational choices prompted by fear, by community or familial pressure or by the fact that the women were isolated and had no resources (pp 21 and 29).[125] The best thing for these women, say Hoyle and Sanders, would be to help them to change their circumstances so that they can make different choices (p 21). To this end, they say, a range of measures is necessary. Arrest only helped to reduce violence if combined with other measures such as perpetrator programmes (p 30).[126] They assert that the pro-arrest stance is mainly of symbolic value (p 30),[127] although it is useful in giving the women time and space to decide what to do. Support from domestic violence officers and the use of bail conditions could help to ensure that the time is used constructively (p 31). Pro-arrest policies, on their own, then, may fail some women.[128] In particular, the utility of such policies must be questioned in the light of the way the Crown Prosecution Service and the courts deal with domestic violence cases.

## 1. The Crown Prosecution Service

The Crown Prosecution Service revised its policy on prosecuting domestic violence in 2001 in a way that accords some recognition to the interests of victims (CPS 2001 para 5.1–5.2). The Crown Prosecution Service decides upon the charge to be pursued (CPS 2001 para 6.1–6.3) and, whereas in the past, reduced charges were common,[129] charging is now, it has been said, generally appropriate (HMcpsi and HMIC 2004 para 7.53).[130] In deciding whether to proceed with the case, the prosecutor has to apply two tests. Crown prosecutors must be satisfied that there is enough evidence to provide 'a realistic prospect of conviction'. If the case satisfies this requirement they must go on to consider whether the prosecution is necessary in the public interest. When considering the public interest test, the prosecutor should always take into account 'the consequences for the victim of the decision whether or not to prosecute, and any views expressed by the victim or the victim's family' (CPS 2001 paras 3.2–3.5). If the evidential test is passed and the victim is willing to give evidence, a prosecution will 'almost always' be mounted (para 5.3).

Where the victim withdraws support for the prosecution, and where it is suspected that she has been pressured to do so, the police will be asked to investigate (para 4.9). If

---

124 This was usually because the arrest had had the desired effect on the assailant's behaviour or because of fear that prosecution would not end the violence and could even provoke more (Hoyle and Sanders 2000 p 23). The main reason women did not want to make a statement or wanted to withdraw a statement was fear of retaliation. Others did not want to pursue the legal route because they had separated. Some, however, said they wanted to save the relationship (p 24).

125 See Hester, *et al*, (2000) para 1.11. See also Richards (2004) paras 4.3.3 and 5.3.3.

126 See below.

127 But see Dobash (2003) p 316 who emphasises both the symbolic force and the 'real' consequences of the use of the criminal law.

128 Indeed, there is evidence from the USA and Canada that mandatory arrest policies have resulted in increased rates of arrest of both men and women. See Chesney-Lind (2002) p 83.

129 See Paradine and Wilkinson (2004) para 6.1. A survey carried out as recently as 2001 amongst workers in the domestic violence sector, such as refuge workers, evoked complaints about the down-grading of charges from an 'overwhelming majority' of respondents (Barron 2002 p 17).

130 But see Barron (2002) p 17. Her respondents reported that charges were often downgraded or dropped.

the victim insists on withdrawing the complaint, the prosecutor is required to consider whether the case can proceed in her absence and whether it is in the public interest to proceed (para 4.10). In serious cases the prosecution may consider requiring the victim to give evidence or using Section 23 of the Criminal Justice Act 1988[131] (paras 4.4–4.15).

Complainants wishing to drop charges are obliged to do so formally. In the past, they were expected to make a statement to the police or to the court, sometimes in the witness box (Cretney and Davis 1996 p 169). This practice was criticised as operating punitively rather than helping complainants. Cretney and Davis maintained that it did not identify those cases where women were coerced into retracting. Rather it functioned to protect the police and the court if serious violence occurred at a later date (1996 p 169). Moreover, it was suggested that the ability to drop charges is an important bargaining chip for women negotiating safety and that they should not be deprived of it (Morley and Mullender 1992 p 272). It has since been decided that, although the police should take a statement to determine whether the victim had been put under pressure,[132] prosecutors should no longer require victims to attend court to explain why they wish to withdraw their allegations (HMcpsi and HMIC 2004 para 1.25).

Finally, measures have been put into place to improve witness care. Victims are supposed to be encouraged to articulate the effects on them of the violence in personal statements. Also, victims are supposed to be kept informed about the progress of their cases; the CPS is responsible under the Direct Communication with Victims Scheme for communicating directly with victims to explain decisions such as a decision to discontinue a prosecution (HMcpsi and HMIC 2004 para 1.4).

The CPS has been found wanting in fulfilling this role (HMcpsi and HMIC 2004 para 3.28) as well as in other respects. The joint inspectorate made a number of criticisms: the majority of CPS files do not include personal statements from victims (HMcpsi and HMIC 2004 para 2.44); section 23 of the Criminal Justice Act 1988 is seldom used (HMcpsi and HMIC 2004 para 7.3); some prosecutors continue the practice of requiring the victim to appear in court to explain why she does not wish to proceed (HMcpsi and HMIC 2004 para 7.27); breaches of bail conditions are not acted on (HMcpsi and HMIC 2004 para 7.5); and prosecutors still appear to accept bind-overs in some cases when it would be more appropriate to pursue criminal proceedings (HMcpsi and HMIC 2004 para 7.68).

Overall, it seems from the findings of the joint inspection report that it is only a small proportion of domestic violence incidents that lead to prosecution and conviction. The report estimates that approximately 5% of incidents reported to the police resulted in a conviction (HMcpsi and HMIC 2004 para 6.11).[133] However it seems that the CPS does not necessarily drop charges if the victim does not want to proceed.[134] In 44% of cases dealt with by the CPS, the victim made a withdrawal statement and in about a third of

---

[131] Which provides that in certain circumstances, such as fear on the part of a witness, a statement can be admitted without the witness having to appear. S 80(3) of the PACE 1984 made a wife a compellable witness in cases of domestic violence. However this power is rarely used.

[132] Police shortcomings in this regard have been noted (HMcpsi and HMIC 2004 para 2.45).

[133] See also Hester, *et al*, (2003).

[134] The CPS is often unwilling to proceed with a prosecution if the victim indicates that she does not wish to co-operate. There are a number of reasons for acceding to the woman's wishes. Her failure to co-operate is seen as making a conviction unlikely. In addition, it is recognised that the victim may be put at risk as a result of a prosecution. Cretney and Davis (1997b p 88), while suggesting that failure to proceed on the part of the CPS means that the symbolic force of the law is not being deployed to condemn domestic violence, nevertheless take the view that compelling women to testify is not helpful. Victims should, however, receive the support and encouragement that would enable them to go through with the prosecution process. This would produce a higher conviction rate which, coupled with appropriate penalties, would convey the message that domestic violence cannot be tolerated.

these, the CPS summonsed the victim to appear in court or proceeded on the basis of evidence other than the victim's (HMcpsi and HMIC 2004 para 6.15).[135] The low conviction rate may be attributable at least in part to the attitude of the courts.

*2. The Courts*

High acquittal rates, the frequent use of bind-overs, the use of plea-bargaining and the leniency of sentences have been observed by a number of researchers and, it has been suggested, these practices make victims feel let down by the court process.[136] Edwards (1996 p 208), for example, noted that sentences were reduced where the assailant was not considered a danger to the public. Courts also took into account matters such as the victim's infidelity. Hester, *et al*, (2003) found that sentences were more lenient when reference was made to contact between offenders and their children.[137] Cretney and Davis found that there was less likely to be a conviction where the couple were still together and, when there was a conviction, the penalty was likely to be lower (1997a p 153). Serious violence, they say, attracts a low level of punishment because it takes place in a domestic context (1997a p 153). Cases, they say, are still viewed 'through the lens of "the couple" or the "family"' (1997a p 147); domestic violence is still not regarded as 'fully criminal' (Cretney and Davis 1996 p 171).

The government, at the time of writing, is considering whether specialist domestic violence courts would 'offer more effective protection for victims' (Home Office 2003 p 28).[138] A number of pilot schemes are already in operation, emphasising co-operation between all relevant agencies. It is also envisaged that there will be an 'improvement of the civil/criminal interface' in these courts (Home Office 2003 pp 28–29). A recent American study suggests that specialised domestic violence courts focusing on victim safety and offender accountability may contribute to a reduction in repeat violence. They also appear, by taking domestic violence seriously, to encourage the police to arrest more readily (Gover, MacDonald and Alpert 2003).

## XI. THE PROTECTION FROM HARASSMENT ACT 1997

This Act, initially introduced to deal with 'stalking', covers a broad range of conduct and one of its main uses has been in relation to domestic violence.[139] The legislation is dealt with more comprehensively in chapter 12 but some aspects of its operation are covered here.

The statute prohibits the pursuit of a course of conduct that amounts to harass-

---

[135] Compare Hoyle and Sanders (2000) p 16. They found that '[f]or police officers and prosecution, victim withdrawal marked the end of the case' (p 17). See also Hoyle (1998).

[136] See Hester, *et al*, (2003); Hoyle (1998) pp 191–93; Humphreys and Thiara (2002) p 51. The joint inspectorate found that some cases were discontinued when a bind-over was ordered (HMcpsi and HMIC 2004 para 6.15). The acquittal rate was significantly higher than the national average (HMcpsi and HMIC 2004 para 6.17).

[137] See, on domestic violence and contact, ch 14.

[138] For an evaluation of specialist courts, see Cook, *et al*, (2004). The authors observed that more custodial sentences and community penalties were being imposed. Victim satisfaction increased but the specialist courts had no effect on the level of charges or the rate of victim withdrawals.

[139] See Harris (2000) p 9. However Humphreys and Thiara (2002 p 51) report little use of the Act in relation to women in their sample. Barron (2002 p 18) also found the Act to be under-used.

ment[140] and creates two offences: harassment contrary to this prohibition[141] and putting a person in fear of violence.[142] According to Section 7, a 'course of conduct' must involve conduct on at least two occasions. 'Harassment' is not defined, save that Section 7 provides that it includes alarming or causing distress to a person and that harassment may take the form of either words or conduct. This is taken to encompass 'unwanted telephone calls, letters or gifts, vandalism of property or harassment of family and friends' (Harris 2000 pp 1–2). These types of conduct may be accompanied by threats and are often linked to controlling behaviour and abuse (Harris 2000 p 2). Conviction may result in imprisonment or a fine. In addition, the court can make a restraining order[143] prohibiting certain kinds of behaviour, such as contacting the victim or visiting her home.[144] Breach of an order can carry a prison sentence. The Act also makes provision for a civil remedy for harassment in the form of damages.[145]

Harris' research into the use of the legislation revealed that some 41% of cases involved parties who were intimately known to each other, usually ex-partners. In 94% of cases in her sample involving 'intimates', the suspect was male (2000 p 11 and Table 2.2). The most common reason for harassment was that the complainant had decided to end the relationship with the suspect (p 17).

**Q** Do you consider that Harris' findings mirror the findings of researchers attributing domestic violence to male proprietary control?

In her evaluation of the operation of the legislation, Harris found support for its use among the police, the CPS and magistrates; it was seen providing the possibility of prosecuting cases that were not adequately covered previously by the criminal law (2000 p 41). However she also found similar problems to those identified in relation to the operation of the criminal justice system in domestic violence cases generally. She found that the police did not have background information when they attended an incident (pp 21–22), information that could be relevant to establishing a course of conduct. There was some confusion among the police as to what the requirements of the Act are (p 20). There was extensive use of bail conditions but suspects were simply re-bailed where these conditions were breached (p 34). The attrition rate was high as a result of lack of evidence and the decisions of complainants not to proceed (pp 29–30). Bindovers were common (p 31) and there was some evidence of down-charging (p 46). The most common sentence was a conditional discharge although this was often combined with a restraining order (p xviii and p 37). But while complainants were generally kept informed of developments by the police (p 26), they were not told of the outcome of a trial or whether a restraining order had been made (p 38). Harris suggests that restraining orders should be made in far more cases than they are (p 56) but notes that breaches of such orders were not acted on by police (p 43). This is in contrast to Barron's finding that restraining orders are 'quite effective' (2002 p 18).

There was some disagreement among those surveyed by Harris as to whether it was appropriate to use the criminal rather than the civil provisions in the Act. The police tended to be willing to use the criminal law but complained of being thwarted when cases reached the CPS or the courts. The judiciary, in particular, seemed to assume that

[140] S 1.
[141] S 2.
[142] S 4.
[143] S 5.
[144] See Harris (2000) p 5.
[145] S 3.

harassment should be dealt with as a civil matter (p 48). Some magistrates in turn felt that criminalising harassment could lead to unfounded and vindictive accusations. Police and prosecutors were also wary of what they termed 'paranoid' women who 'read more into another's behaviour than was perhaps warranted' (p 42). This view is somewhat surprising in the light of the fact that Harris found that few women knew of the Act or what to expect when they made a report to the police. And about half of the victims interviewed had 'endured the unwanted behaviour for a significant period before they decided to report it' (2000 p 19). The fear of vindictive women is also surprising given the high attrition rate noted by Harris.

**Q** Can you think of other areas of the law where women have traditionally assumed to be irrational, untrustworthy or vindictive?

## XII. CRIMINAL OR CIVIL PROCEEDINGS?

The criminal justice system has been criticised both for failing to be sufficiently punitive towards offenders whose victims pursue criminal proceedings and for being punitive to women who do not wish to do so. The Law Commission, reviewing the role of the law in domestic violence cases, expressed the view that the criminal law, being primarily concerned with punishment, might be inappropriate in many cases; most victims simply 'want the violence to stop and they want protection' (1992a para 2.9). Civil law, it thought, could be framed to provide a flexible framework enabling account to be taken of the different needs of different victims (*ibid*). Cretney and Davis, in turn, point out that the criminal law, with its focus on discrete incidents, is not always appropriate for dealing with what may have been a long history of violence (1995 p 84).

Feminist commentators[146] have expressed unease at giving priority to civil remedies for domestic violence, suggesting that this approach reinforces the notion that it is not a criminal matter and that it diverts attention away from necessary reform of the criminal process. Nevertheless, there is research indicating that women feel that they have benefited from using the civil law. In addition, there are advantages in the lower standard of proof and in the fact that orders can be tailored to meet a variety of problems (Humphreys and Kaye 1997 p 405).

**Q** What role do you see for the criminal justice system in domestic violence cases? Why?

## XIII. CIVIL LAW

The High Court has always had jurisdiction to grant injunctions where it is just and expedient to do so[147] and the County Court acquired the same powers through statute.[148] However, the exercise of these powers was subject to limitations.[149] Pursuant to

---

[146] For an overview of the literature, see Humphreys and Kaye (1997) p 405.
[147] S 37(1) of the Supreme Court Act 1981, declaratory of the existing law.
[148] S 38(1) of the County Court Act 1984.
[149] See p 456 n 5; p 461 n 43.

the recommendations made in 1975 by the Select Committee on Violence in the Family, legislation designed specifically to improve the civil law protection of victims of domestic violence was passed.[150] These laws enabled women to seek injunctions without first instituting divorce or separation proceedings. An order could be sought to prevent one partner molesting the other or the children. In addition it was possible to apply for an ouster[151] order excluding the abuser from the common home and even from the area in which it was situated. A power of arrest could be attached by the court to an order, authorising a police constable to arrest without warrant a person whom he or she had reasonable cause to suspect was in breach of an injunction.

However a number of problems were identified in relation to the scope of the civil law and its implementation.[152] In 1992, the Law Commission described the then existing civil remedies as complex, confusing and lacking integration (1992a para 1.2). Post-separation violence was not adequately addressed.[153] The law governing ousters, orders that could be especially useful for abused women, was thought to be too restrictive. The Law Commission noted that the criteria for the award of ouster orders placed too much emphasis on the seriousness of the conduct of the abuser rather than on its effects on the applicant. Also children's interests were given insufficient weight (1992a para 2.26).

Barron (1990), reporting on an empirical study investigating the effectiveness of legal protection for victims of domestic violence, found deficiencies in the remedies and services provided. She criticised the way in which the legislation relating to ousters was being applied, observing that, whereas non-molestation orders were granted fairly readily, anything more than that could be difficult to obtain. Courts were reluctant to deprive a man of 'his' home, she said, quoting one judge as saying that ousters 'are remedies of the last resort' (p 50). Courts frequently referred to such orders as 'Draconian'[154] and a Practice Direction was issued indicating that an ouster should not last longer than three months.[155] Limitations were also placed on the granting of *ex parte* orders in order to protect the rights, especially the property rights, of respondents.[156]

**Q** What does the emphasis on property rights tell us about the seriousness with which the courts have tended to view domestic violence?

Barron reported that once obtained, orders often proved ineffective.[157] Neither the police nor the courts, she observed, provided the back-up necessary to enforce them (1990 p 65). Often, orders, especially *ex parte* orders, had no power of arrest[158] attached (p 55) and, in the absence of a power of arrest, the response from the police was found

---

[150] The Domestic Violence and Matrimonial Proceedings Act 1976 and the Domestic Proceedings and Magistrates Courts Act 1978. The Matrimonial Homes Act 1967 (incorporated in and extended by the Matrimonial Homes Act 1983), although not designed primarily to provide remedies for victims of abuse, came to be designated the principal Act governing ousters.

[151] Or in the magistrates' court, an exclusion order which was somewhat more limited in scope.

[152] See, generally, Edwards (1996) p 213ff.

[153] See, eg, Peacock (1998) p 629. Post-separation violence is common. For example in a study undertaken by Humphreys and Thiara, more than three quarters of the women surveyed suffered post-separation violence (2003 p 199).

[154] Law Commission (1992a) para 2.26.

[155] Practice Note [1978] 2 All ER 1056.

[156] See *Ansah v Ansah* [1977] 2 WLR 760; Practice Note (Matrimonial Cause: Injunction) [1978] 1 WLR 925.

[157] But see Humphreys and Kaye (1997) p 405.

[158] In *Lewis v Lewis* [1978] 2 WLR 644, the Court of Appeal stated that a power of arrest should not be regarded as a routine remedy.

to be particularly weak. Courts in turn were reluctant to send men to prison for breach of an injunction or undertaking (p 69).[159] Instead, judges appeared to stress the need for amicable agreement (p 123; p 69).

## XIV. THE FAMILY LAW ACT 1996

In the wake of considerable criticism of the law, Part IV the Family Law Act 1996 was enacted, with the intention of addressing the difficulties identified.[160] While the provisions of the legislation are discussed more fully in chapter 12,[161] a brief outline is provided here.

There are two basic types of remedy, 'non-molestation orders' and 'occupation orders', and eligibility for either order is restricted to 'associated persons'. This category of persons is defined in Section 62(3) and reflects the underlying principle that persons who have, or have had, a family or domestic relationship should be protected (Cretney, *et al*, 2002 p 252–54).[162]

As regards occupation orders, the Act draws a distinction between persons who are 'entitled' and those who are not. Entitlement can derive either from possession of matrimonial home rights, arising automatically out of marriage, or from an interest in the property.[163] This will change when the amendments to the 1996 Act embodied in the Civil Partnership Act 2004 come into force. Matrimonial home rights will be substituted by home rights and those rights will be vested in civil partners as well as spouses.

The policy seems to be that the courts should have more extensive powers to protect an applicant who is 'entitled' than one who is not. Moreover, a distinction is drawn within the category of non-entitled applicants between former spouses and cohabitants or former cohabitants; the law affords greater protection to former spouses (and in future, former civil partners) than to cohabitants and former cohabitants.

**Q** What is the purpose of these distinctions?

A 'balance of harm test' was introduced to determine whether an occupation order should be granted. Broadly, the court must decide whether to make an order by balancing the extent of the harm likely to result if the order is not granted against the extent of the harm likely to result if it is granted.

---

[159] This attitude may be changing. In *Neil v Ryan* [1998] 2 FLR 1068 it was held that a serious attack in breach of a non-molestation order warranted immediate committal to prison. In *Hale v Tanner* [2000] 2 FLR 879 the court said that while it is not usual to imprison on the first breach, there is no rule preventing this (para 26). In *Lomas v Parle* [2003] EWCA Civ 1804; [2004] 1 FLR 812, the Court of Appeal increased the sentence imposed in committal proceedings under the 1996 Act. The husband had repeatedly disobeyed court orders and the appeal judge commented that it was a case with an appalling history of intimidation and abuse' (para 41). He was sentenced to eight months' imprisonment concurrent on each of the admitted breaches. The sentence would have been at least ten months but the court took into account the fact that there were also criminal proceedings and there was an element of double jeopardy. See also *Wilson v Webster* [1998] 1 FLR 1097.

[160] Some modifications to the Law Commission's recommendations were necessitated by a campaign by a tabloid newspaper and a minority of Conservative MPs alleging that the original Bill (the Family Homes and Domestic Violence Bill 1995) undermined 'family values' (Murphy, 1996) p 845).

[161] And see, for detailed discussion, Cretney, *et al*, (2002) pp 235ff; Bird (1996a).

[162] For a critique of this reasoning in relation to non-molestation orders, see Hayes (1996). 'Associated persons' is defined to include, eg, persons who are or have been married to each other, cohabitants or former cohabitants and relatives. See further ch 12.

[163] S 33(1)(a).

The law governing *ex parte* applications has been relaxed and the procedure is no longer considered exceptional, whether in relation to non-molestation orders or occupation orders.[164]

Powers of arrest are no longer discouraged and are even obligatory in some cases.[165] Where a power of arrest is not attached, a warrant of arrest can be sought in terms of which the police are involved in enforcement.[166] And when a respondent is arrested, the court is empowered to remand him in custody so that he is not free to exact his revenge on his partner.[167]

Section 60 also provides a potential source of help for women afraid to proceed themselves but who want a remedy; rules of court may provide for third parties to act for her.[168] This section has not yet been implemented but there is strong support for it to be put into effect. It has even been suggested that it could lead to better protection: 'if the police are seen to be applying for orders on a woman's behalf, the courts are less likely to disregard the seriousness of the situation' (Barron 2002 p 10).

> **Q** The changes to policies within the criminal justice system and the reform of the legislation governing the civil law appear to be intended to increase protection for victims of abuse. How do you reconcile these changes with the changes designed to encourage mediation on divorce (see chapter 11) and the emphasis on the 'implacably hostile' mother in contact cases (see chapter 14)?

Researchers have sought to evaluate the Family Law Act and the results suggest qualified approval. In a study conducted among domestic violence workers (Barron 2002), the majority of those surveyed thought that the 1996 Act had improved protection (p 5). However, the general view was that orders are only effective if the perpetrator has some respect for the law and if the police are prepared to enforce the order (p 9). Powers of arrest are seen to be crucial to effectiveness.[169]

These conclusions are mirrored in Humphreys and Thiara's research. They report that the orders available under the civil law have been found to be helpful in many cases:

> The [quantitative] data suggest that there was a group of women who found protection orders effective. In fact, over one-third (36%) of those who used protection orders said that they were very helpful and the abuse stopped. A further 39% said that they were of some help; that although they were breached, the abuse may have been less or they felt more protected … .
>
> There is evidence in both the quantitative and the qualitative data that a significant group of women are finding effective (or some) protection using civil remedies. A total of 73% of this sample of women said that they would apply for an order if they needed one in the future, though many (60% who answered the question) said that they would have preferred a third

---

[164] See s 45. In the county court in, 2003, 12,414 applications for non-molestation orders were made *ex parte*, while only 4612 were made on notice. For occupation orders the figures were 7207 applications made *ex parte* and 3372 made on notice (DCA 2003b Table 5.9).

[165] See s 47(1). In 2003 in the county court, powers of arrest were attached to 19,112 non-molestation orders and 2706 orders had no power of arrest attached. Powers of arrest were attached to 7826 occupation orders and 1491 orders had no power of arrest attached (DCA 2003b Table 5.9).

[166] S 47(8).

[167] Ss 47(10)–(11), read with Sch 5. There were 515 remands in custody and 369 remands on bail in 2003 in the county court (DCA 2003b Table 5.9).

[168] It remains unclear who will be authorised to act in terms of such rules. It could be the police, the CPS or organisations such as Women's Aid. For discussion of third-party applications, see Humphreys and Kaye (1997); Burton (2003).

[169] See Bossy and Coleman (2000) para 3.3.

party to take the order on their behalf to relieve them of the dangers and responsibilities of invoking legal proceedings against their partner or ex-partner … .

[H]owever … for those women who were suffering chronic post-separation violence, civil protection orders had little impact. Over a third of the women (36%) completing the question-naire found that abuse was continuing. Twenty five per cent of those who used orders found them of no help; the abuse continued and police or the courts were unhelpful in acting upon breaches. These women experienced themselves to be outside protection, a finding mirrored in other research which indicates significant disillusionment with the effectiveness of orders … .

Women who were unable to access orders also failed to gain protection. This included women who found them too expensive, who lacked knowledge of the orders, who were afraid to take court proceedings for fear of making the abuse worse, and whose immigration status pre-cluded them from access. Interestingly, the data on the use of non-molestation orders shows that in spite of significant improvements to protection orders under the Family Law Act, 1996, and a very substantial increase in orders with a power of arrest, there has not been an increase in the actual number of civil protection orders granted under the legislation … . The increasing financial cost of legal services is posited as a significant factor inhibiting use.[170]

(2003 pp 203–5, references omitted)

Humphreys and Thiara conclude that:

The effectiveness of protection orders for some women suggests that there is a group of men who respond to cultural norms and the legislative framework and who do not want to be seen to step outside the law. The shame brought to the family or the impact on employment provide significant restraining factors. More assertive action on breaches could impact relatively quickly on making more of these orders effective It is also important to recognise that all the women in this study had the support of outreach services and that they therefore had access to information, advocacy and on-going support. … [I]t is difficult in the extreme for women to take legal action and give evidence about violence and abuse without support. (2003 p 209)

The authors go on to consider the law in general and its effect on determined abusers:

[A] smaller group of chronic and serious offenders were unresponsive to normative frame-works. 'Brushes' with the law which result in being charged with minor offences, cautions, binding over or short custodial sentences had no effect and in fact served to reinforce the abuser's belief that there are no effective constraints or sanction on his behaviour. They can increase the dangers to women, who will be seen to have 'transgressed' by having called the police or given evidence against the abuser. Moreover poor and ineffective action from law enforcement and prosecution services may serve to confirm a woman's belief that she is outside help and, therefore, has no option other than to seek to appease the abuser. (2003 p 210)

Humphreys and Thiara suggest that the new policy developments in the police service and CPS might be helpful but that a co-ordinated response with community support, civil protection and criminal justice is needed (2003 p 210).

## XV. A CO-ORDINATED RESPONSE

Some indication of what might be included in such a response can be seen in the priori-ties enumerated by the domestic violence survivors who participated in an internet

---

[170] *Ibid*, para 3.4.

consultation (Bossy and Coleman 2000). They made it clear that they wanted domestic violence to be treated seriously by the criminal justice system. They also wanted changes made to the law relating to contact with children to ensure that women and children were not endangered post-separation.[171] In addition to legal measures, they wanted more publicity and information to be made available about sources of support. Finally, they wanted better access to accommodation as well as more support services in the form of refuges, outreach services and advocacy.

Steps have already been taken to promote a more co-ordinated response.[172] Multi-agency partnerships are encouraged[173] and there are now Domestic Violence Fora intended to promote a multi-agency approach. Their membership comprises statutory, non-statutory and voluntary representatives such as Women's Aid, housing departments, social services, the health service, Victim Support and criminal justice agencies (HMcpsi and HMIC 2004 para 10.9). Within agencies, such as social services and the health service, policy, guidance and training are receiving attention.[174] Agencies such as the benefits agency and the Child Support Agency are expected to provide information on domestic violence. Publicity and information are also made available through help lines and poster campaigns.[175]

As part of the wide-ranging effort to tackle domestic violence, a number of offender programmes have been set up, run by voluntary organisations or incorporated into probation work with offenders (Dobash, *et al*, 2000 p 295).

*Perpetrator Programmes*

Perpetrator programmes vary in their approach depending on what are identified as the 'causes' of domestic violence. In those programmes where it is defined it as a 'clinical condition',[176] typified by a faulty personality,[177] personality disorder or substance misuse, a therapeutic approach is adopted. In those that espouse systems theory, family systems counselling is used, involving the whole family 'system'. Other programmes, characterised as pro-feminist, are designed to challenge men's violence and to hold perpetrators responsible for their actions.[178] Violence is perceived as 'intentional behaviour chosen by men as a tactic or resource associated with attempts to dominate, control and punish women' (Dobash, *et al*, 2000 p 293).

Mullender and Burton (2000) say that research in these programmes shows no conclusive evidence of success. But Dobash, *et al*, take a more positive view. Their research into two pro-feminist programmes revealed that, while a 'concerted criminal justice response involving arrest and prosecution may affect the subsequent violence of men' (2000 p 300), 'in comparison with other criminal justice sanctions, participation in one of the programmes is more likely to reduce the incidence and frequency of violence and

171 See further ch 14.
172 See Home Office (2003) p 14.
173 See Cabinet Office and Home Office (1999).
174 For discussion of women's varied experiences with these services, see Humphreys and Thiara (2002).
175 See Cabinet Office and Home Office (1999).
176 See Dobash, *et al*, (2000) pp 291–293.
177 The courts appear to favour anger management programmes: see *Lomas v Parle*, n 159 above, para 51. These may fail to address the question of why the man is angry and the appropriateness of the anger (Dobash, *et al* 2000 p 45).
178 For example, they must stop minimising the violence, stop blaming their partners and recognise the effects of their violence (Adams 2000 p 315). See further Mullender and Burton (2000).

associated controlling behaviours' (p 301). The authors point out (p 304), however, that programmes must be integrated into the criminal justice mechanisms dealing with domestic violence. The use of programmes within that context reinforces the message that there are costs for using violence. The process of being arrested, charged, prosecuted and sentenced to attendance at a programme, with the threat of increased sanctions in the event of failure, provides an incentive to change.[179] By contrast, there is a high attrition rate in relation to voluntary attendance at programmes. For example, some abusers enter voluntary counselling in order to persuade their partners to return home or not to leave home. They drop out when they achieve this aim (*ibid*). Without court sanctions, most perpetrators do not attend for long enough to make any lasting changes (Adams 2000 p 315).

Women's Aid (2003 pp 11–12) criticises existing programmes such as those run by the National Probation Service and Prison Service; the safety of women and children is not sufficiently prioritised. In addition, sanctions for non-attendance, failure to participate or repeat violence are not enforced and cases are not returned to court. It says that what is needed is intervention by the criminal justice system and attendance by offenders at 'proven'[180] re-education programmes with sanctions for non-compliance. In the meanwhile, offenders should have no access to victims and children until they can prove that they are not violent.

## XVI. FURTHER REFORM

The Domestic Violence, Crime and Victims Act is intended to address a number of problems identified within the law. It deals with both the criminal and the civil law, expanding the scope of protection and strengthening enforcement mechanisms. This is covered in chapter 12 but a brief overview will be provided here.

The government observed that the majority of domestic violence cases involve common assault[181] but that there is uncertainty among the police as to their powers of arrest in such cases. In addition, what powers they do have do not cover situations commonly encountered when attending the scene of domestic violence incidents (Home Office 2003 p 26). Section 10 of the Act therefore amends the Police and Evidence Act 1984 to make common assault an arrestable offence. This means that the police do not need a warrant in order to arrest.

The government thought that restraining orders under the Protection from Harassment Act 1997, currently available on conviction for offences under that Act, should be available in a wider range of circumstances (Home Office 2003 p 35). These orders may be used to prohibit the offender from engaging in conduct that amounts to harassment or causing fear of violence.[182] Section 12 amends the 1997 Act to extend the court's power to make a restraining order to cases where there has been a conviction for any offence. It also introduces a new Section 5A which empowers the court to make an order when the defendant is acquitted of an offence if the court considers this to be necessary

---

[179] See also Dobash (2003) pp 316–17.
[180] Those that comply with the standards set by RESPECT (the National Association for Domestic Violence Perpetrator Programmes and Associated Support).
[181] Women's Aid disputes this (Women's Aid 2003 p 13).
[182] See further ch 12.

to protect a person from harassment. The order would prohibit the defendant from doing anything specified in the order.

The Act is aimed also at broadening the scope of the civil law. It amends the Family Law Act 1996 so that same-sex cohabitants are treated in the same way as heterosexual cohabitants as regards occupation orders.[183] It also to makes non-molestation orders available to those people, currently excluded, who are or were in an intimate relationship but who never lived together or married.[184]

In order to ameliorate the difficulties involved in enforcing orders, the government proposed making breach of an order an offence (Home Office 2003 pp 33–34). This was intended to avoid the victim having to seek a warrant in the absence of a power of arrest, a step that could place her at risk. In addition, it would deal with the problem that the police are not always clear about the scope of the power of arrest in cases where it is attached to part of an order. A new s. 42A is therefore to be introduced into the 1996 Act which makes breach of a non-molestation order an arrestable offence.[185] Breach of an occupation order has not been made an offence as a history of violence or molestation is not a prerequisite for an order.[186] However the court is obliged to consider making a non-molestation order when considering whether to make an occupation order.[187] Also the Act prohibits the court from accepting an undertaking where a non-molestation order, with arrest as a means of enforcement, is necessary for the protection of the applicant or a child.[188]

In addition to these legislative reforms, the government is contemplating a number of other measures. One priority is education. It is suggested that there should be education in prisons about domestic violence (Home Office 2003 p 17) and that, in schools, Personal, Social and Health Education should cover anger management and negotiating within relationships (Home Office 2003 p 16). Education should also focus on 'risk factors' such as substance misuse and early pregnancy (pp 18–20). The health service and schools are seen as having a role to play in identifying abuse (pp 20–22). Schemes to inform victims of sources of help are discussed (pp 22–23). Offender programmes will be implemented and monitored (pp 32–24).

> **Q** Can you identify the 'causes' of domestic violence that are apparently accepted by the government in suggesting some of these 'solutions'?

As regards the legal system, education is again central. Training for prosecutors and the judiciary is singled out as an important measure (pp 26–27). Specialist domestic violence courts are being considered (p 28).[189] Better co-operation and information sharing between criminal and civil courts is recommended, so that, for example, bail conditions[190] should not undermine arrangements for contact made by family courts (p 28). Better information for victims is also considered necessary to reduce risks where a

---

[183] S 3.

[184] S 4.

[185] Under s 24(1) Police and Criminal Evidence Act 1984.

[186] Domestic Violence, Crime and Victims Bill [HL], Explanatory Notes, para 26.

[187] Para 36, Sch 10, creating a new s 42(4A) and s 42(4B) FLA 1996.

[188] Para 37, Sch 10, creating a new s 46(3A) FLA 1996.

[189] See, for criticism of the present 'interface' between the criminal and civil courts, *Lomas v Parle*, n 159 above, para 51. Thorpe LJ recommended a reconsideration of the present dual system in favour of integrated courts.

[190] Women's Aid recommends that bail should be refused where the perpetrator is in close contact with the victim and is likely to interfere with her or commit further offences. Where bail is granted, it should be subject to conditions that should be robustly enforced. Perpetrators often use the opportunity afforded by bail to 'terrorise the woman into dropping charges' (2003 p 14).

perpetrator is released (p 28).[191] The Sentencing Advisory Panel is to be asked to provide sentencing guidelines (p 29). A register of civil orders is being considered so that police and prosecutors are aware of the offender's previous history (p 36). A register of domestic violence offenders is also being mooted (p 36). Measures are put forward to ensure that child contact is safe, chiefly by means of the use of supervised contact centres (pp 38–40).

The government states that it is concerned to provide support for victims of domestic violence. It refers, for example, to the aim of increasing accommodation options, including more refuges, outreach and resettlement services, enabling victims to stay in their own homes if appropriate, and better advice and information (pp 42–44).

## XVII. FAMILY PRIVACY REVISITED

The law, and increasingly government policy, clearly countenance intervention in the family but commentators have observed that implementation of both law and policy has remained marked by a persisting reluctance to interfere or to interfere decisively. This is something that the Law Commission has referred to with concern; it remarked that legal remedies can be undermined by the way the law is implemented in practice; women may be deterred from proceeding and the law can be made ineffective if the reactions of those working in the area are 'affected by particular perceptions of male and female roles or an ambivalence about the propriety of legal or police intervention in the family' (1992a para 2.8).

Some of this reluctance to take domestic violence seriously may be attributable to a continuing perception of the family as private. Schneider asserts that the 'rhetoric of privacy has masked inequality and subordination' (1994 p 39) and continues[192]:

> The rationale of privacy legitimates and supports violence against women; woman abuse reveals the violence of privacy. Privacy justifies the refusal of the state to intervene, of judges to issue restraining orders,[193] of neighbours and friends to intervene or to call the police, of communities to confront the problem. (p 53)

But, she says, there are aspects of the concept of privacy that abused women may not wish to relinquish. While they want to be free of abuse, they also want the freedom to choose whether to continue with or end their intimate relationships (1994 p 53). Similarly, it has been argued that women should not be compelled to testify against their wishes[194] and that third party applications should not be made possible without the victim's consent.[195] At present, however, women who do not go through with legal proceedings attract criticism. The question often asked is why the woman does not simply leave. Yet not all women seeking help want to leave (Stanko, *et al*, 1998 p 43).

Mahoney (1994 p 59) contends that the preoccupation of the law with exit from the relationship ignores the dangers and difficulties associated with leaving; it assumes that

---

[191] There is a limited right to receive information and make representations in s 35 of the Domestic Violence, Crime and Victims Act 2004.
[192] See also Pahl (1985c) p 191.
[193] The US equivalent of injunctions.
[194] See Ellison (2003) pp 767–68.
[195] See Burton (2003) pp 146–47; Barron (2002) p 10.

leaving both is possible and will bring safety. On the contrary, she says, the violence may continue as part of an attempt to reassert control over the woman. Moreover for women to redefine their loved ones as batterers is a difficult decision, particularly if there are children; the welfare of children is widely believed to be bound up in their relationships with their fathers. To many women, the best course appears to be to seek to improve the relationship with their partners. Mandatory participation in legal proceedings or discounting victims' wishes can, it is argued, be coercive and have the effect of disempowering or even re-victimising the women concerned.[196] Nor does prosecution necessarily offer a solution:

> While it is important that improvements in the prosecution process and the legal system as a whole should continue to be made, domestic violence cannot be dealt with by the criminal justice system alone. Many women, for good reasons, avoid it altogether; and for all women, protection from danger will always be the most important consideration. A universal response of prosecution does not always achieve that object. (Barron 2002 p 19)

So, while it is widely thought that women who seek help from outside agencies should not be denied it, feminist writing brings into question the desirability of intervening against the victim's wishes. This approach, it might be suggested, may not be appropriate in cases of serious violence where the public interest demands the intervention of the criminal law and where the matter cannot be seen through the 'lens of the "couple"'. Stanko refers to the variations of violence, in arguing that the law should provide a flexible range of resources for abused women. It appears to be in this context that she contends that the law should leave to those women the decision as to whether and to what extent the abuse should become a matter for public concern:

> It is essential that we begin to explore the variations and nuances of men's violence to women. ..[M]en's dangerousness varies. ..[T]his demands flexible services to women at various stages of exiting from violence. It means that we take seriously the hold of emotional attachments (Ellis and DeKeseredy (1997) call this loyalty/love) and be willing to work with and through these attachments without losing patience with women for not leaving. Moreover, we must promote a variety of mechanisms that support women's own voices, which guide them and us through that crucial and dangerous stage of separation. (1997 p 634)

## XVIII. CONCLUSION

Abuse of women, through the efforts of the early 'moral entrepreneurs', and more recently, feminists, has come to be constructed as a social problem[197] demanding a response from government and from various public agencies. The 19th century campaigns began the process by making the phenomenon of wife abuse visible and by challenging long-held convictions about the appropriate status of women; for change to be possible, women had to be seen not simply as adjuncts to the patriarch but as meriting protection in their own right. In the 20th and 21st centuries, the process has also

---

[196] See Ellison (2003) pp 767–68; Burton (2003) pp 146–47.
[197] See, eg, Dobash and Dobash (1992) pp 285 and 288.

been characterised by an emphasis on gender inequality, and researchers and commentators have sought to reconceptualise domestic violence as an abuse of power and an expression of possessiveness. The efforts of the reformers have been successful, in that abuse in intimate relationships is now less likely to be seen by the police and by the courts as an excusable lapse. Moreover, the explanation of domestic violence in terms of power and control has now gained widespread acceptance. However feminist efforts to establish gender inequality as the 'cause' of the problem have been less successful; it is still primarily conceived of as a problem of individuals. Despite the new emphasis on education, the 'solution', for government, the police and professionals in the field, therefore lies primarily in the treatment and/or punishment of those individuals rather than in (significantly less manageable) far-reaching social change.

Perhaps one of the most crucial factors in the construction of domestic violence as a social problem has been the challenge to the conception of the family as a private haven. Although this is still the most potent image of the family, the home is now also perceived as a potentially dangerous place, especially for women and children, and, as such, it is not immune to outside intervention.

Yet the ideal of family privacy, it is said, has continued to inhibit those charged with implementing measures to protect women. The civil and criminal justice systems in particular have come in for criticism for failing to help those seeking protection from domestic violence. In response to these criticisms, policies have changed and the law has been reformed to increase levels of intervention and to toughen the measures available to combat domestic violence. Yet some changes, namely the introduction of pro-arrest and no-drop policies, have provoked yet more criticism. These policies, it is said, do little to support women or to protect them, and at the same time they fail to accommodate the diversity of cases and operate punitively in relation to victims. Women who bring violence into the public arena, sometimes because seeking outside intervention is the only way they can attempt to renegotiate their relationships, are unable to retreat easily back into privacy.

To refuse to intervene and to withhold help from abused women on the grounds of family privacy clearly leaves them exposed to risk. In addition, non-intervention is symbolically damaging for all women. Yet to force victims into the public arena of the criminal law or to insist that they leave their abuser before taking them seriously can also have damaging consequences. It is argued that when and the extent to which violence is made public should be a decision for the woman and not for outside agencies. Whether to invoke the criminal law or civil law or both should be the woman's choice. And women who choose to remain with their violent partners should be able to receive safe, confidential advice and support.[198] What is needed are mechanisms that make it easier and safer for abused women who wish to do so to obtain advice, to seek legal remedies and to access support networks and housing.[199] These needs are currently being addressed to some extent by the government's initiatives. However it remains a matter for concern that the new policies, as well as the law, will not always be implemented in practice.

---

[198] See Women's Aid (2003) p 25.
[199] See Morley and Mullender (1992) p 271.

## FURTHER READING AND SELECTED RECENT REFERENCES

M BARNISH, *Domestic Violence: A Literature Review* (London, HM Inspectorate of Probation, 2004).

J BARRON, *Five Years On: A Review of Legal Protection from Domestic Violence* (Bristol, WAFE, 2002).

P BART and E MORAN, (eds), *Violence Against Women: The Bloody Footprints* (London, Sage, 1993).

J BOSSY and S COLEMAN, *Womenspeak. Parliamentary Domestic Violence Internet Consultation: Report of the Main Findings* (Bristol, WAFE, 2000).

A BROWNE, *When Battered Women Kill* (New York, NY, Free, 1987).

M BURTON, 'Third Party Applications for Protection Orders in England and Wales: Service Provider's Views on Implementing Section 60 of the Family Law Act 1996' (2003) 25 *JSW&FL* 137.

D COOK, *et al*, *Evaluation of Specialist Domestic Violence Courts/Fast Track Systems* (London, Crown Prosecution Service and Department of Constitutional Affairs, 2004).

A CRETNEY and G DAVIS, 'Prosecuting Domestic Assault' (1996) *Crim L Rev* 162.

——, 'Prosecuting Domestic Assault: Victims Failing Courts, or Courts Failing Victims?' (1997a) 36 *Howard Journal* 146.

——, 'The Significance of Compellability in the Prosecution of Domestic Assault' (1997b) 37 *Brit J Criminal* 75.

——, *Punishing Violence* (London, Routledge, 1995).

RE DOBASH, 'Domestic Violence: Arrest, Prosecution and Reducing Violence' (2003) 2 *Criminology & Public Policy* 313.

RE DOBASH and RP DOBASH, 'Violent Men and Violent Contexts' in RE Dobash and RP Dobash, (eds), *Rethinking Violence Against Women* (London, Sage, 1998).

——, 'The Politics and Policies of Responding to Violence Against Women' in J Hanmer, *et al*, (eds), *Home Truths About Domestic Violence: Feminist Influences on Policy and Practice: A Reader* (London, Routledge, 2000).

——, 'Women's Violence to Men in Intimate Relationships. Working on a Puzzle' (2004) 44 *Brit J Criminol* 324.

RE DOBASH, *et al*, 'Confronting Violent Men' in J Hanmer, *et al*, (eds), *Home Truths About Domestic Violence: Feminist Influences on Policy and Practice: A Reader* (London, Routledge, 2000).

D ELLIS and W DEKESEREDY, 'Rethinking Estrangement, Interventions, and Intimate Femicide' (1997) 3 *Violence Against Women* 590.

L ELLISON, 'Responding to Victim Withdrawal in Domestic Violence Prosecutions' (2003) *Crim LR* 760.

MA FINEMAN and R MYKTIUK, (eds), *The Public Nature of Private Violence: The Discovery of Domestic Abuse* (London, Routledge, 1994).

D GADD, *et al*, *Domestic Abuse against Men in Scotland* (Edinburgh, Scottish Executive, 2002).

J HANMER, *et al*, (eds), *Home Truths About Domestic Violence: Feminist Influences on Policy and Practice: A Reader* (London, Routledge, 2000).

J HARRIS, *An Evaluation of the Use and Effectiveness of the Protection from Harassment Act 1997*: Home Office Research Study 203 (London, Home Office, 2000)

N HARWIN and J BARRON, 'Domestic Violence and Social Policy: Perspectives from Women's Aid' in J Hanmer, *et al*, (eds), *Home Truths About Domestic Violence: Feminist Influences on Policy and Practice: A Reader* (London, Routledge, 2000).

J HEARN, *The Violences of Men: How Men Talk About and How Agencies Respond to Men's Violence to Women* (London, Sage, 1998).

M HESTER, *et al*, *Domestic Violence: Making it Through the Criminal Justice System* (University of Sunderland, Northern Rock Foundation and International Centre for the Study of Violence and Abuse, 2003).

M HESTER, C PEARSON and N HARWIN, *Making an Impact: Children and Domestic Violence: A Reader* (London, Jessica Kingsley, 2000).

C HOYLE, *Negotiating Domestic Violence: Police, Criminal Justice and Victims* (Oxford, OUP, 1998).

C HOYLE and A SANDERS, 'Police Response to Domestic Violence: From Victim Choice to Victim Empowerment?' (2000) 40 *Brit J Criminol* 14.

C HUMPHREYS, *Child Protection and Woman Protection: Links and Schisms: An Overview of the Research* (Bristol, WAFE, 2000).

C HUMPHREYS and R THIARA, *Routes to Safety: Protection Issues Facing Abused Women and Children and the Role of Outreach Services* (Bristol, WAFE, 2002).

——, 'Neither Justice nor Protection: Women's Experiences of Post-separation Violence' (2003) 25 *JSWFL* 195.

C ITZIN, 'Gendering Domestic Violence: The Influence of Feminism on Policy and Practice' in J Hanmer, *et al,* (eds), *Home Truths About Domestic Violence: Feminist Influences on Policy and Practice: A Reader* (London, Routledge, 2000).

F KAGANAS, 'Domestic Homicide, Gender and the Expert' in A Bainham, S Day Sclater and M Richards, (eds), *Body Lore and Laws* (Oxford, Hart Publications, 2002).

R LEWIS, RE DOBASH and K CAVANAGH, 'Law's Progressive Potential: The Value of Engagement with the Law for Domestic Violence' (2001) 10 *Social and Legal Studies* 105.

A MCOLGAN, 'In Defence of Battered Women who Kill' (1993) 13 *OJLS* 508.

C MCGEE, *Childhood Experiences of Domestic Violence* (London, Jessica Kingsley, 2000).

J MOONEY, 'Revealing the Hidden Figure of Domestic Violence' in J Hanmer, *et al,* (eds), *Home Truths About Domestic Violence: Feminist Influences on Policy and Practice: A Reader* (London, Routledge, 2000).

A MULLENDER, *Reducing Domestic Violence … What Works? Meeting the Needs of Children,* Policing and Reducing Crime Briefing Note (London, Home Office, 2000).

A MULLENDER and S BURTON, *Reducing Domestic Violence … What Works? Perpetrator Programmes*, Policing and Reducing Crime Briefing Note (London, Home Office, 2000).

A MULLENDER and R MORLEY, (eds), *Children Living with Domestic Violence: Putting Men's Abuse of Women on the Child Care Agenda* (London, Whiting & Birch, 1994).

A MULLENDER, *et al*, Children's Perspectives on Domestic Violence (London, Sage, 2002).

K O'DONOVAN, 'Law's Knowledge: The Judge, The Expert, The Battered Woman, and the Syndrome' (1993) 20 *JLS* 427.

K PARADINE and J WILKINSON, *Research and Literature Review: Protection and Accountability: The Reporting, Investigation and Prosecution of Domestic Violence Cases* (London, Her Majesty's Crown Prosecution Service Inspectorate (HMCPSI), Her Majesty's Inspectorate of Constabulary (HMIC), Centrex, 2004).

E STARK and A FLITCRAST, *Women at Risk: Domestic Violence and Women's Health* (London, Sage, 1996).

S WALBEY and J ALLEN, *Domestic Violence, Sexual Assault and Stalking: Findings from the British Crime Survey*: Home Office Research Study 276 (London, Home Office, 2004).

## Reports

Cabinet Office and Home Office, *Living Without Fear: An integrated approach to tackling violence against women* (London, Cabinet Office, 1999).

DCA (2003) Judicial Statistics.

Her Majesty's Crown Prosecution Service Inspectorate (HMcpsi), Her Majesty's Inspectorate Of Constabulary (HMIC), *A Joint Inspection of the Investigation and Prosecution of Cases Involving Domestic Violence* (2004).

Home Office, 'Domestic Violence: Revised Circular to the Police', Home Office Circular No 19/2000 (London, Home Office, 2000b).

Home Office, *Justice for All* (London, HMSO, Cm 5563, 2002).

Home Office, Safety and Justice: *The Government's Proposals on Domestic Violence* (London, HMSO, Cm 5847, 2003).

Law Commission, *Partial Defences to Murder. Consultation Paper No 173* (London, The Law Commission, 2003).

Women's Aid Federation of England, *Response to 'Safety and Justice', the Government's Consultation Paper on Domestic Violence* (Bristol, WAFE, 2003).

# 11

# A Public or Private Matter—Alternative Dispute Resolution and Negotiation

## I. INTRODUCTION

We have discussed elsewhere[1] the dilemma that the liberal state faces in seeking to regulate the family while at the same time preserving, or at least appearing to preserve, family privacy. Divorce, like marriage, has long been regarded as a public matter and as necessitating legal intervention. However, recent decades have seen a gradual move to the partial privatisation and de-legalisation of the process. The introduction of no-fault divorce, the special procedure for undefended divorces[2] and the growth of mediation, for example, evidence this trend.[3] And, while further reform to the divorce law proved very contentious, there is a remarkable degree of consensus about the limitations of law and the courts in dealing with family disputes, particularly disputes about children. There is a widely held view that, wherever possible, cases should be kept out of the courts and that the parties should be encouraged to reach their own agreements. The most well-established mechanisms for achieving settlements are lawyer negotiation,[4] mediation and in-court conciliation.[5] However, new schemes are currently being piloted or have already been implemented. Even before these latest developments, Davis wrote that it was becoming increasingly difficult to distinguish between 'legal services and mediation, between the mainstream and the "alternative"' (2000 p 3). He went on:

> Any applicant to the court in respect of children or money will now be deflected to one of a variety of negotiating opportunities. These may or may not be on court premises, and the mediation label may or may not be attached. ... [C]ustomers of mediation services may find that their mediator is in fact a lawyer ... . Even if the mediator's academic antecedents are impeccably 'social' it is likely that he or she will be a good deal preoccupied with achieving agreements which can be presented to the court as constituting formal legal settlement. So we have mediation in the law, and we have law in mediation; or to put this another way, we have deflection from the formal and formalisation of the informal. That is either an impressive convergence of practice and of principle, or it is a very fine mess, depending on how one looks at it.
>
> (Davis 2000 p 3)

---

[1] See ch 9.

[2] Almost all divorces are undefended (see p 514 below) and public funding is not available to defend a divorce petition.

[3] See ch 14.

[4] This crucial means of resolving disputes is often omitted in the discourse surrounding alternative dispute resolution, which generally focuses on processes such as mediation.

[5] The term 'conciliation' was originally used to refer to both in-court and out-of-court schemes. It was then replaced by the term 'mediation'. Now it appears that the term 'conciliation' has been resurrected in relation to in-court schemes, while 'mediation' is used to refer to independent schemes.

Here, we trace the development of alternative dispute resolution as the 'officially' approved means of settling practical arrangements when partners separate. We focus primarily on mediation and settlement through negotiations by lawyers. We also consider, more briefly, the new mechanisms. In the course of examining all these forms of private ordering,[6] we highlight the problems that can arise out of the privatisation of decision-making.

## II. ALTERNATIVE DISPUTE RESOLUTION

### *The Background to the Rise of Mediation and ADR*

The seemingly inexorable rise in divorce rates since World War II led to a re-evaluation of both the grounds for divorce and the procedures by which divorces were granted.[7] Initially, efforts at reform were directed at promoting reconciliation between spouses as well as at reducing costs to public funds and relieving pressure on the legal system.

This preoccupation with marriage saving was reflected in the Divorce Reform Act 1969. Section 3 required solicitors to certify whether or not they had discussed the possibility of reconciliation with their clients and had offered to refer them to counselling. In addition, courts were empowered to adjourn proceedings while parties attempted reconciliation. However, as Eekelaar and Dingwall have observed, in the context of a legal system intent on expediting cases and containing costs, these provisions were 'an almost immediate dead letter' (1988 p 11). Attention shifted instead, during the 1970s, to what was then called 'conciliation'. This term is now used in relation to in-court services but other schemes are generally referred to as 'mediation'.

Rather than concentrating on trying to save marriages, reformers became concerned with facilitating the settlement of disputes arising on marriage breakdown with as little conflict as possible. The increase in divorce was acknowledged to be the product of apparently irreversible social change such as the economic emancipation of women through participation in employment; the availability of social security support to those women who would otherwise be unable to leave their marriages; and a growing perception that the purpose of marriage should be emotional fulfilment.[8] Preserving unhappy marriages was no longer the main priority for the state. Equally important, it was thought, was the provision of a means by which relationships could be dissolved and differences settled with as little acrimony as possible.

Since the mid-1970s, when the first conciliation services were established,[9] mediation has increasingly come to be seen as an appropriate forum for the settlement of family disputes.[10] The Family Law Act 1996 placed enormous emphasis on mediation. Part III, dealing with funding, has now been repealed and there are plans to repeal Part II, which was intended to govern the divorce process but was never implemented. Nevertheless, it is still government policy that family disputes about property, finance and especially

---

[6] For a discussion of family group conferences in the context of child protection, see pp 364–5.

[7] See, generally, Eekelaar and Dingwall (1988); ch 14 below.

[8] See, eg, Eekelaar and Dingwall (1988) p 15.

[9] For an account of the history of mediation in England and Wales, see the Newcastle Conciliation Project Unit Report (1989) para 2.21 ff.

[10] See Walker, *et al*, (1994) pp 5–6; Piper (1993) pp 11–12.

children should be diverted from the court-room wherever possible and should be resolved by means of mediation or other alternative dispute mechanisms.

### Alternative Dispute Resolution: Government Policy

While mediation is currently the most favoured mechanism for settling, or managing, family disputes, the government plans to extend the use of alternative dispute resolution even further. It aims to encourage separating parties, particularly parents, to learn about the effects that separation can have upon their children, and then to use this knowledge to settle, rather than litigate any disagreements they may have about their children. The government's plans are sketched out in the Green Paper, *Parental Separation: Children's Needs and Parents' Responsibilities* (DCA, DfES and DTI 2004) and reiterated in the White Paper, *Parental Separation: Children's Needs and Parents' Responsibilities: Next Steps, Report of the responses to consultation and agenda for action* (DCA, DfES and DTI 2005). The proposals in these documents are directed at children cases rather than finances and are aimed at:

- minimising conflict and supporting good outcomes both for children and their parents, preferably without recourse to the courts;
- improving parental access to those services which will enable them to reach agreements; and
- improving legal processes and service delivery for those who do go to court.

(DCA. DfES and DTI 2004 p 2, Ministerial Foreword)

The White Paper re-states the now received wisdom that, '**Collaborative agreements** made between parents should be favoured, as they are likely to work better than those arrangements that flow from court-based resolutions' (DCA, DfES and DTI 2005 para 2, emphasis in original).

A range of services and measures is canvassed in the Green and White papers.[11] Parents are to be given information and advice about how to deal with the consequences for their children of relationship breakdown. They will have access to 'practical/emotional advice on how to handle and resolve disputes' via telephone and websites (DCA, DfES and DTI 2004 p 5; DCA, DfES and DTI 2005 para 42). Parenting plans[12] showing what arrangements work for parents and children will be available to help parents reach 'reasonable agreements' (DCA, DfES and DTI 2005 para 31). Solicitors will be expected to promote 'resolution rather than conflict' (DCA, DfES and DTI 2004 p 5) and an accreditation scheme for them will be introduced (DCA, DfES and DTI 2005 para 45). Early resolution will be facilitated through the introduction of FAInS (Family Advice and Information Service). Mediation will be supported and the potential of 'collaborative law' explored (DCA, DfES and DTI 2004 p 6; DCA, DfES and DTI 2005 para 46). For cases that do go to court, the government will develop and implement nation-wide an in-court conciliation system. The Family Resolutions Pilot Project may lead to this service being rolled out nationally as well. CAFCASS will focus more on dispute resolution than on report writing (DCA, DfES and DTI 2004 p 6).

The new measures are all aimed at providing parents, who might otherwise engage in contested court hearings, with an alternative route (DCA, DfES and DTI 2005 para 47).

---

[11] See also ch 14.
[12] See also p 323 above and ch 14.

Government policy is that parties should be 'strongly encouraged to attend mediation and other alternative dispute resolution sessions' (DCA, DfES and DTI 2005 para 51). A funding code consultation paper sets out a proposal that '[m]ediation and other forms of ADR be considered routinely in publicly funded litigation' (DCA 2004 p 6) and supports awards of costs against parties who are not in receipt of public funding and who 'unreasonably' refuse to take mediation 'seriously' (p 9).

The government yet again re-iterates its determination to promote alternatives to court proceedings in *The Government Response to the Constitutional Affairs Select Committee Report: Family Justice: the Operation of the Family Courts* (DCA and Lord Chancellor 2005). However it has rejected suggestions, which appear to be based on the defunct provisions of the Family Law Act 1996, that all parties be required to attend a meeting to consider the benefits of mediation.[13]

The suggestion favouring the adoption of such a measure was somewhat surprising given the findings of the researchers whose evaluations of the impact of information meetings held under the Family Law Act 1996 contributed to the abandonment of the provisions dealing with divorce and mediation.[14] Walker and her team found that information 'may' have encouraged some people to attempt mediation or counselling (Walker 2004 p 123). However most recipients of information about mediation still consulted a solicitor and 85% engaged one (p 123). The Family Law Act 1996 was intended to make mediation an 'integrated part of the divorce process' (LCD 1995a p 42) and one of the factors that led the Lord Chancellor to announce he would ask for the repeal of Part II was the fact that greater numbers of people were not encouraged to attend mediation as a result of the information meetings (p 131). What is more, to his disappointment, the research studies indicated that 39% of people were more likely to consult a solicitor after attending an information meeting (Diduck 2003 p 111).

Walker suggests that recommendations by solicitors are more effective in getting people to attend mediation than the provision of information about it (Walker 2004 p 132). In any event, she remarks, 'most people will choose not to use mediation' (p 131). Only 10% of those responding to the survey carried out by Walker and her co-researchers had attended mediation and a further 2% had gone to a preliminary meeting with a mediator but did not engage in the mediation process (p 131). Walker speculates that 'there is little prospect of increasing the use of mediation so long as attendance remains voluntary' (p 134). And she does not think the solution lies in compulsion; mediation has little prospect of success in cases where parties with little faith in the process are forced to participate.[15]

Before going on to discuss in a little more detail how other methods of alternative dispute resolution, both established and new, operate, we will first consider mediation at some length. As Davis has observed: 'The main "story" of private family law over the past two decades has been the emergence of mediation. This has attracted massive interest in its own right, and it has also greatly influenced the work of family lawyers and the family courts' (Davis 2000 p 1).

---

[13] Nevertheless, it proposed altering the Draft Children (Contact) and Adoption Bill to allow courts to direct parties in contact disputes to attend such meetings (DCA and Lord Chancellor 2005 paras 27–28). However there is nothing to that effect in the Children and Adoption Bill at the time of writing.

[14] The legislation required a party embarking on the divorce process to attend an information meeting at least three months before making a statement of marital breakdown. The other party, if applying to court regarding a child, property or finance, or if contesting an application, was also supposed to attend a meeting. One of the purposes of this meeting was to inform the parties about mediation.

[15] See Walker (2004) p 140.

*What is Mediation?*

Mediation is intended to facilitate joint decision-making by the parties. It was used in the UK, initially, primarily in seeking to resolve disputes about children. However its scope has been broadened to address issues of property and finance[16] as well as 'other practical issues' and the question of how the parties will communicate in the future (CLS 2004 p 3). Mediation is described in a report by Walker, *et al*:

> Family Mediation is a process in which an impartial third person, the mediator, assists couples considering separation or divorce to make arrangements, to communicate better, to reduce conflict between them, and to reach their own agreed joint decisions. The issues to be decided may concern separation, the divorce, the children, finance and property.
> The mediator has no stake in any disputes, is not identified with any of the competing interests, and has no power to impose a settlement on the participants, who retain authority to make their own decisions.
> Couples enter mediation voluntarily, to work together on the practical consequences of family breakdown, and to reach proposals for settlements which may then be endorsed by their legal representatives and the court, wherever appropriate. Mediation offers an alternative to negotiation by solicitors and to adjudication through the court, but is not a substitute for legal advice and representation. (1994 facing page)[17]

The main objectives of the process were enumerated prior to the enactment of the Family Law Act 1996 as:

> to help separating and divorcing couples to reach their own agreed joint decisions about future arrangements; to improve communications between them; and to help couples work together on the practical consequences of divorce with particular emphasis on their joint responsibilities to co-operate as parents in bringing up their children. (LCD 1995a para 5.6)

The process of mediation is shaped by a number of underlying ideas, the most prominent among which have been described by Simon Roberts as follows:

> that family disputes should be approached in a spirit of restraint rather than antagonism; that those in dispute should retain responsibility for decision-making rather than surrender this to third parties; that there are advantages in informality of process; that the focus of third-party intervention should be upon relationships rather than specific issues and vice versa; that outcomes should be founded in agreement and compromise rather than coercion; that the handling of disputes should be taken out of the hands of specialists; that there should be a move from state ordering to private ordering, from a legal to a non-legal world. (1983 p 538)[18]

---

[16] Mediation involving only property and finance tends to be more formal and oriented towards fact finding than child-related mediation (Dingwall and Greatbach 2000 p 233). In the study conducted by Davis and colleagues, which began in 1997 and which was published in 2000, 85% of cases referred for mediation concerned disputes about children and 33% of cases had a financial or property dispute as a component (Davis *et al* 2001b p 111). Of those cases that were actually mediated, 67% involved an attempt to resolve issues about children (p 112). Walker (2004) found that 38% of mediation users were hoping to resolve child-related and financial issues. 28% were concerned only about finances and 20% only about children. 14% were not clear about why they had been referred to mediation at all (pp 131–32). 38% of those who attended mediation did so on the advice of their solicitors (p 132).

[17] See also CLS (2004) p 3.

[18] See also Davis and Roberts (1988) p 6.

Mediation therefore differs from forms of alternative dispute resolution such as arbitration where the final decision is made by a third party, the arbitrator. It is also distinguished from other forms of intervention to deal with family breakdown.

It differs from the process of financial dispute resolution (FDR).[19] This is restricted to financial matters and the parties' representatives attend together with their clients. FDR is in effect an attempt, normally before a district judge, to reach a negotiated settlement. FDR does not require the consent of the parties,[20] whereas mediation in Britain is voluntary.

Mediation is different from the process of negotiation and dispute settlement often conducted by lawyers because, in mediation, the negotiation is undertaken by the parties themselves. Although they are assisted by the mediator, it is the parties, it is said, who control the outcome. By contrast, when cases are settled by lawyers, it is the lawyers who conduct negotiations, often in the absence of their clients (Davis and Roberts 1988 p 8).

Mediation must also be distinguished from family therapy or counselling.[21] Whereas therapeutic intervention is predicated on the assumption that the parties or the family suffer from a disorder requiring treatment, mediation proceeds from the assumption that the parties are competent to define the issues and to arrive at a negotiated solution (Davis and Roberts 1988 p 8). According to the advice provided to the public, mediation can be used to help parties decide whether their relationship is over (CLS 2004 p 3). But if the parties wish to reconcile, they should attend counselling. The same applies if a party wishes to talk to someone about how he or she is feeling (p 5).

Moreover, since mediation does not concern itself with delving into the psyche[22] but is rather concerned with managing practical arrangements, it is essentially forward-looking. Since, in general, it is less concerned with *why* the relationship has broken down than with the consequences of that breakdown, it is usually not conducted in a way that encourages parties to rehearse the past and to express their hurt and resentment.[23] As Marian Roberts says, 'excessive or prolonged' excursions into such matters may 'seriously impede rational exchange and lead to a deterioration of relations, rather than any improvement' (1997 p 25). Indeed, Dingwall and Greatbach (2000 p 251) remark that mediation is often seen as a 'quasi-legal, dispute resolving intervention'.

While the characteristics mentioned above are common to almost all forms of mediation, the ways in which mediation is carried out vary. Most schemes can be categorised as either in-court conciliation or out-of-court mediation.

In-court conciliation is carried out on court premises by court personnel. CAFCASS officers attend at directions appointments where a decision is made about how the case in question should proceed. It may be possible at that stage for the parties to agree an outcome. Alternatively the parties may be given the opportunity to attend a conciliation session with the CAFCASS officer.[24] The conciliation schemes staffed by CAFCASS do

---

[19] See below.

[20] See, further, Coleridge, *et al*, (1996); Singer (1996).

[21] Roberts (1983 p 552) points out, however, that it is not always possible to draw a clear line between intervention in the form of giving advice and counselling and intervention to facilitate joint decision-making.

[22] See Booth (1985) para 3.11.

[23] The White Paper preceding the Family Law Act 1996 (LCD 1995a para 5.4) suggested that mediation might be better suited than the legal process to identifying those marriages which might be saved; to enable parties to 'deal with their feelings of hurt and anger' and to address matters such as the conduct of a spouse. None of these functions is currently prioritised by most mediation services. That mediators are not concerned about reconciliation was observed by Dingwall and Greatbach (2000 p 241).

[24] CAFCASS (2003) paras 3.21–3.29. See, on the scheme operated in the Principal Registry of the Family Division, District Judge Brasse (2004).

not conform to a uniform model and not all schemes involve sessions being conducted on court premises. An inspection revealed eight different models and found that there was no common definition describing or delimiting the schemes. It was not even possible to identify a clear purpose for each different scheme (MCSI 2003 para 4). It remains to be seen whether more clarity will emerge as a result of the government's plan to extend in-court conciliation[25] by CAFCASS at the first appointment and the issuing of a *Model Scheme for In-Court Dispute Resolution*.[26]

Out-of-court mediation is conducted off court premises. Services[27] are staffed mainly by professionals with counselling, social work or legal backgrounds. Lawyers, however, operate primarily in the private profit-making sector, rather than in the not-for-profit, sector.

Comprehensive mediation[28] was developed in response to the growing perception that issues around children cannot be sensibly dealt with without also addressing questions of finance and property. Each impacted on the other. In addition, it was thought, the benefits of mediation over children might be lost if parties were left to deal with disputes over assets through traditional adversarial channels.

## A Voluntary Process?

The government has announced that it does not intend to make mediation compulsory.[29] 'An essential part of the process', it says, 'is that people come to it voluntarily and are therefore willing to participate' (DCA, DfES and DTI 2005 para 50). However, it does intend to promote and extend in-court conciliation nationwide and to ensure that schemes are introduced where none exist.[30] In addition, the role of CAFCASS is expected to change to concentrate more on conciliation and less on report writing. Even in cases where a report is ordered, while the focus of the CAFCASS officer is expected to be on what is in the child's best interests, consideration should also be given to reducing conflict and seeking agreements (DCA, DfES and DTI 2005 para 71).[31]

---

[25] See DCA (2002) Recommendation 16.

[26] Published in the Private Law Programme—Guidance Issued by the President of the Family Division (2004).

[27] The UK College of Family Mediators was formed to validate professional standards in the private and not-for-profit sectors. Many not-for-profit mediation services are affiliated to National Family Mediation (NFM). The Family Mediators' Association (FMA) is an association of individual practitioners. Both NFM and FMA undertake training of mediators. See Davis, *et al*, (2000d) for a description of different procedures adopted in mediation.

[28] Services have adopted differing models of comprehensive mediation. A lawyer might act as a co-mediator together with a welfare professional, eg, or might act as a consultant who is not directly involved in mediation sessions. See, further, Walker, *et al*, (1994) pp 15–16; Roberts (1997) pp 34–37. Dingwall and Greatbach comment that mediators in their study showed limited abilities to advise on financial matters and frequently referred issues to solicitors (2000 p 233; Dingwall and Greatbach 2001 p 379). While solicitor mediators do deal with both children and finance, they deal mainly with finance and property (Davis *et al* 2000d p 36).

[29] This has long been the preferred approach. See also University of Newcastle's Conciliation Project Unit's report (1989 para 20.19); the Law Commission (1990); and the Lord Chancellor's Department (1995a). Among the cases where mediation was considered potentially unsuitable by the Law Commission were cases involving exploitation of the weaker party by the stronger, cases where this would lead to delay and also where courts might postpone difficult and painful cases which ought to be decided quickly. See Law Comm (1990) paras 5.34–5.7.

[30] See DCA, DfEs and DTI (2005) paras 55–58.

[31] Concern has been expressed that CAFCASS may have neither the resources nor the skills for this new role. See DCA, DfEs and DTI (2005) para 68. However it is not an entirely new role. It was observed some years ago that court welfare officers (as they were then known) sometimes adopted a conciliatory approach in the course

Although mediation is and will continue to be voluntary, disputing parties may find themselves under pressure to avoid litigation. Even mediators in the independent not-for-profit sector, who operate outside the court arena, may strongly influence clients to undergo mediation. There are, say Davis, *et al*, (2000f) 'hidden pressures' because clients are in 'advice-seeking mode' and they fear that they might be 'ill-advised' not to accept the mediator's suggestions (p 214).[32]

If parties do get as far as the court, the pressures may be even greater. In the Newcastle study, it was found that those using court-based services, especially women, felt under even greater pressure to attend than those going to independent services (CPU 1989 p 286). The involvement of a judge or a representative of a court-based service in referring the client to conciliation was perceived as introducing an element of 'obligation and formality' (*ibid*). This is unlikely to have changed and the pressure from court personnel may even be greater nowadays.

The judiciary are clearly in favour of mediation and may be willing to exert some pressure on the parties to consider participating. In one unusual case[33] where mediation was resumed with the 'encouragement' of the court at appellate level, Thorpe LJ observed that, under the supervision of the court, 'there is no case, however conflicted, which is not potentially open to successful mediation, even if mediation has not been attempted or has failed during the trial process'.[34] In this case, the appeal court demanded an explanation for the initial failure of mediation and, finding that this was in part attributable to the administration of the court's ADR scheme, a 'fresh endeavour was made to persuade the parties' that 'the mediation road offered much better prospects'.[35] With the agreement of counsel, there was an adjournment for further mediation and the court appointed the mediators, one of whom was a spiritual leader of the Muslim community.

In the more usual type of case, parties are expected to reach agreement without a full hearing having to take place at all. To this end, the court may require the parties to attempt in-court conciliation. For example, District Judge Brasse reports that, in the Principal Registry of the Family Division, a conciliation appointment can only be dispensed with by order of the district judge[36] and that such orders are only made in cases where there are allegations of serious domestic violence or child abuse. And, he says, while agreement, once conciliation has commenced, 'must be reached voluntarily', the CAFCASS officer might consider it necessary to adopt a 'forceful directive attitude' (2004 p 723). Indeed the voluntary nature of this process may also be questioned in the light of the fact that the Practice Direction extending the scheme to *all* Section 8 and Section 13 applications under the Children Act 1989 states that such applications will be placed on a conciliation list unless the district judge directs otherwise.[37] The parties and

---

of compiling welfare reports and brought about settlements in that way. See further Roberts (1997) pp 31–34. In addition, as the government has pointed out, the service already conducts a large number of dispute resolution appointments. It conducts 38,000 of these per year. In contrast, there are 12,000–14,000 mediations undertaken each year by the independent and voluntary sector (DCA, DfES and DTI 2005 para 70). The government says CAFCASS will simply be 'developing what is already a substantial aspect of its current service' (DCA, DfES and DTI 2005 para 70).

[32] Davis, *et al*, (2001a) report that, from their research, it is apparent that giving people a choice of processes at a time of crisis is to expect them to focus on matters they do not understand (pp 266–67).

[33] *Al-Khatib v Masry* [2004] EWCA Civ 1353; [2005] 1 FLR 381. See para 17.

[34] On the difficulty of determining at what stage a case may be 'ripe' for mediation, see Wilson (2005).

[35] Para 9.

[36] See *District Judge's Direction. Children Conciliation* [2004] 1 FLR 974.

[37] *Ibid*, paras 1; 2.1 and 2.2.

their legal advisors must attend the appointment and the 'conciliation appointment will be conducted with a view to the parties reaching an agreement'.[38]

In the *Private Law Programme—Guidance Issued by the President of the Family Division* (2004), the President sets out the 'principles' to be adhered to by courts dealing with applications under Part II of the Children Act 1989. The first of these is that there should be 'Dispute resolution at First Hearing' (p 5). This means that in every case there has to be an early First Hearing dispute resolution appointment which should normally be attended by a CAFCASS officer[39] whose function is to 'facilitate early dispute resolution rather than the provision of a formal report' (para 1). Save in exceptional cases, namely where there are safety concerns or there is immediate agreement, the court must direct that the family attend a Family Resolutions Pilot Project,[40] where available, or some other service, which could be therapeutic or be a form of 'ADR, including mediation and conciliation' (para 1). The hearing can be adjourned to enable the parties to attend conciliation. In effect, this programme will place an expectation on all judges countrywide hearing children disputes to direct the parties to attend some form of ADR except in exceptional circumstances.

There are also financial incentives designed to persuade people to engage in mediation to resolve their disputes before they ever get to court. Those who can afford to pay for representation are free to decide on the manner in which they wish to proceed.[41] But for those seeking public funding, it is necessary to consider mediation before legal funding can become available. The incentives to consider mediation were introduced in the Family Law Act 1996 and survive the demise of Parts II and III in a slightly different form.

Community Legal Services funding is regulated by the Legal Services Commission Funding Code Criteria (LSC 2000) and Funding Code Guidance (LSC 2003b).[42] Section 8 of the Access to Justice Act 1999 specifies the principles that must shape the criteria for funding and subsection (3) states that '[t]he criteria set out in the code shall reflect the principle that in many family disputes mediation will be more appropriate than court proceedings'.[43]

The Funding Code Guidance (LSC 2003b para 20.6) states that the intention behind the code is to 'limit work in family cases to pre-proceedings work unless and until it has become clear that the matter cannot be resolved either through mediation or negotiations without the issue of proceedings'. All applications for General Family Help[44] (para 20.8.6) or Legal Representation (para 20.11.1)[45] must be assessed for suitability

---

[38] *Ibid*, para 4.2.

[39] See also the Model Scheme for In-Court Dispute Resolution included in the Private Law Programme.

[40] See below.

[41] But see above on the possibility of penalties in the form of costs being introduced. Mediation clientele was in any event, found to be largely white (p 50) and middle class by Davis, *et al*, (2000e p 49). It seems that those eligible for public funding, less likely to be middle class, manage to avoid mediation despite all the measures designed to get them to go.

[42] The Decision Making Guidance should be considered together with the provisions of the Funding Code Criteria and the Funding Code Procedures, the Access to Justice Act 1999, directions, orders and regulations made under the Act and the provisions of the Human Rights Act 1998 (www.legalservices.gov.uk. Accessed 16 May 05). The Guidance is set to change; a draft Restructured Family Guidance has been published (LSC 2004).

[43] See also ss 4 which states that it is the most appropriate service that must be funded if more than one is available.

[44] General Family Help covers assistance with things like investigation, disclosure and negotiation (LSC 2003b para 20.8). The plan is to abolish this and help with mediation around 2006 (or 2007) and to create a single level of service called Family Help which would be the vehicle for funding non-adversarial resolution of family disputes (LSC 2004 para 20.9.4).

[45] See also LSC (2003a) C27.

for mediation unless any of the exemptions apply (para 20.8.6). It is only if a case falls within the exceptions, if a mediator has assessed the case as unsuitable for mediation or if mediation breaks down that General Family Help is available (para 20.8.7).[46] Legal representation is not available unless it can be demonstrated that there has been a genuine attempt[47] to resolve the case by means of negotiation or, in ancillary relief applications, the Financial Dispute Resolution procedure has failed (para 20.8.9).

So, in effect, those seeking public funding must be assessed to determine whether mediation is suitable and they cannot access funding for other services unless mediation has been ruled out or it has failed.[48] Even then, funding for representation in court proceedings will be refused unless there has been an attempt to negotiate. Clients must accordingly attend an assessment meeting with a mediator to determine suitability and mediation will be provided if the mediator is satisfied that mediation is appropriate (para 20.10).[49] The exemptions to this are set out in the Procedures (LSC 2003a C29). These include cases where mediation is not suitable because the other party is unwilling to attend an assessment and to consider mediation. Also exempt are cases where the client is afraid of domestic abuse from the other party and is in consequence unwilling to participate in mediation. Where the client is willing to participate despite suffering domestic violence in the past, then mediation can proceed. However the mediator retains the right to refuse to conduct a mediation where there are concerns about safety (LSC 2003b para 20.11.5). If the case is considered suitable for mediation, then the parties are permitted access to family mediation and to funding in the form of Help with Mediation (LSC 2003b para 20.11.28).

Research conducted in the late 1990s when equivalent rules existed requiring attendance at a meeting to consider mediation showed that, while there was an increase in these intake assessments, the significant number of cases deemed unsuitable meant that the number of mediations proper did not grow noticeably (Davis, *et al*, 2000c).[50]

> **Q** Consider the conditions upon which the availability of public funding for legal services depends. Do you think their effect is simply that of encouraging mediation or do you think they could have the effect of putting pressure on the parties to mediate?

## *Why Mediation?*

A number of diverse needs and pressures led to the development of mediation as a 'better' way of dealing with the consequences of family breakdown.

The notion of family privacy was significant in explaining early support for mediation. According to Parkinson (1985 p 245), for example, mediation reinforced the private family against threatened intrusion by the 'powerful system of state control'. Party control was seen as central, with disputants being able to shape their own outcomes.[51] And Mnookin saw liberal philosophy as fundamental to support for private ordering:

---

[46] See also LSC (2003b) para 20.8.14–15.
[47] This could be difficult to interpret.
[48] Walsh (2004) suggests that funding may determine the fate of family law and mediation. The poor will have no choice and only the rich will have recourse to the courts.
[49] See also LSC (2004) para 20.12.
[50] See also Davis, *et al*, (2000d) p 33.
[51] See CPU (1989) p 276.

*The advantages of private ordering*

Let me begin with the arguments supporting the presumption in favour of private ordering. The core reason is rooted in notions of human liberty. Private ordering is supported by the liberal idea that individuals have rights, and should largely be left free to make of their lives what they wish. (1984 p 366)

However, there were also a number of other pressures at work. One factor,[52] particularly prominent in the debates leading up to the enactment of the Family Law Act 1996,[53] was financial. The soaring legal aid bill for divorce provided the impetus to look for cheaper alternatives to lawyers and courts (Piper 1996a p 64; Davis and Roberts 1988 p 10).[54] So, for instance, the White Paper setting out the government's proposals for reform leading up to the Family Law Act 1996 anticipated that 'family mediation [would] ... prove to be more cost effective than negotiating at arms [*sic*] length through two separate lawyers and even more so than litigating through the courts' (LCD 1995a para 5.20). In addition, courts were struggling under the burden of the growing number of cases. It was thought that court time could be saved if there were a higher number of settlements (Davis and Roberts 1988 p 10). In fact, research conducted by Bevan, *et al*, (2001) calls both these supposed advantages into question. They found that mediation had almost no effect on the likelihood of a full legal aid certificate being awarded (p 187) and there was almost no effect on legal costs (p 188).[55]

There were other arguments in favour of mediation, however. The effectiveness of court intervention was thought to be limited. Pressure of time meant that courts were unable to enquire into arrangements for children. More significantly, there were doubts whether it was appropriate for courts even to attempt to make such enquiries; parents were more likely to know what was best for their children.[56] In any event, court ordered arrangements were frequently found to break down (Gingerbread and Families Need Fathers 1982 pp 19–21) and it was thought that agreements voluntarily reached by the parties themselves would be more likely to endure than arrangements foisted on them from an external source.[57]

So, mediation came to be regarded not only as the solution to political, financial and administrative problems, it also came to be seen as better for the parties and their children. The benefits believed to flow from mediation are encapsulated in the recent White Paper:

The successful involvement of mediators enables parents to resolve their differences outside of the court room. This helps to minimise the negative impact of parental separation on children and maximise the making of enduring arrangements between the parents that are responsive to children's interests and wishes. (DCA, DfES and DTI 2005 para 51)

**Q** Can the preference for mediation be reconciled with the welfare principle?

---

[52] Another factor, which will not be dealt with here, was pressure coming from various professional groupings such as probation officers. For details see Piper (1996a) p 66; Davis and Roberts (1988) p 11.

[53] But see also the Report of the Interdepartmental Committee on Conciliation (1983); Newcastle Conciliation Project Unit Report (1989).

[54] From the Government's point of view, funding litigation is increasingly costly; the number of applications over contact and residence has grown from 52,924 in 1992 to 94,598 in 2002 (Langdon-Down 2005 p 20).

[55] But see Fisher and Hodson (2001).

[56] See Piper (1993) p 12; Piper (1996a) pp 65–66.

[57] See Parkinson (1983) p 23. See also Piper (1993) p 12.

As Piper (1996a p 65) notes, proponents of mediation have tended to rely chiefly on arguments focusing on the welfare of children. Children are seen as the victims of divorce and the divorce system, with its adversarial, conflictual character, is thought to exacerbate the damage caused to them.[58] In contrast, mediation is thought to encourage parents to put the needs of their children first. Davis and Roberts explain:

> [C]onciliation has been identified with a greater concentration on the needs of children, bringing home to parents the hurt and perhaps even the long-term damage that may result from their continuing quarrelling, or the abandonment of all links between the children and the non-custodial parent. ...Many mediators are motivated, at least in part, by a perception that conflict between separated parents is bad for children; indeed, this is a quite explicit part of the case advanced on behalf of conciliation services. (1988 pp 10–11)

This focus on reducing conflict[59] is given expression in the Code of Practice of the UK College of Family Mediators (2000) which states:

> 2.2 Mediation ... aims to assist participants to communicate with one another now and in the future and to reduce the scope and intensity of dispute and conflict within the family.
> 2.3 Mediation should have regard to the principles that where a marriage or relationship has irretrievably broken down and is being brought to an end it should be brought to an end in a way which minimises distress to the participants and any children, promotes as good a relationship between the participants and any children as possible, removes or diminishes any risk of violence to any of the participants or children from the other participants, and avoids unnecessary cost to the participants.[60]

The aim of reducing conflict and the emphasis on co-operative parenting is apparent also in an advice leaflet published by the Community Legal Service:

> Mediation aims to help you find a solution that meets the needs of you, your partner and any children, and that you all feel is fair. ...
> Mediation can help to reduce tension, anger and misunderstandings, and improve communication between you and your partner. This is especially important if you have children, because you will probably have to co-operate over their care and upbringing. (CLS 2004 p 3)

This case for mediation has proved very persuasive. As we have seen, the White Paper maintains that is has the potential to 'minimise the negative impact of parental separation on children' (DCA, DfES and DTI 2005 para 51). The earlier White Paper that preceded the Family Law Act 1996 was even more explicit:[61]

> Conflict is harmful to children and the Government is of the view that the reduction of conflict should be high on the list of objectives for a good divorce process. ...
> It is also important that, where there are children, parents learn early to communicate during the process of making arrangements for a life apart. ...Research shows that the children who do best are those whose parents are able to talk together. ...
> Research has established that communication between a couple is improved by their being able to say things face to face in mediation. (LCD 1995a paras 5.16–5.18)[62]

---

[58] See, eg, LCD (1995a) para 5.2.

[59] Mediation and other forms of ADR are perceived as means of managing conflict (see eg, Smart and May 2004b pp 358–59). References to party control and autonomy are now rare.

[60] These aims echo the general principles set out in Part I of the Family Law Act 1996.

[61] See also LCD (1993) para 4.5); Home Office (1998) para 4.41.

[62] See also para 5.11. See also DCA DfES and DTI (2004) p 2 (Ministerial Foreword).

Mediation, then, is regarded as a 'civilising'[63] process, reducing conflict, facilitating communication, promoting agreement and safeguarding the best interests of children. However the talk about mediation, according to Davis, *et al*, (2001a), conflates two different kinds of activity. The first is that of 'mediation as an aid to private communication' (p 265). The outcomes are meant to be 'better understanding, agreement on a variety of specific issues, and improved capacity to negotiate in future, and less conflict' (p 265). The second 'involves the attempted settlement of contested legal proceedings'. This latter activity, the authors suggest, is best regarded as part of the court procedure, intended, to 'divert cases from trial' (Davis, *et al*, 2000e p 136), and, like most procedural devices, to minimise legal costs and 'advance the settlement process' (Davis, *et al*, 2001a, p 265). And, now, it seems that keeping cases out of the court room through alternative dispute resolution is coming to be seen as having the added advantage of deflecting the criticisms of the legal system and its role in contact disputes that fathers groups have been publicising in the media.[64]

Not all the professed aims and outcomes rank equally in importance. Mediation appears nowadays to be focusing less on the relationships between the parties or empowerment of clients and more on the aims of settlement and diversion from court. Dingwall and Greatbach, for example, report a higher degree of formality than was apparent in earlier research and observe that this could be evidence of a more 'professional' approach. They go on to say:

> However, from a different perspective, it could be argued that mediation is being bureacratized and incorporated into the legal system in a way that compromises its founding ethos of empowerment and client control. Mediators have become much more sophisticated and subtle than in the 1980s in their management of process and the guidance of clients towards preferred outcomes. Their work is becoming complementary to the legal process rather than an alternative to it. There may be some debate, though, about whether the legal process should use such indirect means, and about its implications for clients. (Dingwall and Greatbach 2000 p 232).

'Client empowerment' they say, has given way to 'managed settlement seeking' (Dingwall and Greatbach 2001 p 379). So, on one hand commentators have observed of mediation that the autonomy it purports to confer on the parties is illusory; the assumptions underlying mediation, its focus on settlement and the norms espoused by mediators permeate the mediation process and influence its outcome. On the other hand, fears have been expressed that, in the absence of partisan representation by lawyers and of formal legal safeguards, imbalances of power between the parties remain unchecked because of mediator non-intervention and the welfare of children is jeopardised.

*Autonomy and Control*

The potential for mediator influence in the process and outcome of mediation was highlighted some years ago by Simon Roberts.[65] He suggested that the mere presence of the mediator must have an impact on negotiations and that this impact is likely to be amplified by the activities of the mediator; minimal intervention by mediators is rare:

---

[63] See Walker, *et al*, (1994) p 9; CPU (1989) p 276.
[64] See The Hon Mr Justice Munby (2004).
[65] See also Grillo (1991).

Once the mediator goes on to provide a normative framework for discussion, however sparse, the universe within which bilateral negotiation would have taken place is profoundly changed. This transformation is taken further if he helps to clarify issues and demands, or offers advice on matters outside the knowledge of the disputants (such as points of law, or the probable action of judicial agencies under different circumstances). Many mediators will see it as necessary to a settlement that the disputants' view of their predicament be transformed; and so deliberately set out to do this, offering evaluations of past conduct or future options, and identifying what they consider to be the appropriate outcome.

In so far as the mediator succeeds in transforming the disputants' view of the quarrel, he comes to share with them control over the outcome. (1983 p 549)

The UK College of Family Mediators Code of Practice states that mediators should be neutral as to the outcome of mediation (2000 para 4.2). Similarly, the Law Society's Code of Practice for Family Mediation, which binds members of the Family Mediation Panel (who are solicitor mediators accredited by the Law Society), stresses that the mediator 'must not seek to impose his or her preferred outcome on the parties' (The Law Society 2004 Annex A para 5.5).[66] Yet research suggests that neutrality may be difficult to achieve. Certainly, Piper's empirical study of child-focused mediation revealed considerable mediator control:

What became apparent was that the 'facts' supplied by parents were used by mediators with prior beliefs, stemming from a normative framework, about the problem and its solution. Full parental responsibility for the process and outcome could then be possible only in the hypothetical case where what was supplied by parents was acceptable to mediators. (1993 p 190)

And Marian Roberts has warned mediators against adopting a directive role:

Mediators are not neutral. ...They have their own values and attitudes. Influenced by prevailing research findings, they are likely to adopt a strong pro-contact stance in the belief that it is better, on the whole, for children to have a continuing relationship with both parents after separation and divorce. In most cases, these values are shared by parents themselves. However, mediators should not brow-beat parents with research evidence or with warnings of emotional damage or of the harmful effects of litigation. The exertion of overt influence is incompatible with the facilitating role of the mediator. (1997 p 124)[67]

Dingwall and Greatbach (2001 p 380) report that the mediation clients in their sample considered mediators impartial.[68] But what they go on to say bears out the view that mediators are not neutral as to outcome:

Mediators, however, clearly had views about outcomes. We have called these 'the parameters of the permissible'. Within these, clients were left to work out their own deals, but the client who

---

[66] However mediators must have regard to Pt 1 of the Family Law Act 1996 (The Law Society 2004 Annex A para 8.1). The UK College of Family Mediators also imposes such a duty (2000 para 2.3 quoted above p 428). How this requirement can be reconciled with the idea of non-directive mediation is not clear. It may be that in the case of solicitor mediators it is relevant in relation to another part of the Law Society Code which states that it is permissible for mediators to inform the parties if their proposed arrangements are in his or her view, likely to fall outside the parameters of what the court would consider acceptable (para 5.10). The UK College, however, limits the circumstances in which mediators may do this (UK College of Family Mediators 2000 para 4.2). Also, if the arrangement appears 'unconscionable or fundamentally inappropriate, the mediators may terminate the mediation' (The Law Society 2004 Annex A para 5.10) See also UK College of Family Mediators (2000) para 4.7.5.

[67] See also Roberts (1997) p 84; Dingwall and Greatbach (2000).

[68] This means that they did not favour one party over the other.

stepped outside could face heavy mediator pressure. For example, mediators may not be greatly concerned whether a contact agreement specifies one weekend in three or one weekend in four. A residential parent who refuses any contact, however, has breached the parameters and will be pressed to return to them. The parameters seemed to be broader for financial issues, probably because houses and cash are more easily divisible than children.

The mediators' view of permissible agreements seemed to vary somewhat, as did the amount of pressure they were willing to apply. (Dingwall and Greatbach 2001 p 380)[69]

Neale and Smart too point out that:

Mediation is not value-free. It operates (at present) only marginally in the shadow of the law but centrally in the shadow of social welfare ideology. Indeed it may operate as 'a cover for value laden tampering with family life', with mediators exerting subtle pressure on clients to conform to current welfare notions. (1997 p 383, footnote omitted)

Walker, *et al*, found that even in relation to money matters, mediators deployed various strategies to get parties to re-think arrangements they disapproved of (1994 p 106). It appears that the process the researchers refer to as 'coming round' (1994 p 97) involved, at least to some extent, a transformation in the perceptions of the parties to accommodate ideas more acceptable to mediators (Piper 1996a p 77).

Clearly then research suggests that the parties are not necessarily empowered by mediation and that the norms of the mediators tend to shape the agreement forged between the parties. Some commentators who have observed the process have also identified an element of control.[70] Bottomley, for instance, contended that the privatisation of family disputes masks continuing supervision of families which is rendered benevolent by notions of welfare (Bottomley 1985 p 163): 'the process of de-legalization is not one of de-regularization but is a shift from one form of social discipline to another' (1984 p 300). Her critique points to the potency of mediation in purveying particular norms and underwriting particular images of the family.

*Dominant Norms*

Because mediation can be used to promote particular ideologies of the family, it can be viewed as a means of social control. And the ideology that has been observed to be dominant in mediation has, it is argued, potentially damaging implications for women. The focus on children is seen as a denial of women's identities distinct from motherhood. It also leads to a preference for a particular model of joint parenting and a presumption in favour of contact, an approach that helps to perpetuate the power of fathers.[71] Several women told Walker and her colleagues, for example, that they felt pressured to come to an agreement (2004 p 138) and, we can surmise, although the researchers do not tell us so, that these women agreed to contact; usually, mothers are expected by professionals, including mediators, to agree to contact.[72] The emphasis on

---

[69] See further, Dingwall and Greatbach (2000) pp 242–45.

[70] See Sanders (1997) p 8.

[71] See Roberts (1996). See also Pickett (1991) pp 29–33. Davis, *et al*, (2000e p 100) speculate that that the slight preference for mediation over solicitor negotiation by the men in their research sample might suggest that mediators might be more supportive of the arguments advanced by non-resident parents, who are usually fathers.

[72] See, for example, Dingwall and Greatbach (2001) p 380, quoted above.

jointness ignores the unequal contributions of fathers and mothers to parenting prior to separation. It also places the burden of absorbing any strain and inconvenience caused by contact on mothers (Piper 1988 pp 491–92). For, although Smart (1999) in her study found that some fathers became more involved in child care after divorce, the reconstruction of the family in the mould of the 'continuing-but-separated' family leaves intact in many cases the traditional divisions of labour, enabling fathers to continue as decision-makers while leaving mothers as primary caretakers.[73]

**Q** Read the chapters on residence and contact. Do you think that courts might be said to espouse the same familial ideology as mediators?

*Power and Mediation*

While interventionism by mediators is seen by some as opening the way to social control and as disempowering the parties, particularly mothers, non-interventionism can present dangers for the weaker party: '[t]he stronger party may be enabled to force a coercive settlement on the weaker' (Roberts 1983 p 557). This is a problem that has frequently been adverted to by feminist writers warning that women are often in the weaker bargaining position and that to ignore this perpetuates inequalities in power.[74]

Bryan (1992), writing in the United States, has asserted that women are disadvantaged in numerous ways.[75] They tend to earn less than men; they are less likely to be employed in jobs that develop negotiating skills; they have lower self-esteem; and they are more care oriented, focusing on relationships and sacrificing other goals in order to keep the peace. Men's greater status promotes dominant behaviour and their experience in the public sphere enhances their authority and their ability to negotiate. These disadvantages are compounded by the familial ideology informing mediation:

> Mediation proponents seductively appeal to women's socialized values by speaking softly of relatedness. Yet mediation exploits wives by denigrating their legal entitlements, stripping them of authority, encouraging unwarranted compromise, isolating them from needed support, and placing them across the table from their more powerful husbands and demanding that they fend for themselves. The process thus perpetuates patriarchy by freeing men to use their power to gain greater control over children, to implant more awareness of male dominance into women's consciousness, and to retain more of the marital financial assets than men would obtain if lawyers negotiated divorce settlements. (Bryan 1992 p 523)

Although concerns about adequate representation arise also in the legal arena,[76] the problems are more acute in mediation because the process occurs in private, without the presence of partisan lawyers and without access to appeal (Bruch 1988 p 120).

**Q** Do you agree that women are more likely to be in a weaker bargaining position than men?

---

[73] See Pickett (1991) p 32.

[74] See Bottomley (1985) p 179; Hilton (1991) p 29.

[75] Davis, *et al*, (2000e p 85) report that a higher proportion of women found mediation about children matters upsetting than found solicitor negotiations upsetting. However a significant proportion of women found mediation satisfactory overall. See below.

[76] Indeed, Roberts (1997 p 158) has pointed out that new inequalities may be created. The parties' resources might be unequal as might be the skill of their lawyers.

Roberts does not recommend mediation in cases where there is a serious imbalance in bargaining power such as those involving domestic violence, those where a sense of guilt makes a party liable to agree to prejudicial arrangements and those where cultural norms deny women decision-making authority (1997 p 129). However Davis and Roberts found the feminist critique relating to power to be largely unsubstantiated in an early study. The mediators they observed 'controlled the ebb and flow of negotiation' and 'in some cases, the "weaker" party did, indeed, feel empowered' (1989 p 306).[77] Moreover, Marian Roberts has argued in the past that bargaining power involves a complex interplay of forces and is constantly shifting. 'Rarely are the disadvantages or advantages stacked all one way, nor should it be assumed, either, that where one party has superior "endowments" of one sort or another that power will necessarily be used, let alone exploited'. (1996 p 239)

Nevertheless, the feminist critique has had an impact. The Law Society's Code of Practice for accredited solicitor mediators requires them to be alive to the possibility of power imbalances including, for instance, 'behaviour which is controlling abusive or manipulative' as well as imbalances arising from financial position, 'status; communication and other skills; possession of information; [and] the withholding of co-operation' (The Law Society 2004 Annex A para 6.1). If power imbalances threaten to make mediation unfair, the mediator should takes steps to prevent this (para 6.2). If that is not possible, the mediation should be terminated (para 6.4).[78]

The power of mediators to control the process of mediation is not perceived as a source of reassurance by some critics. Grillo (1991 p 1592), for example, has suggested that the mediator may not have sufficient understanding of the power dynamic in the relationship to know whether or how to intervene. More recently, Davis, *et al*, (2000f p 217) have suggested that oppression or undue pressure could be problems and they remarked that some mediators in their study found this difficult to handle. They report that there was generally no exploration by mediators of the clients' emotional state other than in relation to violence (p 216).[79] Little regard was paid to intellectual capacity or articulacy *(ibid)*. Some of the women clients questioned indicated that they felt intimidated whatever strategy they used to resolve the outstanding issues; whatever they did could lead to punitive consequences (2000f p 217). This finding brings into question claims that mediators can redress serious imbalances of power.

The issue is particularly troubling in cases where there has been a history of domestic violence. Such instances present the starkest examples of inequality of bargaining power and the greatest likelihood that power will be exploited.

*Domestic Violence and Mediation*

*1. Outlining the Problems*

The prevalence of domestic violence should not be underestimated.[80] Davis, *et al*, (2000c) state that in their sample, mediation suppliers reported being aware of allegations of domestic violence in 31% of cases (p 28). There were also reports of fear of

---

[77] See further Roberts (1997) pp 120–21; 160–62.

[78] See also UK College of Family Mediators (2000) para 4.3.2.

[79] The main cause for unsuitability relied on was violence or intimidation (Davis, *et al*,2000f p 216) However not all cases involving violence were excluded (p 217).

[80] See Kaganas and Piper (1994) p 268.

violence in 19% of cases (p 29). These percentages are slightly higher, perhaps because screening is better, than the 23% noted by Walker, *et al*, some years earlier (1994 p 62). That such cases can be dealt with easily is belied by the evidence of at least one of their interviewees, who said:

> Signals were being given to [the mediator] which he didn't take up. I was too afraid of my husband to state the nature of my anxieties—mentioning it would have prompted more. [The mediator] was asking us to go away and discuss the very things which provoked him to violence—the children and the house ... on our own when in fact that's what we'd gone there for.
>
> (1994 p 62)

**Q** Do you think the problem in this case was that the mediator apparently was not aware of the history of violence? Do you think mediation could have been made fair and safe for the wife if he had been aware?

There are strong arguments for saying that mediation is not appropriate where relationships have been characterised by sustained violence. These were summarised by Kaganas and Piper:

> The basic elements of mediation have been described as voluntary participation, equality or rough parity of bargaining power, neutrality on the part of the mediator, and confidentiality. ... It has been pointed out that these fundamental principles are in the main incompatible with protecting the interests of victims of abuse. ...
>
> First, it is argued that the existence of a violent relationship undermines the voluntary nature of mediation. Victims have no real choice. They are not free to act contrary to their partner's wishes in either electing or rejecting mediation. Nor are they really free to terminate it once it has commenced ... . Secondly, it is said that, in the context of abuse, mediation cannot achieve its principal aim: co-operation for mutual benefit. Because an abuser devalues his victim ... he is able to dismiss her point of view ... . Thirdly, it is feared that in place of co-operation, mediation might lead to capitulation by the weaker party. Disputes over matters such as child custody can form part of an ongoing effort to assert control and exact concessions from the other party ... . Victims may be unable even to articulate their wishes and needs and may, through fear or to avoid conflict, yield to their husbands' demands. Seen in this light, it becomes clear that 'mediation empowers only the already more powerful husband' ... and is detrimental to the interests of abused women ... .
>
> The ability of mediators to redress the balance is doubtful. In the first place the mediator may not even be aware of the dynamics of the parties' relationship: 'Even the most sensitised mediator cannot be expected to identify and interpret the ... innuendo of threat or coercion' which might be present in a look or gesture ... . Where mediators do intervene, their efforts are generally confined to promoting procedural equality and this does not redress the power imbalance ... . The substantive inequality remains and, in circumstances of this kind, mediation does not result in genuine agreement.
>
> The concerns of mediators to remain neutral and to avoid allocating blame not only leads to a failure to confront problems of power and domination, it can have the effect of exacerbating them. The absence of any challenge to the abuser's conduct can be interpreted as condoning it. ...
>
> That this might have the effect of compounding the danger to the victim becomes evident when it is remembered that violence often escalates during and after separation.
>
> (1994 pp 266–67, references omitted)

The authors concluded that, while those victims of violence who feel sufficiently confident to participate in mediation should be given the opportunity to do so, mediation should not be extended to cases in which the impact of violence on the victim negates any benefits of the process. It is crucial that services devise methods to determine not only whether abuse has occurred but also the levels of fear experienced by the victim and whether that fear leads her to modify her behaviour to placate the abuser (Kaganas and Piper 1994 pp 272–73). In order to determine whether the effect of violence is such that the victim is rendered unable to assert herself and to negotiate effectively, the authors adopted the concept of a culture of battering developed by Fischer, *et al*, (1993). Three elements need to be present for a culture of battering to be established: actual abuse of whatever type; a systematic pattern of domination; and the victim's denial and minimisation of abuse:

> [W]here a relationship is characterised by these features, mediation holds no promise of a satisfactory outcome for the victim. Mediators cannot compensate, however well trained and aware, for the damage done to anyone who has not only suffered the direct effects of abuse but who has also been systematically controlled over time and who has not been able to acknowledge the abuse. (Kaganas and Piper 1994 p 271)

Screening for violence is important as information about a background of violence may not emerge in other ways. Victims of domestic violence are often reluctant to seek court orders or even to reveal their plight.[81] As Kaganas and Piper point out:

> Victims as well as abusers tend to minimise or deny violence: voluntary disclosure is relatively unusual. Researchers have advanced a number of possible explanations for this. First, to acknowledge violence by disclosing it, is to acknowledge that the relationship in which so much has been invested cannot continue. Disclosure may therefore signify too much personal loss for it to be psychologically possible. Moreover, while some victims may refrain from seeking help for fear of retaliation, others may still be emotionally bound to their partners; Ellis and DeKeseredy refer to the loyalty/love that victims often feel. The possibility that victims do not disclose during the course of their relationships is significant on divorce: it means that there is no 'official' evidence in the form of court orders or criminal proceedings that abuse occurred. This, in turn, makes it less likely that the abuse will be discovered on divorce.
>
> Secondly, even on divorce the victim/survivor may not expect to be believed or taken seriously. Thirdly, she may fear being labelled a failure—a misplaced sense of shame therefore inhibits disclosure. Fourthly, she may have fears that she will lose her children. Fifthly, it may be difficult for her to redefine an intimate partner as an abuser, particularly if he is the father of her children. Finally, she may not disclose because she does not conform to her own stereotypes of battered women. (1999 p 188, references omitted)

Ellis and Stuckless (1996 pp 77–80) have suggested that mediation services that employ screening, coupled with, in the cases they do take on, support for the party with weaker bargaining power and monitoring for abusive behaviour, may mitigate the effects of power imbalances. They also have said that voluntary mediation can play a part in reducing 'postprocessing abuse' (1996 p 58). However mediation can be inappropriate and even dangerous in cases where mediators do not ask about violence, do not understand its impact and do not have the skill to deal with the issues (Young 1996, cited in Hester, *et al*, 1997 pp 59–60).

---

[81] See further Women's Project (1998) pp 9–12.

## 2. Professional Practice

Official documentation giving information and advice to the public makes it clear that mediation should not be conducted where one party feels 'threatened or pressured' by the other (CLS 2004 p 3):

> Mediators must make sure that mediation discussions are fair, and that you and your partner feel safe. So the mediator will check with each of you separately before and during mediation to see whether there is a problem of violence or abuse.
>
> If you are worried about your safety or your children's safety, you should tell the mediator. In that case, the mediator will probably say that you should see a solicitor ... .
>
> If you decide to use mediation but do not want your partner to know your address or phone number, you should tell the mediator. You can also ask for separate waiting areas when you come to mediation discussions. (CLS 2004 p 4)

Mediators are not only required to screen for violence but also to counter its effects in mediation.[82] The UK College of Family Mediators' Code of Practice, for example, states:

> *4.8 Abuse within the family*
>
> 4.8.1 In all cases, mediators must seek to discover through a screening procedure whether or not there is a fear of abuse or any other harm and whether or not it is alleged that any participant has been or is likely to be abusive towards another. Where abuse is alleged or suspected mediators must discuss whether any participant wishes to take part in mediation and information about available support services should be provided.
>
> 4.8.2 Where mediation does take place, mediators must uphold throughout the principles of voluntariness of participation, fairness and safety and must conduct the process in accordance with this section. In addition, steps must be taken to ensure the safety of all participants on arrival and departure.
>
> (UK College of Family Mediators 2000)

The screening policy document issued by the UK College defines abuse widely and focuses on the perspective of the victim:

> [B]ehaviour that seeks to secure power and control for the abuser and the impact of which is to undermine the safety, security, self esteem and autonomy of the abused person. Domestic violence contains elements of the use of any or all of physical, sexual, psychological, emotional, verbal or economic intimidation, oppression or coercion.
>
> (UK College of Family Mediators 1999 C)

> *D Principles of Screening for Domestic Abuse*
>
> 1.1 Mediators must routinely screen for abuse before a decision is taken to proceed with mediation.
>
> 1.2 Screening must take place separately with each participant.
>
> 1.3 In reaching a decision about whether to proceed, priority should be given to the individual's perception of abuse over any judgement about levels of severity or types of abuse.
>
> 1.4 If in any doubt about the appropriateness of mediation the mediator could consult with his/her supervisor and if doubt still remains, must not proceed ... .

---

[82] See, for example. The Law Society (2004) Annex A para 6.3; LSC (2002) F1.1.

4 Whether or not domestic abuse emerges as an issue at an initial screening, continued screening must take place throughout mediation ...

(UK College of Family Mediators 1999)

The Legal Services Funding Code Guidance (LSC 2003b) seeks to put in place screening measures for those seeking public funding who are normally obliged to consider mediation. Solicitors have the initial responsibility to screen for domestic violence and mediators continue to be required, in accordance with the Family Mediation Code of Practice, to identify cases where either party may be influenced by fear of abuse. Domestic abuse screening must be conducted by the mediation service as soon after the initial contact with the client as possible (LSC 2003b 20.11.17; LSC 2003a D5). Mediators should give the parties the option of being seen separately and, if they are seen together, screening must be conducted with the parties separately and prior to the meeting (LSC 2003b 20.11 19–23).[83]

The duties resting on mediators to guard against the problems created by domestic violence were tightened up in the wake of research showing its prevalence and effects. Screening policies were put in place by services but later research showed that these had limited impact on the attitudes and practices of a large proportion of mediators. Hester, *et al*, (1997) reported that not all of the mediators in their study knew whether their service had a screening policy and only a minority used mainly a 'safety-oriented approach' which involved some form of screening and a readiness to intervene rather than remain impartial (p 37). None mentioned the risk to abused mothers that might arise in the context of contact between abusive men and their children (p 53). Court welfare officers (as they were then termed) also failed to take safety measures, assuming that domestic violence cases were screened out by the clients themselves and/or by earlier court processes (pp 21–22).

More recently, Dingwall and Greatbach (2000, 2001), evaluating their research carried out in 1998–99,[84] raised doubts about the effectiveness of Codes of Practice. Their conclusions suggest that mediators may still not be taking domestic violence seriously enough. The authors observed that there was little clarity as to the stage at which screening was meant to take place (2000 pp 251–52).[85] Moreover, violence was not treated as being of much significance when the issue was raised in actual mediation sessions:

[F]ew mediators routinely asked whether violence was an issue. When the issue arose it tended to be marginalised, as found in previous research. No case was terminated on this ground. Mediators clearly had some difficulty in knowing where to draw a line between 'acceptable' and 'unacceptable' levels of conflict in the relationship. (Dingwall and Greatbach 2001 p 381)[86]

Davis, *et al*, (2000f p 216) report that if violence was revealed, mediators still encouraged people to consider mediation, although they did suggest some safety measures. However '[i]n order for mediation to be ruled out on the grounds of past violence, clients had to make quite strong claims that they were in fear of the other party' (Davis, *et al*, 2000f p 217).

---

[83] See also LSC (2004) para 20.12.12.
[84] See Dingwall and Greatbach (2000) p 230.
[85] Most of their research focused on FMA, which, like the UK College of Family Mediators, requires its members to screen for domestic violence. Usually, screening is meant to take place at the initial meeting.
[86] See further, Dingwall and Greatbach (2000) pp 245–48.

Conciliation appointments conducted by CAFCASS appear to be perhaps even less influenced by power and safety concerns. An inspection into the (mainly in-court) services provided by CAFCASS concluded that officers had insufficient knowledge at the directions stage about service users to be sure that they had given informed consent to participate. Even if consent had been given, officers did not know whether there were safety issues that needed to be addressed (MCSI 2003 para 4.36 and p 49). The inspectors also noted with disapproval that officers adopted the practice of asking the parties in each others' presence, and in a public area, whether they objected to a joint interview (para 4.44).[87] *The Model Scheme for In-Court Dispute Resolution*[88]requires only that the CAFCASS officer dealing with the First Hearing dispute resolution should conduct a paper risk assessment. The officer may undertake further assessment, seeing the parties separately prior to a joint meeting (paras 11 and 16). The requirements in this document, apart from the mention of separate interviews, are unlikely to change practice.

Solicitors appear to be no more adept at identifying cases involving violence.[89] The Legal Services Funding Code Guidance (LSC 2003b para 20.11.5) points out that research has shown that 'a considerable number of clients' who are referred to an assessment meeting are not suitable because they are unwilling to mediate due to fear of domestic abuse. And Davis, *et al*, (2000f p 217) observed that solicitor mediators barely touched on the question of violence.

In spite of their criticisms of the professionals participating in the pilot studies, Davis, *et al*, (2000e p 58) are not entirely convinced of the dangers posed by domestic violence in the context of mediation. They report that in 57% of cases in which a mediation client referred to fear of violence, mediation was nonetheless considered suitable by the mediator. 71% of clients who said they feared violence reported that they had felt able to say what they wanted to say in mediation: 'Reported fear of violence was not on this evidence associated with reduced ability to communicate freely' (p 70). They conclude that the view that a history of violence should preclude mediation is not a view held by mediators or by their clients (p 58). They also say that although fear of violence featured in a great many of the cases they surveyed, it appeared, 'for the most part to be overcome in mediation' (p 137). Women's responses to mediation were, 'on the whole', slightly more positive than those of men' (p 137).

Nonetheless, even they found that those clients who feared violence were about twice as likely to find mediation upsetting than those who did not (p 75). And Walker's informants provided even less reassuring information. They did not necessarily find that fear of violence was overcome and some reported feeling intimidated (2004 p 138).

*Mediation and Children's Welfare*

Not only does mediation have the potential to mask inequalities between the participants, the privatisation of divorce also has the effect of removing from public scrutiny the issue of the best interests of the children concerned.

---

[87] Davis, *et al*, (2000d) found that, of cases where parties attended the intake meeting together, a background of violence was reported by service providers in 11%. Where there were separate meetings, and where the wife alone attended, the figure was 29%. The authors speculate that it is probably the case that parties are less likely to attend together where there has been a history of violence. They also suggest that joint attendance has the effect that it is less likely that violence will be revealed (2000d p 31).

[88] See above.

[89] See also Kaganas and Piper (1999).

Mediation, like other forms of private ordering, is premised on the assumption that parents know what is best for their children and fails to acknowledge that the needs of parents and children are not always synonymous; [90] parents might reach an agreement that does not best serve their children's best interests. Moreover, the child's views and wishes are usually not canvassed.

Harold and Murch express concern that the increased emphasis on mediation and ADR may marginalise the child. Unless mediators and in-court conciliators involve children directly, they will often have to rely on parents' perceptions of their children and these may not be reliable (2005 p 199).

Article 12 of the UN Convention on the Rights of the Child gives the child a right to express an opinion and have it taken into account. Some mediators do consider direct participation by children but most tend to rely on the adults concerned to relay children's views. The UK College of Family Mediators policy stipulates:

> The UK College has a positive policy that family mediators should actively encourage parents and/or other participants[91] in mediation:
>
> to talk with and listen to their children so that the decisions parents make about arrangements for their children are reached in the light of an understanding of each child's perspective
>
> to consider the different ways in which children may be involved or consulted, including, when appropriate, offering opportunities for them to take part directly in discussions with the mediator/s.[92]
>
> (UK College of Family Mediators 2002 para 1)

Dingwall and Greatbach (2001) found that in their study, there were no cases where children were seen by the mediator, although the 'idea' was discussed in two cases.[93] They did observe a focus on children's interests, however:

> [T]he children's perspectives were distinguished and discussed in 52 of the 56 cases where they were relevant. Since the 1980s mediators seem to have become much better at separating what might in general be good for children[94] and what parents claim would be good for children and in dealing with these separately. (Dingwall and Greatbach 2001 p 381)[95]

Harold and Murch also argue that the change in CAFCASS practice proposed by the government to move away from report writing to concentrate on conciliation and support (DCA, DfEs and DTI 2005 paras 66–67) could deprive children of an opportunity to express their views to a CAFCASS officer (Harold and Murch 2005 p 201).

In fact, the inspection of CAFCASS services found that officers were divided on the desirability of involving children and that there was very little provision for their systematic inclusion. Some schemes did make provision for interviewing children at the request of the parents or the court, however. (MCSI 2003 p 49).[96] The scheme in the Principal

---

[90] See Piper (1994) p 101; Richards (1995b); Douglas, *et al*, (1996) p 130.

[91] It seems that family members other than the couple are beginning to be included (Kleanthous 2003 p 849).

[92] Mediators affiliated to the UK College (UK College of Family Mediators 2002 para 4) are instructed not to involve children directly unless they have been trained to do so as are those accredited to the Law Society (The Law Society 2004 Annex A para 8.3).

[93] See also Douglas, *et al*, (2000) p 191.

[94] This would appear to embrace an assumption that contact is good for children. See above pp 314ff.

[95] See further, Dingwall and Greatbach (2000) pp 248–49.

[96] The *Private Law Programme—Guidance Issued by the President of the Family Division* (2004) does not mandate attendance by children at the First Hearing dispute resolution meeting. The document states that children aged 9 and over can attend where the resources are available and the local scheme allows attendance. They

Registry of the Family Division is different in that children are routinely seen.[97] Children aged 9 years or over must be brought to the conciliation appointment and, if there is more than one child and at least one is 9 or older, the younger children can also attend. The children are interviewed separately by the CAFCASS officer (District Judge Brasse 2004 pp 722–23). Their involvement is regarded as useful because their wishes and feelings appear to be a factor in bringing about an agreement (p 724).[98]

A number of suggestions have been made in the past to increase the focus on children's interests and wishes.[99] The government has now indicated that this is one of its priorities:[100]

> 52. We are ... looking at other ways of involving children and developing new models of child focussed mediation and dispute resolution. This may involve mediators in meeting with children. Alternatively, it may involve the mediator in helping the parents to focus on their child or children and more fully to consider their wishes and feelings in the process of separation.
>
> (DCA, DfES and DTI 2005)

### The Harmonious Divorce/Separation?

As we have seen, mediation is conceived of primarily as a means of reducing conflict, facilitating settlement and, to some extent, as a way of improving communication between warring parties. Since the early days of its deployment in family disputes, efforts have been made to differentiate it from other forms of intervention. In 1989, for instance, the Newcastle study into conciliation stated that the objectives of conciliation, as it was then generally termed, 'are not reconciliation, adjudication, arbitration or counselling as such although each of these may play a part in the settlement of a dispute' (CPU 1989 p 276).

Mediation and conciliation are premised on the ability of the participants to negotiate in a rational way, unclouded by hostility, and, particularly in the case of child related issues, to put the interests of the children first. The assumption is that, not only is it more cost-efficient than the traditional legal route to dispute resolution, it is better at reducing conflict and promoting co-operation.

Day Sclater, however, raises the question whether the harmonious divorce can be promoted by removing it from the realm of the adversarial system or whether, to some extent, polarisation, opposition and conflict may be part of the psychology of divorce (Day Sclater 1999a p 162) (and, presumably, separation). She goes on to suggest that, not only are negative emotions an undeniable reality in many family break-ups, but that the drive to reduce conflict and the refusal to countenance expressions of anger and hostility in dispute resolution processes may be detrimental to participants. Exhortations to co-operate can be experienced as persecutory (1999b p 183). Conflict may be implicated in the process of rebuilding of the self (1999a p 176). And the ideal of

---

should not attend unless the environment is child friendly (pp 7 and 11). Attendance at the joint meeting with the CAFCASS officer for conciliation is limited to the parents, unless the officer advises otherwise and the parties agree (*Model Scheme for In-Court Dispute Resolution* para 16).

[97] See *District Judge's Direction. Children Conciliation* [2004] 1 FLR 974.

[98] See also *Al-Khatib v Masry* [2004] EWCA Civ 1353; [2005] 1 FLR 381.

[99] See on training schemes for mediators to get them to help parents to consult their children or for mediators to consult children directly, Fisher 1996 p 14; Piper 1994; Piper 1996 p 375; Roberts 1997 pp 141–42; Piper 1999b pp 91–92.

[100] See also in relation to in-court conciliation, DCA, DfES and DTI (2005) para 57.

parental harmony for the sake of the children operates to delegitimise feelings of anger that could be important for survival and recovery (see 1999a p 170; 1999b p 180). A refusal to allow parties to dwell on past wrongs could also deprive parties of a helpful strategy: the re-interpretation of the past (1999a p 173; 1999b p 150). Often the marriage is viewed negatively from the vantage point of the present, so making it possible to see the break-up more positively and as a route out of an oppressive relationship (1999a p 175). A focus on the future 'sits uneasily with the need to revisit and reinterpret the past' that is essential to recovery (1999b p 177).

Day Sclater found that those who underwent mediation fared less well psychologically than those who relied on a solicitor from the start. She speculates that one explanation for this could be that 'the barrier to the expression of hostile emotions, posed by the discourses of welfare and harmony, runs counter to ordinary coping strategies, thus militating against the achievement of psychological separation and emotional resolution' (Day Sclater 1999b p 149).[101] The participants are not given the opportunity to tell their stories. Instead these stories are 'reframed' during the course of mediation to fit in with the discourse of welfare and harmony (1999b p 150).

She comments that our

> inability to accept the emotional complexities of divorce … lead us either to trivialise it (as in booklets distributed to divorcing parents which tell them that they must 'put their feelings to one side for the children's sake'), or to pathologise it, as when 'conflict' is regarded as a dangerous, abnormal and avoidable (1999a p 180).

In both cases, she says, we try to render emotions manageable and we 'deny the realities of family breakdown' (1999a p 180).

Other commentators seem now to be suggesting that mediation be adapted to take account of emotion. Dingwall and Greatbach (2000 p 251), for example, suggest that mediators probably require training in counselling or related skills to deal with clients' distress. And it seems that some mediators too are suggesting that clients' emotions should be acknowledged. Also, they say, that this 'emotional work' has the added advantage of helping to achieve settlements (Wilson 2004).[102]

**Q** Consider the description of the FAInS pilots below. Is this a more coherent way of accommodating clients' varied needs?

## III. NEGOTIATING THROUGH LAWYERS

Solicitors frequently refer clients to mediation.[103] However, often, rather than do that and rather than litigate, they negotiate agreements on behalf of their clients.[104] Lawyers

---

[101] See also Day Sclater (1999a p 177).

[102] This appears to be a return to a position rejected in earlier years. See, for example, Roberts (1997) p 25, referred to above, p 422.

[103] Solicitors who were obliged to refer clients to mediation resented doing so, considering that they should be trusted to assess the suitability of their cases for the process (Davis, *et al,* 2001a p 266).

[104] See Bailey-Harris, *et al,* (1998), ch VII. The majority of ancillary relief applications lead to a negotiated outcome. See Davis, *et al,* (2000b). It is claimed that solicitors settle at least 90% of their cases (Davis, *et al,* 2001a pp 265–6). Only 10% of contact arrangements are court ordered. See DCA, DfES and DTI (2004) p 1.

play a pivotal role in dealing with disputes arising on divorce and separation. Walker (2004 p 122), reporting on the results of a large study into the information meeting pilots, says that over 80% of those in the research sample who applied for divorce consulted a solicitor.[105] Whether or not people had received information about services such as mediation beforehand made little difference to the statistics. And solicitors will play an even more prominent role in the context of FAInS (p 121).

Traditionally lawyers are seen as implicated in fomenting conflict through partisanship and adversarialism. This view is apparent in a government document published in 1998, which announced a commitment to ensuring that the divorce process 'does not make the situation worse for the family … by for example encouraging litigation or making children pawns in a fight between parents'. To that end, it said, it is important to reduce conflict and to strengthen mediation as an alternative to lawyer negotiation (Home Office 1998 para 4.41). However it is questionable whether the dichotomy set up between lawyer negotiation and mediation is defensible.

Within the context of family break-up most lawyer negotiations no longer take the form of 'a bipartisan process involving constructive but hard bargaining to secure the client's interests' (Neale and Smart 1997 p 383). The chair of Resolution (previously the SFLA), for instance, has recently said that:

> There has been a huge drive on the part of practitioners to behave more responsibly. This is partly … because people have become more aware of how traumatic family breakdown is for children. On the client's side there is the fear of legal costs and litigation. Fewer people are eligible for public funding, while many middle income families simply cannot afford solicitors.
>
> (Langdon-Down 2005 p 20).

Neale and Smart (1997 p 383) observed, as long ago as 1997, that conceptions of 'good' legal practice had changed to emphasise the welfare principle in the law and the growth of mediation. In line with the Resolution Code of Practice (undated), which enjoins solicitors to seek agreements and to persuade their clients of the advantages of a constructive and non-confrontational approach,[106] 'good' lawyering has come to resemble mediation.[107] Moreover, the Legal Services Commission Draft Restructured Family Guidance describes specialist family practice as dealing not only with legal issues but also as fulfilling the role of identifying the 'social welfare and practical issues' that clients may present (LSC 2004 para 20.2.2).

The Law Society's Family Law Protocol (2002a)[108] was published in 2002 with the support of the SFLA (now Resolution), the LCD (now the DCA) and the Legal Services Commission.[109] It specifies its purpose as follows:

The protocol is intended to

- encourage a constructive and conciliatory approach to the resolution of family disputes
- encourage the narrowing of the issues in dispute, and the effective and timely resolution of disputes
- endeavour to minimise any risks to the parties and/or the children and to alert the client to treat safety as a primary concern

---

[105] Most respondents did likewise (Walker 2004 p 122).

[106] See paras 2, 3, 11 and 20.

[107] King (1999) observed, eg, that clients were encouraged to be 'sensible'. Lawyers try to reduce tensions and try to achieve the best deal for clients only within the confines of the normative standards of the law (Eekelaar, *et al*, 2000 pp 184–85).

[108] www.lawsociety.org.uk (accessed 16 May 2005).

[109] See LSC (2004) para 20.1.4.

- have regard to the interests of the children and long-term family relationships[110]
- endeavour to ensure that costs are not unreasonably incurred

Advanced members of the Family Law Panel are expected to comply with the requirements of the protocol.

Davis, *et al,* (2000e) suggest that solicitors dealing with disputes about contact or residence do not follow 'unreasonable' or confrontational instructions. In their sample,

> 66% of informants said that their solicitor had acted 'completely' in their interests. This is a lower percentage than one might expect given that the solicitor is, after all, a partisan who acts on his client's instructions. It reflects the fact that family lawyers temper their partisanship quite considerably. They also see themselves as representing the children's interests, as sponsoring 'reasonable' solutions, and as having a responsibility to rein in their client's worst excesses.
>
> (Davis, *et al,* 2000e p 85)

Neale and Smart's research led them to conclude that the image of the 'good' lawyer has become that of the welfarist, impartial and conciliatory practitioner (1997 p 378). This, they said, has led many lawyers to focus on the welfare of the child, as they understand it, and joint parenting and agreement as opposed to litigation. Practice among the solicitors participating in their study varied, with some adopting a traditional adversarial approach and others being flexible, steering a middle course between traditional lawyering and 'good' lawyering. Yet others adhered rigidly to the approaches characterising 'good' lawyering. This inflexible 'good' lawyering can, the authors contended, be 'bad' for clients in some cases: 'The "good" solicitor who is more concerned about enforcing [*sic*] co-parenting and avoiding litigation may not be disposed to accept that some parents have good grounds for denying contact. In fact the sympathies of such solicitors may well lie with the parent who has been denied contact'. (1997 p 393).

Clients, they suggested, could be left unsupported and vulnerable.[111] In support of their argument, they quoted a family law specialist describing his approach to contact disputes:

> I think the only time that I lay down the law and I'm heavy handed is if I've got a mother whose [*sic*] not allowing contact … *I try to beat everybody into submission* … . The prospect of the court ever backing [a contact order] up with [committal proceedings] is very unlikely, but *I would never tell the mum that* … What you hope is that the judge will be strong enough *to frighten the socks off mum* … I've got a particularly difficult case at the moment where the mother has … been subject to *what seems to be some nasty incidents of violence and fled the area specially to get away* … . There's been no contact for eight months in respect of a child who's just two … . Now persuading her to get contact up and running again is very, very difficult. And, in fact, we [the two lawyers] were able to arrange that … .
> Q:  Who were you acting for?
> A:  I was acting for mum. …
>
> (1997 p 394, emphasis in original)

---

[110] Yet Piper (1997) reports that solicitors do not wish to and rarely do ascertain children's wishes. Their main concern is parental agreement.

[111] See also Davis, *et al,* (1994) p 261. The authors point out that inequality between parties is not always redressed in negotiations between lawyers. Much depends on the ability and commitment of the legal advisor. In addition the ability of each party to withstand delay is important. Typically, women need an order resolving the dispute while men are content to allow a stalemate to continue.

This account appears to demonstrate that solicitors, like mediators, put considerable, and perhaps more explicit, pressure on mothers to accede to contact. However, it seems that their understanding of what they consider reasonable may be communicated to fathers as well. Davis, *et al*, (2000e p 99) report that only half the men who reached agreement through a solicitor said that it was in the best interests of the children, compared with two thirds of those who went to mediation. Men (34%) were also far less likely than women (69%) to be satisfied that the agreement reached was 'completely reasonable' (p 100).[112] From this, the authors infer that 'solicitors bring some pressure to bear on their male clients, requiring them to modify their initial stance in order to bring this more into line with norms of settlement in child contact disputes' (p 99).

## IV. THE OUTCOMES AND THE CLIENT'S VIEW

Both mediation/conciliation and solicitor negotiation are aimed at avoiding litigation. Yet it appears that support among professionals for ADR and negotiation is stronger than support among members of the public. Resolution reported that in its survey, only 55% of people thought it was 'very important to avoid a court battle' (Cross 2005 p 168). In particular, public understanding of and support for mediation is limited. Davis, *et al*, (2000f pp 202–3) observed that, whereas those who attended mediation of their own accord or who were referred by solicitors or, in some cases, the court, appeared knowledgeable about the process and came at a time that was right for them, clients who were referred to assessment meetings as a condition of receiving public funding were less knowledgeable, less conciliatory and less motivated. Diduck comments that:

> This finding is significant to the extent that government enthusiasm for mediation was based in large part upon mediators' enthusiasm, which seems now to have been the result of their experience of a self-selecting and unrepresentative clientele. The actual families that they now encounter may represent the less than ideal altruistic, rational and free-willed individuals of government expectations. (Diduck 2003 p 112)

Davis and his colleagues sought to compare client responses to mediation with responses to representation by a solicitor. Their findings indicate that the public do not necessarily find mediation more attractive. They remark that '[f]or mediation to work it is probably necessary that both parties feel able to negotiate directly with each other in good faith' (Davis, *et al*, 2001a p 112). They found that in fact there were high levels of mistrust of former partners among their panel of clients. Those participating in the study also doubted their former partners' commitment to resolving the disputed issues (*ibid*). Similar factors were cited by Walker's informants as reasons for not attending mediation. Some, however, said they did not need mediation as they could make their own arrangements. Others referred to the fear of intimidation by the other spouse. The main reason given was the unwillingness of other party to attend (2004 p 133).

   The experiences of those who did attend mediation were not noticeably better than the experiences of those who went to solicitors. Solicitors were rated as 'very helpful' in

---

[112] Fear of violence did not alter these proportions except very marginally.

explaining options by 60% of clients questioned, compared with 35% of mediators' clients (Davis, *et al*, 2000e p 83). 69% of solicitors were said to have understood their clients' problems 'very well' as opposed to 51% of mediators (p 83). The researchers found that 81% of their sample would recommend seeing a solicitor to others in the same position, compared with 71% of mediation clients (p 86).[113] Of those engaged in financial disputes, 84% said they would recommend seeing a solicitor, compared to 68% of mediation customers who said the same of going to mediation (p 89). Overall solicitors scored higher than mediators.[114] The authors suggest that although, particularly in disputes concerning children, solicitors restrain clients whom they consider unreasonable,

> [a]t the same time they remain partisan and this, probably, is the reason they tend to score higher than mediators on most of these measures. People feel they need partisanship, and even if it is muted, they like it. People who opt for mediation are also positive on the whole, but approval ratings across the board are not quite as high. This is no reflection on mediators, or indeed on mediation. It is just an indication of the kinds of help that people value most highly at this particular time. Some people value both, but there is a tendency to value lawyers more. It might be more accurate to say that they value partisanship more.[115] Mediation, in comparison, is like castor oil—everyone says it is good for you, but that does not mean you have to like it.
>
> (Davis, *et al*, 2000e p 85)

Mediation can only claim limited success when it comes to outcomes as well. Agreement rates in mediation are not very high. In children cases, Davis, *et al*, report a rate of 45%, dropping to 40% where the informant reported fear of violence (2000e p 77). The agreement rate in respect of financial issues was 34% (p 80). Walker reports that only 30% of clients stopped mediation because they felt it had achieved its objectives and 30% said it was not achieving anything (2004 p 135). 46% of users were helped to find solutions to their problems but only about 25% resolved all the issues raised (p 136).[116]

Davis, *et al*, (2000e) also considered the durability of the agreements reached and the likelihood of their renegotiation. Overall, 59% of those who had been in mediation about children said they thought they would be able to modify the agreement when necessary but, for those in the group who feared violence, the percentage was lower: only 43% of those who feared violence thought they could renegotiate (p 80). In fact, when people from the same sample of mediation clients was interviewed a second time, it was only in about 20% of all those cases where the agreement had broken down[117] that the parties had managed to negotiate a new one (p 80). 65% of those who used solicitor negotiations to reach agreement said they thought they would be able to renegotiate when necessary. When interviewed later, 72% said their agreements had lasted and 20% of those that did not were renegotiated (p 106).

Davis, *et al*, suggest that their findings:

---

[113] They caution that, if people were compelled to attend mediation, satisfaction rates with the process would be likely to be lower (Davis, 2000).

[114] Walker reports that 'satisfaction with solicitors was higher than satisfaction with mediators, but not as high as satisfaction with counsellors' (2004 p 130).

[115] See further Walker (2004) pp 127–28. Some people felt that their solicitor was not partisan enough while others said that their solicitor had been too partisan and had caused unnecessary conflict.

[116] The figure of 28% is cited elsewhere (Walker 2004 p 142).

[117] The agreement had broken down in 9 out of 29 cases (Davis, *et al*, 2000e p 80).

cast doubt on one of the central claims made on behalf of mediation, namely that it delivers *durable* agreements and, furthermore, that it improves couples' capacity to negotiate together in future. On this evidence, which admittedly is subject to various possible qualifications, mediation does not deliver this any more effectively than do lawyers. Given that mediation is in so many instances a relatively fleeting intervention, this is hardly surprising.

> (Davis, *et al*, 2000e p 101, emphasis in original)

The research findings of Walker and her colleagues also raise doubts about the durability of agreements. Contact arrangements were particularly prone to break down, 'often because residential parents feel that they [were] pushed into reaching agreements about which they [were] not happy' (2004 p 142). They also found little evidence to support the wider claims often made for mediation. People, particularly if they had failed to reach an agreement, 'did not feel that attending mediation had helped to make divorce less distressing,[118] or that it had helped them to improve communication, share decision-making about parenting, reduce conflict or avoid going to court' (2004 pp 140–41).

Finally, Davis, *et al*, go on to call into question another claim made in favour of mediation, that it saves costs:

> Does mediation, overall, save money on lawyer services? Answer: we do not think so. Engaging in mediation is not of itself associated with reduced legal costs, although there appears on the face of it to be an association between mediation *agreement* and reduced cost.
>
> Is mediation a service which people value? Yes it is, by those who choose to avail themselves of it. However, efforts to shepherd a much larger section of the relevant population into the arms of mediators have not proved cost-effective. This is partly because of client resistance, and partly because the chosen mechanism is so inefficient as a means of securing the engagement of both parties.[119] (Davis, *et al*, 2000e p 138, emphasis in original)

Davis and his colleagues suggest that mediation should be seen as an 'aid to private communication' rather than as a means of saving costs and diverting cases from trial (2000b paras 29–30). We should not, they say, expect mediation to reduce significantly the demand for legal services. Many people simply do not feel that the conditions for fair resolution of their dispute through reasonable discussion exist. They turn to lawyers and the courts as a means of countering strategies such as 'lying, evasion or threat' used by their former partners. Mediation is not seen as being able to respond adequately to such levels of conflict and, therefore, 'there is little prospect of mediation replacing lawyers— or certainly not of its replacing them effectively' (para 30.5).

Walker draws similar conclusions, suggesting that mediation will continue to be used by only a minority, while the majority, including those who go to mediation, will continue to depend on legal services (2004 p 145). If FAInS is successful, she says, this will mean that a more 'holistic' approach will be likely to spread throughout the legal profession 'and keep lawyers to the fore in the process of divorce and ancillary family disputes for many years to come' (p 148).

---

[118] Some of Walker's informants complained that their solicitor had ignored the 'stressful, emotive issues' surrounding divorce (2004 p 128).

[119] The main reasons for cases to be designated unsuitable were that the former partner was unco-operative, unwilling to compromise or didn't attend (Davis, *et al*, 2000a para 15.3). Failure to reach agreement also increases cost (para 31.3).

## V. ALTERNATIVE DISPUTE RESOLUTION: THE OTHER ALTERNATIVES AVAILABLE

*Family Advice and Information Service (FAInS)*

This initiative is being piloted at the time of writing. It is intended to enable those experiencing family problems to use a solicitor as a type of one-stop shop. Research indicates that a significant majority of people who are divorcing or separating consult a lawyer at some time.[120] The solicitors involved in the FAInS project are specialist family solicitors who act as 'case managers', providing not only legal advice and representation, but also directing clients to other services that could be of assistance.[121] These services might offer help in the form of advice about practical matters such as finances and benefits claims. There are also mediation services dealing with financial matters or arrangements for children or both. In addition, emotional needs are addressed though, for example, counselling.[122] This approach of seeking to ensure that parties are referred to appropriate services is, according to the Green Paper, 'expected to assist in diverting families away from adversarial, prolonged court proceedings' (DCA, DfES and DTI 2004 para 60).

The main objectives of the FAInS project are:

(a) To bring together expert services to protect children from harm and the risk of social exclusion;
(b) To facilitate the dissolution of broken relationships, in ways which minimise distress to parents and children, and which promote family relationships and co-operative parenting;
(c) To provide tailored information and access to services that may assist in resolving disputes, or may assist those who are trying to save their relationship ...

(LSC 2004 para 20.2.1)

*Collaborative Law*

This is a relatively recent addition to the ADR mechanisms available to settle family related disputes. It was first introduced into the UK in 2003 and around 100 specialist family lawyers, many trained as mediators, are trained to offer this service.[123] The process is being promoted by Resolution (LNTV 2005a). In this process, both parties are represented by lawyers whose aim is to settle the case. All four participants enter into a participation agreement in which they agree not to go to court while the process is ongoing (LNTV 2005a p 3). The agreement also stipulates that if a settlement is not reached, neither lawyer can take the case to court. The parties have to instruct different legal representatives for that purpose (*ibid*).

The parties set out to negotiate a settlement in a 'series of round table meetings known as "four-way" meetings' (*ibid*). The parties and their lawyers all negotiate face-

---

[120] Genn, *et al*, (1999 Fig 3.7) found that 82% of those in their study consulted a solicitor or law centre. See also Walker (2004) p 122.

[121] Legal Services Commission Website, accessed 9 May 2005: http://www.legalservices.gov.uk/civil/fains. See also LSC (2004) 20.2.

[122] *Ibid.*

[123] Cambridge Collaborative Family Law Group website (www.collabfamilylawcambs.co.uk. Accessed 19/5/05).

to-face. There is no set timetable and the parties negotiate at their own pace (LNTV 2005a p 5). If necessary, other professionals will be asked to assist. These could be pensions advisors, accountants and others who can advise in financial matters. There are also other professionals who can be asked to assist with difficulties engendered by the family dynamics. The role of family consultants is seen as 'crucial' (LNTV 2005a p 3). They are likely to come from 'therapeutic, social work and counselling backgrounds' and many have mediation experience (*ibid*). Their contribution to the process involves helping parties and their lawyers deal with some of the emotional fall-out of the separation or divorce (*ibid*). It is this involvement of a variety of professionals and the therapeutic element that differentiate collaborative family law from lawyer negotiation and mediation. It also differs from mediation in that each party has a lawyer to provide advice and support.

Nevertheless, it is not suitable for everyone and it is up to the practitioners to screen out inappropriate cases (LNTV 2005a p 4). Such cases might involve highly conflicted former partners (LNTV 2005b). Also, cases involving child abuse or domestic violence may not be suitable (LNTV 2005a p 4). How active this screening is, is not clear; one practitioner interviewed on a DVD associated with the College of Law remarked that most unsuitable clients screen themselves out (LNTV 2005b). This may be cause for concern[124] but at least, unlike in the case of mediation, the party who is not the abuser does have a lawyer who should be alert to any prejudice to their interests or to those of the children. Imbalances of power may not be as stark as those that can potentially exist in the context of mediation.

Concerns have also been expressed about other limitations of the process. There is a risk that the lack of a timetable could lead to abuse of the process by means of delay. There is no way of ensuring that honest disclosure of assets or other information is made (LNTV 2005a p 5). Nor is there any way in which the child's wishes and views are being conveyed other than through the parents, although it has been suggested that children's interests might be addressed by referring the case to one of those mediation services which do consult children (*ibid*): 'the voice of the child is very much part of the collaborative process even though children unlikely (sic) to be entering the four-way meetings' (*ibid*).[125]

Despite these drawbacks, it is thought that this method of dealing with disputes will become widely used (LNTV 2005b). However it is not a particularly cheap method of dispute resolution (*ibid*) and the government has announced that a model using the principles of collaborative law is being considered for publicly funded parties (DCA, DfES and DTI 2004 para 63). The Legal Services Commission is planning to run a pilot scheme (Langdon-Down 2005 p 22).

*Financial Dispute Resolution*

This process[126] is designed to facilitate agreement in settling financial matters arising out of divorce. It is triggered when a case is brought to court and it is managed by the district judge. After being piloted in the 1990s, it now forms part of the standard

---

124 Women's Aid has expressed concerns that the emphasis on promoting agreement through collaborative law 'is likely to mean that fears about domestic violence will continue to be minimised or ignored' (DCA, DfES and DTI 2005 para 41).
125 This quote comes from an interview with a collaborative consultant, trainer, and mediator.
126 See further Bird (2002).

procedure. It entails, ideally, strict control by the judge to ensure that matters are resolved as quickly and 'justly'[127] as possible. Justice demands that the parties are on an even footing. The aim is also to save expense and to deal with cases in a manner proportionate to the amounts involved and to the complexity and importance of the issues.[128]

The parties are obliged to attend a first appointment, with their solicitors, before the district judge. This appointment is meant to be used to define the issues and save costs.[129] Unless the court considers it inappropriate to do so, it must then direct that the case be referred for a Financial Dispute Resolution (FDR) appointment. This is held 'for the purposes of discussion and negotiation' and the parties must use the 'best endeavours to reach agreement'.[130] It is only if a consent order is not possible that the case will go on to a final hearing. A different judge must preside over the final hearing.

*Family Resolutions Pilot Project*

This pilot is designed specifically to deal with disputes about children which have led parents to ask for a court hearing (Maclean 2004 p 687). Cases where there is a risk factor are meant to be filtered out (Maclean 2004 p 687). The pilot is, according to the Green Paper, 'based on the key principle ... that the children's welfare is paramount, and that this is best promoted by a continuing relationship with both parents, as long as any safety issues are properly addressed' (DCA, DfES and DTI 2004 para 69).

On application to the court, the parents are sent a letter from the judge explaining the process and advising them to take part. (Maclean 2004 p 687). The information sent is supposed to include 'guidance on how the court operates and how it views contact cases' (DCA, DfES and DTI 2004 para 71). This should make it clear that the court expects there to be a 'meaningful ongoing relationship with both parents' (para 71). The pilot involves a three stage process. First, the parents are directed to attend, separately, group sessions to watch a video where children describe their experience of parental separation (Maclean 2004 p 687). The second session involves separate attendance at conflict management workshops (Maclean 2004 p 688). Finally, both parents must, together, attend parenting planning sessions with a CAFCASS officer and, possibly, the child if appropriate (DCA, DfES and DTI 2004 para 71). Participation in this process is not mandatory but 'there is a strong judicial expectation that parties to cases will participate' (DCA, DfeS and DTI 2005 para 65). Despite this encouragement, in its first nine months of operation the pilot has attracted only 47 couples.[131] This has been attributed to the fact that the scheme is not compulsory and there have been calls, on the part of fathers' groups and the Conservatives, for the scrapping of the scheme in favour of compulsory mediation (Dyer 2005b).

**Q** What, if any, part of the ADR process do you think ought to be mandatory for separating parents?

---

[127] R2.51B FPR 1991/1247.
[128] *Ibid.*
[129] R2.61D FPR 1991/1247.
[130] *Ibid.*
[131] It was expected that 1000 couples would opt to use the system, but as at June 2005, only 47 couples began the programme and only 23 completed it (Dyer 2005b).

## VI. CONCLUSION

Private ordering, in political and professional discourse, is generally considered to be a beneficial development. There is much good practice that bears out this judgement. However there is an element of coercion in some of the schemes to engage in the process of ADR and to agree to the types of post-separation family arrangements preferred by the professionals. While private ordering enables parties to avoid the stress and expense of litigation and while it may often enable parties to retain some measure of autonomy, it may be a far from perfect solution in some cases of family break-up. To speak of family privacy and family autonomy is to assume that the family is capable of making decisions as a unit. However, the interests and desires of different family members may be very different and may even be irreconcilable. To contain decision-making and dispute resolution in the private sphere means that the formal safeguards designed to ensure that each party's case is heard are absent. Imbalances of power may be left unredressed and a party unable to articulate his or her point of view is disadvantaged. In addition, a party may 'agree' out of fear or exhaustion to arrangements that could be damaging. Moreover, the familial norms purveyed by some professionals engaged in mediation, negotiation and other forms of ADR may place pressure on one party, usually the mother, to agree to arrangements that are not in her interests.

### FURTHER READING AND SELECTED RECENT REFERENCES

G DAVIS, 'Introduction' in G Davis, et al, *Monitoring Publicly Funded Family Mediation: Report to the Legal Services Commission* (London, Legal Services Commission, 2000).

G DAVIS, *et al, Monitoring Publicly Funded Family Mediation: Report to the Legal Services Commission* (London, Legal Services Commission, 2000).

G DAVIS, R FITZGERALD and S FINCH, 'Mediation Case Profiles' in G Davis, *Monitoring Publicly Funded Family Mediation: Report to the Legal Services Commission* (London, Legal Services Commission, 2000).

G DAVIS, *et al*, 'The Panel' in G Davis, *et al, Monitoring Publicly Funded Family Mediation: Report to the Legal Services Commission* (London, Legal Services Commission, 2000).

G DAVIS, G BEVAN and J PEARCE, 'Family Mediation—Where do We Go from Here?' (2001) *Fam Law* 265.

G DAVIS, S FINCH and R FITZGERALD, 'Mediation and Legal Services—The Client Speaks' (2001) *Fam Law* 110.

S DAY SCLATER, 'Experiences of Divorce' in S Day Sclater and C Piper, (eds), *Undercurrents of Divorce* (Aldershot, Ashgate, 1999a).

——, *Divorce: A Psychosocial Study* (Aldershot, Ashgate, 1999b).

A DIDUCK, *Law's Families*, ch 5 (London, LexisNexis Butterworths, 2003).

R DINGWALL and D GREATBACH, 'The Mediation Process' in G Davis, *et al, Monitoring Publicly Funded Family Mediation: Report to the Legal Services Commission* (London, Legal Services Commission, 2000).

——, 'Family Mediators—What Are They Doing?' (2001) *Fam Law* 378.

G DOUGLAS, *et al*, 'Safeguarding Children's Welfare in Non-contentious Divorce: Towards a New Conception of the Legal Process?' (2000) 63 *MLR* 177.

J EEKELAAR, M MACLEAN and S BEINHART, *Family Lawyers: The Divorce Work of Solicitors* (Oxford, Hart Publishing, 2000).

K FISCHER, N VIDMAR and R ELLIS, 'The Culture of Battering and the Role of Mediation in Domestic Violence Cases' (1993) 46(5) *SMU Law Review* 2117.

F KAGANAS and C PIPER, 'Divorce and Domestic Violence' in S Day Sclater and C Piper, (eds) *Undercurrents of Divorce* (Aldershot, Ashgate, 1999).

M HESTER, C PEARSON and L RADFORD, *Domestic Violence: A National Survey of Court Welfare and Voluntary Sector Mediation Practice* (Bristol, Policy Press, 1997).

G LANGDON-DOWN, 'Family Fortunes' (2005) 102(8) *Law Soc Gazette* 20.

M MACLEAN, 'The Family Resolutions Pilot Project' (2004) *Fam Law* 687

M MAHONEY, 'Legal Images of Battered Women: Redefining the Issue of Separation' (1991) 90 *Michigan Law Review* 1.

M PAGELOW, 'Effects of Domestic Violence on Children and their Consequences for Custody and Visitation Agreements' (1990) 7(4) *Mediation Quarterly* 347.

C PIPER, 'Divorce Reform and the Image of the Child' (1996) 23 *J of Law and Society* 364.

——, 'How Do You Define a Family Lawyer?' (1999) 19 *Legal Studies* 93.

S ROBERTS, 'Alternative Dispute Resolution and Civil Justice: An Unresolved Relationship' (1993) 56 *MLR* 452.

C SMART and V MAY, 'Why Can't They Agree? The Underlying Complexity of Contact and Residence Disputes' (2004) 26 *JSW&FL* 347.

J WALKER, *Picking up the Pieces: Marriage and Divorce Two Years After Information Provision* (London, Department of Constitutional Affairs, 2004).

*Reports*

CAFCASS, *Service Principles and Standards* (HMSO, 2003).

DCA, *Government's Response to the Report of the Children Act Sub-committee of the Lord Chancellor's Advisory Board on Family Law 'Making Contact Work*, (www.dca.gov.uk) (2002)

——, *A New Focus for Civil Legal Aid: Encouraging Early Resolution; Discouraging Unnecessary Litigation* (London, DCA, 2004).

DCA, DfES and DTI, *Parental Separation: Children's Needs and Parents' Responsibilities* (Cm 6273, 2004).

——, *Parental Separation: Children's Needs and Parents' Responsibilities: Next Steps, Report of the responses to consultation and agenda for action* (London, The Stationery Office, 2005) Cm 6452.

The Law Society, Family Mediation Panel. *Criteria and Guidance Notes* (London, The Law Society, 2004).

Legal Services Commission, *The Funding Code—Criteria* (2000).

——, *Quality Mark Standard for Mediation* (2002) (1) 12/02.

——, *The Funding Code: Procedures* (2003a) (R9 April 2003).

——, *Funding Code Guidance* (2003b) R11: December 2003.

——, *The Funding Code: Restructured Family Guidance* (2004).

Her Majesty's Court Service Inspectorate (MCSI) (2003) *Seeking Agreement. Children and Family Court Advisory and Support Service (CAFCASS). A Thematic Review by MCSI of the Operation of Schemes Involving CAFCASS at an Early Stage in Private Law Proceedings* (www.cafacass.gov.uk).

Resolution (undated) *Code of Practice for Resolution Members*.

UK College of Family Mediators, *Code of Practice for Family Mediators* (2000) (www.ukcfm.co.uk).

——, *Domestic Abuse Screening Policy* (1999) (www.ukcfm.co.uk).

——, *Children, Young People and Family Mediation: Policy and Practice Guidelines* (2002) (www.ukcfm.co.uk).

# Section 3

## Reordering Family Relationships

.

# 12

# Violence and Separation

**Q** Albert and Eve, both 40 years old, have been married for just over 15 years. They bought their home, a two-bedroom bungalow, 10 years ago. The home is registered in their joint names. Eve and Albert are both qualified accountants and both work full time. They have no children living with them. Recently, Albert and Eve have been having difficulties and Eve is becoming frightened of Albert. He has struck her on a number of occasions, the last time bruising her badly. Eve asks him to leave, having decided that she can no longer accept Albert's apologies nor believe his promises that it will not happen again. She has not, so far, contacted the police, but tells Albert that if he does not leave the home by the end of the week she will go to both a solicitor and the police. At the end of two weeks it seems clear to Eve that Albert is not prepared to leave the home. She becomes increasingly fearful for her safety and feels that she should see a solicitor as soon as possible, but does not know whom to approach.

Eve does not, at this time, want a divorce from Albert. She believes he can change his behaviour. She merely wants him to seek help and to stay away from her while he is doing so.

Advise Eve.

## I. ADVICE AND COUNSELLING FOR THOSE EXPERIENCING VIOLENCE

It is not uncommon for those in unhappy relationships to wish to end the unhappiness rather than the relationship. When Eve consults her solicitor, they will discuss the possibility of taking legal proceedings, any costs involved and her eligibility for public funding through the Legal services Commission. If she is fearful for her safety, the criminal law may provide assistance as may the civil law. However there are also other matters on which she needs information. What kind of 'help' could Albert receive for his behaviour, and what kind of 'help' is available for Eve to understand his violence and to deal with her emotions? Will her solicitor be able to advise her on these matters?

The Code of Practice of Resolution, formerly the Solicitors Family Law Association, contains the following paragraph:

11. You should ensure that your clients are aware of other services that may help them to reach a settlement, including counselling and mediation. Where appropriate, you should explore with your client the possibility of reconciliation. (Resolution Code of Conduct 2001)[1]

If Eve's solicitor is a member of Resolution or involved in the FAInS project he or she will be able to provide Eve with information about counselling services.[2] Some solicitors may not perceive their job as including this type of advice, however, as it does not impinge directly upon any potential legal proceedings, and so Eve may have to find out about them from other sources. These include help lines, Citizens' Advice Bureaux, the police, doctors, social workers, local borough council services and Women's Aid. Woman's Aid, for instance, offers outreach services including advocacy, telephone support and the provision of information.[3]

For violent men, there are some organisations which accept self-referrals,[4] but more which accept men who are ordered to attend as a requirement of probation after having been convicted of an offence involving domestic violence or as part of a community sentence.[5]

## II. PROTECTION FROM VIOLENCE—INTRODUCTION

Eve can invoke both the criminal and the civil law as a result of Albert's conduct. He has assaulted her and this is of course an offence. His behaviour probably also constitutes an offence under the Protection from Harassment Act 1997. In addition, Eve can seek a civil remedy under the Protection from Harassment Act 1997 and/or the Family Law Act 1996.[6]

## III. CRIMINAL LAW

Albert has struck Eve, and this constitutes assault occasioning actual bodily harm.[7] The Court of Appeal has indicated that domestic assaults should be treated as seriously as

---

[1] This Code has been incorporated into the Law Society's Family Law Protocol 2002.

[2] On the inappropriateness of mediation in cases of domestic violence, see ch 11.

[3] See, for more detail, Humphreys and Thiara (2002).

[4] See, eg, the Domestic Violence Intervention Project (1998).

[5] See Crimereduction.gov.uk/dv03d.htm; Paradine and Wilkinson (2004) pp 57–58. Many such services are being run by the National Probation Services and the Prison Service, for example. See Women's Aid (2003) pp 11–12 for criticism of existing programmes. See also ch 10.

[6] The High Court has inherent jurisdiction to grant injunctions 'in all cases in which it appears to the court to be just and convenient to do so' (Supreme Court Act 1981 s 37) and the County Court is empowered to do the same (County Courts Act 1984 s 38). The courts have, however, circumscribed their powers to grant injunctions. See, for discussion, Cretney, *et al*, (2002) para 10–026. Cretney, *et al*, remark that the vast majority of cases involving a domestic element are covered by the Family Law Act 1996 and the Protection from Harassment Act 1997.

A 'persistent course of domestic violence' can generate concurrent proceedings in different courts under different legal heads. There may be criminal proceedings as well as civil, and there is no bar to initiating civil proceedings under both the Family Law Act 1996 and the Protection from Harassment Act 1997. See *Lomas v Parle* [2003] EWCA Civ 1804; [2004] 1 FLR 812.

[7] *See R v Miller* [1954] 2 QB 282, 292.

other assaults.[8] Section 10 of the Domestic Violence, Crime and Victims Act 2004, when it comes into effect, will amend the Police and Criminal Evidence Act 1984 to encourage the police to act in domestic violence cases by giving them the power to arrest a person on suspicion of assault and/or battery without an arrest warrant.[9] Even with this additional power, the police may be reluctant to proceed[10] and, even if they do, the Crown Prosecution Service may decide not to do so, either for lack of sufficient evidence or because prosecution is not in the public interest. Should the case get as far as the court, the sentence is likely to be lenient, particularly as this would be a conviction for a first offence.[11]

## IV. THE PROTECTION FROM HARASSMENT ACT 1997

This legislation, while not enacted specifically to deal with domestic violence, is, it seems, potentially useful for that purpose, particularly in cases of post-separation violence.[12] The legislation is potentially very broad in scope and embodies a combination of criminal law and civil law measures.[13]

Section 1 prohibits any person from engaging in a course of conduct which he or she knows, or ought reasonably to know,[14] constitutes harassment. 'Harassment' is not defined, save that Section 7 provides that it includes alarming or causing distress to a person and that harassment may take the form of either words or conduct.[15] According to Section 7, a 'course of conduct' must involve conduct on at least two occasions.[16]

Two substantive offences are created by the statute. Section 2 makes it a summary offence[17] to pursue a course of conduct in breach of the prohibition against harassment in Section 1.[18] Section 4 makes it an offence, triable either way,[19] to pursue a course of conduct that puts a person in fear of violence. This offence is committed where the perpetrator knows or ought reasonably to know that such fear will be induced.[20] Both harassment and the more serious offence of putting people in fear of violence are

---

[8] *R v Cutts* [1987] Fam Law 311.

[9] See House of Lords (Session 2003–4) Domestic Violence, Crime and Victims Bill, Explanatory Notes para 47.

[10] The police already have power to arrest for breach of the peace. See, generally on the power and its compatibility with the European Convention, *Steel v United Kingdom* (1999) 28 EHRR 603; *Chief Constable of Cleveland Police v McGrogan* [2002] EWCA Civ 86; [2002] 1 FLR 707.

[11] See p 401 above.

[12] Harris (2000 p 9) reports that most cases concern 'the unwanted attentions of ex-partners' as well as harassment by neighbours. But see also Humphreys and Thiara (2002 p 51); and Barron (2002 p 18) who found very limited use of the Act in their studies. See, for an evaluation of the legislation, Harris (2000). See also ch 10 pp 401–3.

[13] For a fuller discussion of the legislation, see Cretney, *et al*, (2002) paras 10–002–10–003, 10–025; Lawson-Cruttenden and Addison (1997).

[14] This is an objective test judged by the standard of a reasonable person: *R v Colohan* [2001] EWCA Crim 1251; [2001] 2 FLR 757.

[15] It appears to be similar in scope to the concept of molestation. See below, p 460.

[16] The fewer the incidents and the wider spread they are over time, the less likely it is that a finding of harassment will be made. See *Lau v Director of Public Prosecutions* [2000] 1 FLR 799, 801.

[17] The penalty is a term of imprisonment of up to 6 months or a fine of up to £5000 or both (s 2(2)).

[18] The offence is not committed if the act does not qualify as harassment, for example if it is reasonable (see s 1(3)).

[19] A person convicted on indictment is liable to imprisonment for up to 5 years or a fine or both (s 4(4)(a)). If the offender is convicted in summary proceedings, the penalty is imprisonment for up to 6 months or a fine or both (s 4(4)(b)).

[20] Defences are set out in s 4(3).

arrestable offences.[21] This means that the police can arrest, without a warrant, any person reasonably suspected of committing either offence. The Act also makes provision for orders designed to prevent the offender repeating the offence; Section 5 empowers the court to make restraining orders when dealing with persons convicted under Section 2 or 4. Section 5(5) makes it an offence for a defendant, without reasonable excuse, to do anything in contravention of a restraining order. This, too, is an arrestable offence.[22]

Section 12 of the Domestic Violence, Crime and Victims Act 2004 will, when it comes into force, extend the powers of the court. First, it amends the 1997 Act so that a restraining order can be made on conviction for any offence, not just offences under that Act. Secondly, a new Section 5A has been enacted. This provision will enable the court to make a restraining order even if the defendant is acquitted, as long as the court considers it necessary to do so in order to protect a person from harassment by the defendant.[23] To do anything without reasonable cause that is prohibited in such an order will be an arrestable offence.

In addition to its criminal law provisions, the Protection from Harassment Act also created a tort of harassment; in terms of Section 3, an actual or apprehended breach of Section 1 may form the basis of a civil claim. The court is empowered to award damages and to grant an injunction restraining the defendant from pursuing conduct that amounts to harassment. It is an arrestable[24] criminal offence to breach such an injunction without reasonable cause.[25] An alternative method[26] of enforcing an injunction is for the victim to go to court to apply for a warrant of arrest in terms of Section 3(3).

The 1997 Act has advantages over other available measures in cases of domestic violence. Since the offence of harassment is potentially very broad, the police need not be concerned with determining whether the assailant's act falls within the definition of assault. In addition, because it is the police who take action when an offence under the statute is committed, and not the victim, there is no need for a person subject to violence to finance civil proceedings for a non-molestation order or to apply for legal aid. So, provided the police do not prove reluctant to exercise their powers, and provided the Crown Prosecution Service and the courts take domestic violence seriously,[27] the Act may provide a cheap and quick way for Eve to seek protection should Albert persist in his aggressive conduct.

Eve might not wish to rely solely on the criminal law; she might want to seek an injunction under Section 3 so that she can gain protection without having to have her case proved beyond reasonable doubt. Breach of such an order can be treated either as an arrestable offence or as contempt of court. If the police and the Crown Prosecution Service show themselves willing to proceed down the prosecution route under the Act, it may be that Section 3 will be useful for people in Eve's position. However, if there is a reluctance to prosecute, Eve herself will be responsible for initiating contempt proceedings and she will be better off with a non-molestation order under the Family Law Act 1996 with a power of arrest attached.[28]

---

[21] See s 2(3) and Lawson-Cruttenden and Addison (1997) p 40.

[22] Under s 24(6) of the Police and Criminal Evidence Act 1984. See also s 5(6).

[23] The parties will be permitted to lead the same sort of evidence as would be admissible in injunction proceedings under s 3. See s 5(3A).

[24] Under s 24(6) of the Police and Criminal Evidence Act 1984. See Lawson-Cruttenden and Addison (1997) para 6.2.

[25] S 3(6) and s 3(9).

[26] Criminal proceedings and contempt of court proceedings are mutually exclusive (ss 3(7)–(8)).

[27] See ch 10 on practices within the criminal justice system in relation to domestic violence. See, on sentencing under the Protection from Harassment Act 1997, *Liddle v Hayes* [2000] 1 Cr App R(S).

[28] See below, p 460.

Moreover, Eve could have difficulty in obtaining a remedy under the 1997 Act in the light of the decision in *R v Hills*,[29] given that she and Albert may not have been living sufficiently separate lives. The court in that case was unconvinced that the evidence was enough to link the two incidents relied on so as to show a course of conduct. One of the main considerations in reaching this conclusion appears to have been that the parties' relationship was continuing. Otton LJ remarked that the case before him was remote from the 'stalking' for which he said the Act was intended and he seemed unwilling to include ongoing violent relationships within the scope of the legislation. He said that it could be applied to cases where a person made

> a nuisance of himself to a partner or wife when they have become estranged. However in a situation such as this, when they were frequently coming back together and intercourse was taking place ... it is unrealistic to think that this fell within the stalking category which either postulates a stranger or an estranged spouse. (para 31).

In any event, however useful the Protection from Harassment Act 1997 may be, there is nothing in it that can be deployed to regulate occupation of the home. Eve's best option appears to be to seek protection under the Family Law Act 1996.

## V. THE FAMILY LAW ACT 1996

Part IV of the Family Law Act 1996 deals with domestic violence and makes provision for two types of order: a non-molestation order, which prohibits molestation, and an occupation order, which regulates occupation of the family home.[30] Before going on to discuss these orders, however, it is important to note that, in the past, courts have tended to accept undertakings from alleged abusers rather than make orders.[31] And commentary on the operation of the 1996 Act suggests that this practice is continuing; undertakings are being accepted even in inappropriate cases where there is considerable risk to the applicant.[32] An undertaking is a promise made by a party to the court and is enforceable in the same way as a court order.[33] However, since a power of arrest cannot be attached to an undertaking,[34] Eve would have to return to court in the event of a breach by Albert. Moreover, there is evidence that the police tend not to take any action when called to a domestic violence incident in the absence of a power of arrest.[35] This means that the enforcement of undertakings is slower and less effective than that of court orders, particularly those that have a power of arrest attached.[36]

---

[29] [2001] 1 FLR 580.

[30] The High Court, county courts and magistrates' courts all have jurisdiction under the Act (s 57). However, the jurisdiction of magistrates' courts is limited: see s 59.

[31] The Family Law Act 1996 makes provision for this practice to continue. S 46(1) provides that '[i]n any case where the court has power to make an occupation order or non-molestation order, the court may accept an undertaking from any party to the proceedings'.

[32] See Humphries (2001). See also Humphreys and Thiara (2002) p 54.

[33] S 46(4).

[34] See p 473 below.

[35] See Bossy and Coleman (2000) para 3.3; Barron (2002) pp 8–9.

[36] For fuller discussion of undertakings, see Kewley (1996).

*Non-Molestation Order*

Section 42 of the Family Law Act 1996 defines a non-molestation order and specifies the proceedings in the course of which an order may be made:

42 Non-molestation orders

(1)    In this Part a 'non-molestation order' means an order containing either or both of the following provisions—
(a)  provision prohibiting a person ('the respondent') from molesting another person who is associated with the respondent;
(b)  provision prohibiting the respondent from molesting a relevant child.[37]

(2)    The court may make a non-molestation order—
(a)  if an application for the order has been made (whether in other family proceedings or without any other family proceedings being instituted) by a person who is associated with the respondent; or
(b)  if in any family proceedings to which the respondent is a party the court considers that the order should be made for the benefit of any other party to the proceedings or any relevant child even though no such application has been made.

Nowhere in the Act is the term 'molestation' defined. The Law Commission took the view that a definition was unnecessary and might prove to be over restrictive (1992a para 3.1). It has recently been held that the term implies 'deliberate conduct which is aimed at a high degree of harassment ... so as to justify intervention by the court'.[38] The courts have, over the years, treated a wide range of behaviour as 'molestation':

Examples of ... 'non-violent' harassment or molestation cover a very wide range of behaviour. Common instances include persistent pestering and intimidation through shouting, denigration, threats or argument, nuisance telephone calls, damaging property, following the applicant about and repeatedly calling at her home or place of work. Installing a mistress into the matrimonial home with a wife and three children, filling car locks with superglue, writing anonymous letters and pressing one's face against a window whilst brandishing papers have all been held to amount to molestation. The degree of severity of such behaviour depends less upon its intrinsic nature than upon it being part of a pattern and upon its effect on the victim.[39]
(Law Commission 1992a para 2.3, footnotes omitted)

A non-molestation order may be granted to an 'associated person'[40] in free-standing proceedings, or in the course of family proceedings,[41] whether on application or on the

[37] 'Child' is defined as a person under the age of 18 years (s 63(1)). 'Relevant child' is defined in s 62(2) as: (a) any child who is living with or might reasonably be expected to live with either party to the proceedings; (b) any child in relation to whom an order under the Adoption Act 1976, the Adoption and Children Act 2002 or the Children Act 1989 is in question in the proceedings; and (c) any other child whose interests the court considers relevant.
[38] *C v C (Non-molestation Order: Jurisdiction)* [1998] 1 FLR 554, 556–57.
[39] See, eg, on the meaning of molestation: *Vaughan v Vaughan* [1973] 1 WLR 1159; *Horner v Horner* [1982] Fam 90; *George v George* [1986] 2 FLR 347; *Smith v Smith* [1988] 1 FLR 179; *Johnson v Walton* [1990] 1 FLR 350.
[40] Children under 16 may themselves apply for non-molestation or occupation orders with leave (s 43). See, for criticism of the leave requirement, Murphy (1996) pp 850–51.
[41] S 63(1) defines 'family proceedings' as proceedings related to children under the court's inherent jurisdiction and proceedings under the enactments specified in s 63(2). They include proceedings under Parts II and IV of the Family Law Act 1996 and Parts I, II and IV of the Children Act 1989. Proceedings under Part V of the Children Act are not included but there is one exception. S 42(3) of the Family Law Act 1996 stipulates that 'family proceedings' include proceedings in which the court has made an emergency protection order under s 44 of the Children Act 1989 which includes an exclusion requirement.

court's own motion.[42] Should Eve wish to initiate separation proceedings,[43] she could apply for a non-molestation order in the course of those proceedings. Alternatively, she could make a free-standing application to the court. However, in order to take either of these measures, she must qualify as a 'person associated with the respondent' (who would, of course, be Albert).

### *'Associated Persons'*

The Law Commission took the view that the often intense nature of family or domestic relationships made it necessary to provide special remedies and procedures in cases of violence or molestation.[44] The category of 'associated persons' was accordingly devised to identify those relationships. Section 62(3) provides:

For the purposes of this Part, a person is associated with another person if—

(a)   they are or have been married to each other;

[(aa) they are or have been civil partners of each other][45]

(b)   they are cohabitants or former cohabitants[46];

(c)   they live or have lived in the same household, otherwise than merely by reason of one of them being the   other's employee, tenant, lodger or boarder[47];

(d)   they are relatives[48];

(e)   they have agreed to marry one another (whether or not that agreement has been terminated)[49];

[eza] they have entered into a civil partnership agreement (as defined by section 73 of the Civil Partnership Act 2004) (whether or not that agreement has been terminated);[50]

---

[42] See, Law Commission 1992a para 5.2. In its *Report to the Lord Chancellor on the Question of Parental Contact in Cases Where There is Domestic Violence*, the Children Act Sub-Committee of the Advisory Board on Family Law recommended that courts ordering interim or longer direct contact between parents and children in cases involving domestic violence should consider exercising this power (1999 paras 5.4(d) and 5.7(c)).

[43] See below, pp 481ff.

[44] See, Hayes (1996); Law Commission (1992a) paras 3.8–3.27. It was thought inappropriate in such cases to require victims to rely on the court's jurisdiction under s 37 of the Supreme Court Act 1981, or s 38 the County Courts Act 1984. These provisions provide limited assistance to those who fall outside the scope of the Family Law Act 1996. Because injunctions are generally only granted in support of an existing legal right (but see *Burris v Azadani* [1995] 1 WLR 1372), the victim normally has to prove that the respondent's behaviour amounts to a tort such as battery, assault, trespass or nuisance. See *Wilkinson v Downton* [1897] 2 QB 57; *Siskina (Owners of cargo lately laden on board) v Distos Compania Naviera SA* [1979] AC 210.

[45] To be added when the Civil Partnership Act comes into force.

[46] 'Cohabitants' are, in terms of s.62(1)(a), 'a man and a woman who, although not married to each other, are living together as husband and wife'. 'Former cohabitants' should be read accordingly, but the term 'does not include cohabitants who have subsequently married each other' (s.62(1)(b)) and, according to the Civil Partnership Act 'or become civil partners of each other'. The Civil Partnership Act will amend the definition of cohabitants to include same sex couples who are not in a civil partnership.

[47] This covers partners in same sex relationships who live together.

[48] This term is very widely defined in s.63(1) as:

(a) the father, mother, stepfather, stepmother, son, daughter, stepson, stepdaughter, grandmother, grandfather, grandson or granddaughter of that person or of that person's spouse of former spouse, or

(b) the brother, sister, uncle, aunt, niece or nephew (whether of the full blood or of the half blood or by affinity) of that person or of that person's spouse or former spouse,

and includes, in relation to a person who is living with or has lived with another person as husband and wife, any person who would fall within paragraph (a) or (b) if the parties were married to each other.

This will be amended. The words 'husband and wife' will be replaced by references to cohabitants and former cohabitants (Domestic Violence, Crime and Victims Act 2004) and the words civil partner, former civil partner, and partnership wil be added wherever reference is made to spouse, former spouse, affinity or marriage (Civil Parternship Act 2004).

[49] There is a time limit of 3 years after termination of the agreement; no application for either a non-molestation or an occupation order can be made after this period has elapsed (s.42(4) and s33(2)).

[50] To be included when the Civil Partnership Act 2004 comes into effect. There will be a three year time limit after termination of the agreement (s.33(2A) and s.42(4ZA) FLA as amended by the Civil Partnership Act).

[(ea)  they have or have had an intimate personal relationship with each other which is or was of significant duration][51]
(f)   in relation to any child, they are both persons falling within subsection (4)[52]; or
(g)   they are parties to the same family proceedings (other than proceedings under this Part).

The definition of cohabitants and former cohabitants in s.62 will be amended to include same sex couples.[53]

The concept of 'associated persons' has been interpreted by the courts to take account of the Law Commission's concern to deal with the heightened stresses engendered by disputes between those in close relationships. In *Chechi v Bashier*[54] the Court of Appeal held that a dispute between brothers and their families fell within the ambit of the Act because, although the quarrel was about land, the family relationship fuelled it and kept it alive. In *G v G (Non-Molestation Order: Jurisdiction)*,[55] the court held that the parties qualified as former cohabitants under Section 62(3)(b) even though the relationship had not been stable (p 543). Wall J took the view that:

> where domestic violence is concerned, they [the justices] should give the statute a purposive construction and not decline jurisdiction, unless the facts of the case before them are plainly incapable of being brought within the statute. Part IV of the 1996 Act is designed to provide swift and accessible protective remedies to persons of both sexes who are the victims of domestic violence, provided they fall within the criteria of S 62. It would, I think, be most unfortunate if S 62(3) was narrowly construed so as to exclude borderline cases where swift and effective protection for the victims of domestic violence is required. This case is, after all, about jurisdiction; it is not about the merits. (p 543)

Clearly, since Eve and Albert are married to each other, Eve qualifies as a person associated with Albert in terms of Section 62(3)(a). She is therefore eligible to apply for an order, but whether or not the court grants her one is within its discretion. Because the consequences of a non-molestation order are less serious for the respondent than an order excluding him from the home, the courts have tended to grant non-molestation orders quite readily.[56]

Section 42(5) sets out in broad terms the matters to which the court should have regard:

[51] Added by the Domestic Violence, Crime and Victims Act 2004 s 4. This may or may not be a sexual relationship. The provision does not cover platonic relationships or one-night stands (House of Lords (2003–4) Domestic Violence, Crime and Victims Bill, Explanatory Notes, para 31)
[52] A person falls within subs. (4) if he or she is a parent of the child or has or has had parental responsibility for the child. Since the enactment of the Family Law Reform Act 1987 s 1, the term 'parent' has included the unmarried father; he is a parent even if he does not have parental responsibility. An order may be sought against an unmarried father by the mother of the child irrespective of the fact that the parents have never lived together. The Act also makes provision for the situation where an adoption agency has the power to place a child for adoption, where a placement order has been made or where a child has been adopted. Two persons are associated with each other if one is the natural parent or grandparent and the other is the child or an adoptive parent, a person who has applied for an adoption order or a person with whom the child has been placed for adoption (s 62(5)).
[53] The definition set out in the Domestic Violence Crime and Victims Act 2004 is: 'two persons who, although not married to each other, are living together as husband and wife or (if of the same sex) in an equivalent relationship'. Note, however, that the Civil Partnership Act 2004 provides for a further amendment when it comes into force: 'two persons who are neither married to each other nor civil partners of each other but are living together as husband and wife or as if they were civil partners'.
[54] [1999] 2 FLR 489.
[55] [2000] 2 FLR 533.
[56] See Cretney, *et al*, (2002) p 258.

In deciding whether to exercise its powers under this section and, if so, in what manner, the court shall have regard to all the circumstances including the need to secure the health,[57] safety and well-being—

(a)  of the applicant, [or in a case falling within subsection (2)(b), the person for whose benefit the order would be made]; [58] and

(b)  of any relevant child.

The intention behind the wording of the section is to ensure that the courts focus on the effects of the respondent's behaviour on those around him rather than on the nature of the conduct itself. This approach, said the Law Commission, is consistent with the 'trend in family law towards providing protection from harm rather than punishment or blame' (1992a para 3.6).[59]

**Q**  Why should family law not be concerned with punishment or blame?

Should the court decide that the circumstances warrant a non-molestation order against Albert, it will go on to consider the scope and duration of an appropriate order. The order 'may be expressed so as to refer to molestation in general, to particular acts of molestation, or to both'.[60] Typically, courts will frame orders to prohibit the respondent from intimidating, harassing or pestering the applicant and from encouraging someone else to do so (Platt 2000 p 908). If specific acts are complained of, these are likely to be referred to in the order as well.[61] The order 'may be made for a specified period or until further notice'.[62]

*Occupation Order*

Eve may wish to seek, in the course of separation proceedings or as a free-standing application,[63] an occupation order excluding Albert from the family home or part of it, or even from the area in which the home is situated. As the Law Commission pointed out, these orders are particularly important in domestic violence cases where the parties

[57] Defined in s 63(1) as including physical or mental health.

[58] Bracketed words to be deleted in terms of the Domestic Violence, Crime and Victims Act 2004, Sched 10, para 36(3).

[59] The court may refuse an injunction where it considers it would have undesirable consequences. In *Chechi v Bashier* [1999] 2 FLR 489, the judge was held to have been justified in refusing a non-molestation order because granting such an order would have meant that he would have had to attach a power of arrest under s 47(2)(b). In the circumstances, this would have given the applicant unacceptable power over the respondents which he would be likely to abuse. In *Banks v Banks* [1999] 1 FLR 726 the court refused to make a non-molestation order because the wife's abusive behaviour was a result of her mental condition. She had no control over her conduct and so the order would serve no purpose. However it is not necessary that the person subject to the injunction has a detailed understanding of the court's powers. It suffices if he understands that he is not permitted to do the act concerned and that he will be punished if he does (*P v P (Contempt of Court: Mental Capacity)* [1999] 2 FLR 897).

[60] S 42(6).

[61] See Freeman (1996b) p 86. His Honour Judge John Platt suggests that if a power of arrest is attached to an injunction framed only in general terms this may contravene Art 8(2) of the European Convention on Human Rights; powers of arrest should be attached only to specific prohibitions (2000 p 908).

[62] S 42(7). It is not exceptional to make a non-molestation order for an indefinite period. The court should first decide whether a non-molestation order is warranted and, if so, what its duration should be. Then the court should consider the necessity of a power of arrest. The power of arrest may be for a shorter period than the order if this is appropriate (*Re B-J (Power of Arrest)* [2000] 2 FLR 443).

[63] See s 39(2).

live together: 'an occupation order ousting the respondent from the home will often be the only way of supporting a non-molestation order and giving the applicant effective protection' (Law Commission 1992a para 4.6). By contrast, the utility of occupation orders was doubted by many of those from within refuge organisations who responded to Barron's questionnaire. These orders were relatively rarely sought by women entering refuges, many of whom wish to be re-housed where they cannot be traced by their abusers (Barron 2002 p 7).

In relation to occupation orders the Act draws a distinction between an applicant who qualifies as a 'person entitled' and one who does not. The powers of the court differ according to which category the applicant falls into and are more extensive where she has some interest recognised in law or in equity in the property. Moreover, the categories of non-entitled persons eligible to seek an occupation order are restricted to former spouses (and eventually, former civil partners), cohabitants and former cohabitants.[64] Partners in existing or former same sex relationships are not at present included and would only be able to seek an occupation order if entitled to occupy the home.[65]

The Law Commission (1992a para 4.7) favoured drawing a distinction between entitled and non-entitled applicants for two reasons. First, an occupation order can 'severely restrict the enjoyment of property rights' and this interference is 'more difficult to justify' where the applicant has no right to occupy the premises. Secondly, it was said, the purpose of an occupation order is generally different in the two cases. In the case of an applicant who is entitled, an order has a purpose beyond short-term protection; it regulates occupation of the home until a decision is made as to the medium- or long-term disposition of the property and, in some circumstances, lasts indefinitely. In the case of non-entitled applicants, an order is 'essentially a short term measure of protection intended to give then time to find alternative accommodation or, at most, to await the outcome of an application for a property law remedy' (*ibid*).

### *'Person Entitled'*

A person falls into this category either by virtue of an interest recognised by the general law or by virtue of matrimonial home rights under Section 30 of the Family Law Act 1996. Section 30 comes into operation where one spouse is entitled to occupy the home, whether by reason of a beneficial estate or interest, contract or statute, and where the other spouse is not so entitled. The spouse who is not so entitled[66] is given matrimonial home rights.[67] These comprise the right, if in occupation, not to be excluded from the

[64] The term 'cohabitant' will be defined to include same sex couples when the amending legislation comes into force.

[65] See Bailey-Harris and Wilson (2003).

[66] S 30(9) provides that a spouse with an equitable interest should be treated, for the purposes of determining matrimonial home rights, as if she is not entitled to occupy the home. In relation to former spouses, see s 35(11). In relation to cohabitants and former cohabitants, see s 36(11).

[67] No such rights arise if the home has at no time been, and which at no time was intended to be, the parties' matrimonial home (s 30(7)). However, if the relationship breaks down before the parties move into a home which they intended to be their matrimonial home, the non-entitled spouse does gain matrimonial home rights. If only one spouse, say the non-entitled spouse, intended the home to be the matrimonial home and the other did not, it is not clear whether matrimonial home rights will arise. The fact that subs (7) stipulates that no such rights arise if the home was at no time intended by 'the spouses' to be a matrimonial home suggests that as long as one spouse had this intention, this suffices to create matrimonial home rights. Yet s 33(1)(b) makes it clear that, for an occupation order to be granted, both spouses must have intended the home to be their common home. So if matrimonial home rights could be said to arise under s 30, s 33 would make it impossible to enforce them.

house, or any part of it, without the leave of the court and the right, if not in occupation, to enter and occupy the property with the leave of the court.[68]

Importantly, the Civil Partnership Act 2004 (Schedule 9) will give registered civil partners the same rights in the family home, to be called 'home rights', as spouses currently have with 'matrimonial home rights', and thus automatically give them the status of 'entitled applicants'. The term 'home rights' will replace the term 'matrimonial home rights' whether the parties are married or in a civil partnership.

If the applicant is a 'person entitled', she can seek an occupation order against anyone with whom she is associated, provided the home is or has been or was intended to be their common home:

**Occupation orders where applicant has estate or interest etc. or has matrimonial home rights**[69]

33. (1) If—

(a)    a person ('the person entitled')—
        (i)  is entitled to occupy a dwelling-house by virtue of a beneficial estate or interest or contract or by virtue of any enactment giving him the right to remain in occupation, or
        (ii)  has matrimonial home rights in relation to a dwelling-house, and
(b)    the dwelling-house—
        (i)  is or at any time has been the home of the person entitled and of another person with whom he is associated, or
        (ii)  was at any time intended by the person entitled and any such other person to be their home,

the person entitled may apply to the court for an order containing any of the provisions specified in subsections (3), (4) and (5) ... .

...

(3) An order under this section may—

(a)    enforce the applicant's entitlement to remain in occupation as against the other person ('the respondent');
(b)    require the respondent to permit the applicant to enter and remain in the dwelling-house or part of the dwelling-house;
(c)    regulate the occupation of the dwelling-house by either or both parties;
(d)    if the respondent is entitled as mentioned in subsection (1)(a) (i), prohibit, suspend or restrict the exercise by him of his right to occupy the dwelling-house;
(e)    if the respondent has matrimonial home rights in relation to the dwelling-house, and the applicant is the other spouse, restrict or terminate those rights;
(f)    require the respondent to leave the dwelling-house or part of the dwelling-house; or
(g)    exclude the respondent from a defined area in which the dwelling-house is included.

(4) An order under this section may declare that the applicant is entitled as mentioned in subsection (1)(a) (i) or has matrimonial home rights.

---

[68] Ss 30(2)(a) and (b). A spouse with matrimonial home rights may pay rent, mortgage payments or other outgoings and these payments are as good as if made by the other spouse (s 30(3)).

[69] The Civil Partnership Act 2004 will change all references to 'matrimonial home rights' to 'home rights' and will add to all references to 'spouse', the words 'or civil partner'. It will add to all references to 'marriage' the words 'civil partnership'.

(5) If the applicant has matrimonial home rights and the respondent is the other spouse, an order under this section made during the marriage may provide that those rights are not brought to an end by—

(a)   the death of the other spouse; or
(b)   the termination (otherwise than by death) of the marriage.

The court can, therefore, make a declaratory order in terms of Section 33(4) or a regulatory order in terms of Section 33(3).[70] A declaratory order simply states that the applicant is entitled to occupy the home and, presumably, declares the nature of the interest from which that entitlement flows.[71] To enforce the right to occupy, or to exclude the respondent, an applicant must look to the provisions governing the regulatory orders.

The court has wide powers under Section 33(3). An order under Section 33(3)(a) could be combined with a declaratory order and would be appropriate where the respondent interferes or threatens to interfere with the applicant's right to occupy under the general law or Section 30.[72] Section 33(3)(b) applies where the applicant has been excluded from the home[73] or part of it. The power under Section 33(3)(c) to make an order regulating occupation of the home enables the court to direct which parts of the home may be used by each party and to prescribe those parts of the home that one or other party may not enter.[74] Section 33(3)(d) empowers the court to override the respondent's property rights and deny, suspend or restrict the exercise of those rights. A respondent's matrimonial home rights can be restricted or terminated in terms of Section 33(3)(e). In addition, the respondent may be excluded from the home or from a specified area surrounding it.

As the matrimonial home is registered in Albert's and Eve's joint names, Eve has a claim to the legal estate in the property and therefore qualifies as a 'person entitled'.[75] In addition, she and Albert fall into the category of persons associated with each other. It follows that Eve is eligible to apply for an order prohibiting, for example, Albert from exercising his right as joint owner to occupy the home and requiring him to vacate it. The duration of any order made under Section 33 is at the court's discretion; an order may be made for a specified period or until the happening of a specified event or until further order.[76]

In deciding whether to make an order in Eve's favour, the court is required to have regard to a number of factors enumerated in Section 33(6):

---

[70] See Law Commission (1992a) para 4.1.

[71] See Cretney, *et al*, (2002) p 241.

[72] See Bird (1996a) para 3.3.

[73] Or has been threatened with exclusion (Bird 1996a para 3.3).

[74] See Bird (1996a) para 3.3. See, for example, *G v G (Occupation Order: Conduct)* [2000] 2 FLR 36.

[75] If the property were registered in Albert's sole name, Eve would still qualify as a 'person entitled' by virtue of her matrimonial home rights or if she could show an equitable interest in the property.

[76] S 33(10). Because matrimonial home rights cease to exist when a marriage is terminated, a spouse who is otherwise not entitled to occupy the home would then be restricted, as a non-entitled former spouse, to a remedy under s 35. S 33(5) accordingly provides that an order made during the marriage may stipulate that the matrimonial home rights are not brought to an end by termination of the marriage. The court may exercise its powers under ss (5) 'where it considers that in all the circumstances it is just and reasonable to do so' (s 33(8)). Normally, should the parties divorce, questions concerning the matrimonial home will be finalised by means of a property adjustment order rather than under this jurisdiction (Bird 1996a para 3.4). In relation to orders extending rights of occupation beyond the death of the other party, the Law Commission commented that, generally, a time limit would be appropriate (Law Commission 1992a para 4.3).

In deciding whether to exercise its powers under subsection (3) and (if so) in what manner, the court shall have regard to all the circumstances including—

(a) the housing needs and housing resources of each of the parties and of any relevant child[77];
(b) the financial resources of each of the parties[78];
(c) the likely effect of any order, or of any decision by the court not to exercise its powers under subsection (3), on the health, safety or well-being of the parties and of any relevant child[79]; and
(d) the conduct of the parties in relation to each other and otherwise.[80]

However, in certain circumstances, specified in Section 33(7), the court has no discretion whether to make an order; it is required to do so:

If it appears to the court that the applicant or any relevant child is likely to suffer significant harm attributable to conduct of the respondent if an order under this section containing one or more of the provisions mentioned in subsection (3) is not made, the court shall make the order unless it appears to it that—

(a) the respondent or any relevant child is likely to suffer significant harm if the order is made; and
(b) the harm likely to be suffered by the respondent or child in that event is as great as, or greater than, the harm attributable to the conduct of the respondent which is likely to be suffered by the applicant or child if the order is not made.[81]

These tests replace the criteria contained in earlier legislation[82] which were described by the Law Commission as being 'unsatisfactory' in that they did not afford adequate protection to victims of violence and gave insufficient weight to the interests of children (1992a para 4.23). The 'balance of harm test' now incorporated in the Family Law Act 1996 was designed to remedy the situation:

In cases where the question of significant harm does not arise, the court would have power to make an order taking into account the … factors set out above[83]; but, in cases where there is a likelihood of significant harm, this power becomes a duty … . It is likely that a respondent threatened with ouster on account of his violence would be able to establish a degree of hardship (perhaps in terms of difficulty in finding or unsuitability of alternative accommodation or

---

[77] In *G v J (Ouster Order)* [1993] 1 FLR 1008, 1018–19, Purchas J expressed the view that the court should not regard its task as solving a housing problem. However, the courts have in the past tended to be more ready to exclude a party who has alternative accommodation (see *Scott v Scott* [1992] 1 FLR 529). Moreover, an application by a wife might be more likely to be refused if the local authority has an obligation to rehouse her but not her husband. See also *Wooton v Wooton* [1984] FLR 871. However, the respondent's conduct may tip the balance in favour of an order despite his lack of alternative housing *(Thurley v Smith* [1984] FLR 875). But see *B v B (Occupation Order)* [1999] 1 FLR 715, where the interests of the abuser's child tipped the balance against an order.
[78] See *Baggot v Baggot* [1986] 1 FLR 377.
[79] See *O'Connell v O'Connell* (28 August 1998).
[80] See *Thurley v Smith* [1984] 1 FLR 875. But see *E v E (Ouster Order)* [1995] 1 FLR 224, where the court refused to exclude a husband from the home despite the fact that he had attempted to rape his wife. On the facts, it was decided that it would suffice to order that the wife should have exclusive use of a bedroom and that the husband should be prohibited from entering it. In *Scott v Scott* [1992] 1 FLR 529 it was held that, since an ouster would be the only way of preventing the husband from breaching a non-molestation order, it was correct to grant one.
[81] The Act does not, however, restrict the court's discretion as to the type of order it makes.
[82] The Matrimonial Homes Act 1983. See *Richards v Richards* [1984] 1 AC 174.
[83] These factors are now contained in ss 33(6)(a)–(c). Conduct was not included in the criteria recommended by the Law Commission.

problems in getting to work). But he is unlikely to suffer significant harm, whereas his wife and children who are being subjected to his violence or abuse may very easily suffer harm if he remains in the house. In this way the court will be treating violence or other forms of abuse as deserving immediate relief, and will be directed to make an order where a risk of significant harm exists.[84] (Law Commission 1992a para 4.34).

Since there are no relevant children to consider in this case, all will depend on the balance of harm as between Eve and Albert. If Eve cannot show significant harm attributable to Albert's conduct, the case falls to be decided on the basis of subsection 6.[85] If she does succeed in showing significant harm then the court must grant an order unless Albert can show that the harm he will suffer as a result of an order being granted is equal to or greater than the harm to Eve if the order is not granted. If he can show this, the case falls to be decided under subsection 6.

'Significant harm' is a concept derived from the Children Act 1989.[86] While 'harm' is defined in both the Children Act 1989 and the Family Law Act 1996, neither statute contains a definition of 'significant'. The term has been interpreted in the context of the Children Act 1989 as 'considerable, noteworthy or important'[87] and it is appears that this definition is being applied in interpreting the Family Law Act 1996 too.[88] 'Harm' is defined in Section 63(1) of the Family Law Act 1996 and a distinction is drawn between persons who are under and over the age of 18:

'harm'—

(a)  in relation to a person who has reached the age of eighteen years, means ill-treatment or the impairment of health; and
(b)  in relation to a child, means ill-treatment or the impairment of health or development;

'health' includes physical or mental health;

'ill-treatment' includes forms of ill-treatment which are not physical and, in relation to a child, includes sexual abuse.

**Q** Would sexual abuse of an adult constitute 'ill-treatment'?

In the case of the applicant, the harm must be attributable to the conduct[89] of the respondent whereas the harm to the respondent that may be taken into account is 'harm in the widest sense, for example, the harm which might be suffered as a result of being evicted' (Bird 1996a para 3.8). Whether or not the harm suffered by an applicant or relevant child engendered by having to live in unsuitable accommodation after fleeing the violence of the respondent can be attributed to the respondent's conduct is open to

---

[84] Compare *B v B (Occupation Order)* [1999] 1 FLR 715. This was an unusual case in that the respondent was the primary caretaker of his child by a previous relationship. The wife, who had been subjected to severe violence, had moved out of the home with the child of the marriage. The court paid little attention to the risks of violence if, say, the wife and child returned. While emphatically declaring that the purpose of the legislation is to secure safe occupation of previously shared property, the court was unable to do this because the harm to the husband's child if required to move outweighed the harm to the wife and child if they stayed away.

[85] *Chalmers v Johns* [1999] 1 FLR 392, 396; *G v G (Occupation Order: Conduct)* [2000] 2 FLR 36, 41.

[86] See ss 31 and 105 Children Act 1989.

[87] DoH (1991c) para 3.19; *Humberside County Council v B* [1993] 1 FLR 257, 263.

[88] *Chalmers v Johns* [1999] 1 FLR 392, 398.

[89] Conduct that is unintentional can cause harm within the meaning of the section. What matters is the effect of the conduct on the applicant or children rather than the intention of the respondent. *G v G (Occupation Order: Conduct)* [2000] 2 FLR 36, 40.

question.[90] Arguably it is not solely attributable to the lack of suitable housing but also to the conduct that forced them to occupy inadequate accommodation.

In the light of the definition of harm, any upset or inconvenience to Eve by, for instance, having to leave the home is unlikely to qualify as significant harm. Even if Eve is likely to suffer so much stress as a result of having to leave the home that, say, her mental health is significantly impaired, this may or may not be considered attributable to Albert's conduct in terms of Section 33(7). The court may, however, find, in the light of Albert's violence[91] towards Eve, that she is likely to suffer significant harm if the order is not granted, and it is clear that this harm is attributable to Albert's conduct.

The next step is to determine whether Albert is likely to suffer significant harm. In his case, the court could, it seems, consider any harm including, say, any impairment to his physical or mental health that might be caused by having to leave the home.[92] The court then has to consider whether the harm likely to be suffered by him if the order is granted is equal to or greater than the harm likely to be sustained by Eve if it is not.

If it is found that it is Eve who is likely to suffer the greater harm, the court is obliged to make an order. If not, the court has a discretion and will exercise this in the light of all the circumstances, including the specific matters referred to in Section 33(6). Factors such as the availability of alternative accommodation and financial resources will be relevant. However, they will probably not prove to be decisive, particularly in view of the fact that both Albert and Eve are full-time accountants and are both likely to be able to afford adequate accommodation. The more important considerations are likely to be Albert's conduct and Eve's safety.

Under the old legislation, courts were reluctant to exclude parties (usually men) from their homes, stressing the 'Draconian'[93] nature of such an order. In *Wiseman v Simpson*,[94] for example, the Court of Appeal declared that, although violence or molestation was not a prerequisite for making an ouster order, it was not just or reasonable to make such a Draconian order simply because the applicant had a greater need for accommodation.[95]

While the criteria in Section 33(6) are somewhat broader than those applied previously, it appears that courts regard occupation orders in the same light as they did ousters—as drastic measures to be used sparingly. In *Chalmers v Johns*[96] Thorpe LJ described the new occupation order as 'Draconian' like its predecessors and continued, '[i]t remains an order that overrides proprietary rights and ... it is an order that is only justified in exceptional circumstances'. What would qualify as exceptional is not clear (Humphries 2001 p 544). However the judgment in *G v G (Occupation Order: Conduct)*[97] seems to imply that little other than violence will suffice. Upholding a decision to refuse an occupation order and confirming an order regulating shared occupation of the home, Thorpe LJ said:

---

[90] See Lowe and Douglas (1998 p 202). See also *B v B (Occupation Order)* [1999] 1 FLR 715.

[91] The adverse effects on the health of the applicant of the violence would be taken into account. See *O'Connell v O'Connell* (28 August 1998).

[92] *Ibid.*

[93] See *Davis v Johnson* [1979] AC 264, 302–3. Indefinite exclusion of a sole owner from his property has been seen as particularly drastic. See *Wiseman v Simpson* [1988] 1 WLR 35, 44.

[94] [1988] 1 WLR 35.

[95] See also *Blackstock v Blackstock* [1991] Fam Law 415.

[96] [1999] 1 FLR 392, 397. See, for critical comment, Kaganas (1999a).

[97] [2000] 2 FLR 36.

This was not a case in which the wife had suffered any violence at the hands of the husband. It has been said time and time again that orders of exclusion are draconian and only to be made in exceptional cases. Add to that the judge's assessment that the friction between the parties was only the product of their incompatible personalities and the heightened tensions that any family has to live with whilst the process of divorce and separation is current, and the judge's conclusion is plainly justified. (p 41)

And even if there has been violence, the court will not necessarily grant an order. *Chalmers v Johns* was a case involving violence but was, in the view of Thorpe LJ, 'in the range of domestic violence a slight case'.[98] Decisions, it seems, are being made in the same way that they were before the 1996 Act (Humphries 2001 p 544).

### *Ancillary Provisions*

A court, when making an occupation order[99] or at any time after doing so, is empowered to make an ancillary order imposing obligations on either party regarding maintenance and repair of the property[100]; payment of rent, mortgage and other outgoings[101]; and the payment of what amounts to occupation rent to a party excluded from a property which he or she would otherwise have been entitled to occupy.[102] In addition, the court may grant either party possession of the furniture or other contents of the home.[103] Eve may wish to apply for one or more of these orders. However, it seems that there is no way to enforce an order made under Section 40 for payment of money to a third person, such as a mortgagee. In *Nwogbe v Nwogbe*,[104] the husband was ordered to pay the rent, water rates, council tax and certain arrears relating to the property. He failed to do this and the wife applied for his committal for contempt of court. The court held that it did not have the power to commit him to prison. Nor could it make an attachment of earnings order. The court remarked that this is a serious omission from the statute requiring urgent attention.

### *Ex Parte Orders*

Normally, an applicant must comply with rules of court specifying the notice to be given to the respondent of proceedings. The general rule is that a court should not make an order without giving those likely to be affected by it the opportunity to be heard. However, in some circumstances the court may grant an *ex parte* order even though the necessary notice has not been given.[105] The situations in which this step might be necessary are, according to the Law Commission, where the remedy is needed urgently or where the applicant, although she may not need the order itself as a matter of urgency, is so frightened of the respondent that she needs protection in order to pursue her remedy.[106]

---

[98] P 397.
[99] Whether under ss 33, 35 or 36 (see s 40(1)).
[100] S 40(1)(a)(i).
[101] S 40(1)(a)(ii).
[102] S 40(1)(b).
[103] S 40(1)(c).
[104] [2000] 2 FLR 744.
[105] The potential difficulties of effecting service are described by Barron (1990) pp 22–23.
[106] Law Commission (1992a) paras 5.6 and 5.8.

Prior to the Family Law Act 1996, it was clear that *ex parte* orders would be granted only in limited circumstances.[107] However, although under the new legislation, the remedy of an *ex parte* order remains discretionary, its wording leaves open the possibility that the courts could grant such orders more readily. Section 45(1) provides that both occupation and non-molestation orders may be made *ex parte* where the court considers it 'just and convenient to do so'. In deciding whether to make such an order, the court must, in terms of Section 45(2), have regard to all the circumstances including any risk of significant harm to the applicant or a relevant child, attributable to the respondent's conduct, if the order is not made immediately; whether, unless the order is made immediately, it is likely that the applicant will be deterred or prevented from proceeding; and whether there is reason to believe the respondent is evading service and the applicant or child will be prejudiced by delay. If Eve fears that Albert will react violently to being served with her application, she can apply for an *ex parte* order. Barron maintains that occupation orders are not very often made without notice (Barron 2002 pp 7–8) but the figures for the county courts in 2003 show that about twice as many applications were received *ex parte* as were received on notice (DCA 2003b Table 5.9).[108]

## Enforcement

Should Eve succeed in obtaining an order, there is no guarantee that Albert will abide by it. Breach of a court order constitutes contempt of court, punishable by imprisonment.[109] The court in *Hale v Tanner*[110] set out guidelines for dealing with such cases:

(26) [T]hese cases have to come before the court on an application to commit … . Not surprisingly, therefore, the court is directing its mind to whether or not committal to prison is the appropriate order. But it does not follow from that that imprisonment is to be regarded as the automatic consequence of the breach of an order. Clearly it is not. There is, however, no principle that imprisonment is not to be imposed at the first occasion … . Nevertheless, it is a common practice, and usually appropriate in view of the sensitivity of the circumstances of these cases, to take some other course on the first occasion … .

(29) [T]he length of the committal has to depend upon the court's objectives. There are two objectives always in contempt of court proceedings. One is to mark the court's disapproval of the disobedience to its order. The other is to secure compliance with that order in the future. Thus, the seriousness of what has taken place is to be viewed in that light as well as for its own intrinsic gravity … .

(36) An important part of the exercise is that the contemnor should understand[111] the importance of keeping court orders, of not breaking them and the likely consequences if they are so broken … .

(38) It is rare, when one looks at the reported cases, to find sentences of 6 months' imprisonment in the context of much more serious breaches than took place in this case. One tends to find, even in cases of violence causing quite significant injury, a shorter sentence.

---

107 See *Ansah v Ansah* [1977] 2 WLR 760; Practice Note (Matrimonial Cause: Injunction) [1978] 1 WLR 925. The Law Commission noted that in practice, *ex parte* ouster orders were particularly rare (1992a para 5.5).

108 See ch 10.

109 It appears that the courts may be more willing now to imprison for breach of an order than they have been in the past, at least where a serious attack is involved. See *Neil v Ryan* [1998] 2 FLR 1068; *Wilson v Webster* [1998] 1 FLR 1097; *Hale v Tanner* [2000] 2 FLR 879. See also *Lomas v Parle* [2003] EWCA Civ 1804; [2004] 1 FLR 812.

110 [2000] 2 FLR 812.

111 See, on capacity to understand, *P v P (Contempt of Court: Mental Capacity)* [1999] 2 FLR 897.

There are difficulties and delays involved in enforcing orders through civil contempt proceedings,[112] and the Family Law Act was framed to include significant reforms. First, it makes provision for greater use to be made of powers of arrest.[113] Secondly, it provides for the involvement of the police in enforcing orders even where there is no power of arrest.[114] Thirdly, it gives the courts the power to remand[115] and, if bail is granted, to require compliance with requirements considered necessary to prevent interference with witnesses or to prevent the obstruction of justice by other means.[116]

### Power of Arrest

Eve can seek to have a power of arrest attached by the court to one or more provisions of the order. If a power of arrest is attached, a constable may arrest Albert without warrant if he or she has reasonable cause to suspect that Albert is in breach of any provision to which the power is attached.[117] Albert would then have to be brought before the court within 24 hours of his arrest[118] and the court may punish him for contempt. The power of arrest serves the purpose of providing a short route to the power to commit for contempt of court and also has the effect of removing the abuser from the scene.[119]

The court is obliged to attach a power of arrest in certain circumstances:

47. Arrest for breach of order

(1) In this section a 'relevant order' means an occupation order or a non-molestation order.[120]

(2) If—

(a)    the court makes a relevant[121] order; and
(b)    it appears to the court that the respondent has used or threatened violence against the applicant or a relevant child,

it shall attach a power of arrest to one or more provisions of the order unless satisfied that in all the circumstances of the case the applicant or child will be adequately protected without such a power of arrest.

It seems that courts may not be willing to interpret 'violence' as including emotional abuse[122] but it appears that any physical violence[123] suffices to satisfy subsection 2(b).[124]

---

112 See Women's National Commission (1985) para 108ff; Barron (2002) p 8.
113 Prior to the Family Law Act 1996, the courts were reluctant to attach powers of arrest. See *Lewis v Lewis* [1978] 1 All ER 729. They were normally limited to 3 months in duration: Practice Note (Domestic Violence: Power of Arrest) [1981] 1 WLR 27.
114 In the past, those engaged in putting committal orders made by the High Court and the county court into effect were the officers of those civil courts, and they were not available outside working hours. It was only the magistrates' courts that could involve the police.
115 S 47(7)(b) and (10). This power was previously restricted to magistrates courts.
116 S 47(12).
117 S 47(6).
118 S 47(7)(a).
119 *Re H (Respondent Under 18: Power of Arrest)* [2001] 1 FLR 641.
120 This subsection is to be deleted (Domestic Violence, Crime and Victims Act 2004 Sched 10, para 38. S 47 will deal with breaches of occupation orders and breaches of non-molestation orders will be covered in the new s 42A.
121 Subsections (2)–(5) will be amended to refer to an 'occupation order' instead of a 'relevant order' (Domestic Violence, Crime and Victims Act 2004 Sched 10, para 38).
122 See Barron (2002) p 8; Humphries (2001) p 542.
123 Other than those forms considered socially acceptable such as reasonable chastisement of children (see Freeman 1996b p 93).
124 See Bird (1996a) para 5.3

The court would therefore be required to attach a power of arrest unless satisfied that Eve would be adequately protected without one. If a power of arrest were attached, it would be registered at a local police station.[125]

There is a view that orders without a power of arrest are so difficult to enforce that they are 'virtually useless' (Barron 2002 p 8). Nevertheless there are a number of situations in which no power of arrest is attached. First, the court retains complete discretion in cases that do not fall within Section 47(2), such as those where there has been no actual or threatened violence. Secondly, a power of arrest will not be attached where, in terms of Section 47(2), the court is satisfied that the applicant or child is adequately protected without one. Thirdly, in the case of *ex parte* orders the presumption in favour of a power of arrest does not operate and the court's discretion is limited; it may make an order if violence has been used or threatened and there is a risk of significant harm if the power of arrest is not attached immediately.[126] Fourthly, the power of arrest might be attached only to certain provisions of the order. Finally, it is not possible to attach a power of arrest to an undertaking[127] and the courts still appear to be accepting undertakings readily. However the Act does provide that if a power of arrest is appropriate, the court cannot accept an undertaking instead of making an order.[128]

Although the number of orders with powers of arrest attached has increased,[129] Barron (2002 p 8) reports that they are 'by no means universally obtainable, and are noticeably less likely to be attached to occupation orders than to non-molestation orders'. If no power of arrest is attached, then, in the event of breach, the court is empowered to issue a warrant for arrest.[130]

## *Warrant for Arrest*

The court is empowered under Section 47(8), on application, to issue a warrant of arrest if satisfied that the respondent has breached an order or an undertaking.[131] If a court does decide to issue a warrant of arrest, this would enable the court to involve the police in the enforcement process.

## *Offence of Breaching a Non-Molestation Order*

The difficulties of enforcing orders were noted by the government:

---

[125] R 3.9A(1) of the Family Proceedings (Amendment No 3) Rules 1997 SI 1997/1893 (L29); R 20(1) of the Family Proceedings Courts (Matrimonial Proceedings etc) (Amendment) Rules 1997 SI 1997/1894 (L30).

[126] S 47(3). The violence as well as the risk of significant harm must relate to the applicant or a relevant child.

[127] S 46(2). Barron (2002) p 8 suggests that powers of arrest are not normally attached to *ex parte* orders. Arrest of a person before the order has been served on him may be unlawful and a breach of his human rights (Platt 2000 pp 907–8).

[128] S 46(3). To be amended to preclude acceptance of an undertaking instead of making of an occupation order (Domestic Violence, Crime and Victims Act 2004 Sched 10, para 37(2). A new s 46(3A) will be inserted stating that the court shall not accept an undertaking instead of making a non-molestation order in cases where it appears to the court that the respondent has used or threatened violence against the applicant or relevant child and, for the protection of the applicant or child it is necessary to make a non-molestation order so that breach will be punishable under s 42A (Sched 10, para 37(3)).

[129] See Home Office (2003) para 46.

[130] Committal proceedings may also be used. See R 3.9A(5) of the Family Proceedings (Amendment No 3) Rules 1997 SI 1997/1893 (L 29); R 20(5)–(13) of the Family Proceedings Courts (Matrimonial Proceedings etc) (Amendment) Rules 1997 SI 1997/1894 (L30).

[131] S 46(4) provides that an undertaking is enforceable as if it were an order of court.

[G]iven that the power of arrest is often only attached to specific parts of an order, police officers may be unclear whether they can arrest the respondent or not. Moreover, information on orders and powers of arrest is not recorded centrally, and the arrangements for passing such information between police forces can be inconsistent. If no power of arrest was attached, the victim has to apply to the civil court for an arrest warrant, which can put the victim at risk of further violence until the warrant is issued. (Home Office 2003 para 46)

In order to ameliorate the problems,[132] the Domestic Violence, Crime and Victims Act 2004[133] will amend the 1996 Act, inserting a new Section 42A to make breach of a non-molestation order an arrestable[134] offence:

42A Offence of breaching non-molestation order

(1)   A person who without reasonable excuse does anything that he is prohibited from doing by a non-molestation order is guilty of an offence.
(2)   In the case of a non-molestation order made by virtue of section 45(1),[135] a person can be guilty of an offence under this section only in respect of conduct engaged in at a time when he was aware of the existence of the order.
(3)   Where a person is convicted of an offence under this section in respect of any conduct, that conduct is not punishable as a contempt of court.
(4)   A person cannot be convicted of an offence under this section in respect of any conduct which has been punished as a contempt of court.

The effect of this will be that the police can arrest without a warrant or a power of arrest. Alternatively the victim can apply for a warrant of arrest for contempt of court.[136] The Act does not make breach of an occupation order an offence because a history of violence or molestation is not required for such an order (House of Lords Session 2003–04 para 26). However it does insert[137] a new Section 42(4A) which is intended to ensure that those victims who need the protection that an immediate arrest offers will be given it. The court is required, when considering whether to make an occupation order, to consider whether it should exercise its power to make a non-molestation order of its own motion. In addition, the Act introduces a measure designed to prevent the court accepting an undertaking in a case where an arrest power is warranted. Section 46(3A) will provide:

The court shall not accept an undertaking under subsection (1) instead of making a non-molestation order in any case where it appears to the court that—

(a)   the respondent has used or threatened violence against the applicant or a relevant child; and
(b)   for the protection of the applicant or child it is necessary to make a non-molestation order so that any breach may be punishable under section 42A.

---

[132] But see McCulloch (2004). The SFLA argues that making breach of a non-molestation order an offence may deter victims from applying for such an order.
[133] S 1.
[134] See House of Lords (Session 2003–4) para 23.
[135] This deals with *ex parte* orders.
[136] See House of Lords (Session 2003–4) paras 23–25.
[137] See Sch 10, para 36.

## Applications by Third Parties

Should a victim of violence such as Eve be unable to bring proceedings herself because, for example, she feels too vulnerable, there is provision for rules of court to prescribe persons or categories of persons who may act on her behalf. This provision had not yet been implemented at the time of writing but it is thought that if it is, the main designated category will be the police.[138]

> **Q** What remedies would be available to Eve if she and Albert were divorced and Eve had no legal or beneficial interest in the property?

## Non-Entitled Former Spouse

The category of 'associated persons' includes former spouses[139] and Eve's position regarding a non-molestation order would be no different. However, as she would have no recognised interest in the home and her matrimonial home rights would have terminated when the marriage ended,[140] she would not qualify as a 'person entitled' and Section 33 would not apply. Her application for an occupation order would be dealt with under Section 35 instead. That section makes provision for cases involving former spouses where one is entitled to occupy the home[141] and the other is not.

The court, in relation to non-entitled persons, has to engage in a two-stage decision-making process.[142] First, it has to decide whether the applicant should be granted 'occupation rights'.[143] If it decides in favour of the applicant, it then goes on to consider whether to make a regulatory order.

The first stage is dealt with under subsections (3) and (4). Before considering the possibility of a regulatory order, the court must make what is in effect a declaration that the applicant is entitled to occupy the home. If she is in occupation, the order must include provision giving her the right not to be evicted or excluded from the home or any part of it for the period specified in the order. It must also prohibit the respondent from excluding her.[144] If she is not in occupation, the order must give her the right to enter and occupy the home for the period specified and it must require the respondent to allow her to exercise that right.[145]

In deciding whether to make an order making provision of the kind mentioned in subsection (3) or (4), the court must, in terms of Section 35(6), have regard to all the circumstances including:

(a)  the housing needs and housing resources of each of the parties and of any relevant child;

(b)  the financial resources of each of the parties;

---

[138] See ch 10.

[139] S 62(3)(a). It will also include former civil partners when the Civil Partnership Act 2004 comes into force.

[140] S 33(5) can be used to avoid this happening if an order is made during the marriage. See above.

[141] It must have been, at any time, or have been intended to be their matrimonial home (s 35(1)(c)). The new s 35(1)(c) FLA 1996, inserted by the Civil Partnership Act 2004, will include a reference also to the civil partnership home.

[142] In practice, the process may often be telescoped (Law Commission 1992a para 4.18).

[143] See Law Commission (1992a) para 4.18.

[144] S 35(3).

[145] S 35(4).

(c)    the likely effect of any order, or of any decision by the court not to exercise its powers under subsection (3) or (4), on the health, safety or well-being of the parties and of any relevant child;
(d)    the conduct of the parties in relation to each other and otherwise;
(e)    the length of time that has elapsed since the parties ceased to live together;
(f)    the length of time that has elapsed since the marriage was dissolved or annulled; and
(g)    the existence of any pending proceedings[146] between the parties—
    (i)   for an order under section 23A or 24 of the Matrimonial Causes Act 1973 (property adjustment orders in connection with divorce proceedings etc);[147]
    (ii)  for an order under paragraph 1(2)(d) or (e) of Schedule 1 to the Children Act 1989 (orders for financial relief against parents); or
    (iii) relating to the legal or beneficial ownership of the dwelling-house.

The court, if it decides to make an occupation rights order, must then go on to consider whether a regulatory order is appropriate. Under Section 35(5), it has the power to make an order regulating the occupation of the house; prohibiting, suspending or restricting the exercise by the respondent of his right to occupy; requiring the respondent to vacate the home or part of it; or excluding the respondent from a defined area in which the home is situated.

Section 35(8) places an obligation on the court to make an order under subsection (5) in certain circumstances. Such an order is mandatory if it appears to the court that, unless provision is made under subsection 5, the applicant or a relevant child is likely to suffer significant harm attributable to the respondent's conduct unless the harm suffered by the respondent or child as a result would be as great or greater.

If the court is not obliged to make an order under Section 35(8), then, as under Section 33, it still has the discretion to make one. It may find, for example, that the harm to the respondent if it did exclude him would be as great as the harm to the applicant if it did not. In deciding whether to include a subsection (5) provision in its order, the court must have regard to all the circumstances including the matters referred to in subsection 6(a)–(e).[148]

An order in favour of a former spouse, unlike one in favour of a spouse, cannot exceed six months in duration. The reason for this appears to be that occupation remedies for non-entitled parties are seen as 'a relatively short term measure of protection, just to give sufficient time to find alternative accommodation or to await the outcome of property proceedings' (Law Commission 1992a para 4.19). However, an order may be extended for further periods of up to six months each.[149]

**Q** What remedies would be available to Eve if she had no legal or equitable interest in the home and she and Albert had never married?

---

[146] If an order settling the financial and property arrangements between the parties is to be made in the near future, the court is less likely to make an occupation order. See *Chalmers v Johns* [1999] 1 FLR 392; *G v G (Occupation Order: Conduct)* [2000] 2 FLR 36.

[147] A new s 35(6)(g)(ia) FLA 1996 will be inserted by the Civil Partnership Act 2004. This refers to a property adjustment order under Part 2 of Schedule 5 of the Civil Partnership Act 2004.

[148] S 35(7).

[149] S 35(10).

*Non-Entitled Cohabitant or Former Cohabitant*

Cohabitants and former cohabitants qualify as 'associated persons' in terms of Section 62(3)(b). Whether or not Albert and Eve were still living together, Eve could seek redress under Section 36. That section applies in cases where the parties are cohabitants or former cohabitants, and where one party is entitled to occupy the home[150] and the other is not. The provisions of Section 36 are identical to those of Section 35 in many ways. The two-stage process is common to both sections. The court, must decide whether to give the applicant occupation rights[151] and then consider whether to make a regulatory order in terms of subsection (5). And in deciding whether to make provision for occupation rights under subsection (3) or (4) many of the matters which the court is directed to consider under Section 36(6) are the same as those specified in Section 35(6). The court must have regard to the housing needs and resources[152] and the financial[153] resources of the parties and relevant children; the likely effects of its decision on their health, safety and well being[154]; the conduct of the parties[155]; the length of time that has elapsed since the parties lived together[156]; and the existence of pending proceedings between the parties.[157]

However, there are significant differences. First, Section 36(6) also provides that the court must have regard to:

(e)   the nature of the parties' relationship;[158]
(f)   the length of time during which they have lived together as husband and wife; [159]
(g)   whether there are or have been any children who are children of both parties or for whom both parties have or have had parental responsibility.[160] ...

> **Q** Why should a person be more or less deserving of the right to occupy the home depending on the duration of the relationship or on whether the parties have had children together?

Section 41 elaborates on the instruction to consider the nature of the parties' relationship:

41 Additional considerations if parties are cohabitants or former cohabitants

(1)   This section applies if the parties are cohabitants or former cohabitants.
(2)   Where the court is required to consider the nature of the parties' relationship, it is to have regard to the fact that they have not given each other the commitment involved in marriage.

---

[150] It must be the home in which they live or have lived or intended to live as husband and wife, s 36(1)(c). This will be amended to refer to same sex relationships. See Domestic Violence Crime and Victims Act 2004 Sched 10, para 34.
[151] S 36(3) and (4).
[152] S 36(6)(a).
[153] S 36(6)(b).
[154] S 36(6)(c).
[155] S 36(6)(d).
[156] S 36(6)(h).
[157] S 36(6)(i).
[158] The Domestic Violence Crime and Victims Act 2004 (s.2) will add the following words at the end of this subsection: 'and in particular the level of commitment involved in it'.
[159] This will be amended to accommodate same sex relationships. See Domestic Violence, Crime and Victims Act 2004 Sched 10, para 34.
[160] The wording suggests that children who have grown up are intended to be covered.

The second difference is that an order containing a subsection 5 provision is entirely within the court's discretion; there are no circumstances in which it is obliged to make one. The court is simply directed,[161] in exercising this discretion, to have regard to all the circumstances, including the factors listed in subsection 6(a)–(d), and to apply the balance of harm test.[162] There is no duty on the court to make an order even if the applicant or relevant child would suffer considerably more harm by its failure to do so than the respondent or child would suffer if it did make an order.

> **Q** Why is the need for an occupation order apparently less pressing in a case involving cohabitants or former cohabitants than in a case involving spouses or former spouses?

> **Q** Bailey-Harris and Wilson (2003) suggest that Section 36, in distinguishing between parties on the basis of marital status, may fall foul of the Human Rights Act 1998. Do you agree?

Finally, the duration of an order is limited to six months and it can be extended only once for up to six months.[163]

> **Q** Why is the duration of occupation orders in favour of cohabitants limited to a maximum of 12 months?

If Eve were to fall into the category of non-entitled cohabitant, rather than that of either spouse or non-entitled former spouse, she might find it more difficult to exclude Albert from the home. And if she did succeed in obtaining an order, it would have effect for a shorter period than if she were married to him or had been married to him.

The legislation appears to be designed to offer protection more readily to those cohabitants who can produce evidence of commitment to the relationship. An applicant who has lived with the respondent for a long time or who has had children or shared parental responsibility with him would, it seems, find it easier to obtain an order than one who has not. However, as Section 41 so clearly shows, the law views cohabitants as being, by definition, not committed to their relationships in the way that those who marry are.[164]

The effect of Section 41 is not clear. It is, says Freeman (1996b p 83), 'an ideological statement' stemming from the *Daily Mail*-inspired opposition to the 1995 Family Homes and Domestic Violence Bill.[165] He doubts its significance in practice but expresses concern that cohabitants might be labelled uncommitted if, for example, they keep separate bank accounts. Cretney, *et al*, also suggest that it might be having little effect in practice. The section, they point out, 'was clearly intended to satisfy those MPs perturbed by the spectre of the erosion of the institution of marriage. Its linguistic and logical inelegance is as open to doubt as its impact on the everyday practice of the courts' (2002 para

---

161 In terms of s 36(7).

162 Contained in s 36(8).

163 S 36(10). While a year may be sufficient time to find alternative accommodation in most cases, this limitation may prejudice a cohabitant with special needs for whom the home has been purpose-built or specially adapted (Murphy 1996 p 849).

164 A subsequent divorce does not detract from the initial commitment.

165 A group of Conservative MPs opposed that Bill on the ground that it undermined marriage because, they said, it improved the position of cohabitants. As Freeman wryly comments, '[t]hat some of the provisions they identified had been the law since 1976 either escaped their attention or was deemed irrelevant' (1996b p 4).

10–017). That the section is to be repealed makes sense. However, the court will still be expected to take cognisance of the level of commitment of the parties in terms of the amended s 36(6)(e).

> **Q** What remedies would be available to Eve if neither she nor Albert were entitled to occupy the home?

*Neither Party Entitled to Occupy*

This situation could arise where, for example, the parties are squatters, where their right of occupation has been terminated,[166] where neither party wishes to assert a right to occupy or where such a right cannot be proved.[167] Section 37 deals with spouses and former spouses[168] while Section 38 deals with cohabitants and former cohabitants.[169]

Both sections empower a court to make an order requiring the respondent to allow the applicant to enter and remain in the home[170] or part of it; regulating the occupation of the home; requiring the respondent to leave the home or part of it; or excluding the respondent from a defined area in which the home is situated.[171]

In deciding whether to make an order in cases involving spouses or former spouses, the court is required to apply Sections 33(6) and (7).[172]

In deciding whether to exercise its powers in a case involving cohabitants, the court must have regard to all the circumstances including housing needs and resources, financial resources, the effect of its decision on the health, safety and well being of those concerned and the conduct of the parties.[173] It is also required to apply the balance of harm test[174] but is not mandated to make any order.

An order under Section 37 cannot be made for a period exceeding six months but may be extended for one or more periods of up to six months.[175] An order under Section 38 may not exceed six months in duration but may be extended once for up to six months.[176]

> **Q** What if Eve and Albert had a daughter aged 14?

[166] See Bird (1996a) para 3.27.

[167] See Freeman (1996b) p 78.

[168] The Civil Partnership Act 2004 amends this provision to include civil partners and former civil partners (Sched 9 para 8).

[169] The Domestic Violence, Crime and Victims Act 2004 amends this provision to include same sex cohabitants (Sched 10 para 35).

[170] In relation to spouses or former spouses it must be or have been the matrimonial home (s 37(1)(a)). In relation to cohabitants or former cohabitants it must be the home in which they live or have lived together as husband and wife (s 38(1)(a)). These provisions will be amended to accommodate same sex relationships. See Domestic Violence, Crime and Victims Act 2004 Sched 10 and Civil Partnership Act 2004 Sched 9.

[171] Ss 37(3) and 38(3).

[172] S 37(4).

[173] S 38(4).

[174] Contained in s 38(5).

[175] S 37(5).

[176] S 38(6).

*Children*

A daughter aged 14 would qualify as a 'relevant child' and would have to be considered in applying any provisions, such as the balance of harm test, which make reference to such a child.[177]

If Eve did not wish to apply for an order ousting Albert, her daughter might be able to do so as parent and child are 'associated persons'.[178] However, as she is under 16 years of age, she would need the leave of the court.[179] This would be granted only if she were adjudged to have sufficient understanding under Section 43 to make the application and even if the court were satisfied that she does, it is still at liberty to refuse leave.

Should a child[180] make an application for an occupation order, it is not at all clear from the legislation what criteria the court should apply in deciding whether to grant it. As we have seen, an occupation order is defined in Section 39 as an order made under a number of specified sections, all but one of which refer to spouses or cohabitants. The one exception refers to parties who are 'entitled' to occupy and, presumably, a child with, say, a beneficial interest in property would qualify. Other than that, the Act is silent on this matter.[181]

In addition, the Children Act 1989[182] was amended by the 1996 Act to create a new power to include an exclusion requirement in an emergency protection order or an interim care order. This permits the removal from the home of a suspected abuser instead of the child. Exclusion requirements are considered in more detail in chapter 17.

## VI. HOUSING

Eve might decide to leave the home. Often, victims of abuse who lack resources flee the home to stay with friends or family or in a refuge. Some may not wish to return home even if the abuser is ousted because they fear that the abuse will continue as long as their abusers know where they are. The question that arises is how they can secure for themselves long-term accommodation. Housing and homelessness are dealt with in detail in chapters 3 and 13 and Eve's situation will be covered in brief.

Eve can apply to the local housing authority for accommodation if she is eligible.[183] Provided she can show that she is unintentionally homeless and in priority need, the authority has a duty to house her.[184] She will qualify as homeless if she has nowhere to

---

[177] If an applicant is not eligible under the Family Law Act 1996 to apply for an occupation order, it is nevertheless possible to exclude a respondent to protect children's interests. It was held in *C v K (Inherent Powers: Exclusion Order)* [1996] 2 FLR 506 that the court's jurisdiction under s 37 of the Supreme Court Act 1981 or under s 38 of the County Courts Act 1984 can be invoked in support of the rights and duties conferred by a residence order. A person may be restrained from interfering with the exercise of parental responsibility of a person who has a residence order.

[178] S 62(4). A step-child does not appear to qualify under this provision unless the step-parent has acquired parental responsibility.

[179] See R 3.8(2) of the Family Proceedings Rules 1991.

[180] Whether under 16, with leave of the court, or between the ages of 16 and 18, as of right.

[181] Murphy appears to think that the courts may develop their own grounds for granting orders: '[t]he basis on which children's petitions will be considered is therefore left to judicial exegesis' (1996 p 851).

[182] Ss 38A and 44A Children Act 1989.

[183] See ch 13 for a fuller discussion of housing.

[184] S 193 Housing Act 1996.

stay.[185] The fact that she has fled from a violent relationship means that she could not reasonably have been expected to remain in the home with Albert.[186] She is therefore not intentionally homeless.[187] She will be able to show priority need if she has a dependent child who is living with her or who could reasonably be expected to live with her. Alternatively she might qualify as vulnerable[188] as she has fled to escape violence. However, given that she has the financial resources to house herself in the private sector, she may well fail the vulnerability test.

Even if she does not fall within the category of priority need, she is not necessarily precluded form being allocated accommodation through the housing scheme. Eve will fall within Section 167(2) and should be given reasonable preference within any housing scheme if she is homeless. However the scheme may take into account factors set out in Section 167(2A) which include financial resources. This means the housing authority could give less priority to someone who is in a position to secure accommodation at market rent or who is in a position to buy a home (ODPM 2002 para 5.23).

Since it appears that she is likely to be able to afford to do so, Eve will probably have to seek accommodation in the private sector. Should she decide to seek a court order formalising the separation, she might have the matrimonial home reallocated to her alone: in the event of divorce or judicial separation, the court can make a property adjustment order under the Matrimonial Causes Act 1973.[189]

# VII. JUDICIAL SEPARATION

Because one's legal status does not change upon separation, one is not required to obtain the sanction of the court in order to separate from a spouse and of course, many spouses live apart without attending court for an order. However, for those who do need

---

[185] See s 175 Housing Act 1996 and p 498.

[186] See s 177 Housing Act 1996 and p 501.

[187] See s 191 Housing Act 1996.

[188] See Code of Guidance paras 8.12–8.13 and 8.27. See pp 503–4 below.

[189] See ch 14. This power of re-allocation exists not only in relation to owner-occupied property but also in relation to public sector housing (see *Thompson v Thompson* [1975] 2 WLR 868, decided under the Matrimonial Causes Act 1973). For a more detailed discussion, see Bird (1996a) ch 8. The court has the power to transfer protected, statutory, secure and assured tenancies in terms of s 53 of and Sch 7 to the Family Law Act 1996. Sched. 7 will be amended by the Civil Partnership Act 2004 to include civil partners. Significantly, Sched. 7 applies also to cohabitants and will be amended to cover same sex relationships by the Domestic Violence, Crime and Victims Act 2004. Bailey-Harris and Wilson (2003 p 578) contend that the exclusion of same sex relationships renders the current law susceptible to a declaration of incompatibility under the Human Rights Act 1998.

The effect of Sch 7 is that the court can make an order transferring a tenancy, whether sole or joint (para 6, Sch 7), including a tenancy of local authority housing. The power to do so exists provided the property is or was the matrimonial home (or, when amended, civil partnership home) or in the case of cohabitants, the home in which they lived together (para 4, Sch 7). It exists in addition to the courts' powers to make occupation orders (para 15(2), Sch 7). It is useful in cases of violence, enabling the court to transfer the right to occupy the home from the abuser, or the abuser and victim jointly, to the victim alone.

However, the remedy provided under Sch 7 is available only once the relationship is over and in the case of spouses (or civil partners), legal proceedings are instituted (para 2(2), Sch 7); the court is empowered to make an order at any time after a decree of divorce (on amendment on dissolution of civil partnership), judicial separation or nullity. In relation to cohabitants, the court may make an order transferring a tenancy if they cease to cohabit (para 3(2), Sch 7). It is, therefore, not appropriate in all cases.

An alternative course of action is available if the parties are joint tenants of a local authority property: the housing authority may agree to rehouse one of them if he or she terminates the joint tenancy by giving notice to quit (*Hammersmith & Fulham London Borough Council v Monk* [1991] 3 WLR 1144; *Harrow London Borough Council v Johnstone* [1997] 1 FLR 887; *Bater v Greenwich London Borough Council* [1999] 4 All ER 944).

to make their separation formal, the law makes provision for an order currently termed a 'judicial separation' decree.

The Matrimonial Causes Act 1973 provides in Section 17 that a petition for a decree may be made on the grounds of the existence of any of the facts mentioned in Section 1(2).[190]

The Civil Partnership Act 2004 also provides for judicial separation,[191] allowing either civil partner to make an application for a separation order on the ground that certain facts exist.[192] Further, the court shall grant a decree of judicial separation (under the MCA; a separation order under the CPA) if it is satisfied on the evidence of any of those facts and that there are no children to whom consideration of a s 8 (Children Act 1989) order ought to be given.[193] The court is not concerned to establish that the marriage (or the civil partnership) has broken down irretrievably.[194] The same provisions for the special procedure in considering petitions apply in separation cases as in divorce cases.[195] In separation cases under either the MCA or the CPA, just as in divorce or dissolution cases, there are provisions also relating to the solicitor's and the court's exploration of reconciliation[196] and the court's acceptance of negotiated settlements.[197] Unlike in the case of divorce (or dissolution), the petition (or application) is not barred during the first year of marriage (or civil partnership), and the decree (or order) takes effect immediately on being granted. The main difference between a judicial separation and a divorce or dissolution is, of course, that the marriage or civil partnership continues. This obviously has implications for matters such as pensions and other financial obligations.[198]

If one is not concerned to maintain one's legal status as a husband, wife or civil partner, for religious reasons for instance, why would one seek a judicial separation? Relief such as the protection from violence and occupation of the home with which Eve is concerned may be granted without a judicial separation. However there are certain financial remedies which only become available once a petition is filed and a decree granted. Financial provision orders, property adjustment orders or orders for the sale of property under the Matrimonial Causes Act 1973 can only be made after a decree of separation,[199] and under the Civil Partnership Act only on making a separation order.[200] Another reason one might wish to petition for judicial separation is that proof of the fact in the separation proceedings may be relied upon in subsequent divorce or

---

[190] S 17(1). The facts are adultery, behaviour, desertion, two-year separation with consent and five-year separation without consent. For interpretation of these facts see ch 14.

[191] S 37(d) CPA

[192] S 56(1). The facts are behaviour, two-year separation with consent, desertion and five-year separation without consent. It is likely that the court will interpret these facts as it did under the MCA 1973.

[193] S 17(2) MCA; s 56(3) CPA

[194] S 17(2) MCA; s 56(2) CPA

[195] See ch 14.

[196] S 17(3) MCA referring to s 6 MCA; s 42 CPA.

[197] S 17(3) MCA referring to s.7 MCA; s.43 CPA.

[198] Although the provisions relating to devolution of estates on intestacy do not apply if one spouse dies while living separate under an order: s 18(1) or one civil partner dies while separated from the other (s 57 CPA).

[199] Although interim orders are available once the petition is filed, and s 27 provides that maintenance may be ordered in situations where one spouse has failed to provide reasonably for the other: see ch 5. Further, one may wish to rely upon the more limited jurisdiction of the magistrates in the DPMCA 1978 to make financial provision orders.

[200] Schedule 5 of the CPA 2004 makes provision for financial relief, including property adjustment orders and sale of property orders, that corresponds to provision made in connection with marriages under the MCA 1973; schedule 6 makes provision that corresponds with relief available under the Domestic Proceedings and Magistrates' Courts Act 1978 in connection with marriages. See s 72 CPA.

dissolution proceedings.[201] This means that Eve may obtain financial relief along with a judicial separation in the hope that a reconciliation is possible, but leave the way open to petition for divorce on the same ground if all hope fails (Conway 1997; Lowe and Douglas 1998 p 258).

> **Q** Why do you think parties may not obtain a separation order by consent rather than having to establish one of the specified facts?

## VIII. CONCLUSION

Eve may wish to invoke the criminal law as Albert has assaulted her. Any future assaults or even harassment will also constitute offences. However, Eve wants to keep Albert out of the home and, to achieve this objective, she will need to look to the civil law. She should apply to court both for a non-molestation order and an occupation order. If she is afraid to return to the home, even under the protection of court orders, because she fears that Albert will pursue her and subject her to violence or harassment if he knows of her whereabouts, she will have to find alternative accommodation. Ultimately, however, she may wish to institute separation proceedings, if not divorce proceedings, so that property[202] and financial matters can be permanently resolved.[203]

### FURTHER READING AND SELECTED RECENT REFERENCES

R BIRD, *Domestic Violence: The New Law: Part IV of the Family Law Act 1996* (Bristol, Jordan, 1996a).

M HUMPHRIES, 'Occupation Orders Revisited' (2001) *Fam Law* 542.

J McCULLOCH, 'Protection Before Punishment' (2004) *Fam Law* 64.

F KAGANAS, '*B v B (Occupation Order)* and *Chalmers v Johns*: Occupation Orders Under the Family Law Act 1996' (1999) 11 *CFLQ* 193.

T LAWSON-CRUTTENDEN and N ADDISON, *Blackstone's Guide to the Protection From Harassment Act 1997* (London, Blackstone, 1997).

---

[201] S 4 MCA; s 46(3) CPA
[202] This could involve a reallocation of property or a transfer of a tenancy.
[203] Although an occupation order if Eve is a 'person entitled' can potentially be indefinite.

# 13

# Making Ends Meet

**Q** 24-year-old Cathy and her 4-year-old son James moved last year to London from her parents' home in Blackpool. After completing her studies, Cathy, a newly graduated trained librarian, is now having difficulty finding a job which would accommodate her responsibility for James. She approaches the local authority enquiring about housing while she continues looking. Since having to move out of accommodation provided by the college a few weeks ago, she and James have been sleeping on the sofa in a friend's studio flat. The friend has told Cathy that she is finding the crowded conditions difficult and that she and James should find somewhere else to stay by the end of the month. Cathy also approaches a Jobcentre for financial help and help finding employment and is told to expect to receive a letter from the Child Support Agency requesting details about James' father. Cathy is quite distressed about her housing situation, and the advice about the CSA, as she wants to keep Rob, James' father, out of the picture. She and James haven't seen him for 3 years. She wants to know what help she and James are entitled to receive.

Cathy is one of a growing number of never-married lone mothers.[1] The broad question raised in this scenario is who has responsibility for helping her and James. Again, we can reflect on the roles of the private family and the public sector in answering this question.

In the private sphere, we could suggest that Cathy's parents ought to take some responsibility for her and their grandson, James. There is no legal obligation upon grandparents to support grandchildren or on parents to support their adult children, however.[2] Any assistance Cathy's parents give to her, then, including accommodation, is entirely voluntary. Cathy may, however, obtain financial assistance from the state and from James's father. She may also receive assistance in finding housing, a suitable job and childcare for James. We shall deal with each of these sources of help for Cathy, starting with child support.

Cathy was never married to James' father Rob, and so he owes no legal duty to contribute to Cathy's support. He does, however, have a legal obligation to contribute to James' support. This obligation can be found in the Children Act 1989[3] and the Child Support Act 1991 (CSA),[4] both of which place responsibility upon parents to support children. It is the Child Support Act that applies to Cathy's and James' situation, how-

---

[1] According to the General Household Survey 2003 (ONS 2005, p 2), never married lone mothers accounted for 1% of households in 1971 and 11% in 2003. See also ch 3.
[2] The position under the Poor Laws was different. See MacLean and Eekelaar (1997) pp 41–44 and ch 5.
[3] Sch I s 1.
[4] S 1(1).

ever, because Cathy, James and Rob meet the definitions of 'person with care',[5] 'qualifying child'[6] and 'non-resident parent'[7] respectively, and the jurisdiction given to the Child Support Agency (CSA) to make a maintenance calculation ousts the jurisdiction of the court to do so.[8] Either Cathy or Rob may apply to the CSA for a maintenance calculation,[9] but James himself may not do so. Cathy's application for benefit is treated as an automatic application to the CSA. Where a decision under the Child Support Act 1991 involves the exercise of discretion, the officer of the CSA must have regard to James' welfare; indeed to the welfare of any child likely to be affected by his or her decision.[10] Before we examine how the Act will apply to Cathy and James, let us look at its provenance.

## I. THE CHILD SUPPORT ACT 1991: BACKGROUND[11]

In chapter 5 we saw that one of the policies driving the Child Support Act was the privatisation of individual responsibility for child support and we examined the role that that policy generally, and private maintenance in particular, play in the broader social context of support for a family's overall welfare. In this section we shall focus more closely on the way the Child Support Act operates as between parents and between parents and children.

Historically, it was a father's obligation to support his legitimate children, but, as there was no procedure in private law to enforce that obligation until the 19th century, it remained in practice more of a moral one.[12] Although the Poor Law Amendment Act 1834 allowed magistrates to make financial orders against non-married fathers, those affiliation proceedings were difficult procedures for the woman concerned (Finer and McGregor 1974; Barton and Douglas 1995 p 197). In the period immediately before the CSA 1991 came into effect in 1993, a parent of a child who was not able to agree the

---

[5] S 3(3) reads:

A person is a 'person with care' in relation to any child, if he is a person–
(a) with whom the child has his home;
(b) who usually provides day to day care for the child (whether exclusively or in conjunction with any other person); and
(c) who does not fall within a prescribed category of person.

[6] S 3(1) reads:

A child is a 'qualifying child' if–
(a) one of his parents is in relation to him, a non-resident parent; or
(b) both of his parents are in relation to him, non-resident parent.

[7] S 3(2) reads:

The parent of any child is a 'non-resident parent' in relation to him, if–
(a) that parent is not living in thsame household with the child; and
(b) the child has his home with a person who is in relation to him, a person with care.

[8] S 8(3).
[9] S 4(1).
[10] S 2.
[11] See also ch 5.
[12] The Divorce and Matrimonial Causes Act 1857 was the first authority for a court to award maintenance for children of divorced or separated parents. See Finer and McGregor (1974); Barton and Douglas (1995); Cretney (2003a); and MacLean and Eekelaar (1997) on the history of child support. See also the dissenting opinion of Baroness Hale in *R v Secretary of State for Work and Pensions ex parte Kehoe* [2005] UKHL 48.

issue with the other parent could apply for support from the other parent under the
Domestic Proceedings and Magistrates' Courts Act 1978,[13] the Children Act 1989[14] and
the Matrimonial Causes Act 1973.[15] The court reserved a wide discretion for itself in
making these awards, and Eekelaar's study of registrars reported in 1991 that one half
of them felt they did not need to use any sort of guidelines in making their awards; they
felt it was a matter of 'experience' (1991b pp 94–96). The system was criticised as being
'unnecessarily fragmented, uncertain in its results, slow and ineffective' (*Children Come
First* 1990 p 1). The other problem with the system of child support identified by the
government was the dramatic increase in the numbers of lone parent families in receipt
of state benefits (p 1).

Clarke, Craig and Glendinning summarise the situation in these rather understated
terms:

> There was certainly justifiable concern over the efficiency and equity of the previous mainte-
> nance system. The 1980s saw a trend towards 'clean break' divorce, in which the parent with
> day-to-day responsibility for children was awarded full rights to the family home. This was off-
> set by nominal or token cash payments towards the ongoing maintenance of children. As a
> consequence growing numbers of lone parents received little or no maintenance from former
> partners towards their children's care and increasingly relied on social security benefits for the
> whole of their day-to-day income. Considerable differences in the treatment of lone parent
> families resulted from the adversarial nature of negotiations between former partners, the dis-
> cretion which was widely used to determine maintenance awards, the absence of regular
> up-rating of maintenance payments in line with inflation or improvements in a former partner's
> earnings, and the apparent ease with which former partners avoided compliance with court
> maintenance orders. The courts also tended to protect the living standards of 'second' families
> of a former partner in assessing maintenance, whereas the majority of 'first families'—lone
> mothers and their children—lived on means-tested benefits. All these concerns added to argu-
> ments within and outside government (Dennis and Erdos 1992; Davies 1993), that action was
> needed to enforce the responsibilities of *both* parents to provide adequate financial support for
> their children. (1996 p 8)

The White Paper on which the 1991 Act was based proposed to remedy the problems as
follows:

> 2.1 The Government proposes to establish a system of child maintenance which will be equally
> available to any person seeking maintenance for the benefit of a child which will:
> —ensure that parents honour their moral and legal responsibility to maintain their own chil-
> dren whenever they can afford to do so. It is right that other taxpayers should help to maintain
> children when the children's own parents, despite their own best efforts, do not have enough
> resources to do so themselves. That will continue to be the case. But it is not right that taxpay-
> ers, who include other families, should shoulder that responsibility instead of parents who are
> able to do it themselves;
> —recognise that where a liable parent has formed a second family and has further natural chil-
> dren, he is liable to maintain all his own children. A fair and reasonable balance has to be
> struck between the interests of the children of a first family and the children of a second;

---

[13] Ss 1 and 2. The Act is applicable to married parents only and gives the court power to order unsecured
periodical payments and lump sum orders only.
[14] S15 and Sch 1. The CA 1989 applies to all parents, guardians and persons with residence orders, married
or unmarried.
[15] Ss 21 to 24A, as amended by the Family Law Act 1996. A married parent can apply under this Act on
divorce or separation.

—produce consistent and predictable results so that people in similar financial circumstances will pay similar amounts of maintenance, and so that people will know in advance what their maintenance obligations are going to be;

—enable maintenance to be decided in a fair and reasonable way which reduces the scope for its becoming a contest between the parents to the detriment of the interests of the children;

—produce maintenance payments which are realistically related to the costs of caring for a child;

—allow for maintenance payments to be reviewed regularly so that changes in circumstances can be taken into account automatically;

—recognise that both parents have a legal responsibility to maintain their children;

—ensure that parents meet the cost of their children's maintenance whenever they can without removing the parents' own incentives to work, and to go on working;

—enable caring parents who wish to work to do so as soon as they feel ready and able;

—provide an efficient and effective service to the public which ensures that:

(a) maintenance is paid regularly and on time so that it provides a reliable income for the caring parent and the children and

(b) produces maintenance quickly so that the habit of payment is established early and is not compromised by early arrears;

—avoid the children and their caring parent becoming dependent on Income Support whenever this is possible and, where it is not possible, to minimise the period of dependence.

*(Children Come First* 1990 para 2.1 pp 5–6)

The resulting Child Support Act 1991 was intended also to 'effect a cultural change in attitudes towards maintenance' so that it would no longer be regarded as optional (Keating 1995 p 30). The Act created a formula by which maintenance was to be assessed,[16] an agency and officers to administer the assessments[17] and required all 'persons with care'[18] on state support to co-operate with the Agency or risk a reduction in benefits,[19] while allowing the reduction to be avoided if the Child Support Officer considered that 'there are reasonable grounds for believing that, if she were required to comply, there would be a risk to her or any of her children living with her suffering harm or undue distress as a result of complying'.[20] The Act also removed jurisdiction from the courts to make child support orders where the Child Support Agency has jurisdiction.[21]

The 1991 Act came into effect in April 1993, and difficulties became apparent almost immediately. A series of reports, including the Social Security Select Committee Report

[16] S 11(2); Sch 1. See also Parker (1991) pp 36–48; and Eekelaar (1991b) pp 105–11 for a discussion of different models of child support which could have been employed.

[17] S 11(1), and see also s 13. As a result of 1994 amendments, the Child Support Officer became entitled to make interim assessments: s 12(1) and (1A).

[18] S 3(3): 'A person is a "person with care" in relation to any child, if he is a person—(a) with whom the child has his home; (b) who usually provides day to day care for the child (whether exclusively or in conjunction with any other person); and (c) who does not fall within a prescribed category of persons'. See *C v Secretary of State for Work and Pensions and B* [2002] EWCA Civ 1854; [2003] 1 FLR 829, where being defined as an absent parent or a person with care was not to be considered merely by reference to a family proceedings order, but was considered to be a matter of fact. In this case, the mother had a residence order, the child was in boarding school and the father had roughly shared contact with the child on weekends and during school holidays. The determination should have been based on the level and frequency of care that would have been provided had the child not been in boarding school.

[19] Ss 6 and 46.

[20] S 46(3). On considering the 'risk of harm or undue distress' exemption to the s 6 requirement to co-operate a Child Support Commissioner stated that 'although the risk must be real as opposed to fanciful, the question is not whether the harm or undue distress would actually happen' (Knights 1997 p 121). See also Provan, *et al*, (1996).

[21] S 8(3). See also ch 5.

on the first year of the 1991 Act's operation (HC Social Security Committee 1993) and a second report on operation and proposals for change (HC Social Security Committee 1994) revealed deficiencies in implementation and administration and a lack of public confidence in the scheme. Indeed, the Act was the subject of angry, sometimes violent public reaction, when (mostly) non-resident fathers and their 'new families' objected to the increased levels of maintenance they were ordered to pay and to the formula's disregard for 'clean break' property settlements effected in the past.[22] In addition, lone mothers and their children did not appear to be benefiting from the Act. Clarke, Craig and Glendinning reported on the agency's apparent inability actually to collect maintenance for lone mothers from absent[23] parents (1996 p 16) and found that for none of the 53 lone mothers they interviewed in 1995 did the CSA result in a net gain in income (Clarke, *et al*, 1996 p 23).

> For mothers on income support, the lack of a maintenance disregard meant that any maintenance paid had no effect on their income. Indeed, where mothers were just lifted off income support by maintenance, it might drop them into a 'poverty trap'. For some of the mothers who were themselves on family credit, this entitlement had been reduced because they received higher maintenance, but the latter was rarely paid both regularly and at the correct level. Some mothers preferred to suffer the additional hardships of a benefit penalty rather than face the disruption of the assessment process … . (Clarke, *et al*, 1996 pp 23–24)

In many cases these financial losses were compounded by indirect losses, particularly of gifts of cash from fathers for the benefit of their children. Further:

> [t]here was no evidence that the Act had had the effect of encouraging any lone mothers to enter employment or to increase their hours of work so that they moved off income support onto family credit. This appeared to be partly because other obstacles to work, such as child care, were a more immediate issue, but also partly because the Agency was unable to guarantee the payment of maintenance to those not on income support. (Clarke, *et al*, 1996 p 24)

Non-resident parents, who are overwhelmingly fathers, objected to the act as well. Many claimed that the detailed calculations required by the Act insufficiently took account of their new family responsibilities and they objected also to the element in the calculation designated to meet the costs of child care, believing that it amounted to support for the caretaking parent herself. They felt generally that the formula was inflexible, failing to take account adequately of debts, liabilities and agreements assumed after the breakdown of the relationship.[24] As a result of criticism from many sources, changes to the administration of the Act were made after its first year of operation which eased absent parents' transition to making higher payments and raised their 'protected income' level to take into account their 'new' families.[25] The second Select Committee report also led to a Government White Paper in 1995 proposing further changes to the Act. *Improving Child Support* (1995) indicated that the government supported the principles behind the child support scheme of the 1991 Act, but proposed further changes to the formula for assessing maintenance by raising the absent parent's protected income level more

---

[22] See, on the public reaction to the CSA 1991, Collier (1994); Wallbank (1997); Diduck (1995).

[23] The legislation prior to 2000 referred to non-resident parents as 'absent' parents. This terminology is used in the literature of the time as well.

[24] See generally, Diduck (2003) ch 7; Wallbank (1997); Bradshaw, *et al*, (1999).

[25] Child Support (Miscellaneous Amendments and Transitional Provisions) Regs 1994 SI 1994/227. See also chs 5 and 15.

dramatically, by raising the level of exempt income for an absent parent, and for taking into consideration, in certain circumstances, previous 'clean break' settlements.[26] In addition, the White Paper resulted in the Child Support Act 1995 which amended the 1991 Act to allow for discretionary 'departure directions' to be made (allowing departure from the formula) in appropriate circumstances on application by either of the parties[27] and for introducing a whole new scheme whereby the person with care in receipt of income support (IS) or income-based Jobseeker's Allowance (IJSA) would build up 'credits' of £5 per week, towards a maximum £1000 lump sum, which she would be eligible to redeem on taking up employment of over 16 hours per week.[28]

It could be argued that the majority of changes made to the scheme in 1995 improved the situation of absent parents, while doing relatively little for persons with care. Nonetheless, a report published in the *Observer* newspaper in 1997[29] indicated that absent parents continued to ignore Child Support Agency payment orders on a wide scale, including almost total non-compliance with interim maintenance assessments which are imposed when required information is not provided.

The policy underlying the child support scheme is based upon the individualisation and privatisation of responsibility for children. Although children's welfare was considered briefly in *Children Come First* (1990), it is arguable that alleviating child poverty was not the main impetus behind the scheme,[30] and it is significant that the welfare of the child is not a factor in determining child support.

Q Recall that earlier proposals for reform suggested by the Finer Committee (1974) envisaged a degree of state responsibility for assisting one parent families living in poverty. The main features of the 'guaranteed maintenance allowance' proposed by the committee were to provide a non-contributory fixed benefit to all one-parent families which would substitute for maintenance payments. Maintenance would be collected by the authority administering the allowance (Finer 1974 vol I para 5.104 pp 295–96).

Compare and contrast the CSA 1991 provisions with Finer's proposal. Which do you prefer?

In 1998 the then new government proposed to amend the CSA further. As part of its 'modernisation' project, it proposed a complete overhaul of the system while leaving its basic framework intact. It published a Consultation Paper (Department of Social Security 1998) which emphasised that parents must take their responsibilities seriously.[31]

---

[26] SI 1995/1045, which took effect from April 1995 applied a 'broad brush provision for capital and property and capital settlements' where a 'qualifying transfer' (ie, before 5 April 1993 pursuant to a court order) had been made. The Child Support (Miscellaneous Amendments) Regs 1996 also amended earlier regs to ensure that an absent parent was always to be left with at least 70% of his net income after maintenance was deducted.

[27] Ss 28A–F and Sch 4B The Child Support Departure Direction and Consequential Amendments Regs SI 1996/2907 (amended further by SI/1998/58) implements the 'departures' scheme that was provided for by the CSA 1995. Applications for departures from the formula were allowed on 3 categories of grounds: special expenses (including high travel to work costs); property or capital transfers; and 'additional cases' (which included unreasonably high housing costs for absent parents). In all cases, the CSO was to decide whether it was 'just and equitable' to give a departure direction and take into account, among other things, whether making a direction would be likely to result in the absent parent or parent with care ceasing to work.

[28] S 10 was put into effect by the Social Security (Child Maintenance Bonus) Regs SI 1996/3195 and came into effect in April 1997. See also SI 1997/454, SI 1998/563, chs 3 and 5.

[29] 15 June 1997.

[30] See Eekelaar (1991b) for different ideological foundations of child support schemes, and ch 3.

[31] See Diduck (2003) ch 7.

Conceiving of child support as a personal responsibility was not new, but the 1999 White Paper which followed (DSS 1999) also framed the issue in language that included children's welfare and rights. The Prime Minister's Foreword made this agenda clear:

> [N]o one should be able to duck their responsibilities for their families and their children.
>
> Over half of all children living in poverty in Britain today live in single-parent families. If every absent parent paid the maintenance they owe, more than a million children would face a brighter future. Not only because they would be financially better off, but when a child knows the non-resident parent is still helping to pay for their food, clothes and shoes, they understandably feel more secure and more loved. (DSS 1999 p 2)

The government recognised the failures of the system in achieving behavioural change: 'It has not in practice helped responsible parents—or forced those who had no intention of supporting their children to act responsibly' (DSS 1999 ch 1 para 2). Further, it failed to benefit children on income support because of the pound for pound reduction in benefit (para 3) and, overall, only 40% of non-resident parents were actually paying all that was owed (*ibid*).[32] The fault for all of these failures was seen to lie primarily in the complicated calculation of maintenance assessments.

> CSA staff spend on average 90% of their time making assessments, keeping them up to date and making initial payment arrangements. Only 10% of the Agency's resources are left for chasing up the many parents who are behind with their maintenance payments. And, since parents have to supply information before maintenance can be arranged, the process is too easily delayed—or derailed altogether—by parents who are unwilling to cooperate fully.
>
> (DSS 1999 ch 1 para 8)

The result was the Child Support, Pensions and Social Security Act 2000, and as far as child support is concerned, its main features are a simplified formula for calculating maintenance liability, introduction of a child maintenance premium which allows families in receipt of benefit to keep up to £10 per week of any maintenance paid before their benefits are reduced, and tougher sanctions for parents who avoid their 'responsibilities'.[33] The 2000 Act does not repeal the 1991 one, but uses it as a framework for the new provisions.[34]

Based upon the assumptions that '[w]hen parents live together, they normally share family expenses' (DSS 1999 ch 2 para 2), they expect to meet their children's needs first (para 3) and they spend roughly 30% of their income on a child (para 5), the level of child maintenance owed by a non-resident parent is now set at 15% of his net income for

---

[32] Enforcement of payments and of arrears remains a serious issue. It is hoped that the new enforcement mechanisms will assist the CSA in timeously enforcing payments. If the person with care experiences undue delay in the Agency's taking action, however, she may not personally enforce arrears. This bar on a client's ability personally to enforce arrears is said to be the essence of the Child Support Act, meaning that she has no right in domestic law to do so. Consequently, the right under Article 6 of the ECHR to access to a court to enforce one's rights at law is not engaged. See *R v Secretary of State for Work and Pensions ex parte Kehoe* [2004] EWCA Civ 225. Baroness Hale in dissent, held that the right to obtain maintenance is the right of the child, that the Child Support Act 1991 charged the Agency with securing that right on behalf of the child, and that the Agency therefore had an obligation to do so in compliance with Article 6 ECHR The House of Lords upheld, for different reasons, the decision of the Court of Appeal [2004] EWCA Civ 225; [2004] 1 FLR 1132.

[33] In order to collect payments or arrears, the CSA may obtain a deduction from earnings order (CSA 1991 s 31). To collect arrears, after obtaining a liability order (CSA 1991 s 33), the CSA may levy a distress warrant and the defaulter's goods can be sold (CSA 1991 s 35); register a county court judgment (CSA 1991 s 36); or commit the defaulter to prison or disqualify him from driving for a specified period of time (CSA 1991 s 39A; 40 and s 40A).

[34] For detail of the mechanics of the Act and commentary upon it, see Diduck (2003); Pirrie (2002a); (2002b); (2002c); Wikeley (2000a); (2000b); Wikeley, *et al*, (2001).

one child, 20% for two children, and 25% for three or more children.[35] A non-resident parent's net income is his income remaining after deduction of national insurance, tax and pension contributions, as well as a deduction of 15%, 20% and 25% as above for any children with whom he is currently living in a new relationship. This assessment may be reduced further if the qualifying child stays with the non-resident parent for more than 52 nights per year. That is, if the child stays with the payer 52–103 nights per year, or 1 or 2 nights per week, his payments are reduced by $^1/_7$, if 104–155 nights by $^2/_7$, if 156–174 nights by $^3/_7$ and if 175 nights or more by $^1/_2$. It was hoped that the ease and transparency of the much simplified calculation would increase compliance and collection rates and that the linking of assessments to overnight contact or 'shared care' would increase both those rates and incidences of shared care (DSS 1999 ch 7 paras 11–12).

Let us consider the implications of these changes. First, in the light of the research that illustrates a gender difference in how family income is allocated and parental roles are played out, it could be argued that the assumptions both about how 'intact' families allocate income and that this allocation will continue on separation are unrealistic (chapter 5). Because the primary responsibility for child rearing tends to fall upon women, they are usually more in tune with the day to day financial requirements of child care (Neale and Smart 2002 pp 191–95) and exhibit stronger preferences for spending to benefit children (Pahl 1989; Ringen and Halpin 1997; Lister, *et al*, 1999). Further, because the consequences for many families of the gendered division of child care is that for fathers, child care consisted mainly of days out or 'fun' times with their children, they may remain happy to buy large items of clothing for school, pay for treats or for one-off presents, but may balk at knowing about or paying for the day to day 'maintenance costs' of child care (Diduck 2003 p 168; see also Bradshaw, *et al*, 1999). To many, child support, even under the new regime, is still something to 'beat'.

Research in 2002 into how parents perceived the then forthcoming provisions indicated that the formula's disregard of the income of the person with care was seen as a source of injustice by non-resident parents (Gillespie 2002). In contrast, they thought that the deduction for shared care might encourage them to think about seeking more staying contact with their children (*ibid*). As Herring (2004) puts it, 'a one-seventh reduction in child support for the cost of a burger and a video is a bargain' (p 178 fn 133), while the person with care's financial responsibility is not significantly reduced if the child spends one or two nights away from home. Whether the link drawn between staying contact and support will benefit children is open to debate.

Procedurally, the emphasis remains upon coercing responsible behaviour; according to government, the new provisions are designed to help responsible parents and force irresponsible ones to act responsibly (DSS 1999 ch 1 para 2). Responsible non-resident parents pay and responsible persons with care seek payment. The government reiterated its view that 'applying for child support is not a matter of choice for parents on income support' (DSS 1999 ch 4 para 21), and now the child support claim flows directly from the benefits claim. Even parents who do not receive benefit are encouraged to use the CSA. While they do not have to apply to the Agency and can negotiate their own

---

[35] Sch 1 Child Support Act 1991. This is the basic rate and is assessed if the non-resident parent's income is between £200.00 and £2000.00 per week. £2000.00 is the maximum assessable income. If his income is between £100.00 and £200.00 per week, a reduced rate applies. If he earns less than £100.00 per week or receives benefit or allowance, a standard £5.00 per week payment is required. Exceptional claims for costs or for amounts in excess of the maximum can be made to a special tribunal.

agreement, either parent may apply to the CSA for a reassessment of the maintenance one year after the agreement has been registered in the court or made into a consent order by the court.

Finally, while much of the language of the White Paper (DSS 1999) was framed in terms of children's welfare and rights, welfare was not prioritised in the new legislation, and children's rights were not adverted to at all.[36]

The new scheme was to come into effect in 2001, but difficulties with implementing it lead to successive delays, and it eventually came on track, for new cases only, in March 2003. As at October 2004, there were about 1.2 million cases under the two schemes—old and new (HC Work and Pensions Committee 2005 para 13). Government optimism about the efficiency of the new formula soon dissipated, however; the CSA was still thought to be failing its clients. In 2004 a Parliamentary Inquiry was launched so that Parliament could be 'properly and fully informed of the alarming situation' (HC Work and Pensions Committee 2005 para 30). The resulting report called the CSA a 'failing organisation which is currently in crisis' (*ibid*, Report Highlights, p 3). It highlighted service failures to persons with care in the areas of delay, poor communication and inaccurate information provided to clients by staff, inaccurate maintenance calculations, failure to chase up arrears, lack of enforcement activity, and failing to pass on payments to clients (para 22). From the perspective of the non-resident parent, things were no better. The inquiry found deductions from earnings orders inaccurately applied, arrears recovered at unrealistic rates, enforcement action taken without adequate consideration, and general problems concerning correspondence being mislaid (para 23). No ministerial targets were achieved (para 30). Government, however, maintains its faith in the legislation and in the Agency, and, while acknowledging that 'the early experience of the new scheme has been 'unsatisfactory', it hopes that a new Chief Executive and improved IT arrangements will result in the change that is necessary (Select Committee on Work and Pensions First Special Report 2005).

> **Q** Review the material both supporting and criticising the Child Support Acts, and
> their effect upon the day-to-day material conditions of the person with care, the
> non-resident parent and any new families these parents have.[37] Review also
> the effect of these Acts on the continued privatisation of families and the role of
> the state (chapters 3 and 5).[38] How, if at all, would you reform the child support
> system further?

## II. THE CHILD SUPPORT ACTS: APPLICATION[39]

As soon as Cathy applies for either income-based Jobseeker's Allowance or Income Support, an application will be made to the Child Support Agency. Because she has been a full time student until recently, she is likely to apply for one of these benefits, as it is unlikely that she will qualify for contribution-based Jobseeker's Allowance (see below).

---

[36] See on maintenance as the right of the child, the dissenting opinion of Baroness Hale in *R v Secretary of State for Work and Pensions ex parte Kehoe*, above.

[37] See, eg, Burgoyne and Millar (1994); Collier (1994); Boden and Childs (1996); Wallbank (1997).

[38] See Diduck (1995); Clarke, *et al*, (1995). On history see Lewis (1991); Bastin (1996); Eichler (1990).

[39] See also ch 15.

Unless she can show that she or James will suffer harm or undue distress, she is required to co-operate with the CSA by providing information about herself and James and by providing information about Rob, James's father. If she refuses without good cause to do so her benefits will be cut. If Cathy does not know how or where to contact Rob, the CSA can search for him through other government departments such as the Driver and Vehicle Licensing Agency, the Prison Service or Inland Revenue. While Cathy does not have to provide information about her finances, on being contacted by the CSA Rob must provide his employment details, including income and pension contributions as well as details about bank accounts and about any other children with whom he lives. It is a criminal offence for him to refuse to provide this information or knowingly to provide false information.[40] If he delays or withholds information, the Agency can order a rate of payment based on an average salary. It was hoped originally that a maintenance calculation would be able to be made four to six weeks from the initial application, but recent evidence indicates that throughput is now at 15–22 weeks (HC Work and Pensions Committee 2005 para 78). Rob's liability for maintenance begins as soon as the Agency contacts him, so he may wish to begin to make voluntary payments in order to avoid building up arrears before the final calculation is made. These can be made directly to Cathy, or through the CSA.

If Rob disputes James' parentage, the CSA may still make a maintenance calculation against him if it can presume that he is the father. The situations in which such a presumption arises are listed in Section 26 of the Child Support Act 1991. For Cathy's purposes, the relevant ones are if he is registered as James' father; if a scientific test shows that he is the father; if he refuses to take such a scientific test; or if he has been declared to be the father in other proceedings.[41] Scientific tests must include tests of Cathy and James as well, and if Cathy refuses to take the test or to make James available for it, her benefits may be cut.

If everyone cooperates with the agency, Cathy should begin to receive payments for James' support at an amount (roughly) equal to 15% of Rob's net income. Rob can pay by direct debit, standing order or a voluntary deduction from earnings order and the CSA will then pass on the payments to Cathy by credit to her bank account. The CSA will take into account the wishes of both parents to decide how maintenance will be paid. They may be encouraged to take advantage of Maintenance Direct, a new service in which payments are made privately and directly between the parties, but are monitored by the CSA. Finally, if Cathy begins to receive income-based JSA or IS, she will only be entitled to keep up to £10.00 per week of any maintenance paid.

If Cathy is successful in obtaining employment which provides her with sufficient income to live without income support or income-based jobseeker's allowance, the Child Support Agency will not *require* her to make an application. In such a case, she has that option, but she may, if she wishes, make a private agreement with James's father regarding child support. She may then register that agreement with the court in order to obtain the court's assistance with its enforcement, but even then she or Rob will be at liberty after one year to apply for a maintenance calculation by the CSA.

**Q** If she is not required to do so, would you advise Cathy to apply for a CSA maintenance calculation? Why or why not?

---

[40] S 14A Child Support Act 1991.
[41] See eg, *Secretary for Work and Pensions v Jones* [2003] EWHC 2163; [2004] 1 FLR 282.

## III. STATE SUPPORT[42]

As Cathy is unemployed and has no income she is entitled to some assistance from the state both financially and in finding employment. As we have seen (chapters 3 and 5), the basic state provisions for people with no income or on low income are Income Support and Jobseeker's Allowance. Entitlement to Income Support can be found in the Social Security Contributions and Benefits Act 1992[43] and related regulations and entitlement to both contribution-based (CJSA)[44] and income-based jobseeker's allowance (IJSA)[45] in the Jobseekers Act 1995.

No one can claim both JSA and IS. Assuming she has been out of work while a student, Cathy is not entitled to claim contribution-based jobseeker's allowance because she cannot satisfy the contribution conditions set out in Section 2 of the Jobseekers Act 1995.[46] On the face of it, however, Cathy may be entitled to claim IJSA. She is capable of work, available for work and actively seeking work. On making a claim, Cathy will attend an interview at which time she will get information about jobs and assistance with filling in her forms. She will be required to make a Jobseeker's Agreement with her adviser. The agreement will include details of the type of work she wants, her availability for it and the steps both she and the Jobcentre will take to help her find it. These requirements are strictly enforced; no benefit will be paid unless an agreement is reached, Cathy attends regular (usually every two weeks) meetings with her advisor and is taking active steps to find employment.[47] The amount she will receive is the same as that which she would receive through Income Support, and because Cathy is a new claimant (that is, a post April 2004 claimant) it will not include any family premiums. Rather, she will be eligible to claim Child Tax Credit which includes family and child elements.[48]

---

[42] See also chs 3 and 5 and Wikeley (2002).
[43] S 124(1).
[44] S 1 establishes general entitlement:

> 1—(1) An allowance, to be known as jobseeker's allowance, shall be payable in accordance with the provisions of this Act.
> (2) Subject to the provisions of this Act, a claimant is entitled to a jobseeker's allowance if he—
>   (a)  is available for employment;
>   (b)  has entered into a jobseeker's agreement which remains in force;
>   (c)  is actively seeking employment;
>   (d)  satisfies either—
>       (i)   the conditions set out in section 2 [contribution based conditions]; or
>       (ii)  the conditions set out in section 3 [income-based conditions];
>   (e)  is not engaged in remunerative work;
>   (f)  is capable of work;
>   (g)  is not receiving relevant education;
>   (h)  is under pensionable age;
>   (i)  is in Great Britain.
>
> S 2 establishes the contribution-based conditions.

[45] S 3 establishes the income-based conditions.
[46] Basically, she must have made National Insurance Contributions in respect of one of the immediately preceding two years.
[47] There is provision for reduced benefits to be paid if regular IJSA cannot be paid if, among other reasons, one makes one's self unavailable for work, fails to agree a Jobseeker's Agreement or is not actively seeking work. Hardship provision will be paid after a two week waiting period unless one is in a vulnerable group in which case it will be paid on the next regularly scheduled payment date. One is a member of a vulnerable group if one or one's partner is pregnant or cares for a child or for someone who is long-term disabled, for example.
[48] See discussion in chs 3 and 5.

Because Cathy wants to find a job as a Librarian, she may wish to take advantage of the help that her advisor and the Jobseeker's agreement will give her. If she is not able to find suitable childcare for James while she looks for work and attends at all her required interviews, however, she may not be considered to be 'available for work' or to be 'actively seeking work', and thus not eligible for IJSA at all. In that case, she may claim Income Support. Because as a lone parent of a child under the age of 16 she is exempt from the JSA requirements actively to seek work, she will not need to attend the Jobcentre for regular appointments. When she makes her claim for IS she will, however, have to attend a work-focused interview (or WFI, also known as a Personal Advisor Meeting).[49] The WFI itself is required, but taking up work is not. The interview is designed to encourage lone parents to work[50] and must be repeated regularly, usually every six months. If she refuses without good cause to attend the WFI, her benefit claim, if new, will be withdrawn, and if ongoing, will be cut.

An application for IS will also make Cathy eligible to join the New Deal for Lone Parents.[51] Because the goal of this programme is to help lone parents into work, it provides financial and other incentives, including assistance with childcare, which might be beneficial to Cathy. Finally, while on IS (or IJSA) Cathy is also entitled to claim housing benefit[52] to cover rent, council tax benefit[53] and 'passported' benefits such as free prescriptions.

If Cathy is later successful in obtaining employment, she is allowed to earn a small amount per week before her IS, housing benefit (HB) and council tax benefit (CTB) begin to be reduced. If she obtains employment of at least 16 hours per week, she ceases to be eligible for IS (or IJSA, for that matter), but becomes able to claim the Working Tax Credit.[54] The amount of tax credit she would be entitled to would depend upon her income. The tax credit includes a childcare element to help her pay for 'approved' or 'registered' childcare.

The policy behind the government's 'modernisation' of the welfare system is clear. It is interesting that it is also the same policy that was behind the changes to unemployment benefit and income support made by the Jobseeker's Act in 1995 by the previous government. The aims proposed in the 1994 White Paper *Jobseeker's Allowance* were as follows:

(1) to improve the operation of the labour market by helping people in their search for work, while ensuring that they understand and fulfil the conditions for receipt of benefit;

(2) to secure better value for money for the taxpayer by a streamlined administration, closer targeting on those who need financial support and a regime which more effectively helps people back to work;

(3) to improve the service to unemployed people themselves by a simpler, clearer more consistent benefit structure, and by better service delivery. (para 1.5)

As is noted by other commentators,[55] these objectives reflect a continuing governmental concern with the 'personal motivation' of unemployed people, and places more responsibility upon them actively to seek work, including low paying work. The changes also represent a policy to reduce, in the name of more efficient targeting of resources, both

---

[49] S 2A Social Security Administration Act 1992.
[50] See discussion in ch 3.
[51] See discussion in ch 3.
[52] SSCBA 1992 s 130.
[53] *Ibid,* s 131.
[54] See generally ch 5; and Tax Credits Act 2002.
[55] See, eg, Wikeley (1995) and (2002).

the number of eligible claimants and the actual value of the benefit. While the current government proposals aim to provide 'work for those who can and government support for those who cannot', the list of those who cannot is small and getting smaller (Bennett 2002). Cathy is in a difficult position in the light of these policy imperatives. As a single parent, she is deemed to be the proper caretaker for her child and thus is excused from the requirement to seek work, but at the same time she is encouraged to take on part time or low paying work to supplement the (at least temporary) state assistance she requires to care for James.

**Q** The government states its policy to be one of providing choice for lone parents, so that those who wish to work can do so without remaining in a 'poverty trap' of low wages. Review the policies and initiatives outlined in chapters 3 and 5 and assess the success of their meeting this policy objective from Cathy's perspective.

## IV. CHILD CARE[56]

We noted earlier that Cathy's position is complicated by her role as sole carer of James. She must be able to ensure his welfare while at the same time work outside her home, ideally as a librarian. Full time nursery or pre-school places for 4-year-olds are not now universally available, but part time early years education is. As a part of the Sure Start programme and the National Child Care Strategy, both launched by the government in 1998, children aged 3 and 4 are entitled to five two and one half hour sessions of early education for 33 weeks per year (HM Treasury, *et al*, 2004 para 3.14). As the government has noted, however, this may not be sufficient help for someone like Cathy.

> Although the number of childcare places has increased significantly since 1997, some parents are still not able to find the childcare that they need. Places for pre-school children are more expensive than for school-aged children, and places for school-aged children are not always available in a way that fits conveniently with the school day and around parents' work patterns.
> (HM Treasury, *et al*, 2004 para 3.17)

> Some parents face problems in co-ordinating different types of provision to fit with each other. For pre-school children, the most frequent problem is being unable to find a childcare place that 'wraps around' the free 12.5 hours per week of early education. Local authorities have an obligation to deliver the free early education places, but they do not have an obligation to provide childcare around this that would help parents who work or train. Too often parents are left to find what childcare provision they can. (*Ibid* para 3.20)

To meet these challenges, Government policy is a long term one. Its stated 'vision' is that by 2010 all families with children under 14 will have access to affordable, flexible high-quality childcare that meets their circumstances (HM Treasury, *et al*, 2004 p 33; ch 3). Until then, however, from Cathy's perspective, free or subsidised places are difficult to find, many being available only to children in need as defined by the Children Act

---

[56] See also chs 3 and 5.

1989.[57] Finally, if her income allows for it, she may be able to pay market rates for nursery places. Her other option is to engage a child-minder or to make alternative arrangements for private, in-home care, while she is at work until James begins attending school full time. Then she may require before and after school care, which currently is provided only by some schools. Once she obtains work, she will be able to claim Working Tax Credit, which contains a childcare element to cover 70% of her childcare costs[58] and is currently set at a maximum of £175.00 per week.

## V. HOUSING[59]

The local authority has a duty to provide temporary housing[60] for people who are eligible[61] for assistance, unintentionally homeless or threatened with homelessness and who have a priority need. Settled housing is allocated through the local authority housing allocation scheme.[62]

The Housing Act 1996, as amended by the Homelessness Act 2002 provides as follows:

193 Duty to persons with priority need who are not homeless intentionally

(1)   This section applies where the local housing authority are satisfied that an applicant is homeless, eligible for assistance and has a priority need, and are not satisfied that he became homeless intentionally.

(2)   Unless the authority refer the application to another local housing authority (see section 198), they shall secure that accommodation is available for occupation by the applicant ... .

195 Duties in case of threatened homelessness

(1)   This section applies where the local housing authority are satisfied that an applicant is threatened with homelessness and is eligible for assistance.

(2)   If the authority—
(a) are satisfied that he has a priority need, and
(b) are not satisfied that he became threatened with homelessness intentionally.
they shall take reasonable steps to secure that accommodation does not cease to be available for his occupation ... .

(3)      Where in pursuance of the duty under subsection (2) the authority secure that accommodation other than that occupied by the applicant when he made his application is available for occupation by him, the provisions of section 193(3) to (9) (period for which duty owed) ... apply ... .

---

[57] If James were considered a 'child in need' the local authority would have a duty to provide care or supervised activities for him after school or in the school holidays (s 18). How the local authority fulfils this duty is left to its discretion. Additionally, para 8, Pt 1, of Sch 2 to the Children Act 1989 sets out other services for children in need, including home help, holidays, travel and recreational activities. James is a 'child in need' if he 'is unlikely to achieve or maintain or to have the opportunity of achieving or maintaining a reasonable standard of health or development without the provision for him of services by a local authority under this Part' (s 17(10)).

[58] Rising, from April 2006, to 80%.

[59] See also ch 3 and 12.

[60] From its own stock or by ensuring that someone else provided accommodation.

[61] See ss 160A(1) and (3); and ODPM (2002) ch 4. See further ch 3 above. The exclusion of those subject to immigration control has been criticised as having the effect of excluding many women fleeing domestic violence.

[62] See Arden and Hunter (2003) para 2.3.

Section 175 contains the definition of homelessness:

> 175 Homelessness and threatened homelessness
>
> (1)  A person is homeless if he has no accommodation available for his occupation, in the United Kingdom or elsewhere, which he—
>      (a) is entitled to occupy by virtue of an interest in it or by virtue of an order of court,
>      (b) has an express or implied licence to occupy, or
>      (c) occupies as a residence by virtue of any enactment or rule of law giving him the right to remain in occupation or restricting the right of another person to recover possession.
> (2)  a person is also homeless if he has accommodation but—
>      (a) he cannot secure entry to it, or
>      (b) it consists of a moveable structure, vehicle or vessel designed or adapted for human habitation and there is no place where he is entitled or permitted both to place it and to reside in it
> (3)  A person shall not be treated as having accommodation unless it is accommodation which it would be reasonable for him to continue to occupy.
> (4)  A person is threatened with homelessness if it is likely that he will become homeless within 28 days.

A person becomes intentionally homeless, in terms of Section 191(1), 'if he deliberately does or fails to do anything in consequence of which he ceases to occupy accommodation which is available for his occupation and which it would have been reasonable for him to continue to occupy'.

Cathy then, may be statutorily homeless. Cathy has to show that she has no licence to remain in her friends' home or that it would not be reasonable to expect her to continue to stay there. Considerations of reasonableness[63] in this context include the general housing conditions in the authority's area compared with the accommodation vacated by the applicant, the physical conditions of the accommodation,[64] overcrowding,[65] the financial resources available to the applicant and the cost of housing, as well as the employment and financial conditions of the area.[66] The permanence or otherwise of accommodation is not relevant to whether it is reasonable to leave it.[67] Nevertheless, some types of accommodation such as a refuge, which is intended to provide temporary shelter in a crisis should not be regarded as accommodation which it is reasonable to occupy in the medium or long term.[68]

---

[63] See for more detailed discussion, Arden and Hunter (2003) paras 5.84–5.130. See Code of Guidance para 6.22ff.

[64] According to *R v South Hertfordshire District Council, ex parte Miles* (1983) 17 HLR 71 a hut 20 feet by 10 feet, infested by rats and with no direct mains services was held to be reasonable accommodation for two adults and two children. In *Pulhoffer and Another v Hillingdon LBC* [1986] AC 484 one room in a guest house with no cooking or laundry facilities was not unreasonable for two adults and two children to occupy, especially in the light of the lengthy waiting list for two-bedroomed accommodation.

[65] Code of Guidance para 6.26; Arden and Hunter (2003) para 3 5.103–5.104.

[66] In *In re Islam* [1983] 1 AC 688 the House of Lords found that in the interests of the mobility of labour local authorities must accept that sometimes it will not be unreasonable for an applicant to leave accommodation.

[67] *Tower Hamlets LBC v Begum* [2000] 1 WLR 306.

[68] See the Code of Guidance para 6.26. *R v London Borough of Ealing ex p Sidhu* [1982] 2 HLR 45 established that accommodation of a purely temporary or emergency nature such as in a refuge did not mean that a person was not homeless.

Cathy and James are living in cramped conditions and have been told that they cannot stay beyond the end of the month. Cathy might also try to argue that she is homeless because the overcrowded conditions of their current accommodation are unsatisfactory. The House of Lords has stated that '[i]f the accommodation is so bad that leaving for that reason would not make one intentionally homeless, then one is in law already homeless'.[69] The conditions may not, however, be bad enough for Cathy to be able to rely on this line of argument. In any event, she is, at the very least, threatened with homelessness,[70] and at the end of the month will be in fact homeless. She also has a priority need because she has a dependent child.[71]

The local authority may contend that Cathy is not homeless because she and James can return to stay with Cathy's parents in Blackpool.[72] Cathy would have to show either that her parents will not permit them to stay or that it is not reasonable[73] to expect her to live with them.

If Cathy can show that she falls within the criteria of Section 193 or Section 195, the local housing authority has a duty to house her and James. This accommodation will be temporary and they will be allocated settled accommodation through the housing scheme. The duty to house them terminates if Cathy refuses either temporary accommodation that the authority considers suitable[74] or a final offer of accommodation under the scheme, if the accommodation is considered suitable by the authority.[75] The duty also ceases if she accepts an offer of housing allocated under the scheme.[76]

For the purposes of allocating housing under the local housing authority scheme, the legislation sets out priorities.

167 Allocation in accordance with allocation scheme

(2)  As regards priorities, the scheme shall be framed so as to secure that reasonable preference is given to—
  (a) people who are homeless (within the meaning of Part 7); [77]
  (b) people who are owed a duty by any local housing authority under section 190(2), 193(2) or 195(2) ... or who are occupying accommodation secured by any such authority under section 192(3);
  (c) people occupying insanitary or overcrowded housing or otherwise living in unsatisfactory housing conditions;
  (d) people who need to move on medical or welfare grounds; and
  (e) people who need to move to a particular locality in the district of the authority, where failure to meet that need would cause hardship (to themselves or to others).

---

[69] *R v LB of Brent, ex parte Awua* [1996] 1 AC 55, 67–68.

[70] *See R v LB of Brent, ex parte Awua* [1996] 1 AC 55.

[71] S 189(1) states: 'The following have a priority need for accommodation—(a) a pregnant woman or a person with whom she resides or might reasonably be expected to reside; (b) a person with whom dependent children reside or might reasonably be expected to reside; (c) a person who is vulnerable as a result of old age, mental illness or handicap or physical disability or other special reason, or with whom such a person resides or might reasonably be expected to reside; (d) a person who is homeless or threatened with homelessness as a result of an emergency such as flood, fire or other disaster.'

[72] *See Tower Hamlets LBC v Begum* [2000] 1 WLR 306.

[73] She might try to argue that her employment prospects in London are significantly better. She would, however, be in a stronger position if she already had a job offer. See *R v Winchester CC ex p Ashton* (1991) 24 HLR 520.

[74] S 193(5). The housing authority's designation of the accommodation as suitable is subject to review. There are various other circumstances in which the duty to house ceases. See ss 193 and 195(4).

[75] Ss 193(7) and 195(4).

[76] Ss 193(6)(c) and 195(4).

[77] See s 175 above.

The scheme may also be framed so as to give additional preference to particular descriptions of people within this subsection (being descriptions of people with urgent housing needs).

(2A) The scheme may contain provision for determining priorities in allocating housing accommodation to people within subsection (2); and the factors[78] which the scheme may allow to be taken into account include—

(a)   the financial resources available to a person to meet his housing costs;
(b)   any behaviour of a person (or a member of his household) which affects his suitability to be a tenant;
(c)   any local connection (within the meaning of section 199[79]) which exists between a person and the authority's district.

So, if Cathy is allocated accommodation under Section 193 or Section 195, the duty to house her will, in the normal course of events, only cease when she has been given a home under the housing scheme and she, as someone who falls within Section 167(2)(b), would be given reasonable preference under such a scheme. However, if she finds employment with remuneration sufficient to enable her to pay for private sector accommodation, she may find that she ranks very low in the order of priorities for settled accommodation under 167(2A).

Although the Children Act 1989 requires local authorities to provide housing for children in need,[80] Cathy may not rely upon this section to help her if to do so would be incompatible with the housing authority's duties.[81]

**Q** What if Cathy were living with and caring for her elderly mother instead of James?

Cathy may still be eligible for income support in this situation, as she may qualify as a person with significant caring responsibilities and her IS would include a carer's premium.[82] If not, she may be eligible for income-based jobseeker's allowance, which provides the same level of benefit, but requires her to meet the conditions set out earlier, and to comply with the jobseeker's agreement she must sign.

She may also be eligible for carer's allowance if her mother is severely disabled and she provides care for at least 35 hours per week.[83] She would likely still qualify for local authority housing,[84] housing benefit and council tax benefit.

**Q** What if Cathy had fled from her home in Blackpool because of the violent behaviour towards her of James' father, with whom she was living?

In this case, Cathy may be exempted from her obligation to co-operate with a child support officer if the officer feels that she or James would be at risk of harm. If so, James' father would not contribute to his support and Cathy would not lose any of her benefit. Her entitlement to other benefits would remain the same.

---

[78] The Revision of the Code of Guidance suggests that another indicator of priority between households with similar levels of need could be waiting time (ODPM 2002 para 5.24).).
[79] For example, through being normally resident or employed in the area.
[80] S 27.
[81] See ch 3 and *R v Northavon DC, ex parte Smith* [1994] 2 AC 402.
[82] Regs made under the Social Security Contributions and Benefits Act s 124.
[83] Social Security Contributions and Benefits Act 1992, s 70.
[84] She may have a priority need under s 189(1)(c). The housing authority has a discretion under s 192 to provide accommodation to those who are unintentionally homeless but who do not have a priority need.

The local authority's duty to house Cathy and James would likely remain the same; even though Cathy may have an interest in her home in Blackpool[85] or a licence to occupy it, she is still statutorily homeless if it is not reasonable for her to continue to occupy it. Section 177 of the Housing Act 1996 states:

177 Whether it is reasonable to continue to occupy accommodation

(1)   It is not reasonable for a person to continue to occupy accommodation if it is probable that this will lead to domestic violence or other violence[86] against him, or against—
(a) a person who normally resides with him as a member of his family, or
(b) any other person who might reasonably be expected to reside with him.

(1A) For this purpose 'violence' means—
(a) violence from another person; or
(b) threats of violence from another person which are likely to be carried out;
and violence is 'domestic violence' if it is from a person who is associated[87] with the victim.

This means, strictly speaking, that, if Cathy can show that to return home would expose her or James to probable violence or to threats that are likely to be carried out, she is homeless, irrespective of any rights that she might have to occupy the property. As Arden and Hunter point out, it is not necessary to show a history of actual violence; threats by someone likely to carry them out suffice (2003 para 5.74). The Code of Guidance makes this clear:

The fact that violence has not yet occurred does not, on its own, mean that it is not likely to occur ... [H]ousing authorities ... should not necessarily expect evidence of violence as such from the applicant. And an assessment of the likelihood of a threat of violence being carried out should not be based solely on whether there has been actual violence in the past.

(para 6.18)

Nevertheless many authorities, say Arden and Hunter, require evidence of actual violence in the past and also insist on a high standard of proof (2003 para 5.74). Women's Aid (2003 p 22) reports that, while some local authorities accept the woman's statement in the absence of other evidence,[88] many ask for 'substantial proof' of domestic violence and will not accept a statement as evidence.

Moreover, local authorities have in the past sometimes adopted a requirement that an applicant, in order to qualify as homeless, had to show that she had exhausted her legal remedies under domestic violence legislation.[89] Arden and Hunter point out that the only relevant question in deciding whether it is reasonable to continue to occupy under Section 177 is whether it is probable that continued occupation of the property would lead to violence or the threat of violence (2003 para 5.76). Whether the victim took steps to protect herself such as calling the police or obtaining an injunction is not relevant.

---

[85] See ch 5.
[86] The reference to other forms of violence is designed to cover cases such as racial harassment (Arden and Hunter 2003 para 1.98).
[87] Defined in terms similar to those in the Family Law Act 1996. The category includes spouses, former spouses, cohabitants, former cohabitants, parents of the same children, relatives and members or former members of the same household. See s 178 of the Housing Act 1996.
[88] See also Humphreys and Thiara (2002) pp 75 and 77.
[89] See Cowan (1997) pp 128–29.

Moreover, if a woman has taken such measures, it cannot be assumed that they will be effective, so reducing the risk below the standard of probability.[90] The Code of Guidance states that, 'Applicants should not automatically be expected to return home on the strength of an injunction' (para 6.20).[91]

In addition to showing that she is homeless, Cathy will also have to convince the authority that she has not become homeless intentionally.[92] She cannot be classified as intentionally homeless unless it would be reasonable to expect her to have remained in her home. Clearly, it is not reasonable to expect someone to remain in a home where she is being subjected to violence and abuse. In addition, the victim should not be expected to seek court orders against her abuser. The Code of Guidance states that, generally, it should not be considered a deliberate act or omission where 'the applicant has fled his or her home because of violence or threats of violence likely to be carried out, and the applicant has failed to pursue all legal remedies against the perpetrator(s) because of fear of reprisal or because he or she was unaware of the remedies available' (para 7.12).

Finally, Cathy also has to show that she has a priority need.[93] Domestic violence does not, in itself, require a victim to be categorised as being in 'priority need' under the Act. However Cathy, like many women, falls within the scope of the Section 189(1)(b) because she has a dependent child living with her.

So, provided Cathy can convince the housing authority that she has left her home as a result of violence or threats, she should in principle qualify under Section 193 for temporary accommodation. As someone who is owed a duty under Section 193, she should also be given reasonable preference under the housing scheme when it comes to allocating settled housing. Moreover she should be given additional preference over and above this if the scheme allows for such a category of people. Section 167(2) as amended gives housing authorities the power to design their housing allocation schemes so as to give additional preference to certain types of people within the 'reasonable preference' groups who have urgent housing needs. The Revision of the Code of Guidance specifically recommends that housing authorities should consider giving additional preference to 'those owed a homelessness duty as a result of violence or threats of violence likely to be carried out and who as a result require urgent rehousing, including victims of domestic violence ...' (ODPM 2002 para 5.18).

While Cathy's position appears reasonably straightforward in principle, she may in reality face a number of obstacles. Local authority housing policies and practices have attracted considerable criticism for making it difficult for abused women to obtain housing.

In some areas, says Women's Aid (2003 p 22), housing officers actively discourage women experiencing domestic violence from applying as homeless. They also provide inaccurate information to potential applicants. Humphreys and Thiara report that a number of the women in their survey said that they were pressured to return home (2002 p 76). They also found that many women experience interviews conducted by housing

---

[90] *Bond v Leicester CC* [2001] EWCA Civ 1544; [2002] 1 FCR 566.

[91] Government policy states that women who refuse to return home with the protection of a court order should not be treated as if it is safe for them to return and therefore that they not homeless or that they are intentionally homeless (Home Office 2000 para 2c.iii.2).

[92] Defined in s 191(1) Housing Act 1996. See above.

[93] The guidelines suggest that in order to distinguish between different people within the same category, housing authorities might consider banding applicants into groups reflecting different levels of housing need, with prioritisation within these groups being determined by waiting time (ODPM 2002 para 5.11).

officers as an interrogation (2002 p 77).[94] These are sometimes so upsetting that women consider going back home, feeling that they are to blame for the violence (Women's Aid 2003 p 22). Women who attend housing departments alone are often treated worse than women who go with an advocate or support worker (*ibid*).[95] And women who allege psychological or emotional abuse seem to encounter even greater problems than those who can show physical abuse.[96]

Housing authorities seem to interpret the legislation strictly and at times appear to pay little heed to the Code of Guidance.[97] It seems, for example, that housing departments try to 'evade [their] responsibilities towards women experiencing domestic violence' by classifying them as intentionally homeless (Barron 2002 p 11). In spite of the instruction in the Code of Guidance to the contrary, some authorities term women intentionally homeless where they refuse to apply for a court order. Women are also treated as intentionally homeless if they do get an injunction or occupation order but do not return to the home. Women who owe rent on a property or are liable for repairs are penalised by some authorities. Some authorities class women as intentionally homeless if they leave temporary accommodation with friends or relatives.[98] Despite these problems, however, research has elicited praise for many housing departments. Barron found that the practice of deeming women to be intentionally homeless was rare (2002 p 14) and most authorities seemed to recognise that the existence of an injunction or occupation order was not a good reason to refuse help to a woman who felt that she was still in danger.[99] Nor did they tend to expect women to apply for orders if the women considered this inappropriate (Barron 2002 p 12).

It seems that some housing authorities also interpret the statutory provisions on priority need narrowly. Abused women who are not pregnant and who do not have dependent children experience problems in obtaining accommodation. In seeking to establish a priority need, they have to rely on Section 198(1)(c) and seek housing as persons who are 'vulnerable' for a 'special reason'. However, in the past, not all local authorities have accepted that domestic violence constitutes a 'special reason'.[100] The Code of Guidance states that a person has a priority need if she is vulnerable as a result of 'ceasing to occupy accommodation because of violence from another person or threats of violence from another person which are likely to be carried out' (para 8.12).[101] It goes on to stress that the safety of the applicant and the maintenance of

---

[94] The Code of Guidance exhorts authorities to handle cases of domestic violence with care and some sensitivity (para 3.14).

[95] See also Humphreys and Thiara (2002) p 78.

[96] See Bossy and Coleman (2000) para 5.1. Government policy directs that local authority housing policies should provide for the recognition of psychological abuse as satisfying the requirements for being found to be statutorily homeless where it would be not be reasonable for the person to continue living at home (Home Office 2000 para 2c.iii.2).

[97] The Code of Guidance is not binding.

[98] The Code of Guidance refers to the possibility of family mediation in cases where friction between the applicant and family or friends with whom she is staying might lead to homelessness. But it specifically cautions against the risks of returning home in cases of violence or abuse (para 6.8).

[99] See Bossy and Coleman (2000) para 5.4.

[100] See Malos and Hague (1993 para 3.16); Murphy (1996 p 855); Cowan (1997 p 137). The Law Commission noted in 1992 that some local authorities, despite *dicta* to the contrary in *R v Ealing London Borough, ex parte Sidhu* [1983] 2 HLR 41, 45, required women to seek a custody order (now called a residence order) before they could be treated as being in priority need (Law Commission 1992a para 2.16 n. 50).

[101] The test for vulnerability that must be satisfied is 'whether, when homeless, the applicant would be less able to fend for himself than an ordinary homeless person so that he would be likely to suffer injury or detriment in circumstances where a less vulnerable person would be able to cope without harmful effects' (Code of Guidance para 8.13). Housing authorities should provide that women fleeing domestic violence may be vulnerable and have a priority need even if they do not have children and are not pregnant (Home Office 2000 para 2c.iii.2).

confidentiality are of 'paramount concern' (para 8.26). In assessing whether it is likely that threats will be carried out, authorities should consider the probability of violence and not measures that the applicant could take, such as obtaining an injunction (*ibid*). The factors an authority might take into account in assessing vulnerability are set out in paragraph 8.27.[102]

In keeping with the Code, women in some areas who have experienced domestic violence are routinely treated as vulnerable, irrespective of whether they have dependent children with them (Barron 2002 p 11).[103] Yet Women's Aid (2003 p 23) reports that significant numbers of single women and women without dependent children still face difficulties in finding a home because they cannot establish that they are 'vulnerable'.

Women fleeing domestic violence often attempt to move to another area. The duty under Section 193 of the Housing Act 1996 does not normally apply[104] where there is no local connection, such as prior residence, and the authority is permitted to refer the case to a district where there is one.[105] However referral is not appropriate where the applicant, or a person who might reasonably be expected to reside with her, has suffered violence[106] in the past, and where it is probable that a return to the district with which there is a local connection will lead to further violence.[107] The authority's discretion to refer can only be exercised if it takes the view in a particular case that the risk is no longer present in the other area.[108] Conversely, if the woman applies within her home area, the authority is expected to have her housed in a different area if there is a risk and it is necessary to reduce the potential for contact with a violent partner (Code of Guidance para 12.10). Nevertheless, some authorities refer women back to the areas with which they have a local connection (Arden and Hunter 2003 para 8.36).

The duty to provide accommodation ceases if a person turns down accommodation considered suitable by the housing authority.[109] In particular, the duty ceases where an applicant refuses a final offer of accommodation allocated under Part 6 of the Act, provided that applicant has been advised in writing of the possible consequences of refusal and of the right to request a review of the suitability of the accommodation.[110] Section 193(7F) provides that a local authority should not make a final offer of accommodation under Part 6 unless they are satisfied that the accommodation is suitable for the applicant and that it would be reasonable for the applicant to accept the offer. ODPM (2002 para 5.3) states that allocation policies should give applicants a choice of accommodation wherever possible and where there is no choice, consideration should be given to allowing applicants an opportunity to express a preference (para 5.6).

The right to request a review of any offer and the obligation on housing authorities to make appropriate final offers were introduced by the Homelessness Act 2002; it remains to be seen what effect they will have. Research carried out before these provisions were enacted showed that most housing authorities refused further help if a woman turned

---

[102] These are: the nature of the violence or threats; the impact and likely effect of the violence or threats on the applicant's physical and mental health and well-being; and whether the applicant has any support networks.

[103] See also Women's Aid (2003) p 23.

[104] A housing authority cannot adopt a position that all those who have a local connection elsewhere should automatically be referred back (*R v Harrow LBC ex p Carter* (1992) 26 HLR 32).

[105] S 198 Housing Act 1996.

[106] This includes threats.

[107] S 198(2)(c) Housing Act 1996.

[108] See Arden and Hunter (2003) paras 8.36–8.38.

[109] S 193. See above pp 497–500.

[110] S 193(7) Of the Housing Act 1996 as amended.

down an offer of temporary accommodation (Barron 2002 p 11). And often, the accommodation offered was in 'hard to let' areas[111] or unsuitable.[112] The study by Women's Aid (2003) suggests that this continues to be the case in some areas. For instance, a woman might be offered a space in a local refuge as the only option, even when it may not be safe to stay locally. Some women face financial difficulty in seeking to travel to a refuge in a different area. Some authorities do not refer women to refuges at all; they offer only unsupported temporary accommodation which does not meet the women's need for safety and support. And, say Women's Aid, women leaving home often still have difficulty safeguarding their possessions and pets (2003 p 22).[113]

Women may be forced to wait for long periods in refuges.[114] This means that women may feel impelled to return home or that they and their children become institutionalised (Women's Aid 2003 p 22).[115] It also means that spaces in refuges are not freed for new arrivals. At the other extreme, women are re-housed too quickly, without adequate support being put in place. Many of these women also return to their violent partners (Women's Aid 2003 p 22).

In some areas, it has been observed, there is good practice; a domestic violence panel fast tracks housing applications and resources are available to provide long-term support in the community (Women's Aid 2003 p 22). However there remains the perennial problem that there is a shortage of suitable affordable social housing and, in addition, reliance on the private sector may lead to women suffering financial hardship[116] and insecurity.[117] The lack of appropriate housing can create a serious impediment to women who want to leave violent relationships. For example, one worker quoted by Bossy and Coleman said, 'I believe that the problem of housing is one of the greatest inhibiting factors in women's choice to leave an abusive relationship' (2000 para 5.1).

## VI. CONCLUSION

We see in the regulation of Cathy's situation the relationship between the public and the private spheres. Public assistance regarding finances and housing is highly regulated and geared to subsistence levels on the assumption that individuals will not otherwise 'take responsibility' for themselves. Cathy's situation demonstrates the paradox inherent within the public support system, as on the one hand she is encouraged by the inducements in the benefit, housing and child support schemes to take responsibility for herself (or to require James' father to take responsibility for their son), yet on the other she is discouraged from work through lack of child care and the inducements only towards low-paying work.

---

[111] See Barron (2002) p 11.

[112] See Humphreys and Thiara (2002) pp 77–78.

[113] See also Bossy and Coleman (2000) paras 5.5–5.6.

[114] Women with insecure immigration status experience particularly severe difficulties in accessing temporary accommodation and they find it 'almost impossible' to get 'move-on' accommodation (Women's Aid 2003 p 22).

[115] See also Charles (1994) p 465. The Code of Guidance directs that refuge accommodation should be used only in the short term and states that 'housing authorities should not delay in securing alternative accommodation in the hope that the applicant might return to her partner' (para 11.33).

[116] See Bossy and Coleman (2000) para 5.3.

[117] See Women's Aid (2003) p 23.

# FURTHER READING AND SELECTED RECENT REFERENCES

A ARDEN and C HUNTER, *Homelessness and Allocations: A Guide to the Housing Act 1996 Parts VI and VII*, 6th rev edn, (London, Legal Action Group, 2003).

F BENNETT, 'Gender Implications of Current Social Security Reforms' (2002) 23 *Fiscal Studies* 559.

J BRADSHAW, *et al*, *Absent Fathers?* (London, Routledge, 1999).

D CHATTERTON, 'The Cost of the Single Parent' (1994) *Fam Law* 23.

J EEKELAAR, 'A Child Support Scheme for the United Kingdom' (1990) *Fam Law* 15.

C HUMPHREYS and R THIARA, *Routes to Safety: Protection Issues Facing Abused Women and Children and the Role of Outreach Services* (Bristol, WAFE, 2002).

B NEALE and C SMART, 'Caring, Earning and Changing: Parenthood and Employment after Divorce' in A Carling, S Duncan and R Edwards, (eds), *Analysing Families: Morality and Rationality in Policy and Practice* (London, Routledge, 1999).

J WALLBANK, 'The Campaign for Change of the Child Support Act 1991: Reconstituting the "Absent" Father' (1997) 6 *Social and Legal Studies* 191.

N WIKELEY, *Wikeley, Ogus and Barendt's: The Law of Social Security* (London, Buterworths, 2002).

## *Reports*

Department of the Environment, Transport and the Regions and Department of Social Security (2000) *Quality and Choice: A Decent Home for All: The Housing Green Paper* (London, DETR and DSS, 2000).

Women's Aid, *Response to 'Safety and Justice', the Government Consultation Paper on Domestic Violence* (Bristol, WAFE, 2003).

Department of Social Security, *A New Contract for Welfare: Children's Rights and Parents' Responsibilities* (London, The Stationery Office, 1999).

HM Treasury, DfES, DWP and DTI, *Choice for Parents, the Best Start for Children: A Ten Year Strategy for Childcare* (London, HM Treasury, 2004).

# 14

# Dissolution of Legal Relationships: The Process and its Consequences

**Q** Steve and Jenny have been married for eight years. They have been living in the same Housing Association flat for the past seven years since the birth of their daughter Barbie. Jenny has worked part-time for her local council, and Steve is a part-time sales assistant currently looking for full-time work. Due to financial difficulties, their relationship in the last two years has become strained, and finally things become so difficult that both agree that despite their attempts to make the marriage work, they should divorce. Steve moves out.

Steve works most weekends, and also every afternoon, and has not had much opportunity to spend time with Barbie since she started school two years ago. He tried to take an active role in her upbringing, especially when Barbie was small and while Jenny was at work three mornings per week, but gradually the day-to-day care for Barbie has been left more and more to Jenny. Jenny and Steve feel that they will have no difficulty agreeing financial arrangements; however, they disagree on what would be best for Barbie.

Steve and Jenny need advice concerning divorce and its consequences, which include arrangements about finances, housing and Barbie's future. The only matters in question for this particular couple are the divorce itself and Barbie's care. Part I of this chapter will deal with the legal dissolution of relationships, and part 2 with residence and contact orders concerning children.

## I. DIVORCE—INTRODUCTION

As we saw in chapter 2, entry into marriage is considered to be a private and voluntary matter, and marriage has always been regarded as a sort of hybrid, resembling both a contract and a binding vow. The state's regulation of marriage takes many forms, and it relies upon social and ideological forces.[1] Perhaps surprisingly, however, regulation occurs also through divorce law. In any event, while entering into marriage is relatively easy as long as both partners satisfy the formal requirements,[2] ending a marriage has never been quite so simple. We will explore not only whether and, if so, how Steve and

---

[1] See ch 2.
[2] See ch 2.

Jenny can divorce, but will also present different views of the moral, religious, economic and social policies behind these legal questions.

## II. THE HISTORY OF DIVORCE

The early history of formal divorce[3] in England and Wales begins with Canon law and is discussed by Finer and McGregor (1974 pp 85–87). The ecclesiastical courts treated marriage as indissoluble and, in the case of validly contracted marriages, granted only a limited form of relief in certain circumstances. A divorce *a mensa et thoro* could be granted on proof of a matrimonial offence, but had the effect only of a modern judicial separation. However, the law of nullity was developed in order to 'provide a legitimate avoidance of the rigours of the doctrine of indissolubility' (Finer and McGregor 1974 p 86).

So, until the 17th century those who could afford to had to petition the ecclesiastical court for divorce. Although, theologically, this court could not break the bond that God had created, it could declare that that bond had never existed in the first place and grant a divorce *a vinculo*. The impediments to a validly contracted marriage usually dealt with lack of capacity to marry or lack of proper consent to marriage.[4] Successfully challenging the validity of the marriage in one of these ways meant, of course, that any children were rendered illegitimate and their entitlement to property defeated. But it did have the effect of allowing the parties to marry again.

The first 'modern' way to escape from a valid marriage was the development in the 17th century of what became known as Parliamentary divorces (Stone 1990 pp 309–11). Finer and McGregor (1974 p 92) explain that this new remedy was developed primarily to secure succession to peerages and property but later filtered down from the aristocracy to the merchant class.[5]

Adultery was the sole ground for parliamentary divorce and, for a wife's petition to succeed, her husband's adultery had to be 'aggravated' by bigamy, incest or an unnatural vice. It was thought that '[s]hort of this, she suffered no "very material injury" and she ought not to resent her husband's unfaithfulness' (Cornish and Clark 1989 p 379).[6] Husband petitions, on the other hand, became so common and the rules so routinised that, in 1840, a select committee of the House was set aside to hear divorce petitions. However ecclesiastical proceedings and parliamentary divorces were still meeting the needs only of the propertied classes.[7] For those who were not wealthy there was no legal exit from marriage.

---

[3] See, for the history of divorce law generally, Stone (1990); McGregor (1957); Cornish and Clark (1989); Cretney (2003a); summaries in Finer and McGregor (1974); Royal Commission Report (1956); Hoggett, *et al*, (1996); Cretney, *et al*, (2002).

[4] Some of the more enduring impediments to capacity are still reflected in the Matrimonial Causes Act 1973. They include an existing marriage or too close a family relationship between the parties and impotence at the time of marriage (See s 11 of the MCA). Impediments based upon lack of consent or non-consummation are also still a part of the law of England and Wales (See s 12 of the MCA). See also ch 2.

[5] See also Anderson (1984).

[6] Cornish and Clark (1989 p 379) go on: '[i]n the period to 1857, only four women would ever succeed in securing a divorce Act'. See also Finer and McGregor (1974 p 94).

[7] For those who did not wish to litigate at all but for whom property was of some concern, settlements drafted by conveyancers were available to deal with separation and property matters, if not full divorces. See Stone (1990 Part VII).

Yet just as the poor symbolically challenged the laws of church and state in their means of marrying, they often did the same in their means of divorcing. One of the most popular means of 'divorce' was desertion. For others, ritual was important. Jumping backwards over the broom symbolised to the couple and to the community that the 'marriage' was over by mutual agreement of the parties. In some parts of England the custom of wife-selling was practised in which a man put a halter around his wife's neck and led her to the open cattle market to 'auction' her to the highest bidder. Usually, these auctions were prearranged, and by agreement between the husband, wife and new partner. They represented an important symbolic end to one relationship and beginning of another (O'Donovan 1984). Folk custom served the same purpose for the poor as parliamentary divorce did for the rich; it served as public notice of the end of a marriage.

For many, however, desertion was the route out of marriage. It was relatively easy for a migrant worker or man who wished to enlist to get 'lost' in pre-industrial England, and deserted wives accounted for about 6% of all women in south east England who applied for Poor Relief in the 18th century (Stone 1990 p 142). However, by the 19th century, the large number of deserted wives posed problems for the parishes which became responsible for them. In addition, the influence of liberals such as Mill and Bentham, the lobbying of women and reforms directed at the separation of Church and state led to the press taking up the cause of divorce reform (Cornish and Clark 1989 p 383).[8] A Royal Commission was set up in 1852 to investigate the matter.[9] The history of divorce from that time to the present becomes the history of proposals for reform countered by resistance to reform based upon fears for the health of society caused by an increasing divorce rate and the undermining of the institution of marriage.

While the government argued publicly in the 1850s that divorce reform would promote equality by bringing divorce from the door of only the rich man to the 'humblest classes' (Stone 1990 p 371), Stone argues that this was a fallacious claim; the government had no intention of creating equality in accessibility of divorce. It seems that the motives and the morals of the 'humbler' classes were always suspect.

> To virtually all legislators, the poor were seen as a threatening, immoral, dissolute mass of people to whom it would be extremely dangerous to extend the facility of easy divorce ... [It] might, it was argued, undermine what elements of stability existed in working-class families. In any case, there was no evidence at all that the poor were demanding divorce. (Stone 1990 p 374)

Rather, the object of reform was to abolish the separate and 'chaotic' distribution of jurisdiction over separation and divorce among Parliament, Church courts and common law courts. The real significance of the first Act relating to divorce, passed in 1857, was, then, that it met this object; it made divorce a secular matter. The law, in reality, however, did not change that much. The Divorce and Matrimonial Causes Act 1857 removed the procedure from the ecclesiastical court and Parliament to the common law courts—a process that was cheaper but not cheap, thereby allowing divorce a little lower

---

[8] Cretney (2003a p 162) observes that the impetus for change also came from the review of the probate jurisdiction of the Ecclesiastical Courts, resulting in the creation of the Court of Probate in 1857 and questions about what to do with the courts' remaining jurisdiction over matrimonial causes.

[9] It was chaired by Lord Campbell. It reported in 1853 (*Royal Comm. on Divorce and Matrimonial Causes* 1853).

down the social scale—while keeping in place the old grounds for obtaining a divorce.[10] Divorce *a mensa et thoro* was similarly transformed into judicial separation. Collusion and connivance were absolute bars to divorce. The Act did not, in the end, achieve the equality of accessibility it apparently promised to the poor, and it never was intended to achieve complete equality between men and women, but it did probably address some of the concerns of the middle classes.[11]

Divorce reform did not reappear as a political issue until 1909 when another Royal Commission was convened.[12] According to Stone, there were three stimuli to demands for further reform: the increasing erosion of beliefs in general religious 'truths' and the general secularisation of society; the scandals and absurdity of the collusion required by so many in order to obtain a divorce; and the growing movement, particularly among middle class women, for women's equality in the public sphere, and also a move towards greater equality between the classes (1990 pp 391–92). The Commissioners, reporting in 1912, were split.

> A Majority Report advocated reform of the legal machinery for divorce and offered reasons to justify it. A Minority Report, signed by three members, opposed all the important proposals on the grounds that they would make divorce easier; that this would merely create more divorces; and that any extension of the causes for divorce beyond female adultery were against the express words of Christ.
>
> The Majority Report was a remarkable document for its day. It set out three principles. The first was that there should be equality of access between both rich and poor and men and women. Over this there was ostensibly not much dispute. The second was that divorce should be regarded as merely a legal mopping-up operation after the spiritual death of a marriage. The third was that in any society there is no necessary correlation between the number of divorces and the level of sexual immorality. (Stone 1990 p 393)

While pressure for reform continued (Cretney 2003a pp 214–16), political debate was interrupted by the War and only continued after 1918. In 1923 the next piece of legislation was passed.[13] The only amendment it made to the law was to equalise the ground of adultery as between men and women. 'So, in an age which was doing a good deal formally to give women equality with men, there passed away the notion of the husband's "accidental adultery" and with it the most egregious application of the double standard' (Cornish and Clark 1989 p 397).

In 1937 yet another divorce reform Act was passed,[14] this time extending the grounds for divorce beyond adultery to include desertion for three years, cruelty, habitual drunkenness and incurable insanity. The preamble to the Bill reveals the changes in perception of the 'problem' of divorce which allowed such provisions to pass into law:

> The preamble to the act, written by AP Herbert, stated that its object was to offer true support for marriage; protection for children; the removal of hardship for the unhappily married; the

---

[10] A husband could petition on the ground of adultery and a wife could petition on the grounds of incestuous adultery; bigamy with adultery; rape; sodomy; bestiality; adultery with such cruelty as would have entitled her to a divorce *a mensa et thoro*; or adultery with desertion for two years. See the Divorce and Matrimonial Causes Act 1857, s XXVII.

[11] See generally Cretney (2003a) ch 5.

[12] The Gorrell Commission's terms of reference were to inquire into the present state of the law and the administration thereof in Divorce and Matrimonial Causes, and Application for Separation Orders, especially with regard to the position of the poorer classes in relation thereto' (Cretney 2003a p 209). See on this period generally, Cornish and Clark (1989) pp 393–98; Cretney (2003a) ch 6.

[13] Matrimonial Causes Act 1923.

[14] Matrimonial Causes Act 1937. On this Act generally, see Cretney (2003a) ch 7.

reduction of illicit unions; the elimination of unseemly litigation; the relief of consciences of the clergy; and the restoration of due respect for the law. (Stone 1990 p 401)

Herbert thus presented his Bill not as a force for change but as a source of stability (Cretney 2003a p 51). And, while the law now appeared to grant formal equality between spouses with regard to grounds for divorce, Smart argues that that goal was undermined by differential interpretations in the courts: women were often held to higher moral and sexual standards than men and grounds for divorce often were interpreted differently for men than for women (1984 pp 27–53). Rather than divorce legislation, it was probably the introduction of Legal Aid in 1948 which did most towards achieving greater practical equality in divorce, given the differences in men's and women's incomes and wealth.[15] Certainly, statistics show a great increase in the rate of divorce after the extension of legal aid in 1949 (Smart 1984 p 33), though the end of the Second World War was another influence.

In the 1950s another Royal Commission on Marriage and Divorce was struck to consider and explain the reasons for the higher, though stable, rate of divorce[16] while having 'in mind … the "need to promote healthy and happy married life and to safeguard the interests and well-being of children"' (Royal Commission 1956 p 7).

**Q** Review the mandates and objectives of the various commissions and reports on divorce. What themes do you see emerging in divorce reform debate?

While the Commission had a very wide remit, the main issue before it was the ground for divorce, and on this question it was divided. Only one Commissioner recommended that divorce be available in the absence of any 'matrimonial fault'. The remaining 18 signatories to the 1956 Report were split nine members to nine on whether divorce should be granted on the ground only of the 'irretrievable breakdown of the marriage' (provable by separation for seven years or more, with some adding the proviso that divorce would not be available if one of the spouses objected and others adding the proviso that the separation be attributable to the unreasonable conduct of the respondent spouse), rather than on the ground of one spouse having committed a matrimonial offence. Cretney, *et al*, characterise the outcome as designating the role of law as being to 'give relief where a wrong had been done', rather than to provide a 'dignified and honourable means of release from a broken marriage' (2002 p 273). Those in favour of the new ground argued their case as follows:

70. (vii) We think that the time has come to recognise that matrimonial offences are in many cases merely symptomatic of the breakdown of marriage, and that there should also be provision for divorce in cases where, quite apart from the commission of such offences, the marriage has broken down completely … .

(ix)      … We do not believe that the introduction of this new principle of divorce into the law will lessen respect for marriage and undermine it as an institution. On the contrary, by basing dissolution of marriage on a complete breakdown of that union, we are, we think, heightening

[15] See also Cretney (2003a) pp 306–18.

[16] The Morton Commission discussed factors such as the 'complexity of modern life'; the conditions of modern life including scarce housing, earlier age at marriage and the 'greater demands made of marriage, consequent on the spread of education, higher standards of living and the social and economic emancipation of women'; newer attitudes towards sex and modern psychology which encouraged 'self-expression'; and a general 'dangerous' tendency to take the responsibilities of marriage less seriously (Royal Commission, 1956 paras 43–49, pp 8–10). See also Smart (1984) pp 36–38; Cretney (2003a) pp 327–43.

the respect for true marriage, for the emphasis is then placed on marriage as a real union for life. It is impossible to ignore the fact that at the present time the matrimonial offence is in very many cases only a means of obtaining a dissolution of marriage desired by both parties. Our proposal avoids the distasteful expedient of committing a matrimonial offence to give cause for divorce, lessens undesirable publicity and dispenses with the often unwarrantable assumption that one spouse is more to blame than the other ... . (Royal Commission 1956 pp 23–24).

The contrary view was expressed as follows:

69. (ii) We believe that the consequences of providing the 'easy way out' afforded by divorce by consent would be disastrous to stability in marriage. The inevitable result would be the granting of divorces in cases where no real necessity for the remedy had arisen ... . People would then come to look upon marriage less and less as a life-long union and more and more as one to be ended if things began to go wrong, and there would be a real risk that widespread divorce would come to be an accepted feature of our society. As those attitudes spread they would undermine, and ultimately destroy, the concept of life-long marriage.

(iii)      ... We are deeply concerned about the effect on children of the present divorce rate; their suffering would be multiplied if divorce were to become more widespread. The best home for children is of course a happy home, but in our opinion (and most of our 'expert' witnesses confirmed this) children can put up with a good deal of friction between their parents so long as the home remains intact ... .

...

(vii) ... But whether there are children or not, the State must be concerned in the maintenance of a marriage and in its dissolution, because the state has an overriding responsibility to ensure, in the interests of the community, that the institution of marriage is upheld.

(viii) ... [To] give people a right to divorce themselves would be to foster a change in attitude to marriage which would be disastrous for the nation ... . (Royal Commission 1956 pp 14–15)

**Q** Note that each 'side' argues that its position buttresses, rather that undermines, marriage as an institution. Which argument do you favour? Smart characterises the question as whether the law ought to see marriage as a contract between the spouses and the state, or as one simply between the spouses (1999b).

Note also that the religious aspects of divorce were no longer argued by either side, but that recourse is had to morals, to the interests of children and to the interests of society. Children are considered seriously for the first time in the divorce reform debate and, yet again, the dependence of the stability of society upon the institution of marriage is assumed rather than argued for.

Nothing was to come of this Royal Commission Report for several years, but Stone suggests that it presented the germ of the idea of no-fault divorce to an increasingly secular society (Stone 1990 p 409). Interestingly, the idea was taken up by a group set up by the Archbishop of Canterbury—concerned at the rate of illegitimacy—which produced its own report in 1966 favouring no-fault divorce and suggesting that irretrievable breakdown of marriage be the only ground for divorce (Archbishop of Canterbury's Group 1966). The newly created Law Commission supported this proposal in its report also published in 1966. Some of the Law Commission's conclusions are summarised as follows:

120. (1) The objectives of a good divorce law should include (a) the support of marriages which have a chance of survival, and (b) the decent burial with the minimum of embarrassment,

humiliation and bitterness of those that are indubitably dead.

...

(3) Four of the major problems requiring solution are:

(a)   The need to encourage reconciliation. Something more might be achieved here; though little is to be expected from conciliation procedures after divorce proceedings have been instituted

(b)   The prevalence of stable illicit unions. As the law stands, many of these cannot be regularised nor the children legitimated

(c)   Injustice to the economically weaker partner—normally the wife

(d)   The need adequately to protect the children of failed marriages.

(Law Commission 1966 pp 53–54)[17]

**Q** Do you agree with these objectives? Note their similarities and differences from previous commissions and reports.

The time appeared to be right for change, and the result of the two reports was a compromise position: while irretrievable breakdown should be the sole ground for divorce, breakdown would be proved by evidence of one or more of five facts, three of which were, in effect, the matrimonial offences of adultery, cruelty and desertion.[18] Marriage-saving remained important, though, and it was thought that the parties should be encouraged to attempt reconciliation wherever possible. Thus, the Divorce Reform Bill did not remove fault from divorce law entirely. And, its long title stated that its purposes included facilitating reconciliation.

Arguments in favour of the no-fault provisions of the Bill included claims that it did no more than reflect changes already occurring in society, and that rather than undermining family life and marriage, it strengthened both by allowing the many stable but illegitimate unions to become legitimate (Stone 1990 p 407). Indeed, Smart asserts:

Arguably, this legislation marked a shift away from the traditional method of controlling family life through restriction and limitation on movement and change, towards regulating it by providing directions for this movement and change. The direction in which individuals were invited to go was away from an unsatisfactory marriage towards a second more satisfactory one. Quite simply, the solution to the divorce problem was seen as (re)marriage. ... In the debates in the House of Commons, MPs spoke of divorce as the process by which individuals could leave miserable relationships in order to start new, legitimate, fulfilling ones. Moreover, although there was concern over the effects of divorce on children at this time, this concern was also submerged by the faith in the stabilising power of the re-constituted family. (1999b pp 7–8)

One can view the Divorce Reform Act 1969, with its at least symbolic acknowledgement of marriage breakdown as the only ground for divorce, as a remarkable piece of legislation. It can also be seen as remarkable in the way in which it reconciles the competing ideas of marriage as *both* a contract between individuals and between the individuals and the state, and in the way in which it continues to promote marriage-saving as an appropriate part of divorce law.

The Act was subsequently consolidated with other legislation, including the Matrimonial Proceedings and Property Act 1970, into the Matrimonial Causes Act 1973, and is the law pursuant to which Steve and Jenny may divorce. The history of divorce reform

---

[17] See also Cretney (1996b).
[18] See generally Cretney (2003a) pp 355–75.

does not end here, though. These substantive changes were followed by procedural changes that have had an equally—if not more—dramatic effect on the availability and nature of divorce. Both the Law Commission and the Archbishop's group envisaged that a court would examine the evidence and only then determine whether the marriage had indeed irretrievably broken down. This vision has been gradually abandoned and a 'special procedure' was first established in 1973 for the simplest of the undefended divorce cases, and then extended in 1977 to all undefended divorce cases. The special procedure means that the parties do not have to appear in court, but their documents are scrutinised by a district judge who then satisfies her—or himself that the petitioner is entitled to a decree of divorce.[19] The documents are checked for procedural as well as substantive regularity.[20] Very little opportunity is provided to the parties or the court to query any of the allegations in the documents and in effect this means that divorce has become an administrative rather than judicial procedure.[21] In practice, about 99% of divorces are undefended and granted under the special procedure rules (LCD 1993 para 2.7).

## III. STEVE, JENNY AND THE MATRIMONIAL CAUSES ACT 1973

The Matrimonial Causes Act 1973:

1. (1) Subject to section 3 below, a petition for divorce may be presented to the court by either party to a marriage on the ground that the marriage has broken down irretrievably.[22]

(2) The court hearing a petition for divorce shall not hold the marriage to have broken down irretrievably unless the petitioner satisfies the court of one or more or the five following facts,[23] that is to say—

(a) that the respondent has committed adultery and the petitioner finds it intolerable to live with the respondent[24];

(b) that the respondent has behaved in such a way that the petitioner cannot reasonably be expected to live with the respondent[25];

---

[19] Family Proceedings Rules 1991, R 2.36.

[20] *Santos v Santos* [1972] Fam 247; *Pounds v Pounds* [1994] 1 FLR 775.

[21] Cretney (2003a p 383) suggests that rather than minimising the bitterness and distress of divorce, the special procedure may have increased them, because parties no longer have the opportunity of answering allegations made in the petition or venting their grievances in court.

[22] See *Pheasant v Pheasant* [1972] 1 All ER 587.

[23] It is not necessary to show that the fact relied upon caused the irretrievable breakdown: *Buffery v Buffery* [1988] 2 FLR 365. Evidence of breakdown is insufficient if one of the facts is not proved: *Stringfellow v Stringfellow* [1976] 2 All ER 539, and evidence of one of the facts is insufficient if irretrievable breakdown is not proved: *Buffery v Buffery* [1988] 2 FLR 365.

[24] Note that the petitioner may not rely upon his or her own adultery, and that *both* adultery and intolerability have to be proved. The intolerability need not be because of the adultery: *Cleary v Cleary* [1974] 1 All ER 498 (CA). Adultery requires some element of penile-vaginal penetration: *Sapsford v Sapsford and Furtado* [1954] P 394; [1954] 2 All ER 373; *Dennis v Dennis* [1955] P 153; [1955] 2 All ER 51 (CA). It may be proved by the respondent's admission on the prescribed form in the special procedure and the co-respondent need not be named. Note s 2(1): if the parties live together for more than six months after the adultery, the Petition cannot be based on that act of adultery.

[25] Once again, the petitioner cannot rely upon his or her own behaviour, and note also that proof of this fact has both a subjective and an objective element. The court must make a value judgement and determine if a reasonable person would think it was reasonable for that petitioner to continue to live with that respondent (*Pheasant v Pheasant* [1972] 1 All ER 587) taking into account the temperament of the parties and in that case, the mental illness of the respondent.

Behaviour, then, need not be intentional. See also *O'Neill v O'Neill* [1975] 3 All ER 289; *Ash v Ash* [1972]

(c)  that the respondent has deserted the petitioner for a continuous period of at least two years immediately preceding the presentation of the petition[26];

(d)  that the parties to the marriage have lived apart for a continuous period of at least two years immediately preceding the presentation of the petition ... and the respondent consents to a decree being granted[27];

(e)  that the parties to the marriage have lived apart for a continuous period of at least five years immediately preceding the presentation of the petition ... .[28]

(3) On a petition for divorce it shall be the duty of the court to inquire, so far as it reasonably can, into the facts alleged by the petitioner and into any facts alleged by the respondent.[29]

(4) If the court is satisfied on the evidence of any such fact as is mentioned in subsection (2) above, then, unless it is satisfied on all the evidence that the marriage has not broken down irretrievably, it shall, subject to [section 5] below, grant a decree of divorce.

(5) Every decree of divorce shall in the first instance be a decree nisi and shall not be made absolute before the expiration of six months from its grant unless the High Court by general order from time to time fixes a shorter period ... .[30]

**2.** (1) One party to a marriage shall not be entitled to rely for the purposes of section 1(2)(a) above on adultery committed by the other if, after it became known to him that the other had committed that adultery, the parties have lived with each other for a period exceeding, or periods together exceeding, six months.

(2) Where the parties to a marriage have lived with each other after it became known to one party that the other had committed adultery, but subsection (1) above does not apply, in any proceedings for divorce in which the petitioner relies on that adultery the fact that the parties have lived with each other after that time shall be disregarded in determining for the purposes of section 1(2)(a) above whether the petitioner finds it intolerable to live with the respondent.

---

Fam 135; [1972] 1 All ER 582. The value judgement of the court in illustrated in *Thurlow v Thurlow* [1975] 2 All ER 979 where the husband petitioned on the basis of his wife's volatile and increasingly violent behaviour. The court said its job was to take into account all the obligations of the married state including the normal duty to accept and share the burdens of ill-health, and here it was above and beyond reasonable expectations for Mr Thurlow to stay with his mentally ill wife. Contrast this with the *Richards* decision in which it was not unreasonable to expect Mrs Richards to continue to live with Mr Richards' moodiness, spells of silence and staring and occasional violence. In *Richards v Richards* [1972] 3 All ER 695, 701, notwithstanding irretrievable breakdown, the behaviour was not such that she could not reasonably be expected to live with him. See more recently, however, *Birch v Birch* [1992] 1 FLR 564 where the husband's dogmatic and chauvinistic behaviour towards a sensitive wife was held to be behaviour with which she could not reasonably be expected to live. Note s 2(3) which allows the court, for the purposes of determining the reasonableness of the expectation that the Petitioner ought to continue living with the Respondent, to take into account the continued cohabitation of the spouses after the last incident relied upon in the petition only if the cohabitation lasts for more than six months.

[26] This fact is rarely used. Desertion requires an unjustified withdrawal from the married state without the consent of the other spouse and with the intention to remain permanently separated. But, note s 2(4), which states that intention may be inferred by the court in certain circumstances if the respondent was incapable of continuing it. Note also s 2(5) which states that the continuous period of two years desertion, or two years (s 1(2)(d)) or five years (s 1(2)(e)) living apart will not be interrupted by the parties resuming cohabitation for up to six months, but that those periods of cohabitation shall not count as part of the time of desertion or living apart. This appears to encourage attempts at reconciliation.

[27] Living apart means not living in the same household s 2(6) and can occur if the parties are living under the same roof: *Mouncer v Mouncer* [1972] 1 All ER 289.

[28] No consent is required for this separation. This provision was originally described as a 'Casanova's Charter' and so protection for innocent deserted spouses was put into place in s 5.

[29] Undefended divorces now proceed according to the special procedure: see above.

[30] The period of time between the decree nisi and decree absolute is now six weeks.

(3) Where in any proceedings for divorce the petitioner alleges that the respondent has behaved in such a way that the petitioner cannot reasonably be expected to live with him, but the parties to the marriage have lived with each other for a period or periods after the date of the occurrence of the final incident relied on by the petitioner and held by the court to support his allegation, the fact shall be disregarded in determining for the purposes of section 1(2)(b) above whether the petitioner cannot reasonably be expected to live with the respondent if the length of that period or of those periods together was six months or less.[31]

(4) For the purposes of section 1(2)(c) above the court may treat a period of desertion as having continued at a time when the deserting party was incapable of continuing the necessary intention if the evidence before the court is such that, had that party not been so incapable, the court would have inferred that his desertion continued at that time.

(5) In considering for the purposes of section 1(2) above whether the period for which the respondent has deserted the petitioner or the period for which the parties to a marriage have lived apart has been continuous, no account shall be taken of any one period (not exceeding six months) or of any two or more periods (not exceeding six months in all) during which the parties resumed living with each other, but no period during which the parties lived with each other shall count as part of the period of desertion or of the period for which the parties to the marriage lived apart, as the case may be.

(6) For the purposes of section 1(2)(d) and (e) above and this section a husband and wife shall be treated as living apart unless they are living with each other in the same household, and references in this section to the parties to a marriage living with each other shall be construed as references to their living with each other in the same household.

...

**3.** (1) No petition for divorce shall be presented to the court before the expiration of the period of one year from the date of the marriage.

(2) Nothing in this section shall prohibit the presentation of a petition based on matters which occurred before the expiration of that period.

...

**5.** (1) The respondent to a petition for divorce in which the petitioner alleges five years' separation may oppose the grant of a decree on the ground that the dissolution of the marriage will result in grave financial or other hardship to him[32] and that it would in all the circumstances be wrong to dissolve the marriage.[33]

(2) Where the grant of a decree is opposed by virtue of this section, then—

(a)    if the court finds that the petitioner is entitled to rely in support of his petition on the fact of five years' separation and makes no such finding as to any other fact mentioned in section 1(2) above, and

(b)    if apart from this section the court would grant a decree on the petition, the court shall consider all the circumstances, including the conduct of the parties to the marriage and

[31] This section appears to encourage parties to attempt reconciliation without fear that such an attempt would make it more difficult to establish the behaviour fact if the attempt fails.

[32] Financial hardship includes loss of pension rights. Other hardship can include social and religious hardship: see *Banik v Banik* [1973] 3 All ER 45; but note now s 10A which allows the court to withhold the decree absolute until both parties have declared that they have taken all steps required to dissolve the marriage in accordance with their religious practices.

[33] '[A]ll the circumstances' includes the wishes of the parties and the children. Note that this is the second part of a two part test. Both must be proved. Further protection is provided between the decree nisi and the decree absolute by s 10, under which the court must in separation fact cases, be satisfied that reasonable financial provision is made by the petitioner to the respondent or that no financial provision is to be made.

the interests of those parties and of any children or other persons concerned, and if of opinion that the dissolution of the marriage will result in grave financial or other hardship to the respondent and that it would in all the circumstances be wrong to dissolve the marriage it shall dismiss the petition.

(3) For the purposes of this section hardship shall include the loss of the chance of acquiring any benefit which the respondent might acquire if the marriage were not dissolved.

**6.** (1) Provision shall be made by rules of court for requiring the solicitor acting for a petitioner for divorce to certify whether he has discussed with the petitioner the possibility of a reconciliation and given him the names and addresses of persons qualified to help effect a reconciliation between parties to a marriage who have become estranged.

(2) If at any stage of proceedings for divorce it appears to the court that there is a reasonable possibility of a reconciliation between the parties to the marriage, the court may adjourn the proceedings for such period as it thinks fit to enable attempts to be made to effect such a reconciliation.

Steve and Jenny both want a divorce. However, as there is no provision for joint petitions, one of them will have to petition the court and designate the other as respondent. Whoever petitions must establish that his or her marriage has broken down irretrievably and prove that one of the five facts applies to him or her.

The petitioner's first step will probably be to obtain information about how to proceed. He or she could attend at a Citizen's Advice Bureau or see a solicitor to get this information, but if they live in one of the areas that is currently piloting a new system, the Family Advice and Information Service (FAInS),[34] they will be able to access a 'one-stop shop' intended to provide legal advice and representation as well as information about a range of other specialist services including marriage support, counselling and mediation. In the current Legal Services Commission pilot projects, solicitors act as case managers, tracking and supporting the client through the various stages of the separation and divorce process (Walker 2004). The results of the pilots will be evaluated in 2005–06, but it is that anticipated a FAInS or some form of it will eventually become established nationally, as government policy is to provide information and support to divorcing couples, with a view to decreasing acrimony and conflict. This policy was made clear in the statutory provisions, which never came into force, contained in Part II of the Family Law Act 1996. The legislation required a party considering divorce to attend an information meeting before he or she was able to present a petition for divorce.[35] The results of the pilot projects on those information meetings indicated that while parties wanted and appreciated receiving information about divorce, they were unhappy about the 'one-size-fits-all' nature of the information provided at the meetings (Walker 2001; and 2004). The new service is intended to tailor information to individual clients.

The results of the information meeting pilots also indicated that parties were just as likely, if not more so, to seek the advice of a solicitor after attending the meeting (Walker 2001). People overwhelmingly see divorce as a legal matter as much as an emotional and social one (Walker 2001; 2004; and Genn 1999), and so either Steve or

---

[34] See ch 11.
[35] See below pp 523–26.

Jenny will be likely to want to consult a solicitor about their divorce.[36] While public funding is not available for a solicitor's services regarding the divorce itself, some funding might be available for resolving any issues about residence or contact or finances. Steve and Jenny must note, however, that the Legal Services Commission Funding Code (LSC (2000) Section 11; LSC (2003a) C27–9)[37] requires all who apply for funding for legal representation or general family help first to attend a meeting with a mediator who will determine if mediation is suitable to their dispute. If the mediator determines that it is not, then funding for representation or general family help is available (LSC 2000 Section 11; LSC 2003a C27–9). If the determination is positive, however, then funding may be available for full mediation (*ibid*). So, if either Steve or Jenny cannot afford the services of a lawyer, he or she must attend this meeting in order to determine if their questions about Barbie's care are suitable for mediation, so opening the way to public funding.[38] Steve and Jenny should note also, however, that even if they do not require public funding for their case, they will be encouraged to mediate rather than litigate any disputes they may have over finances or Barbie's care. (DCA, DfES and DTI 2005).[39]

As they have been married for over one year, Steve and Jenny are not affected by the bar under Section 3(1). Provided none of the other bars applies and provided one of the five facts and irretrievable breakdown are established, a decree of divorce will be granted. However, on the information available, it is not obvious that any of the five facts is appropriate. There is no suggestion of adultery, although adultery need not occur during the cohabitation of the parties in order to be relied upon. If they wish to divorce quickly, they may rely upon the behaviour fact, but one of them will have to prove behaviour which has made it unreasonable for him or her to live with the other. That unreasonableness will be considered from both an objective and subjective point of view. What has to be established is whether it is unreasonable to expect Steve to continue to live with Jenny or Jenny to live with Steve. The older cases indicate that the behaviour needs to be fairly serious, but the more recent evidence is that the court will not judge too strictly that which one partner claims is unreasonable for him or her. The Law Society has suggested that 'virtually any spouse can assemble a list of events, which, taken out of context, can be presented as unreasonable behaviour sufficient on which to found a divorce petition' (The Law Society, Family Law Sub-Committee 1979, in Law Commission 1988a para 3.8). The fact remains, however, that one partner will have to allege such behaviour on the part of the other, and so one of them will have to provide evidence of incidents probably pointing to more than merely a 'strained' relationship, and allege that they constitute behaviour on the part of the other with which it unreasonable to expect them to live. However, as the Law Commission's comments suggest, it would probably be possible to devise an appropriate list of to support a petition.

Steve and Jenny are now separated. After they have been apart for two years, and assuming, as is the case here, the other consents to the divorce, one of them could instigate divorce proceedings on the basis of the separation fact in Section 1(2)(d).

---

[36] The Legal Services Commission will launch a pilot telephone helpline service in March 2006. It will aim to help people avoid using the courts by directing them towards other services which might help them to resolve their disputes. The pilots will be evaluated after one year (DCA, DfES and DTI 2005 para 43).

[37] See further ch 11.

[38] See below p 531. As at March 2005 the government was considering restructuring the levels of service for private family law cases, replacing the current three levels of service with one (DCA, DfES and DTI 2005 para 43). Further, the government will pilot a 'collaborative law' model to operate where cases are publicly funded. In this model both parents' solicitors are committed to promoting settlements and they cannot take the case into court if it fails. Another solicitor will have to be instructed (DCA, DfES and DTI 2004 para 62).

[39] See discussion below, p 531; see also ch 11.

Separation need not be physical separation, however, and if they can show that for the past two years they have lived separately under the same roof, they may be granted an immediate divorce. In order to establish that their households have been separate for two years, they will need to show that they have not been sharing a common life together, in that they have not, for example, been sharing meals, finances, affection or other incidents of cohabitation. It is doubtful whether they will be able establish this state of affairs, once again, as a difficult or strained relationship probably would not constitute living in separate households.

It seems that despite Steve and Jenny's common desire to divorce in the light of their assessment that their marriage is over and their unsuccessful attempts to work things out, they will not be able to obtain a divorce unless they live separately for two years or establish that it is unreasonable to expect one to live with the other in the light of his or her behaviour. Because the divorce will proceed on an undefended basis, any allegations made will not be challenged or scrutinised too closely. If they are successful in establishing the ground for divorce, the court will not grant the decree nisi unless it is also satisfied that satisfactory arrangements have been made for Barbie's welfare, including arrangements regarding where she lives, her education and financial support.[40]

In conclusion, as Steve and Jenny do not appear to be in rush to divorce, waiting for the separation fact may not be a hardship to them. To others, however, it may be.

> **Q** What purpose, if any, is served by requiring proof of one of the facts in addition to the irretrievable breakdown of Steve and Jenny's marriage? How would you advise Jenny? Would your advice to Steve be different?

## IV. DIVORCE REFORM 1969–2005

While the MCA 1973 remains the law, the issue of divorce reform has continued to vex the government. Perhaps the compromise nature of the 1969 reforms made continuing debate inevitable. Smart suggests also that by the 1980s the 'optimistic scenario in which families happily re-constituted themselves did not materialise' (1999b p 9). In the light of cultural shifts in the meanings of parenthood and shifts in patterns of employment, it became evident that, 'for many women with children, remarriage was unlikely, unattractive or even financially irresponsible' (*ibid*). But in the 1980s and 1990s context of increased public spending on divorced spouses and their children, increased expenditure on legal aid, perceptions of the effects of conflict and divorce on children and the former Conservative government's 'back to basics' and 'family values' political rhetoric, a moral panic of sorts appears to have been created by the increase in the rate of divorce.[41] In 1988 the Law Commission presented a discussion paper proposing further reform of divorce law (1988a), and followed this paper with a Report (1990) in which it presented the view that divorce ought to be treated in law as a process over time rather than as a single event. The particular proposals could also be seen as a means of reducing the upwardly spiralling legal aid budget in family matters. The government therefore adopted the Report in a Consultation Paper issued by the Lord Chancellor's Department (LCD 1993) and followed this with a White Paper (LCD 1995a). A Bill[42]

---

[40] S 41 MCA 1973.

[41] In 1971 there were 73,666 decrees absolute granted in England and Wales; in 1981 144,763; in 1991 158,301; and in 1996 156,692 (Population Trends 117, 2004 p 74).

[42] The Family Law Bill 1995.

was published in 1995 and the Family Law Act was passed in 1996. Parts II and III of the Act dealing with divorce and legal aid will not become law, but in many ways their legacy lives on in policy and procedural reform.

Before we examine this legacy, let us first look at the criticisms of the existing law. Are they still valid? The Law Commission, like other commissions before it, agreed that its brief was twofold: to buttress rather than to undermine the stability of marriage and to allow the 'empty shell' of an already broken down marriage to be destroyed with maximum fairness and a minimum of distress and bitterness (1990). While the objectives had not changed much from previous commissions, this time it was also suggested that there was an overwhelming belief that the current law was confusing and unjust. The Law Commission's (1990) six main criticisms of the 1973 Act were:

*(a) It is Confusing and Misleading*

2.8 There is a considerable gap between theory and practice, which can lead to confusion and lack of respect for the law. Indeed, some would call it downright dishonest. There are several aspects to this. First, the law tells couples that the only ground for divorce is irretrievable breakdown, which apparently does not involve fault. But next it provides that this can only be shown by one of five 'facts', three of which apparently do involve fault ... .

2.9 Secondly, the fact which is alleged in order to prove the breakdown need not have any connection with the real reason why the marriage broke down ... .

2. 10 The behaviour fact is particularly confusing. It is often referred to as 'unreasonable behaviour', which suggests blameworthiness or outright cruelty on the part of the respondent; but this has been called a 'linguistic trap'[43] because the behaviour itself need be neither unreasonable nor blameworthy: rather its effect on the petitioner must be such that it is unreasonable to expect him or her to go on living with the respondent, a significantly different and more flexible concept which is obviously capable of varying from case to case and court to court ...

2.11 Finally, and above all, the present law pretends that the court is conducting an inquiry into the facts of the matter, when in the vast majority of cases it can do no such thing. (pp 5–9, emphasis in original))

**Q** Do you agree that the current law is confusing and misleading? What arguments would you make against this accusation?

*(b) It is Discriminatory and Unjust*

...

2.13 The fault-based facts can ... be intrinsically unjust. 'Justice' in this context has traditionally been taken to mean the accurate allocation of blameworthiness for the breakdown of the marriage.[44] Desertion is the only fact which still attempts to do this ... . A finding of adultery or behaviour certainly need not mean that the respondent is any more to blame than the petitioner for the breakdown of the marriage. ...

---

[43] *Bannister v Bannister* (1980) 10 Fam Law 240, *per* Ormrod LJ.
[44] See on this Whelan (1995) and particularly in that volume N Barry. For a contrary view, see Ellman (1997). One must also ask whose sense of justice is being denied. If the majority of divorces are instigated by wives, it is usually husbands who feel that, because the decision to leave was not theirs, they should not be punished by sharing any of 'their' assets with their wives (Davis, et al, 1994 pp 51–53). Indeed, Ellman (1997 p 227) indicates that wives usually feel satisfied with their divorces and the results of their divorces.

2.14 This inherent potential for injustice is compounded by the practical problems of defending or bringing a cross-petition of one's own … .

> **Q** Do you agree that 'justice' includes the allocation or recognition of blame in divorce cases? The Law Commission's earlier paper (1988a) reported that usually both parties were equally to blame for the end of the marriage. Do you agree?

*( c ) It Distorts the Parties' Bargaining Position*

2.15 … Questions of the future care of children, distribution of family assets, and financial provision are all governed by their own legal criteria … . Yet negotiations may also be distorted by whichever of the parties is in a stronger position in relation to the divorce itself.[45] The strength of that position will depend upon a combination of how anxious or reluctant that party is to be divorced and how easy or difficult he or she will find it to prove or disprove one of the five facts … .

*( d ) It Provokes Unnecessary Hostility and Bitterness*

2.16 A law which is arbitrary or unjust can exacerbate the feelings of bitterness, distress and humiliation so often experienced at the time of separation and divorce. Even if the couple have agreed that their marriage cannot be saved it must make matters between them worse if the system encourages one to make allegations against the other … .

> **Q** Is there anything the law can or should do to ease the pain of relationship breakdown?

*( e ) It Does Nothing to Save the Marriage*

2.17 None of this is any help with the law's other objective, of supporting those marriages which have a chance of survival. The law cannot prevent people from separating or forming new relationships, although it may make it difficult for people to get a divorce. The law can also make it difficult for estranged couples to become reconciled. The present law does make it difficult for some couples—in practice a very small proportion—to be divorced, but it does so in an arbitrary way depending upon which facts may be proved. It also makes it extremely difficult for couples to become reconciled … .

2.18      … An undefended decree can be obtained in a matter of weeks. If both parties are contemplating divorce, the system gives them every incentive to obtain a 'quickie' decree based on behaviour or separation, and to think out the practical consequences later.[46]

*( f ) It Can Make Things Worse for the Children*

2.19 … The children themselves would usually prefer their parents to stay together. But the law cannot force parents to live amicably or prevent them from separating. It is not known whether children suffer more from their parents' separation or from living in a household in conflict where they may be blamed for the couple's inability to part … . Children who suffer most are those whose parents remain in conflict.

---

[45] See Ellman (1997).
[46] *Ibid.*

2.20 ... [T]he present law can, for all the reasons given earlier, make the conflict worse. It encourages couples to find fault with one another and disputes about children seem to be more common in divorces based on intolerable behaviour than in others ... .

**Q** Do you accept these criticisms of the current law? If so, what options for reform are there? Some jurisdictions chose to adopt a divorce system based on separation of the parties for a minimum period. This option is said to have the advantage of requiring the parties to experience living apart from each other, with all of the financial and emotional consequences that entails, before they divorce.[47] Other options are to allow divorce by consent of the parties or divorce on the unilateral demand of one party, as in Sweden (Bradley 1996). These options were rejected by the Law Commission because, among other things, it was said that to adopt either would allow the state to abdicate its interest in sustaining marriage and determining when marriages should be ended. In your view, are these compelling interests that the state should accommodate in its divorce law? See Ellman (1997) and Whelan (1995) for contrary views on this question.

Deech argues:

[E]very 20 years or so, we ease divorce law, claiming that marital breakdown is attributable to changing social factors and not to the law. Every successive attempt during this century to bring statute law into line with 'reality' has resulted in an increase in the divorce rate. The increased divorce rate results in greater familiarity with divorce as a solution to marital problems, more willingness to use it and to make legislative provision for its aftermath. The resultant pressure on the divorce system leads to a relaxation of practice and procedure ..., then to a call for a change in the law in order to bring it into line with 'reality', and then to yet another increase in divorce. (1994 p 121)

Richards (1996) takes issue with Deech's correlation between divorce reform and the rate of marriage breakdown. He argues:

There is a widespread view that the number of those who divorce is determined by the ease or difficulty of the legal process. In the widest sense this is, of course, true—if divorce is not possible, it cannot happen. However, as the example of Ireland shows, the absence of a divorce process does not ensure that all couples remain living together or, indeed, married. The process of marital breakdown should be distinguished from the various legal processes that those whose marriages have ended use (or do not use) to regularise their situation ... .

The views in Phillips (*Putting Asunder: A History of Divorce in Western Society* (CUP, 1988)) represent a consensus among researchers and informed commentators:

divorce law reforms had little or nothing to do with setting off the most recent [ie 1960–70s] divorce rate increases. In almost all countries divorce rates had begun to rise before legal reforms were enacted or came into force, and the widespread introduction of no-fault divorce legislation during the 1970s was partly a response to increased divorce, not a cause of it. (p 620)

... There are those who have, and will, argue that the proposed legislation [the Family Law Act 1996] will make divorce 'easier' and so increase the numbers. Such arguments miss the point; for most couples the difficulty or ease of divorce lies not in negotiating the legal procedures but in the inevitably painful process of reaching a decision to end a relationship and the enormous emotional, social and economic upheavals that are involved in uncoupling. (1996 pp 151–53).

---

[47] See eg, Canada, The Divorce Act 1985; and Davies (1993).

**Q** Do you find Richards' arguments convincing? Do the debates confuse rates of marital breakdown with rates of divorce? Is there anything that law can do about marital breakdown? Can it be argued that the symbolic value of the law is as important as its practicalities, so that the message law gives to the public about the 'ease' or 'difficulty' of divorce must not be ignored?

The option chosen by the Law Commission and implemented in the Family Law Act 1996 was said to make divorce both 'easier' and 'more difficult'. A 'process over time' option was said best to meet the government's objectives of a new divorce law:

> to support the institution of marriage; to include practicable steps to prevent the irretrievable breakdown of marriage; to ensure that the parties understand the practical consequences of divorce before taking any irreversible decision; where divorce is unavoidable, to minimise the bitterness and hostility between the parties and reduce the trauma for the children; and to keep to the minimum the cost to the parties and the taxpayer. (LCD 1995 para 3.5 p 18).

**Q** Note the similarities and differences between these objectives, written in 1995, and those in 1912, 1937, 1956 and 1966.

## V. THE LEGACY OF THE FAMILY LAW ACT 1996

Section 1 FLA sets out a number of general principles designed to provide guidance to courts and professional personnel involved in the divorce process. It is in force, and despite its specific reference to Parts II and III which are not in force, sets out clearly the current policy with respect to divorce.

> 1. The court and any person, in exercising functions under or in consequence of Parts II and III, shall have regard to the following general principles—
>
> (a) that the institution of marriage is to be supported;
> (b) that the parties to a marriage which may have broken down are to be encouraged to take all practicable steps, whether by marriage counselling or otherwise, to save the marriage;
> (c) that a marriage which has irretrievably broken down and is being brought to an end should be brought to an end
>     (i) with minimum distress to the parties and to the children affected;
>     (ii) with questions dealt with in a manner designed to promote as good a continuing relationship between the parties and any children affected as is possible in the circumstances; and
>     (iii) without costs being unreasonably incurred in connection with the procedures to be followed in bringing the marriage to an end; and
> (d) that any risk to one of the parties to a marriage, and to any children, of violence from the other party should, so far as reasonably practicable, be removed or diminished.

We immediately see that this part of the Act has a dual focus: both to end and to save marriages, and it is arguable that these dual, indeed, conflicting goals contributed to the unworkability of the divorce parts of the Act and to their eventual repeal (Walker 2004).

We shall provide an overview of the statutory provisions rather than their details[48] and suggest that their vision of the good divorce and the good divorcing subject continues to drive reform, now, however, of divorce policy and procedure (Diduck 2003).[49]

The sole ground for divorce under FLA 1996 was irretrievable breakdown of marriage, which was to be evidenced by one or both parties lodging with the court a 'statement of marital breakdown', waiting a prescribed period of time for 'reflection and consideration' (at least nine months) beginning two weeks after making the statement, and then, having reflected upon the breakdown and considered arrangements for their future, lodging with the court a further statement that the marriage had irretrievably broken down. The court would then grant the divorce if it was satisfied that the parties had made satisfactory arrangements for the future, including arrangements settling financial matters between them and for any children of the marriage. No party, however, was entitled to make the initial statement of marital breakdown, unless he or she had first attended an 'information meeting', that had two principal objectives: '[t]he first was to direct attention to the issues which it was felt people contemplating taking steps to end their marriage needed to consider. The second was to ensure that these people were given information on the various options for the resolution of difficulties, including the availability of marriage support services, mediation and legal services' (Walker 2004 Executive Summary).

There are novel aspects of both the procedure and the 'message' (Eekelaar 1999) of the 1996 Act. Procedurally, 'fault' was finally removed from the law; irretrievable breakdown was to be evidenced solely by living apart. The second novel aspect of the legislation was that divorce was to be a decision taken solely by the parties; the Act provided, in effect, for divorce by consent. These two changes supported a revised vision of marriage: that it is about the relationship between the individuals concerned rather than about the relationship between them and the state. The third novel procedural aspect of the Act was the way in which it directly promoted, indeed required, the previously only implicitly encouraged relationship between law and applied social work (Cretney 2003a p 390) at various stages of the process. This last element of the Act was important in order to give effect to a number of new 'messages' the Act was designed to 'radiate' (Eekelaar 1999),[50] including the idea that divorce was not a one-off event, but rather was to be seen as part of a family's life course; it was a transition rather than an ending. Further, the message was that parties ought to be able to manage that transition in a responsible way if sufficient information and counselling were provided to them (at the information meetings and meetings with a marriage counsellor) and that they would then reflect upon it (during the period of reflection and consideration) and see that the responsible divorce was one which was conflict-free and harmonious (and so choose to mediate rather than litigate outstanding issues between them). In general the 'FLA 1996 was intended to do more than simply provide a new framework for divorce. It was intended to effect a cultural shift in how people view marriage and divorce, and also to effect behavioural change' (Diduck 2003 p 58).

One of the ways in which that change was to be encouraged was through the provision of information at the mandatory information meetings. We have seen that the results of the information meeting pilot projects indicated that while people do want information about divorce law, they want information that is relevant to them and their

---

[48] For a detailed discussion of the provisions and how they would have applied to Steve and Jenny's marriage, see the first edition of this volume pp 427–35.

[49] See also Walker (2004).

[50] See also Dewar (1998).

circumstances (Walker 2004) and that while they thought information about the importance of reducing conflict and its effects on children was 'useful' (Walker 2001 p 829), having that information did not necessarily translate into the 'crude behavioural changes anticipated by government' (Diduck 2003 p 59). And yet, while the mandatory information meetings are being consigned to history (for now), government seems to retain its belief that people's behaviour can be influenced by providing them with the 'right' information, now by solicitors through the FAInS.

Under FLA 1996 people were to take personal responsibility for acting on the information they received. They were to reflect upon it, consider it and, ideally, in its light, either to choose a therapeutic intervention for their marriage, or choose to divorce responsibly by submerging conflict. In this way, the Act has been described as radiating another 'message': in this case a new social and individual moral agenda around divorce (Reece 2003; Diduck 2003; Eekelaar 1999) that provides a new way of regulating it (Smart 1999b; Reece 2003). Rather than imposing upon divorcing couples a morality of externally defined obligation or duty (such as a law based upon punishment and matrimonial fault) the Act redefined as moral those choices people take reflectively and responsibly (Reece 2003) so as to produce the 'good', harmonious divorce. Engaging in counselling and particularly in mediation were two of the ways in which their moral choices were to be exercised under FLA 1996, and we can see that these messages remain in current marriage and divorce policy and procedure.

Finally, the message that divorce is a transition in family life rather than a one-off event is also one which has remained beyond the 1996 Act. Imperatives directed toward saving marriages are now recast into saving families, and the conflict-free divorce is designed to do this by producing the harmonious 'post-divorce family' (Day Sclater 1999; Smart 1999b).

Although Part II of the 1996 may not be with us, therefore, through procedural changes designed to provide information, to encourage mediation and counselling and to 'save' families, its ideal divorce may be.

> The ideal divorce manages families, it brings new forms of families into the ideal family net—in this case a post-divorce family which must take up where the pre-divorce one failed and be forever stable, co-operative and harmonious. It is a non-threatening family (Day Sclater 1999 p 15) and it can be achieved by the 'good' divorce which is harmonious and characterised by rational appraisal and behaviour which plans properly for the future … [i]t keeps families together' (Day Sclater 1999 p 177). It is a bad divorce that tears families apart—it is 'conflict ridden, accusatory, costly … and associated with the legal process' (Day Sclater 1999 p 176).
>
> (Diduck 2003 p 66)

Current divorce law is thus in many ways contradictory. It expresses the preoccupations and compromises of both the 1960s and the new millennium. It displays a tension between theory and practice about whose interests are to be protected by divorce law: the state's or the individual's (Cretney 2003a p 391). Further, its substantive provisions about fault, for example, contrast with its procedural ones about harmony. The effect of this tension can be serious for divorcing individuals.

> The dominant saving marriages [and reducing conflict] agenda points to—indeed it requires—a focus on the 'we' at a time when, psychologically, many spouses are concerned primarily, for a host of complex reasons, with a project of (re)development, (re)assessment and defence of the 'me', of the divorcing self. (Collier 1999 p 261)

The way in which divorce law and practice deal with the 'we' and the 'me' can have profound consequences for divorcing individuals. Day Sclater's (1999) study of the psychodynamics of divorce demonstrates that 'emotions, conflicts and anger are normal psychological parts of coping with loss, separation and reconstruction of identity, yet divorce law and process reject the relevance of feelings, or at least assume they are 'manageable' (Diduck 2003 p 65). Further, while an opportunity to revisit and understand the past is an important part of an individual's building of his or her post-divorce identity, the process allows only a focus on the future of the 'new' family.[51]

## VI. THE CIVIL PARTNERSHIP ACT 2004

As we saw in chapter 2, The Civil Partnership Act 2004 provides for the creation of a new legal status for same-sex partners, and regulates acquisition of that status in ways that are very similar to that of marriage. The Act provides also for the dissolution of civil partnerships, and in this section we outline those provisions and how they might apply to a couple we shall call Stephanie and Jenny, who wish to dissolve their partnership.

> **Q** Stephanie and Jenny were living together for eight years, when in December 2005, they registered their partnership under the Civil Partnership Act 2004. It is now June 2006, and they have been living in the same Housing Association flat for the past seven years since the birth of their daughter Barbie who was conceived with sperm from an anonymous donor received through a licensed fertility clinic. Stephanie and Jenny agreed that Jenny would be the birth mother. On Barbie's birth, they applied for, and received from the court, a shared residence order. Jenny has worked part-time for her local council, and Stephanie is a part-time sales assistant currently looking for full-time work. Due to financial difficulties, their relationship in the last two years has become strained, and finally things become so difficult that both agree that despite their attempts to make the relationship work, they should seek a dissolution. Stephanie moves out.
>
> Stephanie works most weekends, and also every afternoon, and has not had much opportunity to spend time with Barbie since she started school two years ago. She tried to take an active role in her upbringing, especially when Barbie was small and while Jenny was at work three mornings per week, but gradually the day-to-day care for Barbie has been left more and more to Jenny. Jenny and Stephanie feel that they will have no difficulty agreeing financial arrangements; however, they disagree on what would be best for Barbie.

Section 37(1)(a) empowers the court to make a dissolution order, which dissolves a civil partnership. Section 37(2)(a) states that such an order is a conditional order and Section 38(1)(a) that it may be made final after six weeks. Section 41(1) states that no application for a dissolution order may be made within the first year of the civil partnership. We see so far the same provisions as those which apply in divorce proceedings, and

---

[51] On the different experiences of men and women of divorce, see Day-Sclater (1999); Smart and Neale (1999).

indeed Secion 42 imposes on both solicitors and the court the same requirements to take measures to encourage reconciliation of the civil partners as are imposed in divorce proceedings. The similarities with divorce continue:

44

(1) Subject to Section 41, an application for a dissolution order may be made to the court by either civil partner on the ground that the civil partnership has broken down irretrievably.

(2) On an application for a dissolution order the court must inquire, so far as it reasonably can, into—
(a) the facts alleged by the applicant, and
(b) any facts alleged by the respondent.

(3) The court hearing an application for a dissolution order must not hold that the civil partnership has broken down irretrievably unless the applicant satisfies the court of one or more of the facts described in subsection (5)(a), (b), (c) or (d).

(4) But if the court is satisfied of any of those facts, it must make a dissolution order unless it is satisfied on all the evidence that the civil partnership has not broken down irretrievably.

(5) The facts referred to in subsections (3) and (4) are—
(a) that the respondent has behaved in such a way that the applicant cannot reasonably be expected to live with the respondent;
(b) that—
  (i) the applicant and the respondent have lived apart for a continuous period of at least 2 years immediately preceding the making of the application ('2 years' separation'), and
  (ii) the respondent consents to a dissolution order being made;
(c) that the applicant and the respondent have lived apart for a continuous period of at least 5 years immediately preceding the making of the application ('5 years' separation');
(d) that the respondent has deserted the applicant for a continuous period of at least 2 years immediately preceding the making of the application.

45

(1) Subsection (2) applies if—
(a) in any proceedings for a dissolution order the applicant alleges, in reliance on Section 44(5)(a), that the respondent has behaved in such a way that the applicant cannot reasonably be expected to live with the respondent, but
(b) after the date of the occurrence of the final incident relied on by the applicant and held by the court to support his allegation, the applicant and the respondent have lived together for a period (or periods) which does not, or which taken together do not, exceed 6 months.

(2) The fact that the applicant and respondent have lived together as mentioned in subsection (1)(b) must be disregarded in determining, for the purposes of Section 44(5)(a), whether the applicant cannot reasonably be expected to live with the respondent.

(3) Subsection (4) applies in relation to cases where the applicant alleges, in reliance on Section 44(5)(b), that the respondent consents to a dissolution order being made.

(4) Rules of court must make provision for the purpose of ensuring that the respondent has been given such information as will enable him to understand—
(a) the consequences to him of consenting to the making of the order, and
(b) the steps which he must take to indicate his consent.

(5) For the purposes of Section 44(5)(d) the court may treat a period of desertion as having continued at a time when the deserting civil partner was incapable of continuing the necessary intention, if the evidence before the court is such that, had he not been so incapable, the court would have inferred that the desertion continued at that time.

(6)  In considering for the purposes of Section 44(5) whether the period for which the civil partners have lived apart or the period for which the respondent has deserted the applicant has been continuous, no account is to be taken of—
(a) any one period not exceeding 6 months, or
(b) any two or more periods not exceeding 6 months in all,
during which the civil partners resumed living with each other.

(7)  But no period during which the civil partners have lived with each other counts as part of the period during which the civil partners have lived apart or as part of the period of desertion.

(8)  For the purposes of Section 44(5)(b) and (c) and this section civil partners are to be treated as living apart unless they are living with each other in the same household, and references in this section to civil partners living with each other are to be read as references to their living with each other in the same household.

...

47

(1)  The respondent to an application for a dissolution order in which the applicant alleges 5 years' separation may oppose the making of an order on the ground that—
(a) the dissolution of the civil partnership will result in grave financial or other hardship to him, and
(b) it would in all the circumstances be wrong to dissolve the civil partnership.

(2)  Subsection (3) applies if—
(a) the making of a dissolution order is opposed under this section,
(b) the court finds that the applicant is entitled to rely in support of his application on the fact of 5 years' separation and makes no such finding as to any other fact mentioned in Section 44(5), and
(c) apart from this section, the court would make a dissolution order.

(3)  The court must—
(a) consider all the circumstances, including the conduct of the civil partners and the interests of the civil partners and of any children or other persons concerned, and
(b) if it is of the opinion that the ground mentioned in subsection (1) is made out, dismiss the application for the dissolution order.

(4)  'Hardship' includes the loss of the chance of acquiring any benefit which the respondent might acquire if the civil partnership were not dissolved.

48

(1)  The court may, on an application made by the respondent, rescind a conditional dissolution order if—
(a) it made the order on the basis of a finding that the applicant was entitled to rely on the fact of 2 years' separation coupled with the respondent's consent to a dissolution order being made,
(b) it made no such finding as to any other fact mentioned in Section 44(5), and
(c) it is satisfied that the applicant misled the respondent (whether intentionally or unintentionally) about any matter which the respondent took into account in deciding to give his consent.

(2)  Subsections (3) to (5) apply if—
(a) the respondent to an application for a dissolution order in which the applicant alleged—
(i) 2 years' separation coupled with the respondent's consent to a dissolution order being made, or
(ii) 5 years' separation,

has applied to the court for consideration under subsection (3) of his financial position after the dissolution of the civil partnership, and

    (b) the court—

        (i) has made a conditional dissolution order on the basis of a finding that the applicant was entitled to rely in support of his application on the fact of 2 years' or 5 years' separation, and

        (ii) has made no such finding as to any other fact mentioned in Section 44(5).

  (3)    The court hearing an application by the respondent under subsection (2) must consider all the circumstances, including—

    (a) the age, health, conduct, earning capacity, financial resources and financial obligations of each of the parties, and

    (b) the financial position of the respondent as, having regard to the dissolution, it is likely to be after the death of the applicant should the applicant die first.

  (4)    Subject to subsection (5), the court must not make the order final unless it is satisfied that—

    (a) the applicant should not be required to make any financial provision for the respondent, or

    (b) the financial provision made by the applicant for the respondent is—

        (i) reasonable and fair, or

        (ii) the best that can be made in the circumstances.

  (5)    The court may if it thinks fit make the order final if—

    (a) it appears that there are circumstances making it desirable that the order should be made final without delay, and

    (b) it has obtained a satisfactory undertaking from the applicant that he will make such financial provision for the respondent as it may approve.

We can see that the law to be applied in Stephanie and Jenny's case is virtually the same as that in Steve and Jenny's. The only difference is that Steve and Jenny, like all heterosexual spouses, have a possibility of proving irretrievable breakdown of their marriage by reason of adultery, while Stephanie and Jenny do not have this option. The DTI (2003b) stated that adultery was not included among the dissolution facts, but sexual infidelity could found an application for dissolution proceedings by amounting to behaviour:

> Adultery has a specific meaning within the context of heterosexual relationships and it would not be possible nor desirable to read this across to same-sex civil partnerships. The conduct of a civil partner who is sexually unfaithful is as much a form of behaviour as any other. Whether it amounted to unreasonable behaviour on which dissolution proceedings could be grounded would be a matter for individual dissolution proceedings. (DTI 2003b p 36)

**Q** Do you agree that adultery has a very specific meaning in heterosexual marriage that does not apply in civil partnerships? What is that meaning? Do you agree that it would not be desirable to extend it to same-sex civil partnerships?

Stephanie and Jenny, then, could have difficulty in establishing that their partnership had broken down irretrievably. It might be possible to establish the behaviour fact if one of them can find sufficient 'bad' behaviour on the part of the other. If this is not possible, however, like Steve and Jenny, they would have to wait until the two year separation fact could be established. In addition, whichever of them chose to bring the application would have to wait until one year after the civil registration to do so, as they are barred from initiating proceedings within the first year of the registered partnership.

## VII. CONCLUSION (1)

What does the history of divorce tell us about the way in which law and society regulate our relationships? Indeed, what effect *can* the law regulating dissolution of relationships have upon the breakdown of some relationships and the creation of new ones? Many, including sociologists, historians and psychologists, have attempted to explain rising rates of marriage breakdown, but no conclusive answers have been agreed (Stone 1990 pp 410–16). Stone suggests that a combination of factors, including 'changes in social, religious, and moral values, which seem to have been permanently affected by two world wars, together with the by-products of medical and contraceptive technologies, the rise of service economies, and the opening of the labour market to married women' (p 416), have contributed to increased rates of marital breakdown. Richards (1995a) suggests that the nature of marriage itself has changed making relationships more vulnerable. People now expect their marriage partners to meet their emotional, sexual and companionate needs, and women, at least, are more prepared to leave a marriage that does not fulfil these expectations. Yet, perhaps these explanations are less relevant when it comes to same-sex relationships. Given their freedom from socially ascribed gender roles, same-sex partners often have different expectations of each other and of the relationship from those of opposite-sex partners.[52] The statistics that are sure to be compiled eventually on the formation and dissolution of civil partnerships may tell us more about the role that law can and does play in those relationships.

> **Q** 'In 2003, 69% of divorce decrees were granted to the wife in England and Wales. The most frequent fact on which divorce was granted to a woman was the unreasonable behaviour (sic) of her husband, while for a man it was separation for two years with consent' (Office for National Statistics 2004). What explanation can you give for this?

> **Q** Stone suggests that comparisons of current divorce rates with past times may be misleading because of the failure to realise the role played in the past by premature death in dissolving marriages (1990 p 421). Stone's figures show that the proportion of marital dissolutions by death or divorce in England and Wales at the early stages of marriage was much the same for the cohort marrying in 1826 as for that marrying in 1980 (1990 p 410). What conclusions can you draw from this suggestion?

> **Q** Are marriage and divorce two sides of the same coin? Is divorce law the best place for implementing state policy on marriage? Why is this policy implemented at this stage? Would we tolerate any more regulation of our relationships? Finally, why does state policy on civil partnerships appear to mirror almost exactly that on marriage?

---

[52] See eg Weeks (2002); Weeks, *et al*, (1999); Dunne (1999). See also Giddens (1992), Beck and Beck-Gernsheim (1995) and discussion in ch 1 about the changing nature of relationships generally.

## VIII. RESIDENCE AND CONTACT—INTRODUCTION

The breakdown of the relationships in our scenarios raises questions concerning the arrangements to be made for Barbie's care. In Steve and Jenny's case, because they are married to each other, both automatically have parental responsibility and they retain it beyond divorce.[53] In Stephanie and Jenny's case, the joint residence order gives Stephanie parental responsibility with Jenny as long as the residence order remains in force.[54] In both cases, however, there remains a need to decide with whom Barbie should live and what arrangements should be made, if any, for contact with the non-resident parent. It may be necessary for the court to make a residence order to settle the former issue and a contact order to settle the latter. To ascertain the law concerning these orders, it is necessary to refer to the Children Act 1989. It is also necessary to consider certain provisions in the Matrimonial Causes Act 1973 for Steve and Jenny, and in the Civil Partnership Act 2004 for Stephanie and Jenny. These statutes provide the framework for addressing questions of contact and residence in the context of divorce or dissolution proceedings. Before we do this, though, we must review the procedure for obtaining public funding for assistance with any dispute about residence or contact, and the procedures to which parents will be directed for resolving those disputes.

Recall that parents may be eligible for public funding for legal representation or general family help only if their dispute is deemed not suitable for mediation. If it is suitable, they may obtain funding for mediation.[55] The government is committed to promoting alternatives to the court as the primary mechanism for resolving disputes about children. Its main focus is on mediation,[56] but it also plans to develop court-based directions for alternative resolution schemes, including in-court conciliation.[57] In order to help parties reach agreements, the government also intends to develop Parenting Plans. It describes these as:

> a set of templates which seek to show the sort of contact arrangements that work well for children at different ages and who are living in a range of circumstances. These will be made widely available in solicitors' offices, as well as through advice and mediation services. They will describe, in practical terms, arrangements that are generally beneficial for children. They are intended to be used as practical aids, both by parents themselves and by solicitors, conciliators and mediators, to help parents to reach reasonable agreements.
>
> (DCA, DfES and DTI 2005 para 31)

The likelihood of a dispute about Barbie's care reaching court is, therefore, low, but the legal principles developed by courts will form the context in which any mediation or negotiation takes place.

---

[53] See chs 4 and 7.

[54] See *Re C* [1994] Fam Law 468; and chs 4 and 7 on the rights and responsibilities of parenthood, and how Stephanie might otherwise acquire parental responsibility for Barbie. See also Children Act 1989 s 12(2). Because Barbie was conceived using donor sperm from a registered clinic, she is legally fatherless. If the sperm was obtained some other way, she might have a legal father who, by virtue of that status would be entitled to make an application for a s 8 order. We shall not pursue this scenario here, but for a discussion on the position of such fathers, see chs 4 and 7.

[55] See ch 11.

[56] See pp 425–26.

[57] DCA, DfES and DTI 2005.

## IX. THE POWER OF THE COURT TO MAKE SECTION 8 ORDERS

Residence and contact orders, along with prohibited steps and specific issue orders, are designated as Section 8 orders under the Children Act 1989.[58]

Section 10[59] deals with Section 8 orders collectively and sets out the circumstances in which a court is empowered to make such an order. A parent, who falls within the ambit of Section 10(4)(a), is entitled as of right to apply for any s.8 order.[60] This capacity will be extended to step-parents and to civil partners who have attained parental responsibility under s.4A.[61] A civil partner or former civil partner who has treated the child as a child of the family will, when the Civil Partnership Act comes into force, be able to apply for a residence or contact order as of right.[62] Anyone who does not fall within the scope of the definition of a person who is entitled to seek an order is obliged to apply for the leave of the court to make an application.[63] In addition, whether or not a particular person is entitled to seek an order, and irrespective of whether an application has been launched, a court may, of its own motion in family proceedings,[64] make an order in favour of any person. Proceedings under the Matrimonial Causes Act 1973 and Civil Partnership Act 2004 are included in the definition of 'family proceedings'.[65] So, while it is open to any of our parties to institute proceedings for a Section 8 order at any time, once divorce or dissolution proceedings commence the court also has the power to make such an order of its own motion.

Even if parents agree on the arrangements for their children, the court has a part to play. In terms of Section 41 of the Matrimonial Causes Act 1973, and Section 63 of the Civil Partnership Act 2004, it has a duty in divorce and dissolution cases, lest unsatisfactory arrangements be permitted to go by default in the absence of parental opposition,

---

[58] See s 8(2).

[59] Ss 10(4) and (5) provide:

(4) The following persons are entitled to apply to the court for any s 8 order with respect to a child—
(a) any parent or guardian [guardian or special guardian] of the child;
[(aa)any person who by virtue of s 4A has parental responsibility for the child];
(b) any person in whose favour a residence order is in force with respect to the child.
(5) The following persons are entitled to apply for a residence or contact order with respect to a child—
(a) any party to a marriage (whether or not subsisting) in relation to whom the child is a child of the family;
[(aa)any civil partner in a civil partnership (whether or not subsisting) in relation to whom the child is a child of the family] (These words were inserted by the Civil Partnership Act 2004 and are to come into force in December 2005).
(b) any person with whom the child has lived for a period of at least three years;
(c) any person who—
(i) in any case where a residence order is in force with respect to the child, has the consent of each of the persons in whose favour the order was made;
(ii) in any case where the child is in the care of a local authority, has the consent of that authority; or
(iii) in any other case, has the consent of each of those (if any) who have parental responsibility for the child.
[(5A) A local authority foster parent is entitled to apply for a residence order with respect to a child if the child has lived with him for a period of at least one year immediately preceding the application.]

[60] A step-parent falls within the scope of ss 10(5)(a) and (aa) and is therefore entitled to apply for a residence order as of right.

[61] Not in force at the time of writing. S 4A was amended by the Civil Partnership Act.

[62] S 10(5)(aa).

[63] Ss 10(1)(a)(ii), 10(2)(b). The child concerned may apply for a s 8 order with leave of the court in terms of s 10 of the Children Act 1989.

[64] S 10(1)(b). For the definition of 'family proceedings', see s 8(3)–(4).

[65] S 8(4) of the Children Act 1989.

to consider whether the court should exercise any of its powers under the Children Act with respect to any children involved.[66]

> **Q** Do you think it necessary to give the courts the power to reject the arrangements made by parents on divorce or dissolution? If so, do you think the courts should have similar powers when cohabiting couples separate?

*Restricting Access to the Court*

Section 91(14) of the Children Act 1989 makes provision for the restriction of access to the court so that families can be shielded from repeated applications for orders.[67] It states that when the court disposes of an application under the Act, whether or not it makes an order as a result of the application, it can make an order that no application at all, or no application of a specified type, can be made by the person named in the order in respect of the child named unless the court gives leave.

The judgment in *Re P (Section 91(14) Guidelines) (Residence and Religious Heritage)*[68] sets out guidance for the way in which this provision should be used. Firstly, it should be read in conjunction with Section 1(1) which makes the child's welfare paramount. Second, the power to restrict the right of a party to bring proceedings should be used only in exceptional circumstances. It is generally a last resort to be used in cases of 'repeated and unreasonable' applications.[69] However the court can impose the leave restriction if the welfare of the child requires it to do so, even in cases where there is no past history of unreasonable applications.[70] There would need to be a serious risk that, without the imposition of the restriction, 'the child or the primary carers will be subject to unacceptable strain'. The court will also need to be satisfied that the facts go beyond the need for time to settle into the regime ordered by the court. Animosity between the adults will not suffice either. Finally, a restriction may be imposed with or without a time limit, but should be proportionate to the harm it is intended to avoid.

The court in *Re P* also considered whether Section 91(14) might contravene the Human Rights Act 1998 and the ECHR and concluded that it does not. The applicant is not denied access to the court; the effect of the legislation is to create a partial restriction that prevents the applicant from getting the right to an immediate *inter partes* hearing. Moreover, the court said:

> On an application for leave, the applicant must persuade the judge that he has an arguable case with some chance of success. That is not a formidable hurdle to surmount. If the application is hopeless and refused, the other parties and the child will have been protected from unnecessary

---

[66] The court may direct that a dissolution, divorce or separation order is not made until the court orders otherwise if it appears that its powers under the Children Act should be exercised; that they cannot be exercised or that further consideration is needed before they are exercised; and that there are exceptional circumstances making it desirable in the interests of the child that such a direction be made (s 41(2) of the Matrimonial Causes Act 1973; s 63(2) of the Civil Partnership Act). S 41 is under review at the time of writing: see DCA (2002) Recommendation 13. Quaere how this review will affect the CPA 2004 provisions.

[67] The court has the power to do this of its own motion. See *Re C (Prohibition on Further Applications)* [2002] EWCA Civ 292; [2002] 1 FLR 1136.

[68] [1999] 2 FLR 573, 592–93.

[69] See also *Re G (Child Case: Parental Involvement)* [1996] 1 FLR 857; *B v B (Residence Order: Restricting Applications)* [1997] 1 FLR 139.

[70] See *Re M (S 91(14) Order)* [1999] 2 FLR 553; *Re F (Children) (Restriction on Applications)* [2005] All ER (D) 42 (Apr).

involvement in the proposed proceedings and unwarranted investigations into the present circumstances of the child. (pp 593–94)

What the court will be looking for in deciding whether to grant leave is whether an arguable case has been made out that there is a need for renewed judicial investigation.[71]

An order imposing an absolute prohibition does not fall under the section and would have to be made under the court's inherent jurisdiction.[72]

## X. THE WELFARE PRINCIPLE

The Children Act 1989 is cast very firmly in the welfare mould. As we have seen, the welfare of the child is paramount in decisions relating to his or her upbringing.[73] This principle, as we have observed,[74] is not susceptible of easy application in any particular case. The problem of indeterminacy, as well as all the other difficulties surrounding the welfare test that we have considered, is imported into the legislation.

The 1989 Act seeks to reduce indeterminacy and to make explicit certain values by codifying 'what society considers the most important factors in the welfare of children' (Law Commission 1988b para 3.19). A checklist of these factors was incorporated into the statute in the hope that this would provide greater consistency and clarity and to promote a more systematic approach to decision-making by courts. CAFCASS (Children and Family Court Advisory and Support Service) officers, such as the children and family reporter, are also required to give consideration to the checklist when carrying out their duties.[75] Section 1(3) provides:

In the circumstances mentioned in subsection (4), a court shall have regard in particular to—

(a)   the ascertainable wishes and feelings of the child concerned (considered in the light of his age and understanding);
(b)   his physical, emotional and educational needs;
(c)   the likely effect on him of any change in his circumstances;
(d)   his age, sex, background and any characteristics of his which the court considers relevant;
(e)   any harm which he has suffered or is at risk of suffering;
(f)   how capable each of his parents, and any other person in relation to whom the court considers the question to be relevant, is of meeting his needs;
(g)   the range of powers available to the court under this Act in the proceedings in question.[76]

**Q** Do you agree that there is a consensus that these are the most important factors? What would you include in such a checklist?

While the checklist provides some guidance for the courts and furnishes the backdrop for private negotiations, it is of limited use. As Cretney, *et al*, (2002 p 651) observe, it

---

[71] *Re A (Application for Leave)* [1998] 1 FLR 1.
[72] *Re P (S 91(14) Guidelines) (Residence and Religious Heritage)* [1999] 2 FLR 573, 593.
[73] S 1(1) of the Children Act 1989.
[74] See ch 8.
[75] FPR 1991 R 4.11(1); FPC 1991 R 11(1).
[76] At the time of writing, consideration was being given to amending the checklist to 'ensure that the courts have regard to the importance of sustaining a relationship between the children and the non-resident parent (House of Commons, House of Lords 2005 para 121).

merely lists the factors to be considered and does not indicate *how* they should be viewed. It does not prioritise the criteria and courts are still obliged to carry out a difficult balancing exercise. Dewar says that 'the checklist will not eliminate subjective value judgements about parenting and child care arrangements, but may serve to immunise them from challenge on appeal' (1992 p 366)[77]; it may be difficult to overturn a decision reached after consideration of all the criteria (Eekelaar 1991b p 127).

## XI. THE NON-INTERVENTION PRINCIPLE

Section 1(5) of the Children Act 1989 stipulates that the court should not make an order unless there is some positive advantage to doing so. The courts in dissolution or divorce proceedings do not have a general supervisory role in relation to all arrangements for children on divorce; intervention should be limited to those cases where it is thought necessary.

Evidently, the intention behind the legislation is to encourage agreement, to limit judicial intervention[78] and to foster the perception that recourse to the courts should be a last resort. However, the retreat of the courts[79] does not mean that the law becomes insignificant. As Mnookin and Kornhauser say, bargaining takes place 'in the shadow of the law' (1979 p 968).

The 'shadow of the law' loomed particularly large under the ill-fated Family Law Act 1996. The statute promoted private settlement and also contained provisions that would have impacted on the negotiating process. While almost nothing remains of the radical new scheme, Section 1, setting out the general principles, remains in force. It has no legal effect because it was intended to govern the decision-making of judges and 'any person, in exercising functions under or in consequence' of Parts II and III. This would have included solicitors, mediators and children and family reporters, who are officers of the Children and Family Court Advisory and Support Service (CAFCASS).[80] All were expected to have regard to the principle that marriages that have irretrievably broken down should be brought to an end in a way that promotes 'as good a continuing relationship' as possible between the parties and their children. Part II, covering divorce, will never be brought into force and Part III, dealing with legal aid for mediation, has been repealed. Nevertheless, as we saw above, the endorsement of continuity in relationships between parents and children and, as we saw above, the rejection of conflict are principles that permeate government policy, professional practice and legal decision-making relating to separation and divorce. As Walker (2004) observes, there is general agreement on a number of principles:

---

[77] Eekelaar contends that the heavily subjective nature of the power granted to the judge means that, so long as he does not claim to be applying it as a conclusive rule of law, a judge can consider almost any factor which could possibly have a bearing on the child's welfare and assign to it whatever weight he or she chooses (1991b p 125).

[78] See Law Commission (1988b paras 3.3–4).

[79] Indeed, whether the attempt to reduce litigation has been successful is open to doubt; Bailey-Harris, *et al*, (1998) p 16 report a steady increase in the number of the cases going before the courts. The new measures described in DCA, DfES and DTI 2005 above may have a more direct effect, however.

[80] Prior to the establishment of CAFCASS as a result of the Criminal Justice and Court Services Act 2000, the officer acting in private law proceedings would have been a court welfare officer.

These are: that the law has a responsibility to protect the best interests of children; that parents should be encouraged to reduce any conflict between themselves in order to minimise distress to their children; and that, other than in exceptional circumstances, the relationships children have with both their parents should be maintained and fostered during the upheavals and transitions, and on into post divorce family life. (Walker 2004 p 149)

Should our parties reach an agreement about Barbie's upbringing, perhaps through mediation or perhaps with the help of lawyers, that agreement, subject to the court's supervisory role (s.41 MCA and s.63 CPA), will stand. Should they fail to agree, litigation may ensue, but, as we discussed earlier, court proceedings do not signal unconstrained adversarialism.[81] It is worth bearing in mind that the law is influenced by child welfare knowledge and that the legal process has come to share certain values with mediation; professionals and courts alike increasingly deplore any show of hostility by one parent to the other. According to Pickett, '[n]ot only does law cast its shadow over mediation, but mediation also casts its shadow over law' (1991 p 28). And both, she argues, are implicated in reinforcing a familial ideology.

It is against this background that we now turn to the task of advising our parties.


## XII. RESIDENCE

In many cases, parents reach agreement on the question of where the child is to live. The Law Commission (1988b para 3.2) noted that the number of contested cases is small[82] so that orders are generally not necessary to settle disputes. In the event of a dispute, however, or when certainty is considered desirable, it may be necessary to seek a residence order from the court.

A residence order is defined in Section 8 of the Children Act 1989 as 'an order settling the arrangements to be made as to the person with whom a child is to live'. Usually residence is ordered in favour of one parent with contact in favour of the other. A residence order does not have the effect of re-allocating parental responsibility between parents; both retain it and the non-resident parent keeps the right to deal directly with third parties such as schools and hospitals (Bainham 1990 p 210). Therefore, each parent is, on divorce or dissolution, legally entitled to exercise parental responsibility as before, except to the extent that to do so would conflict with a residence or any other court order.[83] While the scope of a residence order in this respect was the subject of some

---

[81] See Bailey-Harris, *et al*, (1998) p 24. Further, Eekelaar, Maclean and Bienart (2000) note that most family law solicitors prefer to promote settlement rather than adversarialism. See also Piper (1999d).

[82] See, eg, Eekelaar and Clive (1977) para 13.3; Priest and Whybrow (1986) para 4.10. Simpson, *et al*, (1995 p 25) report that the majority of non-custodial fathers in their sample accepted the *status quo* regarding residence; approximately 1 in 5 was involved in a dispute about it. In 2003, the number of residence orders granted was 31,966, while only 202 orders were refused (DCA (2003b para 56)).

[83] See s 2(8) of the Children Act 1989. A residence order does not entitle the person in whose favour it is made to change the child's surname or remove the child from the UK without the written permission of every person with parental responsibility or the leave of the court (s 13(1)). This does not prevent a person with a residence order from removing the child from the UK for a period of less than one month (s 13(2)). A residence order significantly weakens the position of the non-resident parent in cases where the caretaking parent wishes to place the child in local authority accommodation. Normally, a local authority may not provide accommodation if there is someone with parental responsibility able and willing to provide accommodation or to arrange for it to be provided for the child (s 20(7)). Also, if a child is being accommodated, he or she may be removed by any person with parental responsibility (s 20(8)). However, these provisions do not apply if there is a residence order in force (s 20(9)).

uncertainty,[84] *Re P (A Minor) (Parental Responsibility Order)*[85] establishes that a residence order precludes the non-resident parent from interfering with the arrangements for the day-to-day life of the child.[86]

> **Q** If Jenny applied for and were granted a residence order, who would be entitled to make decisions regarding Barbie's bedtime? Her schooling? Whether she should be allowed to smoke cigarettes?

Bainham (2005) comments that:

> In most cases, therefore, despite theoretical equality and the ethos of continuing parental responsibility, it is the resident parent who, for practical purposes, will exercise parental powers. The legislation may, notwithstanding, have some influence on the way in which the role of parents is perceived following divorce. It might even be viewed as an attempt at social engineering. It is statutory recognition that ex-spouses remain parents and are expected to be able to distinguish between termination of their own legal and factual relationship and their continuing moral and legal obligations to their children. There is a clear expectation in the legislation that these obligations should not simply be off-loaded onto the other parent or the State. (p153)

Bainham (1990 p 212) has in the past expressed regret at what he perceived to be a legislative failure to promote dual parenting. He took the view that the Children Act should have focused more closely on the concept of time-sharing in the form, perhaps, of a presumption in favour of joint residence. Leaving decisions to parents or, in the event of disagreement, the courts, without establishing a statutory norm of joint parenting, he said, allows many parents to relinquish their parental role (p 213); there is nothing in the legislation to prevent parents continuing 'to agree in droves that mothers should have sole responsibility for the post-divorce care of children' (p 217).

The Children Act does leave open the possibility of shared residence orders on separation: Section 11(4) states that where a residence order is made in favour of two or more persons who do not live together, the order may specify the periods of time during which the child is to live in the different households concerned. It appears that this statutory provision has not, in the past, prompted the judiciary to embrace enthusiastically the possibility of shared residence when parents do not live together.[87] However, judicial pronouncements of late suggest that things might be changing. This may be in part a response to the calls being made by fathers' rights groups for the enactment of a presumption of shared parenting. Certainly, the government does not appear to be averse to court ordered shared parenting.[88]

> **Q** Read chapter 8. What arguments are there in favour of a presumption of shared residence? What arguments are there against it?

---

[84] See Bainham (1993) p 128 n 89.
[85] [1994] 1 FLR 578, 585.
[86] What qualifies as 'day-to-day' is itself not beyond dispute.
[87] See Baker and Townsend (1996).
[88] See DCA, DfES and DTI (2004 paras 42–43).

## XIII. APPLYING THE WELFARE PRINCIPLE

Section 1(3) applies to contested Section 8 cases[89] so any advice to our parties has to be based on a consideration of the welfare checklist[90] and the way it is likely to be applied by a court in this situation. While much of the case law applying the welfare principle pre-dates the Children Act 1989,[91] it remains relevant in carrying out this exercise,[92] even with respect to Stephanie and Jenny's case. Although there is very little case law on residence[93] and contact disputes between same-sex parents, the principles that have developed in the context of opposite-sex parenting will, no doubt, apply to Stephanie and Jenny and to those in their position.

Apart from the fact that it introduces a new emphasis on the child's wishes, the checklist, in effect, codifies previous practice. The courts continue to give weight to the same kinds of factors in deciding residence cases as they did in the past when settling custody disputes. They are reluctant to disturb existing arrangements for the care of the child[94]; they tend to try to ensure that siblings are not separated[95]; they consider which parent is more likely to facilitate contact with the other[96]; they consider material wealth but do not regard this as very important[97]; and they disregard matrimonial misconduct that does not affect parenting capacity.[98] A useful encapsulation of the priorities embodied in the welfare test is provided by a New Zealand court:

> Welfare is an all-encompassing word. It includes material welfare, both in the sense of an adequacy of resources to provide a pleasant home and a comfortable standard of living and in the sense of an adequacy of care to ensure that good health and due personal pride are maintained. However, while material considerations have their place, they are secondary matters. More important are the stability and the security, the loving and understanding care and guidance, the warm and compassionate relationships, that are essential for the full development of the child's own character, personality and talents. (*Walker v Walker and Harrison*)[99]

---

[89] See s 1(4)(a) of the Children Act 1989. Precisely how the courts are using the checklist is not entirely clear. It appears that something less than meticulous adherence to the checklist is required: *B v B (Minors) (Interviews and Listing Arrangements)* [1994] 2 FLR 489, 500. In *B v B (Residence Order: Reason for Decision)* [1997] 2 FLR 602, which concerned a contested residence order, Holman J said that, while it is not necessary to go through it laboriously, the checklist is important in ensuring that all the relevant factors in a case are considered. Strictly speaking, the checklist applies in s 8 proceedings only in contested cases but it seems to influence decision-making generally. Indeed in *Re B (Change of Surname)* [1996] 1 FLR 791 the court held that, although application of the checklist was not mandated in the circumstances before it, nevertheless it remained a 'useful aide mémoire of the factors that may impinge on the child's welfare' (p 793).

[90] However, as the Law Commission indicated (1988b para 3.19), it is not intended to be exhaustive.

[91] See, for a review of the application of the welfare principle in pre–1989 cases, Law Commission (1986) para 6.38.

[92] See *C v C (A Minor) (Custody: Appeal)* [1991] 1 FLR 223, 230. For a discussion of the checklist, see Bainham (2005) pp 40–42. See also Cretney, *et al*, (2002) para 20–011ff.

[93] The court has awarded shared residence to a former partner when a lesbian relationship ended in order to ensure that she had parental responsibility (*G (Children)* [2005] EWCA Civ 462). See ch 7.

[94] *Stephenson v Stephenson* [1985] FLR 1140, 1146; *Re A (A Minor) (Custody)* [1991] 2 FLR 394, 402–3; *Re B (Residence Order: Status Quo)* [1998] 1 FLR 368.

[95] *C v C (Minors: Custody)* [1988] 2 FLR 291; *Re A (A Minor) (Custody)* [1991] 2 FLR 394.

[96] *D v M (A Minor: Custody Appeal)* [1983] Fam 33, 41. See, also, eg, the comments made in *Re A (A Minor) (Custody)* [1991] 2 FLR 394, 403. But see *Re B (Residence Order: Status Quo)* [1998] 1 FLR 368.

[97] *Stephenson v Stephenson* [1985] FLR 1140, 1148. See also *D v M (A Minor) (Custody Appeal)* [1983] Fam 33.

[98] See *Re K (Minors) (Children: Care and Control)* [1977] Fam 179; *S (BD) v S (DJ) (Children: Care and Control)* [1977] Fam 109.

[99] [1981] NZ Recent Law 257, cited with approval by the Law Commission (1986) para 6.10.

In assessing where the child's best interests lie, the courts often rely heavily on the opinions of child welfare professionals.[100] The parents might decide to call their own expert witnesses and the court itself can call for a welfare report.[101] This report is compiled by the children and family reporter (CFR). The CFR[102] should normally see all those concerned in the case and the report must include recommendations, or explain why recommendations cannot be made, drawing on the 'relevant aspects of the welfare checklist' (CAFCASS 2003 para 3.11). A court is not bound to follow the recommendations of the CFR. However if it does decide to depart from the recommendations, the court should hear evidence from the reporter and provide an opportunity to address the court's concerns,[103] and it should give reasons.[104] Failure to consider the CFR's evidence or to give reasons constitutes ground for appeal.

We will now proceed to consider those factors enumerated in the checklist that would be most important in evaluating what would be considered best for Barbie.

*The Child's Wishes*

The court is obliged to have regard to the 'ascertainable wishes and feelings of the child concerned (considered in the light of [her] age and understanding)'.[105]

This item on the checklist echoes the mature minor test deployed in the *Gillick* case.[106] There, the House of Lords emphasised the significance of children's views and accorded to some young people limited autonomy in decision-making, subject to their age and ability to understand the relevant issues.

In the context of Section 8 proceedings, the child's wishes do not determine the outcome of the case; the welfare of the child may be found to dictate that an entirely different course be taken. James, *et al*, found that CFRs 'attach greater importance to their own judgements about the welfare of the child, which are based on a range of professional principles and personal considerations, than to the child's wishes and feelings' (2003 p 893). The authors state that even if a practitioner considered a child competent to express a view, this view might not be reported if the practitioner felt it conflicted with the child's best interests (*ibid*).

The Law Commission saw potential pitfalls in eliciting children's wishes at all. For example, it said, although the wishes of older children cannot be ignored, children should not be made to feel responsible for the eventual decision, and in any event, a child's views may be unreliable (1988b para 3.23).[107]

---

[100] See Buchanan, *et al*, (2001) p 1. See, on the use of experts, King and Kaganas (1998).
[101] S 7 Children Act 1989. The court is not obliged to request a welfare report.
[102] For a critique of the practice of CFRs, see James, *et al*, (2003).
[103] *Re A (Children: 1959 UN Declaration)* [1998] 1 FLR 354.
[104] *W v W (A Minor: Custody Appeal)* [1988] 2 FLR 505; *Re W (Residence)* [1999] 2 FLR 390.
[105] S 1(3)(a).
[106] See ch 16.
[107] See also Cantwell and Scott (1995); Trinder (1997). However, there is research indicating that children do want to be consulted, particularly about residence. See Smart, *et al*, (2001); Hawthorne, *et al*, (2003). Gollop, *et al*, (2000), who carried out research in New Zealand, found that parents rarely discussed arrangements with their children. In the UK, Buchanan, *et al*, found that most children wanted to be more involved in the decision-making process but fewer than half of those interviewed felt they had been heard by the court and their parents (2001 p 92). They also found that few children were asked with whom they wanted to live, although more than half were consulted about contact (2001 p 64). However, more and more significance is being accorded to children's views and *Making Contact Work* (The Advisory Board on Family Law 2002 para 3.2.3) states that parents should be advised to inform and consult their children. See, generally, Kaganas and Diduck (2004). For moves to involve children more in mediation, see ch 11.

In *B v B (Minors) (Interviews and Listing Arrangements)*,[108] the court was clearly alive to these difficulties. While affirming that it was within the judge's discretion to see the children concerned, it commented that this discretion should be exercised cautiously and not as a matter of routine.[109] Wall J went on to observe, *obiter*, that the ascertainment of children's wishes and feelings is normally the province of the welfare professionals advising the court. So, in the context of private law cases, the children and family reporter[110] would normally be expected to speak to the child and include an account of the child's wishes and feelings in the report compiled for the court. Judges who do speak to children are expected to be mindful of their vulnerability: '[W]hen the court does exercise its discretion to see a child it is of the utmost importance to make it clear to the child ... that it is the court which has to make the decision and that the responsibility for the decision is in no sense that of the child.' (pp 496–97)

The Human Rights Act 1998, together with the UN Convention on the Rights of the Child 1989,[111] has led to a heightened consciousness of children's rights, however, and this appears to be prompting the courts to accord greater significance to consultation with children.[112] And there is also a more general view within the courts that 'children should be seen and heard in child cases'.[113] What is more, it is clear that, in some cases, the child's wishes are crucial. In *M v M (Transfer of Custody: Appeal)*,[114] the court observed that to ignore the wishes of a 12–year-old and to impose an order to which she was implacably opposed, would provoke her to resist and, possibly, run away.[115] In *Re S (Contact: Children's Views)*,[116] the court attached considerable importance to the views of teenagers.

> **Q** Why might it be important to take cognisance of Barbie's wishes? Would her wishes be taken into account if her parents were in agreement?

*The Likely Effect of Any Change*

The checklist instructs the court to consider the likely effect on the child of any change in his or her circumstances. This reflects the long-standing practice of applying what is known as the '*status quo* principle'. Courts are very reluctant to disrupt children's lives by moving them from one home to another.[117] As a result, the parent who takes on the care of the children when a relationship breaks down may have an advantage should a dispute over residence arise.

---

108 [1994] 2 FLR 489.

109 P496.

110 See CAFCASS (2003 para 3.5).

111 Art 12.

112 See *Re A (Contact: Separate Representation)* [2001] 1 FLR 715. Depending on the circumstances and the age and maturity of the child, Art 8 of the ECHR may require courts to ensure that they hear children involved in disputes between their parents. Otherwise a parent could claim that the procedural requirements implicit in Art 8, that there should be adequate protection of the parent's interests in the decision-making process, have not been met. See *Sahin v Germany*; *Sommerfeld v Germany* [2003] 2 FLR 671, para 73.

113 *Re A (Contact: Separate Representation)* [2001] 1 FLR 715, para 22. See Kaganas and Diduck (2004) pp 974ff.

114 [1987] 2 FLR 146.

115 Pp 152–53. See also *Re F (Minors) (Denial of Contact)* [1993] 2 FLR 677; *Re P (A Minor) (Education)* [1992] 1 FLR 316, *M v M (Defined Contact Application)* [1998] 2 FLR 244.

116 [2002] 1 FLR 1156.

117 See Eekelaar and Clive (1977) paras 5.3–5.4.

The importance attributed to continuity is evident in *Dicocco v Milne*,[118] where the Court of Appeal reversed a decision to award custody[119] to the father. Ormrod LJ stated:

> [I]t is generally accepted by those who are professionally concerned with children that, particularly in the early years, continuity of care is a most important part of a child's sense of security and that disruption of established bonds is to be avoided whenever it is possible to do so. Where, as in this case, a child of 2 years of age has been brought up without interruption by the mother (or a mother substitute) it should not be removed from her care unless there are strong countervailing reasons for doing so. (pp 259–60)

Of course, the court might decide to move a child if it considers that the existing childcare arrangements are unsatisfactory. As Ormrod LJ said in *S v W*: '[T]he status quo argument depends for its strength wholly and entirely on whether the status quo is satisfactory or not. The more satisfactory the status quo, the stronger the argument for not interfering. The less satisfactory the status quo, the less one requires before deciding to change.' (p 82)[120]

Not surprisingly, in heterosexual relationships such as Steve and Jenny's, it is mothers who tend to benefit from the *status quo* principle. The Office for National Statistics reports that, in its research sample, 93% of resident parents were female while 89% of non-resident parents were male (Blackwell and Dawe 2003 para 1.3).[121] When relationships break down, it is mothers who most often take, or continue to take, responsibility for the care their children.[122] It seems that not many fathers seek residence orders. Smart and May[123] found that, in their study, most applications for residence orders were made by mothers fearing that their children might be removed from their care or attempting to recover a child who had already been removed (2004 p 37):

> It was also nearly always the case that the person applying for residence already had the child living with them. When fathers applied for residence, it tended to be in circumstances where the mother was said to be incapable of caring for the child because of mental health problems or substance abuse. Similarly, when grandparents applied for residence, it was in cases where neither parent was able to care for the child.
>
> It was rare to find cases where a parent was applying for a change in the physical residence of the child … . However, in the 33 cases[124] where the courts in the study sample did order a change in residence, 22 were in favour of fathers and seven were in favour of a grandparent. The study concluded from this that the courts tend to favour a solution that preserves the status quo and that children are moved from one carer to another in fairly exceptional cases.
>
> (Smart and May 2004a p 37)[125]

---

[118] (1983) 4 FLR 247. See also *Re B (Residence Order: Status Quo)* [1998] 1 FLR 368; *Re M (Residence)* [2004] EWCA Civ 1574; [2005] *Fam Law* 216.

[119] Note that cases which refer to 'custody' pre-date the Children Act 1989. Custody orders are no longer part of the court's repertoire. Instead, courts now have the power to make contact and residence orders.

[120] [1981] Fam Law 81.

[121] See also Walker (2004) Table 7.1.

[122] See Walker (2004) p 156ff.

[123] See also Smart, *et al*, (2003).

[124] But see *Re K (Residence Order: Securing Contact)* [1999] 1 FLR 583. In this case it was the father who was granted a residence order because the mother could not be trusted not to take the child to India, and so obstruct contact. The order was granted in spite of the fact that the 2–year old child had always been brought up by the mother, albeit with the help of the grandmother. On the question of abduction or snatching of children, see *Townson v Mahon* [1984] FLR 690; *Re J (A Minor) (Interim Custody: Appeal)* [1989] 2 FLR 304; *Re B (Minors) (Residence Order)* [1992] 3 All ER 867; Bainham (2005) p 742ff.

[125] The sample comprised 430 cases of which 59% involved residence disputes.

It seems that nothing has changed since Brophy's (1989 p 220) work under the pre-Children Act regime. She explained the predominance of custody orders in favour of mothers in terms of maternal caretaking and rejected allegations of discrimination against fathers by the courts. First, she noted, the children's appointment under the old Section 41 procedure[126] was used largely to rubber-stamp the decisions already made by parents. Secondly, parents rarely contested custody in court.[127] And thirdly, in both contested and uncontested cases, custody orders tended to be made on the basis of the *status quo* principle, with the court electing to leave children with the parent who was caring for them at the time of the proceedings.[128]

## The Child's Needs

The court has to consider the physical, emotional and educational needs of the child and assess how capable each parent is of meeting those needs. In doing so, it will take into account factors such as the strength of the bonds between the child, the parents and other members of the household.[129] Where a parent has re-partnered, the suitability, in the court's view, of the new partner as a step-parent as well as the child's relationship with him or her will be significant; fathers who can offer a satisfactory mother substitute, for example, tend to be considered better placed than lone fathers to obtain a residence order.[130]

In *Stephenson v Stephenson*,[131] the Court of Appeal reversed an order placing a child in the care of her mother. The child had been cared for primarily by her father's cohabitant before being removed by the mother. She was found by the court to have a happy and secure life with the father and his cohabitant. The mother had had limited contact with her and, despite the fact that the father was 'awkward' about it, was said to have abandoned her child. The mother's cohabitant had a criminal record, and was unemployed and had uncertain prospects. Moreover, the court doubted the stability of the mother's relationship with him.

In *Re DW (A Minor) (Custody)*,[132] however, it was a step-mother who, although she had been an exemplary carer, was thought to have become an unsuitable candidate for a custody order. This unsuitability was attributable to the fact that her marriage to the father had ended and that she would be a lone parent. The child was moved to the biological mother and her husband.

In *Re DW*, the court may have been prompted by a preference for biological parenthood or by a preference for the nuclear family. In other reported cases, judges may have been influenced by traditional gender roles and the values associated with these.

*May v May*[133] seems to have accorded precedence to those values traditionally associated with the paternal role. The court dismissed an appeal against an order awarding the father care and control of his children. It was thought that he would raise them in a more disciplined way than their mother and her new partner would and that he would

---

[126] S 41 of the Matrimonial Causes Act 1973.
[127] See also Priest and Whybrow (1986) para 4.10.
[128] See also Eekelaar and Clive (1977) para 5.3; Priest and Whybrow (1986) para 4.11.
[129] *Stephenson v Stephenson* [1985] FLR 1140; *Re A (A Minor) (Custody)* [1991] 2 FLR 394.
[130] See *Stephenson v Stephenson* [1985] FLR 1140.
[131] *Ibid.*
[132] [1984] Fam Law 17.
[133] [1986] 1 FLR 325.

provide more stimulation from an educational point of view. The mother lavished affection on the children but her home was more easy-going.

Other decisions have stressed the roles of fathers as earners and of mothers as carers. The courts tend to prefer a parent who is not working full time to one who is.[134] However the prospect of a man, who is capable of working, relying on social security in order to become a full-time carer was apparently anathema to the court. In *B v B (Custody of Child)*,[135] the father had cared for the child. When asked by his employer to go on shift work, he demurred and became unemployed. It was decided that the father should retain custody, with the court emphasising that he had not deliberately given up work in order to go on social security.

In *B v B (Custody of Children)*,[136] a 4½ year-old child had been in the father's care since the breakdown of the marriage over two years earlier. The father was able to devote his time to his son largely because he had lost his job. The court *a quo* had ordered that the child be given into the care of his mother, relying heavily on the father's joblessness. The decision was overturned on appeal, with Oliver LJ stating:

> I find myself in the end unable to resist the conclusion that in exercising his discretion in this case the judge allowed the principal and only question of what the welfare of the minor demanded to be influenced by a consideration of the moral duty of the father not to take advantage of the benefits provided by the welfare state, and I think that must vitiate the balancing exercise in this particular case. I do not wish to suggest for a moment that the prospect of an able-bodied man being permanently unemployed is not a relevant consideration, but it does seem to me that in this particular case the judge's emphasis on it showed that he regarded it ultimately as the conclusive consideration. ... (p 179)

Cumming-Bruce LJ concurred, remarking obiter:

> I agree with the judge that as a matter of common sense it must usually be sensible to place a small child in the care of an affectionate and sufficiently capable mother who is available to give full-time care, rather than placing the child with a father who, in order to attend the needs of the infant, will have to give up work either altogether or to a great degree. (pp 183–84)

**Q** Why was it considered not only acceptable, but desirable, for a mother to be available as a full-time carer but not for a father? How might these gendered assumptions be disrupted in same-sex relationships?

A subsequent case[137] suggests that the courts' dislike of reliance on state benefits may extend also to mothers who wish to be full time carers. In a situation where the man apparently cannot support the post-separation family alone, the court appears to jettison traditional roles rather than countenance the possibility of a drain on the public purse.

*Re DW, May* and both *B v B* decisions reflect outmoded prejudices and assumptions; similar cases might be decided very differently on the basis of different criteria today. Perhaps one of the most striking changes is that the courts now seem to be paying more attention to the question of which parent is most likely to facilitate contact. In *V v V*

---

[134] See *Re M (Residence)* [2004] EWCA Civ 1574; [2005] Fam Law 216.
[135] [1985] FLR 462.
[136] [1985] FLR 166.
[137] *Re R (Residence Order: Finance)* [1995] 2 FLR 612.

*(Contact: Implacable Hostility)*[138] the most important factor in transferring residence from the mother to the father appears to have been that the mother was found to have been unreasonably obstructing contact with the father, whereas he would be likely to encourage contact with the mother if the children moved. Also, the father was found to be committed to his children; he could offer 'reasonable' accommodation; he would provide a private education; he had a network of close family members who would help him with childcare; and his working hours were adaptable.[139]

More generally, as Cretney, *et al*, observe, courts nowadays rely far more on assessments informed by child welfare knowledge (2002 p 656). It seems that a court, faced with a decision about so important a matter as the relationship between a parent and child, is now expected to seek expert opinion. The European Court of Human Rights indicated, in *Elsholz v Germany*,[140] that the national court's refusal to order an independent psychological report in a contact dispute was a factor in its finding that both Article 8 and Article 6 had been breached. Article 8 had been violated because the father had not been sufficiently involved in the decision-making process and Article 6 had been violated because, in the absence of expert evidence, questions of fact and law raised by the case could not be adequately resolved on the basis of the material at the disposal of the German court. The requirements of a fair and public hearing in terms of Article 6 had not been satisfied.

### The Child's Age, Sex, Background and Any Characteristics of His Which the Court Considers Relevant

In the past, courts tended to place young children and older girls in the care of their mothers, while older boys were placed with their fathers.[141] However, recent reported judgments have been, in general, careful to avoid explicit application of the old rules of thumb although there is still a tendency to award residence orders to mothers in cases where the child is very young. This preference was articulated in very clear terms by the House of Lords in *Brixey v Lynas*,[142] a Scots case. The court asserted that, while there is neither a presumption nor a principle that very young children should be with their mothers, the advantages of maternal care must be taken into account.[143]

## XIV. SHARED RESIDENCE

In chapter 8 we referred to the efforts of fathers' rights groups to have the law changed to introduce a presumption of shared parenting. The Government rejected this proposal in its Green Paper (DCA, DfES and DTI 2004). However, the Government's Parenting Plans—a set of templates seeking to show the sort of arrangements that work well for

---

[138] [2004] EWHC Fam 1215; [2004] 2 FLR 851.

[139] Para 42.

[140] [2000] 2 FLR 486.

[141] See Priest and Whybrow (1986) para 4.24.

[142] [1996] 2 FLR 499, 505.

[143] See, further, pp 580ff. See also *Re S (A Minor) (Custody)* [1991] 2 FLR 388; *Re A (A Minor) (Custody)* [1991] 2 FLR 394; *Re A (Children: 1959 UN Declaration)* [1998] 1 FLR 354.

children (DCA, DfES and DTI 2005)—include one scenario involving shared residence, with the children spending half the week with each parent. The guidance does however acknowledge that arrangements like this can be difficult and depend on the parents' jobs, locations and whether they have space in the home (DfES 2005c Template 4).

The courts are becoming increasingly willing to make shared residence orders when parents separate. These orders are not necessarily confined to cases where children spend equal amounts of time with each parent, but they are meant to be used in cases where the children spend substantial periods of time with each.

In the past, the courts tended to shy away from joint orders as being contrary to the well-being of children.[144] They conceded that Section 11(4) of the Children Act envisaged shared residence orders but maintained a circumspect attitude towards granting them.[145]

For example, the Court of Appeal in *A v A (Minors) (Shared Residence Order)*[146] dismissed an appeal against a shared residence order relating to two girls, aged 10 and 7. But it clearly regarded such an order as inappropriate in 'normal' circumstances. Connell J stated that shared residence orders should only be made in 'unusual' cases where an order would give rise to a 'positive benefit for the children'[147]

Butler-Sloss LJ, in turn, sketched examples of such 'unusual' circumstances:

[A] shared residence order would, in my view, be unlikely to be made if there were concrete issues still arising between the parties which had not been resolved, such as … contact … .

If a child, on the other hand, has a settled home with one parent and substantial staying contact with the other parent, which has been settled, long-standing and working well, or if there are future plans for sharing the time of the children between two parents where all the parties agree and where there is no possibility of confusion in the mind of the child as to where the child will be and the circumstances of the child at any time, this may be, bearing in mind all the other circumstances, a possible basis for a shared residence order, if it can be demonstrated that there is a positive benefit to the child. It does not mean it will be; it may be. (pp 677–78)

Butler-Sloss LJ accepted that the 'wisdom' that a child should have one home was likely to be applicable in many cases.[148] And she reiterated that the 'usual' order would have been a sole residence order and that a positive benefit has to be demonstrated to justify a shared order. Consequently, she observed, 'a shared residence order is an unusual order which should only be made in unusual circumstances'.[149]

In *D v D*, however, instead of stressing the unusual nature of the order,[150] the court indicated that shared residence would be appropriate provided it reflected the 'reality of [the] children's lives'; this would be sufficient benefit to justify an order.[151] This shift in emphasis was highlighted by the Court of Appeal in *Re A (Children) (Shared Residence)*:

[10] As I have indicated from the outset, I am very doubtful as to whether the judge in the county court has sufficiently reflected in his approach the shift of emphasis signalled by the decision of this court in *Re D*. There is no doubt at all that there is a need for courts of trial to

[144] See *Riley v Riley* [1986] 2 FLR 429. Compare *J v J (A Minor) (Joint Care and Control)* [1991] 2 FLR 385.
[145] See *Re H (A Minor) (Shared Residence)* [1994] 1 FLR 717.
[146] [1994] 1 FLR 669.
[147] See pp 672–73.
[148] P 677.
[149] P 678.
[150] See *D v D (Shared Residence Order)* [2001] 1 FLR 495, para 41.
[151] *D v D (Shared Residence Order)* [2001] 1 FLR 495, para 34.

recognise that there may well be cases that are better suited by a joint residence order than by residence orders to one parent alone. Where there is a proximity of homes and a relatively fluid passage of the children between those two homes, the judicial convention that the welfare of children demanded a choice between one parent or the other as a guardian of the residence order to promote the welfare of the children no longer runs as it used to run. I am in no doubt at all that orders made in the courts of trial should above all reflect the realities.[152]

In *Re F (Shared Residence Order)*[153] Wilson J made it clear that an equal division of time is not necessary: 'Any lingering idea that a shared residence order is apt only where, for example, the children will be alternating between the two homes evenly, say week by week or fortnight by fortnight, is erroneous'.[154] In addition, the element of proximity was abandoned. Thorpe LJ said:

[21] ... The fact that the parents' homes are separated by a considerable distance does not pre-clude the possibility that the children's year will be divided between the homes of the two separated parents in such a way as to validate the making of a shared residence order ... . Of course the residence order reflects just that—the place of the children's residence. It is not intended to deal with issues of parental status.

Yet Wilson J pointed to the symbolic significance of a shared residence order:

[32] Speaking for myself, I make no bones about it; to make a shared residence order to reflect the arrangements here chosen by the judge is to choose one label rather than another. Her cho-sen arrangements for the division of the girls' time could also have been reflected in orders for sole residence to the mother and generous defined contact with the father. But labels can be very important.[155]

And in *A v A (Shared Residence)*[156] Wall J seemed to regard the symbolic function of a shared residence order as important. Making an order in a case involving considerable conflict[157] between the parents he said:

[124] If these parents were capable of working in harmony, and there were no difficulties about the exercise of shared parental responsibility, I would have ... made no order as to residence ... . Here the parents are not, alas, capable of working in harmony. There must, accordingly, be an order. That order, in my judgment, requires the court not only to reflect the reality that the children are dividing their lives equally between their parents, but also to reflect the fact that the parents are equal in the eyes of the law, and have equal duties and responsibilities towards their children.

[125] In addition, there is the risk, in my judgment, that a sole residence order in Mr A's favour is likely to be misinterpreted ... . Whilst ... I regard him as an honourable man, and one who will implement the 50/50 living arrangement, I have no doubt that he wishes to be in control....

[126] ... Control is not what this family needs. What it needs is co-operation. By making a shared residence order the court is making that point.[158]

---

[152] [2002] EWCA Civ 1343; [2003] 3 FCR 656.
[153] [2003] EWCA Civ 592; [2003] 2 FLR 397.
[154] Para 34.
[155] The symbolic impact of an order is referred to also in guidance to the Children Act 1989 (DoH 1991c para 2.28).
[156] [2004] EWHC Fam 142; [2004] 1 FLR 1195.
[157] Compare *Re O (Contact: Withdrawal of Application)* [2003] EWHC Fam 3031; [2004] 1 FLR 1258 para 8.
[158] Compare *Re M (Children) (Residence Order)* [2004] All ER (D) 44.

The question that is raised by these cases is the extent to which shared residence orders might be being used by the courts not so much because they benefit children but because they benefit parents and because they 'radiate'[159] the message of co-operation and shared parenting. Bridge (1996 p 22) asserts that the benefit must surely be 'parental appeasement, the idea that the "other" parent who none the less cares for the children on a regular basis should not be left feeling he is the loser'. She argues that shared residence may simply be a 'symbolic resolution of parental conflict' (p 13), affording comfort to parents but not necessarily serving the child's best interests:

> The increase in shared parenting agreements can be attributed, at least in part, to the ideological attractiveness of sharing as a way of resolving custody issues at the time of separation. Sharing the physical care of the children appears to be a straightforward and fair solution, lessening anxiety and loss for parents, increasingly acceptable to fathers, and reducing the burden of day-to-day care for mothers. For the child, it can be perceived as maximising time with each parent and thereby avoiding the sense of loss the child might otherwise experience. Some American studies have asserted that parents believe shared custody is in their children's best interests because it closely models the nuclear family situation, while other commentators have highlighted the normality of day-to-day living and avoidance of the artificiality of access that shared residence brings … . However, is the child's welfare truly paramount in such an arrangement or is it designed to provide a 'feel good factor' for parents?
>
> After all in any sharing agreement it is the child who has to move, often on a weekly basis, pack and unpack, and have the wrong clothes in the wrong home at the wrong time. Possibly the only true shared arrangement which has a chance of enhancing the child's welfare is the 'bird's nest' scheme where the child remains in the home and the parents flit in and out on an alternate basis. (p 17, footnotes omitted)

Neale, *et al*, report findings from their empirical research that, to some extent, bear out Bridge's concerns.

> From the child's perspective … this is not shared residence so much as dual residence and, arguably, this is a much more accurate term. Thus, it should be acknowledged that, when using the term 'shared residence', one is adopting the perspective of adults rather than children … . Shared residence is … not the same thing as shared parenting. Shared parenting does not require the children to have to spend an equal amount of time with each parent. Shared parenting is defined by degrees of emotional support and collaborative working, not by hours and days. In the studies, it was found that children who have one 'home' can easily feel that they enjoy shared parenting. So it is important that one does not, in policy terms, allow a slippage in terminology that makes it appear that only shared residence can achieve shared parenting … .
>
> [A] regular routine for some [of the children in the authors' sample] meant they knew exactly what to expect but for others it meant an unbearable and inflexible regime. Some of the children relished the feeling of being loved by both parents and understood shared residence as a manifestation of this, but others felt that this was a terrible burden because they became responsible for the emotional well-being of both their parents. Finally, some children thought the arrangement was excellent because it was fair for their parents, but others thought it was dreadful because it was incredibly unfair on them … .
>
> [D]rifting towards, or even legislating for, a particular arrangement …, or assuming that shared residence is a simple solution to a knotty problem, may be very problematic for the lives of some children and young people. Our research suggests …that solutions to these problems need to be based on a knowledge of the parties involved, rather than adherence to a single principle or rule (such as equality or equal shares). This is most definitely a situation where one size does not fit all. (Neale, *et al*, 2003 pp 904–5)

---

[159] See Dewar (1998) p 483.

Neale, *et al*, found that shared residence works best where the children's needs are prioritised, arrangements are flexible and the children feel at home in both households. Children, particularly pre-teens, could be 'very content' with shared residence (2003 p 908). But if parents refused to modify the arrangements, this could become an 'intolerable' situation for teenagers who wanted greater freedom from both parents (p 906). The authors also point out that the assumption that shared residence promotes shared parenting is not always well-founded: 'Parents who use their children as pawns or who treat them as matrimonial property when the children are 8 or 9, will not necessarily change when the children are 14 or even 18' (p 908).

> **Q** Would a shared residence order be appropriate in relation to Barbie? Why/why not?

## XV. CONTACT

Should the court decide on a sole residence order in favour of one of the parties, it may also need to make a contact order. A contact order is defined as 'an order requiring the person with whom a child lives, or is to live, to allow the child to visit or stay with the person named in the order, or for that person and the child otherwise to have contact with each other'.[160] The provision is therefore wide enough to encompass visits, staying contact or, where those direct forms of contact are thought inappropriate, telephone calls, letters, cards and gifts. Direct contact which is supervised is also a possibility. The supervision might be undertaken by family member or friends or contact could take place at a contact centre.

As Maidment (1984 p 253) noted, many professionals agree that 'the closer and more normal [the] relationship can be, for example through staying contact, the better it is for the child'.[161] In *Surviving the Breakup*, Wallerstein and Kelly clearly subscribed to this view, commenting that: 'Successful outcome at all ages, which we have equated with good ego functioning, adequate or high self-esteem and no depression, reflected a stable, close relationship with the custodial parent and the non-custodial parent'. (1980 p 215)

They were of the opinion that irregular or infrequent contact damages children and that children are best served by an arrangement that provides them with the supports they would enjoy in an intact family. Co-operation between the parents was found to be crucial to their children's well-being. Richards (1982 p 143) pointed to other benefits thought to result from the preservation of ties with both parents: children gain a wider variety of experience and are not deprived of the role model important to the development of gender identity. Freeman (1983 p 216) referred to yet another expected advantage, suggesting that a father who has contact with his child is more likely to be willing to support that child financially. *The Exeter Family Study* (Cockett and Trip 1994, 1996 pp 62–63) asserted that one of the ways to reduce the adverse outcomes for children whose parents part is to facilitate contact, but only if the child desires it. More recently, Sturge and Glaser (2000 p 3) described the benefits of contact as meeting a number of the needs of the child. These include the need for

---

[160] S 8(1).
[161] See further, ch 8.

- warmth, approval, feeling unique and special to a parent;
- extending experiences and developing (or maintaining) meaningful relationships;
- information and knowledge;
- reparation of distorted relationships or perceptions.

Not all the available research points to a need for contact between children and non-resident parents however. Maclean and Eekelaar note that: 'What has not been established is whether a child whose separated parents behave gently and reasonably to her and to one another, but who sees the outside parent rarely or never, somehow does 'less well' than a child of similar parents who sees the outside parent often'. (1997 p 55)

Moreover, Sturge and Glaser advert to a number of possible disadvantages of contact and to the risks associated with it. They mention, for instance, the potential for an escalation of conflict, divided loyalties and the undermining of children's stability and emotional well-being (2000 p 3).

Hunt, in a comprehensive review of research into contact, observes that the evidence of links between contact and children's well-being is contradictory (2003 p 7).[162] In particular, she points out that most studies show no relationship between frequency of contact and children's well-being (p 8). Other factors might be more important. These include the nature of the arrangements; whether the contact is regular; whether there is a good relationship between the contact parent and the child; the financial position of the resident family; and the degree to which the child is caught up in conflict between the parents (*ibid* and p 13).[163] Hunt concludes:

> The question of whether contact itself is of value would seem increasingly to be fairly meaningless.
>
> The key questions to address would seem to be what kind of contact, in what circumstances, is good for children and in what ways? What are the disadvantages of contact for children? How do these balance out? Where there is conflict between parents, what form of contact arrangement is least detrimental? (2003 p 66)

Maclean and Eekelaar suggest that the priority accorded to contact is based less on empirical evidence of its beneficial effects on children than on a belief that 'it is wrong to deny children the opportunity to develop a relationship they might possibly value and also wrong to deny the same opportunity to a parent who wanted it' (1997 p 148).[164]

The attitude of the courts to contact is consistent with the view that contact with their non-resident parents is beneficial, or at least potentially valuable, for children generally. By the early 1970s, the judiciary was endorsing the 'immense value'[165] of contact to children and in *M v M (child: access)*,[166] with a rhetorical flourish that has echoed down the years, Wrangham J declared it to be a right of the child:

> I for my part would prefer to call it a basic right in the child rather than a basic right in the parent. That only means this, that no court should deprive a child of access[167] to either parent unless it is wholly satisfied that it is in the interests of that child that access should cease, and that is a conclusion at which a court should be extremely slow to arrive. (p 85)

---

162 She also reports conflicting research findings on levels of contact but suggests that 'the proportion of children with no contact is decreasing' (Hunt 2003 p 14). See also ch 8.
163 See also Maclean and Eekelaar (1997) pp 53–57.
164 See further ch 8; Bailey-Harris, *et al*, (1998) pp 34–35; 41–44; Kaganas (1999).
165 *M v M (Child: Access)* [1973] 2 All ER 81, 85.
166 [1973] 2 All ER 81. See also *Re W (A Minor) (Contact)* [1994] 2 FLR 441, 447.
167 The term 'access' pre-dates the Children Act 1989 and has been replaced by the term 'contact'.

This right, said Butler-Sloss LJ in *Re R (A Minor) (Contact)*,[168] is endorsed both in the United Nations Convention on the Rights of the Child[169] and in Section 2(1), the parental responsibility provision, of the Children Act 1989.[170] Subsequent judgments have tended to avoid the language of rights[171] but have instead articulated a 'very strong presumption in favour of maintaining contact between a child and both parents'.[172] Balcombe LJ stated in *Re H (Minors) (Access)*[173] that the court should ask the question: 'Are there any cogent reasons why this father should be denied access to his children; or putting it another way: are there any cogent reasons why these two children should be denied the opportunity of access to their natural father?' (p 152)

There is no need to show any positive advantage in contact; this is presumed to exist, although in *Re M (Contact: Welfare Test)*,[174] the court proposed a balancing exercise relying on the welfare checklist. Wilson J said:

> I personally find it helpful to cast the principles into the framework of the checklist of considerations set out in s 1(3) of the Children Act 1989 and to ask whether the fundamental emotional need of every child to have an enduring relationship with both his parents (s 1(3)(b)) is outweighed by the depth of harm which, in the light, inter alia, of his wishes and feelings (s 1(3)(a)), this child would be at risk of suffering (s 1(3)(e)) by virtue of a contact order.
>
> (pp 278–79)

However this approach was not followed[175] and later decisions reiterated the presumption. It was said in *Re O*, for instance, that it is 'almost always' in the interests of the child to have contact with the non-resident parent.[176]

The terminology appears to be changing again but the view articulated in *Re O* persists. In *Re L*,[177] Thorpe LJ declared that the existence of a presumption might 'inhibit or distort the rigorous search for the welfare solution' and that a presumption might be too easy a solution in cases where the decision-maker is unsure what to do. Instead, he said, the word 'assumption' was preferable. He did, however, refer to the 'universal judicial recognition of the importance of contact to a child's development'.[178] And Butler-Sloss P in turn endorsed the 'principles' set out in *Re O*.[179] These pronouncements, together with the fact that the court required the application of the welfare checklist, as suggested in *Re M*, only in cases where there is evidence sufficient to 'offset'[180] the assumption,[181] suggests that the change in terminology is of little practical

---

[168] [1993] 2 FLR 762, 767.

[169] See Art 9 of the UN Convention on the Rights of the Child which sets out the child's right to contact on a regular basis with both parents if separated from one or both, except where this would be contrary to his or her best interests.

[170] See, further, p 297.

[171] See *Re L (Contact: Domestic Violence); Re V (Contact: Domestic Violence); Re M (Contact: Domestic Violence); Re H (Contact: Domestic Violence)* [2002] 2 FLR 334, 359ff. But see, for example, *V v V (Contact: Implacable Hostility)* [2004] EWHC Fam 1215; [2004] 2 FLR 851 para 47.

[172] *Re M (Contact: Welfare Test)* [1995] 1 FLR 274, 281.

[173] [1992] 1 FLR 148.

[174] [1995] 1 FLR 274.

[175] Except, some years later in relation to domestic violence and, possibly, other cases involving severe parental deficits. See *Re L (Contact: Domestic Violence); Re V (Contact: Domestic Violence); Re M (Contact: Domestic Violence); Re H (Contact: Domestic Violence)* [2002] 2 FLR 334. See further below pp 568–70.

[176] *Re O (Contact: Imposition of Conditions)* [1995] 2 FLR 124, 128.

[177] *Re L (Contact: Domestic Violence); Re V (Contact: Domestic Violence); Re M (Contact: Domestic Violence); Re H (Contact: Domestic Violence)* [2002] 2 FLR 334, 364.

[178] P 364.

[179] P 343.

[180] Pp 367, 371.

[181] Butler-Sloss P restricted its application to cases involving domestic violence. See pp 342–43.

significance. This view is borne out by an examination of the words used by a judge in a subsequent case. In *V v V (Contact: Implacable Hostility)*[182] Bracewell J said: 'It is for the mother to establish by credible evidence any basis for denying or restricting contact'

Not only is contact deemed to be beneficial for children, it is assumed that to deny contact would be to jeopardise the child's welfare.[183] So in *Re F (Minors) (Contact: Mother's Anxiety)*,[184] the court refers to 'the risk, well documented by medical and legal literature and cases, that the children could be damaged by not having the right to know their own father'. That this harm might be counterbalanced by other harms which could arise if contact were ordered is not easy to establish. The Court of Appeal in *Re O*[185] indicated that courts should 'not at all readily' accept that the child's welfare might be injured by direct contact and that the likelihood of short-term problems should not be given excessive weight.

> **Q** Do you think that assumptions in favour of contact with non-resident parents, developed in the context of non-resident fathers' claims, can be generalised to same-sex parents? Is there something about the biological relationship between fathers and children that may underlie some of the strength of the assumption? Are there other factors related to the sex of the parents and the 'politics' of motherhood and fatherhood that may be important? See chapter 8. Can you think of any situations in which it might be better for a child not to have contact with a non-resident parent?

The strength of the presumption/assumption in favour of contact has grown in recent years[186] and, with the advent of the Human Rights Act 1998, it has been considered necessary to strengthen the law supporting contact even further.[187] A useful survey of the relevant law under the European Convention on Human Rights is provided by Munby J in *Re D (Intractable Contact Dispute: Publicity)*:[188]

> [26] ... It suffices for present purposes if I merely extract a few of the most important points that emerge from the authorities. The first is the principle, long recognised, that, as it was put in Kosmopoulou v Greece [2004] 1 FLR 800 at para [47} :

>> ... the mutual enjoyment by parent and child of each other's company constitutes a fundamental element of family life, even if the relationship between the parents has broken down, and domestic measures hindering such enjoyment amount to an interference with the right protected by Art 8 of the Convention.

> [27] The second is the principle, also long recognised and most recently stated in *Hoppe v Germany* [2003] 1 FLR 384 at para [54], that, '... in cases concerning a person's relationship with

182 [2004] EWHC Fam 1215; [2004] 2 FLR 851, para 47. See also *Re O (Contact: Withdrawal of Application)* [2003] EWHC Fam 3031; [2004] 1 FLR 1258 para 4.
183 It has been argued that conflict and denial of contact have been constructed as the primary risks to children in the context of divorce; other risks have been largely discounted: Kaganas (1999).
184 [1993] 2 FLR 830, 834.
185 *Re O (Contact: Imposition of Condition)* [1995] 2 FLR 124, 129.
186 Compare Weyland (1992) with Weyland (1995). Of course, the existence of a contact order does not guarantee that contact will take place. Often, either fathers cease maintaining contact for various reasons or mothers will not permit it to take place. While courts may threaten mothers with imprisonment or the loss of their status as resident parents, fathers still seem to feel that mothers have the upper hand (Simpson, *et al,*1995 pp 34 and 69). See also Geldof (2003); Kaganas (2005 forthcoming); ch 8.
187 See *Re D (Intractable Contact Dispute: Publicity* [2004] EWHC Fam 727; [2004] 1 FLR 1226 paras 35ff.
188 [2004] EWHC Fam 727; [2004] 1 FLR 1226.

his or her child, there is a duty to exercise exceptional diligence in view of the risk that the passage of time may result in a de facto determination of the matter'... .[189]

[28] The third is the principle that in private law cases, just as much as in public law cases, Art 8 includes what was described in *Hokkanen v Finland* [1996] 1 FLR 289 at para [55] as: '... a right for the parent to have measures taken with a view to his or her being reunited with the child and an obligation for the national authorities to take such action.'

The court has repeatedly stressed that, as part of their 'obligation ... to take measures to facilitate contact by a non-custodial parent', national authorities 'must do their utmost to facilitate' co-operation between the parents: see *Hokkanen v Finland* at para 58 ... .[190]

[29] The fourth is the general principle enunciated in *Hornsby v Greece* (1997) 24 EHRR 250 ...: '... [T]he right to a court as guaranteed by Art 6 also protects the implementation of final, binding judicial decisions, which, in states that accept the rule of law, cannot remain inoperative to the detriment of one party. Accordingly, the execution of a judicial decision cannot be unduly delayed.'

[30] These positive obligations extend in principle to the taking of coercive measures not merely against the recalcitrant parent but even against the children ... .

The court [said] in *Hansen v Turkey* [2004] 1 FLR 142 at para [106]: 'Although measures against the children obliging them to reunite with one or other parent are not desirable in this sensitive area, such action must not be ruled out in the event of non-compliance or unlawful behaviour by the parent with whom the children live.'

[31] ... This was elaborated in *Kosmopoulou v Greece* [2004] 1 FLR 800 at para [45]:

> the national authorities' obligation to take measures to facilitate reunion is not absolute, since the reunion of a parent with children who have lived for some time with the other parent may not be able to take place immediately and may require preparatory measures to be taken ... . Whilst national authorities must do their utmost to facilitate ... co-operation, any obligation to apply coercion in this area must be limited since the interests as well as the rights and freedoms of all concerned must be taken into account, and more particularly the best interests of the child and his or her rights under Art 8 of the Convention. Where contact with the parent might appear to threaten those interests or interfere with those rights, it is for the national authorities to strike a fair balance between them.

[32] The test was set out in *Sylvester v Austria* ... [2003] 2 FLR 210 at paras 59–60:

> In cases concerning the enforcement of decisions in the realm of family law, the court has repeatedly found that what is decisive is whether the national authorities have taken all the necessary steps to facilitate execution as can reasonably be demanded in the special circumstances of each case. In examining whether non-enforcement of a court order amounted to a lack of respect for the applicant's family life the court must strike a fair balance between the interests of all persons concerned and the general interests in ensuring respect for the rule of law ... .[191]

---

[189] Munby J also cited, on this point, *Glaser v United Kingdom* [2001] 1 FLR 153, para 93; *Sylvester v Austria* [2003] 2 FLR 210, para 69.

[190] Other cases cited by Munby J on this point included *Glaser v United Kingdom* [2001] 1 FLR 153, para 66; *Hansen v Turkey* [2004] 1 FLR 142, para 98; *Kosmopoulou v Greece* [2004] 1 FLR 800, para 45.

[191] See also *Maire v Portugal* [2004] 2 FLR 653, paras 70–71.

[35] Not least in the light of the Strasbourg jurisprudence there is no room for complacency about the way in which we handle these cases.

Before going on to examine the proposals for reform, we now turn to the English case law to ascertain what factors the courts take into account in deciding contact cases.

## Lack of Contact in the Past

The fact that the child has no recollection of the absent parent or that there has been a long period without contact does not preclude an order.[192] Indeed, that a father had refrained from attempting to see his children when they visited his parents was said to be to his credit in *Re F (Minors) (Contact: Mother's Anxiety)*.[193] He had been a 'very unsatisfactory young man'[194] and had stopped seeing his children after the mother sought an injunction against him.[195] However, in *Re L*,[196] Thorpe LJ suggested that existing relationships should be treated differently from potential relationships:

> I doubt that sufficient distinction has been made between cases in which contact is sought in order to maintain an existing relationship, to revive a dormant relationship or to create a non-existent relationship. The judicial assumption that to order contact would promote welfare would surely wane across that spectrum. I would not assume the benefit with unquestioning confidence where a child has developed over its early years without any knowledge of its father, particularly if over those crucially formative years a psychological attachment to an alternative father has been achieved. (p 364)

## Disruption for the Child

It appears that the absence of a bond between the non-resident parent and the child may be a significant factor where the possibility of disruption to the child's life is raised. However, the courts seem to be growing reluctant to regard the potential for disruption as decisive. The court in *Re SM (A Minor) (Natural Father: Access)*[197] allowed an appeal against an order in favour of the father. Although the father had had contact with the child regularly in the past, the court placed considerable weight on the fact that the child's bond was not with the biological father but with the mother and step-father. In addition, there was a risk of destabilising the family if contact took place. Yet more recently, in a case with comparable facts, the court adopted a somewhat different approach. In *Re R (A Minor) (Contact)*,[198] the court seemed to accept that contact would lead to disruption but adjourned the father's application with a view to having the child introduced to her father when the risks posed by contact diminished.

---

[192] See *Re D (Contact: Reasons for Refusal)* [1997] 2 FLR 48. See also *Re W (A Minor) (Contact)* [1994] 2 FLR 441. Compare the earlier case of *Re SM (A Minor) (Natural Father: Access)* [1991] 2 FLR 333.
[193] [1993] 2 FLR 830, 833.
[194] P 831.
[195] Compare *Re M (Contact: Welfare Test)* [1995] 1 FLR 274, 280, where it seems the court had different expectations of a mother; she was criticised for not persevering with contact even though she had been advised by a court welfare officer to withdraw.
[196] *Re L (Contact: Domestic Violence); Re V (Contact: Domestic Violence); Re M (Contact: Domestic Violence); Re H (Contact: Domestic Violence)* [2002] 2 FLR 334.
[197] [1991] 2 FLR 333. See also *Re W (A Minor) (Access)* [1989] 1 FLR 163.
[198] [1993] 2 FLR 762. See also *A v L (Contact)* [1998] 1 FLR 361.

The courts have, however, taken into account the negative effects on the family of contact in cases where the child needed a great deal of care and medical attention.[199] They have also done so where the potential disruption was very severe. *In Re H (A Minor) (Parental Responsibility)*[200] provides an extreme example.[201] There the step-father objected so strongly to any contact between father and child that he wrote to the father indicating that his marriage to the mother would be jeopardised if contact continued. The court refused contact in order to preserve the child's home-life.[202] In *Re H (Contact Order (No 2)*[203] the father, who suffered from Huntington's disease which affected his personality, had threatened suicide and had made preparations to kill the children. The mother testified that she could not cope with the prospect of a contact order and that she had made contingency arrangements for the children lest she suffer a breakdown. The court refused to order direct contact, finding that the effect of an order on the mother's ability to parent and the need to promote her physical and mental health out-weighed the need of the children to have direct contact.

> **Q** Read the cases on transfer of residence referred to below. Consider the relative importance accorded by the courts to the risk of disruption and to the aim of achieving contact.

## The 'Implacably Hostile' Parent

It is sometimes the case that the resident parent (who is usually the mother in cases of heterosexual parents) seeks to prevent contact between the child and the non-resident parent. It has also been suggested by some commentators that there is a problem of parental alienation syndrome (PAS) that needs to be addressed.[204] This refers to the situation where a resident parent has influenced a child to the point where the child refuses contact with the other parent. However, PAS is not recognised as a disorder in the UK. In the Sturge/Glaser report, compiled for the court in *Re L*[205] by child psychiatrists, the authors preferred the term 'implacable hostility', a state of affairs that can arise for a variety of reasons, some justifiable (2000 pp 7–8). The Court of Appeal relied on the report and commented that, while 'some parents, particularly mothers, are responsible for alienating their children from their fathers without good reason',[206] this is a long way from a 'syndrome' requiring the help of mental health professionals. Nevertheless, these

---

[199] *Re F (Contact: Enforcement: Representation of Child)* [1998] 1 FLR 691; *Re C and V (Contact and Parental Responsibility)* [1998] 1 FLR 392.

[200] [1993] 1 FLR 484.

[201] See also *M v M (Parental Responsibility)* [1999] 2 FLR 737. Note, however, that despite the father's condition, he was granted indirect contact. In *M v A (Contact: Domestic Violence)* [2002] 2 FLR 921, it was held that direct contact would adversely affect the emotional stability of the home. However, the father, whose conduct was criticised, and who had convictions for manslaughter and rape as well as dishonesty, was given indirect contact.

[202] See also *Re B (Contact: Stepfather's Opposition)* [1997] 2 FLR 579. See also *Re M (Contact: Violent Parent)* [1999] 2 FLR 321, 332.

[203] [2002] 1 FLR 22.

[204] See, for example, Willbourne and Cull (1997) p 807.

[205] *Re L (Contact: Domestic Violence); Re V (Contact: Domestic Violence); Re M (Contact: Domestic Violence); Re H (Contact: Domestic Violence)* [2002] 2 FLR 334.

[206] *Re L (Contact: Domestic Violence); Re V (Contact: Domestic Violence); Re M (Contact: Domestic Violence); Re H (Contact: Domestic Violence)* [2002] 2 FLR 334, 351.

mothers are seen as creating an 'insoluble problem'[207] and are regarded as selfish and short-sighted.[208]

Certainly mothers who oppose contact feel that they are put under considerable pressure from solicitors, court welfare officers and mediators to withdraw their objections.[209] And the courts, in particular, have taken an increasingly censorious view of mothers who resist contact.[210] There are, it is true, instances where the mother's opposition to contact has been treated as a reason for denying contact. For example, the court in *Re P (Contact: Discretion)*[211] indicated that contact might be refused if a mother has good reason for her hostility and, even if she does not, where her attitude would make contact damaging for the child. But although the court might refuse contact, the unsatisfactory nature of this situation is often remarked on. *Re D (A Minor) (Contact: Mother's Hostility)*[212] was one such case. The mother said that the father had been violent towards her, drank excessively and took drugs. The judge thought he was now a reformed character although he had certainly behaved in an intimidatory fashion towards the mother and her parents. He had caused a disturbance at the mother's home on more than one occasion at night; he had slashed the mother's clothes before delivering them; and he had arrived in court with 12 associates, intimidating the mother and her family to the extent that they left by a private door. He had had no contact with his child, aged almost 3, and the mother opposed the application on the grounds that the hatred and fear she felt for him would make contact unworkable and that it would be upsetting and detrimental for the child. On appeal against an order refusing contact, Waite LJ said:

> It is now well settled that the implacable hostility of a mother towards access or contact is a factor which is capable, according to the circumstances of each particular case, of supplying a cogent reason for departing from the general principle that a child should grow up in the knowledge of both his parents. I see no reason to think that the judge fell into any error of principle in deciding, as he clearly did on the plain interpretation of his judgment, that the mother's present attitude towards contact puts D at serious risk of major emotional harm if she were to be compelled to accept a degree of contact to the natural father against her will … .
>
> I share the hope of the trial judge that matters may change for the future, and that the mother herself will come in time to realise that for the long-term benefits of D an upbringing in the knowledge of both his parents may prove to be to his advantage. (pp 7–8)

On other occasions the courts have simply refused to countenance mothers' objections. And at times, the expectations they appear to have of mothers seem oppressive. In *Re P (Contact: Supervision)*,[213] the stress occasioned to the mother by contact was held insufficient reason to deny the father supervised contact. The father was violent, racist, anti-semitic and had in the past threatened to strangle the mother and kill the children. Yet, far from justifying the mother's opposition to contact, the mother's mental state and the history of abuse was treated as placing a 'special burden'[214] on her to accede to

---

[207] *Ibid.*
[208] See Ingman (1996) p 617.
[209] See Smart and Neale (1997), Piper (1993).
[210] See, generally, Piper (1995). It has been argued that in constructing resident parents as having the power and responsibility for decisions concerning contact, the law has succeeded in characterising unco-operative mothers as posing the main risk to children; they have to be persuaded or compelled to make the 'right' decision: Kaganas (1999) p 115.
[211] [1998] 2 FLR 696.
[212] [1993] 2 FLR 1. See also *Re J (A Minor) (Contact)* [1994] 1 FLR 729.
[213] [1996] 2 FLR 314.
[214] P 332.

contact so that her children could know their father. If she impeded contact, the court said, the children would blame her in later years.

In addition, the courts regard it as imperative not to allow resident parents to defy them. In *Re W (A Minor) (Contact)*,[215] the mother indicated that she would disobey an order, contending that the father was incapable of looking after the child and that an order would have a deleterious effect on the stability of the child. The appeal court described the failure of the court below to make an order as an abdication of responsibility and said that the mother had no right to deny the child contact with his father.[216] Moreover, intervention is regarded as essential in some cases to ensure that the passage of time does not become a reason for deciding that it is too late to rescue the relationship between the child and the non-resident parent.[217]

*Re O (Contact: Imposition of Conditions)*[218] provides a clear statement of the courts' refusal to be dictated to by the resident parent:

> The courts should not at all readily accept that the child's welfare will be injured by direct contact. ..Neither parent should be encouraged or permitted to think that the more intransigent, the more unreasonable, the more obdurate and the more unco-operative they are, the more likely they are to get their own way. (pp 129–310)

The court went on to recommend that if direct contact were not possible, there should be indirect contact[219] to ensure that, until direct contact could take place, the child would grow up knowing of the absent parent's love and interest.[220]

Where resident mothers disobey or undermine contact orders, the courts are beginning to adopt an increasingly hard line. In a recent development, the courts have come to see some tactics used by mothers resisting contact as so damaging for children that they warrant a care order. In *Re M (Intractable Contact Dispute: Interim Care Order)*,[221] the mother had persuaded the children, falsely, that the father and the paternal grandparents had abused them.[222] As a result, Wall J made an order under Section 37 of the Children Act 1989 instructing the local authority to consider whether care proceedings might be appropriate. He had come to the conclusion that the children were suffering significant harm in the mother's care. They were suffering emotional harm because, in particular, the mother was seeking to instil in them the false belief that their father had sexually abused them.[223] The local authority agreed and an interim care order was made. Residence was then transferred to the father, with a two-year supervision order made in favour of the local authority. The purpose of the care proceedings, said the judge, was to

---

[215] [1994] 2 FLR 441.

[216] See also *Re F (Minors) (Contact: Mother's Anxiety)* [1993] 2 FLR 830; *Re H (A Minor) (Contact)* [1994] 2 FLR 776.

[217] See *Re S (Unco-operative Mother)* [2004] EWCA Civ 597; [2004] 2 FLR 710, para 17. See also, for a similar pronouncement by the European Court of Human Rights, *Maire v Portugal* [2004] 2 FLR 653, para 74.

[218] [1995] 2 FLR 124. See also *V v V (Contact: Implacable Hostility)* [2004] EWHC Fam 1215; [2004] 2 FLR 851 para 47.

[219] See also *Re M (Contact: Supervision)* [1998] 1 FLR 727.

[220] P 130. This case clarifies the nature of the conditions that can be imposed in terms of s 11(7) of the Children Act 1989. The court has jurisdiction to compel a mother to send photographs, medical reports and school reports in order to promote meaningful contact between father and child. In addition, the mother could be ordered to write reports to the father. See also *Re M (Contact: Supervision)* [1998] 1 FLR 727.

[221] [2003] EWHC Fam 1024 ; [2003] 2 FLR 636.

[222] There were also allegations of physical assault and verbal abuse but these were never adjudicated as injunction proceedings were compromised (para 46). The court declined to give any weight to the allegations of domestic violence (para 48).

[223] Para 29.

protect the children from significant harm and to restore their relationship with the father. 'In the longer term', he said, 'the aim was to enable the children to retain a good relationship with both parents'.[224] His judgment, he added, should not be seen as either pro-father or anti-mother.[225]

Wall J warned that before invoking Section 37, the court must be satisfied that there are reasonable grounds for believing that the children are suffering or likely to suffer significant harm in terms of Section 31 of the Children Act 1989. He went on:

[11] Although this case is but an example, it does seem to me that it is possible to extract some general considerations of wider application from it … .

(1)  The court must be satisfied that the criteria for ordering a s 37 report are satisfied … .
(2)  The action contemplated (removal of the children from the residential parent's care either for an assessment or with a view to a change of residence) must be in the children's best interests. The consequences of the removal must be thought through. There must, in short, be a coherent care plan of which temporary or permanent removal from the residential parent's care is an integral part.
(3)  Where, as here, the allegation is that the children have been sexually or physically abused by the absent parent, the court must have held a hearing in which those issues were addressed, and findings made about them … .
(4)  The court should spell out its reasons for making the s 37 order … .
(5)  The children should be separately represented … .
(6)  Preferably, the s 37 report should be supported by professional or expert advice … .
(7)  Judicial continuity is essential … .
(8)  Undue delay must be avoided … .
(9)  The case may need to be kept under review … if the decision of the court is to move the children from one parent to the other … .

The court also made a finding of abuse, but transferred residence immediately rather than invoke Section 37, in *V v V (Contact: Implacable Hostility)*.[226] The mother had stopped contact on several occasions, alleging that there had been sexual, physical and emotional abuse of the children, aged 8 and 6, by the father and his relatives. These allegations had led to the involvement of the police, doctors and social services. The court decided that the allegations were unfounded or exaggerated. It also considered the mother responsible for an anonymous campaign to discredit the father and his family. The court said that she had involved the children in false allegations and that she had abused them emotionally by subjecting them to four interviews with the police and visits to hospital which were unnecessary.[227] The mother, it said, was 'twisted'.[228] Her concern about the children was feigned and was being used as an excuse to oppose contact. She presented herself as supporting contact but, in reality, was storing up ammunition against the father.[229] The children had been coached to make allegations[230] and their wish to remain with their mother, with whom they had always lived, could not determine the outcome. This was partly because they were young and partly 'because they

---

[224] Para 20. In fact the children were no longer seeing their mother and the court commented that the father and his parents were communicating their hostility to the children. He urged them not to fall into the same 'trap' as the mother had. See para 173–76.
[225] Para 23.
[226] [2004] EWHC Fam 1215; [2004] 2 FLR 851.
[227] Para 53.
[228] Para 23.
[229] Paras 22–23.
[230] Para 22.

have become so enmeshed in the parents' problems and have learnt to say what they think is expected of them'; they were 'tainted by the influence of the mother'.[231] The court granted a residence order to the father, saying:

[45] If the children move to the father they would be uprooted from the mother's daily care, where they have lived all their lives. They would have to change schools and settle in a new environment with the father and extended family. The mother has more than adequately provided for their needs, except in the relationship with the father. The change would be traumatic … . If the children stay with the mother … [t]here would be … a real risk that the father would become battle-weary and withdraw from the children's lives defeated and demoralised.

[46] If the children move to the father I am satisfied he would actively support generous contact to the mother … but there is the emotional upheaval for the children to consider … .

**Q** What did the court consider to be the greatest risk for the children? Why?

Bracewell J severely criticised those mothers who resist contact and called for more effective measures to enforce orders:

[4] There is a perception among part of the media, and some members of the parents' groups, as well as members of the public, that the courts rubber-stamp cases awarding care of children to mothers almost automatically and marginalise fathers from the lives of their children. There is also a perception that courts allow parents with care to flout court orders for contact and permit parents with residence to exclude the parent from the lives of the children so that the other parent is worn down by years of futile litigation which achieves nothing and only ends when that parent gives up the struggle, or the children are old enough to make their own decisions, assuming they have not been brainwashed in the meantime … .

[6] … Unreasonable parents, by definition, are difficult to deal with, and the most intractable situation is undoubtedly the unreasonable mother, but judges currently do not have the tools with which to make progress with the unreasonable mother or sometimes the unreasonable father who can flout or frustrate orders with impunity unless sent to prison.

[7] It appears to me that there are ways in which the problems can be addressed ….They consist of case management …, judicial continuity, timetabling to suit the needs of the case…, proactive orders …, and attaching conditions to residence orders under Section 11(7) of the Children Act 1989 … . CAFCASS officers, in addition to writing reports … will be there to monitor the initial stages of contact, help with hand-over arrangements and, if necessary, bring the case back to court … .

[10] The second way in which improvements can be effected requires legislation … .Currently, there are only four options available to the court [to enforce orders] and each is unsatisfactory: one, send the parent who frustrates contact to prison, or make a suspended order of imprisonment. This option may well not achieve the object of reinstating contact; the child may blame the parent who applied to commit the carer to prison; the child's life may be disrupted if there is no one capable of or willing to care for the child when the parent is in prison; it cannot be anything other than emotionally damaging for a child to be suddenly removed into foster care by social services from a parent, usually a mother, who in all respects except contact is a good

---

[231] Para 44. The evidence on which the court based this conclusion appears to have been that it considered the allegations unfounded or 'exaggerated'. There may therefore, it seems, have been some deficiencies in the care afforded by the father.

parent. Two, impose a fine on the parent. This option is rarely possible because it is not consistent with the welfare of the child to deprive a parent on a limited budget. Three, transfer residence. This option is not necessarily available to the court, because the other parent may not have the facilities or capacity to care for the child full-time, and may not even know the child … . Four, give up. Make either an order for indirect contact or no order at all. This is the worst option of all and sometimes the only one available. This is the option which gives rise to the public blaming the judges for refusing to deal with recalcitrant parents. This option results in a perception fostered by the press that family courts are failing in private law cases and that family judges are anti-father. The truth, however, is that without the weapons to use against what is in essence a small group of obdurate mothers, the ability of judges to do better for fathers is strictly limited.

**Q** Is the court primarily concerned with the children's best interests in designating the 'do nothing' option as the 'worst'? To what extent is it concerned with countering fathers' rights campaigns and media criticism?

Bracewell J went on to call for legislative reform. She suggested that judges and magistrates should be empowered to refer parties to mediation. The law regarding family assistance orders should be changed.[232] These orders should be directed at CAFCASS instead of at the local authority and the six month time limit on orders should be removed. Orders should not be limited to exceptional circumstances and parties should not be allowed to veto the making of an order.[233] The powers to enforce court orders should be augmented. There should be a power to refer a defaulting parent to resources such as information meetings, meetings with a counsellor, parenting programmes and to classes dealing with contact disputes. There should be a power to refer a parent to a psychologist or psychiatrist. There should be a power to order community service and probation. There should be the possibility of ordering financial compensation in cases where, for example, a holiday has to be cancelled. Non-resident parents who are violent might be referred to perpetrator programmes.[234]

Similar calls for reform in the light, apparently, of the European jurisprudence among other things, had previously been made by Munby J in *Re D (Intractable Contact Dispute: Publicity)*.[235] The judge also referred to media coverage, presumably of fathers' rights campaigns, and said: 'There is much wrong with our system and the time has come for us to recognise that fact … . If we do not we risk forfeiting public confidence. The newspapers … make uncomfortable reading for us. They suggest that confidence is already ebbing away. We ignore the media at our peril' (para 4).

He too favoured removing as many cases as possible from the court arena.[236] He stressed tackling the problem of delay affecting those cases that do go to court and the need for judicial continuity. He also advocated 'swift, efficient, enforcement of existing court orders … at the first sign of trouble'.[237] Moreover, he said, committal might be

---

[232] See s 16 Children Act 1989. These orders can require that a CAFCASS or Local Authority officer be made available to 'advise, assist and (where appropriate) befriend any person named in the order'.

[233] Para 11.

[234] Para 12.

[235] [2004] EWHC Fam 727; [2004] 1 FLR 1226.

[236] See also the view of Thorpe LJ that the capacity of the family justice system to produce good outcomes in contact disputes is limited. He suggested that investment in therapeutic services might be beneficial (*Re L (Contact: Domestic Violence); Re V (Contact: Domestic Violence); Re M (Contact: Domestic Violence); Re H (Contact: Domestic Violence)* [2002] 2 FLR 334, 366–67).

[237] Para 56.

appropriate, particularly if the sentence is short and will not impair the mother's parenting capacity.[238]

The Government response was to publish a White Paper (DCA, DfES and DTI 2005) declaring its intention to review Family Assistance Orders, to develop Parenting Plans, to encourage mediation strongly and to improve services such as contact centres. It records that CAFCASS is shifting its focus from report writing to conciliation and that the Private Law Framework will improve case management by the courts. It also refers to proposed legislation to improve enforcement.

This legislation is currently in the form of the Children and Adoption Bill of 2005. Clause 1 is designed to amend the Children Act 1989 to empower the court to make contact activity directions[239] or to attach contact activity conditions to contact orders. Contact activity directions and conditions require parties to 'take part in an activity that promotes contact with the child concerned'.[240] Contact activities include 'programmes, classes and counselling or guidance sessions that may assist a person as regards establishing, maintaining or improving contact with a child'.[241] Provision is also to be made for directing parents to attend information or advice sessions to assist them to make arrangements, possibly through mediation, and to operate contact arrangements.[242]. Also, the Bill[243] makes provision for the monitoring of contact orders as well as contact activity orders and directions. Finally, it broadens the court's power to enforce contact orders.[244] It will be possible to make an unpaid work requirement under an enforcement order [245] and an order for financial compensation.[246] When the court makes or varies a contact order, it has to attach a notice warning of the consequences of failure to comply.[247] Family assistance orders[248] will no longer be reserved for exceptional cases; they can be made for up to a year and the order may, if a contact order is in force, direct the officer dealing with the family to give advice and assistance regarding contact . The officer may also be required to report to the court about contact.

---

[238] See paras 56–57.

[239] As long as the court considers making, varying or discharging a contact order, a contact activity direction can be made even if no contact order is made (House of Lords, Children and Adoption Bill Explanatory Notes para 9). Contact activity conditions can be made only where a contact order is made or varied (proposed s 11C).

[240] Proposed s 11A(3) and s 11C(2) of the Children Act 1989.

[241] Proposed s 11A(5) Children Act 1989 contained in the Children and Adoption Bill, Cl 1.

[242] *Ibid.* It will not be possible to compel parents to attend mediation or medical or psychiatric treatment or assessment (proposed s 11A(6)).

[243] Cl1 (proposed s 11G) and Cl 2 (proposed s 11H). See further ch 8, p 323.

[244] These powers are in addition to powers relating to contempt of court and the power to alter contact and residence arrangements (House of Lords, Children and Adoption Bill, Explanatory Notes para 11). To obtain an enforcement order, it is necessary to prove beyond reasonable doubt that a contact order has been breached. Breach of a contact activity condition constitutes breach of a contact order. The court may not make an order if it is satisfied that there is a reasonable excuse for non-compliance. See House of Lords, Children and Adoption Bill, Explanatory Notes para 28.

[245] Cl4 (proposed s 11J–M). In deciding whether to make an enforcement order, the court must be satisfied that an order is necessary to secure compliance with the order in question and that the order is proportionate to the seriousness of the breach (proposed s 11L(1)) The draft Bill included provision for a curfew requirement and an electronic monitoring requirement. Both have been dropped. A committee of MPs and peers called the electronic monitoring requirement humiliating and recommended that it be omitted (House of Commons, House of Lords 2005 para 89).

[246] Cl 5 (proposed s 11O–P). This will compensate a party financially prejudiced by non-compliance eg wasted holiday expenses where the child is not made available to go on the holiday.

[247] Cl 3 (proposed s 11I). Such a notice must also be attached to an enforcement order (Cl 4, proposed s 11N).

[248] See Cl 6.

Undoubtedly resident and non-resident[249] parents alike could be required to attend information sessions, guidance and counselling. In addition, the Bill provides that the resident parent may seek an enforcement order in the same way that a parent seeking contact may.[250] The White Paper states:

> [C]hanging social expectations, as well as Government action, are both needed. In time, it needs to become socially unacceptable for one parent to impede a child's relationship with its other parent wherever it is safe and in the child's best interests. Equally, it should be unacceptable that non-resident parents absent themselves from their child's development and upbringing following separation. Friends, relatives, the legal profession and the media all have a role to play in emphasising that children require a good and lasting relationship with both their parents whenever it is safe and in the child's best interests to do so.
>
> (DCA, DfES and DTI 2005, Ministerial Foreword)

This document was developed in the context of heterosexual parenting disputes and the 'gender wars' they have been reported to have inspired. However, it is assumed that its principles will be applied in cases of same-sex parenting disputes. In both situations, though, there can also be little doubt that it is against resident parents (and in the paradigm heterosexual cases specifically resident mothers)[251] that the contact activity provisions and the enforcement mechanisms will primarily be used. It is difficult at present to conceive of a court ordering a reluctant father to attend counselling about how to improve contact or punishing a father who does not visit his children.

So, the fathers' rights campaigns[252] appear to have had the effect of galvanising the government and the courts into action against mothers whom they see as obstructive. More punitive as well as therapeutic measures are to be deployed against them. We may well see more cases like *A* v. *N (Committal; Refusal of Contact),*[253] where the mother was committed to prison for refusing to allow supervised contact with a violent father. The Court of Appeal has even gone so far as to make a suspended committal order where the mother, in its view, was 'communicating her views about the father and her hostility to contact to the children'[254] so that they refused contact. The court stated that there was 'a clear obligation upon the mother to assist the children to come to terms with having contact with their father'.[255] So, it seems, not only are caretaking mothers to be punished for defying contact orders, they may be punished for exposing their children to their negative feelings towards the non-resident parent. And not only are they expected to obey contact orders, it seems they have a positive duty to see to it that their children want contact. It remains to be seen whether courts will apply the same presumptions to same-sex parents who are in dispute.

---

[249] The Joint Committee Report recommended that the government give consideration to allowing resident parents to apply to court to impose a contact activity on non-resident parents who fail to discharge their responsibilities to the children (House of Commons, House of Lords 2005 para 38). The language of the Bill admits of an interpretation consistent with this.

[250] Cl 4 (proposed s 11J(5)).

[251] See, for criticism of a mother's resistance to undergoing therapy, *Re S (Unco-operative Mother)* [2004] EWCA Civ 597; [2004] 2 FLR 710.

[252] And, perhaps, to some extent, the European cases on swift enforcement. However, these, of course all refer to a balancing exercise, reasonableness and to the undesirability of proceeding against children's wishes.

[253] [1997] 1 FLR 533.

[254] *F v F (Contact: Committal)* [1998] 2 FLR 237.

[255] P 242.

The new measures in the Bill are likely to be deployed punitively against resident mothers but therapeutic intervention[256] may be useful in some instances. Trinder, *et al*, (2005) found that parents in dispute were experiencing multiple problems. Resident parents tended to say they wanted more contact rather than less. When they wanted contact curtailed, this was because of the perceived lack of commitment of the non-resident parent or, more commonly, because of distress to children and fear of violence. Parents exhibited high levels of anger and distrust, linking children's distress to the other parent's behaviour. The research shows that these cases are not, as non-resident parents characterised them, single issue disputes about one parent's obstruction of contact. Resident parents saw the contact issue in the context of other concerns.

Rhoades (2002) however sees little merit in the planned reforms. She warns that measures such as those already being implemented in the UK, together with the new proposals, divert attention from poor parenting during contact visits by non-resident fathers. Her research in Australia shows fathers failing to care adequately for their children or failing to turn up for contact visits at all. These fathers can and do 'breach the terms of contact orders with impunity' (p 78). Moreover, she found that few mothers flouted contact orders and that the most common source of conflict was the resident parent's concern about domestic violence. There were mothers who disobeyed consent orders but in many of these cases the order was amended to place greater restrictions on the father (pp 84–85). It may be, then, that at least some of these mothers had been persuaded or pressured into agreeing to inappropriate contact arrangements to begin with.

> **Q** In the cases discussed above, what do the courts appear to consider the primary impediment to beneficial contact? Is it conflict between the parents? The non-resident parent's conduct? The mother's 'implacable hostility'? Smart and Neale (1997) point out that little attention is paid to the 'damage' to children resulting from their fathers failing to take responsibility for them. They argue that contact has become an ideological issue; the 'implacably hostile mother', in refusing to share her child with the father is 'obstructing the new ideal of the post-divorce family' (p 335). Do you agree? Are not fathers who fail to maintain contact also undermining the ideal?

> **Q** Read chapter 8. Do you think the proposed new measures will lead to more and better contact?

*Child's Wishes*

Proponents of 'parental alienation syndrome' would argue that in some cases, children's opposition to contact stems from the influence of their resident parent. In any event, since contact is assumed to be overwhelmingly beneficial for children, courts[257] are reluctant to allow a child's resistance to it to be decisive.[258] In *Re H (Minors) (Access)*[259] it was said that courts should not be unduly perturbed by the prospect of

---

[256] In particular, it could be helpful to require abusers to attend perpetrator programmes in cases where there is a history of violence. Presumably the references to programmes in the Bill could include such programmes.
[257] See also James, *et al*, (2003).
[258] See *M v M (Defined Contact Application)* [1998] 2 FLR 244.
[259] [1992] 1 FLR 148.

some distress being caused to children by contact. Balcombe LJ cited[260] with approval the judgment of Latey J in *M v M (Child) (Access)*:

> [W]here the parents have separated and one has the care of the child, access by the other often results in some upset to the child. Those upsets are usually minor and superficial. They are heavily outweighed by the long-term advantages to the child of keeping in touch with the parent concerned so that they do not become strangers, so that the child later in life does not resent the deprivation and turn against the parent who the child thinks, rightly or wrongly, has deprived him, and so that the deprived parent loses interest in the child and therefore does not make the material and emotional contribution to the child's development which that parent by its companionship and otherwise would make. (p 88)[261]

However, long-term emotional injury caused by forcing children to see a parent will militate against contact. In *Re M (Contact: Welfare Test)*[262] the distress of the children, aged 8 and 9, at contact with their mother and their express wish not to see her was crucial to the decision to refuse an order. Considerable weight was also given to the children's steadfast refusal to see their transsexual father in *Re F (Minors) (Denial of Contact)*.[263] In *Re S (Contact: Children's Views)*,[264] the court refused to make a contact order in respect of a girl aged 16 and made orders for contact by negotiation and agreement in relation to her brothers, aged 14 and 12. These were not, in the end, children, said the court. They were teenagers and the two older ones were, in reality, young adults and should be treated as such; they could make decisions without being pressurised and the 12–year old should be given some choice commensurate with his age. Young people, the court said, have to be brought up to 'respect the law' and so 'the law must respect them and their wishes, even to the extent of allowing them, as they occasionally do, to make mistakes'.[265] To make an order for contact contrary to their wishes would be counter-productive and the quality of the contact foisted upon them might be poor.[266]

## XVI. CONCLUSION (2)

In relation to residence and contact, the court will make its decision in accordance with what it perceives to be the child's best interests. There are no presumptions in respect of residence and the court will use the checklist as a guide. As far as young children are concerned, in cases with heterosexual parents, it appears that the mother may well be considered to be the 'natural' carer unless there are indications to the contrary. Shared residence orders are becoming less unusual.

Since Barbie is no longer very young, in Steve and Jenny's case, less weight will be given to the 'natural' role of the mother as carer. In Stephanie and Jenny's case, this factor will not be considered relevant at all, although the court might favour the biological mother. In addition, Barbie may be considered old enough to have her wishes taken into

---

[260] P 151.
[261] [1973] 2 All ER 81.
[262] [1995] 1 FLR 274.
[263] [1993] 2 FLR 677. See also *Re C (Contact: No Order for Contact)* [2000] 2 FLR 723.
[264] [2002] 1 FLR 1156.
[265] *Ibid* 1171.
[266] P 1169.

account, although they will not be decisive. Given that Barbie's day-to-day care has largely been Jenny's responsibility and there is no indication that Jenny will not be in a position to provide her with acceptable accommodation, the *status quo* principle points to a residence order in favour of Jenny in both cases. Also, in Steve and Jenny's case, because it is anticipated that Steve will be in full-time work and cannot offer a mother substitute who will be responsible for child care in his absence, it is unlikely that he would succeed in obtaining an order. In Stephanie and Jenny's case, Stephanie will have to show that she will be able to offer some form of care for Barbie while she, Stephanie, is in full-time work. Should Steve abandon his plans to find full-time employment, this may be frowned on by the court, particularly if this step would entail reliance on state benefits. The court may not take the same view of Stephanie abandoning her plans to obtain full-time employment, but it may if she has to rely on state benefits.

A shared residence order is a possibility in both cases since the parents seem to be able to co-operate with each other, but it would have to be shown to be a workable arrangement, reflecting the reality of the parties' lives.

With regard to contact, there is a strong presumption or assumption that it is in the child's best interests to have contact with the non-resident parent. So strong is this presumption/assumption that there would have to be very cogent reasons for denying contact. Steadfast opposition and distress on the part of the child may suffice. So might severe disruption to the child's life. However the resident parent's opposition, even if founded on the past conduct of the other parent, is unlikely to be seen by the courts as furnishing a sufficiently compelling reason.

Since the relationship between Steve and Barbie appears to be a relatively close one, and since there are no cogent reasons to deny contact, it seems certain that, should a residence order be made in favour of Jenny, and if in spite of Section 1(5) an order is considered necessary, Steve would be awarded an order for direct contact. The same position can be taken with respect to any application Stephanie might take for contact.

**Q** Jenny tells you that she wishes to move with Barbie to a distant part of the country as she has been offered a better paid part-time job there. The school which Barbie could attend is a good one and suitable housing is available. Advise Jenny.

## XVII. RELOCATION

The priority accorded to contact has led courts on occasion to deny resident parents permission to relocate with their children. For instance, in *Tyler v Tyler*,[267] the court refused the mother permission to emigrate because the move would deprive the children of a relationship with their father.

In deciding whether to grant an application to relocate, the court applies the welfare principle and also considers whether the resident parent's proposals are reasonable; they must be practical in the sense of being realistic, and they must be genuine and not motivated by a selfish wish to exclude the other parent.[268] The reasons for the non-resident

---

[267] [1989] 2 FLR 158. See also *Re T (Removal from Jurisdiction)* [1996] 2 FLR 352. On same sex parents, see *G (Children)* [2005] EWCA Civ 462. The court below refused permission for the move.

[268] *Payne v Payne* [2001] EWCA Civ 166; [2001] 1 FLR 1052; *Re C (Permission to Remove from Jurisdiction)* [2003] EWHC Fam 596; [2003] 1 FLR 1066.

parent's opposition must also be appraised. One question to consider is whether he or she is motivated by 'genuine concern' for the child's welfare or by some 'ulterior motive'.[269] Another is the potential damage to the non-resident parent's relationship with the child should the move be allowed. If the refusal of an application is likely to have a detrimental impact on the care that the primary carer will be able to give to the child, this consideration will usually outweigh the detrimental impact on the relationship with the other parent if the application is granted.[270] Where the resident parent cares for a child or proposes to care for the child in a new family, the impact of a refusal on the new family or step-parent must also be examined; normally the welfare of the child cannot be secured unless the new family can pursue its goals without unreasonable restrictions.[271]

However, where the resident parent's primary motive is to get away from the non-resident parent in order to reduce or terminate contact, the court is likely to refuse the application.[272] And in one unusual case, a request to remove a child was denied because the child was being cared for in a shared care arrangement and, even if the mother did leave the country, it would be in the child's best interests not to experience the disruption of a move.[273]

## XVIII. CONCLUSION (3)

Jenny's proposals to move seem reasonable; they are realistic and do not appear to be motivated by a wish to exclude the other parent. The court may well grant an application to relocate provided the disruption for Barbie and damage to her relationship with her other parent do not outweigh any detriment that would follow should the application be refused.

**Q** Would it affect your advice regarding contact with Steve if there were evidence that Steve had abused Jenny and/or Barbie?

## XIX. VIOLENCE AND CHILD ABUSE

Buchanan, *et al*, (2001 p 17) report that one of the main reasons that led mothers in their research sample to oppose fathers' proposals about child care was domestic violence. Mothers' fears might relate to their own safety[274] and to that of their children. Similarly, Trinder, *et al*, (2005) found that mothers in their sample reported high levels of domestic violence, with some violence beginning after separation. Women referred to

---

[269] *Re C (Permission to Remove from Jurisdiction)* [2003] EWHC Fam 596; [2003] 1 FLR 1066, para 40.

[270] *Ibid,* para 24(9).

[271] *Re B (Removal from Jurisdiction); Re S (Removal from Jurisdiction)* [2003] EWCA Civ 1149; [2003] 2 FLR 643.

[272] See *B v B (Residence: Condition Limiting Geographic Area)* [2004] 2 FLR 979.

[273] *Re Y (Leave to Remove from Jurisdiction)* [2004] 2 FLR 330.

[274] Buchanan, *et al*, (2001 p 15) found high levels of violence in their sample. This was frequent in many cases and often severe. For some mothers in the study the fear still persisted a year after court proceedings began (2001 p 61).

risks to both themselves and their children. Nevertheless contact was seldom supervised.[275] Hester and Radford (1992) point to studies indicating that children who witness violence inflicted on their mothers suffer profound effects[276] and that men who are violent to their partners may also be violent to their children. In their own research, carried out between 1992 and 1995, they found that the children of half the women in their sample[277] had been physically and/or sexually abused by the women's partners and most had witnessed violence to their mothers (Hester and Radford 1996 pp 5 and 9). Often, abuse or neglect occurred during contact visits (pp 10–11; p 22).[278] Yet many of the professionals interviewed 'had a strong commitment to the idea of maintaining contact for children with non-resident fathers, even where there had been child abuse and the children were afraid' (p 23).

Their study also confirms that there is a risk that contact may be used by fathers as an opportunity to continue harassment or abuse of their partners. The majority of women in their sample were assaulted by their husbands or partners after separation and '[a]ll of the post-separation violence was linked in some way to child contact' (p 3).[279] In some instances, children were forced to aid their fathers in abusing their mothers (p 10).

In spite of this, they found, most mothers did not hamper, and even facilitated, contact with violent partners provided they believed that it would benefit their children (pp 24–25). Nevertheless, when women did oppose contact, the problem was predominantly defined by professionals and courts alike as the mothers' hostility rather than the violence of their partners and its effect on the children.[280] Professionals failed to see any link between the welfare of children and the safety of their caretaking mothers.

Similar findings are reported in relation to a study conducted in 1995 by Rights of Women (Anderson 1997b). Mothers who had been abused were not generally opposed to contact but the wishes of those who were, and the wishes of their children, appeared to have little impact on outcomes. The author of the report comments that, '[i]t seems that the ideological assumption of the importance of contact with the father is so strong that cases are rarely dismissed as being without merit, however extreme the circumstances' (p 8).[281]

**Q** Consider the cases concerning the 'implacably hostile' parent above. Do they bear out Hester and Radford's contention that it is the mother's hostility that is defined as the problem rather than the violence?

---

[275] The Joint Committee recommended that courts be obliged to consider the safety implications before ordering a contact activity or making an enforcement order (House of Commons, House of Lords 2005 paras 45 and 101). There is currently nothing in the Bill dealing with safety. The Bill merely stipulates that in deciding whether to make a contact activity direction, the court must treat the child's welfare paramount (Cl 1, proposed s 11A(8)).

[276] See also Humphreys and Harrison (2003b) p 240.

[277] See also McGee (2000) who interviewed women and children who had experience of domestic violence. In over 70% of cases the children had witnessed their mothers being physically assaulted. Over half the children were found to have been physically abused themselves and emotional abuse was found in almost two-thirds of the families. A significant proportion of the children had been subjected to controlling behaviour and some had been sexually abused.

[278] For an example of such a case, see *G v C (Residence Order: Committal* [1998] 1 FLR 43.

[279] See also pp 8, 26–27.

[280] See pp 23–26. But see also *Re T (A Minor) (Parental Responsibility: Contact)* [1993] 2 FLR 450.

[281] See also Buchanan, *et al*, (2001). Parents reported being placed under pressure to settle by lawyers, and there was also reference to pressure being exerted by the judge, the court welfare officer and the former partner (p 24).

Subsequent to the publication of research studies such as these and partly as a result of their findings,[282] concern about violence to women and children in the context of divorce has increased. Mediators and the court welfare service, now CAFCASS, began to address the problem.[283] Legislation was also introduced acknowledging the need for protection. After initial opposition from the government on the ground that it was not relevant to divorce and separation,[284] a provision dealing with domestic violence was inserted into the 'general principles' contained in Section 1 of the Family Law Act 1996.[285] However this provision is of no obvious effect, given the fate of the 1996 Act. Possibly more significant is the amendment of the Children Act 1989, although this change is not directly applicable to Section 8 proceedings. After consultation[286] the definition of 'harm' in Section 31 was expanded to include 'impairment suffered from seeing or hearing the ill-treatment of another'.[287] Of more direct relevance to contact disputes is the fact that reported judgments on contact have also begun to reveal a growing awareness of the risks to mothers and children.

In *Re D (Contact: Reasons for Refusal)*[288] the Court of Appeal dismissed an appeal against a refusal to order direct contact.[289] The court accepted that the father presented a risk of physical harm to the child, or of physical harm to the mother to an extent that the child would be indirectly harmed. The court declined to treat this case simply as one involving an implacably hostile mother. Hale J remarked that the way in which that term is used is sometimes misleading and continued:

> It is … an umbrella term that sometimes is applied to cases not only where there is hostility, but no good reason can be discerned either for the hostility or for the opposition to contact, but also to cases where there are such good reasons. In the former sort of case the court will be very slow indeed to reach the conclusion that contact will be harmful to the child. It may eventually have to reach that conclusion but it will want to be satisfied that there is indeed a serious risk of major emotional harm before doing so. It is rather different in the cases where the judge or the court finds that the mother's fears, not only for herself but also for the child, are genuine and rationally held; as indeed the court did in this case. (p 53)

There developed a greater readiness to accept that experiences of violence can have a lasting and traumatising effect so that mothers' opposition to contact becomes explicable and justifiable (Kaganas and Day Sclater 2000 p 633).[290] And, in taking mothers' fears more seriously, the courts also began to examine the behaviour of the fathers concerned (*ibid*); 'violent fathers are now expected to deal with drink and drug problems and to confront their violence in counselling or therapy' (*ibid*). In *Re M (Contact: Violent Parent)*,[291] for example, Wall J stated:

> Often in these cases where domestic violence has been found, too little weight … is given to the need for the father to change … a father, like this father, must demonstrate that he is a fit

[282] See *Re L (Contact: Domestic Violence); Re V (Contact: Domestic Violence); Re M (Contact: Domestic Violence); Re H (Contact: Domestic Violence)* [2002] 2 FLR 334, 369.
[283] See ch 11.
[284] See Bird and Cretney (1996) para 1.17.
[285] S 1(d) Family Law Act 1996.
[286] See CASC (1999) and CASC (2000).
[287] This notion of harm will, presumably, influence courts hearing contact disputes.
[288] [1997] 2 FLR 48. See, for the law in Scotland, *S v M (Access Order)* [1997] 1 FLR 980.
[289] See also *Re M (Contact: Family Assistance: McKenzie Friend)* [1999] 1 FLR 75.
[290] See *Re K (Contact: Mother's Anxiety)* [1999] 2 FLR 703, 708.
[291] [1999] 2 FLR 321. See also *Re H (Contact: Domestic Violence)* [1998] 2 FLR 42, 57.

person to exercise contact, that he is not going to destabilise the family, that he is not going to upset the children and harm them emotionally. (p 333)

The new focus on violence is central to the decision of the Court of Appeal in *Re L*.[292] Dame Butler Sloss P said:

The family judges and magistrates need to have a heightened awareness of the existence of and consequences (some long term), on children of exposure to domestic violence between their parents or other partners. There has, perhaps, been a tendency in the past for courts not to tackle allegations of violence and to leave them in the background on the premise that they were matters affecting the adults and not relevant to issues regarding the children. The general principle that contact with the non-resident parent is in the interests of the child may some-times have discouraged sufficient attention being paid to the adverse effects on children living in the household where violence has occurred. It may not necessarily be widely appreciated that violence to a partner involves a significant failure in parenting[293]—failure to protect the child's carer and failure to protect the child emotionally.

In a contact or other s 8 application, where allegations of domestic violence are made which might have an effect on the outcome, those allegations must be adjudicated upon and found proved or not proved. It will be necessary to scrutinise such allegations which may not always be true or may be grossly exaggerated.[294] If however there is a firm basis for finding that vio-lence has occurred, the psychiatric advice becomes very important.[295] There is not, however, nor should there be, any presumption that, on proof of domestic violence, the offending parent has to surmount a prima facie barrier of no contact. As a matter of principle, domestic vio-lence of itself cannot constitute a bar to contact. It is one factor in the difficult and delicate balancing exercise of discretion … . In cases of proved domestic violence, as in cases of other proved harm or risk of harm to the child, the court has the task of weighing in the balance the seriousness of the domestic violence, the risks involved and the impact on the child against the positive factors (if any), of contact between the parent found to have been violent and the child. In this context, the ability of the offending parent to recognise his past conduct, be aware of the need to change and make genuine efforts to do so, will be likely to be an important consideration. (pp 341–42)

Dame Butler-Sloss P found that in the cases before her, the mothers' fears were 'reason-able' and that this distinguished them from 'implacable hostility' cases.[296] In reaching her conclusions she endorsed Wilson J's approach in *Re M (Contact; Welfare Check-list)*,[297] which involved using the Section 1(3) checklist. This, she said, was 'a useful sum-mary of the proper approach to a contact application where domestic violence is a factor'.[298]

Thorpe LJ, like Dame Butler-Sloss P, was careful not to elevate domestic violence cases to a special category, 'Domestic violence', he said. 'is one of a catalogue of factors that may operate to offset the assumption for contact but it has not been separately

---

[292] *Re L (Contact: Domestic Violence); Re V (Contact: Domestic Violence); Re M (Contact: Domestic Vio-lence); Re H (Contact: Domestic Violence)* [2002] 2 FLR 334.

[293] This phrase echoes the word used in the Sturge/Glaser report that was before the court.

[294] In the research conducted by Buchanan, *et al*, (2001), half of the mothers interviewed reported violence or fear at the time proceedings commenced (p 15) and for some, the fear persisted a year later (p 61). Only a quarter regarded domestic violence as an issue in the proceedings (p 15). So, rather than mothers making false allegations in proceedings, it seems that many mothers who have suffered abuse do not raise the matter in court.

[295] But see Saunders and Barron (2003) p 8 on the appropriateness of this kind of expert evidence.

[296] P 343.

[297] [1995] 1 FLR 274, 278–79. See above p 580.

[298] *Re L* 342–43.

categorised ..., nor ... should it be'.[299] Like Butler-Sloss P, he rejected the recommendation in the Sturge/Glaser report that, where a parent is or has previously been violent, there should be an assumption against contact. Instead he said: 'In my opinion the only direction that can be given to the trial judge is to apply the welfare principle and the welfare checklist, Section 1(1) and (3) of the Children Act 1989, to the facts of the particular case'.[300] The effect of domestic violence, along with other serious misconduct or deficiencies, would be to 'offset' the 'assumption' in favour of contact and to activate the checklist:

> [T]he factors that may offset the assumption in favour of contact are probably too legion to be either listed or categorised. Abuse must form the largest compartment: as well as physical abuse of the other parent and/or the child there is equally sexual and emotional abuse within the family. Then there is the self abuse of either drugs or alcohol and the failure to maintain sexual boundaries appropriate to the development of the child. Additionally mental illness or personality disorder may be a dominant factor as may be malign motives prompting the applicant to pursue a seemingly justifiable application for the covert purpose of threatening or dominating the primary carer. This uncomprehensive catalogue only demonstrates that the factor of domestic violence must be kept in proportion (p 370)

So, on the basis of the President's judgement, the checklist must be used in cases where domestic violence has been proved. Thorpe LJ.'s obiter dictum appears more wide-ranging; it enumerates a number of factors that would invite the application of Section 1(3). Nevertheless, both judges agree that the court should have discretion to award contact in cases of violence and, it seems, it is only in the exceptional cases that the assumption is offset; in cases not covered by the exceptions, the presumption/assumption in favour of contact persists.

The Government has made it clear that it has no plans to introduce a presumption of no contact in cases where it has not been established that contact will be safe for all involved (DCA, DfES and DTI 2005 preamble to para 20).[301] There are however guidelines for the courts:[302] *Guidelines for Good Practice on Parental Contact in Cases where there is Domestic Violence* (CASC 2002). These substantially reflect the judgments in *Re L*. The court is required to make findings on allegations of domestic violence that could affect its order. In deciding on interim contact, it must use the welfare checklist and also give particular consideration to the risks to the child. Where the court orders a welfare report, this will address the child's wishes as well as issues of risk and harm to the resident parent and the child (para 1.3). The court should consider whether any contact ordered should be supervised. It should endeavour to ensure that risks to the child are minimised and that the safety of the child and the resident parent is secured before, during and after contact (para 1.4). At the final hearing, the court should make findings of fact and apply the checklist in the light of those findings, giving particular consideration to the risks to the child. An order for contact should only be made if the court is satisfied that the safety of the resident parent and the child can be secured before, during and after contact (para 1.5). The court has to consider the effect of any violence proved on

---

[299] P 367.
[300] P 370.
[301] Compare s 16B of the New Zealand Guardianship Act 1968; s 68F of the Australian Family Law Reform Act 1995. The New Zealand legislation contains a presumption against unsupervised contact in cases of violence. See, further, Kaye (1996). See also Radford, *et al,* (1999) p 33; Saunders (2001); Saunders and Barron (2003) p 61.
[302] Extracted from CASC (2000) and endorsed by the government in 2001. See Saunders (2001). The Guidelines are not binding.

the child and the resident parent. It must also have regard to whether the non-resident parent's motivation is to continue his violence, or his intimidation or harassment of the other parent. It must consider what the contact parent's behaviour is likely to be like during contact and its effect on the child. Whether the contact parent appreciates the effect of the violence on the other parent and the child is also relevant, as is the attitude of the contact parent to past violence and whether he has the capacity to change (para 1.6).

When contact is ordered in cases involving domestic violence, the court has to consider whether it should be supervised, whether conditions should be attached (such as seeking treatment or advice) and whether a non-molestation order should be made.

> **Q** Do these guidelines operate where there is no proof of past violence but there is nevertheless evidence of a future risk of violence? In implementing these guidelines, to what extent is the court's assessment of risk significant? To what extent is its understanding of the nature of domestic violence important?

### *Harm to the Child*

Where it is alleged that a child has been sexually[303] or otherwise[304] abused by the non-resident parent, the court may deny contact altogether. According to Thorpe LJ in *Re L*,[305] proof of abuse serves to 'offset' the 'assumption' in favour of contact. However, abuse is not necessarily a bar to contact and, in order to avoid terminating contact completely, the court has in the past sometimes ordered supervised contact. In *L v L (Child Abuse: Access)*,[306] for example, the court allowed supervised contact, finding that there was a close bond between father and daughter, that she showed no ill-effects and that contact was in her best interests.[307] In *Re L*,[308] the Court of Appeal refused to allow direct contact in any of the four cases before it. In the first case, *Re L*, the father had engaged in serious and sadistic violence to the mother and there were risks of emotional harm to the child.[309] In the second, *Re V*, the child continued to be distressed and traumatised by the experience of having witnessed a knife attack on his mother.[310] In the third, *Re M*, the court found that if the child were forced to have contact, this would have a detrimental effect on him.[311] And in the fourth, *Re H*, the father had made serious threats against the mother who was afraid of him and feared he would abduct the children. In addition, contact could expose the children to a clash of cultures.[312] Nevertheless, the orders for indirect contact[313] made by the lower courts were considered appropriate in all four situations.

---

[303] *S v S (Child Abuse: Access)* [1988] 1 FLR 213.

[304] See *In re A (Contact: Domestic Violence)* [1998] 2 FLR 121 where the father's assault on one of the children as well as his violence against the mother were relevant to the court's decision to deny contact.

[305] *Re L (Contact: Domestic Violence); Re V (Contact: Domestic Violence); Re M (Contact: Domestic Violence); Re H (Contact: Domestic Violence)* [2002] 2 FLR 334.

[306] [1989] 2 FLR 16.

[307] See also *Re H (Minors) (Access: Appeals)* [1989] 2 FLR 174. For a critical appraisal of the courts' reluctance to deny contact, see Jones and Parkinson (1995).

[308] *Re L (Contact: Domestic Violence); Re V (Contact: Domestic Violence); Re M (Contact: Domestic Violence); Re H (Contact: Domestic Violence)* [2002] 2 FLR 334.

[309] Pp 345–46.

[310] P 348.

[311] P 353.

[312] P 357.

[313] See also in the context of care proceedings, *Re G (Domestic Violence: Direct Contact)* [2000] 2 FLR 865.

Although the courts do restrict contact in cases of violence or abuse, research suggests that there is a possibility that if the court does make a contact order, even a supervised contact order, it will not necessarily ensure that either the resident mother or the child will be safe.

### The Effects of Re L and of the Guidelines

Kaganas (2000), commenting on *Re L*, suggested that whether it will help victims of violence and abuse will depend on whether the courts develop better knowledge about the dynamics of domestic violence. In *Re L* itself, it appears from the President's judgment that, in order to avoid being labeled 'implacably hostile', the resident parent may need to show not only that her fears are 'genuine' but also 'reasonable' (pp 318–19).[314] This, arguably, does not take sufficient account of the experiences of some victims. Cessation of violence does not automatically bring women's fears to an end and some abused women may suffer post-traumatic stress giving rise to disproportionate anxiety. In any event, whether fears are regarded as reasonable depends on the court's understanding of violence and awareness of post-separation violence. It also depends on the court's assessment of the seriousness of the violence. Also relevant is whether the court sees domestic violence in terms of mutual combat: 'Fears are less likely to be perceived as "genuine" if the parties are seen as equals engaged in a fight. Fears are also less likely to be seen as "genuine" if it is assumed that they cease once the violence has stopped' (p 319). In addition, the fact that only proof of violence rather than evidence of risk suffices to 'offset' the assumption may leave women and children vulnerable. This restrictive test is, Kaganas argues, consistent with a 'general reluctance to curtail contact' (p 318). Butler-Sloss P, for instance, warns in *Re L* of the danger of the 'pendulum swinging too far against contact where domestic violence has been proved'.[315] There is, therefore, a possibility that 'the balancing exercise which the court is required to undertake under Section 1(3) might be deployed in a way that continues to accord contact greater weight than other considerations, such as the impact on resident mothers of past violence' (Kaganas 2000 p 318).

Subsequent research examining the impact of *Re L* and of the Guidelines suggests that, while there have been some improvements, courts are indeed still prioritising contact and failing to protect abused women and children. A survey conducted by Women's Aid Federation of England (Saunders 2001) asked 127 refuge projects about the experiences of abused women and children in the period of approximately one year after *Re L* had been decided. Only 11 (8%) thought court practice had generally improved, while 66 (50%) said it had stayed the same. 47 said courts were not holding hearings to determine whether allegations of domestic violence were proved. 61 (48%) said that, if contact was ordered despite allegations of abuse, adequate measures were not being taken to ensure the safety of the child and resident parent, while only 3 projects said they were. Most projects said their local contact centre provided only 'low vigilance' contact, as opposed to supervised contact. Nearly half reported that they knew of cases where a man used contact proceedings to track down his former partner. 30 (23%) said that they knew of abused women who were ordered to hand over their children for contact visits even though they were on the Child Protection Register as a result of abuse by the father. 45 projects reported that children had been harmed during contact visits.

---

[314] See also *Re H (A Child: Contact: Mother's Opposition)* [2001] 1 FCR 59.
[315] P 342.

Similar results emerged from a subsequent survey by Women's Aid (Saunders with Barron 2003).[316] This involved sending questionnaires in 2003 to refuges and domestic violence services, asking about their views concerning contact and residence proceedings since the Guidelines were first introduced in 2001.[317] There were 178 responses. One of the findings reported is that women were frequently threatened with a change in residence to the abusive parent or with other enforcement proceedings. These threats, usually made by solicitors and judges, had the effect of pressurising women into handing their children over for contact (p 53). The key findings of the study were as follows:

- *Only 3% of respondents think that appropriate measures are now being taken to ensure the safety of the child and the resident parent in most contact cases involving domestic violence.* This is a clear indication that the good practice guidelines on child contact and domestic violence are not working.
- *Only 6% believe that children who say they do not want contact with a violent parent are being listened to and taken seriously in most cases; 57% say that this happens in some cases but not all, and 13% say children's views are never taken into account.* This is very worrying as the failure to listen to children has been highlighted in several child homicide reviews.
- *Respondents reported cases since April 2001, where a total of 18 children were ordered to have contact with parents who had committed offences against children and where a total of 64 children were ordered to have contact with parents whose behaviour previously caused children to be placed on the Child Protection Register. 21 of these children were ordered to have unsupervised contact with the abusive parent.*
- *Respondents reported cases where a total of 101 children were ordered to live with an abusive parent, often because he was living in secure accommodation in the former family home.*
- *46% of respondents knew of cases where a violent parent has been able to use contact proceedings to track down his former partner.*
- *83% of respondents say that young children who have been abused are not likely to disclose this during a one-off interview with a professional.* This shows that the standard procedures for investigating allegations of abuse in private law family proceedings urgently need to be reviewed. (p 5, Emphasis in original)

Smart and May (2004a p 41) conclude from the study that they conducted that, 'the courts operate under an assumption in favour of contact and it appears that, before the courts take the step of denying or restricting contact, they require substantial proof of harm potentially caused to the child by contact'. And where courts do restrict contact, recent research findings raise questions about the safety of the measures currently being used to do so.

*Contact Centres*

Contact centres were introduced largely in response to the perception that family breakdown was increasing and that fathers were losing contact with their children, particularly when they had no suitable place to meet (Humphreys and Harrison 2003b p 239). Some contact centres offer high vigilance supervision while others are low-vigilance supported centres.[318] A source of concern for commentators is that supported contact centres are being inappropriately used for families with a history of severe domestic violence

[316] See also Humphreys and Thiara (2002) pp 87ff.
[317] See CASC (2001a).
[318] Humphreys and Harrison (2003b) pp 241–42. Some supported centres do provide high levels of observation. See Humphreys and Harrison (2003a) p 421.

(Humphreys and Harrison 2003a pp 420–21). These cases, if the Guidelines were being followed, ought to have been using indirect contact (p 422). What is more, the courts, centre co-ordinators and fathers all put pressure on mothers to shift to more open arrangements (p 422), which might be even less safe.

New standards for safety in contact centres are being implemented but, say Humphreys and Harrison, the ways in which violence becomes minimised or is made invisible may persist (2003b p 244). One problem is that centre coordinators are not always aware of the history of violence. This could be because the woman never reveals it or because professionals, such as CFRs and solicitors, do not pass on any information about violence that they may have (p 245). Another problem is that perpetrators deny or minimise violence and, often, there is no evidence corroborating the woman's allegations (pp 246–47). And even if there is evidence of violence, it was not always assessed by professionals and coordinators as relevant to contact (p 248). Risks are not adequately investigated (pp 249–50) and, in any event, a pro-contact stance might override concerns about safety (p 250).

Even if new high vigilance contact centres are opened, this will not help, say the authors, if mothers and children are rapidly moved on to unsupervised contact. There is also the risk that such centres will be used in cases where contact is so dangerous that it would otherwise have been refused (p 252).

## XX. CONCLUSION (4)

If there is evidence that Steve has been violent to Jenny, this will not necessarily deter the court from making a contact order in his favour if it considers contact to be in Barbie's best interests. However, there is a possibility that an order may be made for supervised or, possibly, indirect contact. Evidence of abuse of Barbie or of other harm to her may lead the court to refuse an order, to order indirect contact or to make an order for supervised contact. Whether the contact will be safe for either Jenny or Barbie is open to question.

## FURTHER READING AND SELECTED RECENT REFERENCES

A BAINHAM, *et al*, (eds), *Children and Their Families: Contact, Rights and Welfare* (Oxford, Hart Publishing, 2003).

A BUCHANAN, *et al*, *Families in Conflict: Perspectives of Children and Parents on the Family Court Welfare Service*, (Bristol, Policy, 2001).

R COLLIER, 'The Dashing of a "Liberal Dream"?—The Information Meeting, the "New Family"and the Limits of Law', (1999) 11 *Child and Family Law Quarterly* 257.

S CRETNEY, *Family Law in the Twentieth Century: A History* (Oxford, OUP, 2003a).

S DAY SCLATER and C PIPER, (eds), *Undercurrents of Divorce* (Aldershot, Ashgate, 1999).

S DAY SCLATER, *Divorce: A Psychosocial Study* (Aldershot, Dartmouth, 1999).

J DEWAR, 'The Normal Chaos of Family Law' (1998) 61 *MLR* 467.

GA DUNNE, 'A Passion for "Sameness"? Sexuality and Gender Accountability' in EB Silva and C Smart, (eds), *The New Family?* (London, Sage, 1999).

J EEKELAAR, 'Family Law: Keeping Us "On Message"' (1999) 11 *CFLQ* 387.

M FREEMAN, (ed), *Divorce: Where Next?* (Aldershot, Dartmouth, 1996).

M GOLLOP, AB SMITH and N TAYLOR, 'Children's Involvement in Custody and Access Arrangements After Parental Separation' (2000) 12 (4) *CFLQ* 383.

WJ GOODE, *World Changes in Divorce Patterns* (New Haven, CT, Yale Univeristy Press, 1993).

J HAWTHORNE, et al, *Supporting Children through Family Change: A Review of Interventions and Services for Children of Divorcing and Separating Parents* (Cambridge, Centre for Family Research, University of Cambridge; York, Joseph Rowntree Foundation, 2003).

M HESTER, *et al*, 'Domestic Violence and Access Arrangements for Children in Denmark and Britain' (1992) *JSW & FL* 57.

M HESTER and L RADFORD, *Domestic Violence and Child Contact Arrangements in England and Denmark* (Bristol, Policy, 1996).

C HUMPHREYS and R THIARA, *Routes to Safety* (Bristol, WAFE, 2002).

C HUMPHREYS and C HARRISON, 'Squaring the Circle—Contact and Domestic Violence' (2003a) *Fam Law* 419.

——, 'Focusing on Safety—Domestic Violence and the Role of Child Contact Centres' (2003b) 15 *CFLQ* 237.

J HUNT, *Researching Contact* (London, One Parent Families, 2003).

AL JAMES, A JAMES and S MCNAMEE, 'Constructing Children's Welfare in Family Proceedings' (2003) *Fam Law* 889.

F KAGANAS, 'Contact, Conflict and Risk' in S Day Sclater and C Piper, (eds), *Undercurrents of Divorce* (Aldershot, Ashgate, 1999).

——, '*Re L (Contact: Domestic Violence; Re V (Contact: Domestic Violence); Re M (Contact: Domestic Violence); Re H (Contact: Domestic Violence)*: Contact and Domestic Violence' (2000) 12 *CFLQ* 311.

F KAGANAS and S DAY SCLATER, 'Contact and Domestic Violence—The Winds of Change?' (2000) *Fam Law* 630.

F KAGANAS and A DIDUCK, 'Incomplete Citizens: Changing Images of Post Separation Children' (2004) 67 (6) *MLR* 959.

M KING and F KAGANAS, 'The Risks and Dangers of Experts in Court' (1998) *Current Legal Issues* 221.

C MCGEE, *Childhood Experiences of Domestic Violence* (London, Jessica Kingsley, 2000)

A MULLENDER and R MORLEY, 'Context and Content of a New Agenda' in A Mullender and R Morley, (eds), *Children Living With Domestic Violence: Putting Men's Abuse of Women on the Child Care Agenda* (London, Whiting & Birch, 1994).

B NEALE, J FLOWERDEW and C SMART, 'Drifting Towards Shared Residence?' (2003) *Fam Law* 904.

J PEARCE, G DAVIS and J BARRON, 'Love in a Cold Climate—Section 8 Applications under the Children Act 1989' (1999) *Fam Law* 22.

C PIPER, 'How Do You Define a Family Lawyer?' (1999) 19 *Legal Studies* 93.

——, 'Ascertaining the Wishes and Feelings of the Child' (1997) *Fam Law* 796.

L RADFORD, S SAYER and AMICA, *Unreasonable Fears? Child Contact in the Context of Domestic Violence: A Survey of Mothers' Perspectives of Harm* (Bristol, WAFE, 1999).

H RHOADES, 'The "No-Contact Mother": Reconstructions of Motherhood in the Era of the "New Father"' (2002) 12 *Int J of Law, Policy and the Family* 71.

H SAUNDERS, *Making Contact Worse?* (Bristol, WAFE, 2001).

H SAUNDERS and J BARRON, *Failure to Protect? Domestic Violence and the Experiences of Abused Women and Children in the Family Courts* (Bristol, WAFE, 2003).

C SMART, 'Divorce in England 1950–2000: A Moral Tale', paper prepared for CAVA Workshop, *Frameworks for Understanding Policy Change and Culture* (1999).

C SMART, *et al, Residence and Contact Disputes in Court* (London, Department for Constitutional Affairs, DCA Research Series No 6/03, 2003).

C SMART and V MAY, 'Residence and Contact Disputes in Court' (2004) *Fam Law* 36.

C SMART and B NEALE, 'Arguments Against Virtue—Must Contact be Enforced?' (1997) *Fam Law* 332.

——, *Family Fragments?* (Cambridge, Polity, 1999).

C SMART, B NEALE and A WADE, *The Changing Experience of Childhood* (Cambridge, Polity, 2001).

L TRINDER, et al, A Profile of Applicants and Respondents in Contact Cases in Essex (London, DCA Research Series 1/05, 2005).

J WALKER, *Information Meetings and Associated Provisions within the Family Law Act 1996: Summary of the Final Evaluation Report* (London, The Stationery Office, Lord Chancellor's Department, 2001).

——, *Picking up the Pieces: Marriage and Divorce: Two Years after Information Provision* (London, Department of Constitutional Affairs, 2004).

J WEEKS, 'Elective Families: Lesbian and Gay Life Experiments' in A Carling, S Duncan and R Edwards, (eds) *Analysing Families: Morality and Rationality in Policy and Practice* (London, Routledge, 2002).

J WEEKS, C DONOVAN and B HEAPHY, 'Everyday Experiments: Narratives of Non-heterosexual Relationships' in EB Silva and C Smart, (eds), *The New Family?* (London, Sage, 1999).

## Reports

CAFCASS, Service Principles and Standards (2003).

Children Act Sub-Committee Of The Advisory Board On Family Law, A Report to the Lord Chancellor on the Question of Parental Contact in Cases where there is Domestic Violence, (London, The Stationery Office, 2000).

Children Act Sub-Committee Of The Lord Chancellor's Advisory Board On Family Law, Guidelines for Good Practice on Parental Contact in Cases where there is Domestic Violence. Section 5 of Report of Children Act Sub-committee to Lord Chancellor on the Question of Parental Contact in Cases where there is Domestic Violence (London, Lord Chancellor's Department, 2001).

——, *Guidelines for Good Practice on Parental Contact in Cases where there is Domestic Violence* (London, DCA, 2002).

DCA, DfES and DTI, *Parental Separation: Children's Needs and Parents' Responsibilities. Next Steps. Report of Responses to Consultation and Agenda for Action* Cm 6452 (London, The Stationery Office,

——, *Parental Separation: Children's Needs and Parents' Responsibilities* Cmd 6273 (2004).

DTI (Women and Equality Unit), *Responses to Civil Partnership* (London, The Stationery Office, 2003b).

# 15

# Children in Non-Marital Relationships and Financial Adjustment on the Breakdown of Marital Relationships

**Q** Evelyn, as a result of a brief relationship with Richard, has a son, Jeremy, now aged 5. Evelyn and Richard have never lived together and Jeremy has always stayed with his mother. Evelyn works as a teacher. Two years ago Richard married Jane, a former bank cashier, and moved with her to Manchester. He visits Jeremy occasionally when he is in London and contributes to Jeremy's keep when he feels able to spare any money. He is always sure to send Christmas and birthday gifts to Jeremy. Richard works full-time as a bus driver in Manchester while Jane stays at home to care for their 1-year-old daughter, Molly.

A year ago, Evelyn began a lesbian relationship with Phoebe, who has now moved in with her and Jeremy. Richard strongly disapproves and wishes to seek a residence order in relation to Jeremy. Failing that, he feels that, at the very least, he ought to have some say in the way Jeremy is brought up. Complicating matters further, Richard's and Jane's relationship is in difficulty, and although they are attempting to work things out, Richard is worried about how he will cope financially in the event of a separation or divorce.

This scenario raises issues concerning Jeremy's care and Richard's and Jane's finances. We will deal first with Richard's relationship with Jeremy.

## I. STATUS OF UNMARRIED PARENTS

While parents who are married to each other are both automatically vested with parental responsibility,[1] the legal status of parents is different if they do not marry.[2] Section 2(2) of the Children Act 1989 states:

---

[1] S 2(1) of the Children Act 1989. For further discussion of parental responsibility, including the position of married parents, see chs 4, 7, 14 and 16.

Special guardians have parental responsibility automatically (s 14C(1)(a) Children Act 1989). This parental responsibility can be exercised to a large extent to the exclusion of any other person with parental responsibility, such as the parents (s 14C(1)(b) Children Act 1989). Prospective adopters also have parental responsibility (s 25 Adoption and Children Act 2002. Not in force at time of writing).

[2] The distinction between married and unmarried fathers has been held to be compatible with Arts 8 and 14 of the European Convention of Human Rights. See further chs 4, 7.

Where a child's father and mother were not married to each other at the time of his birth—

(a)    the mother shall have parental responsibility for the child;
(b)    the father shall have parental responsibility for the child if he has acquired it (and has not ceased to have it) in accordance with the provisions of this Act.

The ways in which the Act permits an unmarried father[3] to acquire parental responsibility are set out in Section 4.

Section 4 provides:

Acquisition of parental responsibility by father.
4(1) Where a child's father and mother were not married to each other at the time of his birth, the father shall acquire parental responsibility for the child if—

(a)    he becomes registered as the child's father under any of the enactments specified in subsection (1A);
(b)    he and the child's mother make an agreement (a 'parental responsibility agreement') providing for him to have parental responsibility for the child; or
(c)    the court, on his application, orders that he shall have parental responsibility for the child.

(1A) The enactments referred to in subsection (1)(a) are—

(a)    paragraphs (a), (b) and (c) of section 10(1) and section 10A(1) of the Births and Deaths Registration Act 1953 … .

(2) No parental responsibility agreement shall have effect for the purposes of this Act unless—

(a)    it is made in the form prescribed by regulations made by the Lord Chancellor; and
(b)    where regulations are made by the Lord Chancellor prescribing the manner in which such agreements must be recorded, it is recorded in the prescribed manner.

(2A) A person who has acquired parental responsibility under subsection (1) shall cease to have that responsibility only if the court so orders.

(3) The court may make an order under subsection (2A) on the application—

(a)    of any person who has parental responsibility for the child; or
(b)    with the leave of the court, of the child himself,

subject, in the case of parental responsibility acquired under subsection (1)(c), to section 12(4).

(4) The court may only grant leave under subsection (3)(b) if it is satisfied that the child has sufficient understanding to make the proposed application.

Section 12 stipulates:

12 Residence orders and parental responsibility
(1) Where the court makes a residence order in favour of the father of a child it shall, if the father would not otherwise have parental responsibility for the child, also make an order under section 4 giving him that responsibility.
(2) Where the court makes a residence order in favour of any person who is not the parent or guardian of the child concerned that person shall have parental responsibility for the child, while the residence order remains in force

---

[3] See, for a summary of the debates concerning the desirability or otherwise of granting unmarried fathers automatic parental responsibility, Herring (2004) pp 320ff. See also ch 7 above.

(3) Where a person has parental responsibility for a child as a result of subsection (2), he shall not have the right—

...

[(b)   to agree or refuse to agree, to the making of an adoption order, or an order under section 84 of the Adoption and Children Act 2002 with respect to the child];[4] or
(c)   to appoint a guardian for the child.

(4) Where subsection (1) requires the court to make an order under section 4 in respect of the father of a child, the court shall not bring that order to an end at any time while the residence order concerned remains in force ... .

At present, the only ways in which a step-parent can get parental responsibility is by adoption or by obtaining a residence order. However the Act has been amended, and when the changes come into effect, it will extend the possibility of gaining parental responsibility to step-parents and to registered civil partners. The change does not apply to a cohabitant who is not the child's parent, however.

4A Acquisition of parental responsibility by step-parent
(1) Where a child's parent ('parent A') who has parental responsibility for the child is married to [or a civil partner of][5] a person who is not the child's parent ('the step-parent')—

(a)   parent A or, if the other parent of the child also has parental responsibility for the child, both parents may by agreement with the step-parent provide for the step-parent to have parental responsibility for the child; or
(b)   the court may, on the application of the step-parent, order that the step-parent shall have parental responsibility for the child.

(2) An agreement under subsection (1)(a) is also a 'parental responsibility agreement' and section 4(2) applies in relation to such agreements as it applies in relation to parental responsibility agreements under section 4.

(3) A parental responsibility agreement under subsection (1)(a), or an order under subsection (1)(b), may only be brought to an end by an order of the court made on the application—

(a) of any person who has parental responsibility for the child; or
(b) with the leave of the court, by the child himself.

(4) The court may only grant leave under subsection (3)(b) if it is satisfied that the child has sufficient understanding to make the proposed application.

If Richard wants the right to have his son live with him, he has to seek a residence order. Should he succeed, the court will be obliged in terms of Section 12(1), as he does not already have parental responsibility, to make a parental responsibility order in his favour as well. The reasoning behind this provision is that the parent with day-to-day responsibility for a child's care ought to be endowed with the legal status necessary to enable him to make decisions concerning that child's upbringing. The result would be that Richard would be entitled to have Jeremy live with him and he would share parental responsibility with Evelyn. Moreover, once he has parental responsibility, it can only be terminated in accordance with Section 4(2A); the order will remain in force during Jeremy's minor-

---

4 Not in force at the time of writing.
5 Inserted by the Civil Partnership Act 2004.

ity even if the residence order is subsequently brought to an end.[6] Should he fail to secure a residence order, Richard will still be able to have some say in Jeremy's upbringing if he and Evelyn enter into a parental responsibility agreement or if he can obtain a parental responsibility order from the court.[7] Because the amendment of Section 4 of the Children Act 1989 came into force on 1 December 2003, and because it does not have retrospective effect,[8] Richard will not have parental responsibility automatically even if he and Evelyn registered Jeremy's birth jointly.[9]

## II. DETERMINING A CHILD'S RESIDENCE

The fact that Evelyn and Richard were not married to each other is very unlikely to be a crucial factor in the court's deliberations; cases on residence do not generally turn on marital status. For a full discussion of the court's approach to disputes over residence and the application of the Section 1(3) welfare checklist, you should refer to chapter 14. However, there are two significant additional factors in this case that require consideration. The first is that Jeremy is still very young and the second is that Evelyn is involved in a lesbian relationship.

### Young Children—a Maternal Preference?

We have noted that the courts in the past tended to award care of young children to their mothers while older boys went to fathers and older girls to mothers.[10] However, the courts have indicated that rules of thumb of this kind cannot now serve as a legitimate basis for judicial decision-making.[11]

In *Re S (A Minor) (Custody)*,[12] the Court of Appeal was faced with a dispute concerning a 2–year-old girl. The mother had left when the child was aged 9 months, leaving her with the father. The mother had had a miscarriage and was apparently suffering from depression. In addition, she had been assaulted by the father at the time that she was leaving. By the time the case came before the Court of Appeal, the mother had taken the child and the child had been with her for several months. There was concern on the part of the court welfare officer that the child had suffered severe nappy rash while with the father and also that it appeared that if returned to him, the child's care was going to be left to other family members. Butler-Sloss LJ, remitting the case for rehearing, stated:

> The welfare of the child is the ... paramount consideration ... . It used to be thought many years ago that young children should be with mother, that girls approaching puberty should be with mother and that boys over a certain age should be with father. Such presumptions, if they

---

[6] Compare the position, in terms of s 12(2), of those other than parents or guardians.

[7] Maclean and Eekelaar noted that parental responsibility was acquired only by a 'tiny proportion' of unmarried fathers (1997 p 146). See also Pickford (2003).

[8] S 111(7) Adoption and Children Act 2002.

[9] See further ch 7.

[10] See ch 8.

[11] See, for example, *Re W (A Minor) (Custody)* [1983] 4 FLR 492, 504. Note that terms such as 'care and control', 'custody' and 'access' pre-date the Children Act 1989.

[12] [1991] 2 FLR 388.

ever were such, do not, in my view, exist today. There are dicta of this court to the effect that it is likely that a young child, particularly perhaps a little girl, would be expected to be with her mother, but that is subject to the overriding factor that the welfare of the child is the paramount consideration ... . I would just add that it is natural for young children to be with mothers but, where it is in dispute, it is a consideration but not a presumption. (p 390)

Lord Donaldson added:

[I]t is natural for young children to be with their mothers. Given that situation, if you take enough cases, you will almost certainly find that, in the majority of them, it is in the interests of the child that he or she should be with the mother. Whether or not this amounts to a presumption, I know not.

What is clear is that there is a change in the social order, in the organisation of society, whereby it is much more common for fathers to look after young children than it used to be in bygone days. It must follow that courts could more readily conclude in an individual case that it was in the interests of a young child that it be with its father than it would have done previously. (p 392)

**Q** Why is it natural that children, especially young children, are looked after by their mothers? What does Butler-Sloss LJ mean when she says that this should be a 'consideration but not a presumption'? To what extent do you agree with Lord Donaldson's comment in *Re S* that it is now far more common for fathers to care for their children? What criteria would you use in assessing which parent would be the better carer for the child?

In *Re A (A Minor) (Custody)*,[13] Butler-Sloss LJ elaborated on the views she had expressed in *Re S*:

In cases where the child has remained throughout with the mother and is young, particularly when a baby or toddler, the unbroken relationship of the mother and child is one which it would be very difficult to displace, unless the mother was unsuitable to care for the child. But where the mother and child have been separated, and the mother seeks the return of the child, other considerations apply, and there is no starting point that the mother should be preferred to the father and only displaced by a preponderance of evidence to the contrary. (p 400)

**Q** Is Butler-Sloss LJ saying that if a very young child has been in the continuous care of the mother, the court should adopt as its 'starting point' the position that the mother should be preferred to the father except where there is 'a preponderance of evidence to the contrary'? Would this be the same as saying there is a presumption in favour of the mother in those circumstances? Is this merely an application of the *status quo* principle?

In *Brixey v Lynas*[14] the House of Lords, hearing a Scots case, and applying a Scots statutory provision which, like the Children Act 1989, makes the child's welfare the paramount consideration, cited *Re A* with approval. It held:

---

[13] [1991] 2 FLR 394. See also *Re W (A Minor) (Residence Order)* [1992] 2 FLR 332.
[14] [1996] 2 FLR 499.

[T]he advantage to a very young child of being with its mother is a consideration which must be taken into account in deciding where lie its best interests in custody proceedings in which the mother is involved. It is neither a presumption nor a principle but rather recognition of a widely held belief based on practical experience and the workings of nature. Its importance will vary according to the age of the child and to the other circumstances of each individual case such as whether the child has been living with or apart from the mother and whether she is or is not capable of providing proper care. Circumstances may be such that it has no importance at all. Furthermore it will always yield to other competing advantages which more effectively promote the welfare of the child. However, where a very young child has been with its mother since birth and there is no criticism of her ability to care for the child only the strongest competing advantages are likely to prevail. (p 505)

The courts are even less likely now to talk in terms of a presumption in favour of the mother. In *Re L*[15] Thorpe LJ remarked that there is a danger that the identification of a presumption in deciding a Section 8 case might 'inhibit or distort the rigorous search for the welfare solution'. Instead, he preferred to speak of an 'assumption' in favour of contact in contact disputes. In *Payne v Payne*[16] he gave a further explanation of his misgivings:

[25] ... Generally in the language of litigation a presumption either casts a burden of proof upon the party challenging it or can be said to be decisive of outcome unless displaced. I do not think that such concepts of presumption and burden of proof have any place in Children Act 1989 litigation where the judge exercises a function that is partly inquisitorial. ...

Moreover, he said, to elevate a consideration to a presumption could constitute a breach of a party's rights under Article 8 ECHR and Article 6 ECHR.[17]

In *Re X and Y (Leave to Remove from Jurisdiction: No Order Principle)*[18] the judge raised a different objection to the use of presumptions, arguing that their application is incompatible with Section 1(5) of the Children Act 1989. Munby J was of the opinion that, when it comes to decisions hinging on children's best interests, the burden rests on the person seeking a court order to make out a positive case for it. Unless the order would contribute to the child's best interests, no order should be made: 'The proper application of Section 1(5) [of the Children Act 1989] is inconsistent with identifying any particular factor(s) as giving rise to a presumption in favour of making an order or as being all important or only to be displaced by strong countervailing considerations.' (p 148)

There might be factors that are regarded as carrying great weight, he went on. But whether any particular factor might tip the balance one way or another had to be decided on an evaluation of the circumstances rather than by applying a presumption.

## Parent's Sexual Orientation

This is an issue that the courts found particularly troubling over the past two decades or so.[19] The reported cases provide some indication of the approach taken in dealing with

---

15 *Re L (Contact: Domestic Violence), Re V (Contact: Domestic Violence), Re M (Contact: Domestic Violence), Re H (Contact: Domestic Violence)* [2000] 2 FLR 334, 364.
16 [2001] EWCA Civ 166; [2001] 1 FLR 1052.
17 Para 40.
18 [2001] 2 FLR 118.
19 See Tasker and Golombok (1991); Bradley (1987).

it[20] but, as Bradley remarked, they reveal a diversity of judicial opinion (1987 p 187). The courts, he said, eschewed an 'abstract moral perspective' (p 188) in evaluating alternatives through the prism of the welfare test. But this, of course, does not denote neutrality; while a parent's homosexuality has not constituted a bar to the success of an application, parental sexual orientation has been perceived as having a significant impact on children's well-being. In *C v C (A Minor) (Custody: Appeal)*,[21] the Court of Appeal upheld an appeal by a father against an order awarding custody to the mother on the ground that the trial judge had taken little account of her lesbian relationship. This, according to the court, was plainly wrong as the nature of the relationship was 'an important factor to be put into the balance'.[22]

In *Re D (An Infant) (Adoption: Parent's Consent)*,[23] the adverse consequences for a child of his father's homosexuality were seen as so severe that his consent to the boy's adoption by the mother and stepfather was dispensed with. Lord Wilberforce in the House of Lords warned that courts should be vigilant to guard against: 'the risk of children, at critical ages, being exposed or introduced to ways of life which ... may lead to severance from normal society, to psychological stresses and unhappiness and possibly even to physical experiences which may scar them for life.' (p 629)

Neither the notion that homosexual parents are more likely to expose their children to abuse nor the suggestion of 'corruption', making children more likely to grow up homosexual or lesbian, gained currency in the courts.[24] In the past, however, homosexual and lesbian parents were faced with the argument that children suffer embarrassment and are stigmatised as a result of their parent's sexuality.[25] This argument could be coupled with the assertion, in the case of a contest between a homosexual or lesbian parent and a heterosexual parent, that the latter could offer a more 'normal' lifestyle.

In *B v B (Minors) (Custody, Care and Control)*,[26] Judge Callman addressed the issue of 'whether a child should as a matter of principle be brought up in a lesbian household',[27] relying heavily on the evidence of a mental health expert:

> His opinion and advice basically are that one has to assess the problems of lesbianism and children being brought up in such households under two heads: the sexual identity of the child being brought up in such a household and the stigmatisation. It is very much the same thing as talking about corruption on the one hand and reputation on the other.
>
> The professor came to the conclusion ... that ... there is not an increased incidence of homosexuality among the children of homosexual parents ... .
>
> The second question which was raised was stigmatisation or reputation.  ...
>
> [T]here could be embarrassing conduct and comments, especially amongst the child's friends or schoolmates ... .
>
> Let me say immediately, on the question of stigmatisation, the professor indicated quite plainly that children tend to be teased about matters about which they show sensitivity, and the professor indicated that most of his cases in his experience ... relate to the child personally ... and that in his experience it is very rare for children to show an interest in the background of the parents of other children and that, in fact, children are far more tolerant of their classmates' background and parents than most people give them credit for ... .

[20] See eg, *Re P(A Minor) (Custody)* [1983] 4 FLR 401; *Re H (A Minor) (Section 37 Direction)* [1993] 2 FLR 541, 545.
[21] [1991] 1 FLR 223.
[22] P 229.
[23] [1977] AC 602.
[24] See *Re P* [1983] 4 FLR 401; Bradley (1987) p 192.
[25] For a comprehensive review of the case law and a critical assessment of the literature, see Reece (1996b).
[26] [1991] 1 FLR 402. See, further, Standley (1992).
[27] P 404.

Professor Russell-Davis has said that the fears of psychosexual development being distorted if a child is reared in a lesbian household, or that he will be subjected unduly to taunts and teasing or be ostracised, find no support in the systematic evidence that he has looked at … .[28]

(pp 405–6)

It seems, then, that even in 1991, the stigmatisation argument was not considered a persuasive one for the purposes of removing a child from the mother. The argument invoking the 'normal family', however, was successfully deployed in the same year. In *C v C (A Minor) (Custody: Appeal)*[29] the father appealed against an order that his child should live with her mother. Allowing the appeal and ordering a rehearing, Glidewell LJ commented that:

Despite the vast change over the past 30 years or so in the attitudes of our society generally to the institution of marriage, to sexual morality, and to homosexual relationships, I regard it as axiomatic that the ideal environment for the upbringing of a child is the home of loving, caring and sensible parents, her father and her mother. When the marriage between father and mother is at an end, that ideal cannot be attained. When the court is called upon to decide which of two possible alternatives is then preferable for the child's welfare, its task is to choose the alternative which comes closest to that ideal.

Even taking account of the changes of attitude to which I have referred, a lesbian relationship between two adult women is an unusual background in which to bring up a child. (p 228)

Balcombe LJ added:

In my judgment, [the judge] should start on the basis that the moral standards which are generally accepted in the society in which the child lives are more likely than not to promote his or her welfare.  …

With those preliminary observations I turn to what should be the judicial approach when faced with the problem with which the judge was faced in this case: to which of two parents should the care and control of a 6½ year-old girl be given, where both parents clearly love and are loved by the child, both can give the child good physical care, but the father who has remarried lives with his new wife, while the mother has formed a lesbian relationship with another woman? Of course, the fact that the mother has a lesbian partner is not of itself a reason for denying the mother the care and control of her daughter.  ..I agree with Glidewell LJ that in those circumstances the judge can only start with the approach that in our society it is still the norm that children are brought up in a home with a father, mother and siblings (if any) and, other things being equal, such an upbringing is most likely to be conducive to their welfare. If, because the parents are divorced, such an upbringing is no longer possible, then a very material factor in considering where the child's welfare lies is in which of the competing parents can offer the nearest approach to that norm. In the present case it is clearly the father. (pp 230–31)

While the court in this case made reference to morals, it based its decision primarily on generalised assumptions about the welfare of children. However, it seems that views on same-sex relationships and children's welfare have changed; there is a growing body of case law that does not assume that being brought up by people who are lesbians[30] is inimical to well-being. So, for example, in *G v F*, where a lesbian relationship broke down and one of the women sought leave to apply for shared residence and contact in

---

[28] However the court seemed to think, for some reason, that life in a household of 'militant' lesbians might present significant risks for children. See p 410.

[29] [1991] 1 FLR 223.

[30] There are no reported cases dealing with gay men in the context of residence and contact.

relation to the other's child, the judge said it would be wrong to discriminate against the applicant.[31] And, in *Re G (Children) (Shared Residence Order: Parental Responsibility)*,[32] the court made a shared residence order in relation to children born in the context of a lesbian relationship as a result of artificial insemination. The court was of the view that this was necessary in order to give the biological mother's former partner parental responsibility to prevent her from being marginalised in the future. Thorpe LJ said that there had been judicial recognition of diversity in family forms and that the same importance should be accorded to partners in same-sex relationships as is accorded to fathers in heterosexual ones.[33]

Both these cases involved disputes between the two women involved. There is no recent UK case law involving a dispute, such as that in *C v C*, between, say, a mother and father who are respectively lesbian and heterosexual. It is not inconceivable that, faced with a choice between a same-sex and a heterosexual family, the court would still prefer the more 'normal' family. However this argument, on its own, is very unlikely to succeed now. In *Salgueiro Da Siva Mouta v Portugal*,[34] the ECtHR upheld a claim by a homosexual father under Article 14 ECHR, read with Article 8. He argued that the mother had been given custody of his daughter solely on the ground of his sexual orientation. The Portuguese court had suggested that the father's sexuality presented 'an abnormality' and that the child should not have to grow up in an 'abnormal' situation.[35] The ECtHR concluded that this showed that the father's sexuality had 'swayed the final decision in a decisive manner'.[36] The requirement of proportionality between the means used and the aim of safeguarding the child's interests was therefore not satisfied.[37] One commentator has remarked that this case 'makes it absolutely clear that the sexual orientation of one of the parties to the [contact or residence] proceeding, without more, can no longer be cited as a negative factor' (Wintemute 2000 p 620).[38]

In any event, English courts are beginning to accept far greater diversity when it comes to family forms. In *Singh v Entry Clearance Officer New Delhi*,[39] the court commented at length on the nature of family relationships in the context of the ECHR, noting a growth in diversity and multiculturalism, as well as the increase in cohabitation. The judge went on:

> [62] ... [T]here has been a sea-change in society's attitudes towards same-sex unions. Within my professional lifetime we have moved from treating such relationships as perversions to be stamped out ... . to a ready acknowledgement that they are entitled not merely to respect but also, in principle, to equal protection under the law: see *Ghaidan v Godin-Mendoza* ... [2004] 2 FCR 481, especially the speech of Baroness Hale ... .
>
> [63] The result of all this is that in our multi-cultural and pluralistic society the family takes many forms. Indeed in contemporary Britain the family takes an almost infinite variety of forms. Many marry according to the rites of non-Christian faiths. There may be one, two, three or even more generations living together under the same roof. Some people choose to live on their own. People live together as couples, married or not, and with partners who may not always be of the opposite sex. Children live in households where their parents may be married

---

[31] See *G v F(Contact and Shared Residence: Applications for Leave)* [1998] 2 FLR 799.
[32] [2005] EWCA Civ 462; [2005] All ER (D) 25 (Apr).
[33] Para 24–26. See Gibb (2005).
[34] (2001) 31 EHRR 47.
[35] See para 34.
[36] Para 35.
[37] Para 36.
[38] See also Marshall (2003) pp 831–33.
[39] [2004] EWCA Civ 1075; [2004] 3 FCR 72. See also *M v Secretary of State for Work and Pensions* [2004] EWCA Civ 1343; [2005] 1 FLR 498.

or unmarried. They may be the children of polygamous marriages. They may be brought up by a single parent. Their parents may or may not be their natural parents. Their siblings may be only half-siblings or step-siblings. Some children are brought up by two parents of the same sex. Some children are conceived by artificial donor insemination. Some are the result of surrogacy arrangements. The fact is that many adults and children, whether through choice or circumstance, live in families more or less removed from what until comparatively recently would have been recognised as the typical nuclear family. As Baroness Hale of Richmond observed in *Ghaidan v Godin-Mendoza* … at [141]:

> … If [a] couple are bringing up children together, it is unlikely to matter whether or not they are the biological children of both parties. Both married and unmarried couples, both homosexual and heterosexual, may bring up children together. One or both may have children from another relationship: this is not at all uncommon in lesbian relationships and the court may grant them a shared residence order so that they may share parental responsibility. A lesbian couple may have children by donor insemination who are brought up as the children of them both: it is not uncommon for each of them to bear a child in this way. A gay or lesbian couple may foster other people's children.

[64] Many of these changes have given rise to profound misgivings in some quarters … .All of those views are entitled to the greatest respect but it is not for a judge to choose between them. The days are past when the business of the judges was the enforcement of morals or religious belief … .

[65] The law, it seems to me, must adapt itself to these realities … .

The court in this case declared itself unwilling to be influenced by the moral scruples of some groups in society. Generally speaking, the climate of opinion has changed in relation to same-sex relationships. This is apparent from the passing of the Civil Partnership Act 2004[40] and from the fact that the Adoption and Children Act 2002 makes provision for adoption of unrelated children by same sex couples[41] as well as adoption by one partner of the other's child.[42] That prejudice has been eroded in many respects, including in relation to child care, is clear. Baroness Hale, reviewing the evolution of the law in relation to homosexual rights, comments that 'we have already reached the stage of recognising same sex relationships for what many will think the most important purpose of regulating family relationships: providing for the care and upbringing of the next generation' (2004 p 134).

In deciding the dispute between Richard and Evelyn, the court will undoubtedly give weight to Jeremy's age, the fact that he has always been cared for by his mother, his attachment to each parent, his relationship with his parents' new partners, and the nature and stability of the relationships of both parents with their new partners. It is likely that, instead of considering, as in the past, whether Richard can offer a family life that is closer to the 'norm', the court would probably rely on expert evidence[43] and/or the child and family reporter's report concerning the child's welfare.[44] Should the court decide to award residence to Evelyn, and if she is unwilling to enter into a parental responsibility agreement, Richard may choose to seek a parental responsibility order.

---

[40] The refusal to extend marriage to same sex couples might, however, seen as manifesting a preference for heterosexuality. See Crompton (2004).

[41] S 50.

[42] Ss 51(2) and 144(7).

[43] See *Re M (Sperm Donor Father)* [2003] Fam Law 94.

[44] The ECtHR has held that a refusal to authorise adoption by a homosexual man did not infringe the principle of proportionality, taking into account the child's welfare and the state's margin of appreciation. The court observed that the scientific community was divided over the consequences for children of being adopted by one or more homosexual parents. See *Frette v France* [2003] 2 FLR 9.

## III. PARENTAL RESPONSIBILITY

The need for parental responsibility orders has been reduced by the change in the law to allow for automatic parental responsibility for unmarried fathers who register the birth jointly with the mother. Orders will still be necessary for fathers who were not aware of the pregnancy or birth; for fathers who cannot gain the co-operation of mothers in effecting a joint registration; for fathers whose registration pre-dated the coming into effect of the amendment; and, in future, for step-parents and civil partners who cannot persuade the parent, or both parents if both have parental responsibility, to enter into an agreement.[45]

A parental responsibility order, like the pre-Children Act parental rights order, is currently perceived as conferring a status on unmarried fathers[46] in recognition of their concerned and responsible attitude to their children. As the court pointed out in *Re S (Parental Responsibility)*,[47] the 1989 Act places a greater emphasis on responsibility than on rights. However, it is apparent from the decided cases that what is required of fathers is that they conform to a particular image of the 'responsible' father espoused by the courts. And it emerges that the notion of responsibility deployed by the courts is coloured by traditional conceptions of parenthood; the rhetoric of responsibility has not displaced traditional images of 'good mothers' and 'good fathers'. Butler-Sloss LJ in *Re S* stated that, in seeking a parental responsibility order, the father was asking to assume the 'burden as well as [the] pleasure of looking after his child'; he was showing his willingness to shoulder the weight of his duties by sharing responsibility with the mother.[48] Yet the case law reveals an apparently collective judicial vision of the family in which 'good' fathers still play a limited role in caring for their children. It has been said that 'the demands that parenting put upon a mother are infinite in variety and scale'.[49] In contrast, judicial expectations of fathers are somewhat more modest.

### *The Responsible Father*

As Deech points out, parental responsibilities

> include feeding, washing and clothing the child, putting her to bed, housing her, educating and stimulating her, taking responsibility for arranging babysitting and daycare, keeping the child in touch with the wider family circle, checking her medical condition, arranging schooling and transport to school, holidays and recreation, encouraging social and possibly religious or moral development. (1992 p 8)

---

[45] Masson (2003) argues that there is no logical reason for parental consent rather than notification because the step-parent's acquisition of parental responsibility does not affect the parental responsibility of the biological parent. A system based on notification would have placed the burden of initiating proceedings on the objecting parent instead of the step-parent. Objections by the parent will 'serve to discourage applications, add to the expense and increase bitterness between the parents' (Masson 2003 p 582). In any event, she says, courts will be loath to refuse applications, particularly where the step-parent and step-child have 'family life' for the purposes of Art 8 ECHR (*ibid*). Bainham (2005) takes a different point of view. He says that because parental responsibility will have to be shared between three instead of two people, this would have the effect of weakening the parental responsibility of the objecting non-resident parent (p 236). He observes that an agreement is only likely where there is a high degree of co-operation between all the parties (2005 p 235).

[46] When s 4A Children Act 1989 comes into force, the court will have to consider the merits of both women and men as step-parents and civil partners.

[47] [1995] 2 FLR 648.

[48] P 659.

[49] *Re L (Contact: Transsexual Applicant)* [1995] 2 FLR 438, 442.

She maintains that fathers who do not take on a fair share of these tasks do not know their children sufficiently well to be able to make decisions sensibly about their upbringing. However, it is unlikely that the court in *Re S* envisaged these duties being performed by the non-resident father. Instead, it appears that what is required of 'responsible' fathers is some form of 'commitment'.

This criterion derives from the judgment of Balcombe LJ in *Re H (Illegitimate Children: Father: Parental Rights) (No 2)*.[50] The judge formulated the test to be applied in proceedings concerning parental rights orders under the Family Law Reform Act 1987. This test (often referred to as the CAR test), as well as the case law generally on parental rights orders, has been held to be applicable in interpreting Section 4 of the 1989 Act.[51] Balcombe LJ suggested that:

> In considering whether to make an order under s 4 of the 1987 Act, the court will have to take into account a number of factors of which the following will undoubtedly be material (although there may well be others, as the list is not intended to be exhaustive):
>     (1) the degree of commitment which the father has shown towards the child;
>     (2) the degree of attachment which exists between the father and the child; and
>     (3) the reasons of the father for applying for the order.
>
> (p 218)

The courts do not require a great deal to convince them of a father's commitment. Certainly, where fathers take on the physical care of their children, even temporarily, the courts regard this as exceptionally strong evidence. So, in *Re P (A Minor) (Parental Responsibility Order)*,[52] the court found unanswerable the case for the father of a girl aged 5½:

> The father has shown, to use the words of the magistrates, 'great love and concern' for the child. He has striven successfully for contact with her from 1990 onwards. In 1992 he was looking after her on an extensive basis for more than half the week for some months, even though she was then only 4 years old. Now, under the order of the magistrates, he is to have her to stay with him on alternate weekends and for further periods in school holidays. ...
>
> In the light of the authorities to which I have referred and the far lesser involvement of the fathers in those ... cases in the past and likely future lives of their children, it would seem to me that, subject to the point made by the magistrates to which I will now turn, there is an overwhelming case for an order to be made under s 4 of the Act.
>
> The magistrates based their decision on ... 'the reasons of the father for applying for the order' ... .
>
> Prima facie, if a father is committed to his daughter, as is this father to this daughter, his reasons for applying for an order for parental responsibility will be in order to have his commitment reflected in a formal way ... .
>
> Miss Dooley has to concede that, even if her client was without an order for parental responsibility, he could always apply under s 8 of the Act for a specific issue order or a prohibited steps order relating to matters such as schooling, medical treatment, surname etc; but, says Miss Dooley, that is very much a second best and not properly reflective of the father's position in other respects as an active and committed father. (pp 583–84)

---

[50] [1991] 1 FLR 214.
[51] See *Re CB (A Minor) (Parental Responsibility Order)* [1993] 1 FLR 920, 923.
[52] [1994] 1 FLR 578. See also *Re CB (A Minor) (Parental Responsibility Order)* [1993] 1 FLR 920.

As the judge intimated, the case for an order in these circumstances was exceptionally strong. Generally, where fathers are concerned, the courts do not see commitment and attachment as inextricably bound up with the practical care of children. Fathers who show that they care about their children, support them and, where possible, maintain contact with them stand a good chance of being accommodated within the category of 'committed' fathers. In *Re S (Parental Responsibility)*,[53] the father's application, which succeeded on appeal, was formulated on the basis that 'he is very fond of this little girl, that he has always paid money for her, that he takes her out regularly, he has regular contact and that he is thoroughly committed to her'.[54] What is more, the very act of applying for parental responsibility was taken as evidence of that dedication and served to fortify his case.[55]

That fathers are expected to play only a peripheral part in their children's lives emerges clearly from the case law. The court in *Re E (Parental Responsibility: Blood Tests)*[56] asserted that, where a father has demonstrated constant commitment to his child, has had regular contact and has made financial provision, it is *prima facie* in the child's best interests that a parental responsibility order be made. One of the reasons for this was that, should the mother die, it would be detrimental to the child if the father had no *locus standi*. The father, therefore, although he had never lived in the same household as his daughter, was seen as a 'reserve' carer who had to be granted legal status.

Indeed, it was held in *Re C (Minors) (Parental Rights)*,[57] a case involving an application for a parental rights order, that although, on the facts, there was little prospect of the father's being able to exercise any of his rights, this was not a sufficient reason for denying him the formal status he sought. It would have 'real and tangible value', not only as something he could 'cherish for the sake of his own peace of mind, but also as a status carrying with it rights in waiting' which were of value to him and, potentially, to the children.[58]

Because parental status is seen as divorced from child care,[59] the court was able in *Re C* to make an order in favour of a father who had to be excluded from his children's lives; any involvement would, it was found, have been damaging to the mother and therefore harmful to the children. So even if a father is not in a position to make any practical contribution to his children's lives, the courts see it as imperative to confer on him parental status. The status itself is regarded as important. It is a way of acknowledging paternal concern about, if not actual care of, children. And it is perceived as good for children.

**Q**  Why do you think it might be beneficial for children to confer parental status on absent fathers?

---

[53] [1995] 2 FLR 648.
[54] P 652.
[55] P 659.
[56] [1995] 1 FLR 392.
[57] [1992] 1 FLR 1.
[58] P4. See also *Re H (A Minor) (Parental Responsibility)* [1993] 1 FLR 484. There, the father's case for an immediate order was strengthened by the fact that he would not be able to have contact with the child in the foreseeable future. This was because, should he apply at a later stage, the lack of contact would make his case a weak one.
[59] See also *Re H (Paternity: Blood Test)* [1996] 2 FLR 65, 82.

## IV. THE WELFARE OF THE CHILD

The idea that parental responsibility orders are important for the welfare of children emerges most clearly from the judgments in *Re G (A Minor) (Parental Responsibility Order)*.[60] The child in question was in care as the mother, and to some extent the father, were having problems with alcohol and drugs. It was anticipated that the mother would undergo a detoxification programme and that the child would be returned to her. The father had contact with his daughter but was adjudged by the court of first instance to have little insight into her needs. The Court of Appeal found that, whatever the failings of the father, they were not sufficiently serious to warrant denying him a parental responsibility order:

> I am quite prepared to accept that the making of a parental responsibility order requires the judge to adopt the welfare principle as the paramount consideration.[61] But having said that, I should add that, of course, it is well established by authority that, other things being equal, it is always to a child's welfare to know and, wherever possible, to have contact with both its parents, including the parent with whom it is not normally resident, if the parents have separated.
>
> Therefore, prima facie, it must necessarily also be for the child's benefit or welfare that it has an absent parent sufficiently concerned and interested to want to have a parental responsibility order. In other words, I approach this question on the basis that where you have a concerned although absent father, who fulfils the other test about which I spoke in *Re H* ... then prima facie it would be for the welfare of the child that such an order should be made ... .
>
> At the end of the day, I come back to what is the purpose of a parental responsibility order. It is to give the unmarried father the rights which would have been automatically his by right if he had been married at the time of the child's birth. ...
>
> [L]et me assume against Mr G that he is awkward, difficult, and thoroughly unresponsive to the approaches of the social workers who have the interests of his child at heart: even so I cannot see why that should unfit him to have the order which gives him a locus standi in the life of his child. ... (pp 408–9)

**Q** Why do you think the court regarded it significant that, had he been married, the father would automatically have had parental responsibility? Given the degree of commitment and attachment required by the courts, do you agree that it is *prima facie* in a child's interests that the 'natural father' have a say in his child's upbringing?

There seems to be a feeling among judges that it is natural for biological fathers to be involved in making decisions about their children and that it is almost always best for children that this be so. An order is a means of allowing fathers to discharge their paternal obligations. Certainly, this is the tenor of the judgments in *Re S (Parental Responsibility)*.[62]

The case concerned a child, aged 7, whose parents separated some 18 months after the birth. In the following year, the father was convicted of being in possession of obscene pædophilic literature. As a result, the mother terminated contact. However, when it became apparent that this distressed the child, contact was resumed and eventually staying contact was allowed. The father's application for a parental responsibility order was

[60] [1994] 1 FLR 504.
[61] The statute does not explicitly require the application of the s 1(3) checklist, however.
[62] [1995] 2 FLR 648.

refused on the grounds that it would give him the scope to interfere with the arrangements for the child and would deprive the mother of control over contact. The decision was reversed on appeal. Ward LJ stated:

> It is wrong to place undue and therefore false emphasis on the rights and duties and the powers comprised in 'parental responsibility' and not to concentrate on the fact that what is at issue is conferring upon a committed father the status of parenthood for which nature has already ordained that he must bear responsibility. ...
>
> There is another important emphasis I would wish to make. I have heard, up and down the land, psychiatrists tell me how important it is that children grow up with good self-esteem and how much they need to have a favourable positive image of the absent parent. It seems to me important, therefore, wherever possible, to ensure that the law confers upon a committed father that stamp of approval, lest the child grow up with some belief that he is in some way disqualified from fulfilling his role and that the reason for his disqualification is something inherent which will be inherited by the child, making her struggle to find her own identity all the more fraught.[63] (p 657)

Butler-Sloss LJ agreed, adding that 'this father should be allowed to share the burden of caring for his daughter' by giving him 'the status in which he can share in the responsibility for the child's upbringing and demonstrate that he will be as good a parent as he can make himself to this little girl'.[64]

> **Q** How does the legal status of parental responsibility better enable non-resident or unavailable fathers to fulfil their paternal duties? Do you agree that legal labels have the powerful impact on children that Ward LJ suggests they do? Can you think of other factors that might have a greater influence on the child's image of the father? If judges were not so willing to grant orders to all but those fathers considered seriously deviant, would the refusal of an order carry the stigma referred to by the court?

Ward LJ noted that there are few cases where the refusal of an order has been upheld. In those instances where it was, the fathers were 'cruel and callous'[65] or 'outrageous'; they were violent, 'feckless' or intent on sabotaging adoption plans.[66] In *Re H (Parental Responsibility: Maintenance)* the court commented, '[t]he cases show that when a father shows some devotion to his children he should ordinarily be granted a parental responsibility order in the absence of strong countervailing circumstances'.[67] Even the father's failure to support his children, coupled with a refusal to divulge his telephone number so he could be contacted in an emergency, was insufficient to deny him an order. It was

---

[63] See also *Re C and V (Contact and Parental Responsibility)* [1998] Fam Law 10. Compare *Re H (Shared Residence: Parental Responsibility)* [1995] 2 FLR 883, 887. There, the court commented that a boy of 14½ would not be able to comprehend the implications of a shared residence order and the grant of parental responsibility that would accompany it.

[64] P 659.

[65] *Re T (A Minor) (Parental Responsibility: Contact)* [1993] 2 FLR 450, 456.

[66] See Ward LJ's account in *Re S* at pp 654–55 of *Re T (A Minor) (Parental Responsibility: Contact)* [1993] 2 FLR 450 and *W v Ealing London Borough Council* [1993] 2 FLR 788. See also *Re P (Terminating Parental Responsibility)* [1995] 1 FLR 1048; *Re P (Parental Responsibility)* [1997] 2 FLR 722. See also *Re H (Parental Responsibility)* [1998] 1 FLR 855, where a father who had injured his child in a manner adjudged to be cruel, and perhaps sadistic, was denied parental responsibility. See also *M v M (Parental Responsibility)* (1999) 2 FLR 237 where the father suffered from serious impediments to his intellectual functioning and was violent. The court said that the element of motivation in the CAR test, as well as the relevant provisions in the Children Act 1989, presupposed a capacity to reason. The father lacked this and was refused parental responsibility.

[67] [1996] 1 FLR 867, 872.

enough that he had shown some commitment by attempting to maintain contact and showing an interest in the children's schooling.

In *Re T (A Minor) (Parental Responsibility: Contact)*,[68] however, the father's behaviour was so deplorable that it convinced the court that an order would not be in the child's best interests. He had assaulted the mother while she was pregnant and, on a later occasion, while she had the baby in her arms. He failed to return the child after contact visits, keeping her on one occasion for nine days. He showed no remorse for this action. He failed to discharge his financial obligations to the child and insisted on maintaining control over the expenditure of any money he did provide.

The court's reluctance to deny parental responsibility does not, however, denote the existence of a presumption that a 'devoted father will ordinarily be granted an order'.[69] The three criteria set out in *Re H* were not intended to be the only relevant ones; to adopt that approach would be contrary to the paramountcy principle.[70] In *Re P (Parental Responsibility)*,[71] Hirst LJ said:

> Parental responsibility is not automatically conferred on fathers who are not married to the mothers of their children. There must, accordingly, be criteria against which an application for parental responsibility falls to be judged. The only statutory criteria are (1) that it must be in the interests of the child for such an order to be made, and (2) that the making of a parental responsibility order must be better for the child than making no order. In every case it is a matter of weighing in the balance the various factors ... and deciding, on the facts of the individual case, whether an order for parental responsibility is in the interests of the child ... .
>
> Clearly, where a father has shown commitment to a child, has a good relationship with the child and has sound and genuine reasons for wanting parental responsibility, an order granting him that status will not usually be refused. ...
>
> [I]t is the element of irresponsibility in the father's behaviour, or his abuse or likely abuse of parental responsibility which may disqualify him. (pp 109–10)

## V. EFFECT OF A PARENTAL RESPONSIBILITY ORDER

The courts have been reluctant to accept arguments based on the effects of a parental responsibility order as a reason for refusing applications. Parental responsibility encompasses all the rights and duties that a parent has in relation to his child and, except where there is a residence order in force, the legislation does not limit the independent decision-making powers of a non-resident parent with parental responsibility. In addition, the duty to consult imposed by the court comes into play when each parent has parental responsibility.[72] Nevertheless the courts have striven to minimise the practical significance of an order.

In *Re P (A Minor) (Parental Responsibility Order)*,[73] the court awarded a parental responsibility order to the father of a child aged $5\frac{1}{2}$, rejecting the argument that that this would enable him to interfere in her day-to-day life:

---

[68] [1993] 2 FLR 450.
[69] *Re H (Parental Responsibility)* [1998] 1 FLR 855, 859.
[70] *Ibid.* pp 859–860.
[71] [1998] 2 FLR 96.
[72] See ch 7.
[73] [1994] 1 FLR 578.

It is important to be quite clear that an order for parental responsibility to the father does not give him a right to interfere in matters within the day-to-day management of the child's life. Section 2(8) of the Children Act 1989 provides that:

> The fact that a person has parental responsibility for a child shall not entitle him to act in any way which would be incompatible with any order made with respect to a child under this Act.

There is, of course, an order for residence in favour of the mother under the Act and that invests the mother with the right to determine all matters which arise in the course of the day-to-day management of this child's life. ... (pp 58485)

Wilson J then went on to observe more generally:

> It is to be noted that on any view an order for parental responsibility gives the father no power to override the decision of the mother, who already has such responsibility: in the event of a disagreement between them on a specific issue relating to the child, the court will have to resolve it. If the father were to seek to misuse the rights given him under s 4 such misuse could, as a second to last resort, be controlled by the court under a prohibited steps order against him and/or a specific issue order. The very last resort of all would presumably be the discharge of the parental responsibility order. (p 585)

In *Re S (Parental Responsibility)*[74] Ward LJ stated that the possibility of interference with the day-to-day management of the child's life was irrelevant. In reaching this conclusion he relied on three arguments. First, a parental responsibility order is a mechanism for conferring a status rather than rights; secondly, a non-resident parent has little opportunity in practice to exercise parental responsibility; and, thirdly, any abuse can be restrained by means of a court order.

> It would, therefore, be helpful if the mother could think calmly about the limited circumstances when the exercise of true parental responsibility is likely to be of practical significance. ... There seems to me to be all too frequently a failure to appreciate that the wide exercise of s 8 orders can control the abuse, if any, of the exercise of parental responsibility which is adverse to the welfare of the child. Those interferences with the day-to-day management of the child's life have nothing to do with whether or not this order should be allowed. (p 657)

However, while Section 8 orders[75] are regarded as a useful solution to the problem of interfering fathers, they were considered inadequate to constrain a father who intended 'to use a parental responsibility order for improper or inappropriate ends to try to interfere with and possibly undermine the mother's care of the child'.[76] The court accordingly refused to make an order in favour of a father who planned to use it to monitor the child's health, schooling and arrangements for her care.[77] Similarly, in *Re M (Contact: Parental Responsibility)*,[78] the court denied the father parental responsibility

---

[74] [1995] 2 FLR 648. Compare *Yousef v The Netherlands* [2003] 1 FLR 210, where the recognition sought by the father was considered a prelude to changing the child's living arrangements, contrary to her best interests. The refusal of recognition did not, therefore contravene Art 8 ECHR.

[75] See, on the use of specific issue orders, Gilmore (2004). It seems that each dispute has to be adjudicated separately. There is authority stating that one parent cannot be given in advance, the power to make decisions in a particular category, such as education: *Re P (Parental Dispute: Judicial Determination)* [2002] EWCA Civ 1627; [2003] 1 FLR 286. See Gilmore (2004) who argues for a different interpretation of the case.

[76] *Re P (Parental Responsibility)* [1998] 2 FLR 96, 110.

[77] *Ibid.*

[78] [2001] 2 FLR 342.

in relation to his severely mentally disabled daughter on the grounds that he would be very likely to 'misuse it to lend weight to future interference in her care, thus continuing the stress on the mother and potentially undermining her ability to care properly for KM.'[79] He and his family saw parental responsibility as conferring rights and would interfere even more than they already had. In what the court referred to as an 'extreme' case like this, it would not suffice to put in place court orders specifying what the father could and could not do.[80] The court stated that commitment, attachment and motivation are not the only relevant factors and made it clear that 'parental responsibility is not a reward for the father, but an order which should only be made in the best interests of KM'.[81]

In contrast, the potential for interference was not treated as relevant and the court focused almost exclusively on the CAR test in *Re J-S (A Child) (Contact: Parental Responsibility)*.[82] The court also thought it significant that it was prepared to grant the father contact. Because of that fact and in the light of the good relationship he had with the child, the 'father should be entitled to play the natural role which fatherhood ordains for him by the very fact of his being a father'.[83] It was an 'overwhelming' case for granting parental responsibility.[84]

The courts are generally keen to grant orders except in the most exceptional cases. This approach has attracted some criticism,[85] and it has been suggested that parental responsibility orders should be restricted to those fathers actively engaged in parenting. But the amendment of Section 4 of the Children Act 1989, in extending automatic parental responsibility to most unmarried fathers, has shown that registration of the child's birth is regarded as sufficiently indicative of their commitment (LCD Press Release, 2 July 1998).[86] For those fathers who do not register, however, it may be that the court's willingness to grant orders may be affected Masson (2003) suggests that applicants may, at the very least, be expected to explain why they have not done so (p 581). On the other hand, if this is correct, there is the possibility that we will see the judicial construction of a category of 'implacably hostile' mothers in the context of parental responsibility in the same way as we have seen it emerge in the context of contact disputes.

## VI. CONCLUSION (1)

Richard will face some difficulty in obtaining a residence order. Jeremy is a young child who has always been in the care of his mother. Where other things are equal, the courts tend to prefer to entrust the care of young children to their mothers in such circumstances. In addition, the *status quo* principle would favour Evelyn. Whether her involvement in a lesbian relationship would outweigh these factors, or even be

---

[79] P 365.
[80] *Ibid.*
[81] Pp 365–6.
[82] [2002] EWCA Civ 1028; [2003] 1 FLR 399.
[83] Para 50.
[84] *Ibid.*
[85] See Kaganas (1996).
[86] The LCD Press Release (2 July, 1998) also states that automatic parental responsibility will encourage such fathers to meet their responsibilities.

considered very significant, is doubtful. Richard's chances of success are, however, slightly enhanced by his ability to offer a full-time mother substitute.

Although he might fail to get a residence order, he will almost certainly succeed in obtaining a parental responsibility order. He supports his son financially to some extent, maintains contact and is clearly concerned about his well-being. He can therefore demonstrate his commitment. He would, presumably, be able to persuade a court that there is a measure of attachment between Jeremy and himself. And there is nothing to suggest that his motives in applying for an order are 'improper or wrong'. The court would, in all probability, take the view that it is necessary and in accordance with nature that he be given the formal status he seeks. The court would also see such a step as being *prima facie* in Jeremy's interests.

## VII. CHILD SUPPORT[87]

Richard has an obligation, as Jeremy's parent, to contribute to his support. As we saw in chapter 13, however, because Richard was not married to Jeremy's mother, that obligation did not arise at common law, but was imposed by subsequent legislation.[88] Because Evelyn is not receiving IS, IJSA, Housing Benefit or Council Tax Benefit, she will not be required to seek a maintenance calculation, but she may do so if she wishes.

There appears to be no order currently in effect, no maintenance calculation[89] and no written agreement concerning Jeremy's support. Evelyn and Richard seem to have been satisfied thus far with their informal financial arrangements, and unless either of them makes an application to the Child Support Agency,[90] there is no reason why this arrangement should not continue. Alternatively, they may wish to make a formal maintenance agreement or even to have that agreement confirmed by the court in the form of a consent order, but they must be aware that the existence of an agreement or court order will not oust the jurisdiction of the CSAct 1991.[91] In answer to the question '[i]s Richard meeting his duty of support toward Jeremy?', then, the answer must be yes—legally he is.

Many parents who do not live together make informal arrangements of this type, and experience varying degrees of satisfaction with them. Sometimes, the actual amount of money paid must be balanced against other considerations, such as maintaining a good relationship between the non-resident parent and the child, and mothers often feel that this is their responsibility (Smart 1991 p 498). Therefore Evelyn may feel it is in Jeremy's best interests that she not 'rock the boat' with Richard by requesting further support from him. Clarke, *et al*, (1996) found that lone parents often experienced a strain on

---

[87] See also chs 5 and 13. See also Bainham (2005) pp 378–406; Herring (2004) 161–83; and Cretney, *et al*, [2002] ch 15.

[88] S 15(1) and Sch 1 Ss 1(1) (2) CA 1989; Ss 1(1) Child Support Act 1991.

[89] Prior to the reforms in 2000, they were called 'child support agency assessments'. See S 4(1) Child Support Act 1991.

[90] Either the person with care or the non-resident parent may make the application (s 4(1) CS Act 1991). The Child Support Agency has jurisdiction over a case where there is a 'non-resident parent' (s 3(2) CS Act 1991), a 'person with care' (s 3(3) CS Act 1991) and a 'qualifying child' (s 3(1) CS Act 1991).See also chs 5 and 13.

[91] While s 9(2) CS Act 1991 provides that maintenance agreements are not precluded by the Act, s 9(3) provides that any existing agreement shall not prevent any party from applying for a maintenance calculation. Where there is a court order in effect, the application may not be made within the first year.

relationships with their partners or between fathers and children after completing Child Support Act maintenance assessment forms. Diduck (2003) reviews the other reasons given by lone parents for not wishing to approach the CSA:

> [M]any mothers were happy with informal, extra-judicial arrangements for support agreed with their ex-partners, usually because they conferred greater financial benefit on the children than formal payments would have done. Some of these informal arrangements took the form of money payments and many were help in kind or occasional contributions toward the cost of holidays, presents or toys for the children. Sometimes mothers were content with informal arrangements because it helped to maintain an amicable relationship with their former partner and did not encourage direct attempts to control them in the way that formal arrangements did.
>
> (p 174)

Many mothers did not wish to be financially dependent at all on their former partner:

> Their experience of receiving maintenance was that it conferred power on their former partner … 'he sent me a letter, "I want a list of everything you buy, baby foods, don't put any extra pennies on … ", he wanted a list of everything I bought for her, nappies and things like that'.
>
> (Clarke, *et al*, 1995 p 139)

If Evelyn does wish to apply for a maintenance calculation in relation to Jeremy she will merely have to provide information about Jeremy's age and paternity and Richard's address. The Agency will then contact Richard with a request to provide his financial information and information about any other children with whom he is living—in this case Molly.[92] The formula by which Richard's maintenance obligation will be calculated is found in Schedule 1 to the CSAct 1991. Because he is employed as a bus driver his weekly net income will be likely to fall within the band specified at between £200.00 and £2000.00 per week. If so, his maintenance calculation will be at the basic rate—15% of his net income. His net weekly income will be calculated, however, on a basis that includes a 15% reduction because of his responsibility for Molly. If Richard's net weekly income is lower, ie between £100.00 and £199.00 per week, he will pay a reduced rate. He is not entitled to a further 'shared care' reduction because Jeremy does not spend any nights with him.[93] He may, however, be entitled to a variation of the basic rate on the basis of his 'special expenses', in this case, the costs he incurs in travelling between London and Manchester to maintain contact with Jeremy.[94] The CSA has jurisdiction to vary the calculation in these and other circumstances on application by a non-resident parent.[95]

**Q** Would you advise Evelyn to approach the Child Support Agency?

We see then that there is no role for the courts in relation to child support for Jeremy, unless his parents wish to have an agreement made into a consent order, and even that would only oust the jurisdiction of the CSA for one year. The only role the courts have left in child support matters is if the CS Act 1991 does not apply to the parties because, for example, any of them is not habitually resident in the UK or the child does not qualify by reason of being over the age of 16 and not in full-time education; where a

---

[92] See also ch 5.
[93] See discussion in ch 5.
[94] CS Act 1991 Sch 4B s 2(3)(a).
[95] CS Act 1991 Sch 4B.

non-resident parent earns over the £2000.00 ceiling for the basic rate and a 'top-up' award would be appropriate; where the child is receiving instruction or training and has additional expenses in connection with that training; where the qualifying child has additional expenses as a result of a disability; or if an order is to be made against the person with care.[96] In these cases it is open to a parent or to someone with a residence order to apply under the Children Act 1989 for a maintenance order in respect of the child,[97] or for a transfer[98] or settlement[99] of property for the child's benefit.[100] If Evelyn were to do so the court would consider all of the circumstances including those outlined in paragraph 4(1) of Schedule 1, such as parents' finances:

(a)   the income, earning capacity, property and other financial resources which each person mentioned in sub-paragraph (4) has or is likely to have in the foreseeable future;
(b)   the financial needs, obligations and responsibilities which each person mentioned in sub-paragraph (4) has or is likely to have in the foreseeable future;
(c)   the financial needs of the child;
(d)   the income, earning capacity (if any), property and other financial resources of the child;
(e)   any physical or mental disability of the child;
(f)   the manner in which the child was being, or was expected to be, educated or trained.

## VIII.  FINANCIAL AND PROPERTY ARRANGEMENTS ON DIVORCE OR SEPARATION[101]

Richard is concerned about his financial position if his marriage with Jane ends. While on the basis of the information provided it is not possible to give him figures, we can advise him of the factors a court may take into account in determining any liability he may have to Jane and Molly in the event of a separation or divorce.[102] In all cases, he would be advised that such decisions are within the court's discretion. The broad discretion of the court has advantages and disadvantages. On the one hand, it provides the court with the flexibility to make different orders suited to individual circumstances, but on the other, it means that different judges can legitimately make different orders in similar circumstances and outcomes are difficult to predict (Eekelaar 1998; Ancillary Relief Advisory Group 1998).

The first step in any event would be to identify all Richard's and Jane's assets. All assets, whether acquired before or after the marriage or after any eventual separation, must be accounted for. Both parties are expected to make provide complete disclosure

---

[96] CS Act 1991 s 8. Cretney, *et al*, (2002 p 452) suggest that that the instances when this will happen will be rare.
[97] Sch 1 s 1.
[98] Children Act 1989 Sch 1 para 1(2)(e).
[99] Children Act 1989 Sch 1 para 1(2)(d).
[100] See, eg, *T v S (Financial Provision for Children)* [1994] 2 FLR 883; *A v A (A Minor: Financial Provision)* [1994] 1 FLR 657; *H v P (Illegitimate Child: Capital Provision)* [1993] Fam 515.
[101] See also chs 6 and 11.
[102] The financial provision orders or property adjustment orders available to the court are the same on the granting of a decree of divorce or a decree of judicial separation. The court also may make orders pending suit, that is, interim orders designed to assist a spouse who requires support before the final order can be made (s 22 MCA), and orders varying or discharging final orders (s 31 MCA). There are no specific factors for the court to consider in making an interim order. The factors to which the court is to have regard in considering a variation order are listed in s 31(7)–(7G) MCA.

of their financial information as soon as they consult solicitors (Pre-application Protocol 2000),[103] and certainly if a petition for divorce or judicial separation is later completed.[104] It is only on the basis of full knowledge that they can make any arrangements to settle financial matters between themselves or expect the court to make any order. Rather than litigating, though, Richard and Jane may wish to try negotiating a settlement, and as we saw in chapter 11, current policy is to encourage them to do so.[105] If they are successful, the court will usually abide by their agreement and incorporate it into a consent order if asked to do so.[106] If one of them seeks to resile from an agreement previously made, but not yet incorporated in an order of court, the existence of such an agreement becomes a factor in the court's exercise of its discretion in determining overall ancillary relief. The court in this case will not lightly set aside an agreement made between two competent adults after receiving legal advice, but will retain its duty to ensure the overall fairness of the agreement.[107]

Any bargaining between the parties will be conducted in the light of the legislative principles and the case law,[108] so it is to that law that we, and they, must turn. As we saw in chapter 6, the Matrimonial Causes Act (MCA) 1973 provides guidelines for determining any allocation of property or income between them.

> **Q** Negotiations between spouses or former spouses are often characterised by feelings of pain, blame and guilt—feelings which are not taken into account in law's understanding of a 'freely negotiated contract' between two formally equal individuals. Sometimes the parties' bargaining positions are unequal, affected as they may be by differences in economic power, connection with children, or by a stronger desire to end the marriage or a greater desire to make concessions. Feminist critiques of utilising strict formal equality principles in domestic bargaining situations argue that there is a need to take these considerations into account.[109] How could this be done? Further, Davis, et al, (1994) note that many men negotiating ancillary matters on divorce felt that it was 'their' money that was being dealt with (p 49) and research from the United States found that in divorce 'men discuss with their attorneys ways to 'keep' their property or assets, and women discuss ways to 'get' assets' (Gray and Merrick, 1996, p 243). Finally, mothers' pragmatic but short-term concern for their children often outweighs concerns for their longer-term, personal financial welfare (Douglas and Perry 2001).
>
> What, if anything, can law or lawyers do about these issues?

---

[103] [2000] 30 *Fam Law* 509.
[104] FPR 1991 R2.61B.
[105] See also Diduck (2003) ch 6.
[106] S 33A MCA 1973. The court retains its jurisdiction to examine the agreement, however, and will not simply act as a 'rubber stamp'. *Harris v Manahan* [1997] 1 FLR 205.
[107] See *Xydhias v Xydhias* [1999] 1 FLR 683; *X v X* [2002] 1 FLR 508; *Edgar v Edgar* [1980] 1 WLR 1410; *Smith v McInerney* [1994] 2 FLR 1077; and *Pounds v Pounds* [1994] 1 FLR 775.
[108] See Mnookin (1979). But see also Davis, *et al*, (1994); Sarat and Felstiner (1995); Ingleby (1992); Eekelaar, *et al*, (2000) regarding the actual process of negotiation between a solicitor and his or her client and between them and the 'other side'.
[109] See ch 5 and Diduck (1999b).

The MCA 1973[110] states that the court, once it has made a decree of divorce or judicial separation, may make financial provision orders, property transfer orders or orders for the sale of property either by consent of the parties or on application by one of them. On granting a decree of divorce of nullity, it may also make a pension sharing order.[111]

A financial provision order is:

MCA 1973
23(1)(a) an order that either party to the marriage shall make to the other such periodical payments, for such term as may be specified in the order;
(b) an order that either party to the marriage shall secure to the other to the satisfaction of the court such periodical payments, for such term, as may be so specified;
(c) an order that either party to the marriage shall pay to the other such lump sum or sums as may be so specified;
[(d), (e) and (f) repeat these provisions in circumstances for payments to a person, or to a child of the family, for the benefit of that child.]

A property adjustment order is:

MCA 1973
24(1)(a) an order that a party to the marriage shall transfer to the other party, to any child of the family or to such person as may be specified in the order for the benefit of such a child such property as may be so specified, being property to which the first-mentioned party is entitled, either in possession or revision;
(b)  an order that a settlement of such property as may be so specified, being property to which a party to the marriage is so entitled, be made to the satisfaction of the court for the benefit of the other party to the marriage and of the children of the family or either of them;
(c)  an order varying for the benefit of the parties to the marriage and of the children of the family any ante-nuptial or post-nuptial settlement [...] other than one in the form of a pension arrangement ...
(d)  an order extinguishing or reducing the interest of either of the parties to the marriage under any such settlement other than one in the form of a pension arrangement ... .

An order for the sale of property is:

MCA 1973
24A (1) Where the court makes under section 23 or 24 of this Act a secured periodical payments order, an order for the payment of a lump sum or a property adjustment order, then, on making that order or at any time thereafter, the court may make a further order for the sale of such property as may be specified in the order, being property in which or in the proceeds of sale in which either or both of the parties to the marriage has or have a beneficial interest either in possession or reversion.

An order for sale may contain:

MCA 1973
24A(2)(a) provisions requiring the making of a payment out of the proceeds of sale of the property to which the order relates, and

---

[110] They may also use the Domestic Proceedings and Magistrates' Courts Act 1978 for more limited financial relief if they do not wish to divorce. See ss 1–7.
[111] All of these provisions will also apply to registered civil partners when the Civil Partnership Act comes into effect. (Civil Partnership Act 2004 Sch 5).

(b)   provision requiring any such property to be offered for sale to a person, or class of persons, specified in the order.

Finally, the court may make one or more pension sharing orders.[112]

The matters to which the court will have regard are set out in Section 25.[113] There is no *right* to any support or property; any redistribution is within the discretion of the court. It will consider all the income and assets of the parties and share them out 'fairly',[114] first consideration given to the welfare of any child of the family.[115]

Richard's and Jane's assets include their incomes from whatever source, all of their real property, personal property, bank accounts, shares, etc, and, finally, if either of them has acquired pension rights through employment, the value of these rights must also be taken into account.[116] The court will place all of these assets into a 'pot' and decide how best to distribute them, using the above 'menu' of orders available to it.

Let us consider how a court might deal with Richard's and Jane's situation. Section 25 sets out the factors the court must consider in deciding whether, and if so, how to exercise its powers to make orders for ancillary relief.

25(1) It shall be the duty of the court ... to have regard to all the circumstances of the case, first consideration being given to the welfare of while a minor of any child of the family who has not attained the age of eighteen.

In this section 'child of the family' includes a child of both parties and any child who has been treated by both parties as a child of their family.[117] In *Suter v Suter and another*[118] the court clarified that 'first' did not mean 'paramount' but rather that the child's welfare was the first in the list of factors to consider. This means that any order the court makes, or any agreement Jane and Richard reach, must consider Molly's welfare.

The list of further factors that follows is not meant to be exhaustive, but merely designates those factors to which the court must have 'particular' regard. They are:

25(2)(a) the income, earning capacity, property and their financial resources which each of the parties to the marriage has or is likely to have in the foreseeable future, including in the case of earning capacity any increase in that capacity which it would in the opinion of the court be reasonable to expect a party to the marriage to take steps to acquire;
(b)   the financial needs, obligations and responsibilities which each of the parties to the marriage has or is likely to have in the foreseeable future;
(c)   the standard of living enjoyed by the family before the breakdown of the marriage;
(d)   the age of each party to the marriage and the duration of the marriage;
(e)   any physical or mental disability of either of the parties to the marriage;
(f)   the contributions which each of the parties has made or is likely in the foreseeable future to make to the welfare of the family, including any contribution by looking after the home or caring for the family;

---

[112] MCA 1973 s 24B (1). A pension sharing order is defined as an order which 'provides that one party's–(i) shareable rights under a specified pension arrangement, or (ii) shareable state scheme rights, be subject to pension sharing for the benefit of the other party, and (b) specifies the percentage value to be transferred' (MCA 1973 s 21A(1)(a)).
[113] See ch 6.
[114] See *White v White* [2001] AC 596; [2000] FLR 981 and ch 6.
[115] MCA 1973 s 25(1).
[116] MCA 1973 s 25B. See also chs 5 and 6 and Brindley (2001).
[117] MCA 1973 s 52(1).
[118] [1987] 2 FLR 232.

(g) the conduct of each of the parties, if that conduct is such that it would in the opinion of the court be inequitable to disregard it;

(h) in the case of proceedings for divorce or nullity of marriage, the value to each of the parties to the marriage of any benefit, which, by reason of the dissolution or annulment of the marriage, that party will lose the chance of acquiring.

...

None of these factors is given priority over others, they are not equally weighted and not all are always relevant. Further complicating matters is the court's duty, on granting a divorce, to consider making a clean break between the parties:

> 25A (1) Where on or after the grant of a decree of divorce or nullity of marriage the court decides to exercise its powers [to make a periodical payments or lump sum payment order, a property adjustment order, an order for sale of property or a pension sharing order] above in favour of a party to the marriage, the court shall in particular consider whether it would be appropriate so to exercise those powers that the financial obligations of each party towards the other will be terminated as soon after the grant of the decree as the court considers just and reasonable.
>
> (2) Where the court decides in such a case to make a periodical payments or secured periodical payments order in favour of a party to the marriage, the court shall in particular consider whether it would be appropriate to require those payments to be made or secured only for such term as would in the opinion of court be sufficient to enable the party in whose favour the order is made to adjust without undue hardship to the termination of his or her financial dependence on the other party.

Further complicating matters still is the 'gloss' put on this section by the *White*[119] decision, which suggests that fairness will usually be measured by the yardstick of equality.[120] Recall the court's observations about its duty to achieve 'fairness' in ancillary relief cases:

> Generally accepted standards of fairness in a field such as this change and develop, sometimes quite radically, over comparatively short periods of time. ... These wide powers [conferred by Parliament in s 25 of the Matrimonial Causes Act 1973] enable the courts to make financial provision orders in tune with current perceptions of fairness. Today there is greater awareness of the value of non-financial contributions to the welfare of the family. There is greater awareness of the extent to which one spouse's business success, achieved by much sustained hard work over many years, may have been made possible or enhanced by the family contribution of the other spouse, a contribution which also required much sustained hard work over many years. ... In the exercise of these discretions 'the law is a living thing moving with the times and not a creature of dead or moribund ways of thought'. (references omitted pp 989–90)

And now recall the place of non-discrimination and equality in achieving fairness:

> In seeking to achieve a fair outcome, there is no place for discrimination between husband and wife *and their respective roles*. ... [W]hatever the division of labour chosen by the husband and wife, or forced upon them by the circumstances, fairness requires that this *should not prejudice or advantage* either party when considering para (f), relating to the parties' contributions. ... If, in their different spheres, each contributed equally to the family, then in principle it matters not which of them earned the money and built up the assets. There should be no bias in favour of the money-earner and against the homemaker and the child-carer. (p 989 emphasis added)

---

119 *White v White* [2000] 2 FLR 981.
120 See further, ch 6 and Herring 2004 pp 209–13.

Having made these comments, however, the court was clear that fairness and non-discrimination do not equate with a presumption of equal sharing; they only mean that equality ought to be a starting point: 'a judge would always be well advised to check his tentative views against the yardstick of equality of division. As a general guide, equality should be departed from only if, and to the extent that, there is good reason for doing so.' (p 989). And then, 'The need to consider and articulate reasons for departing from equality would help the parties and the court to focus on the need to ensure the absence of discrimination.' (*ibid*).

While the 'yardstick of equality' is an important new principle in ancillary relief law, however, it is not entirely clear if the House of Lords intended to confine it only to cases like *White,* that is, where there were long marriages (over 20 years) and 'big money' to divide. It may be argued, for example, that it applies only where the issue is the division of assets in excess of those required to meet the parties' immediate housing needs and financial requirements, and that valuing domestic contributions over a shorter period the same as valuing them over a long period is unfair.[121]

Let us now, taking into account the relevant Section 25 factors, the duty to consider a clean break and the potential application of 'the yardstick of equality', try to advise Richard. It is likely that the first concern of the court would be to ensure that Molly and her carer have a home. If Richard and Jane own their home, and there is sufficient equity in it to provide funds[122] on its sale for each of them reasonably to rehouse themselves, the court might order a sale with a direction as to the allocation of the proceeds.[123] In *Piglowska v Piglowski*[124] the House of Lords approved this arrangement, but clarified that there was no right to housing for both parties, particularly where finances did not allow it.

In *M v B (Ancillary Proceedings: Lump Sum)* [1998] 1 FLR 53, 60, Thorpe LJ said:

> In all these cases it is one of the paramount considerations, in applying the section 25 criteria, to endeavour to stretch what is available to cover the need of each for a home, particularly where there are young children involved. Obviously the primary carer needs whatever is available to make the main home for the children, but it is of importance, albeit it is of lesser importance, that the other parent should have a home of his own where the children can enjoy their contact time with him. Of course there are cases where there is not enough to provide a home for either. Of course there are cases where there is only enough to provide one. But in any case where there is, by stretch and a degree of risk-taking, the possibility of a division to enable both to rehouse themselves, that is an exceptionally important consideration and one which will almost invariably have a decisive impact on outcome.

My Lords, I do not doubt for a moment the sound sense of these remarks. That was a case in which the couple had two children aged 10 and six and the question was whether the wife should have a house which cost £210,000, leaving the husband without enough to buy a property of his own, or a house costing £135,000, leaving the husband £75,000 to buy a property of his own. The Court of Appeal held that the second approach was correct. This is a useful guideline to judges dealing with cases of a similar kind. But to cite the case as if it laid down

---

121 In *GW v RW* [2003] EWHC 611; [2003] 2 FLR 108 the court said 'I find it to be fundamentally unfair to be required to find that a party who has made domestic contributions during a marriage of 12 years should be awarded the same proportion of the assets as a party who has made the domestic contributions for a period in excess of 20 years' (para 43). See discussion in ch 6 above.
122 Perhaps with the aid of a mortgage.
123 Eg in *Scallon v Scallon* [1990] FLR 194.
124 [1999] 1 WLR 13670; [1999] 2 FLR 763.

some rule that both spouses invariably have a right to purchased accommodation is a misuse of authority. (Per Lord Hoffman pp 1371–72)

Such an arrangement does have the advantage, say the courts, of furthering 'clean break' principles. If, however, there would not be sufficient proceeds to allow Jane to find suitable accommodation for her and Molly (assuming Molly would stay in Jane's care), the court might protect Richard's interest in the home but allow Jane and Molly to continue living in it for a specified period of time or until the happening of a specified event.[125] In *Clutton v Clutton*[126] the court referred to this arrangement as a deferred clean break. Finally, the court can order an outright transfer of one party's interest in the home to the other, usually in exchange for some concessions with respect to other assets or future support.[127] If they do not own their home but are renting it from the council, the court also has jurisdiction, under the Family Law Act (FLA) 1996, to order the transfer of protected, statutory, secure and assured tenancies.[128]

The court will not deal with the home in isolation, however. In addition to it being a 'home', it is also considered to be one of the assets to be divided fairly, and so arrangements for dealing with it will be taken in the context of the ancillary relief as a whole. In this holistic exercise, the court (and solicitors' negotiations) will usually begin from one starting point or another,[129] taking care to ensure that housing is arranged.

The relevant factors to be considered in Richard's and Jane's case then, are first, subsection (a) resources and earning capacity. Richard has an income from his employment. Jane is currently not employed, but she has training and experience as a bank cashier. While in some cases it might be expected that a full-time mother obtain some form of employment,[130] in cases where there are very young children, such as this one, the court may not expect Jane to seek employment immediately,[131] and indeed, may consider that to predict when she will be able find employment would be too risky.[132]

---

[125] As in *Mesher v Mesher and Hall* [1980] 1 All ER 126 where the wife was to remain in the home until the youngest child attained the age of 17, or in *Martin v Martin* [1978] Fam 12 where the wife remained in the home until she no longer needed it or remarried. See also *Elliott v Elliott* [2001] 1 FCR 477 where the court made a Mesher order on the basis of the equality principles in *White* and contrast this with *B v B (Mesher Order)* [2002] EWHC 3106; [2002] 2 FLR 285 where the court declined to make a Mesher order, saying that it would violate the equality principles in *White*. This was because the wife would be making a substantial contribution in the form of childcare for a number of years in the future and this contribution should be recognised. In addition, her childcare responsibilities would inhibit her capacity to build up capital, whereas the husband would be free to accumulate capital. See discussion in ch 6.

[126] [1991] 1 All ER 340.

[127] See ch 6.

[128] S53, and Sch 7.

[129] Such starting points have included the *Wachtel v Wachtel* ([1973] 2 WLR 366; [1973] 1 All ER 829 (CA)) 'one third rule', (no longer used); equal shares for dual career couples (*Burgess v Burgess* [1996] 2 FLR 34) and now, fairness, which will include the principle of non-discrimination in valuing the parties' contributions to the family and in some cases mean that the division of assets is checked against the yardstick of equality (see discussion in ch 6; *White v White* above and see *B v B (Mesher order)* above, para 32). Fairness might also include a consideration of the way the marriage came about, the way it ended and the legitimate expectations it engendered (*MSM v AJRM* [2005] EWHC 528; approved by CA (*Miller v Miller* [2005] EWCA Civ 984; [2005] 2 FCR 713). See ch 6 above. These must only be starting points or guiding principles, however; the court must also consider all of the circumstances as required by the statute.

[130] *Waterman v Waterman* [1989] 1 FLR 380.

[131] *Ibid.*

[132] *C v C (Financial Relief: Short Marriage)* [1997] 2 FLR 26.

Next, their financial needs and obligations have to be considered.[133] Here is where reasonable housing needs[134] are considered, as well as reasonable[135] requirements for day to day maintenance. Both parties require enough to maintain their (relatively modest, in our case) lifestyles, but given that Jane has no income, or the prospect, at least in the short term, of obtaining an income, Richard may be expected to contribute to her support, either on a periodical basis or by way of lump sum. A lump sum, or a satisfaction of his obligation in the form of a property transfer, may be fair and in the interests of a clean break, but the courts are not anxious to force a clean break upon parties where their future is unclear or where there are young children.[136]

The standard of living of the parties must be taken into account[137] However this factor is less relevant to Richard and Jane than it might be to wealthy couples, as it may combine with the previous one to determine the parties' 'reasonable requirements'. Section 25(2)(d) however, may be important for Richard and Jane. We are not told how old the parties are, but given that they have a one year old child, we can assume they are relatively young, at least not yet close to retirement age. This fact (probably considered in the assessment of their needs and resources), plus the fact that the marriage has lasted only 2 years (if the parties separate now), may mean that it will be relatively easy for the parties to return to their pre-marital positions and thus reduce any award that may otherwise be made. While intuitively one might think the shorter the marriage, the smaller the award, however, this outcome is by no means certain. Even a short marriage may have significantly affected a spouse's health and needs, particularly if there are children.[138] And an interesting question arises as to whether the *White* yardstick of equality applies in short marriages. The cases that have considered it have tended to be of over 20 years duration, and in *GW v RW*[139] the court suggested that it was 'problematic' to apply it to shorter marriages. The question has not yet been resolved.[140]

Section 25(2)(e) is usually considered under other sections and the next important section for Richard and Jane is Section 25(2)(f)—the parties' contributions to the welfare of the family. It is pursuant to this section that the court is able to take account of both financial and non-financial contributions and *White's* presumption that there should be no discrimination between them. This means that in making any order Richard's financial contributions should not be weighted more heavily than Jane's domestic, non-financial contributions.[141]

Section 25(2)(g), the conduct factor, does not appear to have direct relevance to Richard and Jane's circumstances. The type of conduct considered by the courts to be 'inequitable to disregard' can be matrimonial conduct[142] or conduct relating to the family finances or property.[143] It can be conduct which was extremely advantageous for the

---

133 MCA 1973, s 25(2)(b).

134 *Scallon v Scallon* [1990] FLR 194.

135 See *Dart v Dart; Gojkovic v Gojkovic* [1990] 2 All ER 84; [1990] IFLR 140; *White v White* and ch 6, all above, for the court's discussion on reasonable requirements in 'big money' cases. For most cases, needs are not limited to a bare subsistence level, but still must be reasonable. Note that, as a result of cases such as *White*, wives' entitlement under the legislation is no longer calculated exclusively, or even primarily, on the basis of 'reasonable requirements.

136 *C v C* (above); *Suter v Suter* (above).

137 S 25(2)(c).

138 *C v C* (above).

139 [2003] EWHC 611; [2003] 2 FLR 108.

140 See discussion in ch 6.

141 See above pp 600–01 and discussion in ch 6.

142 See *B v B (Financial Provision Welfare of Child and Conduct)* [2002] 1 FLR 555.

143 See *Beach v Beach* [1995] 2 FLR 160. Quare, however, whether *Miller v Miller* (above n 129) may allow conduct to be considered as one of the 'circumstancs of the case' on order to do fairness in some cases.

family,[144] as well as conduct which disadvantages the family or the other party. Finally, Section 25(2)(h) directs the court to consider any benefits that may be lost on loss of one's status as a spouse. It is most clearly directed to pensions.

We saw in chapter 5 the importance of pensions to a family's well-being in later life. Any rights accumulated under occupational pension plans are included in the 'pot' of assets available for distribution on granting a decree of divorce, dissolution or nullity. There are three ways in which the court (or a settlement agreement) can take pensions into account in that distribution. The first is to offset the value of the pension against another asset or a lump sum which the non-pensioned spouse, usually the wife, can invest for her future.[145] The difficulty with this option is that it is only available for wealthy spouses who have other assets of value, or available income against which to set off their pension. The other difficulty is that it gives the non-pensioned spouse the immediate benefit of an asset from which the pensioned spouse may never benefit.[146] Finally, given the need of carers (usually wives) and children in their care for housing and some security in income in the years immediately following their separation or divorce, there is a trend towards offsetting a claim to future pension entitlement against the home. This, however, often results in poverty for women in their retirement (Ginn 2002).[147]

The second option is for the court to order the pension trustees or administrators to earmark a percentage of the pensioner's prospective pension income for the benefit of the non-pensioned party and to make payments to her in that proportion when the sums become payable to him on his retirement.[148] The disadvantage of this type of order is that the parties will not achieve a clean break. Also, if the spouse with the pension dies before it becomes payable, the other spouse will get nothing.

The final main option is pension sharing.[149] The court may make an order splitting the pension into portions representing the proportion it deems fair to allocate to each party. In effect, it creates two pensions out of one and each party becomes responsible to contribute to his or her pension as appropriate from then on. The advantages of this order are that it allows for a clean break, and seems to allow the court to make a fair division of the asset. A disadvantage is that because it requires the parties to continue to build up their separate pensions, it does not resolve the unfair disparities in retirement income between the parties: 'the constraints upon a divorced mother's employment and pension building continue' (Ginn 2002 p 170). Finally, the courts have said that the MCA 1973 does not require them to make a pension sharing order[150] and it is unclear whether *White's* yardstick of equality will apply if they do.

Richard and Jane probably both have some pension credits as a result of their employment. The court will value their pensions and use one of the above means to allocate them fairly.

In general, therefore, we see that welfare, fairness and clean break ideology will combine to influence the determination of Richard's and Jane's financial arrangements should they separate or divorce. In the past, clean break may have carried more weight

---

[144] *Kokosinski v Kokosinski* [1980] 1 All ER 1106.
[145] *Richardson v Richardson* [1978] 9 Fam Law 86.
[146] See discussion in ch 6 however, as to the theoretical basis for these awards.
[147] See also ch 5 and Douglas and Perry (2001).
[148] MCA 1973 s 25B(4) and (5).
[149] MCA 1973 S21A Private occupational pensions can be the subject of this order, as can SERPS or now, S2P pensions. See ch 5.
[150] *T v T (Financial Relief: Pensions)* [1998] 1 FLR 1072.

than it does now, because the availability of income support for the party awarded the home was not affected by its transfer, and income support would pay that party's mortgage interest on the home. Recently, this benefit has been restricted, however, and this restriction, combined with the realisation that capital transfers of this type could not oust the jurisdiction of any subsequent Child Support Act assessment,[151] have meant that clean break orders whereby the home was transferred to the carer in exchange for no order for spouse or child support have become less common. Indeed, any order for ancillary relief the court makes or the parties negotiate should take into account any liability that could be assessed by the CSA.

## IX. CONCLUSION (2)

If there is evidence that Jane can obtain employment, notwithstanding Molly's age, and given the short duration of the marriage, a term order for support for Jane may be considered.[152] The parties (or the court) will want to be sure that each of them will have somewhere to live, however, so these payments may be foregone in exchange for an arrangement enabling Jane and Molly to remain in the home. Richard's share of the home can be transferred to Jane outright, or alternatively he may retain an interest in it but its sale may be deferred until Jane finds employment[153] or until Molly reaches a certain age.[154] If support is ordered, the quantum will depend upon Richard's and Jane's incomes (including benefit and potential CSA maintenance calculation) and their needs.

Child support will be payable by the non-resident parent to the person with care. Assuming that Jane retains care of Molly the Child Support Agency will have jurisdiction over them. If Jane applies for benefit, the Child Support Agency will treat this as an application for a maintenance assessment. If Jane does not apply for benefit, she may still approach the Child Support Agency, or she may wish to include child support in her agreement with Richard.

## FURTHER READING AND SELECTED RECENT REFERENCES

B BRINDLEY, 'Black and White in Pensions' (2001) *Fam Law* 462.
L CROMPTON, 'Civil Partnerships Bill 2004: The Illusion of Equality' (2004) *Fam Law* 888.
G DOUGLAS and A PERRY, 'How Parents Cope Financially on Separation and Divorce- Implications for the Future of Ancillary Relief' (2001) 13 *Child and Family Law Quarterly* 67.
J EEKELAAR, M MACLEAN and S BEINARTS, *Family Lawyers: The Divorce Work of Solicitors* (Oxford, Hart Publishing, 2000).
F GIBB, 'Lesbian's Former Lover Wins Right to Share Child', *The Times*, 8 April 2005.
J GINN, 'Do Divorced Women Catch Up in Pension Building?' (2002) 14 *CFLQ* 157.
S GILMORE, 'The Nature, Scope and Use of the Specific Issue Order' (2004) 16 *CFLQ* 367.
Lady Justice B HALE, 'Homosexual Rights' (2004) 16 *CFLQ* 125.

[151] *Crozier v Crozier* [1994] 1 FLR 126.
[152] *See C v C* [1997] 2 FLR 26.
[153] *Martin v Martin* [1978] Fam. 12 (CA).
[154] *Mesher v Mesher and Hall* [1980] 1 All ER 126 (CA).

F KAGANAS, 'Responsible or Feckless Fathers? *Re S (Parental Responsibility)*' (1996) 8 *CFLQ* 165.

J MASSON, 'The Impact of the Adoption and Children Act 2002: Part 1—Parental Responsibility' (2003) *Fam Law* 580.

R WINTEMUTE, 'Lesbian and Gay Inequality 2000: The Potential of the Human Rights Act 1998 and the Need for an Equality Act' (2000) 6 *EHRLR* 603.

*Reports*

Ancillary Relief Advisory Group, *Report to the Lord Chancellor by the Ancilliary Relief Advisory Group* (London, 1998).

# 16

## Decisions about Children's Upbringing: Parental Responsibility, the Child's Wishes, the Medical Profession and the Court

### PART A

**Q** William and Linda are not married and have not lived together for many years. Linda lives with her mother, Doris, and 15-year-old Cindy, Linda and William's daughter. Cindy spends every other weekend with her father. There is no residence order in force. Linda is concerned that recently Cindy has become too preoccupied with boys and she wants to send her to a religious boarding school. William disagrees, as does Doris. Cindy is totally opposed to the idea. In addition, she has stated that she and the family doctor have discussed cosmetic surgery and that she wishes to undergo an operation to improve the shape of her nose. Both William and Linda are adamant that she should not do so.

Advise Linda, William, Cindy and Doris.

Would your answer be any different if Cindy were aged 16?

### I. INTRODUCTION

The disagreements about Cindy's education and medical treatment raise questions about who is legally entitled to make decisions affecting children's[1] lives and the extent to which children themselves can act as autonomous decision-makers. It is also necessary to consider the extent to which the law plays a part in resolving disputes between family members about children's upbringing. Before going on to consider the legal position of Cindy and her family, we will briefly outline the way in which and the context within which the law has developed.

We have already outlined how the law moved from protecting paternal authority to safeguarding children's welfare,[2] so that child protection came to be seen as a legitimate reason for intervention in the family.[3]

---

[1] In this chap. the terms 'child' and 'minor' are used to denote young people under the age of 18, the age at which majority status is attained.

[2] See ch 8.

[3] See ch 9.

Talk about child protection has at times been couched in terms of children's rights,[4] but since the 1970s a number of commentators have sought to expand the concept of children's rights to embrace the notion of self-determination.[5] The views of the children's liberationists of that era, who advocated the same sorts of rights for children as there are for adults, have not been widely accepted. As Fortin says, 'it appears that few commentators today claim complete personal autonomy for all children, or even for all mature teenagers' (2003 p 19).[6] Instead, autonomy is understood in relation to young people as referring to very limited decision-making rights, mainly within the confines of the home[7] and the school,[8] often concerning health care (*ibid*).

Of course, children's rights/interests need not be promoted and their views can legally be ignored as long as the family's decision-making remains in the private domain.[9] But there is some recognition that it might be beneficial to consult children about matters affecting them[10] and children may be allowed in future have a greater role in the public sphere. Fortin observes that there is a growing view in industrialised nations that children should be given the opportunity to develop their decision-making capacities and their ability to become responsible citizens (2003 p 11). Indeed, the notion of citizenship has become central to government policy in the UK in respect of young people in recent years.[11] In line with this effort to promote responsible citizenship, children are to be given a greater say in the services available to them[12] and they will now have a voice in shaping policy[13] through the creation, by the Children Act 2004, of the office of Children's Commissioner.

Political consciousness of the significance of children and their role in society has been matched by academic interest. There has been a proliferation of research seeking to reveal children's experiences in the context of, for example, domestic violence or parental separation. Sociologists of childhood have recently begun to explore notions of agency in relation to children.[14] Constructions of children and childhood have changed to accommodate images of children as actively influencing the shape of their own lives, the lives of those around them and the societies in which they live. And, for some years now, legal theorists working within a rights framework have been grappling with the competing images of children and young people as rational and competent on the one hand, and, on the other hand, as irrational and vulnerable. They have sought to theorise

---

[4] See Freeman (1983) pp 18–19.

[5] See the discussion in Freeman (1983) pp 22–24. See, for a comprehensive discussion of children's rights, Fortin (2003) chs 1 and 2. See also Herring (2004) pp 383ff; Bainham (2005) pp 97ff.

[6] See also Bainham (2005) p 100.

[7] Parents are not legally obliged to consult children on decisions affecting them. See, eg, on decision-making about relocating the family, Ackers (2000). Compare The Children (Scotland) Act 1995, s 6(1) which requires a parent, on making a major decision involving his or her child's upbringing to 'have regard so far as practicable to the views (if he wishes to express them) of the child concerned', taking into account the child's age and maturity. It also provides that 'a child twelve years of age or more shall be presumed to be of sufficient age and maturity to form a view'. This provision is described as having 'symbolic' significance (Fortin 2003 p 79).

[8] However the UK has been criticised for failing to engage in systematic consultation with children with regard to education. See UN Committee on the Rights of the Child (2002) para 29. See also ch 4 above.

[9] Only a minority of children are consulted about arrangements that affect them when parents separate. See May and Smart (2004) pp 305–6 and references cited there.

[10] See Fortin (2003) p 19. Smart and Neale, for example, found that for many children it was important to be given information and to participate in making arrangements after parental separation or divorce (2000 p 165). See also Buchanan and Hunt (2003) pp 372–73.

[11] See chs 4 and 9 in this volume. See also Kaganas and Diduck (2004).

[12] See, for example, DfES (2005). See also ch 4.

[13] See also the references to increasing participation of children and consultation with them by government, local authorities and civil society generally, UN Committee of the Rights of the Child (2002) para 29.

[14] See ch 4.

ways in which competent young people can be empowered to make their own choices about their lives and, at the same time, can be protected from their own folly and from abuse by others.

Freeman (1983 p 40), for example, has identified four categories of rights. These are rights to welfare; rights to protection; rights which adults have (eg, to vote); and autonomy rights. Children, he said, can be assumed to want to be given the chance to mature into 'a rationally autonomous adulthood and [to] be capable of deciding on [their] own system of ends as free and rational beings' (p 57). They would want to be shielded from decisions that would frustrate this goal and so should not be permitted to exercise their rights in a way that would prevent them from achieving it (*ibid*).

Eekelaar (1986) has spoken of three interests which might be said to form the foundation of rights claims. The 'basic interest' refers to '[g]eneral physical, emotional and intellectual care' (p 170) from immediate caregivers. The second interest, whereby children's capacities should be developed to their best advantage, is termed the 'developmental interest' (*ibid*). Finally, he said, children have an interest in choosing their own lifestyles free of adult control: the 'autonomy interest' (p 171). In the event of the child's autonomy interest conflicting with the developmental or basic interests, the latter interests should prevail. He argued that few adults would retrospectively want to have been allowed to make choices that would have prejudiced their life chances. In a later work (1994a), Eekelaar developed his theory to take greater account of children's interest in making choices. He devised the concept of 'dynamic self-determinism'. This is based on an understanding of children's best interests that allows scope for the child to determine what those interests are. He maintained that the 'very fact that the outcome has been, at least partly, determined by the child is taken to demonstrate that the outcome is in the child's best interests' (p 48). It should be the competent child's decision that should determine the issue under consideration, but this should be subject to two limitations. The child's decision must be compatible with the law and with the interests of others. And the child should not be permitted to make decisions 'contrary to his or her *self-interest*, ... narrowly defined in terms of physical or mental well-being and integrity' (p 57).

We can see in both Freeman's and Eekelaar's analyses of children's rights the difficulties encountered in seeking to reconcile the competing images of children and childhood, the competing imperatives of self determination and protection. The law too has had to confront this dilemma and the issue of children's autonomy has proved particularly problematic (Douglas 1992 p 570). In general, the law continues to maintain a paternalistic stance; children are perceived as being in need of protection both from themselves and from others. They lack full legal capacity and decisions about their upbringing are normally entrusted to the adults who are responsible for them.

Yet the law has increasingly come to treat the child, and the older child in particular, as an individual whose views, which might conflict with those of other family members, should be taken seriously. The *Gillick* case[15] gave us the concept of the competent minor and legislation gives prominence to the wishes of the child. In relation to private law proceedings,[16] relevant statutory provisions include the checklist in Section 1 of the Children Act 1989, requiring that, in opposed Section 8 applications, the court should

---

[15] See below at pp 615ff.
[16] S 1(3) of the Children Act 1989 also applies to child protection proceedings under Part IV See also ss 20(6), 22(5), 26, 46(3)(d), 61(2) and 64(2).

take into account the wishes and feelings of the child.[17] In addition, young people, if of sufficient understanding, can invoke the jurisdiction of the court to oppose parental decisions.[18] The principle of family autonomy continues to find expression in the law,[19] but 'parental power' can now be challenged by children as well as by the child protection machinery (Bell 1993 p 398).

The statutory provisions give children access to legal representation and to the court and, Roche (1995 p 285) suggests, 'can be seen as going some way towards meeting the obligations of the UK government under the United Nations Convention on the Rights of the Child'.[20] Article 12 of the Convention provides:

1.   States parties shall assure to the child who is capable of forming his or her own views the right to express those views freely in all matters affecting the child, the views of the child being given due weight in accordance with the age and maturity of the child.
2.   For this purpose the child shall in particular be provided the opportunity to be heard in any judicial and administrative proceedings affecting the child, either directly, or through a representative or an appropriate body, in a manner consistent with the procedural rules of national law.

This provision is described by Fortin as promoting children's capacity for self-determination and autonomy but, she points out, it does not guarantee autonomy (2003 p 20). It refers to consultation and participation in decision-making, as well as a right to be heard and represented, but there is nothing in Article 12 that says that children have a right to have their choices implemented (*ibid*). Moreover, although children's rights are also protected by the Human Rights Act 1998 and by the ECHR, the Convention is not specific to children and not designed to promote their autonomy.[21] And as far as the Children Act 1989 is concerned, Piper asserts that the introduction of provisions requiring consideration of children's wishes and feelings was mainly intended to add 'the child's perspective to the operation of the welfare test'; the law is primarily concerned with children's welfare (1999b p 79).

The law, like commentaries on children's rights and now also government policy, emphasises children's participation in, rather than control of, decision-making (Roche 1999 p 58). This 'new right to a conversation', Roche (1999 pp 58–59) says, avoids the difficulty of choosing between self-determination and paternalism: the languages of rights and welfare converge. The child's best interests require a consideration of that child's wishes; '[t]he child's right to participate, as opposed to making the decision, is integral to their welfare as well as respectful of their liberty rights' (p 59).

This participation is limited. In particular, although this may be changing somewhat, the courts have tended to seem uncomfortable with the notion of the child as an active participant in decision-making and in legal proceedings.[22] It has often been assumed

[17] S 1(3)(a) of the Children Act 1989.
[18] See below, pp 631ff.
[19] Eg in the non-intervention principle contained in s 1(5) of the Children Act 1989. The emphasis on mediation in relation to decisions about children also supports the idea of family autonomy but it is notable that opinion is moving in favour of involving children in the process. See ch 11.
[20] But see UN Committee on the Rights of the Child (2002) para 29. The Committee states that the obligations under Art 12 have not been consistently incorporated into legislation such as that dealing with divorce and adoption. Also, it says, the right to independent legal representation is not 'systematically exercised'.
[21] See, on children's rights and the ECHR, Fortin (1999). See, on children's rights in the Constitution for Europe, Schuurman (2003). The fate of the Constitution is unclear at the time of writing as it has not met with universal approval within the EU.
[22] See Roche (1995 p 285); Newsline (2003) p 296.

that children should not have the 'burden' of saying what they want and that 'court is a bad place for children' (Piper 1999c p 396). Indeed it seems that in some ways, children's participation may be becoming even more restricted, particularly as a result of the increasing privatisation of disputes between parents about their children on divorce or separation. Increasingly, parents are being encouraged to make their own arrangements when it comes to child care after divorce or separation.[23] If they cannot agree they are exhorted to settle their differences without resorting to court; they are told to attend mediation or ADR. This, say Harold and Murch (2005), may lead to the marginalisation of the child.[24] Unless mediators and in-court conciliators involve children directly, they will often have to rely on parents' perceptions of their children and these may not be reliable (2005 p 199). Moreover, the change in CAFCASS practice proposed by the government to move away from report writing to concentrate on conciliation[25] and support (DCA, DfEs and DTI 2005 paras 66–67) could deprive children of an opportunity to express their views to a CAFCASS officer (Harold and Murch 2005 p 201).

Even if children are permitted to participate in mediation or ADR, the problem remains that the process may fail to check or compensate for power imbalances within the family and, as a result, children could be disadvantaged relative to the more powerful adults involved. Concerns arise also from the fact that the separating or divorcing family is being closed off from public scrutiny.

Arguably, it is the ability to invite this scrutiny that is regarded as the most important aspect of giving children a say. It appears that neither the courts nor Parliament have so much endorsed children's autonomy rights as opened up the private family, and parental conduct, in particular, to 'new forms of surveillance' in some areas, making the family more susceptible to regulation (Lyon and Parton 1995 p 40, quoting Alan Prout). Children's rights can be invoked to intervene in the private family to protect children.[26] Indeed, Nelken has suggested that, whatever the concerns about increasing children's autonomy, in the medium term the idea of children's rights has led to increased control by welfare professionals over the child (and we would say, over the family). This development, he argued, was consistent with what he saw as a trend to undermine the control of parents in favour of the 'psy' professions (1998 p 318).

While Nelken's observations remain valid today, there has recently developed another trend alongside the paternalistic one he noted. Government policy is now placing great emphasis on families and the individuals within them to take responsibility for themselves and for bettering the society in which they live. Increasingly, we think, children's participation is coming to be seen as a way of 'civilising' children, transforming them into responsible citizens and removing the potential threat to society they could pose through delinquency and social exclusion.[27] There is, in some spheres and particularly in relation to the youth justice system, a 'move away from a paternalistic model of regulation that stresses the essential passivity of youth toward the cultivation of a more active subjectivity within young people who will be required to take more responsibility for their lives' (Vaughan 2000 p 348).[28] Yet, at the same time, as we shall see in this chapter, children are still perceived as vulnerable.

[23] See Piper (1999c).
[24] See ch 11. See also Dame Butler-Sloss with Fiddy (2001) p 16.
[25] See ch 11.
[26] See Fortin (2003) p 9. But see Cooper (1998 p 85) who argues that rights can drive a wedge between family members and 'unwisely' cast them in the role of adversaries.
[27] See Kaganas and Diduck (2004).
[28] Vaughan argues that in relation to criminal liability, we are treating children more like autonomous adults but that the effect of this is to enable young people to be regulated more intensively than before (2000 p 359).

## II. PARENTAL RESPONSIBILITY AND DECISION-MAKING

Parental responsibility confers on a person 'all the rights, duties, powers, responsibilities and authority which by law a parent of a child has in relation to the child and his property'.[29] This includes the capacity to make decisions concerning the child's education and to consent to medical treatment.[30] Consequently, the first step in advising the parties in this case is to determine who has parental responsibility for Cindy.

William and Linda have never married and, unless William has acquired parental responsibility under Section 4[31] of the Children Act 1989 through registering as Cindy's father,[32] through a parental responsibility agreement[33] or by means of a court order,[34] Linda alone has parental responsibility.[35] If William has acquired parental responsibility, he holds it concurrently with Linda.[36] Each of them may act independently of the other in meeting his or her responsibility[37] but it appears that parental responsibility confers a right to be consulted or informed about important matters such as education.[38] If William has not acquired parental responsibility, all decision-making power vests solely in Linda.

Parental responsibility does not confer absolute powers on anyone who holds it. The law makes provision for a child as well as other interested parties to challenge parental decisions in court.[39] In addition, young people themselves have limited capacity to make decisions concerning medical treatment. It was in relation to medical decisions that the first significant moves were made to confer on children some autonomy and it is to that subject we now turn.

### Cindy's Medical Treatment

Where adults are concerned, unless there are exceptional circumstances, the consent of the patient is essential to any medical examination or treatment. In the absence of valid consent, any examination or treatment constitutes an assault and renders the doctor liable in tort.[40] The law's emphasis on the autonomy of the individual and the right to physical integrity is reflected in the rule that competent adults have an absolute right to choose whether or not to undergo medical treatment, for any reason, rational or irrational or for no reason at all, even if their decisions lead to their own deaths.[41] Although in

---

[29] S 3(1) of the Children Act 1989.

[30] See pp 169ff above.

[31] Parental responsibility can also be acquired by obtaining a residence order (s 12(1) of the Children Act 1989). In addition, an unmarried father can acquire parental responsibility by being appointed as a guardian (s 5(6) of the Children Act 1989) but an appointment would not take effect while the mother is alive (s 5(8) of the Children Act 1989). See, further, ch 4.

[32] In terms of s 4(1)(a) and s 4(1A) of the Children Act 1989. See p 578.

[33] In terms of s 4(1)(b) and s 4(2) of the Children Act 1989. See p 578.

[34] In terms of s 4(1)(c) of the Children Act 1989. See p 578.

[35] S 2(2) of the Children Act 1989.

[36] S 2(5) of the Children Act 1989.

[37] S 2(7) of the Children Act 1989.

[38] *Re G (Parental Responsibility: Education)* [1994] 2 FLR 964. See p 284.

[39] In some cases, the local authority has instituted proceedings to obtain a ruling on a question relating to a child's medical treatment. See, eg, *Re C (HIV Test)* [1999] 2 FLR 1004.

[40] See *In Re T (Adult: Refusal of Treatment)* [1992] 3 WLR 782, 787; *Re B (Consent to Treatment: Capacity)* [2002] EWHC Fam 429; [2002] 1 FLR 1090.

See *Sidaway v Board of Governors of the Bethlem Royal Hospital and the Maudsley Hospital* [1985] AC 871, 904–5; *Re T (An Adult) (Consent to Medical Treatment)* [1992] 2 FLR 458, 460; *Re MB (Medical Treatment)*

recent years the courts have shown themselves at times ready to find this presumption rebutted,[42] it is presumed that adults are competent to make these decisions.

The position of children is very different, however. The adults responsible for the child are empowered to decide on his or her medical treatment.[43] The Children Act 1989 gives some authority to temporary carers to make such decisions[44] but, apart from this statutory exception and the exception recognised under the doctrine of necessity,[45] the consent of someone with parental responsibility is normally required before a child can be medically examined or treated.[46] Depending on the seriousness with which the treatment decision is viewed, the decision may be one in relation to which each person with parental responsibility is obliged to consult the other.[47] Where the parents are in dispute, one can institute Section 8 proceedings in the form of an application for a specific issue order or a prohibited steps order to challenge the other's decision. The decision of the court is made on the basis of the welfare principle, taking into account any expert evidence before it as well as other considerations.[48]

There are circumstances in which parents have a positive duty to ensure that their children receive medical treatment,[49] but otherwise it is within their discretion to give or withhold[50] consent.[51] However, the law has, consonant with changing perceptions of children, come to embrace the idea that children's wishes should be heeded and, in some circumstances, be allowed, in the event of conflict, to prevail over those of their parents.[52]

---

[1997] 2 FLR 426, 432; *St George's Healthcare NHS Trust v S; R v Collins, ex parte S* [1998] 2 FLR 728; *Re JT (Adult: Refusal of Medical Treatment)* [1998] Fam Law 23; *Re AK (Medical Treatment: Consent)* [2001] 1 FLR 129; *Re B (Consent to Treatment: Capacity)* [2002] EWHC Fam 429; [2002] 1 FLR 1090.

42 See *In re T (Adult: Refusal of Treatment)* [1992] 3 WLR 782; *Re MB (Medical Treatment)* [1997] 2 FLR 426. But see *St George's Healthcare NHS Trust v S; R v Collins, ex parte S* [1998] 2 FLR 728; *Re B (Consent to Treatment: Capacity)* [2002] EWHC Fam 429; [2002] 1 FLR 1090.

43 Where a child is in care, the local authority shares parental responsibility with the parents. See ch 17.

44 S 3(5) enables a temporary carer to arrange for medical assistance in an emergency resulting from an accident, eg, but does not authorise consent to major elective surgery (see Law Commission 1988b para 2.16).

45 A doctor may treat a patient in an emergency without first obtaining the necessary consents if this is necessary to save life or safeguard health. See *F v West Berkshire Health Authority* [1989] 2 All ER 545, 564 and 566.

46 Where treatment is undertaken without consent, the cause of action lies in tort and would have to be based on trespass to the child's person. See further Bainham (2005) p 318.

47 Presumably serious surgery would qualify. The courts appear to be expanding the categories of medical procedures that warrant consultation: eg immunisation (*Re C (Welfare of Child: Immunisation)* [2003] EWCA Civ 1148; [2003] 2 FLR 1095) and circumcision of a boy (*Re J (Specific Issue Orders: Child's Religious Upbringing and Circumcision)* [2000] 1 FLR 571). Female circumcision is illegal: Prohibition of Female Circumcision Act 1985.

48 *Re C (Welfare of Child: Immunisation)* [2003] EWCA Civ 1148; [2003] 2 FLR 1095. See O'Donnell (2004) for a critical appraisal of this exercise in *Re C*.

49 Children and Young Persons Act 1933 s 1. See ch 4 above.

50 O'Donnell (2004) points out that in relation to minor issues, both parents can agree to withhold treatment. In relation to major matters, their decision can be challenged in court. Where the parents are in dispute, even minor matters become justiciable and the courts do not tend to show any preference for endorsing the views of the primary carer.

51 They have the power to consent to therapeutic treatment and, it seems, non-therapeutic treatment where this is for the benefit of the child (Bainham 2005 pp 316–17). Herring suggests that a parent cannot give effective consent to a procedure that is detrimental to the child (2004 p 400). Some procedures, such as sterilisation that is not incidental to other medical treatment, require the consent of the court. See the discussion in *Re HG (Specific Issue Order: Sterilisation)* [1993] 1 FLR 587, 594–95. See further, Bainham (2005) p 319ff; ch 3 above, pp 73ff on reproductive rights.

52 Compare *Nielsen v Denmark* (1988) 11 EHRR 175. The ECtHR held that a 12 year old could be confined to a closed ward on the authority of his mother and against his wishes. His Art 5 rights were not infringed and his mother's Art 8 rights included the right to exercise parental authority. Fortin (2003 p 82) argues that the decision involves an 'immoderate view of the parental role' and that interpretations of the ECHR should be informed by the thinking behind *Gillick* (below).

Older minors are empowered by statute to consent to medical procedures.[53] Section 8 of the Family Law Reform Act 1969 provides that:

> 8(1) The consent of a minor who has attained the age of sixteen years to any surgical, medical or dental treatment.[54] ... shall be as effective as it would be if he were of full age; and where a minor has by virtue of this section given an effective consent to any treatment it shall not be necessary to obtain any consent for it from his parent or guardian. ...
>
> ...
>
> (3) Nothing in this section shall be construed as making ineffective any consent which would have been effective if this section had not been enacted.

It is in the courts, in judgments interpreting the statutory rules and expounding on the common law, that the law on medical decision-making is being shaped. This process began with the landmark decision of the House of Lords in *Gillick v West Norfolk and Wisbech Area Health Authority*.[55]

## III. GILLICK/FRASER COMPETENCE

The *Gillick* case arose out of the decision of the Department of Health and Social Security to issue to area health authorities a memorandum of guidance on family planning which indicated that, in 'exceptional' circumstances, a doctor could lawfully prescribe contraception to girls under 16 without their parents' knowledge or consent. Victoria Gillick, a mother of daughters under the age of 16, objected to the guidance and sought a declaration that it was unlawful. The arguments put forward on her behalf were, first, that a doctor acting on the guidance would be guilty of a criminal offence[56]; secondly, that children under the age of 16 years could not validly consent to medical treatment; and, thirdly, that the guidance could or did adversely affect her rights as a parent. Mrs Gillick failed in the court of first instance but the Court of Appeal allowed her appeal. The case went before the House of Lords, where the majority rejected the argument based on the criminal law and focused on the other two issues. By a majority of three to two, the DHSS' appeal was upheld[57] and a test based on competence rather than chronological age was adopted to determine capacity.

On the question of capacity, Lord Fraser of Tullybelton had this to say:

> The contention on behalf of Mrs Gillick was that section 8(1) [of the Family Law Reform Act 1969] shows that, apart from the subsection, the consent of a minor to such treatment would not be effective. But I do not accept that contention because subsection (3) leaves open the question whether consent by a minor under the age of 16 would have been effective if the section had not been enacted. ... (p 167)

---

[53] See also in the context of public law, ss 43(8) and 38(6) of the Children Act 1989.

[54] It appears that organ donations are not within the scope of this provision. See Fortin (2003) p 127.

[55] [1986] 1 AC 112.

[56] By encouraging the commission of unlawful sexual intercourse contrary to s 28 of the Sexual Offences Act 1956.

[57] Fortin speculates that a mother like Mrs Gillick would not succeed today if she sought to rely on Art 8; the court may well prefer to uphold the adolescent girl's right to respect for her private sexual life (2003 p 135).

It would ... appear that, if the inference which Mrs Gillick's advisers seek to draw ... is justi-fied, a minor under the age of 16 has no capacity to authorise any kind of medical advice or treatment or examination of his own body. That seems to me so surprising that I cannot accept it in the absence of clear provisions to that effect. It seems to me verging on the absurd to sug-gest that a girl or a boy aged 15 could not effectively consent, for example, to have a medical examination of some trivial injury to his body or even to have a broken arm set. Of course the consent of the parents should normally be asked, but they may not be immediately available. Provided the patient, whether a boy or a girl, is capable of understanding what is proposed, and of expressing his or her own wishes, I see no good reason for holding that he or she lacks the capacity to express them validly and effectively and to authorise the medical man to make the examination or give the treatment which he advises. After all, a minor under the age of 16 can, within certain limits, enter into a contract. He or she can also sue and be sued, and can give evi-dence on oath. Moreover, a girl under 16 can give sufficiently effective consent to sexual intercourse to lead to the legal result that the man involved does not commit the crime of rape
... .

Accordingly, I am not disposed to hold now, for the first time, that a girl aged less than 16 lacks the power to give valid consent to contraceptive advice or treatment, merely on account of her age. (p 169)

He then went on to consider the question of parental rights and duties, pointing out that parental rights existed, not for the benefit of the parent, but for the benefit of the child. They were justified, he said, only in so far as they enabled the parent to perform parental duties.[58] He cited[59] with approval the dictum of Lord Denning in *Hewer v Bryant*[60] to the effect that the rights of parents were 'dwindling' rights 'which the courts will hesitate to enforce against the wishes of the child, and the more so the older he is. It starts with a right of control and ends with little more than advice'. Then Lord Fraser continued:

Once the rule of the parents' absolute authority over minor children is abandoned, the solution to the problem in this appeal can no longer be found by referring to rigid parental rights at any particular age. The solution depends upon a judgment of what is best for the welfare of the particular child. Nobody doubts, certainly I do not doubt, that in the overwhelming majority of cases the best judges of a child's welfare are his or her parents. Nor do I doubt that any important medical treatment of a child under 16 would normally only be carried out with the parents' approval. ..But there may be circumstances in which a doctor is a better judge of the medical advice and treatment which will conduce to a girl's welfare than her parents. ...
The only practicable course is to entrust the doctor with a discretion to act in accordance with his view of what is best in the interests of the girl who is his patient. He should, of course, always seek to persuade her to tell her parents that she is seeking contraceptive advice, and the nature of the advice that she receives. At least he should seek to persuade her to agree to the doctor's informing the parents. But there may well be cases, and I think there will be some cases, where the girl refuses either to tell the parents herself or to permit the doctor to do so and in such cases, the doctor will, in my opinion, be justified in proceeding without the parents' consent or even knowledge provided he is satisfied on the following matters: (1) that the girl (although under 16 years of age) will understand his advice; (2) that he cannot persuade her to inform her parents or to allow him to inform the parents that she is seeking contraceptive advice; (3) that she is very likely to begin or to continue having sexual intercourse with or with-out contraceptive treatment; (4) that unless she receives contraceptive advice or treatment her physical or mental health or both are likely to suffer; (5) that her best interests require him to give her contraceptive advice, treatment or both without the parental consent. (pp 173–74)

---

58 P 170.
59 At p 172.
60 [1970] 1 QB 357, 369.

**Q** Who, according to Lord Fraser, should decide whether advice or treatment should be given? Is it the parents, the girl or the doctor? What criteria should form the basis of this decision?

Lord Scarman, like Lord Fraser, rejected the interpretation of Section 8(3) of the Family Law Reform Act 1969 put forward on Mrs Gillick's behalf. And like Lord Fraser, he adopted the view that parental rights existed only for the purpose of fulfilling duties; parental rights, he said, could be challenged or even overridden if not exercised in accordance with the welfare principle.[61] However his judgment can be read as conveying a clearer endorsement of young people's autonomy:

> The underlying principle of the law was exposed by Blackstone and can be seen to have been acknowledged in the case law. *It is that parental right yields to the child's right to make his own decisions when he reaches a sufficient understanding and intelligence to be capable of making up his own mind on the matter requiring decision.* (p 186, emphasis added)

> *I would hold that as a matter of law the parental right to determine whether or not their minor child below the age of 16 will have medical treatment terminates if and when the child achieves a sufficient understanding and intelligence to enable him or her to understand fully what is proposed.* It will be a question of fact whether a child seeking advice has sufficient understanding of what is involved to give a consent valid in law. *Until the child achieves the capacity to consent, the parental right to make the decision continues* save only in exceptional circumstances. Emergency, parental neglect, abandonment of the child, or inability to find the parent are examples of exceptional situations justifying the doctor proceeding to treat the child without parental knowledge and consent. ...
>     When applying these conclusions to contraceptive advice and treatment it has to be borne in mind that there is much that has to be understood by a girl under the age of 16 if she is to have legal capacity to consent to such treatment. It is not enough that she should understand the nature of the advice which is being given: she must also have a sufficient maturity to understand what is involved. There are moral and family questions, especially her relationship with her parents; long-term problems associated with the emotional impact of pregnancy and its termination; and there are the risks to health of sexual intercourse at her age, risks which contraception may diminish but cannot eliminate. It follows that a doctor will have to satisfy himself that she is able to appraise these factors before he can safely proceed upon the basis that she has at law capacity to consent to contraceptive treatment. (pp 188–89, emphasis added)

**Q** How do you interpret the italicised passages in this judgment? In whom does Lord Scarman say the capacity to decide resides? Do you think most adults have the kind of knowledge required of girls under 16? Could a young person who makes a decision that to adult eyes appears detrimental to her interests still qualify as '*Gillick* competent' or, as it is often now termed, 'Fraser competent'? How would you advise a doctor who asked you whether she was required to comply with the clear and confidential request of a mature and intelligent 15-year-old girl for contraceptive treatment, when she was not sure that it would be in the girl's best interests to become sexually active?

---

[61] P 184.

While the *Gillick* case concerned medical decisions, it was interpreted by some commentators as recognising young people's capacity to make their own choices and it was thought that this autonomy might extend to other spheres. John Eekelaar wrote:

The significance of Lord Scarman's opinion with respect to children's autonomy interests cannot be over-rated. It follows from his reasoning that, where a child has reached capacity, there is no room for a parent to impose a contrary view, *even if this is more in accord with the child's best interests.* For its legal superiority to the child's decision can rest only on its status as a parental right. But this is extinguished when the child reaches full capacity. More importantly, the argument catches the court itself … . The inherent jurisdiction of the High Court to intervene in the lives of children rests on the doctrine of the Crown's role as *parens patriae.* But on what principle can the Crown retain the parental jurisdiction when the parent himself has lost it, not through deprivation, but due to the superior right of the child? The primary question … can no longer be: what is in the best interests of the child? It must be, has the child capacity to make his own decisions?

This recognition of the autonomy interests of children can be reconciled with their basic and developmental interests only through the empirical application of the concept of the acquisition of full capacity. This, as Lord Scarman made clear, may be no simple matter. The child must not only understand the nature of the transaction, but be able to evaluate its implications. Intellectual understanding must be supplemented by emotional maturity. It is easy to see how adults can conclude that a child's decision which seems, to the adult, to be contrary to his interests, is lacking in sufficient maturity. In this respect, the provision of the simple test of age to provide an upper limit to the scope of a supervisory, paternalistic power has advantages. … [C]ould we not say that it is on balance better to subject all persons to this potential inhibition up to a defined age, in case the failure to exercise the restraint unduly prejudices a person's basic or developmental interests? It avoids judgments in which question [*sic*] of fact and value will be impenetrably mixed. But the decision, it seems, has been taken. Children will now have, in wider measure than ever before, that most dangerous but most precious of rights: the right to make their own mistakes. (1986 pp 181–82, emphasis in original)

**Q** Explain what Eekelaar means when he refers to the mixing of questions of fact and value.

The concept of '*Gillick* competence'[62] is a flexible one, enabling the courts to demand capacity commensurate with the gravity of the consequences of the decision in question.[63] On occasion, the levels of understanding demanded have been very high. For example, in *Re E (A Minor) (Wardship: Medical Treatment)*,[64] the court overruled the refusal of a Jehovah's Witness, a few months short of his 16th birthday, to accept blood transfusions. Ward J (as he then was) found that the boy, who suffered from leukaemia, was intelligent and realised he might die without transfusions. Nevertheless, he was not sufficiently competent because he did not have a full understanding of the manner of his death and the extent of his own and his family's suffering.[65] Similarly, a Jehovah's Witness aged 15½ was held not to be '*Gillick* competent' because she too had an insufficient understanding of the manner of her death and the pain and distress that would attend

---

[62] See, on the concept of competence in relation to young children and adolescents, Fortin (2003) pp 72ff.

[63] See *Re S (A Minor) (Consent to Medical Treatment)* [1994] 2 FLR 1065, 1076. This test has been applied also in relation to adult capacity. See *In re T (Adult: Refusal of Treatment)* [1992] 3 WLR 782, 799; *Re MB (Medical Treatment)* [1997] 2 FLR 426, 437.

[64] [1993] 1 FLR 386.

[65] This patient, when he reached the age of 18, is reported to have exercised his right to refuse blood and died. See *Re S (A Minor) (Consent to Medical Treatment)* [1994] 2 FLR 1065, 1075.

it. Moreover, she was child-like in hoping for a miracle to save her.[66] In *Re L (Medical Treatment: Gillick Competency)*,[67] another Jehovah's Witness, aged 14, failed the test of *Gillick* competence because she did not have enough knowledge of the details of the 'horrible' way in which she would be likely to die. She did not have the requisite knowledge because the surgeon did not tell her.[68] Nevertheless this contributed to the court's decision. It was also influenced by the fact that she lived a sheltered life among her family and under the influence of a religious congregation.

In *Re M (Medical Treatment: Consent)*[69] the court was faced with the refusal of a 15½ year old girl to consent to a heart transplant. She explained her refusal saying she did not want to have someone else's heart and that she did not want to take medication for the rest of her life. The court was at pains to point out that she was intelligent and that her views should carry 'considerable weight'.[70] Nevertheless, she was judged to be 'overwhelmed by her circumstances and the decision she was being asked to make'.[71] It appears from this, although the court did not rule explicitly on M's competence, that it considered her to be lacking the competence necessary to make the decision. In any event, the girl's mother had consented to the treatment and the court simply went on to state that despite the risks of the surgery and of rejection, and despite the risk that M might resent what had been done to her, the alternative of certain death meant that the operation would be in her best interests and should go ahead.

**Q** Although there is evidence that the courts may on occasion be willing to intervene in adults' decisions to refuse treatment, the way they have applied the '*Gillick*/Fraser competence' test appears to be more rigorous than the test used to determine adult competence. Why do you think this might be? The court in *Re E* remarked that courts 'should be very slow to allow an infant to martyr himself'.[72] Do you think this explains their approach? Do these decisions bear out Eekelaar's concern that the unacceptability of the young person's decision could lead to a finding of incapacity? Do you agree with Bridge (1999 p 591), who suggests that the application of the competence tests is a 'sham' because the court makes its decision on the basis of outcome and its view of the child's welfare?

**Q** Fortin suggests that society has an interest in protecting young people from their own mistakes and that it might be more honest to accept that a patient is *Gillick* competent but to override his or her wishes all the same (2003 p 134).[73] Do you agree?

---

[66] *Re S (A Minor) (Consent to Medical Treatment)* [1994] 2 FLR 1065.

[67] [1998] 2 FLR 810.

[68] Herring (2004 p 395 n 317) reports that the BMA has suggested that doctors should not withhold information for fear of distressing a young patient. See, for discussion of the BMA guidance, Fortin (2003) pp 124–25.

[69] [1999] 2 FLR 1097.

[70] P 1100.

[71] *Ibid.*

[72] P 394.

[73] See also Bridge (1999a) p 594.

## IV. THE COMPETENT CHILD AND MEDICAL DECISIONS

Eekelaar interpreted the *Gillick* decision as giving the competent child the right to make mistakes. However judges in subsequent cases have balked at this prospect and have interpreted the decision restrictively. The Court of Appeal has taken the view that *Gillick* establishes only that a competent child can give valid consent to medical treatment; it does not give the child a right to veto the administration of treatment. A competent child's refusal to undergo treatment can be overridden by a person with parental responsibility. What is more, whether it is a competent minor's consent or refusal that is in question, his or her decision can be overridden by a court exercising its inherent jurisdiction or, it seems, on an application for an order under Section 8 of the Children Act 1989.[74]

In *Re R (A Minor) (Wardship: Medical Treatment)*,[75] the court was asked to consider whether a 15-year-old girl was entitled to refuse treatment in the form of medication. She was admitted to an adolescent psychiatric unit and diagnosed as psychotic. The unit made it clear that, if she was to remain a patient in its care, it should have a free hand in the administration of medication, whether she consented to it or not. During a lucid interval, the girl indicated that she did not wish to take the drugs prescribed for her. A consultant psychiatrist reported that if she failed to continue with the treatment, her more florid psychotic behaviour was likely to recur. The court found that she was not competent, even if she was capable of passing the *Gillick* test on good days; her fluctuating mental disability rendered her incompetent. In any event, whether she was competent or not, the wardship court was empowered to override her decision. Lord Donaldson commented *obiter* on the implications of the *Gillick* case and on the question whether a minor could validly refuse treatment:

> [C]onsent by itself creates no obligation to treat. It is merely a key which unlocks a door. Furthermore, whilst in the case of an adult of full capacity there will usually only be one keyholder, namely the patient, in the ordinary family unit where a young child is the patient there will be two keyholders, namely the parents, with a several as well as a joint right to turn the key and unlock the door. If the parents disagree, one consenting and the other refusing, the doctor will be presented with a professional and ethical, but not with a legal, problem because, if he has the consent of one authorised person, treatment will not without more constitute a trespass or a criminal assault. ... (p 196)

---

[74] The use of the inherent jurisdiction is said to be appropriate at least in relation to older children (CAAC 1992/93 p 68). The wardship jurisdiction was successfully invoked to override a minor's refusal to undergo medical treatment in *Re R (A Minor) (Wardship: Medical Treatment)* [1992] 1 FLR 190. Alternatively, proceedings can be brought under the inherent jurisdiction or under s 8, perhaps in the form a specific issue order (see *Re K, W and H (Minors) (Medical Treatment)* [1993] 1 FLR 854, 859; *Re HG (Specific Issue Order: Sterilisation)* [1993] 1 FLR 587). In *Re O (A Minor) (Medical Treatment)* [1993] 2 FLR 149, the court took the view that applications such as that in question, concerning an infant child of Jehovah's Witnesses requiring blood transfusions, should ordinarily be made under the inherent jurisdiction. Where a local authority is the applicant and is seeking a result that could be achieved by means of a specific issue order, the use of the court's inherent jurisdiction is unnecessary and inappropriate. In any event, cases where the fundamental beliefs of the parents might be overridden should be heard *inter partes* and in the High Court wherever possible *(Re R (A Minor) (Blood Transfusion)* [1993] 2 FLR 757). See further Children Act Advisory Committee Report (1992/93 pp 67–68). See, on the role of the local authority in safeguarding children whose health is at risk, Bainham (2005) pp 323ff.

[75] [1992] 1 FLR 190.

... Lord Scarman [in *Gillick*] was discussing the parents' right '*to determine* whether or not their minor child below the age of 16 will have medical treatment' (my emphasis). ..A right of determination is wider than a right to consent. The parents can only have a right of determination if *either* the child has no right to consent, ie is not a keyholder, *or* the parents hold a master key which could nullify the child's consent. I do not understand Lord Scarman to be saying that, if a child was '*Gillick*-competent', to adopt the convenient phrase used in argument, the parents ceased to have an independent right of consent, as contrasted with ceasing to have a right of determination, ie a veto. In a case in which the '*Gillick*-competent' child refuses treatment, but the parents consent, that consent *enables* treatment to be undertaken lawfully, but in no way determines that the child shall be so treated. In a case in which the positions are reversed, it is the child's consent which is the enabling factor, and again the parents' refusal of consent is not determinative. If Lord Scarman intended to go further than this and to say that in the case of a '*Gillick*-competent' child, a parent has no right either to consent or to refuse consent, his remarks were obiter, because the only question in issue was Mrs Gillick's alleged right of veto. Furthermore, I consider that they would have been wrong.[76]

(pp 197–98, emphasis in original)

**Q** Is the *Gillick* test relevant to determining the capacity of those who are mentally ill?[77]

**Q** Is the interpretation of Lord Scarman's judgment persuasive? Douglas (1992 p 575) suggests that, if a parent has no right to 'determine' whether a child should undergo treatment, it does not make sense to say that that parent can give valid consent to it. She also argues that to override a refusal means having to interfere with a person's intellectual and physical autonomy and that, therefore, a person's refusal should be given greater weight than a consent. Do you agree?

Lord Donaldson went on to consider the power of the court:

In many cases of wardship, the parents or other guardians will be left to make decisions for the child, subject only to standing instructions to refer reserved matters to the court ... and to the court's right and, in appropriate cases, duty to override the decision of the parents or other guardians. If it can override such consents, as it undoubtedly can, I see no reason whatsoever why it should not be able, and in an appropriate case willing, to override decisions by '*Gillick*-competent' children who are its wards or in respect of whom applications are made for, for example, s 8 orders under the Children Act 1989. (p 199)

Lord Donaldson developed this line of reasoning further and applied it to a case involving a girl aged 16 and so competent in terms of the 1969 Act. In *In Re W (A Minor) (Medical Treatment: Court's Jurisdiction)*,[78] the local authority sought authorisation from the court, exercising its inherent jurisdiction, to treat a girl suffering from anorexia nervosa without her consent.[79] This time, however, Lord Donaldson referred only briefly to the position of parents. He conceded that his interpretation of Lord Scarman's judgment in *Gillick* might be wrong and that, as far as the common law was concerned, Lord Scarman might have said that the consent of those with parental responsibility would not be effective in the face of the minor's refusal. However, he went on, the question

---

[76] Staughton LJ doubted this interpretation and, like Farquharson LJ, focused on the minor's competence and the power of the court in wardship proceedings.

[77] Fortin argues that mental health legislation could be seen as providing better safeguards for patients' rights than cases like *Re R* (Fortin 2003 pp 142ff).

[78] [1992] 3 WLR 758.

[79] There was a care order in force which meant that she could not be made a ward of court. See p 762.

before him concerned the power of the court to authorise treatment, something not decided in *Gillick*.

The first question he addressed was whether Section 8 of the Family Law Reform Act 1969 had the effect of depriving those with parental responsibility of the power to consent to the treatment of the young person. His analysis of the wording of the provision and a review of its history[80] persuaded him that it did not and that parents retained the ability to give valid consent. Power to give valid consent may vest concurrently in more than one person:

> On reflection I regret my use in *In Re R* ... of the keyholder analogy because keys can lock as well as unlock. I now prefer the analogy of the legal 'flak jacket' which protects the doctor from claims by the litigious whether he acquires it from his patient who may be a minor over the age of 16, or a '*Gillick* competent' child under that age or from another person having parental responsibilities which include a right to consent to treatment of the minor. Anyone who gives him a flak jacket (that is, consent) may take it back, but the doctor only needs one and so long as he continues to have one he has the legal right to proceed ... .
>
> Hair-raising possibilities were canvassed of abortions being carried out by doctors in reliance upon the consent of parents and despite the refusal of consent by 16- and 17-year-olds. Whilst this may be possible as a matter of law, I do not see any likelihood taking account of medical ethics, unless the abortion was truly in the best interests of the child. ...Despite the passing of the Children Act 1989, the inherent jurisdiction of the court could still be invoked in such a case to prevent an abortion which was contrary to the interests of the minor.
>
> (pp 767–68)

> **Q** Should it be left to medical ethics to curtail legal powers that might be seen as too far-reaching? Who determines whether the abortion is in the child's best interests? Fortin (2003 p 141) suggests that Articles 3, 5 and 8 of the ECHR would probably protect a pregnant teenager from undergoing an abortion against her will. Construct an argument along those lines.

Lord Donaldson went on to affirm the importance of taking into account the wishes of young people. The welfare of young people, he said, requires that they be given 'the maximum degree of decision-making which is prudent'.[81] Balcombe LJ in turn remarked that it would normally be in the best interests of a competent minor to respect his or her 'integrity as a human being and not lightly override its decision on such a personal matter as medical treatment'.[82]

> **Q** How does this rationale for respecting young people's decisions differ from the reasons we respect adult's decisions?

Nevertheless, irrespective of the child's capacity, the court has the power to impose whatever decision best serves the child's interests.[83] Lord Donaldson suggested that

---

[80] For criticism of the court's analysis, see Thornton (1993).

[81] P 770.

[82] P 776.

[83] *In Re W (A Minor) (Medical Treatment: Court's Jurisdiction)* [1992] 3 WLR 758, 776. See also *Re L (Medical Treatment: Gillick Competency)* [1998] 2 FLR 810, 813. Bridge (1999a p 594) suggests that a court would be unwilling to overrule a young person's objections where the proposed procedure is complex, ongoing and would require the patient's co-operation.

anorexia is a condition that is capable of destroying the ability to make an informed choice. But in any event, he held, the court could override W's choice:

> There is ample authority for the proposition that the inherent powers of the court under its parens patriae jurisdiction are theoretically limitless and that they certainly extend beyond the powers of a natural parent. ...There can therefore be no doubt that it has power to override the refusal of a minor, whether over the age of 16 or under that age but '*Gillick* competent'. (p 769)

His summary of his decision included the following points:

> 4. Section 8 of the Family Law Reform Act 1969 gives minors who have attained the age of 16 a right to consent to surgical, medical or dental treatment. Such a consent cannot be overridden by those with parental responsibility for the minor. It can, however, be overridden by the court. ...
> 5. A minor of any age who is '*Gillick* competent' in the context of particular treatment has a right to consent to that treatment which again cannot be overridden by those with parental responsibility, but can be overridden by the court. ...
> 6. No minor of whatever age has power by refusing consent to treatment to override a consent to treatment by someone who has parental responsibility for the minor and a fortiori a consent by the court. Nevertheless such a refusal is a very important consideration in making clinical judgments and for parents and the court in deciding whether themselves to give consent. Its importance increases with the age and maturity of the minor.[84] (p 772)

The 'theoretically limitless'[85] power of the high court exercising its inherent jurisdiction was again successfully invoked in *South Glamorgan County Council v W and B*.[86] In that case, it was held that Section 38(6) of the Children Act 1989, giving children the right to refuse to submit to an examination or assessment, did not in any way affect the inherent jurisdiction of the court. A competent minor subject to an interim care order could be assessed, treated and restrained against her will. The inherent jurisdiction can also be used to authorise the detention of a minor in a clinic and to use reasonable force to do so.[87]

The approach of the court in cases such as *In Re W* meets with the approval of Lowe and Juss (1993): [88]

> After all, it is perhaps all too easily forgotten that, in the final analysis, a child is still only a child. Moreover, the entire thesis based on the premise of Lord Scarman's child of 'sufficient understanding and intelligence' who is able 'to understand fully what is proposed' is, it is submitted, in one sense open to question. Is a child of sufficient understanding and intelligence if he or she acts irrationally? Is autonomy meaningful if it is irrational? ... To those who question how a child can be held able to give a valid consent yet be unable to exercise a power of veto, we

---

[84] In *Re P (Medical Treatment: Best Interests)* [2003] EWHC Fam 2327; [2004] 2 FLR 1117, the court overrode the objections of a 17 year old Jehovah's witness to treatment with blood or blood products. The court declared itself reluctant to overrule his wishes but did so on the basis of his best interests.

[85] For discussion about the inherent jurisdiction and the circumstances in which the court will not exercise its jurisdiction, see Cretney, *et al*, (2002) pp 625–30.

[86] [1993] 1 FLR 574.

[87] *Re C (Detention: Medical Treatment)* [1997] 2 FLR 180. The 16-year-old minor in that case was found to be incompetent under the test set out in *Re C (Refusal of Treatment)* [1994] 1 FLR 31. This test comprises three stages: (1) comprehending and retaining treatment information, (2) believing it, and (3) weighing it in the balance to arrive at a choice. However in the light of the decision in *In Re W*, the court could have made the order even if she were competent. See, on this case, Fortin (2003) pp 150–51.

[88] See also Fortin (2003) pp 128–29.

would reply that there *is* a rational distinction to be made between giving consent and with-holding it. We must start with the assumption that a doctor will act in the best interests of his patient. Hence, if the doctor believes that a particular treatment is necessary for his patient, it is perfectly rational for the law to facilitate this as easily as possible and hence allow a '*Gillick* competent' child to give a valid consent, and also to protect the child against parents opposed to what is professionally considered to be in its best medical interests. In contrast, it is surely right for the law to be reluctant to allow a *child* of whatever age to be able to veto treatment designed for his or her benefit particularly if a refusal would lead to the child's death or perma-nent damage. In other words, the clear and consistent policy of the law is to protect the child against wrong-headed parents and against itself with the final safeguard, as *Re W* unequivo-cally establishes, of giving the court the last word in cases of dispute.

(pp 871–72, emphasis in original)

Bridge, reviewing the case law, also argues that it is right that the courts should be able to override objections by parents and young people to treatment in a life or death situa-tion; as a society, we take the view that a young person should be given the opportunity to grow up to make up his or her own mind. 'In a life and death situation the court, as society's representative, is unlikely to allow parents, or the almost competent teenager, to choose death,' she says (Bridge 1997 p 318). Yet she is very uneasy about the fact that parents can consent effectively to treatment to which the young person objects. She would prefer use of the mental health legislation or court authorisation for secure accommodation to detain a child, for example. As the law stands, she maintains, 'the treatment of young people remains in the hands of parents, health care professionals and ultimately medical ethics' and parents, in particular, occupy too powerful a position (pp 313 and 329).

> **Q** It is established law that the capacity of an adult cannot be impugned solely on the ground that the decision in question is irrational.[89] Why should it be different where a young person is concerned? Who decides whether the parent or child is being 'wrong-headed' as Lowe and Juss call it? Could there be a divergence of opinions on this question?[90]

The effect of the cases is to leave intact the presumption created by Section 8 of the 1969 Act[91] that children over the age of 16 have the capacity to consent to medical treatment, enabling a doctor willing to do so to administer it.[92] However a refusal to undergo treat-ment will be ineffective if overridden by someone with parental responsibility.[93] In the case of a minor under the age of 16, the law does not confer competence unless the child passes the *Gillick* test. If the child is deemed *Gillick*/Fraser competent, he or she is in a

---

[89] See pp 613–614.

[90] See Douglas (1992) p 576.

[91] See Brazier and Bridge (1996) p 90.

[92] But no doctor can be required to treat a child, whether by the court, the parents, the child or anyone else: *Re R (A Minor) (Wardship: Medical Treatment)* [1992] 1 FLR 190, 200; *R v Cambridge District Health Authority, ex parte B* [1995] 1 FLR 1055; *Re C (Medical Treatment)* [1998] 1 FLR 384.

[93] As one commentator observes, however, it is doubtful whether a doctor would be willing to carry out intrusive treatment against the wishes of an articulate and intelligent teenager: Downie (1997) p 500. Fortin reports that, although the law enables them to do so, the medical profession and the BMA are loath to consider treating adolescents against their will (2003 p 130). Legally, a doctor would not be exposed to liability and need not apply to court for authorisation to administer medical treatment to a *Gillick*/Fraser competent minor who refuses consent, provided he or she has the consent of a holder of parental responsibility: *Re K, W and H (Minors) (Medical Treatment)* [1993] 1 FLR 854. Since this case involved authorisation for treatment in a *future* emergency, it is submitted that medical treatment in a non-emergency situation is covered by the judg-ment.

position analogous to that of the competent minor over the age of 16. In either case, an unwilling adolescent can be subjected to treatment pursuant to the consent of a parent who may not be the best judge of that young person's best interests. And not all would assume that doctors always know best. Doctors are, however, unlikely to treat too readily. As Herring says, a doctor can treat a patient only if he or she believes that this would be in the patient's best interests and it would be unusual for a doctor to decide it would be in the interests of a 16 or 17 year old to treat them against their will (2004 p 304). Also, any decision about the medical treatment of a child, whether made by a parent or by the child, can be overturned by the court. In practice, though, most cases where a parent consents to treatment will not be brought before the court.[94]

Fortin (2003) argues that an adolescent forced to undergo treatment may be able to invoke the ECHR successfully. Article 8 guarantees the right to 'physical and moral integrity' but, Fortin says, the medical team could contend that the treatment is necessary to protect the patient's health under Article 8(2) (2003 p 130). She suggests, however, that the patient could rely on Article 3 because forcing treatment on a patient could involve 'inhuman or degrading treatment'. This is the case as regards competent and incompetent adults[95] and, according to Fortin, the same principle could apply to minors (*ibid*).[96] Similarly, it might be possible to rely on Article 5, which protects the right to liberty and security of the person, in cases involving restraint or detention (pp 130–31). She concludes that 'the principle established in *Re R* and *Re W* [and the *South Glamorgan* case][97] might be vulnerable to challenges brought under the Human Rights Act 1998, based on Articles 3 and 5, combined with Article 14, arguing that minors require similar protection from forcible treatment as do adult patients' (p 131). However, she goes on to suggest that courts faced with adolescents refusing to accept life-saving treatment might be able to invoke Article 2, which creates a duty to take reasonable steps to preserve life. This could outweigh the patients' rights under Articles 3 and 5 (*ibid*). However, a court might be circumspect about asserting its duty under Article 2 where the patient is competent in law (p 132).

In summary then, the law recognises, to some extent, the autonomy interests of the minor in the context of medical decisions. However the child's wishes are not decisive. The ultimate arbiter is, in those cases of dispute that are brought before it, the court. And although the court takes cognisance of the child's views, it makes its decision on the basis of the welfare principle. It may, it is true, choose to uphold the child's wishes rather than those of the parent. Yet the effect of the case law, by allowing the mature minor's wishes to be overridden, may be said to entrench paternalism in the law.[98]

If she is *Gillick* competent, Cindy's consent to undergo the proposed surgical procedure cannot be overridden by her mother. Linda[99] may, therefore wish to apply to the court for an order. A court will take account of a competent minor's wishes and

---

[94] Balcombe LJ said in *Re W (A Minor) (Medical Treatment: Court's Jurisdiction)* [1992] 3 WLR 758, 782 that in the event of a conflict, where the child refuses consent but a parent gives it, the jurisdiction of the court should always be invoked. However, it has since been held that a doctor with consent from someone with parental responsibility need not bring legal proceedings (*Re K, W and H (Minors) (Medical Treatment)* [1993] 1 FLR 854, 859).

[95] See *Herczegfalvy v Austria* (1992) 15 EHRR 437.

[96] See *R (On the Application of Burke) v The General Medical Council* [2004] EWHC Admin 1879; [2004] 2 FLR 1121, paras 58, 80 145–49, 178, where the court explicitly refers to babies as well as incompetent adults.

[97] See Fortin (2003) p 150.

[98] See Lowe and Douglas (1998) p 250.

[99] An application to court to resolve a dispute can also be made by the minor concerned. A competent minor can apply to court independently while one who is not competent must do so through a next friend. See below p 631ff.

'approach its decision with a strong predilection to give effect to the child's wishes'. Indeed, courts will also regard an incompetent child's wishes as material.[100] However, in the end the decision will turn on what the court perceives to be Cindy's best interests.

## V. DECISIONS ABOUT EDUCATION—THE COURT'S JURISDICTION

### Cindy's Education

Choice of school falls within the scope of parental responsibility.[101] Linda, because she has Cindy living with her, is in a position to put her decision into effect. Whether or not William has parental responsibility, if he wishes to contest any course of action Linda proposes to take in relation to Cindy's education, he has to seek a court order. Similarly, Cindy or Doris need to invoke the jurisdiction of the court to challenge Linda's decision. The court's decision will be dictated by what it sees as being Cindy's best interests.

### The Court's Jurisdiction

Where a child's upbringing is in question, proceedings may be instituted under the Children Act 1989, under the inherent jurisdiction or in wardship. However, where possible, the procedures available under the Children Act 1989 should be used.[102]

Disputes concerning education can be dealt with adequately by means of an order under Section 8 of the Children Act 1989 in the form of a prohibited steps order or a specific issue order. Section 8 orders may be sought in the course of existing family proceedings or, as would be the case here, in a free-standing application.[103]

### Specific Issue Orders

Section 8(1) provides that: ' "a specific issue order" means an order giving directions for the purpose of determining a specific question which has arisen, or which may arise, in connection with any aspect of parental responsibility for a child.'

The court is empowered to give directions in order to resolve disputes. An order must relate to matters encompassed by parental responsibility such as medical treatment or education.[104] However, an order should be sought only for important matters. In *Re C (A*

---

100 In *Re W (A Minor) (Medical Treatment; Court's Jurisdiction)* [1992] 3 WLR 758, 776.

101 See further on education and parental responsibility, Cretney, *et al*, (2002) pp 537–38. See, on education generally, Fortin (2003) pp 161ff; and on parents' responsibilities to secure their children's education, ch 4 above pp 176ff.

102 For a full discussion of jurisdictional issues, see Gilmore (2004); Bainham (2005) pp 480–83 and pp 532–37; Herring (2004) pp 426–29 and pp 553–54; Cretney, *et al*, (2002) pp 601–2.

103 For full discussion of applications for s 8 orders, see Cretney, *et al*, (2002) p 610ff.

104 *Re R (A Minor) (Blood Transfusion)* [1993] 2 FLR 757; *Re O (A Minor) (Medical Treatment)* [1993] 2 FLR 149; *Re A (Specific Issue Order: Parental Dispute)* [2001] 1 FLR 121. See Cretney, *et al*, (2002) para 19–020). A specific issue order may also be sought in relation to a change of surname: *Re PC (Change of*

*Minor) (Leave to Seek Section 8 Orders)*[105] the court refused an application for leave made by a child wishing to go on holiday against her parents' wishes, indicating that orders should not be sought for trivial matters.[106] Orders can be sought in circumstances that, before the Children Act 1989, would have necessitated wardship proceedings[107]; they can be used to address serious and sensitive questions. In *Re HG (Specific Issue Order: Sterilisation)*,[108] the court was asked to decide whether a young woman with limited mental capacities should be sterilised. Although there was no dispute between the parents, said the court, this was a matter that could and should be brought before it under Section 8.

### Prohibited Steps Order

A prohibited steps order is defined in Section 8(1) as: 'an order that no step which could be taken by a parent in meeting his parental responsibility for a child, and which is of a kind specified in the order, shall be taken by any person without the consent of the court.'

This order is modelled on the wardship jurisdiction.[109] A prohibited steps order is less wide-ranging in nature than wardship, however. Whereas the effect of wardship is to require any important decisions relating to the child to be brought before the court, a prohibited steps order places only those matters named in the order under the court's supervision.

While an order may be directed at any person, not just someone with parental responsibility, it can only be made in respect of those steps that could be taken by a parent in meeting his or her parental responsibility for a child. So, for example, an order can be used to prevent someone, who is not party to the proceedings and who does not live with a child, from having contact with the child.[110] However, it cannot forbid parents to have contact with each other, because contact between parents has nothing to do with the exercise of parental responsibility.[111] It can also be used to prevent a child from being taken out of the jurisdiction[112] or to forbid a change of school (Masson and Morris 1992 p 32).[113]

It has been suggested that, because an order can prohibit only those steps that a parent could take in exercising parental responsibility, it cannot extend into those spheres where the minor is mature enough to make the relevant decision (Cretney, *et al*, 2002 p 595 n 67). For example, Masson and Morris (1992 p 32) contend that 'an order could stop a person allowing a child to have cosmetic surgery or engage in a dangerous sport

---

*Surname)* [1997] 2 FLR 730. In *Re HG (Specific Issue Order: Sterilisation)* ([1993] 1 FLR 587, 593) the court stressed that the notion of parental responsibility should not be interpreted restrictively.

[105] [1994] 1 FLR 26.

[106] See also *Re C (Residence: Child's Application for Leave)* [1995] 1 FLR 927, 931.

[107] Cases where parents withhold consent to medical treatment may be brought before the court by a local authority where the child is at risk. See *Re R (A Minor) (Blood Transfusion)* [1993] 2 FLR 757, where the court held that a specific issue order was the appropriate mechanism for deciding whether the child of Jehovah's Witnesses should receive a blood transfusion. See *Re O (A Minor) (Medical Treatment)* [1993] 2 FLR 149 for a case where the court regarded the inherent jurisdiction as more appropriate.

[108] [1993] 1 FLR 587.

[109] Law Commission (1988b) para 4.20.

[110] *Re H (Prohibited Steps Order)* [1995] 1 WLR 667.

[111] *Croydon London Borough Council v A (No 1)* [1992] 2 FLR 341.

[112] See s 1 of the Child Abduction Act 1984 and s 13 of the Children Act 1989 for consent requirements for the removal of a child from the jurisdiction.

[113] See *Re G (Parental Responsibility: Education)* [1994] 2 FLR 964.

but would not be effective to prevent a mature young person making such a decision for himself'. Yet the wording of the section refers to the steps that could be taken by *a* parent and not *the* parent. This could be interpreted as referring to the parental responsibility of parents generally, rather than to the powers of the particular parent concerned, whose child might happen to be a mature minor. Moreover, in his comments in *Re R*, Lord Donaldson indicated that the court, 'in the exercise of its wardship or statutory jurisdiction', has the power to override the decisions of a *Gillick* competent minor as well as those of parents.[114] This suggests that the courts may be unwilling to accept an interpretation constraining their powers under Section 8 in the manner suggested. If they do, it will remain open to a party to invoke the inherent jurisdiction.

## *Section 8 Orders and Education*

It is clear, then, disputes about education can be dealt with by means of these orders and, as Gilmore (2004) notes, a number of reported specific issue cases are concerned with education. He examines the factors that are taken into consideration by the courts in deciding such cases:

> Each case very much depends on its own facts, but factors that have been highlighted in the case-law as relevant in such cases include: the timing of any proposed change of school and its effect on the child; the distance, and ease of travelling, to any relevant school(s); and, where the dispute is as to whether the education should be publicly or privately funded, the parents' current and ongoing ability to meet any school fees.[115] It has been said that where a child has recently changed school, compelling reasons will be required for further disruption to the child's schooling.[116]
> Some of the disputes have a bicultural dimension, where parents of different nationalities and/or cultures are seeking to ensure that their own culture is reflected in the child's education. In general, the courts appear, in such cases, to have attempted to ensure some balance regarding the child's access to both cultures.[117] (pp 379–80)

Gilmore (2004) raises the question of whether the court awarding a specific issue order has to make the decision itself or whether it can delegate decision-making power to someone else such as one of the parents. The case law on this is not clear.

In *H-D (Children)*,[118] Hale LJ refused permission to appeal against a specific issue order which stated that the mother could control the choice of the children's schools and religious upbringing.[119] Similarly, in *Re W (Children) (Education: Choice of School)*[120] the Court of Appeal approved an order that the children should attend the school of the mother's choice, although Hale LJ remarked that the purpose of specific issue orders is normally to 'decide the issue and not give the right of exclusive decision to one parent or the other'.[121] In *Re H (A Child: Parental Responsibility)*,[122] Thorpe LJ made a specific

---

114 [1992] 1 FLR 190, 200. See also 199.
115 See *Re W (Children) (Education: Choice of School* [2002] EWCA Civ 1411; [2002] 3 FCR 473.
116 *Ibid.*
117 See *Re A (Specific Issue Order: Parental Dispute)* [2001] 1 FLR 121.
118 [2001] EWCA Civ 402.
119 Para 13.
120 [2002] EWCA Civ 1411; [2002] 3 FCR 473.
121 At para 5. Thorpe LJ concurred.
122 [2002] EWCA Civ 542.

issue order saying that the mother should have sole responsibility for any decisions concerning the medical treatment of the child.[123]

Yet Thorpe LJ took a very different position in *Re P (Parental Dispute: Judicial Determination)*.[124] He allowed an application for permission to appeal against an order directing that questions about the children's education arising in the future should be finally determined by the mother following consultation with the father. He took the view that this amounted to 'the plainest failure to adjudicate'.[125] The order was 'unprincipled'[126] and the result an abdication of the court's 'primary obligation to decide'.[127] The final decision had to be made by the judge and it was not permissible to 'appoint one of the parents with more or less absolute responsibility',[128] so empowering one and disempowering the other.[129]

Reviewing these cases and noting the potential for contradictory interpretations of Thorpe LJ's judgments, Gilmore suggests that *Re P* should not be read as precluding entirely an order in the terms granted by the court below. He ventures that the decision was 'unprincipled' because the court below had failed to consider the question before it and simply delegated the decision. He argues that a specific issue order 'can and ought to be able to, empower others to determine a question'. But he concedes that the position is not entirely clear (2004 pp 370–71).

Whether or not the order has to be framed in specific terms or whether it can be framed more generally, a specific issue order (or a prohibited steps order) is available in principle. It remains to consider, however, who has standing to apply for such an order.

*Power to Make Section 8 Orders*

Section 10 of the Children Act 1989 sets out the court's powers:

Power of court to make section 8 orders

10.—(1) In any family proceedings in which a question arises with respect to the welfare of any child, the court may make a section 8 order with respect to the child if—
(a)    an application for the order has been made by a person who—
       (i)   is entitled to apply for a section 8 order with respect to the child; or
       (ii)  has obtained the leave of the court to make the application; or
(b)    the court considers that the order should be made even though no such application has been made.

(2) The court may also make a section 8 order with respect to any child on the application of a person who—
(a)    is entitled to apply for a section 8 order with respect to the child; or
(b)    has obtained the leave of the court to make the application.

(3) This section is subject to the restrictions imposed by section 9.

---

[123] Para 16. A prohibited steps order was also made preventing the father from locating or attempting to locate the address of the mother and child.
[124] [2002] EWCA Civ 1627; [2003] 1 FLR 286.
[125] Para 6.
[126] Para 11.
[127] Para 8. See also para 11.
[128] Para 11.
[129] Para 12.

(4) The following persons are entitled to apply to the court for any section 8 order with respect to a child—

(a)   any parent or guardian [guardian or special guardian] of the child;

[(aa) any person who by virtue of section 4A has parental responsibility for the child];[130]

(b)   any person in whose favour a residence order is in force with respect to the child ... .

(8) Where the person applying for leave to make an application for a section 8 order is the child concerned,[131] the court may only grant leave if it is satisfied that he has sufficient understanding to make the proposed application for the section 8 order.

(9) Where the person applying for leave to make an application for a section 8 order is not the child concerned, the court shall, in deciding whether or not to grant leave, have particular regard to—

(a)   the nature of the proposed application for the section 8 order;

(b)   the applicant's connection with the child; [132]

(c)   any risk there might be of that proposed application disrupting the child's life[133] to such an extent that he would be harmed[134] by it; and

(d)   where the child is being looked after by a local authority—

    (i)   the authority's plans for the child's future; and

    (ii)  the wishes and feelings of the child's parents.

Section 9 limits the circumstances under which and the duration for which an order may be made:

9(5) No court shall exercise its powers to make a specific issue order or prohibited steps order—

(a)   with a view to achieving a result which could be achieved by making a residence or contact order; or

(b)   in any way which is denied to the High Court (by section 100(2)) in the exercise of its inherent jurisdiction with respect to children.

(6) No court shall make any section 8 order which is to have effect for a period which will end after the child has reached the age of sixteen unless it is satisfied that the circumstances of the case are exceptional.

(7) No court shall make any section 8 order, other than one varying or discharging such an order, with respect to a child who has reached the age of sixteen unless it is satisfied that the circumstances of the case are exceptional.

The legislation distinguishes between different categories of applicants for Section 8 orders: those who are entitled to apply as of right and those who can apply with the leave of the court. This distinction is designed to control access to the courts. It makes it possible to screen out unmeritorious applications or potentially disruptive litigation

---

[130] The words in brackets were inserted by the Adoption and Children Act 2002 and were not yet in force at the time of writing.

[131] See, on the European Convention on the Exercise of Children's Rights 1996, which promotes rights of participation in proceedings for children, Bainham (2005) p 577–79. See, on the ECHR, Bainham (2005) pp 579–80; *Sahin v Germany*; *Sommerfeld v Germany* [2003] 2 FLR 671.

[132] The more meaningful and important the connection between the applicant and child, the greater the weight to be given to this factor: *Re M (Care: Contact: Grandmother's Application for Leave)* [1995] 2 FLR 86, 95.

[133] The court has considered not just the effect of the application but also the consequences if the application were to succeed (*Re A (A Minor) (Residence Order: Leave to Apply)* [1993] 1 FLR 425, 428). However in *Re H (Children)* [2003] EWCA Civ 369; 2003 WL 1202504, the Court of Appeal stated that it was the risk of disruption caused by the litigation, and not the possible outcome, that should be considered (para 26).

[134] 'Harm' is as defined in s 31(9): *Re A (Minors) (Residence Order)* [1992] 3 All ER 872, 876; *Re M (Care: Contact: Grandmother's Application for Leave)* [1995] 2 FLR 86, 96.

while at the same time enabling anyone with a genuine interest in the child's welfare to apply for an order.[135] In deciding whether to grant leave, the court should not focus on the merits of the applicant's case; instead it should make its decision on the basis of the checklist in Section 10(9).[136] The court must consider all the factors set out in Section 10(9) and is entitled also to consider the welfare checklist in Section 1(3).[137] Because an application for leave does not fall within Section 1(1), however, the child's welfare is not the paramount consideration.[138] In the case of an application for leave made by a child, the best interests of the child are a significant consideration[139] but Section 10(9) does not apply.

**Q** Under which sections could William apply for an order? Cindy? Doris?

**Q** How would you frame a specific issue order in this case, whether sought by William, Cindy or Doris?

**Q** How would you frame a prohibited steps order in this case, whether applied for by William, Cindy or Doris?

## VI. APPLICATIONS MADE BY CHILDREN[140]

*Party Status and Separate Representation.*

Children can be given party status and separate representation if the court considers this appropriate.[141] Ordinarily, children cannot bring or defend proceedings in their own right; they need to be represented by an adult. If a child is making a claim, the case must be conducted by a next friend and, when a child is defending a claim,[142] the case must be conducted by a guardian *ad litem*,[143] usually a CAFCASS officer or some other person appointed by the court.[144] The functions of these representatives are described in *Re CT (A Minor) (Wardship: Representation)*:

---

[135] See DoH 1991c para 2.43.

[136] Case law has established that s 10(9) governs the decision whether to grant leave rather than the old test of an arguable case: *Re J (A Child) (Leave to Issue Application for Residence Order)* [2002] EWCA Civ 1346; [2003] 1 FLR 114; *Re H (Children)* [2003] EWCA Civ 369; 2003 WL 1202504.

[137] *North Yorkshire County Council v G* [1993] 2 FLR 732; See also *R (On the Application of Burke) v The General Medical Council and Others* [2004] EWHC Admin 1879; [2004] 2 FLR 1121, paras 58, 80 145–49, 178, where the court explicitly refers to babies as well as incompetent adults *Re A (A Minor) (Residence Order: Leave to Apply)* [1993] 1 FLR 425, 428.

[138] *Re A and W (Minors) (Residence Order: Leave to Apply)* [1992] 2 FLR 154; *Re A (Minors) (Residence Order)* [1992] 3 All ER 872; *Re SC (A Minor) (Leave to Seek Residence Order)* [1994] 1 FLR 96. (It appears that *Johnson J in Re C (A Minor) (Leave to Seek S 8 Orders)* [1994] 1 FLR 26 erred on this point.)

[139] Again, the welfare of the child is not of paramount importance. See *Re C (Residence: Child's Application for Leave)* [1995] 1 FLR 927, 931.

[140] See for detailed discussion, Fortin (2003) ch 7.

[141] Family Proceedings Rules 1991, R 9.5.

[142] RSC Ord 80 and Family Proceedings Rules 1991, R 9.2.

[143] This is not to be confused with the children's guardian who is the person, normally a CAFCASS officer, charged with conveying the child's wishes to the court and giving an opinion on the child's best interests in (mainly) public law cases.

[144] See Family Proceedings Rules 1991, R 9.5. The National Youth Advocacy Service (NYAS) has represented children, mainly in relation to residence and contact disputes between parents (Fowler and Stewart 2005).

A next friend or guardian does not in those circumstances act merely as the child's representative. He has an independent function to perform, and must act in what he believes to be the minor's best interests, even if that should involve acting in contravention of the wishes of a minor who is old enough to articulate views of his own … . Those functions can be performed by anyone who has no interest in the proceedings adverse to those of the child: there is no need for a next friend or guardian ad litem in private law proceedings to be professionally qualified … . In practice, however, problems of representation and legal aid make it difficult for a lay person to act … . He owes a loyalty which has by its very nature to be divided: to the child whose views he must fully and fairly represent; and to the court, which it is his duty to assist in achieving the overriding or paramount objective of promoting the child's best interests.

(pp 280–81)[145]

The Family Proceedings Rules have been altered in ways that may make separate representation more common in future,[146] and while there seems to be increasing readiness on the part of the judiciary to hear children's views,[147] courts have tended to use their power to order separate party status sparingly.[148] Although as Fortin says, judges will now be alive to the possibility of a challenge under the HRA if they refuse separate representation (2003 p 213), recent developments appear to be designed to restrict children's participation as separate litigants. In view of the potential for expense and delay resulting from separate representation, the President of the Family Division has issued a Practice Direction[149] which applies in cases involving children who are not judged competent in terms of FPR 1991, r9.2A[150] and whose cases do not qualify within the category of specified proceedings under Section 41 of the Children Act 1989. The Practice Direction sets out the legal position:

[1] The proper conduct and disposal of proceedings concerning a child which are not specified proceedings within the meaning of s 41 of the Children Act 1989 may require the child to be made a party. Rule 9.5 of the Family Proceedings Rules 1991, SI 1991/1247 provides for the appointment of a guardian ad litem (a guardian)[151] for a child party unless the child is of sufficient understanding and can participate as a party in the proceedings without a guardian, as permitted by r 9.2A of the 1991 rules.

[2] Making the child a party to the proceedings is a step that will be taken only in cases which involve an issue of significant difficulty and consequently will occur in only a minority of cases. Before taking the decision to make the child a party, consideration should be given to whether an alternative route might be preferable, such as asking an officer of the Children and Family

---

145 [1993] 2 FLR 278.

146 The Family Proceedings Rules provide that the Child and Family Reporter is under a duty in every family proceedings case to advise the court whether it 'is in the best interests of the child to be made a party to the proceedings' (Family Proceedings Rules 1991, R 4.11B(5) and (6)). In addition, a new s 41(6A) Children Act 1989 (inserted by s 122 Adoption and Children Act 2002) means that some children involved in s 8 cases may have the possibility of separate representation by a children's guardian together with a legal advocate, rather than simply a guardian *ad litem*. See, for discussion, Fortin (2003) p 221–22. See also below p 638.

147 See *Re A (Contact: Separate Representation)* [2001] 1 FLR 715, 721. See also Dame Butler-Sloss with Fiddy (2001). But see Douglas, *et al,* (2000) p 191.

148 See Bellamy and Lord (2003). See also Dame Butler-Sloss with Fiddy (2001 p 14). In *Re A (Contact: Separate Representation)* [2001] 1 FLR 715, Hale LJ stated that in cases where parents are separating, children need to be heard and may need someone 'to orchestrate an investigation of the case on their behalf' (p 721). However this does not, she said, mean that they need separate representation. Often, the parents or the CAFCASS officer can meet their needs (*ibid*).

149 *Practice Direction (Family Proceedings: Representation of Children)* [2004] 2 FCR 124.

150 See below.

151 The Practice direction stipulates that the first choice for guardian *ad litem* should normally be a CAFCASS officer. Only a circuit judge can appoint a guardian. See Harold and Murch (2005) p 203.

Court Advisory and Support Service (CAFCASS) to carry out further work or by making a referral to social services or possibly, by obtaining expert evidence.

Examples given in the Practice Direction of cases where separate representation might be appropriate include those where the CAFCASS officer recommends such a measure; where the child has a standpoint or interests that cannot be represented by the adult parties; where there is an intractable dispute over contact or residence, including where contact has ceased or there is evidence of 'irrational but implacable hostility' to contact or the child 'may be suffering harm associated with the contact dispute'; where the wishes of the child cannot be adequately represented by means of a report; where there are serious allegations of physical, sexual or other abuse of the child or there are allegations of domestic violence not amenable to resolution with the help of a CAFCASS officer; where there is an older child opposed to the court's proposed course of action; or where there are complex issues such as medical or mental health issues.[152]

According to Harold and Murch, the new reluctance to order separate representation evidenced in the restriction of its use to cases involving 'serious difficulty', together with the government's attempt to discourage courts from calling for welfare reports, 'heralds a new low in the official response to the demands of Article 12(2) of the UN Convention on the Rights of the Child' (Harold and Murch 2005 p 203).[153]

### Separate Representation and the 'Mature' Minor

As we have seen above, children themselves may initiate proceedings with the leave of the court under Section 10(8) of the Children Act 1989. Normally they have to be assisted by a next friend or guardian *ad litem* in running their cases. But there is another route to separate representation open to children who are judged sufficiently mature to make choices about important matters in their lives.[154] Under Rule 9.2A of the Family Proceedings Rules 1991, the child can apply to begin or defend proceedings without the guidance of an adult representative or, if one is already in place, to dispense with that person's services.

### a) Leave to Apply for a Section 8 Order

Applications by children for leave to seek Section 8 orders must be heard in the High Court.[155] In order to be granted leave,[156] the child must satisfy the court that he or she has sufficient understanding.[157] And even if the court is so satisfied, it still has a discretion whether to grant leave.[158]

---

[152] See, for what are considered appropriate cases for the involvement of CAFCASS Legal, *CAFCASS Practice Note (6 April 2004)* [2004] 1 FLR 1190.

[153] But see Whybrow (2004) who argues that party status for the child, as opposed to the guardian/CAFCASS officer, serves no purpose unless the child is competent to instruct a solicitor.

[154] See Fortin (2003) p 224.

[155] Practice Direction: Children Act 1989—Applications by Children [1993] 1 FLR 668.

[156] The child does not need a litigation friend or GAL to apply for leave. This can be done by a written request or an oral representation at the hearing (Family Proceedings Rules 1991 R 9.2A(2)).

[157] If the application is made by an incompetent minor through a next friend, there is no need to seek leave: *Re HG (Specific Issue Order: Sterilisation)* [1993] 1 FLR 587, 596. But arguably this view sits uneasily with a case indicating clearly that a competent minor acting through a next friend must get leave. See *Re S (Contact: Application by Sibling)* [1998] 2 FLR 897.

[158] *Re SC (A Minor) (Leave to Seek Residence Order)* [1994] 1 FLR 96; *Re N (Contact: Minor Seeking Leave to Defend and Removal of Guardian)* [2003] 1 FLR 652.

In *Re C (Residence: Child's Application for Leave)*,[159] the court indicated that such cases should be approached cautiously, taking into account the child's best interests but not making them paramount.[160] It is necessary to balance the child's wish to be heard and to have her views taken into account against the possible detrimental effects of, for example, being cross-examined or hearing evidence it would be better not to hear. In addition, judges have declared themselves conscious of the need to protect children from their lack of insight and maturity.[161]

It appears also that the courts are wary of intervening in the relationship between parent and child. In *Re C (A Minor) (Leave to Seek Section 8 Orders)*,[162] a girl of almost 15 sought leave to apply for a residence order to enable her to live with a friend's family rather than with her parents. She also sought leave to apply for a specific issue order allowing her to go on holiday with the friend's family. Johnson J refused leave in relation to the residence order indicating that this was something that would be better resolved through discussion within the family. Moreover, leave to seek a specific issue order might be interpreted by the girl as giving her 'some advantage against her parents' in a situation where she should be dealing directly with her parents rather than seeking the intervention of the court.[163] He also took the view that the jurisdiction was intended to be exercised only in relation to matters of some importance and that a dispute over a holiday was too trivial to warrant the granting of leave.

> **Q** Sawyer writes that '[t]here can be no simple answer as to when and how the child should be heard when the State intervenes in the family'(1995 p 194). She points out that '[t]he empowerment of the child as active participant in proceedings represents a distortion of the usual power-structure of the family which may of itself provoke tension' (p 192).[164] Family stability may be affected as might the child's life within the family (p 193). She concludes that '[a]ny process by which the State or any outside body ... becomes involved in resolving internal family disputes, must recognise the child's subjectivity without ignoring the implications of the child's position of emotional dependency within the family' (p 194). Do you see any similar concerns reflected in the decisions dealing with leave above?

## b) Representation of Children

Whether or not a minor is competent to run a case unassisted by an adult representative, leave of the court to initiate an application must be sought under Section 10(8). Where the minor is competent, however, additional rules apply to allow him or her to run the case without such a representative: rules of court enacted under the Children Act 1989 authorise a minor in certain circumstances to bring or defend certain family proceedings, including proceedings under the inherent jurisdiction and Section 8, without the intervention of a next friend or a guardian. The effect is to enable the child to instruct a solicitor directly. In order to do so, the child must be judged either by the court or by the

---

159 [1995] 1 FLR 927.
160 The court made it clear that s 10(9) of the Children Act 1989 does not apply in the case of an application by the child concerned in the case.
161 See *Re C (Residence: Child's Application for Leave)* [1995] 1 FLR 927, 929, citing *Re S (A Minor) (Independent Representation)* [1993] 2 FLR 437. See also *Re A (Care: Discharge Application by Child)* [1995] 1 FLR 599, 601.
162 [1994] 1 FLR 26.
163 *Ibid*, p 29.
164 See also Sawyer (1999) pp 111–12.

solicitor[165] instructed by the child to have sufficient understanding.[166] The Family Proceedings Rules 1991 state:

> 9.2A Certain minors may sue without next friend etc
>
> (1) Where a person entitled to begin, prosecute or defend any proceedings to which this rule applies, is a minor to whom this Part applies, he may, subject to paragraph (4), begin, prosecute or defend, as the case may be, such proceedings without a next friend or guardian ad litem—
>
> (a) where he has obtained the leave of the court for that purpose; or
> (b) where a solicitor—
>    (i) considers that the minor is able, having regard to his understanding, to give instructions in relation to the proceedings; and
>    (ii) has accepted instructions from the minor to act for him in the proceedings and, where the proceedings have begun, is so acting.

To obtain leave the child must show that he or she has 'sufficient understanding to participate as a party in the proceedings concerned or proposed without a next friend or guardian ad litem'.[167] And the courts have been slow to find this test satisfied; they set a high standard. In *Re H (A Minor) (Guardian ad Litem: Requirement)*[168] the court said:

> Participating as a party ... means much more than instructing a solicitor as to his own views. The child enters the arena among other adult parties. He may give evidence and he may be cross-examined. He will hear other parties, including in this case his parents, give evidence and be cross-examined. He must be able to give instructions ... . Thus the child is exposed and not protected ... . The child also will be bound to abide by the rules ... including rules as to confidentiality.

In *Re S (A Minor) (Independent Representation)*,[169] the court held that *Gillick* competence was the appropriate measure for the child's understanding.[170] But Sir Thomas Bingham said that where 'sound judgement' calls for the kind of insights that only maturity and experience can bring, the court and the solicitor should be 'slow' to conclude that the child's understanding is sufficient.[171] The court went on in terms that clearly convey the tensions between the images of the autonomous and the vulnerable child:[172]

---

[165] It is the court that has the ultimate right to decide whether a child has the capacity to instruct a solicitor (*Re CT (A Minor) (Wardship: Representation)* [1993] 2 FLR 278, 289). The minor must be able not only to instruct the solicitor as to his or her views, but also to give instructions on various matters arising in the course of the case: *Re H (A Minor) (Role of Official Solicitor)* [1993] 2 FLR 552. The court, if it later finds it is not satisfied that the child still has sufficient understanding, can appoint a next friend or guardian (r.9.2A(10)).

[166] If a child already has a next friend or guardian in an ongoing case, the child can seek the leave of the court to continue without the next friend or guardian. Again, the test is whether the child has sufficient understanding to participate as a party in the proceedings without a next friend or guardian (Family Proceedings Rules 1991, R 9.2A). This is the same test as that under s 10 of the Children Act 1989 (*Re N (Contact: Minor Seeking Leave to Defend and Removal of Guardian)* [2003] 1 FLR 652). For a case where the child, aged 7, was considered too young to instruct a solicitor, see *Re W (Contact: Joining Child as a Party)*[2001] EWCA Civ 1830; [2003] 1 FLR 681.

[167] FPR 1991, R 9.2A(6)(b).

[168] [1994] 4 All ER 762, 765.

[169] [1993] 2 FLR 437.

[170] P 447.

[171] P 444. See also *Re N (Contact: Minor Seeking Leave to Defend and Removal of Guardian)* [2003] 1 FLR 652.

[172] See Kaganas and Diduck (2004). Children themselves differ on whether they wish to attend court and whether they wish to speak to the judge (Newsline 2003 pp 295–96).

[C]hildren are human beings in their own right with individual minds and wills, views and emotions, which should command serious attention. A child's wishes are not to be discounted or dismissed simply because he is a child. He should be free to express them and decision-makers should listen. Second is the fact that a child is, after all, a child. The reason why the law is particularly solicitous in protecting the interests of children is that they are liable to be vulnerable and impressionable, lacking the maturity to weigh the longer term against the shorter, lacking the insight to know how others will react in certain situations, lacking the experience to match the probable against the possible ... (p 448)

However there are some cases where the court appears to have come down on the side of autonomy.[173] The most striking declarations in favour of young people's autonomy can be found in *Mabon v Mabon,* a recent Court of Appeal case dealing with residence orders.[174] Thorpe LJ said:

23. There are a number of factors which pointed strongly towards the grant of separate representation in the present case. The applicants were at the date of judgment aged respectively 17, 15, and 13. What remained was a disposal hearing. As Mr Everall eloquently put it without separate representation how were they to know what their parents were contending for: were there cross-applications for residence, what were the contact applications? It was simply unthinkable to exclude young men from knowledge of and participation in legal proceedings that affected them so fundamentally. They had been seen by an experienced family practitioner who had no doubts as to the sufficiency of their understanding: hardly surprising given that they are educated, articulate and reasonably mature for their respective ages ... .
25. ... In our system we have traditionally adopted the tandem model for the representation of children who are parties to family proceedings, whether public or private. First the court appoints a guardian ad litem who will almost invariably have a social work qualification and very wide experience of family proceedings. He then instructs a specialist family solicitor who, in turn, usually instructs a specialist family barrister. This is a Rolls Royce model and is the envy of many other jurisdictions. However its overall approach is essentially paternalistic. The guardian's first priority is to advocate the welfare of the child he represents. His second priority is to put before the court the child's wishes and feelings. Those priorities can in some cases conflict. In extreme cases the conflict is unmanageable. That reality is recognised by the terms of rule 9.2A. The direction set by rule 9.2A(6) is a mandatory grant of the application provided that the court considers 'that the minor concerned has sufficient understanding to participate as a party in the proceedings concerned.' Thus the focus is upon the sufficiency of the child's understanding in the context of the remaining proceedings.
26. In my judgment the Rule is sufficiently widely framed to meet our obligations to comply with both Article 12 of the United Nations Convention and Article 8 of the ECHR, providing that judges correctly focus on the sufficiency of the child's understanding and, in measuring that sufficiency, reflect the extent to which, in the 21st Century, there is a keener appreciation of the autonomy of the child and the child's consequential right to participate in decision making processes that fundamentally affect his family life ... .
28. The guidance given by this court in *Re S* ... on the construction of rule 9.2A is now twelve years old. Much has happened in that time. Although the United Kingdom had ratified the UN Convention some fifteen months earlier, it did not have much impact initially and it is hardly

---

173 See *Re H ( A Minor) (Guardian ad Litem: Requirement)* [1994] 4 All ER 762, especially p 767. See also *Re CT (A Minor) (Wardship: Representation)* [1993] 2 FLR 278 where the court made it clear that a minor's capacity to instruct a solicitor goes beyond the Children Act 1989 to include wardship proceedings; wardship proceedings could not be used to impose a guardian *ad litem* on a competent 13½ year old girl. However, allowing a young person separate representation does not necessarily mean that he or she will be permitted to give evidence in court. See *Re O ( Care Proceedings: Evidence)* [2003] EWHC Fam 2011; [2004] 1 FLR 161.
174 [2005] EWCA Civ 634; [2005] All ER (D) 419.

surprising that it was not mentioned by this court on the 26 February 1993. Although the tandem model has many strengths and virtues, at its heart lies the conflict between advancing the welfare of the child and upholding the child's freedom of expression and participation. Unless we in this jurisdiction are to fall out of step with similar societies as they safeguard Article 12 rights, we must, in the case of articulate teenagers, accept that the right to freedom of expression and participation outweighs the paternalistic judgment of welfare.

29. In testing the sufficiency of a child's understanding I would not say that welfare has no place. If direct participation would pose an obvious risk of harm to the child arising out of the nature of the continuing proceedings and, if the child is incapable of comprehending that risk, then the judge is entitled to find that sufficient understanding has not been demonstrated. But judges have to be equally alive to the risk of emotional harm that might arise from denying the child knowledge of and participation in the continuing proceedings … .

32. In conclusion this case provides a timely opportunity to recognise the growing acknowledgement of the autonomy and consequential rights of children, both nationally and internationally. The Rules are sufficiently robustly drawn to accommodate that shift. In individual cases trial judges must equally acknowledge the shift when they make in individual cases a proportionate judgment of the sufficiency of the child's understanding.

Wall LJ added:

40. The Children Act 1989 and the Family Proceedings Rules 1991 provide the two methods by which children can be separately represented in proceedings relating to their welfare as identified by Thorpe LJ in his judgment. I am in no doubt at all that in the overwhelming majority of cases in which it is appropriate for children to be separately represented, what has become known as the 'tandem model' of representation serves the interests of those children extremely well. The child has the input of expertise from the different disciplines of lawyer and guardian, who are able, with the court's permission, to call on additional expertise and advice where necessary. In public law proceedings, Section 42 of the Children Act 1989 gives the guardian sweeping powers of investigation on the child's behalf. At the same time, the child concerned is protected from the corroding consequences of adversarial litigation. Children are not required to give evidence and be cross-examined: they do not have access to the sensitive documentation generated by the case. This system is, of course, paternalistic in approach, but it usually works well, in my experience, even in cases where the child has sufficient understanding to participate in the proceedings concerned without a guardian.

41. However, the FPR 1991 sensibly make provision for the circumstance in which the guardian and the children concerned fall out, as has happened in this appeal In these circumstances, FPR rule 9.2A(4) gives children the right to apply to the court for permission to prosecute or defend the remaining stages of the proceedings without the guardian, and FPR rule 9.2A(6) makes it clear that the court must grant that permission and remove the guardian if it considers that the children concerned have sufficient understanding to participate in the proceedings concerned without a guardian … .

43. … the judge seems to me, with all respect to him, to have perceived the case from the perspective of the adults. From the boys' perspective, it was simply impossible for the guardian to advance their views or represent them in the proceedings. He would, no doubt, faithfully report to the judge what the boys were saying, but the case he would be advancing to the judge on their behalf would be (or was likely to be) directly opposed to what the boys were actually saying.

44. In these circumstances, I do not agree with the judge that the only advantage from independent representation was 'perhaps the more articulate and elegant expression of what I already know'. That analysis overlooks, in my judgment, the need for the boys on the facts of this particular case to emerge from the proceedings (whatever the result) with the knowledge

that their position had been independently represented and their perspective fully advanced to the judge.[175]

As Fortin says, overall, the ways in which children's wishes are conveyed to the court are 'fragmented and arbitrary' (2003 p 211). The 'tandem model' discussed in *Mabon* applies in cases which qualify as 'specified proceedings' under Section 41 of the Children Act 1989 and has been largely confined to public law cases. But its application has now been potentially extended to Section 8 cases. Section 41 of the Children Act 1989 has been amended by Section 122 of the Adoption and Children Act 2002 to allow for the inclusion of Section 8 applications in the category of 'specified proceedings'. If this enabling provision does result in the inclusion of Section 8 cases, it will put them on a par with public law cases. A guardian, in the form of a CAFCASS officer, will have to be appointed unless the court considers it unnecessary to do so. In addition, the child will have a solicitor to represent him or her.

On the face of it, this change will mean greater participatory potential for children, but whether the 'tandem model' will better enable children to convey their views to the court is open to question. James, *et al*, found that CAFCASS officers in their study operated within the context of a 'universal model of childhood and "the child"' (2003 p 890). They attached more importance to their own judgements about the welfare of the child, which were based on professional principles and personal considerations, than on the children's wishes and feelings (p 893).[176] They also focused on the family as a group as their priority rather than on the individual child (p 894). The authors conclude that there are obstacles in the way of any attempt to 'make real' children's 'rights' to be heard in judicial proceedings (p 895). Masson, in the context of public care proceedings reports that solicitors regard the guardian and not the child as their client and that they spend little or no time with the children concerned (Masson 2000 p 480). Guardians and solicitors are reluctant to view as competent children whose wishes are considered to conflict with their best interests (p 486).

The 'tandem model' is, then, an essentially a paternalistic one and it is not designed to give the child an independent voice. As the court in *Mabon* made clear, it does not preclude the need for allowing the mature minor to act as an autonomous litigant in appropriate cases. An older minor might, for instance, express disagreement with the guardian.[177] *Mabon* may herald a time when greater priority will be given to recognising young people as autonomous.

---

[175] Judges have tended to be reluctant to discuss what children want directly with them. See the discussion in Freeman (2001) p 198.

[176] Compare May and Smart (2004) where children's views were sometimes important in the context of residence and contact. However they note that, while older children did influence outcomes, younger children tended to make an impact only if their views were consistent with other evidence and were in agreement with the welfare professional's assessment. Otherwise their views were disregarded (p 315), although the authors say it is not clear whether this was because of their status as children or because it' would be genuinely unsafe to place too much weight on their views' (*ibid*). They also express concerns elsewhere that assumptions concerning children's welfare take the place of consultation with children (Smart and Neale 2000 p 168). See also Sawyer (2000). See further on children's wishes and feelings in the context of residence and contact, ch 14 pp 539–40.

[177] However, Masson reports that research in relation to care proceedings revealed that guardians were reluctant to express their views to the child concerned or to show the child the report. This meant that the child would not even know whether there was a disagreement (Masson 2000 p 486). Children were also discouraged from seeking separate representation under FPR 1991, R 12 (p 486–87). Children had little influence on the process or the outcome (p 492). The welfare orientation within the proceedings coupled with a belief that legal proceedings are damaging fro children meant that they were excluded from participation (*ibid*).

## VII. CONCLUSION 1

*Cindy's Medical Treatment*

Whether or not Cindy qualifies as a *Gillick*/Fraser-competent minor depends on factors such as her understanding of the nature of the proposed surgery and of any short-term or long-term risks involved. If she is competent in the view of her doctor, her consent may be relied on in carrying out the surgery. Although a competent minor's refusal to undergo medical treatment may be effectively overridden by the consent of a person with parental responsibility, a competent minor's consent to treatment cannot be over-ridden except by a court. Linda or William would have to apply for an order overriding Cindy's consent.

Arguably, the case could be dealt with by means of a specific issue order even if Cindy is *Gillick*/Fraser-competent. In any event, proceedings could be commenced under the inherent jurisdiction. If she is judged competent by the court, Cindy's wishes will be a significant consideration. Even if she is not considered competent, her wishes will be material. In either case, however, the decision of the court would be made in the light of the paramountcy principle.

*Cindy's Education*

Whether or not he has parental responsibility, William is entitled, as a parent,[178] to make an application as of right[179] for a Section 8 order relating to Cindy's education. This could take the form of a prohibited steps order to restrain Linda from changing Cindy's school or a specific issue order to determine where she should be educated. Should Cindy wish to challenge her mother's decision, she could apply for an order her-self but only with the leave of the court. Alternatively Doris, who is determined that Cindy should not have a religious education, may apply to the court with leave.[180] If one of these potential applicants launches proceedings, it is possible for another to seek to be joined as a party to the proceedings, but only if he or she has a separate point of view to put over.[181]

If Cindy wishes to apply for an order without a next friend, she has to satisfy the court that she is of sufficient understanding both for the purposes of seeking leave under Section 10(8) of the Children Act and for the purposes of obtaining leave under the Rules of Court. If she does have sufficient understanding, she need not be repre-sented by a next friend and can instruct her solicitor herself.[182] Given that Cindy is 15 years old, it is likely that she will have sufficient understanding both to make choices concerning her education and to make the decisions necessary for the purposes of the litigation. Even if she does not, and even if it is William or Doris who applies for an

---

178 See s 1 of the Family Law Reform Act 1987; *M v C and Calderdale Metropolitan Borough Council* [1993] 1 FLR 505, 507 and 509.
179 S 10(4)(a) of the Children Act 1989.
180 Grandparents are unlikely to have difficulty obtaining leave (DoH 1991c para 2.44).
181 *North Yorkshire CC v G* [1993] 2 FLR 732, 735.
182 Where a solicitor has accepted instructions from a minor and where the solicitor considers that the child is competent to give instructions, the court may permit the minor to litigate without a next friend or guardian even where leave has not initially been sought to do so (see R 9.2A(1)(b)).

order, the court will take account of Cindy's wishes.[183] However, while orders that run counter to the wishes of older children are unusual,[184] the welfare of the child is paramount and will dictate the court's decision.

*Cindy Aged 16*

If Cindy were aged 16, Section 8 of the Family Law Reform Act 1969 would apply and, in the absence of any evidence that she was incompetent, she would have the capacity to consent to medical treatment. However, her decision could be overruled by the court in the same way that a decision of a minor under the age of 16 might be. A court cannot make a Section 8 order in respect of a minor aged 16 unless the circumstances are exceptional,[185] and it is not obvious that this would be considered a sufficiently exceptional case. In any event, the court's inherent jurisdiction could be invoked, as it was in *In Re W*, to override her decision.

Whether a court would consider itself empowered under Section 8 or be willing to exercise its inherent jurisdiction to make decisions about a competent 16–year-old's education is unclear.

## PART B

**Q** Nazeer and Anji have been married for five years. Anji is a nurse and Nazeer is a youth worker. They have a nine-month-old baby, Ushma. Ushma was born with a defective heart and has remained in hospital since her birth. The doctors treating her have advised Nazeer and Anji that they consider it essential to operate otherwise Ushma will die before her second birthday. There is a 30% chance that the operation will be successful and, if it is, Ushma will be able to lead a relatively normal life. Nazeer and Anji say they are not prepared to put Ushma through the pain and suffering that would attend the surgery and maintain that they want to make sure that whatever the span of her life, it will be as happy as they can make it.

Advise the hospital.

## VIII.   INTRODUCTION

Very sick babies are treated differently from older children; they cannot communicate so others, usually parents, make choices for them. Indeed, Fortin suggests that very small infants have not yet taken on the mantle of 'personhood' (1998 p 414).

---

[183] S 1(3) of the Children Act 1989 applies in contested s 8 proceedings.
[184] *Re B (Change of Surname)* [1996] 1 FLR 791, 794.
[185] S 9(7) of the Children Act 1989.

Section 1 of the CYPA 1933 renders parents liable to criminal prosecution if they fail to provide adequate medical assistance for their children. More often, however, the question of medical treatment arises in the context of civil law when the court may be asked to override the parents' lack of consent to treatment.[186] Conversely, in some cases, the courts are asked for guidance where the doctors do not consider that treatment would benefit the patient but the parents want their seriously ill baby to be treated. The court may make a decision under its inherent jurisdiction, wardship or under Section 8 of the Children Act 1989.

It is largely as a result of technological developments that the courts are being asked to make these difficult decisions. In years gone by, medical science could not help seriously disabled infants. However, babies whose survival in previous years would have been unthinkable, can now be kept alive. But their lives can, in some cases, be painful and dependent on technology (Wells 1988 p 325).

Wells observed in 1988 that non-treatment of severely disabled neonates had become far from uncommon. Fortin (2003 p 315) cites authority suggesting that the same remains true today.[187] This may suggest that, as a society, we view neonates and very young babies in a different light from older children and adults. The sanctity of human life is a principle that informs all decisions about life and death, whether they relate to infants or others, However, as Wells has noted, the principle is not absolute (1988 p 330) and it may be that we are more ready to allow infants to die than, say, older children.[188]

*Infants and 'Personhood'*

Dworkin (1993), although he does not deal specifically with medical treatment, argues that we do see the death of an infant differently from the death of an older child or adult. He espouses a sanctity of life approach, maintaining that we see each human life as being inviolable. This, he says, is because each human is the result of complex creative investments (p 84). Each human life is the product of the creative force of nature[189] and also of human creativity. A life is the sum of natural evolution, of the human intelligence of parents, of self, of other people and of culture (p 82). Any premature end to a life, once it has begun, is intrinsically bad and a waste of the investments made in that life (pp 73–74, 81, 84 and 88).

Most people think that everyone has an equal right to life, says Dworkin (p 85). But, he goes on, we also think that 'some cases of premature death are greater tragedies than others' (pp 84–85). We believe that there is a greater waste of life when a young person dies than when an old person dies (p 85). And he goes on to point out that, 'it is terrible when an infant dies but worse, most people think, when a three-year-old child dies and worse still when an adolescent dies' (p 87). The waste of life is often greater and more tragic because of what has already happened in the past, he says. The death of an adolescent girl is worse than the death of an infant girl because the adolescent's death frustrates the investments she and others have already made in her life in terms of, say,

---

[186] If the threshold conditions are satisfied, a local authority may take the child into care in which case it can consent, or if the child is being accommodated, the local authority can seek a specific issue order under the Children Act for the treatment.

[187] She cites Mason, McCall Smith and Laurie (2002).

[188] Actively taking steps to kill a seriously ill infant is prohibited by the criminal law. But see *Re A (Children) (Conjoined Twins: Surgical Separation)* [2000] 4 All ER 961.

[189] Or, for those who are religious, God.

emotional attachments and future plans (p 87). The 'frustration is greater if it takes place after rather than before the person has made a significant personal investment in his own life, and less if it occurs after any investment has been substantially fulfilled' (p 88)

If one applies Dworkin's reasoning to the case of seriously ill infants, therefore, it could be suggested that it would make the frustration worse if life were allowed to continue because this would add to the wasted investments made by the child and by others in a life that will inevitably end early.[190] In some cases, then, a choice of premature death could minimise the frustration of life and, rather than compromising the doctrine of the sanctity of life, would uphold it.

Other scholars have focused on the notion of personhood. Wells (1988) reviewed various arguments taking this approach. She referred to the view that, although they are human, newborn babies are not 'persons'. According to this thesis, this is because they lack, for instance, an awareness of self as a present and future being (Wells 1988 p 331). They are entitled to protection but the moral obligations owed to them are different and there may be 'less compelling reasons for their full protection than there are for protecting fully-fledged persons' (p 331).[191] Alternatively, she observed, newborns can be seen as being entitled to partial or even full protection, not because they qualify as persons, but because they have the potential to become full persons (*ibid*).

Fortin discusses personhood too but specifically in the context of Article 2 ECHR. She suggests that problems might be avoided if Article 2 were interpreted to confer the full protection of the right to life only on 'persons' and if personhood were confined to those with the 'capacity to value existence'. According to this approach, personhood would be withheld from, among others, anencephalic babies and those who are 'brain-dead' (2003 p 319). She suggests that there are good ethical reasons for distinguishing between babies who have some cognitive awareness and those who have no intellectual capacity (p 316).

The notion that only 'persons' with the capacity for consciousness and rationality command serious moral concern is rejected by other commentators.[192] And whether or not one agrees with the construction of infants as non-persons or potential persons, and whether or not one agrees that they should be treated differently,[193] the question of whether a severely disabled baby should be kept alive at all costs is a very difficult one. It is one that parents, the medical profession and courts are increasingly having to face. For all involved, whether it is an infant or an older person whose life is at stake, the decision is an agonising one.

In all cases involving infants,[194] the test for deciding whether he or she should be treated is the infant's best interests.

---

[190] See Dworkin (1993) pp 90–91. He also argues that ending a life might be a way of upholding the sanctity of life if a person's life would 'go worse' if left alive without being conscious. However this argument relies primarily on judging the situation through the eyes of the patient as a conscious, competent person (see Dworkin 1993 ch 7). To extrapolate this approach to newborns is not possible unless one applies a fictitious version of the subjective test, something which our courts do appear willing to do in cases of non-treatment of infants (see below).

[191] See also Kuhse (1987) who argued that human life is sacred only in that it is a prerequisite for rationality, the holding of ideals and the ability to be a moral being.

[192] See eg, Price (2001) p 640.

[193] Views on disability appear to be changing according to Read and Clements (2004). This in turn could be affecting the way we treat disabled infants.

[194] And incompetent older children and adults.

## IX. THE BEST INTERESTS TEST

There is a strong presumption in favour of preserving life but there are circumstances in which it does not apply. The least contentious of these is where, as in *Re C (a minor) (wardship: medical treatment)*,[195] the child was dying and any treatment could do no more than postpone death for a short while; death was inevitable and life could be only marginally prolonged. It is well-established that the presumption in favour of preserving life does not apply where treatment would be 'futile'.[196] The second category, about which some uncertainty has been expressed,[197] is where a child's faculties have been entirely destroyed.[198] In both these categories of cases the court may well find that it is in the child's best interests to be allowed to die with dignity.[199]

What the courts have found most difficult are cases where the infant, although 'gravely disabled is not dying'.[200] In the case of *Re B*[201] the court was of the view that it should not withhold consent to treatment which could enable a child to survive a life-threatening condition unless the quality of the child's subsequent life would be 'intolerable to the child', 'bound to be full of pain and suffering' and 'demonstrably so awful that in effect the child must be condemned to die'.[202]

These formulations were rejected in *Re J (A minor) (Wardship: Medical Treatment)*.[203] The baby concerned had suffered very severe brain damage. He was likely to develop paralysis of both his arms and legs. He appeared to be blind and was likely to be deaf. He was unlikely ever to be able to speak or to develop even limited intellectual abilities. It was, however, likely that he could feel pain. He was expected to die before his teens.

The court made it clear that the sanctity of life doctrine is not absolute and noted that there are cases in which 'it is not in the interests of the child to subject it to treatment which will cause increased suffering and produce no commensurate benefit'.[204] Instead of using an objective test to decide whether this was such as case, the court looked at the situation 'from the assumed point of view of the patient'.[205] This is referred to as the 'subjective test' or the 'substituted judgement test'.

> I consider that the correct approach is for the court to judge the quality of the life the child would have to endure if given the treatment and decide whether in all the circumstances such a life would be so afflicted as to be intolerable to that child. I say 'to that child' because the test should not be whether the life would be intolerable to the decider. The test must be whether the child in question, if capable of exercising sound judgment, would consider the life intolerable

195 [1989] 2 All ER 782.
196 *Re L (Medical Treatment: Benefit)* [2004] EWHC Fam 2713; [2005] 1 FLR 491 para 12. Any obligation under Art 2 ECHR to provide life-sustaining treatment is subject to this qualification (*R (On the Application of Burke) v The General Medical Council and Others* [2004] EWHC Admin 1879; [2004] 2 FLR 1121 paras 152–62). 'Futile' in this context appears to include cases where death will inevitably ensue soon and where the patient is a PVS patient. But it also seems to include the situation where the intolerability test is satisfied (see below). See also the later Burke case, unreported at the time of writing but discussed by Dyer (2005c).
197 See *Re J (A minor) (Wardship: Medical Treatment)* [1990] 3 All ER 930, 938.
198 *Ibid*, 944–5.
199 See *R (On the Application of Burke) v The General Medical Council* [2004] EWHC Admin 1879; [2004] 2 FLR 1121 para 116.
200 *Ibid*, para 105.
201 [1990] 3 All ER 927; [1981] 1 WLR 1421.
202 See p 929–30.
203 [1991] Fam 33; [1990] 3 All ER 930; [1991] 2 WLR 140. See generally on difficult decisions concerning neonates Mason and McCall Smith (1994), ch 7; Wells (1988); Pearl (1991).
204 *Re J (A minor) (Wardship: Medical Treatment)* [1990] 3 All ER 930, 938.
205 *Ibid*.

... . It takes account of the strong instinct to preserve one's life even in circumstances, which an outsider, not himself at risk of death, might consider unacceptable. (All ER p 945)

The use of this test in cases where the patient has never been competent has been criticised.[206] A New York court, for example, discussing the issue of treatment for a patient with profound learning difficulties, thought it unrealistic to ask what the patient would want if, for a 'miraculous moment', he could comprehend his plight.[207]

English courts have also disapproved of the subjective test in the past[208] yet, in more recent cases, they appear to have been willing to try to apply it. In *Portsmouth NHS Trust v Wyatt and Wyatt, Southampton NHS Trust Intervening*[209] the court described the exercise as 'daunting', if not impossible, but endorsed the use of the subjective approach.[210] However it stressed that the decision must be made on the basis of the child's best interests and it went on to elaborate that concept. The notion of 'intolerability' deployed in earlier judgments could not be used as a test in itself; it was simply a consideration in applying the welfare test.[211] There were also a number of other relevant considerations. The views of the parents would be significant[212] and would have to be weighed in the balance along with the principle of the sanctity of life[213] as well as the child's interest in a 'good death'.[214] Finally, the court emphasised that the 'best interests' of the child are interpreted broadly to include not only medical considerations but also others.[215] The courts take into account also emotional, social, ethical, moral and welfare considerations.[216]

The decisions referred to above clearly place a great deal of importance on the quality of life of the child concerned. If treatment was likely to prolong life, the courts would often weigh this in the balance with the projected quality of life of the child and the suffering treatment might inflict.[217] However the judgment of Ward LJ in *Re A (Children)*

---

[206] See Wells, *et al*, (1990).

[207] See *ibid* p 1545, referring to the case of *Re Storar* 52 NY 2d 353; 420 NE 2d 64 (1981). See also Rhoden (1988).

[208] The test was rejected by the House of Lords in *Airedale NHS Trust v Bland* [1993] 1 FLR 1026, 1043 and Ward LJ doubted whether it was still good law in *Re A (Children) (Conjoined Twins: Surgical Separation)* [2000] 4 All ER 961, 999.

[209] [2004] EWHC Fam 2247; [2005] 1 FLR 21.

[210] Para 30. See also *A National Health Service Trust v D* [2000] 2 FLR 677, 686–87.

[211] Para 24. In *Re J (A minor) (Wardship: Medical Treatment)* [1990] 3 All ER 930, 944 the court said that, 'where the child is terminally ill the court will not require treatment to prolong life; but where, at the other extreme, the child is severely handicapped although not intolerably so and treatment for a discrete condition can enable life to continue for an appreciable period, albeit subject to that severe handicap, the treatment should be given.' See also *A National Health Service Trust v D* [2000] 2 FLR 677, 692. Intolerability is therefore used as a guide to determine whether the quality of life of the patient means that treatment may not be the best option.

[212] *Portsmouth NHS Trust v Wyatt and Wyatt, Southampton NHS Trust Intervening* [2004] EWHC Fam 2247; [2005] 1 FLR 21, para 32.

[213] Sanctity of life has to take second place, in the case of competent patients, to personal autonomy. It may also have to take second place to dignity, and this applies also to those who are not competent, including babies: *R (On the Application of Burke) v The General Medical Council and Others* [2004] EWHC Admin 1879; [2004] 2 FLR 1121, paras 58, 80 145–49, 178. Art 3 can be interpreted as embodying the right to die with dignity (para 130).

[214] *Portsmouth NHS Trust v Wyatt and Wyatt, Southampton NHS Trust Intervening* [2004] EWHC Fam 2247; [2005] 1 FLR 21, para 28. See, on the idea of the right to die, Wilson (1995).

[215] Paras 32 and 39.

[216] *R (On the Application of Burke) v The General Medical Council and Others* [2004] EWHC Admin 1879; [2004] 2 FLR 1121 para 116 and 213, read with *Re L (Medical Treatment: Benefit)* [2004] EWHC Fam 2713; [2005] 1 FLR 491, para 12.

[217] See, for example *A National Health Service Trust v D* [2000] 2 FLR 677, 687.

*(Conjoined Twins: Surgical Separation)*[218] exhibits considerable unease about making this a deciding factor and he attempts to fashion a more rigid version of the sanctity of life principle.

The Court of Appeal was faced here with a very unusual and a very sad case. Jodie and Mary were conjoined twins. Jodie was capable of an independent existence but Mary was dependent on her sister to live. If they were not separated, both would die as Jodie could not support both her own and her sister's life; her heart would fail. If the operation were performed, Mary would certainly die. The doctors caring for the twins wanted to operate to separate the babies but the parents, for religious reasons, refused to consent.

The court found that the operation would allow Jodie to enjoy a normal life expectancy and, in prolonging her life, would be in her best interests.[219] However Ward LJ balked at the suggestion in the court below that Mary's life, if she were not separated from her twin, would be 'worth nothing to her' and espoused what he considered the 'true principle of sanctity of life'.[220] It meant, he said, that 'each life has inherent value in itself and the right to life, being universal, is equal for all of us'.[221] Nevertheless, he acknowledged that the doctrine leaves room for the withdrawal of withholding of treatment in some situations.

Drawing on the work of Keown,[222] an academic in the field of law and medical ethics, Ward LJ argued that there is a distinction between saying that treatment would be worthwhile and saying that the patient's life would be worthwhile.[223] Mary's life, irrespective of how diminished her capacity to enjoy it and how desperate her circumstances, still had its 'own ineliminable value and dignity.'[224] Moreover, it was certainly not in her best interests that she undergo an operation to separate her from her twin, a procedure that would result in her death.[225]

In order to reach a conclusion the court had to strike a balance between the twins. The equal right to life of each of the twins had to be weighed in the balance. But there were other considerations that tipped the scales. Ward LJ said he was precluded by the sanctity of life doctrine from comparing the worth of one life with the other. But he could take into account the worthwhileness of the treatment:

> When considering the worthwhileness of the treatment, it is legitimate to have regard to the actual condition of each twin and hence the actual balance sheet of advantage and disadvantage which flows from the performance or the non-performance of the proposed treatment. Here it is legitimate, as John Keown demonstrates, and as the cases show, to bear in mind the actual quality of life each child enjoys and may be able to enjoy. In summary, the operation will

---

[218] [2000] 4 All ER 961.

[219] P 996.

[220] P 999.

[221] P 1000.

[222] *Ibid.* According to Keown, treatment can be withdrawn where it is 'disproportionate'. This would be where the treatment is futile or excessively burdensome. A treatment is futile if it offers 'no reasonable hope of therapeutic benefit' and excessively burdensome 'if, for example, it would cause great pain' (Keown 2000 p 71). Also, if a proposed treatment offers 'no reasonable hope of improving the patient's condition or "quality of life"', there is no duty to administer it (*ibid*). By this, he says he means that we should not ask whether the patient's life is worthwhile but whether 'Given this patient's quality of life or condition, does this treatment offer a reasonable prospect of improving it?' (*ibid*). See also Keown (1997).

[223] Pp 1000–1.

[224] P 1002.

[225] P 1004. This chapter deals only with the family law aspects of the case. The court also had to make important findings in relation to the criminal law.

give Jodie the prospects of a normal expectation of a relatively normal life. The operation will shorten Mary's life but she remains doomed for death. ... [The] balance is heavily in Jodie's favour. ... [T]he balancing exercise I have just conducted is *not* a balancing of the quality of life in the sense that I value the potential of one human life above another ... . In this unique case it is, in my judgment, impossible not to put in the scales of each child the manner in which they are individually able to exercise their right to life. Mary may have a right to life, but she has little right to be alive. She is alive because, and only because ... she sucks the lifeblood of Jodie and she sucks the lifeblood out of Jodie. She will survive only as long as Jodie survives. Jodie will not survive long because constitutionally she will not be able to cope. Mary's parasitic living will be the cause of Jodie's ceasing to live. (p 1010, emphasis in original)

The best interests of the twins[226] therefore demanded that the chance of life be given to Jodie, who was capable of accepting it, even if that meant sacrificing the life of the other twin, who could not.[227]

Price (2004) comments that Ward LJ has misunderstood Keown's position. Keown is attempting, in Price's view, to confine the decision-making criteria purely to medical questions such as the efficacy of the treatment and the extent of prolongation of life. For Price, Keown's approach cannot be sustained.[228] If one accepts that the sanctity of life principle is not absolute, he says, questions about the patient's quality of life must inevitably come into play. He agrees that it is the treatment rather than the patient that must be evaluated. But whether treatment is worthwhile cannot be assessed without taking into account the patient's overall condition, including any disability (Price 2001 pp 642–43).

He maintains that Ward LJ's formulation of the decision-making criteria does not follow Keown's argument but is in fact in accord with the criteria embodied in the British Medical Association Guidelines. These state that in deciding on treatment, not only medical benefits but also 'other, less tangible benefits' must be considered (Price 2001 p 642). And Fortin (2003 p 318) predicts that, although the judge's emphasis on the right to life might affect medical practice, it is unlikely to change legal decision-making. According to the approach adopted by Ward LJ, quality of life still enters the equation, albeit at a different stage; it has to be considered when deciding whether the treatment is worthwhile.

## X. THE PARENTS, THE DOCTORS AND THE COURTS

We have seen that the courts will apply the best interests test in deciding on the medical treatment of infants. However, the courts are not necessarily involved in such decisions. Where there is no dispute, the case need not be brought before the court. Ward LJ said in *Re A* that despite the fact that the medical team disagreed with the parents' insistence that nature should be allowed to take its course, it would have been open to them to

---

[226] There is some slippage here in Ward LJ's judgment as he had previously indicated that surgery was not in Mary's best interests.

[227] P 1011. For a critique of the rights analysis used, see Munro (2001). See, on the withdrawal of treatment and Art 2 ECHR, *An NHS Trust v M; An NHS Trust v H [*2001] 2 FLR 367.

[228] He also questions whether it is possible to determine sensibly whether treatment is futile or the suffering it creates is excessive.

'bow to the weight of the parental wish'.[229] It was within the hospital's discretion, rather than its duty, to seek a judicial ruling.[230]

Similarly, it is open to the parents to accept medical opinion. The Court of Appeal put it this way in *R v Portsmouth Hospitals NHS Trust Ex Parte Glass*:

> There can be no doubt that the best course is for a parent of a child to agree on the course which the doctors are proposing to take, having fully consulted the parent and for the parent to fully understand what is involved. ... If that is not possible and there is a conflict, and if the conflict is of a grave nature, the matter must then be brought before the court so the court can decide what is in the best interests of the child concerned. (p 910)[231]

In the situation where the doctors wish to treat but the parents do not agree, it is not possible to proceed without parental consent. Doctors cannot, except in an emergency, simply ignore a parent's objections to treatment. The case has to be taken before the court,[232] failing which the treatment will amount to a violation of the patient's rights to respect for private life and physical integrity.[233]

Where the jurisdiction of the court is invoked, ultimately it is the judge who has to decide.[234] But where the medical team do not consider treatment to be appropriate, not even the court can compel them to administer it.[235] If the parents want their child to be treated contrary to their doctors' advice, they will need to instruct another doctor who is prepared to treat. In particular, there is no obligation on the medical profession to treat where treatment would be futile, and so not in the patient's best interests.[236]

As a general rule, the courts places considerable weight on the medical evidence and tend to accede to the clinical judgment of the doctors,[237] although, as we shall see in *Re T* below, the medical position is not determinative. In particular, members of the medical profession have no expertise in assessing the range of non-medical considerations that must inform a decision.[238]

The weight that courts place on parental wishes varies. It is clear that when the court comes to adjudicate, 'there must always be a real possibility of an outcome at variance with parental wishes.'[239] In *Re A*[240] Ward LJ said:

[229] [2000] 4 All ER 961, 987.
[230] The proceedings were initiated under the court's inherent jurisdiction.
[231] [1999] 2 FLR 905. See also *R (On the Application of Burke) v The General Medical Council and Others* [2004] EWHC Admin 1879; [2004] 2 FLR 1121 para 202.
[232] *Re A (Children) (Conjoined Twins: Surgical Separation)* [2000] 4 All ER 961, 987.
[233] *Glass v United Kingdom* [2004] 1 FCR 553.
[234] *Portsmouth NHS Trust v Wyatt and Wyatt, Southampton NHS Trust Intervening* [2004] EWHC Fam 2247; [2005] 1 FLR 21 paras 16 and 33.
[235] See n 92 above. See also the Burke case reported by Dyer (2005c); *A National Health Service Trust v D* [2000] 2 FLR 677, 686.
[236] *Airedale NHS Trust v* [1993] 1 FLR 1026. See also *Re L (Medical Treatment: Benefit)* [2004] EWHC Fam 2713; [2005] 1 FLR 491 para 12.
[237] See eg, *Re J (A Minor) (Wardship: Medical Treatment)* [1991] 1 FLR 366; [1990] 3 All ER 930; *Re C (Medical Treatment)* [1998] 1 FLR 384. In *Airedale NHS Trust v Bland* [1993] 1 FLR 1026, 1042, the House of Lords referred to the greater experience than doctors have in these matters, compared with judges. In *Re L (Medical Treatment: Benefit)*, the court urged the mother to 'listen to what is proposed by those who have a great deal of medical and nursing experience' ([2004] EWHC Fam 2713; [2005] 1 FLR 491 para 32). For a case where the parents were persuaded, see *Re MM (Medical Treatment)* [2000] 1 FLR 224.
[238] *R (On the Application of Burke) v The General Medical Council* [2004] EWHC Admin 1879; [2004] 2 FLR 1121, paras 93, 116 and 213.
[239] *Re Wyatt (No 3)(A Child) (Medical Treatment: Continuation of Order)* [2005] EWHC Fam 693; [2005] All ER (D) 278, para 12. See also *Re A (Children) (Conjoined Twins: Surgical Separation)* [2000] 4 All ER 961, 1010.
[240] *Re A (Children) (Conjoined Twins: Surgical Separation)* [2000] 4 All ER 961, 1006.

Since the parents have the right in the exercise of their parental responsibility to make the decision, it should not be a surprise that their wishes should command very great respect. Parental right is, however, subordinate to welfare … .

[I]t is perhaps useful to repeat the passage in the judgment of Bingham MR in *Re Z (a minor) (freedom of publication)* [1995] 4 All ER 961 at 986 … . Bingham MR said:

> I would for my part accept without reservation that the decision of a devoted and responsible parent should be treated with respect. It should certainly not be disregarded or lightly set aside. But the role of the court is to exercise an independent and objective judgment. If that judgment is in accord with that of the devoted and responsible parent, well and good. If it is not, then it is the duty of the court, after giving due weight to the view of the devoted and responsible parent, to give effect to its own judgment … .

That is the law. That is what governs my decision.(pp 1007–8)[241]

The courts have tended to override parental wishes where they consider that the parent's decision would harm or endanger the child. So, for example, in *Re R (a minor) (blood transfusion)*[242] the court authorised the use of blood products in treating the 10-month-old daughter of Jehovah's Witnesses, whose religious convictions precluded them from countenancing such treatment.[243]

However, in a case that has attracted considerable criticism, the court appeared to be guided primarily by the mother's wishes. In *In Re T (A minor) (Wardship: Medical Treatment)*,[244] the parents, both health care professionals and having jobs in a distant commonwealth country, refused to consent to liver transplant surgery for their 17 month old son, even though unanimous medical opinion said the child would not live beyond the age of two and half without the transplant. The trial judge authorised the treatment, but the Court of Appeal overruled the trial court. Butler-Sloss LJ said that unanimous medical opinion was 'that the prospects of success were good and that this operation was in the best interests of the child' (p 506). The issue before the court was whether it should overrule the decision of the parents and give consent to the operation.

'The judge in a careful, comprehensive and sensitive judgment, reviewed the reasons for the mother's refusal to consent and said … . 'Whilst I can understand her difficulties, I conclude that her refusal to accept the unanimous advice of the doctors is not the conduct of a reasonable parent'. (p 506)

However Butler-Sloss LJ differed:

> A line of cases from 1981 has, in my judgement, clearly established the approach of the court to these most difficult and anxious questions: … [After referring to *Re B (Wardship: Medical Treatment)*,[245] *Re B (A Minor) (Wardship: Sterilisation)*,[246] *Re J (A Minor) (Wardship: Medical Treatment)*[247] and *Re Z (A Minor) (Identification: Restrictions on Publication)*[248]] … .
> From the decisions to which I have referred which bind this court it is clear that when an application under the inherent jurisdiction is made to the court the welfare of the child is the court's

---

[241] See also *J v C [1969]* 1 All ER 788; *Re D (A Minor) (Wardship: Sterilisation)* [1976] 1 All ER 326, 333.
[242] [1993] 2 FLR 757.
[243] See also *Re B (A Minor) (Wardship: Medical Treatment)* [1990] 3 All ER 927; *Re S (A Minor) (Medical Treatment)* [1993] 1 FLR 376.
[244] [1997] 1 FLR 502, and see Michalowski (1997) and Fox and McHale (1997).
[245] [1982] 3 FLR 117.
[246] [1988] AC 199; [1987] 2 FLR 314.
[247] [1991] Fam 33; [1991] 1 FLR 366.
[248] [1997] Fam 1, sub nom *Re Z (A Minor) (Freedom of Publication)* [1996] 1 FLR 191; [1995] 4 All ER 961.

paramount consideration. The consent or refusal of consent of the parents is an important consideration to weigh in the balancing exercise to be carried out by the judge.

... In my view ... the judge erred in his approach to the issue before the court. He accepted the unchallenged clinical opinion of the three consultants and assessed the reasonableness of the mother's decision against that medical opinion. (p 509)

But ... the reasonableness of the mother was not the primary issue. This mother and this child are one for the purpose of this unusual case and the decision of the court to consent to the operation jointly affects the mother and son and it also affects the father. The welfare of this child depends on his mother. The practical considerations of her ability to cope with supporting the child in the face of her belief that this course is not right for him, and the requirement to return probably for a long period to this country, either to leave the father behind and lose his support or to require him to give up his job and seek one in England were not put by the judge into the balance when he made his decision. (p 510)[249]

... The welfare of the child is the paramount consideration and I recognise the very strong presumption in favour of a course of action which will prolong life, and the inevitable consequences for the child of not giving consent. But to prolong life ... is not the sole objective of the court and to require it at the expense of other considerations may not be in a child's best interests ... . I believe that the best interests of this child require that his future treatment should be left in the hands of his devoted parents. (p 512)

Waite LJ stated:

It can only be said safely that there is a scale, at one end of which lies the clear case where parental opposition to medical intervention is prompted by scruple or dogma of a kind which is patently irreconcilable with principles of child health and welfare widely accepted by the generality of mankind; and that at the other end lie highly problematic cases where there is genuine scope for a difference of view between parent and judge ... the greater the scope for genuine debate between one view and the other the stronger will be the inclination of the court to be influenced by a reflection that in the last analysis the best interests of every child include an expectation that difficult decisions affecting the length and quality of its life will be taken for it by the parent to whom its care has been entrusted by nature. (pp 513–14)

> **Q** Is there a difference in the reasoning of Butler-Sloss LJ and that of Waite LJ in *Re T*? Do either or both of them adopt a test different from the other cases we have considered?

Fortin suggests that a court confronted in the future by a similar situation to that which arose in *Re T* might find it more difficult to refuse to authorise treatment in the light of the HRA, which imposes a duty to protect life under Article 2 of the ECHR. This would counter a parent's claim to the right to respect for family life (Article 8), freedom of religion (Article 9) and freedom from discrimination (Article 14) (Fortin 2003 p 324).

O'Donnell maintains that parental qualities, such as reasonableness,[250] are treated as relevant in deciding what weight to ascribe to their wishes (2004 pp 224–25). Commentators have noted that parental objections founded in religious belief appear to be more

---

[249] This approach has been criticised for failing to recognise the independent interests of the child. See Downie (2000) p 200.

[250] See also Fox and McHale (1999) p 702. Ward LJ in *Re A (Children) (Conjoined Twins: Surgical Separation)* [2000] 4 All ER 961, 1009 emphasised that, despite their religious foundation, the parents' objections had some substance; 'this is not a case where opposition [by the parents] is "prompted by scruple or dogma" ' when he declared that their wishes did not accord with the children's best interests.

easily discounted by the courts as 'scruple or dogma'. They are more likely to take seriously any objections voiced by articulate professionals such as the parents in *Re T*.[251] These commentators question whether religious and ethical beliefs ought to be downgraded and also whether it should be so readily accepted that educated parents are being reasonable.[252]

## XI. CONCLUSION 2

The hospital needs the consent of at least one parent with parental responsibility before the operation goes ahead. Since this consent is not forthcoming, the case will have to be taken before the court, perhaps under the inherent jurisdiction.

The court will make its own assessment of the situation, mindful of the presumption in favour of preserving life and its duty under Article 2 ECHR. In making its assessment it will take into account the medical evidence and also the parents' wishes. The weight the court attributes to the parents' wishes will almost certainly be influenced by its opinion as to whether they are reasonable. The views of 'reasonable', 'responsible' and 'devoted' parents are likely to be more influential than those of parents who are judged wanting or who are acting out of religious conviction in a way that the court regards as irrational. Whether the parents are considered reasonable will be judged in the light of the medical evidence.

Ultimately, the decision of the court will turn on its assessment of the child's best interests. This will necessitate consideration of a number of issues and the court is not confined to medical matters. Among the factors to be considered would be the medical prognosis, the child's projected quality of life and whether the treatment is worthwhile in the light of this, the suffering that would be caused by the medical procedures and the willingness and ability of the parents to care for her.[253]

It may well be that in this case, although the parents are professionals and the mother has knowledge of medical matters, if not specifically paediatric medicine, their wishes will be overruled. The courts tend to be guided by medical opinion and, given the grim prognosis if the surgery is not performed and the likely benefits that will follow if it is successfully performed, the court may authorise the operation. This would seem to be in Ushma's best interests and would be the route dictated by the presumption in favour of life.

Undoubtedly, however, the court will be given pause by the unfavourable odds in relation to the likelihood of the operation being successful and the suffering it will entail. There will also be some reluctance to override the parents' wishes. Nevertheless, this is a decision that cannot be kept within the private family.

---

251 Fortin (1998 p 415) points out that the parents in another case, who were asking for treatment to continue as required by their beliefs as orthodox Jews, were treated very differently and their wishes were overruled (*Re C (Medical Treatment)* [1998] 1 FLR 384). In *Re C (HIV Test)* [1999] 2 FLR 1004, however, the parents' wishes were overruled because they flew in the face of accepted medical opinion.

252 See Downie (1999); Fox and McHale (1997); Fortin (1998); Bridge (1999b).

253 Although this would probably carry less weight than it did in *Re T*.

## FURTHER READING AND SELECTED RECENT REFERENCES

A BAINHAM, 'The Balance of Power in Family Decisions' (1985) 45 *CLJ* 262.

District Judge C Bellamy and District Judge Geoff, 'Reflections on Family Proceedings Rule 9.5' (2003) *Fam Law* 265.

C BRIDGE, 'Parental Powers and the Medical Treatment of Children' in C Bridge, (ed), *Family Law Towards the Millennium: Essays for PM Bromley* (London, Butterworths, 1997).

——, 'Religious Beliefs and Teenage Refusal of Medical Treatment' (1999) 62 *MLR* 585.

——, 'Religion, Culture and Conviction—The Medical Treatment of Young Children' (1999) 11 *CFLQ* 1.

J BRIDGEMAN, 'Old Enough to Know Best?' (1993) 13 *Legal Studies* 69.

G DOUGLAS, 'The Retreat from *Gillick*' (1992) 55 *MLR* 569.

C DYER, 'Doctors Win Appeal Over Rights of the Terminally Ill', *The Guardian*, 29 July 2005.

J EEKELAAR, 'The Interests of the Child and the Child's Wishes: The Role of Dynamic Self-determinism' (1994) 8 *Int J of Law and the Family* 42.

J FORTIN, '*Re C (Medical Treatment)*: A Baby's Right to Life' (1998) 10 *CFLQ* 411.

——, 'Rights Brought Home for Children' (1999) 62 *MLR* 350.

——, *Children's Rights and the Developing Law*, 2nd edn, (London, LexisNexis Butterworths, 2003) pt II.

——, 'Children's Rights: Are the Courts Now Taking Them More Seriously?' (2004) 15 *KCLJ* 253.

M FREEMAN, 'The End of the Century of the Child?' (2000) 53 *CLP* 505.

S GILMORE, 'The Nature, Scope and Use of the Specific Issue Order' (2004) 16 *CFLQ* 367.

M GOLLOP, A SMITH and N TAYLOR, 'Children's Involvement in Custody and Access Arrangements after Parental Separation' (2000) 12 *CFLQ* 383.

AL JAMES, A JAMES and S McNAMEE, 'Constructing Children's Welfare in Family Proceedings' (2003) *Fam Law* 889.

F KAGANAS and A DIDUCK, 'Incomplete Citizens: Changing Images of Post-separation Children' (2004) 67 *MLR* 959.

J KEOWN, 'Restoring Moral and Intellectual Shape to the Law After *Bland*' (1997) 113 *LQR* 481.

——, 'Beyond *Bland*: A Critique of the BMA Guidance on Withholding and Withdrawing Medical Treatment' (2000) 20 *Legal Studies* 66.

H KUHSE, *The Sanctity of Life Doctrine in Medicine* (Oxford, Clarendon Press, 1987).

G LANSDOWN, Taking Part: Children's Participation in Decision Making (London, IPPR, 1995).

J MASSON, 'Representations of Children' (1996) *CLP* 245.

V MAY and C SMART, 'Silence in Court?—Hearing Children in Residence and Contact Disputes' (2004) *Fam Law* 305.

V MUNRO, Square pegs in Round Holes; the Dilemma of Conjoined Twins and Individual Rights' (2001) 10 *Social and Legal Studies* 459.

D NELKEN, 'Afterword: Choosing Rights for Children' in G Douglas and L Sebba, (eds), *Children's Rights and Traditional Values* (Aldershot, Ashgate, 1998).

C PIPER, 'Barriers to Seeing and Hearing Children in Private Law Proceedings' (1999c) *Fam Law* 394.

——, 'Ascertaining the Wishes and Feelings of the Child' (1997) *Fam Law* 796.

D PRICE, 'Fairly Bland: An Alternative View of a Supposed "Death Ethic" and the BMA Guidelines' (2001) 21 *Legal Studies* 618.

J READ and L CLEMENTS, 'Demonstrably Awful: The Right to Life and the Selective Non-treatment of Disabled Babies and Young Children' (2004) 31 *JLS* 482.

C SAWYER, 'Conflicting Rights for Children? Implementing Welfare, Autonomy and Justice Within Family Proceedings' (1999) 21 *JSW&FL* 99.

——, 'An Inside Story: Ascertaining the Child's Wishes and Feelings' (2000) *Fam Law* 170.

C SAWYER, 'The Competence of Children to Participate in Family Proceedings' (1995) 7 *CFLQ* 180.

C SMART and B NEALE, ' "It's My Life Too"—Children's Perspectives on Post-divorce Parenting' (2000) *Fam Law* 163.

L TRINDER, 'Competing Constructions of Childhood: Children's Rights and Children's Wishes in Divorce' (1997) 19 *JSW&FL* 291.

B VAUGHAN, 'The Government of Youth: Disorder and Dependence?' (2000) 9 *Social and Legal Studies* 347.

C WELLS, 'Whose Baby is it?' (1988) 15 *JLS* 323.

C WELLS, P ALLDRIDGE and D MORGAN, 'An Unsuitable Case for Treatment' (1990) *NLJ* 1544.

J WHYBROW, 'Children, Guardians and Rule 9.5' (2004) *Fam Law* 504.

W WILSON, 'Is Life Sacred?' (1995) 12 *JSWFL* 131.

## Reports

UN Committee on the Rights of the Child, Concluding Observations of the UN Committee on the Rights of the Child on the United Kingdom's Second Periodic Report (CRC/C/15/Add.188) (www.unhchr.ch) (2002).

# 17

# Child Protection

**Q** A local authority social worker receives a telephone call from Brian and June's neighbour who says he is worried about their 4-year-old child, Amy. He has frequently heard her crying and he has seen her looking dirty and unkempt. The social worker realises that this call refers to the same child about whom she received a call the previous day. That call was from the child's playschool where staff are very concerned. They have observed that Amy has become increasingly withdrawn and tends to recoil from physical contact with adults. On the day of the call, they noticed that she had bruising on her inner thigh. June told them that Amy hurt her leg when she fell. Should the social worker be concerned? If so what should she do?

## I. INTRODUCTION

There may well be cause for concern. Amy's physical state may suggest that she is being neglected and the bruising on the inner thigh, which is probably inconsistent with a fall, could be interpreted as a sign that Amy is suffering sexual or some other form of physical abuse.[1] Her withdrawn manner and the fact that she recoils from physical contact with adults tend to support this interpretation.

The primary agency[2] responsible for child protection, the prevention of abuse and neglect, the investigation of cases and the initiation of court proceedings is the local authority.[3] So, for example, while the Children Act 1989 empowers the police to take children at risk into police protection for up to 72 hours, the local authority has to be notified of such cases and if, after inquiry, the police consider it necessary to apply for an emergency order, this is done on behalf of the local authority.[4] It is, therefore, the local authority that is charged with endeavouring to ensure that Amy is not being abused or at risk of being abused.

---

[1] The most appropriate person to evaluate the parents' explanation is likely to be a paediatrician: *R v Harrow London Borough Council, ex parte D* [1990] 1 FLR 79.

[2] Art 19 of the UN Convention on the Rights of the Child places a duty on states to take measures, including administrative and legislative measures to protect children from violence, injury abuse and maltreatment. There is also a requirement that states provide for social programmes to provide support for the child and the child's carers, as well as forms of prevention and identification, treatment and, if necessary, judicial involvement.

[3] Local Authority Social Services Act 1970, Sch 1. The NSPCC is designated an 'authorised person' and is therefore permitted to initiate care proceedings. However, it rarely does so. For a more detailed description of the child protection service and child protection investigations, see Bainham (2005) chs 10–12.

[4] S 46. Of course, the police would be the principal agency involved in a criminal investigation concerning abuse.

However, it is important to keep in mind that a number of agencies, including NHS trusts, health authorities, police and probation, are all required to have regard to the need to 'safeguard and promote the welfare of children' when carrying out their normal functions. This duty, embodied in Section 11 of the Children Act 2004, rests on both the agencies and those individuals working within them.

According to the DfES, safeguarding and welfare are 'two sides of the same coin':

Safeguarding has two elements:

• protecting children from maltreatment; and
• preventing impairment of children's health or development.

Whereas promoting welfare is a proactive responsibility, ie:

• ensuring that children are growing up in circumstances consistent with the provision of safe and effective care; and,
• creating opportunities to enable children to have optimum life chances such that they can enter adulthood successfully.

(DfES 2005b para 2.1.7)

Principles underpinning work with children and their families should be:

• child centred;
• rooted in child development;
• supporting the achievement of the best possible outcomes for children and improving their wellbeing;
• holistic in approach;
• ensuring equality of opportunity;
• involving children and families;
• building on strengths as well as identifying and addressing difficulties;
• multi/inter-agency in its approach;
• a continuing process;
• designed to identify the services required and monitor the impact their provision has on the child's developmental progress;
• evidence based.

(para 2.2.8)

## II. FROM 'RISK' TO 'NEED'?

We have discussed the concept of child abuse as a social construction and the contingency of the definition of abuse.[5] However, even assuming that, at any one time, child welfare professionals have shared understandings within broad parameters about what is abusive and warrants intervention, there remain enormous difficulties in determining whether a particular case falls within those parameters: '[t]he fact that something has occurred is almost always contestable' (Wattam 1996 p 192).

Professionals dealing with children and charged with child protection are obliged to apply the *Framework for the Assessment of Children in Need and their Families* (DoH, DfEE and Home Office 2000). This identifies three domains that have to be considered:

[5] See ch 9.

the child's developmental needs; the parents' or caregivers' capacity to respond appropriately; and the wider family and environmental factors (para 1.40). In attempting to determine whether a child has been abused, professionals have to rely on evidence[6] such as physical symptoms and injuries as well as the child's development and the adequacy of parental care. They also have regard to factors such as the relationships between the family members, the home environment and the circumstances of the alleged injury. But evidence is often inconclusive and can be interpreted in different ways. Currently, whether cases proceed through the child protection system appears to be dependent on whether certain risk factors are present.[7] For example, Farmer and Owen (1995 chapter 10) observed a preoccupation with risk at child protection conferences and found that certain factors were closely related to the decision to enter a child's name on the child protection register.[8] These were the perceived severity of the abuse or neglect; the existence of secondary concerns such as neglect in a home where physical or sexual abuse was suspected; and the prior involvement of the family with welfare agencies. In addition, registration was more likely when it was the mother who was suspected of abuse.

Cooper, *et al*, observe that social work is characterised by risk assessment and risk avoidance (2003 p 59). They maintain that 'fear of failure has shaped child protection practice in England and Wales for several decades' (p 10) and that 'the system encourages social workers to protect their own position, in a way which runs counter to the lessons and principles they learned during their training' (p 11).

This preoccupation with avoiding risk has also met with criticism from the government: 'risks must be taken in order to get a more successful outcome for the child by keeping various avenues of family support firmly in mind when child protection enquiries are underway' (DoH 1995b p 52).[9] Rather than confining themselves primarily to child protection, workers were being urged to 'tackle the wider welfare requirements of children and families' (p 48). A shift from protection to prevention in the form of increased provision of services was advocated in a Department of Health publication, *Child Protection. Messages From Research*:

> The research studies suggest that too much of the work undertaken comes under the banner of child protection. ...A more useful perspective [is one according to which] much early work is viewed as an enquiry to establish whether the child in need might benefit from services. ...
>     The focus would be on the overall needs of children rather than a narrow concentration on the alleged incident. (1995b pp 54–55)

This message was reiterated in *Working Together to Safeguard Children*, which contains guidance for agencies and professionals working in the field of child welfare and protection. They are instructed to focus on outcomes for children at risk, having regard to issues such as educational achievement (DoH, Home Office and DfEE 1999 para 2.26). The document also refers to the provision of services:

Child Protection in Context

- promote access to a range of services for children in need without inappropriately triggering the child protection processes;

---

[6] See, for factors to be considered, DoH, Home Office and DfEE (1999) para 2.18.
[7] See, eg, DoH (1995b) pp 33–34. Compare earlier research that revealed a 'rule of optimism' (p 356 above).
[8] See pp 662–63.
[9] See also Cooper, *et al*, (2003).

- consider the wider needs of children and families involved in child protection processes, whether or not concerns about abuse and/or neglect are substantiated.

(DoH, Home Office and DfEE 1999 para 2.26).

1.9 Effective measures to safeguard children should not be seen in isolation from the wider range of support and services available to meet the needs of children and their families:

> many of the families who become the subject of child protection concerns suffer from multiple disadvantages. Providing services and support to children and families under stress may strengthen the capacity of parents to respond to the needs of their children before problems develop into abuse … . (DoH, Home Office and DfEE 1999)

**Q** Refer to chapter 9. Why is it important to ensure that the child protection process is not 'inappropriately' triggered?

This guidance reflects government policy, discussed in chapter 9, which emphasises the importance of outcomes and focuses on the provision of universal services for all children in order to achieve these. The aim is to improve the lives of children generally and to provide additional, targeted support for children in need and children at risk. There have been a number of initiatives[10] such as the establishment of Children's Centres, *Sure Start* and *Connexions* to provide services for children and families. Children's Trusts are being created to facilitate 'more integrated service delivery and better outcomes for children and young people' (DfES 2004a para 2.20).[11] And the Children Act 1989 imposes obligations on local authorities to provide services. The nature of these is outlined in Part III of the Act and they include day care and accommodation. In particular, local authorities are required[12] to provide services for 'children in need' and their families:

> Provision of services for children in need, their families and others
>
> 17.—(1) It shall be the general duty of every local authority (in addition to the other duties imposed on them by this Part)[13]—
> (a)  to safeguard and promote the welfare of children within their area who are in need; and
> (b)  so far as is consistent with that duty, to promote the upbringing of such children by their families,
> by providing a range and level of services appropriate to those children's needs.  …
>
> (4A) Before determining what (if any) services to provide for a particular child in need in the exercise of functions conferred on them by this section, a local authority shall, so far as is reasonably practicable and consistent with the child's welfare—
>
> (a)  ascertain the child's wishes and feelings regarding the provision of those services; and
> (b)  give due consideration (having regard to his age and understanding) to such wishes and feelings of the child as they have been able to ascertain.

---

[10] See HM Treasury (2005) paras 5.1–5.21.

[11] See, for discussion of Children's Trusts, pp 373–74 above.

[12] With the help of other authorities, if necessary. See s 27 Children Act 1989; Children Act 2004.

[13] These include duties relating to the provision of day care and of accommodation for children in need. Pt 1 of Sch 2 of the Children Act 1989 also imposes duties on local authorities, including the duty to 'take reasonable steps, through the provision of services under Part III of this Act, to prevent children within their area suffering ill-treatment or neglect' (para 4(1)). They are also obliged to take reasonable steps to reduce the need to bring care proceedings or criminal proceedings in respect of children (para 7). For a detailed discussion of Part III of the Children Act 1989, see Bainham (2005) pp 420ff.

(10) For the purposes of this Part a child shall be taken to be in need if—
(a)  he is unlikely to achieve or maintain, or to have the opportunity of achieving or maintaining, a reasonable standard of health or development without the provision for him of services by a local authority under this Part;
(b)  his health or development is likely to be significantly impaired, or further impaired, without the provision for him of such services; or
(c)  he is disabled,
and 'family', in relation to such a child, includes any person who has parental responsibility for the child and any other person with whom he has been living.

(11) For the purposes of this Part, a child is disabled if he is blind, deaf or dumb or suffers from mental disorder of any kind or is substantially and permanently handicapped by illness, injury or congenital deformity or such other disability as may be prescribed; and in this Part—

'development' means physical, intellectual, emotional, social or behavioural development; and

'health' means physical or mental health.

In practice, the tendency is to define 'appropriate' to match resources rather than need.[14] In the context of limited resources, local authorities seem to have concentrated services on those children deemed to be at risk of abuse or neglect.[15] Cooper, *et al*, for example, remark that 'most resources are still focused on high risk situations and crises. The thresholds for intervention, if anything, are being raised' (2003 p 21). Moreover, it remains the case that professionals have to identify children who are at risk. For one thing, *Working Together* states that compulsory intervention should be confined to 'exceptional cases' such as those where a child has to be protected from significant harm (DoH, Home Office and DfEE 1999 para 1.5).[16]

So, while the local authorities are expected to turn their attention to the provision of services to families and children generally, they are still charged with the duty to protect children at risk and to intervene early to avert that risk.[17]

When referrals[18] are made to local authorities, whether by members of the public, schools or otherwise, these have to be taken seriously (DoH 1995a para 4.10–11) and an appraisal has to be made of the child's safety. If not satisfied that the child will be safe under a voluntary arrangement, the local authority may apply to court for an order empowering it to intervene coercively:

3.8 ... In the great majority of cases, children are safeguarded from harm by working with parents, family members and other significant adults in the child's life to make the child safe, and to promote his or her development, within the family setting. Where a child is at continuing risk of significant harm, social services are responsible for co-ordinating a [sic] inter-agency plan to safeguard the child, which sets out and draws upon the contributions of family members, professionals and other agencies. In a few cases, the social services department, in consultation with other involved agencies and professionals, may judge that a child's welfare can not be sufficiently safeguarded if he or she remains at home. In these circumstances, the social services

[14] See Cretney, *et al*, (2002) pp 704–5 and sources cited there. See also *Report of the National Commission of Inquiry into the Prevention of Child Abuse* (1996) para 5.9.
[15] See Audit Commission (1994) paras 44, 48, 59.
[16] See also DoH, Home Office and DfEE (1999) para 1.8.
[17] See pp 352ff above.
[18] Unlike many US states, the UK does not have laws making the reporting of suspected child abuse mandatory. But see DoH, Home Office and DfEE (1999) paras 5.3–5.4.

department may apply to the courts for a Care Order, which commits the child to the care of the local authority. Where the child is thought to be in immediate danger, the social services department may apply to the courts for an Emergency Protection Order, which places the child under the protection of the local authority for a maximum of eight days.[19]

(DoH, Home Office and DfEE 1999)

## III. LEGAL CRITERIA FOR THE GRANTING OF COURT ORDERS

Court orders permitting compulsory intervention are available only if the statutory criteria centred on significant harm or a likelihood of significant harm are met. In addition, the court must apply the welfare test in Section 1[20] of the Children Act 1989 and must, in accordance with Section 1(5), be satisfied that making the order would be better for the child than making no order.[21] The term 'significant' is not defined in the legislation but is said in the Guidance and Regulations to mean 'considerable, noteworthy or important' (1991c para 3.19).[22] 'Harm' is defined in Section 31:

31(9) In this section—

...

'harm' means ill-treatment or the impairment of health or development including, for example, impairment suffered from seeing or hearing the ill-treatment of another;[23]

'development' means physical, intellectual, emotional, social or behavioural development;

'health' means physical or mental health; and

'ill-treatment' includes sexual abuse and forms of ill-treatment which are not physical.

(10) Where the question of whether harm suffered by a child is significant turns on the child's health or development, his health or development shall be compared with that which could reasonably be expected of a similar child.[24]

---

[19] Renewable for a further seven days. See below pp 668ff

[20] The checklist in s 1(3) applies in relation to care proceedings but not to emergency cases dealt with under Part V of the Act.

[21] See p 359 above.

[22] See also *Humberside County Council v B* [1993] 1 FLR 257, 263.

[23] This is intended to cover cases where children witness domestic violence.

[24] So, eg, a greater degree of care may be expected for a child with brittle bone disease or a disability. The Guidance suggests that cognisance might have to be taken, not only of the child's physical characteristics, but also of 'environmental, social and cultural characteristics' (DoH 1991c para 3.20). See, on the impact of the statutory criteria on different ethnic groups, Brophy, *et al*, (2003). See also Brophy (2003).

## IV. IMMEDIATE PROTECTION AND INVESTIGATION

The first concern of the child protection professionals should be to ensure that the child is safe,[25] and, in appropriate cases, to seek to remove the child pursuant to a voluntary arrangement or an emergency protection order.[26] In other situations, referrals may lead to no further action, to the provision of services from an appropriate agency[27] and/or to a fuller initial assessment of the needs and circumstances of the child, which may in turn be followed by Section 47 enquiries (DoH, Home Office and DfEE 1999 para 5.12).

In this case, the evidence does not appear to demand emergency protection for the child. However it will be necessary to follow up the referral with an initial assessment in order to determine whether the child is in need in terms of Section 17 or whether she is at risk in terms of Section 47 (DoH, Home office and DfEE 1999 para 5.15).[28] The local authority may decide, as a result of its enquiries, that Amy is a child in need and that the family would benefit from services provided under Part III of the Children Act 1989.[29] However, if, as is likely here, there is felt to be cause for concern, a strategy discussion must be held involving all relevant agencies (DoH, Home Office and DfEE 1999 para 5.28). This discussion will address questions such as whether to begin or continue[30] Section 47 enquiries, and it will be used to agree matters such as any measures needed for the immediate protection of the child. Also, a decision will be made as to whether a core assessment[31] will be commenced as a means of carrying out the Section 47 investigation.[32] Such an investigation is obligatory if there is cause to suspect abuse:

47 Local authority's duty to investigate

(1) Where a local authority—
(a)   are informed that a child who lives, or is found, in their area—
         (i)  is the subject of an emergency protection order; or

---

[25] The first enquiry normally involves consulting available records and discussion with professionals or services, such as the police. (DoH, Home Office and DfEE 1999 para 5.10). Permission should be sought from the parents before discussing the referral with other agencies unless this would expose the child to significant harm (para 5.11). A decision about how to proceed must be made within 24 hours (para 5.10).

[26] See DoH, Home Office and DfEE (1999) paras 5.12; 5.23–5.27. See also DoH 1995a paras 5.2–5.3.

[27] Agencies such as housing and education authorities are required to give help when requested to do so by the local authority, provided this is compatible with their other duties and does not unduly prejudice the discharge of their other functions (s 27 Children Act 1989).

[28] See, for details regarding the initial assessment, DoH, Home Office and DfEE (1999) paras 5.13–5.16.

[29] *Working Together* appears to require local authorities to assess needs once there has been a referral and the initial consideration of the case reveals a need for further assessment (DoH, Home Office and DfEE 1999 paras 5.10 and 5.13) However an assessment does not give rise to a right, enforceable by an individual, to services to meet those assessed needs; s 17 merely sets out duties of a general character intended to benefit children in the area generally. In particular, the local authority has no obligation to provide residential accommodation for individual children and their families in cases where the parents are homeless; an authority providing accommodation for a child is not under a duty to accommodate the family as well: *R (on the application of G) v Barnet London Borough Council; R (on the application of W) v Lambeth London Borough Council; R (on the application of A) v Lambeth London Borough Council* [2003] UKHL 57; [2004] 1 FLR 454. On the relationship between local authorities' powers to accommodate and immigration law, see *M v London Borough of Islington and Secretary of State for the Home Department* [2004] EWCA Civ 235; [2004] FLR 867.

[30] If enquiries have already begun.

[31] This is an in-depth assessment of the child's needs and the abilities of the parents or carers to respond appropriately (DoH Home Office and DfES 2003 para 32). A core assessment has to be carried out in accordance with the *Framework for the Assessment of Children in Need and their Families* (DoH, DfEE and Home Office 2000) to determine whether services would be helpful and, if so, what types of services would promote good outcomes for the child (DoH, Home Office and DfEE 1999 para 5.20) Family Group conferences might be used in such cases (*ibid*).

[32] See for further details DoH, Home Office and DfEE (1999) paras 5.28–5.32.

(ii) is in police protection; or … .
(b)     have reasonable cause to suspect that a child who lives, or is found, in their area is suffering, or is likely to suffer, significant harm,

the authority shall make, or cause to be made, such enquiries as they consider necessary to enable them to decide whether they should take any action to safeguard or promote the child's welfare.[33]

Investigations can be made jointly by social services and the police or, as seems more likely in this case, by social services alone. In any event, all investigations should involve gathering information from and liaising with other agencies and professionals.[34] Enquiries should involve separate interviews with the child and, in most cases, interviews with the parents or carers (DoH, Home Office and DfEE 1999 para 5.34). Wherever possible, the professionals are expected to work in partnership with the family although, as the guidance issued by the Department of Health, *The Challenge of Partnership in Child Protection: Practice Guide*, acknowledges, '[s]ometimes the hostility and anger experienced by families may preclude any possibility of partnership and even involvement at this stage' (DoH 1995a para 6.4).

### Impeding Access to the Child

Partnership will be unlikely if the parents obstruct access to the child. Section 47(4) of the Children Act 1989 places an obligation on a local authority conducting enquiries under Section 47(1) to take such steps as are reasonably practicable to gain access or ensure that access is gained to the child, unless satisfied that they already have sufficient information. Section 47(6) provides that where, in the course of Section 47 enquiries, the person conducting the enquiry is refused access to or denied information about the whereabouts of the child, the authority has a duty to apply for an emergency protection order, a child assessment order, a care order or a supervision order unless they are satisfied that the child's welfare can be satisfactorily safeguarded without doing so.

Section 44(b) provides that where Section 47(1) enquiries are being made and those enquiries are being frustrated by access to the child unreasonably being refused, the court may make an emergency protection order. Refusal to allow access at a reasonable time without good reason could be construed as unreasonable (DoH 1991c para 4.39). However, a request that the social worker return later or an undertaking to take the child to be seen at a clinic, for example, may not amount to unreasonable refusal of access. According to Masson and Morris (1992 p 135), the excuse that the child is asleep would probably not be sufficient.

---

[33] The child's wishes and feelings must be taken into account in determining what action should be taken (s 47(5A)). S 47 governs the local authority's duties in cases where it is alerted to the possibility of abuse. Concern about a child might also arise in the course of family proceedings such as s 8 proceedings. S 37 of the Children Act 1989 provides that, where it appears to the court in any family proceedings that it might be appropriate to make a care or supervision order in relation to a child, the court may direct the appropriate local authority to undertake an investigation into the child's circumstances. If the local authority decides, after investigating, not to apply for a care or supervision order, it must inform the court of the reasons for that decision and of the services or assistance they have provided or intend to provide and of any other action taken or proposed to be taken. The court no longer has the power it had prior to the Children Act to commit children to care in matrimonial and domestic proceedings.

[34] See DoH, Home Office and DfEE (1999) para 5.34. For a detailed discussion of the way investigations are expected to be planned and executed, see paras 5.33–5.38.

In addition, the court must be satisfied that the local authority has reasonable cause to believe that access is required as a matter of urgency. Factors such as the child's condition when seen in the recent past, the nature of the suspicions, the child's age and whether there is any opportunity to see the child in other places such as school would be relevant.[35]

Another possibility is that the local authority could apply for a child assessment order.[36] Alternatively, if time is of the essence, the local authority might ask the police to take the child into police protection.[37]

A constable, if he or she has reasonable cause to believe that a child would otherwise be likely to suffer significant harm, can take that child into police protection for up to 72 hours.[38] A constable taking a child into police protection in terms of the Children Act 1989 must inform, as soon as possible, the local authority, the parents and the child about what steps have been taken. The child must be taken to a refuge or local authority accommodation.[39] A designated officer must investigate the case and the child must be then be released unless that officer is satisfied that there is reasonable cause to believe that the child would be likely to suffer significant harm if released. If so satisfied, the designated officer can apply for an EPO on behalf of the local authority, whether they are aware of this or not. Alternatively, the local authority, apprised of the situation and obliged to investigate in terms of Section 47, might apply for an order itself or ask the police to do so on its behalf.[40] The designated officer must, while the child is in police protection, allow reasonable contact between the child and the persons specified in Section 46(10).

Masson, *et al*, report that police protection powers are used primarily when the police 'stumble' on a situation or when they are requested to take action by the local authority. This might be because it is thought that an application for an EPO would be too slow or because the events in question occur outside court hours (2004 pp 6–7).

### The Outcome of the Investigation

Once they have completed an investigation, the professionals may decide that there is no cause for concern, in which case they should consider whether the family needs support and services (DoH, Home Office and DfEE 1999 para 5.46). Alternatively, there may be concerns, but the evidence is lacking. Then the decision may be to monitor the family (DoH, Home Office and DfEE 1999 para 5.47). Or it may be that the child has suffered significant harm but can be protected without the need for compulsory intervention.[41] Where, however, it is judged that the child remains at risk of significant harm, the local authority must call a child protection conference.[42]

---

[35] See Masson and Morris (1992) p 135.
[36] See below pp 667ff.
[37] See, on the use of police protection, Masson (2002).
[38] S 46 Children Act 1989. See also s 17(1)(e) Police and Criminal Evidence Act 1984.
[39] Although Masson, *et al*, report that most are taken initially to a police station (2004 p 7).
[40] S 47(3)(c).
[41] See DoH, Home Office and DfEE (1999) paras 5.48–5.51.
[42] There is no legal requirement to call child protection conferences. However, they are an important part of the child protection process.

*The Child Protection Conference*

The responsibility for convening a child protection conference[43] rests with the children's services authority.[44] The function of the conference is described in *Working Together*:

> 5.53 The initial child protection conference brings together family members, the child where appropriate, and those professionals most involved with the child and family, following s 47 enquiries. Its purpose is:
>
> - to bring together and analyse in an inter-agency setting the information which has been obtained about the child's health, development and functioning, and the parents' or carers' capacity to ensure the child's safety and promote the child's health and development;
>
> - to make judgements about the likelihood of a child suffering significant harm in future; *and*
>
> - to decide what future action is needed to safeguard the child and promote his or her welfare, how that action will be taken forward, and with what intended outcomes.
>
> (DoH, Home Office and DfEE 1999)

Family members and carers may be invited to attend. Parents should normally be invited and helped to participate with the assistance, if they so wish, of a friend, supporter or advocate (DoH, Home Office and DfEE 1999 para 5.57).[45] Children, depending on their age and understanding, may also attend and bring a friend, advocate or supporter (*ibid*). In any event, the child's wishes and feelings should be conveyed to the conference (*ibid*).

The task of the conference is to decide whether the child is at continued risk of significant harm. If the answer is in the affirmative, a formal child protection plan will be needed and the conference must formulate an outline plan (para 5.64).[46] In addition, the child's name will be placed on the child protection register.[47] In future, concerns will be recorded on a database, as provided for in s 12 Children Act 2004. At the time of writing, however, the register continues in operation and the test the conference must apply is set out in *Working Together*:

> 5.64 The conference should consider the following question when determining whether to register a child[48]:
>
> - Is the child at continuing risk of significant harm?
>
> The test should be that either:
>
> - the child can be shown to have suffered ill-treatment or impairment of health or development as a result of physical, emotional, or sexual abuse or neglect, and professional judgement is that further ill-treatment or impairment are likely; or

---

[43] There is no reference to child protection conferences in the Children Act 1989 but they are referred to in many of the guidance documents such as *Working Together*.

[44] The NSPCC also has statutory powers but it is usually the local authority that convenes the conference.

[45] Violence or intimidation are examples of reasons to exclude family members. See DoH, Home Office and DfEE (1999) para 5.58.

[46] See, for the contents of the outline plan, DoH, Home Office and DfEE (1999) para 5.69.

[47] See DoH, Home Office and DfEE (1999) para 5.66, 5.68. The register lists all the children resident in the local authority's area who are considered to be at risk of significant harm and for whom there is a child protection plan (para 5.99).

[48] If the child's name is not placed on the register, the conference must nevertheless consider the family's need for help (para 5.67).

- professional judgement, substantiated by the findings of enquiries in this individual case or by research evidence, is that the child is likely to suffer ill-treatment or the impairment of health or development as a result of physical, emotional, or sexual abuse or neglect.

(DoH, Home Office and DfEE 1999)

If a decision is made to register the child,[49] a key worker is appointed and a core group of professionals and family members is established (DoH, Home Office and DfEE 1999 para 5.68). The key worker is the lead professional in working with the family and is also responsible for developing the outline plan into a detailed inter-agency plan (para 5.76). The core group is also responsible for developing the plan and for implementing it (para 5.77). The plan should 'take into consideration the wishes and feelings of the child, and the views of the parents, insofar as this is consistent with the child's welfare' (para 5.83). If their preferences are not accepted, this should be explained and the family should be advised of their right to complain (*ibid*).

A core assessment must be completed in respect of every child on the register[50] and the assessment should inform the child protection plan.[51] Parents should be made aware of the causes for concern, 'what needs to change, and [be clear] about what is expected of them as part of the plan for safeguarding the child' (para 5.88). A written agreement regarding the implementation of the plan should be produced as part of, or in addition to the plan (*ibid*). Regular child protection reviews have to be held to monitor the case (para 5.90).[52]

Guidance instructs professionals to consider whether it will be possible to work in partnership with some or all family members but warns that partnership may not be an option. In particular, it notes, partnership is impossible if there is continued hostility to professional intervention or lack of motivation to be involved in planning for the child's future. Allegations of sexual abuse; denial of abuse where there is evidence that it occurred; or persistent violence on the part of a man towards the children or his partner may preclude partnership (DoH 1995a paras 8.17–8.20).

*Intervention*

Guidance for professionals states that interventions should address matters such as the child's needs as well as the relationship between the child and the abuser and the parents' capacity to respond to the child's needs (DoH 2003b para 58). Measures taken might include therapy for the child and the abuser (para 59). A key issue is whether the child's developmental needs can be met within the family and within timescales that are appropriate for the child (para 61). Where the family situation does not improve fast enough, the child may be removed (*ibid*). This could be done on the basis of a voluntary arrangement or by means of a court order.

---

[49] A child may be de-registered at a subsequent date, and this possibility should be considered at every child protection review. See DoH, Home Office and DfEE (1999) para 5.91. The criteria for de-registration are set out in *Working Together* (DoH, Home Office and DfEE 1999 para 5.93).

[50] Children in need must also be assessed if their parents want this to be done (DoH, Home Office and DfEE 1999 para 5.85).

[51] See DoH, Home Office and DfEE 1999 paras 5.85 and 5.87.

[52] The review is needed to consider whether the child's name should remain on the register, to review the child's situation against the intended outcomes of the plan, to ensure that the child is being safeguarded and to consider whether any changes are necessary (see DoH, Home Office and DfEE 1999 para 5.90–5.95).

Court proceedings, according to *The Challenge of Partnership*, do not necessarily put an end to partnership. A new kind of partnership may be negotiated in which the worker 'makes explicit her or his control' (DoH 1995a para 8.16). The family can co-operate in building a safer environment for the child or accept the child's long-term or permanent removal (*ibid*).

> **Q** Refer to chapter 9. What does 'partnership' mean in the context of child protection? On whose terms is the partnership?

Provided June and Brian are co-operative, it is likely that the professionals will consider it unnecessary to seek a court order. They may choose to seek to avert any need for compulsory measures by monitoring the family and by providing assistance. Local authorities have a duty to take 'reasonable steps, through the provision of services under Part III of [the] Act, to prevent children within their area suffering ill-treatment or neglect'.[53] In addition, they have a duty to take reasonable steps designed to avoid having to take children into care.[54] Section 17, in turn, imposes duties on local authorities in relation to children in need.

If it is considered too risky to leave the child in the same home as the suspected abuser, the suspected abuser might be persuaded to agree to leave. In that event, the local authority may provide him or her with assistance, if necessary financial, to find alternative accommodation.[55] The more commonly adopted solution, however, is to offer to accommodate the child away from the home under Section 20 of the Children Act 1989:

Provision of accommodation for children: general

20.—(1) Every local authority shall provide accommodation for any child in need within their area who appears to them to require accommodation as a result of—
(a) there being no person who has parental responsibility for him;
(b) his being lost or having been abandoned; or
(c) the person who has been caring for him being prevented (whether or not permanently, and for whatever reason) from providing him with suitable accommodation or care. ..[56]

(3) Every local authority shall provide accommodation for any child in need within their area who has reached the age of 16 and whose welfare the authority consider is likely to be seriously prejudiced if they do not provide him with accommodation.[57]

(4) A local authority may provide accommodation for any child within their area (even though a person who has parental responsibility for him is able to provide him with accommodation) if they consider that to do so would safeguard or promote the child's welfare. ...

(6) Before providing accommodation under this section, a local authority shall, so far as is reasonably practicable and consistent with the child's welfare—
(a) ascertain the child's wishes and feelings regarding the provision of accommodation; and

[53] Sch 2, para 4(1), to the Children Act 1989.
[54] Sch 2, para 7(a)(i).
[55] Sch 2, para 5, to the Children Act 1989.
[56] This would include parents who cannot care for their children as a result of illness and parents who need respite from caring for their child. Respite care is used by parents of children who need constant attention, such as children with disabilities, and by parents of children with behavioural problems.
[57] For discussion of the position of children aged 16 and over, see Bainham (2005) pp 434–35.

(b)  give due consideration (having regard to his age and understanding) to such wishes and feelings of the child as they have been able to ascertain.

Accommodation may be a short-term measure to enable the parents to deal with their problems. In those cases where the child cannot return home, accommodation in a residential establishment or foster home[58] is provided as a 'long-term substitute for home' (Barton and Douglas 1995 p 301).[59] In either event, a child can only be accommodated in terms of Section 20 if those with parental responsibility consent. However, whether consent is always freely given is open to doubt; some parents may be faced with the prospect of a care or supervision order as an alternative.[60]

Accommodation on a voluntary basis may enable the local authority to avoid seeking court orders authorising compulsory intervention,[61] but the Guidance and Regulations state that where there is a risk, the local authority must consider whether this course of action is sufficient to safeguard the child.[62]

Parents retain their parental responsibility while their child is being accommodated, and the voluntary nature of accommodation is evident in a number of the provisions in Section 20. A local authority may not provide accommodation for a child if a person with parental responsibility objects and is willing and able to provide accommodation or to arrange for it to be provided.[63] And once accommodation is being provided, any person with parental responsibility for the child may remove him or her.[64] The only circumstances in which these provisions do not apply are where a child who has reached the age of 16 agrees to the accommodation[65] or where a person who has a residence order, or who has the care of the child pursuant to an order under the High Court's inherent jurisdiction, agrees to it.[66]

While the child is being accommodated, neither the local authority nor a foster parent acquires parental responsibility. However the Act allows for the delegation of parental responsibility in full or in part[67] and provides authority for carers to make routine decisions: Section 3(5) states that a person who does not have parental responsibility but has care of the child may do what is reasonable in the circumstances in order to safeguard or promote the child's welfare.[68] When a child is accommodated, a written agreement is

---

[58] See s 23 for the duties owed by local authorities regarding accommodation of children whom they are looking after. See, on the Care Standards Act 2000 and the regulation of substitute care arrangements such as children's homes and fostering arrangements, Bainham (2005) pp 445ff

[59] The majority of 'looked after' children are the victims of abuse or neglect and about a third of children are 'looked after' pursuant to voluntary arrangements (Creighton 2003). The practice of using accommodation as a substitute for a care or supervision order has been criticised as leading to drift. See the discussion in Bainham (2005) p 431.

[60] See Masson, *et al*, (2004) pp 58–60; Lindley and Richards (2000) p 224; Barton and Douglas (1995) p 302.

[61] See DoH (1991b) para 2.29.

[62] See DoH (1991b) para 2.30. See also DoH (1989a) p 8.

[63] S 20(7).

[64] S 20(8). The statute does not require that the person wishing to remove the child give any notice of that intention but, normally, the ways in which accommodation may be terminated will be incorporated into a written agreement between the parents and the local authority (DoH (1991b) para 3.28). Masson, *et al*, found that, where children at risk were being accommodated, parents who sought to remove their children contrary to an agreement faced the possibility of proceedings for an emergency protection order (2004 p 69). The authors recommend that parents have access to legal advice or independent advocacy before entering agreements (p 77).

[65] S 20(11).

[66] S 20(9).

[67] S 2(9).

[68] It may be that this provision could be used to prevent a parent from removing a child from accommodation, eg, if the parent is aggressive, violent or drunk. See HC Deb, 18 May 1989, Standing Committee B, col 148. But see Cretney, *et al*, (2002) p 710.

drawn up setting out the arrangements for the child's care.[69] It should specify the arrangements for contact, delineate the roles of the various parties in relation to day-to-day decision-making and include the arrangements for rehabilitation of the child with the person with whom he or she has been living.[70] Although the agreement is not legally binding, it forms the framework for the partnerships between all those concerned. In addition, the Act requires the local authority, before making any decisions about a child, in so far as is reasonably practicable, to ascertain and give due regard to the wishes of the child, in the light of his or her age and understanding, and the parents.[71]

> **Q** At a child protection conference, a decision is made to register Amy and a child protection plan is then agreed. Brian and June are instructed to attend a family centre with Amy weekly for counselling and help with parenting skills. They are both busy, however, and miss two sessions in a row. The social worker, when she calls at the house, thinks she can hear Amy's voice but is told by Brian that she cannot see the child because she is at a swimming lesson. When she calls on two subsequent occasions at the appointed times, she is told on the first occasion that Amy is out and, on the second, that she is asleep and cannot be disturbed.

Clearly, a high degree of co-operation is needed between all the parties to sustain partnership relationships:

> Work with parents to achieve an initial agreement to the accommodation of the child by the local authority will usually ensure that the ongoing plan for the child can be operated in partnership with the parents. Where a parent is unwilling to co-operate at the outset or becomes unco-operative or inconsistent in attitude or commitment to the child the nature of the arrangement should be reassessed and the need for care proceedings or emergency protection action should be considered. (DoH 1991b para 2.30)

The fact that the family has failed to attend the appointments coupled with the difficulties faced by the social worker in gaining access to Amy would be likely to heighten concerns about her safety. The social worker should consider the possibility of involving the local authority solicitor with a view to applying for a court order.[72] Consideration might be given to obtaining a child assessment order. Alternatively they might seek the help of the police and have Amy taken into police protection. It might then be possible to seek an EPO.[73]

---

[69] S 3, Arrangements for Placement of Children (General) Regs 1991, SI 1991/890. See DoH (1991b) para 3.32.

[70] Sch 4, Arrangements for Placement of Children (General) Regs 1991, SI 1991/890.

[71] S 22(4) and (5). A local authority refusal to consult with a parent or keep him informed was held to be an irregularity that did not render the decisions made void in *Re P ( Children Act 1989, ss 22 and 26: Local Authority Compliance)* [2000] 2 FLR 910.

[72] Masson, *et al,* found that applications for emergency protection orders were often precipitated by an incident affecting a child about whom there were already concerns (2004 p 51). They also observed that court proceedings might be instituted if parents failed to abide by the terms of an agreement. The breach would be seen as evidence of inadequacy and non-co-operation. It was also easier to establish the need for an order because voluntary arrangements had been tried and had failed (pp 71–72).

[73] Masson, *et al,* found that EPOs followed police protection in about one third to a half of their cases (2004 p 37).

# V. COURT ORDERS

## *Child Assessment Order*

This order[74] is designed to facilitate assessment of children about whom there are concerns and whose parents do not co-operate voluntarily. The child assessment order authorises assessment of the child[75] and requires that any person in a position to produce the child do so and comply with any directions specified in the order.[76]

> 43 Child assessment orders
>
> (1) On the application of a local authority or authorised person for an order to be made under this section with respect to a child, the court may make the order if, but only if, it is satisfied that—
> (a)   the applicant has reasonable cause to suspect that the child is suffering, or is likely to suffer, significant harm;
> (b)   an assessment of the state of the child's health or development, or of the way in which he has been treated, is required to enable the applicant to determine whether or not the child is suffering, or is likely to suffer, significant harm; and
> (c)   it is unlikely that such an assessment will be made, or be satisfactory, in the absence of an order under this section.

An order cannot have effect for more than seven days[77] and the child may be kept away from home only if it is necessary for the purposes of assessment, and then only for the period specified in the order.[78] If the child is to be kept from home, the order should contain directions concerning contact.[79]

Child assessment orders are intended to be used where significant harm is suspected but the child is not thought to be at immediate risk (DoH 1991c para 4.9). The purpose of an order is to enable the local authority (or NSPCC), where the parents or other carers are refusing to co-operate, to ascertain how the child is. A decision can then be made as to what further action, if any, is needed.[80]

The advantage of the child assessment order was thought to be that it is less interventionist than emergency protection orders and interim care or supervision orders (DoH 1991c para 4.6). However it is seldom used, apparently because social workers are reluctant to alienate parents who might otherwise co-operate and because a time limit of seven days is too short to allow for a reliable assessment (Dickens 1993 p 91).[81]

---

[74] This order had no equivalent under the pre-Children Act scheme; it was introduced pursuant to a recommendation in the report of the Kimberley Carlile inquiry, see London Borough of Greenwich (1987) ch 25.

[75] S 43(7) of the Children Act 1989. A child, if of sufficient understanding to make an informed decision, can refuse to submit to the assessment (s 43(8)). But see *South Glamorgan County Council v W and B* [1993] 1 FLR 574.

[76] S 43(6) of the Children Act 1989. Deliberate failure to comply with an order may suffice to satisfy the grounds for an emergency protection order. In cases of extreme emergency, it may be necessary to call on the police to exercise their powers under s 46 of the Children Act 1989 (see p 661) or their powers under the Police and Criminal Evidence Act (s 17(1)(e)) to enter and search premises if there is a threat to life and limb. See DoH (1991c) para 4.19.

[77] S 43(5).

[78] S 43(9).

[79] S 43(10).

[80] See DoH (1991c) para 4.6.

[81] See also Lavery (1996). See also *Re B (A Minor) (Care Order: Criteria)* [1993] 1 FLR 815.

It is said that a child assessment order should not be used when an emergency protection order or an interim care or supervision order would be more appropriate (DoH 1991c para 4.6). Indeed Section 43(4) provides that a child assessment order should not be made if the court is satisfied that there are grounds for an emergency protection order and considers that it ought to make such an order instead.

*Emergency Protection Order*

Prior to the Children Act 1989, it was common to apply for emergency orders, called place of safety orders, as a prelude to full care proceedings.[82] In contrast, the provisions of the Children Act reflect a consensus that the emergency powers of local authorities should be circumscribed. The emergency protection order is designed to 'enable the child in a genuine emergency to be removed from where he is or be kept where he is, if and only if this is what is necessary to provide immediate short-term protection' (DoH 1991c para 4.28).[83]

The Children Act 1989 provides:

Orders for emergency protection of children

44.—(1) Where any person ('the applicant') applies to the court for an order to be made under this section with respect to a child, the court may make an order if, but only if, it is satisfied that—
(a)   there is reasonable cause to believe that the child is likely to suffer significant harm if—
    (i)   he is not removed to accommodation provided by or on behalf of the applicant; or
    (ii)  he does not remain in the place in which he is then being accommodated[84];
(b)   in the case of an application made by the local authority—
    (i)   enquiries are being made with respect to the child under section 47(1)(b); and
    (ii)  those enquiries are being frustrated by access to the child being unreasonably refused to a person authorised to seek access and that the applicant has reasonable cause to believe that access to the child is required as a matter of urgency.[85]

Section 44(1)(a) should normally be used where the child has been seen (DoH 1991c para 4.42) and there is enough information to satisfy the court that there is reasonable cause to believe that significant harm is likely. It may be that in this case, there is insufficient information. One way to get to see Amy would be to ask the police to take her into police protection. However, the police would have to be satisfied that there is reasonable cause to believe that she would otherwise be likely to suffer significant harm. Alternatively, the local authority would have to rely on Section 44(1)(b). The problem is that, in order to do this, they would have to show that they were undertaking a Section 47 enquiry and had been refused access in the course of that enquiry. It may be, however,

---

[82] For criticism of these orders, see DHSS (1985) ch 13; DHSS (1987) paras 45–66; Butler-Sloss (1988) para 4.92.

[83] In 2001, there were about 2127 emergency protection orders and extensions of orders (Masson, *et al*, 2004 p 12).

[84] Eg, a hospital.

[85] S 44(1)(c) contains provisions similar to those in s 44(1)(b) and applies where the application pursuant to an enquiry is made by an authorised person (the NSPCC). Unlike the local authority, however, the applicant must satisfy the court about the existence of reasonable cause for suspicion.

that the social worker was not engaging in an enquiry when she was refused access; it may be that she was merely monitoring the family. A new Section 47 enquiry might have to be commenced and, if the social worker were again refused access, there could be grounds for an EPO.

An application for an EPO may in some circumstances be made *ex parte* and the court will, in making its decision, apply the welfare principle in Section 1(1)[86] as well as the non-intervention principle in Section 1(5). If granted, an order would be made for a period of up to eight days, with the possibility of an extension not exceeding a further seven days.[87] An application to discharge the order may be made after 72 hours, but there is no provision for appeal either against the granting of or refusal of an order.[88]

The order operates as a direction to any person in a position to do so to comply with any request to produce the child.[89] It may authorise the applicant to enter premises to search for the child and any other child thought to be there whom the court is satisfied is at risk.[90] All emergency protection orders authorise, for the purposes of safeguarding the welfare of the child,[91] removal of the child to accommodation provided by the applicant or the prevention of the removal of the child from the place where he or she is.[92] It also gives the applicant parental responsibility for the child.[93] This can be exercised only in so far as is necessary to safeguard or promote the welfare of the child[94] and the parents retain their parental responsibility. The court may give directions with respect to assessment of the child as well as contact.[95] Subject to any such direction, the applicant must allow reasonable contact.[96]

In *X Council v B (Emergency Protection Orders)*,[97] the court urged that decisions to make EPOs should not be made lightly. Munby J acknowledged that the removal of children in terms of such orders is in principle compatible with the European Convention and there may be cases where an *ex parte* application is justified.[98] However, he said, '[a]n EPO, summarily removing a child from his parents, is a terrible and drastic remedy'.[99] He considered that defects in the statutory scheme, such as the absence of a right of appeal, make it all the more important that courts approach applications with 'anxious awareness of the extreme gravity of the relief being sought and a scrupulous regard

---

[86] The checklist in s 1(3) is, strictly speaking, not applicable.

[87] S 45. An extension is permitted only where the court has reasonable cause to believe the child will suffer significant harm if the order is not extended. A children's guardian will be appointed under s 41 to safeguard the interests of the child in the proceedings.

[88] Ss 45(9) and (10). See *Essex County Council v F* [1993] 1 FLR 847. See also *Re P (Emergency Protection Order)* [1996] 1 FLR 482.

[89] S 44(4)(a).

[90] Ss 48(3) and (4). In terms of s 48(9), a warrant may be obtained if it appears to the court that a person trying to exercise powers under an EPO has been frustrated by being refused entry to premises or access to the child or that he or she is likely to be frustrated in this way. The warrant will authorise any constable to assist, using reasonable force if necessary.

[91] S 44(5)(a).

[92] S 44(4)(b). It is an offence intentionally to obstruct the exercise of these powers (s 44(15)).

[93] S 44(4)(c).

[94] S 44(5)(b).

[95] S 44(6). A child, if of sufficient understanding to make an informed decision, may refuse to submit to an examination or other assessment (s 44(7)). But see *South Glamorgan County Council v W and B* [1993] 1 FLR 574. The court also has the power to impose conditions in relation to contact and may direct that there shall be no assessment (s 44(8)).

[96] S 44(13).

[97] [2004] EWHC Fam 2015; [2005] 1 FLR 341.

[98] Para 35. See also, for example, *Haase v Germany* [2004] 2 FLR 39. See also Masson, *et al*, (2004) pp 21–22.

[99] Para 34.

for the European Convention Rights of both the child and the parents'.[100] The judge
went on to comment generally on the way that the law should be applied:

[57] ...

(i) An EPO, summarily removing a child from his parents, is a 'draconian' and 'extremely
harsh' measure, requiring 'exceptional justification' and 'extraordinarily compelling reasons'.
Such an order should not be made unless the FPC is satisfied that it is both necessary and proportionate and that no other less radical form of order will achieve the essential end of
promoting the welfare of the child. Separation is only to be contemplated if immediate separation is essential to secure the child's safety: 'imminent danger' must be 'actually established' ... .

(iii) Any order must provide for the least interventionist solution consistent with the preservation of the child's immediate safety.

(iv) If the real purpose of the local authority's application is to enable it to have the child
assessed then consideration should be given to whether that objective cannot equally effectively, and more proportionately, be achieved by an application for, or by the making of, a CAO
under s 43 of the Children Act 1989.

(v) No EPO should be made for any longer than is absolutely necessary to protect the child.
Where the EPO is made on an ex parte (without notice) application very careful consideration
should be given to the need to ensure that the initial order is made for the shortest possible
period commensurate with the preservation of the child's immediate safety ... .

(vii) Save in wholly exceptional cases, parents must be given adequate prior notice of the date,
time and place of any application by a local authority for an EPO. They must also be given
proper notice of the evidence the local authority is relying upon.

(viii) Where the application for an EPO is made ex parte the local authority must make out a
compelling case for applying without first giving the parents notice. An ex parte application
will normally be appropriate only if the case is genuinely one of emergency or other great
urgency—and even then it should normally be possible to give some kind of albeit informal
notice to the parents—or if there are compelling reasons to believe the child's welfare will be
compromised if the parents are alerted in advance to what is going on.[101]

(ix) The evidential burden on the local authority is even heavier if the application is made ex
parte ... .

(xii) ... The local authority must apply its mind very carefully to whether removal [of the child]
is essential in order to secure the child's immediate safety. The mere fact that the local authority
has obtained an EPO is not of itself enough....The local authority, even after it has obtained
an EPO, is under an obligation to consider less drastic alternatives to emergency removal ... .

(xiii) ... [Sections 44(10)(a) and (11)(a) impose] on the local authority a continuing duty to keep
the case under review day by day so as to ensure that parent and child are separated no longer
than is necessary to secure the child's safety ... .

(xiv) Section 44(13) of the Children Act 1989 requires the local authority, subject only to any
direction given by the FPC under s 44(6), to allow a child who is subject to an EPO 'reasonable
contact' with his parents. Arrangements for contact must be driven by the needs of the family,
not stunted by lack of resources.

(Quotation marks in the original)

---

[100] Para 41.
[101] *In Haase v Germany* [2004] 2 FLR 39, para 95, the ECtHR said that 'it may not always be possible,
because of the urgency of the situation, to associate in the decision-making process those having custody of the
child. Nor may it even be desirable, even if possible, to do so if those having custody of the chid are seen as the
source of an immediate threat to the child'. However it must be shown that there was reason to think that the
circumstances justified removal of the child without prior consultation (*ibid*).

The Children Act 1989 was amended[102] so that, rather than social services having to remove the child from the home, the court can order that the suspected abuser be excluded instead. Section 44A of the Children Act 1989 provides that an exclusion requirement can be included in an emergency protection order. It may exclude a person from the home or a defined area in which the home is situated. It may also prohibit that person from entering the home. In addition, the court may, in terms of Section 42(2)(b) and Section 42(3) of the Family Law Act 1996, make a non-molestation order where this would benefit the child.

An exclusion requirement can be included, in the case of an emergency protection order made under Section 44(1)(a), if there is reasonable cause to believe that, if the relevant person[103] is excluded from the child's home, the child will not be likely to suffer significant harm if not removed from or kept out of the home. In the case of an order made under Section 44(1)(b),[104] there must be reasonable cause to believe that enquiries will cease to be frustrated if the relevant person is excluded. A further condition for the inclusion of an exclusion requirement is that there is someone in the home, whether a parent or not, who consents to it and who is willing and able to care for the child.[105] The exclusion requirement ceases to have effect when the emergency protection order does and may be made for a shorter period.[106] A power of arrest can be attached to it permitting a constable to arrest without warrant any person reasonably believed to be in breach.[107] Alternatively, the court may accept an undertaking which is enforced through contempt proceedings.[108]

In Amy's case, there could be difficulty in obtaining an EPO unless there was a Section 47 enquiry at this stage or unless the police intervened to enable the local authority to see Amy and, if necessary, to invoke Section 44(1)(a). In any event, in the light of the Munby J's opinion in the *X* case, it seems that the local authority might have to consider applying for a CAO as they are in reality seeking to assess Amy.

> **Q** A child assessment order is granted. Amy is removed from the home and, in accordance with a direction from the court, she is examined by a paediatrician. He finds that she has severe bruises of various ages on her legs and abdomen. Amy says she does not know what caused them and her parents say she is clumsy and bumps into things.

It may now be necessary to consider the need for a care or supervision order.[109] The local authority will make an assessment of which order it considers most appropriate and frame its application accordingly. However the court has a discretion under Section 31 and is therefore at liberty to make an order other than that applied for.[110] The court

---

[102] See s 52 of and Sch 6 to the Family Law Act 1996.

[103] In a case where suspicion is not directed at a particular individual such as one of the parents, there is no 'relevant' person who might sensibly be excluded. An exclusion requirement would not, therefore, be appropriate.

[104] Or s 44(1)(c).

[105] S 44A(2)(b) of the Children Act 1989.

[106] S 44A(4).

[107] Ss 44A(5) and (8).

[108] S 44B.

[109] In 2003, 7387 care orders and 2383 supervision orders were made (DfES 2004e p 47).

[110] Although cogent reasons should be given if the court decides to impose an order on the local authority that is different from the order sought: *Re O (Care or Supervision Order)* [1996] 2 FLR 755, 759.

may decide to make a care order,[111] a supervision order, a residence order[112] or, indeed, no order at all.[113] The court should always be alert to the possibility that further intervention may do more harm than good.[114]

**Q** Can the court accurately predict what the outcome would be of each course of action? If so, how?

## VI. CARE PLANS

Before making an order, the court must be satisfied that the order would be in the child's best interests[115] and that to make that order is better for the child than making no order at all.[116] It is therefore imperative that the court is aware of the local authority's proposed course of action should an order be granted. The local authority must present a care plan to the court outlining the child's needs and indicating how these are to be met. The plan should give details of matters such as where the child is to live and what arrangements for contact will be made.[117] Parents who wish to challenge a care plan on human rights grounds should normally do so under Section 7(1)(b) of the HRA 1998 within the context of the care proceedings.[118] Where the court disagrees with the care plan it can refuse to make the order.[119]

## VII. THE CHILDREN'S GUARDIAN

Section 41(1) stipulates that the court must appoint an officer of CAFCASS (Children and Family Court Advisory and Support Service)[120] for the child unless satisfied that it is not necessary to do so in order to safeguard his or her interests.[121] In public law cases, this officer is the children's guardian.[122] The guardian would normally be a qualified and

---

113 A care or supervision order may not be made with respect to a child who has reached the age of 17 (or 16 in the case of a child who is married) (s 31(3)).

114 Eg in favour of a relative.

113 See *Re B (Care or Supervision Order)* [1996] 2 FLR 693, 698.

114 See DHSS (1985) para 15.24. See also DoH (1995b) pp 49–50.

115 Ss 1(1) and (3).

116 S 1(5).

117 The obligation to prepare a care plan is now embodied in statute: s 31A Children Act 1989. The obligation arises where an application is made on which a care order may be made, but not when the application is for an interim care order. No care order may be made until the court has considered a s 31A plan (s 31(3A)). See also DoH (1991d) para 2.62; *Manchester City Council v F* [1993] 1 FLR 419; *Re J (Minors) (Care: Care Plan)* [1994] 1 FLR 253.

118 *Re L (Care Proceedings: Human Rights Claims)* [2003] EWHC Fam 665; [2003] 2 FLR 160. See also *Re V (Care Proceedings: Human Rights Claims)* [2004] EWCA Civ 54; [2004] 1 FLR 944 para 8; *R (CD) v Isle of Anglesey County Council)* [2004] EWHC Admin 1635; [2005] 1 FLR 59. See below, pp 684ff on the failure to implement care plans properly.

119 *Re J (Minors) (Care: Care Plan)* [1994] 1 FLR 253, 258; *Re B (Supervision Order: Parental Undertaking)* [1996] 1 FLR 676. But see *Re M (Care Order: Freeing Application)* [2003] EWCA Civ 1874; [2004] 1 FLR 826 para 20(iv).

120 Established under the Criminal Justice and Courts Services Act 2000.

121 This duty arises in relation to 'specified proceedings' enumerated in s 41(6). These include applications for care or supervision orders, applications to discharge these orders and proceedings under Part V.

122 Prior to the creation of CAFCASS, this role was carried out by a guardian *ad litem*, who was a member of a panel set up by the local authority. CAFCASS is accountable to Parliament through the DfES (www.cafcass.gov.uk, accessed 4 April 2005).

experienced social worker.[123] He or she is under a duty to safeguard the interests of the child[124] and to represent the child. Normally, the child's solicitor is appointed and instructed by the guardian.[125] While the role of the guardian is fairly limited in emergency proceedings,[126] it is very significant in care and supervision proceedings, involving, among other things, an investigation into all the circumstances and the writing of a report for the court.[127]

## VIII. INTERIM ORDERS

An interim order may be needed initially to ensure that Amy is protected after expiry of the child assessment order and while enquiries are completed,[128] the guardian's report is written up and a case is prepared.[129] While this will involve some delay in settling the arrangements for the child's care, and delay is usually considered prejudicial to the welfare of the child,[130] it is justifiable in order to ensure that the court reaches its decision on the basis of the best available information.[131] Section 38(1) provides that the court may make an interim order where proceedings on an application for a care or supervision order are adjourned or where a direction is given under Section 37(1). To make an interim order, the court has to be satisfied only that there are reasonable grounds for believing that the child's circumstances meet the criteria in Section 31(2) for granting a care or supervision order.[132] This test is less strict than that governing the making of a full order; then the court requires proof of the matters referred to in Section 31(2). Interim orders can be made for up to eight weeks and can be extended for four-week periods.[133]

[123] See www.cafcass.gov.uk, accessed 4 April 2005.
[124] S 41(2)(b).
[125] However, if the child is of sufficient understanding to instruct a solicitor and those instructions conflict with the guardian's, the solicitor must follow the child's instructions (Family Proceedings Rules 1991, SI 1991/1247, R 4.12(1)(a); Family Proceedings Court (Children Act 1989) Rules 1991 SI 1991/1395, R 12(1)(a)). See also *Re P (Representation)* [1996] 1 FLR 486.
[126] See DoH (1991f) para 2.69.There may not be a guardian appointed in emergency proceedings. See *X Council v B) Emergency Protection Orders)*[2004] EWHC Fam 2015; [2005] 1 FLR 341, para 37.
[127] For a more detailed account of the guardian's role and that of the child's solicitor, see Bainham (2005) pp 585–93.
[128] The court has the power to order or prohibit assessments of the child (s 38(6) and (7)), although the older child has the capacity to refuse. But see *South Glamorgan County Council v W and B* [1993] 1 FLR 574. The court's jurisdiction extends to all assessments that involve the child and are directed at providing the court with the information it needs in order to reach a proper decision at the final hearing of the application for a full care order. This can entail assessment of the child within the family in a residential institution. The local authority cannot refuse to make such an assessment on the grounds of lack of resources (*Re C (A Minor) (Interim Care Order: Residential Assessment)* [1996] 3 WLR 1098). An application under s 38(6) can engage Arts 6 and 8 of the European Convention. In many cases the parents' only hope of averting a care order and adoption may lie in the successful completion of an assessment. The fate of the child may rest on this (*Re G (Interim Care Order: Residential Assessment)* [2004] EWCA Civ 24; [2004] 1 FLR 876).
[129] See DoH (1991c) para 3.39.
[130] S 1(2).
[131] See Hayes and Williams (1995) p 147.
[132] S 38(2). See *Oxfordshire County Council v S* [2003] EWHC Fam 2174; [2004] 1 FLR 426. The test in s 1(5) also applies.
[133] Ss 38(4) and (5).

If the court makes a residence order, in favour of relatives for example, it must make an interim supervision order unless satisfied that the child's welfare will be safeguarded without it.[134]

Where the court makes an interim care order, it may include an exclusion requirement[135] if satisfied that there is reasonable cause to believe that, if a particular person is excluded from the home, the child will cease to suffer, or cease to be likely to suffer, significant harm. There must be some other person in the home, whether a parent or not, who consents to the exclusion requirement and who is able and willing to care for the child adequately. A power of arrest may be attached. Alternatively the court may accept an undertaking, in which case a power of arrest cannot be attached.[136]

## IX.  CARE AND SUPERVISION ORDERS—THRESHOLD CRITERIA

Where a court is faced with an application for a care order, the court has to determine whether the requirements of Section 31 have been met. If they have, the court has a discretion whether to grant the order or not and must exercise that discretion in accordance with Section 1. These two stages are referred to as the 'threshold' stage and the 'welfare' stage respectively.[137] In addition, the court may not make a care order empowering the local authority to remove the child from the family without considering the European Convention Article 8 rights of the adults and children of the family. The judge 'must not sanction such an interference with family life unless he is satisfied that it is both necessary and proportionate and that no other less radical form of order' would promote the child's welfare.[138] Indeed, it has been said that any application under Part IV of the Children Act 1989 engages Arts. 6 and 8.[139]

Section 31(2) sets out the threshold conditions and provides that:

A court may only make a care order or supervision order if it is satisfied—
(a)   that the child concerned is suffering, or is likely to suffer, significant harm; and
(b)   that the harm, or likelihood of harm, is attributable to—
  (i)   the care given to the child, or likely to be given to him if the order were not made, not being what it would be reasonable to expect a parent to give him; or
  (ii)  the child's being beyond parental control.

The section, then, allows for an order to be made not only in circumstances where the child is already suffering harm but also where there is no evidence of existing or past harm but there is a risk of future harm. It is not sufficient if the 'significant harm'[140] test is met. In addition, the court must be satisfied that the harm is attributable to some parental deficit.

---

134 S 38(3).
135 S 38A.
136 See s 38B.
137 *Re M and R (Child Abuse: Evidence)* [1996] 2 FLR 195, 202.
138 *Re B (Care: Interference with Family Life)* [2003] EWCA Civ 786; [2004] 1 FCR 463 para 34.See also *Re V (Care Proceedings: Human Rights Claims)* [2004] EWCA Civ 54; [2004] 1 FLR 944 para 8. See further on the Human Rights Act, ch 9 pp 365ff above.
139 *Re V (Care Proceedings: Human Rights Claims)* [2004] EWCA Civ 54; [2004] 1 FLR 944 para 8.
140 The meaning of this term is considered on p 658 above.

*'Is Suffering'*

The relevant time for determining whether a child 'is suffering' significant harm was considered by the House of Lords in *Re M (A Minor) (Care Orders: Threshold Conditions)*.[141] When the child concerned in that case, G, was 4 months old, his father murdered his mother and was then sentenced to life imprisonment. The mother's cousin, Mrs W, took over the care of the older children in the family but felt unable to look after G as well. G was accordingly sent to foster parents and the local authority applied for a care order. He later went to live with Mrs W who had changed her mind. With the support of the local authority, she applied for a residence order. However, the child's father argued that G should be adopted. The question that had to be decided was whether the Section 31 threshold test was satisfied, since G was being adequately cared for at the time the court had to make a decision and was not *at that time* suffering significant harm.

Reviewing the provisions of the Act, and Sections 31 and 32 in particular, Lord Mackay LC said:

> Indeed, I think there is much to be said for the view that the hearing that Parliament contemplated was one which extended from the time the jurisdiction of the court is first invoked until the case is disposed of. ..There is nothing in s 31(2) which in my opinion requires that the conditions to be satisfied are dissociated from the time of the making of the application by the local authority. I would conclude that the natural construction of the conditions in s 31(2) is that where, at the time the application is to be disposed of, there are in place arrangements for the protection of the child by the local authority on an interim basis which protection has been continuously in place for some time, the relevant date with respect to which the court must be satisfied is the date at which the local authority initiated the procedure for protection under the Act from which these arrangements followed. If after a local authority had initiated protective arrangements the need for these had terminated, because the child's welfare had been satisfactorily provided for otherwise, in any subsequent proceedings it would not be possible to found jurisdiction on the situation at the time of initiation of these arrangements. It is permissible only to look back from the date of disposal to the date of initiation of protection as a result of which local authority arrangements had been continuously in place thereafter to the date of disposal. It has to be borne in mind that this in no way precludes the court from taking account at the date of the hearing of all relevant circumstances. The conditions in sub-s (2) are in the nature of conditions conferring jurisdiction upon the court to consider whether or not a care order or supervision order should be made. Conditions of that kind would in my view normally have to be satisfied at the date on which the order was first applied for. (p 583)

> It is true that an important change has been made in the statutory provisions in respect that it is now permissible under the second branch of s 31(2)(a) to look to the future even if no harm has already occurred in the past. This is an important difference from the previous legislation but in my opinion to read the present legislation as the Court of Appeal has done [ie, that the harm had to be present at the time of the disposal of the case] is substantially to deprive the first branch of s 31(2)(a) of effect. ..It is also clear that while Parliament added the new provisions looking to the future without any necessary connection with harm already suffered, it wished to retain the first branch in respect of harm which the child is suffering. (p 586)

The court went on to say that whether the criteria for a care or supervision order had been satisfied had to be determined before going on to consider the residence application.

---

[141] [1994] 2 FLR 577.

The court decided that the child was suffering significant harm at the relevant time and held that a care order should be made despite the fact that he was now being well cared for. Although the local authority was right to make arrangements for G to remain with Mrs W, there could be future difficulties. The order would enable the local authority to monitor the situation and, in particular, would empower it to determine the extent to which the father might be permitted to exercise his parental responsibility.

In *Re G (Care Proceedings: Threshold Conditions)*,[142] the Court of Appeal held that although the threshold had to have been crossed at the time of the initial intervention, the local authority was entitled to rely on information obtained after that date, and even on later events, if those later events were capable of proving the state of affairs at the date of the first intervention.

> **Q** In *Re M*, (above) Lord Templeman commented that '[r]estrictions on the right of a local authority to apply for a care order were imposed by Section 31 to prevent a local authority interfering too readily with the rights and responsibility of parents' (at p 589). Refer to chapter 9. Why was this a matter of concern to the legislature?

*'Is Likely to Suffer'*

In chapter 9 we discussed the difficulties of predicting those events that we designate as child abuse. Nevertheless, when the courts decide cases based on the ground that the child is 'likely to suffer significant harm', they are in effect making predictions. And it appears that they may be prepared, in the course of this exercise, to look far into the future.[143] The way in which they establish the boundary between what is sufficiently 'likely' and what is not is through rules of evidence. The date at which this likelihood is assessed is the date on which the local authority initiated protective arrangements, provided these remain continuously in place until dipsosal of the case by the court.[144]

What suffices to prove likelihood was considered by the House of Lords in *In Re H and Others (Minors) (Sexual Abuse: Standard of Proof)* (sometimes called *Re H*).[145] This case concerned four sisters and step-sisters. The oldest, D1, alleged that she had been sexually abused and raped by her stepfather, Mr R, the father of two of her siblings. He was charged and acquitted but the local authority proceeded with applications for care orders for the younger girls. The local authority rested its case solely on the alleged abuse of D1, arguing that there was at least a substantial risk that Mr R had sexually abused her and that the others were likely to be harmed too. The House of Lords held that the threshold criteria were not satisfied.

Delivering the majority judgment, Lord Nicholls first considered the meaning of the word 'likely' in the statute. He concluded that it refers to 'a real possibility, a possibility that cannot sensibly be ignored having regard to the nature and gravity of the feared harm in the particular case'.[146] He then went on to deal with the standard of proof and held that cases must be proved on a balance of probabilities. However, he continued:

---

[142] [2001] EWCA Civ 968; [2001] 2 FLR 1111.
[143] See *Re H (A Minor) (S 37 Direction)* [1993] 2 FLR 541, 548.
[144] *Southwark London Borough Council v B* [1998] 2 FLR 1095.
[145] [1996] AC 563, sub nom *Re H and R (Child Sexual Abuse: Standard of Proof)* [1996] 1 FLR 80.
[146] At p 585.

When assessing the probabilities the court will have in mind as a factor, to whatever extent is appropriate in the particular case, that the more serious the allegation the less likely it is that the event occurred and, hence, the stronger should be the evidence before the court concludes that the allegation is established on the balance of probability. ...A stepfather is usually less likely to have repeatedly raped and had non-consensual oral sex with his under-age stepdaughter than on some occasion to have lost his temper and slapped her. Built into the preponderance of probability standard is a serious degree of flexibility in respect of the seriousness of the allegation.

Although the result is much the same, this does not mean that where a serious allegation is in issue the standard of proof required is higher.[147] It means only that the inherent probability or improbability of an event is itself a matter to be taken into account when weighing the probabilities and deciding whether, on balance, the event occurred.  ... (p 586)

> **Q** Keating (1996 p 160) argues that 'a bald generalisation about levels of abuse in society is not evidence from which the credibility of a particular allegation can be judged'. Do you agree?

Lord Lloyd, dissenting, rejected the majority interpretation of the legislation and said: 'It would be a bizarre result if the more serious the anticipated injury, whether physical or sexual, the more difficult it became for the local authority to satisfy the initial burden of proof, and thereby ultimately, if the welfare test is satisfied, secure protection for the child' (p 577).

Lord Nicholls also addressed the question of what information counts as a 'fact' for the purposes of determining likelihood of harm.[148] He noted that, although the judge in the court below suspected that the abuse did occur, the local authority, on whom the burden of proof rested, had failed to establish that it had. Upholding the decision of the Court of Appeal, he said:

I have indicated that unproved allegations of maltreatment cannot form the basis for a finding by the court that either limb of s 31(2)(a) is established. It is, of course, open to a court to conclude there is a real possibility that the child will suffer harm in the future although harm in the past has not been established. There will be cases where, although the alleged maltreatment itself is not proved, the evidence does establish a combination of profoundly worrying features affecting the care of the child within the family. In such cases it would be open to a court in appropriate circumstances to find that, although not satisfied the child is yet suffering significant harm, on the basis of such facts as are proved there is a likelihood that he will do so in the future.

This is not the present case. The three younger girls are not at risk unless D1 was abused by Mr R in the past. If she was not abused there is no reason for thinking the others may be.  ...To decide that the others are at risk because there is a possibility that D1 was abused would be to base the decision, not on fact, but on suspicion: the suspicion that D1 *may* have been abused.
(pp 591–92)

Lord Browne-Wilkinson, dissenting, said:

---

[147] In *Re ET (Serious Injuries: Standard of Proof)* [2003] 2 FLR 1205, the court suggested that the difference between the civil and the criminal standard is 'largely illusory'. That contention was firmly rejected in *Re U (Serious Injury: Standard of Proof); Re B* [2004] EWCA Civ 567; [2004] 2 FLR 263, where the court reasserted that the standard is the balance of probabilities in accordance with the test set out in *Re H*. See also *Re T (Abuse: Standard of Proof)* [2004] EWCA Civ 558; [2004] 2 FLR 838 para 28.

[148] See also *East Sussex County Council v K and Others* [2005] EWHC Fam 144; [2005] All ER D (201) (Mar).

[T]he facts relevant to an assessment of risk ('is likely to suffer ... harm') are not the same as the facts relevant to a decision that harm is in fact being suffered. In order to be satisfied that an event has occurred or is occurring the evidence has to show on balance of probabilities that such event did occur or is occurring. But in order to be satisfied that there is a *risk* of such an occurrence, the ambit of the relevant facts is in my view wider. The combined effect of a number of factors which suggest that a state of affairs, though not proved to exist, may well exist is the normal basis for assessment of future risk. To be satisfied of the existence of a risk does not require proof of the occurrence of past historical events but proof of facts which are relevant to the making of a prognosis.

Let me give an example, albeit a dated one. Say that in 1940 those responsible for giving air-raid warnings had received five unconfirmed sightings of approaching aircraft which might be enemy bombers ... The facts relevant to the assessment of such risk [of an air-raid] were the reports ..., not the truth of such reports. They could well, on the basis of these unconfirmed reports, have been satisfied that there was a real possibility of an air-raid. ... (pp 572–73)

Lord Lloyd too dissented on this point:

In the usual case, there will be a number of interlocking considerations, all of which will give rise to separate issues of fact, and on all of which, if the Court of Appeal be right, the court would have to make separate findings on the balance of probabilities before proceeding to the second stage.[149] Suppose, for example, there are three or four matters for concern which have led the social services to the belief that a child is at risk, on each of which there is credible evidence, supported, it may be, by evidence from a child psychiatrist, but suppose the evidence is insufficient on any of them to justify a finding that the child has been abused. Is the court powerless to proceed to the second stage? This is not what Parliament has said, and I do not think it was what Parliament intended. (p 581)

In *Re M and R (Child Abuse: Evidence)*,[150] the Court of Appeal held that the approach adopted in the House of Lords in *In Re H* applied at the welfare stage of the court's deliberations in the same way that it did at the threshold stage. An item in the welfare checklist, Section 1(3)(e), refers to any harm the child has suffered or is at risk of suffering. The court, in considering that provision, 'can only have regard to any harm that the child has suffered or is at risk of suffering if satisfied on the balance of probabilities that such harm or risk of harm in fact exists'.[151] Although the judge in the court below had concluded that there was a 'real possibility' that sexual abuse had occurred, the Court of Appeal held that this did not suffice: 'If ... the court concludes that the evidence is insufficient to prove sexual abuse in the past, and if the fact of sexual abuse in the past is the only basis for asserting a risk of sexual abuse in the future, then it follows that there is nothing except suspicion or mere doubts to show a risk of future sexual abuse'. (p 203)

**Q** Keating (1996 p 160) says that *In Re H* 'strikes a balance between the state's interest in protecting vulnerable children and the family's right to privacy'. Which of these is prioritised by the majority judgment and which by the dissenting judges?

Hayes (2004) explains the effect of the reasoning adopted by Lord Nicholls in *In Re H* and argues that a better criterion would be whether there is a real possibility that the past alleged harm occurred. Lord Nicholls' test is too rigid and, according to his approach, she says:

---

[149] To determine whether the facts as proved show that the child is likely to suffer significant harm.
[150] [1996] 2 FLR 195.
[151] At p 205.

The event either happened or it did not. Where the court is not satisfied on the balance of probabilities that an event occurred it must be totally disregarded. Thus a court is prevented from
taking account of all unproven allegations, however many these amount to, and whatever their
nature, where it is assessing whether non-accidental harm to the child did, in fact, occur, and
where it is assessing whether there is any future risk to that child, or to other children ... .

   In the usual kind of case there will be a number of concerns that cumulatively lead a local
authority to believe that a child is suffering, or is likely to suffer, significant harm. However, if
each allegation of fact on its own does not satisfy the balance of probabilities test then, applying Lord Nicholls of Birkenhead's analysis, there are no facts to support a finding of risk of
future harm and the court is powerless to proceed. It is suggested that this is not a safe
approach to risk taking with children. (Hayes 2004 p 66)

Operating a high threshold to establish significant harm ... may satisfy adult concerns about
the niceties of proof and the proper exercise of draconian powers over family life, but it can
also lead to the application of policy values that do not recognise the physical and emotional
consequences to children of the court making errors at any fact-finding stage ... .

   A high threshold that prevents court intervention where proof of child abuse has not been
established to the civil standard protects the rights of parents to respect for their private and
family life under Article 8(1) of the European Convention. However this same high threshold
prevents any exploration by courts into whether the parents' rights should be qualified in order
to protect the health, rights and freedoms of their children, as provided for by Article 8(2).

                                                                                    (p 83)


## Standard of Parental Care

To make an order under Section 31(2)(b)(i), the court must be satisfied that the significant harm or risk of significant harm is attributable to the standard of care given to the
child and that this care is not what would be reasonable to expect a parent to give that
child. The test is not what would be reasonable for the parents in question but for a
hypothetical parent. And the hypothetical parent is a reasonable parent: '[t]he court
must compare the care given to the child in question with what it would be reasonable to
expect a reasonable parent to give him, having regard to his needs' (DoH 1991c para
3.23). The greater the child's needs, the higher the standard of care that would be
expected. Parents whose care falls below the requisite standard and who do not seek or
use appropriate services are covered by the provision, as are parents who unreasonably
fail to protect their child from abuse by a third party (para 3.23). However, this test
should not be regarded as having been satisfied in cases of minor shortcomings; a '*substantial* deficit' in the standard of care must be evident (DHSS 1985 para 5.15).

> **Q** Would the provision cover a blind lone mother? Parents who are poor? A family in
> which the father frequently beats the mother?

There have been a number of cases in recent years in which the court has been faced
with the situation where there is evidence of significant harm but it is not clear who the
perpetrator is. *In Re B (Minors) (Care Proceedings: Practice)*[152] was a case where the
court could not be certain which of the parents had harmed the child. It nevertheless
made a care order: '[a] finding that it must have been either father or mother means ...

---

[152] [1999] 1 WLR 238, p 249.

that the child is at risk from both'. In *Lancashire County Council v B*,[153] the child's care was shared between the parents and a childminder and it was not apparent which of these carers had inflicted the child's injuries. The House of Lords dealt with this problem by adopting a relatively broad interpretation of Section 31(2)(b). Lord Nicholls rejected an interpretation put to him that he said could lead to successful care proceedings in a case where parents temporarily entrust a child to someone they reasonably think is suitable. He also rejected a formulation that would preclude a care order despite repeated abuse of a child, simply because the perpetrator could be one of two or more people and so could not be identified.[154]

> I consider that a permissible and preferable interpretation of s 31(2)(b)(i), between the two extremes, is as follows. The phrase 'care given to a child' refers primarily to the care given to the child by a parent or parents or other primary carers. That is the norm. The matter stands differently in a case such as the present one, where care is shared and the court is unable to distinguish in a crucial respect between the care given by the parents or primary carers and the care given by other carers. Different considerations from the norm apply in a case of shared caring where the care given by one or other of the carers is proved to have been deficient, with the child suffering harm in consequence, but the court is unable to identify which of the carers provided the deficient care. In such a case, the phrase 'care given to the child' is apt to embrace not merely the care given by the parents or other primary carers; it is apt to embrace the care given by any of the carers … .
>
> I recognise that the effect of this construction is that the attributable condition may be satisfied where there is no more than a possibility that the parents were responsible for inflicting the injuries which the child has undoubtedly suffered … . I recognise that this interpretation of the attributable condition means that parents who may be wholly innocent, and whose care may not have fallen below that of a reasonable parent, will face the possibility of losing their child … . [But] it by no means follows that because the threshold conditions are satisfied the court will go on to make a care order … .
>
> But, so far as the threshold conditions are concerned, the factor which seems to me to outweigh all others is the prospect that an unidentified, and unidentifiable, carer may inflict further injury on a child he or she has already severely damaged. (pp 589–90)

Lord Clyde in turn said:

> What the subsection requires is the identification of the incidence of harm, or the risk of harm, attributable to the care of the child, not the identification of the hand which caused, or may be likely to cause, it … .
>
> [T]he function of the section is to define the jurisdiction of the court … . The making of the order requires a much more careful consideration of the case with regard in particular to the matters specified in s 1(3) of the Act, subject always to the paramount consideration of the child's welfare, as specified in s 1(1). So it is reasonable to allow a degree of latitude in the scope of the jurisdictional provision. (pp 592–93)

The test to be applied, both at the threshold stage and the welfare stage, before treating someone as posing a potential risk is 'whether there is a real possibility or likelihood that one or more of a number of people with access to the child might have caused the

---

[153] [2000] 1 FLR 583.
[154] At p 588.

injury to the child'.[155] In other words, 'is there a likelihood or real possibility that A or B or C was the perpetrator or a perpetrator of the inflicted injuries?'[156]

So, although it is not proved as a fact which of the carers caused the harm or is likely to do so, anyone in relation to whom there is a real possibility is designated as posing a risk.[157] This was confirmed by the House of Lords in *Re O and N; Re B*.[158] As in *In Re H*, the court was concerned with the nature of what counts as evidence. But it was doing so at the welfare stage and in the context of an unidentified perpetrator case. Lord Nicholls reiterated the test in *In Re H*; where significant harm or likelihood of significant harm are in question, the court can only have regard to facts proved to the requisite standard.[159] He also went on to comment *obiter*, that in cases where the threshold criteria are satisfied on one ground, but not on another, the unproven allegation cannot be taken into account at the welfare stage under Section 1(3)(e).[160] However, he said, different policy considerations might apply in determining the matters the court can take into account when assessing risk under different statutory provisions. So it appears that the courts take a more flexible approach when it comes to the question of attributing harm. The *Lancashire* case shows that this is so at the threshold stage. And *Re O and N; Re B* shows this is so at the welfare stage:

> [26] The first area concerns cases of the type involved in the present appeals, where the judge finds a child has suffered significant physical harm at the hands of his parents but is unable to say which. I stress one feature of this type of case. These are cases where it has been proved, to the requisite standard of proof, that the child is suffering significant harm or is likely to do so.
>
> [27] Here, as a matter of legal policy, the position seems to me to be straightforward. Quite simply, it would be grotesque if such a case had to proceed at the welfare stage on the footing that, because neither parent, considered individually, has been proved to be the perpetrator, therefore the child is not at risk from either of them. This would be grotesque because it would mean the court would proceed on the footing that neither parent represents a risk even though one or other of them was the perpetrator of the harm in question.
>
> [28] That … would mean that, in 'uncertain perpetrator' cases, the court decides that the threshold criteria are satisfied but then lacks the ability to proceed in a sensible way in the best interests of the child. The preferable interpretation of the legislation is that in such cases the court is able to proceed at the welfare stage on the footing that each of the possible perpetrators is, indeed, just that: a possible perpetrator … .
>
> [33] … The approach adopted in *Re H* … is not apt at the welfare stage in 'uncertain perpetrator' cases.

It appears that Amy may well be suffering 'significant harm' in terms of Section 31. Prior to being removed by the local authority, she suffered injuries consistent with acts that would generally be designated as physical abuse. Moreover, these injuries could be attributable to what could be characterised as unsatisfactory parental care, whether

---

[155] *North Yorkshire County Council v SA* [2003] EWCA Civ 839; [2003] 2 FLR 849, para 26. 'Likelihood' and 'real possibility' were treated as synonymous by the court.

[156] *Ibid.*

[157] Evidence that emerges at a late stage helping to identify the perpetrator may lead to a rehearing; it is in the public interest that the perpetrator be identified (*Re K (Non-accidental Injuries: Perpetrator: New Evidence)* [2004] EWCA Civ 1181; [2005] 1 FLR 285).

[158] [2003] UKHL 18; [2003] 1 FLR 1169.

[159] Paras 16–18. The court also rejected the suggestion that in cases of this type, the court should find one or both parents guilty of failure to protect the child and assess the future risk on that basis: 'Inability to identify the perpetrator is not always accompanied by a finding of failure to protect' (para 30).

[160] Paras 37–38.

Brian or June or both caused the injuries or whether they unreasonably failed to prevent them from being inflicted by someone else.

If proceedings are instituted, a guardian will investigate with a view to representing Amy's best interests to the court. The court will consider the guardian's report as well as any expert evidence[161] explaining the cause of Amy's injuries and assessing her physical and psychological state. There may also be evidence of a statement made by Amy, to a social worker for example, or perhaps there might be a video of an interview conducted with her.[162] There would also be expert evidence addressing matters such as Brian's and June's capacity to parent Amy and the nature of their relationship with her. If the court is satisfied on a balance of probabilities that the threshold criteria are met, and that an order is necessary and proportionate, the court will make the order it considers will best safeguard Amy's welfare.

## X. EFFECTS OF A CARE ORDER

Although many children subject to care orders remain at home,[163] a child may be removed to be cared for elsewhere if this is thought necessary. The aim, however, should be to reunite the family if and when this becomes possible.[164] Care orders invest local authorities with parental responsibility and, although parents retain their parental responsibility,[165] their ability to exercise it is significantly curtailed.[166]

Effect of care order

33—(1) Where a care order is made with respect to a child it shall be the duty of the local authority designated by the order to receive the child into their care and to keep him in their care while the order remains in force.

...

(3) While a care order is in force with respect to a child, the local authority designated by the order shall—
(a)   have parental responsibility for the child; and
(b)   have the power (subject to the following provisions of this section)[167] to determine the extent to which a parent or guardian of the child may meet his parental responsibility for him.

---

161 See *East Sussex County Council v K and Others* [2005] EWHC Fam 144; [2005] All ER D (201) (Mar). See also *Re Y and K (Split Hearing: Evidence)* [2003] EWCA Civ 669; [2003] 2 FLR 273.

162 Hearsay evidence is admissible in cases of this kind. See s 96(3) of the Children Act 1989; The Children (Admissibility of Hearsay Evidence) Order 1993, SI 1993/621. The procedure for interviewing children and recording interviews is set out in Butler-Sloss (1988) ch 12. Failure to observe these guidelines is likely to reduce or undermine entirely the probative value of any conclusions drawn from the interview (*Re E (A Minor) (Child Abuse: Evidence)* [1991] 1 FLR 420; *Re A and Others (Minors) (Child Abuse: Guide-Lines)* [1992] 1 FLR 439). The case must be managed in accordance with the *Protocol for Judicial Case Management in Public Law Children Act Cases* [2003] 2 FLR 719.

163 Such placements are governed by the Placement of Children with Parents etc Regs 1991, SI 1991/893.

164 *Re C and B (Children) (Care Order: Future Harm)* [2001] 1 FLR 611 para 34. See further ch 9 pp 367–68.

165 See ss 2(5) and (6).

166 S 2(8) precludes those with parental responsibility from exercising it in a way that is incompatible with a court order. See also s 33(3)(b) below.

167 These relate to determining the child's religion, consenting to the child's adoption and appointing a guardian (s 33(6)). In addition, consent from every person or the leave of the court is necessary before the child's surname can be changed and before the child can be removed from the UK for a period longer than one month (ss 33(7) and (8)).

(4) The authority may not exercise the power in subsection (3)(b) unless they are satisfied that it is necessary to do so in order to safeguard or promote the child's welfare.

(5) Nothing in subsection 3(b) shall prevent a parent or guardian of the child who has care of him from doing what is reasonable in all the circumstances of the case for the purpose of safeguarding or promoting his welfare.

There is little scope for challenging local authority decisions concerning children in care.[168] However the statute imposes obligations on local authorities designed to promote partnership with parents and children. Sections 22 and 23 apply to all children 'looked after' by local authorities, and this term refers to children in care as well as to children being accommodated. Consultation with parents and children in making decisions is required where reasonably practicable. In addition, the complaints procedures mandated by Section 26(3) are open to children and the parents of children who are being looked after both voluntarily and under care orders.[169] The local authority looking after a child must arrange for that child to live with a parent, a person with parental responsibility, a relative or a friend unless this is not reasonably practicable or consistent with the child's welfare.[170] If this is not possible, although the statute states no preference, foster care is normally be regarded as the best alternative; institutional care has fallen out of favour.[171] Accommodation that is provided must be near the child's home and siblings must be accommodated together whenever this is reasonably practicable and consistent with children's welfare.[172]

Contact with their families is widely regarded as important to children's well-being while in care and it has been found to be a significant factor in facilitating the successful rehabilitation of children with their families.[173] The statute therefore places considerable emphasis on preserving links between children and their families.[174] Schedule 2 paragraph 15 imposes a duty on local authorities, in so far as is reasonably practicable and consistent with the child's welfare, to 'endeavour to promote contact' between a child who is being looked after and his or her family and friends.[175] Section 34 empowers courts to make contact orders[176] and also creates a presumption[177] of contact between children in care and their parents:

34. Parental contact etc with children in care

(1) Where a child is in the care of a local authority, the authority shall (subject to the provisions of this section) allow the child reasonable contact with—

---

[168] See below.

[169] Research suggests that complaints procedures are rarely understood or used (DoH 1995b p 46). See, further, Williams and Jordan (1996).

[170] Ss 23(4) and (6).

[171] See Utting (1997) pp 1–2. However Utting (paras 3.25–3.31) found that abuse occurs in foster care as well as in institutional care. For an extreme case of harsh institutional care, see Levy and Kahan (1991). See further DoH (1998) paras 5.16ff.

[172] S 23(7).

[173] Bullock, *et al*, (1993) p 100; DoH (1991e) p 24ff.

[174] This is in conformity with Art 9(3) of the UN Convention on the Rights of the Child which requires states to respect the rights of a child to maintain personal relations and direct contact with parents unless this is contrary to the child's best interests.

[175] It is for the local authority to justify refusing contact to family members such as grandparents (*Re M (Care: Contact: Grandmother's Application for Leave)* [1995] 2 FLR 86).

[176] If appropriate, the court can impose conditions on contact (s34(7)). If reasonable contact is appropriate, there is no need to make an order (*Re S (A Minor) (Care: Contact Order)* [1994] 2 FLR 222).

[177] See *Re Y (Child Orders: Restricting Applications)* [1994] 2 FLR 699 for an extreme example of circumstances rebutting this presumption.

(a)   his parents;

(b)   any guardian or special guardian of his;

(ba)  any person who by virtue of section 4A has parental responsibility for him;

(c)   where there was a residence order in force with respect to the child immediately before the care order was made, the person in whose favour the order was made; and

(d)   where, immediately before the care order was made, a person had care of the child by virtue of an order made in the exercise of the High Court's inherent jurisdiction with respect to children, that person.

If the local authority[178] wishes to refuse contact to such a person, it has to apply to court.[179] It is only in an emergency that contact can be justifiably denied without the authority of the court and then only for seven days.[180] Any restrictions on contact may damage the parent/child relationship; such measures constitute an interference with family life under Article 8 of the European Convention and so warrant strict scrutiny.[181] In particular, '[c]utting off all contact and the relationship between the child or children and their family is only justified by the overriding necessity of the interests of the child'.[182]

# XI. CHALLENGING LOCAL AUTHORITY DECISIONS IN COURT

While decisions about whether to grant, refuse or discharge a care order, as well as decisions about contact, lie in the hands of the courts, all other decision-making while the child is in care is within the discretion of the local authority.[183] In particular, Section 9(1) prevents parents from seeking to resolve disputes with local authorities by means of prohibited steps or specific issue orders: '[n]o court shall make any Section 8 order, other than a residence order, with respect to a child who is in the care of a local authority'. Judicial review is possible[184] but the court's inherent jurisdiction cannot be invoked to challenge decisions.[185] Moreover, the court cannot make a care order subject to conditions that the local authority implement it in a particular way.[186]

---

178 A child is also entitled to seek termination of contact (s 34(4)).

179 S 34(4). See *Re E (A Minor) (Care Order: Contact)* [1994] 1 FLR 146, where a local authority's application to refuse contact to parents was denied although there was no prospect of rehabilitation. Compare *Re L (Sexual Abuse: Standard of Proof)* [1996] 1 FLR 116, 127. See also *Re S (Care: Parental Contact)* [2004] EWCA 1397; [2005] 1 FLR 469.

180 S 34(6).

181 See ch 9, n 149 and sources cited there.

182 *Re C and B (Children) (Care Order: Future Harm)* [2001] 1 FLR 611 para 34.

183 Decisions about children who are looked after, whether as a result of care proceedings or because they are accommodated, are made by the local authority in consultation with the child and parents. However in the event of a dispute, children who are accommodated can be removed by the parents and the local authority is generally in a weaker position as it does not have parental responsibility. Disputes about children in care are therefore potentially more likely to arise. Some parents of accommodated children might be persuaded to agree to decisions by the threat of care proceedings.

184 But it should not normally be used to seek to prevent proceedings for an emergency or care order from being instituted (*Re M (Care Proceedings: Judicial Review)* [2003] EWHC Admin 850; [2003] 2 FLR 171). See, on the right to complain against a decision not to apply for a care order, *R v East Sussex County Council, Ex Parte W* [1998] 2 FLR 1082.

185 *A v Liverpool City Council* [1982] AC 363. A dispute over the scope of parental responsibility may be resolved under the court's inherent jurisdiction (*Re M (Care: Leave to Interview Child)* [1995] 1 FLR 825).

186 *Re T (A Minor) (Care Order: Conditions)* [1994] 2 FLR 423.

A question that has arisen is whether the court can oversee the activities of local authorities, particularly in the event of a change to the care plan or a failure to implement it. The court cannot make a care order without first considering the care plan.[187] However, once a care order is made, control by the courts is largely lost.

This was the issue before the House of Lords in *Re S (Minors); Re W (Minors)*.[188] There were two appeals. In *Re S*, the care plan was devised to facilitate rehabilitation of the children with the mother but none of the assistance envisaged, such as therapy, was forthcoming. In *Re W*, the judge had described the care plan as 'inchoate' because it involved considerable uncertainty. It was contingent on the outcome of assessments and therapeutic intervention as well as the possibility of the grandparents moving from the United States to care for the children.

When the cases went on appeal, the Court of Appeal introduced two innovations. First, it provided guidelines intended to give courts a wider discretion to make interim, rather than final, care orders. Secondly, it introduced the notion of 'starred' care plans. Once the care order was made, the court said, the essential milestones of the care plan would be identified and starred. If a starred milestone was not reached within a reasonable time, the case could be brought back to court by the children's guardian or the local authority. This, thought the court, would be a legitimate exercise under Section 3 of the Human Rights Act; it would be interpreting the Children Act 1989 so that it would be compatible with the European Convention.

The House of Lords disagreed and said this about the 'starring' of care plans:

> [27] ... [A] court cannot have day to day responsibility for a child. The court cannot deliver the services which may best serve a child's needs. Unlike a local authority, a court does not have close, personal and continuing knowledge of the child. The court cannot respond with immediacy and informality to practical problems and changed circumstances as they arise. Supervision by the court would encourage 'drift' in decision making ... . Nor does a court have the task of managing the financial and human resources available to a local authority ... .
>
> [42] I have ... noted, as a cardinal principle of the [Children] Act [1989], that the courts are not empowered to intervene in the way local authorities discharge their parental responsibilities under final care orders. Parliament entrusted to local authorities, not the courts, the responsibility of looking after children who are the subject of care orders. To my mind the new starring system would depart substantially from this principle ... . In short, under the starring system the court will exercise a newly-created supervisory function.

The court took the view that there was nothing in the Children Act that lent itself to the introduction of the scheme and that the Court of Appeal had gone beyond interpretation. This was not a legitimate use of Section 3 of the Human Rights Act 1998.

The House of Lords went on to point out that the mere failure to adhere to a care plan does not necessarily violate human rights; there might be good reason such a change of circumstances.[189] However, if things go really wrong in the local authority's exercise of parental responsibility, this might entail a violation of Article 8 rights. This

---

[187] S 31(3A) and s 31A Children Act 1989. See further pp 662–63 above.

[188] *Re S (Minors) (Care Order: Implementation of Care Plan); Re W (Minors) (Care Order: Adequacy of Care Plan)* [2002] UKHL 10; [2002] 1 FLR 815.

[189] However, when there is any significant change to the care plan or to the child's living arrangements, the parents must be properly involved in the decision-making and must have an opportunity to put forward their views (*Re G (Care: Challenge to Local Authority's Decision)* [2001] EWHC Fam 551; [2003] 2 FLR 42 para 43). See further on the case law under the Human Rights Act 1998, ch 9, pp 365ff

could be addressed by judicial review or, as a last resort, by proceedings under Section 7 of the HRA.[190]

However, there is a lacuna in the legislation, according to the court. Where decisions vitally affect the parent-child relationship, the scrutiny afforded by judicial review might not be sufficiently strict to satisfy the standards set by the Strasbourg court,[191] although a remedy for breach of Article 8 rights might be available under ss. 7 and 8 of the HRA 1998.[192] There is also another lacuna in that young children, who have no parent or guardian willing or able to challenge local authority decisions, do not have their rights protected.[193]

The court went on to consider the use of interim care orders:

[90] From a reading of section 38 as a whole, it is abundantly clear that the purpose of an interim care order, so far as presently material, is to enable the court to safeguard the welfare of a child until such time as the court is in a position to decide whether or not it is in the best interests of the child to make a care order ... . The corollary to this principle is than an interim care order is not intended to be used as a means by which the court may continue to exercise a supervisory role over the local authority in cases where it is in the best interests of a child that a care order should be made.

[93] [In cases] where the uncertainty needs to be resolved before the court can decide whether it is in the best interests of the child to make a care order at all ..., the court should finally dispose of the matter only when the material facts are as clearly known as can be hoped ... .

[94] More difficult, as a matter of legal principle, are cases where it is obvious that a care order is in the best interests of the child but the immediate way ahead thereafter is unsatisfactorily obscure ... .

[95] ... The uncertainty may be of such a character that it can, and should, be resolved so far as possible before the court proceeds to make the care order. Then, a limited period of 'planned and purposeful' delay can readily be justified ... .

[97] .... Frequently the uncertainties involved in a care plan will have to be worked out after a care order has been made ... . [In such cases] 'the function of the court is not to seek to oversee the plan but to entrust its execution to the local authority'.

[98] ... . Quite apart from known uncertainties, an element of future uncertainty is necessarily inherent in the very nature of a care plan ... . These are matters for decision by the local authority ... .

[99] Despite the inevitable uncertainties, when deciding whether to make a care order the court should normally have before it a care plan which is sufficiently firm and particularised for all concerned to have a reasonably clear picture of the likely way ahead for the child for the foreseeable future ... . If the parents and the child's guardian are to have a fair and adequate opportunity to make representations to the court on whether a care order should be made, the care plan must be appropriately specific.

[102] ... [T]he court must always maintain a proper balance between the need to satisfy itself about the appropriateness of the care plan and the avoidance of 'over-zealous investigation into matters which are properly within the administrative discretion of the local authority'.

(Quotation marks in original. References omitted)

Changes have now been made to the law dealing with reviews of cases and these have the effect of allowing some cases to be referred back to the court. There are now regulations requiring each local authority to appoint an independent reviewing officer to review

---

[190] Para 62.
[191] Para 79.
[192] Paras 80–81.
[193] Para 86.

cases,[194] to monitor the local authority's performance of its functions in relation to reviews. They have the power to refer those cases which cannot be resolved to their satisfaction to CAFCASS.[195] The CAFCASS officer, who would be part of the Legal and Special Casework Team,[196] assesses the case and makes a decision. The options available[197] are to reject the referral; to attempt to resolve the problems through mediation; to refer the matter to another agency such as the local authority legal department, the guardian or the Official Solicitor; or to bring civil proceedings against the local authority.[198] The civil actions available are listed by Hinchcliffe (2004 p 661) as follows: judicial review proceedings; a compensation claim; or a freestanding Human Rights Act 1998 application.

## XII. SUPERVISION ORDERS

A supervision order[199] does not give the supervisor, the local authority,[200] parental responsibility. The effect of an order is to make it the duty of the supervisor to 'advise, assist and befriend the supervised child' and to take such steps as are reasonably necessary to give effect to the order.[201] An order lasts for up to a year but can be extended to cover a total of three years.[202] Orders may affect the child and the 'responsible person', defined as any person with parental responsibility and any other person with whom the child is living.[203]

What might be contained in an order is set out in Schedule 3. It may require the child to comply with directions given by the supervisor about where to live, what places to attend and in which activities to participate.[204] So the supervisor could, for example, require the child to take part in educational activities. The child could also be required to allow the supervisor to visit.[205] However, although the child can be required to undergo psychiatric and medical examination and treatment, this must be specifically

[194] Each case must be reviewed within four weeks of the date on which the child begins to be looked after or provided with accommodation. The second review must take place within three months of the first and subsequent reviews must be carried out within six months of the previous review (Review of Children's Cases Regulations 1991, SI 895 s 3, amended by SI 2004/1419).

[195] Review of Children's Cases Regulations 1991, SI 895 s 2A, inserted by SI 2004/1419; S 26(2A) Children Act 1989.

[196] See Hinchcliffe (2004) p 660.

[197] *Ibid,* p 661.

[198] See Children and Family Court Advisory and Support Service (Reviewed Case Referral) Regulations 2004, SI 2187 Reg 7.

[199] Supervision orders can be granted only when the significant harm test is satisfied. Where concerns about a family emerge in the course of family proceedings, usually in the context of private law proceedings, the court is empowered to make a family assistance order in terms of s 16. This jurisdiction exists in any proceedings in which the court has the power to make a s 8 order, which would include care proceedings as well as various private law proceedings. The court must be satisfied that the circumstances are exceptional and that every person named in the order, other than the child, consents. The order requires an officer of the local authority to be made available to advise, assist and befriend those named. The powers of the officer are very limited but the order can require that visits be allowed.

[200] See Children Act 1989 Sch 3, para 9.

[201] Ss 35(1)(a) and (b).

[202] Children Act 1989 Sch 3, para 6.

[203] Children Act 1989 Sch 3, para 1.

[204] Para 2.

[205] Para 8.

provided for in the order.[206] Obligations can be imposed on the responsible person too if he or she consents. In that event, the order may include a requirement that he or she take reasonable steps to ensure that the child comply with the supervisor's and the court's directions. It may also require the responsible person to attend to take part in specified activities.[207]

There is no prescribed means of enforcing directions given under a supervision order. The statute states only that when the order is not complied with or becomes unnecessary, the supervisor is required to apply to court to vary or discharge it.[208] If the child is considered to be at risk, the local authority would apply for an emergency protection order or a care order in the usual way.

## XIII. CARE ORDER OR SUPERVISION ORDER

In cases where it is thought safe to leave the child in the home, it is open to the court to make either a care order or a supervision order. However, the court should begin with a preference 'for the less interventionist rather than the more interventionist approach'.[209] In *Re W (A Minor) (Interim Care Order)*,[210] the court indicated that wherever possible, a supervision order should be made rather than a care order: '[i]t is only if the supervision order appears unlikely to be sufficient to obviate the risk that the court should go on to make a care order'. This approach has since been endorsed as being in conformity with the HRA 1998. As Hale LJ observed in *Re C and B (Children) (Care Order: Future Harm)*, state intervention in family life is permissible under Article 8 of the European Convention only if it is in accordance with the law; is in pursuit of a legitimate aim; and is necessary in a democratic society. This last requirement is interpreted as emphasising that the intervention has to be proportionate to the legitimate aim.[211] What the court has to decide is whether a supervision order is a proportionate response to the risk presented.[212]

The more 'serious'[213] care order is needed in cases where the risk to the child is grave,[214] where intensive monitoring of the child is needed, where responsibility for safeguarding the child should be entrusted to the local authority under Section 22 and where the local authority needs to have parental responsibility.[215] Other considerations are the extent to which the parents are willing to co-operate and give consent to any 'requirements' under a supervision order as well as whether the court considers that an

---

[206] Paras 2(3), 4 and 5.

[207] Para 3.

[208] S 35(1)(c).

[209] *Re O (Care or Supervision Order)* [1996] 2 FLR 755, 760; *Oxfordshire County Council v L (Care or Supervision Order)* [1998] 1 FLR 70.

[210] [1994] 2 FLR 892, 898. See also *Re B (Care or Supervision Order)* [1996] 2 FLR 693, 698.

[211] *Re C and B (Children) (Care Order: Future Harm)* [2001] 1 FLR 611 paras 33–34.

[212] *Re O (Supervision Order)* [2001] EWCA Civ 16; [2001] 1 FLR 923, para 28. See also *Re C (Care Order or Supervision Order)* [2001] 2 FLR 466.

[213] *Re B (Care or Supervision Order)* [1996] 2 FLR 693, 698.

[214] Where the risk is low, a supervision order will be granted in preference to a care order. See *Re C (Care Order or Supervision Order)* [2001] 2 FLR 466; *Re O (Supervision Order)* [2001] EWCA Civ 16; [2001] 1 FLR 923.

[215] *Re S(J) (A Minor) (Care or Supervision Order)* [1993] 2 FLR 919. See also *Re S (Care or Supervision Order)* [1996] 1 FLR 753 where it was held that a supervision order would not confer on the child the degree of protection considered necessary.

effective sanction in the event of non-compliance is needed.[216] Supervision orders rely on the co-operation of the family, whereas care orders give the local authority coercive powers. In cases where it is not considered safe to leave the child at home, the only option is a care order.[217]

> **Q** Refer to chapter 9. Why should there be a preference for a less interventionist order?

## XIV. EXCLUDING THE ABUSER—THE FAMILY LAW ACT 1996, SECTION 8 ORDERS UNDER THE CHILDREN ACT 1989 AND INHERENT JURISDICTION

There may be cases where one parent abuses the child but the other could, given the opportunity, care for or be helped to care for the child in a manner considered satisfactory. These cases might be best dealt with by leaving the child at home with the non-abusing parent and ousting the abuser. The abuser might be persuaded to leave voluntarily and the local authority may be able assist financially or provide alternative accommodation.[218] It is open to the non-abusing parent, provided he or she qualifies under Part IV of the Family Law Act[219] to seek an occupation order excluding the abuser from the family home so as to protect the child. Indeed Section 43 provides that children themselves may apply for occupation orders with leave of the court. However, the grounds on which occupation orders may be granted in favour of children are not clear from the statute.[220] There is no power to exclude a parent from the family home under the child protection provisions of the Children Act 1989 except under Sections 38A and 44A.

The provisions of Parts IV and V of the Children Act 1989 were intended to set out a comprehensive code for the protection of children at risk. The aim of the legislation was to allow compulsory intervention in the family only where the strict threshold criteria could be satisfied.[221] The use of Section 8 orders was to be confined largely to disputes between private individuals and the extensive use of wardship by local authorities in public law cases to supplement or even circumvent the statutory provisions governing child protection was to be curtailed.

Wardship derives from the *parens patriae* duty of the state to protect minors; the state has an interest in seeing that children are properly brought up and educated.[222] Originally used as a means of protecting the property of wealthy orphans, the wardship

---

[216] *Re V (Care or Supervision Order)* [1996] 1 FLR 776, 786. In *Re O (Care: Discharge of Care Order)* [1999] 2 FLR 119, the mother was co-operative and also the children needed to be relieved of the threat posed by a care order of being removed from their parent.

[217] Once a care order is made, it remains in force until the child reaches the age of 18 unless it is brought to an end earlier by an order of court (s 91(12)). A care order may be discharged on application to the court under s 39. The making of a residence order discharges a care order (s 91(1)). A care order has no effect while a placement order is in force (Adoption and Children Act 2002 s 29(1)).

[218] Children Act 1989 Sch 2 para 5.

[219] See Ch 12.

[220] See p 480.

[221] See Law Commission (1988b) paras 4.51–4.52; DHSS (1987) para 5.

[222] See *Hope v Hope* (1854) 4 De GM & G 328, 344–45.

jurisdiction of the High Court was increasingly invoked in the years prior to the Children Act 1989 in complex cases concerning children.[223] Section 100 was framed to put a stop to this practice although it left the High Court with its inherent jurisdiction, of which wardship is a part. The inherent jurisdiction can be invoked to decide single issue disputes, whereas wardship places the child's life under the supervision of the court; all important decisions must be brought before the court. Local authorities, while they normally cannot seek wardship,[224] are permitted to invoke the court's residual inherent jurisdiction where there are no statutory provisions applicable to the situation in question.

Section 100 states:

100(2) No court shall exercise the High Court's inherent jurisdiction with respect to children—
(a)  so as to require a child to be placed in the care, or put under the supervision of a local authority; or
(b)  so as to require a child to be accommodated by or on behalf of a local authority; or
(c)  so as to make a child who is the subject of a care order a ward of court; or
(d)  for the purpose of conferring on any local authority power to determine any question which has arisen, or which may arise, in connection with any aspect of parental responsibility for a child.

(3) No application for any exercise of the court's inherent jurisdiction with respect to children may be made by a local authority unless the authority have obtained the leave of the court.

(4) The court may only grant leave if it is satisfied that—
(a)  the result which the authority wish to achieve could not be achieved through the making of any order of a kind to which subsection (5) applies; and
(b)  there is reasonable cause to believe that if the court's inherent jurisdiction is not exercised with respect to the child he is likely to suffer significant harm.

(5) This subsection applies to any order—
(a)  made otherwise than in the exercise of the court's inherent jurisdiction; and
(b)  which the local authority is entitled to apply for (assuming, in the case of any application which may only be made with leave, that leave is granted).

Local authorities' use of Section 8 orders is limited by Section 9:

9(2) No application may be made by a local authority for a residence order or contact order and no court shall make such an order in favour of a local authority.  ...
...

(5) No court shall exercise its powers to make a specific issue order or prohibited steps order—
(a)  with a view to achieving a result which could be achieved by making a residence or contact order; or
(b)  in any way which is denied to the High Court (by section 100(2)) in the exercise of its inherent jurisdiction with respect to children.

---

[223] See, generally on wardship, Lowe and Douglas (1998) Ch 16.
[224] But see *Re W and X ( Wardship: Relatives Rejected as Foster Parents)* [2003] EWHC Fam 2206; [2004] 1 FLR 415. There was a need in this case for 'external control' and a care order was not possible in the circumstances.

There have been occasions when local authorities have attempted to protect children by means of Section 8 orders or through the inherent jurisdiction instead of using care or supervision orders. In particular, these cases have raised the issue of whether an abuser can be excluded from the home.

In *Nottinghamshire County Council v P,*[225] the Court of Appeal was faced with a situation where, although the children in question were considered to be at risk of sexual abuse from their father, the local authority declined to seek a supervision or a care order. Instead it applied for a prohibited steps order, requiring the father not to live in the same home as the children and not to have contact with them except under specified conditions. The court held that such an order was precluded by Section 9 as the same results could be achieved by means of a residence and a contact order.[226] Moreover, as a matter of policy, where children are found to be at risk, the court said, local authorities should seek care or supervision orders as only these orders confer those powers necessary to protect children. A prohibited steps order was therefore inappropriate. A residence order in favour of the mother who opposed the exclusion of the father gave the local authority no powers and was also inappropriate. The court expressed concern that where the local authority resists taking steps to obtain a care or supervision order, there is nothing the court can do to protect children.

This case establishes that a Section 8 order cannot be used to remove a parent from the family home. However, it has been held in a much-criticised decision that the inherent jurisdiction can be invoked to this end. In *Re S (Minors) (Inherent Jurisdiction: Ouster)*[227] the court, for the purposes of Section 100(4)(a) found that the result that the local authority wished to achieve was to oust an abuser from the family home. Since there was no statutory power under the Children Act to do so, Section 100(4)(a) was satisfied. However Dewar (1995 p 66) contends that the 'result' that the local authority wanted could have been characterised more broadly as the protection of the children. Section 31 proceedings are designed to accomplish this objective and therefore the inherent jurisdiction should not have been invoked. Moreover, Roberts (1995) says, in the light of the *Nottinghamshire* case, the inherent jurisdiction, like Section 8 orders, should not be used as an alternative to the statutory powers to protect children at risk.

The High Court's inherent jurisdiction and Section 8 have been successfully deployed to prohibit a person outside the family from communicating with or having contact with children.[228] However, while these cases might be interpreted as authority for excluding non-family members by those means,[229] it is questionable whether local authorities will be able in future to obtain orders to exclude parents except as a temporary measure under sections 44A and 38A of the Children Act 1989.

[225] [1993] 2 FLR 134.
[226] An order that there shall be no contact falls within the definition of a contact order (at 143).
[227] [1994] 1 FLR 623.
[228] See *Devon County Council v S* [1994] 1 FLR 355. See also *Re H (Prohibited Steps Order)* [1995] 1 FLR 638 where it was held that a prohibited steps order could be made against the abuser, the mother's former partner, to the effect that he should have no contact with the children.
[229] See M Roberts (1995) pp 247–48.

## XV. CONCLUSION

Once it appears that to provide services for the family will not be enough to keep Amy safe and that voluntary arrangements with the family are not working, the local authority will seek a court order. If the court is satisfied that the monitoring possible under a supervision order will suffice to protect Amy and that Brian and June consent to, and will comply with, any requirements that it is thought necessary to impose on them, this is an appropriate order. Otherwise a care order will be necessary. Depending on the nature and the seriousness of the risk to Amy, she may be left in the home with her parents. If she has to be removed, local authority efforts must to be directed at effecting a successful rehabilitation[230]; Article 8 of the European Convention is understood to require rehabilitation if possible and to require that this should take place as soon as possible.[231] The position should be reviewed every six months.[232] Meanwhile Amy should have reasonable contact with her parents.[233]

If the local authority comes to the conclusion that it is in Amy's best interests to return home[234] and that the care order is no longer necessary, it[235] can apply for the discharge of the order under Section 39.[236] Alternatively discharge of the order can be sought[237] by Brian or June as persons with parental responsibility.[238]

## FURTHER READING AND SELECTED RECENT REFERENCES

J BROPHY, 'Diversity and Child Protection' (2003) *Fam Law* 674.

J BROPHY, J JHUTTI JOHAL and C OWEN, 'Assessing and Documenting Child Ill-treatment in Ethnic Minority Households' (2003) *Fam Law* 756.

S CREIGHTON, *Child Protection Statistics 3: Child Protection Outside the Home* (London, NSPCC, 2003).

C EDWARDS, 'Are Children Better Off Following Protective Interventions?' (1995) 7 *CFLQ* 136.

M HAYES, 'The Proper Role of Courts in Child Care Cases' (1996) 8 *CFLQ* 201.

——, 'Reconciling Protection of Children with Justice for Parents in Cases of Alleged Child Abuse' (1997) 17 *Legal Studies* 1.

——, '*Re O and N; Re B*—Uncertain Evidence and Risk-taking in Child Protection Cases' (2004) 16 *CFLQ* 63.

M HINCHCLIFFE, 'Whatever Happened to Starred Care Plans?' (2004) *Fam Law* 660.

M KING and F KAGANAS, 'The Risks and Dangers of Experts in Court' (1998) *Current Legal Issues* 221.

---

[230] See, on twin track planning, *Re D and K ( Care Plan: Twin Track Planning)* [1999] 2 FLR 872.

[231] See p 682 above and ch 9 pp 367–68. See also s 23(6) Children Act 1989.

[232] Reg 3 of the Review of Childen's Cases Regs 1991 (SI 1991/895). The first review must take place within 4 weeks, the second after 3 months and subsequent reviews must take place at 6–monthly intervals.

[233] As stipulated by s 34 of the Children Act 1989 and in terms of the case law on Art 8 of the European Convention. See pp 683–84 above and ch 9 n 149.

[234] The majority of children do return home (Bullock, *et al,* 1993 pp 64–65).

[235] In the case of a supervision order, as supervisor.

[236] An order can be discharged only if this would be in the child's best interests in terms of s 1.

[237] If an application is refused, no further application may be made within 6 months of the decision without the leave of the court (s 91(15)). The court may impose a requirement, either when the initial order is made or on disposing of an application for discharge, that any application for discharge requires leave (s 91(14)).

[238] Children too are entitled to apply for discharge.

M KING, and J TROWELL, *Children's Welfare and the Law: The Limits of Legal Intervention* (London, Sage, 1992).

J MASSON, 'Police Protection—Protecting Whom?' (2002) 24 *JSW&FL* 157.

J MASSON, M WINN OAKLEY and K PICK, *Emergency Protection Orders: Court Orders for Child Protection Crises* (Coventry, Warwick University, 2004).

M PARRY, 'The Children Act 1989: Local Authorities, Wardship and the Revival of the Inherent Jurisdiction' (1992) 3 *JSW&FL* 212.

*Reports*

DoH, What to Do if You're Worried a Child is Being Abused (London, The Stationery Office, 2003).

DfES, *The Children Act Report 2003* (Nottingham, DfES, 2004).

# BIBLIOGRAPHY

ABORTION RIGHTS (2005) *Abortion: the facts* (London: Abortion Rights).

ACKERS, L (2000) 'From "Best Interests" to Participatory Rights – Children's Involvement in Family Migration Decisions' 12 *CFLQ* 167.

ADAM, BD (2004) 'Care, Intimacy and Same-sex Partnership in the 21st Century' 52 *Current Sociology* 265.

ADAMS, BN (1975) *The Family: A Sociological Interpretation*, 2nd edn, (Chicago, IL, Rand McNally).

ADAMS, D (2000) 'The Emerge Program' in J Hanmer, and C Itzin with S Quaid and D Wigglesworth (eds), *Home Truths About Domestic Violence: Feminist Influences on Policy and Practice: A Reader* (London, Routledge).

ADAMS, L, MCANDREW, F and WINTERBOTHAM, M (2005) *Pregnancy Discrimination at Work: A Survey of Women* (London, Equal Opportunities Commission).

ADVISORY GROUP ON MARRIAGE AND RELATIONSHIP SUPPORT (2002) *Moving Forward Together: A Proposed Strategy for Marriage and Relationship Support for 2002 and Beyond* (Lord Chancellor's Department, London, The Stationery Office).

ALDGATE, J (2001) *The Children Act Now: Messages from Research* (London, The Stationery Office).

ALSTON, P, PARKER, S and SEYMOUR, J (1992) *Children, Rights and the Law* (Oxford, Clarendon Press).

ANCILLARY RELIEF ADVISORY GROUP (1998) *Report to the Lord Chancellor by the Ancilliary Relief Advisory Group* (London).

ANDERSON, L (1997a) 'Registered Personal Relationships' *Fam Law* 174.

—— (1997b) *Contact between Children and Violent Fathers: In Whose Best Interests? Rights of Women Research Report on the Operation of the Children Act 1989 in Circumstances of Domestic Violence* (London, Rights of Women).

ANDERSON, M (1980) 'The Relevance of Family History' in M Anderson (ed), *The Sociology of the Family: Selected Readings*, 2nd edn, (Harmondsworth, Penguin).

ANDERSON, S, (1984) 'Legislative Divorce – Law for the Aristocracy' in GR Rubin and D Sugarman (eds), *Law, Economy and Society, Essays in the History of English Law 1750–1914* (Abingdon, Professional Books).

ANTHIAS F and YUVAL-DAVIS, N (in association with H Cain) (1993) *Racialized Boundaries* (London, Routledge).

ARCHARD, D (1993) *Children: Rights and Childhood* (London, Routledge).

—— (1999) 'Can Child Abuse be Defined?' in M King (ed), *Moral Agendas for Children's Welfare* (London, Routledge).

ARCHBISHOP OF CANTERBURY'S GROUP (1966) *Putting Asunder – A Divorce Law for Contemporary Society* (London, Society for Promoting Christian Knowledge, CUP).

ARDEN, A and HUNTER, C (2003) *Homelessness and Allocations: A Guide to the Housing Act 1996 Parts VI and VII*, 6th rev edn, (London, Legal Action Group).

ARIÈS, P (R Baldick trans) (1962) *Centuries of Childhood* (London, Jonathan Cape).

ASHENDEN, S (2004) *Governing Child Sexual Abuse: Negotiating the Boundaries of Public and Private, Law and Science* (London, Routledge).

ASHWORTH, A (1995) *Principles of Criminal Law*, 2nd edn, (Oxford, Clarendon Press).

ASSOCIATION OF DISTRICT JUDGES (1998) 'Submission of Association of District Judges' Appendix 8 to the *Report to the Lord Chancellor by the Ancillary Relief Advisory Group* (London).

ATWOOD, M (1985) *The Handmaid's Tale* (Toronto, McClelland and Stewart).

AUCHMUTY, R (2003) 'When Equality is not Equity: Homosexual Inclusion in Undue Influence Law' 11 *Feminist Legal Studies* 163.

—— (2004) 'Same-sex Marriage Revived: Feminist Critique and Legal Strategy' 14 *Feminism and Psychology* 101.

AUDIT COMMISSION (1994) *Seen But Not Heard: Co-ordinating Community Child Health and Social Services for Children in Need: Detailed Evidence and Guidelines for Managers and Practitioners* (London, HMSO).

—— (1996) *Counting to Five: Education of Children Under Five* (London, HMSO).

BAAF (2005) British Association for Adoption and Fostering www.baaf.org.uk/info/stats/England

BACCI, CA (1990) *Same Difference* (Sydney, Allen & Unwin).

BACKHOUSE, C (1991) *Petticoats and Prejudice: Women and Law in Nineteenth Century Canada* (Toronto, Women's Press).

BAILEY, MJ (1994) 'England's First Custody of Infants Act' 20 *Queen's L J* 391.

BAILEY-HARRIS, R (1999) 'Third Stonewall Lecture – Lesbian and Gay Family Values and the Law' *Fam Law* 560.

—— (2003) 'Case Comment' *Fam Law* 386.

BAILEY-HARRIS, R and WILSON, L (2003) '*Mendoza v Ghaidan* and the Rights of de Facto Spouses' *Fam Law* 575.

BAINHAM, A (1985) 'The Balance of Power in Family Decisions' 45 *CLJ* 262.

—— (1990) 'The Privatisation of the Public Interest in Children' 53 *MLR* 206.

—— (1993) *Children: The Modern Law* (Bristol, Family Law)

—— (1995) 'Contact as a Fundamental Right' 54 *CLJ* 255.

—— (1999) 'Parentage, Parenthood and Parental Responsibility: Subtle, Elusive, Yet Important Distinctions' in A Bainham, S Day Sclater and M Richards (eds), *What is a Parent?* (Oxford, Hart Publishing).

—— (2005) *Children: The Modern Law*, 3rd edn, (Bristol, Jordan).

BAKER, A. and TOWNSEND, P. (1996) 'Post-Divorce Parenting – Rethinking Shared Residence' 8 *CFLQ* 217.

BALA, N. (1989) 'Recognizing Spousal Contributions to the Acquisition of Degrees, Licences and other Career Assets: Towards Compensatory Support' 8 *Canadian J of Family Law* 23.

—— (1998) 'Canada: Child Support Guidelines, Parental Mobility, and Redefining Familial Relationships' in A Bainham (ed), *The International Survey of Family Law* (London, Martinus Nijhoff).

BANDA, F (2003) 'Global Standards: Local Values' 17 *International Journal of Law, Policy and the Family* 27.

BARLOW, A and DUNCAN, S (2000a) 'New Labour's Communitarianism, Supporting Families and the "Rationality Mistake": Part I' 22(2) *Journal of Social Welfare and Family Law* 23.

—— and —— (2000b) 'New Labour's Communitarianism, Supporting Families and the "Rationality Mistake": Part II' 22(2) *Journal of Social Welfare and Family Law* 129.

——, ——, and JAMES, G (2002) 'New Labour, the Rationality Mistake and Family Policy in Britain' in A Carling, S Duncan and R Edwards (eds), *Analysing Families: Morality and Rationality in Policy and Practice* (London, Routledge).

BARLOW, A and JAMES G (2004) 'Regulating Marriage and Cohabitation in 21st Century Britain' 67 *MLR* 143.

BARN, R (2000) 'Race, Ethnicity and Transracial Adoption' in A Treacher and I Katz (eds), *The Dynamics of Adoption* (London, Jessica Kingsley).

BARNISH, M (2004) *Domestic Violence: A Literature Review* (London, HM Inspectorate of Probation).

BAR-ON, A (1997) 'Criminalising Survival: Images and Reality of Street Children' 26 *J of Social Policy* 63.

BARRETT, B and MELROSE, M (2003) 'Courting Controversy – Children Sexually Abused through Prostitution – Are they Everybody's Distant Relatives but Nobody's Children?' 15 *CFLQ* 371.

BARRETT, M and MACINTOSH, M (1991) *The Anti-Social Family*, 2nd edn, (London, Verso).

BARRON, J (1990) *Not Worth the Paper ...? The Effectiveness of Legal Protection for Women and Children Experiencing Domestic Violence* (Bristol, WAFE).

—— (2002) *Five Years On: A Review of Legal Protection from Domestic Violence* (Bristol, WAFE).

BARRY, N (1995) 'Justice and Liberty in Marriage and Divorce' in R Whelan (ed), *Just a Piece of Paper? Divorce Reform and the Undermining of Marriage* (London, IEA Health and Welfare Unit).

BART, P and MORAN, E (1993) (eds), *Violence Against Women: The Bloody Footprints* (London, Sage).

BARTHOLOMEW, BW (1958) 'Legal Implications of Artificial Insemination' 21 *MLR* 236.

BARTON, C (1997) 'When Did You Next See Your Father? Emigration and the One-parent Family – Re T ( Removal from Jurisdiction); Goertz v Gordon (formerly Goertz)' 9 *CFLQ* 73.

—— (1998) 'Third Time Lucky for Child Support?—The 1998 Green Paper' *Fam Law* 668.

—— (2000) 'Adoption – The Prime Minister's Review' 30 *Fam Law* 731.

—— (2001) 'Adoption and Children Bill 2001—Don't Let Them Out of Your Sight' 31 *Fam Law* 431.

BARTON, C and DOUGLAS, G (1995) *Law and Parenthood* (London, Butterworths).

BASTIN, G 'Europe and the CSA' (1996) *Fam Law* 678.

BBC News Online (2005) 'Call for women-friendly pensions' April 21 2005 http://news.bbc.co.uk/1/hi/business/4469405.stm .

BECK, U and BECK-GERNSHEIM, E (1995) *The Normal Chaos of Love* (Cambridge, Polity).

—— and —— (2002) *Individualization* (London, Sage).

BECKER, HS (1963) *Outsiders: Studies in the Sociology of Deviance* (New York, NY, Free Press).

BELL, V (1993) 'Governing Childhood: Neo-liberalism and the Law' 22 *Economy and Society* 390.

BELLAMY, C, District Judge and GEOFF, District Judge (2003) 'Reflections on Family Proceedings Rule 9.5' *Fam Law* 265.

BENNETT, F (2002) 'Gender Implications of Current Social Security Reforms' 23 *Fiscal Studies* 559.

—— (2005) *Gender and Benefits, Equal Opportunities Commission Working Paper Series No 30* (London, Equal Opportunities Commission).

BENNETT, M (1997) 'Life After Dart' *Fam Law* 79.

BERGER, PL and KELLNER, H (1980) 'Marriage and the Construction of Reality' in M Anderson (ed), *The Sociology of the Family*, 2nd edn, (Harmondsworth, Penguin).

BEST, R (1995) 'Direct Consultation with Children: A Progress Report on Training Modules' 5 *Fam Mediation* 8.

BEVAN, G, DAVIS G, and FENN, P. (2001) 'Can Mediation Reduce Expenditure on Lawyers?' *Fam Law* 186.

BEVERIDGE, Sir WILLIAM (1942) *Social Insurance and Allied Services* (London, HMSO, Cmd 6404).

BIRCHALL, E, (1989) 'The Frequency of Child Abuse – What do We Really Know?' in O Stevenson (ed), *Child Abuse: Public Policy and Professional Practice* (Hemel Hempstead, Harvester Wheatsheaf).

BIRD, R (1996a) *Domestic Violence: The New Law: Part IV of the Family Law Act 1996* (Bristol, Jordans).

—— (1996b) *Child Maintenance*, 3rd edn, (Bristol, Family Law, Jordans).

—— (2000) 'Ancillary Relief Outcomes' 30 *Fam Law* 831.

—— (2002) 'Newsline – Ancillary Relief Procedure – A Reply' *Fam Law* 164.

BISSET-JOHNSON, A and BARTON, C (1995) 'The Divorce White Paper' *Fam Law* 349.

BLACKSTONE, W (1778) *Commentaries on the Laws of England*, 8th edn, (Oxford, Clarendon Press).

BLACKWELL, A and DAWE, F (2003), *Non-Resident Parental Contact* (London, ONS).

BOCK, G (1991) 'Antinatalism, Maternity and Paternity in National Socialist Racism' in G Bock and P Thane (eds), *Maternity and Gender Policies: Women and the Rise of the European Welfare States* (London, Routledge).

BODER, R and CHILDS, M (1996) 'Paying for Procreation: Child Support Arrangements in the UK' 4 *Feminist Legal Studies* 131.

BOND, A (1996) 'Working for the Family? Child Employment Legislation and the Public/Private Divide' 4 *JSW & FL* 291.

BOOTH, Mrs Justice (1985) *Report of the Matrimonial Causes Procedure Committee* (London, HMSO).

BORKOWSKI, M, MURCH, M, and WALKER, V (1983) *Marital Violence: The Community Response* (London, Tavistock).

BOSELY, S (1996) 'Labour Floats Plans to Improve Parenting', *The Guardian,* 14 November.

BOSSY, J and COLEMAN, S (2000) *Womenspeak. Parliamentary Domestic Violence Internet Consultation: Report of the Main Findings* (Bristol, WAFE).

BOTTOMLEY, A (1984) 'Resolving Family Disputes: A Critical View' in M Freeman (ed), *State, Law and Family: Critical Perspectives* (London, Tavistock and Sweet & Maxwell).

—— (1985) 'What is Happening to Family Law? A Feminist Critique of Conciliation' in J Brophy and C Smart (eds), *Women in Law: Explorations in Law, Family and Sexuality* (London, Routledge and Kegan Paul).

BOWLBY, J (1953) *Child Care and the Growth of Love* (Harmondsworth, Penguin).

BOYD, D (1990) 'Blaming the Parents' 2 *J of Child Law* 65.

BOYD, S (1991) 'Some Postmodernist Challenges to Feminist Analyses of Law, Family and State: Ideology and Discourse in Child Custody Law' 10 *Canadian J of Family Law* 79.

—— (1994) '(Re)Placing the State: Family, Law and Oppression' 9 *Canadian J of Law and Society* 39.

—— (1996) 'Is there an Ideology of Motherhood in (Post) Modern Child Custody Law?' 5 *Social and Legal Studies* 495.

BRADLEY, D (1987) 'Homosexuality and Child Custody in English Law' 1 *Int J of Law and the Family* 155.

—— (1996) *Family Law and Political Culture* (London, Sweet & Maxwell).

BRADLEY, H (1997) 'Gender and Change in Employment: Feminization and its Effects' in RK Brown (ed), *The Changing Shape of Work* (Basingstoke, MacMillan).

BRADNEY, A (1994) 'Duress, Family Law and the Coherent Legal System' 57 *MLR* 473.

BRADSHAW, J and MILLAR, J (1991) *Lone Parent Families in the UK* (DSS Research Report No 6, London, HMSO).

BRADSHAW, J, STIMSON, C, SKINNER, C and WILLIAMS, J (1999) *Absent Fathers?* (London, Routledge).

BRANNEN, J et al (1994) *Employment and Family Life: A Review of Research in the UK (1980–1994)* (Department of Employment Research Series No 41, London, University of London).

BRASSE, G, District Judge (2004) 'Conciliation is Working' *Fam Law* 722.

BRAZIER, M and BRIDGE, C (1996) 'Coercion or Caring: Analysing Adolescent Autonomy' 16 *Legal Studies* 84.

BRAZIER, M, CAMPBELL, A and GOLOMBOK, S (1998) *Surrogacy: Review for Health Ministers of Current Arrangements for Payments and Regulation, Report of the Review Team* (Cmd 4068, London, HMSO).

BREUGEL, I (1994) 'Sex and Race in the Labour Market' in M Evans (ed), *The Woman Question,* 2nd edn, (London, Sage).

BRIDGE, C (1996) 'Shared Residence in England and New Zealand – A Comparative Analysis' 8 *CFLQ* 12.

—— (1997) 'Parental Powers and the Medical Treatment of Children' in C Bridge (ed), *Family Law Towards the Millennium: Essays for PM Bromley* (London, Butterworths).

—— (1999a) 'Religious Beliefs and Teenage Refusal of Medical Treatment' 62 *MLR* 585.

—— (1999b) 'Religion, Culture and Conviction – The Medical Treatment of Young Children' 11 *CFLQ* 1.

—— and SWINDELLS, H (2003) *Adoption: The Modern Law* (Bristol, Jordans).

BRIDGEMAN, J (1993) 'Old Enough to Know Best?' 13 *Legal Studies* 69.

BRIGGS, F (1995) *From Victim to Offender: How Child Sexual Abuse Victims Become Offenders* (Australia, Allen & Unwin).

BRINDLEY, B (2001) 'Black and White in Pensions' *Fam Law* 462.

BROPHY, J (1985) 'Child Care and the Growth of Power: The Status of Mother in Child Custody Disputes' in J Brophy and C Smart (eds), *Women in Law: Explorations in Law, Family and Sexuality* (London, Routledge and Kegan Paul).

—— (1989) 'Custody Law, Child Care, and Inequality in Britain' in C Smart and S Sevenhuijsen (eds), *Child Custody and the Politics of Gender* (London, Routledge).

—— (2003) 'Diversity and Child Protection' *Fam Law* 674.

BROWNE, A (1987) *When Battered Women Kill* (New York, The Free Press).

BRUCH, C (1988) 'And How Are the Children? The Effects of Ideology and Mediation on Child Custody Law and Children's Well-Being in the United States' 2 *Int J of Law and the Family* 106.

BRUSH, LD (1993) 'Violent Acts and Injurious Outcomes in Married Couples: Methodological Issues in the National Survey of Families and Households' in P Bart and E Moran (eds), *Violence Against Women: The Bloody Footprints* (London, Sage).

BRYAN, P (1992) 'Killing Us Softly: Divorce Mediation and the Politics of Power' 40 *Buffalo Law Review* 441.

BUCHANAN, A, HUNT, J, BRETHERTON, H and BREAM, V (2001) *Families in Conflict: Perspectives of Children and Parents on the Family Court Welfare Service*, (Bristol, Policy).

BUDGEON, S and ROSENEIL, S (2004) 'Editors' Introduction: Beyond the Conventional Family' 52 *Current Sociology* 127.

BULLOCK, R, LITTLE, M and MILHAM, S (1993) *Going Home: The Return of Children Separated from their Families* (Aldershot, Dartmouth).

BURGHES, L (1993) *One-parent Families: Policy Options for the 1990's* (York, Joseph Rowntree Foundation).

BURGOYNE, C (2004) 'Heart-strings and Purse-strings: Money in Heterosexual Marriage' 14 *Feminism and Psychology* 165.

—— and MILLAR, J (1994) 'Enforcing Child Support Obligations: The Attitudes of Separated Fathers' 22 *Policy and Politics* 95.

BURGOYNE, J, ORMROD, R and RICHARDS, M (1987) *Divorce Matters* (Harmondsworth, Penguin).

BURTON, M (2003) 'Third Party Applications for Protection Orders in England and Wales: Service Providers' Views on Implementing Section 60 of the Family Law Act 1996' 25 *JSW&FL* 137.

BURTON, S and KITZINGER, J with KELLY, L and REGAN, L (1998) *Young People's Attitudes Towards Violence, Sex and Relationships: A Survey and Focus Group Study* (Edinburgh, Zero Tolerance Charitable Trust).

BUTLER, B (1989) 'Adopting an Indigenous Approach' 13 *Adoption and Fostering* 27.

BUTLER-SLOSS, E (1988) *Report of the Inquiry into Child Abuse in Cleveland 1987* (London, HMSO) Cmd 412.

—— and FIDDY, A (2001) 'The ChildRIGHT Interview' December *Childright* 14.

CABINET OFFICE AND HOME OFFICE (1999) *Living Without Fear: An integrated approach to tackling violence against women* (London, Cabinet Office).

CAFCASS (2003) *Service Principles and Standards* (London, HMSO).

CAIRNS, J (ed.) (1965) *The Nineteenth Century 1815–1914* (New York, NY, Free Press).

CAMPBELL, JC (1992) ' "If I Can't Have You, No One Can": Power and Control in Homicide of Female Partners' in J Radford and DEH Russell (eds), *Femicide: The Politics of Woman Killing* (Buckingham, Open University Press).

CAMPION, MJ (1995) *Who's Fit to Be a Parent?* (London, Routledge).

CANAAN, C (1992) *Changing Families, Changing Welfare* (Hemel Hempstead, Harvester Wheatsheaf).

CANTILLON, S and NOLAN, B (1998) 'Are Married Women More Deprived than their Husbands?' 27 *J of Social Policy* 151.

CANTWELL, B and NUNNERLY, M (1996) 'A New Spotlight on Family Mediation' *Fam Law* 177.

CANTWELL, B and SCOTT, S (1995) 'Children's Wishes, Children's Burdens' 17 *JSW&FL* 337.

CARBONE, . (1996) 'Feminism, Gender and the Consequences of Divorce' in M Freeman (ed), *Divorce: Where Next?* (Aldershot, Dartmouth).

CARLING, A (2002) 'Family Policy, Social Theory and the State' in A Carling, S Duncan and R Edwards (eds), *Analysing Families: Morality and Rationality in Policy and Practice* (London, Routledge).

CASC (Children Act Sub-Committee of the Advisory Board on Family Law) (1999) *Consultation Paper on Contact Between Children and Violent Parents*, (London, The Stationery Office).

—— (2000) *A Report to the Lord Chancellor on the Question of Parental Contact in Cases where there is Domestic Violence*, (London, The Stationery Office).

—— (2001a) *Guidelines for Good Practice on Parental Contact in Cases where there is Domestic Violence. Section 5 of Report of Children Act Sub-Committee to Lord Chancellor on the Question of Parental Contact in Cases where there is Domestic Violence* (London, Lord Chancellor's Department).

—— (2001b) *Making Contact Work. A Report to the Lord Chancellor on the Facilitation of Arrangements for Contact Between Children and their Non-residential Parents and the Enforcement of Court Orders for Contact* (London, LCD).

—— (2002) *Guidelines for Good Practice on Parental Contact in Cases where there is Domestic Violence* (London, DCA).

CAWSON, P, BROOKER, S and KELLY, G (2000) *Child Maltreatment in the United Kingdom: A Study of the Prevalence of Abuse and Neglect: Executive Summary* (London, NSPCC).

CHARLES, N (1994) 'The Housing Needs of Women and Children Escaping Domestic Violence' 23 *J of Social Policy* 465.

CHESNEY-LIND, M (2002) 'Criminalizing Victimization: The Unintended Consequences of Pro-arrest Policies for Girls and Women' 1 *Criminology & Public Policy* 81.

CHODOROW, N (1978) *The Reproduction of Mothering: Psychoanalysis and the Sociology of Gender* (Berkeley, CA, University of California).

CHOUDHRY, S (2003) 'The Adoption and Children Act 2002, The Welfare Principle and the Human Rights Act 1998—A Missed Opportunity?' 15 *CFLQ* 119.

CLARK, A (1992) 'Humanity or Justice? Wife Beating and the Law in the Eighteenth and Nineteenth Centuries' in C Smart (ed), *Regulating Womanhood: Historical Essays on Marriage, Motherhood and Sexuality* (London, Routledge).

CLARKE, K, GLENDINNING, C and CRAIG, G (1994), 'Child Support, parental responsibility and the law: An Examination of the implications of recent British legislation' Ch 10 in J Brannen and M O'Brien (eds), *Childhood and Parenthood* (London, University of London Institute of Education)

CLARKE, K, CRAIG, G and GLENDINNING, C (1995), 'Money Isn't Everything. Fiscal Policy and Family Policy in the Child Support Act' 29 *Social Policy and Administration* 26

——, ——, and —— (1996) *Small Change: The Impact of the Child Support Act on Lone Mothers and Children* (London, Family Policy Studies Centre).

CLARKE, L (1989) 'Abortion: A Rights Issue?' in D Morgan and WR Lee (eds), *Birthrights: Law and Ethics at the Beginning of Life* (London, Routledge).

CLARKSON, C and KEATING, H (1994) *Criminal Law: Text and Materials*, 3rd edn (London, Sweet & Maxwell).

CLIVE, E (1980) 'Marriage: An Unnecessary Legal Concept?' in J Eekelaar and S Katz (eds), *Marriage and Cohabitation in Contemporary Societies* (Toronto, Butterworths).

CLYDE, J (1992) *The Report of the Inquiry into the Removal of Children from Orkney in February 1991* (Edinburgh, HMSO).

COBBE, FP. (1878) 'Wife Torture in England' 32 *Contemporary Review* 55.

COCKETT, M and TRIPP, J (1994, 1996) *The Exeter Family Study: Family Breakdown and its Impact on Children* (Exeter, University of Exeter Press).

COLERIDGE, *et al,* (1996) 'FDR – the Pilot Scheme' *Fam Law* 746.

COLLIER, J, ROSALDO, M and YANAGISAKO, S (1982) 'Is There a Family? New Anthropological Views' in M Thorne and M Yalom (eds), *Rethinking the Family: Some Feminist Questions* (London, Longman).

COLLIER, R (1994) 'The Campaign Against the Child Support Act, "Errant Fathers" and "Family Men"' *Fam Law* 384.

—— (1995a) ' "Waiting Till Father Gets Home": The Reconstruction of Fatherhood in Family Law' 4 *Social and Legal Studies* 5.

—— (1995b) *Masculinity, Law and the Family* (London, Routledge).

—— (1999) 'The Dashing of a "Liberal Dream"?—The Information Meeting, the "New Family"and the Limits of Law', 11 *CFLQ* 257.

—— (2001) 'A Hard Time to Be a Father? Reassessing the Relationship between Law, Policy and Family (Practices)' 28 *J of Law and Society* 520.

COMMISSION FOR RACIAL EQUALITY (1994), *Annual Report*.

—— (2005) Statistics Labour Market http://www.cre.gov.uk/duty/reia/statistics_labour.html.

COMMUNITY LEGAL SERVICE (2004) 'Family Mediation: Dealing with Relationship Breakdown without going to Court' 24 *CLS Direct Information Leaflet*.

CONWAY, HL (1996) 'Presumption of Legitimacy and Blood Tests' *Fam Law* 228.

—— (1997) 'The Future for Judicial Separation' *Fam Law* 48.

COOK, D, *et al* (2004) *Evaluation of Specialist Domestic Violence Courts/Fast Track Systems* (London, Crown Prosecution Service and Department of Constitutional Affairs).

COOK, R, DAY SCLATER, S and KAGANAS, F (2003a) 'Introduction' in R Cook, S Day Sclater and F Kaganas (eds), *Surrogate Motherhood: International Perspectives* (Oxford, Hart Publications).

——, —— and —— (eds) (2003b) *Surrogate Motherhood: International Perspectives* (Oxford, Hart Publications).

COOPER, A, HETHERINGTON, R and KATZ, I (2003) *The Risk Factor: Making the Child Protection System Work for Children* (London, Demos).

COOPER, D (1998) 'More Law and More Rights: Will Children Benefit?' 3 *Child and Family Social Work* 77.

COOPER, D and HERMAN, D. (1991) 'Getting "The Family Right": Legislating Heterosexuality in Britain, 1986–1991' 10 *Canadian J of Family Law* 41.

CORNISH, W and CLARK, G (1989) *Law and Society in England 1750–1950* (London, Sweet & Maxwell).

COSSMAN, B (1990) 'A Matter of Difference: Domestic Contracts and Gender Equality' 28 *Osgoode Hall Law Journal* 303.

—— and RYDER, B (2001) 'What is Marriage-like Like? The Irrelevance of Conjugality' 18 *Canadian Journal of Family Law* 269.

COWAN, D (1997) *Homelessness: The (In-)Appropriate Applicant* (Aldershot, Dartmouth).

—— and FIONDA, J (1994) 'Housing Homeless Families under the Children Act 1989: W(h)ither the Housing Act 1985, Part III?' 6(2) *Journal of Child Law* 62.

—— and —— (1995) 'Housing Homeless Families – An Update' 7(2) *CFLQ* 66.

COX, C (1990) 'Anything Else is not Feminism: Racial Difference and the WMWM' 1 *Law and Critique* 237.

COX, EW, (1984) *The Principles of Punishment, as Applied in the Administration of Criminal Law, by Judges and Magistrates* (New York, NY, Garland).

COX, R (1996) *Shaping Childhood: Themes of Uncertainty in the History of Adult – Child Relationships* (London, Routledge).

CREIGHTON, S (2003) *Child Protection Statistics 3: Child Protection Outside the Home* (London, NSPCC).

—— (2004) 'Prevalence and Incidence of Child Abuse: International Comparisons' NSPCC Information Briefings.

—— and TISSIER, G (2003) 'Child Killings in England and Wales' NSPCC Information Briefings.

CRETNEY, A and DAVIS, G (1995) *Punishing Violence* (London, Routledge).

—— and —— (1996) 'Prosecuting Domestic Assault' *Crim L Rev* 162.

—— and —— (1997a) 'Prosecuting Domestic Assault: Victims Failing Courts, or Courts Failing Victims?' 36 *Howard Journal* 146.

—— and —— (1997b) 'The Significance of Compellability in the Prosecution of Domestic Assault' 37 *Brit J Criminology* 75.

CRETNEY, S (1989) 'Privatizing the Family: The Reform of Child Law' *Denning Law Journal* 15.

—— (1990) 'Divorce and the Low Income Family' *Fam Law* 377.

—— (1995a) ' "Tell Me the Old, Old Story" – the Denning Report, 50 Years On' 7 *CFLQ 163*

—— (1995b) 'The Divorce White Paper – Some Reflections' *Fam Law* 302.

—— (1996a) ' "What Will the Women Want Next?" The Struggle for Power Within the Family 1925–1975' 12 *LQR* 110.

—— (1996b) 'Divorce Reform in England: Humbug and Hypocrisy or a Smooth Transition' in M Freeman (ed), *Divorce: Where Next?* (Aldershot, Dartmouth).

—— (1997) *Family Law*, 3rd edn, (London, Sweet & Maxwell).

—— (2003a) *Family Law in the Twentieth Century: A History* (Oxford, OUP).

—— (2003b) 'The Family and the Law – Status or Contract?' 15 *CFLQ* 403.

—— (2003c) 'Community of Property Imposed by Judicial Decision' 119 *Law Quarterly Review* 349.

——, MASSON, J and BAILEY-HARRIS, R (2002) *Principles of Family Law* (London, Sweet & Maxwell).

CROMPTON, L (2004) 'The Civil Partnerships Bill 2004: The Illusion of Equality' *Fam Law* 888.

CROSS, L (2005) 'New Year's Resolution for the SFLA' *Fam Law* 167.

CROW, G and MARSH, P (1997) *Family Group Conferences, Partnership and Child Welfare: A Research Report on Four Pilot Projects in England and Wales* (Sheffield, University of Sheffield Partnership Research Programme).

CUNNINGHAM, H (1995) *Children and Childhood in Western Society Since 1500* (London, Longman).

CYPU (2001) *Learning to Listen: Core Principles for the Involvement of Children and Young People* (London).

DALY, C (1997) 'Too Little Too Late' 135 *Childright* 14.

DALY, M (1994) 'A Matter of Dependency: Gender in British Income Maintenance Provision' 28 *Sociology* 779.

DAVIDOFF, L, DOOLITTLE, M, FINK, J and HOLDEN, K (1998) *The Family Story: Blood, Contract and Intimacy, 1830–1960* (London, Longman).

DAVIES, C (1993) 'Divorce Reform in England and Wales: A Visitor's View' *Fam Law* 331.

DAVIES, J (ed), (1993) *The Family: Is it Just Another Lifestyle Choice?* (London, IEA Health and Welfare Unit).

DAVIS, G and ROBERTS, M (1988) *Access to Agreement* (Milton Keynes, Open University Press).

—— and —— (1989) 'Mediation and the Battle of the Sexes' *Fam Law* 305.

DAVIS, G, CRETNEY, S and COLLINS, J (1994) *Simple Quarrels: Negotiating Money and Property Disputes on Divorce* (Oxford, Clarendon Press).

DAVIS, G and PEARCE, J (1999) 'The Welfare Principle in Action' *Fam Law* 237

DAVIS, G (2000) 'Introduction' in G Davis, G Bevan, S Clisby, Z Cumming, R Dingwall, P Fenn, S Finch, R Fitzgerald, S Goldie, D Greatbatch, A James and J Pearce, *Monitoring Publicly Funded Family Mediation: Report to the Legal Services Commission* (London, Legal Services Commission).

DAVIS, G, PEARCE, J, BIRD, R, WOODWARD, H and WALLACE, C (2000a) Ancillary Relief Outcomes' 12 *CFLQ* 43.

DAVIS, G, BEVAN, G, CLISBY, S, CUMMING, Z, DINGWALL, R, FENN, P, FINCH, S, FITZGERALD, R,

GOLDIE, S, GREATBATCH, D, JAMES, A and PEARCE, J (2000b) *Monitoring Publicly Funded Family Mediation: Report to the Legal Services Commission* (London, Legal Services Commission).

DAVIS, G, FITZGERALD, R and FINCH, S (2000c) 'Monthly Monitoring' in G Davis, *et al*, *Monitoring Publicly Funded Family Mediation: Report to the Legal Services Commission* (London, Legal Services Commission).

——, —— and —— (2000d) 'Mediation Case Profiles' in G Davis, *et al*, *Monitoring Publicly Funded Family Mediation: Report to the Legal Services Commission* (London, Legal Services Commission).

DAVIS, G, FITZGERALD, R, FINCH, S and BEVAN, G (2000e) 'The Panel' in G Davis, G Bevan, S Clisby, Z Cumming, R Dingwall, P Fenn, S Finch, R Fitzgerald, S Goldie, D Greatbatch, A James and J Pearce, *Monitoring Publicly Funded family Mediation. Report to the Legal Services Commission* (London, Legal Services Commission).

DAVIS, G, PEARCE, J and GOLDIE, S (2000f) 'An Analysis of Intake' in G Davis, *et al*, *Monitoring Publicly Funded family Mediation. Report to the Legal Services Commission* (London, Legal Services Commission).

DAVIS, G, BEVAN, G and PEARCE, J (2001a) 'Family Mediation – Where do We Go from Here?' *Fam Law* 265.

DAVIS, G, FINCH, S and FITZGERALD, R, (2001b) 'Mediation and Legal Services – The Client Speaks' *Fam Law* 110.

DAY SCLATER, S (1999a) 'Experiences of Divorce' in S Day Sclater and C Piper (eds), *Undercurrents of Divorce* (Aldershot, Ashgate).

—— (1999b) *Divorce: A Psychosocial Study* (Aldershot, Ashgate).

—— and PIPER, C (eds), (1999) *Undercurrents of Divorce* (Aldershot, Ashgate).

—— and —— (2000) 'Remoralising the Family?—Family Policy, Family Law and Youth Justice' 12 *CFLQ* 135.

—— and KAGANAS, F (2003) 'Contact Mothers: Welfare and Rights' in A Bainham, *et al* (eds), *Children and Their Families: Contact, Rights and Welfare* (Oxford, Hart Publishing).

DE GLANVILLE, R and BEAMES J (tr),(1812) *A Treatise on the Law and Customs of the Kingdom of England* (London, Valpy).

DEAKIN, S and MORRIS, G (1998) *Labour Law*, 2nd edn, (London, Butterworths).

DECALMER, P and GLENDENNING, F (eds), (1993) *The Mistreatment of Elderly People* (London, Sage).

DEECH, R (1977) 'The Principles of Maintenance' 7 *Fam Law* 229.

—— (1992) 'The Unmarried Father and Human Rights' 4 *Journal of Child Law* 3.

—— (1994) 'Comment: Not Just Marriage Breakdown' *Fam Law* 121.

—— (1996) 'Property and Money Matters' in M Freeman (ed), *Divorce: Where Next?* (Aldershot, Dartmouth).

DENNIS, N and ERDOS, G (1993) *Families Without Fatherhood* (London, IEA Health and Welfare Unit).

DEPARTMENT OF CONSTITUTIONAL AFFAIRS (2002) *Government's Response to the Report of the Children Act Sub-committee of the Lord Chancellor's Advisory Board on Family Law 'Making Contact Work*, (www.dca.gov.uk (29 12 04))

—— (2003a) *Involving Children and Young People: Action Plan 2003–04.*

—— (2003b) *Judicial Statistics* (London, The Stationery Office).

—— (2004) *A New Focus for Civil Legal Aid: Encouraging Early Resolution; Discouraging Unnecessary Litigation* (London, DCA).

—— and Lord Chancellor (2005) *The Government Response to the Constitutional Affairs Select Committee Report: Family Justice: the Operation of the Family Courts Cm 6507* (London, HMSO).

——, DFES and DTI (2004) *Parental Separation: Children's Needs and Parents' Responsibilities.* (London, The Stationery Office) Cm 6273.

——, DFES and DTI (2005) *Parental Separation: Children's Needs and Parents' Responsibilities:*

*Next Steps, Report of the responses to consultation and agenda for action* (London, The Stationery Office) Cm 6452.

DEPARTMENT FOR EDUCATION AND SKILLS (2003) *Every Child Matters* Cm 5860 (London, The
Stationery Office).

—— (2004) Local Authority Circular LAC (2004) 27.

—— (2004a) *Every Child Matters: Next Steps* (London, The Stationery Office).

—— (2004b) *Statistics of Education: Referrals, Assessments and Children and Young People on
Child Protection Registers: Year Ending 31 March 2004* (London, TSO).

—— (2004c) *Every Child Matters: Change for Children in Social Care* (London, The Stationery
Office).

—— (2004d) *Every Child Matters: Change for Children* (London, the Stationery Office).

—— (2004e) *The Children Act Report 2003* (Nottingham, DfES).

—— (2005a) *Youth Matters* (London, the Stationery Office) Cmd 6629.

—— (2005b) *Consultation Document: Draft Section 11 Statutory Guidance on Making Arrangements to Safeguard and Promote the Welfare of Children* (London, The Stationery Office).

—— (2005c) *Putting Children First. A Guide for Separating Parents* (London, The Stationery
Office.

—— DOH and HOME OFFICE (2003) *Keeping Children Safe: The Government's Response to the
Victoria Climbie Inquiry Report and Joint Chief Inspectors' Report Safeguarding Children* Cmd
5861 (London, The Stationery Office).

DEPARTMENT OF THE ENVIRONMENT (1993) *Housing Consequences of Relationship Breakdown*
(London, HMSO).

DEPARTMENT OF THE ENVIRONMENT, TRANSPORT AND THE REGIONS AND DEPARTMENT OF
SOCIAL SECURITY (2000) *Quality and Choice: A Decent Home for All: The Housing Green Paper*
(London: DETR and DSS).

DEPARTMENT OF HEALTH (1989a) *The Care of Children: Principles and Practice in Regulations and
Guidance* (London, HMSO).

—— (1989b) *An Introduction to the Children Act 1989* (London, HMSO).

—— (1991a) *Working Together Under the Children Act 1989: A Guide to Arrangements for
Inter-agency Co-operation for the Protection of Children from Abuse* (London, HMSO).

—— (1991b) *The Children Act 1989: Guidance and Regulations, Vol 2 Family Support, Day Care
and Educational Provision for Young Children* (London, HMSO).

—— (1991c) *The Children Act 1989: Guidance and Regulations, Vol 1, Court Orders* (London,
HMSO).

—— (1991d) *The Children Act 1989: Guidance and Regulations, Vol 3, Family Placements* (London, HMSO).

—— (1991e) *Patterns and Outcomes in Child Placement: Messages from Current Research and
their Implications* (London, HMSO).

—— (1991f) *The Children Act 1989: Guidance and Regulations, Vol 7, Guardians Ad Litem and
Other Court Related Issues* (London, HMSO).

—— (1991g) *Child Abuse: A Study of Inquiry Reports 1980–1989* (London, HMSO).

—— (1995a) *The Challenge of Partnership in Child Protection: Practice Guide* (London, HMSO).

—— (1995b) *Child Protection – Messages from Research* (London, HMSO).

—— (1996) *Allocation of Housing Accommodation: Homelessness: Code of Guidance on Parts VI
and VII of the Housing Act 1996* (London, HMSO).

—— (1998) *Working Together to Safeguard Children: New Government Proposals for Inter-Agency
Co-operation: Consultation Paper* (London, The Stationery Office).

—— (2000a) *Protecting Children, Supporting Parents* (London, The Stationery Office).

—— (2000b) *Framework for the Assessment of Children in Need and their Families* (London, The
Stationery Office).

—— (2001), *National Adoption Standards for England* (London, The Stationery Office).

—— (2002) *Protecting the Public* (London, The Stationery Office) CM 5668.

—— (2003a) *Getting the Right Start: National Service Framework for Children: Emerging Findings* (London, The Stationery Office).

—— (2003b) *What to Do if You're Worried a Child is Being Abused* (London, The Stationery Office).

—— (2004) *National Service Framework for Children, Young People and Maternity Services* (London, The Stationery Office).

—— HOME OFFICE and DFEE (1999), *Working Together to Safeguard Children* (London, The Stationery Office).

—— and WELSH ASSEMBLY GOVERNMENT (2003) *Adoption: National Minimum Standards* (London, The Stationery Office).

—— and WELSH OFFICE (1992) *Review of Adoption Law: Report to Ministers of an Interdepartmental Working Group* (London, HMSO).

—— and WELSH OFFICE (1996) *Adoption – A Service for Children: Adoption Bill, A Consultative Document* (London, Department of Health).

—— and WELSH OFFICE, HOME OFFICE, LORD CHANCELLOR'S DEPARTMENT (White Paper) (1993) *Adoption: The Future* (London, HMSO), Cmd 2288.

DEPARTMENT OF HEALTH AND SOCIAL SECURITY (1985) *Review of Child Care Law: Report of Ministers of an Inter-departmental Working Party* (London, HMSO).

—— (1987) *The Law on Child Care and Family Services* (London HMSO) Cmd 62.

DEPARTMENT OF SOCIAL SECURITY (1997) *Statistics 1997* (London, The Stationery Office).

—— (1998) *Children First: A New Approach to Child Support* (London, The Stationery Office) Cmd 3992.

—— (1999) *A New Contract for Welfare: Children's Rights and Parents' Responsibilities* (London, The Stationery Office)

DEPARTMENT OF TRADE AND INDUSTRY (1998) *Fairness at Work* (London, The Stationery Office) Cmd 3968.

—— (WOMEN AND EQUALITY UNIT) (2003a), *Civil Partnership: A Framework for the legal recognition of same-sex couples* (London, DTI Home Office)

—— (2003b) *Responses to Civil Partnership* (London, The Stationery Office).

—— (2005) *Work and Families, Choice and Flexibility: A Consultation Document* (London, The Stationery Office).

DEWAR, J (1989) 'Fathers in Law? The Case of AID and Fatherhood' in D Morgan and WR Lee (eds), *Birthrights: Law and Ethics at the Beginning of Life* (London, Routledge).

—— (1992) *Law and the Family*, 2nd edn, (London, Butterworths).

—— (1995) 'Local Authorities, Ouster Orders and the Inherent Jurisdiction – *Re S (Minors) (Inherent Jurisdiction Ouster)*' 7 *Journal of Child Law* 64.

—— (1998) 'The Normal Chaos of Family Law' 61(4) *MLR* 467.

—— (2000) 'Family Law and its Discontents' 14 *Int J of Law, Policy and the Family* 59.

DICKENS, B (1987) 'Legal Aspects of Surrogate Motherhood: Practices and Proposals', Paper presented at the UK national Committee of Comparative Law 1987 Colloquium 'Legal Regulation of Reproductive Medicine', Cambridge, UK, 15–17 September.

DICKENS, J (1993) 'Assessment and Control of Social Work: An Analysis of Reasons for Non-Use of the Child Assessment Order' *JSW&FL* 88.

DICKSON, DT (1968) 'Bureaucracy and Morality: An Organizational Perspective on a Moral Crusade' 16 *Social Problems* 143.

DIDUCK, A (1990) '*Carnigan v Carnigan*: When is a Father Not a Father?' *Man Law Journal* 580.

—— (1993) 'Legislating Ideologies of Motherhood' 2 *Social and Legal Studies* 461.

—— (1995) 'The Unmodified Family: The Child Support Act and the construction of Legal Subjects' 22 *J of Law and Society* 527.

—— (1997) 'In Search of the Feminist Good Mother' 7 *Social and Legal Studies* 129.

—— (1998) 'Conceiving the Bad Mother: "The Focus Should be on the Child to be Born"' 32 *University of British Columbia Law Review* 1999.

—— (1999a) 'Justice and Childhood: Reflections on Refashioned Boundaries' in M King (ed), *Moral Agendas for Children's Welfare* (London, Routledge).

—— (1999b) 'Dividing the Family Assets' in S Day Sclater and C Piper (eds), *Undercurrents of Divorce* (Aldershot, Ashgate).

—— (2001a) 'A Family by Any other Name... or Starbucks Comes to England' 28 *J of Law and Society* 290.

—— (2001b) 'Fairness and Justice for All? The House of Lords in *White v White*' 9 *Feminist Legal Studies* 173.

—— (2003) *Law's Families* (Cambridge, CUP).

—— (2005a) 'Shifting Familiarity' 58 *Current Legal Problems 235*.

—— (2005b) 'There's no place like home' unpublished paper presented to LSA Annual meeting, Chicago, USA.

—— and ORTON, H (1994) 'Equality and Support for Spouses' 57 *MLR* 681.

DINGWALL, R and EEKELAAR, J (1988) 'Families and the State: An Historical Perspective on the Public Regulation of Private Conduct' 10 *Law and Policy* 341.

DINGWALL, R, EEKELAAR, J and MURRAY, T (1983) *The Protection of Children: State Intervention and Family Life* (Oxford, Blackwell).

DINGWALL, R and GREATBACH, D, (2000) 'The Mediation Process' in G Davis, *et al, Monitoring Publicly Funded Family Mediation: Report to the Legal Services Commission* (London, Legal Services Commission).

DINGWALL, R and GREATBACH, D, (2001) 'Family Mediators – What are They Doing?' *Fam Law* 378.

DNES, AW (1997) *The Division of Marital Assets Following Divorce with Particular Reference to Pensions* (LCD Research Series No 7/97) (London, Lord Chancellor's Department).

DOBASH, RE (2003) 'Domestic Violence: Arrest, Prosecution and Reducing Violence' 2 *Criminology & Public Policy* 313.

—— and DOBASH, RP (1979) *Violence Against Wives* (New York, NY, Free Press).

—— and —— (1992) *Women, Violence and Social Change* (London, Routledge).

—— and —— (1998) 'Violent Men and Violent Contexts' in RE Dobash and RP Dobash (eds), *Rethinking Violence Against Women* (London, Sage).

—— and —— (2000) 'The Politics and Policies of Responding to Violence Against Women' in J Hanmer, *et al* (eds), *Home Truths About Domestic Violence: Feminist Influences on Policy and Practice: A Reader* (London, Routledge).

—— and —— (2004) 'Women's Violence to Men in Intimate Relationships. Working on a Puzzle' 44 *Brit J Criminology* 324.

DOBASH, RP, DOBASH, RE, CAVANAGH, K and LEWIS, R (2000) 'Confronting Violent Men' in J Hanmer, *et al* (eds), *Home Truths About Domestic Violence: Feminist Influences on Policy and Practice: A Reader* (London, Routledge).

DOGGETT, ME (1992) *Marriage, Wife-Beating and the Law in Victorian England* (London, Weidenfeld & Nicolson).

DONZELOT, J and HURLEY R (tr), (1980) *The Policing of Families* (London, Hutchinson).

DOUGLAS, G (1991) *Law, Fertility and Reproduction* (London, Sweet & Maxwell).

—— (1992) 'The Retreat from *Gillick*' 55 *MLR* 569.

—— (1993) 'Assisted Reproduction and the Welfare of the Child' 46 *Current Legal Problems* 53.

—— (1994) 'The Intention to be a Parent and the Making of Mothers' 57 *MLR* 636.

—— (1996) 'Comment on *Re Q*' *Fam Law* 207.

—— (2004) *An Introduction to Family Law*, 2nd edn, (Oxford, OUP).

—— and LOWE, NV (1992) 'Becoming a Parent in English Law' 108 *LQR* 414.

——, MURCH, M, SCANLAN, L and PERRY, A. (2000) 'Safeguarding Children's Welfare in Non-contentious Divorce: Towards a New Conception of the Legal Process?' 63 *MLR* 177.

—— and PERRY, A (2001) 'How Parents Cope Financially on Separation and Divorce – implications for the Future of Ancillary Relief' 13 *CFLQ* 67.

—— and SEBBA, L (1998) *Children's Rights and Traditional Values* (Aldershot, Ashgate).

DOWNIE, A (1997) 'The Doctor and the Teenager – Questions of Consent' *Fam Law* 499.

—— (1999) 'Consent to Medical Treatment – Whose View of Welfare?' *Fam Law* 818.

DUNCAN, S and SMITH, DP (2004) 'And then the Lover, can we all now choose individual fulfilment?' in *Seven Ages of Man and Woman, A Look at Life in Britain in the Second Elizabethan Era* (London, ESRC).

DUNCAN, S, EDWARDS, R, REYNOLDS, T and ALLDRED, P (2003) 'Motherhood, Paid Work and Partnering: Values and Theories' 17 *Work, Employment and Society* 309.

DUNN, J (2003) 'Contact and Children's Perspectives on Parental Relationships' in A Bainham, *et al* (eds), *Children and Their Families: Contact, Rights and Welfare* (Oxford, Hart Publishing).

DUNNE, G (1999) 'A Passion for "Sameness"? Sexuality and Gender Accountability' in EB Silva and C Smart (eds), *The 'New' Family?* (London, Sage).

—— (2000) 'Opting into Motherhood: Lesbians Blurring the Boundaries and Transforming the Meaning of Parenthood and Kinship' 14 *Gender and Society* 11.

DWORKIN, R (1995) *Life's Dominion: An Argument about Abortion and Euthanasia* (London, Harper Collins).

DYER, C (2005a) 'Breaking Uneven' *The Guardian*, 15 March.

—— (2005b) 'Divorce Mediation Scheme Flops' *The Guardian*, 27 June.

—— (2005c) 'Doctors Win Appeal Over Rights of the Terminally Ill' *The Guardian*, 29 July.

EAGLETON, T (1991) *Ideology: An Introduction* (London, Verso).

EAST, E.H. (1972) *Pleas of the Crown*, vol 1 (P.R. Glazebrook (ed)) (London, Professional Books).

EASTON, S (1976) 'Explaining Ideology' 2 *Sociological Analysis and Theory* 187.

EATON, M (1994) 'Abuse by Any Other Name: Feminism, Difference, and Intralesbian Violence' in MA Fine and R Myktiuk (eds), *The Public Nature of Private Violence: The Discovery of Domestic Abuse* (London, Routledge).

EDWARDS, R and DUNCAN, S (1996) 'Rational Economic Man or Lone Mothers in Context? The Uptake of Paid Work' in EB Silva (ed), *Good Enough Mothering? Feminist Perspectives on Lone Motherhood* (London, Routledge).

EDWARDS, R, GILLIES, V and RIBBENS MCCARTHY, J (1999) 'Biological Parents and Social Families: Legal Discourses and Everyday Understandings of the Position of Step-Parents' 13 *Int J of Law, Policy and the Family* 78.

EDWARDS, S (2004) 'Division of Assets and Fairness – "Brick Lane" – Gender, Culture and Ancillary Relief on Divorce' 34 *Fam Law* 809.

EDWARDS, SSM (1989) *Policing Domestic Violence* (London, Sage).

—— (1996) *Sex and Gender in the Legal Process* (London, Blackstone Press).

EEKELAAR, J (1984) ' "Trust the Judges": How Far should Family Law Go?' 47 *MLR* 593.

—— (1985) 'Custody Appeals' 48 *MLR* 704.

—— (1986) 'The Emergence of Children's Rights' 6 *OJLS* 161.

—— (1988) 'Equality and the Purpose of Maintenance' 15 *J of Law and Society* 188.

—— (1991a) 'Parental Responsibility: State of Nature or Nature of the State?' *JSW&FL* 37.

—— (1991b) *Regulating Divorce* (Oxford, Clarendon Press).

—— (1994a) 'The Interests of the Child and the Child's Wishes: The Role of Dynamic Self-determinism' 8 *Int J of Law and the Family* 42.

—— (1994b) 'Third Thoughts on Child Support' *Fam Law* 99.

—— (1996) 'The Family Law Bill – The Politics of Family Law' *Fam Law* 45.

—— (1998) 'Should Section 25 be Reformed?' *Fam Law* 469.

—— (1999) 'Family Law: Keeping Us "On Message" ' 11 *CFLQ* 387.

—— (2000) 'Uncovering Social Obligations: Family Law and the Responsible Citizen' in M Maclean (ed), *Making Law For Families* (Oxford, Hart Publishing).

—— (2001a) 'Back to Basics and Forward into the Unknown' *Fam Law* 30.

—— (2001b) 'Asset Distribution on Divorce – The Durational Element' 117 *Law Quarterly Review* 552.

—— (2001c) 'Rethinking Parental Responsibility' *Fam Law* 426.

—— (2002a) 'Beyond the Welfare Principle' 14(3) *CFLQ* 237.

—— (2002b) 'Contact – Over the Limit' *Fam Law* 271.

—— (2003a) 'Asset Distribution on Divorce – Time and Property' 33 *Fam Law* 838.

—— (2003b) 'Contact and Adoption Reform' in A Bainham, *et al* (eds), *Children and Their Families: Contact, Rights and Welfare* (Oxford, Hart Publishing).

—— (2005) 'Shared Income After Divorce: A Step Too Far' 121 *LQR* 1.

EEKELAAR, J and CLIVE, E (1977) *Custody after Divorce: The Disposition of Custody in Divorce Cases in Great Britain* (Oxford, Centre for Socio-legal Studies, Oxford University).

EEKELAAR, J, DINGWALL, R and MURRAY, T (1982) 'Victims or Threats? Children in Care Proceedings' *JSWL* 68.

EEKELAAR, J and MACLEAN, M (2004) 'Marriage and the Moral Bases of Personal Relationships' 31 *J of Law and Society* 510.

EEKELAAR, J, MACLEAN, M and BEINART, S (2000) *Family Lawyers: The Divorce Work of Solicitors* (Oxford, Hart Publishing).

EICHLER, M (1990) 'The Limits of Family Law Reform or, The Privatization of Female and Child Poverty' 7 *Canadian Family Law Quarterly* 59.

ELLIS, D and STUCKLESS, N (1996) *Mediating and Negotiating Marital Conflicts* (London and California, Sage).

ELLISON, L (2003) 'Responding to Victim Withdrawal in Domestic Violence Prosecutions' *Crim LR* 760.

ELLISON, R (1996) 'Pensions and Divorce – the New Regulations' *Fam Law* 502.

ELLMAN, IM (1997) 'The Misguided Movement to Revive Fault Divorce and Why Reformers Should Look Instead to the American Law Institute' 11 *Int J of Law, Policy and the Family* 216.

ENGELS, F (1978) *The Origin of the Family, Private Property and the State* (Peking, Foreign Language Press).

EQUAL OPPORTUNITIES COMMISSION (1979) *Health and Safety Legislation: Should we distinguish between men and women?* (Manchester, EOC).

—— (1995) *The Life Cycle of Inequality: Women and Men in Britain* (Manchester, EOC).

ERIKSON, EH (1980) *Identity and the Life Cycle* (London, Norton).

FAMILY POLICY STUDIES CENTRE (1995), *Families in Britain, Family Report 3*.

FARAGHER, T (1985) 'The Police Response to Violence against Women in the Home' in J Pahl (ed), *Private Violence and Public Policy: The Needs of Battered Women and the Response of the Public Services* (London, Routledge and Kegan Paul).

FARMER, E and OWEN, M (1995) *Child Protection Practice: Private Risks and Public Remedies: A Study of Decision-making, Intervention and Outcome in Child Protection Work* (London, HMSO).

FERRI, E and SMITH, K (1996) *Parenting in the 1990s* (London, Family Policy Studies Centre).

FINCH, J (1989) *Family Obligations and Social Change* (Cambridge, Polity Press).

FINEMAN, MA (1989) 'The Politics of Custody and the Transformation of American Custody Decision Making' 22 *University of California, Davis* 829.

—— (1991) *The Illusion of Equality: The Rhetoric and Reality of Divorce Reform* (Chicago, IL, University of Chicago Press).

—— (1995) *The Neutered Mother, the Sexual Family and Other Twentieth Century Tragedies* (London, Routledge).

—— (2004) *The Autonomy Myth* (New York, The New Press).

—— and KARPIN, I (eds) (1995), *Mothers in Law: Feminist Theory and the Legal Regulation of Motherhood* (New York, NY, Columbia University Press).

FINER, M (1974) *Report on the Committee on One Parent Families* (London, HMSO) Cmd 5629.

—— and MCGREGOR, OR (1974) *History of the Obligation to Maintain*, Appendix 5 in M Finer, *Report of the Committee on One Parent Families* (London, HMSO) Cmd 5629.

FINKELHOR, D (1986) 'Abusers: Special Topics' in D Finkelhor, *et al* (eds), *A Sourcebook on Child Sexual Abuse* (CA, Sage).

—— and BARON, L (1986) 'High Risk Children' in D Finkelhor, *et al* (eds), *A Sourcebook on Child Sexual Abuse* (CA, Sage).

FIONDA, J (ed) (2001a) *Legal Concepts of Childhood* (Oxford, Hart Publishing).

—— (2001b) 'Youth and Justice' in J Fionda (ed), *Legal Concepts of Childhood* (Oxford, Hart Publishing).

FISCHER, K, VIDMAR, N and ELLIS, R (1993) 'The Culture of Battering and the Role of Mediation in Domestic Violence Cases' 46 *SMV Law Review* 2117.

FISH, DG (1997) 'Child Abuse – A Legal Practitioners' Guide' *Fam Law* 665.

FISHER, T (1996) 'The Rights of the Child in Mediation and Divorce' *Child Care Forum* No 9.

—— and HODSON, D (2001) 'Family Mediation – Did it Make Things Better?' *Fam Law* 270.

FLETCHER, R (1973) *The Family and Marriage in Britain: An Analysis and Moral Assessment,* 3rd edn, (Harmondsworth, Penguin).

FLOOD-PAGE, C and TAYLOR, J (eds), (2003) *Crime in England and Wales 2001/2002: Supplementary Volume* (London, Home Office).

FORTIN, J (1994) '*Re F*: "The Gooseberry Bush Approach"' 57 *MLR* 296.

—— (1998) '*Re C (Medical Treatment)*: A Baby's Right to Life' 10 *CFLQ* 411.

—— (1999) 'Rights Brought Home for Children' 62 *MLR* 350.

—— (2003) *Children's Rights and the Developing Law* 2nd edn (London, Butterworths).

—— (2004) 'Children's Rights: Are the Courts Now Taking Them More Seriously?' 15 *KCLJ* 253.

FOSTER, H (1976) 'A Review of "Beyond the Best Interests of the Child"' 12 *Williamette Law Journal* 545.

FOVARGUE, S (2002) 'The Law's Response to Pregnancy and Childbirth: Consistency, Conflict or Compromise?' *MLR* 290.

FOWLER, E and STEWART, S (2005) 'Rule 9.5 Separate Representation and NYAS' *Fam Law* 49.

FOX, L (2003) 'Reforming Family Property – Comparisons, Compromises and Common Dimensions' 15 *CFLQ* 1.

FOX, M and McHALE, J (1997) 'In Whose Best Interests?' 60 *MLR* 700.

FOX, R (1992) *Reproduction and Succession: Studies in Law, Anthropology and Society* (London, Transaction).

FOX-HARDING, L (1996) *Family State and Social Policy* (Basingstoke, MacMillan).

FRANCOME, C (2004) *Abortion in the USA and the UK* (Aldershot, Ashgate).

FREDMAN, S (1994) 'A Difference with Distinction: Pregnancy and Parenthood Reassessed' 110 *LQR* 106.

—— (1997) *Women and the Law* (Oxford, Clarendon Press).

FREEMAN, MDA (1979) *Violence in the Home* (Aldershot, Gower).

—— (1981) ' "But If You Can't Rape Your Wife, Who[m] Can You Rape?": The Marital Rape Exemption Re-examined' 15 *Family LQ* 1.

—— (1983) *The Rights and Wrongs of Children* (London, Frances Pinter).

—— (1985) 'Towards a Critical Theory of Family Law' 38 *Current Legal Problems* 153.

—— (1989a) 'Is Surrogacy Exploitative?' in S McLean (ed), *Legal Issues in Human Reproduction* (Aldershot, Gower).

—— (1989b) 'Cleveland, Butler-Sloss and Beyond – How are we to React to the Sexual Abuse of Children?' 42 *Current Legal Problems* 85.

—— (1995) 'The Morality of Cultural Pluralism' 3 *The Int J of Children's Rights* 1.

—— (ed) (1996a) *Divorce: Where Next?* (Aldershot, Dartmouth).

—— (1996b) *Current Law Statutes: Family Law Act 1996* (London, Sweet & Maxwell).

—— (2000) 'The End of the Century of the Child?' 53 *CLP* 505.

—— (2001) 'The Child in Family Law' in J Fionda (ed), *Legal Concepts of Childhood* (Oxford, Hart Publishing)

—— and LYON, C (1983) *Cohabitation without Marriage* (Aldershot, Gower).

FREUD, A, SOLNIT, AJ and GOLDSTEIN, J (1973) *Beyond the Best Interests of the Child* (New York, NY, Free Press).

FREUD, S (1905) *Three Essays on the Theory of Sexuality,* vol VII in J Strachey (ed and tr), *The Standard Edition of the Complete Psychological Works of Sigmund Freud* (London, Hogarth).

FROST, N and STEIN, M (1989) *The Politics of Child Welfare: Inequality, Power and Change* (London, Harvester Wheatsheaf).

FRUG, MJ (1992) *Postmodern Legal Feminism* (London, Routledge).

FUDGE, J and GLASBEEK, HJ (1992) 'The Politics of Rights: A Politics with a Little Class' 1 *Social and Legal Studies* 45.

FURNISS, T (1991) *The Multi-Professional Handbook of Child Sexual Abuse: Integrated Management, Therapy and Legal Intervention* (London, Routledge).

GADD, D, FARRALL, S, DALLMORE, D and LOMBARD, N (2002) *Domestic Abuse against Men in Scotland* (Edinburgh, Scottish Executive).

GALLAGHER, B, CHRISTMANN, C, FRASER, C and HODGSON, B (2003) 'International and Internet Child Sexual Abuse and Exploitation – Issues Emerging from Research' 15 *CFLQ* 353.

GEIS, G (1978) 'Rape-in-Marriage: Law and Law Reform in England, the United States, and Sweden' 6 *Adelaide LR* 284.

—— and BINDER, A, (1991) 'Sins of their Children: Parental Responsibility for Juvenile Delinquency' 5 *Notre Dame Journal of Law Ethics and Public Policy* 303.

GELDOF, B, (2003) 'The Real Love that Dare Not Speak its Name' in A Bainham, *et al* (eds), *Children and Their Families: Contact, Rights and Welfare* (Oxford, Hart Publishing).

GELLES, RJ (1973) 'Child Abuse as Psychopathology: a Sociological Critique and Reformulation' 43 *American Journal of Orthopsychiatry* 611.

—— (1975) 'The Social Construction of Child Abuse' 45 *American J of Orthopsychiatry* 363.

—— (1979) *Family Violence* (CA, Sage).

—— (1992) *The Violent Home: A Study of Physical Aggression between Husbands and Wives* (California, Sage).

GENN, H (1999) *Paths to Justice* (Oxford, Hart Publishing).

GEORGE, P (1997) 'In All the Circumstances – Section 25' *Fam Law* 729.

GHANDHI, PR and MACNAMEE (1991) 'The Family in UK Law and the International Covenant on Civil and Political Rights' 5 *Int J of Law and the Family* 104.

GIBB, F (2005) 'Lesbian's Former Lover Wins Right to Share Child', *The Times*, 8 April.

GIBBONS, J, CONROY, S and BELL, C (1995) *Operating the Child Protection System: A Study of Child Protection Practices in English Local Authorities* (London, HMSO).

GIDDENS, A (1992) *The Transformation of Intimacy* (Cambridge, Polity).

GILBERT, G (1993) 'Housing for Children' 5 *Journal of Child Law* 166.

GILLESPIE, G (2002) 'Child Support – When the Bough Breaks' *Fam Law* 528.

GILLIGAN, C (1982) *In a Different Voice* (Cambridge, MA, Harvard University Press).

GILLIS, J (1985) *For Better or for Worse: British Marriages 1600 to the Present* (Oxford, OUP).

—— (1997) *A World of Their Own Making, A History of Myth and Ritual in Family Life* (Oxford, OUP).

GILMORE, S (2004) 'The Nature, Scope, and Use of the Specific Issue Order' 16 *CFLQ* 367.

GINGERBREAD and FAMILIES NEED FATHERS (1982) *Divided Children: A Survey of Access to Children After Divorce*.

GINN, J (2002) 'Do Divorced Women Catch Up in Pension Building?' 14 *CFLQ* 157.

—— (2003) 'Parenthood, Partnership Status and Pensions: Cohort Differences among Women' 37 *Sociology* 493.

—— and ARBER, S (1996) 'Patterns of Employment, Pensions and Gender: The Effect of Work History on Older Women's Non-State Pensions' 10 *Work, Employment and Society* 469.

GIOVANNONI, JM and BECERRA, R (1979) *Defining Child Abuse* (New York, NY, Free Press; London, Collier Macmillan).

GITTINS, D (1993) *The Family in Question: Changing Households and Familiar Ideologies*, 2nd edn, (Basingstoke, Macmillan).

GLASGOW, JM (1979-80) 'The Marital Rape Exemption: Legal Sanction of Spousal Abuse' 18 *J of Family Law* 565.

GLENDINNING, C, CLARKE, K and CRAIG, G (1996) 'Implementing the Child Support Act' 18 (3) *JSW&FL* 273.

GLENDON, MA (1989) *The Transformation of Family Law* (Chicago, IL, University of Chicago Press).

GLENNON, L (2000) 'Fitzpatrick v Sterling Housing Association Ltd – An Endorsement of the Functional Family?' 14 *International Journal of Law, Policy and the Family* 226.

GOLDSTEIN, J (1980) *Before the Best Interests of the Child* (London, Burnett Books).

——, FREUD, A and SOLNIT, AJ (1980a) *Beyond the Best Interests of the Child* (London, Burnett Books).

——, —— and —— (1996) *The Best Interests of the Child: The Least Detrimental Alternative* (New York, NY, Free Press).

GOLLOP, M, SMITH, AB and TAYLOR, N (2000) 'Children's Involvement in Custody and Access Arrangements After Parental Separation' 12 (4) *CFLQ* 383.

GOODE, J (1993) *World Changes in Divorce Patterns* (New Haven, CT, Yale Univeristy Press).

GORDON, L (1989) *Heroes of their Own Lives: The Politics and History of Family Violence: Boston 1880–1960* (New York, NY, Penguin Books).

GOVER, A, MACDONALD, J and ALPERT, G (2003) 'Combating Domestic Violence: Findings from an Evaluation of a Local Domestic Violence Court' 3 *Criminology & Public Policy* 109.

GOVERNMENT STATISTICAL OFFICE (1998) *Population Trends, 91* (London, The Stationery Office).

GRACE, S (1995) *Policing Domestic Violence in the 1990s* (Home Office Research Study No 139) (London, HMSO).

GRAND, A (1994) 'What is this Thing Called Parental Responsibility?' *Fam Law* 586.

GRASSBY, M (1991) 'Women in their Forties: The Extent of the Right to Alimentary Support' 30 *Reports of Family Law 3d* 369.

GRAY, C and MERRICK, S (1996) 'Voice Alterations, Why Women Have More Difficulty than Men with the Legal Process of Divorce' 34 *Family and Conciliation Courts Review* 240.

GREGSON, N and LOWE, M (1994) *Servicing the Middle Classes: Class, Gender and Waged Domestic Labour in Contemporary Britain* (London, Routledge).

GRIFFITHS, DL and MOYNIHAN, FJ (1963) 'Multiple Epiphysial Injuries in Babies ("Battered Baby Syndrome")' *British Medical Journal* 1558.

GRILLO, T (1991) 'The Mediation Alternative: Process Dangers for Women' *Yale Law Journal* 1545.

GUSFIELD, JR (1975) 'Categories of Ownership and Responsibility in Social Issues: Alcohol Abuse and Automobile Use' 5 *Journal of Drug Issues* 290.

HALE, Dame B (1996) *From the Test Tube to the Coffin: Choice and Regulation in Family Life* (London, Sweet & Maxwell).

—— (1998) 'Private Lives and Public Duties: What is Family Law For?' 20 *JSW&FL* 125.

—— (2004) 'Homosexual Rights' 16 *CFLQ* 125.

HALE, Sir MATTHEW (1971) PR Glazebrook (ed), *Historia Placitorum Coronae,* vol 1 (London, Professional Books).

HALL, JG and MARTIN, DF (1990) 'Child Delinquency and Parental Responsibility' 154 *Justice of the Peace* 604.

HAMILTON, AC and SINCLAIR, M (1991) *Report of the Aboriginal Justice Inquiry of Manitoba* (Winnipeg, Province of Manitoba).

HAMILTON, C (1996) 'Marriage, Wardship and "Best Interests"' 123 *Childright.*

—— and WATT, B (2004) 'The Employment of Children' *CFLQ* 135.

HANCOCK, E (1982) 'Sources of Discord Between Attorneys and Therapists in Divorce Cases' 6 *Journal of Divorce* 115.

HANMER, J, GRIFFITHS, S and JERWOOD, D (1999) *Arresting Evidence: Domestic Violence and Repeat Victimisation: Police Research Series, Paper 104* (London, Policing and Reducing Crime Unit).

HANMER, J and ITZIN, C with QUAID, S and WIGGLESWORTH, D (eds), (2000) *Home Truths About Domestic Violence: Feminist Influences on Policy and Practice: A Reader* (London, Routledge).

HARCUS, J (1997) 'Periodical Payments – End of Term?' *Fam Law* 340.

HARNE, L and RADFORD, J (1994) 'Reinstating Patriarchy: The Politics of the Family and the New Legislation' in A Mullender and R Morley (eds), *Children Living with Domestic Violence* (London, Whiting & Birch).

—— and —— (1997) *Valued Families: The Lesbian Mothers' Legal Handbook* (London, Women's Press).

HAROLD, G and MURCH, M (2005) 'Inter-parental Conflict and Children's Adaptation to Separation and Divorce: Theory, Research and Implications for Family Law, Practice and Policy' 17 *CFLQ* 185.

HARRIS, J (2000) *An Evaluation of the Use and Effectiveness of the Protection from Harassment Act 1997: Home Office Research Study 203* (London, Home Office)

HARRIS, N (1993) *Law and Education: Regulation, Consumerism and the Education System* (London, Sweet & Maxwell).

HARRISON, K (1995) 'Fresh or Frozen: Lesbian Mothers, Sperm Donors and Limited Fathers' in M Fineman and I Karpin (eds), *Mothers in Law: Feminist Theory and the Legal Regulation of Motherhood* (New York, NY, Columbia University Press).

HARTRAIS, L (1994) 'Comparing Family Policy in Britain, France and Germany' 23(2) *J of Social Policy* 135.

HARWIN, N and BARRON, J (2000) 'Domestic Violence and Social Policy: Perspectives from Women's Aid' in J Hanmer, *et al* (eds), *Home Truths About Domestic Violence: Feminist Influences on Policy and Practice: A Reader* (London, Routledge).

HATTEN, W, VINTER, L and WILLIAMS, R (2002) *Dads on Dads: Needs and Expectations at Home and at Work* (London, Equal Opportunities Commission).

HAVAS, E (1995) 'The Family as Ideology' 29 *Social Policy and Administration* 1.

HAWTHORNE, J, JESSOP, J, PRYOR, J and RICHARDS, M (2003) *Supporting Children through Family Change: A Review of Interventions and Services for Children of Divorcing and Separating Parents* (Cambridge, Centre for Family Research, University of Cambridge; York, Joseph Rowntree Foundation).

HAYES, M (1994) ' "Cohabitation Clauses" in Financial Provision and Property Adjustment Orders – Law, Policy and Justice' 110 *LQR* 124.

—— (1996) 'Non-molestation Protection – Only Associated Persons Need Apply' *Fam Law* 134.

—— (2004) '*Re O and N; Re B* – Uncertain Evidence and Risk-taking in Child Protection Cases' 16 *CFLQ* 63.

—— and WILLIAMS, C. (1999) *Family Law: Principles, Policy and Practice* (London, Butterworths).

HAYES, P (2003) 'Giving due consideration to ethnicity in adoption placements – A principled approach' 15 *CFLQ* 255.

—— (1995) 'The Ideological Attack on Transracial Adoption in the USA and Britain' 9 *Int J of Law and the Family* 1.

HEARN, J (1998) *The Violences of Men: How Men Talk About and How Agencies Respond to Men's Violence to Women* (London, Sage).

HENDRICK, H (2003) *Child Welfare: Historical Dimensions, Contemporary Debate* (Bristol, Policy).

HENRICSON, C and BAINHAM, A (2005) *The Child and Family Policy Divide, Tensions, Convergence and Rights* (York, Joseph Rowntree Foundation).

HM COURT SERVICE INSPECTORATE (HMCSI) (2003) Seeking Agreement. Children and Family Court Advisory and Support Service (CAFCASS). A Thematic Review by MCSI of the Operation of Schemes Involving CAFCASS at an Early Stage in Private Law Proceedings (www.cafacass.gov.uk accessed 6 June 2005).

HM CROWN PROSECUTION SERVICE INSPECTORATE (HMCPSI),

HM INSPECTORATE OF CONSTABULARY (HMIC) (2004) *A Joint Inspection of the Investigation and Prosecution of Cases Involving Domestic Violence.*

HM INSPECTORATE OF PROBATION (1997) *Family Court Welfare Work: Report of a Thematic Inspection* (London, Home Office).

HM Treasury (1998) *The Modernisation of Britain's Tax and Benefit System; Number 3; The Working Families Tax Credit and work incentives*, Paper published as part of *Budget 98* (London, HM Treasury).

—— (2004) *Child Poverty Review* (London, The Stationery Office).

—— (2005) *Budget 2005: Investing in our Future: Fairness and Opportunity for Britain's Hard-working Families*. HC 372 (London, The Stationery Office).

—— DFES, DWP and DTI (2004) *Choice for parents, the best start for children: a ten year strategy for childcare* (London, HM Treasury)

Herring, J (1998) ' "Name this Child" ' *Cambridge Law Journal* 266.

—— (1999) 'The Human Rights Act and the Welfare Principle in Family Law – Conflicting or Complementary?' 11(3) *CFLQ* 223.

—— (2003) 'Connecting Contact: Contact in a Private Law Context' in A Bainham, *et al* (eds), *Children and their Families: Contact, Rights and Welfare* (Oxford, Hart Publishing).

—— (2004) *Family Law*, 2nd edn, (Harlow, Longman).

—— (2005) 'Why Financial Orders on Divorce Should be Unfair' 19 *Int J of Law Pol and the Fam* 218.

Hester, M, *et al* (1992) 'Domestic Violence and Access Arrangements for Children in Denmark and Britain' *JSW&FL* 57.

—— and Radford, L (1996) *Domestic Violence and Child Contact Arrangements in England and Denmark* (Bristol, Policy).

—— *et al* (1998) 'Domestic Violence and Child Contact' in A Mullender and R Morley (eds), *Children Living with Domestic Violence* (London, Whiting & Birch).

——, Pearson, C and Harwin, N (2000) *Making an Impact: Children and Domestic Violence: A Reader* (London, Jessica Kingsley).

——, Hanmer, J, Coulson, S, Morahan, M and Razak, A (2003) *Domestic Violence: Making it Through the Criminal Justice System* (University of Sunderland, Northern Rock Foundation and International Centre for the Study of Violence and Abuse).

Hetherington, EM (1979) 'Divorce: A Child's Perspective' 34 *American Psychologist* 851.

Hibbs, M, Barton, C and Beswick, J (2001) 'Why Marry?—Perceptions of the Affianced' *Fam Law* 197.

Hill, M (1980) *Understanding Social Policy* (Oxford, Robertson).

Hilton, N (1991) 'Mediating Wife Assault: Battered Women and the New "Family" ' 9 *Canadian J of Family Law* 29.

Hinchcliffe, M (2004) 'Whatever Happened to Starred Care Plans?' *Fam Law* 660.

Hoggett, B (1994) 'Joint Parenting Systems: The English Experiment' 6 *J of Child Law* 8.

—— *et al*, (1996) *The Family, Law and Society: Cases and Materials*, 4th edn, (London, Butterworths).

Holcombe, L (1983) *Wives and Property: Reform of the Married Women's Property Acts* (Toronto, University of Toronto Press).

Holgate, G (1993) 'Intentional Homelessness: Applications for Accommodation, Priority Need and Eligibility' *Fam Law* 487.

Home Office (1990a) *Crime Justice and Protecting the Public* (London, HMSO) Cmd 965.

—— (1990b) *Domestic Violence*, Home Office Circular 60/1990 (London, Home Office).

—— (1993) *Information on the Criminal Justice System in England and Wales, Digest 2*.

—— (1994) *National Standards for Probation Service Family Court Welfare Work* (London, HMSO).

—— (1997) Press Release, 5 June.

—— (1998) *Supporting Families: A Consultation Document* (London, The Stationery Office).

—— (1999) *Supporting Families: Responses to the Consultation Document* (London, The Stationery Office)

—— (2000a) *Domestic Violence: Break the Chain Multi-Agency Guidance for Addressing Domestic Violence* (London, HMSO).

—— (2000b) 'Domestic Violence: Revised Circular to the Police', Home Office Circular No 19/2000 (London, Home Office).

—— (2000c) *A Choice by Right. Report of the working group on forced marriage* (London, Home Office).

—— (2002) *Justice for All* (London, HMSO) Cm 5563.

—— (2003) *Safety and Justice: The Government's Proposals on Domestic Violence* (London, HMSO) Cm 5847.

HOOPER, C (1994) 'Do Families Need Fathers? The Impact of Divorce on Children' in A Mullender and R Morley (eds), *Children Living with Domestic Violence* (London, Whiting & Birch).

HOUSE OF COMMONS SELECT COMMITTEE ON VIOLENCE IN THE FAMILY (1975) *Report from the Select Committee on Violence in Marriage, Vol II, Report, Minutes of Evidence and Appendices* (London, HMSO).

HOUSE OF COMMONS SELECT COMMITTEE ON SCIENCE AND TECHNOLOGY (2004) Written Evidence, May 2004; *Memorandum from the Department of Health* www.publications.parliament.uk/pa/cm200405/cmselect/cmsctech/7/7we02.html

HOUSE OF COMMONS SELECT COMMITTEE ON WORK AND PENSIONS (2005a) First Special Report.

—— (2005b) *The Performance of the Child Support Agency: Second Report of Session 2004–05* Volume 1 HC 44–1

HOUSE OF COMMONS, SOCIAL SECURITY COMMITTEE (1994) *The Operation of the Child Support Act: Proposals for Change* (HC 470 1994–95) (London, HMSO).

—— (1993), *The Operation of the Child Support Act* (HC 69) (London, HMSO, 1993–94).

—— (1998), *Pensions on Divorce* (HC 869) (London, The Stationery Office)

HOUSE OF COMMONS AND HOUSE OF LORDS (2005) *Joint Committee on the Draft Children (Contact) and Adoption Bill, Session 2004–05, Volume 1: Report* HC 400–I, HL Paper 100–I (London, The Stationery Office).

HOWITT, D (1993) *Child Abuse Errors – When Good Intentions Go Wrong* (NJ, Rutgers University Press; Harvester, Wheatsheaf).

HOYLE, C (1998) *Negotiating Domestic Violence: Police, Criminal Justice and Victims* (Oxford, OUP).

—— and SANDERS, A (2000) 'Police Response to Domestic Violence: From Victim Choice to Victim Empowerment?' 40 *Brit J Criminology* 14.

HUDSON, P and LEE, WR (1990) 'Women's Work and the Family Economy in Historical Perspective' in P Hudson and WR Lee (eds), *Women's Work and the Family Economy in Historical Perspective* (Manchester, MUP).

HUMAN FERTILISATION AND EMBRYOLOGY AUTHORITY (2003) *Code of Practice* (London, HFEA).

—— (2005) *Tomorrow's Children; a Consultation on Guidance to Licensed Fertility Clinics on Taking in Account the Welfare of Children to be Born of Assisted Conception Treatment* (London, HFEA).

—— (Undated) Response to the Department of Trade and Industry Women and Equality Unit Consultation, 'Civil Partnership: A Framework for the Legal Recognition of Same Sex Couples' (London, HFEA, undated, accessed 2005).

HUMPHREYS, C (2000) *Child Protection and Woman Protection: Links and Schisms: An Overview of the Research* (Bristol, WAFE).

HUMPHREYS, C and HARRISON, C (2003a) 'Squaring the Circle – Contact and Domestic Violence' *Fam Law* 419.

—— and —— (2003b) 'Focusing on Safety – Domestic Violence and the Role of Child Contact Centres' 15 *CFLQ* 237.

HUMPHREYS, C and THAIRA, R (2002) *Routes to Safety: Protection Issues Facing Abused Women and Children and the Role of Outreach Services* (Bristol, WAFE).

—— and —— (2003) 'Neither Justice nor Protection: Women's Experiences of Post-separation Violence' 25 *JSW&FL* 195.

HUMPHRIES, M (2001) 'Occupation Orders Revisited' *Fam Law* 542.

HUNT, A (1985) 'The Ideology of Law: Advances and Problems in Recent Applications of the Concept of Ideology to the Analysis of Law' 10 *Law and Society Review* 11.

HUNT, J (2003) *Researching Contact* (London, One Parent Families).

INDUSTRIAL RELATIONS SERVICES (1995) 596 *Employment Trends*, (London, Industrial Relations Services).

INGLEBY REPORT (1960) *Report of the Committee on Children and Young Persons* (London, HMSO) Cmd 1191.

INGLEBY, R (1992) *Solicitors and Divorce* (Oxford, OUP).

INGMAN, T (1996) 'Contact and the Obdurate Parent' *Fam Law* 615.

INTERDEPARTMENTAL COMMITTEE ON CONCILIATION (1983) *Report* (London, HMSO, 1983).

ITZIN, C (2000) 'Gendering Domestic Violence: The Influence of Feminism on Policy and Practice' in J Hanmer, *et al* (eds), *Home Truths About Domestic Violence: Feminist Influences on Policy and Practice: A Reader* (London, Routledge).

JACKSON, E, *et al* (1993) 'Financial Support on Divorce: The Right Mixture of Rules and Discretion?' 7 *Int J of Law and the Family* 230.

—— (2001) *Regulating Reproduction: Law, Technology and Autonomy* (Oxford, Hart Publishing).

—— (2002) 'Conception and the Irrelevance of the Welfare Principle' 65 *Modern Law Review* 176.

—— (2006) 'What is a Parent?' in A Diduck and K O'Donovan (eds), *Feminist Perspectives on Family Law* (London, Cavendish).

JAMES, A (1992) 'An Open or Shut Case? Law as an Autopoetic System' 19 *J of Law and Society* 271.

—— (1999) 'Parents: A Children's Perspective' in A Bainham, S Day Sclater and M Richards (eds), *What is a Parent?* (Oxford, Hart Publishing).

JAMES, AL, JAMES A and MCNAMEE, S (2003) 'Constructing Children's Welfare in Family Proceedings' *Fam Law* 889.

JAMES, S (1994) 'Women's Unwaged Work – the Heart of the Informal Sector' in M Evans (ed), *The Woman Question*, 2nd edn, (London, Sage).

JENKS, C (1996) *Childhood* (London, Routledge).

JOHNSON, L (1997) 'Expanding Eugenics or Improving Health Care in China: Commentary on the Provisions of the Standing Committee of the Gansu People's Congress Concerning the Prohibition of Reproduction by Intellectually Impaired Persons' 24 *Journal of Law and Society* 199.

JOLLY, SC (1994) 'Cutting the Ties – the Termination of Contact in Care' 16 *JSW&FL* 299.

—— and SANDLAND, R (1994) 'Political Correctness and the Adoption White Paper' 24 *Fam Law* 30.

JONES, E and PARKINSON, P (1995) 'Child Sexual Abuse, Access and the Wishes of Children' 9 *Int J of Law and the Family* 54.

JOSEPH ROWNTREE FOUNDATION (1996) 'The Relationship between Family Life and Young People's Lifestyles' *Social Policy Research* 95

JOSHI, H and DAVIES, H (1992) 'Pensions, Divorce and Wives' Double Burden' 6 *Int J of Law and the Family* 289.

KAGANAS, F (1995) 'Partnership under the Children Act 1989—an Overview' in F Kaganas, M King and C Piper (eds), *Legislating for Harmony: Partnership under the Children Act 1989* (London, Jessica Kingsley).

—— (1996) 'Responsible or Feckless Fathers? *Re S (Parental Responsibility)*' 8 *CFLQ* 165.

—— (1999a) 'Contact, Conflict and Risk' in S Day Sclater and C Piper (eds), *Undercurrents of Divorce* (Aldershot, Ashgate).

—— (1999b) '*B v B (Occupation Order)* and *Chalmers v Johns* Occupation Orders Under the Family Law Act 1996' 11 *CFLQ* 193.

—— (2000) '*Re L (Contact: Domestic Violence; Re V (Contact: Domestic Violence); Re M (Contact: Domestic Violence); Re H (Contact: Domestic Violence)*: Contact and Domestic Violence' 12 *CFLQ* 311.

—— (2002) 'Domestic Homicide, Gender and the Expert' in A Bainham, S Day Sclater and M Richards (eds) *Body Lore and Laws* (Oxford, Hart Publishing).

—— (2006) 'Domestic Violence, Men's Groups and the Equivalence Argument' in A Diduck and K O'Donovan (eds), *Feminist Perspectives on Family Law* (London, Cavendish, 2006).

—— and DAY SCLATER, S (2000) 'Contact and Domestic Violence – The Winds of Change?' *Fam Law* 630.

—— and —— (2004) 'Contact Disputes: Narrative Constructions of "Good" Parents' 12 *Feminist Legal Studies* 1.

—— and DIDUCK, A (2004) 'Incomplete Citizens: Changing Images of Post-separation Children' 67(6) *MLR* 959.

—— and MURRAY, CM (1991) 'Law, Women and the Family: The Question of Polygyny in a New South Africa' *Acta Juridica* 116.

—— and PIPER, C (1994) 'Domestic Violence and Divorce Mediation' *JSW&FL*, 265.

—— and —— (1999) 'Divorce and Domestic Violence' in S Day Sclater and C Piper (eds), *Undercurrents of Divorce* (Aldershot, Ashgate).

—— and —— (2001) 'Grandparents and Contact: "Rights v Welfare" Revisited' 15(2) *Int J of Law, Policy and the Family* 250.

—— and —— (2002) 'Shared Parenting – A 70% Solution?' 14(4) *CFLQ* 365.

KAHN FREUND, O (1955) 'Matrimonial Property in England' in W Friedmann (ed), *Matrimonial Property Law* (Toronto, Carswell).

KANDEL, RF (1994) 'Which Came First: The Mother or the Egg? A Kinship Solution to Gestational Surrogacy' 47 *Rutgers Law Review* 165.

KATZ, I (2000) 'Triangles of Adoption The Geometry of Complexity' in A Treacher and I Katz (eds), *The Dynamics of Adoption* (London, Jessica Kingsley).

KAYE, M (1996) 'Domestic Violence, Residence and Contact' 8 *CFLQ* 285.

KEATING, H (1995) 'Children Come First?' 1 *Contemporary Issues in Law* 29.

—— (1996) 'Shifting Standards in the House of Lords: *Re H and Others (Minors) (Sexual Abuse: Standard of Proof)*' 2 *CFLQ* 157.

KEMPE, CH *et al*, (1962) 'The Battered Child Syndrome' 181 *Journal of the American Medical Association* 17.

KEOWN, J (1997) 'Restoring Moral and Intellectual Shape to the Law After *Bland*' 113 *LQR* 481.

—— (2000) 'Beyond *Bland*: A Critique of the BMA Guidance on Withholding and Withdrawing Medical Treatment' 20 *Legal Studies* 66.

KEWLEY, A (1996) 'Pragmatism Before Principle: The Limitations of Civil Law Remedies for the Victims of Domestic Violence' 18 *JSW&FL* 1.

KING, M (1981) 'Welfare and Justice' in M King (ed), *Childhood, Welfare and Justice* (London, Batsford Academic and Educational).

—— (1987) 'Playing the Symbols – Custody and the Law Commission' *Fam Law* 186.

—— (1995a) 'Essay Review; *Child Abuse Errors; When Good Intentions Go Wrong*: by Dennis Howitt (New York: Harvester Wheatsheaf 1992)' 86 *British J of Psychology* 437.

—— (1995b) 'Partnership in Politics and Law: A New Deal for Parents?' in F Kaganas, M King and C Piper (eds), *Legislating for Harmony: Partnership under the Children Act 1989* (London, Jessica Kingsley).

—— (1997) *A Better World for Children* (London, Routledge).

—— (1999) ' "Being Sensible": Images and Practices of the New Family Lawyer' 28 *J of Social Policy* 249.

—— and KAGANAS, F (1998) 'The Risks and Dangers of Experts in Court' *Current Legal Issues* 221.

—— and PIPER, C (1995) *How the Law Thinks about Children*, 2nd edn, (Aldershot, Arena).

KINGDOM, E (1991) *What's Wrong with Rights* (Edinburgh, EUP).

KINSEY, A, *et al* (1953) *Sexual Behavior in the Human Female* (Philadelphia, PA, WB Saunders).

KLEANTHOUS, V (2003) 'SFLA Mediation Annual Conference' *Fam Law* 849.

KLINE, M (1995) 'Complicating the Ideology of Motherhood: Child Welfare Law and First

Nation Women' in M Fineman and I Karpin (eds), *Mothers in Law: Feminist Theory and the Legal Regulation of Motherhood* (New York, NY, Columbia University Press).

KNIGHTS, E (1997) 'Child Support Update' *Fam Law* 120.

KOHLBERG, L (1984) 'The Psychology of Moral Development: The Nature and Validity of Moral Stages' in *Essays on Moral Development*, vol 2 (London, Harper and Row).

KURZ, D (1993) 'Social Science Perspectives on Wife Abuse: Current Debates and Future Directions' in PB Bart and EG Moran (eds), *Violence Against Women: The Bloody Footprints* (London, Sage).

KUHSE, H (1987) *The Sanctity of Life Doctrine in Medicine* (Oxford, Clarendon Press).

LACLAU, E and MOUFFE, C (1985) *Hegemony and Socialist Strategy: Towards a Radical Democratic Politics* (London, Verso).

LAFAUCHEUR, N (2004) 'The French "Tradition" of Anonymous Birth: The Lines of Argument' 18 *Int J of Law, Policy and the Family* 319.

LAMING, Lord (2003) *The Victoria Climbie Report* (London, The Stationery Office).

LANGDON-DOWN, G (2005) 'Family Fortunes' 102(8) *Law Soc Gazette* 20.

LANGDRIDGE, D and BLYTHE, E (2001) 'Regulation of assisted conception services in Europe: implications of the new reproductive technologies for "the family"' 23 *Journal of Social Welfare and Family Law* 45.

LANSDOWN, G (1995) *Taking Part: Children's Participation in Decision Making* (London, IPPR).

LAVERY, R (1996) 'The Child Assessment Order – A Reassessment' 8 *CFLQ* 41.

LAW COMMISSION (1966) No 6, *Reform of the Grounds of Divorce – The Field of Choice* (London, HMSO) Cmd 3123.

—— (1969) No 25, *Financial Provisions in Matrimonial Proceedings* (London, HMSO).

—— (1978) No 86, *Third Report on Family Property: The Matrimonial Home (Co-ownership and Occupancy Rights) and Household Goods* (London, HMSO).

—— (1979) No 74, *Illegitimacy* (London, HMSO).

—— (1980) No 103, *The Financial Consequences of Divorce: the Basic Policy* (London, HMSO).

—— (1981) No 112, *The Financial Consequences of Divorce: the Response to the Discussion Paper* (London, HMSO).

—— (1982) No 118, *Illegitimacy* (London, HMSO).

—— (1985a) No 91, *Guardianship: Working Paper* (London, HMSO).

—— (1985b) *Review of Child Law: Guardianship* (London, HMSO).

—— (1986) No 96, *Family Law: Review of Child Law: Custody* (London, HMSO).

—— (1988a) No 170, *Facing the Future: A Discussion Paper on the Grounds for Divorce* (London, HMSO).

—— (1988b) No172, *Family Law: Review of Child Law: Guardianship and Custody* (London, HMSO).

—— (1988c) No 175, *Family Law: Matrimonial Property* (London, HMSO).

—— (1990) No 192, *Family Law: The Ground for Divorce* (London, HMSO).

—— (1992a) No 207, *Family Law: Domestic Violence and Occupation of the Family Home* (London, HMSO).

—— (1992b) No 205, *Criminal Law: Rape Within Marriage* (London, HMSO).

—— (1995) No 139, *Criminal Law: Consent in the Criminal Law, Consultation Paper* (London, HMSO).

—— (1996) *The Treatment of Pension Rights on Divorce, Consultation Paper* (London, HMSO).

—— (2002) No 278, *Sharing Homes: A Discussion Paper* (London, The Stationery Office) Cmd 3345.

—— (2003) No 173, *Partial Defences to Murder. Consultation Paper* (London, The Law Commission).

LAW COMMISSION OF CANADA (2002) *Beyond Conjugality: Recognizing and supporting close personal adult relationships* (Ottawa, Law Commission of Canada).

LAW SOCIETY, Family Law Sub-Committee (1979) *A Better Way Out: Suggestions for the Reform of the Law of Divorce and Other Forms of Matrimonial Relief; for the Setting Up of a Family Court; and for its Procedure* (London, The Law Society).

——, Family Law Committee (1998) *Maintenance and Capital Provision on Divorce, The Family Law Committee's Submission to the Ancillary Relief Advisory Group*, Appendix 10 to *Report to the Lord Chancellor by the Ancillary Relief Advisory Group* (London, The Law Society).

—— (2002a) *Family Law Protocol* (London, The Law Society)

—— (2002b) *Cohabitation: The Case for Clear Law* (London, The Law Society).

—— (2003) *Financial Provision on Divorce: Clarity and Fairness, Proposals of* Reform (London, The Law Society).

—— (2004) *Family Mediation Panel. Criteria and Guidance Notes* (London, Law Society).

—— (Undated) 'What is the Family Law Protocol?' www.lawsociety.org.uk (accessed 24 December 2004).

LAWSON, A (1996) 'The Things we do for Love: Detrimental Reliance in the Family Home' 16 *Legal Studies* 218.

LAWSON-CRUTTENDEN, T and ADDISON, N (1997) *Blackstone's Guide to the Protection From Harassment Act 1997* (London, Blackstone).

LEGAL AID BOARD (1995) *Family Transaction Criteria*, Issue no 2.

LEGAL SERVICES COMMISSION (2000) *The Funding Code – Criteria*.

—— (2002) *Quality Mark Standard for Mediation* (1) 12/02.

—— (2003a) *The Funding Code: Procedures* R9 April.

—— (2003b) *The Funding Code: Decision Making Guidance* R11 December.

—— (2004) *The Funding Code: Restructured Family Guidance*.

LEMMINGS, D (1996) 'Marriage and the Law in the Eighteenth Century: Hardwicke's Marriage Act 1753' 39 *The Historical Journal* 339.

LEVY, A and KAHAN, B (1991) *The Pindown Experience and the Protection of Children: The Report of the Staffordshire Child Care Inquiry 1990* (London, HMSO).

LEWIS, J. (1980) *The Politics of Motherhood: Child and Maternal Welfare in England 1900–1939* (London, Croom Helm).

—— (1991) 'Models of Equality for Women: The Case of State Support for Children in Twentieth Century Britain' in G Bock and P Thane (eds), *Maternity and Gender and Policies: Women and the Rise of the European Welfare States* (London, Routledge).

—— (1992) 'Women and Late-Nineteenth Century Social Work' in C Smart (ed), *Regulating Womanhood: Historical Essays on Marriage, Motherhood and Sexuality* (London, Routledge).

—— (1996) 'Marriage Saving Revisited' *Fam Law* 423.

—— (1999) *Marriage, Cohabitation and the Law: Individualism and Obligation* (Lord Chancellor's Department Research Series No 1/99) (London, The Stationery Office).

—— (2002) 'Individualisation, assumptions about the existence of an adult worker model and the shift towards contractualism' in A Carling, S Duncan and R Edwards (eds), *Analysing Families: Morality and Rationality in Policy and Practice* (London, Routledge).

—— (2004) 'Adoption: The Nature of Policy Shifts in England and Wales 1972–2002' 18 *Int'l J of Law, Policy and the Family* 235.

LEWIS, J, DATTA, J and SARRE, S (1999) 'Individualism and Commitment in Marriage and Cohabitation' in *Lord Chancellor's Department Research Series No 8/99* (London, Stationery Office).

LIDDLE, AM (1993) 'Gender, Desire and Child Sexual Abuse: Accounting for the Male Majority' 10 *Theory, Culture and Society* 103.

LIM, H (1996) 'Messages from a Rarely Visited Island: Duress and Lack of Consent in Marriage' 4 *Feminist Legal Studies* 195.

LINDLEY, B (1997) 'Open Adoption – Is the Door Ajar?' 9 *CFLQ* 115.

—— and RICHARDS, M (2000) 'Working Together 2000—How will Parents Fare under the New Child Protection Process?' 12 *CFLQ* 213.

——, RICHARDS, M and FREEMAN, P (2001) 'Advice and Advocacy for Parents in Child Protection Cases – What is Happening in Current Practice?' 13 *CFLQ* 167.

LINTON, R. (1949) 'The Natural History of the Family' in R Anshen (ed), *The Family: Its Function and Destiny* (New York, NY, Harper & Bros).

LISTER, R, GOODE, J and CALLENDER, C (1999) 'Income Distribution within Families and the Reform of Social Security' 21(3) *JSW&FL* 203.

LITTLETON, C (1987) 'Reconstructing Sexual Equality' 75 *California Law Review* 1279.

LNTV (2005a) 'Family Law: Collaborative Family Law' Programme 1125, LNTV Times.

—— (2005b) 'Family Law: Collaborative Family Law' Programme 1125, LNTV DVD.

LONDON BOROUGH OF BRENT (1985) *A Child in Trust: Report of the Panel of Inquiry Investigating the Circumstances Surrounding the Death of Jasmine Beckford* (London, London Borough of Brent).

LONDON BOROUGH OF GREENWICH (1987) *A Child in Mind: Protection of Children in a Responsible Society: The Report of the Commission of inquiry into the circumstances surrounding the death of Kimberley Carlile* (London, London Borough of Greenwich and Greenwich Health Authority).

LONDON BOROUGH OF LAMBETH (1987) *Whose Child? The Report of the Panel Appointed to Inquire into the Death of Tyra Henry* (London, London Borough of Lambeth).

LONDON STRATEGIC POLICY UNIT, POLICE MONITORING AND RESEARCH GROUP (1986) *Briefing Paper No1: Police Response to Domestic Violence* (London, London Strategic Policy Unit).

LORD CHANCELLOR'S DEPARTMENT (1993) *Looking to the Future: Mediation and the Ground for Divorce: a Consultation Paper* (London, HMSO) Cmd 2424.

—— (1995a) *Looking to the Future: Mediation and the Ground for Divorce: The Government's Proposals* (London, HMSO) Cmd 2799.

—— (1995b) *Legal Aid: Targeting Need: The Future of Publicly Funded Help in Solving Legal Problems in Disputes in England and Wales; a Consultation Paper* (London, HMSO) Cmd 2854.

—— (1996) 'Introduction', in *Marriage and the Family Law Act 1996: The New Legislation Explained* (London, LCD).

—— (1997) Press Release, 13 June.

—— (1998) *Consultation Paper 1: Court Procedures for the Determination of Paternity, 2: The Law on Parental Responsibility for Unmarried Fathers* (London, HMSO).

—— (1999) *Settling Finances on Divorce: Modernising The Role of the Court* (London, The Stationery Office).

—— (2002) *LCD Guidelines for Good Practice on Parental Contact in Cases where there is Domestic Violence* (LCD).

LOVELAND, I. (1996) 'The Status of Children as Applicants under the Homelessness Legislation – Judicial Subversion of Legislative Intent?' 8 *CFLQ* 89.

LOWE, NV (1997) 'The Meaning and Allocation of Parental Responsibility – A Common Lawyer's Perspective' 11 *Int J of Law, Policy and the Family* 192.

—— (2001) 'Children's Participation in the Family Justice System – Translating Principles into Practice' 12 *CFLQ* 137.

—— and DOUGLAS, G (1998) *Bromley's Family Law*, 9th edn, (London, Butterworths).

—— and JUSS, S (1993) 'Medical Treatment – Pragmatism and the Search for Principle' 56 *MLR* 865.

LUHMANN, N (1993) *Risk: A Sociological Theory*, Barrett R. (tr) (New York, NY, Walter de Gruyter).

LUPTON, C, BARNARD, S and SWALL-YARRINGTON, M (1995) *Family Planning? An Evaluation of the Family Group Conference Model, Report No 31* (Portsmouth, Social Services Research and Information Unit, University of Portsmouth).

LYON, C and PARTON, N (1995) 'Children's Rights and the Children Act 1989' in B Franklin (ed), *The Handbook of Children's Rights: Comparative Policy and Practice* (London, Routledge).

MAAS, R (1997) 'What God has Joined …' *Taxation* 387.

MACCOBY, E and MNOOKIN, R (1992) *Dividing the Child: Social and Legal Dilemmas of Custody* (Cambridge, MA, Harvard University Press).

MACEY, M (1995) ' "Same Race" Adoption Policy: Anti-racism or Racism?' 24 *J of Social Policy* 473.

MACKAY, Lord (1989) 'Perceptions of the Children Bill and Beyond' 139 *NLJ* 505.

MACLEAN, M (1994) 'The Making of the Child Support Act of 1991: Policy Making at the Intersection of Law and Policy' 21 *J of Law and Society* 505.

—— (2004) 'The Family Resolutions Pilot Project' *Fam Law* 687

—— and EEKELAAR, J (1993) 'Child Support: The British Solution' 7 *Int J of Law and the Family* 205.

—— and —— (1997) *The Parental Obligation: A Study of Parenthood Across Households* (Oxford, Hart Publishing).

—— and —— (2004) 'The Obligations and Expectations of Couples Within Families: Three Modes of Interaction' 26 *JSW&FL* 117.

—— and —— (2005) 'Taking the Plunge: Perceptions of Risk Taking Associated with Formal and Informal Partner Relationships' *Social Contexts and Response to Risk Network Working Paper 2005/7* (Canterbury, University of Kent School of Social Policy, Sociology and Social Research).

—— and KURCZEWSKI, J (eds), (1994) *Families, Politics and the Law* (Oxford, OUP).

MACLEOD, M and SARAGA, E (1988) 'Challenging the Orthodoxy: Towards a Feminist Theory and Practice' 28 *Feminist Review* 16.

MAHONEY, M (1991) 'Legal Images of Battered Women: Redefining the Issue of Separation' 90 *Michigan Law Review* 1.

—— (1994) 'Victimization or Oppression? Women's Lives, Violence and Agency' in MA Fineman and R Myktiuk (eds), *The Public Nature of Private Violence: The Discovery of Domestic Abuse* (New York, NY, Routledge).

MAIDMENT, S (1975) 'Access Conditions in Custody Orders' 2 *British J of Law and Society* 182.

—— (1984) *Child Custody and Divorce: The Law in Social Context* (London, Croom Helm).

—— (1998) 'Parental Alienation Syndrome – A Judicial Response?' *Fam Law* 264.

—— (2001) 'Parental Responsibility – Is there a Duty to Consult?' *Fam Law* 518.

MAINE, HS (1917) *Ancient Law* (London, Dent).

MALOS, E and HAGUE, G (1993) *Domestic Violence and Housing: Local Authority Responses to Women and Children Escaping Violence in the Home* (Bristol, Women's Aid Federation England, and School of Applied Social Studies, University of Bristol Press).

MAMA, A (1989) *The Hidden Struggle: Statutory and Voluntary Sector Responses to Violence Against Black Women in the Home* (London, London Race and Housing Research Unit).

MAMASHELA, M (2003) *The Practical Implications and Effects of The Recognition of Customary Marriages Act No 120 of 1998 School of Development Studies University of Natal – Durban Research Report No 59* (Pietermaritzburg, Law School University of Natal).

MANNING, N (1985a) 'Constructing Social Problems' in N Manning (ed), *Social Problems and Welfare Ideology* (Aldershot, Gower).

—— (1985b) 'Reconstructing Social Problems: Policy Failure, Ideology and Social Knowledge' in N Manning (ed), Social Problems and Welfare Ideology (Aldershot, Gower).

MARCHANT, R and KIRBY, P (2004) 'The Participation of Young Children: Communication, Consultation and Involvement' in B Neale (ed), *Young Children's Citizenship* (York, Joseph Rowntree Foundation).

MARSHALL, A (2003) 'Comedy of Adoption – When is a Parent not a Parent?' *Fam Law* 840.

MARSHALL, S (1994) 'Whose Child is it Anyway?' in D Morgan and G Douglas (eds), *Constituting Families* (Stuttgart, Franz Steiner Verlag).

MARTIN, A. (1996) 'Pensions and Divorce' *Fam Law* 432.

MASON, JK and McCALL-SMITH, A (1994) *Law and Medical Ethics* 4th edn, (London, Butterworths).

——, —— and LAURIE, G (2002) *Law and Medical Ethics* 5th edn, (London, Butterworths, 2002).

MASSON, J (1989) 'Old Families into New: A Status for Step-parents' in MDA Freeman (ed), *State, Law and Family* (London, Tavistock).

—— (1995) 'Partnership with Parents: Doing Something Together Under the Children Act 1989' in F Kaganas, M King and C Piper (eds), *Legislating for Harmony: Partnership under the Children Act 1989* (London, Jessica Kingsley).

—— (1996a) 'Right to Divorce and Pension Rights' in M Freeman (ed), *Divorce: Where Next?* (Aldershot, Dartmouth).

—— (1996b) 'Representations of Children' *CLP* 245.

—— (2000) 'Representation of Children in England: Protecting Children in Child Protection Proceedings' 34 *Fam LQ* 467.

—— (2002) 'Police Protection – Protecting Whom?' 24 *JSW&FL* 157.

—— (2003) 'The Impact of the Adoption and Children Act 2002: Part 1—Parental Responsibility' *Fam Law* 580.

—— and MORRIS, M (1992) *Children Act Manual* (London, Sweet & Maxwell).

——, WINN OAKLEY, M and PICK, K (2004) *Emergency Protection Orders: Court Orders for Child Protection Crises* (Coventry, Warwick University).

MAXWELL, CD, GARNER, JH and FAGAN, JA (2002) 'The Preventive Effects of Arrest on Intimate Partner Violence: Research, Policy and Theory' 1 *Criminology & Public Policy* 51.

MAY, V and SMART, C (2004) 'Silence in Court?—Hearing Children in Residence and Contact Disputes' *Fam Law* 305.

MAYHEW, P, MAUNG, MA and MIRRLEES-BLACK, C (1993) *The 1992 British Crime Survey* (London, HMSO).

MAYHEW, P and PERCY, A (1996) *The 1996 British Crime Survey: England and Wales* (London, HMSO).

MCCULLOCH, J (2004) 'Protection Before Punishment' *Fam Law* 64.

MCGEE, C (2000) *Childhood Experiences of Domestic Violence* (London, Jessica Kingsley).

MCGLYNN, C (1996) 'Pregnancy Dismissal and the *Webb* Litigation' 2 *Feminist Legal Studies* 220.

MCGREGOR, OR (1957) *Divorce in England* (London, Heinemann).

MCLEAN, S (ed), (1989) *Legal Issues in Human Reproduction* (Aldershot, Dartmouth).

MCLELLAN, D (1996) 'Contract Marriage – The Way Forward or Dead End?' 23 *J of Law and Society* 234.

MCCOLGAN, A (1993) 'In Defence of Battered Women who Kill' 13 *OJLS* 508.

MEREDITH, P (2001) 'Children's Rights and Education' in J Fionda (ed), *Legal Concepts of Childhood* (Oxford, Hart Publishing).

METROPOLITAN POLICE (2004) 'The Met's Response to Domestic Violence' (press release, 19 February).

MICHALOWSKI, S (1997) 'Is it in the Best Interests of a Child to Have a Life-saving Liver Transplantation? *Re T (Wardship: Medical Treatment)*' 9 *CFLQ* 179.

MILES, J (2003) 'Property Law v Family Law: Resolving the Problems of Family Property' 23 *Legal Studies* 624.

MILL, JS (1975) 'The Subjection of Women' in JS Mill, *Three Essays* (London, OUP).

MILLAR, J and WARMAN, A (1996) *Family Obligations in Europe* (London, Family Policy Studies Centre).

—— (1996) 'Mothers, Workers, Wives: Comparing Policy Approaches to Supporting Lone Mothers' in EB Silva (ed), *Good Enough Mothering?* (London, Routledge).

MIRRLEES-BLACK, C (1999) *Domestic Violence: Findings from a New British Crime Survey Self-completion Questionnaire: Home Office Research Study 191* (London, Home Office).

MITCHELL, J, District Judge (2004) 'Contact in Practice' *Fam Law* 662.

MNOOKIN, RH (1975) 'Child Custody Adjudication: Judicial Functions in the Face of Indeterminacy' 39 *Law and Contemporary Problems* 226.

—— (1979) 'Bargaining in the Shadow of the Law: The Case of Divorce' *CLP* 65.

—— (1984) 'Divorce Bargaining: The Limits on Private Ordering' in J Eekelaar and S Katz (eds), *The Resolution of Family Conflict: Comparative Legal Perspectives* (Toronto, Butterworths).

—— and KORNHAUSER, L (1979) 'Bargaining in the Shadow of the Law: The Case of Divorce' 88 *Yale LJ* 950.

MOONEY, J (1994) *The Hidden Figure: Domestic Violence in North London* (London, Islington Council).

—— (2000) 'Revealing the Hidden Figure of Domestic Violence' in J Hanmer, *et al* (eds), *Home Truths About Domestic Violence: Feminist Influences on Policy and Practice: A Reader* (London, Routledge).

MORE, G (1993) ' "Equal treatment" of the Sexes in European Community Law: What does Equal Mean?' 1 *Feminist Legal Studies* 45.

MORGAN, DHJ (1996) *Family Connections* (Cambridge, Polity).

—— (1999) 'Risk and Family Practices: Accounting for Change and Fluidity in Family Life' in EB Silva and C Smart (eds), *The 'New' Family?* (London, Sage).

MORGAN, D (1989) 'Surrogacy: An Introductory Essay' in D Morgan and R Lee (eds), *Birthrights: Law and Ethics at the Beginnings of Life* (London, Routledge).

—— (1990) *Discovering Men* (London, Routledge).

MORGAN, P (1995) *Farewell to the Family? Public Policy and Family Breakdown in Britain and the USA* (London, IEA Health and Welfare Unit).

—— (1996) *Who Needs Parents? The Effects of Childcare and Early Education on Children in Britain and the USA* (London, IEA Health and Welfare Unit).

MORLEY, R (1993) 'Recent Responses to "Domestic Violence" Against Women: A Feminist Critique' 5 *Social Policy Review* 177.

—— and MULLENDER, A (1992) 'Hype or Hope? The Importation of Pro-arrest Policies and Batterer's Programmes from North America to Britain as Key Measures for Preventing Violence against Women in the Home' 6 *Int J of Law and the Family* 265.

MORRIS, A. and NOTT, S. (1995) *All My Worldly Goods: A Feminist Perspective on the Legal Regulation of Wealth* (Aldershot, Dartmouth).

MOSTYN, N (1999) 'The Green Paper on Child Support – Children First: A New Approach to Child Support' *Fam Law* 95.

MOUNT, F (1982) *The Subversive Family: An Alternative History of Love and Marriage* (London, Cape).

MOWAT, C (1961) *The Charity Organization Society 1869–1913: Its Ideas and Work* (London, Methuen & Co).

MULLENDER, A (1994) 'Domestic Violence and Children: What do We Know From Research?' in A Mullender and R Morley (eds), *Children Living with Domestic Violence: Putting Men's Abuse of Women on the Child Care Agenda* (London, Whiting & Birch).

—— (2000) *'Reducing Domestic Violence … What Works? Meeting the Needs of Children' Policing and Reducing Crime Briefing Note* (London, Home Office).

—— and BURTON, S (2000) *'Reducing Domestic Violence … What Works? Perpetrator Programmes' Policing and Reducing Crime Briefing Note* (London, Home Office).

——, HAGUE, G, IMAM, U, KELLY, L, MALOS, E and REGAN, L (2002) *Children's Perspectives on Domestic Violence* (London, Sage).

—— and MORLEY, R (eds), (1994) *Children Living with Domestic Violence: Putting Men's Abuse of Women on the Child Care Agenda* (London, Whiting & Birch).

—— and PASCALL, G (1996) 'Women and Homelessness: Proposals from the Department of the Environment' 18 *JSW&FL* 327.

MUNBY, J (The Hon Mr Justice) (2004) 'The Family Justice System' *Fam Law* 574.

MUNRO, V (2001) 'Square pegs in Round Holes; the Dilemma of Conjoined Twins and Individual Rights' 10 *Social and Legal Studies* 459.

MURPHY, J (1996) 'Domestic Violence: The New Law' 59 *MLR* 845.

—— (2000) 'Child Welfare in Transracial Adoptions: Colour-Blind Children and Colour-Blind Law' in J Murphy (ed), *Ethnic Minorities their Families and the Law* (Oxford, Hart Publishing).

—— (2004) 'Same-sex Marriage in England: A Role for Human Rights?' 16 *CFLQ* 245.

MURRAY, C (2004) 'Same-Sex Families: Outcomes for Children and Parents' *Fam Law* 136.

NASH, M (1991) 'Pronatalism and Motherhood in Franco's Spain' in G Bock and P Thane (eds),

*Maternity and Gender and Policies: Women and the Rise of the European Welfare States* (London, Routledge).

NATIONAL CHILDREN'S BUREAU (1994) *Statistics: Under Fives and Pre-school Services in England and Wales 1994* (London).

NATIONAL COMMISSION OF INQUIRY INTO THE PREVENTION OF CHILD ABUSE (1996) *Childhood Matters: Volume 1: The Report* (London, The Stationery Office)

NATIONAL FAMILY CONCILIATION COUNCIL (1986), *Code of Practice for Family Conciliation Services.*

NATIONAL STEPFAMILY ASSOCIATION (1996), 1 *Stepfamily Matters* Spring/Summer.

NEALE, B. (2004) 'Executive Summary' in B Neale (ed) *Young Children's Citizenship* (York, Joseph Rowntree Foundation, 2004).

—— and SMART, C (1997) ' "Good" and "Bad" Lawyers? Struggling in the Shadow of the New Law' 19 *JSW&FL* 377.

—— and —— (2002) 'Caring, Earning and Changing: Parenthood and Employment after Divorce' in A Carling, S Duncan and R Edwards (eds), *Analysing Families: Morality and Rationality in Policy and Practice* (London, Routledge).

——, FLOWERDEW, J and SMART, C (2003) 'Drifting Towards Shared Residence?' *Fam Law* 904.

NEIL, E (2003) 'Adoption and Contact: A Research Review' in A Bainham, *et al* (eds), *Children and their Families: Contact, Rights and Welfare* (Oxford, Hart Publishing).

NELKEN, D (1998) 'Afterword: Choosing Rights for Children' in G Douglas and L Sebba (eds), *Children's Rights and Traditional Values* (Aldershot, Ashgate).

NEWCASTLE CONCILIATION PROJECT UNIT REPORT (1989) *Report to the Lord Chancellor on the Costs and Effectiveness of Conciliation in England and Wales* (London, Lord Chancellor's Department).

NEWSLINE (2003) 'President's Address' *Fam Law* 294.

NORRIE, A (1993) *Crime, Reason and History* (London, Butterworths).

O'BRIEN, M and SHEMILT, I (2003) *Working Fathers: Earning and Caring* (London, Equal Opportunities Commission).

O'DONNELL, C and CRANEY, J (1982) 'The Social Construction of Child Abuse' in C O'Donnell and J Craney (eds), *Family Violence in Australia* (Cheshire, Longman).

O'DONNELL, K (2004) 'Case Commentary – Re C (Welfare of Child: Immunisation)—Room To Refuse? Immunisation, Welfare and The Role Of Parental Decision Making' 16 *CFLQ* 213.

O'DONOVAN, K (1984) 'Wife Sale and Desertion as Alternatives to Judicial Marriage Dissolution' in J Eekelaar and S Katz (eds), *The Resolution of Family Conflict* (Toronto, Butterworths, 1984).

—— (1985) *Sexual Divisions in Law* (London, Weidenfeld & Nicolson).

—— (1993a) 'Law's Knowledge: The Judge, The Expert, The Battered Woman, and the Syndrome' 20 *JLS* 427.

—— (1993b) *Family Law Matters* (London, Pluto).

—— (2000) 'Constructions of Maternity and Motherhood in Stories of Lost Children' in J Bridgeman and D Monk (eds), *Feminist Perspectives on Child Law* (London, Cavendish).

O'NEILL, O (1979) 'Begetting, Bearing and Rearing' in O O'Neill and W Ruddick (eds), *Having Children* (New York, NY, OUP).

OAKLEY, A (1985) *The Sociology of Housework* (Oxford, Blackwell).

OFFICE FOR NATIONAL STATISTICS (2004) *Population Trends 117* (London, the Office for National Statistics).

—— (2005a) *Population Trends, Spring 2005* (London, Office for National Statistics).

—— (2005b) Annual Online edition, *General Household Survey.*

OFFICE OF THE DEPUTY PRIME MINISTER (2002) *Revision of the Code of Guidance on the Allocation of Accommodation* (London, ODPM)

OKIN, SM (1989) *Justice, Gender and the Family* (New York, NY, Basic Books).

OLSEN, F (1983) 'The Family and the Market: A Study of Ideology and Legal Reform' 96 *Harvard Law Review* 1497.

—— (1992) 'Children's Rights: Some Feminist Approaches to the United Nations Convention on the Rights of the Child' in P Alston, S Parker and J Seymour (eds), *Children, Rights and the Law* (Oxford, Clarendon Press).

PAGELOW, M (1990) 'Effects of Domestic Violence on Children and their Consequences for Custody and Visitation Agreements' 7(4) *Mediation Quarterly* 347.

PAHL, J (1985a) 'Introduction' in J Pahl (ed), *Private Violence and Public Policy: The Needs of Battered Women and the Response of the Public Services* (London, Routledge and Kegan Paul).

—— (1985b) 'Marital Violence and Marital Problems' in J Pahl (ed), *Private Violence and Public Policy: The Needs of Battered Women and the Response of the Public Services* (London, Routledge and Kegan Paul).

—— (1985c) 'Violence Against Women' in N Manning (ed), *Social Problems and Welfare Ideology* (Aldershot, Gower).

—— (1989) *Money and Marriage* (Basingstoke, MacMillan).

PARADINE, K and WILKINSON, J (2004) *Research and Literature Review: Protection and Accountability: The Reporting, Investigation and Prosecution of Domestic Violence Cases* (London, Her Majesty's Crown Prosecution Service Inspectorate (HMCPSI), (Her Majesty's Inspectorate of Constabulary (HMIC), Centrex).

PARENTLINE PLUS (2005) *Stepfamilies: New relationships new challenges* (London, Parentline Plus).

PARKER, S (1987) 'The Marriage Act 1753: A Case Study in Family Law-making' 1 *Int J of Law and the Family* 133.

—— (1990) *Informal Marriage, Cohabitation and the Law 1750–1989* (Basingstoke, MacMillan).

—— (1991) 'Child Support in Australia: Children's Rights or Public Interest' 5 *Int J of Law and the Family* 24.

PARKINSON, L 'Conciliation: Pros and Cons (I)' (1983) 13 *Fam Law* 22.

—— (1985) 'Conciliation in Separation and Divorce' in W Dryden (ed), *Marital Therapy in Britain*, vol II (London, Harper & Row).

PARKINSON, P and HUMPHREYS, C (1998) 'Children who Witness Domestic Violence – The Implications for Child Protection' 10 *CFLQ* 147.

PARRY, ML (1993) *The Law Relating to Cohabitation* 3rd edn, (London, Sweet & Maxwell).

PARSONS, T (1949) 'The Social Structure of the Family' in R Anshen (ed), *The Family: Its Function and Destiny* (New York, NY, Harper).

—— (1992) 'The Contemporary Politics of Child Protection' *JSW&FL* 100.

PARTON, N (1985) *The Politics of Child Abuse* (Basingstoke, Macmillan Education).

—— (1991) *Governing the Family: Child Care, Child Protection and the State* (Basingstoke, Macmillan Education).

PASCALL, G (1997) *Social Policy: A New Feminist Analysis* (London, Routledge).

—— and MORLEY, R. (1996) 'Women and Homelessness: Proposals from the Department of the Environment' 18 *JSW&FL*, 189.

——, LEE, S, MORLEY, R and PARKER, S (2001) 'Changing Housing Policy: Women Escaping Domestic Violence' 23 *JSW&FL* 293.

PATEL, P (2000) 'Southall Black Sisters: Domestic Violence Campaigns and Alliances Across the Divisions of Race, Gender and Class' in J Hanmer, *et al* (eds), *Home Truths About Domestic Violence: Feminist Influences on Policy and Practice: A Reader* (London, Routledge).

PATEMAN, C (1988) *The Sexual Contract* (Cambridge, Polity).

PAYNE, J (1976) 'Family Property Reform as Perceived by the Law Reform Commission of Canada' 9 *Chitty's Law Journal* 289.

PEACOCK, G (1998) 'Domestic Abuse Research' *Fam Law* 628.

PEARCE, J, DAVIS G and BARRON, J (1999) 'Love in a Cold Climate – Section 8 Applications under the Children Act 1989' *Fam Law* 22.

PEARL, D (1991) 'Thou Shalt Not Kill ... But Need'st not Strive Officiously to Keep Alive' 3 *Journal of Child Law* 51.

PERFORMANCE AND INNOVATION UNIT (2000) *Prime Minister's Review of Adoption* (London, Cabinet Office).

PETCHESKY, R (1987) 'Foetal Images: The Power of Visual Culture in the Politics of Reproduction' in M Stanworth (ed), *Reproductive Technologies: Gender, Motherhood and Medicine* (Cambridge, Polity).

PHILIPPS, L (2002) 'Tax Law and Social Reproduction: The Gender of Fiscal Policy in an Age of Privatization' in J Fudge and B Cossman (eds), *Privatization, Law and the Challenge to Feminism* (Toronto, University of Toronto Press).

PHOENIX, A (1996) 'Social Constructions of Lone Motherhood: A Case of Competing Discourses' in EB Silva (ed), *Good Enough Mothering? Feminist Perspectives on Lone Motherhood* (London, Routledge).

PIAGET, J, COOK, M (trans) (1952) *The Origins of Intelligence in Children* (New York, NY, International Universities Press).

PICKETT, E (1991) 'Familial Ideology, Family Law and Mediation: Law Casts More than a "Shadow"' 3 *Journal of Human Justice* 27.

PICKFORD, R (1999) 'Unmarried Fathers and the Law' in A Bainham, S Day Sclater and M Richards (eds), *What is a Parent? A Socio-Legal Analysis* (Oxford, Hart Publishing).

PINCHBECK, I and HEWITT, M (1973) *Children in English Society*, vol II (London, Routledge and Kegan Paul).

PIPER, C (1988) 'Divorce Conciliation in the UK: How Responsible are Parents?' 16 *Int J of the Sociology of Law* 477.

—— (1993) *The Responsible Parent: A Study in Divorce Mediation* (Hemel Hempstead, Harvester Wheatsheaf).

—— (1994) ' "Looking to the Future" for Children' 6 *Journal of Child Law* 98.

—— (1995) 'Court of Appeal: *In Re O (A Minor) (Contact: Imposition of Conditions)'*, *The Times*, 17 March 1995; 17 *JSW&FL* 355.

—— (1996a) 'Norms and Negotiation in Mediation and Divorce' in MDA Freeman (ed), *Divorce: Where Next?* (Aldershot, Dartmouth).

—— (1996b) 'Divorce Reform and the Image of the Child' 33 *J of Law and Society* 364.

—— (1997) 'Ascertaining the Wishes and Feelings of the Child' *Fam Law* 796.

—— (1999a) 'Moral Campaigns for Children's Welfare in the 19th Century' in M King (ed), *Moral Agendas for Children's Welfare* (London, Routledge).

—— (1999b) 'The Wishes and Feelings of the Child' in S Day Sclater and C Piper (eds), *Undercurrents of Divorce* (Aldershot, Ashgate).

—— (1999c) 'Barriers to Seeing and Hearing Children in Private Law Proceedings' *Fam Law* 394.

—— (1999d) 'How Do You Define a Family Lawyer?' 19 *Legal Studies* 93.

—— (2000) 'Historical Constructions of Childhood Innocence: Removing Sexuality' in E Heinze (ed), *Of Innocence and Autonomy: Children, Sex and Human Rights* (Aldershot, Ashgate).

—— (2006) 'Feminist Perspectives on Youth Justice' in A Diduck and K O'Donovan (eds), *Feminist Perspectives on Family Law* (London, Cavendish)

—— and KAGANAS, F (1997) 'Family Law Act 1996, Section 1(d) – How Will "They" Know if there is a Risk of Violence?' 3 *CFLQ* 179.

PIRRIE, J (2002a) 'Child Support Update, Part I' *Fam Law* 195.

—— (2002b) 'The CSA Process' *Fam Law* 290.

—— (2002c) 'Time for the Courts to Stand up to the Child Support Act? – An Address to District Judges' *Fam Law* 114.

PITT, G (1997) *Employment Law*, 2nd edn, (London, Sweet & Maxwell).

PIZZEY, E (1974) *Scream Quietly or the Neighbors Will Hear* (Harmondsworth, Penguin).

—— and SHAPIRO, J (1982) *Prone to Violence* (Hamlyn Paperbacks).

PLANT, R. (2003) 'Citizenship and Social Security' 24(2) *Fiscal Studies* 153

PLATT, J (HH Judge John) (2002) 'Human Rights and Part IV of the Family Law Act 1996' *Fam Law* 905.

POLK, K (1994) *When Men Kill: Scenarios of Masculine Violence* (Cambridge, CUP).

POND, C and SEARLE, A (1991) *The Hidden Army: Children at Work in the 1990s* (London, Low Pay Unit).

PRICE, D (2001) 'Fairly Bland: An Alternative View of a Supposed "Death Ethic" and the BMA Guidelines' 21 *Legal Studies* 618.

PRIEST, J (1993) *Families Outside Marriage*, 2nd edn, (Bristol, Family Law, Jordan).

—— (1997) 'Capital Settlements and the CSA – Part I' *Fam Law* 115.

PRIEST, J and WHYBROW, JC (1986) *Custody Law in Practice in the Divorce and Domestic Courts*, Supplement to Law Commission WP No 96 *Family Law Review of Child Law: Custody* (London, HMSO).

PRIOR, G and FIELD, J (1996) *Department of Social Security Research Report No 50 Pensions and Divorce* (London, HMSO).

PROBERT, R (2002) 'When are we Married? Void, Non-existent and Presumed Marriages' 22 *Legal Studies* 398.

—— (2004) 'Families, Assisted Reproduction and the Law' 16 *CFLQ* 273

PROUT, A (2005) *The Future of Childhood* (London, Routledge Falmer).

—— and JAMES, A (2003) 'A New Paradigm for the Sociology of Childhood? Provenance, Promise and Problems' in A James and A Prout (eds), *Constructing and Reconstructing Childhood* (London, Routledge).

PROVAN, B *et al* (1996) *The Requirement to Co-operate: A Report on the Operation of the "Good Cause" Provisions*, In-house report 14 (London, Department of Social Security Research Branch).

PRYOR, J and RODGERS, B (2001) *Children in Changing Families: Life after Parental Separation* (Oxford, Blackwell).

PTACEK, J (1988) 'Why Do Men Batter Their Wives?' in K Yllo and M Bograd (eds), *Feminist Perspectives on Wife Abuse* (London, Sage).

PURVIS, T and HUNT, A (1993) 'Discourse, Ideology, Discourse, Ideology, Discourse, Ideology...' 44 *British Journal of Sociology* 473.

RADFORD, J (1992) 'Retrospect on a Trial' in J Radford and DEH Russell (eds), *Femicide: The Politics of Woman Killing* (Buckingham, Open University Press).

RADFORD, L, SAYER, S and AMICA, (1999) *Unreasonable Fears? Child Contact in the Context of Domestic Violence: A Survey of Mothers' Perspectives of Harm* (Bristol, WAFE).

RAGONE, H (2003) 'The Gift of Life: Surrogate Motherhood, Gamete Donation and Constructions of Altruism' in R Cook, S Day Sclater and F Kaganas (eds), *Surrogate Motherhood: International Perspectives* (Oxford, Hart Publishing).

RANDALL, V (1996) 'Feminism and Child Daycare' 25 *J of Social Policy* 485.

READ, J and CLEMENTS (2004) 'Demonstrably Awful: The Right to Life and the Selective Non-treatment of Disabled Babies and Young Children' 31 *J of Law and Society* 482.

REECE, H (1996a) 'The Paramountcy Principle: Consensus or Construct?' 49 *Current Legal Problems* 267.

—— (1996b) 'Subverting the Stigmatization Argument' 23 *J of Law and Society* 484.

—— (2003) *Divorcing Responsibly* (Oxford, Hart Publishing).

REEVES, J (1993) 'The Deviant Mother and Child: The Development of Adoption as an Instrument of Social Control' 20 *J of Law and Society* 412.

REGAN, MC (1999) *Alone Together: Law and the Meanings of Marriage* (Oxford, OUP).

RESOLUTION (undated) *Code of Practice for Resolution Members*

REYNOLDS, J and MANSFIELD, P (1999) 'The Effect of Changing Attitudes To Marriage on Its Stability' *Lord Chancellor's Department Research Series* 2/99 vol 1, (London, The Stationery Office).

RHOADES, H (2002) 'The "No-Contact Mother": Reconstructions of Motherhood in the Era of the "New Father"' 12 *Int J of Law Policy and the Family* 71.

RHODEN, NK (1988) 'Litigating Life and Death' 102 *Harv LR* 375.

RICHARDS, L (2004) *Getting Away with It': A Strategic Overview of Domestic Violence Sexual Assault and 'Serious' Incident Analysis* (London, Metropolitan Police Service).

RICHARDS, M (1982) 'Post-divorce Arrangements for Children: A Psychological Perspective' *JSWL* 133.

—— (1987) 'Children, Parents and Families: Developmental Psychology and the Re-ordering of Relationships at Divorce' 1 *Int J of Law and the Family* 295.

—— (1996) 'Divorce Numbers and Divorce Legislation' *Fam Law* 151.

—— (1994) 'Divorcing Children: Roles for Parents and the State' in M Maclean and J Kurczewski (eds), *Families, Politics and the Law: Perspectives for East and West Europe* (Oxford, Clarendon Press).

—— (1995) 'Private Worlds and Public Interests – The Role of the State in Divorce' in A Bainham, D Pearl and R Pickford (eds), *Frontiers of Family Law* (Chichester, John Wiley and Sons).

RIGHTS OF WOMEN (1996), *Summer Bulletin*.

RINGIN, S and HALPIN, B (1997) 'Children, Standard of Living and Distributions in the Family' 26 *J of Social Policy* 21.

ROBERTS, D (1993) 'Racism and Patriarchy in the Meaning of Motherhood' 1 *J of Gender and the Law* 1.

ROBERTS, M (1995) 'Ousting Abusers – Children Act 1989 or Inherent Jurisdiction? *Re H (Prohibited Steps Order)*' 7 *CFLQ* 243.

—— (1996) 'Family Mediation and the Interests of Women – Facts and Fears' *Fam Law 239.*

—— (1997) *Mediation in Family Disputes: Principles of Practice*, 2nd edn, (Aldershot, Arena).

ROBERTS, S (1983) 'Mediation in Family Disputes' 46 *MLR* 537.

—— (1993) 'Alternative Dispute Resolution and Civil Justice: An Unresolved Relationship' 56 *MLR* 452.

ROCHE, J (1991) 'The Children Act 1989: Once a Parent Always a Parent?' *JSW&FL* 345.

—— (1995) 'Children's Rights: In the Name of the Child' 17 *JSW&FL* 281.

—— (1999) 'Children and Divorce: A Private Affair?' in S Day Sclater and C Piper (eds), *Undercurrents of Divorce* (Aldershot, Ashgate).

RODGER, J (1995) 'Family Policy or Moral Regulation' 15 (1) *Critical Social Policy* 5.

ROSE, N (1987) 'Beyond the Public/Private Division: Law, Power and the Family' 14 *J of Law and Society* 61.

ROSENEIL, S (2004) 'Why we should care about friends: An Argument for Queering the Care Imaginary in Social Policy' 3(4) *Social Policy and Society* 409.

—— and BUDGEON, S (2004) 'Cultures of Intimacy and Care Beyond "the Family": Personal Life and Social Change in the Early 21st Century' 52 *Current Sociology* 135.

ROTHMAN, BK (1989) *Recreating Motherhood: Ideology and Technology in a Patriarchal Society* (New York, NY, WW Norton).

ROWE, J (1966) *Parents, Children and Adoption* (London, Routledge and Kegan Paul).

—— and LAMBERT, L (1973) *Children Who Wait: A Study of Children Needing Substitute Families* (London, Association of British Adoption Agencies).

ROYAL COMMISSION ON DIVORCE AND MATRIMONIAL CAUSES (1853) *Report*, Parliamentary Papers 1852–53, vols 40–2.

—— (1912) *Report*, Parliamentary Papers 1912–13, vols 18–20.

—— (1992) No 135, *Report on Family Law* (Edinburgh, HMSO).

ROYAL COMMISSION ON MARRIAGE AND DIVORCE (1956) *Report*, Parliamentary Paper 1951-56 (London, HMSO) Cmd 9678.

RUDDICK, S (1997) 'The Idea of Fatherhood' in HL Nelson (ed), *Feminism and Families* (London, Routledge).

RUMNEY, P (2003) 'Progress at a Price: The Construction of Non-stranger Rape in the Millberry Sentencing Guidelines' 66 *MLR* 870.

RUSSELL, DEH (1990) *Rape in Marriage* (Bloomington and Indianapolis, IN, Indiana University Press).

SACHDEVA, S (1993) *The Primary Purpose Rule in British Immigration Law* (Stoke-on Trent, Trentham Books).

SALFORD, H (2002) 'Concepts of Family under EU Law – Lessons from the ECHR' 16 *Int J of Law, Policy and the Family* 410.

SALTER, D (1996) 'Pensions and Divorce – Where Now?' *Fam Law* 574.

SANDERS, A. (1997) 'First Principles Revisited' 7 *Family Mediation* 8.

SANDLAND, R (2003) 'Crossing and Not Crossing: Gender, Sexuality and Melancholy in the European Court of Human Rights' 11 *Feminist Legal Studies* 191.

SARAT, A and FELSTINER, WLF (1995) *Divorce Lawyers and their Clients* (Oxford, OUP).

SAUNDERS, H (2001) *Making Contact Worse?* (Bristol, WAFE).

—— with BARRON, J (2003) *Failure to Protect? Domestic Violence and the Experiences of Abused Women and Children in the Family Courts* (Bristol, WAFE).

SAWYER, C (1995) 'The Competence of Children to Participate in Family Proceedings' 7 *CFLQ* 180.

—— (1999) 'Conflicting Rights for Children? Implementing Welfare, Autonomy and Justice Within Family Proceedings' 21 *JSW&FL* 99.

—— (2000) 'An Inside Story: Ascertaining the Child's Wishes and Feelings' *Fam Law* 170.

—— (2004) 'Equity's Children – Constructive Trusts for the New Generation' 16 *CFLQ* 31.

SCHECHTER, M and ROBERGE, L (1976) 'Sexual Exploitation' in R Helfer and C Kempe (eds), *Child Abuse and Neglect: The Family and the Community* (Cambridge, MA, Ballinger).

SCHNEIDER, EM (1994) 'The Violence of Privacy' in MA Fineman and R Myktiuk (eds), *The Public Nature of Private Violence: The Discovery of Domestic Abuse* (London, Routledge).

SCHUURMAN, M (2003) 'Children's Rights in the Constitution for Europe' *Childright* 10.

SCOTTISH LAW COMMISSION (1981) Report no 67, *Aliment and Financial Provision* (Edinburgh, HMSO).

SCT (1996) 'Test case: gay men appeal against refusal to let them adopt', 10 May.

SCULLY, A (2003) '*Parra v Parra*: Big money cases, judicial discretion and equality of division' 15 *CFLQ* 205.

SCUTT, JA (1976) 'Reforming the Law of Rape: The Michigan Example' 50 *The Australian LJ* 615.

SECRETARY OF STATE FOR HEALTH (2000) *Adoption: A New Approach – A White Paper* (London, The Stationery Office) Cmd 5017.

SECRETARY OF STATE FOR SOCIAL SERVICES (1974) *Report of the Committee of Inquiry into the Care and Supervision Provided in Relation to Maria Colwell* (London, HMSO).

SEV'ER, A (1997) 'Recent or Imminent Separation and Intimate Violence Against Women: A Conceptual Overview and Some Canadian Examples' 3 *Violence Against Women* 566.

SEVENHUIJSEN, S (1998) *Citizenship and the Ethics of Care* (London, Routledge).

—— (2002) 'A Third Way? Moralities, Ethics and Families' in A Carling, S Duncan and R Edwards (eds), *Analysing Families: Morality and Rationality in Policy and Practice* (London, Routledge).

SHARP, D (2001) 'Parental Responsibility – Where Next?' *Fam Law* 606.

SHAW, C (2004) 'Interim 2003-based national population projections for the United Kingdom and constituent countries' *Population Trends* (London: Office for National Statistics) 118.

SHELDON, S (1993) 'Who is the Mother to Make the Judgment? The Construction of Woman in English Abortion Law' (1993) 1 *Feminist Legal Studies* 3.

—— (1996) 'Subject Only to the Attitude of the Surgeon Concerned: The Judicial Protection of Medical Discretion' 5 *Social and Legal Studies* 95.

—— (1997) *Beyond Control: Medical Power and Abortion Law* (London, Pluto).

—— (1999) '*Re*Conceiving Masculinity: Imagining Men's Reproductive Bodies in Law' 26 *J of Law and Society* 129.

—— (2001) 'Unmarried Fathers and Parental Responsibility: A Case for Reform?' 9 *FLS* 93.

—— (2004) 'Gender Equality and Reproductive Decision-Making' 12 *Feminist Legal Studies* 303.

SHERMAN, LW and BERK, RA (1984) 'The Specific Deterrent Effects of Arrest for Domestic Assault' 49 *American Sociological Review* 261.

SHULTZ, M (1982) 'Contractual Ordering of Marriage: A New Model for State Policy' 70 *California Law Review* 227.

SILVA, EB (ed), (1996) *Good Enough Mothering? Feminist Perspectives on Lone Motherhood* (London, Routledge).

SIMEY, M (1951) *Charitable Effort in Liverpool in the Nineteenth Century* (Liverpool, University Press).

SIMON, Sir J (1996) *With All my Worldly Goods*, Holdsworth Club, Presidential Address, University of Birmingham in B Hoggett, *et al, The Family, Law and Society: Cases and Materials*, 4th edn, (London, Butterworths).

SIMMONS, J *et al*, (2002) *Crime in England and Wales 2001/2. Home Office Statistical Bulletin*.

SIMPSON, B, JESSOP, J and MCCARTHY, P (2003) 'Fathers after Divorce' in A Bainham, *et al* (eds), *Children and Their Families: Contact, Rights and Welfare* (Oxford, Hart Publishing).

SIMPSON, B, MCCARTHY, P and WALKER, J (1995) *Being There: Fathers after Divorce* (Newcastle upon Tyne, University of Newcastle upon Tyne, Relate Centre for Family Studies).

SINCLAIR, R and BULLOCK, R (2002) *Learning from Past Experience – A Review of Serious Case Reviews* (London, DoH).

SINGER, L (1996) 'FDR and the Holy Grail' *Fam Law* 751.

SMART, C (1984) *The Ties That Bind* (London, Routledge and Kegan Paul).

—— (1987) ' "There Is, Of Course, the Distinction Dictated by Nature": Law and the Problem of Paternity' in M Stanworth (ed), *Reproductive Technologies: Gender, Motherhood and Medicine* (Cambridge, Polity).

—— (1989a) 'Power and the Politics of Child Custody' in C Smart and S Sevenhuijsen (eds), *Child Custody and the Politics of Gender* (London, Routledge).

—— (1989b) *Feminism and the Power of Law* (London, Routledge).

—— (1991) 'The Legal and Moral Ordering of Child Custody' 18 *J of Law and Society* 485.

—— (1992) 'Disruptive Bodies and Unruly Sex: The Regulation of Reproduction and Sexuality in the Nineteenth Century' in C Smart (ed), *Regulating Motherhood: Historical Essays on Marriage, Motherhood and Sex* (London, Routledge).

—— (1999a) 'The "New" Parenthood: Fathers and Mothers after Divorce' in EB Silva and C Smart (eds), *The 'New' Family?* (London, Sage).

—— (1999b) 'Divorce in England 1950–2000: A Moral Tale', paper prepared for CAVA Workshop, *Frameworks for Understanding Policy Change and Culture*).

—— (1999c) 'A History of Ambivalence and Conflict in the Discursive Construction of the "Child Victim" of Sexual Abuse' 8 *Social and Legal Studies* 391.

—— and MAY, V (2004a) 'Residence and Contact Disputes in Court' *Fam Law* 36.

—— and —— (2004b) 'Why Can't They Agree? The Underlying Complexity of Contact and Residence Disputes' 26 *JSW&FL* 347.

—— and NEALE, B (1997) 'Arguments Against Virtue—Must Contact be Enforced?' *Fam Law* 332.

—— and —— (1999) *Family Fragments?* (Cambridge, Polity).

—— and —— (2000) ' "It's My Life Too"—Children's Perspectives on Post-divorce Parenting' *Fam Law* 163.

—— and SEVENHUIJSEN, S (eds), (1989) *Child Custody and the Politics of Gender* (London, Routledge).

——, NEALE, B and WADE, A (2001) *The Changing Experience of Childhood: Families and Divorce* (Cambridge, Polity).

——, MAY, V, WADE, A and FURNISS, C (2003) *Residence and Contact Disputes in Court* (London, Department for Constitutional Affairs, DCA Research Series No 6/03).

SMITH, C (2000) 'The Children (Protection from Offenders) (Miscellaneous Amendments) Regulations 1997: New Alliances in the Management of Risk and Uncertainty' 22 *JSW&FL* 367.

—— and LOGAN, J (2002) 'Adoptive Parenthood as a "Legal Fiction" – Its Consequences of Direct Post-adoption Contact' 12 *CFLQ* 281.

SMITH, DK (2001) 'Superannuating the Second Sex: Law, Privatisation and Retirement Income' 64 *MLR* 519.

SMITH, LJF (1989) *Domestic Violence: An Overview of the Literature* (Home Office Research Study No 107) (London, HMSO).

SMITH, M (2003) 'New Stepfamilies – a Descriptive Study of a Largely Unseen Group' 15(2) *CFLQ* 185.

SMITH, R (2004) 'Hands-off Parenting? – Towards a Reform of the Defence of Reasonable Chastisement in the UK' 16 *CFLQ* 261.

SOCIAL SERVICES INSPECTORATE, DEPARTMENT OF HEALTH (1990), *Inspection of Child Protection Services in Rochdale* (Manchester, DoH).

SOCIAL TRENDS (1996) 26 (London, HMSO).

—— (1997) 27 (London, The Stationery Office).

—— (1998) 28 (London, The Stationery Office).

—— (2004) 33 (London, The Stationery Office).

SOCIAL WORK IN EUROPE (1995) 2(3) Special Edition on Elder Abuse.

SOCIETY FOR PROMOTING CHRISTIAN KNOWLEDGE (1966) *Putting Asunder – A Divorce Law for Contemporary Society* (Cambridge, CUP).

SOLICITORS FAMILY LAW ASSOCIATION (1997) *Code of Practice.*

—— (1998) 'Proposals for Reform of Ancillary Relief Law', Appendix 11 to *Report to the Lord Chancellor by the Ancillary Relief Advisory Group,* (Orpington, SFLA).

SPENSKY, M (1992) 'Producers of Legitimacy: Homes for Unmarried Mothers in the 1950s' in C Smart (ed), *Regulating Womanhood: Historical Essays on Marriage, Motherhood and Sex* (London, Routledge).

STAINTON ROGERS, R and STAINTON ROGERS, W (1992) *Stories of Childhood: Shifting Agendas of Child Concern* (London, Harvester Wheatsheaf).

STANDLEY, K (1992) 'Children and Lesbian Mothers: *B v B* and *C v C*', *Journal of Child Law* 134.

STANKO, E (1985) *Intimate Intrusions: Women's Experience of Male Violence* (London, Routledge and Kegan Paul).

—— (1988) 'Hidden Violence Against Women' in M Maguire and J Pointing (eds), *Victims of Crime: A New Deal?* (Milton Keynes, Open University Press).

—— (1997) 'Should I Stay or Should I Go? Some Thoughts on the Variants of Intimate Violence' 3 *Violence Against Women* 629.

—— et al, (1998) *Counting the Costs: Estimating the Impact of Domestic Violence in the London Borough of Hackney* (Wiltshire, Crime Concern).

STANWORTH, M (1987) 'Reproductive Technologies and the Deconstruction of Motherhood' in M Stanworth (ed), *Reproductive Technologies: Gender, Motherhood and Medicine* (Cambridge, Polity in association with Blackwell).

STARK, E and FLITCRAFT, A (1996) *Women at Risk: Domestic Violence and Women's Health* (London, Sage).

STEPHEN, Sir JAMES FITZJAMES (1883) *A History of the Criminal Law of England,* vol III (London, Clay Sons & Taylor).

STONE, L, (1977) *The Family, Sex and Marriage in England, 1500–1800* (London, Weidenfeld & Nicolson).

—— (1979) *The Family, Sex and Marriage in England 1500–1800* (London, Harper & Rowe).

—— (1990) *Road to Divorce* (Oxford, OUP).

STRATHERN, M (1992) *Reproducing the Future: Anthropology, Kinship and the New Productive Technologies* (Manchester, MUP).

STRAUS, M (1993) 'Physical Assaults by Wives: A Major Social Problem' in R Gelles and D Loseke (eds), *Current Controversies on Family Violence* (London, Sage).

—— and GELLES, R (1990) 'Societal Change and Change in Family Violence from 1975 to 1985 as Revealed in Two National Surveys' in M Straus and R Gelles (eds), *Physical Violence in American Families* (New Brunswick, NJ, Transaction).

——, GELLES, R and STEINMETZ, SK (1981) *Behind Closed Doors: Violence in the American Family* (New York, NY, Anchor/Doubleday).

STURGE, C and GLASER, D (2000) 'Contact and Domestic Violence – The Experts' Court Report' *Fam Law* 615.

STYCHIN, C (2006) 'Family Friendly? Rights, Responsibilities and Relationship Recognition' in A Diduck and K O'Donovan (eds), *Feminist Perspectives on Family Law* (London, Cavendish).

SUPPERSTONE, M and O'DEMPSEY, D (1994) *Immigration: The Law and Practice*, 3rd edn, (London, Longman).

SUTTON, A (1981) 'Science in Court' in M King (ed), *Childhood, Welfare and Justice* (London, Batsford Academic and Educational).

SYMES, P (1985) 'Indissolubility and the Clean Break' 48 *MLR* 44.

TALBOT, C and KIDD, P (2004) 'Special Guardianship Orders – Issues in Respect of Family Assessment' 34 *Fam Law* 273.

TALLIN, GPR (1956) 'Artificial Insemination' 31 *Canadian Bar Review* 1.

TASKER, FL and GOLOMBOK, S (1991) 'Children Raised by Lesbian Mothers: The Empirical Evidence' *Fam Law* 184.

TEN BROEK, J (1963-64) 'California's Dual System of Family Law: Its Origin, Development and Present Status' 16 *Stanford Law Review* 257.

THÈRY, I (1989) ' "The Interest of the Child" and the Regulation of the Post-Divorce Family' in C Smart and S Sevenhuijsen (eds), *Child Custody and the Politics of Gender* (London, Routledge).

THOBURN, J (2003) 'The Risks and Rewards of Adoption for Children in the Public Care' 15 *CFLQ* 391.

THOMAS, P and COSTIGAN, R (1990) *Promoting Homosexuality: Section 28 of the Local Government Act 1988* (Cardiff, Cardiff Law School).

THOMPSON, EP (1972) 'Rough Music' 27(1) *Annales: ESC* 286.

THOMPSON, JJ (1977) 'In Defence of Abortion' in RM Dworkin (ed), *The Philosophy of Law* (Oxford, OUP).

THOMPSON, M (1996) 'Employing the Body: The Reproductive Body and Employment Exclusion' 5 *Social and Legal Studies* 243.

THOMPSON, M, VINTER, L and YOUNG, V (2005) *Dads and their babies: leave arrangements in the first year: Working Paper Series No 37* (London, Equal Opportunities Commission).

THORNTON, R (1993) 'Minors and Medical Treatment – Who decides?' 52 *CLJ* 34.

TONNIES, F and JACOBY, EG (ed and tr) (1974) *On Social Ideas and Ideologies* (New York, NY, Harper & Row).

TRINDER, L (1997) 'Competing Constructions of Childhood: Children's Rights and Children's Wishes in Divorce' 19 *JSW & FL*, 291.

—— (2003) 'Working and Not Working Contact after Divorce' in A Bainham, *et al* (eds) *Children and Their Families: Contact, Rights and Welfare* (Oxford, Hart Publishing).

——, CONNOLLY, J, KELLETT, J and NOTLEY, C (2005) *A Profile of Applicants and Respondents in Contact Cases in Essex* (London, DCA Research Series 1/05).

TRISELIOTIS, J (2000) 'Identity Formation and the Adopted Person Revisited' in A Treacher and I Katz (eds), *The Dynamics of Adoption* (London, Jessica Kingsley).

——, FEAST, J and KYLE, F (2005) *The Adoption Triangle Revisited. A Study of Adoption, Search and Reunion Experiences (Summary)* (London, BAAF).

UK COLLEGE OF FAMILY MEDIATORS (1999) *Domestic Abuse Screening Policy* (www.ukcfm.co.uk accessed 6 June 2005).

—— (2000) *Code of Practice for Family Mediators* (www.ukcfm.co.uk accessed 6 June 2005).

—— (2002) *Children, Young People and Family Mediation: Policy and Practice Guidelines (2002)* (www.ukcfm.co.uk accessed 6 June 2005).

UN COMMITTEE ON THE RIGHTS OF THE CHILD (1995) *Consideration of Reports of States Parties: United Kingdom of Great Britain and Northern Ireland*, CRC/C/15 (Geneva, Centre for Human Rights).

—— (2002) *Concluding Observations of the UN Committee on the Rights of the Child on the United Kingdom's Second Periodic Report* (CRC/C/15/Add.188) (www.unhchr.ch).

UN DEPARTMENT OF PUBLIC INFORMATION (1996), *Platform for Action and the Beijing Declaration*.

UNIVERSITY OF EAST ANGLIA IN ASSOCIATION WITH THE NATIONAL CHILDREN'S BUREAU (2005) *Children's Trusts: Developing Integrated Services for Children in England*, Research Report No 617 (Norwich, University of East Anglia).

URSEL, J (1992) *Private Lives, Public Policy: 100 Years of State Intervention in the Family* (Toronto, Women's Press).

UTTING, Sir W (1997) *People Like Us: The Report of the Review of the Safeguards for Children Living Away From Home* (London, The Stationery Office).

VAUGHAN, B (2000) 'The Government of Youth: Disorder and Dependence?' 9(3) *Social and Legal Studies* 347.

VEITCH, E (1976) 'The Essence of Marriage – A Comment on the Homosexuality Challenge' 5 *Anglo-American Law Review* 41.

WALBY, C and SYMONS, B (1990) *Who am I? Identity, Adoption and Human Fertilisation: Discussion Series no 12* (London, British Agencies for Adoption and Fostering) in Hoggett, *et al, The Family, Law and Society* (London, Butterworths,1996).

WALBY, S and ALLEN, J (2004) *Domestic Violence, Sexual Assault and Stalking: Findings from the British Crime Survey: Home Office Research Study 276* (London, Home Office).

WALKER, J (1996) 'Is There a Future for Lawyers in Divorce?' 10 *Int J of Law, Policy and the Family* 52.

—— (2001) *Information Meetings and Associated Provisions within the Family Law Act 1996: Summary of the Final Evaluation Report* (London, The Stationery Office, Lord Chancellor's Department).

—— *et al*, (2004) *Picking up the Pieces: Marriage and Divorce: Two Years After Information Provision* (London, Department of Constitutional Affairs).

——, MCCARTHY, P and TIMMS, N (1994) *Mediation: the Making and Remaking of Co-operative Relationships – An Evaluation of the Effectiveness of Comprehensive Mediation* (Newcastle Upon-Tyne, Relate Centre for Family Studies, University of Newcastle).

WALL, The RT Hon Lord Justice (2005) 'Enforcement of Contact Orders' *Fam Law* 26

WALLBANK, J (1997) 'The Campaign for Change of the Child Support Act 1991: Reconstituting the "Absent" Father' 6 *Social and Legal Studies* 191.

—— (2002) 'Clause 106 of the Adoption and Children Bill: Legislation for the 'Good' Father?' 22 *Legal Studies* 276.

—— (2004) 'Reconstructing the HFEA 1990: Is Blood Really Thicker than Water?' 16 *CFLQ* 387.

WALLERSTEIN, JS (1991) 'The Long-term Effects of Divorce on Children: A Review' 30 *Journal of the American Academy of Child and Adolescent Psychiatry* 349.

—— and LEWIS, J (1998) 'The Long-term Impact of Divorce on Children: A First Report From a 25-Year Study' *Family and Conciliation Courts Review* 368.

—— and KELLY, JB (1980) *Surviving the Breakup: How Children and Parents Cope with Divorce* (London, Grant McIntyre; New York, NY, Basic Books).

—— and BLAKESLEE, S (1989) *Second Chances* (London, Bantam).

WALSH, E (2004) 'Only Connect' *Fam Law* 703.

WALSH, K (1995) 'The Mandatory Arrest Law: Police Reaction' 16 *PACE L Rev* 97.

WARIN, J, SOLOMON, Y, LEWIS, C and LANGFORD, W (1999) *Fathers, Work and Family Life* (London, Family Policy Studies Centre, Joseph Rowntree Foundation).

WARNOCK, Dame Mary (Chair) (1984) *A Question of Life: The Warnock Report on Human Fertilisation and Embryology*, Report of the Committee of Inquiry into Human Fertilisation and Embryology (Oxford, Blackwell).

WARREN, T (2003) 'Working Part-time: Achieving a successful 'work-life' balance?' 55 *Sociology* 99.

WATTAM, C (1996) 'The Social Construction of Child Abuse for Practical Policy Purposes – A Review of *Child Protection: Messages from Research*' 8 *CFLQ* 189.

WEEKS, J (2002) 'Elective Families: Lesbian and gay life experiments' in A Carling, S Duncan and

R Edwards (eds), *Analysing Families: Morality and Rationality in Policy and Practice* (London, Routledge).

WEEKS, J, DONOVAN, C and HEAPHY, B (1999) 'Everyday Experiments: Narratives of Non-hetero-sexual Relationships' in EB Silva and C Smart (eds), *The 'New' Family?* (London, Sage).

WEITZMAN, L (1985) *The Divorce Revolution: The Unexpected Social and Economic Consequences for Women and Children in America* (New York, NY, Free Press).

WELLS, C (1988) 'Whose Baby Is It?' 15 *J of Law and Society* 323.

——, ALLDRIDGE, P and MORGAN, D (1990) 'An Unsuitable Case for Treatment' *NLJ* 1544.

WEYLAND, I (1992) 'Contact within Different Legal Contexts' *Fam Law* 138.

—— (1995) 'Judicial Attitudes to Contact and Shared Residence since the Children Act 1989' *JSW&FL* 445.

WHEELER, D (2004) 'Can We Make Contact Work?' *Fam Law* 601.

WHELAN, R (1995) (ed), *Just a Piece of Paper? Divorce Reform and the Undermining of Marriage* (London, IEA Health and Welfare Unit).

WHINCUP, M. (1991) *Modern Employment Law*, 7th edn, (Oxford, Butterworth-Heinemann).

WHYBROW, J (2004) 'Children, Guardians and Rule 9.5' *Fam Law* 504.

WICKS, The RT Hon Malcolm, MP, Minister of State for Pensions (2004) Speech to TUC Conference Women and Pensions

WIKELEY, N (1995) *Jobseekers Act 1995,* Current Law, 1, c 18 (London, Sweet & Maxwell).

—— (2000a) 'Child Support – The New Formula, Part I' *Fam Law* 820.

—— (2000b) 'Compliance, Enforcement and Child Support' *Fam Law* 888.

—— (2001) 'Children and Social Security Law' in J Fionda (ed), *Legal Concepts of Childhood* (Oxford, Hart Publishing).

—— (2002) *Wikeley, Ogus and Barendt's: The Law of Social Security* (London, Butterworths).

——, BARNETT, S, BROWN, J, DAVIS, G, DIAMOND, I, DRAPER, T and SMITH, P. (2001) *National Survey of Child Support Clients, Research Report No 152* (London, Department for Work and Pensions) (Summary of Report: http://www.dwp.gov.uk/asd/asd5/152summ.html).

WILLBOURNE, C and CULL, L (1997) 'The Emerging Problem of Parental Alienation' *Fam Law* 807.

WILLIAMS, C and JORDAN, H (1996) 'Factors Relating to Publicity Surrounding the Complaints Procedure under the Children Act 1989' 8 *CFLQ* 337.

WILLIAMS, F (2004) *Rethinking Families* (London, Calouste Gulbenkian Foundation).

WILLIAMS, G (1983) *Textbook of Criminal Law*, 2nd edn, (London, Stevens & Sons).

WILLIAMS, PJ (1991) *The Alchemy of Race and Rights* (Cambridge, MA, Harvard University Press).

—— (1994) 'Spare Parts, Family Values, Old Children, Cheap' 28 *New England Law Review* 913.

WILLOW, C (2004) 'Consulting with Under 12s: A Mapping Exercise' in B Neale (ed), *Young Children's Citizenship* (York, Joseph Rowntree Foundation).

WILSON, B (2004) 'Emotion, Rationality and Decision-making in Mediation' *Fam Law* 682.

—— (2005) 'Dispute "Ripeness", Timing and Mediation' *Fam Law*162.

WILSON, M and DALY, M (1992) 'Till Death do Us Part' in J Radford and DEH Russell (eds), *Femicide: The Politics of Woman Killing* (Buckingham, Open University Press).

WILSON, W (1995) 'Is Life Sacred?' 12 *JSW&FL* 131.

WINDEBANK, J (1996) 'To What Extent Can Social Policy Challenge the Dominant Ideology of Mothering? A Cross-national Comparison of Sweden, France and Britain' 6(2) *Journal of European Social Policy* 147.

WINTEMUTE, R (2000) 'Lesbian and Gay Inequality 2000: The Potential of the Human Rights Act 1998 and the Need for an Equality Act' 6 *EHRLR* 603.

WOMAN'S OWN (1987) 31 October.

WOMEN'S AID FEDERATION OF ENGLAND (2003) *Response to 'Safety and Justice', the Government's Consultation Paper on Domestic Violence* (Bristol, WAFE)

WOMEN'S LEGAL EDUCATION AND ACTION FUND (1996) *Equality and the Charter: Ten Years of Feminist Advocacy before the Supreme Court of Canada* (Toronto, Emond Montgomery).

WOMEN'S NATIONAL COMMISSION (1985) *Violence Against Women*, Report of an *ad hoc* Working Group (London, Cabinet Office, 1985).

WOMEN'S PROJECT (1998) *Bridges or Barriers* (Weston-super-Mare, Women's Project).

WONG, S. (2003) 'Trusting in Trust(s): The Family Home and Human Rights' 11 *Feminist Legal Studies* 119

YNGVESSON, B (1997) 'Negotiating Motherhood: Identity and Difference in "Open" Adoptions' 31 *Law and Society Review* 33.

YOUNG, I.M. (1990) *Justice and the Politics of Difference* (Princeton, NJ, Princeton University Press).

YOUNG, K (1996) *Research Evaluation of Family Mediation Practice and the Issue of Violence* (Attorney-General's Department, Australia).

ZIFF, B (1990) 'The Primary Caretaker Presumption: Canadian Perspectives on an American Development' 4 *Int J of Law and the Family* 186.

ZIPPER, J and SEVENHUIJSEN, S (1987) 'Surrogacy: Feminist Notions of Motherhood Revisited' in M Stanworth (ed), *Reproductive Technologies: Gender, Motherhood and Medicine* (Cambridge, Polity).

*Newspaper Articles*

'Parent's role a model for life', *The Guardian*, 7 November 1996.
'Single Mothers' Benefit to be Slashed', *Sunday Telegraph*, 21 July 1996.
'Who Does What?' (2005) www.sociology.org.uk
'Blair Puts Focus on Family Friendly Reforms', *The Guardian*, 28 February 2005.

# Index